DATE DUE			
Mar 8 '76			
Mar 22 '76			
Apr 7 '76			
Apr 26 '77			

NATO

The Entangling Alliance

NATO
The Entangling Alliance

BY ROBERT ENDICOTT OSGOOD

THE UNIVERSITY OF CHICAGO PRESS

CHICAGO & LONDON

LIBRARY OF CONGRESS CATALOG CARD NUMBER: 62-8348

THE UNIVERSITY OF CHICAGO PRESS, CHICAGO & LONDON
THE UNIVERSITY OF TORONTO PRESS, TORONTO 5, CANADA

 PUBLISHED 1962. THIRD IMPRESSION 1966.
PRINTED IN THE UNITED STATES OF AMERICA

DESIGNED BY ADRIAN WILSON

For Eleanor

Foreword

NATO was created as, and is still today officially considered to be, the shield that protects Western Europe from a Soviet attack on land. Yet it has never been clear how NATO could perform that function with the forces actually at its disposal or how it could have performed that function even with the much larger forces which its official spokesmen from time to time declared to be indispensable. Nor has it been clear how such a military organization, top heavy as it is with collective agencies for the making of decisions, would operate effectively in case of war.

These are some of the doubts which arise from within NATO itself. There are others which concern the relations between NATO and the over-all political and military purposes of the Western alliance and, more particularly, of the United States. What is the place of NATO within the over-all military strategy of the United States? What functions could NATO perform for the European communities and a more closely integrated Atlantic community? What impact is the impending diffusion of nuclear weapons likely to have upon the policies and the very existence of NATO? And what of the probable replacement of the manned bomber and bases supporting it by long-distance missiles?

These are some of the questions which the Western governments should have raised long ago and answered. If they have been raised, they certainly have not been answered. It is the great merit of Professor Osgood's book that he raises these questions and tries to answer them. As he did before in his book on *Limited War,* which has had a salutary influence upon our military thinking, he puts these questions in the over-all context of the political and military situation as it exists today and as it is likely to exist in the foreseeable future. Professor Osgood does not suggest spectacular patent solutions. Rather he reasons as the political and military statesmen ought to reason. Starting with certain fundamental political and military principles and purposes, he analyzes the possibilities which the actual situation provides and selects those which are most likely to conform to the principles and achieve the purposes.

HANS J. MORGENTHAU

Preface

This book is a study of contemporary American foreign policy as it has been transformed by the radically new conditions of the postwar period. Specifically, it examines the novel military-strategic issues that challenge the viability of the United States outstanding instrument of security in the cold war, the North Atlantic alliance.

More generally, this is a study of the role of military power in the nuclear age—of the pervasive, diverse, complex, and subtle influence of military strategies and capabilities upon international politics. In particular, it explores the political and psychological ramifications of the unprecedented task of peacetime military-strategic collaboration in NATO—the interaction of strategic logic with the demands of allied cohesion, political warfare, and diplomacy.

I have not, however, presented a comprehensive description or analysis of either the military or non-military aspects of America's relationships with her NATO allies. I have tried only to elucidate those aspects that seem to me most directly related to NATO's past, present, and future utility as a regional security alliance in the cold war.

I completed this book in the early months of 1961; thus most of its observations are cast in the perspective of events as they seemed up to the end of the Eisenhower administration. However, before the manuscript went to press later in the year, I entered a few revisions and additions, chiefly in the concluding chapter, to make the narrative as current as possible.

Throughout this rather hazardous venture in contemporary history I have been sustained by the guidance of a master in interpreting the present in lasting perspective: Hans J. Morgenthau. For additional enlightenment, based upon reading the entire manuscript in one version or another, I am grateful to my discerning colleague George Liska, to Colonel W. M. M. Minton of the office of the United States Representative in NATO, and to Seyom Brown, graduate student at the University of Chicago. For secretarial assistance far beyond the line of ordinary duty and competence I wish to thank Margaret Harrison Case.

CHICAGO

Contents

1
Introduction

1. THE NEED AND CAPABILITY OF COLLABORATION

No feature of the cold war more clearly marks the revolution in America's foreign policy than the North Atlantic alliance, which was created to entangle the United States more firmly in the affairs of Europe. Like America's other alliances, the North Atlantic alliance reflects the fact that American security can be immediately and drastically affected by changes in the overseas balance of power, which the United States cannot unilaterally prevent or counter. But, far more than any other alliance, this European entanglement involves the United States in active military collaboration. In the extent of military co-ordination and political co-operation it demands, NATO is unique among peacetime alliances. In fact, it has assumed tasks of multinational planning, decision, and action that few wartime coalitions have performed.

This extensive collaboration reflects a distinctive need—the need to prevent Communist domination of the single most valuable center of material power, as well as cultural affinity, outside the North American continent—and a distinctive capability of strong and stable nations who share a solid identity of security interests to concert their power.

Soviet leaders have repeatedly acknowledged the pre-eminent importance of this coalition of non-Communist powers as the major obstacle to the creation of a "socialist world system" under Soviet direction. Only the means of eliminating this obstacle have changed. With special emphasis since the death of Stalin, they have pursued the Leninist strategy of undermining the major "capitalist-imperialist" centers in the West by varieties of indirect pressure designed to exploit the "contradictions" among them, to isolate and intimidate them, and to align the colonial and former colonial areas against them. The extension of Communist control and influence outside the NATO area in the Communists' "zone of peace" would constitute a serious blow to American values and security, but the disruption, humiliation, and paralysis of NATO would be a *vital* blow, far more serious than limited Communist territorial gains on the periphery of Eurasia. Furthermore, the demonstrated impotence of NATO would obviate effective resistance to Soviet penetration of the periphery of Eurasia.

At the same time, in its European alliance the United States possesses unique potential for supporting its vital interests through a concert of power with nations who have the political will and capacity to collaborate. No such basis of concerted power exists outside Europe; and outside NATO, America's margin of influence upon nations and events is far narrower than within it. Consequently, of all America's alliances and alignments, NATO represents by far her most vital interest, the most effective instrument of collaboration, and the greatest accretion of her strength.

But extensive collaboration is a source of trouble as well as of strength. The more extensive the collaboration, the more troublesome is the dual task of reconciling the coalition's requirements of internal cohesion with its requirements of external security. For the kinds of commitments and contributions that can elicit co-operation will not necessarily meet the demands of collective security; and the greater the demands of co-operation, the greater difficulty states must encounter in concerting security efforts at an adequate level. In the face of fundamental military and political developments that were not foreseen when the alliance was created, the achievement of this dual task has already occasioned major adjustments in the structure and policies of NATO. It now demands further adjustments of equal significance.

The ascendance of Soviet nuclear power, the prospect of the diffusion of nuclear capabilities among other allies, and the economic and political resurgence of Western Europe now challenge the very foundation of effective collaboration, the basic political and military assumptions upon which the alliance was constructed. At the same time, these portentous developments raise fundamental questions about the utility and the vitality of such a tightly knit regional alliance in the peculiar conditions of the cold war and, more generally, about the capacity of democratic nations to meet the harsh and complex demands of security through close collaboration in peacetime.

2. THE MILITARY CORE OF THE ALLIANCE

This book is concerned primarily with the military-strategic sources of NATO's troubles. It begins with the assumption that NATO is pre-eminently a defensive military alliance and that it must be judged strong or impotent by the extent to which it advances the security of its members.

This is not to say that the central task of NATO can be divorced from its political problems—especially those that concern the division, political ties, and armament of Germany; those that involve allied interests in areas outside Europe; and those that arise from the competition for prestige and influence among the allies. They are inseparable. Nor is it to deny, as many have observed, that NATO has come to be "more than a purely military alliance." It is, indeed, a center of coalition diplomacy vis-à-vis the Soviet bloc and a multilateral framework for interallied diplomacy.

Nevertheless, I take the view that NATO's most crucial problems, whether or not they are manifested directly in a military form, are those that impinge upon its core of mutual security interests, the protection of which remains the chief justification for the alliance, and that these problems, fundamentally, pertain to the task of strategic collaboration. There is a danger of obscuring this troublesome fact in our anxiety to alleviate

NATO's external problems through a direct political resolution of international tensions or to alleviate NATO's internal problems through the elaboration of its non-military functions.

I shall deal with the first expedient in chapter x, on "disengagement." An example of the second is manifested in the report of the Committee of Three on Non-Military Co-operation in NATO, released in December, 1956.[1] This report reflects the common view that, following the Kremlin's tactical shift of pressure to the political realm, the military threat to Europe has ceased to be the foremost problem in the eyes of NATO governments and peoples and that, consequently, NATO can maintain its vitality only through the expansion of political, economic, and cultural co-operation among its members. The underlying assumption here is that during a protracted period of "peaceful coexistence" NATO cannot sustain effective collaboration if its activities pertain solely to its military function and that, therefore, NATO must become something more than a purely military alliance; or, as Secretary of State Dulles put it, "the time has come to advance NATO from its initial phase into the totality of its meaning."[2]

This prescription, without coming to grips with NATO's strategic dilemmas, tries to bolster the alliance by expanding its non-military functions. In distinction to this approach, I shall stress the military-strategic sources of NATO's troubles, on the assumption that, if the alliance fails to find the basis of collaboration in an effective military strategy, NATO's non-military functions will suffer correspondingly and the political problems of its members will be of an entirely different order. But while focusing upon military strategy as the central determinant of NATO's efficacy or impotence, I shall contend that military strategy itself is infused with political significance, because strategic collaboration is a political instrument and depends upon a political process.

3. THE MEANING OF MILITARY STRATEGY

In stressing the strategic sources of NATO's troubles, I am concerned with more than the technical military problems that fall within the special competence of the military profession, for military strategy has become far more than "the science and art of fighting battles." Military strategy must now be understood as nothing less than the over-all plan for utilizing the capacity for armed coercion—in conjunction with the economic, diplomatic, and psychological instruments of power—to support foreign policy most effectively by overt, covert, and tacit means.

The ultimate rationale of military strategy, properly understood, has always been its support of the political purposes of a nation, but the exacting requirements of contemporary deterrence have made the relationship between force and policy both more intimate and more intricate. Efficacious military plans—especially those relating to the development, deployment, command and control, and use of nuclear weapons—now depend upon the most systematic calculation of their psychological impact upon governments and peoples and the most scrupulous attention to their manifold implications for political relations among allies, with the non-aligned, and with adversaries. Indeed, given the present inhibitions against the overt use of armed force, combined with the limitations of diplomacy as an instrument for resolving profound conflicts of national interest, the political and psychological consequences of the nature and disposition of armed forces may be the primary function, not just the by-product, of military strategy. Military policies, like economic policies, have become a delicate and diversified instrument of statecraft.[3]

At the same time, the unprecedented economic and technical demands of military preparedness, combined with the multiplicity of military needs facing a great power, have vastly complicated the problem of strategic choice by putting a new premium upon the systematic allocation of scarce scientific, material, financial, and human resources among a great variety of desirable functions. The profusion of military technology, the rapid rate of technological innovation and obsolescence, the impelling dynamics of the arms race, and the high cost of modern weapons systems require, more urgently than ever before, a continual and studied selection among projects of military research, development, and production. Properly, governments can make this selection only in terms of a coherent over-all strategy that enables them to determine priorities among military functions. But the problem of devising such a strategy is greatly complicated by the diverse and indeterminate nature of the military functions that might be useful to support policy under a wide range of circumstances. For it has become inordinately difficult to anticipate the nature of the contingencies in which the use or threatened use of weapons and forces of certain kinds might serve political objectives. Even if one can identify the potential enemy and the location of the hypothetical conflict, there is considerable diversity in the possible level and scope of violence, the limitations and restraints upon combat, and the political context of anticipated wars; and there is even greater diversity in the circumstances in which one must anticipate supporting policy with military power by means short of war.

The unconscionable human and material cost of a total war fought with nuclear weapons puts a premium upon countering limited and ambiguous forms of aggression with a variety of limited responses. This complicates military planning with an unprecedented problem of combining military effectiveness with the deliberate restraint of the most "efficient" weapons. It expands the range of the forms of conflict that a superpower with global security interests must be prepared to fight and affects all military planning with a crucial interest in the political and physical restraints that are essential to make the resort to war a rational instrument of policy rather than a senseless spasm of violence.

While the diversity of possible military contingencies and political circumstances, combined with the dynamic profusion and costliness of military technology, imposes a severe burden of strategic choice upon military planners, that burden is increased by the greater importance of forces-in-being, as opposed to forces that can be mobilized in weeks or months. For when the forces-in-being may be decisive in preventing war or determining its outcome, this not only increases the cost of military preparedness but also makes more crucial the strategic calculations that determine the selection of weapons systems—beginning with the selection of research and development programs—that will determine the weapons available five or more years ahead.

In enabling governments to discharge this great burden of choice according to some rational plan, military strategy, as I have defined it, is the indispensable bridge between arms and policy. Ideally, military strategy should be constructed of the following interdependent components, logically supplementing each other within a coherent plan: the estimate of the nature, probability, and seriousness of possible military threats to vital political interests; the calculation of the best military methods of responding to these threats in various contingencies in order to deter or resist them; the determination of military capabilities—of the weapons and forces—needed to support these responses; and the formulation of public declarations about responses and the other strategic components.

Actually, strategic logic is something to be approximated but never perfectly achieved. Complete internal consistency among these components is scarcely possible, and not necessarily desirable, where non-strategic values have a legitimate claim upon national policy. In any case, the listing of these components suggests the extent to which military strategy transcends the traditional realm of the military specialist and exceeds the bounds of purely *military* logic. The prior strategic questions—the nature of the threat and the resulting contingencies in which the use of force should be anticipated—are as much matters of political as military judgment. And even the planning of military responses and capabilities, although a highly technical operation, requires, in the absence of battlefield experience with the physical and psychological effects of modern weapons or objective empirical tests of the requirements of deterrence, a novel type of systematic analysis of imponderable and subjective factors.[4]

Indeed, the extramilitary aspects of military strategy are the very essence of the cold war, for the immense destructive power of nuclear weapons has rendered the political and psychological exploitation of military potential a primary means by which the struggle for power and prestige is waged in support of a range of political purposes apart from military security. The situation is analogous to Clausewitz' description of the limited wars of political maneuver in the eighteenth century:

> Thus war became essentially a regular game in which time and chance shuffled the cards; but in its significance it was only diplomacy somewhat intensified, a more forceful way of negotiating, in which battles and sieges were the diplomatic notes. To obtain some moderate advantage in order to make use of it in negotiations for peace was the aim of the most ambitious.[5]

Now it is the *prospect* of war rather than the "battles" and "sieges" themselves that constitutes "diplomacy somewhat intensified."

Of course, there is nothing new about the offensive and defensive manipulation of military power by means short of war, but this manipulation acquires a new significance when it depends, ultimately, upon terrorizing the adversary with the prospect of nuclear obliteration. In the pre-nuclear age it depended primarily upon the capacity of nations to acquire or hold territory, to interdict or keep open lines of supply, to destroy the enemy's capacity to fight by defeating his forces, and, more markedly in the age of aerial bombardment, to destroy the resources of military production. But the possession of nuclear weapons gives nations the capacity to inflict such severe damage upon each other that any but the most carefully restricted use of armed force entails a grave risk of leading to a conflict far more costly than the political objectives at stake would seem to warrant. At the same time, this immense damaging power gives nuclear nations the opportunity to substitute, as a means of armed coercion and persuasion, the threat of civil damage for the actual or threatened destruction of the enemy's capacity to fight. Therefore, the threat of inflicting unacceptable damage upon the adversary—damage that may be unrelated to the capacity to gain or deny immediate territorial objectives at stake—has become the fundamental method, affecting all other methods, by which nuclear powers use their military capabilities as instruments of policy. The two most characteristic manifestations of this method are called "blackmail" and "deterrence." Each has its peculiar and highly developed techniques.

As George F. Kennan has observed, "Armaments are important not just for what could be done with them in time of war, but for the psychological shadows they cast in time of peace."[6] One should add that the psychological shadows that armaments cast in time of peace are shaped largely by what men think could and would be done with them in time of war. Today military strategists must be intimately concerned with viewing and casting these shadows. The best known shadows are in the realm of deterrence, but there are more obscure shadows in the realm of political and psychological warfare that affect interstate relations no less significantly.

4. DETERRENCE AND INTERNATIONAL STABILITY

From the standpoint of the United States and her NATO allies, military strategy serves foreign policy in three principal ways: (*a*) by deterring overt or paramilitary aggression; (*b*) by meeting armed aggression with effective resistance compatible with rational limitations upon warfare if deterrence should fail; (*c*) by supporting political positions and diplomacy vis-à-vis the Soviet Union without the resort to war. The first function is the most fundamental, in the sense that the achievement of deterrence is the prerequisite of effective political relations with the Soviet Union, whereas effective military resistance largely compensates for the failure of deterrence by supporting vital political objectives with overt rather than tacit force. Therefore, quite properly, military strategists have been absorbed in the task of deterrence—although too much at the expense of the other two functions of military power.

The importance of NATO's deterrent power must be understood in the context of the larger objective of stabilizing the over-all competition for power and prestige in international relations, for military deterrence has become the primary mechanism of international stability in the cold war, and NATO plays a crucial part in the efficacy or inefficacy of that mechanism.* Yet deterrence is a delicate mechanism that requires the utmost skill and energy to maintain in working order—and the utmost collaboration within NATO.

The stability of international relations—in the absence of a preponderance of power under supranational control or the hegemony of a dominant state or bloc—implies the moderation and regularization of the competition of power within certain conventional modes of conduct, which the participating states view as reciprocal, self-imposed restraints that work to their mutual advantage while preserving the existing state system. The most stable pattern of international relations in modern times was the balance-of-power system of the eighteenth and nineteenth centuries, which in theory—and, to a notable extent, in practice—deterred the great powers from radical assaults upon each other's interests: on the one hand, by confronting them with the prospect of countervailing alignments and alliances, and, on the other hand, by providing them with the means for limited adjustments of power and interests without the hazards of unrestricted competition. However, the conditions that enabled this system to stabilize international relations as well as it did—principally, a fairly equal distribution of power among several states, a rudimentary moral consensus among rulers and ruling classes, and a war potential of relatively limited destructive capacity—no longer exist. Instead, we live in a largely bipolar political system dominated by superpowers with intensely hostile interests and aims, who could drastically alter the international configurations of power and civilization itself in a single military encounter. And these

* Military deterrence can be defined as the dissuasion of a government from taking a hostile action (in the eyes of the deterring state) by virtue of its fear of the consequences of military counteraction. Clearly, the fear of military counteraction is only one motive among many non-military considerations that may dissuade a government from carrying out a hostile intent. However, in current usage, theories of deterrence are concerned with the calculations of benefit, cost, and risk underlying that kind of dissuasion which is presumed to depend decisively (if only as the marginal factor) upon the fear of an armed encounter. This is the sense in which I discuss deterrence as a mechanism of mutual restraint among powers with strongly antithetical aims and interests.

superpowers do not have access to the balancing mechanisms of the defunct balance-of-power system, even if they should want to use them.

The non-military balancing mechanisms of that obsolete system were primarily territorial acquisitions and compensations and shifts of alliances and alignments. The first mechanism is largely ruled out by the disappearance of the frontier, the rise of nationalism in "backward" countries, and the compelling allegiance of citizens to antithetical ideologies and political systems. The second mechanism is inhibited by the polarization of international power and politics and the over-all antithesis between Communist and non-Communist ideologies and institutions; as a result, the process of balancing power takes place primarily by the accretion of strength through collaboration within the alliance rather than by countervailing adjustments of strength through shifts of states from one alliance to another.

With the disappearance of the non-military balancing mechanisms of the balance-of-power system, the stability of the international competition for power has come to depend more heavily upon the stability of the military balance itself. At the same time, with the revolutionary increase in the destructive capacity of military potential in the last half-century, the resort to armed conflict has become a far more risky and unreliable instrument for maintaining an international equilibrium. Consequently, in the cold war the status quo powers have aspired to construct international stability largely on the foundation of military deterrence, on the assumption that the very capacity of nuclear powers to destroy each other gives them an overriding interest in observing strict restraints on the use or threatened use of armed force.

In large measure, the validity of this assumption has been confirmed so far by the relations between the Soviet bloc and the NATO powers. The Soviet Union has tried to undermine the status quo by rather carefully limited means, and NATO has resisted Soviet incursions by equally limited means. This joint circumspection reflects a kind of tacit agreement upon reciprocal self-restraints, which are greatly reinforced by mutual awareness of the new costs and risks of any armed conflict.

Yet it would be extremely dangerous, when the capacity for devastation is mutual, to underestimate the inherent instability in any military balance and, particularly, in one that depends so heavily upon threats and counterthreats of reprisals intended to constrain the adversary by sheer terror of devastation.

One source of instability is the subjective and imponderable character of the very concept of contemporary deterrence, which puts a premium upon prudent and accurate calculations of the will or intentions of nuclear adversaries to inflict unacceptable damage upon each other, even though neither side would be likely to gain a meaningful advantage if both employed their full capabilities for damage. The dependence of a military balance primarily upon the credibility of essentially punitive reprisals or counterreprisals, rather than upon capabilities to attain or deny military objectives by defeating opposing forces, creates a far more complex and uncertain relationship between military capabilities and the will to use them than existed under the balance-of-power system (which was itself far from being the mechanically predictable regulator of power that its advocates sometimes claimed). Whereas military deterrence under the balance-of-power system depended largely upon estimates of relative military combat capabilities, which, although repeatedly miscalculated, were assumed to have a fairly straightforward relationship to the will to use them in the event of a serious conflict of interests, military deterrence under the balance-of-terror system depends not only upon complicated estimates of relative capabilities but also upon estimates of interacting intentions; that is, upon a complicated process of mutual mind-reading based upon some such speculative calculus as the value of engaging in war for the sake of an objective at stake, considering the estimated effectiveness and costs of military action as opposed to inaction, in the light of the probability of various kinds of military responses.[7] Estimates of the material components of deterrence, such as "missile exchange rates," are at least susceptible to the precise, quantitative calculation of objective, though substantially conjectural, data; but estimates of the crucial non-material components must rest largely on intuitive, qualitative judgments about subjective data. The management and control of deterrence as an instrument of policy is, correspondingly, more unpredictable and subject to miscalculation. At the same time, the consequences of miscalculation could be enormous.

The stability of the military balance is further jeopardized by novel and rapidly changing weapons systems, whose effects must remain speculative in the absence of experience with them in actual battle. Thus, the whole complex calculus of deterrence rests upon assumptions about the consequences of using a military technology that, fortunately, has never been tested in war; and one configuration of capabilities that seems to assure stability can be rapidly supplanted by another that might tempt or provoke war.

Up to a point, the very uncertainty of the requirements of deterrence, combined with the potentially disastrous consequences of miscalculating them, may help stabilize a condition of mutual restraint, since no power will dare upset the balance even at a slight risk of war. But, carried to its full logic, a strategy based upon the stabilizing effect of such uncertainty leads to a dangerous reliance upon the balance of terror to take care of itself and to deter the whole range of possible military threats, from a direct nuclear assault down to conventional limited aggressions.

In reality, the maintenance of the balance of terror, merely in terms of its material components, requires continual, painstaking strategic calculation and continual, expensive technological innovation and production. And in terms of its nonmaterial components, the maintenance of the balance of terror depends on a sensitive and circumspect vigilance that is unremittingly attentive to the vicissitudes of human fears and ambitions, to qualities of judgment and motives of decision, which cannot be comprehended in any "game theory" and which certainly cannot be relied upon to provide a self-sustaining equilibrium.

Furthermore, the stability of the military balance involves more than the balance of terror; it involves the whole spectrum of violence. If a balance of terror succeeds in deterring nuclear strikes (whether offensive or retaliatory) because of the fear of counterstrikes, it only makes more likely the limited and ambiguous non-nuclear forms of aggression, which require a capacity for effective local resistance to deter or counter. Therefore, the over-all stability of the military balance requires a large and diversified military capability, lest stability at the top or most violent end of the spectrum of deterrence lead to instability at the lower end. This requirement is doubly imperative because ordinary prudence demands that nations prepare for the failure of deterrence by having recourse to strategies and capabilities that can wage war within rational constraints.

Viewed in the light of this latter imperative, one of the greatest sources of instability in the contemporary military environment is the proclivity of democratic nations, for the sake of economy, to rely on the threat of nuclear retaliation to deter not only the most catastrophic contingencies but also a wide range of lesser contingencies, while neglecting the requirements of limiting and controlling force, should deterrence fail. The history of NATO's strategy and capabilities affords a dismaying example of this proclivity.

5. THE SOVIET THREAT

The requirements of deterrence and of the other functions of military power should be determined by an integrated assessment of all the components of military strategy. The first component—first in logical sequence and in importance—is the estimate of the nature of the threat to national interests and of the resulting contingencies in which one must contemplate the use or threatened use of armed force. This estimate should originate in a sober appraisal of Soviet ends and means in foreign policy.

The Soviet Union is implacably committed to transforming the world into the Communist image of society, to creating a "socialist world system" of states, with Russia the undisputed leader (or, according to recent formulations, the "vanguard") and all potentially opposing national bases of power under Communist control. At the same time, Soviet leaders are, by doctrine and practice, circumspect and calculating pragmatists in the aggrandizement of Russian power, which they identify with the advancement of their revolutionary goal. Together, these two characteristics make deterrence feasible but preclude its resting on any more stable basis than the will and ability of the prospective victims to make aggression unprofitable. Therefore, deterrence is the condition that enables the United States and her allies to conduct the cold war in an area of political and psychological maneuver, an area in which the Communists operate with all the resourcefulness of practicing revolutionaries exploiting their adversaries' longing for peace and normality.

From NATO's standpoint, the stability of the balance of terror is the prerequisite for protecting the status quo from violent change, but, from the Soviet standpoint, it is the prerequisite for undermining the status quo at a tolerable risk by non-violent means. To the Western powers, international tensions are bad because they disturb normal relations and threaten to erupt in war. These powers yearn to eliminate the specific sources of tension in a step-by-step approach to peace. But, to the Soviet leaders, the raising or lowering of tensions and the threat of war are tools of policy. They regard the underlying source of tensions and war as the existence of the "capitalist camp," a source which is ineradicable until the capitalist states, step by step, are buried. In liberal democratic eyes, war is the opposite of peace, just as conflict is distinguished from the absence of conflict. But in Communist eyes, war and peace are distinguished merely by the method of waging an inexorable class conflict, in which summit conferences, disarmament proposals, peace campaigns, subversion, economic and military assistance, space demonstrations, or war and the threat of war are all tactical parts of an integrated strategy. The Communists will not hesitate to use armed force when other means of pursuing the most vital interests are impractical and the risks of successful opposition seem tolerable, but they also understand and prefer the multifarious uses of military potential in securing peaceful acquiescence.

As long as the Soviet bloc refrains from military incursions, the immediate requirements of deterrence have been met; and the Western powers are therefore inclined to relax their preparedness in the absence of any more tangible test of its adequacy or inadequacy. Yet the most important consequence of a stable or unstable, credible or incredible, posture of deterrence may be, not the prevention or outbreak of overt aggression, but rather the maintenance or loss of prestige and morale, the strength or weakness of political positions and diplomatic maneuvers, or the consolidation or disintegration of the alliance itself. For expectations about the circumstances and consequences of war in the minds of nations and statesmen—Americans, adversaries, allies, and the non-aligned—may affect the fortunes of the cold war no less decisively than war itself. Thus, the necessity of having to choose between nuclear war and ineffective conventional resistance or acquiescence in the event of limited aggressions will weaken the diplomacy and undermine the cohesion of NATO no matter how carefully the Soviet Union may avoid crossing the brink of war.

In Europe the cold war is a struggle for prestige and influence and a test of will and nerves waged against a background of beliefs about the relative military power of the participants, about when and how they might use their power, and about what the results would be if they did. The Soviet objective is to so exploit Russian military power in conjunction with political threats and conciliatory gestures as to exacerbate the "contradictions" among allied states, stimulate neutralism and pacifism among their citizens, convince them that NATO cannot protect them but will only draw them into crises and war, induce them to abandon their collective efforts to build a "situation of strength," and persuade them to accept the Soviet terms of "peaceful coexistence." To these ends, Moscow tries to convince the Western nations that the military balance has shifted drastically against them in favor of the USSR, that they can maintain their "provocative" military bloc and sustain their "untenable" outposts like Berlin only at the risk of a catastrophic war, and that their only reasonable recourse is to accept Russia's conciliatory proposals to relieve international tensions —for example, by making West Berlin a "free city," recognizing

East Germany, withdrawing foreign troops from the Continent, disbanding military bases, abandoning nuclear weapons, and, ultimately, dismantling the alliance. At the same time, they try to demonstrate NATO's impotence by maneuvering the West into tests of will that humiliate the most powerful allies and intimidate the others, while undermining the willingness of all members to support each other's interests at the risk of war.

Clearly, Soviet success in this game heightens the risk of overt conflict by inciting overboldness and miscalculation in Moscow or desperation in the West, but the Soviet objective is to so weaken Western resistance by non-violent means that the extension of Communist power by armed force will be unnecessary. Therefore, the functions of NATO's military strategy are not exhausted with the prevention or defeat of armed aggression. Against the multifaceted Soviet threat allied military power is equally a political weapon, which must be integrally related to diplomacy, propaganda, and other non-violent instruments of policy, in order to obtain the most favorable terms of peaceful coexistence until the threat subsides.

6. THE POLITICAL FUNCTIONS OF COALITION STRATEGY

The realities of the Soviet strategy of inciting political instability mean that, if deterrence can be stabilized, the primary function of military strategy will be to sustain an unrelenting political warfare, which, although it may permit limited accommodations of conflicting interests, will be preponderantly a competition among hostile powers to achieve antithetical political aims. In this political warfare the military posture of the NATO allies can play a central role in conveying the impression and encouraging the reality of confident strength, cultivating a reputation for power combined with restraint, sustaining the morale of threatened peoples (like those in Berlin), promoting a common stand among allies, bolstering resistance to Soviet demands and pressures, and reinforcing political claims and bargaining positions in diplomatic exchanges.

When serious accommodations of political differences with the Soviet bloc are at issue, military strategy will be equally infused with political import. Thus, proposed agreements to relax international tensions through arms control or "disengagement" are inextricably connected with the military balance in Europe. The military posture of the NATO states affects the nature and scope of desirable political accommodations, and the agreement upon a political accommodation logically presupposes an appraisal of its military-strategic implications.

But the political functions of NATO's military strategy embrace relations among the allies as well as with the Soviet Union. In fact, the two are inseparable, for if the alliance is to achieve military security or to support diplomacy and political warfare, it must elicit a certain measure of cohesion among its members—an essentially political task. And allied cohesion should be measured not only by strategic collaboration but also by political co-operation; the two are interdependent.

The dual task of NATO's military strategy is, therefore, on the one hand, to support the security and diplomacy of the allies vis-à-vis the Soviet bloc and, on the other hand, to secure the measure of strategic collaboration and political co-operation that is essential for these purposes. But, as I suggested at the outset, in a multilateral alliance exacting extensive commitments and contributions this is bound to be a delicate and complex task, for the requirements of collaboration do not automatically coincide with the requirements of security. A viable alliance must permit material and political concessions to the requirements of cohesion. Yet it must do so without undermining the common security. The heart of NATO's problems lies in the need to strike a balance between these two requirements through the medium of a military strategy that demands unprecedented peacetime co-operation under revolutionary military conditions.* Naturally, the burden of this task falls

* When I refer to NATO's military strategy I mean more than the plans adopted and the forces controlled by the organization's formal instrumentalities, such as the Council, the Military Committee, and SHAPE. Rather, I refer to the whole complex of member-states' plans and capabilities that bear upon the security of the NATO area. These include, most significantly, America's and Britain's strategic nuclear forces, which are under purely national control.

most heavily upon the most powerful members of the alliance—and, pre-eminently, upon the United States.

NATO's strategic problems would be intractable enough merely as the subject of a logical exercise in military planning for the purposes of deterrence and defense—military strategy has never required such systematic and sophisticated planning on the basis of such imponderable factors. But the task of reconciling allied security and cohesion compounds the inherent complexity of military strategy with domestic and interallied, as well as with external, political considerations. The resulting military-political problems illustrate an important general proposition: In the real world neither national nor coalition strategy can or should reflect a purely military logic. We should not let our fascination with the intricate calculus of deterrence obscure that fact by giving military strategy the illusion of scientific precision.

NATO is built around a solid core of identical security interests, but its members do not always agree upon the means of promoting them or find the political consequences of promoting them mutually acceptable. One reason is that national military strategy affects, and is therefore affected by, strong domestic political, economic, and psychological pressures. Since military power under contemporary conditions depends heavily on the size and composition of forces-in-being, which impose a large and continual drain upon national resources, these domestic pressures are especially marked where strategy impinges upon public expenditures, individual taxes, notions of fiscal soundness, the conscription of manpower, and the allocation of money and manpower to the separate armed services. But there are no less significant pressures of a moral or emotional nature, particularly those that spring from popular reactions to the control of nuclear weapons—reactions that run the gamut from pride and bravado to revulsion and timidity, but that have only a tangential relationship to military logic.

Coalition strategy adds to domestic pressures the complications of foreign pressures, which spring from the requirement that a number of nations with various interests, policies, and levels of power collaborate in a common plan. Since military coalitions are created to promote only a fraction of their members' total interests—many of which interests conflict with each other and even diverge from the central purposes of the alliance—strategic collaboration depends upon a continual process of political accommodation within a field of shifting allied interests and policies, as each of the contracting parties tries to secure the terms of collaboration most compatible with his own objectives.

Military plans—especially as they determine the armament, the economic and military contributions, and the strategic and tactical roles of an ally—can affect the political relations and prestige of that ally in concrete ways that seem of more immediate significance than their conjectural implications for military security. The rearmament of West Germany, the allied force levels recommended by the North Atlantic Council, the deployment of British and American troops on the Continent, the control and command of nuclear weapons on allied soil—strategic issues like these will continue to affect allied political interests that seem more urgent than the hypothetical requirements of security against Soviet aggression. Indeed, in a period of protracted political warfare and maneuver, each member must assess the implications of military strategy for his national interests by broader criteria than deterrence and defense. And the greater the claims of strategy upon his economic and material resources, his manpower, and his independent control of armed force, the more closely he must weigh the alleged security assets of that strategy against the possible liabilities that the terms of collaboration impose upon his ability to support special national interests, which other allies may not share.

In the absence of an actual or imminent overt military threat, the speculative character of military strategic calculations enhances the natural predisposition of democratic states to subordinate the functional requirements of collective security to more urgent and immediate demands of domestic and foreign pressures, which may be only indirectly, if at all, related to security. Consequently, a peacetime alliance like NATO is bound to generate a continual tension between the requirements of security and cohesion almost in proportion to the extent of collaboration it requires.

The extensive collaboration that NATO requires is reflected most concretely in the mutual commitments and contributions it embodies. In order to provide its members with more security than they could obtain outside the alliance, NATO requires from them certain commitments (that is, obligations to participate in common decisions and actions under stated conditions) and certain contributions (principally, money, weapons and equipment, and manpower). But these commitments and contributions also entail liabilities, such as the risks of military involvement, the limitations upon independent action, and economic, material, and manpower costs. Therefore, each ally must predicate his collaboration upon a balance of security advantages that outweighs these liabilities. Yet, since his own security depends upon the effective collaboration of others, each ally who expects a net advantage from the alliance must respect and cultivate the incentives of other allies to collaborate, even while he tries to secure the most advantageous terms of collaboration for himself. For this purpose an ally can grant concessions, by increasing his commitments and contributions; or he can employ sanctions, by reducing or threatening to reduce his commitments and contributions.

Clearly, such concessions and sanctions have political consequences and must therefore become involved in the process of political accommodation. Conspicuously among the North Atlantic allies, the accommodation of divergent foreign interests and policies—especially those that impinge directly upon the configurations of power in Europe—has been an integral part of the process of strategic collaboration. In fact, not only has political accommodation been a precondition of strategic collaboration; strategic collaboration has become an important instrument of political accommodation. For the terms of collaboration have served as a major medium through which the allies have sought to promote their respective political interests. Thus, France's policy toward military integration and the control of nuclear weapons in NATO or West Germany's contribution and commitment to the alliance, although military issues on the surface, have actually pertained at least equally to the political issues of France's prestige and influence vis-à-vis the "Anglo-American bloc" and the place of a resurgent Germany in Europe.

This politicization of allied military policies reflects the limitations that the general military and political environment, as well as the particular constrictions of NATO, impose upon other means by which the allies might exert their political influence. Economically and militarily, the NATO states lack the power to support many of their vital interests independently of the alliance. Politically, they are unable to promote their interests by leaving the alliance or by shifting their weight from one alignment or alliance to another. The commitments and contributions exacted by NATO further constrict their room for independent political maneuver. Therefore, the allies pursue their policy goals, in large measure, by seeking the terms of collaboration that will enhance their influence and promote a favorable configuration of power within the alliance.

At the same time, to further compensate for their loss of political independence, the allies try to retain control over international relations more directly by asserting their voice in the determination of joint allied policies concerning relations with the Soviet bloc. To the extent the allies surrender independent control of their military capacity to support special interests in order to promote, instead, their common interests in a collective effort, they must seek control over foreign policy by political consultation, accommodation, and agreement with their allies instead of by unilateral means. This channel of political influence has become increasingly important as NATO has assumed some of the characteristics of an integrated organization and as the Communist threat in Europe has manifested itself more intensively in political forms. The more dependent the allies have become upon strategic collaboration and military "interdependence," the more compelling their need for political co-operation has grown.

Thus, NATO has become a kind of military-political framework within which its members have pursued a variety of interests transcending military security, and NATO's military strategy has become an inseparable part of this framework. Some observers have contended that the resulting politicization of NATO's functions and the apparent absence of an imminent military threat in Europe mean that NATO must now find its chief purpose and source of cohesion in serving as an instrument of multilateral diplomacy and interallied accommodation. But the matter is not that simple, for as long as Soviet military power constitutes a threat to the allies' vital interests (whether manifested in an overt military form or, less directly, in a political form), the overriding purpose of NATO must be to enhance the military security of its members. That threat persists undiminished. Consequently, whatever non-military interests NATO may serve, outside or inside the alliance, the viability of the alliance depends upon sustaining allied cohesion at a sufficient level of strategic collaboration to meet the requirements of deterrence and defense. Inevitably and properly, the process of eliciting collaboration requires concessions to various domestic and foreign political interests which have little or nothing to do with military security. Yet there are critical limits to which the alliance can afford to sacrifice strategic logic for the sake of achieving political consensus. In the final analysis, the incentives for collaboration must spring from an understanding and acceptance of the concrete requirements of security.

If NATO had remained, as at the outset, essentially a traditional guaranty pact, simply committing its members to come to each other's assistance and calling for minimal peacetime collaboration, the dual task of reconciling the requirements of security and cohesion would not have been so formidable. But since the Korean War and the establishment of a central command shortly afterward, NATO has acquired the characteristics of an integrated military-political organization, exacting unprecedented peacetime contributions and commitments. Therefore, it is not surprising that NATO's strategy contains some logical anomalies that have sprung from the tension between the requirements of security and consensus. It contains disparities between stated objectives and actual capabilities, apparent contradictions between declaratory and operational strategy, and ambiguities in the declaratory pronouncements themselves.

From one standpoint, these contradictions and ambiguities can be regarded as the necessary price of cohesion, insofar as they enable the allies to live with intractable strategic dilemmas and conflicting interests that might disrupt collaboration altogether if they were subjected to the exacting demands of sheer strategic logic. But, from another standpoint, they must be regarded as a threat to both cohesion and security, insofar as they deprive the alliance of coherent rational incentives for effective collaboration and help perpetuate crucial strategic deficiencies.

7. ALTERED CONDITIONS OF SECURITY AND COHESION

In order to understand the way in which novel strategic problems have impinged upon NATO's core of mutual security interests, one must first understand the substance of that core of interests and the function of NATO in protecting it. The North Atlantic allies combined, principally, to protect their common interest in preventing the extension of Soviet control and influence in Europe, and this remains NATO's central purpose. However, other instruments might possibly serve the same purpose; for example, several bilateral pacts or simply a unilateral American commitment like the Monroe Doctrine. Why should there be a multilateral mutual-assistance alliance, let alone one exacting such extensive commitments and contributions?

Proponents of the North Atlantic alliance have attributed two primary advantages to this particular kind of alliance: (*a*) by binding several nations to regard an attack upon one as an attack upon all, it creates a more effective deterrent to aggression; (*b*) by combining the power of several nations, it creates a more effective defense against aggression. The first advantage depends upon the credibility of a joint political commitment.

The second depends upon the efficacy of collective military planning, decision, and action.

However, since the United States has held the preponderance of power in the alliance, the realization of both these advantages has depended largely upon the extent to which this unique kind of military-political instrument augments America's commitment to deterrence and defense in Europe. Yet fundamental changes in the military and political environment and in NATO itself have largely destroyed the original conditions that made this dependence upon the American commitment a satisfactory basis of allied security and cohesion.

From the beginning, the fundamental strength of the North Atlantic Treaty has been thought to lie in the simple commitment of the United States to come to the defense of Europe. Extensive collective military planning and organization arose in response to military and political developments that were not foreseen at the outset. From the beginning, America's allies have been enthusiastic, if occasionally anxious, proponents of the first conception; the United States (together with West Germany) has been the most ardent and active proponent of the second.

The founders of the Treaty, wary of America's history of isolation and conscious of Europe's dependence upon American intervention in two world wars, believed that a truly entangling alliance, formally binding the United States within the mutual obligations of several states, was essential to make America's commitment to come to the defense of Europe convincing to the potential aggressor and to the potential victims of aggression as well.[8] This consideration, combined with the precedent of the Brussels Treaty and the American preference for a regional security organization consonant with Article 51 of the United Nations Charter rather than bilateral pacts resembling "old-fashioned balance-of-power agreements,"[9] accounts for the multilateral character of the North Atlantic Treaty. But it does not account for the fact that the alliance is not only a guaranty pact but also an organization for extensive military collaboration.

As long as the alliance remained, essentially, a multilateral framework for reinforcing America's guaranty to involve herself in the defense of Europe, the problem of strategic collaboration scarcely existed. But, in the course of events which I shall describe in succeeding chapters, the alliance became more than this. Notably, in the aftermath of the North Korean invasion, it began to assume some of the attributes of an integrated military organization, with the establishment at the beginning of 1951 of a central headquarters (Supreme Headquarters Allied Powers Europe) commanded by General Dwight D. Eisenhower as Supreme Allied Commander in Europe (SACEUR), followed in early 1952 by the creation of two other Supreme Commands: one for the Atlantic (SACLANT) and another for the English Channel and southern North Sea (Channel Command).* This development greatly increased the military potential of the alliance, but it also burdened it with an unprecedented task of peacetime strategic collaboration.

Combined with this change in the structure of the alliance, certain radical developments in military technology and the balance of military power—most notably the production of the H-bomb, the growth of Soviet nuclear striking power, and the prospect of several allies building their own nuclear capabilities—have complicated the problem of effective strategic collaboration, while undermining the original basis for dependence upon the American entanglement. The complications are reflected in significant doubts and apprehensions revolving around four central strategic issues: the efficacy of America's capacity for massive retaliation as a deterrent; the function of ground forces; the role of nuclear and conventional weapons; the control of nuclear weapons.

* NATO forces under these central commands are, partly, assigned to NATO under continuous operational control and, partly, earmarked for assignment either on mobilization or the outbreak of war. Generally speaking, SACEUR's tactical air forces and standing land forces are assigned; naval and reserve forces are earmarked. Thus SACLANT, unlike SACEUR, does not have forces permanently assigned to him in peacetime; but the eight maritime powers in the Atlantic Command have earmarked certain of their naval forces for SACLANT in the event of war.

These issues strike at the core of the mutual security interests that bind NATO together as a working defensive alliance. Their resolution is crucial to its security and cohesion. But, beyond their challenge to the viability of NATO strategy, they pose anew the fundamental question of the utility of a multilateral military alliance in an international system sustained by a balance of terror.

2
The Initial Phase

1. THE ALLIANCE AS A POLITICAL GUARANTY

The North Atlantic Treaty, signed in Washington on April 4, 1949, formally registered a widespread belief on both sides of the Atlantic, which had crystallized during the Berlin blockade, that Soviet encroachment upon Europe could be prevented only if the United States associated herself, in a firm and formal entanglement *before* the outbreak of war, with the efforts of Western European nations to defend themselves.

In the spring of 1948 the Soviet Union seemed determined to seize the invaluable prize of Western Europe by political infiltration and subversion on the model of the Czechoslovakian coup, but she confronted the consolidation of an opposing bloc through the Marshall Plan and the Brussels Treaty. Viewing these manifestations of "capitalist-imperialist" solidarity as hostile threats to Russia's natural hegemony in Eurasia, the Soviet leaders were all the more determined to destroy the opposing bloc in order to make the world safe for Soviet Communism. Hence, they decided to apply more intensive pressure against the gathering opposition by isolating and seizing Berlin, which was the key to Germany, the crucial area in Russian plans ever since the Communists came to power in 1917. The Soviet threat against Berlin and West Germany was not a Hitlerian "blitzkreig" but a cautious, well-conceived plan of political and psychological warfare.[1] Nevertheless, in Soviet and Western calculations the conduct of this non-military warfare was closely affected by the general military balance.

There is no indication that Stalin wished to pursue his designs upon Western Europe by engaging Western forces in direct combat. He had gained a healthy respect for the vast and untouched military potential of the United States in World War II, and he evidently believed that another world war would be decided by the same "permanently operating factors."[2] On the other hand, he had demonstrated in the Czechoslovakian coup that he appreciated the utility of superior local forces-in-being as a backstop for political take-over; and he was undoubtedly conscious of similar opportunities in Berlin, which were offered by the disintegration of the Western occupation forces and the precipitant withdrawal and demobilization of American troops. For soon after the war there were only about a dozen scattered, under-strength Western divisions in Europe, while Russia maintained 25 fully armed divisions in Central Europe and, over-all, at least 140 of 175 divisions at battle strength (not counting the numerous satellite divisions).

At the time of the Berlin blockade, the United States, with total ground reserves of about 2⅓ divisions, was unable to send more than a division anywhere without resorting to partial mobilization. In the Department of Defense the West's position in Berlin was considered militarily untenable, and the government soon decided that American forces could not afford to try to break the blockade with an armed convoy. Although the United States enjoyed a monopoly of the atomic bomb and the capacity to deliver it, there were no plans or even inclinations to use the bomb in any contingency short of a massive assault upon Europe, and, in that event, it was generally assumed that Europe (at least to the Pyrenees) would soon be overrun anyway.[3] Only the unexpected success of the airlift—by a very narrow margin, at that—saved the West from the consequences of its local military inferiority.

The effect of this narrow escape was to accelerate the formation of the North Atlantic alliance (which was probably, in itself, an important factor in inducing the Russians to terminate the blockade as a political liability). However, the statesmen who formed the alliance did not generally envisage it as a means of redressing the military imbalance on the Continent but rather as the means of committing America's military potential to the defense of Europe in order to bolster Western European resolution and deter further Soviet incursions with a show of trans-Atlantic solidarity. The deterrent effect was believed to lie chiefly in American and European adherence to Articles 5 and 3, in which the parties agreed "that an armed attack against one or more of them in Europe or North America shall be considered an attack against them all"; that if such an attack occurred, each party would "assist the Party or Parties so attacked by taking forthwith, individually and in concert with the other Parties, such action as it deems necessary, including the use of armed force to restore and maintain the security of the North Atlantic area"; and that, according to Article 3, the parties would undertake "by means of continuous and effective self-help and mutual aid, to maintain and develop their individual and collective capacity to resist armed attack."

Militarily, deterrence was almost completely dependent upon America's Strategic Air Command, which was (and still is) outside allied control, and the combined American-European war potential, especially their superior industrial and scientific capacity. Both of these military resources were expected to perform in another general war the same vital role they had performed in the recent one. Actually, it is quite doubtful that the United States had the bombers, the bomber bases, or even the atomic bombs to stop the Red Army from rolling to the Channel.[4] But NATO was not created to marshal military power, either in being or in potential, in order to deter an imminent attack on Europe. Like Russia's huge army, it was intended to provide political and psychological reinforcement in the continuing political warfare of the cold war. There was no significant fear of a massive Russian invasion.

It was true in 1949, and it is true now, that there would be no compelling reason for this trans-Atlantic alliance if Western Europe could prevent and withstand Communist encroachment by itself. Clearly, this was not the case in 1949. One who appraises the alliance today must ask whether America's formal commitment and tangible contribution to Europe's defense continue to be necessary, militarily and politically. If they are not necessary, then perhaps we need concern ourselves with NATO strategy only as it may facilitate the transition to Western Europe's military self-sufficiency or as it may provide the framework for collective diplomacy and interallied accommodations. But, if they are necessary, we must recognize that the strategic conditions for retaining effective collaboration between the United States and her allies have grown vastly more formidable and complex.

In the initial phase of the North Atlantic alliance, before the Korean War and the emergence of the Soviet Union as a major nuclear power, the alliance embodied an obviously profitable balance of assets over liabilities for all its signatories and a clearly satisfactory distribution of benefits and burdens between the United States and her European partners. For collective defense seemed urgent, while the commitments and contributions it exacted were minimal; and the United States Navy and SAC were virtually the sole and, apparently, sufficient standing military deterrents.

To Britain and France, faced with the threefold problem of achieving a safe military posture in Europe and protecting overseas holdings while regaining their economic strength and meeting the new demands for social welfare programs—a problem compounded in Britain by an expensive atomic weapons program—America's formal political guaranty and her accompanying military and economic assistance seemed the only means of avoiding chronic overcommitment and recovering great-power status. To the other allies, also, NATO seemed to be an essential military and political framework for gaining by collective action the kind of security they could not readily reconcile with economic recovery in a purely European alliance. To the United States, now fully aware that its first line of defense lay overseas, and fully responsive to the European concern that America's political isolation should not again encourage aggression in Europe, the North Atlantic Treaty seemed like an indispensable instrument for extending deterrence and engendering political confidence overseas. Through it, the European states might recover the economic and military strength that would enable them eventually to contain the Soviet menace by themselves.

Despite the expectations of most military men that the alliance would ultimately rest upon a large integrated standing force actually capable of withstanding a Russian onslaught, the alliance was, essentially, in its initial phase, a guaranty pact designed to enhance the credibility of America's commitment to come to the defense of Europe. For psychological reasons the alliance declared itself bound to the objective of local defense, but for internal political and economic reasons it really relied upon America's threat of nuclear retaliation. This contradiction between declaratory strategy and actual capabilities, which was regarded as the price of allied cohesion in the initial phase, subsequently became a source of trouble and confusion when unforeseen developments undermined allied confidence in the original assumptions about the nature of the Soviet threat and the military balance between the Soviet Union and the United States.

2. TWO CONCEPTIONS OF THE ALLIANCE

The alliance in its original form reflected its antecedents in the efforts of Western European countries to organize their own common defense in the face of a succession of hostile Soviet acts. The failure of the Moscow Conference (in March and April, 1947) to reach a settlement of the differences between Russia and the West over Germany, Russia's active opposition to the Marshall Plan, her formation of the Cominform, her clandestine support of Italian and French strikes, and her seizure of Czechoslovakia in 1948—these ominous events moved Britain and France (already allied in the Dunkirk Treaty) to combine with Belgium, the Netherlands, and Luxembourg in the Brussels Treaty of March, 1948: a fifty-year military alliance pledging all its members to meet an "armed attack in Europe" upon any one member with "all the military and other aid and assistance in their power." In September the Brussels Treaty powers decided to form a Western Union Defense Organization, embodying a Consultative Council of Foreign Ministers and a Defense Committee, assisted by joint chiefs of staff (of which Field Marshal Lord Montgomery was appointed chairman).

In the eyes of most of its members—and especially in the eyes of the British, for whom America's commitment to bolster their waning position in the Mediterranean and Europe had become the *sine qua non* of foreign policy—this prototype of the Atlantic alliance was the preliminary step to a wider association which would include the United States.[5] Although at the time the United States was not yet ready for formal alliance with the Brussels Treaty powers, the American government had officially encouraged them to believe that, as in the case of the Marshall Plan, their joint efforts would present the United States with a suitable basis for extending some kind of political support and material assistance;[6] and it continued the same kind of encouragement even more actively after the Western Union was established. In April, 1948, the Canadian Prime Minister, Mr. St. Laurent, suggested that the Brussels powers merge in a single defense system embracing the countries of North America and Western Europe. In July preliminary negotiations leading to the North Atlantic Treaty began in Washington.

Yet, among those on both sides of the ocean who looked forward to the enlargement of the Western Union into a trans-Atlantic pact, there were really two conceptions of the alliance —one largely political and the other envisioning large-scale military collaboration—which coexisted in ambiguous relationship to each other. The military planners in the United States and Europe were the most ambitious proponents of the expansion of Western Union into a full-fledged trans-Atlantic military coalition. After the signature of the Brussels Treaty, the American Joint Chiefs of Staff, convinced by hard professional experience that the American frontier lay on the Elbe, proposed a military alliance with the free nations of Europe, urged the immediate establishment of a central military command for Western

Union, and recommended an American supreme commander in the event of war.[7] When Field Marshal Montgomery of Alamein, an ardent advocate of defending Europe on the ground as far eastward as possible, was appointed commander in chief of the Western Union Defense Organization in September, 1948, his headquarters at Fontainebleau became the center for the formulation of far-reaching joint military plans by representatives from all the signatories in concert with American "observers."[8] American military collaboration proved invaluable in enabling the Brussels Treaty powers to draw up joint strategic plans and a list of military needs to support them, which the American Congress and administration regarded as the prerequisite of closer trans-Atlantic ties.

This joint military planning, looking toward a formal connection of the Western Union with the United States, received congressional approval and encouragement in June, 1948, in the Vandenberg Resolution, which proclaimed as American policy the "association of the United States by constitutional process with such regional and other collective arrangements as are based on continuous and effective self-help and mutual aid and as affect its national security." The approach to an Atlantic alliance was further advanced by Russia's imposition of the Berlin blockade at the end of June, for this crystallized the growing conviction among civilian leaders that the war-weakened European nations could not simultaneously recover their economic and political stability and build the military strength they needed to withstand Soviet pressure unless they received American material help and the assurance of American military support in a showdown.

On the other hand, civilian leaders in 1948 did not necessarily envision an Atlantic alliance as an instrument for constructing the full-scale integrated defense of Europe. Conspicuously, this was not the view of the American Congress, where Senator Vandenberg, one of the principal architects of America's membership in the North Atlantic Treaty, stressed the value of a simple political commitment in encouraging Europe and discouraging the Kremlin, while he explicitly repudiated the idea that the United States should help in building up a sizable force-in-being.[9]

The military planners, impressed by the painful lessons of breaking Germany's hold on the Continent in World War II, were acutely conscious of the West's inability to stop the Russians from rapidly rolling over the whole of Western Europe. They were unwilling to base the defense of Europe solely upon the deterrent effect of an American promise of liberation. Yet with the existing forces in Europe—about 12 ill-equipped and poorly trained divisions and 400 airplanes—they could plan for little more than a rapid withdrawal to the Pyrenees; whereas they looked forward to creating a combined military force of between 80 and 85 divisions (about one-third of which would be reserves capable of mobilization within a period of a few days to a month) to hold the crucial Rhine line and about 15 more to hold the Italian and Scandinavian flanks against a major invasion.[10] Their conception of a massive Continental defense system was also reflected in the United States' insistence, contrary to British civilian opinion, that the proposed Atlantic alliance should include nations outside the Western Union—Canada, Portugal, Denmark, Iceland, Norway, and Italy—who, even if they contributed little or nothing directly to ground defense, could provide valuable bases for American air and sea power.[11]

However, this conception of the proposed Atlantic alliance does not seem to have been fully shared even by all the key civilian planners. Some, in fact, held a conception that could only be regarded as in direct opposition if the underlying issues had been more sharply defined.[12] George F. Kennan, recalling in 1957 his participation as chairman of the State Department's Policy Planning Staff in formulating the terms of the pact, wrote that he conceived the alliance in 1948 and 1949 as simply the means of restoring Western Europe's self-confidence and providing a modest military shield, behind which the West would proceed with the prior task of economic reconstruction and, ultimately, the creation of "a new ordering of international relations . . . so patently worthy and inspiring in itself, and so wholly without menace to anyone anywhere, that peoples could safely repair to it without raising military issues." Despite the adverse military balance in Europe, he said that he never supposed that the alliance was intended to redress the military balance in the face of any imminent danger.

> In all of this NATO had, as a military alliance, its part to play; but I think every one of us hoped that its purely military role would decline in importance as the curse of bipolarity fell from the Continent, as negotiations took place, as armies were withdrawn, as the contest of ideologies took other forms. The central agency in this concept was not NATO but the European Recovery Program; and none of us dreamed at that time that the constructive impulses of this enterprise, which looked to everyone so hopeful in those days, would be overtaken and swallowed up in the space of a mere two or three years by programs of military assistance based on a wholly different concept of the Soviet threat and of Europe's needs.[13]

Certainly, Kennan's conception of European security embodied the profound hopes of many statesmen and political leaders on both sides of the Atlantic. Yet their conception of the alliance was too ambiguous to be so clearly distinguished from that of the military. On the one hand, all shared the hope that President Truman expressed in his inaugural address in January, 1949, that "if we can make it sufficiently clear, in advance, that any armed attack affecting our national security would be met with overwhelming force, the armed attack might never occur."[14] As the British Foreign Minister Ernest Bevin put it:

> I would emphasize . . . that the real purpose of this pact is to act as a deterrent. . . . The situation which we had in 1914 and 1939 and particularly 1940 and 1941, when we had to hold the fort waiting and wondering when other nations would realize the gravity of the aggressive menace, while at the same time we were using up and exhausting our resources—that situation should not be allowed to occur again.[15]

But, on the other hand, allied governments also envisioned the alliance as more than a deterrent commitment disposing only a modest military shield to protect the main task of economic recovery. For they said that they looked forward to the eventual establishment of an armed force capable of redressing the military balance on the Continent and repelling a full-scale invasion. And, although the European allies insisted that economic recovery should have priority over rearmament and welcomed United States indorsement of this axiom,[16] they also pressed the United States with some urgency to remedy their exposed condition as quickly as possible by shoring up their new political commitment with military assistance.

Yet allied governments seem to have regarded this strategy of local defense as more of a political gesture than a military necessity. For insofar as they implicitly subscribed to the military planners' conception of the alliance, it was less from fear of an imminent Soviet attack than from the fear that, if an attack should come, the alliance, instead of protecting them from invasion, could at best only liberate them after another disastrous defeat and occupation. As the French Premier Henri Queuille told an American reporter, in a much-quoted statement:

> We know that once Western Europe was occupied, America would again come to our aid and eventually we would again be liberated. But the process would be terrible. The next time you probably would be liberating a corpse.... The real frontier of Western Europe which must be defended must be moved well beyond the actual frontiers, because once the geographic frontiers of these countries are crossed it will be too late for America to save very much. Even fifteen days after the invasion will be too late.[17]

This did not imply, however, that France foresaw any real likelihood of a Russian sweep through Europe; the fear of Soviet aggression did not seize the European allies until the outbreak of the Korean War, and then only briefly.

The French were particularly articulate in calling for what became known after the Korean War as a "forward strategy." However, this was not because they expected a Soviet attack but rather because they were obsessed with suspicions, stimulated by World War II experience, that, if an attack *did* occur, British and American strategists would be content to conduct the defense of Europe from beyond the Continent or behind the Pyrenees.[18] American planners were attentive to such fears and suspicions and repeatedly declared their determination to protect the homelands of all allies. If the British, like some so-called American isolationists, harbored a traditional preference for a "peripheral" strategy, they officially suppressed it in deference to French sensitivities and, more important, to the requirements of firmly entangling the United States in a commitment to come to their defense. Thus, quite apart from its military feasibility, the repeated indorsement of a forward strategy was conceived to be a political and psychological necessity.

However, the material support of this declaratory strategy was another matter. Since the potential aggressor enjoyed at least a 10 to 1 ratio of numerical superiority in standing divisions and an even greater superiority in trained reserves that could be quickly mobilized, the protection of Europe from another cycle of occupation and liberation would seem to have required the European allies to rearm on a massive scale in order to create and maintain an adequate holding force in a constant state of combat readiness. Yet, as a matter of fact, in the absence of the fear of an imminent attack, neither the European countries nor the United States were remotely prepared to undertake a rearmament effort of this magnitude. The Europeans were unwilling to jeopardize their economic revival or aggravate their political instability; the United States was unwilling to redress the military balance by itself.

In truth, European governments were contending with contradictory popular demands. In order to persuade their parliaments and citizenry to accept the possibly provocative commitments of the North Atlantic Treaty, they felt it necessary to assure them that the alliance could actually protect their countries from invasion. But, in order to persuade them that their commitments would not require intolerable sacrifices, they felt it necessary to assure them that military expenditures would be modest and subordinate to the advancement of their standards of living.[19] Actually, these two assurances could only be fulfilled, if at all, by the participation of West Germany in the alliance, but for political reasons this measure was no more acceptable to the European countries than a massive rearmament effort.

Taking note of the conflict between domestic economic goals and rearmament, the London *Times,* in an editorial on March 11, 1949, saw two choices facing Western leaders.

> In making an Atlantic Pact the leaders of the Western powers had a choice of two methods. They could begin, so to speak, by building the inner keep or fortress and leave the outer walls until this was strong enough to resist assault; or they could start at once with the city walls and hope that these would provide sufficient protection while the main work of fortification went on inside.[20]

The *Times* believed that the United States had chosen the second method, because the assurance that the United States would come to the aid of her allies was not a sufficient guaranty of their security unless she could actually protect them from occupation. However, the truth of the matter seems to be that neither the United States nor her allies saw any such clear-cut choice before them. Rather, they were determined to pursue both goals simultaneously by raising the outer walls just enough to encourage unimpeded progress on the inner keep, while promising to build adequate outer walls for which they had no real plans, in their confidence that American nuclear power would deter an assault on the inner fortress in any case.

In view of the prevailing assumption, then and now, that Western Europe's "outer walls" cannot possibly counterbalance the mobilized masses of the Soviet bloc, it is well to note at the outset that the failure to create forces capable of local resistance has not been dictated by any physical deficiency in war potential; in population, financial resources, and productive capacity, the NATO countries are collectively superior to the Soviet Union and her eastern satellites.[21] It has resulted, in part, from the greater number of military personnel the Western powers employ to support effective fighting divisions (the "division slice," in technical parlance) and the greater expense per man, which result from the extensive service and supply forces attached to Western divisions and the high standard of living that all Western forces enjoy.[22] But, basically, the failure has resulted, first, from the political incapacity of democratic nations to exact the domestic sacrifices and adopt the concerted measures that are necessary to prepare for war during peacetime and, second, from their facility for wishfully believing that what is politically palatable is militarily adequate. Of course, military plans must adjust to the realities of popular will no less than to the realities of manpower, technology, and production; but one must hope that this adjustment will not be made before the real strategic choices are presented and popular will is put to the test of enlightened leadership.

3. AMERICAN MILITARY ASSISTANCE

In the United States the choice between a guaranty pact, such as Kennan envisioned, and an integrated military organization, such as the military planners wanted, was never made so clear as during the debate over military assistance to Europe. But although Congress approved a military assistance program of $1.3 billion, the great bulk of which was earmarked for Europe, the underlying issue of the conception of the alliance that the program was intended to implement remained obscure.

Although the administration considered arms aid to be a necessary complement to the North Atlantic Treaty and encouraged the European governments to think likewise, it decided as a matter of legislative tactics to withhold presentation of this more controversial measure until the Treaty should be approved. In appealing for the approval of the Treaty, the administration denied that it contained any obligation to extend arms aid.[23] It explained that, in any case, rearmament would be limited to strengthening Europe's small existing forces so as to avoid impeding economic recovery, precipitating an arms race, or either provoking or tempting aggression.[24] And it denied that substantial numbers of American troops would be stationed in Europe or that Germany would be permitted to remilitarize, rearm, or contribute to allied forces.[25] To be sure, Secretary Acheson insisted that Europe must be protected from another liberation,[26] and General Bradley stated that "plans for the common defense of the existing free world must provide for the security of Europe without abandoning these countries to the terrors of enemy occupation." "Only upon that premise," he declared, "can nations closest to the frontiers be expected to stake their fortunes with ours in common defense."[27] Yet, insofar as the administration was forced to explain the material implications of these plans, it was content to suggest that the United States role would be merely to speed the process by which a revitalized and, perhaps, reunited Europe, given time, would become capable of defending itself.

Consequently, it is not surprising that this novel entangling alliance seems to have been approved by Congress and the nation with little understanding of its practical military implications, on the general assumption that it would exert a deterrent effect upon the Soviet Union while boosting the morale of Western Europe.[28] Thus Senator Vandenberg, among others, regarded the Treaty as merely a logical extension of the Monroe Doctrine, which was distinguished from old-fashioned military alliances precisely by the fact that its value depended upon the deterrent effect of a formal commitment rather than upon collaboration in building a common armed force.[29] Senator Taft, who opposed ratification of the Treaty, said that he preferred an explicit extension of the Monroe Doctrine to Europe but that he would nevertheless vote for the Treaty, because of its deterrent effect, if the Senate would specifically repudiate any obligation either to build up the armed forces of the eleven allies or to extend them continued aid for the next twenty years "under circumstances of which we have not the slightest conception today."[30]

The administration, while strictly limiting its request for military assistance, neither indorsed nor repudiated the objective of building up an armed force capable of withstanding Soviet aggression. On July 23, 1949, the day President Truman signed the North Atlantic Treaty, he presented a bill for military assistance to Congress. In his letter of transmittal the President described the military objective of American assistance in modest terms.

> The military assistance which we propose for these countries will be limited to that which is necessary to help them create mobile defensive forces. Our objective is to see to it that these

> nations are equipped, in the shortest possible time, with compact and effectively trained forces capable of maintaining internal order and resisting the initial phases of external aggression.[31]

But the President also declared:

> At the present time, the military power which is the greatest deterrent to aggression is centered in the United States, three thousand miles away from Europe. It must be made clear that the United States has no intention, in the event of aggression, of allowing the peoples of Western Europe to be overrun before its own power can be brought to bear. The program of military assistance now proposed is a tangible assurance of our purpose in this regard.[32]

How could a program designed only to equip and bring up to strength Europe's few existing divsions give a "tangible assurance" to the peoples of Western Europe that they would not be overrun by the huge forces available to the potential aggressor? Of course, nobody claimed that Western Europe could become capable of defending itself against an all-out aggression with one American appropriation or in one year. "Our whole contention," General Bradley said, "is that it is going to take time . . . it may take five years, ten years, for these countries to build up their defenses to the point where they can stop an aggressor."[33] But, if the European allies were to become capable of defending themselves even in five or ten years, would this not mean that the Military Assistance Program of 1949 would be only a small down payment on a very large long-term investment in a ground force designed to resist a massive invasion in another large-scale land war? And, if this were not what the government contemplated, then would not the arms aid be only large enough to provoke the Russians and precipitate an arms race without being adequate to keep the Russians from overrunning Europe? These were questions that Senator Taft and other skeptics asked—and with considerable justice.

Secretary Acheson gave perhaps the only plausible answer. He repudiated the possibility of a European army ever approximating the huge Russian forces.[34] Although affirming the necessity of protecting Europe from occupation and liberation, he stressed a far more limited strategic objective of rearmament.

> We do not believe that to discourage military aggression it is necessary to create Western European defense forces which are by virtue of their size capable of successfully resisting an all-out attack. What is required is, rather, sufficient strength to make it impossible for an aggressor to achieve a quick and easy victory.[35]

In other words, he proposed a military shield only large enough to deter limited aggression by convincing the aggressor that he could not obtain his objective virtually unopposed.

This was a strategic objective that might have been consistent with the dimensions of the rearmament effort the United States and her allies were willing to undertake, but it did not meet the problem of defending Europe against an all-out assault if the deterrent should fail. By what strategy did the United States plan to achieve this objective? Published testimony on this question indicates that plans for defending Europe were patterned closely after World War II operations, with the atomic bomb providing an additional element of firepower. However, the congressional hearings of August and October, 1949, which were precipitated by the conflict between the Navy and Air Force over the B-36 bomber program, indicate that there was some difference of opinion among military planners about the capacity of strategic bombing to defeat the enemy without large-scale land operations.

There was general agreement among the military that a Soviet attack would come in the form of a massive blitzkrieg upon Europe and the United States simultaneously, and that Europe would have to be defended initially by a European force that could hold the front long enough for the weight of American military strength to exert a decisive influence. Enthusiasts of airpower, however, were confident that a full-scale atomic counteroffensive against the heart of the enemy's war-making power (first his weapons and bases and then his industry) would secure victory fairly quickly without requiring a costly war of attrition between surface forces;[36] but Army and

Navy planners—of whom General Bradley, the chairman of the Joint Chiefs of Staff, was the most prominent spokesman—anticipated that, despite the great role of airpower, victory would depend eventually upon large-scale land operations, sustained by control of the sea, which would defeat the opposing armies.[37]

Everyone planned to fight World War III on the assumption that the United States would enjoy a virtual monopoly or a meaningful superiority of atomic striking power, and no one anticipated that she might be deterred from employing this power by a Soviet capability to strike back;[38] but it is significant that, nevertheless, there was substantial opposition on political as well as military grounds to the thesis that strategic airpower obviated the need for massive conventional surface operations. In the B-36 controversy naval officers argued against this thesis on the ground that the indiscriminate annihilation of civilians was immoral and contrary to the achievement of a stable peace after the war.[39] But General Bradley, who dissociated himself from the Navy's polemics against civilian bombing, was confirmed in his adherence to the conception of large-scale land warfare by another non-military consideration, which related directly to allied cohesion. As he expressed this consideration in a major address in April, 1949:

> It must be perfectly apparent to the people of the United States that we cannot count on friends in Western Europe if our strategy in the event of war dictates that we shall first abandon them to the enemy with a promise of later liberation. Yet that is the only strategy that can prevail if the military balance of power in Europe is to be carried on the wings of our bombers and deposited in reserves this side of the ocean. It is a strategy that would produce nothing better than impotent and disillusioned allies in the event of war.[40]

General Bradley's statement was directed not only to the allies but also against Senator Taft and other opponents of the military assistance program, with whom the thesis of victory-primarily-through-strategic-airpower was especially popular. Senator Taft saw no reason to build up a large army in Europe, considering the claims of the airpower enthusiasts; and he charged that the administration, in asking for a military assistance program, was really committing the country to a futile, obsolete, and bankrupting strategic concept of defending Europe by large-scale land warfare.[41] Yet Senator Vandenberg, who accepted the military assistance program—although unenthusiastically, after making sure that it would be kept to a minimum—shared Taft's aversion to building sufficient forces-in-being to hold the line against Russia. He conceived the chief function of European forces as assuring adequate defense against internal subversion; he was content to rely upon the "potentials" of the United States and her allies to deter aggression.[42]

Thus both Taft and Vandenberg, although they voted differently on the Military Assistance Act, which was designed to implement the North Atlantic Treaty, vigorously opposed a strategic conception that leading military and civilian officials of the administration said was indispensable to the cohesion of the alliance. In fact, it is doubtful that *any* of the senators who approved the modest arms-aid appropriation accepted the full implications of the strategy that General Bradley advocated. Consequently, the Mutual Defense Assistance Act of 1949 represented a cloudy compromise between divergent conceptions of the alliance, based upon a tenuous connection between strategic objectives and military means. The administration had failed to acknowledge or resolve the contradictions between declared strategic objectives, war plans, and actual capabilities. Congress had indorsed the results.

4. THE STRATEGIC CONCEPT FOR INTEGRATED DEFENSE

It was unanticipated events rather than a coherent design that later transformed the alliance from a multilateral guaranty pact into a semi-integrated military organization. Yet, in one respect, the United States Congress laid the foundation for this transformation when, in order to insure the use of military aid for collective rather than purely national purposes, it injected the statutory requirement that such aid be conditioned upon the development of joint strategic plans by the Treaty's defense committee.

Secretary of State Acheson stated the ultimate rationale of this requirement when he described the basis of allied defense as a revolutionary concept of a division of responsibilities. According to this concept, the allies would no longer maintain complete, balanced defense establishments but would, instead, specialize in the kinds of forces and military production for which each was best suited, within a pattern of integrated defense.[43] This was a concept of integration which not even the smallest allies were ready to carry very far. Yet, to a remarkable degree for a peacetime alliance, it was embodied in the strategic plans that were devised by the military representatives of allied countries and accepted by the civilian representatives of the alliance and the individual countries.

The very requirement of "an integrated defense of the North Atlantic area," which Congress had stipulated, gave impetus to the establishment in September, 1949, of the elaborate structure of civilian and military committees and planning groups that was to make the alliance an organization.* On December 1, 1949, the Defense Committee, composed of allied defense ministers, announced agreement upon a "strategic concept," which was indorsed by the North Atlantic Council on January 6, 1950, and on the basis of which bilateral aid agreements were negotiated.[44] On January 27 President Truman signed these agreements and announced his approval of the recom-

* The central policy-making organs in this structure were the North Atlantic Council, composed of the allied foreign ministers; the Defense Committee, composed of allied defense ministers; the Military Committee, consisting of the chiefs of staff of the member countries; and the Standing Group, the executive committee of the Military Committee, in which representatives of the United Kingdom, France, and the United States supervised the development of military plans by regional planning groups. In November, 1949, the Council established the Defense Financial and Economic Board, composed of allied finance ministers, and the Military Production and Supply Board, which was responsible to the Defense Committee. In May, 1950, the foreign ministers created a permanent civilian body, the Council Deputies, to be responsible for regular political exchanges among the member governments, for the execution of their directives, and for the co-ordination of the work of the subsidiary bodies of the alliance. At the Lisbon Conference in February, 1952, the North Atlantic Council was made a permanent body, with permanent representatives and a secretary general.

mendations for "an integrated defense of the North Atlantic area" based on individual national specialization.[45]

The strategic concept upon which the integrated defense plans were based was not made public, but it undoubtedly followed the outline of the concept that General Bradley had presented to Congress on July 29 after conferring with the Defense Committee of the Western Union.[46] Significantly, this concept involved a type and degree of national specialization of military functions which, under existing or foreseeable capabilities, was far more congruent with a guaranty pact than with an integrated defense system for the protection of Europe; for the United States function was confined to strategic bombing and protecting the naval sea lanes, while Europe was to provide the "hard core of the ground power in being." Nevertheless, at the time, this strategy and its concomitant division of labor seemed to fulfil the imperatives of security and cohesion adequately—or at least as adequately as the burdens of peacetime rearmament and economic recovery permitted.

5. TWO CRUCIAL ASSUMPTIONS UNDERLYING THE TERMS OF COLLABORATION

On the eve of the Korean War, NATO already embodied a degree of military collaboration that was unprecedented among peacetime coalitions. This collaboration was secured at the price of limiting allied contributions to the common defense to a level that was incompatible with NATO's announced strategic objective. However, the alliance so clearly enhanced the security of its members and provided such a satisfactory distribution of military and political benefits among them that the contradiction between declaratory and operational strategy was of little concern.

The United States, sharing an identical interest with the enfeebled countries of Western Europe in their economic recovery and security, extended them the assurance of an entangling alliance, supplemented by material assistance, without which they felt incapable of withstanding the kind of Soviet pressure displayed in the Czechoslovakian coup and the Berlin blockade.

In return, her European allies agreed to strengthen their forces and assume the obligation to defend Western Europe on the ground in accordance with a unified strategic plan. The United States backed up its guaranty to come to the defense of Europe by, in effect, extending the protective umbrella of the Strategic Air Command with the atomic bomb. In return, Europe provided the bases that the United States needed in order to strike effectively at the heart of Russia.

From the standpoint of the European allies these terms of collaboration contained only one significant liability: If America's atomic deterrent should fail and Russia should launch an all-out assault upon Western Europe, they would be overrun and occupied before they could be liberated. To offset this liability the United States assured her allies that NATO would protect every one of them from a Soviet invasion. Yet this assurance was not supported by the projected capabilities or by the strategic concept for the "integrated defense of the North Atlantic area."

The disparity between Russian and Western divisions immediately available for combat along the critical front in the center of Europe was on the order of 100 (including 22 Russian divisions ready on the forward line) to 12; yet it was generally assumed that 50 to 70 divisions would be necessary to defend this front, and the military plans devised by the Brussels Treaty powers in collaboration with the United States apparently called for 80 to 85, including reserves. The strategic conception adopted by the alliance at the behest of the United States Congress prescribed that the "hard core of the ground power in being" should come from Europe. But the European allies said they were incapable of strengthening their forces without jeopardizing their economic recovery and political stability unless the United States granted military as well as economic aid, while the American military assistance program, in accordance with the principle that economic recovery should have priority over rearmament, aimed only to bring existing European forces up to strength. Furthermore, although all military planners agreed that the participation of West Germany in the alliance was essential to the defense of Europe, all governments agreed that this was politically out of the question.

Nevertheless, the contradiction between NATO's declaratory strategy and operational capabilities failed to jeopardize the cohesion of the alliance—in fact, it promoted it—as long as the allies were confident of two crucial assumptions about the nature of the Soviet threat and the means of countering it. The first assumption was that America's capacity to strike at the heart of Russia with the atomic bomb would deter her from pursuing her aims by overt military aggression. The second assumption was that, therefore, Europe might safely proceed with the prior task of economic recovery while undertaking only minimum rearmament and, thereby, reduce her vulnerability to the most serious Soviet threat: subversion and indirect aggression.

The first assumption was based upon the prevailing image of the next war as a more devastating copy of the last, which would be precipitated by an all-out Soviet assault upon Europe and the United States. It was consonant with the general presupposition, as Churchill had declared, that America's monopoly of the atomic bomb, alone, had kept Russia from sweeping over Europe.[47] And it was consonant with the widespread disposition to believe—somewhat inconsistently with the urgency attributed to NATO's commitment to protect Europe from occupation and liberation—that the most serious security threat lay in the capacity of the large Communist parties in Western European countries to exploit economic and social dislocation under the shadow of Soviet military might. The second assumption followed logically from the first and from the more direct impact of known internal problems, as compared to conjectural external dangers.

It is no more demonstrable now than at the time (though it is more dubious in retrospect) that America's possession of the atomic bomb and the means of delivering it played such a decisive role in deterring Russia from sweeping over Europe. Probably Stalin's respect for America's war potential and his consciousness of Russia's great human and physical losses were equally important deterrents in the light of his image of a major war as a protracted massive conflict in which the "permanently operating factors" would be decisive and in the light of his preference for political warfare where war would involve the Red Army in a direct large-scale encounter. The attribution of deterrence must always be a highly conjectural inference about calculations in other minds of which we have no firsthand knowledge, but our own common experience tells us that deterrence is seldom a product of a single factor. Yet, whatever factors may have saved Europe from invasion, as long as the Soviet Union refrained from undertaking or supporting direct military aggression, it was plausible to believe that the Communist threat to Europe lay chiefly in Europe's own weakness. As John Foster Dulles, then a senator, reasoned in approving the military assistance program in September, 1949:

> The information given me, publicly and privately, by our own government and by heads and leaders of European governments, does not indicate that the Soviet Union now contemplates open military aggression in Europe. Direct military aggression is not the preferred weapon of the Communist Party that controls the Russian government. . . . It does not seem likely that Soviet leaders would now switch from methods at which they are superior and with which they have reason to feel they are winning, in order to use methods at which they are inferior.
>
> The time may come when Soviet Communist methods of penetration and indirect aggression cease to be effective, both in the East and the West, and it may be that at that time there will be a critical moment, when open war or peace will hang in the balance. But in the view of the great vista of conquest opened up to the Soviet Union in the Far East by virtue of its present methods, direct military action does not seem to be imminent in the opinion of most competent observers, including the military.[48]

However plausible these two assumptions may have been, two developments combined to undermine allied confidence in them and, correspondingly, in the adequacy of NATO strategy. One was the emergence of the Soviet Union as a nuclear power, marked by the Soviet explosion of an atomic device in August, 1949. The other was the outbreak of the Korean War. The impact of the Korean War was more drastic and immediate but more transitory. The impact of Soviet nuclear power has been more fundamental but more gradual and diffuse. NATO was transformed by the Korean War, and the consequences were soon evident. The full implications of the growth of Soviet nuclear power for the security and cohesion of NATO are still unfolding.

3
The Impact of Soviet Nuclear Power

1. THE STRATEGIC RESPONSE TO RUSSIA'S NUCLEAR EXPLOSION

Logically, the Soviet explosion of an atomic device in August, 1949, some three years ahead of the West's expectation, should have caused a major revision of NATO's strategy and capabilities, if the general belief in the decisive deterrent effect of America's atomic striking power was correct. For, certainly, NATO's overwhelming dependence upon the Strategic Air Command (which was under American, not NATO, control) would become a far less reliable and reassuring deterrent once the United States could no longer devastate Russia with atomic bombs without expecting the atomic devastation of Western Europe and even the United States in return.

A few statesmen followed Churchill's lead in urging that Russia's achievement of an atomic explosion made it imperative to seek a political accommodation of the cold war while America retained a definite atomic advantage.[1] But, so far as strategic implications were concerned, most civilian and military leaders who were in any way alarmed by the Russian achievement simply concluded that the United States had to maintain her nuclear superiority (which was conceived to mean, at that time, her ability to win a nuclear war as well as to deter one) by keeping ahead in the race for nuclear stocks and strategic bombers and proceeding to develop the hydrogen, or "super," bomb. And even those few who were concerned about the inefficacy or immorality of America's strategy of massive nuclear retaliation against non-nuclear aggressions could expect Russia to take about five years to acquire an air-atomic capability that would constitute a significant counterdeterrent by rendering the United States vulnerable to atomic assault.[2]

In any case, the ultimate implications of Russia's nuclear power for the security of Western Europe were too obscure to move allied governments to alter the generally satisfactory terms of collaboration their parliaments had so recently accepted, especially if that meant increasing their contributions to collective defense. Democracies have usually been reluctant to rearm in peacetime, but to adjust military policies and budgets to the hypothetical political and military import of an arms race in a revolutionary weapon system, whose effects would be so terrible as to challenge the rationality and credibility of using them—that is an unprecedented task to levy upon popular governments. It took the explosion of hydrogen bombs and the orbiting of earth satellites to induce the governments of NATO to begin the task of adjusting strategy to the condition of nuclear parity.

2. THE RISING FEAR OF NUCLEAR WARFARE

However, the obscurity of the new military technology's concrete strategic implications did not prevent the advance and spread of nuclear weapons technology from registering upon the consciousness of all governments and peoples in a more general way. In the West, the awesome advances in the technology of nuclear destruction soon created an uneasy balance between the desire to exploit this terrible power for compelling military and political advantages and the gnawing suspicion that the power was too fearful to be an advantageous instrument of policy except in deterring an adversary from using it. The first reaction is, perhaps, typical of nations just becoming, or about to become, nuclear powers; but, particularly in the United States and Great Britain, one can discern a steady trend toward the second reaction, which is reinforced by the apprehensions of non-nuclear powers.

If one were to plot the trend of rising nuclear apprehension on a graph, it would be a gradual slope broken by several steep rises, which mark the dramatic impact of spectacular events —particularly, America's announcement of a thermonuclear explosion at Eniwetok Atoll on November 1, 1952, followed a year and a half later by an official description of the stupendous area of destructive blast and radiation; the Soviet Union's revelation on August 8, 1953, that she had produced a true hydrogen bomb, followed by the Atomic Energy Commission's confirmation of two Soviet thermonuclear explosions in the same month; the unexpected contamination of Japanese fishermen on the "Lucky Dragon," some seventy-five miles from an American thermonuclear explosion in March, 1954; and, on October 4, 1957, Russia's launching of Sputnik, the first artificial earth satellite and the first of a succession of space exploits that dramatized Soviet scientific and military prowess.

In response to the apprehensions created by these dramatic events, the American government for several years continued the policy of strict official secrecy on the nature and effects of atomic weapons. Its reasoning seems to have been based less on the fear of revealing information to the Soviet Union than on the fear that the atomic facts would undermine the psychological basis of its strategy of "massive retaliation" by frightening the American public into defeatism or rashness, alarming allies and neutrals, and stirring up pressure for expansion of the military budget.[3] Nevertheless, even before the Eisenhower administration decided to inform the public about the basic effects of hydrogen bombs and about Russia's parity in this field (in February, 1954, and, especially, in February, 1955),[4] America's own hydrogen explosions and her guarded official admissions of their stupendous destructive effects helped arouse the very fears the government had tried to suppress. And, in the more general statements of American spokesmen about the horrors of nuclear war and the critical need of disarmament, the government, in effect, collaborated with the Soviet Union in crystallizing Western inhibitions against initiating the use of nuclear weapons and in convincing the entire non-Communist world that, as President Truman had said before leaving office in 1953, a thermonuclear war "is not a possible policy for rational men."[5]

3. MUTUAL DETERRENCE

As fear of nuclear war rose and spread throughout the world, abetted as much by the West's anxious advocacy of thermonuclear deterrence and disarmament as by Soviet "peace offensives" and "ban-the-bomb" campaigns, it became increasingly difficult to regard America's nuclear striking power as merely a supplement to the kind of total-war strategy that had defeated the Axis in World War II. Instead, the Strategic Air Command came to be viewed almost exclusively as a punitive deterrent, as a reprisal weapon designed to inflict such horrible damage that the aggressor would not dare launch a military attack, rather than as a means of securing a victory, in the traditional sense, once aggression had occurred.

Yet, as the emphasis shifted to the punitive-deterrent function of America's strategic striking power, the very condition that led to this emphasis—Russia's capacity to strike back at the deterrer—began undermining the credibility of America's resorting to massive retaliation except in response to an attack upon the United States or, possibly, to nuclear assaults upon her allies. In this sense, the basis of the military balance changed from unilateral nuclear deterrence to mutual nuclear deterrence.

It is significant that the depreciation of "massive retaliation" as a guaranty against conventional attacks upon other nations began even before the Soviet Union was presumed to have the capacity to destroy the United States by a surprise attack and before the United States was presumed to lack the capacity to destroy enough of the Soviet Union's strategic force on a first strike to confine her retaliatory damage to an acceptable level.

Surely this indicates that the trend cannot be halted or reversed in the missile age by any accretion of America's strategic striking power or by reaffirmations of America's determination to use it to defend her allies.

4. NUCLEAR DIPLOMACY

The inevitable decline of unilateral nuclear deterrence and the emergence of mutual deterrence gave the Soviet Union significant new leverage in conducting political warfare against the North Atlantic alliance. Even before Khrushchev dramatized Russia's growing nuclear capability, Stalin had played upon the widespread fear of atomic warfare to promote the classic Communist tactic of championing the "cause of peace" against the "warmongers." He had castigated Western moves toward collective defense—especially those leading to German rearmament and membership in NATO—as aggressive acts, which only a renunciation of military preparations, American overseas bases, and atomic weapons and the acceptance of conciliatory Soviet proposals could prevent from resulting in World War III. By alternating manufactured war scares with "peace offensives"—most notably, the world-wide campaign in 1950 to get signatures for the Stockholm Peace Appeal[6]—he had sought to neutralize America's nuclear striking power, the West's one conspicuous military advantage; undermine allied collaboration; and mobilize popular sentiment in favor of Soviet policy. But Khrushchev had new and more powerful cards in his hands, and he played them with greater skill.

Russia's achievement of a hydrogen bomb, her construction of a strategic air force, and, finally, her spectacular progress in ballistic missiles enabled Khrushchev to wage nuclear diplomacy both more boldly and more subtly. Now he could promise that any Western use of nuclear weapons—whether tactical or strategic—would be met in kind and that even the United States could not escape the terrible destruction of Soviet blows. And he could even suggest that the Soviet Union itself might initiate the use of nuclear weapons in sufficiently provocative circumstances. He exploited these new possibilities not only to neutralize America's nuclear guaranty but also to refine and extend the technique of "nuclear blackmail."[7]

In the most direct form of blackmail, Soviet spokesmen on a number of occasions pointedly reminded the United States and her European allies that they would be vulnerable to Soviet-initiated nuclear strikes if they did not cease or abstain from "provocative" acts; but these threats were intermixed with a less direct and more effective form of blackmail, which depended upon maneuvering the Western powers into a position in which the *United States* would have to threaten to initiate nuclear blows.

Some examples of the first tactic were the oblique threats of rocket retaliation against Britain and France during the Suez War of 1956,* the diplomatic notes and public statements about the vulnerability of prospective European missile bases during the NATO discussion of the placement of American IRBM's on the Continent in late 1957, the veiled threat during the Quemoy and Matsu crisis of 1958 to come to the aid of Communist China with nuclear and rocket weapons against American warships if China were attacked by the United States, the similar pledge extended to Cuba in 1960 (although subsequently called "symbolic"), and the threat in 1960 to obliterate European bases from which American espionage planes were discovered to have flown over "socialist" territory. Each of these threats was carefully timed, camouflaged, and qualified so as

* Contrary to a general impression, the Soviet government did not literally threaten to inflict nuclear blows on Britain and France unless they ended the Suez War. In a note to Prime Minister Eden, Marshal Bulganin condemned Britain and France for their Suez attack and asked, "In what position would Britain have found herself if she had been attacked by more powerful states possessing every kind of modern destructive weapon?" He added, "There are countries which need not have sent a navy or air force to the coasts of Britain but could have used other means, such as rocket technique." Then, calling on the British to end the war, Bulganin concluded, "We are fully determined to crush the aggressors and restore peace in the East through the use of force. We hope at this critical moment you will display due prudence and draw the corresponding conclusions from this." He sent a similar note at the same time to Premier Guy Mollet of France (*New York Times,* November 6, 1956, p. 10). However, by this time it was clear that the United States opposed the British and French intervention and would join in calling for its termination. For an analysis of the Soviet threat in its full political and military context, see Hans Speier, "Soviet Atomic Blackmail and the North Atlantic Alliance," *World Politics,* IX (April, 1957), 318–27.

to extract the maximum political advantage with a minimum risk of having to carry it out or seem to back down. Yet they were ominous indications of new Soviet strength and confidence in that they marked Khrushchev's determination to play the game of nuclear blackmail more openly and offensively and reflected his avowed conviction, especially after 1957, that Russia was playing from superior strength now that the military balance had decisively shifted in her favor.[8]

However, even more significant than these incidents as a manifestation of Khrushchev's new confidence in Soviet military ascendance was the subtle intermingling of diplomatic threats and overtures with pointed references to Soviet military strength and the horrors of nuclear war, which sustained the second Berlin crisis, launched in November, 1958.[9] For here it was the United States that was put in the position of threatening to plunge her allies and the whole world into a thermonuclear war in order to resist limited and ambiguous Soviet incursions in Berlin, while the Soviet Union represented her political demands as legitimate, conciliatory offers to stabilize a dangerous situation and remove a source of international tensions and war. As a means of splitting the alliance, weakening Western will and resolution, winning local political gains, and mobilizing the "forces of peace" behind Soviet diplomacy, this was, in the long run, by far the more dangerous form of nuclear blackmail.

The major Soviet political gains in the cold war are not likely to be won by Soviet threats to meet "provocations" with nuclear blows; for, as chapter vii (on the implications of missiles) suggests, in the missile age neither Russia nor the United States is likely to extract much political advantage from a first-strike strategy, however skilfully it may be exploited. On the other hand, if mutual deterrence remains relatively stable against the initiation of nuclear weapons by either side, the military balance will be all the more favorable to Soviet political and even military incursions beneath that threshold of violence, incursions which will put the onus of starting a nuclear war upon the victims of aggression.

In this respect, the Western powers have greatly assisted

Khrushchev's tactics by remaining so dependent upon a nuclear response to non-nuclear aggression. For the disturbing thing about NATO's reaction to Russia's nuclear diplomacy has been that the allied apprehensions it excites are directed less against the serious possibility of Soviet political and military incursions than against the prospect of American nuclear retaliation. Consequently, the growth of Soviet nuclear striking power has tended to undermine confidence in NATO's nuclear strategy and strain allied cohesion without inducing those measures that might mitigate NATO's nuclear dependence.

NATO's nuclear dependence, with Soviet nuclear ascendance, has undermined allied confidence in NATO's strategy in two ways: First, the allies suspect that the United States will *not* resort to massive nuclear retaliation against a less-than-massive aggression in Europe at the staggering cost of a thermonuclear assault upon the United States and that, therefore, America's nuclear striking power is unreliable as a deterrent against contingencies short of a direct attack upon the United States itself. Second, they fear that the United States *will* resort to massive nuclear retaliation against limited aggressions (inside Europe or outside), which NATO cannot effectively counter by less drastic means, and that, therefore, American retaliation will plunge them into a war of annihilation.

Therefore, to the extent that the European allies depend upon America's capacity for massive retaliation, they must anticipate that the United States may either leave them defenseless or drag them into a suicidal war. Both prospects jeopardize the cohesion of the alliance: the first, because it undermines confidence in America's connection with Europe; the second, because it increases the liabilities of Europe's connection with the United States. Moreover, NATO's nuclear predicament renders the allies vulnerable to political pressure, tending to subordinate the fear of aggression to the fear of nuclear war and the longing to relieve the tensions that the Soviet Union manufactures. It enables Moscow to put them in the position of either adhering rigidly to a fixed diplomatic position, backed only by reaffirmations of the nuclear threat, or appearing to resort to appeasement under duress.

5. STRATEGIC IMPLICATIONS

It is easier to discern the adverse military, political, and psychological consequences of Russia's growing nuclear striking power than it is to determine the strategic changes that are necessary to restore the military basis of allied security and cohesion. But among the many controversial strategic implications that have been derived from the changing military environment, the following seem to be the most significant and plausible:

a) As the Soviet capacity to devastate the United States grows, the essential deterrent to a nuclear attack on the United States and her allies is an obvious capability to deliver unacceptable damage to the Soviet Union with a retaliatory blow of massive or, in the event of limited Soviet nuclear strikes, proportionate scope. However, when, if not before, the Soviet Union has also acquired the capacity to deliver unacceptable retaliatory damage after being struck first (and in 1961 that condition already might exist), America's first-strike capability will have ceased to be a reliable deterrent to aggressions short of direct nuclear attacks. To stabilize the resulting "nuclear stalemate" (that is, the mutual deterrence of striking first with nuclear weapons) when both the Soviet Union and the United States can quickly launch a devastating blow permitting little warning, the virtual renunciation of a strategic first strike may become an essential supplement to an "invulnerable" second-strike or retaliatory capability, in order to avoid provoking nuclear attacks launched by fear and misapprehension of being struck first.

During the onset of the missile age the United States placed great emphasis upon stabilizing the nuclear stalemate by retaining an adequate second-strike capability and seeking agreements for mutual protection against surprise attacks launched by misapprehension. However, at the end of 1960 the government still had not fully taken account of the corrosive effect of the stalemate upon its declared strategy of initiating nuclear war against major conventional aggression in Europe.

b) In order to deter and counter less-than-massive aggressions in Europe and relieve the allies of the paralyzing choice between annihilation and capitulation, NATO needs a capacity to resist such aggressions by means short of total war. For, since the growth of Soviet nuclear power tends to deter the United States from initiating strategic nuclear strikes against non-nuclear operations, the temptation for the Soviet Union to instigate limited, indirect, and ambiguous forms of aggression increases, as does her capacity to exert political pressure under the shadow of her vast army.

Soon after the explosion of Russia's first atomic bomb, the State Department Policy Planning Staff concluded that, unless the West substantially increased its ground forces, Soviet nuclear power might reach such proportions by about 1954 as to create a serious danger of conventional aggression or of blackmail that depended on the threat of such aggression. This conclusion was embodied in the National Security Document NSC 68, which President Truman approved early in 1950. However, until the outbreak of the Korean War, budgetary restrictions precluded the government's acting upon it. In a more explicit attempt to counter the threat of local small-scale aggression in Europe, NATO publicly subscribed to a strategy of "intermediate" responses in 1957. But by 1961 the allies still had not provided the capabilities that the military considered necessary to support this strategy, and the American government—at least in its declaratory strategy—continued to rely upon nuclear retaliation rather than on local resistance to deter non-nuclear aggressions. Moreover, even those who accepted this strategic implication of the growth of Soviet nuclear power held differing views about the nature of potential limited wars in Europe and the means of resisting them: Should NATO plan to fight a large-scale limited non-nuclear war in Europe, or should it prepare only to meet border incidents and probing actions by non-nuclear means? Should NATO initiate the use of tactical nuclear weapons against conventional aggressions; if so, could a nuclear war be limited in any significant sense?

c) The protection of Europe from being overrun in a total war is no longer a feasible objective for NATO's ground forces. For since the Soviet Union has a substantial nuclear capability,

America's massive retaliation against a Soviet assault upon Europe would produce a nuclear holocaust that would be more devastating for the European allies than even a Soviet occupation. The logical implication of this is that in a full-scale invasion Europe can secure protection against annihilation or occupation not by relying upon massive land warfare and indiscriminate strategic bombing but only by relying upon the deterrent effect of controlled nuclear retaliation above the threshold of effective resistance by conventional (and, possibly, chemical) limited warfare.

In practice, the negative aspect of this implication was generally accepted by 1954, but NATO's capacity for local resistance continued to dwindle and the concept of tactical nuclear combat, rather than of controlled retaliation, predominated. Yet, in spite of the fact that NATO's original strategic objective of protecting every ally against the dreaded cycle of occupation and liberation by repelling a massive invasion had never been supported by actual capabilities, the psychological and political liability of renouncing it precluded an alteration of this declaratory strategy.

d) To offset the declining credibility of America's commitment to defend Europe at the cost of her own devastation, the United States must keep American troops on the Continent as a visible hostage to her NATO obligations.

This implication was accepted and acted upon. Although they were originally sent as a temporary boost to European rearmament, in 1960, five American divisions remained on the Continent on a semipermanent basis as a reassurance to Europe and a warning to Russia.

e) In order to compensate for the declining credibility of America's willingness to launch strategic nuclear strikes against aggression in Europe and to escape complete dependence upon the decision of the United States to use or not use nuclear weapons, the NATO countries must gain an equitable share of the control of the decision to use nuclear weapons. Some allies might seek this share by acquiring their own nuclear weapons;

others, by participating in a bilateral or multilateral system of control.

Like the other strategic implications of the growth of Soviet nuclear power, the case for sharing control of strategic nuclear capabilities is based on the imperatives of NATO's internal cohesion as well as of its external security. The very prospect of the diffusion of nuclear control, either under independent or joint control, will exert a fateful impact upon the security and cohesion of NATO, since it poses in the most acute form the question of whether an ally needs, or can afford, to base its security upon the decisions of others to go to war. Therefore, by the end of 1960 the control of nuclear weapons had become inextricably connected with NATO's other unresolved strategic issues.

Together, these inferences drawn from the growth of Soviet nuclear power, in spite of all their conjectural and controversial elements, impelled a major revision of NATO's strategy; but their immediate impact upon strategy depended more upon the catalyst of unanticipated crises, dramatic technological developments, and a variety of domestic and foreign political pressures than upon logical strategic analysis and foresight. Of all these immediate influences, the outbreak of the Korean War caused the most drastic revision of NATO's strategy and capabilities.

4
Rearmament and Relaxation

1. ALLIED INDIFFERENCE TO REARMAMENT

On the eve of the Korean War, NATO was already showing some strains from the conflict between its ambitious strategic objective and the natural reluctance of democracies to rearm in peacetime. The basic difficulty was that nations who were unwilling to rearm at the sacrifice of domestic economic and social objectives were, nevertheless, firmly committed to a strategy that called for counterbalancing a vastly larger military machine. But related to this difficulty was the lopsided distribution of power within the alliance, which made the United States the primary counterbalancer, coupled with a distribution of military functions that burdened the European allies and especially France with the unpalatable task of building up the forces-in-being, while the United States merely concentrated upon strategic airpower. The net result of these circumstances was to place the United States in the awkward position of pressing her allies, from the vantage point of her fortress three thousand miles away, to build up a Continental land army for the sake of a strategic objective—the physical defense of every ally—which they proclaimed as indispensable but which their practical preference for relying upon America's atomic deterrent made impossible to support.

European statesmen and politicians continued to call for official American and NATO reaffirmations of the pledge to protect the territory of every ally from Russian occupation.[1] The

United States and NATO continued to oblige.[2] Yet, according to press reports, the allies were planning on no more than 36 divisions in Western Europe by 1955, and by the spring of 1950 they were still unable to field more than 12 in the event of an emergency. France, which was to provide the core of ground forces, had pledged 24 divisions to NATO, but she could dispose only 3 divisions in West Germany and 6 in France, while 10 divisions were tied down in Indochina.[3]

The American government, having assumed the leadership of an effort to redress the dangerous military imbalance in Europe, became increasingly anxious as the cold war grew more intense to see signs of integrated defense planning and rearmament. In asking Congress for $1 billion in new military assistance for Europe, President Truman warned: "The military establishments of Western Europe are below the minimum level consistent with security. Those countries must build up their forces as swiftly as their resources permit, assisted by such help as we can afford."[4] But the European allies, feeling cold war tensions less directly than Russia's major antagonist, were increasingly sensitive to popular apprehensions that the United States concern to contain Russia might be shifting the order of priorities from economic recovery to an arms race just when production, trade, and income had begun to turn upward.

At the meeting of the North Atlantic foreign ministers in May, 1950, the United States urged positive action on new armed force commitments, the co-ordination of defense planning, and a re-examination of the German problem. However, the final communiqué of the conference said nothing of these matters but only emphasized that the "progressive and speedy development of adequate military defense" would be pursued "without impairing . . . social and economic progress."[5] Nevertheless, the more concerned the United States became about building up the defense of Europe, the more concerned an important body of Europan opinion became that the United States might subordinate Western Europe's social and economic progress and its very peace to purely American interests in the cold war.

In order to allay such apprehensions, the United States reaffirmed her belief that there was no imminent danger of overt aggression. Indeed, no event before the Korean War disturbed the general conviction that America's nuclear striking power was a sufficient guaranty of peace unless the United States herself should act rashly. Even Churchill, who was more alarmed than most by Russia's acquisition of nuclear power, said that a situation of "mutual terror" would give the West "the extra time and the new breathing space for the supreme effort which has to be made for a world settlement."[6] Therefore, it was easy to conclude that there really was no overriding need for a "progressive and speedy development of adequate military defense." As the French Socialist André Philip wrote on the eve of the Korean hostilities: "What menaces our existence today is not the immediate danger of war; I have less fear of the atom bomb and the hydrogen bomb than of the misery of the workers —a misery which could erupt into political and social chaos."[7]

2. TWO HOPES FOR RECONCILING SECURITY AND ECONOMY

If civilian goals were granted such a clear priority, if there was no sense of urgency in meeting the rearmament goals which the allies had agreed were essential for their defense, how could NATO ever hope to become capable of withstanding Soviet aggression? How could strategy be reconciled with economy? Two answers were given: (*a*) greater military integration and (*b*) powerful new weapons would enable NATO to get more security for less money.

Under Secretary Acheson, the foreign ministers' meeting in May, 1950, indorsed the principle, which had its legislative origin in the Mutual Defense Assistance Act of 1949, that adequate defense could be achieved only through "the most economical and effective utilization" of available resources by creating "balanced collective forces" on a basis of national specialization.[8] Carried out to its full logic, this principle might have enabled the allies to reconcile their military and civilian requirements, but it also would have made it difficult, if not impossible, for them to maintain independent control of sufficient forces to support purely national interests. It is not surprising, then, that the principle was not carried out sufficiently to reconcile the requirements of security and economy.

In the field of planning and command, the foreign ministers created the Council of Deputies—a permanent civilian body, headed by an American—to correlate the economic and defense planning of subsidiary bodies of the alliance. But the United States, like France, firmly resisted the establishment of a central military command with an American Supreme Commander, which the British were urging largely as a means of binding the United States more tightly to the defense of Europe. Nor was there complete agreement on the disposition and roles of national forces. For example, the French, echoing old complaints about the allegedly faint-hearted British commitment to the defense of the Continent in two world wars, pressed the British to place substantial land forces on the Continent in the event of war, but Britain preferred to limit her contribution to air and naval operations.[9]

In a significant reservation to the principle of balanced collective forces,· the foreign ministers stated that each government was expected to take "fully into consideration the requirements for national forces which arise out of commitments external to the North Atlantic area."[10] In practice, the three NATO countries with the most extensive commitments outside Europe—the United States, Great Britain, and France—followed the principle of balanced *national* forces as far as the pressures toward economy would permit. None felt that the principle of national specialization called for sacrificing the military needs of national policy to those of NATO.

In addition to advocating the principle of balanced collective forces, some American leaders looked hopefully toward wonderful new weapons, which would substitute firepower for manpower, as a means of reconciling security with economy. Thus Secretary of Defense Louis Johnson, in appealing for the Mutual Defense Assistance Act of 1950, assured Congress that a relatively small European ground force could contain the early phases of a Russian invasion and, in collaboration with American long-range bombers using "new weapons," defend the area, if the United States would equip her allies with "the modern weapons and increased firepower made possible by today's science."[11] Johnson's reference to "modern" weapons evidently complemented recent public statements by General J. Lawton Collins and Secretary of the Army Frank Pace, reporting the development of new conventional-warhead antitank and antiaircraft weapons and also artillery and guided missiles for the tactical use of atomic warheads.[12] However, in view of the fact that as late as 1953 military plans still called for about 100 divisions to defend Europe, one must doubt the extent to which the military planners seriously envisioned antitank and antiaircraft weapons as substitutes for mobilized divisions. And as for "tactical" atomic weapons (which, until the late 1950's, used warheads of approximately the explosive power of the Hiroshima bomb), although as early as October, 1949, General Bradley had written about the great advantage they would give a defensive army against a numerically superior invader,[13] they did not begin to become available to American forces assigned to NATO until late 1953. Meanwhile, it was the shock of the Korean War, and not balanced collective forces or "modern" weapons, that momentarily narrowed the gap between strategy and capabilities.

3. REAPPRAISAL OF SOVIET INTENTIONS

The outbreak of the Korean War in June, 1950, temporarily destroyed the West's confidence in the assumption that America's atomic striking power would deter the Soviet Union from instigating overt military aggression. Consequently, it precipitated the first—and only—serious attempt to create the forces which the military had prescribed for withstanding a Soviet attack in Europe. In retrospect, it seems unwarranted to have inferred an imminent danger of Soviet aggression in Europe from the North Korean attack upon a peripheral strategic position in the Far East, especially since the United States had withdrawn her troops from Korea and publicly excluded it from her "defensive perimeter." But the estimate of a potential aggressor's intentions is peculiarly subject to sudden shifts from complacency to alarm. In the absence of conclusive objective tests of intentions, such estimates customarily reflect hopeful assumptions in times of relatively low tension and pessimistic, even alarmist, assumptions during overt crises, according to the margin of safety governments are willing to tolerate in accommodating military needs to civilian demands.

"The attack upon Korea," President Truman proclaimed, "makes it plain beyond all doubt that communism has passed beyond the use of subversion to conquer independent nations and will now use armed invasion and war."[14] Similarly, Secretary of Defense Johnson interpreted the Korean aggression as "undeniable proof" that international communism would invade any free nation within reach if it thought it could get away with it. "The real significance of the North Korean aggression," he charged, "is this evidence that, even at the resultant risk of starting a third world war, communism is willing to resort to armed aggression, whenever it believes it can win."[15] John Foster Dulles, writing a month after the outbreak of the war, saw the arrival of the critical moment, which he had hypothesized some eighteen months before, when international communism felt it had exhausted most of the possibilities of gain by indirect aggression. He warned that the attack on South Korea, combined with the military build-up in the Soviet Union, might mark a new phase of Communist aggression. "It may invalidate the assumption that the Soviet Union would not risk general war for several years to come—the time presumably required for it to develop a large stockpile of atomic weapons. It surely invalidates the assumption that we can continue still for a time to live luxuriously, without converting our economic potential into military reality."[16] Momentarily, Western Europe shared America's drastic reappraisal of Soviet intentions.

4. REARMAMENT

If the West could no longer safely rely upon its military potential and the Strategic Air Command to deter Soviet aggression in Europe, it would have to build up NATO's forces-in-being.

As Secretary of State Acheson warned, "The strength of the free nations is potentially great—more than enough to deal with this threat. But we must translate that potential into defense in being, with the greatest speed." NATO could no longer afford to base its defense policies on surmises about Soviet intentions, he said. "The capabilities of the Communist movement for further acts of aggression must be the measuring rod by which we judge the adequacy of our defensive strength." "By this measurement," Acheson declared, "it is evident that a forced-draft effort on a very large scale is required."[17]

Accordingly, the United States, setting the pattern for her allies, oriented her military plans toward the target date, or "year of maximum danger,"[18] of 1952 and launched an all-out rearmament program, which quadrupled her defense expenditures within three years. Britain raised her conscription period to two years, announced plans to form three new divisions, promised to increase the British contingent in West Germany to five divisions by the end of 1951, and undertook an ambitious arms program that would raise defense expenditures to 12 per cent of the national income. France increased her defense budget by 30 per cent and planned to add fifteen new divisions in three years. All the other European allies, except Iceland and Portugal, announced parallel plans for increasing their defense forces, periods of military service, and military expenditures.

The British and French governments, who were to assume the great burden of the build-up, emphasized that their progress toward achieving these new goals would depend on the amount of American military and economic assistance they received. The British were particularly dependent on this because they, unlike the Continental allies, provided their own heavy defense production. In announcing their dependence on American aid, both governments undertook, in effect, to reverse the subordination of defense goals to economic progress. For the American government made it clear that, henceforth, her aid to Europe would be directed to the support of the military build-up rather than to the promotion of economic expansion, and that it would be contingent on the recipients' progress in that direction.[19]

As a result of this radical shift in allied contributions to collective defense, the United States, even more conspicuously than before the Korean War, assumed the role of prodding allied governments with the lever of military assistance to intensify their rearmament efforts, while, in proportion to the intensity of their efforts, the allied governments demanded adequate military assistance and solid assurances of America's commitment to their defense. Again, France was particularly anxious for assurances that the Anglo-American powers would defend her on the ground and not merely with air and sea power from outside the Continent. Thus, in detailing the sacrifices that the rearmament effort would impose on her people, the French government warned that this effort "would be useless if ground and air forces sufficient to assure the maintenance of peace should not be stationed in Continental Europe" and stated, "It is necessary that the United States and Great Britain, notably, should participate in the defense with a sufficient number of divisions stationed in Continental Europe."[20]

The United States formally recognized the force of this position when President Truman, on the eve of the important meeting of the North Atlantic Council in September, 1950, announced, "On the basis of recommendations of the Joint Chiefs of Staff, concurred in by the Secretaries of State and Defense, I have today approved substantial increases in the strength of the United States forces to be stationed in Western Europe in the interest of the defense of that area." At the same time, the President indicated that he—and, by implication, the American Congress—would regard the contribution of American troops as a prod as well as a concession. "A basic element in the implementation of this decision," he said, "is the degree to which our friends match our actions in this regard. Firm programs for the development of their forces will be expected to keep full step with the dispatch of additional United States forces to Europe."[21]

The *quid pro quo* in the President's offer of troops was reinforced by an increasingly vocal current of American opinion, led by Senator Taft and former President Hoover, which opposed sending military aid or troops until the European allies had created the means of defending themselves and which threatened to resort to a peripheral, as opposed to a Continental, strategy if the allies failed in this effort.[22] Europeans were acutely aware that this sentiment had deep roots in America's historic isolationism and in the widespread opposition, even among those who by no stretch of the word could be called "isolationists," to committing American soldiers to a strategy of massive land warfare on the Continent. Therefore, just as the European governments regarded America's pledge to defend them rather than liberate them as the indispensable condition of popular support for the burdensome commitments and contributions they had undertaken, Hoover and Taft's strictures served to warn them that America's commitments and contributions to their defense depended upon tangible evidence of Western Europe's determination to arm itself.

Thus, the terms of collaboration were changing to meet the new estimate of the nature of the threat, and it seemed that a satisfactory reciprocity between the United States and her allies would be preserved. But that reciprocity called for adjustments in the strategy and even the structure and membership of the alliance.

5. FORWARD STRATEGY

Actually, the outbreak of the Korean War did not so much change NATO's strategy as make its full implications explicit. Military planners had always regarded the integration of German territory and troops in wartime operations as essential to the defense of Western Europe. Civilian leaders had always insisted upon a concept of defense—the protection of every ally from Russian occupation—that could not be supported without German integration, given the proximity of Soviet troops to the Rhine and the unwillingness of the allies to mobilize the required number of divisions by themselves. Therefore, the intensified fear of Russian aggression was merely the catalyst that led the North Atlantic Council, meeting in New York in September, 1950, explicitly to adopt a "forward strategy" of defending Europe as far eastward as possible and, under American pressure, to agree to examine, as a matter of urgency, "the methods by which Germany could most usefully make its contribution" to European defense.[23]

A month earlier the Consultative Assembly of the European Council, following a proposal by Churchill, had adopted a resolution calling for "the immediate creation of a united European army under the authority of a European Minister for Defense, subject to proper democratic European control, and acting in full cooperation with the United States and Canada." At its New York meeting the North Atlantic Council enlarged upon this idea in agreeing to establish "an integrated force under centralized command." The Supreme Commander (who, it was understood, would be an American) would have "sufficient delegated authority to insure that national units allocated to his command are organized and trained into an effective integrated force in time of peace as well as in the event of war."[24] In December, 1950, the Council appointed General Eisenhower as Supreme Commander in Europe (SACEUR) and authorized him to "train national units assigned to his command and organize them into an effective, integrated defense force."[25] In February, 1951, the Supreme Headquarters of the Allied Powers in Europe (SHAPE) was established, and in April it assumed control of the forces which had been assigned by the member nations to the defense of the treaty area.

From the standpoint of NATO's security, these measures merely extended the principle of integration, which had already been recognized in the concept of "balanced collective forces" for the "integrated defense" of the North Atlantic area. From the standpoint of allied cohesion and collaboration, the agreement, in effect, compensated the European allies for bearing the costs of rearmament by binding the United States more tightly to their defense and reassuring them that Germany's participation in the defense of Western Europe would be under collective restraints.

However, the exact formula under which West Germany would collaborate with NATO could not be agreed upon until the Paris treaties were signed in October, 1954; for the European members of the alliance—and most notably France—were not prepared so suddenly to subordinate their fears of a resurgent Germany to the demands of military strategy and American pressure. In the meanwhile, the ceaseless procession of proposals and counterproposals for integrating German troops in NATO was only one manifestation of the difficulties the allies encountered in reaching mutually acceptable terms of collaboration that would be compatible with the radically expanded military requirements they had undertaken to fulfil.

6. NEW COMPLICATIONS AND THE BEGINNING OF RELAXATION

The outbreak of the Korean War completed the transformation of NATO from a multilateral guaranty pact into a semi-integrated military organization designed to redress the military imbalance on the Continent. At the same time, it destroyed the original balance of assets and liabilities for the major allies and drastically altered the original distribution of burdens and benefits, while complicating the task of strategic collaboration.

In seeking new terms of collaboration that would be compatible with the higher level of allied commitments and contributions, the United States, soon after the invasion of Korea, increased her military assistance to the European allies, assumed the central military command of NATO, and promised to place additional American troops on the Continent, while the European allies agreed to put rearmament and the build-up of NATO forces ahead of economic advancement and, in principle, accepted West German participation in the common defense.

In the aftermath of the Korean scare, these new terms of collaboration increased NATO's military strength enough to restore allied confidence in the stability of deterrence against overt military aggression upon Western Europe, but they failed to elicit sufficient contributions to meet the pledged force levels, which the allies had agreed were essential to defend Western Europe if deterrence should fail. Yet, although the alliance had undertaken a military effort that exceeded the willingness of its members to execute, it could not revert to its original form without disrupting the whole enterprise. Therefore, although the gap between strategy and capabilities was somewhat narrowed, the disparity between the pledged and the actual contributions to NATO was greatly enlarged. Now the United States, having firmly committed herself to close the gap between strategy and capabilities, once more assumed the task of inducing her allies—again, with inadequate concessions and sanctions—to fulfil their pledged contributions to collective defense.

At the same time, in the period between the outbreak of the Korean War and NATO's adoption in December, 1954, of a new strategy relying upon tactical nuclear weapons, there arose new political, economic, and military developments to complicate the requirements of allied security and collaboration: the Soviet "relaxation of tensions," the intensification of allied involvements outside the NATO area, the economic strain of rearmament, and the American and Russian achievements of hydrogen explosions. These developments simultaneously increased the hazards of depending upon America's strategic nuclear striking power and reduced allied incentives to build the ground power that might mitigate this dependence.

The decisive factor underlying all NATO's new problems of security and collaboration was the rapid decline of the fear of aggression, which had led NATO to rearm. When it appeared that the Korean War was a limited war confined to the Korean peninsula and not the prelude to other aggressions instigated by the Soviet Union, the fear of imminent aggression in Europe quickly gave way to the fear that the United States might either precipitate a world war or else become so fascinated by the Chinese Communist threat in the Far East as to neglect her European commitments.[26] The long period of stalemate and truce in Korea, starting in the spring and summer of 1951, sapped all sense of urgency.

Prime Minister Churchill, upon assuming office after the defeat of the Labor government, a defeat which was in no small part due to its responsibility for the Korean-inspired rearmament program, expressed the general revival of confidence in the efficacy of deterrence:

> Looking back over the last few days, I cannot feel that the danger of a third world war is so great now as it was at the time of the Berlin Air Lift crisis in 1948, when the Labor Government . . . took great risks in a firm and resolute manner. Of course, no one can predict the future, but our feeling, on assuming responsibility, is that the deterrents have increased and that, as the deterrents have increased, the danger has become more unlikely.[27]

John Foster Dulles, speaking as the prospective Republican Secretary of State early in the presidential campaign of 1952, returned to his pre-Korean estimate of the Soviet military threat. "When we analyze the Soviet military threat," he said, "we can find many reasons to believe that it may not be more than an unused threat, designed partly for defense but chiefly to throw the free world into panic." Disputing the view that the Soviet leaders relied upon overt military force as a means of conquest, he asked why, if this were so, they had not attacked in Europe or Asia, where they would meet no "appreciable opposition," and why they should wait until the West built up its defenses. "One reason," he answered, "is that the Communist leaders of Russia are almost as afraid of the Red Army as we are. . . . A second reason is the supreme skill of the political leaders of Russia in the art of political warfare. A third reason may be that which Mr. Churchill has several times suggested, namely, that they fear the striking power of our atomic weapons."[28]

Both of these estimates of Soviet intentions were the basis, in their respective countries, upon which incoming governments reduced defense expenditures and ground force goals on the supposition that concentration upon strategic airpower would provide more security at a tolerable cost. Throughout Europe, similar estimates assured the restoration of domestic economic priorities over rearmament. To be sure, the European allies—France, in particular—continued to seek and to receive American assurances that NATO was pledged to defend their territories in the event of aggression, but they were impelled more by a desire to satisfy domestic criticisms and suspicions of the alliance than by an active fear of invasion.[29] Feeling incapable of redressing the Continental balance of power by themselves, they were content to rely upon America's atomic might and her immense industrial and military potential to deter aggression and to let the United States, who had the most direct interest in counterbalancing Soviet power, worry about enlarging the ground forces. In the meanwhile, they were more impressed by the burden of rearmament than by the danger of aggression.

7. AMERICAN TROOPS FOR EUROPE

The most important concessions that the United States made as a stimulant to allied rearmament were the appointment of General Eisenhower as Supreme Commander of the NATO forces in Europe and the placement of four more American divisions (making a total of almost six) on the forward line in West Germany. But once these concessions were made, they provided little inducement to further European efforts, while the threat to withdraw them proved worse than useless as a sanction, since these visible symbols of the American commitment came to be regarded as the prerequisites of allied military collaboration.

However, the fundamental obstacle to a vast build-up of NATO forces was not the weakness of American concessions or sanctions but the fact that the announced strategic objectives of the build-up were not sufficiently compelling to warrant the effort. In fact, the same lack of strategic inducement to enlarging ground forces was conspicuous in the defense policies of the United States, who could far better afford the effort. In spite of the greater sense of urgency about rearmament in the American government, the debate over sending additional troops to Europe showed that Americans were no more inclined to adjust their national strategy and capabilities to a conception of massive land warfare than were Western Europeans. Yet, for less ambitious objectives, a much more modest build-up seemed sufficient.

When the Eighty-second Congress convened in January, 1951, Senator Taft reopened a lengthy debate on President Truman's announced intention to send troops to Europe. Taft did not oppose sending a few American divisions to Europe to help the

Europeans build up their armies, providing that they made a sufficient effort of their own. What he objected to was committing the United States to fight the world-wide battle of communism "primarily on the vast land areas of the continent of Europe or the continent of Asia, where we are at the greatest disadvantage in a war with Russia."[30] America's proper strategic role, he insisted, was to provide air and sea power, while the Eurasian countries provided the troops. But, with or without American aid, he could not foresee Europe providing enough troops to withstand a Russian attack. The effort would not only be futile but provocative. This theme was reiterated by Herbert Hoover, Senator Wherry, and other opponents of the President's policy.

Supporters of the President's policy relied heavily upon the persuasiveness of General Eisenhower, who returned from Europe in February in order to testify in its behalf. Yet Eisenhower's testimony fell far short of indorsing the strategic conception Taft criticized. In fact, in some respects it was more like an indorsement of Taft's position. Thus, the Supreme Commander emphasized the contribution of American troops to European morale not to creating a Continental ground force.

> What we are trying to do, ladies and gentlemen, is to start a sort of reciprocal action across the Atlantic. We do one thing which inspires our friends to do something, and that gives us greater confidence in their thoroughness, their readiness for sacrifice. We do something more and we establish an upward-going spiral which meets this problem of strength and morale.[31]

America's role in this enterprise, he said, was to serve as a center of production and inspiration but not as a supplier of troops to the various critical sectors around the vast Sino-Soviet bastion in Eurasia. "Our view in the central position must be directed to many sectors," he said. "We cannot concentrate all our forces in any one sector, even one as important as Western Europe. We must largely sit here with great, mobile, powerful reserves ready to support our policies, our rights, our interests wherever they may be in danger in the world."[32]

When Secretary of Defense Marshall revealed that the United States intended to send no more than four divisions to Europe, this virtually eliminated the immediate issue of America's role in NATO's build-up, but it did not meet the underlying issue of the strategic objective which the build-up was intended to support. Secretary of State Acheson gave the most lucid explanation of NATO's strategy, but the strategic objectives that he emphasized neither required nor inspired the construction of the huge standing army that military plans had specified since pre-NATO days. He said that the first purpose of NATO's forces in Europe was to deter aggression and that, in order to deter aggression, reliance upon retaliatory airpower was not enough. The reason he gave for this conclusion followed the reasoning of NSC 68.

> One reason why we cannot continue to rely on retaliatory air power as a sufficient deterrent is the effect of time. We have a substantial lead in air power and in atomic weapons. At the present moment, this may be the most powerful deterrent against aggression. But with the passage of time, even though we continue our advances in this field, the value of our lead diminishes. In other words, the best use we can make of our present advantage in retaliatory air power, is to move ahead under this protective shield to build the balanced collective forces in Western Europe that will continue to deter aggression after our atomic advantage has been diminished.[33]

Here was, perhaps, the earliest official public statement of the strategic implications of Russia's capacity to neutralize the deterrent effect of America's nuclear striking power, but, pleading security reasons, Acheson declined to elaborate.[34] Moreover, he left somewhat ambiguous the precise strategic conclusion to be drawn from his analysis. If more ground forces were needed to compensate for the declining deterrent power of the Strategic Air Command, what kind of contingencies would they be designed to deter? Here Acheson reiterated his earlier statement of the function of ground forces in deterring limited aggression. He foresaw the possibility not only of indirect aggressions on the Czechoslovakian model but also of direct military incursions by Soviet satellites, which the Soviet Union could disclaim; and he warned that, "in the absence of defense forces-in-being, satellites might be used for such disguised aggression in the hope that they could get away with it, since the free nations could respond only with the weapons of all-out general war, or not at all."[35]

But if the ground forces were intended only to deter limited *fait accompli's*, this would not require building up an army capable of stopping a major Soviet assault on the ground. Should NATO abandon this more ambitious strategic objective? Acheson indicated that it should not. The first purpose of ground forces, he said, was to deter limited and major aggressions, but, if the deterrent failed and Russia launched an all-out assault, the ground forces would have to hold air bases and detain the attack long enough to permit airpower to stem the invasion by striking at the aggressor's homeland before he could consolidate control of the great war potential of Western Europe. Apparently, ground forces were expected to perform the same protective function in a bilateral as in a unilateral nuclear war. "These are the forces," Acheson declared, "that would prevent Europe, in the event of an attack, from having to go through another occupation and liberation."[36]

The European allies might be willing to build a force capable of deterring limited aggression, but would they build a force large enough to prevent Europe from being overrun, especially when they could expect even an unoccupied Europe to be devastated by a Soviet-American nuclear exchange? Everyone avoided a direct answer to this troublesome question. Acheson simply denied any intention of matching the potential aggressor "man for man" or "tank for tank."[37] General J. Lawton Collins, chief of staff of the Army, vigorously denied that Europe need be overrun by an all-out assault, but he did not designate the size of the forces that would be required to protect Europe.[38] However, General Eisenhower, who was urging a rapid build-up by 1952, said he would have to see 40 divisions before he would "feel better"; and he looked forward to 60 fully equipped divisions by 1954.[39]

There is no reason to think that the military planners had abandoned their view that a force approaching 100 divisions would be necessary to withstand a Soviet invasion. Yet in 1951 it was already obvious that only the fear of imminent invasion, and certainly not the temporary placement of six American divisions on the Continent, could conceivably inspire the Europeans to make sufficient contributions of men, money, and equipment to support a strategic objective which the United States herself expected to support primarily with airpower. On the other hand, NATO did seem to be making satisfactory progress toward achieving co-ordinated ground forces, airfields, and a network of supporting communications and supplies, which would be sufficient to support the strategic objective Acheson had emphasized: the deterrence of local *fait accompli*'s.[40] In the aftermath of the Korean scare, Europe's growing confidence in its achievement of this modest deterrent capability sapped the only compelling military incentive for enlarging NATO's standing army.

8. ECONOMIC AND POLITICAL OBSTACLES TO REARMAMENT

While the incentives for expanding allied forces sharply declined, the incentives for cutting back the whole post-Korea defense effort became overwhelming as the strains of rearmament aggravated economic problems and political discontent in the NATO countries. In spite of a general increase in the production and trade of Western Europe, the rearmament programs caused a steep rise in the price of imported raw materials in relation to a slower rise in the price of manufactured exports and thereby created acute balance-of-payments deficits, especially in Great Britain. Concomitant with the balance-of-payments crisis there was a renewal of inflation in the prices of raw materials and foodstuffs in both exporting and importing countries, which, in turn, led Western European governments to pare expenditures for civilian consumption and, in some cases, to impose rationing and price and wage controls, if only to be able to finance rearmament.

These economic repercussions created domestic political problems that were especially galling for governments that had committed themselves to extensive social welfare programs, which now seemed threatened by arms expenditures. On May 15, 1951, French Defense Minister Jules Moch was ejected from the Socialist party's national executive committee for emphasizing the need to sacrifice certain social security benefits for the sake of defense requirements. On September 18, the Netherlands' Foreign Minister, Dr. Dirk U. Stikker, warned the North Atlantic Council that "any further lowering of the present living standard in Europe without the prospect of a rise in the near future will endanger the social peace on the home front which is so essential to our defense effort."[41]

In England the Labor government's arms program, which was expected to cost about 14 per cent of the national income, led Minister of Labor Aneurin Bevan and two of his followers to resign from the government in protest. He and his supporters gave voice to views that were widely shared by politicians in both parties, who hesitated to state them so boldly. They charged that neither England nor the other allied states in Europe could finance rearmament programs of the proposed scale and pace and at the same time maintain their programs for increasing civilian production, building homes, and improving social services. They held that Great Britain, in particular, suffered from carrying a disproportionate share of the West's defense effort, which afforded the United States and other allies a competitive advantage in industrial production and prevented Britain from manufacturing and selling enough export goods to solve its international balance-of-payments problem. Furthermore, they denied the basic strategic premise of rearmament in asserting that the real and sufficient deterrent of aggression in Europe was the American guaranty and not ground forces, while they condemned the American-sponsored build-up as provocative.[42] The victory of the Bevanites and the defeat of the Labor party in the general elections of October, 1951, forcefully demonstrated the political hazards of rearmament.

Against these formidable economic and political obstacles the United States assumed the task of urging her allies to maintain the priority of rearmament over economic advancement in order to create as many battle-ready divisions as possible by 1952, but the European allies responded by beseeching the United States to direct as much foreign aid as possible toward meeting their economic problems in order to mitigate the strains of rearmament. As a French official explained to an American reporter, "With you Americans the big problem is the immediate threat of Russia to our collective security. With us the big problem is the immediate threat to standards of living which cannot be depressed materially without endangering public support for the rearmament program you are demanding of us."[43] The result of this divergence of interests was that the allies made just enough paper concessions to the build-up of ground forces to sustain America's attachment to NATO, while the United States agreed, in principle, that the build-up should not be made at the sacrifice of national standards of living.

At the Rome meeting of the North Atlantic Council, in November, 1951, the allied powers resolved to create a NATO ground force of 43 divisions by 1954 and to accelerate the "short-term" (1952) program of rearmament, subject to the findings of a twelve-nation Temporary Council Committee, which had been charged with determining the defense expenditures that the respective allies were economically capable of contributing to the collective effort.[44] However, the draft report of a working group (the "Three Wise Men"),[45] which was submitted to the TCC in December, proposed levels of expenditure that obviously exceeded the political, if not the economic, capabilities of the allied governments. And the specific distribution of the economic burden among the allies was as disturbing as the magnitude of the assessments. The report urged the European allies to expand production by an average of 14 per cent by June, 1954, and to increase military expenditures by from 5 per cent for France to 50 per cent for Belgium. It assured them that these goals could be achieved without increasing taxation or reducing standards of living, and it suggested that the way to accomplish this feat was for Western Europe to pay for rearmament out of increased production and for the United States to buy more defense supplies abroad. These ambitious recommendations quickly proved to be unrealistic in terms of the willingness of the allies either to subordinate domestic to defense considerations or to subordinate national defense programs to a supranational determination of burden-sharing.

Although the TCC was supposed to indicate to the European allies how they should close the gap between military needs and actual capabilities by their own efforts, it was clear to all the assembled finance ministers that the essential component in the recommended prescriptions for reconciling rearmament with domestic economic goals would have to be a substantial increase in American assistance. Yet the United States secretary of the treasury had already advised the Rome meeting that Europe could not expect increased American aid for defense programs,[46] and the American Congress had reduced the government's requested funds for the Mutual Security Act, cutting most deeply into the appropriations for economic aid for Europe.[47] This tendency to reduce the total Mutual Security Act appropriation for Europe and allocate a greater proportion to military as opposed to economic aid was carried out in the requests and authorizations for fiscal year 1953.[48]

Furthermore, the United States secretary of defense had let the European governments know that the American government intended to pare down its own defense budget (with the exception of airpower) for the sake of the stability of the national economy.[49] And Congress subsequently approved this policy by cutting the administration's total defense budget (although granting generous appropriations to the Air Force, which it had consistently urged the administration to expand). Thus, even while the United States reduced the military and economic assistance that the allied powers in Europe needed in order to fulfil their rearmament pledges without sacrificing their economic and social goals, she provided them, in her own defense policies, with the irresistible formula for squaring economic retrenchment with national security.

9. THE QUESTION OF GERMAN PARTICIPATION IN WESTERN DEFENSE

Before the North Atlantic allies convened in Lisbon in February, 1952, in order to agree upon the force levels required to implement the American-sponsored rearmament program, the United States also encountered allied resistance in pushing another logical concomitant of NATO's forward strategy: the participation of West Germany in the European security system.

In September, 1950, the State Department had proposed incorporating about ten German divisions directly under NATO command. But throughout Western Europe, and especially in France, strong opposition had developed to rushing ahead with German rearmament and membership in NATO before political safeguards against German militarism had been created.

In order to postpone German participation the French Premier, René Pleven, put forward a counterproposal, analogous to the "Schuman Plan" for economic integration through a European Coal and Steel Community. This scheme would so tightly integrate Germany's military contribution in a European framework—chiefly by confining German units to combat teams within international divisions of a European army—as to obviate the danger of independent national action. The "Pleven Plan" was widely regarded as a politically impossible and militarily unfeasible subterfuge for preventing German rearmament. Nevertheless, the United States, after first rejecting the scheme as unrealistic and unfeasible, later indorsed it in order to gain French adherence to a German contribution. She indorsed it, however, in the altered form of a European Defense Community, which would include German divisions integrated on a basis of equality with other national divisions in army groups.[50]

Thus, the French trapped themselves and their allies into accepting, in principle, a European army with supranational features, which it is doubtful that even the United States would have accepted in fact. Yet only the American government regarded EDC as an urgent military necessity, and only the West German government took a keen political interest in the project.

In France the proponents of EDC in the long, intricate debate in the National Assembly argued for the scheme primarily as a means of tying down American troops in Europe, restraining the resurgent Federal Republic within a Franco-German rapprochement, and promoting the grand scheme of European reconstruction through unification. Both sides of the argument displayed almost total indifference to strategic military considerations.[51]

In England the support of EDC as an assurance against American isolation—and as a means of getting Germany to share the burdens of rearmament and compete on more equal terms with British trade—held an uneasy balance over the fear of German ascendance on the Continent and the traditional British opposition to becoming involved in European commitments. But, as in France, the general disposition of proponents and opponents alike was to let America's nuclear power take care of NATO's military security.

In West Germany, Chancellor Adenauer's government, against great popular and political opposition to rearmament, embraced the idea of integrating German troops in a European army—providing they were under national control—as a means of abolishing the restrictions of the Occupation Statute, restoring Germany to equal status among the major powers, laying the ancient ghost of Franco-German hostility, and interlocking Germany's destiny with that of the Western world; in short, for the sake of the larger purpose of restoring German power and prestige within an international framework that would protect Germany and her neighbors from the revival of German chauvinism. But neither inside nor outside the government was there any significant appreciation of, nor concern for, the military implications of EDC.[52]

Thus, on the eve of NATO's adoption of the most ambitious defense program in its history, the two major contributions to this program—rearmament and the participation of West Germany—depended upon the convergence of the contributing nations' disparate political aims and their common interest in securing America's commitment and material support, rather than upon educated convictions about the military requirements of common defense. It is little wonder, then, that the large force goals indorsed at Lisbon turned out to be paper promises. Yet the rearmament effort, which was built upon those goals, eventually led to two other results that were no less important for European security and cohesion: the membership of West Germany in NATO and the further commitment of the United States and Britain to the defense of Continental Europe.

10. THE LISBON GOALS AND THEIR ABANDONMENT

In February, 1952, the North Atlantic Council, meeting in Lisbon, approved the most ambitious force goals of NATO's history: 50 divisions, 4,000 aircraft, and 704 major combatant vessels in 1952 and, provisionally, 75 divisions and 6,500 aircraft in 1953, to be followed by 96 divisions and 9,000 aircraft in 1954, with about 35 to 40 divisions to be ready for combat at all times (including 25 to 30 on the central front) and the rest to be capable of mobilization within a month.[53] The Council approved the contribution of 12 West German divisions to these forces within the framework of the European Defense Community, toward which Great Britain, the United States, and the other NATO countries not participating directly in EDC would assume the same obligations as toward NATO. (The projected force goals did not include the indigenous troops needed to defend Greece and Turkey, whose accession to NATO was now formally recognized.[54]) At the same time, the Lisbon conference took a significant step toward the political integration of the alliance by making the North Atlantic Council a permanent body, with a secretary general as chairman and with permanent representatives, who were to remain in session in the intervals between ministerial meetings.

On the face of things, the force goals indorsed at Lisbon were the consummation of defense plans urged by the military since 1948, but, measured by performance rather than by promise, they turned out to be a mirage on the bleak arms horizon in the aftermath of the Korean stalemate. Statesmen of the member countries hailed the Lisbon agreement as a great achievement, but unofficially it was received with a great deal of skepticism in Europe. The London *Times* regarded the conference communiqué as an unfortunate attempt to combine military planning with political propaganda. "Presumably the announcement was meant to impress someone," its editorial observed, "but it will not impress the Russians, who know very well the true state of affairs and who have the sense to realize that any real plans for real divisions would be kept secret. Indeed this imaginative total [50 divisions], with the still more imaginative promise of 85 or 100 divisions in two years' time, seems to contain the maximum amount of provocation with the minimum amount of deterrent effect."[55]

Nevertheless, NATO did, thereafter, make considerable progress toward achieving the 1952 goal. In the next year or two, NATO forces available for defense of the central front in Western Europe reached a peak of military preparedness in terms of ground divisions—leveling off at about 25 nominally combat-ready standing divisions and about 25 reserve divisions in various states of readiness (before the French and British withdrawals of troops in 1954, 1956, and 1957). Moreover, NATO's "infrastructure" was greatly improved by the construction of over 100 airfields and an extensive network of communications and supply facilities. This put NATO in a fairly good position to prevent the Soviet Union from launching a sudden, unopposed, limited aggression with her 22 divisions in East Germany or from launching a major ground attack without giving the West advance warning.

Yet this level of preparedness was far short of the provisional goals set forth at Lisbon, and every military authority, including General Eisenhower and his two successors, General Ridgway and General Gruenther, had to concede that NATO's forces were insufficient to protect Europe from a major assault.[56] Moreover, it soon became evident that none of the allies was actually willing to increase or even sustain its pace of rearmament in order to create larger ground forces. Indeed, the universal trend was in the opposite direction.

On the very day the Lisbon conference opened, Churchill informed the House of Commons that defense expenditures for the current fiscal year would fall short of the estimate and that the whole program would have to be stretched out beyond the three years planned.[57] This "stretch-out" reflected more than a mere postponement of defense goals. It was the result of a fundamental strategic decision to reconcile economic retrenchment with military security by relying more heavily on strategic airpower and nuclear weapons as opposed to ground power, and by basing defense expenditures on the concept of the "long haul" and the assumption that the danger of war by 1954 had abated.[58] On this strategic basis the Prime Minister announced at the end of July that the whole defense program was under review in order to keep it within limits compatible with the nation's economic welfare.[59] And in September he was reported to have suggested to the American government that concentration upon airpower and nuclear weapons would enable a considerably smaller number of ground forces than 96 divisions to defend Europe.[60] In October the British demonstrated the technological basis of their strategic revision by producing an atomic explosion in the Monte Bello Islands off Australia.

At about the same time that Churchill first announced a "stretch-out," the new French Premier, Edgar Faure, gambling on the provision of substantial additional American aid, submitted to the National Assembly a defense budget somewhat in excess of that suggested by the Three Wise Men for arming 12 divisions, which the Lisbon conference had established as the French contribution; and on his return from Lisbon he proposed a 15 per cent increase in taxation. The National Assembly rejected this proposal, and Faure resigned, to be replaced by Antoine Pinay. The Pinay government sought in vain for assurances of sufficient American aid to permit it, in the light of persistently rising living costs and dwindling dollar reserves, to undertake the defense expenditures projected by its predecessor. The American government declined to supply $600 million previously promised, maintaining that this aid had been contingent upon an adequate French military effort, which had not occurred. The American Congress further prepared the downfall of Pinay's government by making a substantial cut in the annual Mutual Security Program appropriations for military aid and defense support to Europe, to the accompaniment of aspersions about France's efficiency and reliability. Accordingly, Premier

Pinay announced that, in the absence of adequate American aid, France was forced to choose between production goals and manpower goals and would choose the former.[61] In November, 1952, the French government informed NATO that it would be unable to increase its military contribution in 1953 from 12 to 15 divisions in accordance with the Lisbon program.[62]

France encountered a special obstacle to meeting her defense goals in the debilitating warfare in Indochina, which consumed a frightful portion of her professional army and, over a period of five years, more money than the entire amount of all the Marshall Plan aid from the United States.[63] Although in 1952 the United States supported about one-third of the annual financial burden of this war, French authorities did not consider this aid commensurate with the importance of her exertions in the global struggle against international communism.

Britain's and France's abandonment of the Lisbon goals in the face of domestic economic and political obstacles set the pattern for other members of the alliance, who before long reduced their defense budgets and their terms of conscription. At the North Atlantic Council meeting in April, 1953, the foreign ministers formally recognized and sanctioned the relaxation of NATO's defense effort. Although the highest authorities stated then and on other occasions throughout the year that the Soviet threat had not diminished in the slightest,[64] they justified a slackening in the pace of rearmament on the ground that the objective was now to build up NATO's military strength gradually over the "long pull" at a pace compatible with economic welfare, rather than to rearm rapidly in order to achieve full strength by the "year of maximum danger" in 1954. Accordingly, the members of NATO now placed the emphasis on improving the quality of existing forces, while deferring the provisional force goals for 1953 and 1954 to some unspecified date in the future.[65]

Only the Supreme Allied Commander in Europe, General Ridgway, soon to become army chief of staff and to be replaced by General Gruenther, dissented from this formula for abandoning the Lisbon goals. Warning that military plans must be based on Soviet capabilities rather than on attempts to fathom Soviet intentions, he asserted that the scale and burden of NATO's defense effort should actually increase rather than diminish. "Within the strictly military field," he wrote in his annual report as Supreme Commander, "I find the disparity between our available forces and those which the Soviet rulers could bring against us so great as to warrant no other conclusion than that a full-scale attack within the near future would find Allied Command Europe critically weak to accomplish its present mission."[66]

11. GERMANY JOINS NATO

The default upon national force goals was not accompanied by any alteration of the strategy that NATO's forces were intended to serve. NATO and allied spokesmen continued to affirm that NATO's major and indispensable function was the protection of every member against an all-out Russian assault.[67] Therefore, although the pace of rearmament slackened, the fulfilment of NATO's military plans still depended upon reducing the disparity between Soviet and NATO forces. To reduce this disparity, a West German contribution of troops and material resources was indispensable. As General Eisenhower asserted in the First Annual Report of the Supreme Allied Commander, "Even with the maximum potential realized through the collective efforts of member nations, there is little hope for the economical long-term attainment of security and stability in Europe unless West Germany can be counted on the side of the free nations."[68]

West Germany's geographical position alone made her participation a prerequisite of an effective "forward strategy." For, as NATO's military leaders explained, the plans for defending Europe depended upon maintaining combat-ready covering forces to hold the initial onslaught as far eastward as possible, backed by reserve units that could be brought into action within a period of a few days to a month.[69] West Germany's active collaboration with NATO would obviously become essential in implementing this strategic concept.

On May 27, 1952, the European Defense Community Treaty

was signed, and the United States, Britain, and France concluded a Contractual Agreement with the Federal Republic of Germany, ending the occupation. The treaty provided for a German contribution of 12 divisions to an army of initially 43 national divisions, grouped in international army corps under overall control of the Supreme Allied Commander in Europe. West Germany was to receive full sovereignty when all signatories had ratified the treaty. As a special concession to France, the United States and Britain signed a declaration pledging that "if any action from whatever quarter threatens the integrity or unity of the Community, the two Governments will regard this as a threat to their own security" and expressing their "resolve to station such forces on the continent of Europe, including the Federal Republic of Germany, as they deem necessary and appropriate to contribute to the joint defense of the North Atlantic Treaty area."[70]

In the eyes of the military, EDC was a simple strategic imperative, but the subsequent history of the treaty showed that NATO's military security had become inextricably entangled with substantial political issues concerning interallied relations, issues which could be resolved within the new strategic imperatives only by a readjustment of allied commitments. The central feature of this readjustment was the firmer commitment of American and British troops to the Continent in order to counterbalance the accession of West Germany to NATO, especially for the benefit of France. Indeed, in the eyes of its principal architects, EDC became as important as an instrument of Franco-German reconciliation as of military security.

In the United States the signing of the treaty to establish the European Defense Community was hailed, not only as a boon to military security, but also as a giant step toward the ancient ideal of European unification. When the last of the six foreign ministers had signed the last document, Secretary Acheson expressed his "profound conviction that what we have witnessed today may well prove to be one of the most important and most far-reaching events of our lifetime. . . . We have seen the beginning of the realization of an ancient dream—the unity of the free peoples of Western Europe."[71] Undersecretary of State David K. Bruce went further in proclaiming:

> I myself feel that this creation of a European Defense Community is the most significant thing that has happened in western civilization, not in my time, not in our time, but for a period of hundreds of years, because . . . the animosities between nations, these deep-seated hatreds, which are the result of history, not of generations, but of centuries, come to a focus in control over its own armed forces, because there goes with that parting with control over its armed forces a loss of control over its foreign policy, the implementation of its foreign policy, through the force of its own or the disposition of its own armies.[72]

In retrospect, it would seem that Mr. Bruce lauded the very supranational feature that would have doomed EDC to failure even if France had accepted the treaty. However, the world was deprived of this experiment, because the French National Assembly refused to ratify the device that the French government had largely invented, while the United States became increasingly impatient for the acceptance of a scheme it had originally opposed, and the German Federal Republic used the combination of American pressure and French resistance to emphasize her claim to sovereignty and equality.

The French government, fearing a resurgent Germany more than Soviet aggression, tried to gain an EDC formula that would permit greater independent control of the French army, additional guaranties of Britain's commitment to Continental defense, and Germany's renunciation of control over the Saar, contending that these were the minimum conditions for securing the National assembly's ratification of the EDC treaty. The West German government, having persuaded the Bundestag to ratify the treaty largely as the means of achieving full sovereignty, was no less ardent an advocate of EDC than the United States, although it was compelled to be more wary of French apprehensions. But the Adenauer government also had to contend with domestic opposition to the EDC treaty, for, not without reason, the Social Democratic party held that German rearmament in the context of a Western alliance would preclude Russia's agreement to the reunification of Germany. This difficulty prompted the Bonn government to reinforce its claim to American support by letting American observers know that the failure of EDC might bring to power domestic forces that would turn a friendlier eye toward the East.[73]

To allay German domestic opposition, the United States insisted, in support of Chancellor Adenauer, that the best assurance of reunification lay in so strengthening the Federal Republic through EDC as to present Soviet-occupied Germany with an irresistible "attractive power."[74] But stronger inducements were needed to gain French acceptance of the treaty. On the one hand, the United States tried to mollify the French opposition by formally reaffirming her commitments to EDC and NATO and adding a pledge to regard the North Atlantic Treaty as of "indefinite duration,"[75] and by stressing in official statements the value of EDC as a move toward European unity, as a spur to Franco-German reconciliation, and as a protection against the renewal of aggressive German nationalism. Expatiating the latter theme, Secretary of State Dulles told a foreign ministers' conference in January, 1954:

> No more will there be national armies to fight each other and to invade others in a quest for national triumphs. There will be only the common army so interlocked that no single member of the community could in practice commit armed aggression. There would be no more German Army. There would be no German General Staff, and the military service of individual Germans would be closely restricted.
>
> Such a European army could go into action only in response to great and pressing needs of self-defense. It could not be used without the concurrence of countries which themselves have had bitter experience with German militarism and which could never be a party to its revival.[76]

On the other hand, Dulles sought to overcome French opposition to EDC by hinting at a revision of America's commitment to Continental defense and a cessation of American aid unless France joined EDC. Thus he told a meeting of the North Atlantic Council on December 14, 1953, "If . . . the European Defense Community should not become effective; if France and Germany remain apart so that they would again be potential enemies, then indeed there would be grave doubt whether Continental Europe could be made a place of safety. That would compel an agonizing reappraisal of basic United States policy."[77] In January and February, 1953, during a rapid survey of European conditions before drawing up the Mutual Security Program for the next fiscal year, Dulles indicated that further American investments in Western Europe might depend upon Europe's uniting in accordance with the defense treaty.[78] And this warning was underlined by the so-called "Richards Amendment" to the Mutual Security Program appropriation for 1953–54, which made half the military aid for Europe contingent on the adoption of EDC.[79] On June 5, 1954, testifying before the Senate Committee on Foreign Relations, Dulles said, "I would think that it would be acceptable not to make deliveries to [France and Italy] out of next year's [foreign aid] authorizations unless and until they have ratified EDC."[80]

In the end, the French National Assembly refused to be either mollified or frightened into accepting the EDC treaty. Nevertheless, in an atmosphere of crisis that seemed to threaten the very existence of NATO as a military organization, a formula more compatible with traditional national sovereignty was found for securing West Germany's participation in the Atlantic defense system. On August 30, 1954, the National Assembly rejected the EDC treaty by a vote of 319 to 264. On British initiative a new scheme for West German participation in NATO within a restored Western European Union was devised at a nine-power conference in London and embodied in a series of protocols and conventions in Paris, which France joined in signing on October 23.

In the House of Commons Sir Anthony Eden argued for the Paris and London Agreements on broad political grounds. They were essential, he said, to anchor Germany to the West rather than let her drift in the center of Europe, and he emphasized the restraints that WEU would impose upon West Germany, which would prevent her from pursuing an independent military policy. Moreover, he warned that the failure of the British to have taken the initiative in achieving European unity within

WEU after the collapse of EDC might have caused "the complete collapse of that unity and the retirement of the United States into 'Fortress America.' "[81]

The French Premier, Pierre Mendès-France, now advocated WEU before the French National Assembly in equally political terms, arguing that if France turned down a second plan for rearming the Germans, the United States and Britain would arm West Germany anyway and the United States would withdraw from the defense of the Continent in favor of a "peripheral strategy."[82] He persuaded the National Assembly to approve the Paris Agreements on December 28 by a narrow margin of 287 to 260.

In the following four months the legislatures of the other signatories ratified the Agreements, and in May, 1955, over four and one-half years after the NATO members had accepted a German contribution in principle, the Federal Republic joined NATO on terms far more like the original American and German proposals of 1950 than like EDC. Thus, in the end, the North Atlantic allies' concern for the restraint of a resurgent Germany in Europe, for the cohesion of the alliance, and, above all, for America's firm commitment to Continental defense triumphed over their political differences—but only after a new set of commitments had been woven into the tangled strands of allied collaboration.

The demise of EDC meant that national armies under NATO command would remain under national control. In order to make the participation of a German national army acceptable to France, the old Western Union of the Brussels Treaty was revived, linked with NATO, and expanded to include Germany and Italy in a Western European Union, which was empowered to fix the maximum force levels of its members on the recommendation of NATO's military authorities. Germany was to become a member of NATO after all signatories had ratified the new Brussels Treaty and a convention providing for the continued stationing of allied forces in West Germany, subject to German consent. All allied forces on the Continent were placed under the Supreme Allied Commander in Europe (except those recognized by NATO as being properly under national command). These forces were to be located, deployed, and supported logistically by SACEUR according to NATO's strategy and were forbidden to be redeployed or used operationally without SACEUR's consent, subject to "appropriate political guidance" from the North Atlantic Council.

In a unilateral declaration of self-denial Germany undertook (*a*) not to manufacture atomic, chemical, or biological weapons and (*b*) not to manufacture guided missiles, magnetic and influence mines, warships, or long-range bombers, except on the request of SACEUR, approved by a two-thirds majority of the Council of WEU. However, in return for accepting these unique restraints, the Federal Republic gained not only assurances of Western military support but "the full authority of a sovereign state over its internal and external affairs," a national military establishment, and a major voice in the councils of the Western powers.* In short, she gained the attributes of a fully independent state and a position of strength and influence to utilize them, within a political framework acceptable to the major Western powers and compatible with the consolidation of a democratic society.

As a further restraint upon Germany, the United States, Great Britain, and France agreed that any recourse to force which threatened "the integrity and unity of the Atlantic alliance or its defensive purposes" would disqualify the offending government from enjoying its rights "to any guarantee and any military assistance provided for in the North Atlantic Treaty and its protocols." As a counterweight to German power, Great Britain promised to continue to maintain on the Continent the four divisions and the tactical air units already assigned to

* She also gained two commitments of critical importance to any political settlement with Russia involving West Germany. One stated that "the final determination of the boundaries of Germany must await" a peace settlement "for the whole of Germany"—a reference to the Oder-Neisse line. The other pledged the allies to "consider the government of the Federal Republic as the only German government . . . entitled to speak for Germany as the representative of the German people in international affairs"—that is, a pledge not to recognize East Germany.

SACEUR and not to withdraw them against the wishes of the majority of the Brussels powers. Although this pledge added little to existing commitments and was qualified so as not to be binding in case of "an acute overseas emergency" or an excessive financial strain, it was nevertheless a radical departure from Britain's traditional foreign policy and a decisive concession in securing French assent to the Paris Agreements. As a final assurance to France, the United States and Great Britain joined the six WEU countries and Canada in stating that they regarded the North Atlantic Treaty as being "of indefinite duration."

Thus it came about that the effort to obtain West Germany's active participation in a forward strategy led to the further integration of NATO's forces and the further entanglement of the United States and Great Britain in Continental defense, while the proposal for a European army, which had gained much of its impetus from the sentiment for a purely European integration, ended by binding Europe more tightly to a trans-Atlantic framework.

12. THE SOVIET "NEW LOOK" IN FOREIGN POLICY

By the time the Paris Agreements were signed, NATO had become a complex framework of European diplomacy, in which military strategy was inextricably entwined with the delicately balanced configurations of allied power and interests. However, the alliance had to operate in a far different international atmosphere than existed when the plan for securing a German contribution was initiated during the crisis following the outbreak of the Korean War. It was an atmosphere that was anything but conducive to Western rearmament and concerted diplomatic stands.

The new international atmosphere was largely the result of a change in the tactics of Soviet foreign policy in response to the military and political stalemate in Europe and a number of other developments: the growth of nuclear striking power on both sides; the resurgence of West Germany as a major military and industrial power allied with the West; the acceleration of the nationalist, anti-Western, and leftist revolution in the peripheral areas of Asia; and the diffusion of power and influence within the Soviet bloc. The new tactics began to emerge in the midst of the EDC discussions, after the death of Stalin in March, 1953, although there had been signs of them at the Nineteenth Party Congress in 1952 and even before, in June, 1951, when Soviet UN delegate Malik indicated that Russia would support truce negotiations in the Korean War.

In actions, the Soviet "new look" in foreign policy was marked by somewhat better diplomatic manners and by gestures toward a *détente*—the dissolution of the Cominform, the relaxation of controls over domestic economic policy in the satellite states, the return of the Porkkala naval base to Finland, a slight lifting of the Iron Curtain to permit freer East-West communication between scientific and cultural personnel, agreement to the Austrian State Treaty (May, 1955), promotion of the Summit conference in Geneva (July, 1955) to herald the "relaxation of tensions" and "peaceful coexistence," support of its Asian counterpart at Bandung (April, 1955), and announcement of Soviet troop reductions in 1955 and 1956 of 640,000 and 1,200,000, respectively.

Doctrinally, the Soviet "new look," which received its principal formulation at the Twentieth Party Congress in 1956,[83] was marked by a number of propositions defining the new bases of "peaceful coexistence": (*a*) There is no "fatal inevitability" of war as the ultimate precondition of the triumph of international communism, because the united front for peace combined with Soviet nuclear retaliatory power can deter the West from starting such a war in a desperate attempt to prevent the world-wide triumph of communism. (*b*) A "socialist society" has been achieved in the U.S.S.R., and it is advancing much faster than the capitalist societies—which it will eventually surpass—in the decisive area of competition between the two systems: material production and, especially, heavy industry. (*c*) The Soviet Union is no longer encircled by the capitalist-imperialist camp; rather, it is surrounded by allied socialist states and a huge third non-socialist, neutralist camp in the "zone of peace" (including the one-third of mankind living on the periphery of Eurasia), which is destined to enter the Communist camp. (*d*) There are new possibilities outside the major capitalist powers, for the peaceful, even parliamentary transition to communism, although whether the transition is peaceful or violent will depend upon whether the ruling classes resist it. (*e*) The major capitalist powers are experiencing increasing "contradictions"—or political conflicts—among themselves, resulting especially from dissatisfaction with American leadership and the rearmament of West Germany.

These changes in Soviet actions and doctrine encouraged a widespread belief in the West that the hypothetical military threat to Europe was virtually of no practical significance, since Moscow had now abandoned the overt use of armed force because of the hazards of thermonuclear war and had shifted to non-military instruments of policy, such as economic assistance, propaganda, and various forms of political penetration, designed to enhance Soviet influence in the colonial and former colonial areas. To many, an old, enduring hope seemed confirmed: the hazards and expense of the arms race, the pressures of Russian consumer demands, the pragmatism of the new Soviet bureaucracy, the liberalizing tendencies of education, and Russia's fear of Communist China were producing the kind of moderation of Soviet foreign policy that George Kennan had originally anticipated. It seemed to follow, therefore, that the West should encourage these tendencies, adopting a more flexible diplomacy, more responsive to Soviet proposals for disarmament and disengagement in Europe, while meeting the challenge in the underdeveloped areas through enlarged programs of technical and economic assistance and a more favorable attitude toward "neutralism."

Measured by any realistic appraisal of internal developments in the Soviet Union and their relationship to foreign policy or of the altered international military and political environment and its relationship to Soviet *realpolitik*, these popular assumptions were extravagantly optimistic.[84] In the retrospective view of the 1960's it was clearer than in 1955 and 1956 that the Soviet "new look" in foreign policy represented an imaginative effort, not to stabilize the status quo, even in Europe, but to capitalize upon the growth of Soviet nuclear and industrial power, combined with the intensification of the nationalist, economic, and social revolution in the "underdeveloped" areas, to extend Soviet influence and control beyond the bounds consolidated under Stalin while hastening the disintegration of the Western alliance. Khrushchev might accept the existence of a military stalemate insofar as it ruled out the calculated resort to nuclear war or direct armed aggression, but he interpreted this situation of mutual deterrence not as a basis for political accommodation but rather as an opportunity to conduct political and psychological warfare more actively against the Western coalition and its vulnerable outposts like Berlin, while destroying the remnants of Western influence in the "zone of peace" and incorporating the uncommitted nations into a "socialist world system."

In this new phase of the cold war the deterrent to Soviet military adventures was probably as much Russia's opportunities for non-violent aggrandizement as her fear of nuclear retaliation. Yet Khrushchev's growing confidence in the shift of the military balance away from the West toward the Soviet Union and his willingness to play the game of nuclear blackmail and brinkmanship more adventurously in the Middle East and Berlin foreshadowed an increasing danger that Russia might also become engaged in limited military incursions, either deliberately or inadvertently. In any event, by 1954 the range of tactical options for advancing Soviet interests had certainly grown substantially since the death of Stalin, and this foreshadowed a period of intensified Soviet probing and maneuver. Therefore, the post-Stalin phase of the cold war clearly called for new strategic flexibility in order to preserve the military basis of allied security and cohesion.

5
NATO Goes Nuclear

1. THE AMERICAN "NEW LOOK" STRATEGY

As a political arrangement for securing Germany's membership in NATO, the Paris Agreements represented a considerable advancement of NATO as an integrated military organization, but, in themselves, they did not much alter the discrepancy between NATO's declared strategy and its actual capabilities, which could only be rectified by concrete military, economic, and material contributions of the allies. It was several years before the Federal Republic, in the face of domestic opposition to rearmament, managed to contribute any significant number of troops to Western defense. In the meantime, all allied countries were busy once more subordinating their NATO force goals to domestic economic goals.

The logical concomitant of this restoration of the priority of domestic over defense requirements was a revised strategy based on the substitution of nuclear firepower for conventional manpower. In the aftermath of the Korean War, only the United States and Great Britain had the nuclear weapons to carry out this strategy, but their strategic example soon became the model for NATO as a whole; for NATO could not pursue a strategy that its two most powerful members had abandoned.

In the United States the general outline of the "new look" in military strategy was expressed in Dulles' attacks upon "containment" during the presidential campaign of 1952. His views were embraced by President Eisenhower soon after assuming office.[1] In the spring of 1953, the President announced that, in order to bring economic and military necessities "into some kind of realistic focus," defense planning would now be based on maintaining adequate preparedness over a period of years rather than achieving maximum strength by a "magic critical year."[2] However, the actual readjustment of military policies to new economic limitations, for which Dulles had provided the strategic formula, had to await the President's approval of a basic National Security Council decision in October, 1953. This decision authorized the Joint Chiefs of Staff to base their plans on using tactical and strategic nuclear weapons against conventional attacks wherever this was militarily advantageous (although by law the President retained exclusive authority to order their use in any particular contingency). On the basis of this decision the administration gained the approval of the Joint Chiefs for a substantially reduced defense budget, based upon a greater allocation of resources to nuclear striking power at the expense of conventional arms and ground forces. In December Admiral Radford, chairman of the Joint Chiefs of Staff, announced, "Today, atomic weapons have virtually achieved conventional status within our Armed Forces."[3] On January 12, 1954, Secretary Dulles delivered his famous address announcing that the government, in order to get "a maximum deterrent at a bearable cost," had decided to "depend primarily upon a great capacity to retaliate, instantly, by means and at places of our choosing."[4]

Actually, Dulles' pronouncement was not new at all as it applied to the NATO area but only as it threatened nuclear retaliation rather than local conventional resistance against limited aggressions outside Europe.[5] As before, massive retaliation remained the operational strategy in Europe, and massive local defense remained its ghostly partner in declaratory strategy. In fact, to counter any impression that the United States might renounce local defense in Europe, Dulles later stated in a written clarification of his January speech, "Some areas are so vital that a special guard should and can be put around them. Western Europe is such an area. Its industrial plant represents so nearly the balance of industrial power in the world that an aggressor might feel that it was a good gamble to seize it—even at the risk of considerable hurt to himself. In this respect, Western Europe is an exception."[6] And he specifically denied that the government's new strategy foretold a withdrawal of American forces from Europe. If the Continental nations provided "a harmonious nucleus of integrated defense," he said, "the United States would expect to maintain substantial forces of its own in Europe, both in support of the forward strategy of defense and for political reasons."[7]

Nevertheless, the effect of America's "new look" was to discourage rather than encourage Western Europe to build up "a harmonious nucleus of integrated defense." For if the richest and most powerful ally felt compelled to rely more upon nuclear deterrence and less upon ground resistance in order to bring economic and military necessities into "realistic focus," why should her less affluent partners continue to sacrifice their economic advancement for the construction of a large ground force? National specialization between the United States and her allies in the functions of nuclear deterrence and conventional ground resistance might be *militarily* necessary for a while, if only because the allies (except Great Britain) lacked the technological capacity to develop their own nuclear deterrents. But a grossly unequal distribution of sacrifices, such as would be imposed by their continued rearmament for conventional warfare while the United States reduced its conventional forces in favor of a nuclear strategy, would scarcely be compatible with the *political* requirements of allied collaboration. Moreover, if nuclear firepower compensated for conventional manpower in America's armed forces, logically it should do the same for NATO as a whole. The development of tactical nuclear weapons, combined with the continued shortfall in NATO's conventional forces, assured the extension of this logic to the defense of Europe.

2. TOWARD A "NEW LOOK" FOR NATO

The development of compact and relatively low-yield nuclear warheads (10 kilotons and below), which were presumably suitable for discriminating destruction of tactical military targets in the battle zone, had scarcely begun when the Lisbon conference force goals were set.[8] Therefore, these goals were based, essentially, on a World War II concept of strategy with the atomic bombs added to enhance strategic airpower. Although even before the Korean War military and civilian authorities had pointed hopefully to the prospect of using atomic weapons tactically as well as strategically in order to close the gap between NATO's strategy and its capabilities,[9] the first concerted scientific and military study of this prospect—part of the controversial Project Vista, begun in early 1951—grew out of the impact of the Korean War on military thinking, out of the military's desire to increase the West's capacity for local resistance.[10] The failure of the allies to meet the Lisbon goals in the aftermath of the Korean scare, combined with the revision of British and American strategies to take advantage of the purported savings of nuclear deterrents, provided the major impetus for the incorporation of tactical nuclear weapons in NATO's strategic planning.

One of the earliest official intimations that tactical nuclear weapons might enable NATO to achieve its security objectives without meeting the Lisbon force goals came from General J. Lawton Collins, army chief of staff, when he told a press conference on September 6, 1952, that, although tactical nuclear weapons would not decrease "the number of divisions required initially for the defense of Europe," they would "result ultimately in the ability to do the job with a smaller number of divisions."[11] In 1952, however, NATO forces had no tactical atomic weapons, and the American military leaders assigned to Europe had scarcely begun to study the tactics and organization of the forces that might fight with these weapons. Moreover, the Atomic Energy Act of 1946 (or MacMahon Act, as it was popularly termed, after its sponsor, Senator MacMahon), which was enacted when the United States held a monopoly of the atomic bomb in order to prevent the Soviet Union from getting atomic secrets, prohibited the sharing of atomic weapons and atomic information with the European allies. Thus, France's Marshal Juin, commanding allied ground forces in Europe, was forbidden to know the nature and number of atomic arms he might eventually have at his disposal.

Nevertheless, the prospect of at least the American forces in Europe acquiring tactical nuclear weapons made European governments all the more reluctant to exact domestic sacrifices in order to support the Lisbon goals, which had been devised on the basis of conventional military equipment and a World War II strategy that would soon be outmoded. As the British government's statement of defense policy for 1953 put it, "In times of stringency it is specially important to get the fullest possible value for our money; we must avoid overcommitting ourselves too deeply to equipment which will have to be replaced at heavy cost within a relatively short space of time."[12]

Therefore, while the American government held out to her allies the hope of eventually defending Europe with fewer troops by incorporating tactical nuclear weapons in NATO's strategy and tried to loosen up the restrictions that the MacMahon Act imposed on collaborating with them in the development of such a strategy, it was also wary of claiming too much for these weapons, lest it further encourage the allies to relax their defense efforts. Thus, soon after General Collins publicly anticipated that tactical nuclear weapons would ultimately enable NATO's forces to defend Europe with a smaller number of divisions, General Bradley issued a statement warning that these weapons were not sufficiently advanced to justify any slackening in the effort to build up NATO's ground forces to its scheduled goals, which were "essential to collective defense, even with the optimistic estimates of the future capabilities of atomic weapons."[13]

General Bradley's warning was confirmed by the studies and war-gaming of two-sided nuclear warfare that the United States Seventh Army Corps in Europe initiated in the winter of 1952–53. General James M. Gavin, the commander of that Corps, later wrote, "One over-all conclusion stood out clearly, although for several years it was the basis of considerable argument: more rather than less manpower would be required to fight a nuclear war successfully."[14] Similarly, the Supreme Allied Commander, General Ridgway, held that the new tactical nuclear weapons would not only demand more manpower but would also increase the cost of defense to the taxpayer.[15] And his successor, General Gruenther, warned that "new weapons frequently have the effect of adding new problems and new tasks without eliminating those that previously confronted us."[16]

Nevertheless, each new development that facilitated the use of tactical nuclear weapons as an integral part of NATO's military establishment made it increasingly difficult to dampen hopes of substituting technology for manpower and money. In February, 1953, General Sir Richard Gale, commander of the Allied Northern Army Group in West Germany, revealed that in case of war "a certain number of atomic weapons may be available" and that the forces under his command were being trained on the basis of using them.[17] On April 22 the first "low-yield" atomic bomb to be exploded near ground soldiers was tested on the Yucca Flats in Nevada. Shortly afterward, the Defense Department announced that allied officers were to begin taking special instruction in Germany on the use of atomic weapons.[18] In October the first gigantic 85-ton, 280 mm. atomic artillery piece from the United States arrived in Europe, to be followed in 1954 by more maneuverable rockets and missiles (Honest John, Corporal, Matador, and Regulus). At the same time, the American government, acceding to the urgings of Marshal Juin and other allied commanders,[19] sought a relaxation of legislative restrictions upon sharing pertinent operational information on the new weapons.[20] The Atomic Energy Act of 1954 permitted sharing additional information on the external characteristics of these weapons, such as "size, weight, and shape, yield and effects, and systems employed in the delivery or use thereof." However, in provisions apparently designed as much to restrain America's allies as the Soviet Union from developing nuclear capabilities, the Act withheld information that might be useful to the "design and fabrication of the nuclear components," required that the warheads themselves remain under the control of Americans at all times, and gave Congress (through the Joint Committee on Atomic Energy) considerable control over executive agreements to disseminate nuclear weapons information.[21]

As the American government approached its October, 1953, decision to plan on using tactical nuclear weapons against conventional aggressions, top civilian officials in the Eisenhower administration openly advised NATO to adjust its inflated force goals to the capabilities of "radical new weapons" and even indicated their desire to reduce the number of American military personnel in Europe.[22] Although President Eisenhower and Secretary Dulles were quick to calm the resulting French apprehensions by disavowing any existing plan for reducing American combat forces overseas, they did not disavow future plans. At the same time, they affirmed that the need for economy was great and that the new atomic weapons were bound to affect the composition of NATO's forces.[23]

The military justification of this supposition was as popular in Congress as in the Pentagon, and in Congress it was surrounded with fewer qualifications. Thus the Senate report on the 1954 amendments to the Atomic Energy Act stated flatly:

> America's preponderance in atomic weapons can offset the numerical superiority of the Communist forces and serve emphatic notice on the Soviet dictators that any attempt to occupy free Europe or to push further anywhere into the Free World would be foredoomed to failure.[24]

And Representative Sterling Cole, chairman of the Joint Committee on Atomic Energy, declared that

> tactical atomic weapons may confront the Red Army with an impossible operational dilemma. The conventional NATO defenses are already of such a strength that the Soviets could not penetrate them without first massing their ground forces in preparation for a breakthrough. Once the legions of the Red Army are so concentrated, they expose themselves to the mortal peril of counterattack by nuclear weapons.[25]

As for the military planners, by January, 1954, even before a basic military study of the tactics and organization for employing tactical nuclear weapons had been completed, General Gruenther had evidently concluded that these weapons would permit a reduction of forces. Speaking to the American Club in Paris, he explained, "If seventy divisions, for example, are needed to establish a conventional line of defense between the Alps and the Baltic, then seventy minus X divisions equipped with atomic weapons would be needed."[26] However, he also pointed to the need for German troops in order to keep NATO's forward shield strong enough to force the enemy to attack in concentration and thereby offer a profitable target for atomic bombardment.[27]

In July the press reported certain principal features of the "cosmic top secret" study carried out under General Gruenther's direction: (*a*) warfare in the future would inevitably be atomic; (*b*) the first atomic targets would be armed forces and military installations rather than major centers of population; (*c*) the peak of destruction would come at the outset of the war; (*d*) therefore, the outcome would be determined by the active forces-in-being.[28] In August SHAPE was reported to have sent to the NATO Standing Group a three-year plan for completely reorganizing NATO's forces, compensating for the reduction of ground forces by developing air and atomic power.[29] And General Gruenther subsequently stated that this plan would give NATO a "reasonably good chance of defending Europe successfully against an all-out act of Soviet aggression," providing that it could use atomic weapons (which he feared that current Western disarmament plans, leading to the elimination of atomic weapons, might prevent) and count on a German contribution to the forward line.[30]

General Gruenther stated the crucial assumption upon which the whole plan depended when he explained in an interview, "We have determined that our strategy in the center requires the use of atomic weapons, whether the enemy uses them or not, and we must use atomic bombs to redress the imbalance between their forces and ours and to achieve victory."[31] Field

Marshal Montgomery, the Deputy Supreme Commander, stated this assumption even more categorically in a widely quoted lecture to the Royal United Service Institute:

> I want to make it absolutely clear that we at SHAPE are basing all our operational planning on using atomic and thermonuclear weapons in our own defense. With us it is no longer: "They may possibly be used." It is very definitely: "They will be used, if we are attacked." In fact, we have reached the point of no return as regards the use of atomic and thermonuclear weapons in a hot war.[32]

3. THE HYDROGEN BOMB

In 1954 it was widely believed throughout the Western world that the United States could retain its relative military position by maintaining a substantial lead in the atomic arms race and that the introduction of tactical nuclear weapons into NATO's forces would maintain the West's clear-cut military advantage against the masses of conventional forces in the Communist world. To be sure, in 1951 Acheson had warned that "with the passage of time, even though we continue our advances in this field [of atomic weapons], the value of our lead diminishes."[33] But three years later the gradual neutralization of America's nuclear advantage by the growth of Soviet nuclear capacity had exerted little impact upon strategic thinking. Not until March, 1955, did President Eisenhower publicly acknowledge the validity of the proposition that Acheson had suggested, when he told a news conference, "There comes a time, possibly, when a lead [in nuclear weapons] is not significant in the defensive arrangements of a country. If you get enough of a particular type of weapon I doubt that it is particularly important to have a lot more of it."[34] Still, well after 1955 the West's strategic outlook remained under the dominant influence of nostalgic memories of the period of America's atomic monopoly, when it was assumed that every addition to America's nuclear striking capacity gained the West a proportionate increase in military security.

Yet, even while the Western nations looked anxiously toward

tactical nuclear weapons as a deterrent to conventional attacks and a compensation for the shortfall in NATO's ground forces, spectacular evidence of the destructive power of nuclear energy and the capacity of the Soviet Union to utilize it incited powerful inhibitions that would, in time, cast doubt upon the willingness of any nation to use nuclear weapons, whether tactically or strategically, except as a deterrent to nuclear attacks. On November 1, 1952, at Eniwetok Atoll in the Pacific, the United States produced a thermonuclear explosion of such awesome proportions—eyewitnesses described the disappearance of a mile-wide island—as to strike the world's statesmen and military leaders as no less epoch-making than the first atomic explosion in 1945. On August 8, 1953, Soviet Premier Malenkov gave the world another shock with his portentous announcement that "the government considers it necessary to report to the Supreme Soviet that the United States has no monopoly of production of the hydrogen bomb." His boast was confirmed on August 12 and 23, when the Soviet Union exploded thermonuclear bombs that were evidently of a more advanced design than the Eniwetok device.[35] In February, 1954, Sterling Cole, chairman of the Joint Congressional Committee on Atomic Energy, released details about America's first thermonuclear explosion that were as startling as the original announcement.[36] Winston Churchill later told the House of Commons that with the publication of this first comprehensive review of the effects of a hydrogen explosion "the entire foundation of human affairs was revolutionized and mankind placed in a situation both measureless and laden with doom."[37] In another statement he declared, "The advance of the hydrogen bomb has fundamentally altered the entire problem of defense, and considerations founded even upon the atom bomb have become obsolescent, almost old-fashioned."[38]

Nevertheless, it took the radioactive contamination of the "Lucky Dragon" crew in March, 1954, to dramatize for the general public the strange and terrible destructive power of the hydrogen bomb. The Atomic Energy Commission later revealed that the fall-out area from this bomb, which had an explosive power of about twelve megatons of TNT according to unofficial estimates, covered 7,000 square miles in a cigar-shaped area downwind from the explosion.[39] This graphic description and the others that followed it seized the popular imagination with a force unparalleled by the atom bomb.

Merely by demonstrating that the United States was no longer supreme in military technology and general scientific prowess, the Russian thermonuclear explosions undermined allied confidence in America's deterrent capacity in a way the previous atomic explosions had only insinuated. But equally fateful for allied confidence in a strategy based so largely upon nuclear deterrence was the demonstration by America's own explosions that a nuclear war could now result in the sudden virtual annihilation of perhaps all but the largest nations; for ten hydrogen bombs, it was estimated, would turn the British Isles into a radioactive wasteland. Consequently, the fear of America's allies that the United States would not defend Europe at the price of thermonuclear war now began to be overshadowed by the fear that she would.

The mounting sense of vulnerability to national obliteration that underlay European apprehensions was felt even in the United States. Thus President Eisenhower on October 6, 1953, informed the public that "our former unique physical security has almost totally disappeared before the long-range bomber and the destructive power of a single bomb. . . . In its wake we see only sudden and mass destruction, erasure of cities, the possible doom of every nation and society." And two days later, in an official statement confirming reports that the Soviets possessed "a stockpile of atomic weapons of conventional types" and that the August 12 explosion "was produced by a weapon, or the forerunner of a weapon, of power far in excess of the conventional types," he said, "We therefore conclude that the Soviets now have the capability of attack on us, and such capability will increase with the passage of time."[40]

The President's warning seemed especially pertinent when Russia demonstrated in the May Day parade of 1954 that she possessed long-range and medium-range jet bombers comparable to the American B-52 and B-47. This intelligence seemingly (but with some exaggeration, according to subsequent intelligence) confirmed the United States Air Force's fears that Russia was building a huge Strategic Air Command of her own to strike at the United States. The Air Force, committed to the view that America's offensive striking capability was the preeminent deterrent, insisted that the United States should quickly enlarge SAC in order to maintain its supremacy. Outside the Air Force, some scientists and military advisers found a receptive response in the government to the argument that Russia's growing strategic air force increased the urgency of expensive early-warning radar lines and other components of continental defense. In 1953 the administration had already decided to buy this system of continental defense over heavy Air Force opposition, partly on the grounds that it was needed to protect American air bases and limit civilian damage and partly on the ground that the United States might be psychologically disarmed if she could devastate Russia only with the expectation of receiving equal devastation in return.

Actually, neither an increase of America's offensive (that is, "first-strike") nuclear power nor of her capability for continental defense against Soviet bombers was addressed to the more serious military and, especially, political threat to America's deterrent strategy: Russia's intensive ballistic missile program, which was already in progress in 1954. In 1956 evidence of Russian advancement in IRBM's (intermediate-range ballistic missiles) became an instrument of psychological warfare against European allies who harbored American bomber bases, but the full impact of the Russian program did not strike home until Russia's launching of two earth satellites in the fall of 1957; for this achievement suggested that Russia might soon achieve ICBM's (intercontinental ballistic missiles), which no known defense could prevent from devastating the United States.

In 1953 and 1954, despite the President's intimations of America's physical vulnerability, the prevailing atmosphere of military planning in the United States was still, hopefully, that of unilateral nuclear deterrence, but, even then, in Europe's changing assessment of the military gains and risks of the alliance, there were signs of the psychological and political impact of mutual deterrence, which the Sputniks would bring to a head.

4. THE DIVERGENCE OF AMERICAN AND EUROPEAN CONCEPTIONS OF NATO

While the prospect of sudden annihilation was stealthily impressing itself upon the popular imagination in Western Europe, the death of Stalin in March, 1953, and the achievement of a Korean armistice in July opened the way for a new course of "peaceful coexistence" in Soviet policy. As I have suggested, this course acted as an effective supplement to Russia's nuclear might in persuading some allies to subordinate concern about Soviet aggression to the overriding fear that a failure to resolve Soviet-created tensions might lead to a thermonuclear holocaust. It convinced many Western observers that the main thrust of Communist power had shifted to non-military means and to areas outside Europe and raised hopes that diplomacy might now relieve the political tensions which had occasioned the wearying effort to build a situation of military strength on the Continent during the Stalinist era.

In this atmosphere of anxious hope, every indication of America's reluctance to renew the traumatic diplomatic confrontations of 1946 and 1947 and every manifestation of America's determination that the allies should meet their military obligations to collective defense emphasized an important difference in the American and allied conceptions of NATO, a difference which had been of little practical significance before NATO's abortive rearmament effort. In American eyes the alliance, having been transformed from a guaranty pact to an integrated military organization, was the essential instrument for redressing the military imbalance on the Continent; but in the eyes of most European members the major purpose of the alliance remained, as before the Korean War, to commit the United States to come to their defense. To the United States the more taxing terms of collaboration that evolved in the aftermath of the Korean War provided the essential means of supporting a forward strategy, but to her allies in Europe they were more the means of accommodating their political interests and appeasing American pressure than the prerequisites for meeting urgent military requirements.

Consequently, to her allies the United States seemed unnecessarily preoccupied with military considerations at the expense of accommodating divergent political interests in Western Europe and relieving the tensions of the cold war; while to the United States, who had entered the alliance to help Western Europe defend itself, her allies now seemed less interested in assuming the responsibility for their self-defense than she. In truth, the United States, as the principal contender in the cold war, had from the beginning of the alliance implicitly assumed the major responsibility for containing Soviet power in Europe, simply by virtue of her preponderance of power within the alliance. The trouble was that in her eyes the strategic conditions for discharging that responsibility had come to require not merely the extension of America's atomic umbrella but also the creation of a sizable standing army, which, according to the original division of allied labor, should devolve upon the European members. Therefore, the original balance of responsibility and sacrifice between the United States and Europe had grown unsatisfactory to both. Yet the very movement toward a greater reliance upon nuclear weapons, which was intended to render the maintenance of ground forces less onerous, helped discourage the allies from increasing their contributions to a military establishment that would depend upon fantastically destructive and expensive weapons, which only the United States and, to a far lesser extent, Great Britain produced and controlled.

It seems doubtful, under the circumstances, that the United States, by utilizing more drastic concessions or sanctions, could have induced the European allies to support their share of NATO's burdens and strategic functions more fully. The greatest American concession to allied collaboration was the stationing of additional American troops on the Continent, but, once it had been granted, the United States could not threaten to withdraw it without cutting off her nose to spite her face—even though Secretary of State Dulles' threat of an "agonizing reappraisal" of American strategy probably played a part in securing French acceptance of a German contribution. For as the growing nuclear dependence of NATO undermined the credibility of America's commitment to defend Europe, the United States was forced to acknowledge the enhanced psychological importance of her contribution to NATO's ground forces, while her allies confined their contributions to the lowest levels compatible with American political and material support. Thus the principal purpose of America's Continental troops continued to be the promotion of allied collaboration, but their specific function changed from starting a spiral of rising confidence, which would lead Europe to build its own defenses, to stopping a spiral of declining confidence, which would leave Europe helpless in the face of Soviet political and military pressure.

5. NATO ADOPTS A TACTICAL NUCLEAR SOLUTION

By the end of 1954 the shortfall in NATO's post-Korean force goals, combined with the growth of Russia's air-nuclear capacity, had aroused considerable dissatisfaction in the American government with a strategic contradiction—the discrepancy between NATO's declaratory strategy of defending every member on the ground and NATO's actual military capabilities—which all allies had regarded as an acceptable, even indispensable, price of collaboration before the Korean War. Confronted with this contradiction, the United States reaffirmed the essential strategic objective of NATO as the defense of Western Europe by preventing the devastation or occupation of any ally. But, under her leadership, NATO now officially adopted a strategy based upon a tactical nuclear response to conventional aggression in order to support this objective at a level of economic and manpower contributions that the allies were willing to pay. Yet, contrary to original hopes, this strategic expedient, by increasing NATO's dependence upon nuclear weapons against conventional attacks in the face of rising Soviet nuclear power, only compounded the problems of gaining allied collaboration at a level of commitments and contributions compatible with their security.

The North Atlantic Council, at its meeting in December, 1954, refrained from scheduling any significant increase in NATO's forces-in-being during 1955 and contented itself with approving "further improvements in training, equipment, and effectiveness." However, it adopted a composite military report authorizing NATO's military commanders to devise their strategic plans on the basis of using nuclear weapons, whether the aggressor used them or not.[41]

Secretary Dulles hailed this decision as at last providing the means of developing a forward strategy that could protect Western Europe from invasion and liberation and throw back the aggressor "at the threshold."[42] But by this time Dulles' assurances were no longer relevant to the central apprehensions of the European allies. The allies had long ceased to fear a Soviet invasion, and every year that passed without a Soviet attack seemingly confirmed the wisdom of their apathy toward preparing to withstand an all-out attack. On the other hand, they had not ceased to fear the consequences of resisting aggression if it should occur, for each new evidence of rising Soviet nuclear strength emphasized the catastrophic damage that they would incur in a nuclear conflict.

All countries were gratified by official assurances that tactical nuclear weapons would enable them to support NATO's strategic objectives at a saving in manpower and money, but some European members' gratification was tempered by the fact that they had bought an opportunity to defend themselves only at the cost of their obliteration. For, according to the new strategic formula, NATO's forward line was intended primarily to hold long enough to permit the initiation of a nuclear war, which would inflict incalculable damage in Europe even if it remained "tactical" from America's standpoint. On the other hand, some allies feared that the United States, hoping to avoid a nuclear war in which she might be the main target, would withhold the nuclear deterrent while permitting her allies to be subjugated in a local conventional war.

In December, 1956, the North Atlantic Council approved a directive for future military plans based on the concept of forward defense but "taking into account the continued rise in Soviet capabilities and the various types of new weapons available for NATO defense."[43] As a result of this directive the Supreme Commanders made a study of the minimum forces required to carry out their respective missions. In 1957, on the basis of this so-called "minimum-forces" study, the Military Committee adopted a five-year plan (MC–70) to create a NATO force of thirty combat-ready divisions, which were regarded as essentially nuclear forces. If the members of the alliance had actually achieved this force goal, NATO would have been in a much better position to resist any likely aggression short of a massive invasion *without* the use of nuclear weapons, since this new requirement for the forward line was actually greater than under the Lisbon goals (the reduction in the total number of divisions being made in reserves).[44] But, in fact, France's transfer of four divisions from the Continent to Algeria (beginning in 1954), which soon tied down 400,000 troops, and Britain's withdrawal of two divisions in 1957, following her decision to concentrate on building an independent nuclear capability, kept these forces below twenty effective fighting divisions. In the meanwhile, there was no change in NATO's official estimates of the number of Soviet (not including satellite) divisions: 175, of which 140 were operational standing divisions (including 22 in East Germany and Poland and about 80 in the rest of Eastern Europe and in Western Russia), and a capability of mobilizing 400 divisions in thirty days. In this situation, it was questionable whether NATO's ground forces could really do anything more than trip the alarm that would bring the nuclear forces into battle.

6. NATO'S TRIP-WIRE

In the opinion of some military circles, the tactical nuclear strategy adopted in December, 1954, failed to live up to its original promise of providing more security at less cost by substituting nuclear firepower for conventionally armed manpower.

United States Army studies and war games in 1955 and 1958 confirmed the conclusion reached by General Gavin in 1952 that a two-sided nuclear war would require more manpower than a conventional war, chiefly because of the higher rate of casualties, the greater depth of the battle line, and the more complex logistics.[45] Moreover, the progress that the Soviet Union made after 1954 in equipping her own forces with nuclear weapons shook the confidence of military experts in the original assumption that the West would have the advantage in fighting a nuclear war because of the superiority of the nuclear defense over the offense.[46] Certainly, the development and production of tactical nuclear weapons did not turn out to be a financial saving. In fact, they were so expensive that, in the opinion of some Army officers, the "modernization" of ground forces within existing defense budgets dangerously restricted the development and production of conventional weapons without producing sufficient nuclear weapons;[47] consequently, NATO seemed to be losing its capacity to fight a conventional war before it obtained the capacity to fight a tactical nuclear war, which the United States might have no advantage in fighting anyway.

However, this skepticism about tactical nuclear weapons enabling NATO to hold the forward line at less cost in men and money did not persuade the allies of the need to build up NATO's conventional capacity, for they were increasingly inclined to regard tactical, like strategic, nuclear weapons as a *deterrent* to aggression rather than as a *defense* against invasion if the deterrent should fail. This view was encouraged by the development of a widespread belief that the growth of nuclear power in the United States and the Soviet Union had created a "nuclear stalemate" or a stable "balance of terror," which made the outbreak of *any* war in such a vital strategic area as Western Europe extremely unlikely as long as both sides were convinced that any war would become nuclear. Prime Minister Churchill gave the most notable expression to popular confidence in the stability of nuclear deterrence in a speech on March 1, 1955, defending his government's decision to build a hydrogen bomb. Referring to the immense destructive power of the recent thermonuclear explosions, he said:

> The broad effect of the latest development is to spread almost indefinitely and at least to a vast extent the area of mortal danger. This should certainly increase the deterrent upon Soviet Russia by putting her enormous spaces and scattered population on an equality of vulnerability with our small, densely populated island and with Western Europe. Then it may well be that we shall, by a process of sublime irony, have reached a stage in this story where safety will be the sturdy child of terror, and survival the twin brother of annihilation.[48]

Churchill spoke of strategic, rather than tactical, nuclear deterrents, but in the Statement on Defense for 1955 (popularly known as the annual White Paper), which his words were intended to justify, and in the debate on the Statement in the House, tactical nuclear weapons were regarded as part of the general nuclear deterrent.[49] According to this White Paper, the North Atlantic Council decision of December, 1954, assumed the use of nuclear weapons in a "major war"; and in a major war the free nations would have to use the "full weight" of their nuclear power, or "all the weapons at their disposal," in order to counter the Soviet preponderance of conventional power.

Thus, despite an occasional suggestion that tactical nuclear weapons might not lead to an all-out war,[50] the stated official assumption in Britain, as in the United States, was that the use of tactical nuclear weapons in the NATO area would be the concomitant of a thermonuclear exchange, and that this terrible possibility would deter conventional aggression. Presumably—although this point was never publicly explained—tactical nuclear weapons were a useful supplement to massive retaliation because it was more credible that, in the event of a conventional attack, NATO would employ them as a means of resistance on the battlefield than that the United States or Great Britain would immediately drop hydrogen bombs as a means of reprisal on the Soviet Union, even though the employment of tactical weapons would probably lead to a disastrous war of annihilation by a natural process of escalation.

Western leaders were understandably reluctant to define the exact nature and scope of the aggression that would warrant a nuclear response, but, having decided to rely upon nuclear deterrence as a substitute for conventional resistance, they were clearly disposed to assume that the balance of terror would deter the maximum range of contingencies—perhaps all but the smallest police actions and border incidents. This tendency was most pronounced in the United States. In 1956 the basic document for military planning (JSOP 60) followed out the logic of the National Security Council decision of October, 1953 (basing military plans on the use of tactical nuclear weapons against conventional attacks) to its ultimate conclusion by virtually excluding the possibility of a conventional war with the Soviet Union or of another limited war of the scope of the Korean War.[51]

On the basis of this document Admiral Radford, chairman of the Joint Chiefs of Staff, led a major effort in July, 1956, to cut the armed services by 800,000 men, limiting the ground forces primarily to civil defense missions and to token forces abroad, to be supplemented by the indigenous forces.[52] As Walter Lippmann described Radford's basic strategic assumption at the time, any Korean-type limited aggression that concerned the United States and the Soviet Union was expected to lead to the use of small atomic bombs, which, in turn, would lead to the exchange of bigger ones. "The chances of general war would be so great that a local war on the Korean scale would be an incalculable military risk. It is not absolutely certain, but it is very probable, that for the visible future wars of this type will be absorbed into the over-all nuclear stalemate." Therefore, in the future the alternative to general nuclear war would be not local conventional war but guerilla warfare and political intervention and maneuver.[53]

Lippmann's interpretation of Radford's strategic assumption coincided with the reasoning that Secretary of Defense Wilson had conveyed to Congress several months before in explaining why American defense expenditures had been reduced since 1953 while Soviet military strength had been growing.[54] And

Radford's program had been foreshadowed by the testimony of General Nathan Twining, Air Force chief of staff, before the Senate Armed Services Subcommittee on Air Power in June, when he gave the first official confirmation that there had been a top level decision "to develop a new strategy built around the use of atomic weapons in war," which would mean that "we could reduce our forces considerably." The new strategy, he said, "is the only way we can provide the forces for the country within a reasonable standard of financing." "We cannot afford to keep in our armed forces conventional forces for the old type of warfare plus those for atomic warfare. We have got to make up our minds that we have to go one way or the other."[55]

Admiral Radford's proposal to cut the armed forces was rejected, or at least its acceptance was formally postponed, because of the storm it created abroad, but its underlying strategic assumption remained the guiding one in the administration's defense policy. As a matter of fact, in 1956 even few of those who saw a danger of conventional limited wars in peripheral strategic areas considered them a danger worth preparing for in Western Europe.[56] The general assumption was that any war in that area would necessarily implicate the Soviet Union and that the Soviet Union would not dare instigate a conventional attack against NATO forces, because she would thereby lose the indispensable advantage of exercising the initiative and surprise against a superior nuclear force. Thus General Bradley testified in April, 1956, that he did not believe the Russians would attack Europe and touch off World War III without launching a surprise attack on the United States first.[57] Two years earlier Prime Minister Churchill had explained more fully the logic of this assumption.

> Although I have spoken of the overwhelming superiority in conventional weapons of the Soviets, I would mention that I do not believe that a surprise attack with conventional weapons would be made upon the Western front. There would certainly be discernible movements of troops which would raise both the alert and the alarm, and this would certainly bring the use of nuclear weapons into discussion of a decisive character by the heads of all the great States that are involved. If the Soviets, as

> the weaker nuclear Power, resolved to make, which I do not believe they would, a treacherous surprise attack, it is inconceivable, to my mind, that they would begin with ground forces on the Western front and so compromise the advantage of a surprise attack by nuclear weapons.[58]

Thus, as the statement suggests, NATO's limited ground forces were more a device to activate the nuclear deterrent than a means of local resistance. At the most, they would compel the aggressor to mobilize for an attack and thereby give advance warning, hold him until nuclear retaliation could take effect, prevent him from quickly seizing allied territory from which he could be ousted only by subjecting friends to atomic attack, and force him to concentrate for breakthroughs and thereby provide targets for America's nuclear weapons. Thus, unofficially, NATO's ground forces came to be referred to as a "trip-wire" or a "plate-glass," which could not stop aggression but which would touch off the alarm that would bring the West's nuclear forces into action. In effect, they would deter a Soviet attack on Europe by insuring that it would be an all-out nuclear attack, which would be met by massive nuclear retaliation, but, as extra insurance that all aggression would entail the risk of nuclear war, there was NATO's determination to meet conventional attacks with tactical nuclear weapons. Although the trip-wire metaphor was obviously unsuitable for official pronouncements and was, in fact, repeatedly repudiated by the United States, it described operational strategy more accurately than the official declarations of NATO's commitment to a forward strategy designed to protect every ally from the dreaded cycle of occupation and liberation.

7. NUCLEAR INHIBITIONS

In the absence of a controlled experiment, we can only speculate about the effect that NATO's adoption of this nuclear strategy had in deterring the Soviet Union from undertaking military aggression in the NATO area, but we can observe some of the effects of this strategy upon the deterrers; and, as in any strategy of deterrence, the effects upon the subject and the object of deterrence may be closely related. For example, the very nature of the deterrent threat may create attitudes toward the use of military power in the mind of the deterrer that alter the credibility of the threat in the mind of the potential aggressor. Even if the aggressor is not tempted to test the deterrent threat by overt military action, he may try to turn the deterrer's attitudes to his political advantage merely by raising international tensions so as to exploit the deterrer's anticipation of having to carry out the threat. Where there are several deterrers, as in a defensive coalition, this kind of anticipation can exert a serious strain upon their cohesion, which, in turn, can impinge directly upon their diplomatic posture and, ultimately, their security.

The public attitudes toward NATO's tactical nuclear strategy in the major allied countries have been ambivalent, reflecting an uneasy balance between hope and apprehension. Consequently, the positions of allied governments on the use of nuclear weapons have been ambiguous, reflecting their attempt to satisfy popular hopes while appeasing popular apprehensions. On the one hand, tactical nuclear weapons promise to defend Europe at a tolerable cost in men and money. On the other hand, they threaten to obliterate Europe if they have to be used. Unqualified declarations of NATO's determination to turn any overt military aggression into a nuclear war promise maximum deterrence at minimum cost. But the very prospect of having to choose between non-resistance and annihilation, which these declarations seem to assure, erodes the national will to carry out such a strategy.

The difficulty of reconciling the deterrent value of a nuclear threat with the will to carry it out became manifest as soon as NATO adopted its nuclear strategy in December, 1954. Marshal Montgomery's categorical declarations that NATO would use nuclear weapons against conventional attacks aroused considerable consternation—especially in Great Britain—about the possibility of military commanders precipitating a thermonuclear holocaust. Therefore, it became necessary for the North Atlantic Council to emphasize that the decision to use nuclear weapons would be made by civilians. Which civilian representatives of which governments would make this fateful decision by what procedures was not specified, and there was apparently some difference of opinion on this question between the United States, who wanted to centralize and simplify the decision-making process as much as possible, and her allies.[59] But the very acknowledgment that it would be a governmental and not a purely military decision belied the automatic character of a nuclear response, which Marshal Montgomery sought to convey, and raised a question about NATO's collective will to carry out the strategy it had adopted.

Some European allies were, naturally, more sensitive to popular inhibitions against initiating the use of tactical nuclear weapons than the United States, which, in the 1950's, was less vulnerable to sudden annihilation. Therefore, European apprehensions were directed more toward the possibility that the United States might rashly precipitate a nuclear war than toward the possibility that she might be restrained from employing the nuclear deterrent. But these apprehensions were in themselves a restraint upon America's use or threat to use nuclear weapons against a conventional attack. For what if the Soviet Army should overrun part of Europe without using nuclear weapons? As General Collins put it, "We could then imagine their saying to the Americans: 'Now come and get us.' Would we in that case assume the awful responsibility of initiating atomic warfare in order to 'liberate' Europe? Would we bomb Paris, Milan, the Saar, the Ruhr?"[60] Or, as General Taylor wrote in a passage which the State Department considered especially inadvisable to publish, "In Europe, we have some 250,000 soldiers accompanied by thousands of dependents living in close proximity to superior Communist ground forces deployed in the satellite countries. If the latter suddenly advanced west without warning, they would soon be locked in close combat with the NATO armies in such a way as to restrict the employment of atomic weapons against them."[61] Both generals were arguing NATO's need for a substantial capacity to hold on the ground in order to prevent the situation they envisioned from arising. But it is obvious that, even if NATO had the minimum forces specified, the same considerations might restrain the United States from initiating a nuclear war, which would be no less devastating to her allies if their cities were destroyed by Soviet, than if they were destroyed by American, nuclear weapons.

8. GERMANY'S REACTION TO NATO'S NUCLEAR STRATEGY

A vivid suggestion of the kind of destruction that a nuclear war in Europe might inflict was conveyed by the SHAPE war game "Carte Blanche," held in West Germany, the Lowlands and northeastern France in June, 1955. In this game it was announced that, hypothetically, 335 bombs had been dropped on military targets, killing 1,700,000 and wounding 3,500,000, not to mention the numbers affected by radioactivity. Actually, "Carte Blanche" had no relationship to a realistic military contingency, since it was confined to the Western Germany–Northern France area, was waged on a North-South instead of an East-West axis, and involved a quantity of nuclear strikes that was quite superfluous militarily. Nevertheless, the publication of these startling figures aroused, for the first time, wide public concern in Germany about the consequences of NATO's nuclear strategy.[62]

Until this time, Germans who were not opposed to rearmament on moral and political grounds had been generally disposed to accept the assurances of the United States, SHAPE, and their own military and political leaders that German contingents would contribute to a forward strategy, which would spare Germany from becoming a battle zone and military buffer. And, insofar as they had any concrete image of NATO's strategy, they had been led to believe that nuclear weapons would be used primarily against strategic targets in the Soviet Union, while the war in Central Europe would be waged pretty much as a conventional land war, perhaps on the pattern of the Korean War. Therefore, "Carte Blanche" came as a rude awakening to the real risks of NATO's tactical nuclear strategy.

Social Democrats and some independent military experts charged that "Carte Blanche" proved the emptiness of the Adenauer government's previous assurances, which had been presented as an argument for German rearmament and participation in NATO, that Germany would be protected from invasion and from becoming a battlefield.[63] "The strategy of NATO," cried Fritz Erler in the July, 1956, Bundestag debate on the conscription bill, "leaves no room for doubting that an armed conflict in Europe—even with 500,000 German soldiers—will not remain a conventional conflict. The NATO plans are based upon immediate and direct employment of atomic weapons in the event of a conflict in Europe."[64] The conclusion to be drawn from this fact and from "Carte Blanche," said the opponents of rearmament, was that German contingents in NATO would be useless for defending Germany, since they could only collaborate in a strategy that would precipitate a nuclear catastrophe. They expressed no concern about the danger of a Soviet aggression—in fact, German opinion polls showed steadily declining expectations of war throughout the nation after 1950[65] —but they were preoccupied with the popular fear that NATO might turn aggression into a nuclear war.[66]

The government tried to counter this fear by asserting that the best way to save Germany from becoming a nuclear battleground was to contribute German contingents to NATO's ground forces, so that aggression could better be resisted on a conventional basis. It even went so far as to contradict the American and British theory of nuclear deterrence by holding that the advent of Soviet-American nuclear parity would increase the likelihood of local conventional war and give greater weight to conventional armament in the balance of power.[67]

However, the government made its furthest departure from NATO's nuclear strategy when, shortly after the passage of a conscription bill in July, 1956, but before the terms of conscription had been decided, the news of Admiral Radford's plan to reduce the American armed forces by 800,000 leaked out. Throughout Europe this news aroused fears that the United States contemplated withdrawing her troops from the Continent. Although the American government, in public releases and private assurances to German military and civilian officials, quickly denied any intention to reduce or withdraw American forces in Europe immediately or without the approval of the North Atlantic Council, it did not repudiate the central objective of Radford's memorandum: to substitute nuclear deterrence for conventional local resistance.[68] Therefore, in opposition to this objective, Adenauer took the unprecedented step of publicly criticizing American military policy. Writing in the August 21 issue of the Bonn government's official *Bulletin*, he said, "As to the debate which was started by Americans about the relationship between conventional and nuclear weapons, I would like to stress that I regard shifting the principal emphasis to atomic weapons at the present time as a mistake." To counter an East German invasion of West Germany with nuclear weapons would almost certainly "trigger an intercontinental rocket war. . . . I am of the opinion that it is of special importance to localize small conflicts that may occur, and for this we need divisions with conventional weapons."[69]

Nevertheless, Adenauer himself soon decided that Germany's future lay not in bucking the overwhelming trend toward nuclear dependence in defense policies but in joining it. Bowing to popular and political opposition to conscription and blaming it on the effect of the Radford proposal, the Bonn government recommended a twelve-month instead of an eighteen-month period of conscription—the shortest term of any NATO country except Luxembourg—and announced that it could not meet its obligation to raise 500,000 troops by 1959.[70] (By 1958 no more than 125,000 West Germans were in uniform.) Then, in September, following the full logic of this "stretch-out," Chancellor Adenauer and his new defense minister, Franz Josef Strauss, began urging the equipment of the *Bundeswehr* with tactical atomic weapons (though with the warheads under American custody) in order to compensate for its shortage of military manpower.[71]

There are indications that German authorities still did not subscribe to NATO's official position that a substantial local conflict in the center of Europe would necessarily be a nuclear conflict,[72] but West Germany could not very well plan for conventional limited warfare when the alliance as a whole, following the American and British examples, was adopting a strategy of primary reliance upon tactical nuclear weapons. Regardless of whether Adenauer would have adopted the "new look'" strategy for domestic reasons alone, it was necessary that he do so in order to preserve Germany's influence in NATO, for if the other members of NATO were to collaborate with the United States in organizing, equipping, and training their contingents to fight a tactical nuclear war, then as vital a participant as West Germany could hardly retain her voice in allied councils or even support her security by pursuing a strategy of local conventional resistance. By the same logic, the other NATO states were bound to collaborate in a tactical nuclear strategy so long as the United States and Great Britain seemed determined to go ahead with nuclear conversion, for their collaboration was the condition of the Anglo-American commitment to defend the Continent.

Yet collaborating in NATO's strategy was one thing; actually equipping the German army with tactical nuclear weapons was another. Although at the December, 1956, meeting of the North Atlantic Council the defense ministers of France, the Netherlands, and Turkey joined British Defense Minister Anthony Head in requesting that American tactical nuclear warheads be made available to European forces, there was substantial opposition throughout Western Europe, and especially in Great Britain, to any suggestion that the Federal Republic should receive these weapons, even though the United States would have custody of the warheads. Domestic opposition within Germany was equally formidable.[73] Press reports of the NATO Council meeting of December, 1957, which indicated that allied governments had agreed, in principle, to a more extensive sharing of nuclear weapons, touched off a public controversy more widespread and violent than the one precipitated by "Carte Blanche" and the debate on conscription.[74] The most intense opposition to nuclear armament was framed in moral terms, in terms of a blanket repudiation of nuclear weapons, which had no relevance to alternative strategic plans and therefore lacked concrete political impact. In the end, a majority of the voters expressed their confidence in Adenauer's foreign and military policies by giving his party a comfortable victory in the provincial elections, where the opposition had sought to submit the atomic issue to referenda. Nevertheless, the moral and emotional aversion to nuclear strategy in Germany remained a latent threat to Germany's effective collaboration, while informed and responsible criticism of Germany's participation in NATO's strategy actually increased—especially as possible political alternatives, such as disengagement and the "thinning-out" of troops, gained widespread and serious attention throughout the world.

As long as NATO's strategy rendered German forces little more than the instrument for elaborating the cause of a tactical nuclear response, which was expected to lead to general nuclear warfare, popular inhibitions against initiating the use of nuclear weapons seemed likely to grow—that is, if anything could arouse popular concern about external issues amid the preoccupation with internal material advancement. The government, on the other hand, having adopted NATO's nuclear strategy for compelling internal and external reasons, was anxious to minimize these inhibitions and maximize the credibility of the American nuclear threat; and it was determined that German forces should be equipped with nuclear weapons (without warheads) as thoroughly and quickly as possible.

9. FRANCE'S REACTION TO NATO'S NUCLEAR STRATEGY

The intensity of the sporadic German reaction to NATO's tactical nuclear strategy can be attributed to some conditions peculiar to West Germany: her vulnerable geographical position on the forward line; the strength of pacifist and antimilitarist sentiment, associated with the trauma of the Nazi period; the apparent conflict of nuclear armament with reunification. The French reaction, by contrast, was notably bland and formless. From time to time, the general moral issues of the atomic and hydrogen bomb aroused public interest and concern in France, and disarmament attracted special attention; but the implications of nuclear weapons for NATO's strategy and French security caused little popular or political controversy.[75]

Although France had been the most insistent of all allies in urging official reaffirmations of America's and NATO's commitments to defend Europe from a devastating Russian occupation and nuclear liberation, NATO's adoption in December, 1954, of a strategy that promised to turn France into a nuclear battlefield in the event of war occasioned none of the public debate that erupted in Germany. The French were inclined to assume that tactical nuclear warfare would involve only the Germans, and, in any case, they were less impressed than the Germans by the prospect of Soviet aggression.

France readily accepted the view that the development of tactical and strategic nuclear weapons would compensate for a lack of mobilized manpower, since she was particularly conscious of the pressure of military commitments upon domestic economic and social goals. There was no controversy over the strategic concomitant of this view: that nuclear weapons must be used against conventional attacks. Therefore, the more evident NATO's dependence upon nuclear deterrence became, the less reason there seemed to be for France to meet her obligations to maintain ground forces in Europe.

At the same time, if nuclear weapons were to be the decisive measure of military power, French prestige would demand at least equal privileges with Great Britain in receiving nuclear information from the United States. Therefore, as it became apparent that the United States was not going to help France become a nuclear power or give her equal privileges with Great Britain, which was already a nuclear power, it was logical that France should concentrate her military efforts upon becoming an independent nuclear power also. For this reason the government, with little opposition, despite its agreement in April, 1955, to renounce the development of military applications of nuclear energy for at least three years, launched in 1955 a costly military atomic energy program designed to give France membership in the Anglo-Saxon nuclear club.[76] Thus the principal effect of NATO's nuclear strategy upon French military policies was to intensify France's concentration upon developing a nuclear capability instead of collaborating with NATO's forces.

10. BRITAIN'S REACTION TO NATO'S NUCLEAR STRATEGY

The British, more remote than the French from a potential tactical nuclear battlefield but no less vulnerable to annihilation in a general nuclear war, were even more quick than the Germans to debate the strategic implications of NATO's December, 1954, decision. Although the British popular and political reaction to NATO's nuclear strategy was less intense than the German reaction, it was also less emotional and exerted a more coherent impact upon national strategy—or at least upon strategic pronouncements. More clearly than the German reaction, the British government's own qualifying statements about initiating the use of tactical nuclear weapons, which were intended largely to mollify domestic apprehensions, called into question the credibility of the very deterrent it relied upon to compensate for the deficiency of conventional forces in Europe. Nevertheless, Britain's actual dependence on a first-strike strategy of nuclear deterrence proceeded apace with the public depreciation of its credibility.

The White Paper on defense policies that was published in February, 1955, stated that NATO had adopted a strategy that "assumed the use, in a major war, of nuclear weapons," because only with the use of nuclear weapons and with a German contribution could the West protect the Continent from invasion and occupation against the "massive preponderance" of Soviet and satellite forces.[77] When the defense program was debated in Parliament the next month, the Labor opposition, which had already been aroused by Marshal Montgomery's vigorous pronouncements preceding the December, 1954, decision, challenged the government to explain whether it anticipated that any conventional attack in Europe, regardless of its nature and location, would be turned into a thermonuclear war. Such a suicidal strategy, said Denis Healey, would not be credible to the Russians; it would only tempt them to call the West's bluff.[78] In replying to this criticism, the government fell back on the White Paper's reference to a "major war" and said it would be dangerous to be more precise about the circumstances that would activate the nuclear deterrent. "It is important, of course, that the aggressor should know what he may not do," said Minister of Defense Harold MacMillan, "but I think that it is equally important that he should not be told too invitingly what he may do."[79]

A year later, in the parliamentary debates on the White Paper for 1956, another minister of defense, Sir Walter Monckton, went a little further than this statement in conceding that there could be circumstances in which "local aggression might be dealt with quite effectively by local retaliation" and that, if tactical nuclear weapons should be used, it would not be "inevitable that the use of this weapon . . . would necessarily lead to full-scale global war." However, he, too, warned that any attempt to define precisely, in advance, the kind of circumstances in which these weapons would or would not be used "might help others, who may be pondering on the question of whether they could take risks, to see how far they might go without bringing down upon them the ultimate deterrent."[80]

Caught between the conflicting objectives of frightening the Russians and calming the British, the government continued to pursue a military policy of concentrating on nuclear weapons and reducing conventional forces, which could only aggravate the dilemma. This policy reached its logical culmination in the defense program of 1957, presented by the new minister of defense, Duncan Sandys. Pointing to economic stringencies and Britain's disproportionately large share of the burden of Western defense, the 1957 White Paper on defense policies announced that the government would reduce the armed forces from 690,000 to 375,000 by 1962, permitting the abolition of conscription by that time; cut the British Army of the Rhine from 77,000 to 64,000 within twelve months; and rely more heavily upon nuclear deterrent power, to which Great Britain would contribute an appreciable element of her own.

"It must be frankly recognized," the Paper conceded, "that there is at present no means of providing adequate protection for the people of this country against the consequences of an attack with nuclear weapons." But from this crucial premise it drew only the conclusion that "this makes it more than ever clear that the overriding consideration in all military planning must be to prevent war rather than to prepare for it," for "it is unhappily true that, pending international agreement [on disarmament], the only existing safeguard against major aggression is the power to threaten retaliation with nuclear weapons."[81]

Mr. Sandys, anticipating the opposition's criticism of this position, denied that the White Paper assumed that every war would become a nuclear war.

> One must distinguish between major global war, involving a head-on clash between the great Powers, and minor conflicts which can be localized and which do not bring the great Powers into direct collision. Limited and localized acts of aggression, for example, by a satellite Communist state, could, no doubt, be resisted with conventional arms, or, at worst, with tactical atomic weapons, the use of which could be confined to the battle area. If, on the other hand, the Russians were to launch a full-scale offensive against western Europe, it would, I submit, be quite unrealistic to imagine that the issue could be fought out on limited conventional lines and according to rules. In such circumstances ... it is inconceivable that either the Soviet Union or the free world would allow itself to be defeated, with all that that would mean, without throwing everything it had into the battle, including nuclear weapons.[82]

Yet this verbal concession to the fears of nuclear war only drove the opposition to deprecate the credibility of a nuclear response to conventional attacks more categorically. "No human being can be absolutely certain about these matters," said R. H. S. Crossman, "but I am as certain as I can be that, except in the circumstances of the threat of direct Russian attack on this island, those [tactical atomic] weapons would not be used by British forces."[83] The Labor party's chief defense policies spokesman, George Brown, helping to confirm his own prophecy, warned that, unless the government could offer some hope "that we can employ a deterrent without the certainty of being blown up, we may find that we have all the weapons, all the means of delivering the deterrent, and that it will be no deterrent at all because nobody will believe that we would have the will to employ it when the day came." "If we let this backlog of public opinion build up," he declared, "then we may find that we, the Ministers, we, the politicians, have the mechanics but that the people will control the will to make use of them."[84] And to this dire forecast Emmanuel Shinwell, a former Labor party minister of defense, added an ominous preview of an opinion that was to become increasingly articulate in Great Britain. "I can imagine a situation," he said, "where, in a conventional war, it might be more endurable to suffer defeat, even humiliation, even if it means survival on a limited scale, than to use the nuclear weapon and be completely destroyed. After all is said and done, we do not want to commit suicide."[85]

Yet, in spite of this disparagement of the nuclear deterrent, the Labor party in 1957 did not recommend abandoning Great Britain's expensive effort to develop an independent nuclear capability, which would have been a difficult position to take so soon after the Suez War. Nor did it recommend increasing or even maintaining the number of British ground forces, which would have required a continuing commitment to National Service.

Indeed, within NATO's existing strategy the only compelling reasons for maintaining any British troops on the Continent seemed to be to provide the allies with a visible token of Britain's commitment to their defense and to satisfy the conditions of American collaboration. Moreover, just as the announced reduction of British forces served as an additional argument for West Germany to relax her terms of conscription, so Germany's abandonment of the eighteen-month period of conscription increased the reluctance of the British to contribute to NATO's forward line. And America's evident determination to concentrate upon developing nuclear deterrents at the expense of her conventional forces undermined the willingness of the British, as of all allies, to maintain any more non-nuclear forces than were necessary to preserve the American entanglement.

Yet, although all members of NATO became more dependent upon nuclear deterrence, the British government encountered increasing difficulty in maintaining the deterrent value of its nuclear currency in the face of mounting public sentiment against the hazards of a suicidal strategy. Sandys continued to resist opposition to get him to specify the method of response to contingencies between "full-scale" conventional attack, which would be met by massive nuclear resistance, and "very small incidents," which would be handled conventionally.[86] But Labor spokesmen continued to charge that to the extent Britain depended upon a nuclear response in this intermediate realm, the country would prefer surrender to resistance; and this contention began to seem less exaggerated as the advocates of unilateral nuclear disarmament became more numerous and vocal.

Meanwhile, a more moderate and reasoned but no less devastating attack upon the credibility of nuclear deterrence was conveyed in the distinction between "active deterrence" and "passive deterrence," which the *Times*'s anonymous defense correspondent, John Grant, suggested in October, 1958, and which subsequently gained considerable currency among commentators on strategy in parliament and outside.[87] According to this distinction, active deterrence aimed to prevent aggression against other powers and depended upon threatening to strike the aggressor with strategic nuclear weapons if they were attacked; but passive deterrence aimed only to prevent aggression against one's own nation and required employing this threat only against a direct attack upon the homeland. Since carrying out active deterrence would be suicidal for a nation that could not destroy enough of the enemy's strategic striking power to confine his retaliatory damage to an acceptable level (measured in terms of the value of the objective at stake), Grant concluded that Britain would have to stop relying on the American nuclear deterrent to deter aggressions that would not directly involve American territory and stop relying on the British deterrent to deter anything short of a direct attack upon Great Britain.

By 1958 even Marshal Montgomery seemed to be approaching the view that nuclear deterrence should be confined to discouraging direct attacks on the deterrer. In 1954, when the Marshal delivered his categorical declarations that nuclear weapons would necessarily be used against conventional attacks, he had envisaged a general war in Europe proceeding toward a Western victory in three stages: (*a*) the achievement of mastery of the air, while preventing the overrunning of Western bases and territories; (*b*) the destruction of remaining enemy land forces; and, finally, (*c*) the bargaining phase, in which the enemy's homeland would be at the mercy of Western air power, while the West carried the air attack "to the point where the enemy accepts our terms."[88] In 1955, however, he concluded that nobody could win an unlimited war between nuclear nations.[89] In 1956, starting from the premise that such a war would be "suicidal" and speculating about the way it might be fought in 1969, he again envisaged three phases—destruction, exploitation, and reconstruction—but the best outcome he could promise was a kind of stalemate of mutual destruction, in which the West would win only the grim opportunity to begin its own reconstruction. Nevertheless, still speaking as a top NATO official, he reasserted that SHAPE was basing all its plans on using nuclear weapons—and he recognized no distinction between the tactical and strategic varieties—with the sole proviso that "the politicians have to be asked first." "That might be a bit awkward, of course," he added, "and personally I would use the nuclear weapons first and ask afterwards."[90]

In 1958, however, Montgomery's remarks had quite a different ring. Speaking in retirement from his NATO duties, he now foresaw that in due course the United States and the Soviet Union would achieve nuclear sufficiency, and he asked himself how the West would use its nuclear weapons then.

> In the event of minor Russian aggression with conventional forces, do you believe that the West would use its nuclear deterrent *as a weapon* against the cities of Russia and receive in return Russian retaliation which would put the U.K. and the

> U.S.A. out of business? For us to act in this way would be to commit national suicide. I do not believe it will happen. When both sides have nuclear sufficiency, the deterrent will merely serve to deter each side from using it as a weapon.[91]

It should be noted that Montgomery left open the possibility that the West might use the nuclear deterrent as a *threat* against conventional attacks, even though to use it overtly as a *weapon* would be suicidal. This was a possibility that no Western government dared foreclose. For no government could accept the proposition that nuclear weapons served only passive deterrence without conceding, implicitly, that the foundation of NATO's strategy was a gigantic bluff. Therefore, in the absence of a larger capacity for conventional resistance in Europe, the British government, like the American, continued to affirm NATO's determination to meet conventional aggression with nuclear weapons even after it had virtually conceded that the nation would suffer intolerable destruction if the threat were carried out.

Of course, one could still argue that, regardless of the retaliatory damage the Soviet Union would inflict upon Britain, the Kremlin would be deterred from taking a chance that Britain and the United States would not counter aggression with nuclear weapons by the expectation that she would also incur intolerable damage if the West were not bluffing. But even if this were true, the disturbing question remained: If the function of nuclear weapons were reduced to threat and counterthreat, who would win in a test of nerves? In Britain the increasingly articulate public sentiment against the danger and evil of nuclear weapons suggested the liabilities that democratic governments might suffer in this kind of game.

Thus in Great Britain NATO's growing dependence upon a nuclear strategy exerted a dual effect, which was only partially manifested in Germany and France: It stimulated the government to seek its own nuclear capability, at the expense of conventional forces, and it aroused significant popular inhibitions about using nuclear weapons. The net effect was to depreciate the credibility of active nuclear deterrence and undermine its utility as an instrument of policy, while accelerating the tendency in Britain—indeed, in NATO as a whole—to substitute nuclear for conventional capabilities.

11. THE AMERICAN APPROACH TO ACTIVE NUCLEAR DETERRENCE

In the United States, apprehensions about depending upon a strategy that seemed to be based upon the West's threat to start a thermonuclear war were most clearly expressed in the growing number of serious studies of defense policies. The official decision in 1956 to depend more heavily upon nuclear capabilities and the threat of total war to deter conventional aggression coincided with the consolidation in 1956 and 1957 of a consensus among private students of defense policies (especially in academic quarters and in RAND, the independent research organization supported by the Air Force) that the only effective strategy to deter and counter local conventional aggressions, now that the Soviet Union had achieved a substantial nuclear capability, was a strategy of limited war.[92] In these two years a few studies in the United States and England—notably those by Henry Kissinger and Sir Anthony Buzzard—favored a limited-war strategy based primarily upon meeting conventional attacks with the "graduated" use of tactical nuclear weapons, but by 1959 the trend among both private and official students was running strongly against this strategy, in favor of one based primarily on limited conventional resistance even to large-scale conventional aggression, inside as well as outside the NATO area.[93] By 1960, it had become a commonplace view—expressed by congressmen, army and navy officers, newspapers, news commentators, independent studies, and academic students of military policies, too numerous to list—that the credibility of nuclear retaliation against conventional attacks was dangerously declining in the face of growing Soviet nuclear power, and that only a larger capability of local resistance by non-nuclear means could compensate for this loss of credibility.[94]

Nevertheless, even several years after the Soviet launching of the first Sputnik, the nation as a whole did not feel the immediate sense of physical vulnerability to nuclear devastation that had aroused the Germans and the British, and in all the multitude of congressional hearings and special investigations of defense policies there was no counterpart of the efforts of British members of parliament to force the government to elaborate the circumstances under which it would resort to nuclear warfare. Insofar as there was any genuine political debate on military strategy, it revolved largely around the technical and material requirements of weapons systems rather than around the circumstances in which those weapons should be used as an instrument of policy.

Before long, the development of Soviet long-range missiles was bound to undermine official as well as popular confidence in active, first-strike nuclear deterrence, since by 1960 there were already growing doubts about the adequacy of America's strategic striking power even for passive, second-strike deterrence. But the administration that had initiated the "new look" in defense policies on the assumption that nuclear weapons would be used against conventional attacks was no more disposed to renounce this strategy of nuclear retaliation than it was to increase expenditures upon conventional weapons and ground forces. And there was a general disposition among congressmen and their constituents to trust the military judgment of an administration headed by President Eisenhower, while even those who did not share this disposition were reluctant to recommend significantly larger appropriations for conventional limited-war forces when Soviet missile progress seemed to require an intensified program in strategic nuclear striking power.

It is true that, with respect to areas outside the ambit of NATO obligations, Secretary of State Dulles, prompted by domestic and foreign alarm, qualified the implications of his "massive retaliation" pronouncement of January, 1954, soon after he delivered it. He denied that every small aggression would necessarily be turned into a nuclear war, and he emphasized not strategic retaliation but the use of "mobile deterrent power" on a selective basis—by which he evidently meant the dropping of tactical atomic bombs on Chinese Communist staging areas and other military targets related to the area of battle. However, in order to deter conventional aggression in the NATO area, the Eisenhower administration continued throughout its tenure to rely upon the threat of massive retaliation as a concomitant of a tactical nuclear response, on the theory that any aggression in Europe would involve the Soviet Union and that no aggression involving the Soviet Union could be limited. As Secretary of Defense McElroy explained this theory in justifying the reduction of America's limited-war forces, "I do not see how you could have limited warfare between the two major opponents, and if our major opponent is involved . . . they could hardly avoid an all-out military struggle."[95] Any limited war larger than the Quemoy and Matsu or Lebanon incidents of 1958, he maintained, would lead to the use of tactical nuclear weapons and thus become a general war.[96] Therefore, whatever forces were adequate to deter an attack on the United States were also adequate to protect Western Europe. "An attack upon our forces and friends in Western Europe would be an attack upon the United States. It would mean general war."[97] Indeed, the government was logically compelled to affirm this position as the strategic rationale of its policy of economizing on the forces and weapons for local conventional resistance, which it justified on the grounds that the requirements of limited war were covered by the capacity for general war.[98]

From this policy and the strategic assumption upon which it was based, it followed that the more dependent upon a nuclear response Western forces became, the more unequivocally the United States had to indicate that any military incursion beyond the most minor incident would result in a thermonuclear catastrophe. Therefore, although fewer and fewer observers of the changing balance of military power shared the American government's professed belief in the necessary totality of warfare in Europe, and more and more observers were horrified by the prospect, the government seemed determined, in effect, to confirm its prophecy by emphatically declaring that NATO's forces were nuclear forces and denying absolutely that a limited war was possible in Europe. As Secretary McElroy declared, "We better never let anyone get the mistaken idea that we are not going to use our big weapons if they are needed. The free peoples are a minority group in the world, and unless we have serious resolution to use, if need be, the big stuff in order to deter aggression or to protect the free world, you are going to get into a limited war."[99]

Ironically, this declaratory policy of minimizing the chance of limited war in order to maximize the deterrent value of nuclear weapons was one with which Soviet leaders were happy to collaborate at every opportunity. For by consistently denying any distinction between tactical and strategic nuclear weapons, any possibility of limiting a nuclear war, or even a possibility of limiting any kind of war in Europe, they reinforced the insistent Soviet message that the Western powers must disarm, withdraw from their provocative outposts, abandon their "situations of strength policy," and disband the alliance if they wished to avoid a catastrophic thermonuclear war. In other words, they used the West's own deterrent strategy as a potent psychological and political lever against the West.

Yet, unlike the Soviet bloc, democratic nations could not maintain a consistent, monolithic declaratory strategy, if only because their own officials, politicians, and citizenry were free to express divergent views. Thus the more the American and British governments emphasized their dependence upon nuclear deterrence, the more their own citizens sought relief from the risks of this threatening nuclear posture in ways that tended to undermine its credibility. Notably in the United States, even military and civilian officials made public statements that contradicted the official line.

In October, 1958, Vice-Admiral Charles R. Brown, the commander of the Sixth Fleet and about to take over command of allied forces in southern Europe, told the National Press Club that he opposed using even small atomic weapons in limited war because he had no faith in "the so-called controlled use of atomic weapons" or in the distinction between tactical and strategic situations. "I would not recommend the use of any atomic weapon, no matter how small," he asserted, "when both sides have the power to destroy the world,"[100] which, he later stated, would be in the "not too far future," when both the United States and the Soviet Union would have combat-ready ICBM's. In a more guarded statement in April, 1959, General Norstad, who since 1957 had been actively promoting a thirty-division "shield" in order to provide NATO with a capacity for "intermediate responses" between all-out war and acquiescence, told the House Committee on Foreign Affairs that NATO "would deal with any situation that could be dealt with, with conventional weapons, if possible."[101] At about the same time Secretary of State Herter, testifying on his nomination before the Senate Committee on Foreign Relations, said that the West would not be justified in conducting a nuclear war in the initial stages of a Soviet attack before making sure that it was being carried out to the point of an all-out war, and that the President would not involve the United States in an all-out war "unless the facts showed that we were in danger of devastation ourselves."[102]

Army Chief of Staff General Taylor, after his retirement in the spring of 1959, wrote that he had struggled in vain to secure clear official guidance for military planning that would recognize the possibility of limited war in the NATO area, for he believed that "in . . . a situation of nuclear parity, where both sides had the capability of destroying one another, there was no place for a policy of massive nuclear retaliation except as a deterrent to total nuclear war or as a reprisal if one began."[103] In congressional testimony he charged that, because the administration had never resolved the strategic issue between "massive retaliation" and a "flexible response," there had never been any centralized limited-war planning in the government.[104] It is unlikely that the situation changed after General Taylor's retirement. Yet the Eisenhower administration's third secretary of defense, Thomas S. Gates, Jr., once seemed to suggest that a large-scale limited war was a contingency worth preparing for, when he told the annual meeting of the Associated Press in April, 1960, "We must be prepared for military actions of varying degrees and sizes anywhere in the world and be able to contain quickly such action. We must put out the fire of limited war in situations that range all the way from another Korea-sized conflict to one involving a small number of infantry or marines."[105] He said nothing about putting out the fire with nuclear weapons.

The impression of nuclear inhibitions that these statements conveyed was reinforced by the actual record of American policy during crises involving the use or threatened use of armed force. The United States refrained from using nuclear weapons in the Korean War, even when she had a virtual monopoly of them.[106] In the Indochina war of 1954, the President rejected French requests and American proposals to employ nuclear weapons, even though the Chinese had none.[107] In 1955 the President sided with Army Chief of Staff General Ridgway against the other chiefs of staff in opposing the use of nuclear weapons to defend the coastal islands of Quemoy and Matsu against a Communist atack.[108] During the Quemoy and Matsu crisis of 1958, it was the Russians who hinted at using nuclear weapons to defend their Chinese ally against an American attack, while American spokesmen carefully refrained from even suggesting a resort to nuclear weapons, although the United States Navy quietly delivered to Quemoy a number of eight-inch howitzers capable of firing nuclear shells.[109] In the Lebanon landing in 1958, the United States Army was not even allowed to bring an Honest John rocket ashore, because it could fire a nuclear shell.[110]

Of course, all these statements and actions put together did not provide conclusive evidence of the circumstances in which NATO might or might not resort to selective or massive nuclear retaliation; but they did suggest that NATO's nuclear policy was considerably less clear-cut than America's official statements were intended to indicate. This supposition was confirmed by General Taylor's revelation that, despite the government's categorical pronouncements about nuclear retaliation, "the services have never been given a clear-cut statement allowing them to plan with complete confidence on the use or limitation of use of atomic weapons."[111] Yet, in practice, the use or non-use of nuclear weapons seemed destined to be resolved by existing military capabilities, which provided little choice between a nuclear response and non-resistance, even though by 1960 NATO was still far from completing the conversion from conventional to nuclear equipment, organization, and training.

12. THE DILEMMA OF NUCLEAR DEPENDENCE

Within a few years after the United States had encouraged her allies to depend upon a tactical nuclear response to conventional aggressions as the means of meeting the requirements of security at an acceptable level of contributions, it was apparent that this strategic expedient had raised more problems of allied security and collaboration than it had solved. NATO had embraced this nuclear strategy as the means of reducing the discrepancy between existing capabilities and the professed objective of defending Europe against an all-out attack. Yet, with the accumulation of nuclear weapons by the Soviet Union as well as by the United States, this allegedly indispensable objective lost even its theoretical appeal, for even a successful defense of the Continent in a total war would leave allied countries in no better position than if they had been occupied and liberated. As one American observer wrote, "Today one must consider that there is no more point in defending a corpse than there is in liberating it." Therefore, for the purpose of protection in a general war, the allies might better put their money into civil defense instead of ground forces.[112]

Actually, the allies were not willing to buy either form of protection. While they remained completely unprepared to protect their citizens from the consequences of nuclear war, which NATO promised to initiate in order to defend them, they were less interested than ever in spending money and manpower to resist a Soviet attack, which would destroy them in any case. In effect, NATO's ground forces seemed to have become mere accomplices to nuclear deterrence, a kind of trip-wire, with scarcely a pretense to a defensive function. While a trip-wire strategy was consistent with existing capabilities, it provided no incentive for meeting the prescribed minimum requirement of thirty NATO divisions ready for action on the central front in Western Europe. Aside from pleasing the United States, why should the allies go to great trouble to enlarge NATO's ground forces when their primary function was only to offer enough opposition to activate a nuclear war? The question was particularly pertinent in the light of the United States and Great Britain's evident determination to reduce their own forces on the principle that nuclear deterrence was an adequate substitute for mobilized manpower.

Moreover, while NATO's nuclear strategy, reinforced by the American and British examples, further diminished the incentives for fulfilling NATO's minimum-forces goal, it increased the liabilities of strategic collaboration by raising the risks of nuclear obliteration. The general disposition of Western European governments to discount the threat of overt aggression and to let the United States worry about the details of defending the Continent, while they concentrated upon binding her to this commitment, somewhat mitigated their concern about NATO's increasing reliance upon nuclear retaliation, in spite of their awareness of growing Soviet nuclear power. Nevertheless, as the European public became more conscious of the physical consequences of nuclear war, more allied governments, like the British, were liable to come under increasing popular and political pressure to qualify their obligations to resort to nuclear warfare against conventional aggressions. Yet the more dependent on nuclear weapons NATO became, the more imperative it seemed—especially to the American government—to refute any suggestion that the nuclear deterrent might not be used, even though statements by some of America's own officials tended to confirm that suggestion.

Consequently, although NATO's nuclear strategy might help allied governments escape the domestic political difficulties of imposing burdensome defense programs upon the people, it promised to aggravate the larger difficulties that sprang from their growing dependence upon an admittedly suicidal response, the credibility of which they were themselves inclined to call into question in order to appease domestic apprehensions, even while they denied the feasibility of an alternative response.

6
Toward a Strategy of Limited Resistance

1. TWO STRATEGIES OF LIMITED WAR

NATO's increasing dependence on an unlimited nuclear response to conventional attacks at a time of spectacular growth in Soviet nuclear power threatened, in time, to undermine the credibility of the West's deterrent posture, jeopardize allied political cohesion, and weaken NATO's political defenses against Soviet pressure, while blunting allied incentives for collaborating in support of the minimum-forces goal that was held to be essential to Western security. One logical remedy for this predicament was to adopt a limited-war strategy that would provide a rational basis for NATO to equip itself with a capacity to resist limited aggressions effectively by means short of total war; that is, by a local war fought with substantial mutual restraints upon weapons, targets, and other military components of destruction.

By 1957 two strategies designed for this purpose had attracted the attention of military experts. One proposed to rely principally upon nuclear limited warfare;[1] the other, upon conventional limited warfare. Both strategies recognized the need of possessing tactical nuclear weapons, if only because the enemy might use them, but the first strategy favored initiating their use against conventional aggression as the most effective means of local resistance, whereas the second strategy relied upon them principally to deter the enemy from using them, while depending on non-nuclear combat as the most effective means of resistance compatible with limited war.

The first strategy failed to receive official sanction. The second received only ambiguous support. By 1961 neither had been fully adopted. Yet NATO officially and urgently indorsed the objective both were intended to serve: To provide the allies, in the event of limited aggression, with some choice between suicide and surrender.

The argument for a strategy of nuclear limited war started from the same premise as that for a strategy of conventional limited war: With the growth of the Soviet counterdeterrent, the West could not safely rely on the threat of general strategic war to deter and resist a variety of possible conventional aggressions in the NATO area which could not be handled as mere police actions or border incidents. Proponents of both strategies were impressed by the danger of military conflicts in this area which would constitute such an ambiguous and limited threat to Western interests as to provide no suitable or credible cause for a massive response, but which might nevertheless grow into a limited war of considerable dimensions. They pointed to the possibility of probing actions on the northern or southern flank of the forward line, of indirect aggression in Yugoslavia, or of a conflict in the center of Europe growing out of an East German revolt or a disturbance in Berlin. But advocates of a limited-war strategy who were not deeply worried about this prospect nevertheless envisaged likely situations short of war—for example, a manufactured crisis in Berlin—in which the threat of massive retaliation would be a dangerously ineffective and politically disadvantageous instrument of diplomacy in the face of non-military incursions backed by a threat of thermonuclear counterretaliation. The very possibility of the West's having to choose between meeting Soviet terms or turning some limited aggression into a nuclear catastrophe, they feared, would offer the Kremlin a tempting opportunity to test NATO's collective nerve and will.

Of course, the proponents of a nuclear or conventional limited-war strategy for NATO believed that it was not only desirable to be able to fight a limited war in the NATO area but also feasible. They did not all agree on the specific kinds of limitations that might apply. The advocates of a nuclear limited-war strategy had greater confidence in the efficacy of explicit and precise limitations, formulated perhaps in advance of hostilities. The advocates of a conventional limited-war strategy tended to rely upon tacit, *ad hoc* limitations, based on a few simple, inherent, and obvious restraints, which might be reached by a kind of bargaining process. But both strategies assumed that, if neither the U.S. nor the U.S.S.R. was confident that it could deliver a decisive massive strategic blow without receiving unacceptable damage in return, both would have an overwhelming incentive and the rational circumspection to find the means of keeping any military conflict local and well below the level of destruction that they were technically capable of inflicting.

From these common presuppositions, however, the arguments for NATO's depending primarily upon a strategy of nuclear limited war and the arguments for depending primarily upon a strategy of conventional limited war diverged.

2. THE CASE FOR A NUCLEAR LIMITED-WAR STRATEGY

All proponents of a nuclear limited-war strategy claimed that, compared to a conventional strategy, it was a more effective deterrent, and some claimed that it offered more effective resistance if deterrence failed. Some reasoned that, in the light of the unwillingness of the Western powers to maintain a large enough standing force to counteract the numerically superior Soviet-and-satellite divisions on a conventional basis, NATO had to utilize the superior defensive advantages of nuclear firepower—its ability to prevent concentrations for breakthroughs and the seizure of territory. In 1957 Henry Kissinger contended that in nuclear limited war "our superior industrial potential, the broader range of our technology, and the adaptability of our social institutions" would also work to the West's advantage.[2] Furthermore, it was contended, to fight a conventional war with a nuclear power would entail either concentrating forces so that they could operate effectively, in which case one would concede the overwhelming advantage of initiating the use of nuclear weapons to the enemy, or else dispersing them to reduce their vulnerability, in which case they would be ineffective in holding a line against the enemy's concentrations. But the strongest argument for primary reliance upon nuclear limited war was that a strategy of initiating the use of tactical nuclear weapons would be a more effective deterrent than a strategy that assured the aggressor that he need not run the incalculable risks inherent in nuclear war unless he drove the enemy to desperation.

Of course, the case for a strategy of nuclear limited war in the NATO area must rest upon its feasibility as well as its desirability. Here its proponents emphasized that the limitation of political objectives rather than the nature of the weapons used was the fundamental condition for limiting warfare. In answer to those who associated the tremendous destructive power of nuclear weapons with all-out war, they pointed to the development of smaller and "cleaner" nuclear warheads with even less explosive power than some of the conventional TNT bombs and shells of World War II and denied that there was any logical or moral reason to distinguish one kind of explosive from the other, insofar as the intensity and scope of warfare was concerned. Those who advocated basing limited warfare upon the smallest nuclear warheads generally conceded that it would be more difficult for belligerents to observe verifiable distinctions in the destructive power of nuclear than of non-nuclear weapons, but they pointed to a number of possible supplementary distinctions, based on targets and geographical restrictions. And some contended that, given the overriding incentives nuclear powers would have to avoid unrestricted warfare, they might even be expected to establish these distinctions by advance declarations or agreements. The proponents of this nuclear strategy might grant that merely adding tactical nuclear weapons to conventional battlefield operations would probably lead to unlimited devastation, at least in the battle zone;

but they contended, as Kissinger argued in the greatest detail, that the effective utilization of tactical nuclear weapons required new formations, force structures, and tactics. Highly dispersed and self-contained units, he reasoned, need not create excessive destruction and might, in fact, result in even less devastation than a large-scale conventional war.

3. THE CASE FOR A CONVENTIONAL LIMITED-WAR STRATEGY

The case for relying primarily upon a strategy of conventional limited war to deter and resist limited aggressions in the NATO area was based chiefly on the superior feasibility of limiting a conventional war. However, by the late 1950's, partly in response to the growth of the Soviet Union's tactical nuclear capacity, the advocates of a non-nuclear strategy had also concluded that it would be militarily more effective than limited nuclear warfare.[3] The claim of superior feasibility rested mainly upon three contentions:

a) The principal advantage that is attributed to tactical nuclear weapons, their superior military effectiveness, springs from the very characteristic that makes them incompatible with limited war: their great destructive capacity. The blast, heat, and radiation effects of nuclear weapons—especially the larger ones, which might be used against airfields, military bases, etc.—are of such a large order of magnitude, compared to conventional weapons, as to preclude significant physical limitations upon the scope and intensity of warfare. Although limitation of the political objectives of war is an indispensable condition for limiting warfare between nuclear powers, it is not sufficient by itself, considering the dynamic relationship between the ends and means of war and the difficulty of keeping such great destructive potential from escalating.[4] Whereas in an earlier stage of technology the limitation of warfare was greatly facilitated, if not guaranteed, by the sheer physical limits upon the capacity of the belligerents to inflict quick and comprehensive damage upon one another, the peculiar problem of limiting warfare today is the necessity of imposing deliberate restraints upon the most powerful military instruments.[5] This problem can be solved only if military conflict is confined to conventional weapons.

b) The distinction between nuclear and non-nuclear explosions is, by virtue of its uniqueness, simplicity, and the sanction of precedent and popular attitudes, relatively easy to apply and to verify as a basis of reciprocal restraints upon military conflict. Once the precedent is broken and nuclear weapons are used against conventional attacks, there will be no other clear distinctions of comparable stability and reliability to serve as bases of mutual restraint, and it will be virtually impossible to restore confidence in the original distinction between nuclear and non-nuclear explosions. Yet the continuous gradation in the destructive power of nuclear weapons, from the fractional-kiloton shells and grenades to the multimegaton bombs, precludes the fixing of an obvious qualitative "cut-off" point, which the belligerents could readily agree upon, verify, and enforce on their commanders.[6] At the same time, the number of profitable military targets available in Western Europe—such as airfields—would render either "natural" or contrived target distinctions ineffective for the purposes of mutual limitation in a nuclear war. Meaningful geographical restrictions and sanctuaries, in the absence of any other form of physical limitation, would be infeasible because they would require the immediate victim of aggression to accept annihilation while the aggressor struck from his nuclear-exempt tactical air and missile bases.[7]

c) Whatever might be the actual result of new tactics designed, theoretically, to permit use of nuclear weapons within reliable physical limits, in the absence of battlefield experience our military planners have not yet been able to devise any tactics with which they are confident of waging nuclear limited warfare. In the meantime, so far as military foresight can tell, the great pace, fluidity, mobility, and depth of the battle zone that military plans for tactical nuclear warfare envision would be distinctly uncongenial to limitations on the scope and intensity of nuclear conflict, especially in the European zone.

These arguments for the comparative feasibility of limiting conventional warfare are more persuasive in suggesting the difficulty of limiting nuclear warfare than they are in demonstrating the practicability of limiting conventional warfare in the NATO area. Similarly, the arguments for the comparative military and political utility of relying principally on a strategy of conventional limited war (assuming its feasibility) seem stronger in their negative than in their positive thrust. The case for comparative utility rests on the following psychological, political, and military grounds:

a) Subjectively, nuclear weapons are popularly associated with a catastrophic total war. Whatever the objective possibilities of limiting nuclear warfare may be, this popular impression will not be altered by argument, assertion, or analysis, in the absence of actual wartime experience. Therefore, a tactical nuclear strategy will incite much the same apprehensions and inhibitions and suffer almost the same depreciation in credibility as a strategy of massive retaliation, and the Soviet Union will enjoy increasing success in exploiting these subjective attitudes to paralyze and divide the Western powers as she continues to develop a devastating second-strike capability while denying the possibility of a limited nuclear war. Although the threat to initiate nuclear war may be more fearsome, it is a less credible and, in the long run, probably less effective deterrent than the threat of substantial conventional resistance. It is also less prudent because it would be far less useful if the threat should fail to deter.

b) Considering the strength of nuclear fears and inhibitions, NATO's dependence on initiating nuclear warfare against conventional attacks will incur the grave political disadvantage of seeming to leave the allies no choice between suicide and surrender. Even if the allies believe that nuclear warfare could be limited to the extent of confining hostilities to the Continent, they will not be consoled by the thought that extra-Continental powers will be spared while their countries are devastated. On the other hand, some may be equally fearful that the United States will withhold the nuclear deterrent while they are occupied conventionally. In either case, a nuclear strategy entails a differentiation in sacrifices, benefits, and responsibilities among allies that must seriously impair allied collaboration. It enables

Moscow to subject the European "hostages" to pressures that may either hamstring the United States or compel her to act unilaterally. It subordinates the will to meet common military needs objectively to subjective fears and suspicions of American policy.

c) NATO would not derive a military advantage from fighting a limited war with nuclear as opposed to conventional weapons. In fact, the situation is just the opposite. A nuclear limited war would require more manpower, if only to replace the greater number of casualties and handle the more complicated logistics. Since nuclear weapons would seem to be as capable of breaking up a defensive line as an offensive concentration, there is no reason to think that the defending nation in a bilateral nuclear war could offset his numerical inferiority with firepower.[8] Both conventional and nuclear warfare would require highly mobile units capable of rapid concentration and dispersion, simply because of the possibility that nuclear weapons might be introduced. Anyway, if nuclear weapons do favor the defense, NATO forces would be at more of a disadvantage in counterattacking in order to expel the aggressor than the aggressor would be in penetrating allied territory during the initial phase of fluid and far-ranging operations.[9] On the other hand, in conventional warfare, portable antitank weapons and a great range of other non-nuclear devices that are already developed do promise to give the Western powers the generally assumed three-to-one numerical advantage of defending forces and whatever compensation firepower may provide for numerically inferior manpower. Moreover, whereas use of nuclear weapons would tend to neutralize differences in technological and productive strength, in which the Western powers are still supreme, conventional warfare would capitalize upon them. Therefore, if tactical nuclear weapons were reserved as a sanction to enforce the limitations upon conventional conflict, the comparative advantages of fighting limited warfare on a conventional basis would be worth the risk of the enemy's initiating the use of nuclear weapons.

What conclusions emerge from these arguments? The arguments for not relying primarily on a nuclear limited-war strategy have become more persuasive as the objective and subjective obstacles to a useful first-strike tactical nuclear war apparently grow more formidable. Yet the utility of depending heavily upon large-scale conventional resistance in the NATO area has not appeared to grow proportionately. The conjectural advantages of augmenting NATO's capacity for non-nuclear resistance do not strike the European allies as a compelling compensation for the palpable disadvantages of having to contribute more money and troops to an effort that may only provoke the Soviet Union to raise her force levels while further depreciating the credibility of the tactical nuclear threat upon which the allies, in fact, remain heavily dependent. Nevertheless, if a limited-war strategy is advisable at all (as almost all students of the matter contended in 1961), it would seem, on balance, that NATO's military and political advantage lies in depending on conventional weapons to raise the threshold of effective non-nuclear resistance to a level at which the resort to tactical nuclear warfare would constitute a really credible step. It follows that NATO ought to develop its forces—their organization, equipment, and tactics—chiefly for the purpose of supporting local defense with non-nuclear weapons,[10] while relying upon tactical nuclear weapons to deter the aggressor from employing them and to deter him from expanding a conventional war to a scope that might force the West to initiate the limited use of nuclear weapons as a last resort. A thirty-division force would give the West better than a one-to-three ratio in relation to the forces that the Soviet Union might rapidly deploy on the forward line. This would be a ratio adequate for conventional defense, for a limited-war strategy would not require numerically matching the Soviet bloc's standing forces ("man for man and tank for tank," as the opponents of that proposition put it). A limited-war force would not be designed to contain a massive all-out conventional invasion. To prevent a massive assault on the Continent or to counter a major conventional conflict that could not be won or contained by Western conventional forces, NATO would rely primarily upon the deterrent effect of graduated tactical nuclear blows; that is, blows not directed at strategic striking power or civilian and industrial targets but at the enemy's battlefield capabilities, the purpose of which would not be to win a protracted nuclear war—a self-defeating objective—but to raise the level of violence and heighten the risk of strategic nuclear warfare sufficiently to induce the termination of hostilities without at the same time irrevocably committing either side to a war of annihilation.* Since the West cannot afford to lose a conventional war in Europe or relieve the aggressor of the risks of nuclear war inherent in any large-scale conflict, it cannot categorically renounce the first use of tactical nuclear weapons as a last resort, but it should be able to wage effective conventional resistance of a large-scale and protracted nature in order to raise the threshold of violence to a point where limited nuclear resistance would be sufficiently credible to exert its intended political effect.

This last-resort nuclear strategy assumes, of course, that the NATO powers would develop and publicly declare a strategy of limited or graduated nuclear blows as a necessary concomitant to a conventional-resistance strategy, instead of regarding the first use of tactical nuclear weapons merely as a substitute for large-scale conventional warfare and a step on the automatic escalator to massive strategic nuclear exchanges. It also assumes that nuclear weapons will not become so widely diffused throughout NATO's command structure that the central command will be unable to control whether and when they should be employed or unable to limit and proportion their use under political guidance. Perhaps the best way to meet this

* This strategy, like limited strategic nuclear retaliation, aims to persuade the enemy to terminate hostilities on reasonable terms without trying to deprive him of his war-making capability, but it applies persuasion through tactical blows directed at military objectives that serve effective resistance rather than through purely punitive blows designed, not to affect the local balance of military power, but primarily to demonstrate the will to inflict damage that the enemy will consider unacceptable in relation to the value of the objective he seeks. This latter strategy would be far less amenable to meaningful limitation and to the communication and bargaining process it is intended to facilitate. Moreover, a coalition of democratic powers would be at a peculiar disadvantage in engaging in such controlled strategic punitive blows, tit for tat, even if the exchanges did not lead to all-out war. For a full discussion of this and other strategies of limited nuclear reprisals, see Glenn H. Snyder, *Deterrence and Defense* (Princeton: Princeton University Press, 1961), pp. 197–224.

problem is to create a few carefully selected special units primarily equipped and trained to employ tactical nuclear weapons, while the other units are designed to fight conventional war and co-ordinate with the nuclear units when necessary.[11]

Yet, clearly, it will be more expensive for the major allies to maintain any genuine dual capability than to concentrate upon a nuclear capability designed to deter aggressions and leave only a residual conventional capability to resist aggression if the deterrent should fail.[12] This would be especially true if an increase in NATO's forward forces would precipitate a countervailing increase in the Soviet forward forces. Therefore, this raises the question whether the necessarily speculative advantages of creating a sizable conventional capability would really be worth the additional cost. The question can be answered only in terms of the kind of insurance and the margin of safety one seeks in preparing for uncertain contingencies. But, unfortunately, the actuarial figures for this kind of insurance are unknown; and the insurance itself might alter those figures. Even if a dual capability would increase the margin of security, how serious is the threat of limited aggression in the NATO area, and by how much would a larger conventional capability reduce this threat? Might not an explicit conventional limited-war strategy encourage limited aggression by depreciating the deterrent value of nuclear weapons and the threat of total war? How large a conventional war should NATO be prepared to fight on a limited basis? What are the chances of limiting any kind of military conflict in such a vital area and still fighting it effectively, and by what increment might these chances be increased if NATO had a larger conventional capability? What would be the actual physical consequences of a conventional limited war in this area? Would the allies whose homelands were in the battlefield regard such a war as significantly less disastrous than a war in which the West employed graduated nuclear retaliation to secure an armistice? Would their nerves really be any stronger if their military security depended upon a strategy that virtually conceded the first nuclear strike to the enemy?

Considering the imponderability of these questions, it is not surprising that NATO's actual strategy at the beginning of the 1960's was an ambiguous compromise between conventional local resistance, graduated nuclear deterrence, and massive retaliation, reflecting domestic pressures and foreign sensitivities as much as strategic logic.

4. DULLES' BRIEF FLIRTATION WITH NUCLEAR LIMITED WAR

Tactical nuclear weapons were originally adopted by NATO as a substitute for conventional weapons in carrying out the existing strategy of withstanding a Soviet attack in an all-out war, not as a means of resisting aggression effectively by limited means or even of terminating aggression short of total war by graduated nuclear reprisals and bargaining. However, the American government, like the British, could not long ignore the adverse implications of a strategy that would defend the Continental allies by means that promised to destroy them—and, perhaps, the United States, too.

In April, 1957, Secretary of State Dulles, reiterating a favorite theme of President Eisenhower, said, "With modern weapons, any general war could not be won by anybody. It would be a disaster of worldwide proportions, which would threaten indeed the very existence of the human race, certainly in the Northern Hemisphere."[13] The only strategic implication he drew at this time was that "the principal objective now must be not to win war but to prevent war." But two years before he had hinted at another solution to the dilemma of nuclear deterrence and defense: At a news conference in March, 1955, he suggested that the availability of smaller atomic weapons would offer a chance of securing victory on the battlefield without harming civilians, without precipitating a war of mass destruction like World War II.[14] And at other times he implied that nuclear deterrence might rest on the threat of limited, graduated reprisals, not intended to secure victory on the battlefield in the sense of destroying the enemy's fighting capabilities or holding territory but rather to impose unacceptable costs by selective strikes. As he stated in November, 1954:

> We must have the capacity to respond at places and by means of our own choosing. This, however, does not mean that any local war would automatically be turned into a general war with atomic bombs being dropped all over the map. The essential thing is that we and our allies should have the means and the will to assure that a potential aggressor would lose from his aggression more than he could win. This does not mean that the aggressor has to be totally destroyed. It does mean a capacity to inflict punishing damage.[15]

These adumbrations of a strategy of limited nuclear war were made in the context of discussing American policies outside Europe. But in an article published in October, 1957, Dulles applied the strategy more generally—to Europe as well as to peripheral strategic areas.[16] Heretofore, he wrote, our allies have had to depend upon a strategy of deterrence based upon America's great capacity for nuclear retaliation against the aggressor. However, dependence upon a capacity to destroy vast segments of the human race has been acceptable only because there was no alternative. But now, with the development of smaller and cleaner nuclear weapons, "their use need not involve vast destruction and widespread harm to humanity"; their effects can be confined "substantially to predetermined targets." "In the future," he concluded, "it may thus be feasible to place less reliance upon deterrence of vast retaliatory power. It may be possible to defend countries by nuclear weapons so mobile, or so placed, as to make military invasion with conventional forces a hazardous attempt." Nations around the Sino-Soviet periphery could, therefore, possess "an effective defense against full-scale conventional attack" without endangering themselves or friendly peoples in the area, so that "instead of those who are non-aggressive having to rely upon all-out nuclear retaliatory power for their protection, would-be aggressors will be unable to count on a successful conventional aggression, but must themselves weigh the consequences of invoking nuclear war."

This is the nearest that the United States or any of her allies ever came to announcing a strategy of limited nuclear war. Whether the deterrent threat that Dulles had in mind was to punish the enemy by graduated nuclear reprisals against predetermined targets or to fight a limited war of nuclear resistance against opposing forces was never clarified. The American government failed to elaborate or even repeat Dulles' suggestion. By 1957 it did refer to tactical nuclear weapons as though they were designed chiefly for reprisal or punishment, but it left the impression that, whereas in some special cases their use for selective retaliation might not necessarily lead to total war, the United States and her allies were not basing their strategy on this expectation in the NATO area but rather on the probability that any conventional aggression in Europe would lead to nuclear war and any nuclear war would lead to unlimited nuclear war.

Thus in March, 1959, in the midst of a new Soviet campaign of political warfare against West Berlin, President Eisenhower said that the West was determined to defend Berlin but that it certainly would not fight a ground war in Europe because it would be outnumbered. Therefore, he saw no function for a few more thousands, or indeed even a few more divisions, of troops in Europe. Although he was confident that the Soviet Union would not dare to start a war, he implied that, if she did, the United States would defend its interests with nuclear weapons, even though a nuclear war could not "free anything" and would be "self-defeating."[17] Consistent with this reliance upon uncontrolled nuclear deterrence, the President told anxious congressmen that the United States had adequate forces to deal with the Berlin threat, that he intended to go ahead with proposed cuts in American conventional forces, and that any effort to build up conventional or missile forces in response to crises like Berlin would only play into the hands of the Communist strategy of getting the United States to spend itself into bankruptcy.[18]

5. NORSTAD'S RE-EMPHASIS UPON NATO'S SHIELD

While the Eisenhower administration continued to rely primarily upon the threat of a catastrophic nuclear war to deter aggressions in Europe, General Lauris Norstad, who became

NATO's Supreme Allied Commander in November, 1956, conceived his primary strategic task as developing the kind of military plans and forces that could relieve NATO of depending exclusively upon nuclear retaliation.

It was largely under his leadership that NATO adopted the five-year plan, called MC–70, designed to create a standing forward line or "shield" in Western Europe of thirty divisions. In appealing to the allies to support this minimum-force goal, General Norstad set forth three strategic objectives of NATO's shield.[19] Two of these objectives had been recognized in official statements from the beginning of the alliance, although the second was now assigned a relatively higher priority than before: (*a*) to protect all NATO territory against major aggression by holding an attack until the total weight of retaliatory power could be brought to bear; (*b*) to deter a border incident or a limited probing action by making it clear to the potential aggressor that "he would have to use substantial force to breach the shield, an act he knows would bring down upon him the full weight of the deterrent, including our heavy strategic power."

The logical connection between these two objectives and a thirty-division shield was tenuous, since fewer than thirty divisions ought to be sufficient for the second; and, even if thirty were sufficient for the first, NATO would only succeed in "defending a corpse."

On the other hand, Norstad's third strategic objective constituted a coherent justification for the minimum forces he requested. It was specifically aimed at meeting the altered requirements of external security and internal cohesion in the face of Russia's emergence as a full-fledged nuclear power. The third function of the shield, Norstad said, was to provide new military and political flexibility, to relieve the allies of having to choose between total war and passive acquiescence, by enabling NATO to respond to "less than ultimate incidents with something other than massive retaliation"—with some intermediate means. If allied security depended exclusively upon a capacity for massive retaliation, he warned, we would be "piecemealed to death. We wouldn't survive here for six months. This is the most dangerous position we could put ourselves in."

Taking these words at face value, one might suppose that they argued for a strategy of local non-nuclear resistance. But General Norstad stopped short of extending this third strategic function to its full logic. Like spokesmen of American defense policies, he pointedly denied that a limited war was possible in the NATO area, and he emphasized that the shield "can no longer be considered as 'conventional forces,'" although it would retain a "residual conventional capacity." On a conventional level the shield's role would be confined to briefly holding a limited probing action in order to "force a pause" long enough to compel the Russians to make a deliberate decision that they either would or would not go to war while they weighed the costs of the total war that would result from an affirmative decision.

The outsider cannot know to what extent this minimum strategic function coincided with operational plans.[20] Probably, it did not represent the maximum function Norstad looked forward to. Certainly Norstad's reformulation was a compromise between NATO's old strategy and its new imperatives, an attempt to reconcile new strategic requirements with existing capabilities. On the one hand, the Supreme Allied Commander recognized that NATO's dependence on America's threat of massive retaliation had become dangerous to allied security and cohesion. On the other hand, he conceded that NATO was compelled by the minimum number of troops it was willing to raise and support to rely primarily upon the deterrent effect of a nuclear ground force, which could hold an attack only until the full weight of retaliatory power was brought to bear. In order to relieve NATO of the choice between obliteration and occupation, he proclaimed the strategic objective of an alternative intermediate response. But, lest he diminish the deterrent value of the nuclear forces upon which NATO in reality primarily depended, he denied the possibility of a limited war or of a conventional response beyond a brief holding action.

This strategy did not succeed in satisfying the conflicting

demands of more deterrence at less risk and of better defense against limited and major aggressions if deterrence should fail —all at no greater cost in money and men. But no strategy could. The question is whether General Norstad's was the wisest strategic formula, given the limited forces available to him, or whether NATO might meet its minimum force goals and achieve a more satisfactory balance between security and cohesion if it were to clearly embrace a conventional limited-war strategy. As long as NATO was dependent upon forces and weapons that were inadequate for effective local conventional resistance, except to force a pause for decision upon the aggressor, there was a reasonable argument for not depreciating the credibility of the threat of a tactical nuclear response against conventional aggression by openly formulating a strategy of conventional limited war. For to do so might cast doubt upon the West's resolution to initiate the use of nuclear weapons while it lacked a convincing capability of resisting limited aggression by non-nuclear means. On the other hand, NATO might never acquire an adequate shield, which it so badly needed, unless it were openly to adopt a strategy of conventional limited war, since such a strategy might provide the only rational incentive that could induce the allies to enlarge the shield.

Whatever the resolution of this dilemma might be, at the end of 1960 NATO's shield in fact remained at little more than half the operational strength that had been projected in 1957 as a bare minimum. Although ostensibly it contained 21⅓ combat-ready divisions assigned to the central front from Norway to Italy, most observers considered 12 to 16 a more accurate figure and regarded even these divisions as seriously inferior in arms and equipment to the huge Soviet bloc forces facing them in Central Europe.* The numerical gap between the shield's ac-

---

* **In 1959 the Institute for Strategic Studies in London, in an authoritative but unofficial collation of intelligence data, estimated that Soviet force-reductions actually amouted to only 1,100,000 of the more than 2,000,000 claimed, leaving about 2,350,000 in the army and 350,000 security, border, and labor troops. The total number of divisions, it estimated, remained 175, 75 per cent of which were stationed on the western border of the Soviet Union and in Eastern**

tual and required forces might be virtually closed if Germany fulfilled her goal of twelve divisions (only seven of which had been raised by 1961), if France (which maintained only two divisions in Europe) returned the two or more divisions in Algeria, and if Great Britain restored the two divisions she had withdrawn in 1957. But, even so, the task of equipping an enlarged shield with sufficient modern conventional weapons to supplement NATO's capacity for nuclear deterrence with a limited-war capability beyond a mere "residual conventional capacity" would be a far more expensive project than any of the allies, including the United States, seemed prepared to undertake.

In the strategic circumstances of 1960, the only compelling incentive for the European allies to increase their defense budgets was not their concern for enlarging and diversifying collective capabilities but rather, in the case of Britain and France (and, possibly, West Germany before long), their desire to acquire or expand independent nuclear capabilities. If the most powerful members of NATO were to channel their military resources and energy principally into the development of independent nuclear capabilities, to the further neglect of

---

Europe. Equally significant, these Soviet forces were said to have undergone a major reorganization in order to improve atomic capabilities (*NATO Letter*, VII [December, 1959], 22–23). On January 15, 1960, the Supreme Soviet of the U.S.S.R. announced a further reduction of 1,200,000 in over-all forces. However, in his report to the Supreme Soviet on January 14, Khrushchev maintained that the effective fighting power of Soviet forces would actually be increased by modernization and the advancement of nuclear capabilities, including strategic missiles. He also indicated that reserve forces would be enlarged by a "territorial system" of training labor forces (*Current Digest of the Soviet Press*, XII, No. 2, 11). On July 8, 1961, Khrushchev, pointing to the Western build-up during the Berlin crisis, announced the suspension of projected force reductions and a substantial increase in the Soviet budget (*New York Times*, July 9, 1961, pp. 1, 2). At this time Western experts estimated that there were 126 Soviet divisions west of the Urals (including 26 in East Germany, Poland, and Hungary), two-thirds of which were maintained at 70 per cent or more of war strength (*ibid.*, September 10, 1961, p. 6). Administration sources stated that there were about 150 line divisions in the Russian army, with probably fewer than 30 at full strength (located in Eastern Europe and western Russia), but they pointed out that the Soviet Union could put 125 divisions in the field in Europe in thirty days and mobilize 300 divisions in ninety days (*ibid.*, Aug. 13, 1961, p. 4), a capacity that far exceeded that of the NATO powers.

their contributions to local defense, it would be difficult to stop the steady erosion of allied military and political solidarity and the steady deterioration of the West's whole position in the cold war.

6. INTERDEPENDENCE

In 1959 a mounting dissatisfaction with NATO's reliance upon nuclear retaliation, the increasing cost of nuclear and conventional weapons, and a growing technical requirement for military integration stimulated a new interest in some allied quarters in an old solution to the problem of meeting NATO's military needs at an acceptable cost: "Interdependence";[21] that is, a co-ordinated specialization of national forces and arms, matériel, and strategic functions in order to use total resources most efficiently. There is much to be said for greater interdependence on grounds of efficiency and economy, but the pursuit of these objectives is, inevitably, qualified by considerations of separate national interests, by the political requirements of military collaboration. In the light of these considerations, interdependence, while militarily and economically more urgent than ever before, is limited as a solution to NATO's strategic troubles.

Militarily, the need for greater allied interdependence springs, chiefly, from the technical requirements of rapid mobility of ground forces, geographically widespread co-ordination of air and submarine defenses, and central control of tactical nuclear weapons. None of these essential military operations could be performed effectively by national forces without a degree of specialization and co-ordination within a common force that exceeds what De Gaulle has called national "co-operation."[22] Each requires considerable subordination of national to central control of weapons, forces, and logistics.

Economically, the need for interdependence springs from the discrepancy between the cost of strategic flexibility and the price allies are prepared to pay. The less the allies are willing to contribute to meet collective requirements, the greater the need for interdependence. It is true that after 1953 the members of NATO were progressively better able to meet their obligations to the alliance without straining their domestic economies. The substantial economic recovery of Europe by 1953 and then the tremendous growth in per capita gross national product on the Continent (one of the highest rates in the world), as well as the great production of basic industry and consumer goods (greater, in many categories, than in the Soviet Union or even the entire Sino-Soviet bloc),[23] enabled America's allies to assume much larger defense expenditures, both absolutely and in relation to America's expenditures, than ever before.[24] However, the total economic burden of defense had also risen considerably and would rise more if NATO were to create an effective dual-capability force. And, politically, any substantial increase in defense expenditures (say, 5 or 10 per cent) seemed impracticable in the absence of a major crisis or limited war to dramatize the Soviet military threat. Economically, such an increase would exert inflationary and other disturbing effects in many allied countries. Moreover, by 1960 defense expenditures began to compete seriously with the costs of rising foreign economic aid to the underdeveloped areas.

Similarly, there were narrow practical limits within which the allies were willing to increase their contributions of armed forces to NATO. Domestic pressures against conscription itself in Britain and against the numbers of conscripts and period of service in West Germany and elsewhere, along with competing overseas commitments in France, the United States, and Britain, strictly limited the manpower that allied countries would contribute to the common defense in Europe in the absence of war or imminent war.

Therefore, militarily and in terms of money and manpower, it seemed to some that NATO's strategic imperatives in the 1960's, if they could be met at all, would be met not by a massive increase of national contingents and defense budgets but by the more efficient and economical use of total allied resources through specialization and co-ordination of national contributions and strategic functions. The essential thing was that whatever marginal increase in defense expenditures and armed manpower the allies might be induced to contribute should be devoted to NATO's limited-war capabilities and utilized in the most effective way, rather than channeled into purely national forces (especially independent nuclear forces), at the expense of the defense of Europe. Otherwise, NATO would be faced with a growing discrepancy between its requirements of strategic flexibility and its actual capabilities.

By 1952 NATO already embodied a degree of interdependence in defense planning and organization that was unprecedented among peacetime coalitions. To be sure, NATO as such could not control national contributions (or withdrawals) of forces, the length of military service, or other elements of military programs that bore upon its collective capabilities. Nevertheless, through the Annual Review it exerted significant pressure on its members to adjust national contributions and programs to the over-all needs determined by the international staff at SHAPE.[25] SACEUR's authority over the location, deployment, and training of NATO's forces (with the notable exception of American and British nuclear warheads and strategic nuclear forces) made NATO far more than a collection of merely co-operating national armies and navies on the pattern of traditional military coalitions, even though it remained something far less than a united supranational force.

Still, at the beginning of the 1960's, NATO had fallen far short of achieving the ideal of economy and efficiency through interdependence to which its members had been dedicated in principle even before SHAPE was established. Actually, there had been a most inefficient use of combined allied resources, resulting from uneconomical duplication of research, development, and production programs; at the same time, the tendency to create forces, matériel, and weapons for independent national purposes at the expense of an integrated plan showed signs of increasing. Britain's decision in 1957 to reduce her troops in Europe in order to build up her strategic nuclear capability; the pressure in the United States, beginning in 1956, to reduce American troops in Europe in order to implement the "new look" and, after 1958, in order to rectify an adverse international balance of payments; France's decision in 1959 to withdraw her naval units from the Mediterranean Command, her refusal to stockpile nuclear warheads on French soil except under French control, and her determination to follow the American and British lead in giving first priority to an independent nuclear capability—these developments were part of a trend that ran directly counter to interdependence.*

Until 1954 or so, the specialization and integration of allied forces were chiefly products of massive American economic and military assistance and the preponderance of the United States in military production and forces, combined with the inability of her allies to compete or to pursue self-sustaining military programs. Thus America's virtual monopoly of strategic nuclear striking power, though not under NATO command, represented NATO's most notable division of strategic labor, and her pre-eminence as a supplier of the major armaments (most of them without cost) was the primary source of standardization in weapons and equipment. However, this situation changed when the major allies became able to afford diversified arms programs of their own. In Britain and France these programs included even the instruments of strategic nuclear striking power, in addition to the naval power and non-NATO ground forces that they had held from the beginning. The resurgence of allied economic strength, the drive for equality of status, and the reassertion of divergent national foreign policies posed a further threat to the co-ordination of allied strategies, forces, and arms.

NATO's one conspicuous success in interdependence was its "infrastructure" program, that common network of air bases, pipelines, naval facilities, and communication lines created in the aftermath of the Korean invasion for the ground and air defense of Western Europe. However, in 1960 not more than

* On the other hand, in September, 1960, integration was advanced by the establishment of a unified European air defense command, ending France's long refusal to assign her air units to such a command, and the transfer of the Central Army Group in West Germany (composed of German, American, and French troops) to allied command, ending the United States long insistence upon an American command (*New York Times*, September 24, 1960, p. 1).

2 per cent of the total defense expenditure of the NATO powers was channeled through the infrastructure program, and the United States provided 37 per cent of that.

To rationalize the economic and logistic base of NATO's military strategy, the allies needed to standardize weapons and equipment and concentrate their production in countries where it was most economical. In 1960 Alastair Buchan proposed that, instead of relying on bilateral aid agreements, the allies should extend the infrastructure principle—that is, common financing for commonly used facilities—beyond fixed installations to the new weapons systems and facilities (nuclear stockpiles, tactical aircraft, missiles, etc.) on the authority and in accordance with the recommendations of SACEUR.[26] However, these logical expedients were impeded by substantial obstacles of national pride and military tradition, abetted by domestic business and labor pressure. In 1960, despite some indications that the United States and other allies were beginning to move toward greater rationalization of what the French military authority General Gallois called a "strategy of means,"[27] rising nationalist pressures threatened to reverse the trend.

Therefore, there remained a large discrepancy between the generally acknowledged need and the specific implementation of allied interdependence. This discrepancy, however, was not merely a result of the revival of the independent strength and purpose of the European allies. Nor could the allies be expected to regard increased co-ordination and integration purely as military and economic imperatives. The fact is that interdependence has political consequences, which conflict with the oldest and most crucial hallmark of national sovereignty: the ability of a state to support national policy with an independent military establishment. The greater the degree of allied interdependence, the greater the loss of actual (even if not formal) independent national control over military power—especially where interdependence takes the form of the specialization and integration of national forces. Clearly, there are strict limits to the sacrifice of independent military control that allies can be expected to make for the sake of collective defense and, therefore, strict limits to the compatibility of interdependence with allied cohesion. For to sacrifice independent military control is to subordinate national policy to allied policy or, at least, to the policy of the strongest ally.

Furthermore, interdependence may conflict with the configuration of allied concessions and sanctions that sustains the delicate balance of assets and liabilities and the distribution of benefits and burdens that supplement the basic incentives for collaboration. Thus the deployment of American and British troops on the Continent, although an uneconomic use of resources, is a necessary political contribution to collaboration. And what allies may regard as an equitable distribution of the economic burdens and benefits of collective defense may facilitate collaboration even if it is economically wasteful.[28]

Ideally, each ally would be sufficiently farsighted to subordinate his particular interests to the demands of interdependence for the sake of his larger interests in an efficient and economic use of allied resources. But, actually, such subordination depends not simply on states eschewing national parochialism but, fundamentally, on their assessment of the compatibility of their vital interests with the military strategy and foreign policy that interdependence promises to serve. In other words, before accepting the limitations of specialization and integration, each ally must ask, "Interdependence for what?" and assess the answer to that question in terms of the contribution of NATO's strategy to his military security and the compatibility of that strategy with his foreign policy inside and outside the NATO area.

Therefore, the determination of allied strategy and the proper strategic function of each ally within the over-all plan must be prior to the achievement of interdependence, and interdependence must be subordinate to the requirements of allied military collaboration and political consensus. Viewed in this light, one of the greatest obstacles to interdependence has been the failure of NATO's strategy to provide the allies with clear and compelling incentives for subordinating their national defense policies to the kind of co-ordination and integration of functions, forces, and production that their security objectively requires. Because NATO's strategy is an excessively ambiguous compromise between the old concept of nuclear deterrence and the new need for local resistance capabilities, it fails to provide a persuasive reason for enlarging NATO's capacity for fighting conventional limited warfare, which the enhancement of its military flexibility demands. Unless this strategy receives a more coherent formulation, it will offer neither incentive nor guidance for a new pattern of interdependence.

Thus the prospect of integrated forces and supplies in the 1960's depends less upon considerations of military efficiency and economy as such than upon a resolution of the existing ambiguity concerning the kinds of wars the members of NATO intend to fight in various contingencies.[29] Such a strategic clarification would involve an explicit recognition of NATO's primary reliance upon conventional local resistance, supplemented by graduated nuclear deterrence. Otherwise, the European allies will either be content to depend upon America's nuclear deterrent, while contributing only enough to NATO's shield to maintain the American commitment, or else they will insist upon acquiring their own nuclear deterrents, while reducing their contributions to the shield in order to pay for them. Already, by the end of 1960, the issue of the control of nuclear weapons, which is discussed in chapter ix, had emerged as the decisive test of the future of interdependence.

By itself, a reformulation of NATO strategy might still fail to elicit the contributions in money and manpower needed to sustain a dual-capability force of thirty divisions or more, considering the demonstrative reluctance of democratic nations to increase arms and manpower expenditures except under the fear of imminent aggression. But at least it was the prerequisite of a new pattern of interdependence—supplemented, perhaps, by a new configuration of concessions and sanctions, by new terms of collaboration—which could substantially narrow the gap between widely acknowledged strategic needs and NATO's existing capabilities.

7
The Onset of the Missile Age

Just when the preponderant strategic thought in NATO's headquarters and in the United States and Britain (with the conspicuous exception of some top civilian and air force officials in these two governments) seemed to have become convinced of the need of an enlarged and diversified limited-war capability on the Continent, another dramatic technological development in Russia's nuclear striking power called into question the fundamental stability of the strategic nuclear balance, which was by that time generally taken for granted. This was the Russian demonstration in the fall of 1957 that she had achieved a rudimentary intercontinental-range ballistic missile capability that the United States did not yet possess.

The onset of the "missile age" at first distracted allied strategists from the task of building up NATO's limited-war capability, as many realized that the requirements of strategic deterrence were more complex and difficult to achieve than had been generally imagined. But as they recovered from the initial shock of the Russian achievement, they reached a new consensus that the urgent task of maintaining a strategic nuclear balance in the missile age would actually put a greater premium than before upon the development of reliable nonnuclear tactical deterrents. This familiar strategic issue was now complicated, however, with a whole realm of unfamiliar issues relating to arms control, the danger of a pre-emptive strategic attack springing from misapprehension, the diffusion of nuclear control and capabilities to other states, and the intricate requirements of a stable over-all military environment.

These issues added a new dimension of perplexity to the problem of calculating and meeting the requirements of allied security and cohesion. They created a new urgency in the need for a revision of NATO strategy and the terms of allied collaboration. They posed a new challenge to America's strategic and political leadership.

1. THE MISSILE GAP

Well before 1957 many responsible American and allied observers had begun to doubt the credibility of America's threat to meet conventional aggression upon her allies by initiating a nuclear war, which, it was officially conceded, would result in disaster for the United States. The evidence of Soviet missile progress raised doubts about quite another aspect of America's nuclear deterrent capability, the adequacy of which had been generally taken for granted: the deterrence of a massive surprise attack on the United States. To be sure, proponents of a larger strategic air force had been sounding alarms about the inadequacy of this deterrent capability for several years, but they had been preoccupied with the threat of a Soviet long-range air force.[1] Partly in response to their alarms but largely against their original preference for spending limited defense funds on more bombers, the government had constructed a vast continental defense system, complete with early-warning radar stations in Canada. But these countermeasures, like the alarms, were directed at the threat of manned bombers. The problem of deterring a missile attack was quite different and, generally, unanticipated in its details.

Soviet scientists, like their counterparts in the United States, had been developing and refining the German V-2 rocket ever since 1945. However, the Soviet effort to develop a truly long-range missile was more substantial than the American effort, partly because the United States, which already possessed the highly trained and war-tested Strategic Air Command, saw less need for such a missile. Moreover, before the development of a hydrogen or fusion explosion, there was no warhead small enough yet powerful enough to make long-range missiles seem militarily useful, considering their anticipated inaccuracy. The Russians went ahead anyway, developing intercontinental as well as intermediate-range rockets with great thrust. In the United States the long-range ballistic missile project, started in 1948, was canceled in 1950 as impractical and was barely kept alive by the private firm Convair until it was reinstated in 1953.

When fusion explosions were achieved in 1953, the Soviet Union undertook a full-scale, top-priority program to develop and produce intermediate and intercontinental missiles in order to bypass the stage of the manned bomber and gain a technological victory over SAC. The American missile effort, afflicted with budgetary restrictions, administrative confusion, and interservice conflicts, proceeded at a more leisurely pace. By 1956 the Soviet Union was well on the way toward achieving an operational IRBM with a range of 1,500 miles, theoretically capable of wiping out America's overseas bases in the NATO area. Then in August, 1957, the Soviet Union announced a successful test of a "super long-distance intercontinental ballistic rocket," an announcement that was apparently confirmed by American radar observations on the Turkish Black Sea coast. Less than two months later, in October, she used the launching of the first two space satellites to dramatize her claim to have achieved an ICBM of powerful thrust, "a mighty hydrogen warhead of a new design," and "new and improved instruments" for guidance.

American military experts, always quick to respond to developments affecting strategic air power and general-war capabilities, did not conceal their alarm. A number of unofficial reports of official intelligence estimates claimed that the Soviet Union was capable of possessing at least three times as many ICBM's as the United States by 1962 or 1963, and Secretary of Defense McElroy was said to have conceded the possibility of this ratio.[2] From this alleged possibility many concluded that before the late 1960's, when the United States was expected to have quantities of operational solid-fuel missiles placed in protected or mobile bases on land (the Minuteman) and on concealed and mobile bases at sea (the Polaris), the Soviet Union would probably have the capacity to launch a surprise attack that could knock out enough of America's retaliatory power to spare the Russian homeland from unacceptable damage. Military specialists with access to classified information elaborated the complicated mathematics of strategic striking power in the missile age to show what a "delicate balance of terror" America's security against a Soviet "first strike" would depend upon during the critical period of the "missile gap" in the late 1960's, when the Soviet Union would have an impressive numerical advantage in operational ICBM's and the United States would still depend chiefly upon the bombers of the Strategic Air Command.[3]

The administration responded to these critical alarms by assuring the country that, although there might be a temporary "missile gap"—that is, a numerical lead in Soviet over American ICBM's—there would be no "deterrent gap," because American retaliatory power depended, not only upon ICBM's, but upon a variety of strategic weapons systems, including a superior bombing force, which would readily compensate for the missile gap until the United States acquired numerous solid-fuel, mobile, land- and sea-based missiles.[4] Adherents of this position also maintained that before the latter half of the 1960's, even if the Russians did obtain a three-to-one numerical advantage, they would not be sufficiently confident of the reliability of their missiles nor of their mastery of the complicated task of co-ordinating a massive instantaneous salvo to undertake such a fateful act at a tolerable risk of failure.[5] Then, in late 1959, the administration announced that revised intelligence estimates—evidently based largely on radar and plane observations of a very low rate of ICBM test firings[6]—indicated that the Soviet Union probably would not produce nearly as many ICBM's as, theoretically, she might have been capable of producing and that, therefore, the government did not expect the estimated Soviet missile superiority to reach a three-to-one ratio. Furthermore, by the end of 1960 the administration could point to the imminent operational status of the first of several squadrons of submarine-launched Polaris missiles; the operational status of the land-based intercontinental Atlas and its remarkable accuracy (an average two-mile "circle of error probability" under testing conditions); the imminent "hardening" of ICBM bases; the development of electronic and other countermeasures to maintain SAC's ability to penetrate Soviet air defenses; the development of air-launched ballistic missiles; and the deployment before 1962 of new forward radar missile warning systems (especially BMEWS), to be followed by the early-warning and surveillance satellites Midas and Samos.

The critics, in rebuttal, pointed to the comparable accuracy of Russia's ICBM's; her probable achievement of a considerable numerical advantage in operational ICBM's before enough of the solid-fuel and mobile Polaris and Minuteman missiles would become operational to offset them; the vulnerability, in the meantime, of the liquid-fuel, slow-firing, stationary Atlas and Titan; the superiority of Soviet civil- and air-defense measures; the vulnerability of SAC bases and the large percentage of planes that remained on the ground; the absence of early-warning devices during the critical period of the missile gap; and the danger of basing estimates of Soviet ICBM's on calculations of "intentions" rather than capabilities.

And so the missile debate went on, becoming more deeply enmeshed in technical data and speculative calculations, which failed to provide any clear-cut basis of judging where truth lay amidst the disputed mathematics of the balance of terror—until the missile-gap alarms subsided shortly after the presidential election. Yet, from the standpoint of America's contribution to the security of the NATO area, the very terms of the debate about the purported missile gap were more revealing and more disturbing than the assertions and counterassertions about the technical data involved. From this standpoint the most significant aspect of the debate was that it was waged, on both sides, almost entirely in terms of America's ability to deter a direct assault upon the United States (that is, in terms of "passive deterrence"), to the virtual exclusion of any consideration of America's ability to deter aggressions upon her allies (which is the objective of "active deterrence").

There could be no more convincing indication of the serious depreciation of the credibility of America's strategic power as a means of responding to aggressions in Western Europe, even in the eyes of the government that still proclaimed its determination to meet such aggression with nuclear retaliation. For in defending the adequacy of America's strategic nuclear striking force, the American government defined the requirements of this force entirely in relation to the objective of passive deterrence, which depends upon a second-strike capability, and thereby implicitly conceded that this striking force was not designed to meet what would soon be the far more demanding requirements of active deterrence, which depends upon a first-strike capability.* The momentous implications of this strategic emphasis for America's nuclear strategy in Europe, for her monopoly of nuclear control within the alliance, and for the strategy of NATO's shield must be understood in the light of the diverse requirements of deterrence in the missile age.

2. THE REQUIREMENTS OF PASSIVE DETERRENCE

Essentially, passive deterrence—in this context the deterrence of a direct Soviet attack on the United States—requires convincing a potential aggressor that one can inflict unacceptable damage upon him on a second, or retaliatory, strike. As insurance beyond this, especially to prevent uncontrolled destruction and an adverse bargaining position in the event of a failure

---

* In contemporary strategic semantics "first strike" and "second strike" are used in a special sense to distinguish between the initial use of nuclear weapons and the retaliatory use in response to an initial use. Repeated official disavowals of an American first-strike strategy during the Eisenhower administration referred to the initiation of nuclear blows "out of the blue," not to the initiation of nuclear blows in response to aggression. This semantic ambiguity tended to conceal the fact that the United States and NATO were ostensibly committed to a first-strike strategy, in the special sense, in order to defer "major" aggressions in Europe.

of deterrence, some "counterforce" capability* is essential in order not to be compelled to strike only at a fixed number of cities and industrial facilities while the enemy has a large enough capability to strike at some military installations in addition to the major civilian targets.†

At one time, perhaps as late as 1960, it was feasible and conceivably useful for the United States to have a counterforce capability of quite a different sort for passive deterrence: one that could actually blunt a massive Soviet nuclear attack by a pre-emptive blow or, after an attack, win the war by knocking out the enemy's war-making capacity—his striking weapons, command centers, and supporting logistics. But when both the United States and the Soviet Union can be expected to have hundreds of dispersed, hard-based, mobile, and concealed long-range missiles—by 1965 or so—there will be no sense in trying to gain a passive deterrent capability designed either to blunt

* I use "counterforce" capability here in the narrow sense of strategic weapons designed to destroy or damage the opponent's strategic striking power.

† Along with the moral opprobrium attached to a strategy that aims exclusively to inflict unacceptable civilian damage and the immorality as well as irrationality of a strategy of uncontrolled destruction, the great disadvantage of a strategy designed only to annihilate a fixed number of civilian targets is that it would preclude the expedient of responding to nuclear attacks on military targets by countermilitary attacks. Such a response might be the only way to prevent a limited nuclear attack—for example, one springing from miscalculation or accident or the escalation of a more limited conflict—from becoming total. It might also be the only way to prevent the Soviet Union from striking first at American military targets and then extorting surrender under the threat of completely disarming America's strategic force and devastating all of her major cities if she struck at Russian cities with the minimum force remaining. In any case, since the exact nature of a general war or of any war involving strategic nuclear strikes is not predictable, it would be prudent to be prepared to fight a war in which intercontinental nuclear exchanges could be directed at military rather than purely civilian targets, while the residual capacity of the belligerents to obliterate each other's major cities served as an ultimate sanction to limit and terminate the war short of an irretrievable catastrophe for both. The most thorough criticism of "finite" or "minimum" deterrence and the most notable case for the utility of counterforce capability and civil defense in a post-attack situation is Herman Kahn's *On Thermonuclear War* (Princeton: Princeton University Press, 1960), especially pp. 7–116, 138 ff. However, Kahn's argument for counterforce insurance is directed chiefly toward the need for a credible first-strike strategy. For an equally cogent analysis of the uses of counterforce blows in a second-strike strategy, see Glenn H. Snyder, *Deterrence and Defense* (Princeton: Princeton University Press, 1961), pp. 63 ff.

an imminent attack with a pre-emptive blow or to "win the war" through protracted nuclear exchanges. These objectives, barring some truly spectacular unilateral technological innovation, will simply be technically, not to say economically, unfeasible; for one could not even be sufficiently confident of locating the major targets of a pre-emptive strike, and an effort to destroy the enemy's war-making capacity would produce a self-defeating spasm of uncontrolled mutual destruction.

So let us assume that America's chief objective, for the purpose of passive deterrence, is to have a convincing capability to inflict unacceptable second-strike damage on the Soviet Union by controlled nuclear retaliation. What damage will the Kremlin regard as unacceptable? If the objective of a premeditated offensive strike (as distinguished from a pre-emptive strike) were to eliminate the United States as a serious obstacle to Soviet hegemony—and it is difficult to imagine the Soviet Union undertaking the costs of a strategic nuclear war for a lesser objective—conceivably Soviet leaders might be willing to accept tremendous damage if they were quite sure of achieving their objective, although probably not so substantial as to destroy Russia's great-power status in relation to other nations, including Communist China. Since even Khrushchev probably does not know exactly what this minimum level of acceptable retaliatory damage would be in advance of the particular political circumstances that might move him to launch a surprise attack, it is prudent not to assume that the Kremlin would be deterred by anything less than the destruction of at least thirty of Russia's major cities and industrial complexes.

The adequacy of such a second-strike capability will depend heavily upon its degree of invulnerability; that is, its ability to escape or survive a first strike and to strike back. As the accuracy, reliability, penetrating power, and numbers of enemy missiles increase, concealment and mobility will be the most useful attributes of invulnerability.

Conceivably, by the latter half of the 1960's both the United States and the Soviet Union might achieve sufficiently invulnerable second-strike capabilities to compel each other to conclude that it would be materially infeasible or economically disadvantageous to build first-strike capabilities sufficient to confine the other's second-strike to an acceptable level of damage, while, at the same time, both would be confident of maintaining adequate retaliatory power to deter the other from striking first. In this case, the strategic arms race would nevertheless continue, especially qualitatively and in research and development; but the objective of the strategic nuclear powers in this race would then clearly be, not the achievement of a first-strike capability, but rather the maintenance of a second-strike capability against the danger of the adversary's achieving a sudden offensive or defensive advantage that would upset the balance.

Already, by 1959, major spokesmen of the United States Army and Navy had concluded that the United States could not afford to pursue a sufficiently credible first-strike counterforce capability but should concentrate, instead, upon achieving an invulnerable second-strike capability and a larger capacity for local resistance.[7] Moreover, there were signs in 1960 that Soviet leaders were as preoccupied with an invulnerable second-strike capability as the American government. On January 14, the day after Secretary of Defense Gates assured the House Committee on Appropriations that there was no "deterrent gap" because "even a surprise attack by all the missiles the Soviets could muster would not suffice to destroy enough of our retaliatory strike forces to enable him to make a rational decision to attack,"[8] Premier Khrushchev assured the Supreme Soviet that Russia's striking force was adequate for the same reason.

In this speech Khrushchev maintained that missiles and nuclear warheads had become the decisive weapons in warfare (an emphasis subsequently supplanted by a re-emphasis on balanced forces) and that Soviet missile strength and nuclear firepower more than compensated for his announced reduction of 1,200,000 men in the Soviet forces. He conceded that in the event of a general war Russia "would suffer heavy misfortune, would sustain great losses of life"; but he avowed his confidence that, even if some capitalist states were to gain parity with

Russia in modern armaments, they would not rationally launch a first strike, because the Soviet Union had a sufficiently secure retaliatory missile force—by virtue of dispersion, camouflage, and duplication of missiles assigned to targets—to "literally wipe the country or countries that attack us off the face of the earth."[9] It is true that Khrushchev, while proclaiming that the West's first-strike capability had been neutralized, did not explicitly renounce a *Soviet* first strike, but neither did he denigrate the capacity of the capitalist states to maintain an adequate second-strike force. Rather, he conceded that, hypothetically, they might gain "parity" with Russia and that, in any case, Russia would suffer immensely in a nuclear war.

In fact, for several years Soviet spokesmen had been saying that nuclear war would inflict grievous losses on the Communist camp, even though communism would survive and capitalism would perish. But in 1960 this significant admission received new emphasis. For example, the Party's theoretical monthly, *Kommunist* (September, 1960), declared that

> the working class cannot conceive of the creation of a Communist civilization on the ruins of world centers of culture, on desolated land contaminated with thermonuclear fallout, which would be an inevitable consequence of such a war. For some peoples the question of socialism would in general cease to exist: they would physically vanish from the planet. It is thus clear that a present-day nuclear war in itself can in no way be a factor that would accelerate revolution and bring the victory of socialism closer. On the contrary, it would hurl mankind, the world revolutionary workers' movement, and the cause of the building of socialism and Communism back by many decades.[10]

In October, 1960, the leading Soviet military theorist General Nicolai A. Talenski, writing in a prominent Soviet magazine on foreign affairs, indorsed this proposition and reaffirmed Premier Khrushchev's analysis of its strategic implications. In a nuclear war, he contended, "the world population would be reduced by one-half . . . the most active, capable, and civilized portion of mankind would be wiped out . . . the material and technical basis for life would be destroyed . . . humanity would be thrown back and its way to Communism would become immensely longer." Therefore, Talenski concluded, in effect, that no power could derive an advantage from a surprise attack: "The 'saturation level' of nuclear weapons, their disposition, and methods of using them are at present such that the attacked country would always be left with sufficient nuclear means to inflict a counterblow of sufficient proportions to cause tremendous losses and destruction."[11]

The disutility, for Communists as well as capitalists, of a general nuclear war (the only kind of nuclear war that Soviet doctrine acknowledged) was again affirmed in the statement issued by the representatives of eighty-one world Communist parties meeting in Moscow in November, 1960, and in Khrushchev's discussion of this statement in a speech to a meeting of Soviet Communist party organizations on January 6, 1961. The Moscow statement declared:

> Monstrous means of mass annihilation and destruction have developed which, if used in a new war, can cause unheard-of destruction to entire countries and reduce key centers of world industry and culture to ruins. Such a war would bring death and suffering to hundreds of millions of people, among them people in countries not involved in it.[12]

Khrushchev elaborated this proposition in terms of the explosive power and the probable number of deaths resulting from H-bombs dropped on major cities, thereby giving the greatest detail on nuclear destruction that any Soviet leader had yet made public. Although he used Western figures concerning American and British damage in a nuclear war, he did not claim that the Soviet Union would be exempt from comparable damage. Rather, he asserted that nuclear war would not even "spare the people in the countries not directly subjected to the bombing; in particular, millions would die as a result of radiation." Inserting the orthodox Soviet qualification, he said, "We know that if the imperialist madmen were to begin a world war, the peoples would wipe out capitalism." But he added, "We know that the first to suffer in the event of war would be the working people and their vanguard—the working class."[13]

Communist statements about Soviet missile strength at the

beginning of the 1960's were generally made in the context of asserting that, as Khrushchev put it, "The present balance of world forces enables the socialist camp and the other peace forces for the first time in history to set themselves the entirely realistic task of forcing the imperialists to refrain, for fear of seeing their system destroyed, from starting a world war."[14] Significantly, there was no attempt by Khrushchev or his military spokesmen to deny that the military calculus that gave the Soviet Union the power to deter a first strike also gave the West the power to deter a Soviet first strike. Moreover, in 1961 there were no signs that the Soviet Union was undertaking the tremendous missile program that would be needed to acquire an adequate first-strike capability, while there were many signs that her civilian and military leaders understood the requirements of such a capability as well as did Western leaders.

Therefore, at the beginning of the 1960's it seemed very likely that both the United States and the Soviet Union would refrain from trying to build first-strike capabilities adequate to confine retaliatory damage to an acceptable level or second-strike capabilities designed to win the war through protracted strategic counterforce exchanges. Instead, they would probably content themselves with invulnerable second-strike forces adequate for passive deterrence, plus counterforce insurance. This would mean the achievement of that nuclear stalemate that Churchill envisioned in 1955—a "stage in this story where safety will be the sturdy child of terror, and survival the twin brother of annihilation"—although it would probably not lead to complete "saturation," as he called the hypothetical state of nuclear weapons sufficiency; for invulnerability would continually be threatened by technological innovation.

However, as Churchill foresaw, this kind of nuclear stalemate—that is, stable mutual passive deterrence—would not diminish the threat of Soviet aggression upon America's allies, especially aggression of a non-nuclear, limited, and ambiguous nature. In fact, it would tend to encourage such aggression in proportion to Soviet assurance that the United States would not respond with a nuclear attack. So stability of passive deterrence would tend to create instability of active deterrence insofar as active deterrence depended upon the threat of nuclear retaliation. In this way the onset of the missile age aggravated NATO's most serious strategic deficiency: the lack of a sizable conventional limited-war capability.

3. THE REQUIREMENTS OF ACTIVE DETERRENCE

One American reaction to the onset of the missile age—most marked in the Air Force—was to try to maintain the viability of the dominant strategy of "massive retaliation" by enlarging America's counterforce capability. However, this effort ran counter to the prevailing psychology of deterrence and to the technical and economic limitations upon a first-strike strategic striking force.

Theoretically, as a minimum condition, active nuclear deterrence—that is, the deterrence of aggressions upon others by the threat of nuclear attack upon the aggressor—requires a capability to knock out enough enemy retaliatory power to confine one's damage to acceptable levels, unless one can unilaterally develop a substantial defense against incoming missiles (which seems quite improbable, if only because of the relative ease with which the enemy could develop counter-antimissile measures). A comprehensive civil defense program would be a logical concomitant of such a capability.

But will not anything approaching the destruction of thirty or more of America's major cities be considered an unacceptable price to pay for punishing even a "major" aggression in Europe? If so, by the late 1960's a first-strike capability adequate to prevent such damage will require such a vast and effective counterforce capability as to be technically and economically infeasible. For as the numbers, accuracy, dispersion, mobility, concealment, and protection—in short, the relative invulnerability—of Soviet long-range missiles increase (as they must, if only to neutralize America's first-strike capability), it will become prohibitively difficult for the United States to possess the intelligence data and the striking force to give her sufficient assurance of substantially blunting Russia's retaliatory salvos. At the same time, the effort to acquire such a capability would lead to an immensely expensive and, possibly, unstabilizing arms race, if only because both sides would be anxious to protect the threatened invulnerability of their second-strike forces. In any case, even a technically adequate counterforce capability would not guarantee deterrence of a great variety of aggressions upon America's allies, for even when the United States enjoyed a virtual monopoly of nuclear striking power, the credibility of an American first strike began to decline under the influence of growing American and allied inhibitions against nuclear warfare.

The United States might still maintain an adequate first-strike capability if she could safely rely upon either a strategy of limited nuclear war or graduated nuclear reprisals against attacks upon her allies. But, even though these strategies may be credible deterrents and rational responses against Soviet nuclear attacks upon America's allies, they will be no substitute for conventional resistance against conventional attacks. We have already discussed the difficulties and disadvantages of a strategy of limited nuclear resistance. A strategy of graduated nuclear reprisals—that is, a strategy of striking a limited number of selected targets as a means of imposing disproportionate costs in a bargaining process leading to a political settlement[15]—would be no more efficacious as a response to any but the most overt and massive conventional aggression, considering the difficulties of co-operating with the Soviet Union in controlled nuclear reprisals and counterreprisals and the political and psychological liabilities of explicitly relying upon such a strategy.

Therefore, at the onset of the missile age effective active deterrence seemed bound to depend primarily, if not exclusively, upon local resistance forces capable of denying the aggressor the attainment of his immediate objective at an acceptable cost to the defender, rather than upon nuclear forces designed to disarm the aggressor, blunt his attack, or inflict unacceptable damage upon him. If the creation of such denial forces might somewhat hasten the declining credibility of active nuclear deterrence, that would be a price worth paying for relieving one's self of depending upon an obsolescent strategy. On the other hand, if the West neglected its limited-war capabilities, it would remain dependent upon active nuclear deterrence while it lost the first-strike capability required to make its strategy plausible. For this reason, probably the greatest threat to the stability of the military balance in the 1960's, given NATO's lack of local-resistance capabilities, would be limited aggression, which might escalate into unlimited destruction.

Of course, American forces that were incapable of knocking out enough of Russia's second-strike capability on a first strike to confine her retaliatory damage to an acceptable level might nevertheless be an adequate deterrent against aggressions upon the allies, since the potential aggressor might place a very low value on the pursuit of his objectives by military means, in the light of attractive alternative non-military courses of action. As NATO entered its second decade it was generally assumed that the Soviet Union did place some such low value upon military aggression in the NATO area, as she concentrated upon the opportunities for non-military aggrandizement or local "national-liberation wars" outside the area.* However, even if this was a correct estimate, it was dangerous to assume that the Kremlin would not, under changed circumstances—for example, the frustration of Soviet designs in the "zone of peace" or pressure for a more adventurous policy from China or elements within the Soviet Union itself—decide to exploit opportunities for military probes even in Europe, if the "relationship of forces" appeared sufficiently advantageous. The Soviet nuclear

---

* In his speech in Moscow on January 6, 1961, Khrushchev condemned "world wars" and "local wars" (that is, limited wars between states, waged by the "imperialists," like the Suez War of 1956). He said that world wars could be deterred and that local wars must either be deterred or nipped in the bud by Soviet intervention. But he declared that "national-liberation wars," as in Viet Nam and Algeria, "are not only justified, they are inevitable." "The Communists," he said, "support just wars of this kind wholeheartedly and without reservations and they march in the van of the peoples fighting for liberation," while the imperialists are deterred from directly intervening in such wars by the threat of Chinese and Soviet intervention and the danger that the fighting could develop into a world war (text in *World Marxist Review* [London], for January, 1961, reprinted in *Two Communist Manifestoes* [Washington: The Washington Center of Foreign Policy Research, 1961], pp. 48–52).

striking force, which in 1960 might be intended only to deter the United States from launching a massive nuclear strike could, in 1965, embolden the Russians to assume large risks of limited war. In any case, they will be tempted to test Western resolution by limited and ambiguous incursions short of military aggression, and they will certainly try to exploit any deficiency in America's active deterrent capabilities diplomatically and psychologically by convincing America's allies that their dependence on the United States leaves them no choice between catastrophe and capitulation.

4. THE REQUIREMENTS OF MUTUAL ASSURANCE

The onset of the missile age also emphasized another danger that conspired against the efficacy of active nuclear deterrence: the danger of a Soviet defensive first strike, delivered because of a misapprehension of an American first strike. For in order to offset this danger the United States would have to be more concerned about assuring the Russians that it would *not* strike first than about convincing them that it would.

Underlying a growing concern about this new threat to the stability of military deterrence was the anticipation that the United States and the Soviet Union would soon have quantities of long-range missiles of great accuracy and speed, which they might launch, with no more warning than electronics could provide, in a surprise attack that would cripple the other's capability to retaliate effectively. The potential victim of such an attack, to the extent that his striking force was vulnerable, would have to react to a warning of attack as quickly as possible in order to preserve his second-strike capability or, perhaps, to blunt the attack by a pre-emptive blow. Yet, at best, the United States and the Soviet Union could receive scarcely thirty minutes' warning from the time of launching. The reduction of reaction time, in turn, would increase the possibility that the imagined victim might feel compelled to launch a defensive first strike because he mistakenly believed that the adversary was about to launch or had already launched a first strike on him. Such a misapprehension would be most likely to arise from a misinterpretation of warning information, especially during the tension of an international crisis or a limited war.

Like so many other hypothetical military contingencies with which we have no concrete experience, this one seems more logical than likely. But is it so unlikely that, considering its disastrous consequences, one can afford not to plan strategy and capabilities so as to prevent it? That is the insistent question confronting the whole spectrum of military planning. At least a Soviet defensive first strike of this nature seems more likely than the offensive strike "out of the blue"—the Pearl Harbor attack—with which the public debate on the "missile gap" or "deterrent gap" was preoccupied. Nothing that we know of Soviet foreign policy or military thought, or of the trend of the cold war, supports the implicit assumption behind much of this debate that the Kremlin takes such a desperate view of its opportunities for advancement through "peaceful coexistence" and such an optimistic view of its capacity to escape disastrous damage in a general nuclear war as to assume the risks of launching a knock-out blow against the United States on a problematical calculation that Russia's costs might be confined to a certain number of "mega-bodies" or obliterated—even if evacuated—cities. On the other hand, a strategic force perfectly adequate for deterring a Soviet offensive blow would not necessarily deter a defensive strike launched in anticipation of an imminent or actual American attack. For any nation that believed it was about to receive a massive nuclear attack would be under great pressure to launch its striking force before it was hit. Considering America's and NATO's announced strategy of meeting conventional attacks with nuclear retaliation, while both American and Soviet leaders denied the possibility of limiting nuclear warfare, one should not dismiss the danger that Russia might strike first out of fear of being struck first herself, especially during a limited war.

The appearance of a doctrine of pre-emptive attack in Soviet military writings in 1955 lent further credence to the possibility of a Soviet defensive strike.[16] Although some military specialists interpreted this pre-emptive doctrine as the guise for an offensive knock-out strategy, it seems more plausible, in the light of the Soviet preference and opportunities for less drastic forms of offensive action, to suppose that it was aimed, as stated, at deterring or blunting an American first strike, which the doctrine of massive retaliation proclaimed and which NATO strategy embodied.

For that matter, although a pre-emptive doctrine received only partial and unofficial support in American military and civilian circles, the government's frequently proclaimed fear of a Pearl Harbor strike suggests that one cannot dismiss the danger that the United States might also feel compelled during some intense crisis to launch a defensive first strike on the basis of information suggesting an imminent Soviet attack.

Therefore, although neither major nuclear power might wish to launch an offensive first strike, their forthcoming reliance upon long-range missiles created a danger that either might launch a defensive first strike on the misapprehension that the adversary was about to strike first, perhaps because he too feared a surprise attack. The attempt to mitigate this danger led beyond passive deterrence to a strategy of mutual assurance; that is, to a military posture which aims to prevent a first strike by providing potential adversaries with mutual assurance that neither has launched or intends to launch a first strike. Clearly, the search for means to assure the adversary that one will *not* strike first tends to undermine the credibility of active nuclear deterrence, which depends upon convincing the adversary that one *will* strike first.

Officially and unofficially, a number of measures—some unilateral and some requiring international agreement—were suggested to enhance mutual assurance against surprise attack.[17] The most obvious unilateral measure is to abstain from the kind of mobilization, deployments, and maneuvers that might suggest that one is contemplating the initiation of nuclear warfare, such as taking pre-attack civil defense measures or flying formations of bombers across Soviet radar screens.*

---

* The Air Force argued for the continued utility of manned bombers in the missile age partly on the ground that in an air-borne alert they could serve as a

Other unilateral measures would be designed to minimize the chance of touching off nuclear exchanges through miscalculation, accident, or unintentional provocation by developing a second-strike capability that does not depend on a quick, irrevocable, and total reaction to warning of a surprise attack. Essentially, what is needed is a second-strike capability so invulnerable and so susceptible to central control that one need not use it precipitantly or totally—a capability that will relieve a state of the necessity for having such a quick trigger finger as to preclude a thorough and cautious appraisal of the existence or source, scope, and intention of an enemy attack before delivering a controlled counterstrike. Patent invulnerability would compel a state contemplating a defensive first strike to interpret the adversary's *probable* intentions extremely conservatively in the light of the *certainty* of his ability to inflict unacceptable retaliatory damage. It would also avoid giving the impression, which might be conveyed by a vulnerable striking force, that one's striking power was intended *only* to deliver a first strike because it would be useless for a second strike. Moreover, if an enemy strike did occur, an invulnerable second-strike capability that permitted deliberation could at least hold open the possibility of ending hostilities short of a catastrophic sequence of unrestrained nuclear exchanges, which might otherwise be virtually automatic.* As the numbers, accuracy, reliability, and

---

visible sign on Communist radar screens of American preparedness. Chief of Staff General Thomas D. White conceded that this act might be provocative, in that it could suggest that the United States was launching a first strike (testimony on February 3, 1960, Preparedness Investigating Subcommittee, Senate Committee on Armed Services, *Hearings, Missiles, Space and Other Major Defense Matters*, 86 Cong., 2 sess., pp. 137–38). Herman Kahn has argued for a "Preattack Mobilization Base" and a program to evacuate urban populations to fall-out protection partly on the ground that, quickly activated, they would make an American first strike more credible in a tense situation (*On Thermonuclear War* [Princeton: Princeton University Press, 1960]). These examples suggest the difficulty of reconciling a first-strike strategy with mutual assurance against a first strike. The problem is to make a first strike credible enough to restrain the adversary and enhance one's bargaining power but not so credible as to provoke the adversary to strike first himself.

* Of course, it can be argued that the longer the United States took to deliberate about retaliatory blows, the less certain an unacceptable retaliatory blow would become and the better the Soviet bargaining position would be; and that,

penetrating power of missiles increase, concealment and mobility will be not only the most effective attributes of invulnerability; they will also be less provocative than increasing the numbers of missiles and bombers, since they will not so directly threaten the invulnerability of the adversary's striking force.

Let us follow the logic of this position further: If invulnerability were based on sufficient concealment and mobility, as well as upon hardened bases, dispersion, and diversity of strategic weapons systems, the United States would not need to rely so heavily upon early-warning devices, which would be subject to technical failure and misinterpretation and which would put a premium upon quick reaction. With an invulnerable second-strike capability of this kind the United States could be so confident of her retaliatory force surviving a first strike and delivering unacceptable damage in return that she could further reduce the danger of a defensive surprise attack by explicitly renouncing recourse to a pre-emptive blow and publicly adopting a policy of not launching missiles until hostile missiles had actually struck her territory or bases. She might also ask the Russians to adopt the same restraints. Even if the Russians did not reciprocate or did not trust the American renunciation, the policy would be a considerable safeguard against the United States precipitating an all-out nuclear exchange by miscalculation, accident, or (if a number of states had nuclear weapons) anonymous or pseudonymous attack.

Pursuing the rationale of mutual assurance against surprise attack even further, the United States might explicitly renounce a first-strike strategy as an instrument of active as well as passive deterrence—at least to the extent of declaring that she would

---

therefore, an instantaneous and automatic massive retaliatory blow is the most effective deterrent. Theoretically, this is true, although, actually, it seems extremely improbable that the Soviet Union, faced with an obvious American capability to deliver unacceptable retaliatory damage, would strike first in the expectation of securing a bargaining advantage in a limited nuclear exchange. But, in any case, whatever deterrent advantage might have to be sacrificed by renouncing instantaneous, automatic, all-out retaliation, would be well worth the compensating reduction in the risk of miscalculation and provocation and the increase in rational control of strategic nuclear blows.

use nuclear weapons against the Soviet Union only if Soviet nuclear weapons were used against her or her *allies.* To renounce the first use of nuclear weapons in these terms might, in fact, enhance the credibility of a promise to use them in response to nuclear attacks upon allies. She might then seek Soviet indorsement of this policy of self-denial and even make it the subject of an international resolution. To further enhance the credibility of such a renunciation the United States could make it as obvious as possible—for example, by conspicuously foregoing or disclosing certain weapons and their deployment—that she did not possess and did not intend to acquire the kind of capabilities that would be useful for a first strike. Thus, instead of undertaking an ambitious and possibly unstabilizing program of satellite reconnaissance, designed to discover military installations and deployments, the United States might publicly renounce the use of such satellites and invite Soviet inspectors to verify the renunciation.

Consistent with the logic of mutual assurance, the United States might also unilaterally grant the potential *aggressor* an invulnerable second-strike capability—especially since it will be extremely difficult to prevent this anyway. For, logically, mutual assurance is served as well by the adversary's possession as by one's own possession of the kind of striking force that permits the conservative appraisal of intentions, obviates the need for a trigger-quick response, and avoids a provocative posture. It follows that any American capability or action that threatens the invulnerability of Russia's striking power—like great counterforce capabilities, aerial reconnaissance, or harassment of Soviet communications, radar, or missile-launching submarines —works against the stability of the nuclear stalemate. It may not be easy to develop an adequate second-strike capability that would be obviously inadequate for a rational first strike, but the effort demands, at the least, that second-strike capabilities should be maintained by increasing one's own invulnerability, not by trying to decrease the enemy's.

The practical advantage of all these unilateral measures of mutual assurance against surprise attack is that they do not necessarily require the formal collaboration of the adversary in order to achieve their purpose, yet most of them could be the object of an appeal for informal reciprocity based on mutual interest. The complexity and uncertainty of the requirements of deterrence, the dynamic nature of military technology, and the existence of a deep-seated political conflict render any military "co-operation" or mutual restraint between potential belligerents rudimentary, fragile, and tentative. Therefore, the promotion of reciprocal restraints requires the flexibility of informal and tacit agreements, which can be formed, altered, or abandoned without involving the prestige or good faith of the parties too directly. If the West has a suitable second-strike and limited-resistance capability, what is needed to consolidate a basis of mutual interest in avoiding defensive first strikes at this stage of the cold war is not complicated formal schemes of co-operation, verification, and sanctions but, rather, the development of simple, obvious, and reliable informal restraints and the cultivation of purposeful communication between the potential belligerents.[18] Formal procedures, in proportion to their elaborateness, are likely only to multiply the opportunities for, and therefore the suspicions of, both sides dissembling their intentions and manipulating the modes of co-operation for hostile purposes. If only because of their high rate of technological obsolescence, elaborate international inspection and surveillance schemes would be peculiarly susceptible to subversion or simple misunderstanding, so that, in proportion to the co-operation they required, they might actually incite the fear and suspicion they were intended to allay. Nevertheless, one cannot exclude the possibility that there may be mutually acceptable formal bilateral and multilateral agreements that would incorporate adequate methods of disclosure and verification and yet contain sufficient safeguards against deception and subversion to enhance mutual assurance against surprise attack.[19]

But whatever the desirability and feasibility of formal or informal agreements for arms control may be, the point to be made here is that before the West commits itself uncritically to the logic of mutual assurance, it must examine the full implications of the objective itself and recognize that carrying it to its logical extreme would contravene the requirements of active nuclear deterrence and, possibly, even some of the requirements of passive deterrence. If the stability of passive deterrence tends to unstabilize the West's posture of active nuclear deterrence, the mere effort to achieve stable mutual assurance against surprise attack tends to make a first-strike strategy that much more untenable.

If active deterrence depends upon the credibility of one's threat of initiating the use of nuclear weapons against conventional aggressions, and one cannot rely upon limiting nuclear war, the efficacy of this first-strike strategy must certainly depend upon exploiting the advantages of a surprise attack. That is, if there is any advantage in striking first strategically, it must depend on catching the enemy's retaliatory forces unaware and destroying them in a sudden attack. Therefore, only a strategy of active deterrence that does not depend upon the threat of initiating the use of nuclear weapons can be completely compatible with a strategy of providing assurance against surprise attack, unless one can count upon limiting a local tactical nuclear war or a war of strategic nuclear exchanges intended purely for "bargaining" purposes. A nation that wishes to avoid provoking a defensive first strike but does not wish absolutely to renounce its own resort to nuclear war against non-nuclear aggression in extremities must try, somehow, to strike a balance between assuring the adversary that it does *not* intend to strike first in most circumstances and convincing him that it *might* strike first in some circumstances, if only with tactical nuclear weapons. But if at the same time such a nation does not have an adequate capacity to counter conventional aggression without resorting to nuclear weapons, it will de-emphasize its first-strike threat only at the cost of encouraging non-nuclear aggression.

Some measures of mutual assurance might also be incompatible with passive deterrence; for example, those that depend upon the disclosure of strategic forces and their deployment. For, if passive deterrence depends upon an invulnerable second-strike force, and invulnerability depends upon concealing the location and numbers of one's strategic weapons, measures that reveal the location and numbers might actually encourage a surprise attack. This difficulty would be only partially mitigated by agreements designed to disclose positive evidence of peaceful intentions by occasional inspections upon mutual request rather than to provide negative evidence by continual surveillance.*

5. THE NEED FOR AN OVER-ALL STRATEGY OF STABILITY

Let us summarize these observations on the diverse requirements of stable deterrence in the missile age. The stability of military deterrence is not an automatic result of the strategic nuclear arms race. On the contrary, the military balance contains inherent elements of instability, which are aggravated by rapid technological change. To mitigate these elements, stability must be achieved in all sectors of the military environment, lest stability in one sector create instability in another. This means that comprehensive stability can be achieved only at the price of foregoing or de-emphasizing some deterrent capabilities and strategies for the sake of a consistent posture of active and passive deterrence. The most significant price must be paid in terms of decreased dependence upon active deterrence by the threat of initiating the use of nuclear weapons, but this price can purchase stability only if it is accompanied by a substantial increase in local-resistance capabilities by non-nuclear means. If

* It would be easier for states occasionally to prove that they were not about to launch a surprise attack than for them continually to provide such negative evidence, without at the same time jeopardizing the invulnerability of their second-strike capability. However, such selective disclosure schemes assume that states will be completely free to choose the occasion for disclosure in order to prove their peaceful intentions. On the contrary, the very existence of the machinery for disclosure would probably create irresistible pressures—upon the United States, at least—to use it during crises at the request of hostile or neutral states, even though this might interfere with one's desire to enhance the credibility of a first strike or to assure the invulnerability of one's passive deterrent at the moment. Yet to refuse to use the machinery during a crisis would probably destroy its future utility and constitute a serious provocation in itself, in addition to creating a presumption of guilt in the eyes of others.

a stable, consistent posture of active and passive deterrence is achieved, the greatest threat to military stability in the missile age will be the possibility of a defensive first strike. The mitigation of this threat requires measures of mutual assurance against surprise attack. But to achieve their purpose of stabilizing the total military environment against armed conflict, these measures must be consistent with the strategies and capabilities of active and passive deterrence, with which they should be integrated within an over-all strategy of stability.

Considering the complexity of the problem of stabilizing the military environment when deterrence is, essentially, a relationship between two nuclear powers, one must expect the diffusion of independent nuclear capabilities to other powers—especially to powers not aligned with the United States—to create instabilities of a new order of magnitude and complexity. However, the momentous military and political consequences of that prospect is a subject in itself, beyond the scope of this discussion.

This discussion should be sufficient to show that, merely in terms of bipolar deterrence, as the "balance of terror" comes to depend increasingly upon numerous long-range missiles, the diverse requirements of deterrence demand that the United States and her allies make a basic decision whether to try to stabilize the military environment by giving up a first-strike counterforce strategy (except, minimally, as insurance in case of the failure of deterrence), by building up NATO's conventional local-resistance capabilities, and by seeking mutual assurances against surprise attacks or whether to try to achieve and maintain such overwhelming nuclear striking power and such effective civil defense and, possibly, active defense against missiles as to obviate the need for building up NATO's local-resistance capabilities by enhancing the credibility of a first strike, at least on a tactical basis. Any compromise between these two positions that is not purely temporary and transitional seems bound to incur the liabilities of both. If the United States does not make this decision with full recognition of the concrete implications of an over-all strategy of stability, it is in grave danger of drifting into the anomalous position of remaining dependent upon a strategy of active deterrence by nuclear reprisals, while in the name of stability it steadily undermines the credibility of this strategy.

6. THE CONTRADICTIONS IN AMERICAN STRATEGY

At the end of 1960 the American government showed few signs of reconciling the contradictions within its deterrent strategy or the contradictions between its deterrent strategy and its arms control policy. Although it was explicitly concerned with "stabilizing the military environment," it had developed no coherent over-all strategy of stability.

At the onset of the missile age the United States continued to rely primarily upon the threat of nuclear retaliation to deter non-nuclear aggression in the NATO area, for it had declared, in effect, that NATO was dependent upon a nuclear response to any conventional aggression larger than a border incident or a minor probing action and it had denied the possibility of fighting even a *conventional* limited war in the area. Yet President Eisenhower, while proclaiming America's unwillingness—indeed inability—to fight a war of local resistance on the ground and emphasizing his conviction that any war in Europe would become a thermonuclear war, had also declared that such a war would be "self-defeating" and would bring about "the destruction of civilization as we know it."[20]

This declaratory position logically left the United States dependent upon a first-strike strategy for deterring aggression upon her NATO allies, although it is difficult to see what advantage there could be in striking first in a "self-defeating" war. Yet despite certain concessions—chiefly in defense appropriations and in the determination of strategic targets—to the Air Force's appeals for a full-scale win-the-war counterforce strategy,[21] the government did not begin to undertake the massive build up of counterforce capabilities that would soon be necessary to have a chance of knocking out enough of Soviet striking power to confine her retaliatory damage to an acceptable level. Nor did it show interest in the comprehensive civil defense program that could, theoretically, serve the same purpose. Moreover, as if further to depreciate the credibility of its own declaratory strategy, the administration, in the debates of 1959 and 1960 on the "missile gap" or "deterrent gap," as in the debate on air power in 1956, proposed and defended the size and composition of America's strategic striking power entirely in terms of passive deterrence and a second-strike capability.

At the same time, the Eisenhower administration, to the end, remained adamantly opposed to compensating for the declining credibility of active nuclear deterrence by enlarging local resistance forces. Instead, it remained wedded to the thesis—with which neither the Army, the Navy, or any prominent private student of strategy agreed—that nuclear firepower would compensate for a reduction of mobilized manpower, and that the forces that would prevent a big war would also prevent a small war, since the chances of even a limited war growing into a thermonuclear conflagration would deter all overt military aggression.

Actually, the government's strategy was even more contradictory and ambiguous than this, for it appeared not to have secured a strategic consensus within its own councils, even on the strategy and capabilities of passive deterrence. All administration spokesmen, with the occasional exception of Air Force representatives, appeared to regard the sole objective of a strategic nuclear force as passive deterrence, but the representatives of the military services and the Defense Department actually recommended three different kinds of capabilities and concepts of passive deterrence: "finite" or "minimum" deterrence, finite plus some counterforce insurance, and counterforce capabilities to "win the war."

In January, 1959, Secretary of Defense McElroy defended the adequacy of America's deterrent forces against critics of the "missile gap" entirely in terms of deterring an offensive surprise attack on the United States. For that purpose, he explained, "we have enough retaliatory power remaining after we take losses from a surprise attack so that we can still inflict upon [the aggressor] a degree of destruction that will deter him from launching the attack in the first place."[22] This implicit description of general deterrent requirements was the same as SAC Commander Curtis LeMay's before the hearings on air power in April, 1956. "A deterrent force," LeMay had said, "is an effective nuclear offensive force which is secure from destruction by the enemy regardless of what offensive and defensive action he takes against it. The striking force is considered effective if it can still inflict unaceptable damage on the enemy."[23] Evidently, both McElroy and LeMay regarded this kind of deterrent force as equally effective against attacks on America's allies, on the theory that the Soviet Union would not attack any NATO power without attacking the United States;[24] but, since no one raised the question of *active* nuclear deterrence, its strategic requirements were not clarified.

Only Secretary of the Air Force Douglas and General Thomas D. White, chief of staff of the Air Force, indicated that the requirements of deterrence differed, depending upon whether the United States were responding to a surprise attack upon its homeland or to an attack on other powers. In the first case the United States "would turn toward the problem of doing the greatest damage possible to the country as a whole," whereas in the second case the first priority would be to destroy the bases from which the aggressor might destroy the United States.[25] However, these Air Force spokesmen did not directly assert that a first-strike strategy was the nation's actual strategy, and they did not explain specifically the different requirements for a first and second strike. Secretary Douglas implied that far fewer missiles would be needed for passive than for active deterrence and said that for passive deterrence the same number of missiles the Soviet Union could be expected to have would constitute a "wholly unnecessary overkill to accomplish your purpose."[26] But in 1956 General LeMay had described second-strike as well as first-strike requirements in terms of eventually gaining control of the air and then winning the war.[27] And in May, 1959, General White seemed to follow this same prescription when he said that an effective deterring posture, implicitly even for a second strike, required forces with the "capacity to prevail over an enemy" and "selectively and decisively—destroy his military forces and warmaking capacity."[28]

At the other extreme of views on the strategy and capabilities of deterrence, the chiefs of staff of the Navy and Army, Admiral Arleigh Burke and General Maxwell Taylor, testified in 1959 and 1960 in favor of a minimum second-strike capability designed only to inflict unacceptable retaliatory damage by destroying a finite number of civilian targets in the Soviet Union. They said nothing about the requirements of active nuclear deterrence, but implicitly they were in favor of abandoning a first-strike strategy, and explicitly they advocated greater expenditures upon limited-war forces at the expense of the nuclear counterforce capabilities the Air Force was seeking. For the Navy, which saw the Polaris submarine-launched missile as the nucleus of an invulnerable second-strike capability, this conception of minimum deterrence represented a radical shift from the time of the B-36 hearings in 1949, when it had argued against the deterrent strategy of concentrating upon bombing civilian and industrial targets on the grounds that it was ineffective, self-defeating, and immoral. So it was fitting that the Air Force should now adopt the Navy's former arguments and point to the dangers and evils of relying entirely upon countercity instead of counterforce strikes.

At the beginning of the missile debate, in 1957, the Navy had taken the initiative in advocating a strategy of minimum deterrence,[29] but in the congressional hearings of 1959 it was General Taylor who explained most explicitly the requirements of this strategy:

> I would say that it is possible to establish the fact that "X" targets successfully attacked with "Y" megatons is equivalent to the destruction of the enemy. . . . Then, having determined the bombs required on target, you can calculate all the possible losses due to enemy action, aborts, ineffectiveness of the weapons, and so forth, and determine how many delivery vehicles are required.

Taking account of a factor of safety, one would then arrive at the requirements of a strategic nuclear striking force.[30] On the basis of this kind of calculation, both he and Admiral Burke reached the conclusion that the United States was already "overinsured" in strategic retaliatory power, because the United States could "destroy" Russia "many times over" with the weapons she then possessed[31]—although in other contexts General Taylor saw an urgent need for restoring the mobility (under Army control) of the IRBM Jupiter in order to forestall an emerging missile gap,[32] and Admiral Burke stressed the importance of speeding the 40-submarine Polaris program for the same reason.

Whereas Taylor and Burke believed that the United States either had achieved, or readily could achieve, sufficiency in her second-strike capability, they held that the Soviet Union had already achieved, if not sufficiency, at least a measure of invulnerability in her second-strike capability that no American counterforce capability could vitiate.[33] And General Taylor's successor, General Lyman L. Lemnitzer, said that the period in which both the Communist and free world would have a "virtually indestructible nuclear capability" was near at hand.[34]

In response to this attack upon a counterforce capability, Air Force spokesmen charged that Polaris was not invulnerable, that no one, including Khrushchev, knew what retaliatory damage would be unacceptable, that the delicate balance of striking power might easily tilt so as to induce the Soviet Union to launch a first strike, and that a strategy of finite deterrence would be immoral and dangerous because it would deprive the United States of the important option of striking at military targets instead of civilian centers. Yet, like Army and Navy spokesmen, they justified their appeals for weapons and appropriations chiefly in terms of achieving an invulnerable passive deterrent force. Thus General Thomas S. Power, commander of SAC, appealed for a continuous air-borne alert and appropriations for the B-70 bomber as essential contributions to the "survivability" of America's second-strike force. Although he believed that the Soviet-American nuclear balance was currently only in a state of "nuclear stalemate," in which the Kremlin might dare to attack, rather than in a state of "nuclear impasse," in which neither side would have an advantage in striking first, he said that American security demanded reaching the latter state as rapidly as possible.[35] Only General White alluded to other functions of a strategic striking force. Although his statement of the requirements of deterrence, submitted in the hearings of January, 1960, started by discussing deterrence entirely in terms of passive deterrence, two of his specific objections to finite deterrence were set forth in terms of active deterrence. Finite deterrence, he said, disregarded "the possibility of reaction on our part to strategic warning"—a clear reference to a pre-emptive strike on Soviet bases—and conflicted with "broad national policy objectives" that depended on supporting America's allies without leaving the United States subject to a direct attack by unimpaired Soviet striking power—a clear reference to the original strategy of massive retaliation.[36]

However, the civilian branch of the government did not subscribe to this view of the dependence of allied policy upon active nuclear deterrence. It is true that in these same hearings the new secretary of defense, Thomas S. Gates, said in his written statement that the first objective of America's defense program continued to be "to deter the outbreak of general war by maintaining and improving our present capability to retaliate with devastating effectiveness in case of a major attack upon us *or our allies.*"[37] But in the give and take of discussion he, like his predecessor, defined the "deterrent gap" exclusively in terms of passive deterrence:

> It is the situation when your total deterrent force ceases to be sufficient to deter a potential enemy, as contrasted with a simple numerical comparison of a single weapon. . . . If you can be satisfied that your deterrent power exists, is real, and will survive a surprise attack, regardless of what force he can attack you with, then you have no deterrent gap.[38]

As for the material requirements of deterrence, Gates struck a compromise between the Navy-Army and the Air Force positions. He said that it would be hard to tell exactly what targets the United States would go after in a second strike:

> However, it would be correct to say that in order to maintain a valid deterrent we have to maintain a deterrent force capable

> of knocking out [the aggressor's] military power and not just bombing his cities. What we would actually do depends on circumstances, but we are adjusting our power to a counterforce theory; or a mixture of counterforce theory plus attacks on industrial centers and things of that character. We are not basing our requirements on just bombing Russia for retaliation purposes.[39]

Thus, in effect, the administration seemed to be saying through its secretary of defense that the United States was not overinsured in its strategic striking force, because she needed some counterforce insurance in addition to a countercity capability for a second strike, and that she was not underinsured, because the decisive requirement of deterrence was to be able to deliver unacceptable retaliatory damage after a surprise attack on the United States. Although Gates conceded that the Soviet missile force might enjoy at times "a moderate numerical superiority during the next three years," he said this would not constitute a deterrent gap, because "it is the conclusion of those who have analyzed this matter that even a surprise attack by all the missiles the Soviets could muster would not suffice to destroy enough of our retaliatory strike force to enable him to make a rational decision to attack."[40]

General Nathan Twining, chairman of the Joint Chiefs of Staff, voiced an old concern of his when he expressed the fear that charges of a missile gap might "downgrade our capability" so much that "the public will become frightened some day" and the enemy might be encouraged to attack or cause the public to knuckle under to missile-rattling.[41] One does not know how the Russians interpreted the missile debate, but if they interpreted American statements as reflecting the kind of studied indirection they applied in their own esoteric pronouncements, nothing that was said about America's numerical deficiency in missiles could have encouraged them to discount America's threat of nuclear retaliation against aggression in Europe as much as the government's own preoccupation with passive deterrence and a second-strike capability.

More than likely, the American government simply had not managed to resolve the conflicting views and contradictory elements of its deterrent strategy, and as a result the hiatus was filled by strategic pronouncements more representative of the tactics of service competition for appropriations than of concerted official plans, if any such plans existed. How the United States might actually respond to aggression in Europe might have no more relation to plans and pronouncements than its decision to intervene in the Korean War. Yet, in the absence of a test case, not only the Russians but America's allies were bound to draw their own inferences about her strategy and capabilities, and these inferences might have military and political consequences quite beyond American plans or expectations.

7. THE EISENHOWER ADMINISTRATION'S ARMS CONTROL POLICY

While seeming to abandon by default the pursuit of a first-strike capability suitable for active nuclear deterrence, the administration more indirectly cast doubt upon the viability of its strategy of nuclear retaliation in Europe by stressing in its arms control policy the goal of mutual assurance against surprise attack. It cast doubt upon this strategy, not because there was much likelihood of reaching an agreement with the Russians on arms control or even because such a scheme could actually provide mutual assurance if the Russians did agree to it, but because this position indicated that the government, in its concern about the dangers of surprise attack in the missile age, had turned from stressing its determination to deliver a first strike, as at the time of Dulles' "massive retaliation" pronouncement in 1954, to stressing its common interest with the Russians in allaying fears of a first strike. This radical shift of emphasis represented the culmination of the government's implicit acceptance of the psychology of mutual deterrence, reflecting the condition of parity in second-strike destructive capabilities, in place of the psychology of unilateral deterrence, which had reflected America's monopoly of a nuclear first-strike capability. Sooner or later, the credibility of a first-strike strategy is bound to wither in an atmosphere of mutual deterrence.

Ever since President Eisenhower, at the Geneva "Summit" conference in July, 1955, presented the abortive "open skies" proposal for mutual disclosure of military "blueprints" and mutual photo-reconnaissance over national territory, mutual assurance against surprise attack had been a prominent objective of American arms control proposals. In fact, the government seemed to have reached the conclusion that the best hope for disarmament—that is, the reduction and abolition of arms—was not disarmament at all, strictly speaking, but rather the stabilization of the existing balance of terror by arms control, by measures of surveillance and inspection designed to mitigate the risk of wars springing from miscalculation and the fear of attack. Secretary of State Christian A. Herter gave this objective a new emphasis when, on February 18, 1960, he described America's first goal in disarmament policy as the creation of "a more stable military environment" by reducing the risk of war resulting from miscalculation and from the promiscuous spread of nuclear weapons production. To reduce the danger of surprise attack by miscalculation, Mr. Herter suggested aerial and mobile ground inspection, ground observers both inside and outside the zones of inspection, arrangements for the exchange of information about events in outer space, and armament controls. "If these safeguards are effective," he said, "there will be less chance of one side being moved to surprise attack by a mistaken belief that the military moves of the other side portend such attacks. This danger may be particularly acute in a major international crisis, when tensions are high and both sides are moving to heightened readiness."[42]

In May, 1960, the government seemed prepared to pursue this proposal at another summit conference. When Khrushchev torpedoed that conference, following the shooting down of the American U-2 photo-reconnaissance plane deep over Russian territory, President Eisenhower and his secretary of state said the incident pointed up the urgency of an "open skies" agreement to relieve both sides of the fear of surprise attack, a fear which had compelled the United States to fly over Russian territory.[43]

In September, Eisenhower elaborated Herter's February proposal in an address to the U.N. General Assembly. Explaining its purpose, he said:

> The advent of missiles, with ever-shorter reaction times, makes measures to curtail the danger of war by miscalculation increasingly necessary. States must be able quickly to assure each other that they are not preparing aggressive moves—particularly in international crises, when each side takes steps to improve its own defenses which might be misinterpreted by the other. Such misinterpretation, in the absence of machinery to verify that neither was preparing to attack the other, could lead to a war which no one had intended or wanted.

In order to prevent such a war the President proposed to set up a United Nations surveillance body, which would verify the absence of preparations for surprise attack "when requested by any nation seeking to prove its own peaceful intention." Then, continuing his explanation of the rationale of such machinery, he came close to renouncing active nuclear deterrence altogether. "The United States," he said, "wants the Soviet Union and all the nations of the world to know enough about United States defense preparations to be assured that United States forces exist only for deterrence and defense—not for surprise attack." Moreover, he reaffirmed the danger of military secrecy in such absolute terms as to jeopardize even passive deterrence based upon invulnerability through concealment. "In an age of rapidly developing technology," he asserted, "secrecy is not only an anachronism—it is downright dangerous. To seek to maintain a society in which a military move can be taken in complete secrecy, while professing to reduce the risk of war through arms control, is a contradiction."[44]

In practice, it would be extremely difficult for a surveillance body satisfactorily to verify the absence of preparations for surprise attack, especially where such verification would depend upon revealing the numbers and location of air-borne and sea-borne missiles. In any case, the Russians persisted in regarding any such scheme that was not a part of total disarmament as a mere subterfuge for espionage. Nevertheless, the President's apparent renunciation of the initial use of nuclear weapons by surprise and his virtually unqualified indorsement of the principle of mutual assurance through military disclosures were eloquent, if inadvertent, testimony to the obsolescence of the strategy of nuclear retaliation upon which NATO still depended.

8. THE SOVIET VIEW OF STABILITY

At the end of 1960 the United States in its capacity as the leader of the North Atlantic alliance lacked and badly needed an over-all strategy of stability in order to co-ordinate military strategy with arms control and one strategy of deterrence with another. In the absence of such a strategy, NATO could not be expected to resolve its own strategic contradictions and ambiguities, which were largely a reflection of America's military policies. However, an over-all strategy of stability could not properly be formulated merely in terms of the military environment. It would also have to take account of the relation of the military to the political environment. A central element of this relation was the Communist view of stability.

Perhaps, in our conviction of the absurdity or "impossibility" of nuclear war, we tend to exaggerate the autonomous effect of a novel military technology in stabilizing—or, for that matter, unstabilizing—the military environment. After all, military conflicts still arise from political conflicts. They are not created spontaneously by the military configurations of power themselves. Therefore, we should not expect the wisest choice of military deterrents to eliminate all warfare from international relations, especially warfare that springs from political conflicts beyond the control of the major nuclear powers. And, by the same token, we should not expect a common Soviet and American interest in avoiding suicidal war and an unrestricted arms race to engender, by itself, much co-operation in alleviating the political sources of tension and conflict. In short, we should not expect a reversal of the historical relationship between arms and politics, which renders a stable political environment the condition, not the result, of a stable military environment.

For the Soviet Union to accept the complete stability of the military environment would mean for her to give up even the *threat* of war as an instrument of policy. But to give up the threat of war would be to accept the political status quo or else to be content to alter it without reference to the prospect of war as an instrument of coercion and persuasion. As Soviet policies, both courses would be directly contrary to Communist doctrine and practice and to the announced expectations and tactics of Khrushchev and all Communist leaders.

As Khrushchev explained to Walter Lippmann in 1958, he thinks of the status quo as the ineluctable process of revolutionary change, which is leading to the steady erosion of Western power, including its vulnerable forward positions in the North Atlantic area.[45] And, as the statement of the eighty-one Communist party representatives in November, 1960, declared, "The policy of peaceful coexistence is a policy of mobilizing the masses and launching vigorous action against the enemies of peace. Peaceful coexistence of states does not imply renunciation of the class struggle, as the revisionists claim. The coexistence of states with different social systems is a form of class struggle between socialism and capitalism."[46] It is, in Khrushchev's words, "a form of intense economic, political, and ideological struggle between the proletariat and the aggressive forces of imperialism in the world arena."[47] The belief that the Communist bloc is winning this struggle by peaceful means—by sheer economic and scientific progress and appeals to nationalism, neutralism, economic advancement, and peace—makes resort to overt military aggressions like the Korean War unnecessary. In this sense, the vulnerability of the "zone of peace" to Communist pressure and blandishments is the West's greatest deterrent to direct military aggression. However, this situation does not recommend itself as a policy.

Furthermore, the avoidance of direct military aggression does not exclude the indirect and ambiguous support of limited aggression or the political and psychological exploitation of unused military power. Although Khrushchev expects the triumph of the "socialist world system" to come about without war "between states," he considers "national-liberation wars" inevitable and vows to support them. We can take Khrushchev's word for his avowed determination to avoid general war. To this extent he wants to stabilize the military environment, and perhaps the West may even secure Soviet co-operation in elaborating its mutual interest in this objective through tacit understandings and limited agreements to provide mutual assurance against surprise attack and a counterforce arms race. But this does not mean that Soviet leaders perceive a common interest in stabilizing the military environment as a general goal. On the contrary, they manifest a disturbing new confidence in Russia's military ascendancy, which they are eager to exploit for diplomatic and propagandistic purposes. Apparently, they are uninterested in mollifying the West's fears of nuclear war, at least insofar as those fears spring from the prospect of having to counter lesser Soviet incursions. Rather, they show considerable zest and skill in playing upon these fears in order to divide the Western coalition, intimidate allies who provide strategic bases, undermine the uncertain status quo in the center of Europe, seize the propaganda initiative in disarmament discussions, and present Russia to the uncommitted nations as the champion of peace.*

---

* The importance as an instrument of Soviet policy of keeping alive a sense of instability, springing from the fear of thermonuclear war, can be inferred from the previously cited statement of the eighty-one Communist party representatives of November, 1960, and Khrushchev's speech in January, 1961. According to the statement, "The peace movement is the broadest movement of our time, involving people of diverse political and religious creeds, of diverse classes of society, who are all united by the noble urge to prevent new wars and to secure enduring peace." Thus it viewed peace as the principal fighting slogan for gaining broad mass support throughout the "zone of peace" and in other countries for Soviet policy goals in the struggle against the "capitalist-imperialist" states. As Khrushchev explained, "The slogan of the fight for peace by no means contradicts the slogan of the fight for communism. The two go hand-in-hand, for in the eyes of the masses communism appears as a force capable of saving mankind from the horrors of a missile-nuclear war, whereas imperialism is, increasingly, associated with war as a system engendering wars. That is why the slogan of the fight for peace is, as it were, a satellite of the slogan of the fight for communism." But peace is more than a popular slogan; it is a program. Thus the representatives' statement defines the tasks of peace as: "to stop the arms race, ban nuclear weapons, their tests and production, dismantle foreign war bases and withdraw foreign troops from other countries, disband military blocs, conclude a peace treaty with Germany, turn West Berlin into a demilitarized free city, thwart the aggressive designs of the West German revanchists, and prevent the revival of Japanese militarism" (*Two Communist Manifestoes* [Washington: Washington Center of Foreign Policy Research, 1961], pp. 55, 57, 63–64).

Undoubtedly, Moscow was pleased to receive assurance against an American first strike through America's policies, actions, and statements, as well as through the growth of her own retaliatory power. This assurance emboldened her to stir up trouble in the West's forward positions, to take greater chances of "local war," and to support "national-liberation wars." On the other hand, at the beginning of the missile age Soviet leaders showed no signs of wishing to co-operate with the West in providing *mutual* assurance against first strikes. Rather, they remained inveterately suspicious—not without some color of reason—that the proposed co-operative measures to minimize the danger of a defensive first strike were merely devices for redressing America's inferior espionage capabilities in order to facilitate a first strike.* Therefore, in the absence of a convincing posture of active deterrence based upon non-nuclear resist-

---

* The American government gave some credence to Soviet suspicions when, after the U-2 mishap, it argued, on the one hand, that the United States had been compelled to undertake the U-2 espionage program in order to get the kind of intelligence data that the Soviet Union could readily acquire by ordinary means in our open society and, on the other hand, that the unfortunate incident resulting from this necessity demonstrated the urgent need for an "open skies" agreement to secure the same kind of information on an international basis.

The U-2 program was publicly justified in terms of gaining protection against surprise attack. But Khrushchev had a plausible point when he contended that the kind of information the U-2 acquired—for example, the construction of missile bases—could not give tactical early warning of a Soviet surprise attack in the missile age but could have significance only for a state that intended to strike first (*Pravda*, June 22, 1960, p. 31). President Eisenhower gave credence to this contention in his radio and television address to the nation, explaining the U-2 incident and the collapse of the summit conference. For, in comparing the ease with which the Soviet Union could acquire militarily useful information about the United States with the United States difficulty in acquiring such information about the Soviet Union, he referred not only to information about cities but also about such facilities as dams and highways; and, in showing the kind of vital information the U-2 could acquire, he displayed an aerial photograph of an American air base (*New York Times*, May 26, 1960, p. 6). Actually, it is not clear whether the U-2 program, at the time of its demise, was intended to be an instrument of either a counterforce first-strike or second-strike strategy; but, as a general instrument of protection against surprise attack, it was evidently a remnant of pre-missile technology, when surveillance of highways, communications centers, and bases might have given useful tactical warning. Moreover, the program could have been useful for other purposes even in 1960; for example, it could have helped determine whether the U.S.S.R. was building a counterforce striking force or merely concentrating upon building an invulnerable second-strike force.

ance, America's concern to allay mutual fears of surprise attack seemed more apt to encourage Moscow to play an adventurous game than to induce her to co-operate in creating safeguards against the hazards of the missile age.

This is not to say, however, that there is no solid ground of mutual interests upon which the United States might reasonably hope to secure Soviet co-operation in stabilizing the military environment. It is only to say that the Soviet appreciation of this ground, and willingness to act in accordance with it, will depend not upon American ingenuity in devising schemes of formal co-operation but, first, on American resolution in developing with her allies a consistent over-all posture of deterrence that is credible without being provocative and, second, on American skill in utilizing that posture to achieve tacit and informal understandings of reciprocal restraint.

8
The Problem of Nuclear Diffusion

1. THE PROSPECT OF NUCLEAR DIFFUSION

As NATO entered its second decade, it no longer conveyed to its members the simple, compelling relationship between its demands upon them and their security needs that had sustained the vitality of the alliance in a less complicated period—before the Korean War, the emergence of the Soviet Union as a major nuclear power, the post-Stalin departure in foreign policy, and the onset of the missile age. In light of the perplexities of sustaining a common military strategy requiring an unprecedented level of peacetime contributions and commitments for the sake of an esoteric calculus of deterrence and defense, this is not surprising. Consequently, some allies now became receptive to military and political courses that promised to enhance their security by more direct means than delicate adjustments in the terms of strategic collaboration.

In the absence of any large or well-organized support for neutralism in allied countries,* two courses seemed particularly

* Perhaps the most articulate and best-organized minority that favored its nation leaving NATO was the British Campaign for Nuclear Disarmament, beginning in 1958. However, not all those who favored unilateral nuclear disarmament supported British neutralism, and there was overwhelming support for remaining in NATO in Britain as a whole. For, quite apart from NATO's

promising: (*a*) the acquisition of an "independent" (in the sense of independently controlled, not necessarily self-sufficient) nuclear capability or at least a larger share in the control of an American or collective nuclear capability, in order to escape the liabilities of depending exclusively upon the United States decision whether or not to use or threaten to use nuclear weapons; (*b*) an agreement of "disengagement" with the Soviet Union, in order to alleviate the political and military sources of NATO's security problems. The latter course, apart from its absolute unacceptability to West Germany, France, and probably other allies, seemed to be precluded by Russia's complete lack of interest in a genuine political accommodation, but the former course seemed available to several allies by dint of their own efforts and, possibly, American assistance. Although neither course would in itself be an alternative to NATO, both would impinge directly upon NATO's strategy and capabilities—indeed, upon the very core of mutual interests that provides the motive power of the alliance.

Well before 1957 and the launching of the Sputniks, the growth of Soviet nuclear striking power, coupled with the general political and prestige value of nuclear weapons, had fostered in Britain and France some powerful incentives for acquiring nuclear capabilities under independent national control. Technically and economically, probably at least three other allies—West Germany, Italy, and Canada—were capable of producing some kind of rudimentary nuclear warheads by 1965.[1] By 1970 still other allies (at least Belgium and the Netherlands) could join the nuclear club, especially if promising new processes made the production of nuclear warheads easier and cheaper.[2] Acquiring suitable means of delivering nuclear warheads was another matter but—as British, French, and German technological progress indicated—not one that need preclude the production of usable nuclear weapons systems if several

---

contribution to British security, the alliance was seen as an essential means by which Britain could preserve her great-power political status and exert her influence on the United States and other allies in behalf of British views on international questions.

allies independently or in collaboration wanted to allocate enough resources to that end.

These material possibilities raised the disquieting prospect that a number of allies would devote their major defense efforts to the proliferation of independent nuclear capabilities rather than to the integrated conventional forces the alliance so badly needed. This would not only cause a diversion of allied contributions from collective needs; it also seemed likely to arouse distrust and intensify divergencies of interests within the alliance. Furthermore, the spread of independent nuclear production and ownership among NATO members would probably stimulate the proliferation of independent nuclear capabilities among powers outside the alliance, and this development could upset the stability of the whole international military and political environment.

Of course, the technical and economic possibility of several allies building nuclear capabilities of their own did not mean that they would consider such efforts worthwhile—especially in view of the great financial and technical requirements of building a sufficiently invulnerable striking force to constitute a useful deterrent without being provocative. However, the experience of the British and French suggested that allies who had the material means to become nuclear powers would find a net balance of incentives over disincentives to do so, if this appeared to be the only way to avoid leaving the crucial decision of whether or not to use or threaten to use nuclear weapons entirely in American hands.

But there might be another way of avoiding this abnegation of allied to American will. In 1960 the proposal to create a jointly controlled NATO nuclear force received considerable support as the best way to relieve all allies of their exclusive dependence upon America's decision to employ nuclear weapons, without at the same time stimulating the production of independent nuclear capabilities. However, this proposal raised almost as many problems as it was intended to resolve. For one thing, it implied a subordination of national to collective will that challenged the traditional conception of military independence and political sovereignty more radically than simple acquiescence in American control of nuclear weapons. It also implied a severe problem of achieving effective centralized command and control of nuclear weapons and of reconciling the requirements of a multinational decision with the requirements of deterrence. By the end of 1960 the allies had not yet agreed on a procedure for the political control of the decision to use nuclear weapons. This delicate matter could no longer be postponed if the United States were to surrender her *de facto* control of these weapons, through her exclusive custody of the warheads, to NATO. Furthermore, effective joint control of nuclear weapons would absolutely require allied agreement upon a common strategy for the use of nuclear and non-nuclear weapons—a politically sensitive issue that could be left somewhat ambiguous as long as the United States, in effect, exercised exclusive control over nuclear weapons.

Thus the prospect of several allies being able to build their own nuclear capabilities raised the broad problem of nuclear diffusion,* which, in turn, intensified unresolved issues of strategy and interallied relations that underlay the over-all problem of NATO's security and cohesion. As in the case of other issues of allied strategy and politics, American policy toward nuclear diffusion was a key factor. For, despite the economic resurgence and the great scientific and productive power of her allies, the United States continued to be the only ally that could provide in quantity the sophisticated delivery systems that were essential to an invulnerable strategic striking force and a diversified arsenal of tactical nuclear weapons. Equally important, the United States continued to be the only ally that could initiate and carry through the major strategic and political readjustments that either the facilitation or discouragement of nuclear

* Generally, "nuclear diffusion" refers to spreading the control of the decision to use or threaten to use nuclear weapons among states. The most direct means of such control for a state is through physical possession of nuclear weapons, and the most direct means of obtaining physical possession is national production of the weapons. However, nuclear diffusion also embraces arrangements for *sharing* the ownership, production, operation, and decision to use nuclear weapons; and even the diffusion of nuclear information and material is obviously related to the diffusion of actual control of nuclear weapons.

sharing would involve if it were to be compatible with NATO's security and cohesion. At the same time, in shaping her policy toward diffusion, the United States would have to take serious account of allied attitudes and interests; and in all probability, these would compel her to promote a new formulation of NATO's strategy, new terms of allied collaboration, and a new distribution of power between the United States and her allies.

2. AMERICAN POLICY TOWARD NUCLEAR DIFFUSION

From the first relaxation of the Atomic Energy Act of 1946 (the so-called McMahon Act), which had been designed to protect America's atomic monopoly by guarding her nuclear "secrets," the United States government was torn between its desire to promote allied collaboration by sharing nuclear information, material, and weapons control and its fear of undermining allied cohesion and promoting nuclear diffusion among other powers by spreading, or appearing to spread, the independent production and control of nuclear weapons.

The first substantial measure of nuclear sharing came in 1954, when the Eisenhower administration persuaded Congress to liberalize the Atomic Energy Act's restrictions on dispensing information and equipment to the allies. The Atomic Energy Act of 1954 permitted the President to direct the Atomic Energy Commission to deliver atomic weapons to the Department of Defense for such use as he deemed to be in the national interest, but the secretary of defense was not permitted to give the weapons to an ally for training except under the continual custody of American nationals. Nuclear warheads were to remain in the physical possession of Americans. The act also added categories of information on the external characteristics of nuclear warheads that could be imparted to allies in order to facilitate allied training and operations with tactical nuclear weapons without facilitating allied manufacture of nuclear warheads—a dual purpose which, Secretary Dulles conceded, entailed a "difficult task of definition."[3]

The motive for this modest measure of nuclear diffusion arose from the 1954 decision that NATO should plan on the basis of initiating the use of tactical nuclear weapons against conventional attacks in order to compensate for its deficiency in standing forces; if the allies were to be dependent upon this tactical nuclear strategy, they would feel entitled to share at least the essential information for carrying it out. As Dulles told the Joint Committee on Atomic Energy, there was among the allies

> a growing feeling of almost futility on their part unless they can get more information than they now have about tactical weapons. They know we have them and they know the enemy has them, and they stand in between with no knowledge at all at the present time; and it is extremely difficult to retain the morale of the NATO force under the top command of General Gruenther under present conditions. . . . They tend to feel: "what is the use of having any armies at all under the present condition?"[4]

After the passage of the amended Atomic Energy Act, Dulles went to the NATO Council of Ministers meeting in December, 1954, and secured the adoption of a tactical nuclear strategy, in accordance with the "long-haul" concept of cutting back on the rearmament programs undertaken after the outbreak of the Korean War.

But, however much the 1954 amendment facilitated training the allies in tactical nuclear warfare, it did not solve the political problem inherent in America's desire to preserve a monopoly or, strictly speaking, a duopoly of nuclear production and custody within the alliance. On the contrary, it only whetted the allies' appetites for a larger share of the control of nuclear weapons and stimulated the British and French efforts to get American assistance in building independent nuclear capabilities.

At the December, 1956, NATO Council meeting France and West Germany urged greater integration of nuclear weapons with allied forces.[5] The United States promised to speed the distribution of tactical nuclear weapons and warhead stockpiles and accelerate allied training in their use,[6] but she insisted on maintaining exclusive custody of the nuclear warheads. This dual course, inevitably, made the allies more dependent upon weapons which, in effect, the United States alone controlled. Therefore, the logic of a tactical nuclear strategy seemed destined to jeopardize America's relations with her allies unless she would increase their share in the control of the decision to use these weapons (with their warheads, of course), contrary to the letter and spirit of the Atomic Energy Act.

An obvious alternative for some allies was to build their own nuclear weapons. But they would probably want to build *strategic* nuclear weapons, which would presumably give them the most power and status for their money. Strategic nuclear weapons programs, however, would make immense demands on the financial and scientific resources of even the most powerful allies; therefore, American assistance would be extremely valuable to them. Accordingly, the British used their strategic nuclear weapons program as a lever to pry nuclear information and material out of the United States and to persuade the American government to resume the fuller and more confident sharing of nuclear technology of the war period, which had been so abruptly terminated in 1946.[7] Within the tight and detailed restrictions of the McMahon Act and its amendments, Britain did, in fact, succeed in becoming a privileged partner in receiving American nuclear assistance,[8] for every British advance in nuclear technology confronted the United States with a refutation of the basic rationale of the Act: to preserve American secrets. Britain's success in this tactic, in turn, provided an additional incentive for France to develop her own nuclear program, but France's failure to secure equal access to American nuclear technology served as an additional grievance against the special Anglo-American partnership. The Suez War, in which both Britain and France withdrew in the face of American pressure and oblique Soviet threats to drop bombs on London and Paris, strengthened both governments' cases for building independent strategic nuclear forces.

To gain equal status with the Anglo-American bloc, France not only pushed her independent effort to become a nuclear power, but, lacking American assistance, she moved toward forming a consortium with West Germany and the other Common Market states for the development of nuclear technology. One instrument of this consortium was the Euratom (European

Atomic Energy Community) agreement, signed by France and the other members of the "Little Six" on February 20, 1957. Although Euratom was ostensibly created to develop peaceful uses of the atom, those inside and outside the agreement well knew that military and non-military nuclear technology went hand in hand. Moreover, the industrial program that the members of Euratom envisaged was to be based on dual-purpose reactors, capable of large-scale production of plutonium, and on gaseous diffusion plants for the separation of weapons-grade material. And a few weeks after the agreement was signed a West German bulletin summarizing its provisions disclosed that the Federal Republic, like the other members, would have access to the military atomic secrets of all its partners.[9]

German spokesmen properly denied their desire to revoke the WEU restrictions on their military establishment in order to become an independent nuclear power, but, if France were to become a full-fledged nuclear power, then West Germany, whether through a consortium or independently, seemed likely to claim equal privileges, for she was rapidly becoming the most powerful military and industrial member of the alliance in Europe. The prospect of the Federal Republic becoming a nuclear partner of France or an independent nuclear power was particularly disturbing, because of the strongly adverse reaction it caused, not only in the Soviet Union, but among some of America's allies—notably the British.

Faced with the specter of the diffusion of nuclear weapons production and ownership among the allies and beyond, Secretary of State Dulles turned to two major devices to stop this trend: (*a*) international control of nuclear production through the International Atomic Energy Agency and (*b*) joint allied control of the use of nuclear weapons. The first device failed to serve its purpose. The second was not put into effect.

The International Atomic Energy Agency (IAEA), which went into operation in July, 1957, had originated in President Eisenhower's "atoms-for-peace" proposal before the United Nations in 1953.[10] It was intended to promote the development of nuclear energy for peaceful purposes by enabling donor-states to transfer nuclear materials under safeguards, which the agency would establish and administer, against their diversion to military uses. In this respect IAEA was an attempt to internationalize the safeguards provided in America's bilateral agreements for the transfer of nuclear materials. Thus, in appealing for Senate approval of the IAEA statute in May, 1957, Dulles said:

> We must realize that atomic energy materials and know-how will spread, Agency or no Agency. The spread of nuclear technology and facilities is to our interest. But a rapid and unsupervised development of nuclear power around the world raises the specter of nuclear weapons ultimately becoming quite general, the byproduct of nuclear power plants.... These power plants are going to be built. It is just a question of whether their spread around the world will or will not be supervised in the common interest.[11]

However, the IAEA, while undoubtedly helping to spread nuclear technology, proved to be completely ineffectual as a means of dissuading any member-state from continuing to develop its nuclear military program; and it was incapable of deterring any other power from developing a weapons program with fissionable materials acquired through bilateral channels.

In July, 1957, Dulles indicated that he was moving toward a more controversial but, possibly, more effective device for discouraging the spread of nuclear weapons production when he disclosed that the United States was studying a plan for transferring custody of nuclear stockpiles to NATO itself, so that all allies would have equal access to nuclear weapons without having to build their own or remain wholly dependent on the United States.[12] The next day President Eisenhower emphatically indorsed this idea and asserted that the stockpiling proposal would make it unnecessary for others to manufacture nuclear weapons.[13] However, in the face of congressional objections to altering the Atomic Energy Act and the inauspicious circumstance that Harold Stassen was trying at the London disarmament conference to negotiate a ban on transferring nuclear weapons, the administration failed to present the plan for formal allied or congressional consideration at this time.

Then, in October, 1957, a sensational new technological development, Russia's orbiting of the first earth satellites, and her claims of a superior intercontinental missile technology intensified allied pressures for relief from nuclear dependence on the United States. For this development dramatized America's vulnerability to Soviet counter-retaliation and, therefore, deepened the suspicion that America's nuclear striking power was an unreliable basis of allied security. At the same time, it made the allies more vulnerable to nuclear obliteration and blackmail, especially if their territories held American strategic bases. The latter consideration became of immediate practical importance when the United States indicated, in November, 1957, that she hoped to protect herself against a possible "missile gap" —that is, a deficiency in her second-strike capability—by placing medium-range missiles on allied soil.[14]

At the annual North Atlantic Council meeting in December, Secretary Dulles presented the American plan to disperse IRBM's in Europe. He tried to sweeten the pill by promising the dispersion of accessible nuclear stockpiles for tactical as well as strategic weapons, giving assurances that the decision to use the missiles would be bilateral and stating that the United States would, in the future, transmit to any interested ally the secrets of how to build an atomic submarine for a truly invulnerable strategic force, if Congress were willing.[15] France, Italy, and the Netherlands were interested in the submarine offer (Britain was already assured of such American assistance). However, France and other Continental allies expressed doubts and objections concerning the placement of missiles on their soil. As a result, the United States had to be content with an agreement "in principle."

The plan which the Council approved, in principle, entailed the negotiation of bilateral agreements between the United States and her allies for the placement on allied soil of IRBM's, in accordance with NATO plans. The understanding was that the United States would retain custody of the warheads, but the ally would operate the missiles, so that the decision to use the missile would be a joint one, in which both powers retained a veto. In addition, the agreement approved the establishment of stocks of nuclear warheads, for tactical as well as strategic weapons, in places that would be readily available in case of war; but these stocks would be in the custody of the Supreme Allied Commander in Europe, acting in his capacity as an American commander in charge of American forces in Europe (CINCEUR).[16]

Britain and Turkey quickly expressed willingness to accept missiles under this arrangement (indeed, Prime Minister Macmillan and President Eisenhower had already reached an agreement to establish missiles in England at the Bermuda conference in March, 1957); but France, Greece, Belgium, Italy, and the Netherlands refused to commit themselves, and later all but Italy declined, while Norway and Denmark expressed the hope that they would not be asked to accept the missiles and Germany retained a tactful silence. In February, 1958, the United States signed an agreement with Britain to establish missiles in England, to be controlled by a "double-veto" arrangement, which was later revealed to include the installation of the warhead in the missile under a "two-key system."* During 1959 and 1960 four IRBM squadrons were emplaced, containing a total of about sixty above-ground, liquid-fuel Thor missiles. In 1959 the United States negotiated agreements with Italy and Turkey to establish a total of three Jupiter IRBM squadrons, containing a total of about forty-five missiles.

However, these missiles suffered the great military and political liability of being so vulnerable and slow-firing as to be virtually useless for anything except a first strike. Partly for this reason, the United States announced, in October, 1959, that it would not establish any more liquid-fuel missile bases in Europe. Instead, it looked forward to distributing in 1960 and 1961 mobile and solid-fuel Polaris missiles (and, in the case of

* In February, 1960, a number of newspaper and magazine articles disclosed that warheads were actually installed in the Thor missiles in England under a system that required one key, operated by Americans, to be turned in order to activate the warheads and another key, operated by the British, to be turned in order to launch the missile. See, for example, *U.S. News and World Report,* February 29, 1960, pp. 50–51; *Time,* August 8, 1960, p. 21.

Britain, also the air-borne Skybolt missile, which, however, was not expected to be ready until 1964 or 1965). It was later reported that about half of the approximately three hundred Polaris batteries would be based in France.[17]

Meanwhile, France declined to accept missiles or nuclear stockpiles on French soil unless she could control the warheads as well as the means of delivery. She continued to develop her independent nuclear weapons program. And she continued to hold out the possibility of a Continental nuclear consortium as a counterweight to the Anglo-American bloc.

In order to forestall Euratom from becoming the basis of a Continental nuclear weapons consortium, the United States hoped to keep it purely a regional effort to develop power reactors by offering it attractive subsidies and scientific and technical assistance, by promising to buy back plutonium by-products at preferential rates, and by receiving, in return, the right to inspect plants to prevent the diversion of plutonium to weapons manufacture.[18] To help forestall the development of a Franco-German-Italian nuclear axis, Britain took the initiative in establishing a West European Union arms pool for the research, development, and production of various types of arms, including missiles but excluding nuclear weapons.[19] However, the final terms of the American agreements with Euratom, signed in May and June, 1958, and approved by Congress in August, considerably reduced the scope of American assistance and left out the plutonium buy-back provision—both modifications being due to congressional opposition—while leaving all inspection and policing in the hands of Euratom itself, on the insistence of its members.[20] Moreover, neither the subsequent Euratom agreements nor the operations of the WEU arms pool deterred the French from proceeding with their independent nuclear program. General de Gaulle's investiture in June, 1958, guaranteed that.

Thus the other members of the alliance seemed to be faced, not only with nuclear dependence on the United States, but, even more disturbing, with nuclear dependence on Britain, France, and possibly even Germany, unless some means could be found to share the control of nuclear weapons among all the allies. With this in mind, the Dutch parliamentarian J. J. Fens, acting as rapporteur of the Western European Union's Committee on Defense Questions and Armaments in its annual report to the Assembly, called upon the United States and Britain to share the control of nuclear weapons before the diffusion of independent nuclear capabilities destroyed NATO's interdependence:

> As the employment of an A or H weapon by aircraft or missile against a Russian site today spells immediate counter-bombardment on targets in the entire free world, the monopoly of two countries to decide unilaterally on the destiny of themselves and others cannot any longer be maintained lest the alliance be weakened.

If the British argument for an independent nuclear capability were valid, Fens continued, "It is essential that both the technical knowledge required for the production of these weapons, together with the power of decision over their use in a strategic role, should be shared among all member countries." Otherwise, he warned, the trend toward the multiplication of independent nuclear powers would cause "the complete negation of interdependence" to the disadvantage of all.[21]

Faced with mounting pressures within the alliance for relief from the Anglo-American nuclear monopoly, the American government continued to press Congress to relax the restrictions of the Atomic Energy Act in order to satisfy allied demands for a larger share in the management of the tactical nuclear strategy to which they were committed, in the hope that this would stimulate their active collaboration under American leadership and deter them from moving toward either political or military independence. The government explained its reasoning more clearly than before in its appeals for the amendments to the Atomic Energy Act, which became law in July, 1958. Deputy Undersecretary Robert Murphy emphasized the political importance of giving the allies more information about the operation of nuclear weapons in order that they would "have confidence in their ability to meet aggression swiftly and effectively" and in order that there might be "less incentive for additional countries to enter the atomic weapons field."[22] Secretary of State Dulles elaborated the point.[23] The liberalization of American atomic secrecy laws was essential, he said, in order to facilitate allied collaboration in NATO's tactical nuclear strategy:

> Our NATO allies will not feel the strength and confidence needed to pursue vigorous anti-Communist policies if they feel that they are dominated by a Soviet nuclear weapons capability and that we will not share our nuclear capability with them, even to the modest extent required to enable them to share in the planning of a nuclear defense and make them capable of using nuclear weapons received from us if hostilities should occur.

If the United States did not grant her allies a larger share in the operation of her nuclear capability, he warned, they might "either intensively seek to develop nuclear weapons capacity for themselves, or move toward neutrality, or at least nonparticipation, in what should be a common military effort." The first course "would divert the efforts of our allies into a needless and costly duplication." The second would "place a far greater burden on the US and radically alter the power balance with serious damage to our vital security interests." Dulles put his finger on the nature, if not the primary source, of the threat to allied cohesion. But the trouble with his argument was, first, that it was directed only at giving the allies a greater share in the operation of tactical nuclear weapons, when the French and British, at least, were primarily concerned with gaining independent control of strategic nuclear weapons; and, second, that it was applied only to the sharing of operational information, whereas the crucial point of allied dissatisfaction was America's exclusive control of the employment of nuclear weapons, by virtue of her custody of the warheads.

The 1958 amendments to the Atomic Energy Act permitted the United States to give allies additional information on the external characteristics of nuclear weapons, special nuclear material, and certain non-nuclear weapons components and delivery systems. But they retained the requirement of American custody of nuclear warheads. And, so far as information of more direct assistance in the production of weapons was concerned, they merely permitted the United States to extend her discriminatory treatment in favor of Great Britain through a provision that technical information and materials for the manufacture of nuclear weapons should be given only to a nation that had made "substantial progress in the development of atomic weapons."[24]

If it had any effect on the French, this 1958 act must have confirmed their conviction that France could gain equal status with Britain only if she made "substantial progress" in the development of her own nuclear weapons. In July Dulles flew to Paris to confer with De Gaulle on major world problems, but, despite reports of a "large identity of views" on most problems, De Gaulle was said to have reaffirmed "bluntly and unequivocably" his determination to arm France with nuclear weapons, with or without American aid. The Secretary of State was reported to have told the General that, under the Atomic Energy Act, the American government did not have the authority to aid France directly in this objective, but that, instead, the United States might assist France in building a nuclear submarine engine.[25] However, when objections were raised in the Joint Committee on Atomic Energy, and after France decided to withdraw her ships from the NATO fleet and refused to stockpile atomic weapons on her soil, the State Department decided to offer France only enriched uranium fuel but not any data on propulsion reactors. The decision was probably made less for the security reasons that troubled Congress and the AEC than because the department had concluded that such information seemed likely only to help rather than deter an unco-operative France in becoming the fourth nuclear power.[26] (In May, 1960, the State Department, with the support of the Defense Department but the opposition of the Atomic Energy Commission and the Pentagon, revived the submarine plan; but the administration abandoned it after the Joint Committee on Atomic Energy objected.)[27] De Gaulle had made it clear that he intended to use France's nuclear program to support some outstanding national claims, such as equal partnership with the United States and Britain in tripartite consultations on global political problems and the use of atomic weapons anywhere in the world. The United States was not prepared to assist him in revising interallied politics under the threat of his nuclear program.

Even if the American government had been inclined to help France become the fourth nuclear power for the sake of allied cohesion and of mitigating a wasteful duplication of nuclear efforts, it would have been restrained from openly doing so by the growing popular sentiment throughout the world against nuclear testing. By 1958 the fears of nuclear testing, which originally had been directed against radioactive fallout, were focused upon preventing the emergence of the fourth or "*n*th" nuclear power; and the Russians had skilfully transferred the opprobrium of nuclear testing to underground as well as atmospheric tests—even to those undertaken by states who had already acquired nuclear weapons. On March 31, 1958, after a series of tests, the Soviet Union announced that she was unilaterally stopping all nuclear tests. This led to the protracted Geneva test-ban negotiations, beginning in October, and to America's voluntary cessation of all nuclear tests for fear of alienating world opinion or thwarting the chances of achieving an agreement that might prevent the proliferation of nuclear capabilities among states. These developments mobilized domestic and world-wide fears of thermonuclear war, not only against nuclear tests of all kinds, but also against any policy or action that appeared to promote the spread of nuclear capabilities to other states; so that any relaxation of American restrictions upon transmitting nuclear information and material to France would have to bear the onus of seeming to spread nuclear capabilities, unstabilize the military environment, and foster thermonuclear war, contrary to a tacit agreement with the Soviet Union to prevent these evils. President de Gaulle guaranteed this onus by repeatedly proclaiming that France was determined to join the nuclear ranks and would not be bound by a nuclear test ban, formal or informal, unless the cessation of testing were linked with the cessation of nuclear production.

Therefore, in pushing for a nuclear test ban and opposing the transfer of nuclear weapons and weapons production technology to the non-nuclear allies, the United States put herself in the unenviable situation of collaborating with the Russians in preventing her ally France from gaining nuclear equality with Britain, for the sake of the overriding objective of preventing the diffusion of nuclear production, an objective which France was determined to defy in any case. The special irony of this situation was that much of the same opprobrium that was attached to testing and nuclear production assistance was also attached to any plan to share the *control* of nuclear warheads, even though the chief appeal of such a plan in the American and other allied governments was that it might be the only means of discouraging the diffusion of nuclear *production.* Moscow carefully cultivated a suspicion, which was shared by some influential American congressmen and military and civilian leaders, that if the United States abandoned exclusive custody of her nuclear warheads, any scheme for the joint control of the decision to use them would merely be a subterfuge for spreading independent nuclear capabilities, which, in turn, would compel the Soviet Union to give China and her satellites nuclear weapons. Consequently, even if Congress, SAC, France, and the other allies could be satisfied with a system of joint control that technically left the warheads in the custody of Americans (perhaps under the command of an American NATO authority), this would be difficult to represent to the rest of the world as anything but a step toward the spread of independent nuclear capabilities.

To be sure, the French might not forego the production and the completely independent control of nuclear weapons on any condition, but, on the other hand, they surely would not join a nuclear test ban without at least receiving a larger share of the control of nuclear weapons in the alliance. And what good would a nuclear test ban be if France did not adhere to it? Therefore, as long as the United States kept exclusive custody of her nuclear warheads, she seemed bound to get the worst of both positions by simultaneously jeopardizing allied cohesion and promoting the diffusion of nuclear production.

Despite these difficulties of reconciling any plan to share the decision to use nuclear warheads with the objective of preventing or discouraging the diffusion of nuclear production, the United States was under mounting pressure in 1959 and 1960 to share her control of nuclear weapons under some arrangement that would provide a more effective alternative to independent nuclear production and ownership than the "two-key system." Part of this pressure came from NATO itself, in the person of Supreme Commander General Norstad. Thus in a speech in August, 1959, Norstad posed the questions: "How do we meet a growing but still somewhat confused and conflicting desire among our European allies for a broader sharing in the control of nuclear weapons? How can the alliance as a whole be assured that such weapons will be available to them in all reasonable circumstances for their defense, the defense of Europe?" Taking note of France's move toward an independent nuclear capability and the great concern of other allies at the prospect of other states following France's example, he urged, in a tentative manner befitting an exploratory proposition, that the alliance consider transferring the control of nuclear weapons to NATO itself, as the "fourth nuclear power." He warned that this scheme would not necessarily "influence the desire of some nations to pursue their own quest for an atomic weapons capability," but he thought that it "might very well remove a good part of the motivation of others to do so."[28]

In December, 1959, Frederick Mulley, Labor member of the House of Commons and rapporteur of the Western European Union Defense Committee, submitted to the WEU assembly a committee report that recommended meeting these same problems by making the Western European Union the fourth nuclear power, with joint power of decision on the use of strategic weapons. The assembly adopted the recommendation 42 to 9, with 16 abstentions,[29] but this was merely an expression of opinion, since the plan depended on the action of governments, not WEU delegates. In fact, Mulley's proposal that Britain assume the leadership of the plan by placing her nuclear warheads and V-bombers, or some of them, under the joint decision of the seven WEU countries failed to win the approval of either party in his own country.

In Britain, as in the United States, there was bound to be strong opposition to any plan for the joint control of nuclear weapons, if only because it would probably mean transferring custody of symbolically as well as physically potent weapons to other nations. Yet, amid reports that the administration was considering turning over nuclear weapons to certain allies, such as Britain, President Eisenhower, in a press conference on February 3, 1960, seemed to suggest that American laws should be changed so as not to deny America's allies the information and weapons the Russians had.[30] The enthusiastic foreign reaction to the President's statement anticipated a fundamental change in American policy. Western embassies in Paris interpreted it as an effort to persuade De Gaulle to accept the results of a test-ban agreement by assuring him that the United States would end its discrimination against France.[31] However, Senator Anderson and Representative Holifield of the Joint Committee on Atomic Energy warned that the President would not be allowed to violate the 1958 Atomic Energy Act, and soon the White House denied any intention of changing the act or basic American policy toward nuclear sharing.[32]

On February 13 the French exploded their first atomic device in the Sahara and set off a new wave of policy initiatives. As though to precipitate a change, Paul Reynaud, President of the National Assembly Finance Committee, declared, "The young French scientific elite now returns to the place which it held before World War II—in the vanguard of atomic investigation. Now the question is whether Americans will help us take the second step forward. Let them not wait until Mr. K. outdistances them."[33]

On March 2 General Norstad reiterated his suggestion of a NATO nuclear force in the specific form of a highly mobile multinational unit with conventional and nuclear weapons, composed initially of a brigade each from the United States,

Britain, and France, under a single commander, who he hoped would not be an American.[34] American officials in Washington supported the plan but emphasized that the United States would continue to control the nuclear warheads in the multinational units.[35] It was disclosed that State and Defense Department officials were holding exploratory talks with the Justice Department over the legal authority to make a limited transfer of nuclear weapons under existing law, but this transfer apparently applied only to a plan to make nuclear warheads available to Britain for air-to-air missiles under the inherent powers of the President as commander in chief.[36]

The French were cool to Norstad's plan. German Defense Minister Franz Josef Strauss ruled out West German participation in the proposed multinational units, partly, it appeared, because it would obscure French and British refusal to accept full integration of NATO forces.[37] Khrushchev added his dash of cold water on Norstad's plan when he warned President Eisenhower, in a letter on March 8, that it would heighten international tension before the summit meeting in May and compel the Soviet Union to consider giving her allies nuclear weapons.[38]

In any case, the Joint Committee on Atomic Energy was adamantly opposed to any plan that would transfer custody of nuclear weapons to an ally. Representative Holifield, referring specifically to the transfer of custody under the President's inherent constitutional power but bearing in mind Norstad's plan, declared that any such transfer would cause "the greatest debate of our generation. The impact and reverberations of such an act would be calamitous to our international relations." It would

> be used to sustain and prove the Communist charge of imperialistic warmongers. It would destroy our prestige as a proponent of peace and disarmament. It would make a complete farce of our long negotiations for the cessation of nuclear bomb tests at Geneva. It would cut the ground from under our negotiators in the approaching international conference on disarmament in March. It would give Khrushchev a propaganda platform of deadly effectiveness in the scheduled summit conference in April.[39]

The next day General Norstad assured the Joint Committee that there were no plans to turn over American nuclear warheads to the proposed mobile brigades.[40] And President Eisenhower soon assured Khrushchev that American laws prohibited sharing nuclear weapons with her allies and that the United States had no plans to the contrary.[41]

Still, the United States did not abandon her plans to disperse missiles on European—and especially French—soil; and this meant that she could not abandon the effort to find some formula for nuclear sharing that would be equally acceptable to her allies, to Congress and SAC, and to all those who were primarily worried about multiplying the number of nuclear powers in the world. The approaching operational stage of the Polaris missile reactivated the 1957 plan for dispersing IRBM's in Europe, which had been suspended pending the availability of mobile, solid-fuel missiles. At the NATO defense ministers meeting in Paris in April, 1960, Secretary of Defense Thomas S. Gates, Jr., proposed the deployment of hundreds of Polaris missiles on barges and flatcars, when they were expected to become available in a year or two. At the same time, he suggested a modification of the system of dual control which would give NATO's supreme commander the decision to join the missile and activated warhead and send them off.[42]

The British, who were to launch their first nuclear submarine in October, welcomed the forthcoming availability of Polaris, which they looked forward to receiving on a special bilateral basis; and they seized upon this prospect as the occasion to abandon their own program to build the vulnerable and outmoded liquid-fuel Blue Streak.[43] However, De Gaulle would have none of the new version of the 1957 plan. Instead, he was reported to have advised Norstad that he would be prepared to accept Polaris installations in France if one-third of them (about fifty) were given to France for her own use with her own nuclear warheads.[44] In July NATO Secretary-General Paul-Henri Spaak explored the possibilities of such a deal with De Gaulle,[45] but this did not produce an agreement—whether because of French or American opposition, or both, the published information does not reveal.

In September Spaak and General Norstad combined with Chancellor Adenauer to promote the plan of making NATO the fourth nuclear power, which they hoped the United States would indorse at the December meeting of the North Atlantic Council.[46] In October the West German government, consistent with its interest in promoting a tightly integrated alliance and in diverting the pressures leading to independent nuclear programs within the alliance, publicly backed Norstad's plan.[47] By this time Secretary of State Herter was also understood to favor such a plan, against considerable opposition in the Pentagon. But the plan that he was considering proposing to the December Council meeting, now revised by Norstad and supported by a private study for the State Department,[48] depended on American-operated Polaris submarines under NATO command instead of on land- and river-based Polarises or multinational "fire brigades." In November General Norstad, speaking before the annual conference of NATO parliamentarians, publicly urged the alliance to take "a great and dramatic new step" by agreeing upon a NATO-controlled nuclear force.[49] The conference adopted a resolution, interpreted as tacit approval of Norstad's plan, saying that it was "urgent and essential" that the council study the whole question of the "integrated" use and control of nuclear weapons.[50] However, the resolution to study this question reflected considerable uncertainty, already voiced officially in Britain, about the feasibility of sharing the decision to use nuclear weapons among fifteen states—the problem of "fifteen fingers on the trigger," as it was now called.

Finally, on December 16, Secretary of State Herter announced America's indorsement of the "concept" of a NATO-controlled medium-range ballistic missile force to the ministerial council, meeting in Paris.[51] The concept included, first, an offer of five ballistic missile submarines armed with eighty Polaris missiles, to be assigned to NATO before 1963, if the allies would agree on a "multilateral system" of political control; and, second, allied purchase from the United States of 100 more medium-range missiles, to be placed on other kinds of ships, under NATO control.

Some of the members of NATO expressed great interest in

this concept, but their enthusiasm was dampened by its conditional nature. In the first place, agreement upon a multilateral system of political control would be a long and tedious process. In the second place, the whole plan would depend upon congressional approval, which would probably require, as a minimum condition, that nuclear warheads remain in the custody of Americans. And, in the third place, the outgoing Eisenhower administration could not commit the incoming Kennedy administration to any plan; and the incoming administration declined to take a position on this plan in advance. Furthermore, the allies were not eager to buy 100 missiles, and it was not clear whether this was a condition of receiving the five submarines. Nor was it clear who would provide and pay for the special ships to hold these additional missiles. In any case, allied approval of this tentative American plan was not fostered by Herter's concurrent suggestion that the United States might have to "redeploy" some of its Continental troops unless the allies shouldered a greater share of NATO's financial burdens in order to relieve America's balance-of-payments problems.

The final communiqué of the ministerial session noted, simply, that "the United States government suggested the concept of an MRBM [Mid-Range Ballistic Missile] multilateral force for consideration by the alliance. The Council took note of the United States suggestion with great interest and instructed the permanent representatives to study the suggestion and related matters in detail." However, the Council "welcomed the assurance of the United States to maintain in the NATO area United States nuclear weapons made available to NATO."[52] In short, the allies explicitly recognized the problem of the multilateral control of nuclear weapons but suspended a concerted attempt to resolve it until new and firmer initiatives should come from a new American administration.

3. SOURCES OF THE PROBLEM OF NUCLEAR CONTROL

Fundamentally, the problem of the multilateral control of nuclear weapons in NATO arose from the Soviet achievement of a capacity to inflict immense damage upon the United States if the United States were to strike at the Soviet Union in response to an attack upon America's allies. For this undermined allied willingness to remain entirely dependent upon America's decision whether or not to use nuclear weapons, both because of the fear that the United States might *not* use them (and also that the Soviet Union might not believe that she would use them) and because of the fear that the United States *might* use them (and also that the Soviet Union, believing that the United States would use them, might use them first). However, allied dissatisfaction with the American control of nuclear weapons would not have been so marked if the alliance had not been so dependent on a strategy of *initiating* the use of both tactical and strategic nuclear weapons; for it was the threat to initiate the use of nuclear weapons against a Soviet conventional aggression that constituted the least credible, most provocative, and potentially most fateful aspect of NATO's nuclear strategy.

Nevertheless, even if the Soviet capacity to devastate the United States and her allies with nuclear weapons had not become so substantial and the allies had not been so dependent upon a strategy of initiating the use of nuclear weapons, the problem of sharing or not sharing the control of nuclear weapons would have arisen to challenge the cohesion and security of the alliance. It would have arisen because of the growing ability and the actual or potential determination of several allies to produce their own nuclear weapons. For the spread of nuclear weapons technology offered some allies the opportunity to enhance their prestige and reduce their dependence on American control of nuclear weapons by acquiring, at the expense of their contribution to NATO's shield, an independent nuclear capability. And it confronted all the allies with the disturbing political as well as military consequences of nuclear diffusion, including the possible encouragement of nuclear diffusion outside the alliance. Therefore, the technical possibility of independent nuclear efforts added a new incentive for sharing the control of nuclear weapons: to provide an alternative to the contagious multiplication of independent nuclear programs within the alliance.

We have seen how the American government tried to facilitate allied political cohesion and strategic collaboration by measures of nuclear sharing, while simultaneously trying to avoid the disruptive military and political effects of independent nuclear efforts and the diffusion of nuclear control. And we have seen how the creation of a NATO nuclear force emerged as a means of reconciling these two objectives. Yet the tentative plan to make NATO a nuclear power raised almost as many political and military problems as it was intended to solve: for example, the problem of sharing the decision to use nuclear weapons without undermining the military or psychological effectiveness of the deterrent and without encouraging or appearing to encourage the diffusion of nuclear capabilities outside the alliance. Furthermore, there was no guaranty that the creation of a NATO nuclear force would dissuade France or any other ally from developing an independent nuclear force. Consequently, whether or not the allies created or tried to create a NATO nuclear force, the problem of sharing the control of nuclear weapons in such a way as to enhance deterrence and cohesion without fragmenting nuclear control and multiplying nuclear capabilities would remain.

In grappling with this problem the United States, at the beginning of the 1960's, still retained the decisive initiative, if only by virtue of her vastly superior nuclear arsenal and technology compared to her allies. Yet she had only limited control over the basic elements of the problem. The United States could not restore her nuclear monopoly or reverse the Soviet achievement of a devastating second-strike capability. She might diminish or delay the capacity of her allies to build their own nuclear capabilities, but she could not prevent it. The basic elements of the problem, however, were not just the material facts and possibilities but, more important, their impact upon the political interests and attitudes of nations. Consequently, the existence of great Soviet nuclear striking power and the growing capacity of allies to build their own nuclear striking power did not, by themselves, lead inexorably to the diffusion of independent nuclear capabilities or to any other particular disposition of the control of nuclear weapons. That disposition would depend on how the desires, the fears, and the will of allied governments would respond to a variety of possible military strategies and terms of collaboration, which were subject to deliberate control.

To be sure, the United States had only a limited capacity to affect the political interests and attitudes of her allies with respect to the control of nuclear weapons, but this capacity might nevertheless be decisive in determining the future of the alliance. In particular, America's preponderant role in shaping the strategy of NATO and the terms of allied collaboration could determine whether the system of the command and control of nuclear weapons would enhance or undermine the security and the cohesion of the alliance.

However, to exercise this decisive influence wisely the United States would have to appraise correctly the basic interests and attitudes that motivated the policies of her allies toward nuclear control under the existing technological, political, and strategic circumstances. The diversity of allied policies toward the control of nuclear weapons in 1960 indicated that different allies would approach the prospect of nuclear diffusion in different ways, depending on their technological and economic resources, their political status in the alliance, and a number of other considerations; but the British and French experiences suggested that any ally who possessed the necessary resources would have strong incentives to build an independent nuclear capability under existing circumstances. Yet it was necessary to understand the precise relationship between these particular circumstances and allied nuclear policies before one could surmise how a different set of circumstances might alter allied interests and attitudes toward the control of nuclear weapons.

Of course, in the final analysis, the United States would have to determine her policy toward the control of nuclear weapons on the basis of her independent analysis of the merits of the issue; but the merits of the issue could not be divorced from the interests and attitudes of her partners in this entangling alliance.

4. THE BRITISH EXAMPLE

Among America's allies, the British had the most extensive experience with an independent nuclear capability. The British attitude did not necessarily set the pattern for other allies—though it strongly affected French nuclear policy—but it constituted the most complete case study of a major ally's response to the prospect of nuclear diffusion.

From the outset, when the Labor government decided to build a British A-bomb after World War II, national pride was a powerful motive in Britain for developing an independent nuclear capability.[53] Although British scientists had made an important contribution to the Manhattan project during the war, the United States virtually cut off all exchange of information on nuclear weapons with the British after the war. This helped convince politicians and civil servants that Britain could remain a great power and retain a favored position with the United States as a partner in diplomatic and military affairs only by becoming an independent nuclear power. The British correctly calculated that they would secure America's scientific and material assistance in becoming a nuclear power to the extent that their scientists and technicians demonstrated an ability to develop nuclear weapons independently.

This policy met with negligible opposition and was reinforced after the outbreak of the Korean War, when the strains of rearmament gave the Conservative government an additional argument for developing a British nuclear striking force built around the A-bomb (which Britain exploded in 1952) and the V-bombers. This was the argument that nuclear deterrence could provide Britain with greater security without the burdensome costs of maintaining a large ground force on the Continent.[54] Considerations of national prestige and Britain's influence with the United States militated against relying more heavily upon American nuclear striking power. Also, this would have deprived the government of an excuse for not meeting ground force goals. It was also argued that Britain needed her own nuclear striking force in order to be sure of knocking out

Russian bases which would be a threat to Britain but which the Americans might assign a lower priority. This argument, based on a counterforce strategy, became obsolete with the development of H-bombs and the growth of Soviet strategic air power, but it was not abandoned until Russia had begun building long-range missiles.

The 1955 white paper on defense policies dealt largely with the implications of thermonuclear bombs, stating and defending the government's decision to build a British H-bomb. In defending this decision before the House, Prime Minister Churchill argued that an independent air-nuclear deterrent would increase Britain's influence over American policy and actions and would enable Britain to give the proper attention to targets—he mentioned airfields, administrative and industrial centers, submarine bases, and other naval targets—that might be a matter of life and death.[55]

In defending the political grounds for the H-bomb decision, Churchill said, "Personally, I cannot feel that we should have much influence over their [i.e., American] policy or actions, wise or unwise, while we are largely dependent, as we are today, upon their protection. We, too, must possess substantial deterrent power of our own." Although he refrained from elucidating this point in public, the implication was that Britain could not bargain with the United States so effectively unless she could bargain with the Soviet Union effectively by being able to support her policies, when they diverged from American policies, with an independent nuclear striking force.

However, the government did not yet argue for an independent deterrent as a substitute for America's nuclear striking power or as a means of compensating for the declining credibility of America's deterrent. For, although Churchill anticipated that Russia might achieve an H-bomb in two to four years, he did not acknowledge that the Soviet capacity to deliver a thermonuclear attack would unstabilize the existing deterrent balance in any way. Rather, he contended that Britain's nuclear striking power would help deter a Soviet surprise attack during the next three or four years, in which the West would retain an overwhelming superiority in hydrogen weapons, and that after that the nuclear nations would enter a state of "saturation" or nuclear sufficiency, in which surprise attack would be deterred by the certainty that both sides would inflict crippling retaliatory damage upon each other.

The relevance of this argument was, logically, confined to passive deterrence, but at this time the effectiveness of passive nuclear deterrence was not clearly distinguished from the credibility of active nuclear deterrence, upon which the strategy of massive retaliation depended. Consequently, the radical effect of a Soviet thermonuclear capability upon the strategy of initiating the use of nuclear weapons against a Soviet conventional aggression was generally ignored. The distinction between the requirements of active and passive deterrence emerged only with the general recognition that the British Isles could be obliterated by ten to fifteen thermonuclear explosions. But in 1955 the government still maintained that civil defense measures could substantially mitigate the destruction of a thermonuclear attack and argued that the assumption that there was no defense against a thermonuclear attack was merely defeatist.[56]

Some members of the opposition challenged the government's assumption that the credibility of the West's nuclear striking power would remain undiminished in the face of Russia's thermonuclear capacity and charged that, at least in the event of a non-nuclear attack on allied powers, the government would choose appeasement rather than self-destruction, if its only means of countering aggression were to initiate a thermonuclear war.[57] But the 1956 white paper on defense stoutly maintained that "the increased power of the deterrent, that is, the nuclear weapon and the means of delivering it, has made global war more frightening and less likely," and, answering opposition criticism, flatly asserted, "It is sometimes argued that, with the buildup of a stock of thermonuclear bombs by the Russians, the deterrent value to the Western powers of building up a stock of bombs and the means of delivery will diminish. This is not so."[58]

The 1957 white paper, largely the work of Minister of Defense Duncan Sandys, was the logical culmination of the policy of substituting nuclear deterrence for mobilized ground forces, which Prime Minister Churchill had inaugurated in 1953. The policy of concentrating on the construction of a British strategic nuclear force was presented as a necessary corollary to reducing the British forces on the Continent and ending the compulsory conscription of manpower in 1960. In defending this policy, the government strongly emphasized the economic necessity of concentrating resources on building up the nuclear deterrent instead of on maintaining the forces to wage local or general war if the deterrent should fail. It now explicitly recognized that there was no way to protect the country against the consequences of an H-bomb attack, but from this fact it drew the conclusion, not that active nuclear deterrence ceased to be a credible policy for a defenseless island, but rather that "the available resources of the nation should be concentrated not upon preparations to wage war so much as upon trying to prevent that catastrophe from ever happening."[59]

In arguing specifically for an independent nuclear capability, the government no longer contended that it would enable Britain to strike vital targets that SAC might overlook. Instead, it explicitly used a new argument that had arisen in response to the growth of Soviet nuclear striking power, the argument that British striking power was necessary to reinforce the nuclear deterrent as the United States became more vulnerable to direct Soviet attack and less dependent on European bases. Referring obliquely to this argument, Sandys told the House:

> So long as large American forces remain in Europe and American bombers are based in Britain, it might conceivably be thought safe . . . to leave to the United States the sole responsibility for providing the nuclear deterrent. But, when they have developed the 5000-mile intercontinental ballistic rocket, can we really be sure that every American Administration will go on looking at things in quite the same way?[60]

Labor party spokesmen criticized the government's 1957 white paper on the grounds that it would make Britain too dependent on a nuclear response to conventional aggression, and they openly expressed doubts that Britain would use thermonuclear weapons except in response to a direct attack on the British Isles. But they were not in a strong position to challenge the basic policy of substituting nuclear firepower for manpower, since the party had already criticized the 1956 white paper for making "no provision for an immediate cut in the period of National Service nor for any specific plan for its eventual abolition,"[61] and since it had not recommended substituting larger conventional forces for nuclear expenditures. Moreover, the 1957 Labor conference indorsed the decision to build an H-bomb, as the dominant faction argued on political grounds against leftist opponents of a British thermonuclear capability. John Strachey, a former Labor war minister, warned that Britain's abandonment of the H-bomb would make the nation "the wholly dependent satellite of the United States" and render a future Labor foreign secretary "unable even to consider policies which were not approved by the State Department in Washington." And Labor's prospective foreign secretary, Aneurin Bevan, the old left-wing critic of American policy, declared that renunciation of the H-bomb would send a British negotiator "naked into the conference chamber."[62]

This left the opposition approving Britain's program to build an independent nuclear capability but rejecting the government's primary strategic argument for doing so: to provide a more reliable substitute for America's active nuclear deterrent. Needled but undaunted by this criticism, the government reaffirmed the value of Britain's strategic nuclear force for active deterrence but dropped the claim that Britain's force would be more credible than America's. Thus the 1958 white paper stated:

> The democratic Western nations will never start a war against Russia. But it must be well understood that, if Russia were to launch a major attack on them, even with conventional forces only, they would have to hit back with strategic nuclear weapons. In fact, the strategy of NATO is based on the frank recognition that a full-scale Soviet attack could not be repelled without resort to a massive nuclear bombardment of the sources of power in Russia.[63]

At the same time, the government continued to develop a British liquid-fuel IRBM, the Blue Streak, which would be so vulnerable as to be useful only for a first strike.

Having retreated from its military-strategic argument for building a British nuclear striking force instead of relying upon America's, the government came to justify its nuclear program almost entirely on political grounds. Thus, in a television interview in February, 1958, Prime Minister Macmillan explained the need for a British H-bomb entirely in terms of national prestige and influence. "The independent contribution," he said, "gives us a better position in the world, it gives us a better position with respect to the United States. It puts us where we ought to be, in the position of a great power. The fact that we have it makes the United States pay a greater regard to our point of view, and that is of great importance."[64]

As a symbol of national greatness and a psychological reinforcement against Soviet nuclear blackmail, a British nuclear capability needed no military justification. In this respect the memory of the traumatic experience of being "deserted" by the United States in the face of Soviet rocket threats during the Suez War in 1956 was still a powerful argument for an independent nuclear force in 1958. As Randolph Churchill stated before the American Chamber of Commerce in London, in November, 1958, "We are in a very fortunate period when America has absolute air supremacy over the Russians," but even Britain, he declared, could knock out twelve cities in the region of Stalingrad and Moscow from bases in Britain and another dozen in the Crimea from bases in Cyprus. "We did not have that power at the time of Suez," he added. "We are a major power again."[65]

Some members of the opposition drew a different lesson from the Suez incident—that, regardless of an independent nuclear capability, the United Kingdom could not successfully pursue a strong policy even outside the NATO area, at the risk of nuclear war, without American support. But the basic sentiment that an independent nuclear capability was an essential attribute of an independent foreign policy was as strongly indorsed by the

Labor as by the Conservative leadership. Nevertheless, after 1957 affirmations of this basic sentiment had a more shrill and apologetic quality in the face of mounting strategic, economic, political, moral, and emotional counter-arguments.

In the fall of 1958 the *Times* joined opposition critics in charging that Britain's nuclear power contributed nothing to active deterrence, since it was inconceivable that Britain would use it except in response to a direct attack.[66] It continued to maintain that an independent nuclear capability was necessary for passive deterrence, but the opposition began to question whether the second-class striking force that Britain could build was worth the very sizable expenditures it demanded. As R. H. S. Crossman put it, "The trouble about the nuclear deterrent is that if we have one big enough to be militarily significant, we ruin the country, and if we have one within the economic resources of the country, then it is so trivial that it impresses no great power." Therefore, it seemed to him that the British were paying 300 million pounds a year to be a member of a nuclear club they could not afford.[67]

These strategic and economic counter-arguments were buttressed by a more profound, if less coherent, protest against an independent British nuclear force on political and emotional grounds. The 1958 white paper, coming after the announcement in the spring of 1957 of the Anglo-American agreement to base American missiles in England under joint control, raised a protest against Britain's whole nuclear effort on the grounds that it would involve Great Britain in a suicidal thermonuclear war and encourage a disastrous diffusion of nuclear capabilities throughout the world.

The plans for establishing four Thor missile bases in eastern England provoked fears of attracting Soviet H-bombs that far surpassed the fears occasioned by the presence of American bomber bases. Although the bombers made England just as much a target and were under less effective British control (since the United States could operate both the nuclear warheads and the means of delivery out of British bases), the prospect of England suddenly becoming a missile base dramatized the risks of contributing to the nuclear deterrent in a way that the bomber bases, to which the British had become accustomed, had failed to do. Moreover, considering the vulnerability of the liquid-fuel, above-ground Thor missiles to a first strike, they might constitute a greater temptation or provocation for a Soviet attack.

Coupled with the government's announced strategy "based on the frank recognition that a full-scale Soviet attack could not be repelled without resort to a massive nuclear bombardment of the sources of power in Russia," the establishment of missile bases encountered widespread opposition among British of all political complexions.[68] However, the protest against missile bases did not depend on any particular strategic reasoning. For the majority it was not so much a protest against bases as such as against America's share in the control of the missiles. For a vociferous minority it was not only a protest against Britain's dependence on American-controlled missiles but against her dependence on any nuclear weapons. Thus in 1960 the protest against Thor missiles was transferred to the Holy Loch in Scotland, where Britain had granted the United States a base for Polaris submarines—an "invulnerable" sea-borne second-strike weapon, which, nevertheless, in the popular protest it aroused, bore all the psychological liabilities of a vulnerable first-strike weapon.

The Holy Loch sentiment was part of a general moral, political, and emotional protest movement against nuclear deterrence which emerged in late 1957 and 1958 and which became the focus for leftist, pacifist, and neutralist sentiment, opposing not only British production but also British possession and use of nuclear weapons and, soon, Britain's whole involvement in NATO. This was the movement for British unilateral nuclear disarmament. In February, 1958, this movement was organized in the Campaign for Nuclear Disarmament, led by Bertrand Russell and joined by an impressive list of clerics, journalists, literary men, and professional people. The Campaign opposed British ownership and production of nuclear weapons and the establishment of strategic bases on British soil. Most of its proponents also, implicitly or explicitly, opposed Britain's *use* of nuclear weapons. A strenuous expression of these antinuclear sentiments was launched with the first of the annual Easter week-end protest marches from London to Aldermaston, the site of an atomic weapons research laboratory, fifty-four miles away.

This march was probably a more representative expression of the general reformist zeal and fear of nuclear war that motivated the unilateralists than any specific policies or reasoned analysis presented by the Campaign's leadership.[69] But insofar as the movement had an intellectual content, Bertrand Russell set the tone by repeatedly maintaining that disarmament was the only alternative to an otherwise inevitable thermonuclear castastrophe and that, if it came to a choice between disarmament and Communist conquest, he would prefer the latter, since Communist domination would be less of a disaster than the irrevocable extinction of civilization. As immediate measures, however, he put his faith in East-West political and disarmament agreements; and he was content to urge only *British* renunciation of the H-bomb, in the belief that, whereas this would have no measurable effect upon the East-West balance of power, it would exert great moral pressure against the diffusion of nuclear weapons to other powers.[70] Labor party opponents of Russell's position asserted, among other things, that Britain's renunciation of the *use* of nuclear weapons would end her collaboration with NATO and encourage the collapse of the alliance, upon which British security depended. But Lord Russell maintained that a neutral Britain would not only spare the British from nuclear extinction but would also serve the interests of friendly nations and of civilization itself by putting Britain in the vanguard of the uncommitted nations in mitigating the hostility between the Soviet Union and the United States.[71]

The respected military analyst Commander Sir Stephen King-Hall reached similar conclusions on the basis of military-strategic reasoning in his well-publicized book *Defense in the Nuclear Age.* His advocacy of unilateral nuclear disarmament and a strategy of non-violent resistance emerged from an analysis of the futility of NATO's nuclear strategy. Like Lord Russell, he preferred non-violent resistance to nuclear retaliation, not on the traditional pacifist grounds, but "because I am convinced that as between Britain occupied by the Russian army and Britain a smoking radioactive charnel-house the former is the lesser of two great evils."[72]

Although the Campaign for Nuclear Disarmament failed to receive outright Party indorsement, it was strongly supported by the left wing of the Labor party; and the party leadership came under increasing pressure to make concessions to the sentiment for renouncing at least production, if not ownership and control, of nuclear weapons. Nevertheless, in 1958 the party congress, under Mr. Gaitskell's leadership and supported by Aneurin Bevan, voted down resolutions sponsored by pacifist and leftist elements for unilateral renunciation of nuclear weapons and missile bases and accepted the proposition that a future Labor government should be free to continue to manufacture nuclear weapons unless they were banned by international agreement. Gaitskell maintained that unilateral nuclear disarmament would be ineffective as a step toward disarmament and would leave Britain in the cowardly position of sheltering behind American bombs or ceasing to collaborate with NATO altogether. To the view that Britain ought to get out of NATO, he replied that this would cause America to go isolationist, leave Britain defenseless against Soviet pressure and aggression, and deprive her of any influence over American policy.[73]

Instead of advocating unilateral nuclear disarmament, Labor party spokesmen in the House, led by Hugh Gaitskell, George Brown, and Denis Healey, urged reducing the West's reliance upon the employment of strategic nuclear weapons for active deterrence, increasing Britain's and NATO's capacity for conventional resistance, and concentrating upon the achievement of international agreements on disarmament and disengagement.

Nevertheless, in the spring of 1959 the party adopted a proposal that Great Britain should become the charter member of a "non-nuclear club" if she could secure agreements, preferably under U.N. auspices, with other potential nuclear nations to leave the production, testing, and ownership (though not the control and use) of nuclear weapons solely in the hands of Russia and America.[74] This position was not only an intraparty concession; it reflected the party leadership's reasoned resignation to sheltering behind America's nuclear power on the grounds that the political and deterrent value of an independent nuclear capability was not worth the cost, whereas the renunciation of production was a prerequisite to preventing the diffusion of nuclear capabilities. At the same time, the proposal reaffirmed the absolute necessity of collaborating with NATO's strategy, including the acceptance of American missile bases in England, lest America be driven to isolation, the alliance destroyed, and Western Europe left wide open to Soviet pressure. "At best," it claimed, "European independence would be precariously maintained under German leadership and by reliance on an American threat of 'massive retaliation.' At worst the Western community which we have helped to build since 1945 would collapse."

The plan for a non-nuclear club, however, failed to excite interest outside the party or to appease the "unilateralists" inside, and after France succeeded in exploding her first atomic device there was even less reason to think that she might join any such club. Indeed, Labor leaders did not have much enthusiasm for the scheme either. Thus, in the defense debates of March, 1960, Mr. Gaitskell weighed the advantages and the disadvantages of an independent nuclear capability about equally.

On the one hand, he argued that an independent second-strike capability would relieve Britain of excessive military and political dependence on the United States and give her more freedom in standing up to the Russians on matters about which the Americans might not feel so strongly. But, on the other hand, he agreed that there was a case against an independent nuclear capability on the grounds of cost, taking money away from conventional weapons, and encouraging the spread of nuclear weapons. As for the choice between these two positions, he said, "These are matters of balance on which, frankly, I find it impossible to say that it is absolutely clear one way or the other. We have to weigh them." He concluded, "What we have said in our proposals for the so-called non-nuclear club is that we ought to be prepared to give up our own independent nuclear weapon if thereby we can stop the spread."[75]

Yet, despite this luke-warm conditional pledge of nuclear abstinence, when the party conference convened later that spring, Gaitskell led the executive committee to recommend, in effect, that Britain cease the manufacture or ownership of nuclear weapons even if she had to do so unilaterally. "We believe," the committee stated, "that in the future our British contribution to the Western armory will be in conventional terms, leaving to the Americans the provision of the Western strategic deterrent." Although Gaitskell made it clear that Britain would retain a V-bomber force and nuclear bombs as long as they were serviceable and would go on providing American bomber bases as long as they were required, the party's official statement rather ambiguously "opposed" the establishment of Thor missile bases in England but said nothing about the Thors already in place. Although the committee's statement stopped short of renouncing the use of strategic or tactical nuclear weapons and said that Britain should remain a loyal supporter of NATO, it recommended that there be "strict NATO control," that Germany should not manufacture or be armed with nuclear weapons, and that Britain should seek an agreement with the United States that strategic nuclear weapons would not be used without the agreement of NATO. In the most explicit renunciation of active nuclear deterrence by any Western political party, the executive committee rejected the thesis that the West could be defended by threatening to initiate the use of the H-bomb, although it refrained from renouncing the initial use of tactical nuclear weapons. It recommended, instead, that NATO forces should be "armed and trained to defend Western Europe without immediate reliance on nuclear weapons," for which purpose it recommended that Britain return the 22,000 men withdrawn from the British Army of the Rhine.[76]

However, these concessions to antinuclear sentiment did not appease the left-wing unions, who, in October, 1960, succeeded in gaining the annual Labor conference's approval, against Gaitskell's impassioned opposition, of two resolutions demanding the "unilateral renunciation of the testing, manufacture, stockpiling, and basing of all nuclear weapons in Great Britain" and calling for the party's commitment to "a complete rejection of any defense policy based on the threat of the use of strategic or tactical nuclear weapons."[77]

In 1960 there was little evidence that the Labor party's steady disaffection with an independent British nuclear capability forecast a radical change in the attitude of the nation as a whole. The polls indicated that, although a majority opposed the placement of American missiles on English soil, a larger majority continued to favor a British nuclear capability;[78] and, of the minority that wanted Britain to give up her H-bomb unilaterally, almost one-fifth opposed this if it meant going against the wishes of the United States and other NATO countries.[79] An overwhelming majority preferred to rely on nuclear weapons rather than increase conventional forces, but a clear majority also opposed Britain's using the H-bomb against a Russian conventional attack upon the West.[80] These polls and other indications suggest that the British public's chief concern with nuclear striking power was to avoid being too dependent on the United States, on the one hand by building a British strategic force and on the other hand by limiting American control of British-based missiles and missile-submarines. Qualifying this strong sentiment of national pride and independence was a consciousness that Britain could not save herself from annihilation by using her nuclear deterrent and an unwillingness to incur annihilation by using it against a conventional attack on her allies. However, there was no significant public sentiment for trying to escape the risks of annihilation by making Britain neutral. And there was great reluctance to reduce Britain's dependence on nuclear weapons at the cost of increasing conventional forces.

Consequently, the government was under no compelling popular pressure to abandon an independent nuclear effort.

Rather, it was under pressure to maintain that effort but to keep the cost down and to assure the public of British independence of American military and political decisions, on the one hand, and of the compatibility of an independent nuclear effort with the cohesion of NATO and her special relationship with the United States, on the other, while playing down the strategy of initiating tactical nuclear weapons and abandoning the threat of using the H-bomb first. This was, in fact, the course that the popular Macmillan government pursued.

The government stopped justifying a nuclear capability in terms of a first-strike strategy for active deterrence and professed to be completely reassured about America's determination to honor her obligations to defend her European allies. But it continued to regard a British nuclear force as a "contribution" to the general deterrent posture of the West, although the success of the American Polaris submarine program made this argument obsolete; as a necessary instrument of passive deterrence and of protection against Soviet blackmail; and as an essential means of preserving British political influence, especially in the diplomacy revolving around disarmament and political accommodations with the Soviet Union.

In April, 1960, the government announced the abandonment of work on the liquid-fuel missile Blue Streak, which promised to be not only very costly but also too vulnerable and slow-firing to be useful for passive defense by the time it would become operational, in the latter part of 1960. However, it entered into negotiations with the United States for the solid-fuel Polaris, under the same arrangement of joint control that applied to the Thor missiles, and for the air-launched Skybolt, which, when ready (in 1964 or 1965), was expected to give new utility to the independent nuclear deterrent employing Britain's V-bombers, which were to be dispersed among bases overseas. As a further indication of her determination to acquire an independent invulnerable second-strike force, in October, 1960, Britain launched the first of her nuclear submarines, constructed with American co-operation as part of a program expected to lead to British missile-firing submarines.

Nevertheless, the government could not ignore some of the

adverse consequences of persisting in an independent nuclear effort. In particular, it showed increasing apprehension about the eventual diffusion of nuclear capabilities to other nations and the more immediate prospect of West Germany acquiring control of nuclear weapons. This apprehension suggested that the government, like the opposition, *might* be willing to trade the pursuit of an independent nuclear capability for some scheme that promised to halt the trend toward the proliferation of independent capabilities, for which its own policies served as a powerful precedent and stimulant, providing that Britain would not be left entirely dependent upon American control of the nuclear deterrent. And Britain's dependence upon American assistance suggested that the United States *might* still exert considerable leverage in bringing about such a scheme. One result of these two possibilities was that the British government might be persuaded to subordinate its independent nuclear capability to an allied nuclear authority, depending upon the conditions of political control. But, so long as British leaders looked upon their independent "contribution" to the Western deterrent as an essential instrument of both political independence and a privileged interdependence with the United States, they had little incentive to exchange either their "two-key system" or their "one-key system" for a dubious multi-key system.

5. THE GERMAN AND FRENCH ATTITUDES TOWARD NUCLEAR DIFFUSION

Strategically, West Germany and France had better reason than Britain to seek independent nuclear capabilities, since they were more likely to incur direct conventional aggressions in which their threat to initiate the use of nuclear weapons—perhaps in desperation or unreasoning anger—might be more credible to the Kremlin than America's threat. And they were at least as much in need of an independent deterrent to discourage Soviet nuclear attacks or nuclear blackmail. Furthermore, there was no reason that Britain's non-strategic arguments for being a nuclear power—especially, those appealing to national prestige and independent political influence—should not be just as persuasive for Germany and France. Yet, for special political reasons, France was the most outspoken advocate of an independent nuclear force, while Germany became the most outspoken advocate of a joint NATO nuclear force.

After her decision in 1957 to reduce the period of conscription to twelve months and to slow down the pace and scope of rearmament, the Federal Republic, like her senior allies, tailored her military policies to the thesis that nuclear firepower would substitute for conventionally-armed manpower. Therefore, like her other non-nuclear allies, she became progressively more dependent on nuclear warheads and weapons, which she could neither build nor control. However, West Germany was under legal and political constraints against seeking an independent nuclear force that did not apply to Britain or France. Therefore, she staked the enhancement of her military and political influence not on a privileged bilateral partnership with the United States or on an independent nuclear program but on the tight military and political integration of the alliance, within which she pressed for a larger role commensurate with her great power and pivotal position, including a larger share of the control of nuclear weapons.

The Bonn government, conscious of West Germany's proximity and vulnerability to Soviet forces and sensitive to her allies' fears of Germany becoming a major military power again, disclaimed any interest in receiving American IRBM's—at least, until mobile solid-fuel missiles would become available—although it signed the NATO agreement of 1957 that would permit her to receive them and in June, 1959, indicated that it looked forward to the joint production with her allies of IRBM's to replace fighter-bombers.[81] However, the government persistently expressed its strong interest in becoming a full participant in NATO's *tactical* nuclear strategy. Understandably, in the light of NATO's dependence on a tactical nuclear response and the reorganization of the German army to fight a tactical nuclear war, West German leaders after 1957 repeatedly urged the United States to speed the process of arming Germany with nuclear weapons. Under the NATO agreement of 1957 Germany did receive a variety of tactical surface-to-surface and antiaircraft missiles, in addition to the atomic artillery and nuclear-bearing fighter-bombers received and contracted for under regular bilateral agreements. And some of these weapons—particularly, the 600-mile Mace—could be considered strategic as well as tactical.

West German leaders refrained from publicly stating the misgivings about the credibility and reliability of America's control of nuclear warheads that British and French leaders freely voiced. However, there can be no doubt that they were dissatisfied with the extent of their dependence on a unilateral American decision to employ or not to employ tactical nuclear weapons. Being on the front line, and having committed themselves wholeheartedly to tactical nuclear deterrence of conventional attack, they had a special reason to seek equal control of the decision to use these weapons. Although German military and civilian officials pointed to the necessity of deterring limited conventional grabs with conventional forces, far more urgently than any other allied officials they insisted that the Russians must be convinced that NATO would not hesitate to initiate the use of tactical nuclear weapons.

While tactfully pressing for more nuclear weapons, the Bonn government refrained from seeking custody of nuclear warheads or abrogation of the WEU treaty prohibition upon Germany's production of her own nuclear warheads. Nevertheless, as atomic weapons were more widely integrated into NATO's formations and more widely dispersed within these formations (according to some reports, two-man and even one-man nuclear weapons would be available in the 1960's), the technical, as well as political, feasibility of American soldiers remaining the exclusive guardians of the warheads became increasingly doubtful. Under the circumstances, the nuclear armament of Germany might become tantamount to German possession of nuclear warheads.

At the same time, if France remained determined to achieve nuclear parity with Britain, the prospect of collaborating with Germany, who might help provide a much-needed solid-fuel missile, was bound to be tempting. And if France were to gain a substantial nuclear striking force, with or without German help, how long could NATO deny Germany, who of all the European allies had potentially the greatest economic and technical capacity to produce nuclear weapons, the opportunity to join the nuclear club? There was no published evidence that Germany and France agreed to a formal nuclear weapons consortium, although France was apparently interested in a limited nuclear partnership in 1958. In this same year, however, Defense Minister Strauss indicated that if France continued her development of an independent nuclear capability, the Federal Republic might have to follow suit.[82]

On the other hand, the intense popular and partisan reaction to "Carte Blanche" suggested that the domestic opposition to German control and ownership of nuclear weapons might, in some circumstances, become every bit as strong as it was in Great Britain. Certainly, allied opposition was far stronger. Consequently, whatever their private wishes might be, German officials were constrained from seeking unilateral control of nuclear warheads and weapons by their recognition that this might upset the carefully cultivated status of West Germany as a safe and valuable ally, the outstanding proponent of integration and interdependence.

Chancellor Adenauer was sensitive to the dilemma that France's pursuit of an independent nuclear capability posed for West Germany, because of the domestic and foreign opposition to an independent German nuclear force, on the one hand, and the desire not to be excluded from an expanding nuclear club, on the other. Therefore, after the fall of 1960 he and Defense Minister Strauss openly favored an integrated NATO nuclear striking force as an alternative to De Gaulle's policy. But, while emphasizing his opposition to any move that would contravene Germany's consistent promotion of military integration in NATO and indorsing an allied nuclear deterrent, the Chancellor also insisted on equality of arms for all its members. "It would be an intolerable situation," he warned, "to have a force on one side with the most modern weapons confronting forces not similarly armed. We must give all the NATO forces the same arms as are available to the Russians or we might as well give them bows and arrows."[83] By the end of 1960 it began to look as though the creation of an integrated allied nuclear—at least, tactical nuclear—capability, in which Germany would have equal access to nuclear weapons but remain under the restraints of joint control, was the only politically acceptable way to grant equality of arms to the Federal Republic.

While West Germany operated under powerful restraints against seeking nuclear weapons under independent control, France seemed absolutely determined to follow Britain's example in building her own nuclear force. Officially, the French government took the position that only if the nuclear nations should stop nuclear production and enter a general nuclear disarmament agreement would France agree to a test ban or any other restriction that would keep her from becoming a member of the nuclear club. Otherwise, what was good for the United States, the Soviet Union, and the United Kingdom certainly was not to be denied to France. Accordingly, although she was unable to acquire nearly as much American nuclear information and assistance as Britain, France continued from 1952 on to push ahead at great expense in developing nuclear warheads and the means of delivery. The two nuclear explosions in the Sahara early in 1960 were not generally regarded as true warheads, but there was no doubt that France would soon achieve them. Like Britain, France suffered the disadvantage of relying on bombers (principally the Mirage IV) to deliver the warheads, but to overcome this deficiency she invested great money and effort in developing a ram-jet missile and a solid-fuel IRBM and showed considerable interest in building missile-firing nuclear submarines. In 1960, in spite of very strong opposition in the National Assembly, President de Gaulle pushed through a nuclear program costing the equivalent of two billion dollars.

What was the justification for this burdensome effort to make France the fourth nuclear power? French spokesmen said little or nothing about enhancing France's deterrent capacity or military security. In the domestic controversy over France's nuclear program, military strategy was a negligible consideration. Instead, De Gaulle said France must become a nuclear power in order to have the military autonomy that was the prerequisite of political autonomy and an equal voice with the "Anglo-Saxon" nations in diplomacy and discussions of disarmament. In his mind it was an axiom of international relations that military power must have a "national character." Especially considering the fateful consequences of a nuclear war, "France," he proclaimed, "cannot leave her own destiny and even her own life to the discretion of others."[84] Consistent with this notion of national independence, he declared that France wanted allies but not "protectors." Therefore, France must be ready to meet the totalitarian threat, "not as a protégé, but as an ally which has disposal of herself, including her means of defense."[85] In reality, this would strengthen the alliance, not weaken it, he held. Thus Foreign Minister Couve de Murville answered the criticism in the National Assembly that a national nuclear deterrent would isolate France from her allies by asserting that it would strengthen France's voice in formulating NATO's strategic plans in co-operation with the United States and Britain.[86] And President de Gaulle, approving the unity of France, the United States, and the United Kingdom at the abortive summit conference of May, 1960, asserted:

> Our alliance appeared a living reality. In order that it become even more so, France must have her own role in it, and her own personality. This implies that she too must acquire a nuclear armament, since others have one; that she must be sole mistress of her resources and her territory; in short, that her destiny, although associated with that of her allies, must remain in her own hands. It goes without saying that such an autonomy must be coupled with an ever-closer coordination among the Western world powers, regarding their policy and their strategy.[87]

Thus, in his private memoranda to President Eisenhower and Prime Minister Macmillan in September, 1958, General de Gaulle coupled his demand for equal nuclear status with a demand for equal political status. In particular, he suggested that the three allies with interests and responsibilities outside the NATO area should consult regularly, as a kind of tripartite board, on global policies and military strategy.[88] To demonstrate his determination to pursue this policy of independence-with-co-operation, he withdrew French ships from NATO command, refused to accept missiles or nuclear stockpiles on French soil unless France were given control of the warheads, and requested that the United States seek France's consent before using nuclear weapons anywhere in the world.

De Gaulle's juxtaposition of his demand for tripartite nuclear equality with his demand for tripartite political equality within NATO might be an indication that he would accept certain military and political terms of collaboration as a substitute for the pursuit of an independent nuclear capability; that he would, for example, abandon or at least phase out France's nuclear program in return for a special and equal role in controlling a joint nuclear force and an equal voice in regular tripartite political and strategic consultations. However, the sweeping nature of the arguments he used for developing a French nuclear capability might also mean that France's nuclear program was far more than a bargaining lever, a negotiable asset, to be traded in for better military and political terms of alliance. Thus, in a news conference in November, 1959, De Gaulle exclaimed:

> Who can say that if in the future, the political background having changed completely—that is something that has already happened on earth—the two powers having the nuclear monopoly will not agree to divide the world? Who can say that if the occasion arises the two, while each deciding not to launch its missiles at the main enemy so that it should itself be spared, will not crush the others? It is possible to imagine that on some awful day Western Europe should be wiped out from Moscow and Central Europe from Washington. And who can even say that the two rivals, after I know not what political and social upheaval, will not unite?[89]

These did not sound like the words of a man who would trade a unilateral nuclear program for a scheme of joint control under any conditions. Rather, they sounded like the expression of a basic conviction that the only safe and sound condition for pursuing France's historic destiny was an independent nuclear capability, free of the unreliable unilateral control of the United States or of the equally unreliable multilateral control of an integrated NATO deterrent group. Nevertheless, it was possible that as France encountered the difficulties of building a useful nuclear striking force and discovered its limited political efficacy, even De Gaulle might become more receptive to alternative arrangements for the command and control of nuclear weapons, which could actually be more compatible with the equal and effective voice in allied councils that he sought.

6. INCENTIVES AND DISINCENTIVES FOR INDEPENDENT NUCLEAR CAPABILITIES

Clearly, although the problem of sharing or not sharing control of nuclear weapons would exist anyway, it would be less urgent and more tractable if several of the allies did not have the actual or potential capacity and will to build their own nuclear capabilities. Therefore, in order to formulate a policy toward the control of nuclear weapons from the standpoint of the interests of the United States and the alliance as a whole, one must appraise the nature, strength, and validity of both the incentives and disincentives for the individual members of NATO to acquire independent control of a nuclear force.

The most influential reasons for acquiring an independent nuclear capability are probably the following: (*a*) to obtain a more credible and reliable deterrent to military incursions that the United States might not counter with American-controlled nuclear weapons; (*b*) to gain greater protection against "nuclear blackmail"—that is, against various forms of Soviet pressure backed by the threat of nuclear attack or a conventional conflict entailing the risk of nuclear war; (*c*) to contribute to the West's combined deterrent posture by supplementing America's nuclear striking force; (*d*) to support political and military courses of action, including those outside the NATO area, that the United States might not be willing to back at the risk of her own military involvement; (*e*) to enhance bargaining power and influence vis-à-vis the United States and other allies in matters of foreign policy, military strategy, and disarmament; (*f*) to enjoy the most impressive military attribute of national autonomy and prestige and avoid dependence upon another nation's control of this fateful weapon; (*g*) to rationalize economies in other military expenditures, and especially in mobilized manpower, by offering the public military strength at a tolerable cost; (*h*) to avoid being left out of an expanding nuclear club.

The principal reasons for not acquiring an independent nuclear capability are: (*a*) to avoid the great expense and technological effort required, even with American assistance, to develop, produce, and maintain an adequate quantity and quality of nuclear weapons; (*b*) to avoid the increased danger of attracting a Soviet nuclear attack; (*c*) to avoid stimulating the spread of nuclear capabilities and thereby increasing the hazards of joining the nuclear club by impeding disarmament, unstabilizing the military environment, and undermining allied collaboration, while reducing the benefits by diffusing them to other members; (*d*) to avoid contravening a domestic moral and emotional aversion to owning and producing nuclear weapons.

The principal military-strategic justification that allied nuclear aspirants have given for an independent nuclear program rests on the premise that there are circumstances in which an ally's control of nuclear striking power would be a more effective deterrent to Soviet aggression in Europe than America's control. The validity of this assumption depends, in the first place, upon the kind of nuclear force the ally controls and, in the second place, upon the kind of contingency it is intended to deter.

Clearly, a few squadrons of vulnerable liquid-fuel missiles would be worse than useless to an ally as a second-strike force to deter a direct Soviet nuclear attack. They could not survive a first strike, but they might provoke one. And they would be almost equally useless as a first-strike force for deterring a direct non-nuclear attack or an attack upon other allies. During a crisis the ally controlling these weapons would be more likely to go out of his way to assure the Russians that he would not use them than to try to convince them that he would. Therefore, an ally's nuclear striking force must be relatively invulnerable to be useful for either passive or active deterrence. The British experience, and for that matter the American experience, shows how difficult it is for even a great scientific and industrial nation to build or maintain an invulnerable striking force in the face of increasingly numerous and accurate Soviet missiles.[90] Nevertheless, by the 1970's a few allies could probably acquire—especially if they combined resources or obtained American assistance—sufficiently invulnerable nuclear striking forces, based on solid-fuel sea- and air-borne missiles, to inflict extensive damage on the Soviet Union, even on a second strike, without increasing the risk of attracting a Soviet first strike on their homeland. (If inflicting maximum damage were their *only* aim, they might compensate for the relative vulnerability of their striking force by using very dirty bombs.) However, so far as the enhancement of deterrence is concerned, the physical capabilities of an ally's nuclear force would be valuable only insofar as they made the ally's will and capacity to respond to aggression more credible and fearful to the Russians than America's. Under what circumstances, if any, would this be the case?

Would an ally's independent nuclear capability be any more effective than America's nuclear deterrent against a major conventional attack in Europe? There is no reason to think that the United States, faced with the loss of the most vital area among all her overseas commitments, would be any less willing to employ nuclear weapons than her allies, or to suppose that the Russians would count on her being less willing. If it is doubtful that the United States would initiate the use of nuclear weapons in this contingency, it is even more doubtful that any of her allies would prefer obliteration to occupation or some political escape from war, since their resort to nuclear strikes would not spare them from occupation in any case. Of course, the Soviet Union might estimate an ally's response to such aggression more cautiously than she would estimate America's response, on the assumption that a desperate ally would be more likely to resort to an irrational gesture of nuclear defiance. Yet this is certainly a tenuous reason for an ally to seek an independent nuclear capability: that its threat to commit suicide will be a more convincing deterrent than America's capacity to devastate Russia.

But let us suppose that the object of deterrence were a local conventional incursion upon allied territory—say, a seizure of Berlin, a conflict in West Germany growing out of a disturbance in East Germany, or an attack in Norway or Greece—which the United States would regard as limited but which the ally would regard as comparable to a threat to its survival. No ally could build a sufficient first-strike (or antimissile and civil defense) capability to save it from virtual extinction if it launched a nuclear blow. Yet, conceivably, an ally with only a rudimentary nuclear capability might be able to inflict enough damage on the aggressor to deter such an incursion, despite the utter devastation the Soviet Union could inflict in return. In the same situation, the aggressor might take a chance that the United States would be unwilling to incur the penalties of nuclear devastation for the sake of her ally, even if American troops were being killed.

This proposition has a certain plausibility in the abstract. Yet, in reality, the capacity of an ally to exploit a nuclear force for such ends would depend on imponderable factors of national psychology, leadership, and nerve, which must qualify any theoretical calculus of deterrence. It is extremely unlikely that these qualities would be sufficient to embolden nations who are still haunted by the destruction of two world wars and who would be helpless to prevent their annihilation *and* occupation in another one to attempt to stave off the Soviet colossus with a threat to engage him in nuclear war. In any case, the hypothetical credibility of a threat of suicide is not a sound basis for an ally's pursuit of military and political independence.

If there is a case for an ally enhancing its deterrent power with an independent nuclear capability, it must be made in terms of a second-strike capability. But against what contingencies would an ally's retaliatory strike against a nuclear attack be more credible than America's? Certainly not against a general nuclear assault, in which America's nuclear force would be a primary target, but conceivably against a limited nuclear attack confined to the ally in question. Yet it seems most improbable that rational Soviet leaders would ever assume that the nuclear stalemate with the United States were so stable that they could start a nuclear war against America's allies, singly or collectively, without America's nuclear intervention. Such a war would be too direct a threat to a vital American alliance and to American prestige and security in the world at large for Soviet leaders to count on the United States being willing to leave her allies to their fate rather than meet Soviet nuclear attacks with at least a proportionate nuclear response. This would be true even if the United States had withdrawn her troops and bases from Europe, for America's interest in preserving the strength and independence of Western Europe is rooted in considerations of sentiment and security that transcend the protection of American troops or bases.

Nevertheless, the interest of the United States and her allies in resisting Soviet incursions is not identical in all conceivable circumstances. It is, therefore, not certain that the United States would support her allies against all Soviet nuclear threats at the risk of her own involvement. For example, one can imagine that a NATO member's action might provide the Soviet Union with the pretense of a legitimate excuse for striking or threatening to strike with nuclear weapons under circumstances in which the United States might not be willing to respond in kind because she did not support that member's action. But would an ally be any better prepared to withstand such a threat if it had an independent nuclear capability? Or might not its threat to employ nuclear weapons independently of the United States merely reinforce America's unwillingness to become involved in its behalf, without bolstering its position against Russia? Unless the ally were clearly capable of imposing great damage on the Soviet Union, it probably could not credibly threaten to trade nuclear blows, knowing that it would surely be destroyed long before Russia if the game were played out. Therefore, it is quite unlikely that an ally could be more confident of calling a nuclear bluff or deterring a genuine threat by brandishing its own nuclear power than by relying upon the United States, which could both deliver and absorb far more damage. In fact, if an ally could secure American nuclear backing, it might gain more protection against a Soviet nuclear threat by *not* possessing a nuclear striking force (or by prohibiting a foreign-owned force to use its territory) than by threatening to impose unacceptable retaliatory damage independently.

But we have assumed so far that the efficacy of an ally's independent nuclear force as a deterrent depends only on the relation of power and will between that ally and the aggressor, whereas its efficacy may also be affected by the force's influence upon America's nuclear deterrent. Thus an ally might use the threat of its own nuclear response as a threat to involve the Soviet Union in a nuclear war with the United States. For example, it might threaten to launch a nuclear blow or retaliate against a limited Soviet nuclear blow in the expectation that the United States could not fail to back it up with her own nuclear force and that the Soviet Union could not take the chance of acting on the contrary assumption. Or the ally might calculate that because the Soviet Union would not dare to upset the military balance with the United States by expending her striking power on the United States ally, she might either be restrained from attacking the nuclear-armed ally or else be impelled to attack the United States simultaneously. The mere possibility that an ally's striking power might thus act as a trigger on America's striking power might increase the risk and uncertainty facing the aggressor in some circumstances, when there neither existed nor appeared to exist a conflict of interest between the United States and her ally. On the other hand, it might have just the opposite effect in other circumstances. For to the extent that the ally threatened to use its independent nuclear force to trigger off America's force under circumstances in which the United States did not wish to become involved, the United States would have to protect herself from her ally by qualifying her obligation to consider an attack upon one as an attack upon all, thereby leaving the ally in a weaker and more isolated position than before. Moreover, an ally's very possession of an independent nuclear force might depreciate the credibility of an American response by suggesting to the aggressor that the United States had, in effect, turned over her local deterrent responsibilities to her ally.

The British government, faced with the difficulties of enhancing Britain's deterrent power directly by disposing an independent nuclear capability, claimed to enhance that power indirectly, by making an independent contribution to the West's general deterrent posture. But, if it were true that an ally could supplement America's nuclear striking force by providing such values as dispersion, geographical proximity, and a larger number of missiles, that would not be an argument for decentralizing control of nuclear weapons. Quite the opposite. Besides, in 1961 the United States—with the operational status of the Polaris—achieved an adequate second-strike force without allied contributions, and the allies were in no position to enhance America's waning first-strike capability.

The arguments for an independent nuclear capability on grounds of military security are no more applicable to tactical nuclear weapons than to strategic nuclear weapons. For, even if tactical nuclear warfare were regarded as a more effective means of local resistance, an ally upon whose soil such a war would be fought would probably be even more reluctant than the United States to initiate it. In any case, the distinction between tactical and strategic nuclear war had become quite fuzzy by 1961, since tactical nuclear weapons were regarded as instruments of graduated deterrence—as a step up the ladder to massive retaliation—and since some of NATO's nominally tactical planes, rockets, and missiles could reach Soviet territory from the forward line. Indeed, General Norstad regarded the land-based Polaris missiles, which he sought for a NATO nuclear force, as a tactical substitute for medium-range bombers. Of course, if an ally were to completely replace American-controlled tactical nuclear warheads on its territory with its own, that would give the ally a power to *withhold* the use of local nuclear weapons, although the U.S.A. could still employ weapons from outside the territory. But the credibility of the nuclear deterrent would be diminished rather than increased.

There remains the possibility that an ally might increase its military power outside the NATO area by possessing an independent nuclear force. However, the allies with specific interests and commitments outside the NATO area could not protect them with nuclear weapons. The British and French experiences showed that, politically and militarily, the only forces that are useful for this purpose are conventional and paramilitary forces. And, as for resisting Soviet nuclear threats against the use of such forces, the British experience in the Suez War indicated that an independent nuclear capability would be no help if the United States did not support her ally politically.

Therefore—quite apart from the possible liabilities of pursuing an independent nuclear program—on grounds of military security an ally's development and maintenance of an independent nuclear force would not be worth the great effort required. As long as the United States manifested an identical interest in maintaining the basic conditions of allied security, any ally would be better off depending on America's nuclear forces, under assurances that they would be used for the benefit of all the allies, than trying to supplement or supplant those forces with its own. However, like most of NATO's military problems, the problem of the control of nuclear weapons was saturated with political implications, which could not be encompassed within any purely military-strategic calculus.

Then what political value could an ally derive from an independent nuclear capability? If an ally could gain no deterrent power by controlling its own nuclear weapons, it probably could not gain greater protection against nuclear blackmail either; nor could it gain more effective backing for political and military courses of action that the United States was not willing to support. For, like enhancing deterrence, these two political reasons for an independent nuclear capability rest on the dubious assumptions that the Soviet Union would be more fearful of an ally's nuclear power than of America's, and that in the absence of American political support an ally could increase its influence on the Soviet Union by disposing its own nuclear power. Similarly, insofar as an ally's bargaining power with the United States and other allies is a function of its capacity to pursue an independent course with respect to the Soviet

Union, there is no reason to suppose that an independent nuclear force can enhance an ally's bargaining power any more than it can enhance deterrence.

Of course, where the relationship between military power and its objective is so indirect and unspecific and where many other factors must also account for power and influence, it is extremely difficult to calculate the political efficacy or inefficacy of a nuclear force. Perhaps the symbolic value of a nuclear capability can reinforce an ally's influence irrespective of its exact utility if it had to be used. Even the relationship of nuclear weapons to deterrence, which can at least be calculated according to such relatively precise and tangible data as missile exchange rates, is very inexact and speculative. When it comes to national prestige, the military contribution is peculiarly subjective; in a sense, if other powers regard nuclear weapons, for whatever reason, as a potent status symbol, then an independent nuclear capability is an important index of national power.

Yet there is no evidence that permits one to attribute the British, French, or German capacity to resist blackmail, to pursue an independent policy, or to exercise bargaining power inside or outside the alliance to their possession or lack of possession of nuclear weapons. One can more readily attribute their political influence to the quality of their diplomacy, their national leadership, their internal cohesion and economic strength, their geographical position, their historical image, or even to their conventional military power. And, although the possession or non-possession of nuclear weapons may affect their prestige in some general sense, it is difficult to show how it has affected their political influence for specific purposes. The evidence for the influence of an ally's independent nuclear capability upon American policy is equally scant. Surely, Britain's special relationship with the United States—based on a distinctive combination of coinciding interests, shared culture and experiences, and personalties—would have existed whether or not she had become a nuclear power. And it is doubtful that an ally can enhance its influence on the United States merely by demonstrating its will to exploit an independent nuclear force in pursuit of an independent political course. The attempt to do so is more likely to lead to contrary results.

Nevertheless, there are at least two ways in which it is fairly clear that an ally can translate into concrete political results its capacity to build an independent nuclear force: (*a*) by offering to stop or moderate an independent nuclear effort in return for military and political concessions; (*b*) by gaining access to disarmament discussions and influence on disarmament policies. There is little doubt that France, by first developing a significant nuclear capability and then skilfully exploiting it for these ends, could increase her voice in the alliance and in shaping the broad range of militarily and politically significant policies associated with disarmament. Her success in these directions would provide an example for others to follow. So one cannot dismiss the political arguments for an independent nuclear capability as anachronistic appeals to national pride and vanity.

Yet the most persuasive reason for an ally to seek an independent nuclear capability is of a more general and profound nature than any of these. It is simply that military autonomy is the most striking symbol of political autonomy and that the capacity to choose war or peace is the most vital attribute of national sovereignty. Even though military autonomy can only be approximated in reality, a great nation must not surrender any more of it than it can help. Therefore, to leave such fateful decisions as whether or not to use nuclear weapons and how to use nuclear weapons entirely in the hands of another nation amounts to a gross abnegation of national will. No other nation, however mighty and trustworthy it may be, can always be relied upon to make these crucial decisions in a manner completely compatible with a nuclear dependent's own vital interests. The United States is no exception.

Such a patent abnegation of control over one's military fate must be especially galling to an ally when the instruments of its fate are stationed on its own soil. But, in fact, those allies who do not have nuclear weapons on their soil are likely to be as vulnerable to the destruction of a nuclear war as those who do. Therefore, all allies have an interest in avoiding dependence on another nation's exclusive control of nuclear weapons on the simple principle that there should be no annihilation without representation. If they cannot obtain a satisfactory degree of control over the use of these weapons by other means, those allies who have the material capacity will be under some compulsion to secure it by building their own nuclear weapons. At least, the British and French nuclear efforts convey the distinct impression that it is this simple but profound impulse of military and political autonomy, more than any of the specific strategic or political purposes with which they have rationalized it, that has impelled them to seek their own nuclear capabilities at such great expense.

To a lesser extent, the same impulse that impels allies to seek control over the instruments of their national survival or annihilation also leads them to seek nuclear weapons in order to support subordinate national interests. There may be no convincing evidence that an independent nuclear force will enable an ally to support its political objectives more effectively, but there is no conclusive evidence that it will not; for, by its nature, the relationship between military and political power is subtle and indefinite. Under the circumstances, allies may reasonally prefer not to depend entirely on American nuclear power to back their policies if they can help it. In such a crucial yet speculative endeavor as supporting deterrence and diplomacy with military power, it is understandable that governments should want to rely, as much as possible, on their own control of nuclear weapons rather than on the will and ability of the United States to control them in their behalf.

Still, it might be easier for allies to tolerate dependence upon America's nuclear capability than on America's capability *and* the nuclear capabilities of several other allies in addition. For, in a sense, non-nuclear nations would be more nearly equal partners if the United States had a monopoly of nuclear weapons in the alliance than if Britain and France and another ally or two should also possess significant nuclear capabilities. In a situation of rampant or even incipient nuclear diffusion, allies who would not otherwise have chosen to develop independent nuclear forces might do so simply because they did not wish to be left out of an expanding nuclear club. They might wish to control their own nuclear weapons because, although they were willing to depend on the United States to use her nuclear power to their benefit under the existing lines of influence, they were not willing to depend on a number of other nuclear powers doing so when the lines of influence would be more diverse and complicated. Therefore, even if only two or three allies were to act upon the incentives to obtain an independent nuclear capability, the movement might spread by sheer contagion.

On the other hand, any ally contemplating an independent nuclear effort would have to reckon with some formidable liabilities, which might create countervailing disincentives to undertake such an effort. Already, by the time the British canceled their Blue Streak program in 1960, the great expense required to build a useful nuclear capability had dampened one earlier incentive for joining the nuclear club: the desire to get more security for less money. Although this economic motive remained an excuse for not increasing conventional forces and for preserving NATO's nuclear strategy, by 1960 it had ceased to be a convincing justification for an individual ally to try to substitute its own nuclear power for conventional forces.

Soon after the onset of the missile age, allied states also came to understand the modern calculus of deterrence well enough to regard a vulnerable striking force as more of a liability than an asset, since it would be inadequate for a second strike but might attract a pre-emptive attack. Yet it would take any ally, including Britain, a number of years to acquire a sufficiently invulnerable force—especially one based on sea-borne mobility and concealment—by which time that particular weapons system might be obsolescent.

Furthermore, tending to counteract popular sentiment for nuclear autonomy there was the emergence of organized popular sentiment for nuclear abstinence—most notably in Britain, Norway, Denmark, and West Germany. This countervailing sentiment sprang, partly, from a moral and emotional revulsion toward weapons of such terrible destructive capacity and, partly, from a general identification of nuclear abstinence with disarmament and peace. And these motives were powerfully reinforced by the simple fear of physical vulnerability to nuclear obliteration and by the desire to escape obliteration through avoiding the responsibility for deterring it.

At the same time, the possible contagion of an expanding nuclear club was, to some degree, offset by the fear of exacerbating the contagion. The fear was not only that the political advantages of joining the club would diminish with the increased membership but, more important, that the creation of several centers of nuclear control would undermine the cohesion of the alliance and unstabilize the whole international military environment.

To the extent that independent nuclear capabilities actually convinced allies, rightly or wrongly, that they could pursue deterrence, diplomacy, and their separate policies independently, nuclear diffusion would tend to destroy the incentives for military and political co-operation. Supposing a nuclear-armed ally really believed that it had achieved the military autonomy it sought. It would then raise fears in the minds of other allies that it intended to use or threaten to use its nuclear weapons in circumstances that would implicate them in risks of nuclear devastation which they did not wish to incur. These fears would move non-nuclear allies to qualify or rescind their obligations to support this nuclear ally, and it would incite them to seek their own nuclear capabilities in the apprehension that combined forces were no longer a reliable guaranty of their interests. If several allies thereby came to base their security primarily on their independent control of nuclear weapons rather than on the forces and decisions of the alliance as a whole, every ally would be reluctant to commit its armed force for any purpose except opposing blackmail and aggressions that impinged directly and immediately upon its own security or on its exclusive national interests outside the treaty area. In this way the mutual obligations of NATO could readily dissolve in mutual suspicions and fears.

A particularly virulent source of these suspicions and fears would be an independent German nuclear capability, regardless of the restraint with which the German government might exercise this new-found power. But the corrosive effect of nuclear diffusion would be even more serious if it loosened the ties of the United States to her European allies. On the one hand, nuclear diffusion might increase American suspicion, if not the actual likelihood, of some ally involving or threatening to involve the United States in nuclear war under circumstances in which she would not be willing to become involved. After all, to pose a more credible threat of nuclear war than the American threat, to threaten to act when the United States might not, was one of the primary justifications that the British and French presented for their nuclear programs. And, considering the limited nuclear capability that any ally was likely to achieve in the near future, the ability to trigger American nuclear power might appear to be its chief utility. On the other hand, the diffusion of allied nuclear capabilities might lead to a devolution of responsibility for exercising nuclear power, away from the United States and to the allies, which they were not really prepared to assume. And, in that case, the United States would either find herself in the position of acting as the unwanted trigger on *their* nuclear forces; or else, despairing of the task of presenting a common front to Soviet incursions, she would reserve her nuclear power to protect her own most immediate interests. In either case, the effect would be to sever the vital entanglement of the United States and Europe, to drive the United States to do exactly what her allies have always feared: to diminish her obligation to come to the defense of Europe. Since the United States would no longer need strategic bases in Europe, and since her allies would prefer to contribute to their independent nuclear forces rather than to the common defense of Europe on the ground, the United States might even withdraw her troops and return to the position of an overseas guarantor instead of an active European collaborator. But she would be a guarantor under radically different conditions than at the beginning of NATO, before the rise of Soviet nuclear power.

The most immediate and likely consequences of these corrosive effects of nuclear diffusion would not be anything so dramatic as the dissolution of the alliance or an overt armed aggression. Rather, the loosening of allied cohesion would lead to the intensification of the Soviet game of creating crises to test the resolution of the alliance and to exploit political differences, and to more adventurous tactics of subversion and indirect aggression.

Along with these ominous possibilities, prospective nuclear powers would also have to include the following consequences among the hazards of expanding the nuclear club: increasing the risks of a nuclear war by accident or miscalculation, killing the chances of an international agreement to curtail the diffusion of nuclear capabilities, and accelerating the process of nuclear diffusion outside the alliance. Even the diffusion of nuclear capabilities among the allies would tend to unstabilize the military balance by multiplying the sources of potential nuclear mistakes and obscuring the sources of nuclear control and responsibility. But the proliferation of nuclear powers outside the alliance would be vastly more unstabilizing, as new sets of volatile military balances would tempt old rivals and enemies to engage in risky political adventures and pre-emptive or preventive wars, which, in turn, might involve the United States and her NATO allies. As long as there seemed to be any prospect of preventing this development, any ally that feared the contagion of nuclear diffusion could not reasonably claim for itself a privilege of joining the nuclear club that it would deny to others.

Considering the obstacles to America's allies' achieving anything but a token nuclear force in the 1960's and considering the liabilities of their trying to achieve even that, one might expect prospective allied members of the nuclear club to estimate the benefits of membership more modestly than when Britain and France began their nuclear programs, before the implications of the missile age and of nuclear diffusion were understood so well. If the most basic motive for an independent nuclear capability was the compelling impulse to achieve military and political autonomy—that is, the desire to acquire a decent measure of national control over one's military fate—a sober appraisal of the facts of nuclear life in the 1960's should convince allied governments and peoples that an independent nuclear program is not a fruitful investment.

Along with the many costs and liabilities of an independent nuclear program, an ally would have to reckon with the fact that, even if it regarded its nuclear force as a useful supplement to America's second-strike capability, that force would not enhance its control over America's decision to use or not use her own nuclear force. For an ally's nuclear weapons would be no more useful as a safety catch than as a trigger on America's nuclear weapons. They would not meet one of the basic sources of allied dissatisfaction with nuclear dependence on the United States: the fear that the United States might use or threaten to use nuclear weapons under circumstances in which an ally was not willing to incur the risks and costs of nuclear war. Only if an ally could completely supplant America's responsibility for nuclear retaliation with its own, could it gain control over the decision *not* to use nuclear weapons. But, in that case, it could not also expect to enhance the credibility of a positive nuclear decision. More likely, it would be left isolated in the face of Soviet threats, having sacrificed America's nuclear backing for an illusory military autonomy.

In truth, an ally's real guaranty of a decent measure of control over its military fate is not nuclear independence but military and political interdependence. With effective interdependence, based on a strategy compatible with close military and political collaboration, the locus of production, ownership, and custody of nuclear warheads might be dissociated from, or at least subordinated to, the method of making the decision to use them. Then there might be an equitable allied participation in the use of nuclear weapons without a disastrous fragmentation of nuclear control.

9
The Control of Nuclear Weapons

1. POLICY ALTERNATIVES

In the light of the nature and strength of these incentives and disincentives for allies to acquire their own nuclear weapons and the probable consequences of their joining the nuclear club, what policy should the United States adopt toward the control of nuclear weapons in order to advance the security and cohesion of the alliance?* That was the urgent question confronting the United States in the 1960's.

The principal policy alternatives were: (*a*) to keep the existing system of unilateral American control of American- or sea-based nuclear weapons, supplemented by dual control of nuclear weapons on allied soil, with custody of the warheads in American hands; (*b*) to actively assist all those allies who wanted to acquire independent nuclear capabilities to join the

* By "control" I mean the power to govern the use of nuclear weapons, of which physical possession is only one means. The "command and control" of nuclear weapons generally refers to the whole technical and organizational system for co-ordinating the use of weapons under responsible military command, but in this chapter I deal, primarily, with the political locus of the strategy and the decision to use nuclear weapons. On the technical, organizational, and many of the strategic aspects of the problem of maintaining central control over dispersed nuclear weapons, see Thornton Read, *Command and Control* (Princeton University Center of International Studies, Policy Memorandum No. 24 [1961]).

nuclear club; (*c*) to grant the allies a joint share of the control of the decision to use nuclear weapons under a NATO or European command, directed by a joint political body. In reality, these policies were subject to a number of variations and combinations; but, as stated, each represented a distinct strategy for handling the command and control of nuclear weapons, and each would have distinct results.

From the American standpoint there was no *direct* security advantage to be gained by relinquishing custody of nuclear warheads and giving the allies a larger share of their control. On the contrary, sharing nuclear custody and control would complicate the problem of the politically disciplined and responsible employment of nuclear weapons and, possibly, reduce the credibility of nuclear retaliation. *Indirectly,* however, the security of the United States and all the allies might be benefited if nuclear sharing enhanced allied collaboration and directed allied resources toward the support of non-nuclear conventional resistance instead of toward independent nuclear capabilities. Moreover, the cohesion of the alliance had a vital political value in the non-violent struggles of the cold war, quite apart from its contribution to military security.

2. THE EXISTING SYSTEM

The system of nuclear control that existed at the end of 1960 had the virtue of preserving the centralized control of America's nuclear forces, and, in effect, the centralized control of the nuclear weapons in the whole NATO area (except those under British command). But one big disadvantage of this system, which led NATO officials and the American government to explore alternative systems of control, was that it would fail to discourage independent nuclear efforts by other allies—efforts that would reduce their contributions to NATO's shield. In fact, America's Atomic Energy Act provided a positive incentive for nuclear aspirants to make "substantial progress" in the development of nuclear weapons so as to receive more nuclear assistance. And, for France, an independent nuclear program was not only a means of getting more nuclear assistance but also the prerequisite for gaining an equal voice with the Anglo-American bloc in determining matters of military strategy and political policy.

In addition, the existing system incurred the political and psychological liabilities of leaving all the allies dependent on American decisions about if, when, and how to use nuclear weapons—decisions which could be a matter of national survival or extinction for all. Even if this lopsided power of decision within the alliance did not lead to the proliferation of independent nuclear efforts, it tended to blunt the incentives for full military and political collaboration, while stimulating the forces of nuclear pacifism and neutralism.

Nations that could not control the use of the principal weapon upon which their security depended could not be expected to contribute fully to the required build-up of conventional forces, which were intended only to enforce a "pause" and touch off nuclear warfare. Moreover, such dependency grated against the quickening sense of national autonomy on the part of resurgent political communities, which were no longer the weak and devastated states of the Marshall Plan era.

The situation was especially galling to nations upon whose territory American nuclear weapons were deployed. The 1957 system of dual control was intended as a concession to national sentiment in order to make the deployment of missiles and stockpiles on allied soil acceptable, but it was doubtful that it met the problem satisfactorily. For, quite apart from the political acceptability or unacceptability of this compromise, physical separation of the American-controlled warheads from the missiles would create technical problems concerning the combat readiness of the weapons,* yet the placing of the warheads in the missiles under a two-key system as in England would create serious doubts about the effectiveness of American custody, especially in the minds of American congressmen.[1]

* Presumably, in the case of tactical nuclear weapons there would be time to solve this problem in the event of war by a presidential order releasing the warheads from the stockpiles. In any case, worse than any inefficiency in combat readiness would be the chance of accident resulting from numerous widely dispersed tactical nuclear weapons that were "loaded."

In any case, dual control did not seem to be an effective alternative to the push toward unilateral allied control. It was acceptable to Britain only because it was part of a preferential partnership and a close working agreement with the United States on the decision to use the weapons and because Britain had her own nuclear warheads and delivery vehicles anyway. But it was not acceptable to France, who preferred building her own nuclear weapons to accepting any system that denied her custody of the warheads on her soil.

Furthermore, there were more intangible liabilities to the existing imbalance of power in the control of nuclear weapons. It encouraged America's allies to view the crucial problems of military strategy too much through the distorting perspective of their dependence on American responsibility and too little through the perspective of common responsibility. Consequently, allied governments and peoples did not have to face up fully to the real nature and demands of military strategy, especially where they impinged on defense expenditures and conscription. Their nuclear dependency encouraged a kind of innocence and indifference toward these questions, which impeded a concerted and realistic approach to the complex issues confronting the alliance as a whole. Too often the United States took the responsibility for strategic dilemmas and frustrations which she alone could not resolve, while her allies tended to approach these dilemmas and frustrations from the standpoint of influencing American policies rather than solving common problems. The British movement for unilateral nuclear disarmament, which deplored American policy but ignored the real complexities of the hard issues of military power, in the assurance that whatever Britain might do the United States would maintain the balance of terror, was only an extreme manifestation of the psychological aberrations accompanying nuclear dependency.

Yet these adverse effects of the existing system of nuclear control upon allied security and cohesion were the result not only of dependence on America's nuclear weapons but also of NATO's overdependence on nuclear weapons in general, together with considerable ambiguity about the strategy for using them. If there had been an agreed strategy and the capabilities for fighting limited wars in Europe with conventional weapons, distinguishing nuclear counterforce from purely punitive civilian blows, reserving both as second-strike deterrents except in the most extreme and unlikely circumstances, and employing them in a graduated or proportionate manner, there would probably have been less dissatisfaction and anxiety about America's custody of warheads, and there would probably have been more realistic estimates of the military and political utility of nuclear weapons and less incentive for allies to acquire their own.

Therefore, the political liabilities of the existing system of nuclear control might be substantially mitigated if the allies agreed on a military strategy that would delineate more clearly the special and restricted functions of tactical and strategic nuclear weapons. The very process of deliberately and explicitly reaching such a strategic consensus would go far toward giving the allies the needed sense of participation and responsibility. The strategic consensus would, moreover, clear the way for a much-needed measure of concerted political control over nuclear weapons. It would remove a big obstacle to allied agreement on the procedure by which the members of NATO would participate in the decision to use nuclear weapons; for as long as the allies were so dependent on the initiation of nuclear warfare as a substitute for conventional resistance—or, put another way, as long as the threshold between conventional and nuclear war were so low—they would find it extremely difficult to agree, either in advance or *ad hoc,* on the circumstances in which nuclear weapons should be used.

Possibly, with such a consensus the United States might then, with no adverse effects, maintain the custody of her warheads and refrain from assisting her allies in their nuclear efforts, while counting on the sobering facts of nuclear life to discourage them from engaging in burdensome, unnecessary, and futile nuclear programs. With the growth of her Polaris submarine force, the United States would not need to ask her allies to place strategic missiles on their soil and could point to the complete adequacy of her own second-strike strategic force to deter nuclear attacks upon them. If the operational control of tactical nuclear weapons were confined to special interallied battalions or brigades, instead of being diffused throughout all units, and if there were agreed procedures for the political control of the decision to use these weapons according to an agreed strategy, then the formal American custody of warheads might not entail serious technical or political difficulties.

The United States would, of course, continue to keep her troops in Europe and reaffirm her determination to defend Europe by all means necessary, and she would maintain a continuing strategic consensus with her allies on the circumstances in which nuclear and non-nuclear weapons would be used. Implicit in the maintenance of such a strategic consensus and agreement upon the political control of nuclear weapons would be the requirement of continual political consultation about the foreign policies that military power should serve. There would be every reason that France should be granted an equal role with Britain not only on European matters but also on the global strategic and political problems of special concern to France, Britain, and the United States.

The maintenance, by these means, of a strategic and political consensus would be a far better guaranty to an ally of substantive nuclear control—that is, the power to govern use of nuclear weapons—than an independent nuclear force, which, at best, could not control the nuclear forces of the United States or of other allies. If, under all these conditions, France and other allies nevertheless engaged in their own nuclear weapons programs, it should be clear to them and to others that this was for reasons of national prestige, not for valid reasons of security and political autonomy or influence. In this case, they might, at least, have no incentive to try to carry out their nuclear programs beyond the requirements of a token force. And the United States would, at least, have refrained from actively promoting the proliferation of nuclear production and the decentralization of nuclear control.

If the existing system of nuclear control, combined with a strategic revision and an extension of strategic and political consultation, could halt independent nuclear programs, or at least confine them to token efforts, that would be the best alternative. But suppose it could not. Aside from De Gaulle's demanding views of the requirements of political autonomy in the nuclear age, there was the obstacle of the British nuclear force and program. Having achieved a nuclear force at great expense and effort, the British seemed unlikely to give it up—thus trading their special relationship with the United States for equality with France, while granting the United States a monopoly of nuclear production and ownership—merely on the dubious supposition that France might forego her nuclear program in return. Yet as long as Britain retained an independent nuclear force, France would not deny herself the same privilege, merely in return for political concessions or in deference to the American view of strategic logic. And if France joined Britain as a nuclear power, could West Germany be dissuaded from following their example?

3. ACTIVE DIFFUSION OF UNILATERAL CAPABILITIES

If the diffusion of nuclear production and ownership would take place regardless of any plan for the command and control of nuclear weapons that the United States might advance, there was an argument for following the second alternative policy and actively assisting all allies who wished to join the nuclear club to join with a minimum of effort and a maximum of efficiency. At least this policy would relieve the United States of the political liabilities of trying to retain a special nuclear status among allied dependents, and it would save the allies from diverting their economic and scientific resources into wasteful duplication of America's research and development program, enabling them to apply their energies most efficiently to the achievement of invulnerable nuclear deterrents instead of obsolescent weapons. When the United States acquired a sufficient number of nuclear submarines and missiles, she might even offer to sell her allies surplus weapons in this system, so that the process of nuclear diffusion would at least take a less hazardous and possibly useful military direction. At the same time, the United States could positively promote the military posture of the alliance if she could trade her nuclear assistance for increased allied contributions to the conventional forces of NATO's shield.

Perhaps, if the United States stopped opposing her allies' acquisition of their own nuclear capabilities, they would more readily discover, in time, that independent nuclear capabilities would not really give them military and political autonomy, that they were no substitute for military and political interdependence. The nuclear-armed allies might continue to regard their weapons as a gratifying status-symbol and as insurance for the possibility of a serious divergency of interests with their allies; but, like the British, they would go through a process of education that would moderate the extravagant expectations of nuclear newcomers, and, in effect, their nuclear forces would become merely contributions to the general deterrent forces of the alliance.

Yet a policy of actively aiding the diffusion of nuclear capabilities would surely be justified only as a measure of desperation, after all other methods of preserving NATO's security and cohesion by discouraging such diffusion had been tried. For, at best, the multiplication of national nuclear forces would complicate the crucial task of co-ordinating the use of nuclear weapons—especially the use of tactical nuclear weapons. It would also increase the danger of nuclear accidents and foreclose whatever chance there might be to prevent the diffusion of nuclear weapons among non-NATO powers. Its adverse effects upon allied cohesion could only be mitigated to the extent that the nuclear aspirants became disillusioned with their original expectations of military and political autonomy, but this process of education might not come in time to save the alliance from the corrosive effects of fragmenting the control of weapons that could precipitate a common disaster.

4. THE GALLOIS PLAN

A policy of active nuclear assistance at least had the virtue of avoiding some of the liabilities of the existing system of nuclear control while minimizing some of the adverse effects of nuclear diffusion. This was more than could be said for some schemes for combining the two policies. The most prominent scheme of this nature was advanced by General Pierre M. Gallois, former member of the Planning Group at SHAPE, military author, and adviser to the French government under De Gaulle.[2] Gallois proposed that the United States make nuclear weapons available to allied governments (individually or in groups) under dual control, with the agreement that she turn over the "key" to the warheads under critical conditions specified in advance.

General Gallois based his plan on the premise that America's nuclear deterrent was no longer sufficiently credible for her allies to depend on. To overcome this situation, he argued, it was no longer sufficient for the United States to station her armed forces in Europe as a hostage. Consistent with De Gaulle's oft-repeated prediction that American troops would not long remain on the Continent when the United States no longer depended on strategic bases in Europe, Gallois insisted that "such a solution is neither practical nor lasting, for it is subject to limitations which may be imposed by either or both governments involved."[3] According to Gallois, the only way to enhance the credibility of the threat of nuclear retaliation was for the nation whose vital interests were directly threatened to have the power to retaliate. Yet he recognized that, if each ally were to depend entirely upon the independent control of its own nuclear weapons, this would produce a dangerous proliferation of independent nuclear capabilities and would strain mutual-defense obligations. So, to avoid unnecessary risks and to check the proliferation of nuclear weapons at the expense of a considerable duplication of effort in research and production, he proposed that the United States give her allies nuclear weapons under the safeguards of his scheme for combined dual and unilateral control.

Gallois's plan would, purportedly, relieve the allies of exclusive dependence upon America's control of nuclear weapons without requiring them to develop their own nuclear capabilities. It would impose some restraints upon the exercise of independent control without requiring the cumbersome procedures of a collective decision of all the allies. However, the central premise upon which the plan was based is dubious. This premise was that a small nuclear striking force under the control of an ally most directly threatened would be a more credible deterrent than America's striking force or a joint deterrent. Thus, Gallois imagined that a small country—he took Denmark as an example—would enhance the deterrence of a missile strike against one of its cities or of a major conventional aggression across its frontiers if it had a striking force capable only of inflicting enough damage to outweigh the benefits the aggressor could hope to win. He assumed that Denmark would choose annihilation rather than capitulation and that its choice would be automatic, or at least that the aggressor would be deterred by this possibility.

As the preceding discussion has suggested, it is highly questionable, in terms of the operating psychology of the situation, that a single ally will get more deterrence against the threats Gallois envisaged by threatening to hit a few Soviet targets at the cost of certain nuclear obliteration than by relying upon the support of America's striking force. And Gallois conceded that a Soviet threat to hold the United States responsible for a Danish strike "would be meaningless since it could not be carried into effect; the Soviet Union would not consider it worthwhile to risk exchanging ballistic missiles with the United States just for the sake of subjugating Denmark."[4] But, however that might be, an ally that depended upon an independent suicidal counterthreat as a substitute for an American or NATO response would give the Soviet Union dangerous opportunities to isolate and intimidate it by the kind of political and psychological warfare that the Russians would vastly prefer to overt military action anyway. The greatest deterrent to this kind of warfare and, in the long run, to overt military aggression too is the Soviet belief that she cannot exert her military power against one ally without implicating the others. The Gallois plan would create a situation distinctly uncongenial to the credibility of that belief.

Furthermore, it is doubtful that General Gallois's proposal would really avoid the principal political disadvantage of the existing system of dual control, which is that the United States has the exclusive power to decide when to use the nuclear warheads. An advance definition of the special and extreme circumstances in which the United States would release control of the warheads would, indeed, give the ally greater control and responsibility; but it would not make an ally any less dependent upon an American decision than a simple pledge by the United States to use the weapons herself under those same circumstances. Moreover, the very agreement to release control of the warheads to an ally in order to reinforce deterrence might diminish deterrence by indicating so explicitly that the United States regarded her own deterrent threat as deficient. The worst time to transfer nuclear responsibility would be during a crisis.

In short, although the Gallois plan was intended to solve the problems of nuclear diffusion and dependence by combining the military and political advantages of American and independent control, it seemed more likely to combine the disadvantages of both systems.

5. EUROPEAN DETERRENT GROUP

If the existing system of American custody of nuclear warheads —supplemented by a strategic revision, the achievement of a strategic consensus, and the extension of political consultation —would not advance allied security and cohesion and would not confine and moderate the diffusion of independent nuclear efforts, then the best alternative would be some form of joint allied control of nuclear weapons. At the beginning of the 1960's there were, principally, two plans for giving nuclear control to an allied group. One was to create a European group deterrent; the other was to make NATO itself a nuclear power.[5]

In a European nuclear force, several European allies (including at least France, Germany, Italy, Belgium, the Netherlands, and Luxembourg) would jointly own and control combined strategic nuclear forces, separate from the United States SAC and Polaris systems and, if Britain were not a member of the European group, separate from the RAF Bomber Command. These forces would be under central military command and political direction, so that they would be developed, deployed, and used as a unit. The Soviet Union would be likely to treat it as a unit if only because the national identity of nuclear weapons and the decision to use them would be obscure, especially if they were sea-based. Therefore, each member, while avoiding complete dependence on America's nuclear deterrent, would supposedly benefit from the deterrent power of the group's total strategic nuclear forces rather than suffer the handicap of relying upon its own rudimentary and politically isolated force. At the same time, each member would avoid the political and military dangers of fragmenting the control of nuclear weapons.

With American gifts and assistance, combined with its own co-ordinated scientific and production resources, a European group might in time develop a sufficiently large and invulnerable second-strike capability to constitute a truly self-sufficient deterrent. Or, at least, it could be substantial enough to seriously complicate the Soviet calculations that would have to precede a major aggression by confronting the Russians with another large deterrent force in addition to America's. If the full effectiveness of the European deterrent nevertheless depended upon triggering America's deterrent, it would have a considerable advantage over a single nation's nuclear capability for two reasons: (*a*) politically, because the United States would be less apt to dissociate herself from the use or threatened use of strategic weapons by several European nations acting in concert; (*b*) militarily, because in order to knock out a group deterrent the Soviet Union would have to launch a massive attack, which would threaten the whole of Europe, and probably leave the United States with a decisive nuclear advantage if her striking force were spared from attack.

Thus, by combining allied resources and involving all members in an attack upon one, a European group deterrent might eventually contribute more to allied security than either the existing system or the multiplication of independent capabilities, while, at the same time, it would relieve the allies of dependence on America's nuclear weapons without diminishing the credibility of nuclear retaliation. However, the realization of this hypothetical advantage would depend critically upon the willingness of every member to regard an attack on one of the group as an attack upon itself and, more directly, upon the appearance of this willingness in Soviet eyes. Would a European deterrent group manifest sufficient cohesion for this purpose?

There are precedents for European collaboration in the political and military activities of the Western European Union, political consultation and debate in the Council of Europe, scientific co-operation in EURATOM, and economic integration in OEEC, ECSC, and EEC (the European Common Market). However, these organizations have entailed no abdication of national sovereignty comparable to what a European deterrent group would require. That deterrent would require the subordination of the life-and-death decision to wage nuclear war to some central political authority and military command acting, as far as possible, under a pre-arranged set of directives. Could the members of a European deterrent group organize a political consensus sufficient to sustain this degree of military collaboration?

There is one element of such a political consensus in the somewhat nebulous notion that Winston Churchill expounded before the creation of the North Atlantic Treaty and that continues to find ardent and articulate spokesmen among prominent statesmen and journalists in several European countries: the notion that Western Europe is a distinct cultural, economic, and political community, whose destiny is to become a united and independent force in the world. This sentiment has encouraged, and been encouraged by, its most concrete manifestation: the movement toward European economic integration. It has gained vitality from Western Europe's impressive economic resurgence and prosperity, which has largely freed America's allies from their previous dependence upon her aid.

But, clearly, the subordination of national will to joint custody and control of the most powerful instruments of destruction must be sustained by something more compelling than these sentiments and aspirations. It must be sustained by a coincidence of vital national interests. The European allies continue to share the identity of security interests against the expansion of Soviet control that led to the Brussels Treaty and subsequently to the North Atlantic Treaty. But the acceptance of joint control of nuclear weapons implies a close concidence of a wide range of foreign policies that military power might serve, as well as an identity of security interests against hypothetical military threats. Do the prospective members of a European deterrent group have this kind of political consensus? That is a question which each nation would have to answer before deciding whether to join such a group.

The Benelux countries and Italy, who have little opportunity to become independent nuclear powers by their own efforts and who recognize that their political as well as military interests lie in collaborating with the more powerful nations of Europe rather than in pursuing an independent course, would probably participate in a European deterrent group if France and Germany were members. But would France place the fruits of her nuclear effort under joint control after making such a large investment in an independent nuclear capability as the essential condition of her sovereignty, prestige, and political influence in the world?

If France could really achieve such a large and invulnerable nuclear force as to be confident of deterring Soviet aggression independently of the Anglo-American deterrent, there would be little reason to suppose that she would prefer a joint effort. However, Britain's difficulty in developing an independent second-strike force even with American aid might give France a strong incentive to seek the technical and industrial collaboration of Germany and other allies in a joint effort. In that case, France might be content to pursue her overriding goals of national prestige and political influence by assuming the leadership of an independent European deterrent group, which could be the nucleus of a Third Force in the cold war. That prospect would be compatible with De Gaulle's vision of France's destiny, if—and it is a significant "if"—the system of joint control could be reconciled with his general opposition to supranationalism and military integration. It would be compatible with his efforts to consolidate the Franco-German entente, which has been a central feature of France's foreign policy since Germany joined NATO; and it would be a more attractive alternative to an independent German nuclear capability than the more diffuse restraints of a NATO deterrent. If France conceived of a European deterrent group as a counter to Anglo-American power, she might oppose Britain's membership. On the other hand, she might welcome British membership as a means of sharing Britain's nuclear weapons and knowledge, ending her privileged nuclear relationship with the United States, and gaining an additional counter to Germany, as when Britain's association with WEU eased France's acceptance of German rearmament in NATO.

From West Germany's standpoint, sharing nuclear weapons with her European allies under joint control would be acceptable if it appeared to be the fulfilment of Chancellor Adenauer's goal of achieving national equality within a network of obligations binding Germany to the West so closely as to rule out a resurgence of parochial German nationalism. The move would be congenial with his "Europeanism" and his advocacy of greater military integration. However, in reality, German leaders showed a marked preference for NATO-wide integration to any purely European grouping, for they attached special importance to Germany's ties with the United States. Therefore, the Federal Republic would join a European deterrent group, if at all, only on the firmest assurance that this would not weaken America's military and diplomatic support. And, as during the negotiations on Germany's joining a European army, the Federal Republic would greatly value Britain's association with a European deterrent, providing that Britain's policies toward Berlin and the two Germanys were not too divergent.

British participation in an integrated European deterrent

would be very important, materially and politically, to its success; yet Britain is the major European ally least likely to join. Her chief objections would be those she has cited for staying out of European economic organizations with supranational features: Britain's commitments to the Commonwealth and her special relationship with the United States. To be sure, it is difficult to see how Britain's membership in a European deterrent would interfere with meeting her military obligations toward the nations of the Commonwealth, some of whom (conspicuously, Canada, Australia, and New Zealand) now look primarily to the United States for their protection, others of whom (India, Ceylon, etc.) insist upon meeting their defense obligations unilaterally, and few of whom seem as concerned about Britain's becoming politically and militarily entangled on the Continent as the British. And, as for Britain's special relationship with the United States, it is based not only on a transitory technological superiority over other European allies but also on deep cultural and political affinities, which would not suffer from Britain's contribution to Europe's independent strength and unity. Nevertheless, the sentiments opposing tight and exclusively European commitments are strongly rooted in Britain's historical experience as an insular power for many decades before World War II and as a privileged ally aspiring to consolidate an Anglo-American community after World War II. Moreover, like Germany's interests, Britain's special interests, as she conceives them, would in fact be better protected in a NATO-wide military and political grouping, firmly entangling the United States in Europe's affairs, than in a purely European grouping in which she would have to accommodate her interests to those of her major allies without the mediating influence of the American presence.

Of course, with America's blessings and urgings, this view might yield to some countervailing considerations of national interest. And if joining an integrated European deterrent group appeared to be the only alternative to the proliferation of independent nuclear capabilities, Britain might prefer it as the more promising way to maintain a strategic nuclear force independent of America's. Moreover, like her allies, Britain would be subject to inducements. If France and Germany participated in a deterrent group with American support, Britain might find it difficult to remain aloof, just as she was finding it difficult to remain aloof from the thriving Common Market.

But who would command the deterrent group, and how would its members agree on the procedures for giving the command political direction? It is not likely that the political consensus among a purely European group of allies would be strong enough to resolve these awkward questions. Again, the absence of continual American influence would be a crucial obstacle to allied collaboration.

Nevertheless, let us assume that with American backing it is possible, though not likely, that a number of the European allies, including Great Britain, might perceive a sufficient coincidence of vital national interests to assume the collective responsibility of controlling a nuclear capability independent of the United States. Since this step would surely affect the ties between the United States and her European allies, both would have to consider a European deterrent group not only in terms of the cohesion of the group but also in terms of the cohesion of the United States with her NATO allies, which it has always been a dominant objective of the alliance to consolidate. The two considerations are, in fact, related, since it may be that there is a firmer foundation of political consensus for the support of a joint nuclear deterrent in a grouping that includes the United States than in one that is confined to her European allies.

The firm commitment of the United States to the military and diplomatic defense of Western Europe against Soviet pressure seems likely to remain imperative throughout the 1960's and probably far beyond. If Europe were capable of developing not only an adequate nuclear deterrent but also an adequate shield for local resistance without the collaboration of American strategic and tactical nuclear forces and without American troops, weapons, and matériel, there would be no urgent *military* reason to entangle the United States in Europe's defense. But, in fact, it is quite improbable that Western European nations could achieve such a state of military self-sufficiency for a long time, even if they had the collective will to make the effort. At the same time, their concentration upon this effort would surely be at the further expense of their maintenance of adequate conventional forces.

Moreover, as long as American power and diplomacy remain indispensable elements of constraint upon Soviet designs in Europe (as in Berlin), Europe will need America's close collaboration in the political and psychological warfare that will continue to rage beneath the threshold of overt military conflict. For this purpose the European allies have to be able to commit American military power to the support of common interests and policies on the Continent. Therefore, the question is whether the formation of a European deterrent would help or hinder the necessary degree of American military and political collaboration.

Let us posit the most favorable results: The establishment of an independent European deterrent force would not, in itself, lead the United States to abandon her commitment to come to the defense of her allies. Western Europe is too valuable to the United States for too many reasons. Rather, it would relieve the United States of the major responsibility for supporting this commitment with strategic nuclear power, while relieving her allies of depending on the United States to fulfil that responsibility. This might give the Europeans a responsibility for their own destiny that would actually advance the deterrence of aggression and even enhance American-European solidarity.

The creation of an independent European deterrent would probably create pressures on both sides of the Atlantic to turn over the other elements of American- and NATO-controlled military power to the European powers; but, according to the rationale of an independent European nuclear group, this would be a desirable objective, to be promoted for the sake of a strong and united Europe rather than resisted for the sake of preserving the American entanglement.

In the transitional period there would be a problem of co-ordinating a European strategic force with NATO's tactical nuclear force, since any tactical use of nuclear weapons might lead to their strategic use and since the very distinction between tactical and strategic warfare is blurred when "tactical" weapons can reach hundreds of miles outside the area of battle. Moreover, as Alastair Buchan suggests, since the members of the European group probably would not comprise the whole of NATO in Europe, an integrated European deterrent would "cut across the command structures and political arrangements in NATO which have been built up with so much effort over the last ten years."[6] But let us assume that the difficulty of coordination would not be beyond the organizational ingenuity of SHAPE, the United States, and her allies to surmount. Then, eventually, it would be logical for the European group to take over the control of all nuclear weapons in Europe and include all the European members of NATO. Under these circumstances it would be difficult to envision the United States long retaining her troops on the Continent, since they would no longer be needed as a trip-wire on America's nuclear deterrent. But, ultimately, it would be logical anyway for Europe to assume the entire responsibility for a forward shield as well as for the nuclear deterrent. For, ultimately, America's European allies could possess the independent military strength and political cohesion to contain Soviet pressure on Western Europe in a much looser association with the United States, resembling the original conception of a guaranty pact but without the original dependence on American nuclear power. The United States could then follow her original intention of turning over the day-to-day maintenance of Europe's security to Europe, and she could devote more resources and attention to the diverse tasks of her own security outside Europe.

Surely, this happy sequence of developments is not beyond the realm of possibility. But to perceive the formidable obstacles to its fulfilment one has only to think of the crucial matter of timing involved in the devolution of power and responsibility. At the end of 1960 it seemed certain that a European group could not acquire for at least a decade a sufficient strategic nuclear capability to support an independent military and political policy. But the need for an alternative to the proliferation of independent nuclear capabilities was more immediate. Consequently, if the plan for an independent European deterrent were to serve the immediate purposes of nuclear integration, it would run the distinct risk of starting off the devolution of responsibilities from the United States to Europe at a pace that would exceed the actual shift of power to support those responsibilities. Thus the vital ties to the United States might be loosened prematurely, before the European nations actually acquired the power or the cohesion to pursue a strong independent foreign policy. The very agreement to the plan of shifting America's deterrent responsibility to her European allies would jeopardize the credibility of America's nuclear response to aggressions upon them.

But there is a more basic consideration than transition or timing involved in the transfer of power and responsibility to a European group. That consideration is the kind of foreign policy that such a group would pursue if it *did* acquire the military strength and cohesion to act independently of the United States. Would it be a policy compatible with American interests? As a general objective there has been substantial support in the United States for a united, self-sufficient Europe; but, in practice, this sentiment has been sustained by the general desire to see the advancement of international integration or the specific desire to relieve the United States of material burdens, not by the desire to encourage an independent European political policy. Within the context of her entanglement with Europe, the United States has been able to achieve a satisfactory compromise with and among her European allies on somewhat divergent approaches to the political issues at stake in Europe. Would such a compromise be feasible if Europe were to move toward military independence? Would the European allies, free from the entangled strands of American military and political collaboration, enjoy the political cohesion as well as the independent military strength to contain the resourceful Soviet colossus?

6. NATO NUCLEAR FORCE

It was partly an intuitively negative answer to these questions, by American and other allied leaders, that made the creation of a NATO nuclear force seem more feasible and desirable than the creation of a European deterrent group. Like the proposal for a European nuclear force, the plan for making NATO a nuclear power was envisioned as a means of giving America's allies an equitable share in the control of nuclear weapons, consonant with the altered distribution of power within the alliance, while discouraging the spread of independent nuclear capabilities. At the same time, the proponents of a NATO deterrent hoped that it would avoid the dangers of a purely European deterrent by preserving and, in fact, extending the military entanglement of the United States and Europe, so as to enhance the cohesion of the alliance and insure it against Russian attempts to isolate Europe militarily or politically. Thus, through an integrated nuclear force, nuclear sharing could become an instrument of allied consolidation rather than disintegration.

Clearly, the problem of a safe transfer of deterrent responsibility to NATO would be far easier than to a European group. The United States could give or sell the nuclear weapons to be placed under NATO command and political direction at a pace consonant with her independent deterrent requirements without jeopardizing the military balance, for she would retain a large share of the control of these weapons through her voice in NATO. Given the continuation of an American SACEUR, the United States might even preserve formal custody of nuclear weapons while transferring command and control of them to NATO. To establish the joint nuclear force as swiftly and smoothly as possible, the United States would simply earmark for NATO portions of her nuclear forces, including a part of SAC, which are at present obligated to protect the area, while preserving sufficient forces for her independent purposes. The British and French would also be expected to place their nuclear forces under NATO command, except perhaps for token elements.

If this process of nuclear sharing took place within the context of a general plan for the disposition of all kinds of weapons and forces, as it most certainly should, the creation of a NATO nuclear force might then be used to dramatize a readjustment of NATO's entire military posture. In this way it could provide a badly needed initiative and momentum to an overdue revision of allied strategy and capabilities, a revision designed to make the allies less dependent on nuclear responses to conventional aggression, to enlarge their capacity for limited conventional warfare, and to clarify the method of using tactical and strategic nuclear weapons. Having taken the initiative, the United States would be in a position to facilitate this revision. For example, she might adjust the pace of her assignment of nuclear weapons to NATO to coincide with tangible contributions by her allies to the conventional capacity of NATO's shield.

But even if the establishment of a NATO nuclear force took place under these favorable conditions, the problem of nuclear control would still pose a serious difficulty. Could the operational control of nuclear weapons be shared without, in effect, turning them over to national possession under only nominal central command? How could the command and control of nuclear weapons be shared among fifteen nations in such a way as to permit effective political direction and, at the same time, smooth, decisive operation? Would not any arrangement that effectively put "fifteen fingers on the trigger" and on the "safety catch" undermine deterrence? These were questions that worried both the opponents and the advocates of a NATO nuclear force.

In the case of tactical nuclear weapons, the allies had never determined the exact procedure by which fifteen nations would authorize SACEUR to start a nuclear war, but they could no longer afford the resulting ambiguity if the United States were to give her allies an equal share of the control of nuclear weapons. If effective deterrence would demand the capacity to make a quick and concerted decision to use these weapons and the capacity to use them with discrimination in politically as well as militarily appropriate ways, it might be exceedingly difficult to satisfy the formal requirements of political consultation among fifteen states. Of course, a quick response to the *aggressor's* use of tactical nuclear weapons might be authorized in advance by joint contingency directives, but there could be no advance directives to cover the situations in which the *defenders* would choose to initiate the use of nuclear weapons. If a major conventional aggression developed slowly to the point at which the allies would have to choose between using nuclear weapons or accepting defeat on a conventional basis, there would be time enough for full consultation. But, in this event, it is difficult to imagine fifteen nations resolutely reaching such a fateful decision under the pressure of Soviet psychological warfare, backed by the threat of nuclear retaliation and, possibly, accompanied by offers of political settlement.

Similarly, in the case of strategic nuclear weapons, the problem of combining effective military with effective political control on a multilateral basis was not just how to secure time for political consultation but, fundamentally, how to reconcile the requirements of political control with the requirements of deterrence. In the event of a massive enemy first strike, the response would be virtually automatic, regardless of formal requirements of political consultation. But in contingencies short of that, it would be necessary to determine the use of nuclear weapons by deliberation. If NATO had a sufficiently invulnerable strategic striking force (for which the sea-borne Polaris seemed especially well suited in the 1960's), it might afford the time for some sort of political consultation. But the very process of consultation, almost in proportion to the time it consumed, might diminish the certainty of a nuclear response and provide the Soviet Union with dangerous opportunities for nuclear blackmail and division of the alliance.

Nevertheless, the problem of effective military and political control of a joint nuclear capability might be less serious in practice than it seemed in theory. For in any system of joint control the requirements of maximum speed and smoothness of decision would exceed the requirements of deterrence. With so much at stake, the Russians would surely hesitate to act as though the fingers on the safety catch, so to speak, would check the fingers on the trigger, even though they suspected that the process of multilateral decision-making did not permit a quick or certain collective response.

If deterrence failed, however, the problem of using nuclear weapons in a controlled way so as to maximize the chance of terminating the war short of an unmitigated spasm of violence without simply capitulating would be extremely difficult to solve on a multilateral basis. The strategy, technical means, and organization of the system of central command would have to be very carefully prepared in order to preserve effective political direction and yet remain sensitive to multilateral interests. To gain the latter quality, some price would have to be paid in terms of the former.

For that matter, even the existing dual system of control was not foolproof against decentralized national control either before or after an attack. If the men who operate the weapons components and make the decisions to use them are of different nationalities, they will owe their primary allegiance to different national governments. Therefore, under this condition no system can eliminate the possibility that one nation will try to veto the decisions of other nations or of a supranational command, or the possibility that it will try to override the vetoes of others, perhaps even by seizing custody of warheads. The alternative is, of course, to keep the complete operation of the whole weapons system under unified national control; but that is scarcely feasible, either militarily or politically, in the case of NATO's tactical nuclear weapons, which are the primary nuclear deterrent to conventional aggression. At the same time, there is no sure distinction between tactical and strategic nuclear blows.

Consequently, some "slippage" in military and political control would seem to be a necessary cost of an equitable multilateral participation in NATO's nuclear strategy. The basic assurance of nuclear co-ordination would have to be a strategic and political consensus concerning the use of nuclear weapons, without which no system of control could operate effectively.

Beyond this, what is necessary and not impossible is a politically acceptable system of sharing and control of nuclear weapons under central command that would give sufficient promise of a controlled joint response to aggression to deter the Soviet Union from trying to exploit the process of decision-making, militarily or politically, by playing upon allied differences and paralyzing the collective will. This is a problem of organization but also, fundamentally, a problem of strategic and political consensus.

The precise organization of the system for controlling a NATO nuclear force could only be determined on the basis of a period of discussion and bargaining among the allies, since this is an intensely political, not just a complicated technical, question. The rudimentary plans proposed by NATO officials in 1960 would utilize the existing NATO structure by giving SACEUR (as an officer of SHAPE and of American forces in Europe) military command of the nuclear weapons assigned to NATO. There might be a good case for giving command of sea-based striking power to SACLANT or a special naval commander. In any case, an organization that gave command of nuclear weapons, at least initially, to an American officer would be more politically acceptable to the United States and to all her allies than any plan that would give nuclear command to a European officer of a different nationality. On the other hand, Alastair Buchan proposed creating a SACDET (Supreme Commander, Deterrent) and appointing a European senior officer to fill it, partly to avoid adding to SACEUR's burdens and partly to reassure European public opinion.[7] There could, of course, be mixed schemes of organization, such as creating a tripartite or a rotating military command.

But even more important than the organization of the military command would be the organization of the political command of a NATO nuclear force, for it is especially important to preserve civilian control and political direction of such a decisive weapon. For this purpose a much smaller group than the unwieldy North Atlantic Council would have to assume detailed responsibility for the composition, deployment, operation, strategy, and use of nuclear weapons. Henry Kissinger suggested giving these powers to a defense steering committee —composed of four permanent members (representing the United States, Great Britain, France, and West Germany) and three rotating members elected by the council—which would also have broader responsibility for military strategy, defense policies, and disarmament.[8] To further assure effective political control, there was merit in Buchan's suggestion to revitalize the military Standing Group (composed of the representative of the American, British, and French chiefs of staff) as a link between the political and military planners in NATO. With some such organization of centralized political as well as military control of nuclear weapons, the problem of physical custody of warheads would be far less important. If American laws and sentiment or considerations of international politics and arms control still required continued American custody, that would no longer be such a serious obstacle to collective allied participation in the control of nuclear weapons.

Surely, it is not utopian to suppose that there are modes of organization like these—extensions but not supranational transformations of existing modes—which could satisfy the requirements of deterrence and post-attack control without imposing unacceptable deprivations of national sovereignty. After all, the participant in a NATO nuclear force would have no less control over his military fate than if he were to rely on America's and Britain's independent nuclear capabilities, let alone on two or three additional allied capabilities; and, in the end, he would have far more control than if he were to rely on his own nuclear force. But, clearly, no organization of a collective nuclear force would be either efficacious or acceptable unless it were based on a solid strategic and political agreement concerning the circumstances and ways in which the allies would use and threaten to use all kinds of weapons.

The practical importance of achieving allied agreement on a strategy and capability less dependent on nuclear weapons is apparent when one relates the specific circumstances of decision-making to the requirements of political control. There are two ways of providing political control of decisions to use nuclear weapons. One way is to prescribe in advance the contingencies in which the military command would be authorized to employ nuclear weapons in a particular fashion. The other way is to determine the use or non-use of nuclear weapons when the contingencies arise. (The two ways are not, of course, mutually exclusive.) In some circumstances the first method would be essential, even if only one decision-maker were responsible; but in other circumstances the second method would be necessary, especially if a number of decision-makers were responsible. The first method would put no special strain on the political cohesion of allies, but the second method would. Therefore, so far as possible, the common strategy must be designed to avoid putting the allies in situations in which *ad hoc* nuclear decisions would be necessary or in which they would be particularly difficult to reach.

The members of a joint nuclear force should not find it difficult to specify, in advance, the kinds of Soviet nuclear attacks in which the central military command would be authorized to retaliate proportionately without waiting for extensive political consultation, if any. But it would be impossible or irresponsible for them to anticipate in an instrument of authorization the entire range of conceivable circumstances in which nuclear weapons might be used and to specify precisely how they ought to be used. Moreover, the attempt to do so might only help the prospective aggressor circumvent the conditions that would call for a nuclear response and deprive the allies of the necessary flexibility in managing deterrence. Obviously, making an *ad hoc* decision is more difficult and dangerous for a number of governments than for a single government. Yet, within the framework of a strategic consensus, it should not be impossible to reach a multilateral decision on how to respond to a limited nuclear blow or accident. The kind of multilateral decision that *might* be impossible to reach, at least without disrupting the alliance and playing into Soviet hands, would be whether or not to initiate the use of nuclear weapons. Therefore, it is essential for the feasibility of a NATO nuclear force, as it is essential for the maintenance of allied security and cohesion in any case, that NATO have a strategy and capability for non-nuclear resistance that will enable its members to reserve the decision to initiate the use of nuclear weapons for the most extreme and unlikely contingency of a major conventional conflict. To the extent that tactical and strategic nuclear weapons are second-strike rather than first-strike weapons, and therefore confined to the highly specialized functions upon which allies might readily agree, the problems of joint control will be manageable.

If there were an appropriate strategic consensus in the alliance and the military means of supporting it, the creation of a joint nuclear force, separate from but interlocked with America's force, need not diminish the credibility of nuclear deterrence. Those who fear that it would, reason that allied inhibitions would hamstring the operation of a joint force, whereas a unilateral American force, free of allied vetoes, would be less inhibited. It is true that the United States might, in some circumstances, be less reluctant than her allies to initiate the use of nuclear weapons and perhaps more willing to use nuclear weapons against limited nuclear attacks upon an ally, but even in these extreme cases it is not reasonable to suppose that the Soviet Union would defy the threat of nuclear deterrence if the United States had to get the formal consent of her allies in order to use NATO's nuclear force, but not defy the threat if the United States relied entirely upon her own forces. That would suppose that Soviet leaders would attach unusual importance, for enormous stakes, on the efficacy of formal restraints in a capitalist coalition.

Whether or not a system of joint control existed, America's allies could not compel her, any more than she could compel them, to either use or not use nuclear weapons; and this fact, together with the continual need to sustain allied collaboration, would exert a restraining influence on one power or another regardless of the formal requirements of multilateral decision-making. There might always be some differences of opinion among various allies, and between them and the United States, on whether and how to use nuclear weapons. The organization of a joint nuclear force would not eliminate these differences, but it would actually enhance deterrence if it provided a regular and systematic means of resolving and minimizing such differences, an organized means of maintaining a continual strategic and political consensus in which all allies participated and for which all were responsible. Besides, in the give-and-take of this process one need not assume that the allies would always diminish the American will to use nuclear weapons; the United States might also increase allied will.

The most serious temptation to defy the West's nuclear deterrent and to exploit the threat of war for political ends would be a situation in which the Soviet Union believed it could isolate one ally from the others. Throughout the cold war Soviet leaders have tried to divide the alliance—to apply military and political pressure on one or several allies under circumstances in which the others would not support them—and, especially, to divide the United States from her European allies. But the best protection against this tactic is not to keep the deterrent responsibilities in unilateral American control but to present a common front, which, in collaboration with a resurgent Europe, can only come from shared responsibility. The credibility or incredibility of deterrent threats that determine Soviet action will spring from the continuing evidence of a concerted military resolve, or a lack of it, not from Soviet conjectures about the votes in NATO's nuclear control body in the event of aggression.

If the allies exhibited a common will to meet aggression with the appropriate means, the organizational forms for controlling the use of nuclear weapons would be of secondary importance to the credibility of deterrence. On the other hand, the form of organization could affect the strength of that common will by providing a framework conducive to its development and continual cultivation. The existence of a formal institutionalized means for the collective control of nuclear weapons would be an immense asset to deterrence if it focused attention upon the continual need to maintain the kind of strategic and political consensus upon which the security and cohesion of NATO depends. The very process of organizing a NATO deterrent could provide a new incentive and a dramatic occasion to achieve such a consensus.

But is the creation of a NATO nuclear force politically feasible in the first place? This cannot be determined in the abstract but only on the basis of specific initiatives and detailed negotiations. With vigorous and tactful American support, it might prove acceptable to the British and the non-nuclear allies; but, quite possibly, France would decline to participate —at least at first. And even if France did participate, she might not, under De Gaulle, do so at the price of her nuclear program, regardless of what concessions in military command and political consultation the United States might offer. If, because of the contagious effects of France's nuclear effort, the creation of a NATO nuclear force seemed unlikely to achieve one of its major objectives, NATO might be served better by keeping the existing system of nuclear control and extending strategic and political collaboration on a more informal and gradual basis. Nevertheless, the proliferation of independent allied nuclear forces would probably spell the end of NATO as an integrated military and political organization.

Finally, even if a NATO nuclear force were desirable and feasible on all the aforementioned grounds, its utility would also have to be appraised on another ground: Would it stimulate the diffusion of nuclear capabilities outside the alliance? Some opponents of nuclear sharing contended that it would because (*a*) a NATO nuclear force would give the allies access to nuclear weapons, which they would, in fact, use for independent purposes; (*b*) whether or not a NATO nuclear force actually amounted to spreading nuclear capabilities to independent allied control, it would seem this way to the rest of the world; and (*c*) any actual or apparent diffusion of nuclear capabilities among the allies would stimulate the diffusion of nuclear capabilities among other powers and preclude an arms control agreement to prevent such diffusion. On the other hand, the defenders of a NATO nuclear force contended that (*a*) nuclear sharing under joint command and control offered the best opportunity to prevent the proliferation of nuclear production and ownership within the alliance; (*b*) there would be just as effective restraints upon the independent use of nuclear weapons for extra-allied purposes within the framework of central control as under the existing system of dual control; and (*c*) the joint sharing of nuclear control within the alliance would not affect the acquisition of nuclear capabilities outside, but it might be the necessary condition for securing the accession of potential nuclear powers among the allies to a treaty to prevent nuclear testing, production, or lending.

If one regards the spread of nuclear capabilities outside the alliance as a more serious menace to Western security than America's refusal to assist nuclear sharing under joint control within the alliance, the decisive questions upon which the adoption or rejection of a NATO nuclear force should rest are (*a*) whether achievement of an effective international agreement (tacit or formal) to stop the spread of nuclear capabilities would be made likely if the United States were to reject nuclear sharing under either independent or collective control and (*b*) whether creation of a NATO nuclear force would be likely to stop the spread of independent nuclear production and ownership among the allies. If the answer to the first question is affirmative and the second negative, then it would not be worth sharing the control of nuclear weapons by creating a NATO nuclear force, at the risk of spreading or appearing to spread independent nuclear capabilities among the allies and beyond. If the answer to the first question is negative and the second affirmative, it would not be sensible to forego the opportunity of stopping the diffusion of independent nuclear production and ownership among the allies by creating a NATO nuclear force merely in order not to appear to impede nuclear diffusion beyond. If the answer to both questions is negative, then the adoption or rejection of a NATO nuclear force should be based on other grounds than its effect upon nuclear diffusion. But, if the answer to both questions is affirmative, one is indeed faced with a delicately balanced issue, which must be judged on the basis of relative probabilities.

In 1961 the likelihood of an international agreement that

would stop the spread of nuclear capabilities seemed extremely remote. A nuclear test-ban agreement was the most likely of all agreements intended to stop diffusion, but it seemed clearly infeasible. Moreover, even if a formal test ban were achieved and all potential nuclear powers acceded to it, by itself it could have only a slight psychological effect toward stopping diffusion by transfer or production without testing. In any case, Communist China would surely acquire her own nuclear capability regardless of international agreements, world opinion, or any other political obstacle.

The establishment of a NATO nuclear force seemed far more feasible than the achievement of an effective international agreement to stop nuclear diffusion, but it would carry no guaranty of stopping the spread of independent nuclear production and ownership within the alliance. On the other hand, if a NATO nuclear force would be a contribution to allied security and cohesion on other grounds, there was enough of a chance that it might also at least confine and moderate the spread of independent nuclear efforts among the allies to make it unwise to forego this opportunity merely on the tenuous supposition that a joint force would stimulate the diffusion of independent nuclear production and ownership outside the alliance.

Non-nuclear powers outside the alliance would have no additional reason, except the contagion of fashion and relative prestige, to acquire nuclear weapons merely because the NATO allies received them under joint control. Even if these powers did not trust the restraints of joint control, they would not need nuclear weapons to counter allied weapons, since it is quite improbable that the allies would need or want to use nuclear weapons independently against these powers. If an international agreement to stop nuclear diffusion were feasible, a NATO nuclear force would not necessarily be incompatible with it. It would not be incompatible with a nuclear test ban or with a production cutoff; it might, in fact, be the necessary condition for gaining allied adherence to either. It would be difficult to square with an agreement by the nuclear powers not to transfer weapons, even though they would be transferred to the allies under formal joint control. But the Soviet Union would not transfer nuclear weapons to the unilateral control of other powers merely because the United States shared nuclear control with her allies, and neither the United States nor her allies would have any interest in transferring weapons to powers outside the alliance anyway.

The conclusion that emerges from these speculations is that the choice posed for the alliance by the diffusion of nuclear technology was not simply between complete nuclear abstinence and unrestricted nuclear indulgence but rather between the diffusion of nuclear capabilities under independent control and the diffusion of nuclear capabilities under joint control. From the standpoint of the general stability of the military environment as well as from the standpoint of allied security and cohesion, joint ownership and control seemed preferable. It would be an unfortunate irony if the United States and her allies, in order not to jeopardize an international agreement to prevent the spread of nuclear weapons to others, should forfeit the opportunity to check the spread of independent nuclear capabilities among themselves by failing to establish an effective framework of joint control.

But whatever view one might take of the desirability and feasibility of alternative policies for the control of nuclear weapons, at the beginning of the 1960's it seemed that a choice would have to be made, if only by default, on the basis of many uncertainties. For the time to make a choice was probably limited to the few years in which the decision of allies to enter or not enter the nuclear club would still lie in the balance and in which the United States would still retain the preponderant initiative by virtue of her technological supremacy.

10
Disengagement

1. THE NATURE AND PURPOSE OF DISENGAGEMENT

The history of NATO has been one of mounting difficulties in meeting the requirements of allied security and collaboration in the face of political, economic, and military developments (preeminently, the growth of Soviet nuclear striking power) that were not foreseen at the outset. Necessarily, in a defensive alliance entailing a high level of contributions and integration, the chief instrument by which the members of NATO have sought to merge their particular national interests with the mutual advantages of a collective effort, has been military strategy, broadly conceived. Yet, on the threshold of the missile age, there was cause to doubt that the members of NATO would find a satisfactory solution to the problems of security and collaboration within the complex realm of planning, developing, and declaring military capabilities, deployments, and responses. Consequently, the risks, sacrifices, and perplexities of a joint military effort enhanced the appeal of a more direct resolution of the problems of mutual security by a negotiated accommodation with the Soviet Union, intended to mitigate the political source of strategic difficulties. Like the proposals for nuclear sharing, the proposed political accommodations were replete with strategic and political implications that directly affected the core of mutual security interests sustaining the alliance.

Hopes for a political amelioration of the sources of tension and insecurity in the center of Europe have been focused upon a variety of proposals that are commonly subsumed under the general term "disengagement."[1] Some of these proposals have called for nothing more than arms limitation and control in the center of Europe. In this category the most notable were British Foreign Minister Sir Anthony Eden's suggestion at the Geneva summit conference in July, 1955, of "a demilitarized area between East and West" and Polish Foreign Minister Adam Rapacki's proposals in 1957 and 1958 of a "denuclearized zone," prohibiting the production, stationing, and use of nuclear weapons and reducing conventional forces in Poland, Czechoslovakia, and the two Germanys.* However, the most comprehensive proposals have envisaged, in addition to the limitation and control of weapons and forces in a central zone, the withdrawal of foreign troops and the reunification and neutralization of Germany under a mutual security guaranty. The two most in-

* Actually, Eden presented two different plans at different times. On January 29, 1954, at the Four-Power Conference of Foreign Ministers in Berlin, he proposed, simply, the reunification of Germany by free and supervised all-German elections. However, the Eden Plan that was repeatedly referred to in Soviet proposals was the one Eden presented at Geneva on July 18, 1955. The part of this threefold plan that got the most attention and came to be identified with the plan as a whole was the proposal of a demilitarized area between East and West. However, the other parts proposed a supervised limitation of forces and armaments in both Germanys and in the neighboring countries and a mutual security pact to guarantee a united Germany against aggression. Eden said that the whole plan was intended to provide the Soviet Union with reassurances that would make the unification of Germany, free to join NATO, acceptable to the Soviet Union, but Soviet leaders, in their subsequent references to the plan, chose to ignore this aspect.

Rapacki presented his first plan to the United Nations General Assembly on October 2, 1957, and in a memorandum to the powers concerned on February 15, 1958. It proposed an "atom-free zone," to include Poland, Czechoslovakia, and both parts of Germany, in which "nuclear weapons would be neither manufactured nor stockpiled, the equipment and installations designed for their servicing would not be located there, the use of nuclear weapons against the territory of this zone would be prohibited," under a system of ground and aerial control. Rapacki announced the second version of his plan in Warsaw on November 4, 1958. In this he added a reduction of conventional forces in the zone, to go into effect after a first-stage ban on nuclear production and simultaneously with the other denuclearization features.

The complete texts of the two Eden and two Rapacki plans are among the appendixes in Eugène Hinterhoff, *Disengagement* (London: Stevens & Sons, Ltd., 1959).

fluential plans of this scope were presented in 1957 by the British Labor party leader Hugh Gaitskell and by George F. Kennan.*

Kennan's proposal, coming at a time when Russia's launching of the Sputniks had made Europe acutely conscious of the hazards of NATO's nuclear dependence and coinciding with a Soviet diplomatic offensive aimed toward "summit" talks, which were designed in part to forestall the placement of American missiles in Europe, caught the fancy of many Europeans. To them, and especially to the British, it seemed like the basis for a political breakthrough in the menacing perplexities of military security. In the course of 1958, however, Russia's renewed intransigence and her patent opposition to the reunification of Germany, together with the coolness of Western governments to a scheme of such far-reaching implications for the strategic and political bases of the security system they had so laboriously created, rendered disengagement a dormant issue.

Premier Khrushchev, confidently proclaiming that the bal-

---

* Gaitskell first presented his plan on January 11, 1957, in the Golkin Lecture at Harvard, which was published in *The Challenge of Coexistence* (Cambridge, Mass.: Harvard University Press, 1957). Here he proposed the reunification of Germany, the withdrawal of foreign troops, and the limitation, inspection, and control of armed forces in Germany, Poland, Czechoslovakia, and Hungary, and, if possible, Rumania and Bulgaria. He speculated that "the Russians might refuse to contemplate the plan without the neutralization on both sides [of Germany] from the start." He opposed the withdrawal of American troops from the Continent. In an article in *Foreign Affairs* in July, 1958, entitled "Disengagement: Why? How?" he presented a modified version of this plan. Gaitskell's plan was almost identical to the plan formulated by his colleague Denis Healey, who largely devised it.

Kennan made his proposal in the Reith lectures at Oxford in November, 1957, and in BBC broadcasts that December. He published it in his book *Russia, the Atom, and the West* (New York: Harper & Bros., 1957), chaps. iii and iv. It included the reunification and neutralization of Germany and the withdrawal of foreign forces from Germany and Eastern Europe, all under guaranties by the great powers. Germany would be under some kind of military restriction (certainly including the prohibition of nuclear weapons), and the European and NATO countries would depend for local defense on "paramilitary" forces "of a territorial-militia type." In his broadcast on December 20 Kennan said he was prepared to see all American forces withdrawn from the Continent and eventually from Britain. In January, 1959, Kennan defended his original proposal and indorsed the Rapacki Plan but said that Geman security should depend on twelve German divisions instead of on paramilitary forces ("Disengagement Revisited," *Foreign Affairs*, XXXVII [January, 1959], 187–210).

ance of power in the world had shifted to the Soviet Union, now concentrated on getting the West to recognize East Germany and withdraw from Berlin. He regarded the only basis of negotiations as Western accession to such stock Soviet demands as a ban on nuclear armaments and tests, the liquidation of all foreign bases in Europe, and a non-aggression pact between the NATO and Warsaw Pact countries. The principal feature of the disengagement proposals that he formally indorsed was Eden's plan to create a demilitarized area and Rapacki's plan to prohibit the stationing and production of atomic weapons in a Central European zone.* Although the British government favored negotiating on such a plan, the United States, supported by Germany and France, curtly rejected it as disrupting NATO's forward strategy without providing any security against violations by powers outside the proposed zone.

The major Soviet goals in Europe continued to be Western recognition of East Germany, the prevention of West German rearmament, the isolation of West Germany from her allies, the sealing-off of the East-West escape route in Berlin, and the removal of the Western presence in Berlin. However, Khrushchev preferred to pursue these goals by inviting a showdown on Berlin and exploiting Western fears of Soviet missile power in order to exacerbate the "contradictions in the capitalist camp" rather than by negotiating comprehensive disengagement schemes, which, by compelling Soviet withdrawal from East Germany, would deprive the Soviet Union of a valuable forward position, jeopardize Soviet control over the East European satellites, and revive the dreaded specter of German expansion eastward.

Thus, suddenly, on November 10, 1958, he demanded an end of the four-power occupation of Berlin and informed the Western governments that they would have to get out of West Berlin and make it a "free city" within six months or else deal with East

---

* However, during a television interview with American journalists in June, 1957, Khrushchev, in an expansive mood, also suggested that the United States and other countries withdraw foreign troops from Western Europe, in return for which Russia would withdraw her troops from Eastern Europe (Hinterhoff, *op. cit.*, pp. 204–5).

Germany, to which the Soviet Union intended to turn over all her rights in the city. Eventually, through a skilful combination of threats and diplomatic overtures, the Soviet premier first removed President Eisenhower's objections to a summit conference by conceding in the famous Camp David meeting that there would be no time limit on negotiations about Berlin and then succeeded in manipulating an extension of this "slow ultimatum" to get the Western governments, contrary to all their original protestations about the futility of such a vague and unpromising venture, to assemble in Paris in May, 1960, for a four-power conference. Then, when the delegates had assembled in Paris, he dramatically withdrew from the conference before it could convene, while bitterly denouncing the flight of the American U-2 espionage plane shot down over Russia.

Yet, despite this rude end to the disengagement ferment stirred up by Kennan's lectures two-and-a-half years before, there could be little doubt that, if Khrushchev so chose, still another Soviet gesture toward a negotiated "relaxation of tensions" would revive Western interest in the project. For disengagement continued to be the most hopeful political means of relieving NATO's military troubles. And disengagement seemed like the only feasible means of resolving the problem of a divided Germany, which could otherwise ignite the spark of a military conflict that even the most complete military preparation might not prevent or extinguish. Therefore, disengagement deserves serious analysis in a study of the strategic problems of NATO because any plan to mitigate the political source of security problems is intrinsically important, because such plans could someday become mutually acceptable, and because, even if they do not, their mere formulation or lack of formulation will affect one of the primary political issues in the cold war: the place of Germany in Europe.

For the purposes of this analysis we can think of disengagement as including any one or all of the following three components: (*a*) the withdrawal of Soviet and American and other foreign troops from a zone embracing the two Germanys or beyond; (*b*) arms reduction, limitation, and control in such a zone; (*c*) a political settlement unifying Germany and determining the restrictions, if any, upon her armament and upon her political commitments; (*d*) some guaranty by the United States, the Soviet Union, and other powers of these three components.

From the West's standpoint the principal value of any scheme of disengagement will lie in alleviating the military and political sources of tensions that jeopardize the maintenance of security by peaceful means. Through disengagement the West may also seek to strengthen its political position and weaken Russia's, just as Russia would cetainly hope to advance her political ends against the West. But it is unreasonable to expect either of the two competing nations or blocs of nations to enter knowingly into an agreement that would result in a significant accretion of the relative power of the other. On the other hand, disengagement might reasonably require one or both sides to sacrifice something of immediate security, political advantage, or the immediate reduction of tensions and the risk of war in order to promote the achievement of these goals in the long run. Yet there are clearly stringent limits on the extent to which nations can legitimately sacrifice familiar conditions of military security in the short run—which, after all, may be decisive—for the sake of achieving hypothetical military and political advantages in the future. Accordingly, every disengagement proposal should be assessed in terms of a balance of military and political objectives in the short run and long run. With these standards of appraisal in mind, let us consider each of the four components of disengagement to see whether it would be desirable if it could be negotiated. Then we can consider whether a negotiated agreement would be feasible.

2. WITHDRAWAL OF FORCES

Would the withdrawal of Soviet, American, and other forces from a central zone help to reduce tensions and the danger of war in a manner compatible with Western security? The answer would seem to be, "By itself, no," for the proximity of Soviet and American troops is not the source of tensions in Europe.

The real source of tensions is, first, the deep conflict of interests and aims between the NATO powers and a dynamic state moved by a revolutionary ambition to which their very existence is an obstacle and, second, growing out of this fundamental conflict, the explosive political situations, such as the division of Berlin and Germany, from which military conflicts might result. Military disengagement might be the necessary condition for the political amelioration of these situations, for it might adjust the military balance to support a new political configuration; but, in the absence of such amelioration, military *engagement* is probably the best assurance of peace with security.

To be sure, a disturbance in Berlin or East Germany would be less apt to involve foreign troops immediately if they were disengaged; but, if neither the Soviet Union nor the United States wanted to engage in an armed conflict, both powers would have a greater incentive and would be in a better position to control a disturbance and to see that the other side or its allies did not foment or exploit it if their troops were on the forward line. Far from reducing tensions, the withdrawal of foreign troops, in the short run at least, would remove a stabilizing influence from an area that would be inherently unstable politically. A withdrawal of foreign troops that left Germany divided would be especially conducive to tensions and warfare.

But what if there were also some political settlement of the German problem? Let us assume that, as in Kennan's proposal, withdrawal would be a concomitant of the unification and neutralization of Germany. Would it then promote military and political stability?

The process of unification would have to be carefully phased with the process of withdrawal in order to preserve a safe balance of power during the transition; but, at best, withdrawal would create a dangerous period during which rival groups would struggle for political control and try to settle old grievances. A settlement of the Oder-Neisse border would be indispensable if disengagement were not to agitate this old source of German-Polish conflict. Yet, if the zone of withdrawal included the East European satellites, there would be many other ethnic and territorial differences to jeopardize a peaceful withdrawal, and the resulting tensions would be compounded by the internal upheavals accompanying the departure of the Red Army.

The transition to a new military and political order in Europe might well lead to a reintroduction of Soviet forces, for, regardless of Soviet good intentions in withdrawing troops, a violent transition threatening the survival of "friendly" elements might lead Soviet leaders to change their minds. In any case, with a huge Soviet army intact on the border of withdrawal and with Communist agents still active in the satellite states, the Russians would have to exercise unprecedented forbearance to refrain from indirect intervention by subversion, political infiltration, or the support of civil war. Yet the Western powers would find it politically very difficult to intervene to counter Soviet pressure, short of a massive Soviet military reoccupation. And if American forces had been withdrawn from the Continent, even the direct intervention of Soviet forces would be militarily very difficult to counter quickly enough to be effective.

However, we are speaking here of risks, not certainties. It is also possible that the Soviet Union would not withdraw her troops in the first place if she had not correctly assessed the consequences and reconciled herself to the risk of counter-revolutionary regimes or a number of "revisionist" regimes coming to power. It is plausible to suppose that Moscow would undertake such a drastic step as withdrawing the Red Army only in anticipation of securing some general political advantage that would outweigh this risk, and that, having taken this step, it would be prepared to accept reversals in the zone of withdrawal rather than sacrifice the overriding purpose of the withdrawal by trying to restore Russian occupation. It is not inconceivable that the states from which the Red Army was withdrawn would ease the transition to independence by remaining sufficiently friendly to the Soviet Union and sufficiently aloof from the West and by retaining sufficient internal stability, together with adequate conventional resistance strength, to enable the Russians to withdraw gracefully and to discourage them from returning. If so, the risk of inciting new tensions and new dangers of war in the short run might be moderate enough to be a price worth paying for long-run stability.

In estimating the dimensions of this risk, the crushing of the Hungarian revolution in 1956 is not a directly relevant precedent, since Soviet forces had never been withdrawn from Hungary and Hungary's independence was not guaranteed by an East-West agreement. A more relevant precedent might be the experience of Yugoslavia, Austria, Finland, or Sweden, who, even without a specific Western guaranty of their sovereignty, have succeeded in retaining their independence—and, in the case of Yugoslavia and Finland, in the face of great Soviet pressure and the proximity of overwhelming Soviet military strength. The analogy between the position of these neutral states and the hypothetical position of Germany and East European states in a zone of withdrawal is imperfect, since the present neutrals are beneficiaries of a general balance of military power on the Continent that would be substantially altered by Germany's withdrawal from NATO. But the point here is simply that neutral states are not necessarily helpless Soviet pawns, subject to imminent Russian occupation, merely because they are denied ties of military collaboration with NATO. Their independence depends equally upon their internal strength and cohesion, the quality of their diplomacy, and the nature of the general military balance that is maintained by others.

In our preoccupation with the military requirements of containment, reinforced by the oversimple analogy we tend to draw between the problem of containing the Soviet Union and containing Hitler's Germany, we tend to forget that countervailing military power projected abroad by formal commitments to protect territorial boundary lines is only one factor among a variety of non-military factors that may account for the deterrence of aggression. The image of the Soviet Union being restrained from occupying every piece of territory near its borders that is not already under the domination of the Red Army solely by the fear of military resistance or nuclear reprisals is a great oversimplification of the complex motives that actually guide the policy of a regime which by ideology and experience is acutely sensitive to the political and psychological conditions of national power.

Nevertheless, it would be foolhardy for nations who have a choice to intrust their security entirely to non-military deterrents or to ignore the political and psychological conditions of security that depend upon the mere existence of a certain balance of military strength and upon expectations about when and how armed force might be used. In this respect, it is apparent that a withdrawal of foreign troops from the center of Europe would directly contravene the conditions of allied security that previous chapters have discussed.

One essential condition of allied security is the belief which NATO creates in the Soviet mind that one member cannot be attacked without involving the Soviet Union in a war with all members and, especially, with the United States. The neutralization of Germany and the withdrawal of American and other NATO troops could not help but weaken this belief. The withdrawal of foreign forces from the forward line would render Germany more dependent upon the deterrent effect of the West's strategic nuclear power while reducing the credibility of that deterrent in both Soviet and non-Soviet eyes. The Eastern European states, which the United States has clearly considered beyond the sphere of interest that she would protect at the risk of war, would be far more isolated and vulnerable than the Western European states were before the establishment of NATO.

The corrosive impact of disengagement upon the credibility of the American commitment to defend Western Europe, let alone Eastern Europe, would be especially severe if American troops withdrew from the Continent altogether. Perhaps this complete withdrawal would not be inevitable. The insistence of General Norstad and other American military authorities that withdrawal from the Continent would be necessary because of the great expense and difficulty of relocation and the lack of space for realistic training and maneuvers may, as Michael

Howard suggests, be due to "the very natural reluctance of men who have spent nine years in creating a complex and expensive organization to contemplate dismantling their creation and going through the whole business again,"[2] rather than to insurmountable obstacles. The presence of a few American divisions in France and the Lowlands, although foreign troops are never completely welcome anywhere for long, should not prove politically unacceptable, if the host countries regarded them as the price of securing the overriding advantages of the withdrawal of Soviet troops. Nevertheless, at best, even partial withdrawal would tend to undermine the deterrent and resistance functions that NATO's shield is supposed to perform. Certainly, it would put Germany in an intolerably exposed position unless Soviet forces were withdrawn beyond the Polish-German frontier to the borders of Russia.

Mr. Kennan contended that even if American and British troops were withdrawn from the Continent, Europe would not be less secure militarily:

> We must get over this obsession that the Russians are yearning to attack and occupy Western Europe, and this is the principal danger. The Soviet threat . . . is a combined military and political threat, with the accent on the political. If the armed forces of the United States and Britain were not present on the Continent, the problem of defense for the continental nations would be primarily one of the internal health and discipline of the respective national societies, and of the manner in which they were organized to prevent the conquest and subjugation of their national life by unscrupulous and foreign-inspired minorities in their midst.[3]

These words describe a conception of the requirements of cohesion and security which Kennan and many others considered adequate when the alliance was established, but many things have happened since then to enlarge and complicate those requirements. Most important, the growth of Soviet nuclear striking power has made more urgent the need for ground forces capable of an "intermediate response," and this is not a function which could be performed by the "paramilitary" and civil resistance forces which Kennan originally proposed to substitute for "foreign garrisons."[4] Kennan himself eloquently expressed the reason for this need:

> The beginning of understanding rests, in this appalling problem, with the recognition that the weapon of mass destruction is a sterile and hopeless weapon which may for a time serve as an answer of sorts to itself and as an uncertain sort of shield against utter cataclysm, but which cannot in any way serve the purposes of a constructive and hopeful foreign policy.... The suicidal nature of this weapon renders it unsuitable both as a sanction of diplomacy and as the basis of an alliance. Such a weapon is simply not one with which one readily springs to the defense of one's friends. There can be no coherent relations between such a weapon and the normal objects of national policy. A defense posture built around a weapon suicidal in its implications can serve in the long run only to paralyze national policy, to undermine alliances, and to drive everyone deeper and deeper into the hopeless exertions of the weapons race.[5]

Nevertheless, if the allies remain unwilling to increase the capacity of NATO's shield for conventional resistance, and thereby adopt a suicidal defense posture by default, there is merit in Kennan's judgment that it is more desirable to get the Soviet forces out of Central and Eastern Europe than to retain foreign garrisons in Germany and cultivate a German contribution to NATO for the purpose of opposing them while they remain there.[6] Would Western Europe be any less secure from Soviet aggression than at present if Soviet forces were five hundred miles eastward? Surely Western forces on the Continent could return to their former position in the center of Europe before Soviet forces. Suppose, as Mr. Gaitskell and Mr. Healey proposed, that Germany and the other nations in the zone of withdrawal were armed with substantial conventional forces of their own. Could they not perform the functions of NATO's present shield? Assuming the internal stability of these states and their willingness to combine militarily, their conventional forces could at least prevent infiltration, stop the Russians from making a territorial grab without a major effort, and delay a massive invasion. In fact, such a conventionally armed buffer zone might come closer to providing the kind of intermediate response General Norstad has called for than NATO's present forward line, which seems unable to assume any role between that of a conventional police force and that of a tactical nuclear trip-wire. Militarily, at least, the extra space provided by the buffer zone might compensate for the absence of the integration and joint planning with Western forces that NATO's present forward line enjoys.

However, the crucial consequences of a new military balance under disengagement would be its political and psychological effects. Would the nations in the buffer zone, deprived of their formal connections and the ties of collaboration with Western forces, be able to muster the will and common purpose to withstand Soviet pressure backed by an overwhelming military machine designed to isolate and intimidate them? Even within NATO the security and cohesion of the alliance have come to require more than a mere political guaranty. No political guaranty given by NATO to the states in the zone of withdrawal could compensate for the absence of tangible ties of military collaboration. As Michael Howard has observed, "It is one thing to go to the help of a powerful and integrated alliance capable itself of considerable resistance; it is quite another to help effectively a small power whose neighbors have been bribed or intimidated into neutrality and which would probably be overrun in a few hours."[7] Therefore, again, it would appear that disengagement would be compatible with European security only if the nations in the zone of withdrawal had adequate internal stability and the political capacity to present a common front to Soviet blackmail. But these conditions are not likely to exist, especially during the period of transition from engagement to disengagement.

3. ARMS LIMITATION AND CONTROL

Like the withdrawal of foreign troops, a thinning-out or denuclearization of forces in the central buffer zone would fail, by itself, to mitigate the basic cause of tension and the danger of war, which lies in the division of Germany and in other concrete manifestations of the underlying East-West political conflict in

Europe. At the same time, regional arms limitation and control would not help much, if any, to stabilize the military balance, in the absence of a political accommodation.

The prohibition of nuclear arms would somewhat reduce whatever risk there is that states in the zone might stumble into a nuclear war by accident, but it would not impede nuclear weapons from being quickly introduced into a conventional conflict from beyond the zone, whatever formal prohibitions against the use of nuclear weapons there might be.* At the same time, it would deny West Germany access to tactical nuclear weapons on an equal basis with the other NATO members and confine her exclusively to the role of a conventional buffer, while the adversary retained a full arsenal of nuclear and conventional forces beyond the zone of withdrawal.

Nevertheless, a denuclearized zone would not impose a decisive military disadvantage on NATO in protecting Europe if West Germany remained a member of NATO and were permitted to have a conventional force of from twelve to eighteen divisions integrated with other alliance forces under SHAPE. And one can imagine a limitation of conventional forces in the central zone that would also be compatible with Germany's and Europe's military security. In fact, establishment of a suitable ratio of German forces within such a limitation might be a more effective way of meeting the requirements of an intermediate response than trying to build NATO's forward line up

---

* Khrushchev has conceded that any atom-free zone would be within range of Russian and Western nuclear weapons and has said that the guaranty of such an agreement would depend merely on the promise of the nuclear powers not to employ weapons against the zone. Thus, in answering arguments put forward by some Scandinavian politicians for Soviet reciprocity in banning atomic weapons on Soviet territory, he said, "If we consider the range and power of the contemporary rocket and nuclear weapons, a mere 100, 200, or 300 kilometers is of no real importance. Thus rocket- and atom-free zones in a part of Soviet territory will give no guaranty to the Scandinavian countries. If we speak about the problem of guaranteeing the security of the Scandinavian countries in case they are included in an atom- and rocket-free zone, we should take into consideration that both the Western countries and the Soviet Union should undertake to treat the territories covered by this zone as situated beyond the range of rocket and nuclear weapons and to respect the status of that region. The United Nations could be invited to take part, in some form or other, in the solution of the problem" (from a speech in Poland on July 21, 1959, quoted in Hinterhoff, *op. cit.*, p. 294).

to thirty divisions with a dual capability—an effort which, even if it succeeded, might lead the Russians to counteract it with increases in their own conventional forces. On the other hand, if the Federal Republic were deprived of her NATO ties, a ban upon her possession of nuclear weapons would only further isolate and weaken her in the face of Russian pressure. She would be especially susceptible to a Russian offer to grant her reunification on Russian terms.

Nevertheless, a denuclearized zone including Germany might be an indispensable condition for achieving the reunification of Germany through an East-West settlement. Thus Sir Anthony Eden regarded his proposal of a demilitarized zone as a means to "insure that the unification of Germany and her freedom to associate with countries of her choice shall not involve any threat to anybody."[8] Rapacki and Khrushchev, however, regarded a denuclearized zone only as a means of preventing West Germany from acquiring nuclear weapons. They did not couple it with German unification. In addition, they held out the prospect, always appealing in the West, that the achievement of one arms agreement would lead to other arms agreements. Eden also pointed to this prospect in presenting his own plan, when he said that it was, in part, "intended to make a practical experiment in the operative control of armaments" and expressed his hope that "this, if locally successful in Europe, might, as it were, extend outwards from the center to the periphery."[9]

It is reasonable to envisage a plan for a regional nuclear ban and the limitation of conventional forces as the necessary condition for the unification of Germany in a manner compatible with the security of Germany and her neighbors, but it is difficult to see how it might become a first step to broader disarmament agreements, which the great powers have been unable to achieve by more direct means. The reasons that broader disarmament agreements have proved unacceptable are far more deeply rooted than any superficial distrust and suspicion that might be dissolved by a harmonious experience in administering a Rapacki-like agreement. Surely, if the nuclear powers cannot agree on a nuclear test ban or a nuclear production cut-off as a step toward limiting the diffusion of nuclear capabilities and production, a denuclearized zone in the center of Europe would not be a step toward that end. And neither the general problem of reducing armaments nor the more limited problem of providing mutual assurance against surprise attack is analogous to the special problem of limiting and controlling arms in a geographical zone.

Therefore, if there are net advantages to be gained from a plan for nuclear and conventional restrictions in a zone of withdrawal, they are, first, that it might be the necessary condition for securing the unification of Germany and, second, that it might then provide protection against the threat of limited aggression, as a supplement to what would remain of NATO's shield.

4. THE UNIFICATION OF GERMANY

If disengagement is to reduce tensions and the danger of war in a manner compatible with European security, this will be principally because it facilitates a political resolution of the problem of the two Berlins and two Germanys and because it leads to a settlement of the problem of the relation of Germany to the rest of Europe. For these are the basic sources of conflict in Central Europe, not the proximity of foreign troops or their numbers and armament.

The long-run problem of Germany's place in Europe is how to satisfy the legitimate national aspirations and guard the security of a mighty nation in a central strategic position without alarming other European powers and tempting them to make her the object of their diplomatic and military incursions, either to weaken her or to add her power to their own. The more immediate form this problem assumes is how to gain Soviet agreement to the unification of Germany without undermining the security of Germany and Western Europe or, failing that, how to permit the continued division of Germany without weakening Germany's allegiance to NATO or driving her into a bilateral deal for unification with the Soviet Union.

But at the beginning of the 1960's the German problem was posed most directly by the renewed Soviet threat to Berlin. The

Western position in Berlin was a precarious one, which Moscow showed a disturbing determination to make more precarious by a variety of harassing moves directed against the viability and independence of West Berlin. The position of the West in a divided Berlin could not, however, be separated from the position of a divided Germany in Europe.

To appreciate the immense political significance of this dual division, one must first understand that for the present Russian leaders, as for Lenin and the Bolsheviks, the capture of Germany is the key to the domination of all Europe, and that West Germany, next to the United States, is the greatest single national obstacle to Soviet ambitions in the world, as well as the greatest potential asset. If Germany cannot be captured, it must at least be weakened and denied to the West. Second, one must understand that the occupation of East Germany and East Berlin is vital to either the neutralization or the acquisition of West Germany, quite apart from its independent value as a military base and a dependably orthodox adherent of the Soviet bloc. For, since the Russians cannot militarily capture the whole of Germany without precipitating a war they wish to avoid, they must at least consolidate their rule in the Eastern part and exploit the division of Berlin, as means of gaining their dual objectives by diplomacy and subversion.

Yet in this endeavor the Russians encounter major obstacles in the weakness and unpopularity of their East German satellite, in the strength and vitality of West Germany, and in the existence of a free and thriving West Berlin in the midst of Communist territory. They must, therefore, at least secure the West's full recognition of East Germany, because this would bolster the Communist regime, demoralize those who seek self-determination there and in the other satellites, end the free Germans' identification of their hopes for unification with their Western ties, and make it apparent to the Germans and all other parties concerned that the Soviet Union has the sole power to grant or withhold this major national goal. And they must also try to gain control of all Berlin or at least destroy its vitality, because this would eliminate the symbolic capital of an eventually united and free Germany, completely destroy the prospect of deliverance throughout Eastern Europe, close an embarrassing and debilitating escape hatch, and seriously damage confidence throughout the world in the trustworthiness of American and allied guaranties of security. The effect of either the full recognition of East Germany or the capture or emasculation of Berlin would be to demoralize and isolate West Germany, humiliate her allies, and lay the foundation for the Soviet Union to deal with her on a bilateral basis.

It was undoubtedly with these considerations uppermost in his mind that Khrushchev reactivated the Berlin crisis in November, 1958, and began heating it up in the summer of 1961. He was probably emboldened by his interpretation of the favorable shift in the world balance of military power, tempted by signs of Western division, and perhaps prodded by internal pressures and by Chinese disaffection to distinguish himself as the leader of international communism—to make his mark on history as more than just the successor of Stalin—by gaining a victory against the heartland of the capitalist world.

Even if he should not succeed this time, he or some future Russian leader would try again. Therefore, for the West the division of Berlin was a distracting and dangerous source of tension, which could be alleviated, if at all, only by a political settlement. On the one hand, the NATO powers could not afford to let such a powerful symbol of Western vitality, honor, and cohesion come under Communist control. But, on the other hand, they could at best only maintain the status quo against non-military incursions intended to isolate and conquer the city, while they were certainly unable to defend Berlin *with* local military action and probably unable to sustain it against another blockade *without* local military action.*

---

* Although more supplies were stockpiled in West Berlin in 1961 than in 1948, the standard of living there was much higher and the city was much more dependent on outside supplies. Airlift capacity was greater in 1961, but new electronic devices would permit the Communists to interfere with all but visual landings by allied aircraft and so greatly reduce the airlift capacity, which narrowly saved Berlin in 1949. Consequently, if the Russians chose to institute another blockade and maintain it long enough, the West would probably have to supply Berlin on the ground by armed convoy.

Yet it was probably futile to try to remedy the Berlin situation by any diplomatic settlement confined to Berlin itself. For, considering the irreconcilability of the Eastern and Western interests involved, no redefinition of rights would eliminate the source of tension as long as Berlin remained a city under divided control, with its routes of access to West Germany passing through Communist territory; and no system of international control of a united Berlin could supplant the city's direct association with West Germany and her allies as an effective guaranty of its security. Western hopes for this kind of solution betrayed a misapprehension that the Soviet Union had a mutual interest with the West in alleviating a source of tensions in Berlin or that she was in such a weak position that she was compelled to stabilize the local situation. Actually, the Soviet interest lay in exploiting tensions arising from the division of Berlin in order to gain recognition of the East German regime and, if possible, to unify Berlin under Communist control. She was certainly under no compulsion to stabilize the Western position in Berlin. Therefore, from the Western standpoint the resolution of the Berlin problem could come only from the unification of Berlin within a reunified Germany. Otherwise, the Soviet Union could always precipitate a crisis that would compel the NATO powers to go to the brink of war or incur the odium of appeasement.

The desirability and feasibility of reunifying Germany were intimately tied up with disengagement, for if the Russians would agree to the unification of Germany under any circumstances, they would certainly agree to it only if a united Germany's military and political ties with NATO were severed and foreign troops were withdrawn. Whatever else one might say in behalf of the West's insistence that a united Germany should have a free choice in determining its military and political orientation, one could not reasonably maintain that the Soviet Union would ever accept such a provision, since a united Germany with a free choice would join NATO.

But let us assume that military withdrawal and neutralization would make the unification of Germany feasible. Would it also be desirable? I have already discussed the likely effects of disengagement upon the security of a united Germany and the rest of Europe. They would be serious but not disastrous, if the terms of withdrawal were equitable and if the states in the zone of withdrawal were sufficiently stable, militarily strong, and united to protect themselves from indirect aggression and discourage the Soviet Union from attacking one in the expectation that the others would not join its defense. Reunification would be incompatible with German security if Soviet troops withdrew no farther than the Oder or if American troops withdrew from the Continent. A nuclear arms prohibition and a limitation of conventional forces might be necessary for a safe and politically acceptable agreement. Politically, an orderly process of unification consistent with genuine self-determination would have to be based on internationally supervised free elections, not on some kind of "confederation" negotiated by the two German governments. Disengagement would have to be accompanied by recognition of the Oder-Neisse line as the German boundary, so that a united Germany would not be a continual source of political instability in Central and Eastern Europe. (Indeed, there is a good case for the NATO powers, with West German assent, publicly accepting this line as permanent anyway, as a means of improving West German–Polish relations and depriving Russia of a lever to reinforce Polish dependence.)

But even if German unification could be brought about under these optimum conditions, there was a widespread fear in Europe that a united Germany would be a disturbing and dangerous influence because she would return either to an imperial policy or to a policy of collaboration with the Soviet Union. The fear was understandable. Yet, if this was a danger at all, it was less serious than the danger of a divided Germany.

Militating against the resurgence of an imperialist Germany, there would be not only the chastening impact of the Hitler era but also the novel risks of military expansion in the nuclear age. These restraining influences would be reinforced by a nuclear prohibition and a numerical limitation upon German forces. One cannot exclude the possibility of a Russo-German alliance.

But the common analogy of the Rapallo treaty of 1922 is strained, since the Soviet Union would not be a weak state seeking German economic and military assistance, and Germany would not see herself as a nation isolated and suppressed by an unjust Western peace treaty, which she was determined to rectify by turning to the East for help.* If there is a serious danger of a united Germany's severing her ties with the West and joining with the Russians, it lies in the possibility that the division of Germany will lead a desperate and frustrated Federal Republic, unable to get support for her security or for unification from her Western allies, to seek support from Russia.

Nevertheless, an inherently powerful, though formally neutralized, Germany might very well be a disturbing influence in Europe in other ways. It is difficult to imagine such a strong nation in such a crucial geopolitical position placidly playing the non-alignment role of Switzerland or Austria, and it is difficult to imagine the Soviet Union and the United States indefinitely allowing her to play such a role. The question of which way and for what purposes Germany might throw her weight would create a far more fluid and unstable political balance in Europe than the division of Germany permits. Even the most circumspect German diplomacy might not appease the fears and suspicions of her smaller and weaker neighbors. Only if a unified Germany were to become an integral part of a larger European federation, together with neutral East European states, might she mitigate the unsettling consequences of her neutral status; but the political conditions for such a federation scarcely exist.

On the other hand, the continued division of a resurgent

* The Rapallo treaty is commonly regarded as a symbol of the whole development of military, economic, and political collaboration between Germany and the U.S.S.R in the postwar years, culminating in the Nazi-Soviet Nonaggression Pact of 1939. But, actually, it provided merely for the resumption of full diplomatic relations, the mutual cancellation of claims, and most-favored-nation treatment. Secret arrangements for military collaboration had already been made, without the knowledge of German civilian cabinet members. The significance of Rapallo was that it marked the success of Soviet diplomacy in splitting Germany off from the Western community, which had already ostracized her.

Germany could be even more disturbing from the West's standpoint, if, as seems likely, reunification remains a compelling national goal, which the Federal Republic cannot afford to abandon.[10] For, unless the West can convince the Germans that their alliance with NATO is a better assurance of reunification than neutralization and military withdrawal—a proposition that must seem more untenable the longer Germany remains divided—they may conclude some day that the principal obstacle to unity is Germany's membership in NATO, not Soviet imperialism. With a little Soviet encouragement, some future Bonn government might then be tempted to use its economic and military potential (perhaps including a nuclear capability) to bargain directly with Moscow, trading Germany's NATO attachment (and certainly her nuclear arms) for reunification. As Kennan warned, such a bilateral deal, "however innocuous or even constructive in its consequences" it might be, "would set in motion trains of memory, suspicion, and resentment of which only the Communists could be the beneficiaries," if it were made against the wishes of "a Western community which had nailed its flag to the mast of an unconditional capitulation of the Soviet interest in Central and Eastern Europe."[11]

To be sure, in 1961 it was as difficult to foresee conditions under which the Soviet Union would actually grant Germany unification as it was to foresee conditions in which the West German government would accept unification on Soviet terms. But, since Russia was the only country that could grant unification, it would be remarkable if she did not some day, as before the Paris Agreements, use this powerful card in her deck at least to exploit the *prospect* of unification in order to isolate West Germany from the Western community. To offset this danger was one of the best reasons for the NATO powers to formulate and propose a reasonable agreement for German reunification, in order to demonstrate who was to blame for partition. But since such an agreement, to be reasonable, would have to be acceptable not only to the Western powers but also, within some plausible bounds, to the Soviet Union, a proposal of reunification would have to include neutralization (that is, a prohibition upon Germany's joining NATO or the Warsaw Pact), arms limitation, and military withdrawal.

Of course, even to present such a proposal tentatively without assurance that West Germany approved it would defeat its purpose. In 1961, the Bonn government remained adamantly opposed to any disengagement plan. Hence, her allies could scarcely press this major power to contravene her government's conception of a vital interest merely in order to place the onus of German division on Russia. On the other hand, the Bonn government and her allies could not indefinitely pretend that unification might be obtained by integrating West Germany into the Western community. If reunification through comprehensive disengagement were to be ruled out, West Germany would sooner or later have to accept the fact that the implicit condition of her entanglement in NATO is the suspension of her ambition to unite with East Germany. This would not solve the problem of Berlin, but it would at least impede the Russians from exploiting the division of Berlin and Germany to divide the alliance.

As long as the West Germans know that it is the Russians and not their allies who bear the onus of partition, the security of Western Europe will be served better by the Federal Republic's membership in NATO than by her unification with East Germany under the only terms that Russia might conceivably accept. As long as the West German government is not tempted to make a separate deal with the Russians for unification, the liabilities of a divided Berlin and Germany, from the standpoint of NATO as a whole, are counterbalanced by the advantages of West Germany's integration in NATO and by avoiding the risks of reunification through disengagement.

However, Kennan rightly suggested that more is at stake in the issue of German reunification than the welfare of NATO and *Western* Europe; the welfare of Eastern Europe is also involved, and the interests of the United States are bound up with the state of Europe as a whole. For the division of Germany, he said, is inseparable from the larger issue of the division of

Europe. Here he put his finger on a basic difference of outlook that separated him from the opponents of disengagement. The difference sprang from divergent conceptions of NATO's purpose.

What concerned Kennan most deeply was that the division of Germany meant the division of the Continent into two hostile blocs and that, with time, this alienation of the eastern from the western half would become irreparable and the absorption of Eastern Europe into the Russian empire final. This prospect was the antithesis of Kennan's original and abiding conception of NATO's purpose as a political guaranty extended to Western Europe to permit the Europeans to recover their inherent strength and stability and to permit the West to negotiate an all-European settlement with the Russians. Describing his view of the original presuppositions of the North Atlantic alliance, Kennan wrote in 1959:

> There were those of us who, in the inspiring days of the birth of the Marshall Plan and NATO, conceived that the purpose of the cultivation of Western strength was to place the West in a position where it would some day be able to negotiate the liquidation of the vast misunderstanding represented in the division of the continent. What loomed to us at the end of this road we were entering upon was not the crushing of Soviet power by the force of our actions but compromise—compromise on terms more favorable to ourselves than the conditions of that day would have permitted—compromise that would have given not only to a portion of Europe but to the great body of it the possibility to live. Here lay the connection, which so many have found it so hard to discern, between "containment" and "disengagement." And while it did not occur to us that the *substance* of the gains we hoped to see made in Western Europe could ever be regarded as expendable for purpose of negotiation . . . it also did not occur to us that there was to be, in the institutional and particularly the military devices which we were then creating, anything so sacrosanct that these devices could not one day be modified to be exchanged in favor of one with a wider range of relevance and acceptance.[12]

In contrast to this vision of a united Europe, Presidents Truman and Eisenhower and Secretaries of State Acheson and

Dulles were content, for all practical purposes, to look forward to a strong and united *Western* Europe. When they looked beyond the immediate problem of redressing the imbalance of power on the Continent, they were inspired, not by the rather nebulous image of a general European community, but rather by the vision of a united Western Europe tied to the United States in an Atlantic community, including Germany firmly integrated with her democratic neighbors through a network of political, military, and economic strands that permitted her to regain her natural power within the restraints, and for the benefit, of a Western coalition[13]—a vision that coincided with Chancellor Adenauer's eagerness to associate German nationalism with a larger European loyalty. Consequently, whereas Kennan deplored the entanglement of Western European economic collaboration with military obligations, because it would prejudice the extension of the institutions of collaboration to the whole Continent,[14] his opponents applauded the further elaboration of these institutions in a Western European framework and welcomed the entanglement of Western Europe's economic ties with local and transatlantic political and military obligations as one of the most encouraging developments in the cold war. They warned that disengagement would destroy this evolving integration in the Atlantic community and that a neutralized Germany would be a danger to the West, to the Soviet Union, and to the Germans themselves.

As for entering into negotiations to end the division of Germany and Europe, all spokesmen of the Truman and Eisenhower administrations officially looked forward to a negotiated removal of what Kennan called the "great political and military cramp" in the center of Europe, but they professed to believe that this would come about when the West achieved such a powerful political and military posture and when a prospering democratic West Germany exerted such an irresistible "attractive power" that the Soviet government would have no alternative but to accept unification on the basis of Germany's freedom to join NATO. By this formula they paid the verbal price for West Germany's willing collaboration with NATO and perpetuated a delusion, which served, in effect, as a justification for keeping Germany divided.

Secretary Acheson often described the purpose of building "situations of strength" as enabling the West to reach political settlements with the Soviet bloc on outstanding differences. But, typically, he made this point in the context of explaining to those who were urging the American government to enter into negotiations that it was fruitless to expect acceptable accommodations with the Soviet Union until the unfavorable distribution of power on the Continent had been rectified. This was his response to the Soviet proclivity for timing proposals for German unification to coincide with crucial periods of Western integration and military build-up. He believed that when the Russians saw an interest in making some genuine political accommodation, they would do so suddenly and quietly, without regard for the fanfare of negotiations, as in terminating the Berlin blockade of 1949 or signing the Austrian State Treaty in 1955.

In truth, neither Acheson nor Dulles was disposed to sacrifice the tangible progress, so laboriously achieved, in strengthening and knitting together a European-Atlantic community incorporating West Germany, in order to engage in dubious diplomatic ventures directed toward some improbable new European order. They were convinced that the Soviet Union regarded these ventures as only a species of political warfare to confound, divide, and undermine the North Atlantic alliance in order to prevent the Western powers from getting on with the main task of building up the common defense. On this point Dulles differed from Acheson only in emphasis. Secretary Dulles made fewer verbal concessions to the sentiment for negotiated settlements with the Russians than Acheson, openly taking the position that agreements with a state dominated by Lenin's ideology and the Communist party could not be trusted and meeting Soviet overtures for conferences with demands that she first demonstrate "good faith." In Dulles' mind, useful negotiations would have to await not merely a situation of strength but the transformation of Soviet society.

As for the consequences of this NATO-first policy for the future of Eastern Europe, Acheson held that the necessary condition for the Soviet satellites to recover their national identity and keep up their hopes in the meantime was a strong NATO. Anyway, in his view, the Russians could not afford to withdraw their troops as long as withdrawal would lead to the immediate overthrow of Russian-controlled regimes. Therefore,

> A further process of evolution is necessary, both within the Soviet Union and Eastern Europe, before a change to more complete national identity in the latter can take place without erupting into a violence which might engulf the world. When that evolution occurs, Russian and American troop withdrawals may be possible without destroying the basis of American association in the security of Europe.[15]

This was much too indefinite and unlikely a prospect to suit Kennan. "The rosy prospects which Acheson and others discern at the end of the present road of Western policy," he wrote, "seem to rest in general on the possibility for an extensive breakdown of Soviet power," which, in 1959, he regarded as too improbable to figure seriously in the calculations of Western policy.[16] However, Kennan misconceived the nature of the expectations about Soviet power held by the opponents of disengagement, and he exaggerated the significance of these expectations in determining their views on containment.

Kennan himself had once regarded the natural outcome of containment as the "break-up" or "mellowing" of Soviet power.[17] President Truman and Secretary Acheson put more stress on the latter prospect than on the former.[18] Secretary of State Dulles expressed early optimism about the break-up of the Soviet empire in Eastern Europe but later looked chiefly toward the moderation of Soviet policy.[19] Yet there is no evidence that these hopes entered into the calculations of Western policy in any concrete way, any more than hopes for "liberation" affected actual policies.

In the minds of most American policy-makers the task of containment in Europe—building up a strong coalition in which West Germany would be an essential participant—was desirable in itself, for political as well as military reasons, and would have to persist as long as the Soviet threat to Europe remained. But in Kennan's view containment would not achieve its legitimate purpose until a broad European community emerged from the preliminary effort to restore a situation of strength in Western Europe. Having lost his original confidence in the break-up or mellowing of Soviet power in the course of the first decade of the cold war, in the second decade he looked to a negotiated settlement to prevent the irrevocable division of Europe into hostile military coalitions.

Between these two views of the future of Europe, the prevailing one, which underlay the creation and evolution of NATO, is the more promising as a basis of policy. For NATO has consolidated a military and political framework of security in Western Europe that probably could not be achieved in a general European community even if the Soviet Union were to abandon her ceaseless political warfare. Nevertheless, Kennan's proposal was directed toward a serious policy vacuum that needs to be filled by something besides the delusions that Bonn can have both German unification and integration with the West and that Western firmness will lead to a mellowing or break-up of Soviet power. A democratic coalition can acquiesce in the division of Europe and make the best of it, if it has made every reasonable effort to end the deadlock, but it cannot afford simply to adhere doggedly to the status quo, to base its whole security and welfare on the continued partition of Germany and the division of Europe into hostile blocs, on the untenable premise, which most of its members in fact reject, that this will unite Germany and restore peace to Europe. Nor can it afford to seem to have a vested interest, with the Soviet Union, in perpetuating Communist rule over peoples who once were and still yearn to be free.

If a reasonable plan of reunification under comprehensive disengagement remains unacceptable to both West Germany and the Soviet Union—which seems almost certain—the Western powers should, nevertheless, continue to assert their interest in ending the partition of Germany and the Russian occupation of

Eastern Europe. They should assert it, not by mere exhortation and idle demands upon the Russians to remove their troops, but by presenting concrete diplomatic alternatives and taking specific actions which the peoples and even the governments of Eastern Europe will understand as genuine efforts to move toward a viable alternative to their present servitude. The most effective actions would be part of what has been called a policy of "peaceful engagement";[20] that is, actions designed to increase political, economic, cultural, and other informal contacts between the West and Eastern Europe, including those between West and East Germany, toward the end of stimulating further diversity in the Communist bloc and enabling the Soviet satellites to achieve a greater measure of independence within the bloc. The ultimate goal of this policy, as of disengagement, would be not the merging of Western with Eastern Europe and certainly not the sacrifice of Western political, economic, and military integration for the sake of some larger European community, but rather the creation in Eastern Europe of a cohesive group of non-aligned states, enjoying genuine self-determination in their internal affairs—a "cordon sanitaire" that would be neither a threat nor a temptation to the Soviet Union. If such a neutral belt of nations could gain sufficient stature and confidence to be a genuine buffer zone instead of a power vacuum, the Soviet Union might finally see her mutual interest with the NATO powers in bringing about the reunification of Germany under disengagement—a Germany that would retain all her ties to the Atlantic community except those of military alliance but that would no longer be a menace in the eyes of those east of the Oder-Neisse. If Moscow still rejected this solution, the division of Germany would at least be less of a menace to the security and peace of Western Europe.

5. POLITICAL GUARANTY

Any form of disengagement, but especially one embracing political as well as military changes, would be a potentially disturbing alteration of the status quo. The stabilization of the new political and military relationship would require the absolute co-operation of the most powerful signatories. Consequently, many proposals of disengagement have envisaged a formal political guaranty by the signatories to enforce it. Kennan, for example, proposed writing into the treaty sanctions, which, in the event of an infringement by one party of its provisions for withdrawal, would give the other party clearly specified and automatic rights of re-entry.

The only effective guaranty from the West's standpoint would be one whose violation the West could readily redress by political and military counteraction. However, any agreement guaranteeing a zone embracing Eastern Europe would be far easier for the Soviet Union to subvert and violate than for the West to enforce or rectify. Once the United States withdrew her forces and accustomed herself to the new order of things, it would be extremely difficult for her to retain the level of physical and psychological preparedness necessary to deter or counter Soviet-inspired subversion, infiltration, and limited aggression in the Eastern zone. With the present configuration of national power in Europe, NATO can, with difficulty, sustain the preparedness to guarantee its commitments, but with an altered configuration of power, in which West Germany were no longer an ally, it would hardly be prepared to guarantee additional commitments in Eastern Europe without a major reorientation of its political outlook and its military capabilities as well.

The fact is that NATO exhibits the inertia of an organization whose mutual commitments and contributions have become routine. For that reason it is difficult to enlarge those commitments and contributions, but it is also difficult to reduce them, even though, in the absence of NATO, its members would not now undertake the commitments and marshal the joint effort that has grown out of their original perception of an imminent threat to their security. No new political and military order, adopted as a means of relieving tensions and calling for a reduction of NATO's forces and even membership, and yet entailing an expansion of commitments, could readily become the focus of the same degree of organized vigilance as the present alliance. That, in itself, is not sufficient reason for retaining the status quo, but it should warn us against the danger of altering it.

In order to appreciate the danger of entering into an arrangement so dependent upon Soviet co-operation and yet so difficult to enforce, one need not assume that the Soviet Union would accept such a far-reaching agreement with the express purpose of violating it. For regardless of the Kremlin's original intentions, subsequent developments, including those beyond Soviet control, might well confront her with new dangers and new opportunities that would induce her to undermine the agreement. Considering the likely instabilities in the zone of her former satellites, we must not underestimate Soviet incentives and Soviet resourcefulness in subverting disengagement with sufficient deception and ambiguity to avoid a massive, clear-cut violation. Indeed, circumstances might arise that would permit the Soviet Union, with some color of legitimacy, to construe the very terms of a guaranty to provide a right of intervention. Less flagrant transgressions—say, of the terms of neutralization or arms limitation and inspection—would be correspondingly more difficult to counteract, because the remedy would probably always seem more drastic than the violation.

However, just as important as what the United States and her allies actually might or might not do to redress a violation is what the neutral powers in the zone of withdrawal would believe they might or might not do, in the absence of an actual violation. For the Kremlin's penchant for blackmail—for the political exploitation of military power—would be a more immediate threat than an overt attempt to recover physical control of the area. Almost instinctively, Soviet leaders would try to alienate the neutral nations from the NATO powers and, through a combination of conciliation and threat, orient their policies toward the East. According to a long revolutionary tradition and experience, these veterans of political warfare would surely seek to convince the neutrals that they were exposed and helpless and that they must turn to Russia for guidance and protection. By humiliating the Western powers, by demonstrating NATO's inability and unwillingness to protect the neutral states, and by offering these states favored economic and political treatment in return for obedience, the Kremlin would hope to gain political control under the shadow of Russian military might. Against this kind of threat no political guaranty of the independence of a group of neutral nations would be nearly so convincing as NATO's present guaranty to her allies. If Russia's nuclear might and NATO's' weakness in conventional resistance now raise doubts about the efficacy of the present guaranty, how much confidence could any nation place in the proposed guaranty of disengagement? The question is not rhetorical. It implies only that comprehensive disengagement would entail great risks for the West, not that these risks are under no circumstances worth taking or that there are not comparable risks in the status quo.

6. THE RUSSIAN ATTITUDE

One can argue that the West should formulate reasonable proposals of comprehensive disengagement, providing that West Germany is willing to be a partner to them, if only because Moscow itself may some day hold out the prospect of disengagement and German reunification on terms that a West German government would find difficult to refuse. One can argue that the West must demonstrate with its own plan for reunification and disengagement that Russian design, not Western intransigence, blocks German unification in freedom. Yet a sober appraisal of the history of disengagement raises serious doubts about Moscow's interest in any political and military accommodation in the center of Europe that would be compatible with Western interests.

None of the various proposals for disengagement that the Soviet Union put forward in the period from 1947 to 1961 met the minimum conditions of security, stability, and self-determination that the West could safely accept. The closest that Moscow came to indorsing an acceptable comprehensive disengagement plan was in its note of March 10, 1952, which Molotov reaffirmed in about the same form at the four-power

Berlin conference in February, 1954. This note called for four-power talks on a German peace treaty based on a unified and neutralized Germany, the withdrawal of foreign troops within a year, and a limitation on German armed forces (in contrast to earlier Soviet demands for complete demilitarization), and it dropped the standard Soviet demand for the dismantling of all American overseas bases. However, the note said nothing about free and secret all-German elections, which the West considered an indispensable preliminary to unification,* and it included an ominous insistence on "democratic rights" for all Germans. And, of course, it would have left Soviet troops on the eastern border of Germany.

In Western eyes, another basic defect of the note, which in itself presented a significant concession compared to previous Soviet proposals and which might possibly have been improved upon through negotiation, was its obvious timing to coincide with a critical moment in Western negotiations on the European Defense Community. A fruitless attempt to pin Moscow down to a procedure of all-German elections that would not be rigged in favor of the Communists confirmed the Western decision to reject this diplomatic overture as an attempt to forestall E.D.C. Subsequent Soviet proposals of a similar nature were rejected for similar reasons.

---

* Molotov's 1954 version of this plan followed earlier Soviet unification proposals in providing for electoral procedures calculated to assure Communist domination. It called for intrusting responsibility for the conduct of "free all-German elections" to a provisional all-German government, which would be formed from the parliaments of the two Germanys after the withdrawal of occupation forces. Secretary Dulles, at a press conference on January 13, 1959, led some to think that the United States might be abandoning its demand for free elections and moving closer to the Soviet position when he remarked that free elections were not "the only method by which reunification could be accomplished." However, he seems to have intended only to suggest a more flexible approach to the timing of free elections, which the West had until then always put at the beginning of the whole reunification process. At the Geneva conference of May, 1959, Dulles' successor, Christian Herter, put forward a phased plan for reunification, according to which a mixed German committee (twenty-five from West Germany and ten from East Germany) would be responsible for drafting an electoral law for "general, free, and secret elections," to be submitted for approval to an all-German plebiscite. However, the plan called for the reunification of Berlin in the first phase, with Berlin to be governed by a council chosen by free elections under UN supervision (Hinterhoff, *op. cit.*, Appendix 9).

After the ratification of the Paris Agreements in 1955, when the Federal Republic finally joined NATO, the Soviet Union expressed little or no interest in comprehensive disengagement and took the position that unification must be left to negotiations between the two German governments and must take the form of a neutralized confederation in which the "social achievements" of East Germany would be preserved—a formula clearly calculated to lead Germany down the path of previous coalition governments in China, Poland, Rumania, and Hungary.* Separated from this position were several vague and sweeping proposals calling for the withdrawal of all foreign forces and bases from Europe and the dissolution of military blocs. In 1958 Moscow indorsed the Rapacki Plan but did not associate it with the unification of Germany and was not even clear about whether the Red Army would withdraw from East Germany. Thus, although both East and West officially supported the reunification of Germany, the conditions upon which they would accept reunification were totally irreconcilable, and both sides seemed content to leave the situation at that. The Soviet government—with, seemingly, the French and British

---

* In a speech in Leipzig on March 7, 1959, Khrushchev made it clear that the only unified Germany he wanted was a Communist Germany and that he considered Western recognition of the East German regime as a step in that direction: "We stand for the unity of Germany and the German people want unity. But can the peoples of the world exist if the two German states are not unified? They can, and they can exist quite well. Can the Germans live without reunification? They can, and they can even live quite well. Why, therefore, do we attach such importance to the German problem? Because it is a key link in the problem of war and peace and one of the main sources of international friction and conflict. . . . This is why we are pressing and will continue to press persistently for a normalization of the situation in Germany. . . . But how and on what principles can the reunification of Germany take place? We do not favor reunification in just any form . . . the problem of reunification should be approached primarily from class positions. . . . Why not reunify Germany by abolishing capitalism in West Germany and establishing a working class regime there? This is unrealistic at the present time. But it is even more unrealistic to nurture illusions regarding the liquidation of socialist achievements in the G.D.R. . . . I repeat we are for German unity and the German people will be reunited. It is merely a question of time. . . . Therefore, do not be in a hurry. . . . If our grandchildren are to have grateful memories of us, we must fight unremittingly for the conclusion of a German peace treaty, which will be an important step in the reunification of Germany. What must be done now? A peace treaty must be signed with the two German states in actual existence" (*Current Digest of the Soviet Press,* XI, No. 13, 3–5).

governments in tacit agreement—had decided as a matter of national policy to keep Germany divided.

On November 27, 1958, in notes to the United States, Great Britain, France, and the Federal Republic, Moscow turned to a campaign for disengagement from West Berlin alone, calling for the end of the "unlawful occupation of West Berlin" and the establishment of a "demilitarized Free City" there under a rather ambiguous threat to alter the existing procedure for military traffic between West Berlin and West Germany and to bestow full sovereignty upon the East German government in the city if the Western powers did not display sufficient interest in this proposal within six months.[21] Eighteen months of active political warfare waged with this lever won Khrushchev a trip to the United States, President Eisenhower's admission that the situation in Berlin was "abnormal," and a summit conference in Paris but no tangible Western concessions on the Soviet plan to isolate disengagement in Berlin from the problem of disengagement and reunification in Germany. Khrushchev's spectacular torpedoing of the summit conference in May, 1960, ended that particular phase of diplomatic harassment, but with every indication that a new phase would begin with a new President. It did—in August, 1961.

Of course, this unpromising history of disengagement proposals and counterproposals does not prove that the Soviet Union and the Western powers could not have reached at some point—perhaps in 1952 or after the East Berlin riots in 1953 and before the ratification of the Paris Agreements in 1955—a mutually acceptable agreement if the West had really been more anxious to sit down and bargain about the terms; nor does it exclude the possibility in the future. However, the skeptical appraisal of this possibility that emerges from the record of diplomatic parrying is confirmed by the general nature of Russian foreign policy in this period of "peaceful coexistence," as revealed in pronouncements and practice.

Disengagement proposals, like disarmament proposals, presuppose that the Soviet Union has the same interest in reducing international tensions and stabilizing the political and military environment as the non-Communist powers. But there is no indication that the Soviet leaders are frightened of international tensions. Rather, all the evidence indicates that they regard tensions as an instrument of policy to be manipulated so as to overthrow the status quo and advance the predestined triumph of the Communist system. In fact, they regard the status quo itself as the progressive revolution in social and economic relations that is leading to the new world order and resistance to this revolution as a reactionary attempt to change the status quo.[22]

In Khrushchev's view, the proximity of Eastern and Western forces in the center of Europe constituted no danger.[23] The danger to Soviet interests lay in the weakness of East Germany and in the strength of West Germany and the symbolic capital of a reunified Germany, West Berlin. The Soviet forces in East Germany were an essential means of preserving the "achievements of socialism," keeping West Berlin a hostage, and inducing the Western powers to recognize Communist control of East Germany and the other satellites as permanent. International tension was inherent in the opposition of the "capitalist-imperialist warmongers" to these purposes. This tension had to be raised or lowered as the tactical needs of the conflict required.

In the eyes of the Western proponents of disengagement, the terrible possibilities of mutual destruction that lay in such conflicts and tensions made a peaceful accommodation of interests compelling, but in Soviet eyes they made only Western concessions to Communist interests compelling. From Khrushchev's standpoint the spectacular growth of Soviet nuclear striking power could not help but convince the NATO powers that the tensions resulting from their resistance to the progressive alteration of the status quo carried intolerable risks of precipitating a thermonuclear war, which they could avoid only by timely concessions to Soviet demands. For he claimed, and appeared to believe, that Soviet military achievements had effected a fundamental shift in the world balance of power, which had neutralized America's protective nuclear umbrella and rendered her forward positions, as in Berlin, untenable.

But even if Khrushchev had been less confident of the political implications of Soviet nuclear power, he would have had good reasons for preferring the existing political impasse in Europe to any of the schemes for disengagement proposed in the West. The best reason was Russia's inability to withdraw from an area which provided a valuable forward position and a vital buffer zone without a solid guaranty that her satellites would not abandon the "achievements of socialism" and align themselves with the enemy. Developments since the death of Stalin demonstrated that no such guaranty was possible. If Khrushchev had entertained any doubts on the subject, the Berlin riots of 1953 and the Hungarian revolution of 1956 must have convinced him that military occupation by the Red Army was the only safe assurance of friendly Communist regimes in Eastern Europe.

After all, Russia has won no satellite except by military conquest or, as in the case of Czechoslovakia, by subversion under the shadow of conquest; and she has lost the heretical Yugoslavia because she did not occupy it. She has tolerated free, neutral neighbors, like Finland and Austria, but has never withdrawn her forces from an area upon which she had imposed a Communist regime. To do so would be to risk the reversal of the irreversible historical process that prescribes the decay of the capitalist system and the triumph of the socialist system. That would be an intolerable blow to Soviet prestige and to the whole ideological foundation of Soviet authority at home and Soviet influence abroad. Why should any Soviet leader take that risk just when Russia's rising economic, military, and scientific strength and the intensification of the indigenous revolution in Asia, the Middle East, and Africa appeared to promise the extension of Soviet influence and control? What would be the overriding incentives for disengagement?

Fear of unrest in the satellite area might be one of them. For Khrushchev confronted a dilemma in trying to relax the bonds of control over the satellites in order to base Russia's empire on a larger measure of consent than was necessary in Stalin's time, while trying to maintain obedience against the very stirrings of nationalism and freedom that this relaxation encouraged. Yet the more dangerous this predicament might become, the less likely Khrushchev would be to try to resolve it by withdrawing under conspicuous pressure. In any case, the crushing of the Hungarian revolution and the patent unwillingness of the West to intervene seemed to be a decisive reason for restive satellites to seek improvement of their status according to the Polish formula, under Soviet control, rather than the Hungarian formula, against Soviet control. If the Russians ever decided to rid themselves of the burdens of empire in Eastern Europe, it would be because developments in the satellite states themselves gave them assurance of friendly, neutral regimes, which they had no reason to expect in 1961.

Another overriding incentive the Kremlin might have for assuming the risks of disengagement would be the neutralization and denuclearization of Germany. Between Germany's political ties and her nuclear armament, the Russians probably regarded the former as the more fundamental liability, for their overriding objective was to prevent the capitalist adversaries from combining with the United States and with each other, and they considered that Germany's membership in NATO made her an extension of American military power in any case.[24] Yet they would almost certainly prefer a divided Germany with the East firmly under Soviet control to a united Germany whose political orientation was uncertain. For Germany was inherently too powerful and her history too menacing for Russians to trust her as they did Austria or Finland. Consequently, Russia would be extremely unlikely to withdraw her forces unless a Communist or at least a Soviet-oriented regime were assured. Yet there could be no such assurance without the presence of Soviet forces. Under the circumstances, the Russians seemed content to live with the existing division of Europe and to count on time to work in their favor, as they utilized the vulnerable position of Berlin, the threat of German nuclear armament, and the presence of Soviet forces in the center of Europe, backed by Soviet nuclear might, to divide the Western coalition and undermine its will to support an outpost that it could defend only at grave risk of precipitating a nuclear holocaust.

Only if the Soviet Union, pressed by rising unrest in the satellites and thwarted in her ambitions to consolidate Germany under Communist rule, felt compelled to retrench and stabilize her western front in order to contain a threat from Communist China—a contingency that seemed quite remote in 1961—would she be likely to regard the reunification of Germany under comprehensive disengagement as a profitable bargain. But, short of an improbable diplomatic revolution resulting from some such major reversal in Russia's power position, any mutually acceptable disengagement in the center of Europe is virtually precluded.

Yet even if a diplomatic revolution should lead to comprehensive disengagement, this would not eliminate the Communist threat to Europe or the need for NATO to contain it, as long as the Soviet government continued to be moved by a compulsive image of inevitable Western hostility and by a dynamic drive to destroy the centers of Western power. After all, the West's wartime alliance with the Soviet Union did not eliminate that threat. Disengagement would alter—and, in some ways, aggravate—the conditions of tension and conflict in the center of Europe; it would not terminate the cold war. Therefore, insofar as any kind of disengagement is desirable or feasible, it should be viewed as a complement, not as an alternative, to the strategic requirements of allied security and cohesion. In effect, that means that the external and internal strength of NATO is the prerequisite of acceptable disengagement in a general European settlement, just as it is the prerequisite of acceptable engagement in a divided Europe.

11
Conclusion

1. THE MILITARY AND POLITICAL FUNCTIONS OF A TRANSATLANTIC ENTANGLEMENT

The evolution of NATO from a simple guaranty pact to a semi-integrated military organization has been marked by the progressive entanglement of the United States in the military and political policies of Western Europe and by the progressive entanglement of the major European allies in each other's policies. Yet the economic resurgence of Europe and the active reassertion of separate European national purposes, combined with the growth of Soviet nuclear power, the post-Stalinist phase of political warfare, and the prospect of nuclear diffusion, have exerted a centrifugal force within the alliance, while vastly complicating the requirements of collective security. At the root of NATO's resulting troubles is a complex of related strategic issues—all of them revolving around the central issue of the deployment, use, and control of nuclear weapons—which severely taxes the capacity of this peacetime democratic coalition to meet the requirements of allied cohesion with military plans and forces that are adequate for allied security.

For the United States and her allies these issues raise two basic questions, which are crucial to the future of NATO: (*a*) Do their vital interests in the next decade or so require the continued military entanglement of the United States with Europe, or will they be better served by a looser partnership resembling the original conception of a guaranty pact but extended to a more nearly self-sufficient Europe? (*b*) Do their vital interests require the continued development of military integration and interdependence (whether within a European or transatlantic framework), or will they be better served by a looser form of co-operation among nations more reliant upon their independent military policies? This study leads to the conclusion that the best interests of the United States and her allies in the 1960's and into the 1970's—which, in these matters, is the "foreseeable future"—lie in the close entanglement of the United States with Europe and the further development of military integration within the alliance. But within this transatlantic entanglement the European allies must assume a larger share of NATO's collective responsibilities (including the control of nuclear weapons) and material burdens (especially those that support a capacity for non-nuclear resistance) while they continue to increase their political and economic solidarity as a third, but interdependent, force in the world balance of power.

The military and political consequences of the growth of Soviet nuclear power, the need for central but shared control of nuclear weaponry, and the enlarged requirements of a mobile dual-capability ground force have made close military collaboration within a transatlantic framework more important than ever before to all the NATO allies. On the one hand, such collaboration is physically and economically essential in order to meet the expanded and complex requirements of the over-all stability of the military balance. On the other hand, it is politically and psychologically essential, in the face of new centrifugal forces, in order to support allied interests in the continuing political warfare, which is based upon the peaceful exploitation of military power within the framework of mutual deterrence.

The fundamental material fact underlying these two judgments is that no single NATO country can acquire, independently of its allies, and no group of allies can acquire, independently of the United States, an adequate military basis for protecting its vital interests. The fundamental non-material fact underlying the need for close transatlantic collaboration is that there exists a sounder political basis for military collaboration and political co-operation within an alliance in which the United States has a leading role than within any purely European grouping.

In assessing the material and non-material bases of allied security and cohesion, one must reckon with the intimate relationship between military and political factors. It is commonly observed that NATO is more than a purely military organization, but it is not so commonly understood how closely its military and non-military functions are related. Most directly, they are related because the military posture of the alliance is an essential basis of political warfare and diplomacy, affecting the appearance and reality of allied solidarity, determining the anticipated form and consequences of the armed conflict that might grow out of political conflict, and thereby playing a central role in the contest of will and nerves that dominates the cold war. Less directly, NATO's military and non-military functions are related because allied military collaboration calls for consultation and co-operation on the political purposes of the common military effort in order to compensate allies for the sacrifice of independent political control that accompanies the subordination of national to collective military requirements. But, more subtly, the two functions are related because military strategy (in the full sense of the word) is a major medium through which the allies exert their political influence, not only with respect to the adversary but also with respect to each other.

Consider the last point. Obviously, the members of NATO have special as well as common political interests. Yet, under contemporary military and political conditions, they do not have recourse to genuine military independence or to shifts to other alliances as means of pursuing these interests. Instead, a great deal of their effort to promote and safeguard their interests must be transmitted through their influence on the alliance. This influence is, in large measure, a function of their strategic role, which is, in turn, a product of the strategy of the alliance and the terms of allied collaboration. Therefore, by granting or withholding their commitments and contributions in order to get the most favorable strategy and terms of collaboration, the allies try to secure an advantageous strategic role and, through that role, effective political influence.

Thus Britain's independent nuclear program was partly a means of strengthening her special relationship with the United States. West Germany's ardent support of military integration has served as a means of enabling her to become a major power on the Continent without arousing domestic or allied apprehensions, and Germany's allies have regarded her contribution to the alliance as a means of restraining her, not just as a means of enhancing their military security. Avowedly, France's withholding of naval and air units from integration, her insistence on having custody of nuclear warheads on her soil, and her independent nuclear program have been directed toward improving her terms of military and political collaboration and her general status in the alliance. The United States has maintained American troops on the Continent as a means of eliciting allied collaboration, a means more important for its political and psychological than for its military effect. The latent threat of American withdrawal to a peripheral strategy, which is the counterpart of her Continental troops, has exerted a powerful influence on her allies from the beginning. America's policy concerning the control of nuclear weapons and the related problems of nuclear strategy are as important to interallied politics as to collective security.

Of course, all the relationships between the military and political functions of NATO are suffused with another dimension of political influence: the influence of domestic politics. For democratic powers must, in some measure, defer to domestic interests and opinions in pursuing national interests. And the less overt and urgent the threat to allied security, the greater this deference tends to be. A conspicuous example has been the declaratory and operational strategy for the use of tactical nuclear weapons.

These political functions and effects of military strategy emphasize the importance of a transatlantic framework of military collaboration. For America's active and leading role in shaping military strategy and the terms of collaboration has become vital in accommodating the divergent as well as convergent political interests among the European allies. NATO is not only the essential instrument of American entanglement; through that entanglement it is also the essential instrument of European solidarity.

The blending of German, French, and British interests has become so entangled with the terms of military collaboration that to cut or loosen the military ties would be as disruptive to interallied relations as to collective security. Yet, left to themselves, these countries would find such blending far more difficult than within a transatlantic alliance. For American military commitments and contributions exert a preponderant influence upon the terms of allied military collaboration, of which they are an integral part. And American political influence, acting through the leverage of these commitments and contributions, serves as the kind of balance wheel in interallied relations that no other ally could provide.

Therefore, any basic move toward military independence and away from interdependence, particularly the multiplication of independent allied nuclear capabilities or the creation of a European nuclear deterrent group, would tend not only to erode America's commitment to the defense of Europe but also to intensify the divisive and neutralist forces within Western Europe itself. In determining the control of nuclear weapons, as in determining other aspects of NATO's military posture, only the United States has the resources and the political position to elicit the terms of allied military collaboration that will be compatible with both the security and cohesion of the European members. Hence, the advancement of collaboration in NATO and the growth of European solidarity—whether through closer economic co-operation, as in an enlarged Common Market including Britain, or through political and military co-operation—should be considered complementary, not conflicting, processes.

Yet, while the American entanglement is essential to European as well as to American interests, it is equally important that the European members assume, within this transatlantic framework, a larger measure of strategic responsibility, commensurate with the increase of their relative power during NATO's first decade. For the United States will be physically unable and politically unwilling to sustain the military containment of the Soviet Union by itself. If the allies are not given commensurate responsibility, they will not act responsibly; and if they do not act responsibly, the United States will not long discharge the burdens of NATO's strategic tasks for them.

These strategic tasks require hard and unpopular decisions by the allied governments. No member of the alliance is likely to make those decisions unless the other members give tangible evidence of doing the same. But when all members share the burden equitably, governments can appeal for popular support in the name of allied collaboration. Moreover, when there is an equitable division of responsibility, allied governments are more likely to approach the hard decisions squarely on their merits and to educate their citizenry to do the same. Otherwise, they are inclined to play the role of a passive critic of those who seem to control their fate or else to seek control over their own fate by pursuing an illusory course of military independence.

Therefore, a continuation of the dominance of American strategic responsibility in the alliance would be unhealthy. The present dominance is a remnant of a lopsided distribution of allied power that ended with Europe's economic recovery. It becomes more clearly obsolete with every evidence of Western Europe's remarkable economic growth and integration and with every manifestation of the will and capacity of the European allies to assume political initiatives, independently and in concert. Hitherto, the preponderance of American financial, industrial, and military power has served as a substitute for joint planning and multilateral decision-making. Now this preponderance must be altered in favor of a larger and more systematic participation of America's allies in concerting military and political policies.

One striking irony of the cold war is that now the formerly isolationist United States, by virtue of her preponderant power, feels more directly involved in the practical tasks of the power conflict than her front-line allies, who are tempted to view this conflict with something of the disdain, aloofness, and escapism with which Americans once viewed the Old World. Yet the security of the European allies is far more directly and immediately involved in the toils of NATO than the security of the United States was ever involved in the toils of European politics during the heyday of American isolation. What nourishes the illusion of European detachment, as much as any other single factor, is the convenient belief that nuclear deterrence will automatically preserve the military balance and render the collective management of military power unnecessary—a belief for which the United States own strategy is largely responsible. As a result, the alliance suffers from an imbalance of burdens and responsibilities, which impedes a rational response to the objective needs of security and the subjective needs of cohesion.

As James Reston has observed, "The alliance is out of balance mainly because Europe is not doing what it could do, and it is not doing what it could do, partly because it has abdicated and partly because the United States has been willing to carry the load long after Europe was able to do much more in self-defense."[1] It follows that the initiative for a more equitable division of responsibility must come from the United States. Sharing control of the deployment, strategy, and the decision to use nuclear weapons would be a dramatic indication that the United States had assumed that initiative. However, the sharing of military responsibilities cannot be separated from the nature of the whole strategy for which the allies are responsible. Strategically, what is needed, in the first instance, is a less dramatic but more urgent collective effort to relieve defense and diplomacy from the thraldom of inordinate nuclear dependence.

2. THE STRATEGIC BASIS OF ALLIED COLLABORATION

This study stresses the view that allied collaboration can flourish and perform its vital military and political functions only if it proceeds from a continual adjustment of military strategy to meet the changing requirements of allied security and cohesion. At the end of the Eisenhower administration such an adjustment was long overdue. For NATO was becoming more dependent on nuclear weapons, whose warheads were still under independent American (and, to some extent, British) control, while the credibility of a nuclear response and the willingness of allies to remain dependent on American control of a nuclear response was steadily diminishing. At the same time, allied strategy had become permeated with contradictions and ambiguities that prevented the formulation of a coherent military concept, without which there could be no incentive for a basic adjustment.

The history of NATO's strategy (by which I mean the total interaction of allied strategies) demonstrates that perfect strategic logic is precluded by the process of consensus-building among the allies, a process which, quite properly, makes strategy responsive to the non-strategic demands of domestic and foreign pressures. Up to a point, one can regard the resulting strategic contradictions and ambiguities as a necessary concession to the political basis of collective security. However, in the 1950's NATO's strategy exceeded that point; for it no longer provided the minimum conditions of allied security, and it threatened to destroy the incentives for effective collaboration.

As NATO entered its second decade, there was a widespread recognition in all allied countries that the alliance was undergoing some sort of "crisis of confidence" because it had failed to adjust to radically altered conditions. However, in official quarters there was a widespread reluctance to attribute this crisis to serious military-strategic deficiencies or, in any case, to take any measures to remedy such deficiencies. Instead, there was a strong disposition to intrust all security needs to the balance of terror, to turn away from military problems (except for the acquisition or maintenance of an independent nuclear force) and seek salvation in increased political consultation and the further integration of NATO's institutions.

Associated with this disposition, there was a common diagnosis of NATO's troubles which held that its members had been preoccupied with military objectives at the expense of political considerations. But this diagnosis, although substantiated in some instances, missed a more important point: that some kinds of political considerations have exerted too *much* influence, at the expense of military requirements. The diagnosis arose, in part, from a too literal interpretation of superficially military decisions, which, in fact, were made as much on the basis of domestic or interallied political considerations as on the basis of strategic logic. Ostensibly on military grounds, the allies had, in reality, too often sacrificed strategic logic for the sake of domestic and foreign consensus. Hence, in large measure, NATO's military deficiencies and strategic anomalies were the unco-ordinated by-product of an agglomeration of domestic and foreign political pressures, undisciplined by coherent strategic guidance.

In both the cause and cure of NATO's strategic deficiencies, the major role had to be assigned to the United States, who, by virtue of her vast economic and material resources, continued to exert, whether by action or inaction, the preponderant influence on allied military policies. The contradictions between strategic plans, strategic declarations, and actual capabilities for deterring and resisting aggression in Europe; the confusion about the weapons, the targets, and the methods of using nuclear weapons; the indecision and drift concerning the command and control of nuclear weapons; the conflict between military strategy and arms control policy; the ambiguities about the function of local resistance and tactical nuclear weapons in NATO's shield—these deficiencies were, in large measure, a reflection of the contradictions, ambiguities, confusion, and indecision in America's own military strategy. In the absence of an integrated and comprehensive American strategy for stabilizing the whole military environment and an adequate appreciation of the vital role of military power as a political and psychological instrument of foreign policy, the Eisenhower administration was unable to provide the kind of strategic leadership that could orchestrate into some coherent composition the conflicting strategic themes and motifs within the alliance or even within its own government.

3. THE KENNEDY REVISION

The Kennedy administration, in its first eight months, made a start in the right direction toward a comprehensive revision of America's military strategy, a revision which, if carried out in actual capabilities, was bound to have a marked impact on the military posture of the alliance as a whole. Necessarily, the revision began at home. Exactly what it would mean for NATO would become apparent only when America's long-term military program had gained sufficient scope and momentum to permit a range of new decisions and initiatives directly concerning allied strategy and capabilities.

The best-advertised feature of President Kennedy's revision of American strategy was the program to build up non-nuclear limited-war forces, with special attention to guerrilla and "sub-limited-war" forces for use outside of Europe, but also with explicit recognition of NATO's needs. The explicit purpose was to raise the threshold of a limited conventional conflict that the United States and her allies could deter or successfully counter without resorting to the use of nuclear weapons. As the President said in his message on the Berlin crisis, in appealing for an increased defense effort, "We intend to have a wider choice than humiliation or all-out nuclear action."[2] To this end, he requested and received additional appropriations for increasing the Army and Marine Corps combat-ready divisions, the nation's airlift capacity for ground forces, and the development and procurement of advanced conventional weapons. This represented only a minimal rearmament program, but it was, at least, a well-considered step away from the United States overdependence upon nuclear weapons to deter and fight limited wars.

The other aspects of American strategy were not so clearly or completely delineated, but their general nature was foreshadowed at the outset, because it was evident that they would be parts of a comprehensive, integrated strategic concept of achieving stable nuclear deterrence and maximizing the chances of controlling and limiting nuclear warfare if deterrence should fail. In accordance with this concept, the new administration continued but accelerated its predecessor's program to preserve an adequate second-strike force, based primarily on the qualities of concealment and mobility of strategic nuclear weapons. But it also began a real innovation in the strategy and in the command-and-control system of employing nuclear missiles and bombers in order to mitigate the danger that any use of nuclear weapons would lead automatically to an all-out use and in order to provide civilian authorities with new powers of military discretion and discrimination in exercising political control over a nuclear exchange. Consistent with this objective of rationally fighting as well as deterring a nuclear war, the administration also made civil defense an integral part of military strategy, putting it under the Office of the Secretary of Defense and initiating a moderate shelter program designed to reduce civilian damage in the event that nuclear war should occur by irrationality, miscalculation, accident, or escalation.

In the first months of this strategic revision, however, the central matter of the weapons, magnitude, and targets of the strategic striking force and their relationship to the role of a nuclear counterforce capability was not clarified. In its declaratory strategy the administration went further than its predecessor toward ruling out the initial use of strategic nuclear weapons,[3] while it followed its predecessor in publicly formulating the requirements of a strategic striking force entirely in terms of a second-strike force. And, like the Eisenhower administration, the Kennedy administration tried, with partial success, to resist congressional pressure for greater expenditures on the pre-eminent counterforce weapon, the B-70 bomber, while its expenditures on solid-fuel missiles and the bombers already in production did not approach the dimensions that would be required for a useful first-strike capability. But, perhaps because the United States and her allies would not for some time actually possess the conventional capabilities the administration aimed to create, government spokesmen pointedly held open the possibility—while indicating their intention to avoid the necessity—of initiating the use of tactical nuclear weapons, as a last resort, when a major aggression could not be repulsed with non-nuclear weapons.[4] Unlike the previous administration, however, they did not exclude the possibility that a tactical nuclear war might be limited.

Only in the field of disarmament and arms control was there *no* indication of a comprehensive reformulation of a policy that would be integrally related to the nation's total military posture. Here policy remained piecemeal and improvised, a warmed-over version of the incongruous combination of fresh contrivances and stale formulas devised during the previous five years.

Insofar as the administration dealt directly with NATO strategy, it did so largely as an extension of the revision of American strategy. Thus, it explicitly extended the concept of raising the threshold of non-nuclear resistance to the European area, and it urged the major European allies, with little success, to follow America's example in increasing their monetary and manpower contributions to conventional ground forces. At the same time, it indicated that additional American divisions would be prepared to supplement the shield in Germany. On the other hand, in an effort to guard against overdepreciating the credibility of a tactical nuclear response to conventional aggression in Europe and arousing allied (especially German) suspicion that the United States might withhold her nuclear deterrent in an armed clash involving their survival, it joined with allied governments in warning that NATO forces would not refrain from using nuclear weapons rather than suffer defeat without them.[5]

The problem of making the transition from NATO's existing military posture to one that would reserve tactical nuclear weapons as a second-strike and last-resort capability was eased by the renewal of active pressure on Berlin in August, 1961, in that it helped the administration to initiate measures of rearmament it had planned to take anyway. On the other hand, the administration sought to moderate and soft-pedal the transition in order not to appear provocative or militaristic, to avoid starting an arms race in conventional forces, and to allay allied apprehensions that the threat of a tactical nuclear response to conventional aggression might be undermined at a critical moment, while they lacked adequate means of non-nuclear resistance. Yet, despite the difficulty of moving away from NATO's nuclear-bound strategy under the pressure of the Berlin crisis, the Kennedy administration made an important advance by putting prime emphasis on a build-up of non-nuclear capabilities. In time, this initiative might yet overcome the legacy of the past by inducing the allies to abandon their convenient reliance on nuclear deterrence and meet the real military necessities.

On the tangled and sensitive issue of the political and military control of nuclear weapons, however, the new administration retreated from the tentative initiative of the Eisenhower administration, foregoing any action on nuclear sharing at least until more progress should be made toward NATO's non-nuclear goals and until it were satisfied that nuclear sharing could be reconciled with effective and safe central command and control and with congressional sensitivities.

Nevertheless, at the meeting of the NATO foreign ministers at Oslo in May, 1961, Secretary of State Rusk adopted part of Secretary Herter's proposal of the previous December in pledging that the United States would assign Polaris submarines to NATO, evidently under American operational control.[6] And a week later President Kennedy told the Canadian parliament that the United States was looking forward to "the possibility of eventually establishing a NATO sea-borne missile force which would be truly multilateral in ownership and control, if this should be desired and found feasible by our allies once NATO's non-nuclear goals have been achieved."[7]

4. POLITICAL CO-OPERATION

However important the advancement of NATO's military integration and political co-operation might be, the revision of American and allied strategy was surely the first order of business in the 1960's. *Without* the formulation of an internally consistent over-all NATO strategy and the development of suitable military capabilities to support it, military and political interdependence would provide no solution to NATO's problems of security and cohesion. *With* a well-conceived strategy and supporting capabilities, NATO would not need to carry military and political interdependence to the extremes that were required purely by the demands of military and economic efficiency.

NATO is and will remain, so far as one can foresee, a coalition of sovereign nations for the protection of a limited, though vital, core of identical security interests within a mass of convergent and divergent political interests. The effective collaboration of its members depends upon a degree of military independence and, concomitantly, political independence that transcends the requirements of technical efficiency. After all, the nation-state is still—and, in some respects, more conspicuously than ever—the primary focus of political loyalty in human society, even in the advanced industrial democracies, which have cultivated some remarkable new instruments of transnational co-operation.

Nevertheless, it is true that NATO's essential strategic requirements do demand a degree of sustained military integration and collaboration that is unprecedented in peacetime alliances and even in the history of wartime coalitions; and that this degree of integration and collaboration, in turn, demands an unprecedented degree of political co-operation among the allies. The nature, scope, and instrumentalities of political co-operation, however, are things to be developed pragmatically within a pluralistic framework, as the will and habit of interdependence evolve; they are not to be determined mechanically by some doctrinaire conception of unity.

NATO will not elicit the requisite measure of military collaboration if its strategy fails to serve the primary policy goals of the allies, whose freedom of national action it circumscribes. Consequently, military interdependence, in proportion to the restrictions it places on an ally's capacity to support his foreign policy with independent military force, requires that ally's agreement to the political policy for dealing with the central threat that interdependence is intended to counter. In particular, interdependence requires the concerting of allied policy in dealing with the sources of conflict with Russia in Europe, especially because the Soviet threat is posed most directly in non-military forms. Yet political consultation, like interdependence, is no end in itself; its proper form depends on a balance between the theoretical requirements of efficient collaboration and the actual political requirements of blending allied interdependence with national independence.

Despite a tendency to confer verbal indorsement upon the principle of consultation in sweeping terms, the actual approach of the member governments to consultation has been pragmatic and diversified—and properly so. Where they have perceived common interests and dangers, as in their relations with the Soviet Union in Europe and on matters related to the terms of collaboration in the NATO area, they have extensively and effectively used the institutions of NATO not only for military collaboration but also for the co-ordination of foreign policies, a co-ordination which has extended beyond the development of a basic consensus to the formulation of collective positions.[8] Here, what Lord Ismay, the first secretary general of NATO, called "the NATO method"—that is, unanimity through discussion—has worked remarkably well.[9] It must be further cultivated if the reality and appearance of cohesion are to prevail over the centrifugal forces in the continuing political warfare of the future.

Yet the NATO method, carried to extremes, could paralyze allied diplomacy by reducing every diplomatic response and initiative to the lowest common denominator of consensus established by the most obstructionist power, however slight his capacity for coping with the consequences might be. Heretofore, the adverse effects of this method have been mitigated by the reality of American political dominance and by the lack of scope for genuine political maneuver and accommodation with the adversary. But the situation has changed. On the one hand, whether the diplomatic stalemate continues or abates, allied dissatisfaction with American political dominance is bound to increase. On the other hand, whatever may be the disadvantages of dealing collectively with the Soviet Union on European issues, the allies cannot afford to deal with her separately. Therefore, if NATO's collective and internal political necessities are to be reconciled, there must be a more active and purposeful political consultation among the allies, and this consultation must permit a greater flexibility in the modalities of reaching and implementing allied diplomatic positions.

This kind of interallied political activity cannot flourish if it is confined and institutionalized solely within the formal organs of NATO. Actually, the total of allied political co-operation has always far exceeded the sum of political consultation within the organization's regular channels. Collective diplomacy has not prevented political co-ordination bilaterally and within special groupings of allies both inside and outside NATO's auspices. Indeed, it would be unfortunate if the sentiment for multilateral diplomacy, of which the smaller allies (following the lead of Secretary General Spaak) have been, naturally, the strongest advocates, should inhibit individual and bilateral diplomacy in deference to a façade of unity and equality. For, even on matters of common concern in the NATO area, there are important degrees and shadings of interest and responsibility among the allies and obvious limits to the utility of seeking a consensus among fifteen nations.

Presumably, it was to allow proper scope for these political degrees and shadings that the meeting of the NATO foreign ministers at Oslo in May, 1961, rejected the idea of adding any permanent consultative organs to the already complicated bureaucratic apparatus and decided, instead, to rely primarily on *ad hoc* committees, in which only the allies with mutual interests and the most direct commitments with respect to an issue would co-ordinate their policies. On the other hand, if we think of consultation as merely sharing information and explaining and debating policies, the Oslo meeting also indicated a proper and probably inevitable tendency to consult with all allies even on matters outside the NATO area.

The issue of whom to consult, in which way, when, and on what, cannot profitably, at this rudimentary stage of allied integration, be predetermined by fixed institutional arrangements. The allies must, instead, rely primarily upon a few working principles and the informal codification of experience. The greater is the divergence of allied interests and responsibilities on political issues of general concern, the less useful are formal organizational obligations for consultation—especially, consultation leading to decisions. Instead of creating greater unity, such obligations will either create political paralysis or merely aggravate the divisions in the alliance.

Outside the NATO area, where the interests and policies of the allies diverge most seriously, experience demonstrates that there may be no suitable political basis for useful consultation for the purpose of decision-making either inside or outside NATO institutions, except, perhaps, for informal discussions and exchanges of information among the two or three powers with commitments in the area. But this is not the fault of the machinery of consultation, and it cannot be remedied by more machinery. It is the result of the fact that at least three of the major powers in the alliance have important interests in other parts of the world which by no means coincide, even though their pursuit of these interests affects the security and welfare of all the allies.

Clearly, allied foreign policies outside as well as inside the NATO area may impinge upon military interdependence in NATO, and military interdependence in Europe may restrict political independence outside Europe. Therefore, it is true that NATO collaboration would be eased if the allies could accommodate their divergent extra-European policies by political consultation. It is unreasonable, however, to expect allies who have combined to protect a common interest in one crucial area of the world to posit their collaboration within that area upon political agreement in all parts of the world. That is an impossible condition. It is also unnecessary.

Secretary Dulles stated the applicable principle in 1956 when he observed:

> All NATO members would, I think, agree that NATO should not attempt to represent the totality of their policies. . . . Every NATO country . . . has certain vital national interests that may sometimes require independent judgment. Some of us have grave worldwide responsibilities that cannot be effectively discharged unless there is capability of prompt decision and corresponding action. Our consultations must be designed to assure essential harmony in our viewpoints on fundamentals. But the processes of consultation should never enmesh us in a procedural web so that we fall victim to the ability of despotisms to act suddenly and with all their might.[10]

NATO has surmounted major conflicts of interest and policy in the Middle East (especially during the Suez War), North Africa (with respect to Algeria and Tunisia), and Eastern Asia (during the crises in the Formosa Straits and Indochina).* It will continue to surmount similar conflicts as long as the core of mutual security interests that NATO was created to protect seems more important to the key allies with commitments outside Western Europe (particularly, the United States, the United Kingdom, and France) than the divergent extra-European interests that compete for their military support. On the other hand, no measure of allied political consultation can sustain interdependence in NATO if the priorities are reversed, especially in the case of those allies who lack the military power to support both independent and collective commitments.

In this connection, the proposal by President de Gaulle, Viscount Montgomery, and others that the United States, the United Kingdom, and France constitute themselves a political

---

* This is not to say that allied cohesion would not have been benefited by fuller and more candid consultation, if only the exchange of information—especially in the Suez War.

Standing Group in NATO to co-ordinate Western policies throughout the world is unnecessary, unworkable, and perhaps disadvantageous in any case (considering the adverse reaction of extra-European states and of other members of the alliance). In general, all members of the alliance favor consultation; but, in fact, the members of the proposed Standing Group welcome only the *support* of others, not their *advice,* on political problems outside Europe. This situation cannot be altered and might be aggravated by establishing a global triumvirate within the organization. Of course, it is proper and wise that the three allies with the most extensive extra-European commitments should regularly consult each other on global as well as European concerns, but such consultations had better be undertaken informally than institutionalized within the alliance. Actually, in 1960 and 1961, De Gaulle, by virtue of his stature and diplomatic skill, seemed to be achieving the assurance of regular tripartite consultations through conventional diplomatic channels that he had proposed to obtain through NATO.

5. DE GAULLE AND INTERDEPENDENCE

Not only in this respect but in the whole matter of military integration and political co-ordination, President de Gaulle performed the annoying but valuable service of forcing the members of NATO to look again at the fundamental presuppositions of the alliance. He did this by withholding French participation in some aspects of military integration, pursuing an independent nuclear capability, and insisting that France's interdependence with her allies presupposed a larger share in the determination of policy.

These moves were, in part, efforts to restore France's international prestige and national self-esteem. They reflected De Gaulle's particular ambition to gain equality with the Anglo-American entente in the making of strategy and policy and his conviction that NATO integration had been a guise for American dominance.[11] In part, they were also manifestations of his philosophy that national military "co-operation," instead of "co-ordination," is the only relationship compatible with national (or, at least, French) dignity and morale and military efficiency. They sprang, too, from his deeply ingrained view that military power must serve national policy and that, therefore, military interdependence must be based upon a proportionate degree of political consultation.

However, De Gaulle's assertion of France's role in NATO also reflected his assessment of the capacity of NATO to support French security. On this issue De Gaulle seemed to have decided long before he became President that, since NATO could not live up to the pretense of defending France on the ground without obliterating her, France's security would depend almost wholly upon nuclear deterrence. In his view the growth of Soviet nuclear power meant that France could not afford to rely exclusively upon the American deterrent, which might either fail to deter or else rashly precipitate a thermonuclear war. Moreover, in the light of the changing military balance, the United States, he repeatedly predicted (evidently with no tinge of regret), was bound to pull out of Europe and take her warheads with her. Therefore, France needed her own nuclear capability. If France could reinforce deterrence in Europe with her own nuclear capability, then, in De Gaulle's view, the principal task of containment would fall upon France, the United Kingdom, and the United States in areas outside Europe, where Communist advances by military and, especially, non-military means threatened to encircle and isolate the West. As for the limited function of ground defense in Europe, De Gaulle seemed willing to accept the leading role of West German forces on the Continent, which he would reconcile with French power and interests by means of close Franco-German collaboration rather than by the earlier French formula of integration. Therefore, behind De Gaulle's challenge to allied interdependence there lay his reasoned appraisal of strategic as well as political realities.

Considering the critical interest of all the allies in the success of De Gaulle's bold effort to restore France's stability and self-esteem, it seemed expedient and just, at the beginning of NATO's second decade, to give France an equal voice with

Britain in the inner councils of the alliance.* De Gaulle's objectives of political equity for France and mitigation of America's political dominance were compatible with the changes in the modes of political co-operation and the configurations of political influence that were required, in any case, by the general shifts of power inside and outside the alliance. Political equity, however, is a nebulous and subjective thing, which France cannot obtain by mere formal equality; and there may be no concrete concessions in this realm that would induce De Gaulle to alter France's terms of collaboration. Yet, contrary to a general impression, De Gaulle's views on military integration were not inflexible or doctrinaire, as was demonstrated by his acceptance of SHAPE's command-and-control arrangements over French contingents in NATO's shield, France's participation in NATO's air defense system, and her agreement to place German supply and training bases on French soil. With the possible exception of his insistence upon an independent French nuclear force, these views could be reconciled with the imperatives of NATO's security and cohesion, even if not with the aspirations of the most ardent proponents of integration.

However, this reconciliation would depend, not only upon internal political revisions in the alliance, but, equally important, upon a revision of allied strategy to relieve NATO of its paralyzing overdependence on the panacea of nuclear deterrence, a revision which would provide a rational justification for interdependence and assure the firm commitment of the United States to the defense of Europe. Given such a revision, the sharing of nuclear control might be turned toward the consolidation and away from the disintegration of the alliance by offering France, as an alternative to the pursuit of an independent nuclear capability, a share in the control of a NATO

* Inevitably, many aspects of Britain's special relationship would survive any procedural equality of consultation with France on allied strategy and diplomacy. But Britain would have to recognize that, in the long run, she can enjoy no relationship with the United States that impedes the solidarity of NATO, which is America's prior interest; and that her military and political future, like her economic welfare, lies in a closer relationship with the Continental allies.

deterrent that would be compatible with her desire for equal military and political partnership with the United States and Britain.[12] At least one cannot exclude the possibility that France, even under De Gaulle, might prefer to participate in a multilateral system of nuclear control rather than pursue an independent nuclear capability outside the system. Within the framework of a truly flexible military strategy and an integrated NATO nuclear force, the influence of France in the alliance might then be clearly related to her contribution to the needs of collective security rather than to her independent nuclear strength.

But whether or not the joint control of nuclear weapons should prove feasible as an alternative to independent nuclear capabilities, the most important contribution to NATO's security and cohesion would be a strategy that would logically relate the security of all the allies to the compelling advantages of a collective effort instead of one that put a premium upon independent nuclear enterprise. With this kind of strategy the needs of military integration and political co-ordination might readily be met by a degree of interdependence somewhere between De Gaulle's national co-operation and Spaak's supranationalism. Certainly, the alliance could afford to sacrifice something of the efficient and economical use of total resources for the sake of enlisting the collaboration of its members in a strategy more compatible with their security. What it could not afford for long was a military posture so dependent upon nuclear weapons that the members who could acquire them would stake their security primarily upon an independent nuclear effort, while those who could not would seek refuge in political dissociation.

6. NATO IN PERSPECTIVE

In the latter half of 1961, Moscow more openly concentrated its politico-military pressure once again directly against one of the two world centers of non-Communist power, Western Europe, where the cold war had begun. In doing so, it put

NATO back into its proper perspective as the pre-eminent instrument of American security and policy.

This perspective had been somewhat blurred by the apparent achievement of a stalemate in Europe, following the termination of the Berlin blockade, and by the active extension of the cold war into areas outside Europe. It had been partially distorted by a general confidence in the automatic stability of the over-all military balance and by widespread expectations in the United States that the resolutions and operations of the UN, competition for the moral and intellectual allegiance of the new, non-aligned nations, and programs for the economic development of underdeveloped societies would be the dominant instruments of containment in the post-Stalinist phase of the cold war. The turn of events in 1961 did not diminish the importance of the portentous political and social upheavals in the colonial and recently colonial areas. Rather, it emphasized the central significance of the temporarily muted competition of interests and aims that impinged directly upon the area of the advanced industrial democracies.

This change of emphasis in the cold war, in turn, illuminated the crucial, subtle, and pervasive role of military power in the cold war. It demonstrated that, although the balance of terror might have made unlimited war obsolete as a useful instrument of policy, the combination of that balance and the deep-seated political conflict of the cold war had actually enhanced the importance of the *capacity* to wage war, while suffusing it more profoundly with political implications. At the same time, the intensification of the cold war in Europe reinforced the absolute necessity of being able to impose political controls and material limits upon every overt use of armed force if the capacity to wage war should fail to prevent war.

Considering NATO's existing capabilities, together with the irremediable facts of geography, the West operated at a perilous disadvantage in withstanding the calculated piecemeal incursions of the Soviet Union in Berlin. But if this immediate threat could be surmounted with honor and with the alliance intact, the allies might yet profit from the experience by drawing together to buttress the Continent's auspicious economic growth and integration with an integrated military structure of commensurate strength. In the long run, NATO might then make an indispensable contribution to one of the great tasks of modern statecraft: to expand and stabilize an area of mutual restraint upon the use of military power within a hazardous field of antagonistic interests and aims—to achieve essential forms of equilibrium within unavoidable configurations of conflict. Admittedly, in itself the fulfilment of this task would be only a holding action, intended to go as far as possible in civilizing and pacifying the continuing international conflict. But if the NATO nations could achieve that much—if they could develop a military posture that would reliably deter at least the extremities of violence without provoking it and one that could defend free peoples without obliterating them—they might also induce the Russians, and permit themselves, to turn seriously to the task of alleviating the *political* sources of tension and violence, as in the center of Europe. If they could make the military holding action safe enough and reliable enough to remove the constant shadow of catastrophic violence, they might also develop among themselves, as a concomitant of this achievement, new modes of political association, which would show the world that independent nations who concert their arms against the threat of aggression can transcend the limitations of independence by cultivating a broader entanglement for the purposes of protracted peace.

Notes

CHAPTER 1
INTRODUCTION

1. The text of this report appears in the *U.S. Department of State Bulletin* (hereafter cited as *Bulletin*), XXXVI (January 7, 1957), 18–27.

2. *Ibid.,* XXIV (April 30, 1956), 710. Nevertheless, Dulles was careful to qualify the principle of political consultation so as to reserve to the United States the power of independent judgment and action on vital interests requiring prompt decision—especially those interests outside the NATO area that were covered by other political obligations. See the same address, pp. 709–10, and Dulles' news conference on April 24, 1956 (*New York Times,* April 25, 1956, p. 10). On December 12, 1956, Dulles specifically excluded the defense of Taiwan from prior consultation with NATO allies (*ibid.,* December 13, 1956, p. 1). He pledged even more stringent qualifications upon NATO's role in economic co-operation, taking the view that such co-operation was adequately and more properly dealt with through existing organizations created for the purpose. See, for example, his congressional testimony in May, 1956 (House Committee on Appropriations, *Hearings, Mutual Security Appropriations for 1957,* 84 Cong., 2 sess., p. 15). For three analyses of the opportunities and limitations of political consultation in NATO, see Gardner Patterson and Edgar S. Furniss, Jr., *NATO: A Critical Appraisal* (Princeton: Princeton University Conference on NATO, 1957); Ruth C. Lawson, "Concerting Policies in the North Atlantic Community," *International Organization,* XII (Spring, 1958), 163–79; and Carol E. Baumann, *Political Co-operation in NATO* (Madison: National Security Studies Group, University of Wisconsin, June, 1960).

3. For a brilliant analysis of the political role of economic aid in the cold war, see George Liska, *The New Statecraft* (Chicago: University of Chicago Press, 1960).

4. On the most fundamental level of analysis, the outstanding contributions to the systematization of subjective strategic logic are Thomas C. Schelling, *The Strategy of Conflict* (Cambridge: Harvard University Press, 1960), and Glenn H. Snyder, *Deterrence and Defense* (Princeton: Princeton University Press, 1961). The single most extensive application of strategic logic to the determination of military responses and capabilities is Herman Kahn, *On Thermonuclear War* (Princeton: Princeton University Press, 1960).

5. Karl von Clausewitz, *On War,* trans. O. J. Matthijs Jolles (New York: Random House, 1943), p. 580.

6. George F. Kennan, *Russia, the Atom and the West* (New York: Harper & Bros., 1957), p. 93.

7. The novel feature of contemporary military planning is not only the dominant stress upon deterring a potential aggressor from undertaking a variety of military actions, as opposed to defeating him at an acceptable cost if deterrence should fail, but, even more, the stress upon deterring the aggressor by disposing a capacity to inflict drastic and unacceptable costs through reprisals delivered directly upon his homeland, as opposed to relying upon a capacity to deny him his objective by resisting his military effort in the area of battle. The dependence of nations upon deterrence by reprisals means that military plans must largely be based on speculation about what costs, under various circumstances, a potential aggressor will consider disproportionate to the value of his intended objective and his anticipation of achieving it, in the light of the credibility of one's reprisals—a credibility which, in turn, depends upon the aggressor's speculation about one's own balance between expected cost and benefit, in the light of one's anticipation of the probability of aggression and counter-reprisals. Such speculations become especially imponderable when deterrence depends upon such drastic reprisals as to lead to mutual destruction that would be as unacceptable to the deterrer as to the aggressor. For an intensive analysis of the peculiar problems of deterrence by reprisals and by denial in the nuclear age, see Glenn H. Snyder, *Deterrence by Denial and Punishment* (Princeton: "Princeton University Center of International Studies Research Monographs," No. 1, January 2, 1959), and *op. cit.*, especially chaps. i and vi.

8. The mutual obligations of the North Atlantic Treaty are defined primarily in Article 5, which states that the "Parties agree that an armed attack against one or more of them in Europe or North America shall be considered an attack against them all; and consequently they agree that if such an armed attack occurs, each of them . . . will assist the Party or Parties so attacked by taking forthwith, individually and in concert with the other Parties, such action as it deems necessary, including the use of armed force." The British wanted the Treaty to commit the signatories to take military and other action, in accordance with the terms of the Brussels Treaty. But the United States, mindful of constitutional obstacles and senatorial opposition to such a tight commitment, insisted on the less binding terms (*New York Times,* December 1, 1948, p. 13; *The Times* [London], February 11, 1949, p. 4).

9. The regional aspect of the alliance was one of several aspects to which the proponents of the North Atlantic Treaty pointed in order to show that it was different from traditional military alliances, which were associated with an obsolete international system that the United Nations, under American leadership, had supplanted. So great was the interest in this argument that the State Department submitted a memorandum to substantiate it (Senate Committee on Foreign Relations, *Hearings, North Atlantic Treaty,* 81 Cong., 1 sess., pp. 334 ff.).

CHAPTER 2

THE INITIAL PHASE

1. For a detailed reconstruction of Soviet plans and maneuvers and a description of the improvised Western reactions, see W. Phillips Davison, *The Berlin Blockade* (Princeton: Princeton University Press, 1958).

2. In Soviet strategic doctrine under Stalin, a decisive role in war was at-

tributed to the "permanently operating factors" (morale, economic and industrial capacity, command, and qualitative and quantitative military elements), as opposed to the temporary factors, such as surprise. Even after the Soviet Union had become a full-fledged nuclear power and recognized the immense destructiveness of a general nuclear war, military writers continued to stress the importance of war production, large reserves, and other factors they believed to be decisive in a long total war (Raymond L. Garthoff, *Soviet Strategy in the Nuclear Age* [New York: Frederick A. Praeger, Inc., 1958]). According to this view, and especially before Russia acquired a nuclear strategic striking force, the United States must have seemed like a formidable obstacle to direct military aggression in Europe in spite of the disintegration of her forces-in-being, for, although Russia's large submarine fleet might harass the Atlantic lines of supply, the United States itself would remain an invulnerable bastion of war matériel and reserve manpower, as in World War II.

3. The most revealing account of America's military and strategic unpreparedness at the time of the Berlin blockade is Walter Millis (ed.), *The Forrestal Diaries* (New York: Viking Press, 1951), chap. xii, "The Berlin Blockade and the Atomic Bomb."

4. James E. King, Jr., "NATO: Genesis, Progress, Problems," in Gordon B. Turner and Richard D. Challener (eds.), *National Security in the Nuclear Age* (New York: Frederick A. Praeger, Inc., 1960), pp. 150–51.

5. For a description of the British role in promoting Western Union and its enlargement into an Atlantic alliance, see Bernard Law Montgomery, *The Memoirs of Field-Marshal Montgomery* (New York: World Publishing Co., 1958), pp. 447 ff.; and Harry S. Truman, *Memoirs by Harry S. Truman* (New York: Doubleday & Co., Inc., 1956), II, 245.

6. See, for example, Undersecretary of State Lovett's remarks on March 3, 1948 (*New York Times*, March 4, 1948, p. 3), and President Truman's reference to the Brussels Treaty in his address to Congress on March 17, 1948: "I am confident that the United States will, by appropriate means, extend to the free nations the support which the situation requires" (*Congressional Record* [hereinafter cited as *Cong. Rec.*], 80 Cong., 2 sess., 2996–98).

7. Walter Millis, *Arms and the State* (New York: Twentieth Century Fund, 1958), p. 237.

8. Montgomery, *op. cit.*, p. 455. For the plans this group produced, see Roger Hilsman, "NATO: The Developing Strategic Context," in Klaus Knorr (ed.), *NATO and American Security* (Princeton: Princeton University Press, 1959), pp. 13–16.

9. Arthur H. Vandenberg, Jr. (ed.), *The Private Papers of Senator Vandenberg* (Boston: Houghton Mifflin Co., 1952), pp. 419, 495.

10. Hilsman, *loc. cit.*, pp. 14–16.

11. In accordance with this military conception, the State Department, in communications directed especially to the Scandinavian countries, strongly suggested that membership in the North Atlantic alliance was a condition for receiving military assistance (*New York Times*, January 15, 1949, pp. 1, 7). President Truman, responding to the views of the military planners, decided that the State Department should explore the possibility of including in the alliance Sweden, Spain, Germany, and Austria (Truman, *op. cit.*, II, 246). British statesmen and political leaders opposed expanding the membership of NATO for fear that this would spread American military assistance too thin. However, the French government supported the inclusion of Italy, with whom it was promoting a rapprochement as a counterpoise to Germany. Canada's inclusion was assured by her membership in the Commonwealth and her early active role in promoting the expansion of the Brussels Treaty into an Atlantic treaty.

12. While the North Atlantic Treaty was before Congress, James Reston reported confusion in the American government and elsewhere surrounding two conceptions of the alliance. "One is that we were trying to create a military combination so strong, so well armed and so well supplied with actual and potential bases within striking distance of the Soviet Union that the Politburo in Moscow would not dare to risk aggression. The other conception is that we were trying to create an institution that would make clear to our people that certain areas of Europe were vital to our security and provide the machinery for planning the defense of the North Atlantic area." He represented the first conception as being primarily the view of the Pentagon and the latter as primarily civilian but held that the issue between the two was undefined (*New York Times,* February 20, 1949, Sec. 4, p. 3).

13. George F. Kennan, *Russia, the Atom, and the West* (New York: Harper & Bros., 1957), pp. 88–90, 91.

14. *New York Times,* January 21, 1949, p. 4.

15. From a plea for acceptance of the North Atlantic Treaty, delivered to the House of Commons on May 12, 1949 (*Parliamentary Debates* [Commons], CDLXIV, 2016).

16. In testifying for the Treaty before the Senate Committee on Foreign Relations, Secretary of State Acheson asserted that the economic recovery of Western Europe was "the first prime necessity" and would receive a clear priority in providing military assistance. "That means," he said, "that there are very definite limitations on the size of the military forces which Western Europe can maintain, because if you withdraw greatly increased numbers of men from production and put them into military service, you would impair recovery and you would impair the very ability of these nations to resist and to remain as free nations" (Senate Committee on Foreign Relations, *Hearings, North Atlantic Treaty,* p. 37).

17. *New York Times,* March 3, 1949, p. 5.

18. In October, 1948, General de Gaulle sharply criticized the Western Union's military arrangements on this ground (*ibid.,* October 2, 1948, pp. 1, 3).

19. Thus French Foreign Minister Schuman, in hailing the proposed Atlantic pact, said that it would entail no increase of French military expenditures that year and that no extension of military service was contemplated. Yet, as he left for Washington to sign the pact, Paris officials, in emphasizing the urgency of American military assistance, explained that lack of enthusiasm for the alliance in France sprang from doubts that it would protect France in the event of an attack (*ibid.,* March 19, 1949, p. 3; March 31, 1949, p. 3).

20. *Times* (London), March 11, 1949, p. 5.

21. With the addition of Greece and Turkey to NATO, the allied countries contained about 436 million inhabitants to about 300 million for the Soviet Union and its European satellites. In 1959 it was estimated that the Soviet bloc (excluding China) had 58.4 million fit males, whereas the NATO countries had 85.4 million (Foreign Policy Research Institute, *United States Foreign Policy: Western Europe* [Washington, 1959], a study prepared at the request of the Senate Committee on Foreign Relations, 86 Cong., 1 sess. [October 15, 1959], p. 49).

22. F. O. Miksche makes some interesting estimates of relative division slices in *The Failure of Atomic Strategy* (New York: Frederick A. Praeger, Inc., 1958), pp. 60–67. However, in his criticisms of the unfavorable comparison between Western and Soviet division strength he does not take account of the different standards of living, logistics requirements, deployments, and missions of Soviet and Western forces. The Soviet army raises about 175 divisions from an approximate strength of 2,500,000 men, as opposed to the 14 divisions the United

States raises from 870,000 men. However, aside from the relative austerity of Soviet programs in medical care, housing, food, entertainment, etc., the functions of military police and research and development, unlike those in the United States, are performed or strongly supported by outside agencies; and a large portion of American armed strength is allocated to non-divisional combat units in order to provide more flexibility in employment. Moreover, because approximately 40 per cent of the American army is deployed overseas, it requires extensive logistics support.

According to figures published by Hanson Baldwin, in the spring of 1959 the NATO members had earmarked 2,202,000 troops for service under SHAPE, not counting Greek and Turkish troops; whereas 1,770,000 Soviet troops (including 1,250,000 in the Soviet Union) and 1,195,000 satellite troops were assigned to Europe (*New York Times*, March 29, 1959, Sec. 4, p. 1). The NATO troops totaled about 21 divisions; the Soviet troops, about 120. (Baldwin's figures did not make allowance for alleged Soviet troop reductions since 1955, which, if they were actually carried out, would make his estimate of Soviet bloc figures as much as 10 per cent too high.)

23. The question of obligation arose because of Article 3, which stated that the signatories "by means of continuous and effective self-help and mutual aid, will maintain and develop their individual and collective capacity to resist armed attack."

24. Senate Committee on Foreign Relations, *Hearings, North Atlantic Treaty*, 81 Cong., 1 sess., pp. 12–13, 22, 24, 25, 33, 36.

25. *Ibid.*, pp. 47, 57.

26. *Ibid.*, p. 44.

27. *Ibid.*, p. 287.

28. Among other reporters who covered the congressional debate on the Treaty, Marquis Childs and James Reston were struck by the ease and relative lack of excitement with which this radical departure in American foreign policy was accepted, indicating, they thought, that its full seriousness and implications had not been grasped. Childs noted, "I had the impression in talking with members of several foreign delegations present for the signing that it was a foregone conclusion that arms would follow automatically as the implementation of the political understanding expressed in the Pact. But in the Senate one quickly discovered that this was an area of unhappy misgiving. There were Senators who looked rather cynically at the treaty as a bargain if it cost nothing in dollars. Others, sincerely and deeply concerned with the issues of peace or war, were fearful that the shipment of American arms to Europe would only heighten the danger. For still others a major concern was how the Pact and the arms to implement it, if arms were necessary, would impinge on domestic policy" (Marquis W. Childs, "Washington and the Atlantic Pact," *Yale Review*, XXXVIII [June, 1949], 581). Reston summed up the popular and congressional attitude: "In short, there seems to be ignorance about specific parts of the treaty, indifference or a certain fatalistic approach to the future, combined with an acceptance of the idea of 'doing something' about the Russians" (*New York Times*, May 19, 1949, p. 10).

29. *Cong. Rec.*, 81 Cong., 1 sess., pp. 8893–94.

30. *Ibid.*, pp. 9205 ff.

31. *Bulletin*, XXI (August 8, 1949), 188.

32. *Ibid.*

33. Senate Committees on Foreign Relations and Armed Services, *Hearings, Military Assistance Program of 1949*, 81 Cong., 1 sess., p. 108.

34. *Ibid.*, p. 27.

35. *Bulletin*, XXI (August 8, 1949), 193.

36. See the statements by General Hoyt S. Vandenberg (chief of staff, United States Air Force) and Mr. Stuart Symington (Secretary of the Air Force) in House Committee on Armed Services, *Hearings, The National Defense Program—Unification and Strategy,* 81 Cong., 1 sess., pp. 63, 316, 403, 455–56. The same conception of the role of airpower was elaborated by General Carl Spaatz, commander of the Army Air Force, in 1947, before the subcommitte of the House Committee on Appropriations, *Hearings, Military Establishment Appropriation Bill for 1948,* 80 Cong., 1 sess., pp. 401, 601–2.

37. *Hearings, The National Defense Program,* pp. 518 ff. Bradley disagreed with the Navy's estimate of the importance of warfare at sea to secure the lines of communication. He even went so far as to suggest that the atomic bomb made surface fleets en masse "a thing of the past," which precluded the possibility of another large-scale amphibious operation as in World War II. But he did not reconcile this view with his conception of American troops participating in large-scale land warfare in Europe (*ibid.,* p. 525). See also General Bradley's and Admiral Denfeld's descriptions of the Army's and Navy's respective roles in general war in Subcommittee of House Committee on Appropriations, *Hearings, Military Establishment Appropriation Bill for 1950,* 81 Cong., 1 sess., pp. 567 ff. and Part 3, p. 30.

38. Despite the fact that the Russians had already exploded their first atomic bomb, the hearings on military doctrine in October, 1949, were conspicuous for their lack of attention to this event and its strategic implications. Those military experts who took note of the event at all mainly drew the implication that the United States had to reinforce her efforts to preserve her atomic superiority. The only exception was Admiral Blandy (commander in chief of the Atlantic Fleet), who wondered if the American bomb would henceforth retain its deterrent value but, nevertheless, envisioned a European war being fought with the atomic bomb combined with World-War-II-type operations (*ibid.,* pp. 204–5).

39. Admiral Radford presented the burden of the Navy's argument (*ibid.,* pp. 46 ff.).

40. *New York Times,* April 6, 1949, p. 3.

41. Robert A. Taft, *A Foreign Policy for Americans* (New York: Doubleday & Co., Inc., 1951), pp. 97–99.

42. Vandenberg, *op. cit.,* pp. 510–14.

43. Statement on August 8, 1949, before the Senate Foreign Relations and Armed Services Committees, *Bulletin,* XXI (August 22, 1949), 265.

44. *Bulletin,* XXI (December 19, 1949), 948; XXII (January 16, 1950), 104.

45. *New York Times,* January 28, 1950, p. 2.

46. "First, the United States will be charged with the strategic bombing. We have repeatedly recognized in this country that the first priority of the joint defense is our ability to deliver the atomic bomb.

"Second, the United States Navy and the Western naval powers will conduct essential naval operations, including keeping the sea lanes clear. The Western Union and other nations will maintain their own harbor and coastal defense.

"Third, we recognize that the hard core of the ground power in being will come from Europe, aided by other nations as they can mobilize.

"Fourth, England, France, and the closer countries will have the bulk of the short-range attack bombardment, and air defense. We, of course, will maintain the tactical air force for our own ground and naval forces, and United States defense.

"Fifth, other nations, depending upon their proximity or remoteness from the possible scene of conflict, will emphasize appropriate specific missions" (House Committee on Foreign Affairs, *Hearings, Mutual Defense Assistance Act of 1949,* 81 Cong., 1 sess., p. 71).

47. Churchill expressed this oft-quoted opinion on several occasions. At the Massachusetts Institute of Technology convocation in Cambridge, Massachusetts, on March 31, 1949, he said, "It is certain that Europe would have been communized like Czechoslovakia and London would have been under bombardment some time ago but for the deterrent of the atomic bomb in the hands of the United States" (*New York Times,* April 1, 1949, p. 10). Several days later, speaking in the House of Commons, he said, "The situation [in Europe] is . . . from many points of view unprecedented and incalculable. Over the whole scene reigns the power of the atomic bomb, ever growing in the hands of the United States. It is this, in my view, and this alone that has given us time to take the measures of self-protection and to develop the units which make those measures possible" (*Parliamentary Debates* [Commons], CDLXIV, 2030). Cf. Churchill's warning on March 16, 1950, that the Soviet atomic bomb greatly worsened the West's position and made more urgent a political settlement (*ibid.,* CDLXXII, 1297–98).

48. *Cong. Rec.,* 81 Cong., 1 sess., p. 13086; cf. Dulles' estimate of the nature of the Soviet threat in a magazine interview in July, 1949 (*United States News and World Report,* XXVII [July 8, 1949], 31). In 1957 Kennan recalled that in 1948 and 1949 he and others had also believed that the most threatening danger in Europe was not Soviet military aggression but Soviet exploitation of Europe's internal problems—especially her economic weakness and lack of purpose and self-confidence in the wake of World War II (Kennan, *Russia, the Atom, and the West,* pp. 89–90).

CHAPTER 3

THE IMPACT OF SOVIET NUCLEAR POWER

1. Remarks in the House of Commons on March 16, 1950 (*Parliamentary Debates* [Commons], CDLXXII, 1297–98).

2. For a description and analysis of the ambiguous decisions, the arguments and counterarguments, underlying America's hydrogen-bomb program, see Warner R. Schilling, "The H-Bomb Decision," *Political Science Quarterly,* LXXVI (March, 1961), 24–26.

3. Perhaps the most revealing statement of the Eisenhower Administration's reasons for suppressing nuclear information was a talk by Robert Cutler, the President's special assistant on national security affairs, published in the *Harvard Alumni Bulletin* of June 5, 1955, p. 665; cited and quoted in W. W. Rostow, *The United States in the World Arena* (New York: Harper & Bros., 1960), pp. 318–19. Cutler here expounded the arguments against "Operation Candor," the chief proponent of which was Robert Oppenheimer, who published the arguments for releasing more atomic information in his article, "Atomic Weapons and American Policy," *Foreign Affairs,* XXXII (July, 1953), 530–32.

4. In February, 1954, Sterling Cole, chairman of the Joint Congressional Committee on Atomic Energy, released details about America's first thermonuclear explosion at Eniwetok (*New York Times,* February 18, 1954, pp. 1, 8). In March, 1954, Lewis L. Strauss, chairman of the Atomic Energy Commission, released details of the effects of the *Lucky Dragon* shot and information about Soviet progress in multimegaton weapons (*Christian Science Monitor,* February 10, 1955, p. 1; *New York Times,* February 16, 1955, p. 18; February 22, p. 8).

5. In an address on January 7, 1953, explaining the implications of the Eniwetok explosion (*Bulletin,* XXVIII [January 19, 1953], 94).

6. The Stockholm Peace Appeal originated at the third session of the Permanent Committee of the World Peace Congress, held in Stockholm, Sweden, on

March 15–19, 1950. It read: "We demand the unconditional prohibition of the atomic weapon as a weapon of intimidation and mass extermination of human beings. We demand the institution of strict international control to enforce this. We shall consider as a war criminal that government which first employs the atomic weapons against any country. We call upon all people of good will throughout the world to sign this appeal" (*USSR Information Bulletin,* X [April 28, 1950], 234). In August the sponsors of the campaign claimed the implicit support of 600 million men, women, and children and over 273 million actual "mainly adult" signatures (*ibid.,* September 8, 1950, p. 520).

7. For a discussion of the calculated techniques of "nuclear blackmail," with special attention to the Suez War of 1956, see Hans Speier, "Soviet Atomic Blackmail and the North Atlantic Alliance," *World Politics,* IX (April, 1957), 307–28. Speier cogently describes the mingling of threat and conciliation in Soviet blackmail techniques as follows: "In order to exact compliance with an effort at blackmail, the cost of failing to comply must appear disastrously high to the victim. But once fantasies of disaster are aroused, they must be controlled. When they are once aroused, the relatively lesser cost of compliance appears a blessing. This technique corresponds to that of a holdup man who brandishes a gun in front of an armed victim but who, for fear that the frightened man may fight for his life, quickly tells him that he only wants his money" (*ibid.,* p. 323).

8. For a selection of Khrushchev's statements about the shift of the military and political balance toward the Soviet Union, see Senate Document No. 57, a special study prepared by the Legislative Reference Service, *Khrushchev on the Shifting Balance of World Forces,* 86 Cong., 1 sess.

9. For an analytical narrative of this Berlin crisis, see Hans Speier, *The Soviet Threat to Berlin* (Santa Monica: The RAND Corporation, 1960).

CHAPTER 4
REARMAMENT AND RELAXATION

1. For example, Italian Foreign Minister Count Sforza sought and received such reaffirmations in order to counteract repeated reports that the strategic plans of the Atlantic powers called for the abandonment of Italy in case of a Russian attack (*New York Times,* May 24, 1950, p. 15).

2. See, for example, Acheson's testimony before the House Committee on Foreign Affairs in June, 1950 (House Committee on Foreign Affairs, *Hearings, To Amend the Mutual Defense Assistance Act of 1949,* 81 Cong., 2 sess., p. 22).

3. *New York Times,* April 10, 1950, pp. 1, 7.

4. Message of June 1, 1950 (*Bulletin,* XXII [June 12, 1950], 938–40).

5. *Ibid.,* XXII (May 29, 1950), 830.

6. Foreshadowing his famous "balance of terror" statement five years later, Churchill emphasized the deterrent effect of the unprecedented destructiveness of nuclear war and declared that "moralists may find it a melancholy thought that peace can find no nobler foundations than mutual terror" (speech in the House of Commons on March 28, 1950, *Parliamentary Debates* [Commons], CDLXXIII, 197). Cf. Churchill's speech to the House as Prime Minister on March 1, 1955: "Then it may well be that we shall, by a process of sublime irony, have reached a stage in this story where safety will be the sturdy child of terror, and survival the twin brother of annihilation" (*New York Times,* March 2, 1955, p. 8; *Parliamentary Debates* [Commons], DXXXVII, 1894–1905).

7. "France Proves She Is Still a Power," *New York Times Magazine*, June 25, 1950, p. 19.
8. *Bulletin*, XXII (May 29, 1950), 830.
9. *New York Times*, May 16, 1950, p. 23.
10. *Bulletin*, XXII (May 29, 1950), 830.
11. Testimony on June 5, 1950 (*New York Times*, June 6, 1950, p. 3). Also, Joint Senate Committee on Foreign Relations and Armed Services, *Hearings, Mutual Defense Assistance Program*, 81 Cong., 2 sess., p. 22.
12. The modern conventional weapons were designed to check the offensive superiority of the tank-and-tactical-airpower team that had proved so effective in World War II. Their great possibilities were discussed in an Army study during the winter, which had enlisted the assistance of Dr. Vannevar Bush and a group of the Army's leading combat generals and senior planners (Tracy S. Voorhees, "To Prevent a 'Korea' in Western Europe," *New York Times Magazine*, July 23, 1950, pp. 10 ff.). See Hanson Baldwin's skeptical report concerning the publicity releases on the new weapons in the *New York Times*, June 8, 1950, p. 6. The two Senate committees that considered the Mutual Defense Assistance Program for 1950 reported, on the basis of their findings, that the "most modern" weapons would enable Europe to defend herself at less cost in men and money. But the weapons it mentioned specifically were recoilless antitank weapons, shaped charges, non-magnetic mines, and proximity fuses (*ibid.*, June 23, 1950, p. 10).
13. In an article in the *Saturday Evening Post*, dated October 13, and reproduced in House Committee on Armed Services, *Hearings, The National Defense Program—Unification and Strategy*, 81 Cong., 1 sess., p. 320.
14. Statement on June 27, 1950 (*Bulletin*, XXII [July 3, 1950], 5).
15. Statement submitted to Senate Committee on Appropriations, *Hearings, Supplemental Appropriations for 1951*, 81 Cong., 2 sess., p. 272.
16. "To Save Humanity from the Deep Abyss," *New York Times Magazine*, July 30, 1950, p. 35.
17. Senate Committee on Appropriations, *Hearings, Supplemental Appropriations for 1951*, pp. 268–69.
18. The concept of the "year of maximum danger" was originally based on a calculation of the time by which Russia would acquire sufficient atomic capacity to be in a position to utilize her numerically superior manpower to exert intensive political or military pressure on the West. NSC 68, the document that grew out of the State Department Policy Planning Staff's memorandum on the strategic significance of Russia's atomic explosion, set this year as 1954. However, the American Joint Chiefs of Staff apparently regarded the "year of maximum danger" as a convenient guideline for planning rather than as a crucial target date. In the fall of 1950 they moved the guideline date to 1952. Later, when the administration cut their recommended force levels for 1952, the date was extended to 1954. See General Bradley's, General Vandenberg's, and General Twining's explanations of the concept in Senate Committee on Appropriations, *Hearings, Department of Defense Appropriations for 1953*, 82 Cong., 2 sess., pp. 332–35, 385. Roger Hilsman discusses the meaning of the concept in "NATO: The Developing Strategic Context," in Klaus Knorr (ed.), *NATO and American Security* (Princeton: Princeton University Press, 1959), p. 20.
19. Referring to the situation prevailing at the end of the first year of the Mutual Defense Assistance Program in October, 1950, President Truman stated in his semiannual report, "The time for giving economic recovery a clear priority over efforts to build military strength was passing, and the day was fast approaching when all aid to NATO countries, whether military or economic in

nature, would need to be related to, and conditioned upon, the performance by the recipients of the various defense tasks called for by North Atlantic Treaty planning, and upon the undertaking of those complementary measures which were needed, in conjunction with American assistance, to assure attainment of the now inseparable goals of military strength and continuing economic stability" (United States President, *Third Semiannual Report of the Mutual Defense Assistance Program* [Washington: 1950], p. 3).

20. *New York Times,* August 8, 1950, p. 14.

21. *Ibid.,* September 10, 1950, pp. 1, 11.

22. See the statements by Senator Taft on November 10 and 13 (*New York Times,* November 11, 1950, p. 8; November 14, p. 1) and the speeches by Herbert Hoover on October 19 and December 20 (*ibid.,* October 20, 1950, p. 2; December 21, p. 22). Taft challenged the thesis that Europe was America's first line of defense or that it was defensible and urged the 82d Congress to reexamine the scope, methods, and character of American military assistance to Europe. Hoover also doubted that Europe could be defended on the Continent, but he nevertheless insisted that Europe create an army large enough to stop the Russians before the United States sent "another man or another dollar," while maintaining that the United States could defend herself by holding the Atlantic and Pacific Oceans with her sea- and airpower.

23. Communiqué of September 27, 1950, *Bulletin,* XXIII (October 9, 1950), 588.

24. *Ibid.*

25. *New York Times,* December 20, 1950, p. 1.

26. European fears of American action in Korea probably reached a peak when, following the Chinese intervention in the war, President Truman, in response to questions in a press conference on November 30, indicated that the United States might use the atomic bomb if the military situation called for it. This statement aroused such a storm in the House of Commons that Prime Minister Clement Attlee rushed to the United States to seek the President's assurance that the government would not act rashly. The final communiqué of this conference included the statement that "the President stated that it was his hope that world conditions would never call for the use of the atomic bomb. The President told the Prime Minister that it was also his desire to keep the Prime Minister at all times informed of developments which might bring about a change in the situation." For the fullest account of this incident, see Harry S. Truman, *Memoirs by Harry S. Truman* (Garden City, N.Y.: Doubleday & Co., 1956), II, chap. xxv.

27. Speech in the House of Commons on December 6, 1951 (*Parliamentary Debates* [Commons], CDXCIV, 2592).

28. Speech at Des Moines, Iowa, on February 16, 1952 (*Cong. Rec.,* 82 Cong., 2 sess., pp. 1800–1802).

29. In France it was not just the left-wing parties and the Communists who charged that NATO would not and could not defend French territory but also the right-wing elements and the Gaullists. Thus General de Gaulle, looking toward the coming national elections, asserted, "Our Atlantic allies do not contemplate protecting the territory of the old Continent effectively in case of invasion" but, instead, are "disposed to limit their effort to defense of a few points: England, Spain, a 'Breton Redoubt' " (*New York Times,* April 13, 1951, p. 8). He demanded that the cession of bases and communication facilities on French soil should be conditional upon a strategic plan for NATO that would protect Europe from invasion and not undertake an initial retreat (*ibid.,* May 2, 1951, p. 15).

30. *Cong. Rec.*, 82 Cong., 1 sess., p. 52.

31. Address to Congress on February 1, 1951 (*Bulletin,* XXIV [February 5, 1951], 249).

32. *Ibid.*, p. 248. In hearings during July, 1951, General Gruenther, Eisenhower's chief of staff, explained more definitely that Eisenhower conceived the sole purpose of American troops as reviving the confidence of the European countries and that he expected them to be withdrawn "eventually." He represented Eisenhower as believing that airpower would be the dominant element of defense in Europe despite all the talk about divisions (Joint Senate Committee on Foreign Relations and Armed Services, *Hearings, Mutual Security Act of 1951,* 82 Cong., 1 sess., pp. 209 ff.).

33. Joint Senate Committee on Foreign Relations and Armed Services, *Hearings, Assignment of Ground Forces of the United States to Duty in the European Area,* 82 Cong., 1 sess., p. 79.

34. *Ibid.*, pp. 106–7. Acheson's theory of the declining advantage of America's nuclear superiority and the corresponding need for ground troops was developed more fully in an anonymous article, "The Balance of Military Power," *Atlantic Monthly* CLXXXVII (June, 1951), 21–27.

35. Joint Senate Committee on Foreign Relations and Armed Services, *Hearings, Assignment of Ground Forces . . .* , p. 79. Acheson cited a build-up of satellite forces as indicating the danger of proxy aggression. Secretary of Defense Marshall confirmed this intelligence in his testimony of May, 1951, in the so-called "MacArthur hearings": "The impression from the reports that we gather from many sources is there has been a continuous build-up, and not necessarily in strength, though it may be, but particularly in arrangements specifically in the satellite states, and in regard to disposition of Soviet troops in Western Europe" (Joint Senate Committee on Foreign Relations and Armed Services, *Hearings, Military Situation in the Far East,* 82 Cong., 1 sess., p. 593).

36. Joint Senate Committee on Foreign Relations and Armed Services, *Hearings, Assignment of Ground Forces . . .* , p. 80. General Hoyt S. Vandenberg, chief of staff of the Air Force explained that, unless the ground forces could delay the invaders, Russia would gain access to a greater war potential in Western Europe than strategic bombing could knock out in the heartland. Thus, he implied that the Kremlin would be willing to trade a devastated homeland for control of Western Europe (*ibid.*, pp. 222, 227).

37. *Ibid.*, p. 80; also, statement on June 1, 1951 (*Bulletin,* XXIV [June 11, 1951], 926).

38. Joint Senate Committee on Foreign Relations and Armed Services, *Hearings, Assignment of Ground Forces . . .* , pp. 186–88.

39. *Ibid.*, pp. 20, 27; *New York Herald Tribune,* November 27, 1951, p. 1.

40. Reflecting the general optimism about achieving this deterrent capability, Drew Middleton reported in July, 1951, that by the end of the year NATO would have 500,000 soldiers, which would be enough to prevent a *fait accompli* by the 300,000 Soviet troops in East Germany unless they received considerable reinforcement. He said that allied strategists foresaw that the forces available by the spring of 1952 would be strong enough to engage the Russian armies in strength east of the Rhine (*New York Times,* July 25, 1951, p. 6; September 9, 1951, p. 1). Stewart Alsop gave a similarly optimistic report in December (*New York Herald Tribune,* December 26, 1951, p. 21). By the end of 1953 there were 15 allied divisions, with supporting forces, on the front from the Swiss border to the mouth of the Ijssel, over 100 airfields, and an extensive supply and communications network (Roger Hilsman, *op. cit.*, pp. 22–23).

41. *New York Times,* September 19, 1951, p. 6.

42. For representative statements of Bevan's views, see *Parliamentary Debates* (Commons), CDLXXXVII, 34–43, and *One Way Only: A Socialist Analysis of the Present World Crisis,* published in July, 1951. For an analysis of the nature and significance of the entire Bevanite attack upon British and American policy toward NATO, see Leon D. Epstein, *Britain, Uneasy Ally* (Chicago: University of Chicago Press, 1954), chap. xi.

43. *New York Times,* September 17, 1951, p. 5.

44. *Ibid.,* November 28, 1951, pp. 1, 14, 15. The TCC was established in October, at Acheson's suggestion. The actual survey of capabilities was to be made by a three-man committee (dubbed the "Three Wise Men"), composed of W. Averell Harriman of the United States, as chairman, Jean Monnet of France, and Sir Edwin Plowden of Great Britain (replacing Hugh Gaitskell after the defeat of the Labor government).

45. *Ibid.,* December 14, 1951, p. 1.

46. *Ibid.,* November 28, 1951, p. 1.

47. The Mutual Security Act for fiscal year 1952 provided $1 billion for economic aid and $4.8 billion for military aid for Europe. However, it authorized the President to transfer up to 10 per cent of the military funds to economic aid.

48. The administration requested $4.1 billion in direct military aid, arms, and equipment for Europe and $1.8 billion in "defense support," the new name for economic aid, designed to enable recipients to sustain and increase their rearmament programs. Congress authorized $3.4 billion and $1.2 billion, respectively, for these purposes. It cut the appropriation for military aid even further.

49. *New York Times,* November 28, 1951, p. 15. In September, 1951, the administration decided to moderate the pace of rearmament in order to attain peak strength in 1954 instead of 1952. The decision was revealed by Secretary of Defense Lovett in February, 1952 (*ibid.,* February 5, 1952, pp. 1, 8).

50. Secretary of State Acheson gave the concept of a European army qualified indorsement in February, 1951, but international discussions of the French scheme reached a deadlock until General Eisenhower, in July, 1951, accepted the establishment of a European Defense Community as prior to German rearmament and persuaded the French to agree to integration at the army group rather than the divisional level. Soon afterward the North Atlantic allies accepted an interim agreement to this effect, leaving the details to be worked out in the next few months before the Lisbon conference of the North Atlantic Council (Lewis J. Edinger, *West German Rearmament* [Maxwell Air Force Base, Alabama: Air University Documentary Research Study, 1955], pp. 17–21).

51. Daniel Lerner and Raymond Aron, (eds.), *France Defeats EDC* (New York: Frederick A. Praeger, Inc., 1957), pp. 12 ff.

52. Gordon A. Craig, "Germany and NATO: The Rearmament Debate, 1950–1958," in Knorr (ed.), *op. cit.,* pp. 237–39.

53. At the Lisbon conference the North Atlantic Council took the unusual step of publishing the force goals for the end of 1952. Customarily, NATO had not officially released either prospective or actual force levels. The other levels stated here and elsewhere are derived from reports in the press, which show the kind of consistency that could only come from information acquired at SHAPE.

54. The North Atlantic Council had approved the accession of Greece and Turkey, in principle, in October, 1951. However, all the divisions that Greece and Turkey could raise would be needed locally.

55. *Times* (London), February 26, 1952, p. 5.

56. For General Eisenhower's statement, see Supreme Allied Commander in Europe, *First Annual Report* (Paris: SHAPE, 1952), p. 21. For General Ridgway's

statements, see *Times* (London), September 30, 1952, p. 4; SACEUR, *Second Annual Report* (Paris: SHAPE, 1953), p. 21. For General Gruenther's statements see *New York Times,* April 22, 1952, p. 24; address on October 8, 1953, *Bulletin,* XXIX (November 9, 1953), 634; address on September 29, 1954, *Bulletin,* XXXV (October 18, 1954), 563; testimony in March, 1955, Senate Committee on Foreign Relations, *Hearings, NATO and the Paris Accords Relating to West Germany,* 84 Cong., 1 sess., p. 8.

57. Statement on February 20, 1952, *Parliamentary Debates* (Commons), CDXCV, 232. Churchill repeated this explanation on March 5 (*ibid.,* CDXCVII, 433 ff.).

58. *New York Herald Tribune,* November 21, 1952, p. 21. According to Charles Murphy, the underlying strategic reappraisal was produced by the three British military chiefs between January and July, 1952 ("A New Strategy for NATO," *Fortune,* XLVII [January, 1953], 80 ff.; and an unsigned article, "Defense and Strategy: New Accents in Military Thinking and Spending," *Fortune,* XLVIII [December, 1953], 77 ff.).

59. *Parliamentary Debates* (Commons), DIV, 1492–1509.

60. *Economist,* November 22, 1952, p. 539.

61. *New York Times,* August 18, 1952, p. 4.

62. Peter Calvocoressi, *Survey of International Affairs, 1952* (London: Oxford University Press, 1955), pp. 36–41, contains a good summary of the events leading to France's relaxation of her defense effort.

63. According to Acheson's testimony, House Committee on Foreign Affairs, *Hearings, Mutual Security Act Extension,* 82 Cong., 2 sess., p. 11. The annual cost of the Indochinese war was estimated to be $1.25 billion in 1952.

64. Statements by Secretary of State Dulles, *Bulletin,* XXVIII (April 27, 1953), 604; *New York Times,* April 22, 1953, p. 1. North Atlantic Council communiqué, *ibid.,* April 26, 1953, p. 31. Statement by Supreme Allied Commander General Ridgway, *Bulletin,* XXVIII (June 22, 1953), 871–72. President's annual report on the Mutual Security Program, August 17, 1953, *ibid.,* XXIX (September 21, 1953), 385. Statement by Supreme Allied Commander General Gruenther, *ibid.,* XXIX (November 9, 1953), 634. However, speaking in December, 1953, about the recent Council meeting, Dulles said, "At our Paris meeting we discussed the Soviet position and the estimate of the risk. And it was generally judged—I think I can say unanimously judged—by the NATO Ministers that the danger of open military aggression from Soviet Russia was less than it had been a year or two before" (*New York Times,* December 23, 1953, p. 4).

65. Radio-television reports by Secretary Dulles on April 18 and 29, 1953, *Bulletin* XXVIII (April 27, 1953), 599–608; (May 11, 1953), 672. Council communiqué, April 25, *New York Times,* April 26, 1953, p. 1. Dulles' statement on April 30, 1953, House Committee on Foreign Affairs, *Hearings, Mutual Security Act Extension,* 83 Cong., 1 sess., pp. 145 ff.

66. SACEUR, *Second Annual Report,* p. 21; address in New York, May 21, *Bulletin,* XXVIII (June 22, 1953), 863–65.

67. Thus in May, 1953, General Ridgway emphasized in his annual report as Supreme Allied Commander that the military mission intrusted to him remained, first, "In war to defend NATO's European territories. This mission was not qualified in either space or time. It was not merely to defend certain parts of the NATO European area and their peoples. Nor was the responsibility only to become effective in some future year when means might be available. The task was to defend all, at any time, if war should occur" (SACEUR, *Second Annual Report,* pp. 7–8). In April, 1954, President Eisenhower conveyed official as-

surances to the six signatories of EDC that "the United States and its allies are working to build the concrete strength needed to deter aggression and, if aggression occurs, to halt it without the devastation or occupation of any NATO country" (*Bulletin*, XXX [April 26, 1954], 619).

68. SACEUR, *First Annual Report*, p. 2.

69. Statements by Generals Gruenther, Eisenhower, and Ridgway (Senate Committee on Foreign Relations, *Hearings, Mutual Security Act of 1952*, 82 Cong., 2 sess., pp. 203, 218; SACEUR, *First Annual Report*, p. 27; *Bulletin*, XXVII [November 24, 1952], 818).

70. *Bulletin*, XXVI (June 9, 1952), 897.

71. *Ibid.*, p. 895.

72. Senate Committee on Foreign Relations, *Hearings, Convention on Relations with the Federal Republic of Germany*, 82 Cong., 2 sess., p. 64.

73. See, for example, the opinions of German military men cited in Hans Speier, *German Rearmament and Atomic War* (White Plains, N.Y.: Row, Peterson & Co., 1957), p. 57. Dulles indicated that such opinions had had their desired effect when he stated on September 3, 1953, before the German elections, that the failure to retain Adenauer "would be disastrous to Germany and to the prospects of reunification" (*New York Times*, September 4, 1953, p. 1).

74. See, for example, the text of a letter from President Eisenhower to Chancellor Adenauer, dated July 23, 1953, and released on July 25 (*ibid.*, July 26, 1953, p. 20).

75. Message of President Eisenhower to the prime ministers of the six EDC countries, dispatched on April 15, 1954, after consultation with congressional leaders of both parties (*Bulletin*, XXX [April 26, 1954], 619–20). On April 13 the British conveyed the same pledge and similar reaffirmations.

76. *New York Times*, January 31, 1954, p. 4; cf. Dulles' statement on December 22, 1953 (*ibid.*, December 23, 1953, p. 4).

77. *Ibid.*, December 15, 1953, p. 14. In a speech to the National Press Club on December 22, Dulles stated more explicitly that the government's reappraisal would apply to the "forward strategy," which he defined as "a plan . . . to defend the entire area of the prospective EDC countries rather than to contemplate from the beginning the abandonment of advanced positions in Germany, which might make the rest of Europe untenable" (*ibid.*, December 23, 1953, p. 4). Dulles repeated substantially the same warning on June 4, 1954, to the Senate Foreign Relations Committee and on June 10, 1954, in an address in Seattle (*Bulletin*, XXX [June 14, 1954], 922, and XXX [June 21, 1954], 938). President Eisenhower indorsed Dulles' warning in a White House release on December 23, 1953 (*ibid.*, XXX [January 4, 1954], 7).

78. *New York Times*, January 25, 1953, pp. 1, 18; February 13, p. 4; *Manchester Guardian*, February 6, 1953, p. 1; *Bulletin*, XXVIII (February 23, 1953), 287–90.

79. According to the final version of the Richards Amendment, half of American aid would be made available to the Defense Community rather than to individual countries unless the President recommended and Congress authorized otherwise (*Cong. Rec.*, 83 Cong., 1 sess., p. 8683). In a press conference on December 17, 1953, President Eisenhower referred to the Richards Amendment in expressing surprise that Dulles' "agonizing reappraisal" statement should have been considered new or particularly blunt (*New York Times*, December 17, 1953, p. 22).

80. *Ibid.*, June 5, 1954, p. 1. Italy had made her acceptance of EDC contingent upon French ratification.

81. Speaking on November 17, 1954, *Parliamentary Debates* (Commons),

CDLXIII, 400–405, 685. Denis Healey of the Labor party supported Eden's position on the same grounds: "The problem we are now discussing is not simply whether or not Germany is to be rearmed, but whether or not we can fit a resurgent Germany—a great power in Europe, with 50 million people of unexampled energy, intelligence and skill—into the framework of Western unity which we developed in the years following the war" (*ibid.*, p. 504).

82. *New York Times,* October 7, 1954, p. 5.

83. See, especially, Khrushchev's address to the Congress on February 14, 1956 (excerpts in *ibid.,* February 15, 1956, p. 10).

84. See Philip E. Moseley, "Soviet Myths and Realities," *Foreign Affairs,* XXXIX (April, 1961), 341–54; Zbigniew Brzezinski, "The Challenge of Change in the Soviet Bloc," *ibid.,* pp. 430–43; Center for International Affairs, *United States Foreign Policy: Ideology and Foreign Affairs,* study prepared for Senate Committee on Foreign Relations, 86 Cong., 2 sess., pp. 19–36.

CHAPTER 5

NATO GOES NUCLEAR

1. Robert E. Osgood, *Limited War* (Chicago: University of Chicago Press, 1957), pp. 201–3.

2. Statement in a press conference on April 30 (*New York Times,* May 1, 1953, p. 9).

3. In an address on December 14, 1953 (*ibid.,* December 15, p. 31).

4. *Bulletin,* XXX (January 25, 1954), 107–10.

5. Osgood, *op. cit.,* pp. 210–12.

6. "Policy for Security and Peace," *Foreign Affairs,* XXXII (April, 1954), 358.

7. *Ibid.,* p. 363.

8. The United States tested the first small tactical nuclear weapons in the Nevada desert on October 28, 1951.

9. See above, p. 68.

10. The Vista report was submitted to the service secretaries in February, 1952, but encountered great opposition from the Air Force and was never officially approved (James M. Gavin, *War and Peace in the Space Age* [New York: Harper & Bros., 1952], pp. 132–34). See also "The Hidden Struggle for the H-bomb," *Fortune,* XLVII (May, 1953), 109, 110, 230.

11. *New York Times,* September 7, 1952, p. 1.

12. *Statement on Defense, 1953* (February, 1953), Cmd. 8768, p. 3.

13. *New York Times,* September 17, 1952, p. 7.

14. Gavin, *op. cit.,* p. 139.

15. Report of views expressed on February 13, 1953, to visiting NATO information officers (*New York Times,* February 14, 1953, p. 5).

16. Address in New York on October 8, 1953 (*Bulletin,* XXIX [November 9, 1953], 636).

17. *New York Times,* February 25, 1953, p. 5.

18. *Ibid.,* April 29, 1953, p. 16.

19. *Ibid.,* September 2, 1953, pp. 1, 16.

20. *Ibid.,* July 9, 1953, p. 4; December 16, p. 1; December 17, p. 22. President's statement, January 21, 1954. *Bulletin,* XXX (February 1, 1954), 144. Testimony by Secretary of State Dulles and Assistant Secretary of Defense Quarles on June 3 and 4, 1954, Joint Committee on Atomic Energy, *Hearings, To Amend the Atomic Energy Act of 1946,* 83 Cong., 2 sess., pp. 703, 734.

21. Under Section 123 any executive agreement to give such information to another nation had to be submitted to the JCAE, where it was required to lie for a thirty-day review period before it could become effective. Although representatives of the Atomic Energy Commission and the Justice Department publicly complained about this provision, Secretary of State Dulles did not. Later, AEC testimony on the 1958 amendments to the Atomic Energy Act indicated that the government viewed this legislative check on the dissemination of nuclear material and information as a more politically palatable substitute for executive restrictions designed to prevent the spread of nuclear capabilities to the NATO countries while making preferential agreements with the British. See Harold L. Nieburg, "Atomic Secrecy and Foreign Policy" (Chicago, unpublished MS, 1961), pp. 90 ff.

22. *New York Times,* October 17, 1953, p. 3; October 20, p. 1.

23. *Ibid.,* October 21, 1953, p. 1; October 28, p. 19; October 29, p. 26.

24. Senate Report 1699 (Senate Report Amending the Atomic Energy Act of 1946) 83 Cong., 2 sess. (June 30, 1954), in Atomic Energy Commission, *Legislative History of the Atomic Energy Act of 1946,* I, 750–51.

25. Address in June, 1954, in Atomic Energy Commission, *Legislative History . . . ,* I, 1614.

26. *New York Times,* January 18, 1954, p. 2. Casting an apprehensive eye toward current disarmament discussions, Gruenther added, "We must try to determine what X is. But if we build on that basis and then atom bombs are outlawed, where are we?"

27. *Ibid.,* January 12, 1954, p. 3.

28. *Ibid.,* July 25, 1954, p. 1.

29. *Ibid.,* August 14, 1954, p. 3.

30. Address in New York on September 29, 1954, *Bulletin,* XXI (October 18, 1954), 562–66.

31. Interview with Brig. Gen. (ret.) T. R. Phillips, *St. Louis Post-Dispatch,* October 31, 1954, p. C3. Gruenther had earlier stated, in a speech on June 8, that the NATO command was planning on using nuclear weapons (*New York Herald Tribune,* June 9, 1954, p. 9).

32. *Journal of the Royal United Service Institute,* XCIX (November, 1954), 508; cf. lecture at the California Institute of Technology, reported in *New York Times,* November 30, 1954, p. 13.

33. Joint Senate Committee on Foreign Relations and Armed Services, *Hearings, Assignment of Ground Forces of the United States to Duty in the European Area,* 82 Cong., 1 sess., p. 79.

34. *New York Times,* March 3, 1955, p. 1.

35. Evidence later published in the United States tended to confirm the claim of the Soviet atomic scientist Kurchatov that the Soviet thermonuclear device was a true bomb, capable of being transported, whereas the Eniwetok device was too large and heavy to be portable. The Soviet explosion was evidently accomplished with a form of lithium deuteride as a solid, while the American explosion depended upon bulky refrigeration apparatus to keep the heavy hydrogen in liquid form. The evidence suggests that the United States did not succeed in exploding a lithium deuteride bomb until March, 1954 (*ibid.,* February 8, 1960, p. 2).

36. According to Cole's report, the November, 1952, explosion had torn a crater 175 feet deep and a mile wide in the ocean bed, and, if it had exploded in a modern city, it would have created an area of complete destruction six miles in diameter (*ibid.,* February 18, 1954, pp. 1, 8). Churchill, explaining to the House of Commons in April his decision to go to Washington in June, expressed his astonishment at the lack of reaction to this information (*Parliamentary De-*

bates [Commons], DXXVI, 47). In Washington he received further information on the destructive effects of hydrogen explosions.

37. Address on March 1, 1955 (*New York Times,* March 2, 1955, p. 8).

38. Statement to the House of Commons, December 1, 1954 (*Parliamentary Debates* [Commons], DXXXV, 176).

39. *New York Times,* February 16, 1955, p. 18.

40. *Bulletin,* XXIX (October 19, 1953), 507–8.

41. *New York Times,* December 15, 1954, p. 8; December 18, pp. 1, 2.

42. *Ibid.,* December 22, 1954, pp. 1, 4.

43. North Atlantic Council communiqué, December 14, 1956 (*NATO Letter,* V [January 1, 1957], p. 4).

44. See pp. 161–64, below. The reserve forces goal was reported to be 60 divisions, excluding Greek and Turkish forces. As Roger Hilsman has pointed out, the 30 divisions were slightly more than the ready-mobilized divisions required on the forward line according to the Lisbon goals, based on a conventional strategy. However, they constituted a somewhat larger proportion of the total NATO force goals, including reserves (Hilsman, "NATO: The Developing Strategic Context," in Klaus Knorr [ed.], *NATO and American Security* [Princeton: Princeton University Press, 1959], p. 31).

45. See Hanson Baldwin's report on the tactical nuclear war game Operation Sagebrush, *New York Times,* December 5, 1955, p. 12. Conclusions drawn from the 1958 studies and games were reported in *ibid.,* March 14, 1958, p. 1; October 27, p. 1. General Taylor and General Ridgway supported these conclusions in congressional testimony in February, 1956 (Subcommittee of House Committee on Appropriations, *Hearings, Department of Defense Appropriations for 1957,* 84 Cong., 2 sess., pp. 482, 566).

46. For an authoritative exposition of the view that atomic weapons would help the defender more than the attacker, see General J. Lawton Collins, "NATO: Still Vital for Peace," *Foreign Affairs,* XXXIV (April, 1956), 367–79. Collins, who had been Army Chief of Staff from 1949 to 1953, wrote as the United States member of NATO's Standing Group.

47. *New York Times,* May 26, 1958, p. 17. In December, 1958, the Army announced that it was modifying its pentomic infantry divisions to give them greater conventional capacity. The change was attributed to a conviction that nuclear war was less likely than conventional war and to insufficient light dual-purpose missiles (*Washington Post,* December 24, 1958, p. A5).

48. *New York Times,* March 2, 1955, p. 8.

49. *Statement on Defense, 1955* (presented February, 1955), Cmd. 9391; *Parliamentary Debates* (Commons), DXXXVII, 1910 ff.

50. In 1956 British Minister of Defense Sir Walter Monckton said that it did not seem to him that the tactical use of nuclear weapons "would necessarily lead to full-scale global war" (*Parliamentary Debates* [Commons], DXLIX, 1035). On March 15, 1955, Dulles told a news conference that smaller atomic weapons offered a chance of victory on the battlefield without harming civilians, but he was speaking of the doctrine of selective nuclear retaliation as a deterrent against limited aggressions in the Far East (*New York Times,* March 16, 1955, p. 1). Only once, in an article in 1957, did he suggest that the use of these weapons in the NATO area might achieve victory without involving "vast destruction and widespread harm to humanity" ("Challenge and Response in United States Policy," *Foreign Affairs,* XXXVI [October, 1957], 31).

51. According to General Maxwell D. Taylor, this was the gist of the document called the Joint Strategic Objectives Plan for Fiscal Year 1960; that is, the midrange planning document that estimates force requirements four years in

advance and is, theoretically, the basic document by which the Joint Chiefs translate National Security Council guidance into specific plans and programs (Maxwell D. Taylor, *The Uncertain Trumpet* [New York: Harper & Bros., 1960], pp. 38–39).

52. This information was published by Anthony Leviero in the *New York Times*, July 13, 1956, p. 1. The armed forces were to be cut from 2,850,000 to 2,000,000.

53. Lippmann approved the calculation that he attributed to the government as a prudent risk and argued that, as the cost of weapons rose, it would not be possible to keep two military establishments—one for conventional local wars and one for general nuclear war (*Washington Post*, July 19, 1956, p. 13).

54. Testimony on January 24 and July 2, Subcommittee of House Committee on Appropriations, *Hearings, Department of Defense Appropriations for 1957*, pp. 31, 116, 118; Subcommittee on the Air Force, Senate Committee on Armed Services, *Hearings, Study of Airpower*, 84 Cong., 2 sess., pp. 1732–33.

55. *Washington Post*, August 3, 1956, p. 10.

56. One exception was General Maxwell D. Taylor, who denied that an overt military conflict in the NATO area would necessarily be a general atomic war. However, even he did not clearly commit himself to the possibility of a conventional limited war in Europe. See the article he wrote in the spring of 1956, which was denied clearance because of Defense and State Department opposition (Taylor, *op. cit.*, pp. 186–87, 190, 193). The previously cited article by General Collins, which also dealt with NATO's strategy and was published in the same periodical in the spring of 1956, argued that tactical nuclear weapons could save Europe from being overrun and that "it would be unsafe to assume that strategic atomic bombing would not be used by both sides" (Collins, *op. cit.*, pp. 375–77).

57. Subcommittee on the Air Force, Senate Committee on Armed Services, *Hearings, Study of Airpower*, p. 23.

58. Statement to House of Commons, December 1, 1954, *Parliamentary Debates* (Commons), DXXXV, 177.

59. At the Council meeting, representatives of Great Britain and the small powers were reported to have opposed the American position that the decision to use tactical nuclear weapons should be left to the Supreme Allied Commander. The American government agreed that this decision should be made by civilians, but there remained a difference of opinion on whether the deciding body should be the fourteen Council members or the three powers represented on the Standing Committee—a procedural matter that was further complicated by the fact that the United States owned the tactical nuclear stocks, which, by law, could be used only on direct authorization of the President (*New York Times*, December 14, 1954, p. 10; December 15, p. 8; December 18, pp. 1, 2; December 22, pp. 1, 4). Secretary of State Dulles later qualified his concession to governmental decision when he stated that if an attack were made on NATO forces "like that on Pearl Harbor," the decision to shoot back would be made by the commanders on the spot (*ibid.*, November 21, 1957, p. 1).

60. Collins, *op. cit.*, p. 378. British Defense Minister Harold Macmillan raised the same question in arguing for a forward strategy in the Parliamentary debates of March, 1955 (*Parliamentary Debates* [Commons], DXXXVII, 2182–83).

61. From an unpublished article of 1956, reproduced in Taylor, *op. cit.*, p. 190. Although the State Department approved the publication of Collins' query, it commented after Taylor's statement, ". . . it is seriously questioned whether the statement about the restrictions to the use of atomic weapons in relation to the NATO armies should be stated in public."

62. Hans Speier describes and interprets the reaction to "Carte Blanche" on

the basis of his personal interviews as well as his reading of the press in *German Rearmament and Atomic War* (White Plains, N.Y.: Row, Peterson & Co., 1957), pp. 144–47, chaps. x, xi.

63. These assurances were conveyed, most notably, by Chancellor Adenauer himself and by Franz Joseph Strauss, who became his defense minister in October, 1956 (*ibid.*, pp. 161, 169).

64. *Ibid.*, p. 207.

65. *Ibid.*, p. 165.

66. A large majority of West Germans responding to polls in 1954 and 1955 opposed the United States using nuclear weapons to defend Germany against non-nuclear Soviet attack (Karl W. Deutsch and Lewis J. Edinger, *Germany Rejoins the Powers* [Stanford: Stanford University Press, 1959], p. 27).

67. Speier, *op. cit.*, pp. 189, 206.

68. *New York Times*, September 28, 1956, p. 1.

69. Speier, *op. cit.*, p. 15.

70. *Ibid.*, p. 219.

71. Thus Chancellor Adenauer told the Bundestag in March, 1958, "If an important part of NATO doesn't possess weapons as strong as those of its potential opponent . . . then it has neither significance nor importance. If the strategical planning of NATO . . . desires that we too . . . make use of this development of weapons technique, and if we hesitate to do so, then we automatically leave NATO" and are left at the mercy of the Soviet Union (*Das Parliament*, March 26, 1958, pp. 4–5, quoted in Gordon A. Craig, "Germany and NATO: The Rearmament Debate, 1950–1958," in Knorr, *op. cit.*, p. 244).

72. For example, the Committee on Defense Questions and Armaments of WEU reported in December, 1958, that, although British commanders envisaged no war in Europe in which nuclear weapons would not be used, German military authorities could envisage a local conflict, growing out of the political tension in East Germany and Central Europe, in which the aggressor would not employ nuclear weapons and allied forces would not find it appropriate to initiate a nuclear war. Therefore, the German authorities thought that sufficient conventional firepower should be retained in NATO's new formations to deal with limited wars (Assembly of Western European Union, "State of European Security," *Proceedings*, document 105 [December 8, 1958], p. 6).

73. The overwhelming majority of respondents to a poll in 1958 opposed equipping German forces with nuclear weapons or installing launching platforms for missiles in the Federal Republic (Deutsch and Edinger, *op. cit.*, p. 27).

74. Gordon Craig describes this controversy in Knorr, *op. cit.*, pp. 246–49.

75. French attitudes and policies toward nuclear weapons are discussed in Henry A. Kissinger, *Nuclear Weapons and Foreign Policy* (New York: Harper & Bros., 1957), pp. 297–306, and Edgar S. Furniss, Jr., *France: Troubled Ally* (New York: Harper & Bros., 1960), pp. 249–50, 283–88. The most active discussion of the strategic implications of nuclear weapons was carried on, largely by military officers, in the pages of *Revue de Défense Nationale.*

76. On April 13, 1955, the French government renounced the development of military applications of nuclear energy, subject to re-examination in 1958 (*New York Times*, April 14, 1955, p. 6). However, research and development on atomic weapons, which had begun as early as 1952, continued. In April Premier Edgar Faure declared that France had to embark on a research program that would prepare her in two years to manufacture her own nuclear weapons, if that were necessary (*ibid.*, April 6, 1955, p. 5; April 14, p. 6). On May 20, 1955, the first protocol was signed authorizing the Commissariat à l'Energie Atomique (CEA) to carry out a nuclear development program, including

military applications ("France's First Atomic Explosion" [English translation of the French "White Paper"], *Service de Presse et d'Information*, February 13, 1960, pp. 8–9).

77. *Statement on Defense*, 1955, p. 7.

78. *Parliamentary Debates* (Commons), DXXXVII, 1931–37.

79. *Ibid.*, col. 2183.

80. *Ibid.*, DXLIX, 1035.

81. *Defense: Outline of Future Policy* (presented April, 1957), Cmd. 124, pp. 2–3.

82. Statement on April 16, 1957, *Parliamentary Debates* (Commons), DLXVIII, 1765.

83. *Ibid.*, col. 1979.

84. *Ibid.*, col. 1791.

85. *Ibid.*, col. 1966.

86. See Sandys's defense of the 1958 white paper in the House of Commons on February 26, 1958 (*ibid.*, DLXXXIII, 395, 410). The white paper, in a statement that aroused particular opposition, said, "The democratic Western nations will never start a war against Russia. But it must be well understood that, if Russia were to launch a major attack on them, even with conventional forces only, they would have to hit back with strategic nuclear weapons. In fact, the strategy of NATO is based on the frank recognition that a full-scale Soviet attack could not be repelled without resort to a massive nuclear bombardment of the sources of power in Russia. In that event, the role of the allied defense forces in Europe would be to hold the front for the time needed to allow the effects of the nuclear counter-offensive to make themselves felt" (*Report on Defense* [presented February, 1958], Cmd. 363, p. 2).

87. *Times* (London), October 15, 1958, p. 13; October 16, p. 13.

88. Montgomery, "A Look through a Window at World War III," *Journal of the Royal United Service Institute*, XCIX (November, 1954), 510.

89. "Organization for War in Modern Times," *ibid.*, C (November, 1955), 523.

90. "The Panorama of Warfare in a Nuclear Age," *ibid.*, CI (November, 1956), 503–20.

91. "The Present State of the Game in the Contest between East and West, and the Future Outlook," *ibid.*, CIII (November, 1958), 479.

92. On the evolution of strategic thinking about limited war, see Morton H. Halperin, "Limited War: An Essay on the Development of the Theory and an Annotated Bibliography" (Cambridge: Mimeographed MS, Center for International Affairs, Harvard University, 1961).

93. Morton H. Halperin reviewed the literature on the use of nuclear weapons in limited war in "Nuclear Weapons and Limited War," *The Journal of Conflict Resolution*, V (June, 1961), 146–66. The most notable expositions of a strategy of limited nuclear war were by Henry A. Kissinger, "Force and Diplomacy in the Nuclear Age," *Foreign Affairs*, XXXIV (April, 1956), 349–66, and *Nuclear Weapons and Foreign Policy* (New York: Harper & Bros., 1957), and by Rear Admiral Sir Anthony Buzzard, "Massive Retaliation and Graduated Deterrence," *World Politics*, VIII (January, 1956), 228–37. Kissinger publicly revised his views on this question in "Limited War: Conventional or Nuclear? —A Reappraisal," *Daedalus*, LXXXIX (Fall, 1960), 800–818.

94. The earliest reasoned criticism of the doctrine of massive retaliation to present this view and attract widespread attention in the government and press was William W. Kaufmann's memorandum, *The Requirements of Deterrence* ("Memorandum," No. 7 [Princeton: Center of International Studies, 1954]). For a similar contemporaneous analysis, see Bernard Brodie, "Unlimited

Weapons and Limited War," *Reporter*, XI (November 18, 1954), 16–21. It should be noted that in his 1954 memorandum Kaufmann assumed that massive retaliation was still a credible response to "an attack on areas which have come to be regarded as of vital interest to us," since a "majority of people, both here and abroad" would be willing to see nuclear weapons used in such circumstances.

95. Statement in April, 1958 (Subcommittee of House Committee on Appropriations, *Hearings, Department of Defense Appropriations for 1959*, 85 Cong., 2 sess., p. 370).

96. *Ibid.*, p. 378; statement in January, 1959, Preparedness Investigating Subcommittee, Senate Committee on Armed Services and on Aeronautical and Space Sciences, *Hearings, Missile and Space Activities*, 86 Cong., 1 sess., pp. 34, 42).

97. Statement in January, 1959, Subcommittee of House Committee on Appropriations, *Hearings, Department of Defense Appropriations for 1960*, 86 Cong., 1 sess., p. 68. McElroy had stated the same view on May 29 and June 6, 1958 (*New York Times*, May 30, 1958, p. 3; June 7, p. 9).

98. Thus, in a press conference on December 15, 1954, President Eisenhower expressed the view that, in order to preserve the free enterprise system and a level of taxation the people would support, he preferred to plan military policies to meet the great threats and rely on improvisation to handle the small wars, since he believed that if you can win a big war, you can certainly win a little one (*New York Times*, December 16, 1954, p. 24). In slightly qualified form Secretary of Defense McElroy repeated this view in January, 1959, in submitting to the House Committee on Appropriations a prepared statement that limited-war and general-war capabilities were the same thing; that the former was applicable to the latter and the latter, "with a few exceptions," was equally applicable to limited-war situations (Subcommittee of House Committee on Appropriations, *Hearings, Department of Defense Appropriations for 1960*, p. 254). Although this view was openly opposed by the Army and, after 1958, by the Navy, it remained the operational guidance for defense policies and was continually affirmed by Air Force spokesmen. As the chief of staff of the Air Force, General White, put it in 1958, "The real deterrent to significant local conflict is nuclear firepower. The whole of this firepower, up to the total necessary to achieve resolution, is the adequate force for local warfare" (*Air Force*, XLI [January, 1958], 49). In December, 1957, General LeMay, vice-chairman of staff for the Air Force, testified, "I do not understand why a force that will deter a big war will not deter a small one, too, if we want it to and say it will. . . . I think we are going to have to build for the worst cases and then use that for all the others. . . . We have been in some minor skirmishes because we did not make it clear that we would use our full power if necessary. I think that a clarification along that line might be a little helpful, and then I think that a force that would deter a big war will deter a small one" (Preparedness Investigating Subcommittee, Senate Committee on Armed Services, *Hearings, Inquiry into Satellite and Missile Programs*, 85 Cong., 1 sess., p. 913).

99. Subcommittee of House Committee on Appropriations, *Hearings, Department of Defense Appropriations for 1959*, p. 389.

100. *New York Times*, October 8, 1958, p. 12.

101. Statement on April 9, 1959, House Committee on Foreign Affairs, *Hearings, Mutual Security Act of 1959*, 86 Cong., 1 sess., p. 466.

102. *New York Times*, April 21, 1959, p. 1.

103. Taylor, *op. cit.*, pp. 61–62, 64.

104. General Taylor maintained that, as a result of the strategic stalemate

among the Joint Chiefs of Staff, "we have never had any centralized limited war planning at the Pentagon level. Most of the planning was done in the field by the commanders," who usually did not have "enough forces to execute even one of these plans" (Testimony on June 14, 1960, Senate Committee on Government Operations, *Hearings, Organizing for National Security,* 86 Cong., 2 sess., Pt. V, pp. 787–90, 793).

105. *New York Times,* April 26, 1960, p. 26.

106. For a discussion of several likely reasons that the United States did not use nuclear weapons in the Korean War, see Morton H. Halperin, "The Limiting Process" (draft chapter of an unpublished MS on limited war; Center for International Affairs, Harvard University, 1961), pp. 24–27.

107. Robert J. Donovan, *Eisenhower: The Inside Story* (New York: Harper & Bros., 1957), pp. 302, 307; James Shepley, "How Dulles Averted War," *Life,* XL (January 16, 1956), 70 ff.; Chalmers M. Roberts, "The Day We Didn't Go to War," *Reporter,* XI (September 14, 1954), 31–35; Marquis Childs, *The Ragged Edge: The Diary of a Crisis* (New York: Doubleday & Co., Inc., 1955).

108. The specific proposal that the President turned down was, apparently, that the Chinese Nationalist air force should be permitted to bomb targets far inland on the mainland and that, if the Communists launched a retaliatory assault on Quemoy or Formosa itself, American planes should be allowed to join in attacking mainland targets, with nuclear weapons if necessary (Chalmers M. Roberts, "Battle on the Rim of Hell: President vs. War Hawks," *Reporter,* XI [December 16, 1954], 11; *New York Times,* April 7, 1955, p. 15; April 21, p. 1.

109. On September 7, 1958, the Soviet news agency Tass made public a letter, delivered the same day, from Khrushchev to Eisenhower, warning that an attack on Communist China would be an attack on the Soviet Union and that "in the age of nuclear and rocket weapons of unprecedented power and rapid action" warships like those of the seventh fleet were "fit, in fact, for nothing but courtesy visits and gun salutes, and can serve as targets for the right types of rockets." This threat had been preceded by a top-level Sino-Soviet meeting, which had been followed by obviously planted rumors that the Soviet Union had agreed to give the Chinese nuclear weapons and ballistic missiles (Tang Tsou, *The Embroilment over Quemoy: Mao, Chiang, and Dulles* ["International Study Paper," No. 2 (Institute of International Studies, University of Utah, 1959)], pp. 12–14, 31–32).

110. Taylor, *op. cit.,* p. 9.

111. *Ibid.,* p. 117.

112. Malcolm W. Hoag, "The Place of Limited War in NATO Strategy," in Knorr, *op. cit.,* p. 108.

CHAPTER 6

TOWARD A STRATEGY OF LIMITED RESISTANCE

1. In the copious literature on limited war the advocates of a strategy of nuclear limited war were a minority, whose views reached their height of popularity in 1956 and 1957. One analysis received more attention than all the others put together: Henry A. Kissinger, *Nuclear Weapons and Foreign Policy* (New York: Harper & Bros., 1957). See, especially, chap. vi. However, by 1960 Kissinger, without abandoning his advocacy of preparedness for limited nuclear war, had come to regard conventional limited war as the best strategy, reserving nuclear weapons as a deterrent to Soviet nuclear weapons and as a

last resort in case conventional resistance should prove ineffective ("Limited War: Conventional or Nuclear? A Reappraisal," *Daedalus*, LXXXIX [Fall, 1960], 800–817). For a review of the literature on nuclear weapons and limited war, see Morton H. Halperin, "Nuclear Weapons and Limited War," *Journal of Conflict Resolution*, V (June, 1961), 146–66.

2. Kissinger, *Nuclear Weapons and Foreign Policy*, pp. 194 ff.

3. The critique of a strategy of nuclear limited war and the argument for major reliance upon a strategy of conventional limited war were presented most cogently by James E. King, Jr., in "Nuclear Plenty and Limited War," *Foreign Affairs*, XXXV (January, 1957), 238–56, and in a review of Kissinger's book by the same author in two issues of the *New Republic*: "Nuclear Weapons and Foreign Policy," CXXXVII (July 1, 1957), 18–21 and (July 15, 1957) 16–18; and also by William W. Kaufmann, "The Crisis in Military Affairs," *World Politics*, X (July, 1958), 579–603; Arnold Wolfers, "Europe and the NATO Shield," *International Organization*, XII (Autumn, 1958), 425–39; Roger Hilsman, "On NATO Strategy," in Arnold Wolfers (ed.), *Alliance Policy in the Cold War* (Baltimore: Johns Hopkins Press, 1959), pp. 173–77; Malcolm W. Hoag, "The Place of Limited War in NATO Strategy," in Klaus Knorr (ed.), *NATO and American Security* (Princeton: Princeton University Press, 1959), chap. v; P. M. S. Blackett, *Atomic Weapons and East-West Relations* (New York: Cambridge University Press, 1956); and F. O. Miksche, *The Failure of Atomic Strategy* (New York: Frederick A. Praeger, Inc., 1958).

4. See the discussion of this relationship in analytical and historical terms in Robert E. Osgood, *Limited War* (Chicago: University of Chicago Press, 1957), pp. 22 ff. and chap. iv.

5. Bernard Brodie stresses this point in his discussion of limited war in *Strategy in the Missile Age* (Princeton: Princeton University Press, 1959), pp. 309–14.

6. The qualities of weapons systems that facilitate or obstruct agreement on reciprocal restraints are discussed in Thomas C. Schelling, *Nuclear Weapons and Limited War* (RAND Corporation Study P-1620, February 20, 1959). Schelling analyzes the process of "tacit bargaining" in reaching mutual limitations more intensively in "Bargaining, Communication, and Limited War," *Journal of Conflict Resolution*, I (March, 1957), 19–36.

7. One can imagine target and geographical restrictions on nuclear warfare that, theoretically, would be relatively susceptible to mutual verification, but they would seem to place one or the other side at too great a military disadvantage for the belligerents to have a mutual interest in observing them. For example, confining nuclear bursts to antiaircraft shells, to employment at sea, or to use by a belligerent within his own territory would seem to suffer from this difficulty.

8. Roger Hilsman, *loc. cit.*, p. 32.

9. Hoag, *loc. cit.*, p. 119.

10. Most of the considerations that make primary reliance upon tactical nuclear weapons inadvisable also make primary reliance upon biological and radiological weapons inadvisable. However, a strategy for using disabling, as opposed to lethal, chemical weapons might be compatible with the comparative advantages of relying upon conventional resistance, if they could be successfully distinguished from lethal weapons in the eyes of the enemy and allies.

11. Henry Kissinger presents the case against dual-purpose units and for separate nuclear commands in *The Necessity for Choice* (New York: Harper & Bros., 1961), pp. 91–93.

12. As Malcolm Hoag has pointed out, the expense of adding an adequate con-

ventional limited-war capability to a tactical nuclear war capability would depend upon the degree of preparation NATO sought in the latter sphere. To be thoroughly prepared for tactical nuclear warfare (which would include being prepared to fight effectively if one received the first nuclear blow) would entail great expense, but to settle for something like the present inadequate level of preparation for tactical nuclear warfare would not. If the primary function of nuclear weapons were to deter the other side from using them, such a subordination of nuclear to conventional capabilities would be an acceptable compromise between inadequate and thorough preparation for both kinds of warfare (Hoag, *loc cit.*, pp. 121–23); see also, by the same author, "What Interdependence for NATO?" *World Politics*, XII (April, 1960), 369–90.

13. Senate Special Committee To Study the Foreign Aid Program, *Hearings, The Foreign Aid Program*, 85 Cong., 1 sess., p. 402.

14. *New York Times*, March 16, 1955, p. 1.

15. *Ibid.*, November 29, 1954, p. 4. In January, 1955, James Reston reported that a strategy called "2X" was being discussed in the administration. He explained that the strategy meant punishing the aggressor with twice his anticipated gain (*ibid.*, January 9, 1955, Sec. 4, p. 8).

16. "Challenge and Response in United States Policy," *Foreign Affairs*, XXVI (October, 1957), 25–43; see, especially, pp. 30–33.

17. Statement to a press conference on March 11, 1959 (*New York Times*, March 12, 1959, p. 12). When Eisenhower was asked whether, having ruled out a ground war and having said that a nuclear war would not free anyone, he would recommend any intermediate response if the Russians really started something, he replied, "No . . . I didn't say that nuclear war is a complete impossibility. I said it couldn't, as I see it, free anything. Destruction is not a good police force." He concluded that the West had to protect itself and never "back up on our rights and our responsibilities." At another time he said that, since the West would not fight a ground war, it would have to go to "other means" and "think in much, much bigger terms." On the other hand, General Maxwell Taylor, a few hours after General Eisenhower's press conference, told a Senate committee that he could envision the Berlin crisis resulting in a conventional war in which the Soviet Union elected to throw its satellite forces against the West without committing its own power. In this event, he said, the West could win a prolonged conventional ground war in Central Europe (*ibid.*, March 15, 1959, p. 1).

18. *Ibid.*, March 8, 1959, pp. 1, 8.

19. General Norstad's major statements on NATO strategy and forces appear in the *New York Times*, June 25, 1956, p. 22; *Bulletin*, XXXVI (February 18, 1957), 251–55, and XXXVII (December 16, 1957), 952–55; "The Sword and the Shield," *Army*, VIII (December, 1957), 44–47; Senate Committee on Foreign Relations, *Hearings, Mutual Security Act of 1958*, 85 Cong., 2 sess., pp. 185 ff.; Subcommittee of the House Committee on Appropriations, *Hearings, Mutual Security Appropriations for 1959*, 85 Cong., 2 sess., pp. 564–65; House Committee on Foreign Affairs, *Hearings, Mutual Security Act of 1959*, p. 466; and "NATO: Strength and Spirit," *NATO Letter*, VIII (January, 1960), 7–11.

20. One indication that MC–70 did envision a contingency between a brief conventional holding action and a general nuclear war was its requirement for supplies and equipment to keep troops in the field for ninety days. In March, 1960, the British submitted a paper to the Defense Ministers arguing that this requirement should be based on no more than a thirty-day war, since a war in Europe would be either strictly localized or one of total destruction (*Manchester Guardian Weekly*, March 31, 1960, p. 5).

21. The word "interdependence" probably first gained currency when it appeared in the communiqué of October, 1957, following President Eisenhower's and Prime Minister Macmillan's meeting in Washington: "The arrangements which the nations of the free world have made for collective defense and mutual help are based on the recognition that the concept of national self-sufficiency is out of date. The countries of the free world are interdependent, and only in genuine partnership, by combining their resources and sharing tasks in many fields, can progress and safety be found. For our part, we have agreed that our two countries will henceforth act in accordance with this principle." However, here the principle was applied quite narrowly to America's sharing of nuclear information and weapons with Great Britain (*Bulletin*, XXXVI [November 11, 1957], 739–40). "Interdependence" has subsequently been applied to the objectives of strategic, logistical, and political specialization and co-ordination. For analysis of the problems of interdependence in NATO, see Alastair Buchan, *NATO in the 1960's: The Implications of Interdependence* (New York: Frederick A. Praeger, Inc., 1960); Denis Healey, "Interdependence," *Political Quarterly* (January–March, 1960), 46–56; and Hoag, "What Interdependence for NATO?" *World Politics*, XII, 369–90; "On NATO Pooling," *World Politics*, X (April, 1958), 475–83; and "The Economics of Military Alliance," in Charles J. Hitch and Roland N. McKean (eds.), *The Economics of Defense in the Nuclear Age* (Cambridge: Harvard University Press, 1960), chap. xv.

22. For example, in 1960 Alastair Buchan noted that the existing system of ground defense was too unintegrated to permit the necessary mobility. "The present twenty-one divisions in Europe," he stated, "are nearly static, in that they are tied to national lines of communication and have so few standardized components that it would be virtually impossible to despatch, say, two American divisions to Westphalia or a British division to Bavaria" (Buchan, *op. cit.*, p. 97).

23. See the statistical tables on gross national product and production of basic commodities in the study prepared at the request of the Senate Committee on Foreign Relations by the Foreign Policy Research Institute, *United States Foreign Policy: Western Europe* (1959), 86 Cong., 1 sess., pp. 85–86. In part, the tremendous rate of growth reflected the low postwar (1948) base from which it was calculated. However, the growth after 1953 was equally impressive. Buchan noted that industrial production was 52 per cent higher in the six countries of the European Economic Community in mid-1959 that it was in 1953 (Buchan, *op. cit.*, p. 39).

24. In 1958 the Institute of Strategic Studies estimated that the United States, Britain, and France were spending over 8 per cent of their national income on defense, whereas the alliance as a whole was spending only 5.3 per cent. West Germany had never spent over 4 per cent (*ibid.*, p. 39). The Enskilda Bank of Stockholm estimated that the United States spent 10 per cent of its gross national product on defense; Britain, 7 per cent; France, 6 per cent (including Algerian war costs); and the other allies, 3 or 4 per cent (cited in Senate Committee on Foreign Relations, *United States Foreign Policy*, 87 Cong., 1 sess., Part 2, p. 379). At the end of 1959 it was estimated that the re-equipment of NATO forces up to minimum requirements in the next five years would cost the European members about 10 billion dollars more than they were currently spending. This would mean that the European allies would have to increase their defense budgets by 5 to 25 per cent. Yet, since 1952, their defense spending, on the average, had dropped from a peak of 7.6 per cent of total national spending to about 6 per cent in 1959, compared to United States defense spending of about 11.2 per cent of national spending (*U.S. News and World Report*, December 28, 1959, p. 27). On the complexities of reaching an efficient and equitable burden-

sharing formula, see Hoag, *World Politics,* X, 481–83, and Lincoln Gordon, "Economic Aspects of Coalition Diplomacy: The NATO Experience," *International Organization,* X (Autumn, 1956), 531–37.

25. On the process and effect of the Annual Review, see M. Margaret Ball, *NATO and the European Union Movement* (London: Stevens & Sons, 1959), pp. 78 ff.

26. Buchan discusses the opportunities and problems of standardization and common financing in *op. cit.*, chap. viii, "The Underpinning of Interdependence."

27. Gallois advocated greater integration of logistics and of the development and manufacture of weapons, their disposition, emplacement, and maintenance. However, in the "strategy of operations," as opposed to the "strategy of means," he advocated greater national responsibility. To correct the two great weaknesses of NATO's defense posture, an inadequate limited-resistance capability and strategy of means, he contended that "what is now a national concern—namely the assembling of the means required to wage war—must be made a collective one, while responsibility for the use of the arsenal thus assembled must be shifted from the collective to the national level" (Pierre M. Gallois, "New Teeth for NATO," *Foreign Affairs,* XXXIX [October, 1960], 80).

28. Malcolm Hoag noted that the Netherlands' production of British-designed aircraft fitted with Belgian-manufactured engines and Italy's assembling of U.S. Sabres represented uneconomic diversions of aircraft production from the United Kingdom and the United States, although they were examples of international co-operation (*World Politics,* X, 478). However, such dispersal of production is not necessarily intended to economize; it may be intended to distribute economic benefits equitably or, as in the case of Britain's production of V-bombers, to serve as a concession to national pride and independent deterrence. Of course, whether these purposes should take priority over the economic use of over-all resources is not an economic question. Considerations of equity and politics also figure strongly in the much agitated problem of burden-sharing. Thus by 1960 the United States, surveying the increasing expenditures required to expand and re-equip NATO forces and an adverse international balance of payments, was growing increasingly dissatisfied with what she regarded as her disproportionate share of NATO's financial burden, in view of her allies' greatly increased economic capacities and their large share of the benefits of collective defense in comparison to the size of their military efforts (*New York Times,* December 18, 1959, p. 3). See Lincoln Gordon's trenchant discussion of the relationship between the economy, the equity, and the adequacy of allied defense efforts (*op. cit.*).

29. One example of this relation between integration and strategy, with important political overtones, was pointed up by West Germany's move in February, 1960, to acquire supply bases in Spain, which touched off a storm of apprehension and protest in Europe and especially in Great Britain. The German defense minister, Franz Josef Strauss, defended the move as a means of acquiring the necessary rear-area supply bases that NATO had failed to provide according to an earlier NATO plan for a network of such bases. Although NATO had written off this integrated logistics plan on the grounds that it would be unnecessary in the nuclear war that it planned to fight, West German leaders, with NATO encouragement, had continued to plan for a strong conventional resistance on the forward line, for which a rear-area supply system would be essential (*New York Times,* February 25, 1960, p. 3; March 6, p. 5). Before the end of 1960 Germany agreed with France to place German supply bases on French soil.

CHAPTER 7

THE ONSET OF THE MISSILE AGE

1. Intelligence estimates, prompted by the unprecedented appearance of formations of Soviet long-range and medium-range jet bombers in the May Day parade of 1954, led the Air Force to the conclusion that the Soviet Union was producing strategic jet bombers at a rate at least as high as the American rate and was capable of building a bombing force of from 600 to 800 Bison bombers, comparable to the American B-52, by 1959–60. In the spring of 1956 concern over this prospect led to congressional hearings on airpower, in which Air Force officers, Senator Symington, and others expressed alarm about the possibility that the Soviet Union might gain a first-strike capability that could knock out all the United States key bases in a surprise attack unless the B-52's rate of production were increased (Subcommittee on the Air Force, Senate Committee on Armed Services, *Hearings, Study of Airpower,* 84 Cong., 2 sess). A few years later, however, the Soviet Union appeared not to have built more than one-sixth of their estimated theoretical capabilities—perhaps because she decided to put her strategic effort into missiles instead—and the original estimates were revised sharply downward in 1957. Yet another Moscow air show on July 9, 1961, revealed many varieties of new and far-advanced bombers and fighters, which led to a counter-revision.

2. In October, 1959, Joseph Alsop stated that "the best official forecast" of American-Soviet ICBM numbers was 30 to 100 in 1960, 70 to 500 in 1961, 130 to 1,000 in 1962, and 130 to 1,500 in 1963 (*Washington Post,* October 7, 1959, p. A17). For another alarmed account of the "missile gap," based on published accounts and interviews, see Thomas R. Phillips, "The Growing Missile Gap," *Reporter,* XX (January 8, 1959), 10–16. James R. Shepley reported that Secretary McElroy estimated a possible Soviet missile lead of three-to-one ("Life and Death Debate over Missile Program," *Life,* XLVI [March 9, 1959], 116 ff.). This allegation was later widely repeated, but there is no record of McElroy's statement. His successor, Thomas S. Gates, originally accepted the view that McElroy had anticipated the possibility of a three-to-one ratio but later said that, although he assumed from the repeated allegations to that effect that McElroy must have made such a statement, his research staff had failed to verify the assumption (Subcommittee of the House Committee on Appropriations, *Hearings, Department of Defense Appropriations for 1961,* 86 Cong., 2 sess., pp. 476–78). In January, 1960, SAC Commander General Thomas S. Power declared that if the Russians had 300 ballistic missiles, only 150 of which were ICBM's, they could "virtually wipe out our entire nuclear strike capability within a span of thirty minutes" (Senate Preparedness Investigating Subcommittee of the House Committee on Appropriations, *Department of Defense Appropriations for 1961,* pp. 274–79). However, he did not assert that the Russians actually had this number of missiles on launching pads.

3. The most influential statement of this view was written by a RAND specialist, Albert Wohlstetter, "The Delicate Balance of Terror," *Foreign Affairs,* XXXVIII (January, 1959), 211–34. For an equally authoritative and more comprehensive analysis of the implications of missile technology for deterrence, based on unclassified sources, see *Developments in Military Technology and Their Impact on United States Strategy and Foreign Policy,* study prepared at the request of

the Senate Committee on Foreign Relations by the Washington Center of Foreign Policy Research, December, 1959.

4. See, particularly, McElroy's testimony in Subcommittee of the House Committee on Appropriations, *Hearings, Department of Defense Appropriations for 1960,* in January, 1959, and Subcommittee of the Senate Committee on Appropriations, *Hearings, Department of Defense Appropriations for 1960,* in May, 1959.

5. Testimony of administration spokesmen, Senate Preparedness Investigating Subcommittee, Senate Committees on Armed Services and on Aeronautical and Space Services, *Hearings, Missiles, Space, and Other Major Defense Matters,* 86 Cong., 2 sess. Also, Charles J. V. Murphy, "Defense: The Converging Decisions," *Fortune,* LVIII (October, 1958), 230.

6. In May, 1959, McElroy explained that official estimates of Soviet ICBM's were based on the "properly conservative practice" of projecting what the Soviet Union seemed capable of producing and that "it is when the number of ICBM's which the United States actually plans to produce is compared to the number it is estimated the Soviet Union can produce that the so-called missile gap arises." He went on to say that the Soviet Union does not always produce what estimates say it could produce (Subcommittee of the Senate Committee on Appropriations, *Department of Defense Appropriations for 1960,* pp. 9–10). In January, 1960, Secretary of Defense Gates explained that additional intelligence information had enabled the government to downgrade the estimated number of Soviet ICBM's, which had been based on what they theoretically could produce (Subcommittee of the House Committee on Appropriations, *Department of Defense Appropriations for 1961,* p. 24). In an article in April, 1959, Charles J. V. Murphy stated that intelligence estimates were first revised in early 1958, less than a year after the first successful Russian ICBM test in August, 1957, because the ICBM firings came to a long halt and were resumed only at a slow rate thereafter ("The Embattled Mr. McElroy," *Fortune,* LIX [April, 1959], 242).

7. See pp. 200–201, below.

8. Subcommittee of the House Committee on Appropriations, *Hearings, Department of Defense Appropriations for 1961,* pp. 4, 26, 136.

9. *Current Digest of the Soviet Press,* XIV, No. 2, p. 11.

10. Quoted by Zbigniew Brzezinski, "A Book the Russians Would Like To Forget," *Reporter,* XXIII (December 22, 1960), 30.

11. "On the Character of Modern Warfare," *International Affairs,* X (October, 1960), 25, 26.

12. *New York Times,* December 7, 1960, p. 15. The complete text of both the Moscow statement and Khrushchev's speech is reproduced in *Two Communist Manifestoes* (Washington, D.C.: Washington Center of Foreign Policy Research, 1961).

13. *Ibid.*, pp. 53–54.

14. *Ibid.*, p. 15.

15. The most systematic expositions of the strategy of limited nuclear retaliation are Morton A. Kaplan, "The Calculus of Nuclear Deterrence," *World Politics,* XI (October, 1958), 20–43, and "The Strategy of Limited Retaliation" ("Policy Memorandum," No. 19 [Princeton University Center for International Studies, April 9, 1959]). For a balanced appraisal of this strategy, see Glenn H. Snyder, *Deterrence and Defense* (Princeton: Princeton University Press, 1961), pp. 69–75, 193–224. See also Leo Szilard, "How To Live with the Bomb and Survive," *Bulletin of the Atomic Scientists,* XVI (February, 1960), 59–73.

16. The Soviet doctrine of pre-emptive attack is discussed in Raymond L. Garthoff, *Soviet Strategy in the Nuclear Age* (New York: Frederick A. Praeger,

Inc., 1958), and at greater length in Herbert S. Dinerstein, *War and the Soviet Union* (New York: Frederick A. Praeger, Inc., 1959).

17. See Thomas C. Schelling's seminal discussion of different kinds of safeguards against surprise attack: "Surprise Attack and Disarmament," in Klaus Knorr (ed.), *NATO and American Security* (Princeton: Princeton University Press, 1959), and the elaboration and refinement of this discussion in Schelling and Halperin, *Strategy and Arms Control* (New York: Twentieth Century Fund, 1961).

18. Henry A. Kissinger and Thomas C. Schelling have suggested that, physically, such communication could be promoted by the establishment in the United States and the Soviet Union of observation and communications teams with special equipment capable of instantaneous communication to the Soviet and American governments and between the two (Kissinger, "Arms Control, Inspection, and Suprise Attack," *Foreign Affairs,* XXXVIII [July, 1960], 566–67; Schelling, "Arms Control: Proposal for a Special Surveillance Force," *World Politics,* XIII [October, 1960], 11). On the opportunities and difficulties of informal and tacit arms control agreements, see Schelling, "Reciprocal Measures for Arms Stabilization," *Daedalus,* XXCIX (Fall, 1960), 902–10, and Schelling and Halperin, *Strategy and Arms Control,* chap. viii.

19. In the articles and books above, Schelling and Kissinger outline formal agreements designed to enable the parties to provide each other with positive evidence that they are not preparing a surprise attack.

20. Remarks on the Berlin crisis in a press conference, *New York Times,* March 12, 1959, p. 12; and remarks at a state dinner in Manila, *ibid.*, June 16, 1960, p. 14.

21. The Air Force just barely got a budgetary concession to a major counterforce program: the development and production of the B-70 bomber. However, it did better in getting counterforce targets included in the integrated strategic target list. As Hanson Baldwin wrote of the target compromise in 1960, "The nation's current strategic concept is keyed to a target list that includes Soviet cities as well as missile sites and air bases. . . . Any contemporary target list must include both military installations and cities, many high-ranking Pentagon officials maintain" (*ibid.*, January 14, 1961, p. 10).

22. Subcommittee of the House Committee on Appropriations, *Department of Defense Appropriations for 1960,* p. 71.

23. Senate Subcommittee on the Air Force, *Study of Airpower,* p. 10.

24. McElroy testified that "an attack upon our forces and friends in Western Europe would be an attack upon the United States" (Subcommittee of the House Committee on Appropriations, *Department of Defense Appropriations for 1960,* p. 68). LeMay defined the first objective of SAC's role as deterring aggression against the United States and her allies and defined the other objectives—gaining air superiority and winning the war—without distinguishing between first- and second-strike missions (Senate Subcommittee on the Air Force, *Study of Airpower,* p. 102).

25. Subcommittee of the House Committee on Appropriations, *Department of Defense Appropriations for 1960,* p. 929.

26. *Ibid.*, p. 850.

27. Senate Subcommittee on the Air Force, *Study of Airpower,* p. 102.

28. Subcommittee of Senate Committee on Appropriations, *Hearings, Department of Defense Appropriations for 1960,* 86 Cong., 1 sess., pp. 254, 287.

29. The most complete published exposition of the strategy of minimum deterrence by a Navy officer was Cmdr. P. H. Backus' "Finite Deterrence, Controlled Retaliation," *United States Naval Institute Proceedings,* LXXX (March,

1959), 23–29. However, Backus' article was more extreme than official Navy doctrine.

30. Subcommittee of House Committee on Appropriations, *Department of Defense Appropriations for 1960,* pp. 329–30. General Taylor presents a similar formula in *The Uncertain Trumpet* (New York: Harper & Bros., 1960), p. 148.

31. Subcommittee of House Committee on Appropriations, *Department of Defense Appropriations for 1960,* pp. 477, 591, 594.

32. *The Uncertain Trumpet,* pp. 140–42; testimony on February 4, 1960, Senate Preparedness Investigating Subcommittee, *Missiles, Space and Other Major Defense Matters,* p. 194.

33. In his book General Taylor wrote that by 1961 Soviet missiles would be so concealed, dispersed, and mobile that "it will become impossible for our U.S. bombers and missiles to eliminate the Soviet missile threat even by an anticipatory strike" (*op. cit.,* pp. 132–33). Admiral Burke testified on February 8, 1960, that the United States did not have "the least idea" where Soviet missile sites were—except for test sites—and would never know where many of them were (Senate Preparedness Investigating Subcommitte, *Missiles, Space, and Other Major Defense Matters,* pp. 287, 338).

34. *Ibid.,* p. 258. Lemnitzer drew the conclusion that limited war was rendered more likely.

35. From Power's speech to the Economic Club of New York on January 19, 1960, and from his testimony on February 2 (*ibid.,* pp. 7, 1–56).

36. Subcommittee of House Committee on Appropriations, *Department of Defense Appropriations for 1961,* pp. 232–33.

37. *Ibid.,* p. 6. The italics are mine.

38. *Ibid.,* p. 136.

39. *Ibid.,* p. 26.

40. *Ibid.,* p. 4.

41. *Ibid.,* p. 22.

42. *New York Times,* February 19, 1960, p. 4.

43. On May 25, 1960, in his radio and television address to the nation, explaining the U-2 incident and the collapse of the summit meeting, President Eisenhower appealed for a "world of open societies" and an international open skies agreement. After describing the ease with which the Soviet Union could acquire information about American cities, dams, highways, and the like, he said, "Soviet distrust, however, does still remain. To allay these misgivings I offered five years ago to open our skies to Soviet reconnaissance aircraft on a reciprocal basis. The Soviets refused. That offer is still open. At an appropriate time America will submit such a program to the United Nations, together with the recommendation that the United Nations itself conduct this reconnaissance" (*ibid.,* May 26, 1960, p. 6).

44. Address on September 22, 1960 (*ibid.,* September 23, 1960, p. 14).

45. Walter Lippmann, *The Communist World and Ours* (Boston: Little, Brown & Co., 1958), pp. 13–14.

46. *Two Communist Manifestoes,* p. 61.

47. Speech on January 6, 1961 (*ibid.,* p. 56).

CHAPTER 8

THE PROBLEM OF NUCLEAR DIFFUSION

1. According to estimates made by a committee of the American Academy of Arts and Sciences (*The Nth Country Problem and Arms Control* ["National Planning Association, Planning Pamphlet," No. 108 (1959)]). This report con-

cluded that as of 1959 eleven countries could produce nuclear warheads by themselves in five years if they wanted to; eight others could follow shortly; and in a decade at least six others could join the nuclear club.

2. In October, 1960, private firms in West Germany and the Netherlands had advanced so far toward developing a relatively cheap process for producing enriched uranium that the United States induced the West German government to classify the process as a state secret in order to prevent the spread of nuclear production to other nations (*New York Times,* October 12, 1960, p. 1; October 13, p. 18).

3. In his testimony for the 1954 Act, Dulles said, "The art of telling people what a weapon is like, what it can do to others, what it can do to you, how you can protect yourself, and at the same time not tell anybody how you produce the weapon, that undoubtedly is a difficult task of definition" (Joint Committee on Atomic Energy, *Hearings, To Amend the Atomic Energy Act of 1946,* 83 Cong., 2 sess., p. 702).

4. *Ibid.,* p. 703.

5. *New York Times,* December 14, 1956, p. 1.

6. *Ibid.,* February 1, 1957, p. 1; *New York Herald Tribune,* December 15, 1956, p. 8.

7. In 1942 the United States entered into an agreement with Britain and Canada for unrestricted exchange of information on atomic energy. However, British and Canadian scientists complained that Americans (especially the military leadership of the Manhattan project) imposed restrictions upon full nuclear sharing and co-operation. Churchill repeatedly sought the resumption of full exchange of information. Finally, when he threatened to carry out a program of separate research, President Roosevelt arranged a heads-of-government agreement, signed at Quebec in August, 1943, which set up a Combined Policy Committee for the complete interchange of information and ideas and which stipulated that neither power would use the weapons against third parties without the other's consent or communicate any nuclear information to third parties without mutual consent.

After the end of the war the American government treated this wartime agreement as void and stopped exchanging information on atomic weapons developments. The McMahon Act was intended to close the door completely on the sharing of nuclear weapons information, on the supposition that sharing would destroy the secrecy necessary to preserve America's nuclear monopoly against the Russians.

Nevertheless, the Atomic Energy Commission, largely on the initiative of Chairman Lilienthal and Dr. Oppenheimer of the General Advisory Committee, undertook an energetic program of disseminating unclassified atomic information, including a tripartite declassification program with Britain and Canada. In January, 1948, the United States reached a *modus vivendi* whereby the British granted the United States an approximately equal division of uranium produced in the Congo, the United States agreed to disclose nuclear data in nine categories excluding weapons production, and the provision of the Quebec agreement on mutual consultation before using the bomb was explicitly revoked. In 1949 President Truman was even prepared to seek the amendment of the McMahon Act to permit a "full partnership" with Britain in nuclear know-how, including the exchange of information on atomic weapons production. However, the attacks of the congressional Joint Committee on Atomic Energy on alleged AEC security laxness, beginning in 1948, and the objections of Senator Vandenberg discouraged the President from carrying out his plans for nuclear sharing.

In the meanwhile, the British undertook their own nuclear program, while continually urging the United States to negotiate a freer exchange of information (Leonard Bertin, *Atom Harvest* [London: Secker and Warburg, 1955], pp. 5, 70 ff.; Winston S. Churchill, *The Hinge of Fate* [Boston: Houghton Mifflin Co., 1950], pp. 381, 809; Arthur H. Vandenberg, Jr., *The Private Papers of Senator Vandenberg* [Boston: Houghton Mifflin Co., 1952], pp. 252–65; Walter Millis, *The Forrestal Diaries* [New York: Viking Press, 1951], pp. 336–39, 471–72; Harry S. Truman, *Memoirs* [Garden City, N.Y.: Doubleday & Co., Inc.], II, 294–304).

8. British pressure for nuclear sharing won the first amendment of the Atomic Energy Act in 1951, but it was not until after the Russian H-bomb explosion in 1953 had dramatically undermined the original reason for the McMahon Act that the way was opened for substantial sharing with Britain under the 1954 amendment. The provision in this 1954 law (Section 123) that all agreements for nuclear co-operation had to lie before the Joint Atomic Energy Committee for a thirty-day period of review before becoming effective facilitated the government's policy of giving Britain preferential treatment; for, in effect, it enabled Congress to administer the legal criteria for sharing with a discrimination among allies that the executive branch would have found embarrassing. (To reject an executive agreement under this provision, a congressional concurrent resolution would be necessary.) In June, 1956, the Defense Department, with presidential and State Department support but against AEC and JCAE objections, used a legal technicality to conclude an agreement to give the British secrets about the atomic submarine "Nautilus," exchanging information on small military reactors and ship propulsion reactors and sending Britain enriched uranium in return for depleted uranium (*New York Times*, November 16, 1957, p. 1). The United States began to provide information under this agreement in April, 1957.

9. *Ibid.*, March 12, 1957, p. 14; *NATO Letter*, V (April, 1957), p. 22.

10. In his speech on December 8, 1953, the President proposed that the United Nations should sponsor a program for the peaceful application of atomic energy under inspection and control to prevent the misapplication of fissionable and other materials which participating nations would allocate to the international agency.

11. Senate Committee on Foreign Relations, *Hearings, Statute of IAEA*, 84 Cong., 1 sess., p. 4.

12. Dulles said that the administration had considered making fissionable materials available to Britain if she would agree to stop production, but that he thought it would be better to deal with all the allies through NATO in order to avoid "drawing lines of distinction" between them. He pointed out that the nuclear stockpiles might be under the command of NATO's supreme commander in his capacity as the commander of American forces in Europe, but he said that the stockpiling plan might, nevertheless, require a change in the Atomic Energy Act (*Washington Post*, July 17, 1957, p. 1).

13. *New York Times*, July 18, 1957, p. 4.

14. Secretary of Defense McElroy told a NATO parliamentarians' conference that the United States would seek IRBM launching sites in Europe and was considering a plan for giving certain allies control of the warheads as well as the missiles (*ibid.*, November 16, 1957, p. 1; *New York Herald Tribune*, November 17, 1957, p. 1). A few days later Secretary of State Dulles told a press conference that the United States would help establish missile bases in NATO countries that wanted them; that stockpiles of nuclear warheads for both strategic and tactical weapons, under American custody, would be provided at points of ready access during war; and that the United States would give her allies "a deeper sense of responsibility for their safety" by insuring

"a very considerable measure of allied participation" in the handling of the missiles (*New York Times,* November 20, 1957, p. 1).

15. On the submarine suggestion, see *New York Herald Tribune,* December 17, 1957, p. 1; *Christian Science Monitor,* December 17, 1957, p. 1.

16. *NATO Letter,* VI (January, 1958), pp. 11–12.

17. According to C. L. Sulzberger, writing from Paris (*New York Times,* June 25, 1960, p. 20).

18. For the original research and analysis of the military implications of Euratom I am indebted to Harold L. Nieburg for his unpublished doctoral dissertation, "Atomic Secrecy and Foreign Policy" (University of Chicago, 1961).

19. *Times* (London), April 18, 1958, p. 12; *New York Times,* April 15, 1958, p. 1.

20. Atomic Energy Committee, *Twenty-fourth Semiannual Report* (1958), pp. 24–25; Joint Committee on Atomic Energy, *Proposed Euratom Agreements with Associated Documents and Materials,* 85 Cong., 2 sess., p. 21.

21. *Proceedings,* Assembly of Western European Union, Document 87 (June 2, 1958), pp. 120–21.

22. Statement on January 31, 1958, Joint Committee on Atomic Energy, *Hearings, To Amend the Atomic Energy Act of 1954,* 85 Cong., 2 sess., pp. 90–94.

23. Statement on April 17, 1958, before the Joint Committee on Atomic Energy (*Bulletin,* XXXVIII [May 5, 1958], 741–42.

24. The discriminatory intent of this provision was implicit in the report of the Joint Committee on Atomic Energy on the bill, which defined "substantial progress" as follows: "The cooperating nation must have achieved considerably more than a mere theoretical knowledge of atomic weapons design, or the testing of a limited number of atomic weapons. It is intended that the cooperating nation must have achieved a capability of its own of fabricating a variety of atomic weapons, and constructed and operated the necessary facilities, including weapons research and development laboratories, weapons manufacturing facilities, a weapon testing station, and trained personnel to operate each of these facilities" (Senate Report 1654, House Report 1859, 85 Cong., 2 sess., p. 12). The capacity of Congress to discriminate in behalf of certain allies and against others was further enhanced by an amendment to Section 123, which provided that co-operation pertaining to military information or materials could be undertaken only after "the proposed agreement for cooperation, together with the approval and determination of the President . . . has been submitted to the Congress and referred to the Joint Committee, and a period of sixty days has elapsed while Congress is in session, but any such proposed agreement for cooperation shall not become effective if during such sixty-day period the Congress passes a concurrent resolution stating in substance that it does not favor the proposed agreement for cooperation."

25. *New York Times,* July 6, 1958, p. 1. American assistance was said to include development of a propulsion reactor and the transfer of enriched nuclear fuel. Some press reports indicated that Dulles had gone so far as to offer a submarine reactor, as had been promised to Britain (*ibid.,* March 15, 1959, p. 1).

26. Thus the special assistant to the secretary of state for atomic energy and disarmament told the JCAE on June 17, 1959, "The bar to our cooperation with France . . . has not been security in the French defense establishment, but has been our own national policy of not assisting fourth countries to become nuclear powers" (Joint Committee on Atomic Energy, *Hearings, Agreements for Cooperation for Mutual Defense Purposes,* 86 Cong., 1 sess., p. 46). And on June 11 the deputy assistant secretary of state for European affairs said, "In my judgment, France—the De Gaulle administration and De Gaulle specifically—could

not be satisfied with anything short of an agreement which would enable France to become a nuclear power" (*ibid.*, p. 9).

27. *New York Times,* May 15, 1960, p. 4; June 10, p. 3.

28. Speech on December 6, 1959, to the Institute of World Affairs at the University of Southern California, *NATO Letter,* VIII (January, 1960), p. 10.

29. *Times* (London), December 3, 1959, p. 10; December 4, p. 9; *Manchester Guardian,* December 4, 1959, p. 1.

30. When asked by a reporter whether he favored a change in the law so as to provide allies with custody of weapons that Russia already possessed or knew how to make, the President said, "Well, from the very beginning, from what I knew about allied cooperation, and so on, I have always been of the belief that we should not deny to our allies what the enemies, what your potential enemy already has. We do want allies to be treated as partners and allies, and not as junior members of a firm who are to be seen but not heard. So I would think that it woud be better, for the interests of the United States, to make our law more liberal, as long as . . . we are confident, by our treaties and everything else [that the recipient countries would] stand by us in time of trouble" (*New York Times,* February 4, 1960, p. 12).

31. *Ibid.*, February 8, 1960, p. 3.

32. JCAE press release, No. 253–A, February 3, 1960; *New York Times,* February 7, 1960, p. 1.

33. *Ibid.*, February 14, 1960, p. 2.

34. *Ibid.*, March 3, 1960, p. 1.

35. *Ibid.*, p. 1.

36. *Ibid.*, March 8, 1960, p. 13.

37. *Ibid.*

38. *Ibid.*, March 20, 1960, p. 1.

39. Speech on March 9, 1960, *Congressional Record,* 86 Cong., 2 sess., p. 5067.

40. *New York Times,* March 11, 1960, p. 1.

41. *Ibid.*, March 20, 1960, p. 1.

42. *Washington Post,* April 15, 1960, p. A6; *New York Times,* July 23, 1960, p. 1.

43. *New York Times,* April 14, 1960, pp. 1, 3; May 31, pp. 1, 8; June 2, p. 3.

44. C. L. Sulzberger, *New York Times,* June 25, 1960, p. 20.

45. *Ibid.*, July 23, 1960, p. 1.

46. See Sulzberger's account of the meeting of these three leaders at Lake Como on September 9 (*ibid.*, November 23, 1960, p. 28).

47. *Ibid.*, October 20, 1960, p. 13.

48. The private study was undertaken by Robert R. Bowie, director of the Center of International Affairs at Harvard and formerly a member of the State Department's Policy Planning Staff. Although the Bowie study was not made public, its general contents were reported in the press (*ibid.*, October 30, 1960, p. 2; November 24, p. 1; *Chicago Sun Times,* October 13, 1960, p. 1).

49. *Ibid.*, November 22, 1960, p. 2.

50. *New York Times,* November 24, 1960, p. 10; November 27, p. 1.

51. *Ibid.*, December 17, 1960, p. 1; *Washington Post,* December 19, 1960, p. 6.

52. *New York Times,* December 19, 1960, p. 12.

53. See Alastair Buchan, "Britain and the Nuclear Deterrent," *Political Quarterly,* XXXI (January–March, 1960), 36–45.

54. The white paper of 1954 stated, "The primary deterrent . . . remains the atomic bomb and the ability of the highly organized and trained United States strategic air power to use it. From our past experience and current knowledge we have a significant contribution to make both to the technical and to the

tactical development of strategic air power. We intend as soon as possible to build up in the Royal Air Force a force of modern bombers capable of using the atomic weapon to the fullest effect."

"As the deterrent continues to grow it should have an increasing effect upon the cold war by making less likely such adventures on the part of the Communist world as their aggression in Korea. This should be of benefit to us by enabling us to reduce the great dispersal of effort which the existing international tension has hitherto imposed upon us" (*Statement on Defense, 1954,* Cmd. 9075, p. 5).

The implications of this confidence in nuclear deterrence for defense expenditures were logically counteracted by the paper's view that preparations for global war should contemplate a period of "broken-backed" war after the atomic phase, a view that was not abandoned until 1957. However, actual preparations for broken-backed war were largely confined to a moderate continuation of certain naval expenditures.

55. *Parliamentary Debates* (Commons), DXXXVII, 1905.

56. *Ibid.*, col. 1938 ff., 1945–46, 2187.

57. See the statement of Denis Healey, *ibid.*, col. 1931–37.

58. *Statement on Defense, 1956,* Cmd. 9691, p. 4.

59. Statement by Duncan Sandys on April 16, 1957, *Parliamentary Debates* (Commons), DLXVIII, 1759.

60. *Ibid.*, col. 1760–61.

61. Motion presented in parliament on February 28, 1956 (*Parliamentary Debates* [Commons], DLXIX, 1036).

62. *56th Annual Report of the Labor Party* (1957), pp. 177, 181. See also the report of the party conference in the *Times* (London), October 4, 1957, p. 4.

63. *Report on Defense,* 1958, Cmd. 363, p. 2.

64. *Times* (London), February 24, 1958, p. 3.

65. *Ibid.*, November 14, 1958, p. 4.

66. *Ibid.*, October 15, 1958, p. 13; October 16, p. 13.

67. *Parliamentary Debates* (Commons), DLXXXIII, 633–35.

68. A Gallup poll published in December, 1958, reported that 60 per cent of Labor supporters and 54 per cent of Conservative and Liberal supporters, when asked whether the proposed missile bases should be built, answered "No" (Reported in Alastair Buchan, "Britain Debates the 'Balance of Terror,'" *Reporter,* XVIII [April 3, 1958], 8–11). The Labor press, led by the *Daily Herald,* and the Liberal *Manchester Guardian* were especially active in opposing the missile bases. Sixty-nine Labor party members, or about one-quarter of the membership, signed a letter indorsing the *Daily Herald's* position, which included the proposal that Britain renounce the production of nuclear weapons. The official Labor position opposed the installation of missile bases until after Summit talks with the Soviet Union, but did not oppose the H-bomb program.

69. Hedley Bull, in pointing to the emotional content of the unilateralist movement, characterized the campaign as "the inheritor of the radical tradition of dissent from British foreign policy," drawing its support from the desire to revive the "moral enthusiasm and heroic spirit" of the Labor Party and from the desire that "Britain should play once again an independent role on the center of of the World's political stage" ("The Many Sides of British Unilateralism," *Reporter,* XXIV [March 16, 1961], 35–37). For a similar interpretation, stressing also the CND's tone of national self-righteousness and anti-Americanism, see David Marquand, "England, the Bomb, the Marchers," *Commentary,* XXIX (May, 1960), 380–86.

70. *New York Herald Tribune,* February 19, 1958, p. 1; *Christian Science Monitor,* February 19, 1958, p. 6; *New Leader,* XLI (May 26, 1958), 9–10;

Common Sense and Nuclear Warfare (London: George Allen & Unwin, 1959).

71. Bertrand Russell, "The Case for Neutralism," *New York Times Magazine*, July 24, 1960, pp. 10 ff. Hugh Gaitskell argued the case against British unilateral nuclear disarmament and neutralism in *ibid.*, pp. 11 ff.

72. *Defense in the Nuclear Age* (London: Victor Gollancz, Ltd., 1958), p. 141.

73. *New York Times*, October 3, 1958, p. 9.

74. For the full text of this proposal, see the revised joint declaration on nuclear weapons and disarmament issued on June 24, 1959, by the Labor party and the Trades Union Congress, reported in the *Manchester Guardian*, June 25, 1959, p. 2.

75. *Parliamentary Debates* (Commons), DCXVIII, 1136–39.

76. *New York Times*, June 23, 1960, p. 11; *Manchester Guardian*, June 23, 1960, p. 1. The full text of the Labor party's statement on defense and disarmament policies was published on page 3 of the same issue.

77. *New York Times*, October 6, 1960, p. 1.

78. Cited in Buchan, "Britain Debates the 'Balance of Terror,'" *loc. cit.*, p. 10, and in the *Observer*, June 28, 1959, p. 11.

79. Gallup poll of April, 1958, cited in Leon D. Epstein, "Britain and the H-bomb, 1955–1958," *Review of Politics*, XXI (July, 1959), 515 n.

80. Gallup polls in December, 1957, and February, 1958, cited in *ibid.*, notes on pp. 526, 521.

81. Speech by Defense Minister Strauss, *Die Welt*, June 24, 1959, cited in Gerald Freund, *Germany between Two Worlds* (New York: Harcourt, Brace & Co., Inc., 1961), p. 152.

82. In an interview with R. H. S. Crossman in the *Daily Mirror* (London), April 2, 1958, and with Gerald Freund—both interviews in March, 1958 (Freund, *Germany between Two Worlds*, pp. 154–55).

83. *New York Times*, October 20, 1960, p. 13; November 2, p. 7.

84. Press conference on September 5, 1960 (*ibid.*, September 6, 1960, p. 14).

85. Speech of Le Vigan on February 27, 1960 (*ibid.*, February 28, 1960, p. 21).

86. *Ibid.*, October 26, 1960, p. 11; November 11, p. 1.

87. Radio and television address on May 31, 1960 (*ibid.*, June 1, 1960, p. 9).

88. *Ibid.*, June 21, 1959, IV, p. 5.

89. Press conference on November 10, 1959 (*ibid.*, November 11, 1959, p. 10).

90. On the many material, technical, and organizational obstacles to building an adequate strategic nuclear deterrent, see Albert Wohlstetter, "The Delicate Balance of Terror," *Foreign Affairs*, XXXVII (January, 1959), 211–34; and, with special regard to the obstacles facing prospective or aspiring nuclear powers, Wohlstetter, "Nuclear Sharing: NATO and the N+1 Country," *Foreign Affairs*, XXXIX (April, 1961), 361–71.

CHAPTER 9

THE CONTROL OF NUCLEAR WEAPONS

1. *New York Times*, November 22, 1960, p. 13.

2. Gallois, "New Teeth for NATO," *Foreign Affairs*, XXXIX (October, 1960), 67–80.

3. *Ibid.*, p. 74.

4. *Ibid.*, p. 76.

5. The most comprehensive advocacy of the first plan was by Ben T. Moore, in his *NATO and the Future of Europe* (New York: Harper & Bros., 1958), and by TEMPO, in *International Stability: Problems and Prospects* (Santa Barbara, Calif.: General Electric Co., 1961), chap. vii. The most comprehensive advocacy of the second was by Alastair Buchan, in his *NATO in the 1960's* (London: Weidenfield and Nicholson, 1960). For an illuminating discussion of both plans, see Glenn H. Snyder, *Deterrence and Defense* (Princeton: Princeton University Press, 1961), pp. 174–92.

6. *NATO in the 1960's,* p. 70.

7. *Ibid.*, p. 76.

8. Henry A. Kissinger, "For an Atlantic Confederacy," *Reporter,* XXIV (February 2, 1961), 20.

CHAPTER 10
DISENGAGEMENT

1. For a description and analysis of the principal disengagement proposals, see Michael Howard, *Disengagement in Europe* (Baltimore, Md.: Penguin Books, 1958); P. J. D. W., "The Pursuit of Disengagement," *The World Today,* XV (April, 1959), 156–68; Senate Committee on Foreign Relations, Subcommittee on Disarmament, *Handbook on Arms Control and Related Problems in Europe,* 86 Cong., 1 sess.; and, most comprehensive of all, Eugène Hinterhoff, *Disengagement* (London: Stevens & Sons, Ltd., 1959).

2. Howard, *op. cit.,* p. 61.

3. George F. Kennan, *Russia, the Atom and the West* (New York: Harper & Bros., 1957), pp. 62–63.

4. *Ibid.*, p. 63. In a 1959 article Kennan looked forward to the creation of twelve German divisions rather than paramilitary forces as an adequate substitute for foreign garrisons ("Disengagement Revisited," *Foreign Affairs,* XXXVII [January, 1959], 200).

5. Kennan, *Russia, the Atom and the West,* p. 55.

6. In his book of 1957 Kennan wrote, "I would only say that it seems to me far more desirable on principle to get the Soviet forces out of Central and Eastern Europe than to cultivate a new German army for the purpose of opposing them while they remain there" (*ibid.*, p. 45). However, in his 1959 article, in which he placed his hopes for replacing foreign garrisons on twelve German divisions instead of on paramilitary forces, he asked rhetorically, "Is the retention of the foreign garrisons in Western Germany, themselves no longer the essential element in Germany's local protection, of greater value than the strategic advantage to be obtained by the removal of the Soviet divisions now in Eastern Germany to a point several hundred miles further east?" ("Disengagement Revisited," *op. cit.,* p. 200).

7. Howard, *op. cit.,* p. 69.

8. Hinterhoff, *op. cit.,* p. 389.

9. *Ibid.,* p. 389.

10. For a balanced estimate of the strength of West German sentiment for reunification, see Flora Lewis, "The Unstable States of Germany," *Foreign Affairs,* XXXVIII (July, 1960), 588–97, and Gerald Freund, *Germany between Two Worlds* (Harcourt, Brace & Co., Inc., 1961), pp. 94–100. Summing up reunification sentiment, Freund wrote, "Significant forces in the Federal Republic are unenthusiastic about reunification. One finds conflicts of interest, especially

in the commercial world, which dissipate the power behind reunification efforts. Such conflicts are not of lasting importance and in all sectors of society one finds a keen awareness of the partition problem which, as interest in foreign policy increases, will inevitably arouse a more widespread concern" (*ibid.*, p. 100).

11. Kennan, "Disengagement Revisited," p. 205.

12. *Ibid.*, pp. 206–7.

13. Thus, President Eisenhower, commenting on disengagement proposals in a press conference on January 14, 1959, said, "Now as to the different proposals of the Soviets and ourselves respecting Germany and Europe, we think it is just an exercise in futility to try to demilitarize, neutralize, and completely disarm a people as strong, as important and virile as is the German people. On the other hand, that being the general tenor of the Russian proposals, we oppose to that concept this one: that we would say we don't believe in the free arming of Germany in the sense that Hitler tried to rearm it. We would like to see Germany so intertwine itself with other European nations in its economy and its thinking and its defense exercises that it doesn't have to do this. It is a part of a community. Now this has been started so far as the West is concerned in the Euratom, the Coal-Steel Community and the Free Market, that kind of thing. And we think it's a very great development for the benefit and strength of Western Europe. . . . But it's also a development that almost proves they cannot be aggressive. They couldn't move except with the consent of a whole bevy of nations" (*New York Times,* January 5, 1959, p. 18). Dulles, testifying before the Senate Committee on Foreign Relations in 1958, had presented the same argument against German reunification at the price of neutrality in even more unequivocal terms and had identified his views with those of Chancellor Adenauer (Senate Committee on Foreign Relations, *Hearings, Review of Foreign Policy, 1958,* 85 Cong., 2 sess., Pt. 4, pp. 804–5).

14. Kennan, "Disengagement Revisited," p. 197.

15. Dean Acheson, *Power and Diplomacy* (Cambridge, Mass.: Harvard University Press, 1958), p. 93.

16. Kennan, "Disengagement Revisited," pp. 207–8.

17. Thus in his famous "Mr. X" article of 1947, Kennan wrote that, if the Western world could contain Soviet power for ten or fifteen years, the limits to the physical and nervous strength of the Russian people, Russia's economic vulnerability, and the difficulties of transferring power after the death of Stalin might bring about the decline of Soviet power; and that, in fact, the sprouting of the seeds of decay might already be well advanced. The United States, he declared, "has it in its power to increase enormously the strains under which Soviet policy must operate, to force upon the Kremlin a far greater degree of moderation and circumspection than it has had to observe in recent years, and in this way to promote tendencies which must eventually find their outlet in either the break-up of the gradual mellowing of Soviet power" (George F. Kennan, *American Diplomacy, 1900–1950* [Chicago: University of Chicago Press, 1951], pp. 120–26).

18. In 1949 President Truman once spoke of his hope that the "war of nerves" would end in Communist "surrender," just as the shooting war had ended, which was a view consistent with one he was reported to have expressed privately in the same year: that in two years communism would be forced into a great decline and peace and the weight of American policies would be assured (*New York Times,* September 3, 1949, p. 1). However, in later years Truman looked forward not to Soviet decline or defeat but to the moderation

of her policy and a willingness to live and let live. See, for example, his speech on October 15, 1951 (*Bulletin,* XXV [October 29, 1951], 680). Acheson also anticipated that as the free world grew stronger the Kremlin would conclude that Russia's own interests required that she abandon expansionist policies. See, for example, his speeches in 1950 and 1951 (*Bulletin,* XXIII [July 3, 1950], 16; [October 2, 1950], 524; [December 18, 1950], 965; XXV [October 29, 1951], 680.

19. Dulles relied primarily on certain internal developments in the Communist system to bring about a reduction of the Soviet threat—especially a growing critical faculty in the Russian people due to increased education, the moderation of state claims on the individual due to the demands of the people for consumers' goods and for greater personal security, and the dilemma posed by the need to propitiate nationalism and individualism in the satellite countries. See, for example, his statement to the Senate Foreign Relations Committee on June 6, 1958 (*New York Times,* June 7, 1958, p. 8) and also his statements on May 15, 1956 (*ibid.,* May 16, 1956, p. 8) and December 7, 1957 (*ibid.,* December 8, 1957, Sec. 4, p. 5).

20. Zbigniew Brzezinski and William E. Griffith, "Peaceful Engagement in Eastern Europe," *Foreign Affairs,* XXXIX (July, 1961), 642–54.

21. The text of the Soviet note appears in the *New York Times,* November 28, 1958, p. 8. For a critical analysis of the meaning and intent of this note and the subsequent Soviet positions based upon it, see Hans Speier, *The Soviet Threat to Berlin* (Santa Monica: The RAND Corporation, 1960).

22. See Walter Lippmann's reports of his interview with Khrushchev in October, 1958, published in his book, *The Communist World and Ours* (Boston: Little, Brown & Co., 1958), p. 13.

23. In a speech before the Supreme Soviet on January 14, 1960, Khrushchev depreciated the significance of forward troops in the outbreak of a war in the context of denying that Russia would be weakened militarily by the reduction of ground forces: "In present-day conditions wars would not take the course they took in the past and would bear little resemblance to former wars. In the past states tried to keep their armies as close as possible to their frontiers so that a living fence, as it were, of soldiers and cannon could be formed at the needed moment. If a state wanted to invade another country, it had to attack these troops on the border. This is how a war usually started. During the first days the battles would rage on the borders of warring states, and that is where the troops were moved to. If a war should break out today, military operations would take a different course, for the states would have means of delivering weapons over distances of thousands of kilometers. The war would start for the most part deep within the belligerent countries, and not one capital, not one major industrial or administrative center, not one strategic area would escape attack in the first minutes, let alone the first days of the war. Thus war would begin differently, if it began, and would develop differently" (*Current Digest of the Soviet Press,* XII, No. 2, p. 13). However, in a different context, justifying his demand for a peace treaty between the two Germanys, Khrushchev told an East German audience at Leipzig, on March 7, 1959, "Large armed forces of countries of the West and the East are concentrated in Germany. And when two armies confront each other and are in direct contact, any spark may set off a war conflagration and all sorts of unexpected developments may arise" (*ibid.,* No. 13, p. 4).

24. The Russians might correctly calculate that a denuclearized Germany that remained a collaborating member of NATO would constitute more of an obstacle to Soviet political and military pressure than a politically isolated Ger-

many with nuclear weapons. One possible indication of the relative importance that they attached to Germany's armament and her political affiliation was Khrushchev's statement in a press conference on November 27, 1958, that Russia would not change her policy of making Berlin a free city even if West Germany were to give up her rearmament program. "Should Western Germany declare that she will not arm herself, with the occupation regime of Berlin still maintained," he said, "the source of tension and conflict will not be stamped out" (*Soviet News,* November 28, 1958, p. 191, as quoted in Speier, *op. cit.,* p. 26).

CHAPTER 11
CONCLUSION

1. *New York Times,* May 28, 1961, Sec. 4, p. 8.

2. Radio and television address to the nation, July 25, 1961 (*ibid.,* July 26, 1961, p. 10).

3. In a special message to Congress on the defense budget, delivered on March 28, 1961, Kennedy said, "Our arms will never be used to strike the first blow in any attack. . . . We must offset whatever advantage this may appear to hand an aggressor by so increasing the capability of our forces to respond swiftly and effectively to any aggressive move as to convince any would-be aggressor that such a movement would be too futile and costly to undertake. In the area of general war, this doctrine means that such capability must rest with that portion of our forces which would survive the initial attack. We are not creating forces for a first strike against any other nation. We shall never threaten, provoke, or initiate aggression—but if aggression should come, our response will be swift and effective."

These words seemed to rule out a strategic first strike even against major conventional aggression, although they left room for distinguishing a first strike "out of the blue" from a first strike in response to aggression. Yet, clearly, the President did not mean to rule out the initial use of all kinds of nuclear weapons, for he also said, "In the event of a major aggression that could not be repulsed by conventional forces, we must be prepared to take whatever action with whatever weapons are appropriate" (*ibid.,* March 29, 1961, p. 16).

In a television interview shown in Britain shortly before this address, Kennedy said, "We have to assume, after this first blow had been struck against us, what would we have left—with what could we retaliate, and how much of a deterrent, therefore, is there to Russia from making the first strike." "I hope," he continued, "that the people in your country realize that neither we nor they would have any difficulties if it were not that, as a democracy, we will not strike first and that therefore we always have to consider what we have left" (*ibid.,* March 27, 1961, p. 1).

4. Thus, in a speech on April 25, 1961, Secretary of Defense McNamara said, "We have moved to strengthen our non-nuclear limited war forces." But he added, "This does not modify existing national policy to employ nuclear weapons when it is necessary to do so. Rather it is designed to avoid situations in which we might be forced to use nuclear weapons because too narrow a range of non-nuclear weapons were available to us" (*ibid.,* April 24, 1961, p. 29).

5. On May 14, 1961, West German Defense Minister Franz Josef Strauss expressed his government's uneasiness that the new emphasis on conventional weapons would weaken the credibility of the nuclear deterrent (*ibid.,* May 15,

1961, p. 10). On June 1, British Defense Minister Harold Watkinson told the Assembly of the Western European Union that, although Britain recognized the danger of overdependence on nuclear weapons, "On the other hand, we do not believe that NATO can or should provide such massive conventional forces as could hope to deal with any conventional attack, however large, without recourse to nuclear weapons. Such a policy might merely indicate that we should not have the courage ever to use the nuclear weapon in any circumstances. Between these two extremes we must strike a balance on what the alliance can afford without waste of resources" (*ibid.*, June 2, 1961, p. 1). In a news conference at SHAPE on June 4, President Kennedy allayed French and allied apprehensions springing from the new emphasis on limited war by declaring, "We are determined to resist aggression whatever its force and whatever kind of force is needed to resist it" (*ibid.*, June 5, 1961, p. 13). On June 6 the American deputy secretary of defense, Roswell L. Gilpatric, told a news conference, "The current doctrine is that if NATO forces were about to be overwhelmed by non-nuclear attacks from the [Communist] bloc countries, NATO would make use of nuclear arms." And he added that he did not believe in the possibility of limiting a nuclear war (*ibid.*, June 7, 1961, p. 21).

6. *Ibid.*, May 10, 1961, pp. 1, 8.

7. *Ibid.*, May 18, 1961, p. 23.

8. Secretary General Paul-Henri Spaak, speaking in December, 1958, described the extent of political consultation in the following words: "On certain questions, particularly those concerning relations with the East, with the Communist world, for months and months now, not a single initiative has been taken by the more powerful partners in the Atlantic alliance without their having obtained, during preliminary discussion, the agreement and support of all the less large and the smallest partners. The results of this political consultation have, in certain spheres, been perfect. . . . I should like you to realize that these consultations have not been a matter of pure form. Many of the drafts submitted to the Atlantic Council have been not only discussed, but also commented on and criticized and . . . in nearly all cases, I think, the large countries which have submitted the text of their letters or notes have taken the remarks made into account" (*NATO Letter*, VI [December, 1958], 7–8).

For an analysis of the meaning, the extent, and consequences of political consultation among the members of NATO, see Carol E. Baumann, *Political Cooperation in NATO* (Madison, Wisconsin: National Security Studies Group, 1960); and Ruth C. Lawson, "Concerting Policies in the North Atlantic Community," *International Organization*, XII (Spring, 1958), 163–79. For a critical appraisal of proposals to increase political consultation, see Gardner Patterson and Edgar S. Furniss, Jr., *NATO: A Critical Appraisal* (Princeton: Princeton University Conference on NATO, 1957), chap. iv.

9. Lord Ismay, *NATO: The First Five Years, 1949–1954* (Paris, 1954), p. 10.

10. Address to the Associated Press at New York, N.Y., on April 23, 1956 (*Bulletin*, XXXIV [April 30, 1956], 709–10).

11. In a press conference on September 5, 1960, De Gaulle recalled the American dominance and European weakness at the inception of the alliance and said, "So the alliance was set up on the basis of integration, that is to say, of a system whereby the defense of each of the countries of Continental Europe, of Western Europe—not counting England—does not have a national character; a system in which, in fact, everything is under the command of the Americans and in which the Americans decide on the use of the principal weapons—that is to say, atomic weapons." Then he noted, however, that much had changed in the

past ten years. Parts of the world outside the NATO area became danger spots, and the countries of Europe regained their balance and began to prosper, and England built its own nuclear weapons. "Now under these circumstances," he concluded, "France considers that what was done ten years ago within this limited field and on the single exclusive basis of integration must be brought up to date." The two essential points of revision, he declared, were the organization of three-power political and strategic co-operation in areas outside Europe and a change in the integration of European defense to permit the defense of a country, "while being of course combined with that of other countries," to have "a national character" (*NATO Letter,* VIII [November, 1960], 24).

12. As a contribution to this end Alastair Buchan suggested giving the Standing Group more prestige and influence in military planning, partly by increasing the stature of the American, British, and French representatives who composed it (Alastair Buchan, *NATO in the 1960's* [New York: Frederick A. Praeger, Inc., 1960], pp. 78–79). Within a revitalized Standing Group, and with the addition of a German representative, France might no longer find herself in the position of a second-class partner to the Anglo-American entente.

Buchan also suggested assigning command of a NATO nuclear deterrent force to a European officer, rather than to SACEUR. Whether by this means or by some other, it would seem necessary to centralize the military planning and control group for a joint nuclear force. A French representative ought to have a prominent position in such a group, at least equivalent to the position of a British representative.

Similarly, it would be necessary and might be feasible to centralize the political control of a joint deterrent in a way that would recognize France's special and equivalent status. A far-reaching plan for such a political body was made by Henry Kissinger, who proposed the creation of a political mechanism "with the power to make binding decisions for the Western alliance as a whole in certain specified fields, particularly NATO strategy, arms control, and those negotiations with the Soviet Union which affect NATO as a whole, such as the issue of Berlin, German unification, and European security." The political body would also "determine the circumstances in which nuclear weapons would be released to SHAPE" (Henry A. Kissinger, "For an Atlantic Confederacy," *Reporter,* XXIV [February 2, 1961], 20).

Index

To My Mother and Father

This is a Borzoi Book published by Alfred A. Knopf, Inc.

Published in the United States by Alfred A. Knopf, Inc., New York,
and simultaneously in Canada by Random House of Canada Limited, Toronto.
Distributed by Random House, Inc., New York.
ISBN: 0-394-47227-6
Library of Congress Catalog Card Number: 76-171162
Manufactured in the United States of America
First Edition

Owing to space limitations, all acknowledgments of permission for quoting written material in this book have been placed on pp. viii–ix.
All acknowledgments for illustrations will be found at the end of the List of Illustrations.

The Lies of Art

Max Beerbohm's Parody and Caricature

John Felstiner

Alfred A. Knopf
New York 1972

REVISED EDITION

Month-By-Month

WHAT TO DO EACH MONTH TO HAVE A BEAUTIFUL GARDEN ALL YEAR

GARDENING IN FLORIDA

Published by Cool Springs Press, a Division of Thomas Nelson, Inc.,
P. O. Box 141000, Nashville, Tennessee, 37214.

MacCubbin, Tom, 1944-
Month-by-month gardening in Florida : what to do each month to have a beautiful garden all year / Tom MacCubbin.– Rev. ed.
p. cm.
Includes index.
ISBN 1-59186-235-3 (trade paper)
1. Gardening–Florida. I. Title.
SB453.2.F6M23 2005
635'.09759–dc22

2005014741

First printing 1999; First Revised Printing 2006

Printed in Singapore
10 9 8 7 6 5 4 3 2 1

Managing Editor: Billie Brownell
Horticultural Editor: Tom Wichman, Horticulturist, Orange County
Designer: James Duncan, James Duncan Creative
Production Artist: S. E. Anderson

On the cover: Bromeliad, photographed by Thomas Eltzroth

Visit the Cool Springs Press Web site at **www.coolspringspress.net**

REVISED EDITION

Month-By-Month™

WHAT TO DO EACH MONTH TO HAVE A BEAUTIFUL GARDEN ALL YEAR

GARDENING IN FLORIDA

TOM MACCUBBIN

Nashville, Tennessee
A Division of Thomas Nelson, Inc.
www.ThomasNelson.com

DEDICATION

For Mom and Pop, whose nurturing taught me all about gardening and set the good moral examples that have guided me through life, and for my wife Joan, who has waited patiently and provided encouragement while this horticulturist cultivates a garden and works to serve others as a County Extension Agent.

ACKNOWLEDGEMENTS

This book is now ready to help you with your garden, thanks to the assistance of many.

Thanks to my professors who gave me the knowledge needed to pursue a horticulture career, especially Dr. Conrad B. Link, who assisted with my undergraduate and graduate work at the University of Maryland. Thanks to all University of Maryland and University of Florida Extension Specialists who provide knowledge of plant culture and conduct the research needed to grow great gardens and nourish attractive landscapes.

Much appreciation is expressed to Roger Waynick and Hank McBride of Cool Springs Press for their faith in me as the author of a second book published by their company. Thanks especially to Jan Keeling who encouraged and coordinated the writing of this book and then carefully read and edited the many pages. The author is very appreciative of the illustrations by Bill Kersey that help bring many of the techniques to life to make your chores a bit easier, and of the typesetting and formatting by S. E. Anderson, who worked tirelessly to make the information visually appealing and easy to grasp.

A special thanks to Tom Wichman, my good friend and fellow Extension Agent, who spent many hours reading each chapter for horticultural content. A number of his thoughts have been added to each section. Much appreciation is expressed to my wife Joan, who allowed me the time to write this book and took the time to assist with the editing and proofing of each chapter. Many of her ideas have also been added to the book.

Thanks to the residents of Florida who for over thirty years have allowed me to be their Extension Agent, a role which prepared me to write this extensive gardening publication.

CONTENTS

MAR 2006

INTRODUCTION

Welcome to Gardening in Florida!

Whether you are new to the state or just new to gardening, you are about to have lots of fun, enjoy colorful flowers, and reap big harvests from fruit and vegetable plants. Even if you already have some local gardening experience, there is always more to learn and new adventures ahead.

Florida is different from most other states. It's a long state, almost 900 miles from the northernmost point in the Panhandle to the tip of the Keys. There is frost-free growing in the southern part of the state and there are yearly freezes in the north. Before you begin planting, you can learn a little about some other features of our state:

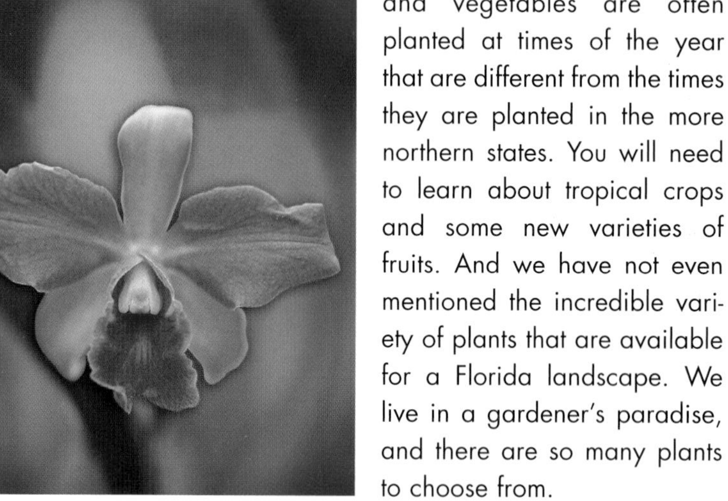

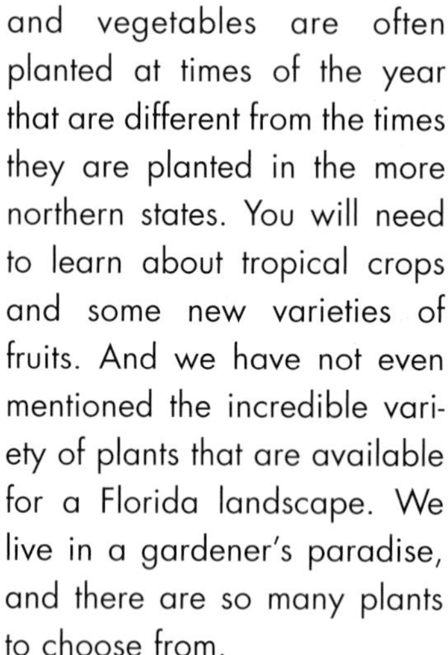

- Most of the soil is sand; gardeners often call it "beach sand." The official state soil is a Myakka fine sand, but there are also areas with clay, rock, and organic soils.
- May through September are very hot months; temperatures often approach 100 degrees Fahrenheit.
- January and February are the coldest months, and only the most hardy vegetables and flowers should be planted then.
- Summer is the rainy season; the rest of the months are relatively dry.
- Fall and spring are times for warm-season plantings, winter is devoted to cool-season plantings, and summer is the time for plants that don't mind the heat.
- Gardeners on the coast and in some isolated inland areas have to deal with salty water and may have to limit landscapes to saltwater-resistant plantings.
- Pest problems are similar to those of other climates, but the pests are active year-round.

By now you have probably gotten the hint that most people can use some help in becoming oriented to Florida growing conditions. Flowers and vegetables are often planted at times of the year that are different from the times they are planted in the more northern states. You will need to learn about tropical crops and some new varieties of fruits. And we have not even mentioned the incredible variety of plants that are available for a Florida landscape. We live in a gardener's paradise, and there are so many plants to choose from.

To gardeners who are new to Florida, palms may be unfamiliar elements in the landscape. Did you know that palms are not really trees, even though the Florida state tree is the cabbage palm? Palms are related to grasses. They make excellent accents and specimens and can even provide shade when clustered. The new gardener should ask for help and advice when growing palms.

All of Florida can enjoy tropical foliage plants. Schefflera, ficus, and crotons can be permanent features of a landscape in South Florida. In Central

Florida, these plants can be grown in the landscape but cannot be counted on to survive many of the colder winters. In North Florida, they are grown in pots and ushered inside when freeze warnings are sounded.

You will be asking lots of questions as you begin gardening in Florida. It's only natural to want to know:

- What citrus plants should I use?
- How should I fertilize the lawn?
- When should I plant the first pansies?
- What water lilies should I plant?
- How can I protect cold-sensitive plants during winter?
- What are the best watering techniques?

This book will help you with finding the best site, preparing the soil, planting, and controlling critters. Unlike many gardener's reference books, we will take you through plant care one month at a time. Just flip through the pages to the current month of the year and learn what you should be doing to make your gardens attractive, produce fruits, and create bouquets.

You will also learn how to share your excitement with friends. When you have a great-looking landscape, others will ask for your advice. You can have fun starting plants for giveaways, sharing your harvests, and helping your neighbors with flower arrangements.

GARDENING IN FLORIDA

On Easter Day, March 27, 1513, Ponce de León arrived off the coast of Florida and declared it the land of flowers. Some suggest he selected the name to honor the feast of the flowers celebrated by the Spanish explorers at about the same time. Others prefer to think the green vegetation and spring blossoms he saw were his inspiration.

Residents like to think of Florida as a land of naturally blossoming plants, but the truth is that a modern well-landscaped home and fruitful gardens do take a little work. Visitors who enter the state are often met by the same soggy swamps, wicked palmettos, and thickets of growth that greeted the early settlers. Much of this land had to be cleared and settled before gardening could begin.

Early Floridians found plenty of critters, including alligators, rattlesnakes, and mosquitos. Perhaps you have heard that one large area in Central Florida—now made of Seminole and Orange counties—was once named "Mosquito County." Early Floridians lived in a state that had numerous battles between nations to settle disputes over the land as well as wars with Native Americans; perhaps this is why much of Florida didn't settle down to real landscaping until the late 1800s. Before this time, most gardening consisted of growing plants for food. We know the first citrus came to the New World with Columbus. But the first fruiting trees are believed to have been brought to the state by Spanish explorers like those who established St. Augustine, the nation's oldest permanent city, in 1565. European visitors found plenty of fruiting citrus trees in Florida, which were likely spread by seeds along the St. Johns River, a major route used by early settlers.

Some plants like the pineapple were already in the New World. One account states that in 1876 there was not a settler from New Smyrna to Jupiter, Florida, who did not have a pineapple patch.

Settlers also brought vegetables to plant, as well as some flowers. Rose enthusiasts sometimes note that long after a house is gone, a lone red 'Louis Philippe' rose may mark the once-flourishing home-

site. This rose is so popular that some have named it the Florida Rose.

Communities sprang up at the crossroads and around coastal ports. In 1819, while Florida was still under Spanish rule, the population consisted of only 4300 inhabitants—but that was to change.

The transfer of Florida to the United States and settling of the wars with the Native Americans made the state much more inhabitable. By the time of statehood in 1845, Florida had 65,500 residents and was growing rapidly. The development of the railroad that began during 1883 also improved Florida's accessibility. And yes, critter control, including that of mosquito populations, helped attract more people as well.

At the turn of the century there were over 500,000 residents, but most had little time to beautify their homes and were more interested in farming and harvesting the lumber from the rich forest lands. Estates with gardens, such as the Brokaw-McDougall House built in 1850 in Tallahassee, and the Arthur Cummer home built in 1903 in Jacksonville, developed first near the state's northern border.

It wasn't until the early 1900s that many gardeners began to set aside land for major plantings. Some of these exist today as examples of early horticulture and many are open to the public. Here is a list of more garden estates along with the date they were built:

- Harry P. Leu Gardens, Orlando, 1936
- Bok Tower Gardens, Lake Wales, 1923
- Maclay State Garden, Tallahassee, 1923
- McKee Botanical Garden, Vero Beach, 1930
- Marie Selby Botanical Gardens, Sarasota, 1920s
- Historic Spanish Point near Osprey, 1910
- Edison's Winter Home,Fort Myer, 1885
- Vizcaya Museum and Gardens,Miami, 1914
- Fairchild Tropical Garden near Miami, 1930s

Gardening interest grew in Florida in the late 1800s with the arrival of new settlers. Three pioneer planters who started or encouraged nurseries were Pliny Ward Reasoner, George L. Tabor, and Dr. H. Harold Hume. Many other horticulturists introduced plants that were needed to develop attractive landscapes, and they also provided encouragement to gardeners and nurseries.

Plants were grown in the ground by early growers. Later in the nineteenth century they were grown in containers as well. The very first containers were oil cans for small plants, Number 10 restaurant cans for gallon-sized plants, and powdered egg cans for 3-gallon plants. (Plastic pots did not arrive at many nurseries until the mid-1970s.)

A sort of horticultural revolution took shape in the early 1900s. Homeowners began to seek out nurserymen to purchase bougainvillea, crotons, tabebuia, caladiums, and other new and different plants. Florida sprouted plant industries in communities that claimed to be plant capitals of the world. Three such communities are Lake Placid, the Caladium Capital; Pierson, the Fern Capital; and Apopka, the Indoor Foliage Plant Capital.

Certainly some of the great gardening interest in our state can be attributed to the University of Florida Institute of Food and Agricultural Sciences. This branch of the University extends research, education, and Extension Services to all areas of the state.

Every county has an Extension Service office that provides horticultural educational services to its residents. Services include formal classes, clinics, free bulletins, telephone consultations, and e-mail information programs. One of the services, the Master Gardener Program, trains gardening enthusiasts to share their knowledge with others in the community. Look in the blue

USDA COLD HARDINESS ZONES

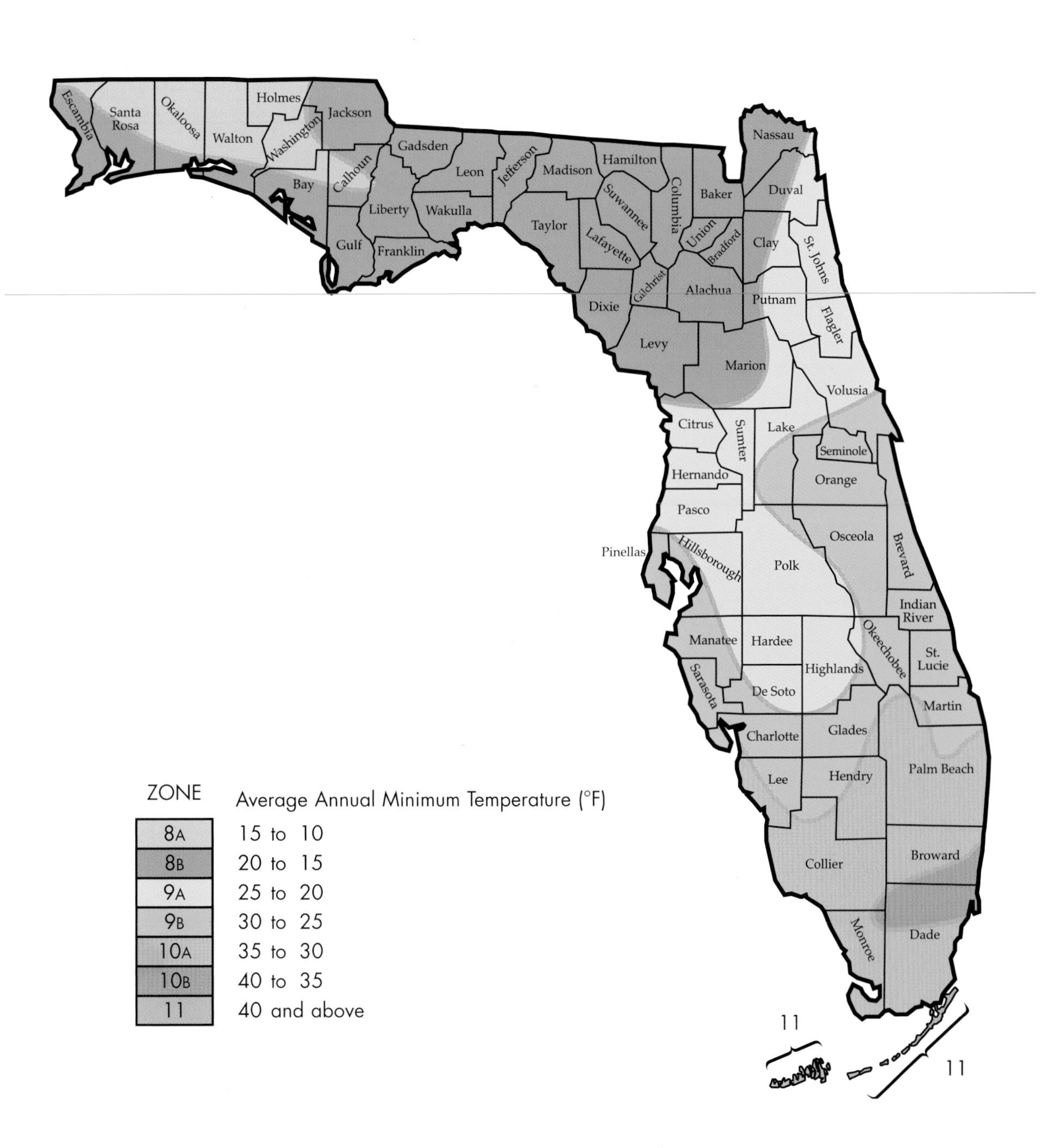

pages of the telephone directory for your local Extension Service office.

There is a strong garden club system in our state. The Federation of Garden Clubs, which has its state headquarters in Winter Park, was started in 1924 and now has over 20,000 members. We also have an active society for horticulture enthusiasts, The Florida State Horticultural Society, which was founded in 1888.

There are societies for those who have a special interest in particular plants such as bromeliads, palms, orchids, herbs, roses, tropical fruits, and many others. Most meet monthly at botanical gardens and community recreation centers.

FLORIDA'S CLIMATE

Enjoy our Florida climate: the living is easy here. Seldom will you need a heavy winter coat, and you can probably sell your snow shovel. Rarely does ice cover the sidewalks and rarely do icicles fill the trees. Most of the state is considered a subtropical climate, although temperate zones sneak down into the more northern regions.

But in spite of the great growing conditions found in most parts of the state, gardeners are often concerned about the weather. After all, most home landscapes contain thousands of dollars worth of plant materials that might be affected by drought, sudden downpours, and even our infrequent freezes. Most gardeners check the paper, television, and radio daily just to stay alert to changing climatic conditions. Many keep track of the rainfall and mark calendars with the daily high and low temperatures. Some consult almanacs to determine weather trends.

Luckily, the weather in many parts of the state tends to be fairly predictable within its climatic zone. On average, spring and fall are warm and dry, summer hot and humid, and winter cool and dry.

Florida is divided into three climatic zones: North, Central, and South. Each is very different from the other when it comes to expected weather. Check out the climate for your area of the state to determine the growing conditions you can expect. (See the map on page 10.)

North Florida

- extends northward from State Road 40.
- has about 60 inches of rainfall per year.
- is sure to get frosts and freezing weather in winter.
- has a first frost by late November and last frost during late February.
- has 350 to 650 annual hours below 45 degrees.
- has summers that are of similar duration to those in more temperate areas but are hotter and more humid.

Central Florida

- lies between State Roads 40 and 70.
- has about 56 inches of rainfall per year.
- has frosts most years and some light freezes in winter.
- has a first frost by mid-December and a last frost during mid-February.
- has 150 to 350 annual hours below 45 degrees.
- has extended summerlike, hot, humid weather in late spring and fall.

South Florida

- extends below State Road 70 across the state.
- has about 56 inches rainfall per year.
- has infrequent frosts and no freezes.
- has 50 to 150 annual hours below 45 degrees.
- has extended, summerlike, hot, humid weather into spring and fall.

GARDENING IN FLORIDA

Our state gets lots of rainfall, but it is not evenly distributed throughout the year. Most of the rain arrives during the summer months. (Some gardeners say you can set your clocks by the daily summer storms that begin arriving off the coasts by 4 p.m. and are over by about 6 p.m.) There are a lot of lightning strikes during summer storms, so take cover at the first sign of rain. It's not abnormal to see some damage to trees after a bout of severe weather.

Some gardeners have a difficult time getting used to the hot and humid summer weather. Here are some tips to help you cope with the heat:

- Work during the cooler morning or early evening hours.
- Find a shady spot for midday gardening.
- Drink lots of water.
- Wear a hat and cover exposed skin with sunscreen that has an SPF of 15 or higher.
- Keep insect repellent handy to ward off biting pests.
- Know your limitations—don't let yourself get exhausted.

Summer may not be your favorite time of the year, but the plants love it. The air is warm, there is plenty of humidity, and it rains almost every day. What more could a plant ask for? This is a great time to grow the tropical gingers, heliconias, bird of paradise, and many others. It's also a good time to move your indoor foliage plants outdoors to recover from their time inside.

Fall and spring are both delightful seasons, even though you will probably have to be careful to keep your plants watered. These are dry times, with about 2 inches of rainfall per month. The rain when it comes usually comes in downpours, so you will have to sprinkle plants between the showers. Many plants like these times of the year, with their temperatures that often fall into the 50s and 60s at night and rise to the 70s to 80s during the day. These are seasons when gardeners can grow both warm- and cool-season flowers, vegetables, and herbs. Many of the fruit trees flower and bear crops. These are good times to be working in the garden, doing some of the heavier chores with little stress. Most Floridians fling open the windows and turn off the air conditioning at this time of the year. It is a good time to take lots of walks to enjoy the flowers and fall color. Maples, dogwoods, sweet gums, and other more-temperate plants display colorful foliage in the central and northern parts of the state.

Winter varies according to the region. If you live in South Florida, you will have a winter that is usually frost- and freeze-free—most of the time it's warm and dry just like spring and fall. You can continue to grow cool- and warm-season flowers and tropical foliage plants in the same garden. Rarely does a frost or freeze sneak into the most southern areas of the state (but it can happen).

As you head north into Central Florida, the winter weather gets a little cooler; to many residents it feels like spring in some of the Northern states. Most days are in the 70s and nights in the 50s or 60s. This is a dry time of year, so some watering will be needed. Because the days are shorter, the plants grow a bit slower and use less water than at other times of the year.

You will need cold protection for your sensitive plants. Every now and then a warm winter occurs during which you don't see a frost or freeze—but that is rare. Often the cold may arrive for only a night or two, but you still should be prepared to protect your crotons, poinsettias, tibouchina, and tomato plants from sudden freezes. The cold winter weather of Central Florida means that tropical fruit production is limited to the warmer areas of the region or to gardeners who are willing to provide protection. But most of time the weather is ideal for gardening.

GARDENING IN FLORIDA

You can count on frosts and freezes to occur in the northern region of the state, and only the more cold-resistant flowers and vegetables should be planted during the fall and winter months. Tropicals are almost out of the picture unless they are grown in pots and can be moved to a warm location when freeze warnings are sounded. On a more positive note, in North Florida you can raise some of the daffodils that cannot be grown in other parts of the state. And oriental magnolias, sweet shrub, and other plants that like a little cool weather can call this area home. North Florida is ideal for gardeners who prefer changing seasons.

WINTER HARDINESS

Here is a good trivia question: *How many USDA plant hardiness zones are found in Florida?* Most gardeners would guess three, but the answer is four. Florida contains zones 8 though 11 (the fourth zone occurs way down in the Keys). See the Cold Hardiness Map on page 10.

Zone	Average Annual Minimum Temperature
8	10 to 20 degrees Fahrenheit
9	20 to 30 degrees Fahrenheit
10	30 to 40 degrees Fahrenheit
11	40 degrees and above Fahrenheit

It would be nice to believe that these temperatures are accurate for all areas of each zone. But Florida is full of microclimates in which the temperatures can be much higher or lower than average during cold weather. Cities are one big factor in determining the amount of cold that plants receive. City locations are often 5 to 10 degrees warmer than country locations. Nevertheless, hardiness zones are good guides and may be used in determining what plants will grow in your area of the state, as long as you recognize that there may be some exceptions.

FLORIDA HEAT

Gardeners often wonder why peonies, forsythia, bearded iris, and lilacs don't grow well locally and why petunias, poppies, and snapdragons give out by early summer. Much of the problem with these plants is the amount of heat received in a warm climate. It may get too hot for good growth and flowering.

If it can be too cold to grow a plant, certainly it can be too hot. Before you make a plant selection, you may want to check to see if a plant can be grown in your part of the state.

SOILS

Understanding soil in Florida is easy: Most landscapes are full of sand. The topsoil in most neighborhoods is like the sand used in an hourglass. But don't be too alarmed—you can grow great plants in sands. You just have to supply water and fertilizer.

Florida also has some pockets of clays, and many areas around lakes are high in organic matter. South Florida between Miami and the start of the Keys is an area of rocky soils. (Gardeners can actually grow very good landscapes in crushed rocks.)

Most of our soils are loose sands, which have a number of advantages:

- Sands are usually well drained, except in lower areas where water accumulates.
- Sands offer good aeration for root growth.
- Because sands offer little resistance to root growth, plants become well anchored in the ground.
- Sands make for easy digging when preparing planting sites.
- Sands can be easily amended to improve water-holding and nutrient-supplying ability.

There are some problems you may have when growing in sands:

• Sands hold very few nutrients and the plants need frequent feeding.

• Sands offer little resistance to pests that move through the soil.

• Sands dry quickly and need frequent watering.

• Sands blow about during windy weather and need covering with vegetation or mulch.

• Sands become hot during the summer if they are not mulched or planted.

• Sandy soils are not suitable for all plants.

Wherever possible, amend your soils with organic matter. These additions help the soils hold moisture and supply some nutrients for plant growth. Have the soil pH tested. The pH helps determine the availability of nutrients to plants. You can perform the test with a pH kit available at garden centers. The test is also performed at many garden centers and through local Extension Service offices.

PLANNING YOUR LANDSCAPE AND GARDENS

A landscape that is well planned and well planted is a wise investment. Many landscapers and real estate agents say a well-planted home can add 15 to 20 percent to the value of a property. Even more important, the landscape is a part of your home. It should be a usable area where you can relax and feel free to invite friends over to visit.

Every landscape needs a plan. It's like a road map that tells you where to go. A landscape plan, often called a design (even if it's just a rough sketch on a pad of paper), helps determine what you have room to grow and the positioning of the plantings.

Here are a few suggestions for gardeners who are just beginning to shape their landscapes, or those who need to make some changes:

• Sketch your homesite on paper. Use a scale that is large enough (for example, 1 inch equals 5 or 10 feet) to allow you to get a feeling for the whole property.

• Walk around the yard and notice good and bad features. Mark these on your sketch, as well as the plants you plan to keep in the landscape.

• Decide on the changes you would like to make in the landscape. Determine where you need screens, shade, flower gardens, and ground covers. Limit turf to the area in which it is really needed. Sketch your ideas on tracing paper placed over the plan of the existing property.

• Make use of books, neighborhood gardens, and botanical gardens to obtain ideas.

Your landscape is an extension of your home. Think of it as several rooms where you perform different activities. You may want a "room" for entertaining, one to do maintenance on equipment, and a room that is a private area. In the "family room" you might have a children's play area, barbecue grill, pool, or badminton court.

You will create the walls that separate the rooms the way a builder does for a house, but you will use plant materials for the most part. Once the "rooms" are created, you will decorate with shrubs, flowers, and garden ornaments. Here are a few thoughts to help you with your planning:

• Use trees to frame the house, enclose the property, and create shade.

• Keep trees at least 15 to 20 feet from the house and septic systems.

• Plan clusters of plants. The magic numbers for groupings are odd numbers: 3, 5, 7, 9, etc.

• Plan for spots of color that can be easily seen from walkways, patios, and windows.

• Use just a few garden ornaments like sundials, birdbaths, statuary, and waterfalls. Too many will clutter your landscape design.

• Keep lower-growing plants under windows.

• Leave the front of the house "open," planting with lower-growing plants so house and entrance can be seen from the road and sidewalks.

• Add walkways of mulch, concrete, or similar materials throughout the landscape. If you have trouble deciding on the shape planted areas should take, use a hose or long extension cord to outline some beds. You might try setting a few containers of plants within the beds to see how they will look before planting.

Learn the ultimate sizes of plants before making final selections. Remember, plants grow tall and wide. Leave enough room between them so they can grow a little. One common mistake is to cram too much into the landscape design.

In general, trees are the taller part of any landscape design. They should be located where you need shade or want to block views. Small trees may be positioned to shade a patio or entrance area. Larger trees might be set to the side of the home or along the property lines to enclose the landscape.

Don't *overplant* the landscape with trees unless you want a forest effect. Leave open spaces with sun to grow flower and vegetable gardens. If there is too much shade, you will greatly reduce the number of plants you can use in your landscape.

Shrubs are the workhorses of any landscape design, and they come in all shapes and sizes. You can find shrubs with foliage that is mostly green, and you can find shrubs that are almost always blooming. Shrubs can perform a number of functions:

• Create view barriers and hedges.

• Form small treelike plantings for walkways, patios, and entrances.

• Create colorful accents.

• Disguise foundations.

• Form backdrops for flower and vegetable gardens.

• Create eye-catching topiaries.

The turf that fills in between the trees and shrubs may be the first ground cover that comes to mind, but many low-growing shrubs and perennials can also be used as ground covers. Once established, they are low-maintenance plants. Use them as a substitute for turf, especially in hard-to-mow areas and naturalistic designs. Ground covers are good for beds where a low-maintenance filler is needed.

Trees or large shrubs usually form a backdrop, then more shrubs can be added to the landscape. You may have several layers of shrubs before you reach the turf or sidewalks. Keep in mind the mature heights of all the plants so as not to have one tree or shrub hiding another.

One more factor you must consider in landscaping is bloom times. Use this guide to determine what is going to give a good show and when. It's a common mistake to load up the later winter and spring gardens with color and forget the rest of the year. In Florida there is no reason not to have something in bloom every month of the year. Many shrubs, trees, annuals, and perennials can bloom year-round. When planning your design, make sure you plan for color in every month.

Flowers are not the only plants that can provide color. Look for fruits, foliage, and barks to provide color interest as well.

GENERAL HORTICULTURAL TIPS

A gardener is always adding plants to the landscape. Sometimes you just have to have a new plant you see at the garden center, or maybe you need to replace a plant that has died for some unknown reason. One of the nice things about living in Florida is that plants can be added to the landscape at any time of the year.

So it's planting time for 12 months out of the year, and most landscape plants have been grown in containers. There are other transplanting techniques utilized in Florida—bare root and balled and burlapped—but they are generally limited to use by nurserymen.

When getting ready to purchase a plant, think about the size you need. Smaller plants may establish just as rapidly as larger ones, so it may make sense to plant small shrubs or trees and just let them grow.

Some of the recommended planting techniques have changed in recent years. Horticulturists are learning new tricks! One research finding is that adding organic matter to the fill soil is of limited benefit. Trees grow too fast from the improved soil and into the surrounding ground to gain much benefit from the additions. Many shrubs grow at the same rate whether the soil has been improved or not. Only the slower-growing shrubs, vines, and ground covers might benefit from improving the fill soil with organic matter and manures.

If you are ambitious and want to help your plants get established, it is beneficial to prepare a large planting site. Work up the entire bed and add lots of organic matter to help especially sandy soils hold moisture and supply some nutrients for plant growth. At this time you can also adjust the soil acidity if needed. Having the right pH is especially important for azalea and blueberry plantings.

Another change in horticultural practice is to set plants with their rootballs a little higher out of the ground than was previously recommended. Sandy Florida soils settle over a period of time, and it's not abnormal to see a tree or shrub that is a few inches deeper into the ground than when it was planted. This encourages trunk and root rot problems in some plants. Just planting with the rootball a little out of the ground and then covering with mulch will help ensure survival.

CONTAINER PLANTINGS

Container-grown plants come in all sizes, from the small annuals in sections of cell-packs to 30-gallon and larger pots at garden centers and nurseries. A plant that has a root system and a soilball firmly anchored to the roots is easy to transport and establish in a new site.

Try to find a plant in a container that you can handle easily. The bigger the pot, the more muscle it will take to move the plant, and the larger the vehicle must be that will take it home.

Now let's begin to plant. Here are a few tips to get your new container-grown plants established quickly:

- Find a site where the plant will have ample room to grow.
- Dig the hole twice as wide as but no deeper than the rootball.
- Position the plant in the center of the hole and at the same depth it was growing or with the top of the rootball 1 to 2 inches above the ground.
- Adding organic matter to the fill soil is optional.
- Fill in around the rootball with soil, adding water as you plant. This will ensure good soil-to-root contact.
- Create a 4- to 6-inch-high berm of soil at the edge of the rootball around the plant to hold water.
- Spread a 3- to 4-inch layer of mulch over the root system.

• If you think larger plants will be affected by winds, add stakes or guy wires to hold them upright.

• Water the planting thoroughly.

BARE-ROOT PLANTINGS

Florida has its own Arbor Day celebration on the third Friday in January. This is the best time of year to plant bare-root plants. Most forest trees are planted at this time, and bare-root trees are shared between friends and community groups. Very few bare-root plants are sold at garden centers, but you may dig a plant with bare roots from the landscape for moving to a new spot. If you do, try moving only small plants. Even the winter season is very warm and dry, and large bare-root plants will have a difficult time when transplanted.

Follow these steps for successful bare-root planting:

1. Dig a planting hole as deep as and twice as wide as the root system. Improving the fill soil is optional.
2. Form a mound of soil in the hole.
3. Spread the root system out and over the mound of soil.
4. Fill the hole with soil and water.
5. Build a 4- to 6-inch berm of soil around the edge of the hole.
6. Add a 3- to 4-inch mulch layer.
7. Stake large plants that might be affected by winds.

BALLED-AND-BURLAPPED PLANTINGS

Balled-and-burlapped techniques work best when plants are grown in clay or loam-type soils, as Florida's sandy soils don't hold together very well. A few plants sold at garden centers, especially palms and trees, are moved in this manner, but the use of balled-and-burlapped plants is mainly a nursery practice; most of the plants handled in this way are quite large and should be planted by professionals.

Gardeners might use the balled-and-burlapped technique when moving a large plant from one area of the landscape to another or when they share plants with friends. Here are a few tips for preparing a balled-and-burlapped plant:

• Tie up the limbs of the plant to make it easier to dig.

• Moisten the soil thoroughly to help the rootball hold together.

• Measure out a foot for each inch of trunk diameter (measured 6 inches above the ground) to determine where to start digging.

• Dig with the back of a rounded-point shovel or nursery spade toward the plant. Avoid applying pressure to the roots or rootball.

• Make downward cuts to form the ball.

• When the ball is shaped, dig under the rootball to loosen the plant.

• Tip the rootball to one side and slide the burlap under the plant. Tip the plant to the other side and pull the burlap the rest of the way under the plant.

• Tie the burlap to the rootball. You are now ready to lift and move the plant by the rootball.

If you cannot immediately replant a balled-and-burlapped plant, keep it in filtered sun, and keep the rootball moist with frequent waterings. If it must be stored for extended periods of time, surround the rootball with mulch.

Planting balled-and-burlapped plants is similar to that of planting container-grown plants. Just make sure that when you are working with the plant you always lift it by the rootball. Grabbing the trunk may cause the soil to fall off the plant, which may cause the plant to decline. Follow these steps to good planting:

1. Dig a hole wider but not deeper than the rootball. Adding organic matter to the fill soil is optional before planting.

2.. Position the burlap-encased rootball at the same depth it was in the ground or an inch or two higher.

3. Fill in around the rootball about halfway with soil and water.

4. Fold down or cut away the upper one-quarter to one-half of the burlap.

5. Finish filling the hole with soil and water.

6. Build a berm of soil at the edge of the rootball.

7. Cover the root system with a 3- to 4-inch mulch layer.

8. Stake plants that might be affected by winds.

PLANTING ANNUALS AND PERENNIALS

Most of Florida's annuals and perennials come in cell-packs with four to six small plants ready to go in the ground or in 1- to 3-gallon containers. It's a good idea to check the rootballs to make sure they are not potbound at purchase time.

If plants have very tightly wrapped root systems, they may not grow out into the surrounding soil and thus will be short-lived. This is especially true of annuals. And many annuals at this stage of growth have completed much of the life cycle. If you do purchase a plant with a tight rootball, pull it apart lightly at planting time.

With annuals, the condition of the rootball is not quite as important as it is with perennials, but it's best to find a plant that is just filling its pot with roots. If you purchase a plant whose roots are tightly bound, pull apart the root system a little to encourage future growth into the surrounding soil. Here are some tips for establishing both annuals and perennials:

- Till the soil for planting, and work in organic matter and manures.
- Till in a light application of a balanced fertilizer.
- Plant at the same depth the plants were growing in their containers.
- Follow spacing instructions on labels or in gardening guides.
- Firm the soil around the root system, and water at the time of planting if you can.
- Add a thin mulch layer, but keep it back from the base of the plants.
- Give the planted site a good soaking.

WATERING NEW PLANTINGS

Just as important as good planting technique is the care a plant receives once it is in the ground. Remember, Florida can have some dry months, and many landscape plantings are made during the spring and fall season when there is little rain and lots of hot weather.

Trees, shrubs, vines, and ground covers all need a good watering program until roots are established in the surrounding soil. It's a common saying: *You don't own an azalea, magnolia, or dogwood for at least two years.* It takes some time to get these and other landscape plants established. Their most important need is good watering or rainfalls. Florida's sandy soils dry very rapidly, so daily watering is needed in the beginning. Some gardeners recommend watering trees once a day for six or more months if they are planted in the very sandy soils that seem to wick the water away from rootballs.

For most plants, however, you will do fine if you just water when the surface soil begins to dry to the touch. Most gardeners water every day for the first few weeks after planting and then back off to an "as needed" schedule, using the surface soil moisture as a guide. (Feel the soil, and if the upper inch is dry, water may be needed.)

Note that it is important to build berms around new plantings. Many plants are grown in highly organic soils and when set in the ground the water tends to run around the rootball. You may think

you are doing a good job of watering but sometimes rootballs remain dry. When you fill a berm around the rootball with water, the moisture has to move down and through the rootball before it goes into the surrounding soil. Here are a few more tips for good watering:

• Don't rely on irrigation systems to water new plantings—do it by hand.

• When watering, thoroughly wet the soil.

• Keep a mulch in place over the root system.

• Where possible, install drip irrigation systems or use soaker hoses.

• Water during the early-morning hours to conserve water and to prevent loss of water due to evaporation and drifting during blowing winds.

• Control weeds that may be competing with the plant for water.

FERTILIZING

Feeding new plants is also part of the establishment program. You may have noticed that no fertilizer was added to the planting hole. There are products available if you want them, but Florida soils are so heavily watered in the beginning that many added nutrients may be lost during the first few weeks of plant care. It is often best to let the tree, shrub, vine, or ground cover plantings get a start on establishment for 4 to 6 weeks, and then make a fertilizer application. The type of fertilizer you use is not that important as long as it's meant for landscape plantings. Many gardeners are using a 16-4-8 or similar product as their main fertilizer.

Slow-release fertilizers are also available—they stretch the time between feedings and your dollars too. Just follow the label instructions.

Most shrubs, vines, and ground covers can be fed lightly every 6 to 8 weeks March through October for the first year. After that a regular maintenance program can be followed.

Give trees their first feeding 4 to 6 weeks after planting, and then feed in March and June for the first three years. After that, no feedings are normally needed for trees except for fruiting trees.

Annual flowers and perennials require a feeding program that is a little different: they are immediately put on a regular maintenance program. Give annuals a monthly feeding year-round, and give perennials a feeding every 6 to 8 weeks during March through November.

SOIL AMENDMENTS

Florida's sandy soils can grow lots of great plants if you add plenty of water and fertilizer, but you can make gardening even easier by improving sandy sites with organic matter. It's almost impossible to add too much organic matter when preparing flower beds, vegetable gardens, and other planting sites. Some of the organic amendments available for use:

• **Compost:** Make your own at home or pick it up at county landfills.

Compost puts to good use the yard trash from your landscape, returning it as an excellent soil amendment. Work 4 to 6 inches into most planting sites including clay soils. Compost produced at landfills is normally alkaline and is not recommended for use with azalea or blueberry plantings.

• **Peat moss:** Florida has local sources of peat moss that can be purchased through landscape supply companies. Canadian peat moss can also be obtained at garden centers.

Work 4 to 6 inches into sandy or clay soils before planting.

• **Manures:** Chicken, cow, and horse manure are all readily available.

Use about 25 pounds for each 100 square feet of bed area to be planted, or follow package instructions.

• **Leaves:** Plenty of leaves are available as soil improvements.

They can be worked into existing soils, but they may tie up nutrients as they decompose. Most gardeners use them as mulch or put them in the compost pile to decompose before adding to the garden.

• **Potting soils:** A potting soil is a good amendment for small garden spots, but it can be costly to use in large beds.

• **Topsoil:** Florida does not have standards for topsoil.

Be careful when ordering to make sure it's not the same sandy soil found in your yard, and that it is free of weeds.

Gardeners with sandy soil may add colloidal phosphate or clays to the ground to improve the water- and nutrient-holding ability. Organic soils are usually not improved with amendments but are ready to plant when tilled. Make sure the organic soils are well-drained, or use raised-bed techniques to prevent root problems.

WATERING ESTABLISHED PLANTINGS

Much of Florida's landscape would shrivel and dry without receiving extra water. Many gardeners are practicing "dryland planting" techniques to reduce water usage. They use trees, shrubs, and other plantings that need very little watering once established. But even water-wise designs usually include an oasis for plants that need more moisture.

The best watering program is one that lets the plants tell you when they need water. Spots in lawns can be used as indicators: when the leaves start to curl, it's time to water. You can also wait until the shrub and perennial foliage shows early signs of wilting—that really won't hurt established plants. Here are some guidelines for conserving water while maintaining a well-kept landscape:

• Turn irrigation systems on manually and only when the plants need water.

• Feel the soil, and if the upper inch is dry, water may be needed.

• Water between 4 and 6 in the morning.

• Apply 1/2 to 3/4 inch of water at each irrigation.

• Water trees and shrubs that use less water separately from lawns and flower beds.

• Use sprinkler heads that keep the water at ground level and off walks and roads.

• Perform monthly tests to make sure the irrigation system is working properly.

• Use miccrosprinklers and soaker hoses in shrub plantings, flower beds, and vegetable gardens.

• Water before freezes are expected.

• Do not water while temperatures are below 32 degrees Fahrenheit.

PROPER FERTILIZATION

Plants need nutrients for growth, especially in Florida's sandy soils. Much of the fertilizer supplied to the plants is quickly gone in a month or two. It's either used for growth or washed deeper into the ground.

There is much concern about groundwater pollution today, and it's important that just the right amount of fertilizer is applied for plant growth and not much more. Many plants actually grow better on a lean fertilizing schedule—they are less likely to have insect and disease problems. Also, you won't have to mow or prune as much.

Where possible, use slow-releasing fertilizers to feed your plants. These supply the nutrients over a period of weeks or months. Many gardeners also like to use manure and sludges that slowly release nutrients for growth.

Use your plant as a guide to when feedings are needed. If it's green and growing, you can skip a scheduled feeding without affecting plant growth. Keep fertilizers off walkways and roads. Try to keep a fertilizer-free zone at least 20 feet wide

around lakes. Here are some suggested feeding times for landscape plantings:

- **Annual flowers:** Monthly
- **Perennial flowers:** Every other month, March through November
- **Citrus trees:** March, May, August, and October
- **Container plantings:** Every other week during warmer months
- **Deciduous fruit trees:** February, June, and August
- **Ground covers:** February, June, and September
- **Lawns:** March and September
- **Orchids:** Every other week, March through November
- **Roses:** Monthly
- **Shade trees:** March and June for three years after planting
- **Shrubs:** February, June, and September
- **Tropical fruits:** March, June, and September
- **Vegetables and herbs:** Monthly

PROPER PRUNING

All plants can benefit from pruning. Sometimes pruning is just a little guidance to keep a tree trunk straight, or pinching out the tips of shrubs to form a compact plant. It's best to learn the natural shape of a plant and then plan its pruning program.

Not all pruning is done at the same time of the year. Plants that bloom in the spring are normally trimmed immediately after flowering. With azaleas, for example, you will have from late March to the end of June to do the pruning—if you wait any longer, you will affect flowering for spring.

Plants that bloom during the late spring and summer can usually be trimmed during later winter. Don't perform the trimming too soon or you could stimulate growth that might be damaged by a late cold snap. Winter pruning is usually performed in January or February, just before new growth begins.

Some plants need constant care. Roses, for example, are always being groomed to remove old flowers and dead stems. Poinsettias are trimmed throughout the spring and summer months to develop into compact plants.

Peaches, pears, figs, and grapes get a yearly pruning. Citrus trees and most tropical fruits just seem to grow themselves (with limited guidance). Check all fruit trees carefully to make sure you perform the pruning that can help promote good production.

Make sure you use good sharp tools when pruning any plant. Jagged cuts only encourage the entrance of pests into the plants. Here are a few pruning tips to help you provide the needed plant care:

- Always prune back to a bud, branch angle, or trunk.
- Remove all dead or declining limbs as needed.
- Clean pruning equipment with a disinfectant after removal of diseased plant portions and after pruning plants of other species.
- Removing just the tips of stems stimulates branching.
- Remove suckers from the base of single-trunk trees.
- Thin out crossing limbs of trees and large shrubs.
- Do not apply pruning paint or sealants to wounds.
- Prune to maintain the shape of your plant or to increase fruit production.
- Avoid pruning plants to rounded or squarish shapes unless you are developing a sheared hedge.
- Not all plants need pruning every year—wait until you have a good reason to prune before doing so.

WINTER CARE

If your plants are chosen properly they will need very little winter care. Most trees, shrubs, vines,

and similar plants go dormant when shorter days signal the end of the growing season.

Plantings in Northern and Central Florida actually benefit from getting a little taste of cooler weather as winter approaches. It slows their growth and makes them much more resistant to frosts and freezes when they arrive. Much of Florida's real plant damage occurs when warm days are followed by sudden freezes that catch plants in active growth. Such freezes devastated home citrus plantings and many ornamentals during the 1980s.

Most winter plant care in Florida means switching to seasonal varieties that won't mind the cooler temperatures. As marigolds fade, they can be replaced with petunias, snapdragons, and pansies. If you are in a really cold pocket, you must pick your plants carefully so they will survive the few days of severely cold weather that might arrive at any time during the winter.

Most gardeners do keep some plantings that could be damaged by cold, usually the tropical plants that cannot be resisted at garden centers during the warmer months. Most landscapes throughout the state include hibiscus, croton, and bird of paradise, all sensitive to temperatures of 32 degrees and below . . . and few planters can resist adding a stand of bananas and pineapples to the landscape. These all need cold protection or they will turn to mush upon freezing.

When cold warnings are sounded, our first urge is to encase plantings with plastic to hold in the heat. But plants are not like people: they do not give off heat. Any heat that can warm a plant must be entrapped before the air cools, come from the ground, or be suppled by a heat source. Plants are often covered with plastic bags by gardeners, but these efforts are futile. The cold quickly passes through the thin films and the plants freeze, and if the wraps are not removed when the sun rises, the plant portions will cook inside the covers.

Another common urge is to quickly harvest all available fruits from citrus trees. In fact, citrus fruits are very hardy. Most can withstand temperatures down to the upper 20s for several hours before they freeze. If they do freeze, you can still turn them into juice over a period of day or weeks.

There are numerous ways to ensure winter survival of cold-sensitive plants:

• Keep the plants in pots that can be moved indoors when cold warnings are sounded.

You can pot some small fruit trees including citrus and mango, or just stick to potted poinsettias, plumeria, tomatoes, and orchids.

• Dig the plants just before the freeze and put them in pots or burlap to move into warmer locations. Many gardeners save their favorite crotons, bromeliads, and heliconias with this technique.

• Mound up soil over the lower stems to protect the buds from freezing temperatures. With some plants the tops can be removed a foot or two above the ground; then the soil is mounded over the stems.

• Cover plants with cloth sheets or quilts draped to the ground to entrap heat from the soil and keep out the cold.

• Surround plants with plastic over stakes held above and back from touching the foliage. Outdoor-approved lights can be added inside the cover to provide heat.

• Construct a plastic or cardboard wind screen several feet high, and add microsprinklers to apply water to the base of the plant. Ten gallons per hour must be uniformly applied to the base of the plant starting before freezing temperatures and continuing until the ice formed melts to protect the lower portion of the plant.

Perhaps the best advice in planning your landscape is to make most of your plantings cold-hardy ornamentals; for interest, add some of the exotics that might not survive the winter. Remember, not all winters bring freezing weather throughout the state. Many years the plants suffer only minor damage that can be pruned away when spring weather arrives.

GENERAL OVERVIEW

Now that you have been introduced to a great gardening state, it's time to create your own experiences. Use this month-by-month guide to begin your landscape activities.

Annuals: Annuals can provide instant color in any landscape. They are so easy to grow that you can germinate them from seeds, or purchase the plants in bloom at garden centers. Use annuals for a bed or a spot of color, in container gardens for the balcony or patio, and in hanging baskets.

Bulbs, Corms, Rhizomes, and Tubers: These may be the most forgotten plants in Florida. Most newcomers don't see their favorite tulips, crocuses, or daffodils at the garden center, and give up on bulbs. But wait—Florida has a wealth of bulbs just waiting to be discovered. You can use them as in-ground accents or in containers. They will bloom just about year-round.

Citrus: If you grow but one fruit, it's got to be citrus. Over half the state can grow a wide selection of oranges, tangelos, tangerines, and grapefruits. And for the colder spots there are some citrus in your future too. Some minimal care is the secret to having fruits ready to eat from September through May every year.

Deciduous and Tropical Fruits: Part of the fun of living in Florida is having an edible landscape. Round out your landscape with some of the additional fruit trees that put food on the table. In Southern and some Central portions of the state this could be tropical fruits like avocados, bananas, and pineapples. And in the Northern and much of Central Florida plant grapes, blueberries, and peaches.

Herbs and Vegetables: Florida has cool, warm, and hot seasons, and not all crops can adapt to every one of them. It's important to follow a guide so that you do not plant out of season—but there is plenty to grow at every season, and you should always have vegetables and herbs for the table.

Lawns: What is the most common gardening activity? Many gardeners would answer *lawn care*. The lawn grows year-round in Florida, but you do get a little break from weekly mowings at certain times of the year. "Go by the book" so you can provide good care that doesn't put too large a dent in your weekends. Learn when to feed and water and about the pests that can attack, and your lawn can be the pride of the neighborhood.

Perennials: As gardeners find other activities that attract their interest, they will have less time to work in their yards. One way to cut down on needed care but keep an attractive yard is to use plants that flower for months and last for years. Florida residents have always used a few perennials, but many more are now being discovered. They make gardening a lot easier when used in flower beds and container gardens.

Shrubs: Shrubs make up most of the plantings in home landscapes. They are used as accents, hedges, space dividers, and foundation plants. One of the first steps to keeping the shrubs attractive is picking the right shrub for the landscape. Some simple care and you can have shrubs with bright green foliage and lots of flowers if you wish.

Trees and Palms: Whether you use trees for shade, to frame the house, or block a view, they are one of the first plants to be added to the landscape. You then want to get them established as fast as possible and with the proper shape. Actually, a good tree is easy to grow and care for in Florida. All you need are a few tips like how to keep a central leader and when to fertilize.

Vines, Ground Covers, and Ornamental Grasses: Fill in the hard-to-mow areas and create great wall coverings from some of these plantings. Perhaps they are the most underused plants in the landscape, but they are growing in popularity. Most fill in quickly in those hard-to-care-for spots. Also, many require minimal maintenance. Learn how to put them to use.

CHAPTER ONE

ANNUALS

Do you need color fast? Planting annuals may be the best and quickest way to brighten your landscape.

This large group of plants includes gardeners' favorites like marigolds, zinnias, petunias, and pansies, which are often used to add color to flower beds and container gardens.

If you have lived in areas that are farther north, you more than likely planted annuals once a year for the spring and summer seasons. In Florida, annuals can be planted year-round.

Annuals last but a short time. Some may grow back from seeds set by the previous year's plants, but most are restarted from fresh grower-produced seed or transplants available at garden centers. You can count on annuals to grow and flower for three to four months. The life cycle includes the following stages:

1. Seeds germinate in 7 to 14 days.
2. Young plants form and flower in 6 to 8 weeks.
3. Plants flower for 8 to 10 weeks.
4. Plantings set seed and decline.

You will notice that some flowers, such as delphiniums, foxgloves, and hollyhocks, that are grown as perennials in cooler climates are grown as annuals in Florida. Plantings such as impatiens, wax begonias, and periwinkles may grow for

more than one year due to our mild climate; such plants are often called long-lived annuals.

Because our weather is so mild, it's common in Florida to make three or four annual plantings a year. But be careful which annuals you grow—some prefer the warm months, others the cooler seasons. Be sure to consult the Annuals chart (page 28) before planting the garden.

PLANNING FOR ANNUAL FLOWERS

Annual flowers are cheery additions to a home landscape. Some gardeners like to plan large beds and others prefer spots of color. A current trend is to use annuals for bursts of color at entrances and along walkways.

If you want to plant a large bed of annuals, there is almost no limit to size. It's probably best to start small until you get the knack of caring for the plants, but you will soon find that growing annuals is easy. When you design the bed, keep these things in mind:

- Decide if you want the bed to be viewed from one side or from many sides.
- Design the bed with tall plants in the center or the back, depending on the viewing angles.
- Select low-growing annuals for the border plantings.
- Decide if you want paths through the bed or if you want to plant it solid.
- Plan to plant the bed in one type of annual flower, or plan for clusters of color.
- Select your flowers according to the light they will receive.
- Use a hose or extension cord to form the outline of the bed during the planning stage.
- Draw lines in the ground with a stick or hoe to show where each flower cluster should be planted.

Perhaps you do not have adequate room for a bed of color but still want to enjoy annual flowers. Container gardens could be for you. How about a big pot of color, maybe a planter box or hanging basket? It can be designed to make the best use of small spaces. You can also move containers around when company arrives to put the color where needed.

PLANTING

Most annuals grow in Florida's sandy soils, but enriching the planting site with organic matter makes care much easier. First eliminate the weeds by digging them out or by applying a nonselective herbicide that allows planting after the weeds decline. Then till the soil, working in any amendments, and you will be ready to plant. Amendments include peat moss, compost, and manures. Most gardeners like to scatter a light amount of a general garden fertilizer over the surface of the soil. When the ground is ready, follow these steps to good planting:

1. Moisten the soil thoroughly a day or two before planting.
2. Loosen the rootballs just a little if any roots are wrapped tightly together.
3. Arrange the plants over the bed at the correct spacing, using labels or charts as a guide.

Sketch out your garden plan.

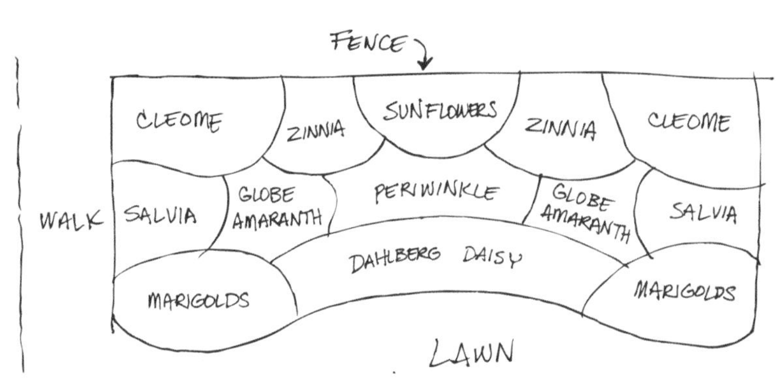

4. Set the plants in the ground at the same depth they were growing in their containers.

5. Spread a thin layer of mulch over the bed, but keep it away from the base of the plants.

6. Water the entire bed of flowers thoroughly.

Gardeners have the option of sowing annual seeds directly into the ground. Unfortunately, Florida soils dry very rapidly, which makes establishing plantings by seed difficult. You will do much better if you sow the seeds in pots or individual cells of market packs and then add them to the landscape as transplants once they have sprouted.

Planting annuals in containers is easy, but be sure to start with a well-drained potting soil. You can make your own by combining equal parts of peat moss, perlite, and compost. Many gardeners prefer to use a potting soil purchased at a local garden center.

Container gardens can be devoted to one type of annual, or you can create the wildflower look by mixing several together. If you use more than one type, keep the tall flowers to the center or back of the container. You may want to use cascading types around the edges.

IN-GROUND ANNUALS

WATERING

Most annual flowers prefer a moist soil. Water annuals daily for the first week or two until the roots begin to grow out into the surrounding soil. Reduce watering frequency gradually until you are watering only when the surface soil is dry to the touch. Learn which annuals tolerate drought if you want to minimize watering chores.

FERTILIZING

Apply a balanced fertilizer monthly to encourage new growth and flowering. If you would like to take some of the work out of plant care, apply one of the slow-release products that can feed your plants for months. Be sure to follow label instructions.

GROOMING

Many annuals benefit from deadheading (the removal of fading flowers) to encourage additional blooms. If you want to develop fuller plants, nip out the tips of new growth. Lanky annuals can also be cut back to shorten the plant, which sometimes encourages new growth and blooms.

CONTAINER ANNUALS

WATERING

Check containers daily and water when surface soil feels dry to the touch. When plants begin to fill their pots, they may need water once or twice a day.

FERTILIZING

Fertilizer solutions are an easy way to feed annuals growing in containers. Apply a balanced fertilizer every other week. Many gardeners prefer to use a time-release fertilizer that is applied every few months.

GROOMING

Deadhead any faded flowers as needed. Remove declining individual annuals and replant as needed.

PEST CONTROL

Annual flowers have very few pests, but check your plantings frequently to prevent major problems. Holes in leaves, yellow spots, and browning plant parts can all mean pests are active. You may notice some of the following problems.

Caterpillars can be up to 2 inches long. They chew holes in leaves, stems, and flowers.

Many gardeners tolerate caterpillar damage and wait for the pests to be transformed into colorful moths or butterflies. Others handpick the insects

from the plants to destroy them, or apply a natural insecticide containing *Bacillus thuringiensis,* or a properly labeled synthetic product.

Aphids are soft-bodied pear-shaped insects about 1/8 inch long. Their colors vary depending on the species and the plants they attack. They attack new growth and flower buds.

Control with a natural soap spray or a properly labeled synthetic insecticide.

Leafminers (immature stages of a moth or fly) tunnel inside the leaves of garden flowers.

Some damage can be tolerated. Control by hanging sticky boards near plantings, or apply a properly labeled synthetic insecticide.

Mites resemble tiny spiders, about 1/50 inch long, and they turn leaves yellow. Some produce a webbing between the leaves.

Control with a soap spray.

Slugs are slimy pests up to 2 inches long that chew flowers and foliage. They can often be detected by slime trails noticeable during the morning hours.

Handpick from the plants or trap in shallow trays of beer or malt beverages, or control with slug baits available from garden centers.

Nematodes are roundworms that live in most Florida soils. They develop large populations that destroy roots among susceptible plants.

Use soil solarization to bake out nematodes during the summer. Plant resistant flowers such as marigolds, ageratum, and zinnias in problem sites.

Root and stem rot problems are caused by several fungal organisms when plants are kept too moist or planted in sites previously infested with these organisms.

Water on an "only-as-needed" schedule once plants are established. Replace the soil in heavily infested sites.

Leaf spots are yellow and brown areas that develop on annual flower foliage because of fungal or bacterial infections.

Keep the foliage as dry as possible. Fungicides are also available at garden centers to apply as needed.

Rabbits can wreak havoc on an annual bed.

Exclude with fencing or apply repellents available from garden centers. Plant varieties which are not a favorite food of rabbits.

Construct a fence to keep rabbits and other unwanted animals from harming your plants.

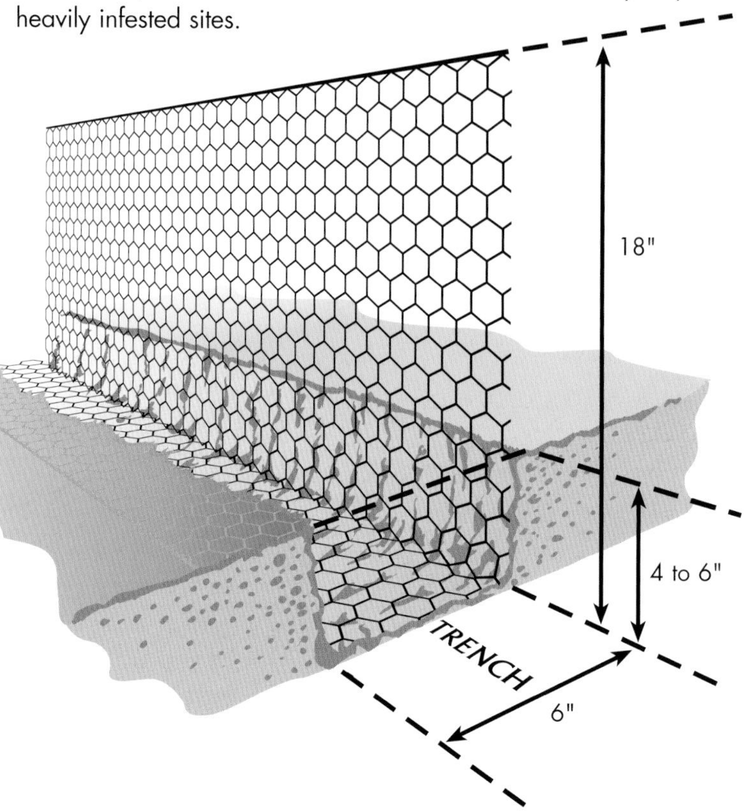

CHAPTER ONE

Annuals

Variety	Flower Color	Height (Inches)	Spacing (Inches)	Cold Hardiness	Light Level
Ageratum	White, blue, pink	6 – 18	10 – 12	Tender	Sun to light shade
Alyssum	White, pink, purple	6 – 12	10 – 12	Tender	Sun to light shade
Amaranthus	Red	36 – 48	12 – 18	Tender	Sun
Aster	White, pink, blue	18 – 24	12 – 18	Tender	Sun to light shade
Baby's Breath	White, pink	18 – 36	18 – 24	Hardy	Sun
Balsam	White, red, purple	18 – 24	12 – 18	Tender	Sun to light shade
Browallia	White, purple	12 – 18	10 – 12	Tender	Sun to light shade
Calendula	Orange, yellow	12 – 18	10 – 12	Hardy	Sun
California Poppy	Yellow, orange	18 – 24	12 – 18	Hardy	Sun
Celosia	Orange, red, yellow	8 – 24	10 – 12	Tender	Sun
Cleome	White, pink	36 – 48	18 – 24	Hardy	Sun
Coleus	Insignificant	12 – 30	12 – 18	Tender	Sun to light shade
Cosmos	White, pink, yellow	18 – 36	12 – 18	Tender	Sun
Dahlberg Daisy	Yellow	6 – 8	8 – 12	Tender	Sun
Delphinium	White, pink, purple	24 – 36	12 – 18	Hardy	Sun
Dianthus	White, pink, red	12 – 18	8 – 12	Hardy	Sun to light shade
Dusty Miller	Yellow	12 – 24	10 – 12	Hardy	Sun to light shade
Foxglove	White, pink, purple	24 – 36	12 – 18	Hardy	Sun to light shade
Gazania	Orange, red, yellow	12 – 18	8 – 12	Tender	Sun
Geranium	White, red, lavender	18 – 24	12 – 24	Tender	Sun
Globe Amaranth	Pink, purple	12 – 24	12 – 18	Tender	Sun
Hollyhock	White, pink, purple	48 – 60	18 – 24	Hardy	Sun
Impatiens	White, pink, purple	12 – 24	12 – 18	Tender	Shade
Lobelia	White, blue, purple	8 – 12	8 – 12	Tender	Sun to light shade
Marigold	Yellow, orange	10 – 36	12 – 18	Tender	Sun
Melampodium	Yellow	18 – 24	12 – 18	Tender	Sun

Variety	Flower Color	Height (Inches)	Spacing (Inches)	Cold Hardiness	Light Level
Mexican Sunflower	Orange	36 – 48	18 – 24	Tender	Sun
Nasturtium	White, yellow, orange	12 – 24	12 – 18	Tender	Sun
Nicotiana	White, pink, red	12 – 24	12 – 18	Tender	Sun
Nierembergia	White, purple	8 – 12	10 – 12	Tender	Sun to light shade
Ornamental Kale or Cabbage	Yellow	10 – 12	12 – 18	Hardy	Sun
Ornamental Pepper	Cream	12 – 18	10 – 12	Tender	Sun
Pansy	Yellow, orange, purple	6 – 8	8 – 10	Hardy	Sun
Periwinkle	White, pink, purple	12 – 18	12 – 24	Tender	Sun
Petunia	White, pink, red, purple	8 – 16	12 – 18	Hardy	Sun to light shade
Phlox (Annual)	White, pink, purple	12 – 18	8 – 12	Hardy	Sun
Purslane	White, yellow, pink	8 – 12	12 – 18	Tender	Sun
Rose Moss	White, yellow, pink, orange	6 – 10	8 – 12	Tender	Sun
Scarlet Sage	White, red, pink, purple	12 – 24	12 – 18	Tender	Sun to light shade
Silk Flower	Pink, red	18 – 24	12 – 18	Tender	Sun
Snapdragon	White, pink, yellow, red	10 – 36	10 – 12	Hardy	Sun to light shade
Stock	White, pink, purple	12 – 24	10 – 12	Hardy	Sun
Strawflower	Red, yellow, orange	18 – 24	10 – 12	Tender	Sun
Sunflower	Yellow, orange	12 – 124	12 – 24	Tender	Sun
Sweet Pea	White, pink, red, purple	18 – 72	8 – 12	Hardy	Sun
Torenia	White, pink, blue, purple	10 – 18	12 – 18	Tender	Sun to light shade
Verbena	White, red, purple	8 – 12	12 – 18	Tender	Sun
Viola	Yellow, pink, blue, purple	8 – 12	6 – 10	Hardy	Sun
Wax Begonia	White, pink, red	12 – 18	8 – 12	Tender	Sun to shade
Zinnia	White, yellow, orange, red	12 – 36	12 – 24	Tender	Sun

CHAPTER ONE

Annual Planting Times by Region

Variety	North	Central	South
Ageratum	March – May September – November	February – May	November – March
Alyssum	February – March September – November	February – April	October – March
Amaranthus	March – May	March – May	October – March
Asters	March – April	February – April	October – March
Baby's Breath	February – March October – December	February – March	August – December
Balsam	March – June	February – June	February – May
Browallia	March – May	March – April	February – March
Calendula	February – April	November – March	November – March
California Poppy	November – January	November – February	November – February
Celosia	March – May September – November	March – May September – November	March – May
Cleome	March – June September – November	March – May	February – May
Coleus	April – September	March – September	March – October
Cosmos	April – May	March – April	November – March
Dahlberg Daisy	April – June	March – June	March – June
Delphinium	February – March	November – January	November – February
Dianthus	November – March	November – March	November – February
Dusty Miller	February – May	November – May	November – April
Foxglove	February – March	December – March	December – February
Gazania	March – May September – November	March – May	November – May
Geranium	March – May	November – April	November – March
Globe Amaranth	March – September September – October	March – May September – November	March – May
Hollyhock	March – April	November – December	Not recommended
Impatiens	March – September	March – November	March – November
Lobelia	March – April	November – March	November – February
Marigold	April – June September – October	March – June	October – March

Variety	North	Central	South
Melampodium	March – July	March – July	February – August
Mexican Sunflower	April – July	March – June	February – June
Nasturtium	March – April	November – March	November – March
Nicotiana	March – May September – October	March – April September – October	February – April
Nierembergia	April – July	March – July	March – July
Ornamental Kale or **Cabbage**	November – February	November – March	November – February
Ornamental Pepper	March – June September – October	March – May	September – April
Pansy	November – February	November – February	November – January
Periwinkle	March – June	March – October	March – October
Petunia	November – March	November – April	November – March
Phlox (Annual)	October – November	October – December	October – December
Purslane	April – July	April – June	April – June
Rose Moss	April – July	March – May	March – May
Scarlet Sage	March – June September – November	March – May September – November	February – May
Silk Flower	April – July	April – July	March – July
Snapdragon	October – March	November – March	November – March
Stock	March – April	November – March	November – March
Strawflower	March – May	March – April	November – March
Sunflower	February – May September – October	February – May	November – April
Sweet Pea	October – February	November – February	November – February
Torenia	March – June September – October	March – June September – October	February – May
Verbena	March – May October – November	March – April October – November	February – March
Viola	November – February	November – February	November – January
Wax Begonia	March – June September – November	March – May	October – April
Zinnia	March – May September – October	March – April September – October	February – March

JANUARY
ANNUALS

PLANNING

Draw a planting plan for annuals. Then take a trip to your garden centers, and look for healthy varieties. Here are a few tips:

1. Select plants that are just starting to form flower buds and have a symmetrical shape.
2. Knock a plant out of its pot and make sure the roots are just starting to form a web around the ball of soil.
3. Make sure the leaves are bright green.
4. Avoid plants with leaf spots and dead stems, as well as those that will need staking as soon as they are planted.

Fill most of the garden with the old reliables, and then add some new selections.

Some annuals that are winter favorites may not be completely hardy. Only **pansies** and **violas** are resistant to hard freezes. Some annuals, including **petunias**, **snapdragons**, and **dianthus**, tolerate light freezes. Consider providing cold protection.

Some of your fall warm-season annuals may be beginning to fade. Replace them with winter annuals.

- Add annuals that require a winter chill to flower well in spring. These include **delphinium**, **foxglove**, and **hollyhocks**.
- Time the completion of **sweet pea** plantings so they will flower during late winter and spring.
- Check seed racks and catalogs for warm-season annuals and place orders.
- Move cold-sensitive flowers that are in containers to a location in a warmer area of the landscape. Be prepared to move them indoors during freezing weather.

PLANTING

It's great planting weather. Sometimes the days are a little cool in the morning, but by midday the air is warm and you won't mind working in the garden. Check the gardens that need replanting and add your favorites to continue the color.

Believe it or not, it will soon be too late for some cool-season annuals. If you are really thinking about planting **pansies** or **violas**, you had better put them in the ground now. They love the cooler temperatures and must have them to survive.

Though a bit risky, it is a good idea to make any **sweet pea** plantings. The young plants are cold sensitive, but if the spring weather is especially warm they will decline quickly. Try getting

Snapdragon

them started now. One trick is to make a shock of dry vines and stems and train the **sweet pea** vines up the sides so they will form a pillar of color.

When warm-season annuals start to fade, it's time to add cool-season color. If frosts and freezing weather have damaged some plants, you may need to make replacements. Here are the steps to preparing new or old planting sites:

1. Till the soil deeply to disperse harmful organisms and weed seeds.
2. Work liberal quantities of organic matter into sandy soils.
3. If the soil is extremely dry, moisten it a day or two before planting.
4. Set new plants in the ground at the same depth they were growing in their containers.
5. Water the soil to ensure good root-to-soil contact.
6. Apply time-release fertilizer.

HELPFUL HINT

Keep a bale of hay handy—not to feed the rabbits or other animals in the landscape, but to protect your annual plantings on cold nights. Much cold protection depends upon holding in heat and excluding frost or freezing temperatures.

- When frosts or freezing temperatures are expected, distribute the hay over the tops of the plantings.
- Form loose layers that hide the foliage and flowers.
- Leave the hay in place until the cold days and nights are over.
- Pull the hay back and remove or use as a mulch.
- Extra hay can be added to the compost pile.

CARE

Annuals grow a little more slowly during the cooler months, but at least once a week you need to check the flower beds for pests and water needs. This is a kind of transition time when some flowers should be finishing growth and others just beginning. Cold weather could appear at any time, so be prepared to protect the plants that need protection.

Plants that have been growing for months may be getting a little lanky. Many may also be forming seedheads. A little help can stretch their life through the winter months. Here are a few tips for winter care:

- Prune off all faded flowers.
- Remove any seedheads that have formed.
- To encourage new growth, cut back stems that become lanky.
- Apply a monthly feeding of general garden fertilizer if not using a time-release product.

January is also one of the dry months of the year. You are sure to need some extra waterings. Just remember, however, it does not hurt to keep the plants a little on the dry side. You are more likely to cause harm by overwatering established plants than by underwatering them.

PROBLEMS

A common misconception is that because it's cold outside, the pests will go away. If you think this, you will be disappointed. One of the pests that is sure to find annuals attractive into the colder months is the caterpillar. Here are a few steps to keeping caterpillars under control:

- Check the plantings once or twice a week for chewed holes that indicate a pest.
- Handpick early infestations, removing leaves if necessary.
- Apply a natural spray of a *Bacillus thuringiensis* insecticide.
- Recheck plants in about a week to confirm control is working.

FEBRUARY

ANNUALS

PLANNING

Even in colder Florida locations, the average last-frost dates occur during the later part of this month. You can begin to add warm-season color to your cool-season plantings of **pansies**, **snapdragons**, and **dianthus**. Choose warm-season **marigolds**, **verbena**, and **salvia**. Here's how to prepare for new plantings:

- Decide where you need new flower beds or which present gardens you want to replace.
- Have the soil pH tested, and adjust with lime or soil sulfur if needed.
- Sketch on paper the new spring plantings.
- Plan a bed with either one type of flower or a collection of different types.
- Where multiple varieties are used, plan to place taller types in the center or back of the bed.
- Select flowers according to the light level in the bed.
- Use lower-growing flowers near the front of the bed.

Your local garden center is always a good source for plants in 4- to 5-inch pots, or gallon containers. In Florida, very few seeds are sown directly in the ground. Some say the local soils eat seeds! What they mean is that seed often fails to germinate due to the dry, sandy conditions, rot organisms, and insects. So start your seeds in a container.

Here are a few tips for ordering seeds or plants from catalogs:

- For the most part, select flowers that are known to grow in your area.
- Try varieties of known flowers with different colors and growth habits.
- Include something new to try in the garden with every order.
- Pick flowers listed for your cold-hardiness zone.
- Place orders a month or more before desired planting dates.

Companies often offer bonuses for early orders, and you are more likely to get your desired selections as well.

- Ask to have the plants shipped on dates when you know beds will be ready.

PLANTING

February is rejuvenation time for most annual flower beds. As you remove the old plants, try to determine if they had any problems. Some things you might notice:

- Nematode damage to the roots.

This is evident as swollen areas along the roots.

- Leaf spot fungal damage that might affect the next crop.
- Rotting stems and roots.
- Cutworms and other plant-destroying insects.
- Perennial weeds that may affect new plantings.

Most of these problems can affect the next flowers you add to a garden. Rejuvenate the beds so they will be ready to provide three to four months of good growth. Here's how:

1. Remove all plant portions from the old flowers. You may want to clean the bed out completely, even if some flowers are still providing good color.
2. Spray green growing weeds with a nonselective herbicide that permits replanting after the weeds turn brown. If you would rather not use a weedkiller, hand-dig the weeds from the garden.
3. When the weeds decline, till the soil deeply and remove any remaining plant portions.
4. Work in liberal quantities of organic matter and manure to enrich the planting site.
5. Adjust the soil acidity if needed and till all amendments into the soil.
6. Smooth out the bed and plant.
7. If nematodes are a major problem, select nematode-resistant plants.

Keep in mind that this is the last time to plant some of the flowers that really need the cool weather. Finish up all **pansy** and **viola** plantings—they will fade from the

garden at the first sign of warm days. Add only large plants of **hollyhock**, **foxglove**, and **delphiniums**—small plants won't have enough time to mature and produce attractive flowers.

CARE

With longer and warmer days, annual flowers should start to make more active growth. Good care is needed now to help old flower beds keep their blooms and to help new beds fill in quickly.

WATERING

This is still the dry-but-cool season. Plants use moisture slowly, but they will need some extra water when the surface begins to dry. Here are some watering tips:

- Water when the plants begin to show a light wilt, or the soil dries to the touch.
- Apply between $1/2$ and $3/4$ inch of water.
- When possible, water during the early-morning hours.
- Use microsprinklers or soaker hoses to wet only the flower bed.
- Check container gardens daily and water when the surface soil feels dry.

Hollyhock

FERTILIZING

If you are using a general garden fertilizer or liquid fertilizer, it's time for the monthly application. Even plants that are in full bloom need nutrients to maintain their green leaf color and the extra nutrients may encourage additional blooms. There is no need to fertilize beds you are about to remove. If you use slow-release fertilizers, note the time that should pass between feedings and apply as needed.

PROBLEMS

Walk the beds at least once a week to look for pests. Check for cutworms when preparing new bed. Caterpillars and mites remain winter problems.

MARCH

ANNUALS

PLANNING

Winter has been over for several weeks in South Florida, but Central and Northern Florida may experience freeze until the middle of March.

If you want to take a chance, you can add spots of color that can be quickly protected with cloth or hay if a late-season frost does occur. Now is the time to renovate your container gardens, for they can be moved to a warmer spot when cold warnings are sounded.

Prepare your planting sites for annual flowers:

1. Decide if you need to plant annuals that need shade, sun, or a little of each.
2. Outline the bed shape with the help of a hose or extension cord.
3. Dig out or spot-kill weeds.
4. Till the soil and work in organic matter including compost, peat moss, and manure.
5. Check the soil acidity and adjust the pH if needed.
6. Work in a light application of a general garden fertilizer.
7. Plant the garden and water.

During the first really warm days, **pansies** and **violas** (often called **Johnny-jump-ups**) will decline. Here are a few tips:

- Remove any planting that is developing leaf spots or other pest problems.
- Plants that have only a few blooms and are mostly seedpods should be removed.
- Take out plants that are growing out of bounds but would look less attractive if cut back.
- Remove plants that will stop flowering and then decline within a few weeks.
- Clean out the entire bed and start over if you have new fresh transplants ready for the garden.

Rethink your planting schedule when the seasons change. Here are some tips:

- Try not to use the same plants in the same spot year after year.

This practice tends to build up pests specific to one plant.

- Vary your planting to try new flowers that have not been available or that are new to you.
- Give the garden a new shape or add some walkways to allow close inspection of the flowers.
- Try mixing some annuals and perennials together to create new interest.
- Vary the height of the plantings to create new interest.

Check for potbound roots before planting.

PLANTING

When you head out to the planting site, make sure you have all the needed materials to get started. Here is your checklist:

- Garden tools: shovel, rake, and trowel
- Fertilizer
- Organic matter: compost, peat moss, and manure
- Plants for the garden
- Trash can
- Hose for watering; sprinkling can
- Gloves

• Hat, sunscreen, and insect repellent

Planting annuals from pots into the garden is simple. First check the annuals to make sure they are not potbound. If they are, break apart the roots just a little. Many gardeners like to fluff apart the roots around the outer portion of the rootball, but resist tearing large sections of the roots from the plant. Follow these steps when putting the new plants in the ground:

1. Open the hole wide, and as deep as the rootball.
2. If the soil is dry, fill the hole with water.
3. As the water starts to drain from the hole, add the plant. Fill in around the rootball with soil.
4. Add a thin mulch of hay, leaves, composted pine bark, or coarse compost.
5. Water the plants to complete the planting.

WATERING

New plantings should be watered daily for a week or two. Don't count on an irrigation system to do a good job. Check the soil, and if it is still dry in some areas after the system stops, it is better to do some hand watering and readjust the sprinkler heads. Here are a few more tips for watering during March:

• Reduce watering to an "as-needed" schedule when the plants start to grow out into the surrounding soil.

For most plantings this is once or twice a week.

• Get to know your drought-tolerant plants—including **portulaca**, **gazania**, **purslane**, and **periwinkle**—that will not want water until the surface soil starts to dry.

Overwatering causes root and stem rots.

• Use soaker hoses and micro-sprinklers to put the water where it is needed.

• Run the irrigation system until it provides 1/2 to 3/4 inch of water.

FERTILIZING

Many gardeners are now taking some of the work out of gardening by using slow-release fertilizers. Some words often seen on the containers are "slow-release," "time-release," or "encapsulated," which let you know they will be feeding your plants for several months. Here are a few tips for using time-release products:

• Check the label for the proper application rate.

• Scatter the proper amount of fertilizer over the bed area before or after planting.

• Note the time the fertilizer is scheduled to be reapplied, and mark the date on the calendar.

• Monitor the plants.

Excessive rain and extremes in temperatures can cause a change in the release rate of a fertilizer. If plants show signs of yellowing or reduced growth before a suggested feeding time arrives, additional fertilizer may be needed.

If you are using a regular granular garden fertilizer or liquid fertilizer, follow a monthly feeding program. Here, too, if the plants do not perform as expected and symptoms point to a lack of fertilizer, make an extra feeding.

PROBLEMS

As the weather becomes warmer, the pest problems will get more intense, and a few new critters may affect the garden. Watch for mites, aphids, leafminers, caterpillars, slugs, and snails.

APRIL

ANNUALS

PLANNING

It's just about the end of the cool-season flower cycle. The rest of your annual planting should be warm-season annuals.

• **Balsam** is a well-known spring flower in the North, but it is often overlooked in Southern gardens. The plants grow over a foot tall and have white, pink, or purple flowers that open along the stems. Some call **balsam lady's slippers** because of the shape of its opening buds.

• **Globe amaranth** is known to many as **gomphrena**, which is also its scientific name. It forms mounds of purple, pink, or lavender blooms. Both low- and tall-growing selections are available.

• **Melampodium** appeared in only a few gardening catalogs for years, and then it became an overnight sensation. It has bright yellow flowers that only frost can stop. As older plants decline, new ones sprout from seeds.

• **Torenia**: Do not miss out on this great warm-season flower for both sun and light shade. In Florida it is often called the **summer pansy**, and is also known as the **wishbone flower**. The latter name is derived from the stamens within the flowers that form a wishbone-like shape. The flowers are small but numerous and come in purple, blue, or pink.

PLANTING

Now is a good time to start **sunflowers** from seed. They are a favorite of many, especially kids. It's fun measuring the weekly height of the **sunflowers**; some grow taller than 10 feet.

1. Find a sunny site and till the soil for planting. Enrich sandy soils with organic matter if you wish.
2. Open up a shallow hole and plant one or two **sunflower** seeds. Make additional plantings 12 to 24 inches apart.
3. Cover the seeds with a layer of soil the same thickness as a seed.
4. Apply a thin layer of hay or compost mulch, and water. Seeds should germinate in seven to ten days.
5. Thin to one seedling per planted site.
6. Water when the soil feels dry to the touch.
7. Feed every 3 or 4 weeks with a garden fertilizer, or as needed to encourage growth.

In addition to special projects like planting **begonias** and **sunflowers**, continue to make use of normal planting techniques to give flower beds and container gardens a good start. Points to remember:

• Select the proper light level.

• Follow the recommended spacing.

• Improve the soil.

• Plant so the rootball is at ground level.

• Water daily until the plants are established.

CARE

Check for any plants that may need staking. It takes **sunflowers** only a few weeks to grow over a foot tall, and it takes only a good wind to blow them over. If these plants or any of the taller-growing **marigold**, **zinnia**, **cleome**, and **nicotiana** start to list to one side, add a stake and a tie to keep each one in an upright position.

Check all the mulches. If any layers are too thin to hold in moisture, add more. To prevent stem rot, make sure the mulch is kept a few inches back from the base of the annuals.

WATERING

It's possible to receive over 2 inches of rain this month, but precipitation is usually not evenly distributed. Temperatures are gradually creeping up into the 80s, and the plants get dry very quickly. Use the following tips to determine when to water:

- Look for signs of wilting plants.
- Feel the soil; if the surface inch is beginning to dry, it's time to water.
- Don't be fooled by light sprinkles; the water may evaporate before getting to the roots.
- Use a rain gauge to determine how much water has been received, and mark it on the calendar.
- Annual flowers can use 1/4 inch or more of water a day; after a few days without water, they will have drained the surface foot of soil of most of the available moisture.

If you side-dress dry fertilizer, scatter it over dry foliage, and then water in.

When you water, apply from 1/2 to 3/4 inch. Run the irrigation system during the early- morning hours. Make a random check of the soil after watering to make sure the ground is moist.

FERTILIZING

Many of the annuals are reaching full size and creating colorful displays. But this is no time to let up on the feeding program. Remember, most plantings need a monthly feeding unless you are using a slow-release fertilizer. If the plants have grown too tall, you might use one of the following suggestions to make sure the fertilizer gets to the soil:

- Scatter dry fertilizer over the dry foliage and water immediately.
- Reach among the leaves and stems with handfuls of fertilizer and place it at ground level.
- Use a liquid fertilizer meant to be sprinkled over the tops of the plants. If you have any suspicion that it is burning the plants, just rinse it off.
- Early in the season, use a slow-release fertilizer that does not need a repeat application.

PROBLEMS

Keep an eye out for mites, garden flea hoppers, whitefly, aphids, slugs, and snails.

MAY

ANNUALS

PLANNING

Summer arrives about a month "early" in Florida, and you have to plan accordingly.

It's time to be thinking about **marigolds**, **portulaca**, **verbena**, **salvia**, **purslane**, and other annuals that don't mind the heat. Some favorites for shade are **coleus**, **impatiens**, **torenia**, and **wax begonias**.

Torenia

Here are a few tips for great **impatiens** plantings in the shade:

• Make sure the site has shade, especially during the midday hours.

• Till the soil as deeply as possible. Tree roots may make only limited turning of the ground possible. In areas with tree roots, up to 2 inches of an enriched soil or potting soil can be added to the site.

• Space the plants so they have at least 6 to 8 inches to grow. It's best to follow seed packet or label information.

• Set the plants in the ground at the same depth they were growing in their containers or a little higher above soil level. **Impatiens** rot easily, so planting them a little higher out of the ground and adding a light mulch won't hurt.

• Water the planting site. Continue with daily waterings for a week, then water as needed to prevent wilting.

• Feed monthly with a granular or liquid fertilizer solution. You may substitute a slow-release fertilizer to eliminate the regular feedings.

• Keep an eye out for snails, and control as needed.

PLANTING

As the cool-season flowers begin to decline, you will be doing plenty of planting. Remember that most annuals last only a few months, set seed, and then decline. When the plants stop flowering and begin to turn brown, follow these steps to replanting:

• Remove top and underside growths. Note any damage to root systems from nematodes.

• If nematodes are present, plant a resistant flower type. For summer, this may be the **marigold**.

• Till the soil deeply and work in lots of organic matter.

• Work in a light feeding of general garden fertilizer.

• Set new plants in the ground at the proper spacing and water.

If you have done your homework and would like to sow some seeds, start with clean pots or cell-packs. Fill the containers with a germination mix available from garden centers. Then do the following:

- Press big seeds into the soil. Sprinkle small seeds on the surface and cover lightly
- Keep the containers moist and in bright light.
- Place in normal growing light, preferably outdoors when the first sprouts are noted.
- Protect from afternoon rains, which could begin this month. Bring them onto a covered patio, or build a transparent cover over the seeded containers to prevent rain damage.
- Feed weekly with a half-strength fertilizer solution
- Transplant to the flower beds or containers when the seedlings are 4 to 6 inches tall, or the size they are found at garden centers. Transplants grow rapidly during the warmer months and can be ready for the garden in 4 to 6 weeks.

CARE

Spend time staking tall plants and pruning off broken portions. Severely damaged plants near the end of their lifecycle should simply be replaced with new flowers.

WATERING

Rain this month is unpredictable, so you have to make independent judgments on when to water. Don't overwater, as this might cause flower damage and stem and root rots. If in doubt, it's best to keep the plants a little dry. Here are a few suggestions:

- Keep track of the rainfall and mark it on the calendar.

Less than 1/4 inch of rain will not significantly wet the ground.

- Water when the surface inch of soil begins to dry. Usually this is a full day or two after a good 1/2 to 1 inch of rain.

Wait until you see some signs of wilting in the plants. Apply 1/2 to 3/4 inch of irrigation.

Take note of the plants that like drier conditions. Watering these plants can be delayed for several extra days.

FERTILIZING

As far as plants are concerned, it doesn't make a difference if you use manure, fish emulsions, or commercial products. They still have to be applied regularly.

Liquid products can be applied through a sprinkling can. Just wet the soil over the root system as you do with any fertilizer. If you would like to try some manure or compost tea, follow these suggestions:

- Fill a 2-gallon or larger container 3/4 full of water.
- Place a quart or more of manure or compost in a large piece of cloth and tie at the top.
- Add a string and suspend the cloth with manure in the water overnight.
- Remove the manure.
- Mix the manure solution with additional water to the color of weak tea.
- Use this as your fertilizer solution every 3 to 4 weeks.

If you are following traditional fertilizer practices with synthetic granules or fertilizer solutions, continue applications once a month. Check your calendar for the next feeding if you are using slow-release products.

PROBLEMS

Keep your fingers crossed, for this month could end much of your mite problem. When the rainy season begins, mites do not cause as much damage. But if the mite threat continues, use a soap spray as needed. Aphids, garden flea hoppers, grasshoppers, whiteflies, and slugs and snails like the hotter weather.

JUNE
ANNUALS

PLANNING

This month, look at the performance of your plantings. Make notes on the varieties and colors you liked.

- Which varieties were poor performers?
- Did some grow taller and wider than you thought?
- Were your color combinations good ones?
- Did the plantings get the care they needed?

Record your observations to guide you in choosing plants for next year.

PLANTING

Do some replanting during the summer months, to correct problems and to replace dying flowers. Warm-season annuals planted in spring may not grow throughout the summer.

If you have to fill in bare spots, follow these steps:

- Remove the declining plant stems, leaves, and roots.
- Trim back surrounding plantings as needed to make room for new transplants.
- Consider adding more of what is already growing well in the bed rather than adding a new selection.
- Till the soil deeply and add organic matter.
- Set the new plants in the hole at the same depth they were in their pots. Add a thin mulch layer, and water.

CARE

Do your weeding after watering. Pulling by hand is a good, quick method. Keep a thin layer of mulch over the soil to discourage weeds. Spot-kill weeds with a nonselective herbicide that permits use around growing plants. Plant the garden through a weed-control fabric to stop weeds before reaching the surface. Lay down multiple sheets of newspaper between the plants to exclude weeds, and cover with a thin mulch. Use a preemergence herbicide in established plantings, following label instructions.

WATERING

Seasonal rains make your work a lot easier. But you still have to determine when plants have enough water. Gardeners are often fooled into thinking plantings have been watered well by the rains. Here are some tips for making sure you have adequate moisture:

- Turn off the sprinkler system during summer; don't waste water or overwater, which will cause rot and leaf spot problems.
- Keep track of the rainfall with a rain gauge.
- Check the soil for adequate moisture after a day or two without at least 1/4 inch of moisture.
- If the upper inch of soil is dry, it's time to water.
- Look for dry spots that appear to repel moisture.

Water these areas separately and as needed. Renew the thin mulch to help them remain moist. Work in lots of organic matter at next plantings.

New beds, of course, need daily watering for a week or two. If rains provide enough moisture, you can skip the daily watering.

FERTILIZING

Keep the summer plantings growing with adequate fertilizer. The summer rains push growth and wash nutrients out of the soil. Keep an eye on the plantings and if growth appears to slow and the foliage turns yellow, they may need an extra feeding. In a similar manner, too much growth and a lack of flowers indicates that the plants have all the nutrients they need and you can skip a feeding. Here are the ways you might feed your plants at this time of the year:

- Granular fertilizers such as 6-6-6, 10-10-10, and similar analysis should be applied at the label rate. Scatter over the surface of the soil and water. If granules adhere to the foliage, wash off during watering.
- Liquid fertilizer solutions can be made from concentrated crystals or bought as liquids to further mix with water. Apply at the label rate (it can be applied over the foliage).
- Manures can be used as sidedressings or made into teas. Water after application.
- Composts are used as sidedressings or mulches.
- Plants absorb the nutrients of slow-release fertilizers over a period of months. Follow the schedule suggested on the label.

PROBLEMS

When the rains pick up, so do the leaf spots. Look for yellow to dark brown spots on some of your annual flowers. Especially susceptible are **impatiens** and **salvias**. Look for stems rots in **periwinkles**, especially if they are getting supplemental irrigation.

Try to reduce the water to an "as-needed" schedule, and keep the foliage as dry as possible. A copper-containing fungicide may help control some leaf spots. Not all brands are labeled for all of the many plants you can grow, but the label will tell you which of the many leaf- and stem-affecting fungal and bacterial diseases it will control. Whether using natural or synthetic fungicides, follow label instructions for safe and effective use.

Water for aphids, garden flea hoppers, grasshoppers, whiteflies, and slugs and snails.

Cut out the bottom of a plastic gallon container to make a protective cover to spot-treat weeds.

JULY
ANNUALS

PLANNING

By now you are surely aware that this is the rainy season. You have probably noticed the **petunias** fading from the landscape and the **celosia** flowers turning brown. Even if some plants can survive the heat, the rains may beat them down. Now is the time to look for more rain-tolerant hot-weather annuals. Some to consider, if only for their quick recovery after a storm:

Coleus
Creeping Zinnia
Globe Amaranth
Impatiens
Melampodium
Periwinkle
Purslane
Rose Moss
Torenia
Wax Begonias

Use July as a time to make a list of plants for the next growing season, and secure the seeds. You may have to act quickly, as most seed supplies at garden centers are removed this month. Florida law dictates that all seed has to be fresh and labeled for the next year starting in August. If you cannot find seeds, hurry and place orders to mail-order seed companies now.

PLANTING

Summer may be one of the more difficult times to establish a new flower bed. The days are hot and the plants dry out very quickly. If you do not keep the soil moist, new plants often use up all available water in their rootballs and then wilt. It's up to you to keep new plants extra-moist for the first few weeks.

Annuals are always ready to fill in the bare spots in a landscape. These can be voids left between new trees and shrubs or produced by plants that suddenly die. You may also want to use annuals during the summer months to fill open spaces in perennial beds as some of the spring bloomers start to decline.

CARE

Summer annuals are often kept either too wet or too dry. We call it the rainy season, but there are times when we have up to a week without rain. Keep your eye out for the dry periods. Annuals are also damaged as the winds blow through the landscape. Keep the pruners handy so you can make repairs by trimming out damaged plants. After a severe storm, an entire bed might need replanting.

Globe amaranth, also known by its botanical name, gomphrena, is a great "heat buster."

WATERING

Turn off the automatic sprinkler and let Mother Nature do the watering. Keep an eye on the rain gauge, and if a day or two passes without at least 1/4 inch of rain, you may have to do some sprinkling. Plants that have deep root systems can survive many more days than those in newly planted gardens. Container gardens need daily attention.

Plants that have filled their pots with roots and shoots can use up all their water in less than a day. If you have a plant that dries before the day is out, set it in a shallow tray. This can hold a little extra water for the roots to draw from during the day. Placing a plant in a tray won't cause root rot if the plant is using water rapidly.

EASY-TO-MAKE POTTING SOIL

Potting soil is needed to fill hanging baskets, planters, and windowboxes. But what do you use? In Florida, do not use the backyard soil unless you are willing to take a gamble. It might contain weeds, insects, diseases, or nematodes. If that is not enough to scare you, it may not have the good drainage needed for container plantings. Here are two formulas you can use to make your own pest-free, well-drained soil at home.

Soil 1

- 1 gallon peat moss
- 1 gallon perlite
- 1 tablespoon dolomitic lime

Soil 2

- 1 gallon peat moss
- 1 gallon perlite
- 1 gallon compost

Mix all ingredients together in a clean container. Use immediately, or store in a plastic trash can or plastic bag. Notice that the second mixture contains no lime: Florida compost is often alkaline, and the absence of lime will help adjust the soil acidity. If in doubt, have the pH of your compost tested.

Potting soils can also be used to improve sandy soils and to replace soils in nematode-infested beds.

FERTILIZING

Growing plants need a constant source of nutrients. Follow your regular feeding schedule, but keep an eye out for nutritional deficiencies. A typical symptom of the need for fertilizer is yellow foliage on the plant. If this appears, one of the following is usually needed:

- Water with a liquid fertilizer solution.
- Apply fertilizer granules.
- Check the slow-release feeding schedule and reapply if needed.

PROBLEMS

Rot problems should be your biggest concern during the summer season. Very few annuals can stand "wet feet." Some annuals that are especially sensitive are **periwinkles** and **wax begonias**.

Garden spots that you thought were well drained will often have standing water after rains. If you notice spots like these that have too much water, make a note on your gardening schedule to mound up the soil or establish raised beds for the next plantings.

Look for garden flea hoppers (which will suck the juices from **marigold**, **globe amaranth**, **verbena**, and similar flowers), grasshoppers, whiteflies, nematodes, and slugs and snails.

AUGUST

ANNUALS

PLANNING

Even though it is a hot month, this is a good time to start the first of the fall warm-season flowers. Some to sow now: **marigolds**, **salvia**, **nicotiana**, **verbena**, **ornamental peppers**, and **sunflowers**. Wait until the middle of the month to begin planting.

Early in the month you probably noticed that the seeds are gone from most garden centers. Only businesses that sell seeds in bulk will still have a supply. The seed packets start reappearing at garden centers after August 15—by Florida law, all seeds have to be removed from the shelves at the end of July and fresh seeds labeled for next year restocked in August. Purchase your seeds as soon as they arrive so you will have annuals for early fall.

PLANTING

Many gardeners take a break at this time of the year and allow their gardens to gradually decline. Other gardeners continue with full replacement. Add new plants as the older ones decline, using good gardening practices. Inspect plant roots for nematodes, as these pests can linger in the soil. If infestations are heavy, you many need to plant resistant plants for the rest of the summer. One plant in particular, the **French marigold**, has been credited with decreasing nematode populations. You might consider planting an entire bed of these plants in nematode-infested soils to reduce the population by cool-season planting time.

CARE

Some of the long-lived annuals, including **wax begonias, impatiens**, and **coleus**, may become lanky and overgrown. These can be trimmed back a foot or more to let new shoots sprout from the base. Most of these also root rapidly from cuttings if you want to enlarge your collection.

WATERING

August can be one of the wettest months, and rains come fairly regularly in the afternoon hours. Often there is no need for special watering of flower beds. Just turn off the irrigation systems and let Mother Nature do the watering for you.

If you do have several days without water, you will have to manually turn on the watering system. Make sure that the plants that have lower water requirements do not get any extra at this time.

Hanging baskets and similar container gardens may be exceptions: they may need daily watering. This is especially true when containers are small and plants are extra-large. In fact, some of these plants may need watering more than once a day.

FERTILIZING

Continue the scheduled monthly feedings for flower beds, and check your calender to determine the next time for slow-release fertilizer applications. Some annuals (container plantings, seedlings, and newly planted flower beds) may need special feedings:

- Container plantings: Nutrients are used rapidly, and extra feedings may be needed to replace fertilizer washed from the pots. Try feeding every other week, but extra weekly feedings may be needed. Slow-release fertilizers can be used to help reduce needed feedings.

• Seedlings: Feed weekly with a half-strength fertilizer solution. Plants making rapid growth can have a full-strength solution applied as needed to maintain leaf color.

• Newly planted flower beds: These beds may need the time between feedings shortened if there is extra rainfall and rapid growth. Shorten the feeding interval to every 2 to 3 weeks if needed for regular fertilizers.

PROBLEMS

Leaf spots and stem disease continue to be a problem with some annual flowers. Consider changing to other selections in problem areas of the landscape, and consider using soaker hoses for watering (they are less likely to wet the plant foliage).

Keep watering in these areas to a minimum...but you cannot stop the rains.

Root rots are usually found in wet areas of the flower bed or are a result of overwatering.

Reduce watering. If replanting, till the soil deeply and enrich sandy sites with organic matter. Fungicides are available but relatively expensive to use with small flower beds.

Watch for garden flea hoppers, grasshoppers, whitefly, nematodes, and slugs and snails.

DEADHEADING AND MUDDING-IN

Some horticulture terms are quite descriptive. One of those terms is deadheading, which refers to the removal of old flower heads (the blooms that have faded and are turning brown). Here is how to put deadheading to use:

• Wait until the blossoms fade; you do not have to wait until they turn brown.

• Remove the flower portions and any forming seedpods with a knife or with your thumb and forefinger.

Is deadheading worth it? Well, it can extend the blooming season for **petunias**, **snapdragons**, **dianthus**, **pansies**, and similar flowers. But after a while you may get tired of deadheading. Mudding-in can be put to use immediately. Mudding-in is adding water at the time of planting to make a muddy planting hole. It is of great benefit when soils are dry and repel water. Here is how to do it:

• Carry a sprinkling can of water to the garden.

• Open a planting hole for the transplant.

• Fill the hole with water.

• Plant the annual just as the water begins to drain from the hole and the soil has a mud-like consistency.

• Add more soil to the hole, and more water if needed.

Mudding-in takes a little extra time, but it guarantees moist soil around new transplants for a day or two.

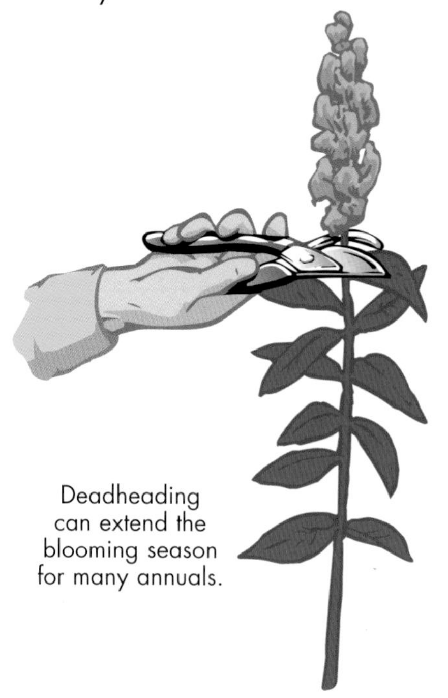

Deadheading can extend the blooming season for many annuals.

SEPTEMBER

ANNUALS

PLANNING

Now is the time to do all your planning for the fall season. Many gardeners relocating to Florida can't wait to plant the first **pansies**. But it's not **pansy** weather yet. Just begin thinking about where you would like to grow these cool-season annuals, and you can start gathering seeds to sow in about a month.

At this between-the-seasons time of the year, you have three choices:

- Let the remaining flowers linger on, and add some additional warm-season color to fill in the voids.
- Remove all fading flowers, and let the beds remain empty until cool weather.
- Replant entire beds with fresh annuals.

Flowers that can be added to the early-fall annual gardens include **celosia**, **cleome**, **nicotiana**, **gazania**, **marigolds**, **scarlet sage**, and **wax begonias**.

Container gardens may also begin to decline after the long summer growing season. Many have run out of growing room and have set seed. They are best replanted as soon as they begin to decline.

Now is the time to plan and dig new annual beds.

PLANTING

Now is the time to carry out major bed renovation. This begins with the removal of all old plants and debris. Check the roots for signs of root rots and nematodes that might be a problem for the next plantings. Look for cutworms and caterpillars that may have been feeding on the remaining foliage. Take the following steps to complete soil preparation for fall:

1. Where possible, use a roto-tiller to turn the soil 4 to 6 inches deep.
2. Till liberal quantities of organic matter into sandy soils. Some easy-to-obtain sources are compost, manures, and peat moss. Leaves can also be used, but plants may require extra fertilizer during plant culture to prevent nutrient deficiencies.
3. Check soil acidity and adjust the pH if needed. Use dolomitic lime to raise the soil pH and soil sulfur to lower the pH. Treatments are best made following the results of a soil test available through your garden center or extension service office.
4. Scatter a light application of fertilizer across the surface of the soil and till it into the ground.
5. If cutworms are a concern, treat the soil with an appropriate preplant insecticide.

Now is a good time to start seeds of the quick-growing warm-season annuals. Try to start them at the beginning of the month so you will have transplants in 4 to 6 weeks. Here are a few seedling-producing tips:

• Use clean pots or cell-packs to start the seeds.

• Grow only the number of seedlings you plan to use.

• Use a potting soil or seedling starting mix to grow the transplants.

• Sow one or two seeds per pot or cell.

• Keep the seeded containers moist.

• Grow in the light level that is appropriate for the crop.

• Feed weekly with a half-strength 20-20-20 or similar fertilizer solution.

• Transplant to the garden when the plants are the size usually seen at garden centers.

CARE

Much of September gardening is a matter of keeping the existing plants growing until new beds can be planted. Sometimes just a little staking makes the plants look better by removing the overgrown, lanky look. A little trimming can also be used to revive **impatiens**, **begonias**, and **coleus**. Sometimes this is all that is needed to encourage the growth that can keep the plants attractive for another season.

And don't forget the weeds. Summer rains and heat encourage lots of crabgrass, spurge, and similar unwanted greenery. Keep up the weeding and edging of beds even if they are to be replaced shortly.

WATERING

Early September is a damp time of year, with summer rains that are usually still present through the early part of the month. By the end of September the rains can quickly taper off, and dryness can catch your plants by surprise. Make sure you are keeping track of the rainfall, and water when needed. Right now is a good time to check out your irrigation system to make sure it properly wets your flower beds.

Gardeners need to follow the general rule for watering: Moisten the soil when the surface inch begins to dry. Remain aware of the garden areas that may dry more quickly than others and will require hand watering. Container plantings should be checked daily and watered when the soil becomes dry to the touch.

FERTILIZING

Fertilizer can be used to encourage growth from maturing plants just a little while longer. Use the following recommendations as a guide to September feedings. Apply general granular fertilizers monthly. Apply side dressings of manure as fertilizer substitutes monthly. Apply liquid fertilizer solutions every three to four weeks. Check calendars to determine the time for the next slow-release fertilizer application.

Container gardens may need increased feedings. Large maturing plants use more nutrients, and much of the fertilizer not used for growth may be washed out by seasonal rains. Applications can be increased to once a week if needed.

PROBLEMS

Expect leaf spots and root rots to continue at their summer pace until the rains start to subside. As the rains taper off, so will much of the leaf spot and stem rots. If lots of rot problems are detected during bed renovation, try different annuals so you will not plant the same susceptible varieties. Watch for garden flea hoppers, grasshoppers, nematodes, slugs and snails, and whitefly.

OCTOBER

ANNUALS

PLANNING

Cooler weather should start arriving in northern areas, but don't expect a drastic change until later. In this in-between time, warm- and cool-season flowers will mingle. Plan the transition between the seasons. Here are some different ways to do it:

- Continue planting the warm-season annuals during the early part of the month. Work in the cool-season flowers gradually.
- When warm-season flowers finish, let the beds lie fallow until mid- to late October. Then plant the cool-season flowers.
- Take a chance on the month being pretty cool; start early with the cool-season flowers, as soon as the beds are ready.
- Continue to plant warm-season annuals throughout the month and wait until November or December to make the change.

This month is also the time to begin sowing some of your favorite cool-season seeds such as **pansies**, **dianthus**, **snapdragons**, **petunias**, **dusty miller**, and **hollyhocks**.

PLANTING

You can work in the garden at almost any time of day as we head into the cooler months. The plants will enjoy the break, too, and establish much faster. Now is a good time to think about the best planting techniques. Working in a prepared soil:

1. Open a hole big enough to contain the rootball.
2. If the roots are wrapped tightly together, fluff them apart just a little.
3. If the soil is extra dry, add water to the planting hole.
4. Set the plant in the ground at the same depth it was growing in the container.
5. Add a thin layer of mulch, but keep it back from the base of the plants.
6. Thoroughly moisten the planting site.

There you are: that is all there is to planting. Now it is up to you to keep the soil moist for the next week or two. As the plants begin to root out into the surrounding soil you can start an "as-needed" watering schedule.

If you will be starting many of your own plants from seed, you can use one of two techniques, depending on the size of the seed:

- Large seeds can be sown directly into pots or cell-packs.

Just use a good potting soil and the plants should be ready for the garden in 4 to 6 weeks.

- It's hard to sow just one or two small seeds in a pot or a single section of a cell-pack.

Small seeds are best started in a community pot and then transplanted. Here's how to do it:

1. Add germination mix to a tray or a 6-inch pot.
2. Scatter the small seeds across the surface. You do not have to sow the entire pack, and you may wish to use more than one container.
3. Water to wash small seeds into the growing mix.
4. Keep the containers in bright light.
5. When the seeds sprout, move them into the proper light for growth of the flowers.
6. Keep sprouts moist and feed weekly with a half-strength 20-20-20 or similar fertilizer.
7. Transplant to small pots or cell-packs when two or three true leaves are present.

CARE

October is an easy month to care for new plantings. Most of the care involves keeping weeds out of the garden. A daily walk is recommended to check for special water needs and pest problems . . . and you don't want to miss the first blooms you can cut for a few bouquets!

WATERING

All of a sudden it's the dry season again. That doesn't mean there won't be showers, but they will occur less frequently. The good news is that plants will not need water as often as the days become cooler. Here are three different ways to determine when it is time to water established plantings:

1. Wait until a few plants begin to show signs of wilting.

2. Feel the soil. When the surface inch begins to feel dry, it's time to water.

3. Put the plants on a watering schedule of every 3 or 4 days.

Methods 1 and 2 are best, as they help conserve water and encourage deep rooting.

FERTILIZING

As the weather turns cool, the plants will not use as much fertilizer. Plants tend to grow a little more slowly, and nutrients are not washed out of the ground as much. Here are some guidelines for fall feedings:

- In-ground plantings: Feed every 3 to 4 weeks with a general garden fertilizer. If you use a slow-release fertilizer, follow label instructions.
- Hanging baskets: Feed every other week with a 20-20-20 or similar fertilizer solution. If you use a slow-release fertilizer, follow label instructions.
- Planters and large pots: Feed every 7 to 14 days with 20-20-20 or a similar fertilizer solution. If you use a slow-release fertilizer, follow label instructions.

As the plantings grow during the fall and the weather becomes even cooler, the time between feedings can be lengthened by a week or more.

PROBLEMS

Mites, one of the garden's real problems, are back. They are as small as a pinpoint and sometimes create webs among affected annuals. There is good news, though: Root rots and leaf spots should decrease, and nematodes are much less active during the cooler months. Watch for garden flea hoppers, grasshoppers, whitefly, and slugs and snails.

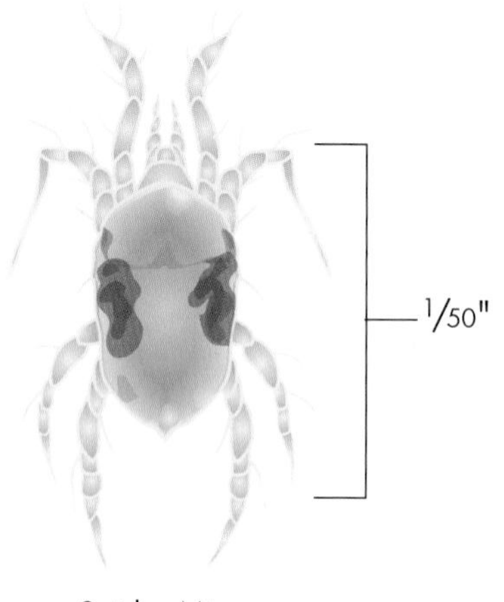

Spider Mite

NOVEMBER

ANNUALS

PLANNING

What is the most eagerly awaited annual in Florida? Probably the **pansy**. November is the earliest you can count on these annuals to beat the heat and survive through late winter into the early spring months. Plant entire beds, spots of color, or a few containers. Here's how to grow great **pansies**:

- Add the plants to a prepared garden site or container of potting soil.

Set the plants in the soil at the same depth they were growing in their original containers. If planted too deep, they may rot.

- Space the **pansies** close together for an efficient garden look.

A spacing of 6 to 8 inches is really not too close.

- Keep the soil moist and feed in-ground plantings every 3 to 4 weeks, container plantings every other week.
- Remove flowers for bouquets, or cut faded blooms from the plants as needed to encourage new growth.

Gardeners should get their **pansies** in the ground soon, since they will have only a few months of enjoyment. **Pansies** and their relatives, the **violas**, also known as **Johnny-jump-ups**, are the most frost- and freeze-resistant of all common winter annuals. Look for other annuals that grow well during the cooler months.

PLANTING

Adding flowers to the garden just got easier when the weather got cooler. Just remember these planting tips:

- Loosen soil before planting.
- Add liberal quantities of organic matter to sandy soils.
- If needed, adjust soil acidity with dolomitic lime or soil sulfur.
- Scatter a light application of garden fertilizer over the surface of the soil before planting.
- Control cutworms with a soil insecticide if needed.
- Plant annuals at the same depth they were in containers.
- Add a thin layer of mulch, but keep it back from the base of the plants.

Thoroughly moisten new plantings, and water every day for the first week. Thereafter, reduce the watering to every other day. If the soil is moist and the plants are growing normally, reduce watering to an "as-needed" schedule. Overwatering can cause root rots.

CARE

Most cool-season annuals are frost-resistant unless they are making a lot of tender growth. If there is any doubt about the hardiness of any annual flowers, it's best to provide some protection when a frost occurs. Here are some tips.

- Avoid the use of plastic covers that touch the plant foliage.

Plastic that touches the plants will conduct the cold to the plants.

- Water the plants to moisten the soil before frost is expected.

Cold weather is often accompanied by drying winds.

- To protect the annuals from a light frost, cover the plants with newspaper, and then with plastic.

You can also use sheets or blankets laid over the plants to keep frost off the foliage, or lightly cover them with hay.

- Remove all coverings when the danger of frost is over or before sun hitting the cover might cause heat damage to the plants.

Any one of the quick covers mentioned above can protect your plants from frost or a few degrees below freezing for a short period of time. It is important to allow plants that need coolness to flower to experience some of the cooler temperatures but not freezing weather.

Johnny-jump-ups

WATERING

Cooler temperatures mean that annuals will not use as much water, but you have to remember that this is also the beginning of the drier time of year. It's very important that all flower beds and container gardens be checked for water needs.

- Water ground beds when the surface inch of soil becomes dry to the touch.
- Water container gardens when the surface soil begins to dry.
- Keep a thin layer of mulch over ground beds to stretch the time between waterings.
- Apply 1/2 to 3/4 inch of water to ground beds. Water hanging baskets and pots until water runs from the bottom. Moisten above-ground planters with up to 3/4 inch of water.

FERTILIZING

The plantings will begin to slow their growth a little during cooler weather, and intervals between fertilizer applications can be lengthened. The following schedules are suitable for most flowers.

In-ground plantings: Feed monthly with a general garden fertilizer. Use a slow-release fertilizer as suggested on the label.

Hanging baskets: Feed every other week with a 20-20-20 or similar fertilizer solution. Use a slow-release product added to the container as recommended on the label.

Planters and large pots: Feed every other week with a 20-20-20 or similar fertilizer solution. Use a slow-release product added to the container as recommended on the label.

Sometimes the weather is warmer than expected, or the plants make exceptional growth, using nutrients faster than normal. Any indication of nutrient deficiency is reason to make an extra feeding.

PROBLEMS

Garden insect populations tend to grow less during the cooler months. They don't go away, but populations are smaller or do not develop as quickly. Keep up frequent visits to the garden and check for pests and other problems that might affect the plantings. Usually diseases are minor problems unless the garden is receiving too much water. Check for root rots, garden flea hoppers, grasshoppers, whiteflies, nematodes, and slugs and snails.

DECEMBER

ANNUALS

PLANNING

With the holiday season just ahead, you might think of getting a little festive. Here are a few suggestions for combinations to use when planning new flower beds and container gardens:

- Red **petunias**, including entire beds and containers
- Combinations of anything red and white: red and white **petunias**, red **petunias** with white **alyssum**, red and white **dianthus**, and red **petunias** with white **lobelia** (pink or purple flowers can be substituted for the red)
- Red, pink, or purple flowers against silvery **dusty miller**
- Red **poinsettias** with white flowers or silvery **dusty miller**

Now is the time to be adding plantings of **sweet peas**. You can get the bush types, but the climbing varieties give the best displays. They need cool weather to be good performers. Keep the soil moist, and fertilize monthly the first month or two after planting. **Sweet peas** are legumes that take some of their nitrogen for growth from the air, with the help of soil bacteria.

PLANTING

Don't delay filling empty spots in the flower garden with cool-season color. You may want to start early in the month. Garden centers begin to concentrate on holiday plants around Christmas time, and they seem to forget about annual flowers. If you wish, you can purchase the annuals even though they may not be needed right away and keep them healthy with the following practices:

- Place them in a space that has the appropriate light level for growth.
- Feed weekly with a 20-20-20 or similar fertilizer solution.
- Check water needs daily. Moisten as needed until water runs from the bottom of the pots.
- Keep the plants no more than a month before adding them to gardens or containers.
- Check the rootballs at planting time, and loosen if needed.

CARE

Be on guard for cold weather. Very few freezes arrive at this time of the year, but frosts are common. Control winter weeds in the flower beds, and start staking taller-growing plants if needed.

WATERING

Keep the soil moist, watering when the surface begins to be dry to the touch. Most in-ground plantings can last three or four days or more between waterings. Check hanging baskets daily. You may be able to skip a day or two between waterings for some.

FERTILIZING

Feed according to schedule to meet plant needs. Most feeding schedules can be lengthened by a week or more during the cooler weather.

PROBLEMS

Pests are less active this month, but some still affect annual flowers. Check for aphids, whiteflies, caterpillars, mites, and slugs and snails.

CHAPTER TWO

BULBS, CORMS, RHIZOMES, & TUBERS

Close your eyes, and think of some plants that grow from bulbs. What immediately comes to mind? Admit it: you see tulips, daffodils, crocus, and hyacinths.

Now erase that image, because most Northern bulbs don't grow well in Florida. You can force a few—and we plan to tell you how—but forcing is a chore. You are about to discover a wide selection of bulbs that you can grow easily right in your own landscape.

We use a broad definition of **bulb** in this chapter. A true bulb resembles an onion, has some residual roots, a small stem portion, and lots of leaves packed closely together. (Can you think of some true Florida bulbs? You would be right if you thought of amaryllis, crinum, and rain lilies.) Many other plants that we call bulbs are technically classified as *stems* and include corms, tubers, tuberous roots, and rhizomes.

Corms: These are tightly compressed, often flattened, stems. If you look closely, you will see the plant portion has a central bud, and there are many smaller buds around the stem portion. The gladiolus is a corm.

Tubers: Look for the buds of this stem on the surface. There is a central bud and many

smaller buds. The skin of the tuber is leatherlike. The caladium is a tuber.

True Bulb

Tuberous roots: These are swollen, fleshy, usually underground roots, such as the sweet potato. The buds that develop into new plants from most tuberous roots are present only at the stem end. An example of a flowering plant we grow from a tuberous root is the dahlia.

Rhizomes: Plants that grow from rhizomes come from thickened horizontal stems. Some grow just at the surface of the soil, while others form slightly underground. The roots grow from the bottom of the rhizomes. Plants that grow from rhizomes include canna, calla lily, and daylily.

Now that you have become acquainted with the different kinds of plants in this group, let's settle on just one term: *bulb.* All these plants grow in a similar manner, forming a clump or cluster from which arise attractive foliage and, often, colorful flowers. Happily, you will find that some of our Florida favorites rival their Northern relatives. Some can be in bloom at just about any time of year. You can have pretty orange lapeirousia in late winter; calla, crinum, and daylilies for spring; caladiums and blood lilies for summer; rain lilies and tuberose for fall. Many of these have extended flowering seasons in our state, so you might see them in bloom several times a year.

You can plant entire beds of bulbs, or use them for small spots of color. A few kinds grow very well in containers and can be moved into the home or to patios, porches, or balconies when in bloom. Only a few lend themselves to naturalization. If you want them to naturalize, do not mow the areas until flowering and foliage growth is over.

PLANTING

Most Florida bulbs can stay in the ground for several years before being replanted. While some grow well in sandy soils, all seem to prefer an improved planting site. A few like damp, poorly drained soil, but most do not like to have their roots in water.

Check to make sure the bulbs you plan to add to the garden will receive appropriate light. Some, like caladiums, grow in either sun or shade, but Amazon and blood lilies prefer some shade. You might change your bulb or the planting site just to ensure a good display.

You should also select a planting site that is free of noxious weeds. It is very difficult to pull Bermudagrass, sedge, Florida betony, and other weeds out of the planting site year after year. One of the best ways to start any new bed is by controlling perennial weeds. They can be hand dug, but you will never really get many of the underground shoots this way. The best way to prepare the bed is with a nonselective herbicide that allows replanting after the weeds decline.

Once the weeds are under control, you are ready to prepare the bed for your next bulb planting. Follow these few steps to getting the soil ready:

1. Remove all weeds and associated debris.
2. Till the soil deeply. If you have a power tiller available, use it to turn the soil 6 to 8 inches deep.
3. Check the soil acidity and adjust if needed. Most bulbs grow well at the 5.5 to 7.5 pH range. If a soil test indicates that pH correction is needed, dolomitic lime or soil sulfur can be used to make the correction.
4. Enrich sandy and clay soils with liberal quantities of organic matter. Some good

sources are compost, peat moss, and manures.

5. Apply up to 2 pounds of a 6-6-6 or similar fertilizer to the soil surface, and work it into the ground lightly. Some gardeners prefer to add bonemeal, a traditional product for bulb plantings. It contains some quickly available nitrogen and lots of slowly available phosphorus.

You are now ready to plant. Florida bulbs come in different forms. A single bulb may come in a mesh bag; some bulbs are sold in plastic bags. Some local bulbs can be purchased in pots; many have flowers already and buds that are ready to open. Some are dug up in clumps or separated into individual plants and shared between friends. It really does not matter how you obtain your bulbs. But if you obtain growing plants, be sure to give them water and the proper light level until the ground is ready for planting.

The best planting recommendation may be to read and follow the label that comes with the bulbs—or consult our planting chart on pages 58 to 59. Learning proper spacing and planting depth is important. Some bulbs do not flower or multiply well if planted too deep. Many like to grow close to the soil line. Keeping the proper planting depth in mind, follow these final planting suggestions:

1. Dig a hole or trench to receive the bulbs.

2. Fill in around the bulbs with soil and water. If the soil is extra dry, make a muddy paste out of the fill soil.

3. Finish filling in around the bulbs.

4. Add a thin mulch layer over the planting site or around bulbs that might be added in containers.

5. Water well.

6. Mark and label the planting site so you will know where the bulbs are growing before they begin to sprout. Include the variety and the planting date on the label.

CARE

It's easy to care for the bulbs you can easily see. They will need watering to prevent the loss of leaves during drought, feeding to encourage growth, pest control, and some grooming as leaves yellow and fruiting structures begin to mature. But some bulbs won't really be noticed until they begin to grow and flower; this doesn't mean they should be forgotten. They are living plants that need some care, including water, weed control, pest prevention, and sometimes cold protection.

WATERING

Most bulbs prefer a uniformly moist soil, and this means you must water during the drier months of the year. A mulch helps to stretch the time between waterings. Use hay, coarse compost, bark, pine straw, or similar mulch to help hold in moisture and reduce weeds. You can also cover the soil with a landscape fabric, but leave room for the bulbs to grow up within the soil covering. You can make an "X" or cut out a circle for the bulbs to grow up through the fabric. Louisiana iris, native iris, and some cannas like a damp-to-wet soil. These plants grow best in bog conditions, which may have to be created in Florida's sandy soils.

FERTILIZING

Most bulbs are not heavy feeders. Two or three applications per year of a complete fertilizer is normally adequate. Perhaps the real secret of Florida bulb care is to feed when the bulbs are making active growth and can use the nutrients.

Any general garden fertilizer can be used. Many gardeners use a balanced fertilizer at the annual flower or perennial rate. Some bulb products are also available—these usually contain a little less nitrogen in the analysis and more phosphorus and potassium. Here are a few tips for fertilizing different types of bulbs:

- **Spring-flowering bulbs and those that lose their foliage after**

flowering: Feed once in March and once in June.

• **Tropical bulbs that grow spring through fall:** Feed lightly every 6 to 8 weeks. Gardeners can also apply a slow-release fertilizer at the perennial planting rate and repeat as recommended on the label.

• **Container plantings during periods of active growth:** Feed every other week with a 20-20-20 or similar fertilizer solution.

Some gardeners like to use natural fertilizers. Organic products including manure tea, composts, and manures can be substituted for synthetic fertilizer products. Some may have to be applied more frequently to properly feed bulb plantings.

PEST CONTROL

Bulbs have only a few pests. Luckily, most bulbs seem to be resistant to nematodes—but it is still a good idea to plant them in soils as free as possible of these roundworms. The best advice is to control other pests as noted. Just check the foliage and flowers during garden walks and handpick the pests from the plants (you may first apply a natural control if you like). If needed, synthetic pesticides are available for insect and disease control.

Bulbs, Corms, Rhizomes, & Tubers

Variety	Area of Florida	When to Plant	Depth Inches	Spacing Inches	Light Needs	Blooms
Achimenes	NC	Feb.– April	1	2 – 3	Light shade	June – Sept.
African Lily	NCS	Year-round	Tip at soil	12 – 14	Sun to light shade	May – July
Alstroemeria	NCS	Jan. – Mar.	4 – 6	10 – 12	Sun to light shade	June – July
Amaryllis	NCS	Year-round	Tip at soil	12 – 14	Sun to light shade	Mar. – June
Amazon Lily	CS	Feb. – June	Tip at soil	10 – 12	Light shade	Dec. – Mar.
Anemone	NC	Oct. – Dec.	1	6 – 8	Sun to light shade	Mar. – April
Aztec Lily	NCS	Year-round	3–4	8 – 10	Sun	April – Aug.
Blackberry Lily	NCS	Feb. – Oct.	1	6 – 8	Sun	May – July
Blood Lily	NCS	Mar.– May	Tip at soil	8 – 10	Light shade	June – July
Caladium	NCS	Feb. – May	2 – 3	12 – 14	Sun to light shade	Insignificant
Calla Lily	NC	Sept. – Mar.	3 – 4	12 – 24	Sun to light shade	Mar. – May
Canna	NCS	Feb. – Aug.	1 – 2	12 – 18	Sun to light shade	April – Nov.
Crinum	NCS	Year-round	Neck at soil	18 – 24	Sun to light shade	Mar. – Nov.
Crocosmia	NCS	Feb. – Oct.	1 – 2	3 – 4	Sun	May – Sept.

Variety	Area of Florida	When to Plant	Depth Inches	Spacing Inches	Light Needs	Blooms
Dahlia	NC	Feb. – May	4 – 6	12 – 24	Sun	May – Aug.
Daylily	NCS	Year-round	Stem at soil	12 – 24	Sun to light shade	April – June
Elephant Ear	NCS	Mar. – Nov.	3 – 4	24 – 48	Sun to light shade	Insignificant
Gladiolus	NCS	Year-round	2 – 3	4 – 6	Sun	In 3 months
Gloriosa Lily	NCS	Feb. – April	2 – 4	12 – 18	Sun to light shade	April – Sept.
Hurricane Lily	NC	Dec. – Feb.	3 – 4	8 – 10	Sun to light shade	Sept. – Oct.
Kaffir Lily	NCS	Year-round	Tip at soil	12 – 18	Light shade	Mar. – May
Lapeirousia	NCS	Oct. – Dec.	1	3 – 4	Sun to light shade	Feb. – Mar.
Lilies	NC	Feb. – April	4 – 6	10 – 12	Sun to light shade	April – July
Louisiana Iris	NC	Year-round	1 – 2	10 – 12	Sun to light shade	April – June
Moraea	NCS	Year-round	1 – 2	6 – 8	Sun	April – Aug.
Narcissus	NC	Sept. – Dec.	2 – 4	6 – 8	Sun to light shade	Mar. – April
Pineapple Lily	NCS	Oct. – Nov.	5 – 6	10 – 12	Sun	June – July
Rain Lily	NCS	Feb. – Sept.	1 – 2	4 – 6	Sun to light shade	May – Sept.
Shell Ginger	CS	Year-round	1	12 – 24	Sun to light shade	April – Oct.
Society Garlic	CS	Year-round	1 – 2	6 – 8	Sun	Mar. – Nov.
Spider Lily	NCS	Year-round	3 – 5	12 – 18	Sun	April – Aug.
Tiger Flower	NC	Feb. – Mar.	3 – 4	4 – 8	Sun to light shade	June – Aug.
Tritonia	NCS	Jan. – Mar.	2 – 3	2 – 3	Sun	April – Aug.
Tuberose	NC	Jan. – Mar.	1 – 2	10 – 12	Sun	April – Aug.
Tuberous Begonia	NC	Jan. – Mar.	1 – 2	10 – 12	Light shade	May – July
Voodoo Lily	NCS	Jan. – Mar.	4 – 6	12 – 24	Sun to light shade	May – June
Walking Iris	NCS	Year-round	Stem at soil	12 – 14	Light shade	April – Oct.
Watsonia	NCS	Oct. – May	3 – 4	6 – 8	Sun to light shade	In 3 months

N = North Florida C = Central Florida S = South Florida

FEBRUARY

BULBS, CORMS, RHIZOMES, & TUBERS

PLANNING

Most of Florida starts to get spring fever in mid-February. The weather is getting warmer, and some serious bulb planting can begin.

Firm up plans for your new bulb plantings. You may need to take out some older plantings and prepare new beds, so add these chores to the work list for this month.

Look for bulbs that need replanting. Keep in mind that tropical types do not like to be out of the ground when temperatures are below 55 degrees Fahrenheit. If they are lifted at this time of year, they should be dried and stored in a warmer location before resetting in the ground. Here are a few tips for digging bulbs:

• Use a digging fork to loosen the soil so to cause minimal plant damage to bulbs.

• Allow dormant bulbs to air-dry in a shady location with temperatures above 55 degrees Fahrenheit.

Separate into individual portions when dry.

• Separate growing plants with bulbs into individual portions at the time of digging or shortly after.

Allow the wounds to air-dry before replanting.

PLANTING

Most garden center racks are starting to fill with bulbs, including **amaryllis**, **crinums**, **rain lilies**, **calla lilies**, **gloriosa lily**, and many more. And don't forget, there may be some bulbs to relocate from one area of the landscape to another, or you may obtain some from friends. Here are some tips for adding the new plantings to the landscape:

• Space the bulbs over the surface of the prepared soil, following the correct spacing according to the label.

• Open up a hole at the proper depth in the soil.

• Fill in around the bulb with soil. Water the planting site.

• If growing plants are added at this time, some staking may be needed. Foliage that has grown too tall and lanky can be cut back to a more reasonable length.

CARE

If winter cold did strike your landscape, some of your bulbs may have been damaged. Prune out the declining foliage as needed. Examine bulbs with necks out of the ground that may have been damaged. If rotting is noticeable, they may have to be lifted and separated to remove the affected portions.

WATERING

The weather is gradually becoming warmer. This means that growing bulbs are going to need extra moisture. Better check your planting sites about twice a week to determine when irrigation is needed. Here are a few watering tips.

• Water as needed when the surface inch of soil begins to be dry to the touch.

• Apply 1/2 to 3/4 inch of water each irrigation.

• Maintain a 2- to 3-inch mulch layer over the root system.

• Hand-pull or dig out weeds that may be competing for the moisture.

FERTILIZING

When growth begins, you can start the spring feeding program. Most bulbs need only a light scattering of a general garden fertilizer. Here are a few feeding tips that can be used early in the season:

• Feed bulb plantings that are beginning growth first. You can feed entire beds, or you can apply the fertilizer to small plots.

• Use granular fertilizers, liquids, or manures for bulbs or perennials, at the rates specified on the labels.

• Water the beds after a feeding to move the nutrients into the root zone.

PROBLEMS

Most pests are just getting used to the warmer days. Aphids are small, soft-bodied, pear-shaped insects that suck juices from new growths.

Control as needed with a soap or synthetic spray available from garden centers.

Mites are pinpoint-sized arachnids that suck juices from foliage and buds. Some are red and some form webs.

Control with a soap spray as instructed on the label.

Thrips are hairlike insects that rasp plant foliage, buds, and flowers, causing browning of the surface tissue.

Apply a synthetic insecticide as instructed on the label.

NATURALIZING BULBS

Creating waves and spots of color with bulbs in lawns and on hillsides is a tradition for Northern bulb growers. Northern bulbs normally sprout leaves and produce flowers only during the spring months. Unfortunately, very few Florida bulbs have this growth pattern. If you want to enjoy this traditional type of spring flowering, choose your bulbs very carefully and use them in perennial or annual flower beds. It's not a very good idea to plant Florida bulbs in with the turf. A few that look good in naturalistic plantings with wild flowers and similar plants are **amaryllis**, **caladiums**, **hurricane lily**, **lapeirousia**, **rain lilies**, and **spider lily**. Here are a few tips for maintaining these plantings.

• Allow seasonal rains to do the watering except during periods of severe drought.

• Feed lightly once in March, June, and September.

• Check for pests and control only when the problem is severe.

• Remove dead or declining foliage only as needed.

• Divide and replant only when clusters become too congested to permit good flowering.

Rain lily

MARCH

BULBS, CORMS, RHIZOMES, & TUBERS

PLANNING

Step up your bulb planning, because planting time is here. Sometimes bulbs can be the answer to the question of what to plant in difficult locations:

• Use bulbs in shady areas. **Achimenes**, **blood lily**, **Amazon lilies**, **caladiums**, and **walking iris** all prefer lower light levels.

• Add bulbs to small, difficult-to-care-for areas where grass won't grow.

• Some bulbs, like **elephant ears**, **Louisiana iris**, some **canna** varieties, and **walking iris**, like the moist areas.

• Use bulbs in planters where you want a different accent.

• Plant some bulbs, like **amaryllis**, **daylily**, **blackberry lily**, **crinum**, **lapeirousia**, **rain lilies**, **society garlic**, and **spider lily** in the drier spots where received water is mostly rains.

PLANTING

Some bulbs need very good timing for transplanting within the landscape. If you have **canna**, **caladiums**, **blood lilies**, or similar bulbs that need transplanting, now is the time. Try to complete the plantings early in the month so they will be ready to bloom on time. Always follow the steps to good planting.

CARE

Spring care begins to intensify during the month of March. Some bulbs (including **amaryllis**, **crinums**, **lapeirousia**, **anemone**, and **narcissus**) will be in full bloom. Decide if you want the flowers to go to seed. It can be fun to collect seeds of a few, but in general this is just wasting energy that could be going into the bulbs. Most gardeners cut off the old seedpods after flowering.

WATERING

It's a dry time of year, and bulbs, like other flowers, need good moisture in the soil to bloom and reproduce. Keep the soil moist by watering when the surface soil begins to be dry to the touch. Some like the **Louisiana iris** need almost bog conditions to be good performers. These areas have to be kept on the wet side.

FERTILIZING

This month is one of the major feeding times for all bulbs that were not fed earlier in the year. You can purchase a special bulb product at the local garden center, or use one of the general garden products. Here are a few fertilizing tips to keep in mind:

• Scatter the fertilizer over the surface of the soil.

• Keep the granules away from the foliage to prevent burns.

• It's fine to start the feeding near the base of the bulbs, but do not allow it to accumulate next to the green stems.

• Water immediately after the feeding.

• Manures and slow-release products can be substituted for general garden fertilizers.

• Bonemeal can be used as part of a feeding, but it's not a complete fertilizer product.

PROBLEMS

As the weather grows warmer, many pests begin to hatch and to feed on the plants. A common pest on **amaryllis**, **crinums**, **spider lilies**, and similar thick-leaved plants is the lubber grasshopper. When the grasshoppers first hatch, they are black with a yellow to reddish line down their sides. They are very

CALADIUM TRICKS

The University of Florida has performed a lot of research on **caladiums** to see if they can encourage more colorful leaf production from the tubers. They knew that the plant portions being set in a pot or the ground are stem portions with leaf buds. As is true of any stem, removing the central bud will encourage more leaves to form. Here is what you can do to get more leaves from one tuber:

Locate the most central bud on the tuber. It will be larger than the rest and may be starting to grow. Using a knife or spoon, scoop out the bud (Figure 1). Allow the wound to air-dry (Figure 2). Plant the tuber in a container of soil, or in the ground to sprout more of the sidebuds (Figures 3 and 4).

The tubers take a little longer to sprout their sidebuds, but you get much more color from one plant. Many of today's growers don't use this technique when starting **caladiums** in containers, but instead add two or more smaller tubers to the pot to get more leaves faster—you can do this too.

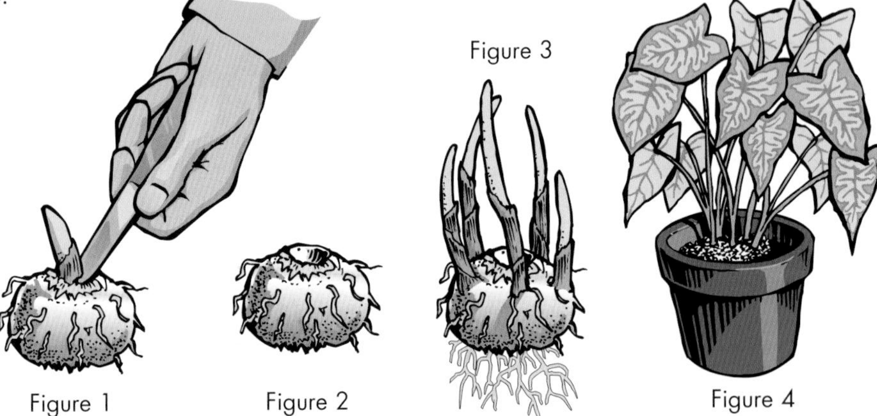

Figure 1 Figure 2 Figure 3 Figure 4

hungry, and they take large hunks out of leaves. If left to develop, they grow into a yellow-and-brown grasshopper over 2 inches long. Here are some of the best controls:

- Handpick clusters of the young insects and destroy.
- To control early, apply a synthetic insecticide that is labeled for grasshoppers.
- Catch and destroy the grown grasshoppers later in the season to prevent them from laying eggs.

Pesticides are of very little help when the grasshoppers are this large.

Lubber grasshoppers are just one of several pests you might see:

Aphids are small, soft-bodied, pear-shaped insects that suck juices from new growths.

Control as needed with a soap or synthetic spray available from garden centers.

Mites are pinpoint-sized arachnids that suck juices from foliage and buds. Some are red and some form webs.

Control with a soap spray as instructed on the label.

Thrips are hairlike insects that rasp plant foliage, buds, and flowers, causing browning of the surface tissue.

Apply a synthetic insecticide as instructed on the label.

APRIL

BULBS, CORMS, RHIZOMES, & TUBERS

PLANNING

Buy new bulbs now. The longer bulbs sit at garden centers, the more vigor they lose. Knowing when to divide is always a problem. Here are a few tips that may keep you from interrupting the flowering cycle:

- True bulbs usually form their flower buds for next year shortly after they bloom.

You may want to leave these in the ground to continue growth.

- After a bulb dies back, it is always a good time to divide and store or replant the bulbs.

Some, like **amaryllis**, that never lose the foliage except during freezes, are best divided during late fall.

- Species that are not true bulbs can be divided at almost any time except while flowering.

Daylilies and **Louisiana iris**, for example, are often dug and divided as soon as the last flowers fade.

Daylilies are divided when the last flowers fade; the rootball can be split in half.

PLANTING

If buying from a garden center, choose bulbs in the dormant stage. Bulbs grown in containers give you a quick start and allow you to be sure of flower color before planting. Here are a few tips to get container plantings established:

1. Prepare the site as for normal bulb plantings. Till in organic matter and a little fertilizer. Remove problem weeds as well.
2. Position the containers in the beds or planters. Rotate the plants so the flowers and best sides will face any visitors.
3. Give them the proper spacing. You may be able to increase the distance between the plants (saving some money), especially if the plants are large.
4. Water the plants in and keep the soil moist. These plants could dry out easily until the roots grow out into the surrounding soil.
5. Remove any faded flowers or damaged plant portions. Stake the plants if needed.
6. Apply the first feeding a week or two after planting.

Continue adding other bulbs, following good planting procedures. Many are sprouting at this time, and good watering is important. Be careful not to damage the tender portions of new shoots. Position bulbs so the shoots will not have any trouble reaching the surface.

CARE

As the blossoms fade, most flower stalks should be removed. A few gardeners may want to allow the pods to fill with seeds, but it takes energy from the plants.

When the foliage starts to fade, this is also the time to do a little trimming. Cut the old leaves back to the main stem or to the ground. Declining leaves are of no value to the plants and may encourage pests. Some plants, like **crinums**, often need to have red-blotch-affected leaves pruned out.

GIVING BULBS A START IN CONTAINERS

Here are the steps to having bulbs ready for the garden in about 60 days:

1. Select a pot that has plenty of room for growth. A 6-inch to 1-gallon container is best. Fill with loose potting soil.
2. Set bulbs at the same depth they would be grown in the ground.
3. Keep bulbs moist and at the proper light level for growth. Feed every other week with 20-20-20 or similar fertilizer solution.
4. Allow to grow to a size that is suitable for planting in the landscape or a planter.

WATERING

Bulbs are tough and can go a few days without water, but it is best not to let them reach the wilt stage. Some in-ground planting tips:

- When the surface of the soil is dry to the touch, it's time to water.
- Apply 1/2 to 3/4 inch water at each watering.
- Keep a light mulch over in-ground plantings.

Tips for container plantings:

- Water when the surface soil just starts to be dry to the touch. Some will need daily watering.
- Apply enough water so that moisture runs from the bottom of the container.
- Plants that frequently wilt between watering may need a bigger container.

FERTILIZING

Warm-season bulbs are making a lot of growth at this time of year. You need to keep the plantings supplied with nutrients for new foliage and for growing new and bigger bulbs.

- Feed in-ground plantings every 6 to 8 weeks with a general garden or bulb fertilizer.

A slow-release fertilizer can be substituted for the scheduled feedings. Follow the recommendations on the label.

- Feed container plantings every other week with a fertilizer solution, or use a slow-release fertilizer.

PROBLEMS

Slugs and snails can be a major pest problem on some bulb plantings. They seem to like **Amazon lilies**, **blood lilies**, **caladiums**, **calla lilies**, **Louisiana iris**, and **tuberous begonias** a lot, but any plant can be attacked. You can usually see the slime trails early in the morning. Slugs grow up to 2 inches long. Snails have a shell on their backs and can be of varying sizes.

Slug and snail controls include handpicking, use of shallow trays of beer or malt beverage to drown the pests, and applications of slug and snail baits.

Other pests are also beginning to enter the garden. Watch for aphids, grasshoppers, and mites.

May

BULBS, CORMS, RHIZOMES, & TUBERS

PLANNING

Many bulbs will be blooming, **Aztec lily**, **blackberry lily**, **crocosmia**, **gloriosa lily**, and **rain lilies** will bloom, just to mention a few. Take a look at your bulb plantings, and plan for the future. Here are some things to consider:

- Decide which plantings will need dividing and mark your calendar for the proper times of the year for these activities.
- Determine which are good performers in your landscape and which should be eliminated. (For example, **narcissus** and **anemones** may not flower as expected.)
- Maybe you would like some new bulbs. Consider which varieties are best for the sun or shade in your yard.
- Decide which bulbs should be moved due to changing light levels.
- Learn which pests to expect, and resolve to be better prepared for them next season.

PLANTING

Begin transplanting. If you have **narcissus** that grow well in your area of the state, wait until the tops die back and dig up the bulbs to divide. You can also divide and replant **daylilies**, **gladiolus**, **Louisiana iris**, **Kaffir lilies**, **lapeirousia**, **shell ginger**, **society garlic**, **watsonia**, and **walking iris**. Use these tips to help make transplanting easy:

- Determine which bulbs can be stored if needed and those that must go immediately back into the ground.

Generally, if the plant dies back, it can be stored for several months before replanting.

- Dig the bulbs or plants.

Allow bulbs without leaf portions to air-dry in a shady location. Break or cut growing bulb-type plants into clumps or individual plants.

- Replant growing bulbs in prepared gardens or containers at the appropriate depth.
- Store dormant bulbs in trays or boxes of dry peat moss or vermiculite until ready to plant, or add them to the garden without storing.
- Keep growing bulbs moist. Apply the first feeding in 2 to 3 weeks.

Louisiana iris

CARE

If the weather turns windy, you may notice the flowering stalks of the **African lily**, **amaryllis**, **blackberry lily**, **gladiolus**, and similar plants blown over after a storm. Keep some stakes and tape handy to give these plants a little support. When the stems are severely damaged, you will find that most bulbs make lovely cut flowers.

WATERING

Keep your eye on these bulbs: **Louisiana iris**, **caladiums**, and

some selections of **cannas**. Even **daylilies** prefer moist soils. If you want good flowers, keep them moist. Some, like the **Louisiana iris**, almost need bog conditions. You may want to grow them in a water garden or plastic-lined bog environment.

Pay special attention to bulbs in pots or planters; they can become dry in a day.

FERTILIZING

Stay on schedule with your fertilizer applications. If the weather is exceptionally dry, you might delay feeding until the rains return. Follow these feeding tips for actively growing bulbs:

• Apply a balanced fertilizer every 6 to 8 weeks, or use a slow-release fertilizer as instructed on the label.

• Feed plants in containers every other week with a 20-20-20 or similar fertilizer solution at the label rate. A slow-release product can also be applied following label recommendations.

You do not have to feed dormant bulbs at this time of year. Feedings can be delayed until growth begins.

PROBLEMS

Red blotch is a major problem with bulbs such as **amaryllis** and **crinums**. The disease, which always seems to be present somewhere in the landscape, appears on foliage as dark-brown to red areas. Severely affected leaves turn yellow and decline. When possible, red blotch is best pruned from the foliage. Much of it may have to be tolerated, but you can try applying a thiophanate methyl-containing fungicide available at garden centers. Repeat application are usually necessary. Now keep your eyes open for the following pests.

Aphids are small, soft-bodied, pear-shaped insects that suck juices from new growths.

Control as needed with a soap or synthetic spray available from garden centers.

Grasshoppers may be bright green to brown and yellow in color. They chew plant portions.

Handpick from the plants and destroy, or apply a synthetic insecticide following label instructions.

Mites are pinpoint-sized arachnids that suck juices from foliage and buds. Some are red and some form webs.

Control with a soap spray as instructed on the label.

Thrips are hairlike insects that rasp plant foliage, buds, and flowers, causing browning of the surface tissue.

Apply a synthetic insecticide as instructed on the label.

STARTING DORMANT BULBS

A few bulbs may be dug up and stored until planting time: **caladiums**, **dahlias**, **gladiolus**, **true lilies**, **tuberous begonias**, and **watsonia**. The shorter the time in storage, the better. Here are a few tips to help prevent rotting and maintain plant vigor:

• Remove the bulbs from the ground when the tops decline or growth is finished. Move them to a shady, dry area with good ventilation.

• Separate soil from the bulbs when dry. Remove unnecessary roots and old bulb portions.

• Separate into individual bulbs. Allow all cut or damaged portions to air-dry.

• Store in well-ventilated boxes or trays in dry peat moss or vermiculite. Keep most bulbs as cool as possible to delay growth. Refrigeration is not necessary. Some, like the caladium, need warm storage.

• Check for rotting bulbs and remove as needed.

• Replant as soon as possible at the proper time of year.

JUNE

BULBS, CORMS, RHIZOMES, & TUBERS

PLANNING

Make plans to add some of the more tropical bulbs to the summer landscape—these bulbs can provide the basics for any good flower garden. Most are tough and durable, surviving in all but the coldest areas of the state. These fairly exotic bulbs are not the only bulbs for summer, of course, but they can make the garden very exciting. Many are available at garden centers as container-grown plants for your summer enjoyment.

PLANTING

Now is the time to add **daylilies** to the landscape. Shop for **daylilies** while they are in bloom. Catalog pictures can never do them justice—you have to see the real flowers. Did you know there are **daylilies** that grow in light shade as well as in sun? And that some are miniature plants? Here are a few tips for adding **daylilies** to the landscape:

- Select a sunny area.

Some tolerate light shade, but all appear to do best in sun.

- Enrich sandy soils with organic matter and manure.
- Transplant **daylilies** into your garden anytime (but if you wait to transplant **lilies** that have just flowered, you will be sure of the color).
- At transplanting time, you can add individual plants or clumps of **daylilies** to the garden.
- If you wish, the tops can be cut back to within 6 to 8 inches of the base.
- Plant the **daylilies** at the same depth they were in their containers or in the ground.
- Keep **daylilies** moist.

While they can survive droughts, they grow and flower best with plenty of water.

- Feed during growth periods.

Once in March, June, and August is usually adequate.

As some of the other flowering bulbs die back, it is transplant time for them. You may want to divide and replant **gladiolus**, **true lilies**, **lapeirousia**, **narcissus**, and **watsonia**.

CARE

Cutting bouquets of **gladiolus**, **dahlias**, **tuberose**, and other **lilies** for the home can be fun at this time of year. It's a good way to enjoy the blooms without having to worry about removing the spent flowers later on.

WATERING

You often won't have to do any watering, as afternoon showers that occur almost daily can provide an inch or more of moisture. Most bulbs don't mind extra water, but a few can drown if they don't have well-drained soil. This is the time to give **tuberous begonias** a protected location so they will not rot. Here are a few watering tips:

- Use a rain gauge to keep track of the rainfall.

Only a daily rainfall of 1/4 inch or more wets the soil enough so you can skip a watering.

- After a few days without rain, check bulb plantings for needed moisture.
- If the surface soil is dry, it's time to water.
- Apply between 1/2 and 3/4 inch of water at each irrigation.
- Renew mulches to help conserve moisture.

FERTILIZING

Keep to a schedule of regular feedings. Review calendar days for your last fertilizer applications. Here are some ways to determine if your growing bulbs need fertilizer:

• Look for plant portions that appear healthy but are a lighter green than expected.

• If growth slows and there is plenty of time left in the season ahead, it could mean a lack of nutrients.

• When plants are not producing new bulbs, it could mean a lack of fertilizer.

• Stunted plantings that lack vigor may need a feeding.

PROBLEMS

Watch for grasshoppers, mites, thrips, and slugs and snails. Aphids are a special problem for **daylilies**.

Red blotch forms dark-brown to red areas on the leaves of **amaryllis**, **crinums**, and other bulbs.

Control by removing severely affected leaves from plantings and applying a fungicide that contains thiophanate methyl, following label instructions.

Control severely affected leaves with an appropriate fungicide.

TROUBLE-SHOOTING BULB PLANTINGS

Many bulbs seem to run out of energy after a while, and stop flowering. It's a common complaint: "They flowered last year, but not this year." Sometimes the flowers just seem to get smaller. Here are a few possible causes and the corrections:

Light too low: Trees and shrubs grow larger over the years, and your bulbs may not be in their original light conditions. Just dig up the bulbs and move them to a better site with the proper light.

Crowded growing conditions: We should be thankful the bulbs are growing so well, but sometimes congested conditions reduce flowering. Dig and divide.

Inadequate water: Sometimes when bulbs start to deteriorate and do not flower well, it just means they lack the water needed for growth. Stay alert to water needs.

Too little fertilizer: Inadequate fertilizer may result in lack of good color and growth. Check your feeding schedule and the amounts being applied.

Insects and diseases: If leaves turn yellow and growth is stymied, look for insects and diseases that drain the plant of vigor. Apply the appropriate control.

Some bulbs stop flowering . . .

JULY

BULBS, CORMS, RHIZOMES, & TUBERS

PLANNING

It's time to take a survey of the landscape to decide where you might add some new plantings. Once you have the spots in mind, it's time to visit the garden center. You might pass by any prepackaged bulbs that have been sitting in displays since spring. Instead, look for bulbs growing in containers. Most will be in bloom and ready to add instant color to the garden. Here are a few suggestions for placing them in the landscape:

• Give them a spot where you want instant color.

• Check the spacing. Since they are full grown, you may be able to give them the maximum recommended spacing, or even a little more than that.

• If you wish, they can be temporary additions that can be moved when other plantings are needed. Many bulbs can be used as fillers until nearby shrubs or trees fill a space.

PLANTING

Don't be afraid to move bulbs that are making full growth or even flowering. You will not severely damage the plants (although you could affect flowering). If the bulbs are in the way or need to be divided, summer is a good time. Most make very rapid growth after being divided.

CARE

Your **gloriosa lily** would probably like a little help climbing a trellis. This is a bulb that can get out of control, so keep it off the nearby shrubs and trees. **Gingers**, including the **butterfly lilies** and **shell ginger**, grow very rapidly. They often encroach upon other plantings. They can be dug and shared with friends, you can prune out the new shoots, or they can be dug and discarded. Don't let any plants take over the garden.

WATERING

Summer rains should do most of your watering, but there may be some dry times. Check bulb plantings frequently to find dry spots. Just stick your finger in the ground and feel the surface soil. If the soil feels moist, the rains have done the job.

Here are a few tips that can help with necessary watering:

• Keep a 2- to 3-inch layer of mulch over bare soil or root systems.

Use loose mulches that encourage good water movement into the soil.

• Add a tablespoon of mild dish detergent to a gallon of water, and sprinkle it over the soil before watering for better moisture penetration.

• Schedule digging and dividing of dense plantings for the proper times of the year.

• Improve soils with lots of organic matter to help loosen the ground and allow water penetration.

FERTILIZING

Check your calendars to keep up with scheduled feedings. The bulbs are making maximum growth at this time of year. Tropical plantings are the real plant food hogs; if they show signs of slowing growth, you can give them an extra feeding. Consider the use of slow-release products that gradually feed the plants throughout the growing season.

PROBLEMS

With all the summer rains, it's not uncommon for some bulbs to have rot problems. Keep your eye out for bulbs that may be planted in an area that is too low; if they appear to have growth problems, they may have to be moved. The **tuberous begonias** need a drier location during the heavier rains.

If bulbs start to rot due to too much water it's better to change the location than to try to correct the problem with fungicides.

Red blotch forms dark-brown to red areas on the leaves of **amaryllis**, **crinums**, and similar bulbs.

Control by removing severely affected leaves from plantings, and applying a fungicide containing thiophanate methyl when needed, following label instructions.

Watch for aphids, grasshoppers, mites, thrips, and slugs and snails.

OFFSHOOTS: A GREAT WAY TO START DAYLILIES

Many **daylilies** form plants that resemble small **daylilies** along their flowering stems. These are ready-to-grow plants that can be removed and will grow on to produce plants just like the parent. Here's how:

- Wait until the small plants have several leaves and some rudimentary roots starting to form, then snap the small plants from the stem.
- Plant each new plant in a 4- to 5-inch container filled with a potting mix. Just push the small plant into the soil so that it stands upright.
- Thoroughly moisten the newly planted **daylilies**.

Give the young plants a full-sun exposure, and check daily for water needs. The new roots will continue to grow rapidly to form the root system. Begin feedings with a liquid fertilizer solution two weeks after adding the plants to the containers. With good growth, they should be ready for the garden or to share with a friend by fall or early spring.

Snap off small daylily offshoots to root more plants.

AUGUST

BULBS, CORMS, RHIZOMES, & TUBERS

PLANNING

You may notice that many of Florida's bulbs flower right through the summer season, which helps make up for the fact that we lack the great Northern-type displays that cannot be reproduced in a warmer climate. Many local bulbs give almost continuous color for months at a time.

PLANTING

Container bulbs may need transplanting. When roots fill the pots, plants use water quickly, so rewet the soil several times a day. You may need to transplant bulbs such as **achimenes**, **amaryllis**, **blood lily**, **caladium**, **Kaffir lily**, **society garlic**, and **voodoo lily**. Do not transplant bulbs that may be going dormant, like the **tuberous begonias**.

Continue digging **gladiolus**, **watsonia**, and other bulbs that go dormant after flowering so you can divide and transplant them if needed. Allow **calla lilies** to go dormant by withholding water and fertilizer. Keep container-grown **calla lilies** on the dry side when they go dormant until growth resumes.

CARE

Many plants have developed older yellowing leaves. This is normal, but the leaves should be removed to make plants more attractive and keep down diseases. Remove faded flowers and old flower stalks as well. If you are not going to start bulbs from seed, remove old seedpods.

WATERING

If the rain gauge receives less than one-quarter inch, check container bulb plantings for moisture. It takes only a few days without water during the hotter months for wilting to begin.

FERTILIZING

Keep feedings on schedule. It's easy to forget time-release fertilizer applications that only have to be applied every few months. Here are a few summer feeding tips:

- Do not feed bulbs that are completing their life cycle.
- Look for signs of nutrient deficiencies like yellow leaves, and feed more if needed.
- Keep granular applications away from the lower stems.

Wash off fertilizer lodged in foliage after an application.

- Water immediately after all feedings to get nutrients to the roots.

Kaffir lily

PROBLEMS

A few bulbs, like **canna**, suffer from rust, a disease that forms red pustules on the foliage. If you run your finger over the rust it leaves orange spores on your finger. Severely affected leaves turn yellow and decline prematurely.

Light infestations can be tolerated, but heavy fungal damage requires a fungicide. Very few fungicides are labeled for rust on **canna**, but gardeners can use Bayleton®-containing sprays available from garden centers, fol- lowing label instructions.

Red blotch forms dark-brown to red areas on the leaves of **amaryllis**, **crinums**, and other bulbs.

Control by removing severely affected leaves from plantings and applying a fungicide that contains thiophanate methyl, following label instructions.

Aphids are small, soft-bodied, pear-shaped insects that suck juices from new growths. Control as needed with a soap or synthetic spray available from garden centers.

Caterpillars are the immature stages of moths or butterflies. One of the worst is the canna leaf roller, which resembles a slug. Look among the leaves to find this caterpillar. Handpick from the plants, or treat with a natural insecticide that contains *Bacillus thuringiensis*.

Grasshoppers may be bright green to brown and yellow in color. They chew plant portions. Handpick from the plants and destroy, or apply a synthetic insecticide following label instructions.

Mites are pinpoint-sized arachnids that suck juices from foliage and buds. Some are red and some form webs.

Control with a soap spray as instructed on the label.

Thrips are hairlike insects that rasp plant foliage, buds, and flowers, causing the surface tissue to brown.

Apply a synthetic insecticide as instructed on the label.

Slugs and snails are slimy garden pests with or without shells. They can often be detected by slime trails, may grow to 2 inches long, and chew holes in foliage.

Control where needed by handpicking from plants. Slugs can be controlled by placing shallow trays of beer or malt beverages in the garden where the pests climb in and drown. Both can be controlled with slug and snail baits, following label instructions.

STARTING BULBS FROM SEED

If you want to start bulbs from seeds, allow seedpods to form on your plants.

When the pods turn brown or start to crack open, collect the seeds. You can put the pods in a paper bag for a few days—most will pop open and the seeds will come out. A few may have a covering that needs to be removed.

- Sow the seeds in trays or pots with good drainage.
- Use a germination mix or potting mix to start the seeds.
- Cover the seeds with a soil layer equal to their thickness.
- Keep moist and in a bright location to begin growth.
- When the seed germinates, usually within 2 to 3 weeks, move the containers to the proper light level for growth.
- Begin feeding with a half-strength fertilizer solution every other week.
- Allow the plants to form 3 to 4 true leaves, and then transplant to cell-packs, individual pots, or rows in the garden.

Give young plants extra attention when applying the water needed to continue growth. Place container plantings on an every-other-week feeding program, using a fertilizer solution at normal rates. Feed in-ground plantings every 4 to 6 weeks with a general garden fertilizer at label rates. Transplant maturing plants to the garden as needed.

SEPTEMBER

BULBS, CORMS, RHIZOMES, & TUBERS

PLANNING

Gardeners can look for fall-blooming **rain lilies** to make an appearance as summer starts winding down. All summer long these bulbs have been providing grasslike greenery as edging for walkways and lower-growing ground cover for perennial beds. Now they will begin to bloom. They come in three colors: pink, yellow, and white. They are in bloom during the rainy season and often pop into bloom after a summer shower. The care that is required is minimal, and the bulbs are often used in naturalistic plant settings.

• Plant these true bulbs just about anytime of year.

Most are available from garden centers and mail-order companies during the fall through spring months. **Rain lilies** grow best in sun but can tolerate light shade.

• Set the bulbs in sandy or enriched garden sites 1 to 2 inches deep and 4 to 6 inches apart.

• Mother Nature does most of the watering, but moisten the soil during periods of drought.

The plants often go dormant during periods of drought and lose their leaves.

• Use no more than a thin, loose mulch among the plantings, as the leaves are quite narrow.

• Very little fertilizer is needed.

A light feeding in June and August is usually adequate.

PLANTING

A few **daffodils** give a good performance in Central and North Florida. To be most successful, look for varieties that are listed for your zone 8 or 9 location. A few that have been tested and give good performance include: 'Golden Perfection', 'Carlton', and 'Silver Chimes'.

It may be best to stick with the good Florida bulbs for the most part. These will be displayed shortly at local garden centers. Fall normally starts off with **amaryllis**, **anemone**, **narcissus**, and **rain lilies** for early plantings.

Continue your transplanting as needed. If you create wounds during digging, allow the spots on the bulbs to dry before replanting. Only a few hours to a day or two are usually needed. Then follow these steps:

1. Prune off any top portions that might be damaged or in the way during planting.
2. Make sure the planting site is well prepared.
3. Set the bulbs in the ground at the proper depth.
4. Keep the soil moist and apply a light mulch.
5. Give growing bulbs a light feeding a week or two after planting.

CARE

A walk through bulb plantings will always result in something for you to do. You can remove declining blooms, or even cut a bouquet for the home or to give to a friend. Many bulb plantings may be overgrown. Don't be afraid to do some rejuvenation pruning.

WATERING

Early September normally offers adequate rainfall for bulb gardens. Then, all of a sudden, the rains stop and you have to be ready to turn on the irrigation system. Use early September to make sure the irrigation system in the gardens is working properly and will be ready when needed.

FERTILIZING

You can reduce the feedings to an "only-as-needed" basis to

keep the foliage green and the flowers coming:

- Make final slow-release feedings of the year.
- Stretch container feedings to every 2 to 3 weeks with a fertilizer solution.
- Use general garden fertilizer only on actively growing bulb plantings, and at longer intervals of up to 8 weeks.
- Instead of using a synthetic fertilizer, apply manures that will slowly meter fertilizer to the bulbs.

PROBLEMS

Stay alert and keep checking for feeding damage on foliage and flowers. With drier weather ahead, expect mites to become more active. Following are some prevalent pest problems.

Red blotch forms dark-brown to red areas on the leaves of **amaryllis**, **crinums**, and other bulbs.

Control by removing severely affected leaves from plantings and applying a fungicide that contains thiophanate methyl, following label instructions.

Watch for aphids, caterpillars (one of the worst is the canna leaf roller, which resembles a slug), grasshoppers, mites, thrips, and slugs and snails.

STARTING BULBS FROM CUTTINGS

A few bulbs can be rooted from cutting to form new plants. These include **achimenes**, **dahlia**, and **tuberous begonia**. **Walking iris** and **daylilies** form little plants on the flowering stem with preformed roots that are ready to grow too. Cuttings may be a way to reproduce bulbs just like the original plant without waiting to divide the bulbs at the end of the growing season:

- Fill shallow pots or a tray with vermiculite and moisten.
- Make cuttings 4 to 6 inches long.

Where little plants have started to form, remove then from the stems to root.

- Place the base of the cutting or small plant in the vermiculite, deep enough so it stands in an upright position.
- Keep moist and in a filtered-sun location.

Some gardeners encase the containers of cuttings in plastic to maintain the high humidity that promotes rooting.

- Roots should form in a matter of weeks.

Well-rooted cuttings can be potted and grown until ready for a larger container or the garden.

Fill shallow trays with potting medium (vermiculite is good) and root cuttings.

OCTOBER

BULBS, CORMS, RHIZOMES, & TUBERS

PLANNING

Perhaps Northern catalogs have tempted you with pages of attractive bulbs and you would like to force a few. Florida does not receive enough cold weather to grow any but a few of the **daffodils**. But if you want to try forcing, follow these steps:

1. Check the catalogs for bulbs recommended for forcing.
2. Force the bulbs in shallow pots. You can grow one bulb per small pot, or several in a container that is 6 inches or larger. Fill the containers with potting soil.
3. Push the bulbs into the soil so the tops of the bulbs are just below the surface. Use a close spacing, with just an inch or two between the bulbs.
4. Thoroughly moisten the containers.
5. Place the containers in a refrigerator. Now here is the secret: There can be no vegetables or fruits in the same refrigerator. These give off a gas that causes flower buds in the bulbs to abort.
6. Leave the containers in the refrigerator for 10 to 12 weeks, keeping them moist.
7. After the cold treatment, bring out the bulbs and grow them to flower in a sunny site.

You can keep the bulbs in a sunny window or on a porch, or sink the pots in the ground. Decide when you want the bulbs to begin growth and determine when they should be given the cold treatment. This way you can create an outdoor bulb display for the late-winter or early-spring months.

PLANTING

A few true **daffodils** do grow and flower in Central and Northern Florida, including the varieties 'Carlton', 'Golden Perfection', and 'Silver Chimes'. Add these selections (and others that need just a short period of cold) to the landscape during the fall months, starting in October. Many of the **paper-white narcissus** selections also flower well in these cooler locations. Follow these steps to success:

1. Select a sunny to lightly shaded site.
2. Loosen the soil and work in liberal quantities of organic matter. Many gardeners also like to add manure and bonemeal to the planting sites.
3. Plant the bulbs 3 to 4 inches deep and 8 inches apart in the garden.
4. Water after planting to thoroughly moisten the soil.
5. Add a thin layer of mulch.
6. Give the garden site normal care.

The bulbs should send up shoots during the spring months, and they will be followed by foliage. Allow the foliage to grow until it naturally declines during late spring. Many give repeat blooms for years.

Use this time to check your other bulb plantings. Many may have filled the beds with new plants and can be divided and transplanted. Outdoor temperatures are a lot better for working at this time of year.

Some narcissus are good candidates for forcing.

EASY-TO-FORCE PAPER-WHITE NARCISSUS

Just about everyone likes the cheery **narcissus** flowers. They are very fragrant and give a fresh garden smell to the home, patio, or landscape. A few gardeners do find the fragrance a little overpowering and display them in areas with adequate air movement.

The bulbs are ready to grow when received in the mail or obtained from local garden centers. Follow these steps for planting.

1. Use a shallow bowl without drainage for forcing. Add an inch or two of small stones to the bowl.
2. Set the bulbs upright on the stones, and add a few more stones to hold them in place. Add water so it just touches the bulb's base.
3. Set the planted containers in the refrigerator for 3 to 4 weeks while the bulbs grow roots and begin growth. Add water to the bowl as needed to keep the level at the base of the bulbs.
4. Bring out the bulbs after the cold treatment, and place them in a sunny window to grow.

CARE

As many bulbs decline, they leave behind old stems and flower portions that should be removed and added to the compost pile. Mark these bed areas so you will not disturb the bulbs except when they need dividing. These areas can be planted with annual flowers if needed for temporary color.

WATERING

It's the dry time of year, but fortunately the temperatures are cooler, which means bulb plantings need minimal waterings. Several days to a week can usually pass between good soakings. Check the soil every 3 to 4 days.

FERTILIZING

If you have not provided growing bulbs with a fall feeding, now is the time in the Central and Northern regions. A general garden fertilizer will do just fine.

Many bulb plantings in South Florida may continue growth. Those maintaining active green foliage and producing flowers can be kept on normal feeding schedules until winter weather arrives.

PROBLEMS

Red blotch forms dark-brown to red areas on leaves of **amaryllis**, **crinums**, and other bulbs.

Control by removing severely affected leaves from plantings and applying a fungicide that contains thiophanate methyl, following label instructions.

Do the pests know it's fall? Some do. Grasshoppers should be starting to decline, and slugs and snails will not be as active. Continue to keep an eye out for these pests, and treat only as needed. A few that are more persistent into the fall months are aphids, caterpillars, mites, and thrips.

NOVEMBER

BULBS, CORMS, RHIZOMES, & TUBERS

PLANNING

A walk through the landscape can tell you that most bulb plantings have stopped flowering or shriveled into dormancy. This is a time for you to think of new plantings.

Here are some areas that may benefit from bulb plantings:

- small areas along walkways that are lacking greenery or seasonal color
- flower beds that need a backdrop of taller-growing bulbs for months of greenery or color
- entrance areas and spots near patios that need a major accent
- empty containers and planters in need of some seasonal interest

PLANTING

Some bulbs that can be planted at this time of year, including the **crinum**, **daylily**, **Kaffir lily**, **lapeirousia**, **Louisiana iris**, and many more. Almost any bulb growing a clump of foliage can be divided and moved as needed. Here are some late-fall planting tips:

- Remove weeds and old plant portions from the bulb beds.
- Trim back trees and shrubs that may be interfering with the new bulb plantings.
- Improve the planting sites with organic matter.
- Set the bulbs in the ground at the proper planting depth.
- Add a 2- to 3-inch layer of mulch over the soil surface.
- Moisten the planting site thoroughly.

Gardeners complain quite often that **amaryllis** does not flower well during the spring months in Florida landscapes. This is partially due to the almost continuous growth of the bulbs in the warm climate. Withholding water from these plantings during the fall can encourage late-winter flowering. The University of Florida has also developed another technique to help the plants come into bloom:

1. Dig up the **amaryllis** in fall, leaving the roots intact.
2. Place the bulbs in a dry shady location for 6 to 8 weeks.
3. Remove any declining foliage.
4. Replant the bulbs after the treatment period, and give normal care to encourage late-winter blooms.

Improve plant beds wih compost and amendments.

CARE

Cleaning up the declining bulb portions may be your biggest chore at this time of year. You can also take down the old stakes used to support tall-growing bulbs and the trellis near the **gloriosa lily**. Keep these handy, however, as new growths are only a few months away.

Bring the container plantings of **achimenes**, **caladiums**, and similar bulbs inside. Give them a shady but well-ventilated spot. Keep them from temperatures below 50 degrees Fahren- heit. They can be left in the soil in their pots or dug and stored in peat moss or vermiculite.

Check on any bulbs that are in storage. Look for bulbs that may be rotting, and remove them immediately. If some are starting to sprout, try to find a storage area that is a little cooler. As a last resort, they can be potted and grown in a protected area of the landscape. Since many of these are cold sensitive, they have to be protected from freezing temperatures.

WATERING

It's a dry-but-cool time of year. For the most part, seasonal rains provide adequate moisture. Keep checking the beds and bulbs that have green foliage. Most can go several days to a week without additional water. If the soil is dry to the touch, you had better give them a good soaking.

FERTILIZING

Feedings are just about over for all but the active tropical bulbs. It may be best to check the plantings and fertilize only as needed. If growths become yellow-green due to a lack of nutrients, give light feedings with a general fertilizer. Most bulb plantings do not need another feeding until late winter.

FORCE AN AMARYLLIS FOR THE HOLIDAYS

It's fun to give a friend a blooming **amaryllis**. Large bulbs with preformed buds are available at local garden centers. All they need is a little care to bring them into bloom.

You have to plan ahead. It takes 4 to 6 weeks to establish bud-bearing bulbs in a pot. This means you have to begin the plantings in mid-November. Follow these steps:

1. Select a 6-inch pot for the bulb. Choose a colorful container to make it a festive gift.
2. Fill the pot to within 2 to 3 inches of the rim with potting soil.
3. Position the bulb in the center so its neck is level with the rim.
4. Add extra soil to within 1 inch of the rim.
5. Place the bulb in a bright-to-sunny location, and keep the soil moist. Good light on all sides will encourage uniform growth. Don't fertilize.
6. Give the plant as a gift when the buds swell.

After flowering, the **amaryllis** can be added to the landscape in spring.

PROBLEMS

Seen any pests lately? Some are active, but you can spot the populations quickly and get them under control by hand-picking or using natural sprays. Here are a few that may still be causing some plant damage:

Aphids are small, soft-bodied, pear-shaped insects that suck juices from new growths.

Control as needed with a soap or synthetic spray available from garden centers.

Mites are pinpoint-sized arachnids that suck juices from foliage and buds. Some are red and some form webs.

Control with a soap spray as instructed on the label.

Thrips are hairlike insects that rasp plant foliage, buds, and flowers, causing browning of the surface tissue. Apply a synthetic insecticide as instructed on the label.

DECEMBER

BULBS, CORMS, RHIZOMES, & TUBERS

PLANNING

Happy holidays! It's a great time to share your love of bulbs with friends. You might give a friend a bulb-planting kit. Think of some of the things you need for growing bulbs, and put them in a big pot or planter box. You might include a large bag of potting soil, trowel and other gardening tools, bulb fertilizer, marking stakes, watering can, and bulbs or started plants of **amaryllis**, **Kaffir lilies**, **gladiolus**, **narcissus**, **rain lilies**, **gingers**, and **tuberous begonias**.

PLANTING

This is a very good time to begin new beds. The weather is cool and the digging is easy.

• Control perennial weeds with a nonselective herbicide that permits replanting.

• Till the ground deeply to 6 to 8 inches.

• Work in liberal quantities of organic matter and manure.

• Test the soil acidity and adjust with dolomitic lime or sulfur if needed.

Let the bed sit. The organic matter will break down a little further to release some nutrients, and the lime or sulfur can begin adjusting the soil acidity if needed. Plan to make your new plantings after the first of the year.

CARE

Take walks through the landscape to check for declining plant portions and pests. The amount of work should be minimal. Check bulbs in storage. You may use this month to remove adhering soil or damaged or unwanted portions.

• Grade the quality of the bulbs.

Small **gladiolus** bulbs might be separated from the large types that are sure to flower.

• Look for bulbs that are starting to sprout, and put these in a separate container to be planted when winter weather warms.

• Remove and discard rotting bulbs.

• Look for signs of pest damage and control as needed. (Cockroaches and similar insects find bulbs tasty.)

• Maintain dry, well-ventilated storage conditions.

Keep **caladiums** in storage at about 70 degrees Fahrenheit. Other bulbs can be stored in the 40- to 60-degree range.

WATERING

It's still the drier time of year, but it is fairly cool in all areas of the state. Check the soil every three or four days for moisture. Most bulb plantings can go a week or more without water now.

FERTILIZING

Skip feedings of all but the tropical and actively growing bulbs in the southern parts of the state. Even these require only light feedings to maintain green foliage and minimal growth.

PROBLEMS

Inspect foliage every week or two. You don't have to make frequent inspections as you do in the hotter months. Aphids, mites, and thrips may still be active.

Caladium

CHAPTER THREE

CITRUS

If you plant only one fruit tree, make it a citrus. There is no fruiting plant that is so adaptable and reliable. Citrus trees almost grow themselves, with just a little care from you.

Citrus were first introduced to Florida during the mid- to late 1500s by Spanish explorers and settlers. They were planted among the early settlements and then transported along the waterway to the rest of the state. The trees grew up in clusters that were eventually called groves. Many fruit trees are said to grow in orchards, but Florida's citrus plantings are still called groves.

Maybe Florida was a little warmer when the early settlers arrived, and they were able to grow citrus in the more northern parts of the state. But freezes have affected the groves, and today most citrus is cultivated in the central and southern portions of the state. The citrus industry has gradually moved from St. Augustine southward to below Route 50, an east-west highway across the state directly through Orlando.

This does not mean you cannot grow citrus in Tallahassee or Ocala, but you do have to be more selective about the variety and be ready to provide some cold protection. In the planting chart

(pages 88 to 89), the hardiness zones of Florida have been noted as a guide.

- **North Florida:** Very few citrus are planted in this portion of the state. Only the very hardy types can survive the cold years. Citrus can always be grown in containers and moved to a warm protected area if needed.
- **Central Florida:** This is a rather long zone extending northward from just above Lake Okeechobee to the Ocala area. Some of the more northerly parts of this zone will be subject to freeze damage. Check with your local Extension Service office or garden center to make sure the varieties you want to grow can withstand the winters. All areas may have trouble growing the more cold-sensitive lemons and limes during the cold years. Where needed, citrus can be grown in containers and protected from cold.
- **South Florida:** This is usually the frost- and freeze-free area of the state. Every few years groves and home plantings are damaged by cold, but usually only the ends of branches are damaged, and new growth is produced in spring. Lemons and limes can be produced with little worry in the most southern portions of this zone.

PLANNING

Most citrus trees grow quite large. The orange, grapefruit, tangerine, tangelo, and similar trees can grow 30 feet tall and wide. Only the lemons, limes, kumquats, and calamondins can be called small trees. You need adequate room for most citrus plantings.

Use the citrus trees as a major planting. They make excellent accent trees with fragrant flowers and colorful fruits. Here are some ways to use the citrus plantings in your landscape:

- Add a tree near the patio. It can cast shade and be used to hang orchids and similar low-light-requiring plants.
- Create a view barrier along the edge of the landscape. Most citrus trees keep their limbs to the ground. The green leaves create a dense evergreen screen.
- Plant citrus trees as a grove of your own. Make plantings so you will have fruits throughout most of the year.
- Use citrus trees along walkway to provide shade and create interest. Plant them far enough back so not to drop fruits on the walk areas.
- Add a citrus tree as a focal point at the end of a view. Both the flowers and fruits attract attention.
- Use a citrus tree as an espalier on a wall or fence.
- Plant a tree in a container for a little patio shade or position one at an entrance.

Planning involves a lot more than just deciding where you would like citrus. You have to select a variety. There is so much to choose from. Often you have a lot more to pick from than what is obvious in our citrus chart. For example, there is more than one navel. To be honest, most gardeners would just be happy with one navel, but if you want, there are numerous selections including named and numbered varieties. These might be studied by the real connoisseurs. There are lots of lemons and kumquats. Check these out at your local garden centers or citrus nurseries.

Determine which rootstock you want for your tree. Just about all citrus tree are sold with a root system called the rootstock that has the desirable variety budded on to the top. The rootstock provides vigor and ability to grow in certain soils, may add hardiness, and is often resistant to prevalent diseases. Some rootstocks you may hear of are sour orange, Cleopatra, mandarin, trifoliate orange, swingle citrumelo, rough lemon, and carrizo citrange. Unless you want to undertake a course of study, it's

really best to allow the garden center or citrus nursery make the rootstock decision for you. Gardeners in North Florida will probably want their trees on the most hardy rootstock: the trifoliate orange.

The union of the rootstock and desirable top of the tree called the scion can be seen within 6 inches of the ground on all budded trees. Make sure the union is healing properly at the time of purchase. Remove any shoots growing from below the budded area. A few citrus trees are sold on their own root systems and will not have a budded area.

PLANTING

Here is the easy part of growing a citrus tree: just make sure you have a sunny location. All citrus need a full day of sun to give good production. They should be located away from older trees of any type and buildings. If planted too closely to large plants or objects, the shade may cause the citrus trees to produce thin growth and fruit very poorly if at all.

Make sure the planting site is well drained. Citrus trees like sandy soils; there is no need to add organic matter to the planting site. Try to find a site where the water table is at least 4 feet below the surface of the ground. If water can be found closer to the surface of the ground, either locate a better site or plant the tree in a mound of soil or raised bed to add extra drainage.

Citrus trees supplied to the home gardening market are usually in 3-gallon containers. Sometimes stores obtain trees in smaller citrus pots—these trees have a smaller ball of soil and are planted like any potgrown plant. A few trees may be obtained bare root and can be planted during the more dormant time of the year (November through February). Planting a citrus tree is easy:

- Open a hole a little wider than the rootball, but no deeper.
- Set a container-grown tree in the ground at the same level it was in the pot.

Position a bare-root tree so the trunk is at the same level it was in the ground at the nursery. Use the change in bark color as a guide.

- Fill in around the roots or rootball with soil removed from the hole, watering as the soil is added.

For bare-root trees, create a 4- to 6-inch berm of soil around the edge of the rootball or edge of the hole.

- Fill the berm-formed area with water. Do not add a mulch to citrus plantings.

CARE

Unlike most fruiting trees and shrubs, citrus needs very little pruning. Most trees tend to assume a rounded shape if left to grow on their own. They usually keep their lower limbs to the ground for years. There is no special pruning for increasing fruiting or ensuring better pest control. Just a little periodic trimming is all that is needed.

- Remove any quick-growing sprouts, often called suckers, from below the budded area. Remove similar limbs that often sprout from among the permanent limbs if in the way.
- Trim off any limbs that may be in the way of good tree maintenance.
- Cut back outer limbs that appear to be growing way beyond the normal limits of the tree as needed.
- Remove limbs that may be interfering with other landscape plantings or irrigation systems.
- Trim all dead or declining limbs as noticed.
- Do not paint pruning wounds but leave them to heal naturally.

WATERING

Young trees need the most attention to watering. After planting, fill the basin formed by the berm of soil daily with water for the first few weeks. Then water every other day to every third

day as needed to keep the soil moist. Citrus trees are tough and very drought tolerant. But you get the best growth from a new fruiting tree with good watering practices. Care is especially needed during the dry spring months after planting. When the summer rainy season arrives, the frequent storms usually supply the needed moisture. Older trees are watered as needed.

- Most established trees need water during the drier months.
- Water once or twice a week for trees in sandy soils. Check the soil, and when the surface starts to dry, provide the needed moisture.

Apply 1/2 to 3/4 inch water at each irrigation.

- Water is best applied by soaker hoses or microsprinklers that put the water where it is needed under the spread of the trees. Conventional irrigation can also be utilized.
- Operate the watering system during the early morning hours to conserve moisture.

Making sure the trees have an even moisture supply ensures good growth and prevents some physiological problems. A problem known as fruit splitting is often increased by intermittent periods of moisture. Maintaining a good watering program minimizes the splitting caused by a sudden swelling of the fruits.

FERTILIZING

Encourage good growth and fruiting habits with frequent but light feedings. Most gardeners shop for a citrus fertilizer that supplies the nutrients needed for good growth. If you wish, a 6-6-6 with minor nutrients can be substituted. New trees are given a first feeding four to six weeks after planting or when the weather warms during the spring. The trees are then fed every six to eight weeks with a light fertilizer application, March through early September. Start with 1/2 pound of fertilizer at the first feeding. Apply a pound of fertilizer at the next feeding. Gradually increase the rate during successive feedings to provide 1 1/2 pounds at the end of the first year, 2 1/2 pounds at the end of year two, and 4 pounds at the end of year three. All fertilizer is scattered under the spread of the trees and watered.

Feeding Citrus Trees

After three years, the tree is placed on a mature-tree feeding program. Most gardeners use a citrus fertilizer or a similar product with minor nutrients included.

- Measure the trunk circumference of the tree 6 inches above the ground.
- For each inch of circumference, weigh out 1/4 pound of fertilizer.
- Apply the fertilizer once in March, May, August, and later September or early October.
- Distribute the fertilizer evenly under the spread of the tree and out past the dripline.
- Water the fertilized area to begin moving the nutrients into the root zone.

Sometimes you have to judge the needs of the tree. Plantings not growing vigorously or damaged in some way may not need a full feeding. When necessary, reduce the quantity of fertilizer applied to the trees.

PEST CONTROL

Most citrus gardeners practice very little pest control even when they notice lots of pests. This may seem a little odd, but citrus trees really are very resistant to insects and diseases. You may see some of the common insects that affect other trees and shrubs, but damage is probably minimal. Citrus has its own diseases too, but they cause little harm. Some more good news: when you think a pesticide is needed, natural controls are usually very effective. Don't get too concerned when you see some of the common problems.

Insects: Aphids, often associated with ant populations, are small pear-shaped insects that suck juices from new growths. They can cause the curling of new citrus leaves.

Where needed, apply a soap spray, or allow the naturally-occurring ladybugs or lacewings to provide control.

Caterpillars eat large sections of leaves but are usually not very numerous. The most common is the orange dog caterpillar, which is the immature stage of the swallowtail butterfly.

Where needed, they can be handpicked or treated with an insecticide containing *Bacillus thuringiensis*.

Citrus leaf miner is a small moth that lays eggs that hatch into a tunneling larva that lives within the leaves. No control is normally applied for mature trees even though leaves become contorted and damaged.

If needed, an oil spray can be applied to new leaves under 1 inch long on young trees.

Grasshoppers and katydids are long-legged chewing insects that are brown to green in color. Damage is usually minimal, but they can remove a lot of foliage from young trees.

Control by handpicking as needed.

Scale are various insects with white to dark coverings that suck juices from the leaves, stems, trunks, and fruits. Mature scale insects develop a pesticide-resistant covering.

Apply an oil spray to obtain control, but avoid pesticide treatment as harvest time draws near.

Whiteflies are small white-winged insects that live on the underside of leaves. They produce a greenish immature stage that is hard to see on the underside of leaves. Whiteflies reduce tree vigor and often encourage sooty mold. They can usually be ignored.

If needed, control with an oil or soap spray.

Mites: Spider mites are small arachnids that attack citrus foliage during the dry months. They may turn leaves yellow and cause them to drop.

Apply an oil or soap spray to control.

Rust mites are extremely small arachnids which cause the surface of fruits to turn brown. The damage is most apparent during the summer and fall seasons. Rust mites also cause fruits to look bad on the surface, but this does not affect internal quality.

Control as needed with an oil or soap spray.

Diseases: Foot rot is a trunk disease that causes bark to

come loose at or near ground level.

The best control is to keep the base of the tree free of vegetation and mulch.

Greasy spot is a fungal disease that produces yellow spots on leaves that gradually turn from brown to black.

Where severe, apply an oil spray or copper-containing fungicide during mid-June to mid-July.

Melanose is a fugal disease that produces rough small brown or purple spots on the surface of foliage and fruits.

Control by pruning out dead wood and, if needed, apply a copper fungicide in late April.

Scab is a fungal disease which produces bumps of scab-like tissue on fruits and leaves during the warm months. Scab causes minimal damage but makes fruits and foliage look bad.

Control where needed by applying a copper-containing fungicide to young fruits and foliage.

When applying pesticides, follow all label instructions. Pay careful attention to the time that must pass before using fruits. Note any precautions as to time of the year and temperatures that might affect the health of the trees when applying pesticides.

Selected Citrus Plantings

Name	Area of Florida	Ready to Eat	Seeds per Fruit	Fruit Size (Inches)	Remarks
ORANGES					
Ambersweet	CS	Oct. – Dec.	0 – 15	3 – 3½	Easy to peel, good juice quality
Cara Cara	CS	Oct. – Jan.	0 – 6	3 – 3½	A red-fleshed navel selection
Gardner	CS	Jan. – Mar.	6 – 24	2½ – 3	Good juice quality
Hamlin	CS	Oct. – Jan.	0 – 6	2¾ – 3	Early juice orange
Midsweet	CS	Jan. – Mar.	6 – 24	2½ – 3	Good juice quality
Navel	CS	Oct. – Jan.	0 – 6	3 – 3½	Very popular, eat fresh or juice
Parson Brown	CS	Oct. – Jan.	10 – 20	2½ – 2¾	Low fruit yields but early
Pineapple	CS	Dec. – Feb.	15 – 25	2¾ – 3	Excellent juice but seedy
Rhode Red	CS	Mar. – June	0 – 6	2¾ – 3	A red-fleshed Valencia selection
Sunstar	CS	Jan. – Mar.	6 – 20	2½ – 3	Good juice quality
Valencia	CS	Mar. – June	0 – 6	2¾ – 3	Excellent juice quality
GRAPEFRUIT AND RELATED FRUITS					
Duncun	CS	Nov. – May	30 – 70	3½ – 5	An old variety, white flesh
Flame	CS	Nov. – May	0 – 6	3¾ – 4½	Most popular, dark red flesh
Foster	CS	Nov. – May	30 – 50	3½ – 5	Good older variety, pink flesh
Marsh	CS	Nov. – May	0 – 6	3½ – 4½	Very popular, white flesh
Pink Marsh	CS	Dec. – May	0 – 6	3¾ – 4½	Also called Thompson, pink flesh

Name	Area of Florida	Ready to Eat	Seeds per Fruit	Fruit Size (Inches)	Remarks
GRAPEFRUIT AND RELATED FRUITS					
Pummelo	CS	Nov. – Feb.	50	5 – 7	May be a parent of the grapefruit
Ray Ruby	CS	Nov. – May	0 – 6	3 1/2 – 4	Dark red flesh
Redblush	CS	Nov. – May	0 – 6	3 1/2 – 4 1/2	Also called Ruby Red, red flesh
Star Ruby	CS	Dec. – May	0 – 6	3 1/2 – 4	Dark red flesh
MANDARINS AND HYBRIDS					
Dancy	CS	Dec. – Jan.	6 – 20	2 1/4 – 2 1/2	Easy-to-peel-and-section tangerine
Fallglo	CS	Oct. – Nov.	30 – 40	3 – 3 1/2	Easy-peeling Temple hybrid
Minneola	CS	Dec. – Jan.	7 – 12	3 – 3 1/2	A tangelo, often called Honeybell
Murcott	CS	Jan. – Mar.	10 – 20	2 1/2 – 2 3/4	A hybrid with a unique flavor
Nova	CS	Nov. – Dec.	1 – 30	2 3/4 – 3	A hybrid with good flavor
Lee	CS	Nov. – Dec.	10 – 25	2 3/4 – 3	A hybrid with good flavor
Orlando	CS	Nov. – Jan.	0 – 35	2 3/4 – 3	A heavy producing tangelo
Osceola	CS	Oct. – Nov.	15 – 25	2 1/4 – 2 3/4	A hybrid with good flavor
Ponkan	CS	Dec. – Jan.	3 – 7	2 3/4 – 3 1/2	Good flavor, easy-to-peel tangerine
Robinson	CS	Oct. – Dec.	1 – 20	2 1/2 – 2 3/4	Good flavor, tangerine
Satsuma	NCS	Sept. – Nov.	0 – 6	2 1/4 – 2 1/2	A hybrid with sweet taste
Sunburst	CS	Nov. – Dec.	1 – 20	2 1/2 – 3	A tangerine with sweet taste
Temple	CS	Jan. – Mar.	15 – 20	2 1/4 – 3	Sweet, easy to peel
ACID CITRUS					
Calamondin	CS	Year-round	6 – 10	1 – 1 1/2	A heavy producing small tree
Key Lime	CS	Year-round	12 – 20	1 – 1 1/2	A small tree with good production
Kumquat	NCS	Year-round	6 – 10	3/4 – 1	A small tree, several varieties
Lemon	S	July – Dec.	1 – 6	2 – 2 1/2	Numerous varieties
Limequat	CS	Year-round	0 – 16	1 – 1 1/2	Hybrid of key lime and kumquat
Meyer Lemon	CS	Nov. – Mar.	10	2 1/2 – 3	Grows as a bush
Ponderosa Lemon	S	Year-round	20 – 30	4 – 5	A hybrid to grow as a small tree
Tahiti Lime	S	June – Sept.	0	1 3/4 – 2 1/2	A hybrid also called Persian lime

N = North Florida   C = Central Florida   S = South Florida

PLANNING

You are now at the height of the citrus season, when many fruits in the home landscape are ripening. You do need to finish up the **navels**, ['Hamlin'], and other early-fruiting **oranges**. Most of the **mandarins** and related hybrids are also finishing production. For a true Florida resident, the **grapefruits** are just starting to get sweet. The 'Temple' and 'Murcott' **oranges** are ready to pick too.

If you do not have a lot of citrus, now is a good time to decide which trees you would like to plant. Obtain some of the different varieties of fruit from friends, a roadside stand, or the grocery store. Let the taste test be your guide. If you like the fruit, you may want to add it to the landscape. Garden centers will be getting trees to plant very soon.

- Try not to plant too many trees in a crowded landscape, as citrus trees grow quite large.
- Allow at least 15 to 20 feet between trees.
- Keep citrus trees away from buildings and other landscape trees.
- Make sure the soil is well drained.

PLANTING

Most citrus trees are purchased in containers ranging in size from small pots to 3-gallon or larger containers. If you make a purchase at this time of the year, you may want to delay the planting if you live in a cold location. Young trees are more susceptible to freezing weather than well-established citrus plantings. Gardeners in the warmer locations can add new citrus anytime.

- Keep trees in containers in a sunny location until you are ready to plant.
- Keep the soil moist by watering when the surface starts to dry.
- Most trees do not need a special feeding at this time.
- Protect the tree from freezing.

CARE

Delay all major trimming in the cooler locations for another month. If it's a warm winter and trees in more southern regions begin to bloom, you can give the trees any needed trimming. Most major pruning in home yards is delayed until the trees are about to bloom. Otherwise, dormancy may be affected in a way that adversely affects hardiness.

WATERING

Winter is a cool but dry period of the year. In order to continue production, the trees need adequate water. Most trees in a well-drained sandy soil need watering once or twice a week. Trees growing in the heavier clay or organic-matter-enriched soil need water only when the surface inch begins to dry to the touch.

- Apply 1/2 to 3/4 inch water each irrigation.
- Water during the early-morning hours.
- Consider using microsprinklers to put the water where it is needed.

Two or more sprinklers may be needed for large trees.

- Do not run sprinklers during freezing conditions. Do make sure the soil is moist before freezing weather arrives.

FERTILIZING

Delay fertilizer applications for another month or two. Citrus trees are usually dormant at this time of the year and are not using available nutrients. You could select a fertilizer and have it ready when citrus feeding time arrives, especially if

QUICK CONTROL OF WINTER DAMAGE

Home gardeners are much luckier than grove owners. They can wait until the cold warnings are sounded to protect their trees from possible freezes. Most citrus trees are quite cold resistant until the temperatures drop down into the upper 20s Fahrenheit. Then some protection is needed. Only **lemons** and **limes** will need protection when temperature is expected to drop to 30 degrees. Just a mound of soil may be all that is needed to protect the budded area of the tree and lower trunk. The soil provides insulation that prevents the cold from reaching the trunk.

• Use any available soil in the landscape.

• Form a foot-high or higher mound around the base of the tree.

• Create the mound a day or two before the cold if possible.

• Leave the mound in place until all threats of cold are over.

Unfortunately, mounds of soil do not protect upper portions of the tree. Any part of the tree could be damaged. But if you protect the base where the graft union is located, a damaged tree can regrow limbs of the desirable variety so you won't have to plant another tree.

garden centers are offering a bargain. A number of products are available.

• Most gardeners look for a standard citrus fertilizer with all major nutrients as well as the minor nutrients (also called trace elements).

• A 6-6-6 that contains minor nutrients can be substituted.

• New products containing slow-release fertilizer are also available. Follow label recommendations.

• Gardeners can also use fertilizer spikes available at garden centers. Follow label instructions as to the number needed per tree.

PROBLEMS

Citrus have very few pests that attack during the cooler weather. To avoid root rot and foot rot problems, make sure you are not overwatering the trees. It's better to underwater a little than keep the trees too wet. You may notice a number of pests already on the trees, perhaps leaf spots and scale insects. Make a note and apply a control at the proper time later in the year.

Protect vulnerable lemon and lime trees from freezes by piling a foot-high mound of soil at the base.

FEBRUARY

CITRUS

PLANNING

In early spring, citrus trees are very susceptible to the cold. Plan to provide winter protection early in the month, although trees may bloom before the end of the month.

When planning, select varieties that fruit at different times of the year. By carefully selecting the trees, you can harvest citrus fruit September through June.

• Pick a tree that ripens early like the 'Ambersweet', 'Satsuma', or 'Hamlin'. These can be eaten fresh or used as juice.

• Next look for a midseason selection. Some are the **navels**, **tangelos**, and juice **oranges**.

• Add a **grapefruit** for a midseason to late-in-the-year fruit. They only get sweeter as the season progresses.

• Your late-season orange is the 'Valencia'. Several selections are available that can still be producing fruits in June, and there are many varieties that ripen during midseason. Plant only a favorite or two—otherwise, you may find yourself with too many fruits at one time.

PLANTING

If daytime temperatures reach the 70s Fahrenheit and nights are above freezing, you can plant. Begin transplanting citrus trees from containers to the landscape. There is still a little frost risk, so you may have to provide protection in colder locations.

1. Select an appropriate site.
2. Open a hole that is larger but no deeper than the rootball.
3. Position the tree so the top of the rootball is at or slightly above the soil line.
4. Fill in around the rootball with soil and water.
5. Build a 3- to 4-inch berm of soil around the edge of the rootball.
6. Do not add mulch, but fill the berm with water.

CARE

Prune before trees jump into spring growth. There is no need to let the tree produce lots of flowers and new shoots during the spring months that might only be pruned off later in the year.

• Remove limbs that may be in the way of maintenance.

• Reshape trees as needed to keep them in-bounds.

• Lower tree height if needed. Most citrus trees give best production when allowed to grow 12 feet or taller.

• Remove shoots, often called suckers, arising from below the graft.

• Shorten limbs that may be overloaded with fruits and susceptible to breakage.

WATERING

Keep up a steady watering program. Citrus trees are drought tolerant but need adequate water to produce fruits. As trees begin to flower and form new shoots, it's an important time to make sure the soil is moist.

• Most trees need an inch of water per week.

• Keep track of rainfall and provide extra water when the soil starts to dry.

• Apply 1/2 to 3/4 inch water each irrigation.

FERTILIZING

Trees coming into growth are ready for a feeding. In the warmer locations, this could be by the end of the month. There is no rush to feed the trees, however. The first feeding can be delayed until March. Newer cit-

It's time to fertilize citrus trees. Determine the amount by measuing the circumference of the tree.

rus feeding programs developed by the University of Florida feed the established trees more frequently but at a lower rate per application.

• Measure the tree circumference 6 inches above the ground.

• Use 1/4 pound fertilizer for each inch of the circumference.

• Spread the fertilizer under the tree and out past the dripline.

• Water to begin moving the nutrients into the soil

CITRUS DOES NOT RIPEN OFF THE TREE

Florida growers often make the claim their fruits are tree ripened. That's because the taste does not improve once the fruit is picked from the trees. Leave your fruit on the tree until you are ready to use it in the home.

Most citrus fruits can be stored on the trees for an extended period of time. Actually, the flavor usually improves as the sugar content increases and the acidity drops. By leaving some fruits on the tree you can have **grapefruits** November through May and **Valencia oranges** into June.

• Give citrus fruits a little twist as they are harvested. Invert the fruit and pull it down to prevent tearing the rind that could cause more rapid deterioration.

• Do not wash the fruits until they are ready for use. Removing the natural wax on the skin causes them to dry more rapidly.

• Do not gather a fruit that has fallen to the ground. It may already have started to deteriorate.

PROBLEMS

As new growth begins, you will likely notice aphids feeding in the new shoots. They affect only the young leaves and can cause them to curl. Control is often applied to new trees which have aphid problems, while aphid damage in older trees is often ignored. You may find ladybird beetles and lacewings giving good control of aphids in citrus trees. Where needed, a soap spray usually gives good aphid control.

MARCH

CITRUS

PLANNING

Which **grapefruit** should you plant? **Grapefruits** come in many colors, sizes and flavors, so experiment to determine which variety your family will like best.

PLANTING

Now is a great time to move a container-grown citrus tree to the landscape. Here's how:

• Keep the trees at least 10 to 15 feet from the home or another building.

• Do not plant citrus trees over septic systems, as the roots could clog drain fields.

• Set the tree in the ground at the same depth it was in the container.

Planting deeper can lead to trunk and root rot problems.

• Create a 4- to 6-inch berm of soil at the edge of the rootball.

• Do not add mulch.

New trees require frequent watering. Citrus is very drought tolerant, but young trees have a limited root system. Keep the soil moist to encourage new root growth into the surrounding soil. The new tree gets its first feeding four to six weeks after planting.

CARE

Native Floridians wouldn't touch a **grapefruit** until around March when the fruits really get sweet. The sugars have been increasing during the fall and winter months, and the acidity has been dropping. Harvest your **grapefruit** now.

Trim lower limbs as needed, and cut away shoots arising from below the graft. The graft union is easy to see: look for a change in bark characteristics within 6 inches of the ground. You may see a bulge, the remains of a wound, or just a color change to indicate where the tree was budded. Any shoots coming from below the graft will grow shoots that compete with the desirable variety and bear inferior-tasting fruits.

If March winds bend a new tree, add a stake. Here is the hard part: it's usually recommended that the first fruits on new trees be removed for two to three years. The tree is not large enough to support a crop, and keeping the fruits delays limb development.

WATERING

Citrus trees need frequent watering during the drier months. This is an important time of year as the crop begins to form. A tree starved for water many drop many of the potential fruits and be more susceptible to pests. New trees get more frequenting watering. Water daily the first few weeks or more as needed to keep a moist soil. Make sure the water wets the rootball.

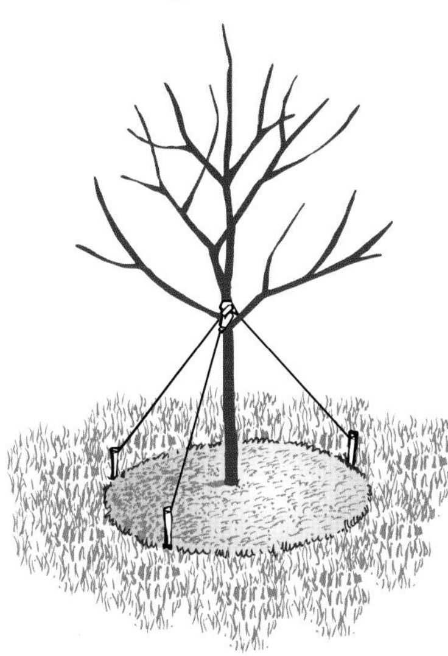

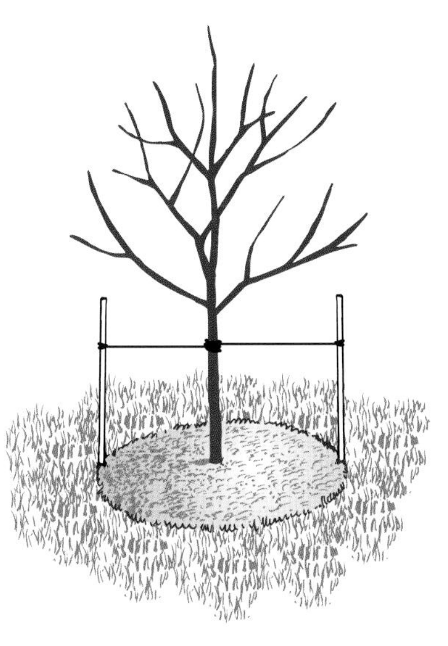

Staking may be necessary for some citrus trees.

WHAT IS A ROOTSTOCK?

The rootstock consists of the roots and a little bit of trunk that is within 6 inches of the ground. A desirable citrus variety is grafted onto this root portion. It's a very important portion of the tree and is selected for a number of different reasons:

- Rootstocks often affect the vigor and fruit quality of a tree.
- Some root systems grow better in different soils.
- A specific rootstock can help increase winter hardiness.
- Rootstocks can affect drought tolerance.
- Different rootstocks offer resistance to various pests.

You may find more choice of rootstocks if you visit a citrus tree nursery to make a purchase.

FERTILIZING

If you are feeding your trees this month, you are on schedule. The trees won't get upset or starve if you are a few weeks or a month off the feeding program. But for good production, it's important that the trees have fertilizer for growth and for the formation of fruits.

With older trees, follow a program of fertilizing lightly about four times a year. The months of March, May, August, and early October are best. Don't get upset if you miss a feeding or are a little off schedule. Young trees are given more-frequent feedings but at a very light rate.

- Give new trees the first feeding four to six weeks after a spring planting, using about $1/2$ pound citrus fertilizer.
- Make additional feedings at six- to eight-week intervals, March through early September, starting with a 1-pound rate per tree.
- Continue the above schedule for the first three years of growth in your yard. Gradually increase the rate to four pounds per feeding by the end of three years.
- Scatter the fertilizer under the spread of the trees and out past the dripline.
- Water after feeding to move the nutrients into the ground.
- After three years, place the young citrus on an established tree-feeding schedule.

PROBLEMS

Some citrus trees have problems with scab, a fungal disease. It may be noted on a number of the hybrids, the **lemons** and the **grapefruits**. It attacks new fruit and foliage, causing a growth. It is mainly a cosmetic problem, but when severe it can lead to fruit drop. Many gardeners just ignore the minor damage often caused to the trees. Where needed, apply a copper-containing fungicide as new leaves begin to open and fruits just start to form. Repeat sprays may be needed to fully protect new foliage forming during the growing season.

Gardeners are sure to notice aphids and some citrus leaf miner damage at this time of the year. Both can cause contorted leaves but are usually ignored. Where needed, controls can be applied to the trees. Also look for sooty mold and the first hint of scale and whitefly infestations. Apply controls as needed.

APRIL

CITRUS

PLANNING

If you live in an urban setting or a colder location, plan to grow citrus in a container. Kept in a large pot, the plant can be moved to a warmer spot when frost threatens.

Even if the temperature drops only a little below 32 degrees Fahrenheit, **lemons** and **limes** may suffer. So even residents living in Central Florida may want to consider a container planting.

Container-grown citrus trees add shade, beauty, and fun to patios and walkways, as well as balconies or rooftop garden areas.

- Give container-grown trees an open area to fully develop.
- Make sure they receive six to eight hours of full sun.
- Use the trees as shade for shrubs, flowers, and ground covers that need shade.
- Pick the fresh fruit to eat fresh or turn into juice.
- Use a tree that has attractive flowers and fruits as an accent.

PLANTING

For citrus, choose well drained containers such as half-barrels, tubs, large pots, or wooden boxes. Your container should hold at least 15 to 30 gallons of soil and be easy to move with a handcart or dolly, or be on wheels. Check the drain holes to ensure they will remain clog-free. Add extra holes if needed. Then choose the right spot for your new tree.

- Obtain a loose potting soil and fill the container about half full.
- Slip the tree out of the nursery pot and position it in the container so the top of the rootball is 1 to 2 inches below the rim.
- Fill in around the rootball with additional potting soil and water.
- If you wish, a slow-release citrus fertilizer can be added to the top of the soil in the container. Follow label instructions. If a surface fertilizer is not used, apply a liquid fertilizer every other week from March through October. No fertilizer is needed during the colder weather. If winters remain warm and the trees appear to need fertilizer, a monthly liquid feeding may be applied.

CARE

Older trees usually need very little pruning in April. Remove dead limbs and shoots growing out-of-bounds. Major pruning will limit fruit production.

If you have a small space, you can still grow many types of citrus in containers.

If young trees under three years of age are holding fruits, remove them. Leave one or two fruits to make sure you have the right variety.

Check young trees for growth from below the graft. When present, the growths should be removed. New shoots can usually be rubbed off with your fingers.

WATERING

New trees need a daily watering for the first few weeks. Then water as needed to maintain a moist soil. Fill the berm of soil forming the basin around the tree to thoroughly wet the soil.

Older trees need water when the surface inch of soil begins to dry. Most should be watered once or twice a week at this time of the year.

Check container plantings for water needs daily. They are going to dry much faster than trees in the ground due to the limited amount of soil for root growth.

FERTILIZING

Feed container plantings and new trees. Older established trees should have been fed in March or February. If not, apply a light application now, then resume the normal feeding schedule in May.

- Feed container plantings every other week with a liquid fertilizer solution, or use a slow-release product as instructed on the label.
- New in-ground plantings are fed every six to eight weeks with a citrus fertilizer. Rates are gradually increased from 1 pound per tree per feeding for new trees to 4 pounds per tree per feeding for trees near the end of the three-year establishment schedule.

PROBLEMS

Perhaps you have noticed leaves that are misshapen and contorted. This is the work of the citrus leaf miner. The insect is active when trees of any age are producing new growth. It tunnels between the layer of the leaves; at one time, it was thought this insect damage could be devastating. But citrus leaf miner damage does not seem to significantly affect fruit production. Although most gardeners ignore the damage, new leaves under 1 inch long can be treated with an oil spray to help control this pest if desired.

Other active pest problems this month include aphids, citrus scab, scale insects, whitefly, and mites. Luckily, most trees can tolerate these pests. Where severe, apply controls.

CITRUS TREES GROWN FROM SEED

Citrus trees grown from seed tend to be larger and thornier than the parent tree, and take eight to nine years to bear the first fruit. You have about a 75 percent chance of getting a tree that produces fruit just like the one you remember eating. Even so, it is just fun to grow a tree from seed.

- Save the larger seeds and let them air-dry for a day or two in a shady spot.
- Plant several of the seeds in a 4- to 6-inch container. Fill as many containers as you wish.
- Cover the seeds with a layer of soil equal to the thickness of the seed, and moisten.
- Keep the container in a sunny location and keep the soil moist. Germination should occur in a few weeks.
- Pinch out all but the strongest citrus shoots.
- Keep the soil moist, transplant as needed, and feed with a liquid 20-20-20 fertilizer solution.

CITRUS

PLANNING

Now is the time to consider new plantings. For a late-spring harvest of **oranges**, plan to select 'Valencia' or related varieties. Most garden centers market a selection of the 'Valencia' that provides spring production if you store the fruits on the tree. You can also look for the variety 'Lue Gim Gong', said to be a seedling of the 'Valencia', and the 'Pope Summer', similar in appearance to the 'Valencia'.

Other fruits that could be in production at this time include the **calamondin**, **Key lime**, **kumquat**, **limequat**, and **Ponderosa lemon**. Some are cold-sensitive citrus and best grown in containers in central and northern portions of the state.

PLANTING

With the start of the rainy season, the soil will be moist and require little watering. Planting citrus trees is easy:

1. Open a hole in a well-drained soil. Remember, citrus trees do not like wet feet. Make sure there is about 4 feet of well-drained soil to contain the roots.
2. Do not add organic matter to the fill soil or planting site. Most rootstocks have adapted to the Florida sands.
3. Add water and existing soil to fill in around the root system.

Make sure the top of the rootball is even with the surface of the soil. Do not add mulch.

You have to be the judge when watering new trees. For the first few weeks a daily watering is probably best. Then water as needed to keep the soil moist.

CARE

Extra-long shoots can be tipped back during early summer. Seldom do citrus trees need major pruning. They usually grow well rounded, even with no pruning at all.

Most gardeners practice clean cultivation at the base of their trees, keep soil bare from the trunk to the dripline. This makes care easier and prevents disease.

- Areas under the citrus trees can be kept free of weeds and other vegetation by hand removal or by the use of herbicides which are safe for use under citrus. Follow label instructions.
- Remove at least a foot or more of vegetation surrounding the trunk to help reduce foot rot, a fungal disease.

Many gardeners find clean cultivation makes it easier to maintain the trees. You don't have to be worried with limbs during mowing, and you can just toss fertilizer on the bare ground without fear of burning turf.

Kumquat

WATERING

Until the rainy season returns you have to do the watering for in-ground plantings. Most trees need a watering once or twice a week at this time of the year.

FERTILIZING

According to the University of Florida schedule, May is feeding time. This approach keeps fertilizer available to the tree throughout the growing season. Measure the trunk circumference 6 inches above the ground. Weigh out $1/4$ pound of a standard citrus fertilizer for each inch of trunk circumference. Scatter the fertilizer under the tree and out past the dripline. You can use fertilizer sticks or slow-release products as substitute feeding methods, following the label instructions.

PROBLEMS

Foot rot is a devastating disease caused by a fungus which damages the base of the trunk near the ground. The fungus causes the tissue near the ground to die and the bark to peel off. Symptoms of decline include loss of leaves and sometimes out-of-season flowering. Just look near the ground line around the trunk to spot the disease. Unfortunately, most gardeners notice foot rot too late and a new tree has to be added. Prevention is the best cure.

Check for whiteflies on the undersides of the leaves, caterpillars, grasshoppers, aphids, citrus leaf-miner, and scab. Most are not that damaging and a control is seldom applied. If necessary, control with an oil spray in June or July.

BUDDING IS EASY

Some gardeners talk about making a cocktail tree, a citrus tree which bears more than one variety of fruit. The technique of adding a new variety to any tree is called budding. Budding is easy, but takes a little practice.

- Budding can be performed at any time of the year but is most successful when new growth is occurring.
- Locate a tree with a desirable variety and remove a stem with buds present. A bud is present at the base of each citrus leaf where it attaches to the stem.
- Remove the bud and insert it into a small stem on the tree where you want the new variety.
- Wrap the bud with a plastic strip to hold it in place. Remove the plastic strip in three to four weeks and wait for the bud to grow. You can cut off the limb above the bud to force out growth.

JUNE

CITRUS

PLANNING

Don't be surprised if you see a citrus tree open a few blooms in June. A June bloom is normal but not desirable because the fruits are often atypical. A June bloom often comes after a cold winter damages spring blooms—so the tree uses its energy to produce a few more buds.

Which citrus trees are missing from your landscape? Give consideration to adding **mandarins** and hybrids. The term **mandarin** is often used to describe any fruit with a loose skin, or one that is easy to peel. It includes the **tangerines**, **tangelos**, and related fruits. There are many reasons you might want to add a few of these fruit trees to your landscape:

- The fruits are easy to eat. Many divide easily into sections.
- Most have a taste that is unique, differing from that of **oranges** and **grapefruits**.
- They are usually good producers.
- This group has many varieties that are cold tolerant.
- The juice of these fruits may be used alone or added to blends.
- Some produce early when other citrus is not available.
- Many produce in midseason and provide great gift fruits.

Mandarin

PLANTING

It's not too late to add any citrus tree to your yard. In fact, the rainy season may help with watering. Garden centers reduce inventory for the summer, so check with local citrus nurseries for a complete selection.

Citrus needs good drainage, so check for well-drained soil as the rains return. Here are some tips for drainage problems:

- Transplant new trees to a better-drained site.
- Use raised beds built a foot or more above the ground to ensure good drainage.
- Consider growing citrus trees in containers.

CARE

Some fruits drop at this time of the year. It's normal, as the tree regulates what it can support. There are three major fruit drops. One occurs immediately after flowering, another in June, and one more in September. Don't be concerned, as the tree is just thinning the crop so it can mature

what is left on the tree. Check your care program to make sure the trees have adequate water and fertilizer to support the fruits.

Some limbs may be overloaded with fruit. This is often the case with **grapefruits** and **tangelos**. They can get so heavy that the limbs crack. If you notice overloaded limbs, you can thin out the fruits or prepare props to hold them up.

Keep the weeds out from under the trees. As the rainy season returns, the weeds can grow out of control. Hand remove or spot-kill with an appropriate herbicide as needed.

WATERING

Take a break from your normal watering schedule with in-ground plantings. Mother Nature will probably do the watering for you. If a week passes without significant rainfall, be ready to turn on the irrigation system.

- Measure rainfall in a rain gauge, and record the daily accumulations.
- If you do not get an inch of water a week during the summer, check the soil under the trees for adequate moisture.
- Apply 1/2 to 3/4 inch of water whenever the surface inch of soil begins to dry.
- Trees in containers are likely to need daily waterings. When the surface soil dries to the touch, give the soil a good soaking.

FERTILIZING

If you missed the May feeding, you are not too late to make a fertilizer application. Just apply the light feeding as recommended by the University of Florida. You have two additional feedings to apply this year, one in August and one in early October.

Trees in containers can receive a slow-release fertilizer application following the product's label, or a liquid feeding twice a month. Use a 20-20-20 fertilizer solution or similar product mixed according to the label instructions.

PROBLEMS

Some gardeners are bound to notice a browning on the surface of their fruits. It's usually on the side facing the sun and resembles a burn. This is rust mite damage caused by the arachnids feeding on the surface of the fruits. June is one time of the year you can clean up this and other insect problems if needed. There is no need to apply the oil spray unless scale insects, whitefly, leaf miner, or similar pests are causing major damage to the trees. The oil will also help control a disease called greasy spot.

- Use oil sprays available from garden centers and labeled for use with citrus. Some may also contain a synthetic insecticide.
- Make sure the trees have adequate water at the time of spraying.
- Note the maximum temperature at which an oil spray can be applied. Usually it must be below 85 degrees Fahrenheit.
- Follow all label instructions.

POLLINATION OF HYBRIDS

Sometimes it pays to plant trees of different varieties. The **tangelos**, some **tangerines**, and related hybrids often need a different citrus variety as a pollinator in order to produce a good crop. These are called self-incompatible varieties. Examples include the 'Orlando', 'Sunburst', 'Page', 'Nova', 'Osceola', 'Robinson', and 'Minneola' varieties. Planting two of these different types can usually provide all the cross-pollination that is needed.

Some other good pollen-supplying trees include the 'Lee', 'Fallglo', and 'Temple' varieties.

PLANNING

Plan where you'll plant **lemon** and **lime** trees for homemade lemonade or limeade during the hot summer season. It's not too late to add them now. **Lemons** and **limes** are the least-hardy trees, but they are usually smaller in size and can be used in spots where other citrus might not fit.

- Add a **lemon** or **lime** tree to a warm patio.
- Use them in a courtyard where they might get warmth from the house.
- Grow one of the more-tender selections in a container that might be moved in when the cold warnings are sounded.
- In the warm locations of South Florida, citrus can be planted in any landscape where a tree is needed.

Within the acid-type citrus group are a number of interesting varieties. Try some of the fruits from a friend's yard, a roadside produce stand, or grocery store Don't go overboard with the plantings. After all, how many **lemons** can you use? And speaking of **lemons**, there are a number of varieties. Gardeners can pick from the 'Avon', 'Bearss', 'Eureka', 'Havey', 'Lisbon', and 'Villafranca' selections. Fruits of the **Ponderosa lemon** and **Meyer lemon** are not true **lemons**, but their fruit may be used in a similar manner.

Limes are also fun to grow, but again, one tree normally supplies all you need. The **Key lime**, which produces small fruit, is a favorite. Who can turn down Key lime pie? The **Tahiti lime**, also known as the **Persian lime**, is ideal for juice and is grown commercially in South Florida. **Limes** are very cold sensitive and need protection from Central Florida northward.

PLANTING

Continue planting all the container-grown citrus trees at this time of the year. They are easy to add to the landscape, following good planting procedures. Just remember, citrus trees need lots of sun.

- Find a spot that receives a full day of sun. Any less will reduce fruit production.
- Locate trees 15 to 20 feet from buildings or other trees.
- Keep the trees away from septic systems and sidewalks.
- Trees may be added to a trellis or trimmed to shapes, but this limits fruit production.
- It's best to add irrigation at planting time. Soaker hoses or microsprinklers can be used to meet water needs during the drier seasons.

Trim off damaged branches, suckers, and limbs that interfere with mowing.

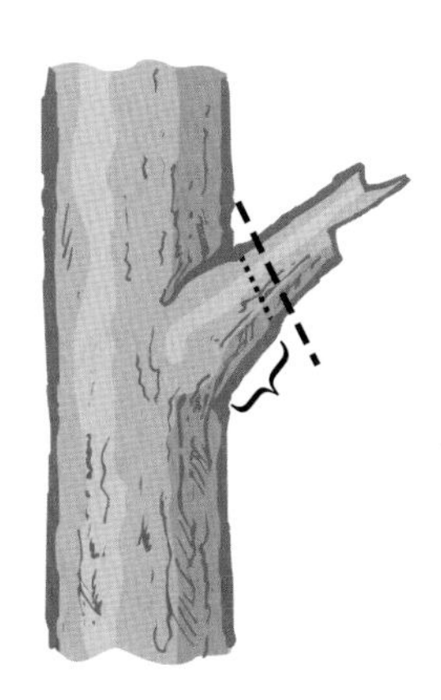

CARE

Get the props ready for heavy-bearing citrus trees. Sometimes gardeners cannot pick enough of the extra fruits to lighten the load. If the limbs have already started to crack under the weight, you may have to do some trimming.

1. Remove limbs damaged by heavy fruiting.
2. Trim off limbs damaged during storms.
3. Remove limbs interfering with mowing and traffic flow through the landscape.
4. Break or cut off suckers growing from below the graft.
5. Cut back the ends of limbs growing out-of-bounds. Every so often you get a shoot that is out of control. It can be cut back as needed.

CONTROL YOUR SOIL pH

University studies show increasing the soil pH to around 7 improves citrus fruit production. Test pH every few years, and make soil adjustments according to the test results.

- Test kits are often available at garden centers. Some garden centers offer the test for a small fee as a service to their customers. Tests results can also be obtained through your local Extension Service office.
- To test your pH level, gather a pint sample of soil from under the citrus trees. Include soil from the surface to a depth of 4 to 6 inches. It's best if you mix several smaller samples together to form a composite sample for the test.
- Follow test results to adjust the soil acidity if needed. In Florida, lime is used to raise the pH and soil sulfur to lower the pH. Follow label instructions.
- Water after the supplements are added. Retest treated sites in four to six months to determine if more adjustments are needed.

Sooty mold is a black substance often seen on citrus foliage. Though it looks scary, the fungus itself is not harmful. Sometimes it can indicate that your tree also has a piercing sucking insect infestation, such as scale, mealybugs, or whitefly. If the infestation is not serious, these insects can be ignored. In the case of a serious infestation, apply an oil spray according to label instructions.

WATERING

With the frequent summer rain, there should be little need for watering. Test the sprinkler system periodically, and check for grass and limbs that might prevent sprinkler heads from popping up. Make sure soaker hoses are intact and working properly.

Check trees in containers for water needs. They may not be able to utilize as much rainfall as trees planted in the ground. If the surface soil is moist to the touch, they probably have adequate moisture.

FERTILIZING

Only trees in containers need a July feeding. Check the schedules of slow-release citrus fertilizer and fertilizer sticks for application times. Otherwise, keep up the normal feeding schedule, applying a fertilizer solution to container plantings about twice a month.

PROBLEMS

If you notice rounded brown spots in the top of your citrus fruits, watch for birds that peck at the fruits. The damage is usually minimal, and the fruits continue to ripen.

AUGUST

CITRUS

PLANNING

It's hot outside, and few gardeners are adding trees to their landscape. But if you are a new homeowner, start planning for citrus. Draw a planting plan, and make sure you have room for all the trees you might like. Remember, some citrus trees grow up to 30 feet tall and 30 feet wide.

- Plan for trees along the sides of your property. They create a good view barrier when spaced appropriately, 15 to 25 feet apart.
- Add a citrus tree near the vegetable garden for easy picking.
- Grow a tree near the patio as an accent. Use a smaller variety if you don't have a lot of room.
- Plant a citrus tree in a container to place in a courtyard or on the patio.

PLANTING

Planting time is anytime you find the citrus variety you like. Don't forget to make a 4- to 6-inch berm of soil at the base of the tree. This helps hold water and directs moisture down through the rootball and out into the surrounding soil. Give your trees a good start:

- Make sure the tree is watered daily for the first few weeks to keep the rootball moist. Then water when the surface soil begins to dry to the touch.
- Do not add fertilizer when planting your citrus tree. Apply the first feeding four to six weeks after the tree is planted. Then follow a regular feeding program for young trees.
- Make sure the tree has good drainage. They love the sandy soils that drain water away quickly. Too much water can rot the roots and slow growth.
- Check the light level. To grow well, citrus trees need full sun and no competition from nearby plants.

If after a year your citrus is still nearly the same size, consider lifting and resetting the tree. You may need to select a new location.

CARE

Control the weeds under your trees by hand pulling, hoeing, or herbicides for spot control. Be sure to follow label instructions. Remove limbs that might be in the way of maintenance and foot traffic within the landscape. Support young limbs that are loaded with fruits to prevent breaking. Removing fruit from trees under three years of age will encourage faster growth.

Sometimes micronutrients are missing from your soil and must be added.

WATERING

August can be one of the wettest months, but keep alert for dry spells. If several days pass without rain, you have to supply the needed moisture. As we approach ripening time, trees need evenly applied moisture. Run your sprinklers manually and only as needed. Too much water is as bad as not enough water and can lead to poor-quality fruits.

FERTILIZING

The University of Florida schedule calls for an August feeding to keep the tree fertilized throughout the growing season.

• Measure the trunk circumference 6 inches above the ground. Note this is not the diameter, which often used for other tree measurements.

• Weigh out 1/4 pound of a standard citrus fertilizer for each inch of trunk circumference.

• Scatter the fertilizer under the spread of the tree and out past the dripline.

Other fertilizer techniques can also be utilized. Gardeners may use fertilizer sticks or a slow-release product as a substitute feeding method. Be sure to follow label instructions.

NUTRITIONAL SPRAYS

Sometimes certain minor nutrients are missing from the soil, or an improper pH level prevents the tree from absorbing these nutrients. If leaves turn yellow in spite of good feedings, you may have a minor-nutrient deficiency. Eliminate the possibility of disease by checking for trunk damage. If the tree looks healthy otherwise, a minor-nutrient spray may help.

• Obtain the minor-nutrient or trace-element spray at a local garden center.

Some are applied to the soil and others are sprayed on the foliage. Follow label instructions.

• One treatment should help regreen a portion of the leaves or prevent further decline in new growths.

If no benefit from the nutritional spray is noted, some other problem is likely to be the cause of the decline.

• If the tree improves after one nutrient treatment, an additional treatment may be beneficial if you think you have problem soils.

PROBLEMS

Grasshoppers, katydids, and caterpillars leave noticeable holes in citrus tree foliage. The damaged leaves are generally only of concern on small or unhealthy trees. Try to determine which insect is causing the problem. Often these pests can simply be handpicked and destroyed.

But wait! Consider leaving the caterpillars alone. The orange dog caterpillar will become a swallowtail butterfly. This caterpillar looks like a bird dropping with a red sensing device and is harmless to humans. If an orange dog caterpillar is damaging the foliage of a small tree, maybe you could find it a spot to complete its life cycle on a larger tree.

Most insects and leaf diseases can be spotted on the trees in your landscape at any time. Unless they are causing major decline, spraying is usually unnecessary. If you do find it necessary to use a pesticide spray, use only the low-toxicity products which are safe to use on citrus trees.

SEPTEMBER

CITRUS

PLANNING

What is your favorite type of citrus? Most gardeners choose the **navel orange**, but when it come to commercial juice production, other varieties are more popular. **Navel orange** trees have a bitter component called limonin that flavors the juice and makes the fruit less enticing to processors.

Orange

You will probably want a **navel orange** tree or two for fresh eating, but there are a number of better juice varieties. Choose juice varieties that produce an early-, mid-, or late- season harvest. The most popular for early to midseason is the 'Hamlin', but some of the newer varieties like 'Gardeners' and 'Midsweet' are excellent. 'Valencia', a longtime standard, is by far the year-end favorite.

• If you live in a colder location, plant a majority of early to midseason varieties. These can produce a harvest before a freeze. Trees holding fruits are more susceptible to the cold.

• Plan enough different types to have juice from October to June.

• Give citrus trees plenty of room to grow. Most **orange** trees grow to 30 feet tall and 30 feet wide.

If you have never grown **oranges** before, you will really enjoy sampling the fruit as different varieties begin bearing. Taste-test the **oranges** over a period of a few months because the flavor improves with the season.

PLANTING

It's never too late to add a citrus tree. There is only one thing to keep in mind. The later in the year the tree is planted, the more attention must be paid to cold protection. Use good planting practices when putting the tree in the ground.

• Open a hole that is wider but no deeper than the rootball.

• Save the fill soil, but there is no need to add organic matter.

• Position the tree so the top of the rootball is level with the ground.

• Fill in around the rootball with water and soil.

• Build a 4- to 6-inch berm of soil around the edge of the rootball and water.

Do not add a mulch.

CARE

Fall care is rather easy. Inspect the fruits and overall condition of the tree. Here are a few chores to perform at this time:

• Prop up limbs overladen with fruits to avoid limb breakage. If needed, some fruits can be removed and added to the compost pile.

• Control weeds under the spread of the trees. Where needed, pulling or light hoeing is best at this time.

• Trim back any ornamental plants that may be affecting the citrus tree growth, including vines attempting to climb the trunk.

• Remove limbs arising from below the graft.

• Cut back any citrus tree limbs that have grown out-of-bounds. Remove any dead wood found in the tree.

WATERING

The rainy season should continue into the early days of September. But by the end of the month, you will probably be doing the watering. Sometimes gardeners notice a lot of fruit splitting at this time of the year. This is usually due to uneven watering or a sudden overabundance of water as the fruits start to mature. Young trees are likely to split fruits more than older trees. Good watering practices can help prevent the splitting and fruit drop often found at this time of the year.

• Water when the surface of the soil feels dry to the touch. Don't water every day or on a schedule.

• Most trees will need water once or twice a week at this time of the year depending on rains and daily temperatures.

• When water is needed, apply 1/2 to 3/4 inch water each irrigation.

• Apply the water during the early-morning hours.

• Where possible, use soaker hoses or microsprinkler irrigation systems.

FERTILIZING

You have two fertilizing choices at this time of the year. Either apply the fertilizer toward the end of the month or wait until early October. If you live in a northern area of Florida, September is best for the final feeding of the year. Ideally, citrus trees should be dormant as they enter late fall. An October feeding may result in some late-season growth. The following are three feeding options available at garden centers:

1. Use a standard citrus fertilizer or 6-6-6 with minor nutrients.
2. Select a slow-release fertilizer and follow label instructions.
3. Add fertilizer sticks or spikes to the ground. Use the number and technique recommended on the label.

After each feeding, be sure to water the trees to begin moving the nutrients into the root zone.

PROBLEMS

You may notice more blemishes on your citrus fruit now that it is late in the season. Don't worry if you find peck marks from birds, rust mite damage, melanose, and citrus leaf miner damage. These pests will only affect the appearance of the fruit and not the flavor. It's too late in the season to apply a chemical control. If your citrus trees have a severe pest problem, mark it on your calendar and use pest controls earlier next year.

Mites can become active on the foliage as we head into the drier months. Mites will cause the leaves to curl up from each side, turn yellow, and drop from the trees. You may apply a soap spray as needed.

OCTOBER

CITRUS

PLANNING

Fall has arrived and it's time to harvest. 'Satsuma', 'Ambersweet', **navels**, 'Hamlin', 'Fallglo', 'Robinson', and 'Osceola' varieties may be ripening. The real question is: how do you tell when a citrus fruit is ripe? Do you tell by the color, or is there some other special way?

- Note the general ripening season for your zone. (Remember that ripening can occur a few weeks earlier or later.)
- The fruit's color is just a hint of its ripeness. Some fruits remain quite green even though they are ready to eat. Others may turn orange as they ripen and then change back to green.
- Use the taste test as the final determination of when the fruits are ripe. It does not hurt to eat an immature fruit, but it may not be very tasty.
- Do not pick fruits off the ground to eat. Bacteria or even insects may have entered these fruits to cause spoilage.
- Don't be in a hurry to eat all the fruits early. Leave some on the tree to continue to mature. They are usually the sweetest at the end of their ripening time.

PLANTING

Now make a taste test and determine which of the fruits you like best; add these to the landscape. If you want, a variety can be added to the landscape or kept in the container until late winter. If added now, you will have to provide winter protection in the colder climates. If kept in a container, the tree can be given good care and a warm location when freezing weather approaches.

- Give containerized trees a full-sun location.
- Check water needs daily.
- Water when the surface soil begins to dry to the touch. During the hotter weather they may need daily watering.
- Water until moisture runs out of the bottom of the container.
- Feed every other week with a 20-20-20 or use a slow-release fertilizer as instructed on the label. Discontinue all feedings during the winter weather.
- Plant the tree in the landscape when consistently warm spring weather returns.

CARE

Minimal care is needed at this time. There are always limbs that break during storms and dead wood that should be trimmed from the trees. Most major pruning is over, however, as the trees enter the dormant period of late fall and winter.

WATERING

Now we leave the rainy season and enter a much drier time of the year. Expect no more than 2 inches of rain this month. Often it comes all at once. You will have to do some watering in-between the storms. Keep track of the amount of rainfall each week and provide the rest needed through irrigation. Most trees will need water once or twice a week depending on the temperature and wind conditions. When watering, apply $^1/_2$ to $^3/_4$ inch each irrigation.

FERTILIZING

If you delayed the fall feeding until now, it's time to make a fertilizer application. Apply this feeding early in the month to pro-

vide needed nutrients before cooler weather arrives. The amount of fertilizer needed is determined by measuring the circumference of the tree trunk:

- Measure the trunk circumference 6 inches above the ground. Note this is not the diameter of the tree as is often used with tree measurements.
- Weigh out 1/4 pound of a standard citrus fertilizer for each inch of trunk circumference.
- Scatter the fertilizer under spread of the tree and out past the dripline.
- Water after feeding to begin moving the nutrients into the root zone.

Other fertilizer techniques can also be utilized to feed your tree. Gardeners may use fertilizer sticks or a slow-release product as a substitute feeding method. Follow label instructions.

PROBLEMS

For the most part, pest control time is over. You will see some aphids at work and maybe some grasshopper, caterpillar, and katydid holes in the leaves. But these can generally be ignored. Try not to apply sprays to your trees at this time of the year when you are starting to consume the fruits. If you do need a spray, use a natural product.

One pest that likes the fruits as much as you do is the roof rat. Your first sign of these pests is hollowed-out fruit on the tree. Roof rats seem to know when citrus is at its peak—just when you would like to do some picking too. If roof rats are feeding in your trees, some control may be needed.

- Harvest and use your fruits to deprive them of a feeding ground.
- Keep all garbage, dog food, and bird food out of the area to discourage the rats from entering your yard.
- Isolate your trees so rats cannot jump onto them, and apply rat guards to the trunks. The guards are made of sheet metal 18 to 24 inches high and fastened around the trunk so rats cannot climb the trees.
- Use trigger traps to catch the rats. Set the traps only during the evening hours so not to harm other animals. Some gardeners use "have-a-heart" traps, available at many hardware stores, to control the rat population.
- If you use poisoned bait, be sure it is in tamper-resistant feeding stations to protect children, pets, and other animals.

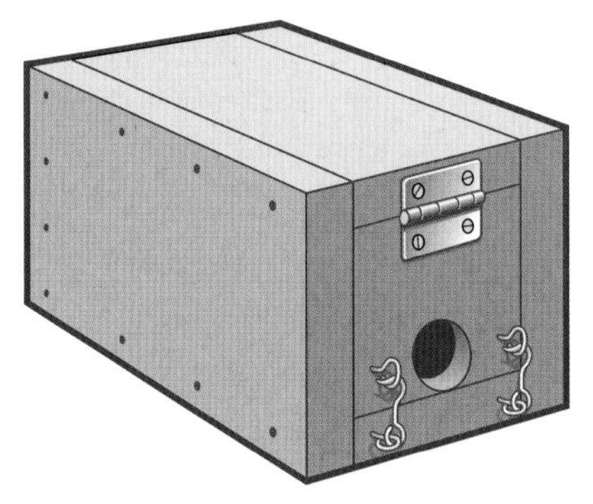

Construct tamper-proof poison bait boxes so only the pests can enter, not pets or children.

NOVEMBER

CITRUS

PLANNING

Many a grove has been planted with bare-root trees at this time of the year. You may find some citrus nurseries offering these plants for sale. A more modern trend is to market trees in citrus pots. These are long and narrow and provide the tree with a good root system. There is no problem adding trees to the landscape as the days grow cooler, but you will most likely have to provide some cold protection. This can be as simple as a mound of soil up over the graft union. Usually the mounds are made a foot high up the trunks.

In recent years growers have been encasing citrus trunks in foam coverings. These provide a few degrees of freeze protection and can include a microsprinkler to keep the trunk warm. Home gardeners can protect their tree trunks with an insulating wrap during the very cold weather. Again, this gives only a few degrees of freeze protection.

PLANTING

Bare-root trees are dug fresh from the nursery. They are 2 to 3 feet tall and very tough and durable. They have been grafted with the desirable variety on the best rootstock for your area.

- Open a hole larger than the root system but not much deeper.
- Create a mound of soil in the center of the hole and rest the bare-root plant on the mound. Spread the roots out over the mound and into the hole. Position the tree so that it is at the same depth it was in the nursery.
- Fill the hole with water and soil until level with the ground.
- Construct a 4- to 6-inch berm of soil around the edge of the hole, and fill with water.
- Do not add a mulch.

CARE

Citrus trees need minimal care at this time of the year. Your major job is harvesting the fruit needed in the home and to be shared with friends. Pull citrus from the trees by bending the fruit up and inverting it before giving it a little twist and pulling down. Try to pick most of the fruit by the end of the normal harvest season. Fruit left on the tree too long may decline in quality and encourage rats.

WATERING

Keep the citrus plantings moist by watering when the surface soil begins to dry. As the days get shorter and cooler, less water will be needed. Most plantings need water once or twice a week. Trees in containers need water whenever the surface soil first begins to dry. This may be daily during the hot weather. As the weather cools, watering every other day may be adequate.

FERTILIZING

Feeding is over for the year for in-ground plantings. Even container plantings may not need another feeding until late winter. If container-grown trees begin to yellow, a feeding can be applied. If the trees begin growth, they will need protection from winter cold.

PROBLEMS

Very few pests are active, but as you harvest the fruit you may find some residual insects and diseases from the growing season. Many fruits may have sooty mold. This is a fungus that lives on the excreta of some piercing sucking insects. Do not try to remove the sooty mold at this time. Wait until you harvest the fruits and wash it from the peel just before the fruits are used or shared with friends. Washing the fruits to remove the sooty mold can remove a protective waxy coating and cause the fruits to dry sooner.

VISIT THE FLORIDA CITRUS ARBORETUM

The best selection of citrus varieties in the world is found in Florida. A citrus arboretum is maintained by the Florida Department of Agriculture and Consumer Services in Winter Haven, Florida.

Established in 1975, the arboretum contains over 250 varieties of citrus and their relatives. The arboretum was established to make sure propagation material would always be available for the breeding and marketing of new trees.

The citrus arboretum is open to the public Monday through Friday, 9 a.m. to 4 p.m. Tours through the plantings are self-guided. The best time to observe the trees in fruit is November through March. The arboretum is located at 3027 Lake Alfred Road, Winter Haven, Florida, 33881-1438.

If fruits are hollow, a rat population is probably feeding in the tree. Harvest the fruit as soon as possible. When necessary, some gardeners control the rats with traps or poisoned bait. Be sure to take all precautions to protect people, pets, birds, and other animals in your landscape.

Leave fruits on the tree to mature as long as possible.

DECEMBER

CITRUS

PLANNING

Giving citrus fruit for Christmas is an old tradition, and if you planned ahead, you can pick it fresh from your trees. Plan to add trees you can harvest in December, such as the Dancy **tangerine**, **navel oranges**, **grapefruit**, and many others.

PLANTING

It's not too late to plant citrus trees. Consider the bare-root selections available from some nurseries. Remember, you may have to provide cold protection. Follow good planting procedures when adding any tree to the landscape.

CARE

Does cold weather make citrus fruit sweet? No, the cold can improve fruit color, but it does not add sweetness. Sweet flavor depends on temperatures during late-summer and fall as well as the amount of water the trees receives. So don't count on cold weather to add sugar.

To protect the trees from cold, mound soil at the base and wrap insulation around the trunks. Citrus growers use water to warm the trees, but this is not practical in home landscapes.

If you think a freeze is coming, leave the fruit on the tree. If it freezes, you still have several weeks to make juice or use the fruit before it deteriorates.

- The rule for fruit on the tree is to consider it edible if it looks, smells, and tastes good.
- Fruit that has been frozen will develop white spots on the membranes between the sections and should be used as soon as possible.
- Do not consume any fruit that has fallen to the ground.

WATERING

Keep the soil moist for all new plantings. Water when the surface of the ground begins to be dry to the touch. Plants in containers need similar watering. Most established trees can usually go up to a week without rain or watering at this time of the year.

FERTILIZING

All feedings are over until late February.

PROBLEMS

Very few pests are active except the roof rats. If you use traps or poisoned bait, take special precautions to protect family members, pets, birds, and other animals in the landscape. Check for pest problems as you harvest fruit, such as heavy scale insect buildup and foliage diseases. Mark your calendar to apply controls at the proper time.

CHAPTER FOUR

DECIDUOUS & TROPICAL FRUITS

You can really make your Florida landscape pay by adding fruiting trees, vines, and shrubs that can provide food for the table. It's easy to replace some or all of the ornamental plants in any design. Just look for fruiting plants with similar growth habits.

Consider how much room the plantings need to be productive. Most require adequate space for the limbs and shoots to branch out and absorb the sunlight. Leave extra room between the trees and shrubs. Give vines a trellis where they can spread out to obtain the needed light.

- Use trees to create shade, screen a view, block winds, and still bear a good crop.
- Create accents with fruiting plants so you can enjoy the flowers and colorful fruits.
- Plant fruits to attract wildlife to the yard.
- Create natural hedges and other space dividers with shrubs and small trees.
- Hide a wall or conceal a fence with vines.
- Create a ground cover with the rambling or lower-growing perennials.

CHAPTER FOUR

PLANNING

Determine what your family likes. Then, unless the plants have other features that make them good landscape additions, plan to plant only what your family is likely to use as food. You may select a fruiting tree, shrub, or vine just because it's a favorite even if it doesn't give very high yields. But to really make the additions worth the effort, most of the plantings should produce a bumper crop each year.

• Consider the hardiness and heat tolerance of the plants. Plants that grow only in the northern or central regions of the state probably cannot stand intense heat or extended periods of warm weather. Many have to have some cold. Others, limited to central and southern zones, are usually damaged by winter cold. These freeze-sensitive plants can be protected from cold or sometimes grown in containers and moved to a warm location.

• Take a look at the pest problems associated with the crop.

You may want to check out Extension Service bulletins to learn of special pests. Most have the common problems, but some have pests that need special sprays.

• Make sure you have the needed room. Don't cram the plants close together just because you want the fruits.

You may be better off selecting only one or two favorites and getting good production.

• Realize there may be pruning, thinning, and other chores needed. If you have only a limited amount of time, pick the plants that need the least amount of extra care. Take a good look at our fruiting plant list (pages 116 to 117). Note the harvest times and plan a year- round fruit planting. You don't want too much in production at one time of the year.

Most fruits have numerous varieties that can be planted to get production over the entire harvest time. Review some of your other plantings that may be providing food, including vegetables and citrus.

PLANTING

Normal planting procedures are used to set fruiting trees, shrubs, vines, and perennials into the ground. Actually, the work is probably a bit less than we perform for some of our ornamentals. A few have some special soil needs. Blueberries require a very acid pH of between 4.5 and 5.2, and figs usually grow best when plenty of organic matter is added to the soil. Most fruiting plants grow fine in any well-drained Florida soil. A good sandy soil found in most Florida landscapes seems to be quite satisfactory.

If the site is not immediately ready for your new plant, it can be grown for a while in the nursery container. Most want a full-sun location. You'll also have to check daily for water needs. Nursery-grown plants usually have enough fertilizer to last for a month or more. If the plants must be held longer, use either a liquid fertilizer or slow-release product to provide some nutrition. It is best if the wait is not too long and you can proceed with the plantings.

• Find a spot with the proper light level.

Check to make sure there is plenty of growing room and no overhead wires in the case of large trees.

• Dig a hole that is one to two times wider but no deeper than the rootball.

• Set the plant in the ground at or slightly above the ground line.

• Fill in around the rootball with water and soil. There is no need to work organic matter in the soil except for figs. Adjust the soil for blueberries to an acid pH if needed.

• Build a berm of soil 4 to 6 inches high around the edge of the rootball to hold water.

• Water the planting and add a mulch to the surface of the soil.

Some fruiting plants are received bare root, especially through mail-order sales. These

should be timed to arrive during the winter months so they can become established before hot spring weather. Planting is similar to that of container plants, except the roots are spread out over a mound of soil as the plant is positioned so it sets at the same level it grew in the nursery.

CARE

Some fruiting plants have very specific pruning needs. The yearly "as needed" trimming is usually performed to improve fruit production and keep the crop within reach. Get familiar with each crop to know the care needed to provide the best yields. Most major care is mentioned in the monthly care schedules.

It's suggested that some form of weed control be practiced. With trees, it may be keeping the weeds and grass away from the base by a foot or two. Shrubs, vines, and perennials may be clean-cultivated. With in-home landscapes, you can add a landscape fabric to prevent weeds. All can be mulched.

WATERING

Young plantings need a good start, and this includes plenty of water. For the first few weeks, water daily. Then gradually taper off the waterings, but keep the soil moist until the plantings are well established. Most fruiting plants are very drought tolerant. Deep-rooted types can go weeks without rain or irrigation. When water is lacking, however, the plantings may start to drop their fruits. It's best to provide water to all established fruits when the surface inch of soil begins to dry to the touch. Some, like figs, need a constantly moist soil.

- When watering, apply 1/2 to 3/4 inch of water.
- Use soaker hoses or microsprinklers when possible.
- Water during the early-morning hours.
- Keep plantings moist to conserve moisture.

FERTILIZING

Fruiting plants vary as to fertilizer needs. You can develop special schedules or stick to a general feeding program. All appear to grow best when fed more than once a year. If the plants are growing among turf, flowers, or shrubs, they may receive an adequate nutrient supply with the feedings given these plants. In general, gardeners like to give the fruiting plants special feedings. Unless you work out a special schedule for your plantings, a two-to-three-times-a-year feeding schedule is fine.

- Apply a 6-6-6, 8-8-8, or similar fertilizer that also contains minor nutrients.
- Feed new plantings lightly every six to eight weeks from March through September. Use 1/4 pound of fertilizer per plant, scattered under the spread of the branches.

This may be gradually increased to 1/2 pound as the plants begin to grow.

- Feed established plantings in March, June, and September at the rate of 1 pound for each 100 square feet of area. Scatter fertilizer under the spread of the planting and out past the branches.
- Apply the fertilizer over mulches.
- Water after applying the fertilizer to begin moving the nutrients into the root zone.

Some other fertilizing techniques are used by growers of fruiting plants. One is to apply manure to the surface of the soil. Fresh manure is often obtained with animal bedding of straw, hay, or sawdust. This provides a source of nutrients and mulch. Fertilizer stakes are also available to feed the plants. Follow manufacturer instructions when determining the number of stakes needed per plant.

PEST CONTROL

Fruiting plants are no different from other landscape additions. They all have pests that can cause decline. In this case, the pests may also affect the harvests. Most fruiting plants are

tough, however, and can tolerate some damage without a significant reduction in yield. Keep your eye out for insects or diseases, and apply controls as needed.

Aphids are small pear-shaped insects of numerous colors that mainly feed in new growths. They cause stems and leaves to become contorted and may reduce flowering. Control as needed with a soap spray.

Trunk borers are prevalent in some deciduous fruit trees but can affect any tree. The larva of an adult beetle completes its life cycle in the trunk, causing death of the tissue. Damage is indicated by sap oozing from the trunks.

The larvae can be dug out, or apply a synthetic insecticide as needed following the label instructions.

Scale insects are various piercing, sucking insects. Adults are covered with a soft or hard waxlike coating, usually white, green, or brown in color. Scale insects reduce plant vigor and can cause death.

Control as needed with an oil spray, following the label instructions.

Twig girdlers are large grayish beetles that girdle limbs up to 1/2 inch or larger in diameter and cause them to fall from the trees.

Damage is minimal, but limbs should be removed from the area. Insects lay the eggs for the next generation in the limbs.

Just a few fruits, including apples, plums, peaches, nectarines, and grapes, may only give good production if routine sprays are provided. The sprays needed can often be purchased as a combination spray for fruit trees.

A few pests are very difficult to control. Papayas, guavas, Surinam cherries, and peaches are just a few that can be attacked by fruit flies, for which there are no sprays. After cool winters that reduce fruit fly populations, gardeners often get good crops—but there are no guarantees. You have to decide if these fruits are worth the risks of limited production due to pests in your landscape.

Leaf spots are caused by a fungus. Almost all fruiting plants can get some fungal leaf spotting, which ruins the appearance of the foliage. Most damage is minor and can be tolerated.

When needed, use a copper fungicide or other synthetic fungicide, following the label instructions for your fruit.

Sooty mold is a black fungus that feeds on plant sap and excreta of piercing sucking insects. It does not cause major plant damage, but is associated with insects that may need control.

An oil spray usually controls both the sooty mold and insects.

Selected Citrus Plantings

Name	Growth Habit	Height (Feet)	Area	Harvest Time	Best Use of Fruits
Apple	Small tree	20 – 25	NC	May – June	Fresh, juice, baking
Atemoya	Small tree	15 – 20	S	Aug. – Oct Nov. – Jan.	Fresh, drinks, ice cream
Avocado	Large tree	40 – 50	CS	May – Mar.	Fresh, salads, sauces
Banana	Large perennial	12 – 15	CS	Year-round	Fresh, baking, ice cream
Barbados Cherry	Shrub	15 – 20	S	April – Oct.	Fresh, juice, jelly
Blackberry	Perennial	4 – 6	NCS	April – May	Fresh, jelly, baking
Black Sapote	Large tree	40 – 50	S	Dec. – Mar.	Fresh, desserts
Blueberry	Large shrubs	5 – 15	NC	May – June	Fresh, salads, baking

Name	Growth Habit	Height (Feet)	Area	Harvest Time	Best Use of Fruits
Canistel	Small tree	15 – 25	S	Year-round	Fresh, baking
Carambola	Medium tree	25 – 35	CS	June – Oct Nov. – Feb.	Fresh, salads, juice
Carissa	Shrub	8 – 10	CS	Year-round	Jelly, juice
Cattley Guava	Large shrub	15 – 20	CS	July – Aug.	Fresh, juice, jelly
Coconut	Palm	50 – 60	S	Year-round	Fresh, baking
Feijoa	Large shrub	12 – 15	NCS	July – Aug.	Fresh, preserves
Fig	Small tree	10 – 15	NCS	June – Aug.	Fresh, salads, baking
Grapes	Vines	15 – 20	NCS	June – Aug.	Fresh, juice, jelly, wine
Guava	Medium tree	20 – 30	CS	Aug. – Oct Nov. – Feb.	Fresh, salads, jam
Jaboticaba	Medium tree	20 – 30	CS	Year-round	Fresh, jelly, wine
Jackfruit	Large tree	40 – 50	S	Year-round	Fresh
Longan	Large tree	40 – 50	S	July – Aug.	Fresh, dried
Lychee	Large tree	35 – 45	S	June – July	Fresh, salads
Macadamia	Large tree	40 – 50	CS	Aug. – Oct.	As nuts, baking
Mamey Sapote	Large tree	40 – 50	S	May – July	Fresh, jelly, ice cream
Mango	Large tree	40 – 50	S	May – Oct	Fresh, salads
Miracle Fruit	Shrub	4 – 6	S	Year-round	Fresh
Monstera	Vine	15 – 20	CS	Aug. – Oct.	Fresh, salads
Nectarine	Small tree	15 – 20	NC	May – June	Fresh, salads
Papaya	Tree-like	15 – 20	CS	Year-round	Fresh, salads, juice
Passion Fruit	Vine	15 – 20	CS	June – Dec.	Fresh, juice
Peach	Small tree	15 – 20	NCS	May – June	Fresh, salads, baking
Pear	Medium tree	20 – 30	NC	July – Aug.	Fresh, canned, cooked
Pecan	Large tree	50 – 60	NC	Oct. – Nov.	As nuts, baking
Persimmon	Small tree	15 – 20	NC	Sept. – Oct.	Fresh, baking
Pineapple	Perennial	2 – 3	CS	Year-round	Fresh, salads, baking
Plum	Small tree	15 – 20	NC	May – June	Fresh, baking
Pomegranate	Large shrub	10 – 15	NCS	Year-round	Fresh, juice, jelly
Prickly Pear	Cactus	4 – 6	NCS	Aug. – Sept.	Fresh
Sapodilla	Large tree	40 – 50	S	Feb. – June	Fresh, juice, jelly
Sea Grape	Large shrub	15 – 20	CS	July – Aug.	Fresh, jelly
Star Apple	Large tree	40 – 50	S	Feb. – May	Fresh
Sugar Apple	Small tree	15 – 20	S	July – Sept. Nov – Jan.	Fresh, ice cream
Surinam Cherry	Large shrub	10 – 15	CS	May – Aug.	Fresh, salads, jelly
Tamarind	Large tree	40 – 50	S	April – June	Drinks, sauce, chutney
Wampee	Small tree	15 – 20	S	June – Aug.	Fresh, pie
White Sapote	Medium tree	25 – 30	S	May – Aug.	Fresh

N = North Florida C = Central Florida S = South Florida

JANUARY

DECIDUOUS & TROPICAL FRUITS

PLANNING

If you need new trees, shrubs, or vines, consider the delicious flavors and enjoyment you'll receive from ornamental fruiting plants. Just about all have attractive features and are sure to be conversation starters. Here are some suggestions:

- Select the taller wide-spreading types for shade trees, such as **avocado**, **macadamia**, **longan**, **lychee**, **tamarind**, **pecan**, and **mamey sapote**.
- Use the smaller trees for the patio or along walkways. These include the **atemoya**, **apple**, **fig**, **nectarine**, **plum**, **peach**, **persimmon**, and **sugar apple**.
- Add some color with accent trees of attractive **flowering apple**, **jaboticaba**, **nectarines**, **peach**, and **plum**.
- Create a hedge with the **blueberry**, **carissa**, **feijoa**, **sea grape**, and **Surinam cherry**.
- **Blackberries** and **pineapples** make a ground cover.
- Cover a wall with **grapes** and **passion fruits**.

Now all you have to do is make sure they can survive in your location. Check with your garden center and local extension service. Some cold-sensitive plants might grow in the warmer parts of your neighborhood or could be grown in containers to move indoors if winter freezes are expected.

Drape the roots of bare-root plants over a mound of soil in the bottom of a planting hole.

PLANTING

Garden centers are filling with cold-tolerant selections. Many deciduous plants arrive without foliage but will soon jump into growth. This is a good time to mail-order plants for early planting. Most will arrive dormant and bare root. Check the trees, and if they are not starting to make growth, they can be stored in a cool spot for a few days before planting. Otherwise, get the bare-root plants in the ground as soon as possible.

- Open a hole twice the size of the spread of the roots but no deeper.
- Make a mound of soil in the center of the hole.
- Spread the roots of the bare-root plants over the mound of soil.
- Position the plant at the same depth it was in the nursery.
- Fill in with soil and water.
- Complete the planting by building a 4- to 6-inch berm of soil around the edge of the hole, and add a 3- to 4-inch mulch layer.

Keep the mulch back about 6 inches from the trunk.

- Water soil thoroughly.

CARE

Prune deciduous plants during the dormant time. In warmer parts of the state, **peaches** and **nectarines** are beginning to bud, and they need pruning.

• Prune the tops out of new **peach** and **nectarine** trees at planting time. Leave a major portion of the stem and three well-spaced limbs around the tree. Remove the top 3 feet above the ground.

• Train mature **peach** and **nectarine** trees to a bowl-like shape with an open center and uniformly spaced limbs forming the sides.

• Each year, remove up to one-third of the new growths. Prune the shoots back to limbs that are developing outwards and not straight up. Other trees trained to an open center include the **atemoya**, **sapodilla**, **guava**, **mango**, and **sugar apple**. Prune these trees only as needed to keep their shape.

WATERING

Keep young trees moist after planting. Water daily the first few weeks filling the berm to overflowing. Then gradually decrease the watering to only what is needed to keep the soil moist. Mature trees need limited watering during the winter months. Due to the cool weather, most can go a week or more without rainfall or irrigation. If the soil dries in the surface inch, apply up to 3/4 inch of water.

FERTILIZING

Wait another month or longer to provide the first feedings. Most trees are not making active growth and can meet nutrient needs from decomposing mulch or residual fertilizer. The new feeding time is late February or March. Gardeners can obtain needed fertilizers as stores restock their shelves. Select a general garden fertilizer with minor nutrients, or a fertilizer specifically designed for your fruit tree.

PROBLEMS

Check for scale insects during winter. Many white, green, or brown areas become evident on leaves and stems as growth slows. The scale insects may range in size from pinhead to dime. Sooty mold fungus sometimes lives off scale excreta and plant sap. If needed, apply an oil spray, following label instructions. Be sure to note the temperature range at which the spray can be applied.

BLUEBERRIES NEED ACID SOILS

Of all the fruit plantings, only one has to have a very acid soil. Have your soil tested if you are planning a **blueberry** planting. You'll need a 4.5 to 5.2 range to grow this crop. Soil-test kits are available at local garden centers, or you can have the soil tested at garden centers for a small fee, or through your local extension service.

1. Adjust the soil pH to the acid level with soil sulfur as recommended by the soil test.

2. Spread the sulfur over the soil and till it in 4 to 6 inches. The sulfur takes several months to make the pH change, but the **blueberries** can be planted while it adjusts the acidity.

3. Have the soil pH-tested in three or four months. If needed, reapply the sulfur.

4. Use an acid-forming fertilizer to help keep the soil acid. These are often sold as azalea-camellia fertilizers.

Some soils have an ability to resist a pH change. These may not be good **blueberry** soils.

FEBRUARY

DECIDUOUS & TROPICAL FRUITS

PLANNING

Some fruit trees need cold weather to produce fruit. These include **apples**, **blueberries**, **peaches**, **pears**, **nectarines**, and **persimmons**. The number of hours below 45 degrees Fahrenheit determines how well they will flower and fruit. When selecting your trees, make sure you choose varieties that will fruit in your area.

PLANTING

Most plants purchased at Florida garden centers are available in containers and will relocate to your soil very easily. Some, like **pecans**, have very deep root systems and will need an extra-deep hole (but no deeper than the depth of the rootball). Select a plant that is well rooted in the pot. Check the root system at the garden center, and if the ball is just starting to develop a web of roots around the soil, the plant is ideal for transplanting.

- Open a hole that is several times wider than the rootball but no deeper.
- Save the soil on a tarp nearby. No organic matter is needed with most fruiting plants, but it can be added to the fill soil.
- Position the rootball so the top is at ground level or slightly above.
- Fill in around the rootball with soil and water.
- Create a 4- to 6-inch berm of soil around the outer edge of the rootball.
- Add a mulch and water one more time.

CARE

Prune **grapes** before the vines sprout new buds. Florida has two main types of **grapes**, and each has a different pruning system. One is the bunch type that includes such varieties as 'Blue Lake', 'Conquistador', and 'Stover'. The second major **grape** is the **muscadine**, often call the **scuppernong**, with varieties 'Dixie', 'Southland', 'Summit', and 'Triumph'. Be sure you train each to a trellis or overhead arbor. It's best to have one main trunk and four to six main canes to produce the crop. Each is pruned differently.

- **Bunch grapes**:

Each year, prune off the old fruit-bearing canes. Keep just the four to six new canes to bear the new crop. Limit these new canes to eight to twelve buds, then cut off the ends. Leave a short shoot called a spur branch with two or three buds at the end of each cane near the trunk. These buds will grow new canes next year.

- **Muscadines**:

Maintain four to six permanent canes. Each year, prune all side shoots that develop back to two or three short stems of buds. Remove stems that might be congested to leave the remaining stems evenly spaced along the permanent canes.

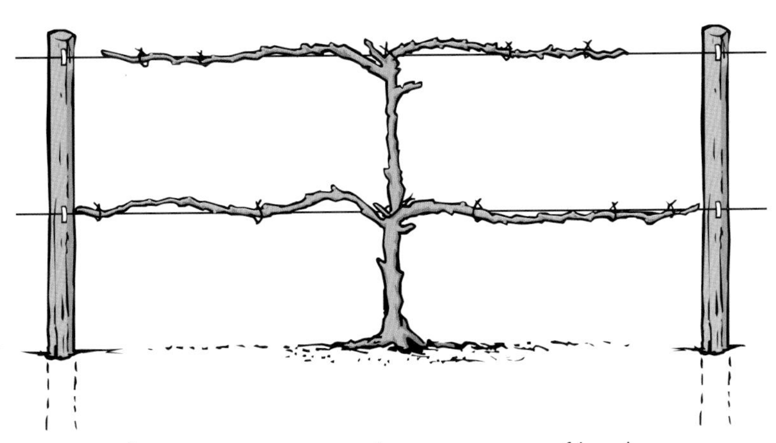

Keep four to six new canes to bear a new crop of bunch grapes.

WATERING

February is still a cool month, and water usage is minimal. Still, this is a good time to test out irrigation systems.

FERTILIZING

Some gardeners will begin spring feedings as the weather warms during late February—but there is no rush. You have all of March for the first-of-the-new-year feedings. You may consider giving some trees a special fertilizer instead of a general garden product. Most fruiting plants have special needs that are considered when formulating these products.

- **Avocado**, **mango**:

Special products for these and other fruits usually contain minor nutrients that are missing or tied up in the more alkaline Florida soils.

- **Blueberries**:

Select a product that promotes an acid soil. An azalea-camellia fertilizer is usually ideal.

- **Grapes**:

Many growers use a 12-4-8 or similar analysis to promote better growth and fruiting.

- **Pecan**:

Special blends consider zinc needs of **pecan**. Look for 1 percent zinc in the formula.

PROBLEMS

As new growths form, look for aphids among the foliage. It's not uncommon to find them in the ends of the shoots sucking juices from unfolding leaves. The aphids are small and of many colors. Where needed, a soap spray available from garden centers usually gives good control. Check for lady beetles and lacewings—if present, no control is normally needed. Some trees may need scale insects controlled with an oil spray. Leaf spots may be noted on trees starting to drop their leaves. This is normal and can usually be ignored.

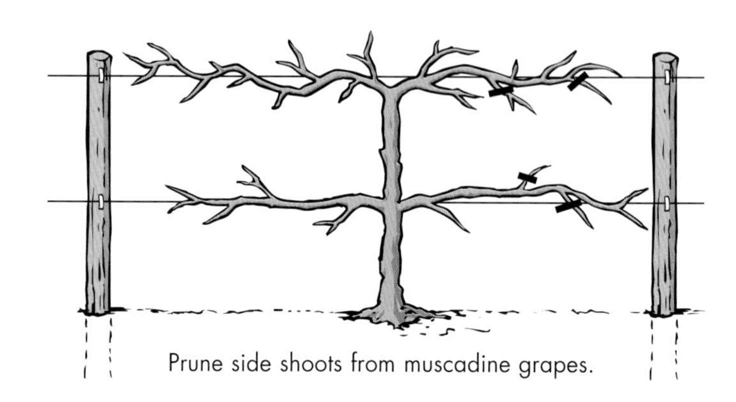

Prune side shoots from muscadine grapes.

CROSS-POLLINATION NEEDED BY SOME VARIETIES

Better check the **grapes**, **blueberries**, **avocados**, **pecans**, **pears**, and other varieties to see if they need to grow near a pollinator selection.

Some **grapes** are female-only plants and need a variety with male flowers nearby. These pollinator plants also have a female flower, so you will get grapes from both varieties.

With some fruits, there may be a compatibility problem. Sometimes the pollen is not released in time or in adequate quantities for proper pollination. This is when a compatible partner is needed. It's as simple as planting another of the proper type. Ask your garden center about the tree's need for a pollinator, or consult your local Extension agent.

MARCH

DECIDUOUS & TROPICAL FRUITS

PLANNING

Every region of the state has its popular fruits. In the southern areas, they are the **mango**, **avocado**, **coconut**, and **guava**. In the central and northern areas, gardeners enjoy the **peaches**, **pears**, and **blueberries**. Actually, many types can be grown in each region.

- Determine which fruits your family likes and how much room you have for planting. If you don't have a lot of space, consider small trees or shrubs for the landscape.
- Keep tall trees and large shrubs away from septic systems and walkways.
- Choose fruiting plants that will give a succession of production throughout the year.
- Decide how the plantings will be used in the landscape—as space dividers, shade trees, or accents.

Most plantings like sandy well-drained soils. **Blueberries** need a very acid soil, and the rest appear to grow in a pH range between 5.5 and 7.5. Last, check with your Extension Service or garden center for weather information. Even in a central zone, a winter of colder-than-normal temperatures can damage many plants.

PLANTING

Start by improving your soil. Some crops like added organic matter. Some, like **bananas**, **blueberries**, **figs**, and **monstera**, seem to benefit from the added water-holding ability supplied by porous sands. With **blueberries**, acidic organic matter helps adjust soil pH.

Thinning—especially of peaches and nectarines—improves fruit production.

- Till a large planting site.

Work in liberal quantities of compost, manure, and peat moss.

- Test the soil acidity and adjust to the proper level if needed.

Check with your extension service or garden center for weather information. Proceed with the planting of your new fruiting crops.

- Dig a hole wider than the rootball.
- Set the top of the rootball level with the soil or slightly above.
- Fill in around the rootball with soil and water.
- Construct a 4- to 6-inch berm of soil around the edge of the rootball and add mulch.

CARE

Trim your **fig** trees if needed. Removing some of the older wood will increase new growth.

Most gardeners grow **figs** as multitrunk trees.

- Prune out all dead or declining stems.
- Limit main trunks to three to five main stems. Remove all small competing stems from the base.
- Thin out limbs that may be crisscrossing.
- Remove up to one-third of the previous season's growth during the pruning process.

Renew the mulch layer. **Figs** need thicker mulch than other fruit plantings. A 6-inch-thick layer is a source of nutrients and helps reduce nematodes. Many gardeners like to add a manure at this time too.

WATERING

March is a dry month, and watering is important to help mature the crops.

New plantings: Keep the soil moist until roots begin growing out into the surrounding soil. Water recent transplants daily for the first few weeks, and then as needed to keep the soil moist.

Established plantings: Maintain a moist soil by watering when the surface inch begins to dry to the touch. Renew the mulch layer as needed. When watering, provide 1/2 to 3/4 inch water at each irrigation. Keep **bananas** and **figs** a little more moist, and keep the soil on the dry side with the **prickly pear**.

FERTILIZING

Give all fruiting plants a fertilizer application. If you are following a special feeding program, continue with your schedule. Otherwise, most fruiting plants grow well on a general fertilizing schedule.

TRICK TO GROW BIG PEACHES

Growers never tell you how they get their big **peaches**. Some of the varieties just normally produce a larger fruit, but the really big ones that fill the palm of your hand are produced by thinning the trees. **Peaches** and **nectarines** set more fruit than they can mature to a good size. For extra-large fruit, remove some of the little **peaches** when they are the size of a quarter. Leave a **peach** about every 6 inches along the branch. Then watch them grow!

- Apply a 6-6-6, 8-8-8, or similar fertilizer that also contains minor nutrients.
- Feed new plantings lightly every six to eight weeks March through September. Scatter 1/4 pound of fertilizer per plant under the spread of the branches. This may gradually be increased to 1/2 pound per plant as the plants begin to grow.
- Feed established plantings in March, June, and September. Scatter 1 pound per 100 square feet under the spread of the planting and out past the branches.
- Apply the fertilizer over mulches.
- Water after applying the fertilizer to begin moving the nutrients into the root zone.

Plantings in alkaline soils may also need a minor-nutrients spray or soil injection at this time to help maintain good color and steady fruit production.

PROBLEMS

Begin a spray program for **apple**, **peach**, **nectarine**, and **plum** production. Many leaf diseases, fruit rot, and insects can affect these trees. Spray programs usually begin as the fruits form and continue almost up to harvest time. Follow all instructions on product labels. Garden centers usually have a home fruit tree spray available to use specifically with these crops.

Watch for leaf spots, aphids, and scales. Treat only as needed to protect the tree. Also look for declining limbs caused by fungal cankers. The dieback may be removed by pruning. Sterilize pruners with alcohol between prunings.

DECIDUOUS & TROPICAL FRUITS

PLANNING

Many gardeners may not know the **persimmon** fruit, or may avoid trying it because of stories they've heard about the fruit's astringent qualities. The stories are true if you eat unripe native **persimmon** fruits or one of the astringent **Oriental persimmons**. But you can avoid the experience by planting one of the non-astringent types. The non-astringent types also have the advantage of being ripe when they are as hard as an apple. No more soggy **persimmons**! Some of the non-astringent types are 'Fuyu', 'Hanafuyu', and 'O'Gosho'.

PLANTING

Continue with planned plantings from container-grown nursery stock during spring. Bare-root plantings are generally discontinued until next December or January. Some trees, like the **pecan**, have a very deep root system. Don't be surprised if the root system is three times deeper than the height of the tree. The young trees invest their time in good roots for the first year or two. It is important the root system is properly set in the ground.

- Dig a hole that is deep enough to accept the roots.

Estimate the depth of the hole needed by the size of the container.

- Carefully remove the tree from the container so as not to loosen the rootball.
- Position the tree in the ground so the top of the rootball is level with the top of the soil.
- Fill in around the rootball with soil and water.
- Create a berm of soil around the edge of the rootball, and add mulch.

Keeping the soil moist is a big part of establishing a new pecan tree. Make sure the rootball does not dry during the spring months. Also, do not expect a lot of growth the first year while the tree reestablishes a root system.

CARE

Your fruit trees love to grow during the spring months, but so do weeds. One of your spring chores is to keep unwanted vegetation out of the plantings. Some chemical controls are available, but most gardeners use other techniques to keep down the weeds.

- Handpull or hoe out as needed.
- Use string trimmers periodically to remove weeds under trees and shrubs.
- Add a landscape fabric to the surface of the soil.
- Maintain mulch layers under your plantings.

WATERING

It's a dry month, and water is important. Make sure the irrigation system is working properly. Look for dry spots that the sprinklers are missing. Use soaker hoses and microsprinklers where possible. Water only during the early-morning hours. Adjust sprinklers to water the plantings only. Apply $^1/_2$ to $^3/_4$ inch at each watering.

FERTILIZING

If you missed the spring feeding, there is still time during April. Actually, the timing of fertilizer applications is somewhat arbitrary. Most plantings need three to four equally-spaced feedings during the year to keep a constant nutrient supply to the plants as they grow and develop fruit. Some gardeners like to use a traditional fertilizer like manure. There are many to pick from

including cow, horse, chicken, and others. They often come with bedding that will provide mulch under the plantings.

• Spread manure under the plants over the root systems.

• Make applications several times a year to meet the nutrient needs of the plants.

Manure is applied at the rate of 15 to 25 pounds for each 100 square feet of area under the plantings. Manure mixed with bedding may be used to replenish the normal mulch layer.

• Keep the manure back from the base of the planting to discourage disease organisms.

GROWING PERSIMMONS

To get a good crop, you need to give **persimmons** a little special care.

• Space trees twenty feet apart.

• Prune an open center to allow good air movement and easy picking.

• Feed new trees every six to eight weeks March though September for the first three years. Use a general garden fertilizer.

• If you fertilize other trees in the landscape, discontinue future feedings. The **persimmon** trees will get adequate feedings from the other applications. Overfeeding can cause fruit drop in established trees.

• Keep the soil moist to help the trees hold their crop.

• **Persimmon** foliage and fruits may develop spotting due to minor diseases. These blemishes are usually ignored and don't seem to affect fruit quality.

PROBLEMS

Some evergreen trees drop much of their foliage during the spring months. It's often a shock when gardeners see their **avocado** trees drop foliage. But don't worry—the new leaves quickly follow. Some of the leaves may have leaf spots and other pests, but no control is needed.

Bunch grapes may need a spray program as the plants begin growth. It is really up to you. Some varieties are susceptible to anthracnose, a stem and fruit disease that can cause a crop loss. Where needed, a copper fungicide may be applied following label instructions. There is good news: **muscadine grapes** generally do not need a spray program in home landscapes.

Pests appearing among the fruit plantings include aphids, leaf spots, caterpillars, grasshoppers, and scales. Control only as needed. Keep up any spray programs that have been started for **apple**, **peach**, and **nectarine** plantings.

Persimmon

DECIDUOUS & TROPICAL FRUITS

PLANNING

Think **blackberries**. The **blackberry** is one of the easiest fruits to grow throughout the entire state. Two varieties, 'Flordagrand' and 'Oklawaha', are best adapted to Central and South Florida. They are planted in pairs for cross-pollination, and they need a trellis. The variety 'Brazo' is usually preferred, as it grows throughout the state and does not need staking. It is grown as a rambling shrub. There are other varieties, including thornless types, but success varies. **Blackberries** take little care. Plants are set in the ground from containers or offshoots dug from existing plants. Set the plants 4 to 6 feet apart to grow in a garden, use as a space divider, or to create a ground cover. They will send up plenty of shoots to expand your collection. Care is simple.

- Keep the soil moist by watering once or twice a week during periods of drought.
- Feed new plants lightly every six to eight weeks from February through September. Feed mature plants with 1/2 pound of general garden fertilizer for each 100 square feet of bed area once in February, June, and late August.
- **Blackberries** ripen April through May and should be harvested to keep animals out of the garden.
- After the plants finish production, cut them back to the ground. They regrow rapidly and produce stems that are ready to open spring flowers by fall.
- Sprays are seldom needed.

PLANTING

Continue planting trees, shrubs, and vines from containers. Hurry to get a good selection from local garden centers before supplies dwindle. If you plan to add just one plant to the landscape, there is no need to prepare a large site. You can take some shortcuts:

- Control weeds and other unwanted vegetation in the area with a nonselective herbicide that permits replanting.
- Clear away the brown vegetation to create a planting site just two to three times larger in diameter than the rootball of the fruiting plant.
- Open the hole and plant.
- Finish by adding a mulch layer and watering.

CARE

Some plants send up suckers that need to be removed during the growing season. Check on your **lychee**, **mangoes**, **peaches**, **per-**

Blackberry

simmons, and similar plants for shoots rising from beneath the graft union. These can usually be rubbed off or trimmed back flush with the trunk. Also control weeds and trim off branches that may have been damaged by storms.

WATERING

May can be very dry, with hot days. Pay special attention to the water needs of all new plantings. Older fruiting plants are usually very drought tolerant, but they may drop the crop if left too dry. It's best to water when the surface inch of the soil begins to be dry to the touch. Most need water once or twice a week at this time of the year.

FERTILIZING

Wait one more month for a major feeding. Fertilizer applications for new plantings should continue on an every-other-month schedule. All fruits growing in containers need every-other-week to monthly feedings, unless you use a slow-release fertilizer. The next major feeding time is June.

WHY NO RASPBERRIES?

Raspberries grow in Florida, but not very well. It's either too cold or too hot. If you want to give them a try, plant the 'Dorma Red' variety in the north and 'Mysore' selection in central and southern portions of the state. Nematodes are a major problem with the 'Mysore' plantings, so pick a pest-free site. When they are able to produce, all varieties give a good-tasting harvest.

- Plant in a sunny location.
- Add a trellis to help keep the canes upright.
- Feed new plantings lightly every six to eight weeks; mature plants in February, June, and late August. Use a general garden fertilizer.
- Keep the soil moist and mulched.
- Prune bearing canes to the ground after harvests. Allow new canes to continue growth to produce next year's crop.

Some gardeners are obtaining new plants of the Northern varieties and growing them as annuals in their landscape. These should be planted in spring. After the plants grow and produce a crop, they are destroyed.

PROBLEMS

Some gardeners notice lace bugs on their **avocado** foliage. These insects also affect ornamental plants by sucking juices from the leaves. The damage appears as a yellow spot on the leaves that gradually turns brown. If you turn the leaf over, you can often see the insects with lacy wings. Some damage may be ignored, but when needed, an oil spray can provide good control.

Caterpillars may also be chewing holes in the leaves of many plantings. These are the immature and larva stages of either moths or butterflies. The damage is unsightly but often minimal. The caterpillars can usually be picked off. If needed, a natural spray containing an extract of the *Bacillus thuringiensis* organism can be applied.

Follow label directions if you use a chemical control. Many must be stopped a week or more before harvest. Keep all sprays locked in a child-proof location.

DECIDUOUS & TROPICAL FRUITS

PLANNING

If your region is too cold for **carambolas** or **mangoes**, plan to use attractive containers. Shop for a container just a size or two larger than your tree's rootball. If it's a large-growing shrub or tree, you will eventually need at least a 20-gallon pot. You may want to select a pot with rollers or add a dolly.

• Make sure the container has plenty of drainage holes.

• Fill the container part of the way with a good potting soil.

• Position the plant so the top of the rootball is about 2 inches below the edge of the rim.

• Fill in around the rootball with soil, and water until moisture runs out of the bottom of the container.

• To make feeding easy, add a slow-release fertilizer to the surface of the soil. Otherwise, feed every other week during the warmer months with a 20-20-20 or similar fertilizer solution. Keep your container plantings in full sun. They make ideal patio plants and focal points in the landscape. If the plant naturally grows tall, you can prune it a manageable size.

PLANTING

All fruiting plants may be transplanted from containers at this time. First check for drainage. Most don't like to sit with their roots in wet soil. As the rainy season begins, look for problem areas.

Many gardeners are tempted to start new **avocados**, **mangoes**, **grapes**, and other fruits from seed. It's a fun project, but there are no guarantees of fruit. Here's a tip: Warm-region fruits usually sprout after planting, but cold-region seeds need a cold treat- ment. These include **nectarines**, **peaches**, **persimmons**, and **apples**.

• Fill a container with potting soil and add your seed. Most can be laid flat in the soil and covered with a soil layer once their thickness. A few, like the **avocado**, are placed with the pointed side up.

• If the seed needs a cold treatment, moisten the soil and place the container in the refrigerator for 120 days. Then remove the container and start the seed germinating.

• Set all containers with seeds ready to grow in an area with bright light, and keep the soil moist.

• When growth is noted, move the plants to the light level normally needed for growth.

• Sometimes more than one seed sprouts from a seed. Keep the best and strongest seedling to grow into a fruiting plant.

Check the drainage of a potential planting site.

CARE

By now many plantings have finished fruiting and have produced a lot of new growth. In home landscapes you can evaluate the plants and decide if some pruning is needed. Most commercial growers prune only once a year if at all, but home gardeners can give their plantings just a little extra care. Remove limbs that may be overhanging walkways and affecting traffic. Prune back plant portions that may be competing with others nearby. Thin out limbs that are becoming congested. Remove all dead or declining portions. Direct growth to produce the desired shape needed for good production.

WATERING

With seasonal rains, established fruiting plants can go a few days without extra waterings. If a week passes without significant rainfall, you will have to water. New plantings and plants in containers usually need daily watering by rain or irrigation.

FERTILIZING

If you are following a general fertilizer schedule, the start of the rainy season is a good time to apply another fertilizer application.

• Apply a 6-6-6, 8-8-8, or similar fertilizer that also contains minor nutrients.

• Feed new plantings lightly every six to eight weeks with a quarter pound of fertilizer per plant From March through September, scatter it under the spread of the branches. This may be gradually increased to a half pound as the plants grow.

• Feed established plantings at the rate of one pound for each 100 square feet of area under the spread of the planting and out past the branches.

• Apply the fertilizer over mulches.

• Water after applying the fertilizer to begin moving the nutrients into the root zone.

PROBLEMS

When the **peach**, **nectarine**, and **plum** crops are harvested and general spraying stops, stay alert to borers affecting the trunks of the trees, damage that is indicated by sap flowing from the bark. If only a few areas of borer activity are noted, the larvae feeding under bark can be dug out with minimal damage to the trees. If necessary, synthetic insecticides are available at garden centers for borer control in fruit trees. Follow label instructions.

Caterpillars may be heavy in many fruiting plants. Trees seem to be especially susceptible. Most gardeners ignore the insects, as it's quite difficult to spray large trees. If needed, the natural *Bacillus thuringiensis* insecticide can be applied to obtain control. Other pests likely to be present are aphids, scale insects, and leaf spots.

SQUIRREL CONTROL

Squirrels will be oggling your **pecan** crop, waiting for nuts to ripen.

• Try to plant nut trees and fruit trees in an open area away from buildings and overhead wires.

• Trim off the lower branches 4 to 6 feet above the ground.

• Surround the trunk of the trees with a 3-foot or higher sheet of metal so the squirrels cannot climb the tree.

• Where trees cannot be isolated, try repellents available at local garden centers as fruits and nuts start to ripen.

JULY
DECIDUOUS & TROPICAL FRUITS

PLANNING

Over half the state can produce **avocados**, and people say Florida residents buttered their bread with **avocados** during World War II.

These handsome trees can grow over 40 feet tall.

The tricky part comes in picking the right **avocado** for your location. Some are hardy and can stand temperatures in the teens (Fahrenheit), but others freeze in the high twenties. If you live in a colder location, better choose from the 'Brogdon', 'Gainesville', 'Lula', 'Mexicola', 'Taylor', 'Tonnage', and 'Winter Mexican' selections. It's usually best to have more than one variety in your yard or neighborhood to ensure good cross-pollination.

Find an open area in the landscape, because the **avocado** tree grows tall and wide. Keep it away from buildings, sidewalks, and septic systems. Most grow well in sandy soil and need good drainage. Here are some tips for successful culture:

- Keep the trees moist by watering when the surface inch of soil begins to dry.
- Maintain a 3- to 4-inch mulch layer.
- Feed young trees every other month with a light scattering of a garden fertilizer from March through September.
- Feed older trees in March, June, and September with 1 pound of fertilizer for each 100 square feet of area under the tree. In some areas, **avocado** fertilizers are available.
- Keep the trees 12 to 15 feet in height by removing the top and pruning all side branches to buds that point outwards.

Major pruning is usually performed after harvests, but expect reduced production for a year or more.

PLANTING

All container-grown fruiting plants can be transplanted in summer, although their fruits may be lost or damaged due to transplant shock.

Make sure the soil stays moist. Plantings can be lost for a variety of reasons. The plant may have lacked the vigor needed to establish a new root system, or maybe it was attacked by pests. If you plan to replace the plant, some care is needed in preparing the site.

- Remove the old dead or declining plant and as much of the root system as possible.
- If possible, move over a few feet or more to some fresh soil.
- When you must plant in the same area, replace as much soil as you can. Just trade it out with other soil from another area of the landscape.

You may also want to till the ground extra-deep and add organic matter.

- Plant at the proper depth, add a 4- to 6-inch berm of soil, and add mulch. Keep the new plant moist.

CARE

Try to finish up needed pruning this month so the stems can mature during the remaining summer season. Control all weeds that have begun to sprout. Be sure to harvest fruits as they ripen, and remove those that have fallen on the ground. Decomposing fruits encourage rodents and fruit flies.

WATERING

With a little luck, the summer rains will do most of the watering. If several days pass without the rains, check the soil to make sure it's not becoming excessively dry. Plantings in pure sand dry quickly. Even though the plants may be drought-tolerant, their fruiting habits may be affected.

FERTILIZING

If you missed the June feeding, there is still time for a summer feeding. Young trees are generally on an every-other-month schedule. Use a fertilizer made for your crop, or select a general garden fertilizer with minor nutrients. Plants in containers need a monthly feeding if you are following a liquid fertilizer program. Otherwise, you might use a slow-release granular product that allows several months between feedings. Follow the label directions.

PROBLEMS

Ripening **nectarines**, **peaches**, **Surinam cherries**, and **guavas** are the favorite food of the Caribbean fruit fly, and you may also find the papaya fruit fly active at this time. No good control exists for any of these pests. Cool winters help reduce the fruit fly activity. **Papaya** can be covered with paper bags to allow the fruits to grow in a pest-free environment. The bags have to be replaced as the fruits become larger.

Watch for leaf spots, aphids, scales, lace bugs, caterpillars, and trunk borers. Control only as needed to prevent major plant decline.

Avocado

WHEN ARE AVOCADOS RIPE?

Avocados reach maturity on the tree but must be harvested and ripened in the home. If left on the tree, **avocados** eventually drop to the ground and will be bruised.

- Determine your variety and the approximate time the fruit is ready to pick.
- Remove the fruits even though they are hard, and bring them indoors to soften.
- Taste-test the softened fruit. If it's suitable, you are ready to harvest and eat the rest of the crop.
- **Avocados** can be stored on the tree and used as needed for a month or so. If you do not know your variety, harvest time will be a guessing game. When the fruit reaches what appears to be a usable size, pick one or two to ripen indoors. Taste-test to determine if they are ready, and note the harvest time on the calendar. If the softened **avocados** are not fit to eat, wait a few weeks longer and repeat the test.

AUGUST

DECIDUOUS & TROPICAL FRUITS

PLANNING

Perhaps you would like to plant a **pineapple** patch as the early settlers did. **Pineapple** is one of the easiest fruits to grow, but you must have patience—plants can take eighteen months to three years to bear fruit.

You can root a **pineapple** top by removing some of the lower leaves and then pushing the top into a container of soil so it stands upright. Some gardeners move their potted **pineapple** plants as needed around the landscape.

Any temperature of 32 degrees Fahrenheit or below will damage **pineapples**, so move your containers into a warm spot if there's a risk of frost.

• Root the **pineapple** plants in a filtered-sun location. They will develop roots in four to six weeks. Then place them in a full-sun location.

• Keep the soil moist and feed every other week from March through October. Use a 20-20-20 or similar fertilizer. Plants kept in the ground can be fed with a general garden fertilizer monthly at the rate of 1/2 pound per 100 square feet of bed area.

• Add a mulch to in-ground plantings to conserve moisture.

• Keep plants in containers or in the ground moist, watering when the surface inch of soil feels dry to the touch. Container plants may need water daily during the dry season. All need less water during winter.

• **Pineapples** usually start to bloom twelve to eighteen months after planting. The fruits mature about five months later.

• Old plants produce offshoots that will produce more fruit. Usually one offshoot is left on each older plant. Other shoots are removed and treated as additional plantings.

PLANTING

You can plant vining fruits this month. Choose plants that are not heavily entwined, or prune them back and wait for new shoots to develop. Transplant container plants to larger pots as the soil fills with roots.

• Select a new container several inches larger in diameter.

• Add fresh potting soil to the bottom.

• Ease the plant out of the old container.

Loosen roots that might be tightly woven around the outside of the rootball.

• Set the plant in the new container so that the top of the rootball is about 2 inches below the rim of the pot.

• Water thoroughly. If using a slow-release fertilizer, apply a normal feeding to the surface of the soil.

Some container plantings may not need a new pot, just some additional soil. Organic matter in soil breaks down, and the plants may sink lower into the pot. Lift it and add a fresh layer of soil to the bottom. Then reset the plant and add more soil around the sides.

CARE

Immediately after fruiting, **blueberries** and **blackberries** need pruning. All pruning should be finished early this month.

• Thin out **blueberries** and trim the plants back to about 4 to 6 feet, depending on the variety. Pruning encourages new growth that bears the fruit in future seasons.

• Trim **blackberries** to the ground. Allow the new shoots to grow and become next year's fruiting canes.

Other plantings may need pruning too. Remove stems growing out-of-bounds or damaged by summer storms. You can also remove the lower limbs which inhibit good maintenance.

WATERING

Summer rains should continue for another month or more. Make sure plantings get needed moisture if the rains fail. Water new plantings and container plantings to keep the soil moist.

FERTILIZING

Only container and new plantings receive a fertilizer application at this time. Some gardeners do vary from general schedules a little and give **grapes**, **peaches**, and **nectarines** their last feeding of the year. These plants often run out of the nutrients needed to maintain their leaves heading into fall.

HOW TO HARVEST PEARS

Most of Florida's popular **pears** were called **sand pears** by pioneer settlers, because they contain grit cells, hard grains in the ripe fruits. When canned, the grit cells disappear, but when eaten fresh they can be very noticeable. **Pears** also break down internally as they ripen during the hot weather. An early harvest will reduce grit cells and internal browning.

1. Pick fruits when they begin to change color during the normal ripening period of summer to early fall.
2. Wrap each in paper, and store in a cool location.
3. Remove the paper, and enjoy them as they soften.

Another way to avoid grit cells is to plant a variety such as 'Flordahome', available for planting in north and central zones.

Pear

PROBLEMS

Caterpillars may be noticeable in the taller trees. It's just about impossible to reach the tops with spray. Where needed, the sprays containing natural *Bacillus thuringiensis* are usually effective.

Check for grasshoppers, katydids, lace bugs, scales and trunk borers. Follow all label instructions when using pesticides.

DECIDUOUS & TROPICAL FRUITS

PLANNING

Plan to harvest **papayas** this month. **Papayas** ripen on the tree, turning from dark green to bright yellow. The color depends on the variety, but they all soften when ripe.

Papayas need a warm climate or a stretch of consistently warm weather to ripen. To get a crop of **papayas** next year before damaging weather arrives, you must sow the seed now to produce transplants for next fall.

Few named **papaya** varieties are recognized as pure strains. You may find many local names. If the **papaya** is known to have a good consistency and flavor, it is probably worth planting. Two varieties marketed through seed dealers are 'Cariflora', developed by the University of Florida, and 'Solo', an older selection.

No matter where you find the seeds, now is the time to sow them in containers.

PLANTING

Plant two or more **papaya** seeds per container. When they germinate, thin to one plant per pot.

- Keep the seedlings in a sunny location and protect from freezing weather.
- Feed monthly with a 20-20-20 or similar fertilizer.
- Add the transplants to the landscape around mid-March.
- Keep the soil mulched.
- Maintain a moist soil by watering when the surface inch of soil is dry to the touch.
- Feed each month with 1/2 pound of a general garden fertilizer for each 100 square feet of area under the plants.
- Harvest fruits when ripe to prevent pests.

As cooler weather moves in, plant new fruit trees. Avoid trees susceptible to cold damage, but hardy plants can become well established in fall and winter.

- Select a tree with a straight trunk and shrubs that are well branched.
- Open a hole that is wider than the rootball but no deeper.
- Set the plant in the ground so the top of the rootball is even with the top of the soil.

Fill in around the rootball with water and soil.

- Construct a 4- to 6-inch berm around the edge of the rootball.
- Add mulch, and water to complete the planting.

CARE

You may have noticed that many commercial **avocado**, **longan**, **lychee**, and **mango** plantings are pruned 12 to 15 feet in height to make harvesting easier. It does reduce the yield, but growers are able to pick most of the fruit. Home gardeners usually allow their trees to grow as tall and wide as shade trees, but if you wish, you can do some trimming.

- Prune back the trees immediately after fruiting.
- Either top and trim the sides, or selectively remove limbs.
- Trees may be pruned yearly or every few years as needed.

Trees generally produce growth to yield a crop the season after pruning. Expect a lower yield per tree, but easier-to-harvest fruits.

WATERING

During early September, you can expect good rains but later in the month you may have to do some watering. Each year is a little different. Just keep checking the soil. When the surface inch feels dry to the touch, it's time to water.

FERTILIZING

Now is the time to apply the last feeding of the year. If you apply the fertilizer now, the plants will have a chance to make growth that can mature before the cooler winter weather.

• Apply a 6-6-6, 8-8-8, or similar fertilizer that also contains minor nutrients.

• Feed new plantings lightly every six to eight weeks from March through September. Scatter 1/4 pound of fertilizer per plant under the spread of the branches. This may be gradually increased to 1/2 pound as the plants begin to grow.

• Feed established plantings at the rate of 1 pound for each 100 square feet of area under the spread of the planting and out past the branches.

• Apply the fertilizer over mulches.

• Water after applying the fertilizer to begin moving the nutrients into the root zone.

Continue to feed container plantings with a liquid fertilizer solution, or use a slow-release granular product.

PROBLEMS

Watch for the papaya fruit fly. The adult resembles a wasp as it lays eggs on the fruit. When they hatch, they enter the fruit and bore throughout the flesh. No good control for the papaya fruit fly is available to home gardeners. If you have enough trees, some will generally remain pest-free. But if you have only a few, try bagging some of the fruits to keep out the flies.

Many fruits have yielded this year's harvest and are making the final growth of the year. Look for caterpillars and end-of-the-season grasshoppers feeding on the foliage. Also check for scale buildups. As the weather becomes dry, mites could affect the foliage. Apply pesticides only as needed.

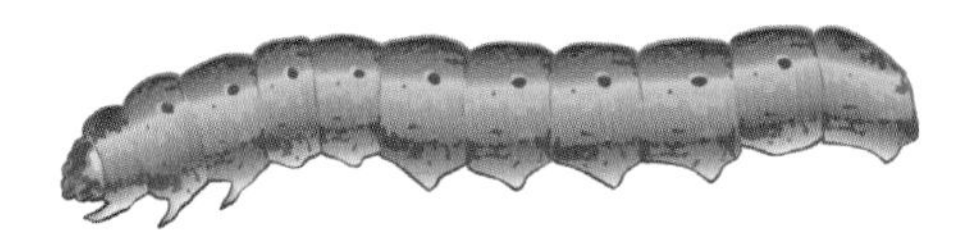

There are many caterpillars that develop into butterflies; know what you are treating before applying pesticides.

TELLING THE GIRLS FROM THE BOYS

Just about everyone has heard that **papaya** plants are male, female, or bisexuals. Actually, it's a confused group of plants, and sometime the plants even seem to change sexes. If you want fruit, you'll need some of each. Here is how to tell the difference:

• Male flowers are produced on long stalks held away from the trunks. Some male plants eventually produce a few fruits.

• Female and bisexual flowers are held flush with the trunk. Look for pollen sacks to determine if the flowers are bisexual.

• You will need one male to about ten female plants for good cross-pollination.

DECIDUOUS & TROPICAL FRUITS

PLANNING

Do you have fruit for the table at this time of the year? You might if you were growing the **Barbados cherry**, **carambola**, **guava**, **passion fruit**, **papaya**, or **persimmon**. And these are just a few of the fruits that can help make the landscape pay its way. It takes a little planning to figure out what you like and what can fit on your piece of property. Now is a good time to do the planning and begin adding some of the fruits your family might enjoy.

- Begin with a simple sketch of your yard. Decide where you need shade and then draw in the trees.
- Next, plan for view barriers to define property lines and block objectionable views.
- Now add accents. Fruiting plants can add flowers, a different leaf shape, and, of course, the colorful edible portions.
- You may also be able to use some of the fruiting vines as ground covers.

Don't cram the landscape too full of fruits. Space them out as you would other plantings. Allow room to grow with time. Make sure your choices are cold hardy and note that some will lose their leaves during the winter months. If you are counting on a plant with foliage year-round, you had better choose an evergreen.

Once you have the plan on paper, or at least a mental picture, determine the best time to plant.

PLANTING

Most fruiting plants can be added to the landscape at any time. But if they are likely to be affected by cold, now may not be the right time for planting. You will have to provide cold protection if frost or freeze warnings are sounded. You can plant any of the temperate plants that won't mind the chill. It is most likely that anything that grows from Central Florida northward can be planted at this time.

- Find a location with the proper light level. Just about all fruiting plants do best in full sun.
- Check for good drainage. Fruiting plants usually like a well-drained soil. They like sands that have been improved with organic matter.
- Check the soil acidity. **Blueberries** need a very acid soil with a pH of 4.5 to 5.2.
- Make sure you set the plant in the ground with the rootball even or slightly above the soil line.
- Build a berm around the edge of the rootball to hold water.

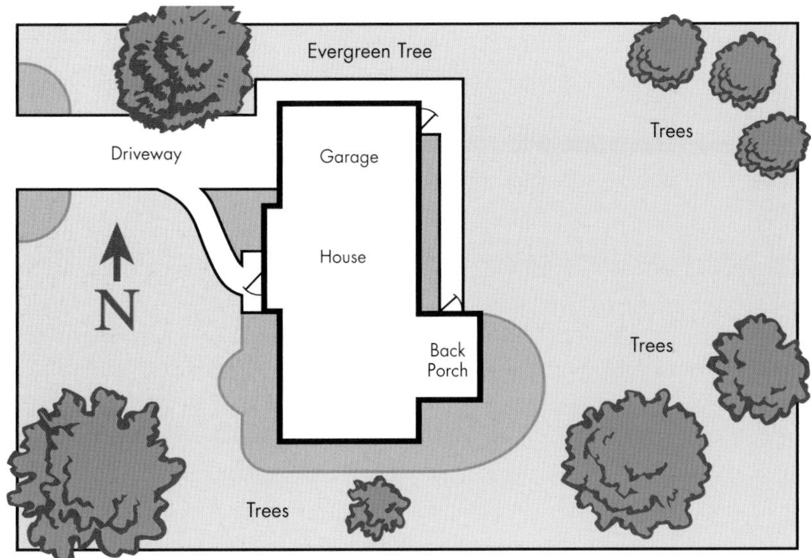

Sketch a layout of your yard to plan tree additions.

• Add mulch to help conserve water and control weeds.

CARE

Make the final check for weeds sprouting among the plantings. Florida has cool-season weeds that begin their growth at this time of the year. It's best to pull them or hoe them out from among the plantings.

• For more permanent weed control, add a landscape fabric to the clean beds.

• Use a preemergence herbicide that permits use with fruiting plants. Follow label instructions.

• Chemically spot-kill sprouting weeds with a nonselective herbicide that permits use with your fruit types.

• Maintain a 3- to 4-inch mulch layer to reduce weed growth.

WATERING

This is the dry time of year. Check established fruit plantings every few days to determine moisture needs. Luckily, the day temperatures are a little lower and the days are growing shorter, both of which help reduce moisture needs. Feel the soil under the mulch; if it's beginning to dry, it's time to water.

Container-grown fruits will most likely need daily waterings. Stick your finger in the soil about an inch; if it's on the dry side, it's time to water. Apply water until it runs out of the bottom of the container.

FERTILIZING

Feeding time is over unless you forgot the fall feeding. If you did, you must hurry to apply the needed fertilizer early in the month. We want the plantings to utilize the fertilizer to complete fall growth and then get ready for winter. The slower and tougher the growth, the less likely the plants are to suffer winter injury.

Plants growing in containers should still be fertilized. Use either a 20-20-20 or similar fertilizer solution or a slow-release fertilizer product available from garden centers. Follow label instructions.

PROBLEMS

Notice any twigs on the ground, especially around the larger trees? If you do, the twig girdler may be at work. This is a large brown to gray beetle that chews off smaller limbs. It does have a plan in mind: eggs are laid in the limbs, and when the limbs fall to the ground, the larvae enter the soil and complete the life cycle. Damage to the tree is minimal, but collect the limbs and send them to be composted, which destroys the immature stages.

Lots of deciduous trees will have leaves with spots. Don't worry, this is normal. In just a few more weeks you will be getting some fall color from **apple**, **grapes**, **peaches**, **pecans**, and **pears**.

NOVEMBER

DECIDUOUS & TROPICAL FRUITS

PLANNING

Every landscape needs some shrubs. They divide spaces, serve as view barriers, and can be attractive accents. Instead of the usual ornamental types, pick a few with fruiting features. Just make sure they are hardy and keep their leaves if you want total privacy.

• **Carissa** is a great evergreen shrub for the warmer locations. The starlike flowers are snow white. The fruits are bright red and very ornamental. Low-growing selections are also available.

• **Feijoa** is a very hardy, drought-tolerant shrub. The flowers are white with red stamens and the petals may be eaten in salads. The green fruit ripens during summer. The shrub grows wide and tall. It can be trimmed to form a treelike plant.

• **Figs** grow as multistem shrubs or small trees. Everyone wants to grow one for its exotic leaves and good eating. Find a nematode-free planting site. Figs make a great accent near a patio.

Pineapple guava (also called by its botanical name, feijoa), has lovely edible flowers.

• **Miracle fruit** is a tender evergreen shrub that should be kept in a container in cooler locations or used in foundation plantings in South Florida. Take just a taste and everything you eat afterwards will be sweet for a while.

• **Pomegranates** often get leaf spots, but they are still attractive shrubs for the patio. They are good accent plants with orange flowers and large orange fruits.

• **Surinam cherry** is often used by gardeners as a hedge. It can be kept sheared for a small hedge, or let it grow to 15 feet tall. The white flowers are small but noticeable. You can't miss the bright-orange to almost-maroon fruits shaped like little pumpkins and contrasting with the deep-green foliage.

Treat fruiting shrubs just like any ornamental planting, but don't do as much trimming. If you do trim, schedule it for after fruiting or during the dormant period.

PLANTING

Continue planting the cold-tolerant fruits in the central and northern portions of the state. Add the cold-sensitive plants only in the southern locations, where the chance of freeze damage is less likely. Follow good planting procedures. If

you need to move any fruiting plants, now is the best time to begin. Digging and moving the plants can continue through February in most locations.

- Make sure the soil is moist before digging.
- Form a large rootball by making downward cuts into the ground.
- Dig under the ball to sever the roots still holding the plant in the soil.
- Place burlap or cloth under the plant, and move to a new location.
- Set in the ground at the same depth it was in the original location.
- Create a 4- to 6-inch berm of soil around the edge of the rootball to hold water.
- Add a 3- to 4-inch mulch layer.

CARE

Besides harvesting fruits still ripening, there is limited work needed to care for your plantings as they head into the dormant season. You should still take weekly walks among the plants to determine any needs.

- Remove limbs that might be damaged by late-season storms.
- Trim back branches that might be interfering with maintenance and traffic.
- To discourage pests, gather and remove any fruits that may have fallen to the ground.
- Control cool-season weeds and renew mulches.
- Check for animal damage and repair as needed.

WATERING

It's a cooler time of the year, and many plants are entering a dormant period. This means they need less water. Still, if the soil becomes dry in the upper inch, it's time to apply 1/2 to 3/4 inch of water. Container plantings need water when the surface of the soil becomes dry to the touch. With most container plants, you can begin to skip a day or two between waterings during the cooler weather.

FERTILIZING

Feeding time is over for all but the container plantings. And if these plants are dormant or making little growth, feeding time is over for them too. Where needed, use a fertilizer solution to keep the leaves green. Follow label instructions.

PROBLEMS

Pests are less active in the cooler portions of the state, but you might find aphids, lace bugs, and similar pests feeding where the temperatures are warm. This is also a good time to check for scale insects on foliage and limbs of dormant plants. If needed, apply an oil spray to obtain control.

- Follow all label instructions on the oil spray container. Check to make sure your fruiting plant is listed.
- Note the temperature range for applying the spray.
- Mix only the amount needed for one application.
- Treat all portions of the plant to coat scale insects. Scale insects loosen and fall from the plants slowly even when under control.
- Spray sooty mold-coated leaves and stems. The oil loosens sooty mold from the plants.

DECIDUOUS & TROPICAL FRUITS

SPRAYING SAFETY TIPS

- Store sprays in locked cabinets.
- Keep sprays from freezing.
- Rinse and dry equipment before storage.
- Replace leaking gloves and boots.
- Wash clothing thoroughly.

PLANNING

A few fruits in the cooler locations are ripening, but most fruiting is over. Plan to protect cold-sensitive fruits.

Move plants in containers to a warm location when cold warnings are sounded. Mound up soil around the bases of tree trunks to protect graft unions from freezing. Some plants suffer leaf damage when temperatures reach the 40s Fahrenheit, but they recover when warmer weather returns.

PLANTING

Continue to move plants from one area of the landscape to another. Add cold-tolerant plants to your collection. Follow good planting procedures. Make sure you have the proper light level. Remember that light patterns change during winter. The sun dips lower in the horizon, and plants in the sun now may be in shade during spring and summer.

CARE

Limbs may get broken at any time and need removal. You may also notice that some trimming will be needed during late winter. Some deciduous fruit trees, including the **peaches** and **nectarines**, may be starting to bloom-—still, delay their pruning until January.

WATERING

It's a dry time of year, but luckily, the weather is cool. Use the touch test to determine when to water. If the surface inch of soil becomes dry, add $^1/_2$ to $^3/_4$ inch of water.

- Water during the early-morning hours.
- Do not water during freezing conditions. Make sure the soil is moist before freezing weather.

Also water as plants begin to recover from freezes.

- Make sure all sprinklers are operating properly.
- Check for limbs that may be affecting the watering patterns.

Plants growing in containers will still need your attention. Better check the soil daily.

FERTILIZING

Feeding time is over by this time of the year. Even container plants are dormant in most locations. Some growth may continue in the most southern portions of the state, and plants will benefit from light feedings. If needed, apply a liquid fertilizer solution to the container plants. Most won't need another feeding until late February or March.

PROBLEMS

The insects know it's winter. A few in the warmer locations that may be found feeding include the aphids, lace bugs, and scales. Where needed, apply a pesticide following label instructions. Most spraying can be discontinued until spring.

CHAPTER FIVE

HERBS & VEGETABLES

Most gardeners will say there is no better tomato than the one you produce at home. And that is true of just about all vegetables. Corn is never sweeter than when it is picked from the stalk and dunked immediately in boiling water. The same is true of herbs. Stems, with their spicy flavors, are best when gathered right from your own patch.

Most plantings need a sunny location. The general rule: If the plant produces a fruit, pod, or similar edible portion, it needs six to eight hours of sun a day. Herbs and vegetables with roots can often get by with four to six hours of sun, or a day of lightly filtered sun.

PLANTING

Florida has a year-round season, but you have to select the proper times to plant the various crops. If you don't plant at the right time you could face failure. First look at our planting chart on pages 143 to 145, then decide what to plant.

It's a good idea to sketch the planting plan on paper. Decide what you are going to plant, when, and where in the garden site, using traditional in-ground or raised-bed plantings.

1. Make beds 6 inches above the ground or higher with lumber, plastic beams, concrete blocks, or similar materials. In Florida, use materials that are resistant to rot and termites. A convenient size is four feet wide and as long as you like

2. Fill the beds with soil. You can use existing landscape soil or mix organic matter, including compost, peat, and manure with sand and clay soils. Many gardeners also like to fill small beds with potting soils that are pest-free.

3. To avoid compaction and the introduction of pests, avoid walking on the soils.

For in-ground plantings:

1. Select a predominantly sunny site. Check for possible shade at different times of the year. In Florida, the sun dips way to the south by midwinter.
2. Till the soil deeply and work in liberal quantities of organic matter with sand and clay soils.
3. Scatter a light application of garden fertilizer over the site and till into the ground
4. Test the soil acidity and adjust the pH with lime or soil sulfur if needed.

If you are using containers, make a list of what you want to grow and when. Then follow these steps:

1. Select a container big enough to accommodate the root system of the plants. Small herbs can grow in 4- to 5-inch pots, but most vegetables need gallon containers. The containers can be fairly shallow, as most roots only grow 6 to 8 inches deep.
2. Fill the containers with a pest-free potting soil. Don't risk bringing in soilborne organisms with these small gardens. After preparing your beds or containers, you will be ready to plant the vegetables and herbs. Use our table as a guide for spacing and planting techniques. If you are cramped for space, use the closer spacings.

CARE FOR YOUR GARDENS

If you set out on a five-minute walk in the garden, you will often end up actually spending thirty minutes to an hour. It's just fun to watch the plants grow. Here are some things to think about during your strolls:

- Use the walks to decide what to plant next.
- Check to see when to harvest the plantings.
- Do minor staking and training along the way.
- Decide when to water and feed.
- Spot pests and beneficial insects.

Decide if a control is needed.

WATERING

Good gardens need plenty of water, but that doesn't mean you should not conserve. Just by enriching sandy soil with organic matter prior to planting, you reduce the need for moisture. Keeping a good mulch over the soil also helps. Here are some tips to stretch the time between waterings:

- Water deeply at each irrigation.
- Feel the soil.

When the surface inch begins to dry, it's time to water.

- Apply 1/2 to 3/4 inch of water at each irrigation.

Use microsprinklers and soaker hoses where possible.

- Control weeds that use water and compete with the crops.
- Adjust your watering schedule to the time of the year.

Hot, dry spring and fall months use more water than the cooler winter and rainy summer months.

- Water during the early-morning hours to prevent loss due to evaporation and winds.

FERTILIZING

Productive gardens need regular feedings to produce lots of foliage, fruits, and root crops. Most plantings tell you when they have run out of nutrients with yellowing leaves and little growth. Often by the time you notice the deficiency symptoms, it's too late to help this season's crop. It's usually best to get on a regular feeding program with most crops.

Liquid fertilizers provide instant food for the plantings. Most need to be reapplied every two to three weeks.

Granular feedings can offer both quick- and slow-release nutrients. Most general garden fertilizers are applied every three to four weeks. Slow-release products may last for months.

Manures have both slow- and quick-release qualities. They are of a low analysis and must be applied frequently in large quantities to be effective. They can be made into a tea for drenching around plants.

PESTS

Florida vegetable and herb plantings have the same types of pests found in most other areas of the world. Here they remain active for longer periods and the numbers can be greater than those found in a cooler climate. They tend to be most active during warmer times of the year.

One pest that is new to many gardeners is the root knot nematode. All nematodes that affect gardens are microscopic roundworms that live in the soil. The root knot nematode causes roots to swell and become ineffective at absorbing water and nutrients. Some controls include planting resistant varieties, using pest-free soils, planting nematode-retarding cover crops, and practicing soil solarization during the summer.

Herbs

Name	Time to Plant	Height (Inches)	Growth Habit	Spacing (Inches)	How to Start	Part Used
Anise	Oct. – May	18 – 24	Spreading	18	Seeds	Seeds when ripe
Basil	Oct. – May	18 – 24	Rounded	12	Seeds	Leaves any stage
Bay Laurel	Year-round	60 – 72+	Upright	48	Cuttings	Leaves any stage
Borage	Oct. – May	18 – 24	Sprawling	24	Seeds	Leaves and flowers
Caraway	Oct. – May	18 – 24	Upright	12	Seeds	Seeds
Cardamom	Oct. – May	36 – 48	Clumping	24	Divisions	Seeds
Chervil	Oct. – May	18 – 24	Spreading	12	Seeds	Leaves any stage
Chives	Oct. – May	12 – 18	Clumping	10	Seeds, division	Leaves any stage
Coriander	Oct. – May	12 – 36	Spreading	12	Seeds	Leaves and seed
Cumin	Mar. – April	8 – 12	Spreading	4	Seeds	Seeds
Dill	Oct. – May	48 – 60	Upright	12	Seeds	Leaves and seed
Fennel	Oct. – Mar.	24 – 36	Upright	12	Seeds	Leaves and seed
Garlic	Oct. – Dec.	24 – 30	Upright	6	Cloves	Bulbs and leaves
Ginger	Year-round	24 – 36	Clumping	12	Rhizomes	Rhizomes
Horehound	Year-round	12 – 24	Spreading	12	Seeds, cuttings	Leaves before flowers
Lemon Balm	Oct. – May	18 – 24	Clumping	12	Seeds, cuttings	Leaves any stage
Lovage	Oct. – Mar.	24 – 36	Upright	12	Seeds	Leaves any stage
Marjoram	Oct. – May	6 – 8	Spreading	12	Seeds	Leaves any stage
Mint	Year-round	12 – 24	Spreading	18	Seeds, cuttings	Leaves any stage
Nasturtium	Nov. – Feb.	12 – 18	Spreading	6	Seeds	Leaves and flowers
Oregano	Year-round	6 – 8	Spreading	12	Seeds, cuttings	Leaves any stage
Rosemary	Year-round	24 – 36	Upright	24	Seeds, cuttings	Leaves any stage
Sage	Oct. – April	18 – 24	Spreading	18	Seeds, cuttings	Leaves any stage
Savory	Oct. – Mar.	10 – 12	Upright	12	Seeds	Leaves any stage
Tarragon	Year-round	24 – 36	Upright	18	Seeds, cuttings	Leaves young
Thyme	Year-round	4 – 12	Spreading	12	Seeds, cuttings	Leaves any stage
Watercress	Oct. – Mar.	6 – 8	Spreading	6	Seeds, cuttings	Leaves young

CHAPTER FIVE

Cool-Season Vegetables

Name	North	Time to Plant Central	South	Planting Method	Spacing (Inches)	Days to Harvest
Asparagus	Year-round*	Year-round		Crowns	12 – 18	2 years
Beets	Sept. – Mar.	Oct. – Mar.	Oct. – Feb.	Seed	3 – 5	50 – 65
Broccoli	Aug. – Feb.	Aug. – Jan.	Sept. – Jan.	Seed, plants	12 – 18	55 – 90
Brussels Sprouts	Sept. – Dec.	Oct. – Dec.	Nov. – Dec.	Seed, plants	18 – 24	75 – 90
Cabbage	Sept. – Feb.	Sept. – Jan.	Sept. – Jan.	Seed, plants	12 – 24	70 – 100
Carrots	Sept. – Mar.	Oct. – Mar.	Oct. – Feb.	Seed	1 – 3	65 – 80
Cauliflower	Jan. – Feb. Aug. – Oct.	Oct. – Jan.	Oct. – Jan.	Seed, plants	18 – 24	55 – 90
Celery	Jan. – Mar.	Sept. – Feb.	Oct. – Jan.	Seed, plants	6 – 10	80 – 125
Chinese Cabbage	Oct. – Jan.	Oct. – Jan.	Nov. – Jan.	Seed, plants	8 – 12	60 – 90
Collards	Feb. – Mar. Aug. – Dec.	Sept. – April	Sept. – Feb.	Seed, plants	10 – 18	40 – 80
Endive/ Escarole	Feb. – Mar. Sept.	Jan. – Feb. Sept.	Sept. – Jan.	Seed	8 – 12	80 – 95
Kale	Oct. – Feb.	Oct. – Feb.	Nov. – Jan.	Seed	8 – 16	50 – 60
Kohlrabi	Mar. – April Oct. – Nov.	Feb. – Mar. Oct. – Nov.	Nov. – Feb.	Seed	3 – 5	70 – 80
Lettuce	Feb. – Mar. Sept.	Sept. – Mar.	Sept. – Jan.	Seed, plants	8 – 12	40 – 90
Mustard Greens	Sept. – Mar.	Sept. – Mar.	Sept. – Mar.	Seed	1 – 6	40 – 60
Onions	Sept. – Dec.	Sept. – Dec.	Sept. – Nov.	Seed, plants	4 – 6	110 – 160
Parsley	Feb. – Mar.	Oct. – Jan.	Sept. – Jan.	Seed	8 – 12	70 – 90
Peas, English	Jan. – Mar.	Oct. – Feb.	Oct. – Feb.	Seed	2 – 3	50 – 70
Potatoes	Jan. – Mar.	Feb. Sept. – Oct.	Sept. – Jan.	Seed pieces	8 – 12	85 – 110
Radishes	Sept. – Mar.	Oct. – Mar.	Nov. – Mar.	Seed	1 – 2	25 – 30
Radishes, Winter	Sept. – Oct.	Sept. – Nov.	Sept. – Dec.	Seed	4 – 6	60 – 70
Rhubarb	Year-round	Aug. – Oct.	Aug. – Oct.	Seed, divisions	24 – 30	100 – 150
Spinach	Oct. – Nov.	Oct. – Dec.	Oct. – Jan.	Seed	3 – 5	45 – 60
Strawberry	Sept. – Oct.	Sept. – Oct.	Oct. – Nov.	Plants	10 – 14	90 – 110
Swiss Chard	Sept. – Mar.	Sept. – Mar.	Sept. – Mar.	Seed, plants	8 – 10	40 – 60
Turnips	Jan. – April Aug. – Oct.	Jan. – Mar. Sept. – Nov.	Oct. – Feb.	Seed	4 – 6	40 – 60

*not recommended for South Florida

Warm-Season Vegetables

Name	Time to Plant North	Central	South	Planting Method	Spacing (Inches)	Days to Harvest
Bean, Lima	Mar. – Aug.	Mar. – June Sept.	Aug. – April	Seed	3 – 4	65 – 75
Bean, Snap	Mar. – April Aug. – Sept.	Mar. – May Sept. – Oct.	Sept. – April	Seed	3 – 4	55 – 70
Cantaloupe	Mar. – April	Mar – April	Feb. – Mar. Aug. – Sept.	Seed, plants	24 – 36	65 – 90
Corn, Sweet	Mar. – April Aug.	Feb. – Mar. Aug. – Sept.	Aug. – Mar.	Seed	12 – 18	60 – 95
Cucumbers	Feb. – April Aug. – Sept.	Feb. – Mar. Aug.–Sept.	Sept. – Mar.	Seed, plants	12 – 24	40 – 70
Eggplant	Feb. – July	Feb. – Mar. Aug. – Sept.	Dec. – Feb. Aug. – Oct.	Seed, plants	24 – 36	75 – 100
Okra	Mar. – July	Mar. – Aug.	Feb. – Mar. Aug. – Sept.	Seed	6 – 12	50 – 75
Peanuts	Mar. – May	Mar. – April	Feb. – Mar.	Seed	24 – 48	75 – 150
Peas, Southern	Mar. – Aug.	Mar. – Sept.	Aug. – April	Seed	2 – 3	60 – 90
Peppers	Mar. – April July – Aug.	Mar. – April Aug. – Sept.	Aug. – April	Seed, plants	12 – 24	60 – 100
Potatoes, Sweet	Mar. – June	Mar. – July	Feb. – July	Plants	12 – 14	120 – 140
Pumpkin	Mar. – April July – Aug.	Mar. – April July – Aug.	Jan. – Feb. July – Sept.	Seed, plants	36 – 60	80 – 120
Squash, Summer	Mar. – April Aug. – Sept.	Mar. – April Aug. – Sept.	Jan. – Mar. Sept. – Oct.	Seed, plants	24 – 36	35 – 55
Squash, Winter	Mar.	Mar. Aug.	Jan. – Feb.	Seed, plants	36 – 48	70 – 110
Tomato	Mar. – April Aug.	Mar. Aug. – Sept.	Aug. – Mar.	Seed, plants	18 – 24	75 – 110
Watermelon	Mar. – April July – Aug.	Feb. – Mar. Aug.	Jan. – Mar. Aug. – Sept.	Seed, plants	15 – 60	75 – 95

JANUARY
HERBS & VEGETABLES

PLANNING

Now you are in the middle of the cool-season gardening period in Florida. All areas of the state can continue to plant the crops that like milder weather. In South Florida you also have the option of sticking with warm-season crops or planting a mixture. Most cool-season crops can withstand frost, and some even a light freeze.

Check the garden and look ahead to the next few months. If a crop will be finishing up soon, replace it with another cool-season planting.

The secret to keeping fresh food on the table is keeping the garden full of productive plants.

If you are just now jumping into planting herbs, you are right on time. Many herbs need the cooler weather to be good producers. Most areas of the state have about five months of good herb season left. Check your spacing of herbs, and make sure they are ones you use or would like to try. Many herbs can be mingled with vegetable plantings and flower beds.

PLANTING

As soon as one crop finishes up, pop in another. Check to see if there were any problems with the crop that might be root-related, like nematodes or cutworms that live in the ground. You will have to protect the next plantings from these pests. When preparing to replant, follow these steps:

1. Remove all remains of old crops, including the roots.
2. Till the soil deeply, to 6 to 8 inches.
3. Enrich sandy and clay soils with liberal quantities of organic matter and manure.
4. Scatter a light application of general garden fertilizer over the surface of the ground and work in lightly.
5. Test the soil pH; adjust with lime or soil sulfur if needed.
6. Apply cutworm treatment if needed, following the label instructions.

Now plant at the correct spacing and depth.

CARE

You have to take almost daily walks to keep up with herb and vegetable plantings now. **Carrots**, **broccoli**, **collards**, **beets**, **lettuce**, and much more can all be maturing at this time. Harvesting will be one of your major chores. Take a basket to the garden and fill it up. If you do not know when to pick a crop, check the displays at the grocery store—when your herbs and vegetables look the same, it's time to harvest.

WATERING

It's a cool but drier time of the year. The crops won't be using a lot of water until they get some size. Your regular walks, however, should still include checking moisture needs. When the surface inch of soil becomes dry to the touch it's time to water. Do not overwater or root rot may result.

FERTILIZING

All plants that produce an edible crop need regular feedings. In general, it is best to mark the calendar and apply fertilizer on a regular schedule. You can also use your judgment. If a plant is not growing vigorously or with a good green color, it probably needs fertilizer.

Pick from the following feeding techniques.

Liquid fertilizer solutions: normally applied once or twice a month. Mix in the proper amount of water and sprinkle over the surface of the soil or mulch. Some can be sprinkled over foliage, if label instructions allow.

QUICK COLD PROTECTION

Most cool-season vegetables are tolerant of frosts and light freezes, but what are you going to do when a heavy freeze is forecast? What about the warm-season crops that are still producing? A little protection may be all that is needed. Here are some ways to save your plantings.

- Cover rows with newspaper, then add a layer of plastic.
- Spread sheets or blankets over the crops. They have to touch the ground to be effective.
- Break open a bale of hay and scatter it over the crops to keep out the cold.
- Turn off all water. Irrigation is used by professionals, but home gardeners cannot provide enough water uniformly over plantings to take advantage of this technique.
- Build a tent over especially cold-sensitive plants and add outdoor-approved electric light as a heat source.

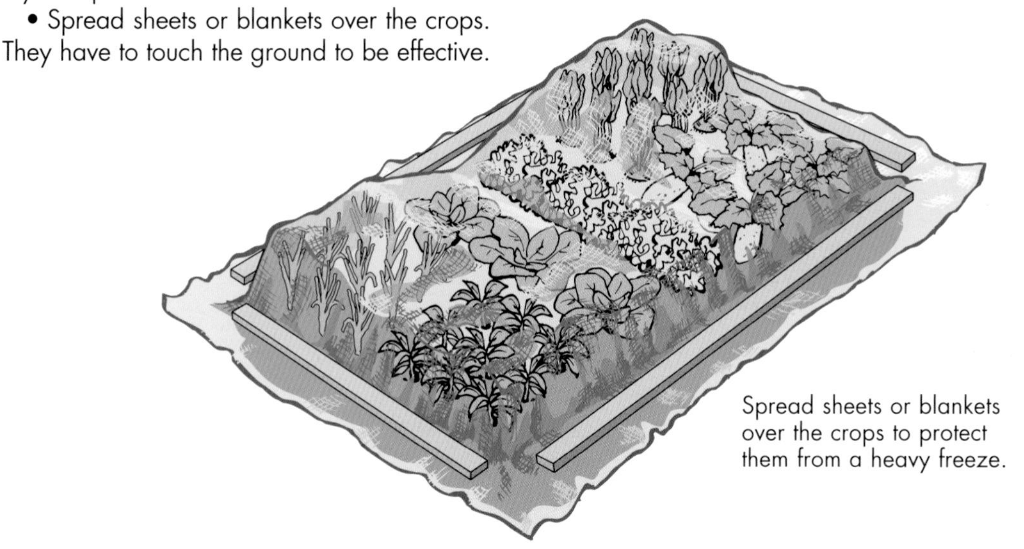

Spread sheets or blankets over the crops to protect them from a heavy freeze.

Granular fertilizers: usually sold as general garden fertilizers or vegetable fertilizers. Scatter around individual plants or along the row. Some may contain slow-release properties. Follow label instructions for the proper rate. They are usually applied every 3 to 4 weeks.

Manure: applied as sidedressing along rows or around plants. All are applied at the rate of 3 to 5 pounds per 100 square feet of planted garden. Manure can also be used as a tea to drench over root systems.

Gardeners may use one technique, or several at different times during the gardening program.

PROBLEMS

Insects and diseases are not a major problem during winter, as only a few stay really active. One is the caterpillar, feeding in leafy crops like **basil**, **mustard**, **greens**, **collards**, and **cabbage**. You may also find them in the **broccoli** and **cauliflower** heads. When present, handpick or apply a natural control, a *Bacillus thuringiensis*-containing insecticide. You might also encounter aphids, nematodes, or whiteflies.

FEBRUARY

HERBS & VEGETABLES

PLANNING

It's last call for many of the cool-season plantings. South Florida gardeners are adding a combination of warm and cool-season crops to their planting sites. Central and North Florida planters have a choice: they can either add some more cool-season crops to the open areas, or prepare the soil for warm-season crops.

PLANTING

Soon it will be time for a warm-season garden, and the soil should be free of unwanted vegetation and pests. Weeds in particular are a problem in the warm-season garden, as they are numerous and make rapid growth. Get some of the real problem types under control now.

- Dig out deep-rooted perennial weeds. Unfortunately, a few always remain to establish regrowth.
- Apply a herbicide to active-growing types. Select a product that permits replanting of vegetables shortly after use.
- Use landscape fabrics over the garden to shut out unwanted weeds.
- Apply thick mulches in the walkways to keep weeds from growing.
- Remove weeds from the garden regularly to keep problem weeds from renewing growth.

Don't wait any longer to start transplants for the warm-season garden. Use cell-packs or small pots to grow the seedlings. Fill the containers and sow the seeds.

- Keep seeded containers moist and in bright light.
- Move them into normal light as the seeds germinate.
- Thin to the desired number of plants. For example, **tomatoes** are normally grown with one to a cell, but you might start three **squash** plants together in a pot to form a cluster.
- Begin feedings when seeds germinate. Use a half-strength liquid fertilizer solution.
- Transplant to the garden when weather warms and plants have four to six true leaves.

CARE

Take some stakes and ties with you when you take walks in the garden. Some crop is always blown by winds or coming off a trellis. You may need to stake blown-about **collards** and **broccoli**. The **peas** may be hanging down from the wire or wood fence. Just a little attention prevents major problems.

This is also the time to renew mulches. Keep a 3- to 4-inch layer over the root system, several inches back from the base of each plant. Many gardeners also like to use a mulch in the rows for easy walking. This also helps to keep down weeds.

WATERING

It's still the cooler time of year. Checking the soil during a walk should be all that is needed to determine if plantings need moisture. You might notice some crops use water faster than others. Taller plants and plants making lots of growth may need extra watering. Don't let seeded containers and in-ground plantings go dry. These must be checked daily. If the soil surface dries, seed germination may be affected. Check seeded containers several times each day.

- Water when the surface soil starts growing dry to the touch.
- Use a misting of water to wet the soil to prevent washing the seeds away.
- Water during the sunny hours to permit moisture to dry from seedling leaves before dark.
- Keep seeded containers in areas with good air movement to prevent diseases.

FERTILIZING

Don't skip a feeding, even if the crop is producing food for the table. Many plants continue to grow and give good yields. This is very important with herbs, **broccoli**, **collards**, **strawberries**, and similar cool- season plantings. Stop the feedings only when you know production is almost over, or when the crop is removed from the ground.

- Most plantings are fed on a monthly basis.
- Extra feedings can be made if the plantings begin to yellow, or if growth slows.
- Water immediately after feeding to move nutrients into the root zone.
- Wash any granular fertilizer from the leaves of plants.
- Mark the feeding date on the calendar and note the next date that a feeding will be needed.

Start feeding seedlings in containers as soon as they sprout. Start with a half-strength liquid fertilizer solution.

- Feed the plantings weekly
- Apply the fertilizer to a moist soil.
- Increase the solution to full strength as the transplants reach garden size.
- Do not allow the new plants to become dry.

PROBLEMS

Whiteflies are a major problem on vegetable garden plantings during the winter months. They especially like **cabbage**, **collards**, **broccoli**, and **cauliflower**. They slowly build up and can cause plants to lose vigor and decline. Control with a soap spray when first noted. Be sure to hit the undersides of the leaves to control the immature stage. You may also see aphids, caterpillars, mites, and root knot nematodes.

Cabbage

CUTWORM CONTROL

Cutworms hide below ground during the day and come out to feed at night. They feed on stems and the foliage of plants. Gardeners notice major damage to transplants shortly after planting in the garden. Here is a good way to get them under control.

1. Punch out the bottom of a paper or styrofoam cup.
2. Make a slit up the side.
3. Use the cup to surround the stem of the transplant.
4. Push the cup about an inch into the soil.

Believe it or not, the cutworms usually will not climb the cup to get to the new plant.

MARCH
HERBS & VEGETABLES

PLANNING

Central and northern growers can plant cool-season crops like **cabbage**, **collards**, **lettuce**, **carrots**, and just about all the herbs. This is really the time for warm-season crops, though, and you had better hurry for them, too. Florida's weather goes from cool to hot rapidly. As early as possible, plant **tomatoes**, **cantaloupe**, **watermelon**, **corn**, and **pumpkins**.

Other warm-season crops can be gradually added through most of April. Next come crops that can really take the heat.

Most seedlings should be ready to transplant. If you have not sown seeds of **peppers**, **tomatoes**, and **eggplant**, make it a first-of-the-month priority.

PLANTING

Follow instructions on the seed packet for most plants. You may need help with **squash**, **cucumbers**, and **melons**. Many gardeners layer manure in the holes and plant these in hills to ensure drainage. Neither is needed in Florida. Here are some tips:

- Till the planting site and add liberal quantities of organic matter and manure to sandy and clay soils.
- Plant each of these crops in groups of three or four seeds, spaced about 1 or 2 inches apart.
- Make the clusters at ground level—no hills are needed.
- Plant additional clusters at the spacing given on the seed packet. Many will be spaced 3 to 4 feet apart or further.
- Keep the seeds extra moist until germination begins, then start normal watering.
- Add mulch between the clusters to stretch the time between waterings, control weeds, and keep the fruits from getting dirty.

CARE

The cool-season garden is finishing up while the warm-season garden is just starting. Keep up with harvests and remove plants when production drops. Use this month and the next to make major decisions on what to keep and what to grow.

Clean seed trays before reusing them.

WATERING

Some plants need lots of water; others need just a little. If you are using microsprinklers, now is the time to make sure they are working. Inspect any soaker hoses as well. These are the two best systems to use in the garden. They conserve water and put it only where it is needed.

Early in the month the weather may still have a little chill, but by the end of March it's almost hot. This is one of the drier months; water use can become heavy at times.

• Keep seeded areas a little extra damp.

You will notice that sandy soils can dry in a matter of hours. If the germinating seeds dry, they may be lost.

• Water established crops only when the soil starts to dry or the plants show signs of wilting. Most can go three to four days without water.

• Add a mulch where possible to extend the time between waterings, and control weeds that use lots of water.

FERTILIZING

Here are a few plants that might need special attention:

• **Corn** is a grass and likes lots of fertilizer. Use a light scattering of a 16-4-8 or similar lawn fertilizer every 3 to 4 weeks, or you will end up with dwarf plantings.

• With the help of bacteria in the soil, all types of **beans** take nitrogen from the air. One or two feedings at 3- to 4-week intervals is all they need to produce a good harvest. Overfertilizing will delay flowering and inhibit fruiting of some types.

• Apply light but frequent feedings to leafy vegetables and herbs to maintain growth. Harvest green leaves while they're young.

PROBLEMS

Pests become more active this month. The leafminer finds **tomatoes**, **basil**, **melons**, **beans**, and **cucumbers** attractive. This moth- or fly-like insect (depending on the species) lays eggs in the leaves that hatch into larvae that tunnel between the leaf surface. Some can be tolerated. Where severe tunneling is noticed, synthetic insecticides labeled for leafminers can be applied following label instructions. Some gardeners also report control by hanging sticky boards near their plants. You may also notice aphids, caterpillars, mites, root knot nematodes, and slugs and snails in the garden this spring.

PLANTING IN A SACK

This is a fun project for kids young and old that starts with a stop at the garden center. Pick up a large bag of good potting soil and some seeds or transplants. Place the sack of soil in a sunny location, following these steps:

• Lay the sack flat on the ground.

• Make two 1- to 2-inch horizontal cuts in the sack near the ground line on each side for drainage.

• Decide where you want to plant the herbs or vegetables in the top of the bag.

• Make an X-shaped slit in the bag, 4 to 6 inches long, at each planting site.

• Plant the seeds or transplant thought the slit and water.

• Keep the soil moist and feed weekly with a fertilizer solution through openings.

Your sack garden will grow just as well as the crops planted in the ground. When the harvest is over, add the soil to your in-ground gardens and start over with another sackful.

HERBS & VEGETABLES

PLANNING

Plan to plant the last of your **corn**, **melons**, and other spring crops. Crops that need only around 50 days can be planted well into the end of the month.

Reliable herbs for hot weather include **basil**, **dill**, **oregano**, **chives**, **thyme**, and **sweet marjoram**. Plan to dry or freeze heat-sensitive herbs.

Plan for more tropical vegetables. **Chayote** and **calabaza squash**, **Southern peas**, **okra**, **Jerusalem artichoke**, **dasheen**, **sweet potato**, and **malanga** can stand the heat and grow on through summer. Starts of these can often be found at the grocery store.

PLANTING

As the cool-season crops finish up, add new plantings. Till the soil and add lots of organic matter. Once the crop is in the ground, keep the soil moist and begin a normal feeding program. Plant **sweet potatoes** from garden centers or mail-order companies. Many gardeners start them at home using a **potato** that is beginning to sprout:

1. Either set an end of the **potato** in a glass of water, or lay it flat in a tray of soil and cover.
2. Keep the glass full of water and the soil moist. New shoots should sprout within two weeks.
3. Allow the shoots to grow to 6 inches long.
4. Look for roots forming on the stems near the **potato**. When the roots appear, remove the shoots, now called slips. Plant them immediately in the ground where they are to grow.
5. Keep them moist. You have started your next **sweet potato** crop.

If you are adding herbs to the garden, plant a few in containers. Plants like **sage**, which have a difficult time getting though the hot rainy season, can often survive in pots of soil that can be moved in out of the weather.

- Use a good potting soil mix in the containers.
- Use a pot 1 to 2 inches larger than the rootball.
- Plant the herb at the same depth it was growing in the original container.
- Keep moist, but protect from heavy rains during summer.

CARE

Control spreading herbs by harvesting what you need and sharing with friends. Add the rest to the compost pile.

WATERING

It's hot and dry. You will see a rainstorm or two, but it could be a week between good drenchings. Keep an eye out for wilting crops. Nothing spoils production more than dry soil. Make sure all irrigation equipment is working properly.

- Crops that are growing tall and wide need more water. You may have to increase watering frequency to every two to three days in sandy soils.
- Maintain a 1/2- to 3/4-inch watering.
- Check the mulch layers. If they are starting to decompose, add a fresh layer. No more than 3 to 4 inches should be kept at any one time.

Mulch that is too thick can keep water from reaching the roots.

- Check vegetables and herbs in containers daily.

The larger plants may need water more than once a day.

FERTILIZING

Maintain your feeding schedule:

• Keep granular fertilizer away from the stems of the plants. Scatter granules over the surface of the root systems.

• Drench liquids over the root systems.

• Water the plantings after feeding to move nutrients into the soil

• Sidedress over the root system with manure, or apply a manure tea drench.

• Make sure **corn** is on a regular feeding schedule. You can use a light scattering of lawn fertilizer if you wish.

• Keep **beans** and their relatives at one or two feedings per crop.

• Give container gardens a weekly feeding with fertilizer solution.

PRESERVING HERBS

Here are some quick ways to preserve a portion of the crop:

• Gather small bundles of herbs and hang them upside-down in a paper bag. The bag will keep the herbs dust-free.

• Strip leaves from the stems and dry them on a screen in a well-ventilated shady spot. Space the leaves so they do not touch. Store in a bottle or plastic bag when dry.

• Microwave between two sheets of paper towel. Dry only four or five sprigs at a time in the oven, for two to three minutes. They will become brittle and flaky.

• Gather herbs to freeze. Wash and pat dry, and store in a plastic bag in the freezer.

PROBLEMS

The plants most affected by insects and diseases are **tomatoes**. The two worst disease problems are wilts and leaf spots (blight).

Wilts is caused by a bacteria or fungus. Plants start to wilt as if they need water, and gradually decline.

The only controls are replanting with resistant varieties, planting in another area, or growing the next crop in containers.

Leaf spots and blight appear as spots on the leaves, often starting with the lower leaves. A fungus or bacteria is usually the cause.

Control with a copper-containing or synthetic fungicide, following label instructions.

You may have seen aphids, caterpillars, mites, slugs, snails, root knot nematodes, and whiteflies in the garden.

HERBS & VEGETABLES

PLANNING

Consider crops that can take the heat, including **cherry tomatoes**, **hot peppers**, **okra**, **Southern peas**, and **sweet potatoes**. Select tropical crops like **dasheen**, **yautia**, **calabaza**, and **chayote** as well.

Herbs have to be tough this month. Lots of them are in full growth, but as hot, rainy weather arrives, they often decline. This is a good time to gather and preserve many of these crops until fall plantings can produce a fresh supply.

Many herbs can be grown in containers. Add pots of **sage** and **thyme**.

Take an inventory of the seeds you will sow later in summer. All packaged seeds are removed from Florida's garden center shelves by the end of July. Here are some storage tips to keep seeds fresh:

- Place the seeds in a plastic bag or a jar with a tight lid.
- When stored in a bag, press out all the extra air.
- Mark the year of storage on the bag or container.

Some gardeners like to categorize the containers according to upcoming sowing dates. Keep different months' sowings in separate containers.

- Keep the seeds in a refrigerator until ready to use. Do not place them in the freezer.
- Most seeds in cool, dry storage remain viable more than a year, but it's still best to plant them during the next available growing season.

PLANTING

Stop warm-season plantings. Rains foster too many diseases, and insects run rampant. You can continue with the hot-season crops, especially **Southern peas**, **okra**, and **sweet potatoes**. One word of warning about **okra**: make sure you have nematode-free soil. **Sweet potatoes** and **Southern peas** are a bit more tolerant of these pests.

When crops finish up, many gardeners give up gardening for the summer. They say it is just too hot outside. If you do this, don't turn the garden over to weeds. Plant a cover crop of **French marigolds**, **legumes**, **hairy indigo**, or **Southern pea** varieties 'Iron' and 'Clay'. This will help reduce nematodes, return nutrients to the soil, and diminish weeds. Here are some care tips:

- Till the soil and remove old crops and weeds.
- Apply a light scattering of general garden fertilizer or manure.
- Scatter the seeds over the soil and lightly rake into the ground.
- Keep the planted site moist to encourage germination.
- Feed **marigolds** each month during growth; feed legumes one time only, a month after germination.
- Mow down and till into the soil when you are ready to plant the fall warm-season garden.

CARE

You should be making daily visits to the garden to perform needed harvests. Crops left in the garden attract critters. Don't worry about how the plants look, as many will be starting to decline. Transfer these to the compost pile.

WATERING

When May showers occur, everyone thinks it's the rainy season—but it's just a tease. Keep watering as needed.

- Feel the soil, and if the surface inch is dry to the touch, it's time to water.
- Give the ground the full 1/2 to 3/4 inch of water.
- Water during the early-morning hours.

HERBS IN A POT

Don't let the rainy weather spoil your herb plantings. Keeping your plants in a well-drained potting mix in a container is a good way to avoid the problem. Growing herbs in containers is also a good way to make use of available patio, balcony, and porch space. The plants can be used as foliage plants to move about as needed. Keeping **mint** plants in containers is a good way of maintaining control. Here are some tips:

- Use a container big enough to hold the plant and allow for some growth.
- Consider planting several different herbs in the same container.
- Use a good potting mix, available from your garden center.
- Set the plants in the soil at the same depth they were growing in their pots.
- Keep the planted container in the proper light for growth.
- Feed every other week with a liquid fertilizer solution.
- Keep the soil moist, but avoid the daily rains of summer.

Mint

- Keep mulches over the root systems.

FERTILIZING

Don't stop fertilizing just because a crop is producing a harvest-wait until the plants are obviously starting to decline. Some crops like **corn** produce only one harvest—when the ears begin to fill, feeding time is over. Also, when **melons** form, no more fertilizer is needed. **Beans** and **Southern peas** are crops that need only one or two feedings each season.

Most remaining warm-season crops like **tomatoes**, **squash**, and **cucumbers** should be fed regularly until production stops. You might stretch the time between feedings just a little bit, as not quite as much fertilizer is needed.

- Apply granular garden fertilizers every 4 weeks.
- Reduce liquid feedings to every 2 to 3 weeks.
- Apply manure every 4 weeks.

PROBLEMS

Insects are one reason many warm-season crops are not planted later in the spring season. Stay alert to pests and control as needed. It's often better to stop planting some of the warm-season crops later in the season than to fight melon worms and leaf spots. Look for aphids, caterpillars, leaf spots, mites, root knot nematodes, slugs, snails, and whiteflies until crop production is finished.

HERBS & VEGETABLES

PLANNING

Keep warm-season crops growing as long as you reap a harvest. **Tomatoes** often continue into the month, as do **lima beans**, **cucumbers**, and a few other vegetables. Most gardeners usually take out the crops when they stop producing.

Continue to plant summer crops. Besides common **okra**, **Southern peas**, **sweet potatoes**, and a few others, there are the real tropical crops. You can often get starts of these plants that flourish in the heat at your local food store.

- **Boniato**: This edible root is often called the **Cuban sweet potato**. It's a true **sweet potato**, but with a red skin and white flesh.
- **Calabaza**: This hard-shell **squash** grows large fruits up to 40 pounds in weight. They appear to have few pests, and the fruits are used like **pumpkins** and other **winter squash**.
- **Chayote**: Let this climbing **squash** cling to a large trellis throughout the summer season. The pear-shaped fruits are produced in the fall and used much like **summer squash**.
- **Dasheen**: The plants look like the perennial **elephant ear**, a relative, and grow from tubers in a moist soil. New tubers mature by fall.
- **Jerusalem artichoke**: Plant the tubers in a moist soil to start this **sunflower** relative. Plants have yellow flowers and grow to 10 feet tall. New tubers are ready in about 130 days.
- **Malanga**: You might find this crop marketed as **yautia** and **cocoyam**. It too has elephant-like ears. Plant the tubers in a moist soil to harvest by fall and eat boiled, baked, or mashed.

PLANTING

All plantings are of the summer crops that won't mind the heat. Give the soil normal preparation, then follow these steps to produce a crop:

1. Remove what remains of older plantings and weeds. Check roots for nematodes.

If affected, avoid the planting site and consider utilizing soil solarization.

2. Till the ground deeply.

Many of the summer crops really like moist soils. Enrich the sites with extra organic matter and manure.

3. Check planting depths for summer crops. Use the following guides:

Boniato: Plant shoots 2 to 3 inches deep.

Calabaza: Sow seeds in clusters of two or three, 1 inch deep.

Chayote: Plant fruits with shoots at soil level.

Dasheen: Set tubers 3 inches deep.

Jerusalem artichoke: Set tuber pieces 2 inches deep.

Malanga: Set tubers 3 inches deep.

4. Keep the soil moist and maintain a 3- to 4-inch mulch. Feed monthly with a general garden fertilizer.

Most of these summer plantings are quite ornamental. They can be grown separately in vegetable gardens or added to flower beds.

CARE

Keep up harvests of warm-season crops. Many are maturing and you do not want ready-to-eat produce declining in the garden. Share some with friends and preserve others to feed the family.

WATERING

It's the rainy season, and you can probably be a little more

relaxed with the watering. But if a day or two passes between rains, check the rain gauge. A quarter-inch or more is considered significant rainfall. Don't let the summer crops become too dry.

FERTILIZING

The organic matter you have been adding to the soil may help feed crops as it decomposes. It may be a good time to add another manure feeding. You can purchase manure from garden centers, or go right to the source. Many stables will let you gather all you want. Other traditional feedings include:

- granular feedings with a garden fertilizer monthly
- liquid fertilizer solutions every other week, or as suggested on the label

Do not feed crops that are just about finished with production.

Consider the use of cover crops in bare garden spots to capture and return nutrients to the soil for future use.

PROBLEMS

What few crops you are producing are normally pretty pest resistant. One pest you might notice on a few of the plantings is the garden flea hopper. These pests are black and less than 1/16 inch long. They suck juices from **sweet potato**, **mint**, **basil**, and similar foliage, causing a yellow dotting of the leaves. Some damage can be ignored. Otherwise, a properly labeled synthetic insecticide will have to be applied. A few of the more common pests you might find in the garden are caterpillars, leaf spots, root knot nematodes, slugs, snails, and whiteflies.

BAKE OUT THE NEMATODES

Use summer heat to bake root knot nematodes out of the ground. If you can heat the soil to the 140-degree range long enough, you will greatly reduce the population. The technique is called soil solarization, which uses the sun's heat during the summer months. It is also a good way to eliminate a few diseases that affect vegetables. The process takes at least six weeks, so start the treatment as soon as possible.

- Prepare the soil as if getting ready to plant. Add needed organic matter and wet the ground.
- Cover the soil with a sheet of clear plastic and anchor it along the edges. An optional cover with a second sheet of plastic can also be added. Lay plastic pipe between the layers to create dead air space.
- Allow the soil to remain covered for 6 to 8 weeks or more.

The longer, the better, to bake out the pests.

- When you are ready to plant, remove the covers and add the crops without significantly disturbing the soil.

JULY
HERBS & VEGETABLES

PLANNING

Soon you will restart your warm-season garden. Plan ahead by removing old plantings and preparing soil for new plantings. Remove unproductive herb or vegetable plants, and enrich the soil with organic matter. Here are some tips:

- Problem weeds may regrow. Either apply herbicides that allow replanting of herbs and vegetables, or dig the weeds from the garden.
- Nematodes: Apply the soil solarization treatments or grow cover crops that reduce these pests.
- Diseases that affect plantings: **Tomatoes** are of major concern. Soil solarization may help, but it is best to plan the plantings for another site.

Assemble the seeds you need for new warm- and early cool-season plantings. Remember, you can still find seeds at bulk stores or order from catalog companies.

Hot season plantings are over. If you hurry, you can make cuttings of growing **sweet potato** vines to start new sites. **Okra** and **Southern peas** can still be added.

Caging tomatoes helps support the fruit to keep it off the ground.

PLANTING

In mid-month, start seeds of **tomatoes**, **eggplants**, and **peppers** for an August planting. Starting seeds may be your only way to grow some varieties, such as older **tomato** varieties, or a selection of **hot peppers**. Seed-starting is fun, and during warmer weather you can usually have a transplant ready in four weeks. **Peppers** may take an extra week or two. Here are the steps to success:

1. Start seeds in small pots or cell-packs.
2. Fill containers with a germination mix available from the garden center, to within 1/2 inch of the top, and moisten.
3. Use your finger to make a 1/2-inch depression where you will plant the seed.
4. Sow one or two seeds per small pot or individual cell.
5. Cover lightly with more germination mix and moisten.
6. Keep the containers moist and in bright light.
7. When the first sprouts are noticed, move the containers to normal light conditions.

The seedlings grow very rapidly and can be fed weekly with a half-strength 20-20-20 or similar fertilizer solution. When garden size, they can be planted in the waiting site or large container. If the transplants have to be held for an extended period of time, consider giving them a larger container, and begin full-strength feedings.

CARE

Don't let summer crops get out of control. It's very easy to allow **sweet potatoes**, **chayotes**, **mint**, and **sweet marjoram** to take over the garden. Use a little pruning to keep the plants in-bounds

and they will still produce a good crop.

WATERING

Summer rains may provide the necessary watering. Look for areas that are too wet. You may need to consider raised beds to ensure good drainage. This would be a good time to plan these gardens and begin construction. If summer rains fail, you will have to provide moisture. Water when the plants show signs of wilting, or if a few days pass without rain.

TRELLISING CROPS

Crops like **tomatoes**, **cucumbers**, **climbing peas**, **pole beans**, and **chayote** grow better and resist disease if they are kept off the ground. Check seed packets to make sure you have a climbing variety.

Tomato fruits that rest on the ground almost always rot. Trellising makes picking easy, saves space, and allows easier spraying when needed. Here are some easy ways to get your plants up off the ground:

- Set up chicken wire between posts. Space the posts 6 to 8 feet apart and use a 4- to 5-foot-high wire netting.
- Make rings of concrete wire up to 2 feet in diameter, and set the plants inside to climb. This is best used with **tomatoes**.
- Buy ready-to-use wire rings to use around plants that need the support.
- Make a teepee of bamboo stakes or wood to support the crop.
- Plant the crops near a chain-link or wooden picket fence.

FERTILIZING

Summer rains may wash out a lot of nutrients. It's best to keep up a normal feeding schedule for the crops left in the garden. Most need a monthly feeding, except **beans** and **Southern peas**. After a feeding or two, they can grow on their own.

Any plantings in containers will need weekly to every-other-week feeding. Use the color and vigor of the plant as a guide. If growth slows or a yellow color develops, increase the frequency of feedings.

PROBLEMS

Pests are still active, but summer crops are very durable. They won't mind a few chewed leaves or some missing sap. One insect you may spot this time of the year is the grasshopper. It is not a major herb and vegetable pest, but it might find the big-leaf **calabaza** and **sweet potato** leaves tasty. Where needed, try handpicking as a control. You may also apply a synthetic insecticide made for the control of grasshoppers in vegetables, following label instructions. During this month, look for caterpillars, garden flea hoppers, leaf spots, root knot nematodes, slugs, snails, and whiteflies in the garden as well.

AUGUST

HERBS & VEGETABLES

PLANNING

Get ready for nine months of great gardening. The first crops are warm- season types, followed by cool-season crops planted during fall, then another round of warm-season crops when spring arrives. South Florida residents may continue warm-season plantings fall through spring.

For gardeners used to planting the first crops in early spring, this is a drastic change. August planting dates are especially important for **corn**, **eggplant**, **pumpkins**, **peppers**, **tomatoes**, and **watermelons**. Each of these crops needs about 90 days to come into production.

- Locate the garden in a sunny spot.
- Remove weeds and till the soil deeply.
- Test the soil and adjust the acidity to the proper pH.
- Work in liberal quantities of organic matter and manure with the soil.
- Plan taller plants for the back of the garden so they won't shade the smaller crops.
- Plant crops that take the most time early in the month.

The weather is still hot, but it's important to start planting the warm-season garden.

PLANTING

Start easy-to-grow crops from seed, including **cucumbers**, **beans**, **squash**, and **corn**.

- Make sure soil is loose and free of debris.
- Open up a row if planting a large garden.
- Set the seeds at the proper depth found on seed packets. Large seeds are normally set 1 inch deep, small seeds 1/2 inch.
- Add a mulch between rows and within a few inches of the seeded areas.
- Keep the soil moist to encourage germination.

If you are growing transplants, try to find varieties with strong stems and bright-green leaves. Avoid plants that are spindly and showing signs of insects or damage.

- Open up a hole in a prepared planting site.
- Fill the hole with water and insert the transplant.
- Set the transplants in the ground at the same depth they were growing in their containers. One exception is the **tomato**, which can be set in the ground to the point where the first leaves are noted on the stems.
- Add a mulch around the plants, but keep it back a few inches from the stem.
- Water thoroughly.

CARE

Explore the garden daily to look for water needs and potential pest problems. If transplants are large, they may even need some staking, or you can add cages around **tomatoes**. If you will be adding a trellis, now is the time to set posts in the ground and string wire.

WATERING

The rainy season may help with watering, but you do not want newly seeded areas or transplants to get dry.

- Water new crops daily for the first week or until seeds begin to germinate.
- As plants root into the surrounding soil, reduce watering to every 3 to 4 days, or as needed to keep the soil from drying.
- Apply 1/2 to 3/4 inch of water each irrigation.
- Be ready to apply extra water as needed to prevent wilting, especially during extra-hot weather.

Crops that are still in the ground will not need frequent watering if rains continue. Maintain a 3- to 4-inch mulch and water when the surface inch of soil begins to dry.

FERTILIZING

Manure, organic matter additions, and fertilizers can help feed crops for the first few weeks of growth. You can also add a little fertilizer to the water used to plant new seeds and transplants; use a manure tea or a weak 20-20-20 fertilizer solution. Then follow these steps:

- Apply the first feedings 2 to 3 weeks after planting.
- Scatter granular fertilizers over the root systems of the plants. Make sure it stays away from stems entering the ground, and new seedlings.

If granules get near stems, wash them back with a stream of water.

- Apply liquid fertilizers over and around the plants, following label instructions. If needed, you can wash fertilizer off the foliage.
- Side-dress with manure along rows or around plants. Keep manure back a few inches from the stems.

SHADING TRANSPLANTS

The hot summer sun can bake the sturdiest transplant before it becomes established. If your homegrown transplants have not been conditioned to the sun, it's important you provide shading for at least a few days:

- Cut a **palmetto** frond with up to a foot or more of stem.
- Position the frond so it casts shade on the new transplant in hot sun.
- Replace the frond if establishment takes more than a day or two. Do not leave the covers in place more than five to seven days, or the plants may become tender and burn.
- Keep the soil moist during the establishment period.

If palm fronds are not available, gardeners can use boards, cardboard, or sheets of plastic to cast the shade.

You can use palmetto fronds to shade transplants.

PROBLEMS

Beware of cutworms. Place a paper collar around the base of transplants to keep these pests from sawing transplants down. If needed, apply a synthetic insecticide as instructed. Other pests to watch for are aphids, caterpillars, mites, slugs, snails, and whiteflies.

SEPTEMBER

HERBS & VEGETABLES

PLANNING

The warm-season gardens started a month ago should be completed as soon as possible in Central and North Florida. These areas of Florida will become too chilly for good production in another month or two. In all areas but South Florida, September has the last dates for planting **tomatoes**, **cucumbers**, **squash**, and **beans**. **Melon-** and **pumpkin**-planting time is over in all areas.

Many containers can be used to plant herbs and vegetables. It is suggested you use a good potting soil. Even though it looks good, soil from the yard may contain insects, diseases, weeds, and nematodes.

PLANTING

Many gardeners continue the tradition of planting in rows. They have seen farmers use this technique for years. You may also have noticed that farmers leave considerable room between the rows to fit in equipment for cultivating and feeding the crops. This is not necessary in home plantings. Many gardeners abandon the wide rows for small paths between the crops. Check plant spacing information on seed packets and use the closest spacing in home gardens.

CARE

Seen any weeds lately? Well, they are part of any garden. It's best to pull them as they are noticed. Many weeds resemble the crops you are growing, so check carefully. How do you determine if sprouting growths are weeds or the seeds you planted? Here are some tips:

- If the plants are growing in rows and the growths look alike, they are probably the crops.
- Check seed packets for pictures of the crops.
- If you have lots of similar plants, they are usually from the seeds you sowed.
- Wait a while and look for identifiable features of the crop: **carrots** with orange roots, **beets** with reddish leaves, or **tomatoes** with the familiar foliage smell.

WATERING

The rainy season may end shortly, leaving watering up to you. Check the irrigation system to make sure it is working. If you water by hand, make sure the sprinklers set in the garden are working. Plastic types can deteriorate and develop cracks. Here are a few more watering tips:

- Consider soaker hoses as a way of watering long rows or clusters of transplants, putting the water right at the root system. You can also put them on a timer to turn off as needed.

Experiment with row gardening to determine the most efficient use of your space.

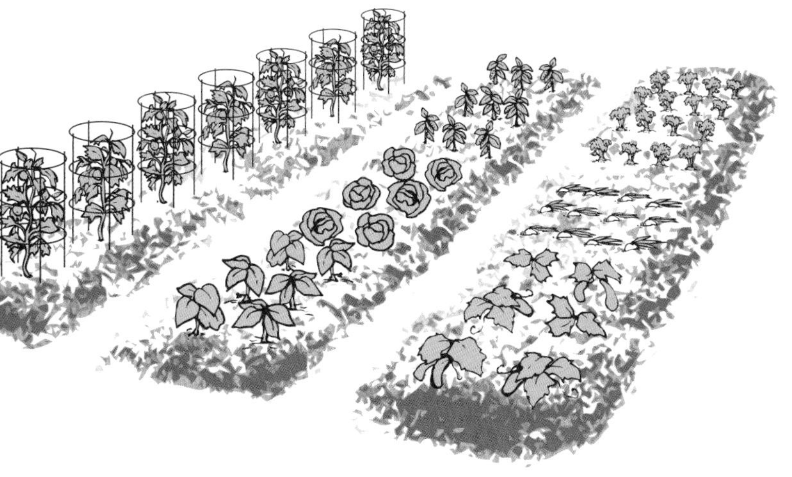

• Use microsprinklers to water small beds. You can often purchase systems that can be adapted to the herb and vegetable garden.

• Regulate overhead sprinklers so they water only the intended plantings.

Make sure they are high enough so as not to batter the plants.

• Operate all systems during the early-morning hours to conserve water, and apply no more than 1/2 to 3/4 inch of water at a time.

FERTILIZING

Feeding schedules are important this time of year. Mark your calendars with the next scheduled feeding. You can always skip a feeding if the plants are growing adequately. Here are some hints to help give your plants the right amounts of fertilizer:

• Follow label rates. Products contain different amounts of nutrients. Use the amounts and frequency of feeding listed on the label as the best guide.

• Plants that are making vigorous growth and have bright-green leaves do not need an immediate feeding. Wait a week or two longer.

THE THREE SISTERS

Here is a fun planting technique that can save space and produce vegetables at the same time. It's a great project for kids, teaching them how the American Indians planted **corn**, **climbing beans**, and **bush squash**. All you need is a sunny garden spot and seeds of each crop. Prepare the soil for planting, with plenty of organic matter and manure, then follow these steps:

1. Form a rounded planting site about a foot or more in diameter. Create as many of the rounded sites as you want, 4 feet apart.
2. Plant seeds of the three crops, spacing them 2 inches apart in the rounded sites. Sow three or four seeds of each.
3. Water the soil and apply a thin mulch layer. Water again whenever the soil begins to dry.
4. While seedlings are still small, remove all but one or two of each crop.
5. Train the **beans** to climb the **corn** stalks, and the **squash** to grow under the corn and beans.
6. Feed the plantings monthly to help produce crops.

The plants should produce **corn**, **beans**, and **squash** at about the same time to complete this enjoyable gardening project.

Overfeeding can reduce production in fruiting crops.

• Wash off granules that lodge among leaves after applications.

• Keep concentrated fertilizers away from stems. Try to get a uniform distribution under the plants.

• Limit **legume** plantings to one or two feedings per crop.

PROBLEMS

Caterpillars may be your major problem this time of year. Populations have had the summer to build up on weeds and other plantings in the landscape. At the first sign of chewing damage, check for these pests. Many can be handpicked from the plants. Others can be controlled with a natural spray of an insecticide containing *Bacillus thuringiensis*. Synthetic products are also available at garden centers. A few more pests found in the fall warm-season garden are aphids, grasshoppers, mites, slugs, snails, and whiteflies.

OCTOBER

HERBS & VEGETABLES

PLANNING

Can you feel the chill in the air? This signals the end of the warm-season planting season everywhere but in South Florida, and the beginning of cool-season crops. **Tomatoes**, **corn**, **squash**, and others are going to continue growing and producing, but you can now concentrate on crops that withstand a light freeze.

Fall also ushers in the herb-growing season. Most herbs prefer cooler weather. Many are sensitive to freezes but can be protected with covers.

PLANTING

Lots of cool-season crops can be planted from seeds, especially **carrots**, **beets**, **turnips**, and similar plants. Use these techniques:

• Plant at the proper depth.

Small seeds are usually sown at a 1/2-inch depth; large seeds, about an inch.

• In dry, sandy soils, sprinkle water over the rows or thoroughly wet the planting site prior to sowing the seeds.

• When seeds are small and the soil may dry quickly, lay a board, piece of cardboard, or newspaper over the row to keep the seeds moist and speed germination. Lift the coverings daily to check for growth, and moisten the soil if needed.

When the first sprouts are noticed, remove the coverings.

• Check growing seedlings for pests. Caterpillars and slugs are a fall problem and may chew the seedling back to the ground.

Handpick, or apply a pesticide as needed.

With some crops, including **broccoli**, **cauliflower**, **collards**, and **onions** you have a choice between seeds and transplants. Transplants are easiest. Start seedlings in pots while other crops are completing production. During cooler months, it takes four to eight weeks to have a transplant ready from seed.

CARE

A thick mulch layer over the soil means reduces the need for ground cultivation. Loosen compacted soils to allow better water absorption. Tilling also helps to release nutrients and stimulate plant growth.

WATERING

Fall begins the drier season that can last until next May. Luckily, plant growth during the cooler months does not require as much water. Check every two to three days for the water needs of growing plants in the ground. Check container plantings daily. Get newly planted crops off the everyday watering schedule as soon as possible. Allowing several days between waterings helps the plants develop deeper pest-resistant root systems.

FERTILIZING

While the weather remains warm, crops need regular feedings. Most growers of herbs and vegetables use a combination of some of the following.

• Granular feedings: usually applied every 3 to 4 weeks. As weather begins to cool, feeding intervals are often lengthened by a week or more.

• Liquid fertilizers: best applied at label rates, usually used every week or two. You can increase the feeding interval by a week during cooler weather.

There are many fertilizing options. You may need more than one type in your vegetable garden.

• Manure and compost: applied as a sidedressing, or a sprinkling of manure tea, over the root system. Feedings are usually made monthly throughout the growing season.

If you use manure, some supplemental feedings with granular or liquid fertilizers may be necessary in sandy soil.

PROBLEMS

Stay alert to mite problems on **tomatoes**, **eggplants**, and **peppers**. Rains are no longer present to wash them off plants. Mites are very small and suck juices from leaves and stems. When populations are large, they may give a reddish color to stems, or form webs, depending on the species. With **peppers**, the tips of stems become contorted. Control with a soap spray or miticide for vegetable use at garden centers. Other pests to watch for include aphids, caterpillars, grasshoppers, slugs, snails, and whiteflies.

STRAWBERRY PYRAMIDS

To have plenty of **strawberries** for the table, a family of four needs between 80 and 100 plants. One way to increase the growing space and intensify the plantings is with a **strawberry** pyramid. Use rot-resistant wood or plastic to build a multilevel planting site. Inch-thick boards that are 6 inches wide are ideal. If you create a planting site 6 feet wide and long, it will hold about 80 plants. Here are the steps:

1. Create the first layer of boards to form the area 6 feet wide and long. Fill the area with soil enriched with organic matter. Compost or potting soil can also be used.
2. Build the next layer a foot in from the sides. Fill with soil mixture.
3. Construct third and fourth layers 1 foot in from the sides in a similar manner, and fill with soil.
4. Plant the **strawberries** 8 to 12 inches apart in each layer of the pyramid.

Keep the plantings moist, and feed monthly with a liquid or granular fertilizer. Some fruiting should begin by January, with peak production during the spring months. Planted pyramids may be kept for two or more years before needing replanting.

NOVEMBER
HERBS & VEGETABLES

PLANNING

It's the cooler time of year throughout Florida. In southern parts of the state, most warm-season crops can still be planted-you can decide if you want **tomatoes** and **beans**, or **broccoli** and **endive** for the garden. Cold damage is possible in these areas, but unlikely most years.

Broccoli

At this time of year in the central and northern portions of the state, it is best to plant mostly cool-season crops, as a frost or freeze is more likely to occur within the next few months. Some of these crops are very cold resistant, and others can only withstand a light frost. Better keep the cold protection handy, starting at the end of the month.

Continue to encourage warm-season crops that are still producing. During a warm winter, even in Central Florida, these plantings may escape major damage. It's not unlikely to have **tomatoes** and **beans** fresh from the garden for the holiday season.

When one crop finishes up, waste no time adding another. If you developed a plan, you'll know exactly where the new plants will go.

PLANTING

Don't let one area of the garden sit without a growing crop. For gardeners who want to take a break for the winter, consider sowing a cover crop of **ryegrass**. Just scatter it over any tilled soil, and water to start the grass growing. It will help hold nutrients in the soil and provide some organic matter for the next planting. It can be mowed down and tilled in at planting time.

As one warm-season crop finishes, have seeds or transplant of the next vegetables ready to put in the ground. Check the roots and above-ground plant portions for pests such as nematodes, cutworms, and mites. If possible, determine a control that can be used before planting.

When one crop follows another very quickly and the problems are minimal, you can use quick transplant techniques:

1. Remove all portions of older crops, including as much of the root system as possible.
2. Move to the area between the rows, or the spots between plantings of the previous crop.
3. Till the ground lightly and work in some manure or compost.
4. Plant to make starting the new garden easy.

Continue planting the herbs in the garden and containers. You should be getting some of the most rapid growth at this time of year. Don't forget, any area in the garden that has even a small open spot is a good place for herbs. A good plant for containers, especially hanging baskets, is **nasturtium**.

1. Fill a hanging basket with a loose potting mix.
2. Place four to six **nasturtium** seeds in the baskets, pushing them 1/2 inch into the soil.

3. Keep the baskets moist and in bright light to encourage germination in about a week.

4. Feed weekly with a fertilizer solution

5. Display in a full-sun to lightly shaded location.

CARE

November should be producing bountiful harvests. Both the warm-season and cool-season crops are starting to mature. Keep the crops picked to encourage new production.

WATERING

It's a dry but cool time of the year. Check established plantings every three or four days to determine water needs. New plantings of herbs or vegetables in containers may need daily watering. Follow good watering practices:

- Water when the surface of the soil is dry to the touch.
- Apply 1/2 to 3/4 inch of water, or moisten the soil until water runs out of the drainage holes in the container.
- Water during the early-morning hours.

FERTILIZING

There is no need to make major adjustments to your feeding program just because the cooler months are here. Keep the following feeding practices in use.

- **In-ground plantings:** Feed monthly with a granular fertilizer or manure sidedressing. Use liquids every 2 to 3 weeks, or as suggested on the label.
- **Container gardens:** Feed every 7 to 14 days with a liquid fertilizer. Some slow-release granular products that allow feedings every few months are also available.
- **Hanging baskets:** Apply a liquid fertilizer every 7 to 14 days, or use a slow-release granular product.

PROBLEMS

Insects are less active during cooler days. A few that you still need to watch for are aphids, caterpillars, slugs, snails, and whiteflies.

QUICK NEMATODE CONTROL

It's no fun finding nematodes in your soil, especially during the winter months. Root knot nematode damage is very obvious, showing up as swollen areas along the roots. When this happens, you have only a few possible controls:

- Take the area out of production and wait until next summer to use soil solarization techniques.
- Find a nematode-resistant crop to plant now or during the spring season and tart plantings in containers.

You can also use this quick and very effective control to get you through the next growing season:

1. Open up a large hole where you want to grow your crops and add nematode-free soil.
2. Make the area for planting 2 to 3 feet in diameter and 6 to 8 inches deep.
3. Fill the hole with potting soil or compost and add the plants or seeds.
4. Make a 4- to 6-inch-high berm around the plantings to catch and hold water. This also prevents soil from the sides with nematodes from contaminating the good soil.

Plantings should remain unaffected by nematodes for one crop or season.

DECEMBER

HERBS & VEGETABLES

PLANNING

Happy holidays! Your garden can add to the big family feast. You can use **mints** in cooking or potpourris for gifts.

While Northern gardens are all but gone, Florida's plantings are still very productive. Keep the garden growing by making replacements as needed. Replace nonproductive warm-season crops with cool-season choices.

Also, think ahead to warm-season gardens for spring. Plan for your winter garden to finish up at the end of February. You might grow quick crops like **lettuce**, **radishes**, and **spinach** in the areas you will want to plant in early spring with **tomatoes**, **melons**, and **corn**.

PLANTING

Use seeds and transplants to keep the garden growing. Use small pots or cell-packs to get them started for when a spot becomes available.

Note which cool-season vegetables take three or more months to produce a crop. These should be started this month. Plant **English peas**, **Brussels sprouts**, and **onions** now.

CARE

Keep protective covers handy, as many areas in North and Central Florida may get a frost or freeze this month. Just a blanket draped over the plants and to the ground may be enough to hold in some heat. A bale of hay may be pulled apart and fluffed over the planting for quick cold protection. Young plants can be protected with an overturned pot, box, or garbage can.

WATERING

Keep checking for water needs of the plants. Moving into the cool months often means less water is being used. Most in-ground plantings can go three or four days or longer between watering. Even plants in containers and hanging baskets can go a day or two.

FERTILIZING

The weather can be cool, but the plants are still active. Maintain feeding schedules with minor variations. If growth seems to be adequate, make the following adjustments.

- For in-ground plantings, increase the time between feedings with granular fertilizers to every 4 to 6 weeks, liquid feedings to monthly.
- For container plantings, apply a liquid fertilizer every 3 to 4 weeks.

PROBLEMS

Most pests don't like the really cool weather. Most active will be caterpillars in the big-leaf crops of **cabbage**, **collards**, **cauliflower**, and **broccoli**. Control caterpillars by handpicking or using a natural insecticide spray containing *Bacillus thuringiensis*. Synthetic sprays are also available.

CHAPTER SIX

LAWNS

What is the number-one gardening activity? According to some surveys, it's caring for the lawn. Some may interpret this finding to mean that lawn care is the most popular of gardening chores. But I suspect surveyors may have simply asked gardeners: "What are you planning for this weekend?" and the answer was often: "We are mowing the lawn!"

Having dense, green grass is a sort of standard for many neighborhoods. In some communities, if the lawn is not of a certain variety or quality, it can be replaced—at your expense.

Not all communities are this tough. But many homeowners would like to have a good, green lawn. Who wouldn't puff out their chest just a little when friends marvel over their green turf?

PLANNING

A good lawn starts from the time you decide to plant grass. First you have to determine what to grow. Here are some questions to ask yourself:

- How much time do I have to care for a lawn?
- Will just any green lawn do, or should it be a fine-bladed, foot-tickling grass?
- Do I have irrigation, or will Mother Nature do most of the watering?
- How much shade do I have?
- Do I want to get to know the pest problems and the controls, or will I have the work done?

These are just a few of the questions you need to ponder. Some lawn types take more work than others. Generally, Bermudagrass and zoysiagrass

need the most maintenance in Florida, St. Augustinegrass gets a moderate rating, and centipedegrass bahiagrass, and carpetgrass, a low-maintenance rating.

Then you have to think about the shade in your lawn. Of all the grasses, St. Augustine can take the lower light levels. It's generally accepted that if you have much more than 25 percent shade, you are better growing some ground cover other than turf. Of the St. Augustine varieties, Bitterblue, Delmar, Palmetto, and Seville are some of the most shade tolerant. Floratam has very little shade tolerance.

All lawngrasses grow best in full sun. Check out our chart on page 173 for other features that can help determine which grass you should grow. Gardeners along the coast should be particularly interested in salt tolerance. If you don't have an irrigation system, select a grass that survives with missed watering.

Due to their durability, pest resistance, and overall easy care, most Florida gardeners select either a St. Augustine or bahia variety. But you be the judge.

• Bahiagrass: A very durable but coarse grass that can be seeded or sodded. Bahia is the second most popular lawngrass and is often selected where the turf cannot always be irrigated. It has an open growth habit and tall seedheads during the summer. The most popular variety is Argentine bahia because it has fewer seedheads and less spring yellowing. Pensacola and Paraguay bahia are also available.

• Bermudagrass: It's the foot tickler of all Florida lawns because of its fine blades and soft growth habit. It's a very high-maintenance grass due to pest control, frequent feeding, and frequent mowing. This is the grass of choice for Florida sports fields and golf greens. Many varieties are available. One variety, FloraTex, has lower maintenance requirements and might be selected for home lawns.

• Carpetgrass: Very few lawns are produced from carpetgrass because of its lack of drought tolerance. It's a medium-textured grass that might be selected for the wetter planting sites.

• Centipedegrass: Often called the "poor man's turf," centipedegrass needs very little fertilizer to produce good growth. In fact, it often declines if it is overfed. Centipede grows close to the ground and forms a dense turf of medium texture. It is very susceptible to nematodes. It is best used in the heavier soils of North Florida.

• St. Augustinegrass: This is the most popular of all Florida turf types for the home lawns with a dense growth habit and good green color. The leaf blades are rather coarse, but durable. It's easy to maintain and has good salt tolerance and relatively few pests. Popular varieties include Bitterblue, Delmar, Floratam, Seville, and Palmetto, Amerishade, and Classic.

• Zoysiagrass: Most gardeners are familiar with the ads promoting zoysiagrass for home lawns. It is a dense, good, green grass with fine blades—but in Florida, it requires a lot of maintenance. One big problem is nematodes, for which there is no easy control in local lawns. Some varieties include Cashmere, Emerald, Empire, and Meyer.

You may find other grasses grown in Florida, but not as permanent turf. Buffalograss has been tried, but it usually declines during summer rains. Ryegrass, along with some other more northern cool-season grasses, can be seeded as a winter ground cover, but it declines during the hot spring and summer weather.

PLANTING

Getting started is about the same for all lawn types. You need to have a well-prepared

planting site. Some people take shortcuts and often fail to get a well-established lawn. Here are the steps recommended to prepare the planting site.

- Control all weeds, especially perennials, with a nonselective herbicide that permits planting shortly after use.
- Remove all brown plant portions after the weeds decline.
- Till the planting site and rake out debris.
- Have the soil tested, and adjust the acidity to the proper pH.

The addition of organic matter is optional and typically skipped in most home plantings.

Now you are ready to start the new lawn with either seed, sod, or plugs. Here are some tips for each.

- **Seeding a new lawn:** Work in a light fertilizer application just prior to seeding. Spread the seed in two directions across the prepared ground. Rake the seed in lightly. Keep the ground moist until the seed is up and the seedlings are well established.
- **Plugging:** Small plugs of turf available at garden centers are usually sold 18 to a tray and set in the ground at about a 1-foot spacing. Keep moist until rooted into the surrounding soil.
- **Sodding a new lawn:** Florida sod is sold in rectangular portions 24 inches long and 16 inches wide. A pallet of sod usually has 400 square feet. Wet the ground before laying the sod and piece it together. Keep the soil moist until the grass becomes rooted in the ground.

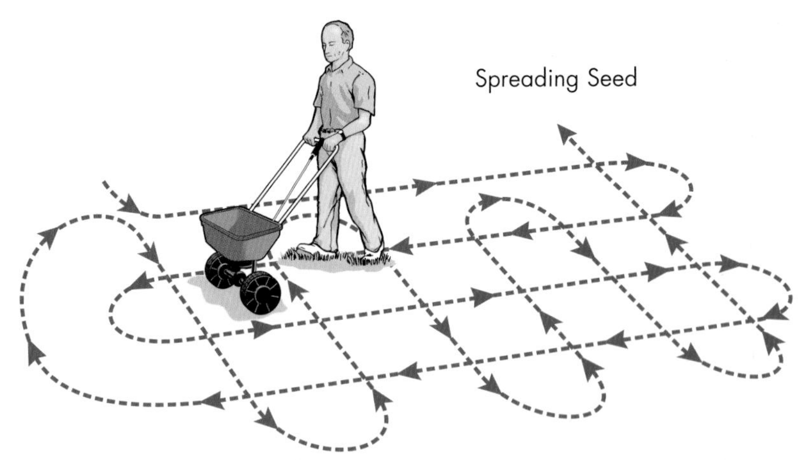

Spreading Seed

CARE

Florida lawns need regular mowing. Very few lawns stop growth except during the winter months. Even then, most lawns just slow down—some mowing is still needed during these cooler months if only to control weeds. A rotary mower can be used with most grasses but if you want a truly fine cut, a reel mower is best for Bermuda and zoysiagrasses. The coarser grasses are usually cut once a week during the growing season. Finer turf types may get a twice-a-week mowing. Keep the blade sharp, and mow at the proper height to have an attractive turf.

WATERING

Let your lawn tell you when it needs water. Where possible, try to avoid putting the lawn on an automatic watering system, which may overwater the turf, encouraging shallow roots, excessive growth, and pest problems. Here are some watering

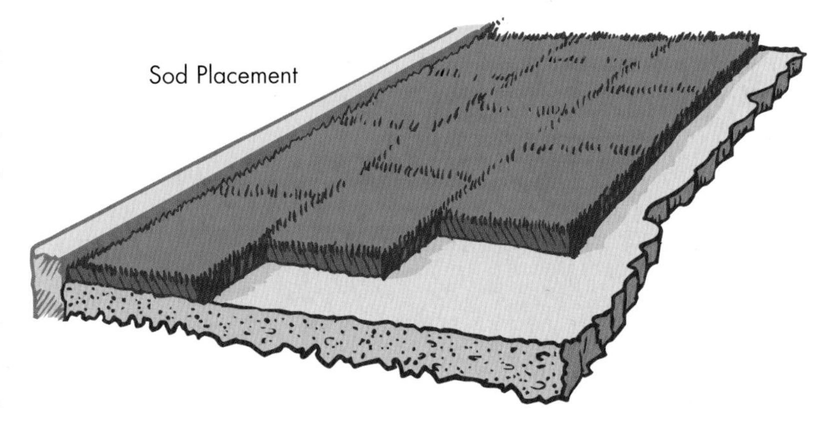

Sod Placement

tips: Water when spots in the lawn show signs of wilting: the grass develops a gray-green color and the leaf blades begin to fold together. Apply 1/2 to 3/4 inch of water to the entire lawn at each watering. Water during early-morning hours. Conserve water by using sprinklers that keep moisture off the streets and sidewalks.

FERTILIZING

All grasses grow best with feedings at least twice a year, once in the spring and once in fall. Use a 16-4-8, 13-3-13, 15-0-15 or similar analysis lawn fertilizer available from your local garden centers. Many communities and counties are considering ordinances that limit phosphorus (the middle number in an analysis) to a range between zero and three percent in lawn products unless a soil test determines more of this nutrient is needed. All gardeners should have a soil test made through the University of Florida IFAS Extension or an independent laboratory to determine the phosphorus level of their soils and plan their lawn feeding programs accordingly.

Lawns may also respond to iron-only feedings during the summer months or when they begin to yellow. Iron is a vital minor nutrient that helps keep grass green. Usually one or two equally spaced iron feedings during the summer (or applied when the lawn begins to yellow) can help regreen the turf without stimulating a lot of growth. Feeding schedules vary greatly and may depend on the type of fertilizer applied to the lawn. Here are some general fertilizer programs:

- Bahiagrass: Complete fertilizer in March and September. Iron during the summer.
- Bermudagrass: Complete fertilizer in March, May, and September. Nitrogen-only in July, October, and December.
- Carpetgrass: Complete fertilizer in March and August.
- Centipedegrass: Complete fertilizer in March and September. Iron during the summer.
- St Augustinegrass: Complete fertilizer in March and September. Iron during the summer.
- Zoysiagrass: Complete fertilizer in March and September. Nitrogen-only in May, July, and November.

PEST CONTROL

Become familiar with the pests that can affect your turf. Try to spot the insects and diseases as they become active, and apply the control only as needed. It may not be necessary to treat the entire lawn. Pick the least-toxic product to apply first. Check for weeds as well, and note the months to make timely herbicide applications.

WEED CONTROL

Weeds are probably the number-one complaint of gardeners. Before you even start a lawn, decide what weed problems exist. If they are perennial weeds, you have just a few choices.

- Try to pull them out to eliminate the top and root growth.
- Dig them out to get all the roots.
- Spot-kill the weeds before planting. This is by far the best technique. Just be sure to use a nonselective weed control product that permits planting shortly after the weeds turn brown.

Other weed problems will pop up throughout the year. Some you can do very little about until the spring or fall months when weeds are more susceptible to controls and grass is more resistant to chemicals. If you have a weed problem, have it identified and then design a control program:

- Many big weeds can be dug or pulled out if they are not too numerous. Just bend over and give them a tug, and you can avoid using chemicals.
- Spot-kill weeds with a nonselective herbicide that allows new growth in the soil. Use a quart sprayer and try to hit only the weed.

CHAPTER SIX

From here on you may have to get tough and use a herbicide over most of the lawn where the weeds are found growing. Here are the major types of weeds and some controls:

Broadleaf weeds have large leaves and often attractive flowers. Use a weed-and-feed product or liquid made for your lawn types as needed; follow label instructions.

Grassy weeds produce narrow and usually long leaves with hollow stems. Prevent seed germination during late winter or spring with a preemergence herbicide, following the instructions on the label.

Sedges resemble grasses but have very shiny leaves. Fruiting stems are solid and triangular. They are often called nut or water sedges. Control with liquid sprays made especially for sedge control.

Lawns

Grass Type	Mowing Height	Method of Establishment	Major Insects	Major Diseases
Bahiagrass	3 – 4 inches	Seed, sod	Mole crickets, caterpillars	Few
Bermudagrass	1/2 – 1 inch	Seed, sod, plugs	Mole crickets, caterpillars	Dollar spot, brown patch
Carpetgrass	1 1/2 – 2 inches	Seed	Mole crickets, caterpillars	Brown patch
Centipedegrass	1 1/2 – 2 inches	Seed, sod, plugs	Ground pearls, caterpillars	Brown patch
St. Augustinegrass	3 – 4 inches*	Sod, plugs	Chinch bugs, caterpillars	Brown patch
Zoysiagrass	1 – 2 inches	Sod, plugs caterpillars	Hunting billbug, brown patch	Dollar spot,

Grass Type	Drought Tolerance	Shade Tolerance	Salt Tolerance	Nematolde Tolerance
Bahiagrass	Very good	Very light	Poor	Very good
Bermudagrass	Very good	None	Very good	Poor
Carpetgrass	Poor	Very light	Poor	Poor
Centipedegrass	Fair	Very light	Poor	Poor
St. Augustinegrass	Good	Filtered	Very good	Good
Zoysiagrass	Very good	Very light	Very good	Poor

* 2 to 2 1/2 inches for semidwarfs

JANUARY
LAWNS

PLANNING

In North and Central Florida, winter grass is often brown due to frost and freezes. In South Florida, the grass is green, but growth is greatly reduced.

Identify where you need new turf. Consider the problems you had with turf last year, and decide on the best action for this year. Here are a few suggestions:

- Turf thinned or dying due to shade: Select a shade-tolerant variety, thin the trees, or use another type of ground cover.
- An area is hard to mow and gets little care: Use mulch or another type of ground cover to fill the area.
- Insects were heavy and the turf declined: Mark your calendar for the time the insects are likely to attack, and be ready with a control.
- Weeds quickly filled the lawn: Remove all live growth, and resod or add plugs. Use a preemergence herbicide just before weed seeds sprout.
- Foot traffic caused the turf to decline: Select a more durable grass, or add a path formed from mulch or steppingstones.

PLANTING

Gardeners usually delay adding new turf to the landscape until the weather is a little warmer; most seed of permanent grasses won't germinate until warmer weather, and if it should freeze, young grass might be damaged. But working outdoors is almost stress-free at this time of year, and you can get areas ready for the spring planting season:

- Remove all weeds. It's usually best to control the weeds with a nonselective herbicide that permits rapid replanting.
- Till the soil and rake out the debris.
- Get a soil acidity test. The test can often be performed at local garden centers or through your Extension Service office.
- Adjust the soil acidity level according to the pH test, using lime or sulfur. Most grasses like a slightly acid soil around pH 6.5. Try to adjust **bahiagrass** to between pH 5.5 and 6.0.
- Rake out the ground and you are ready to seed, sod, or plug.

In the warmer areas of the state there is no reason you cannot begin sodding or plugging at any time now.

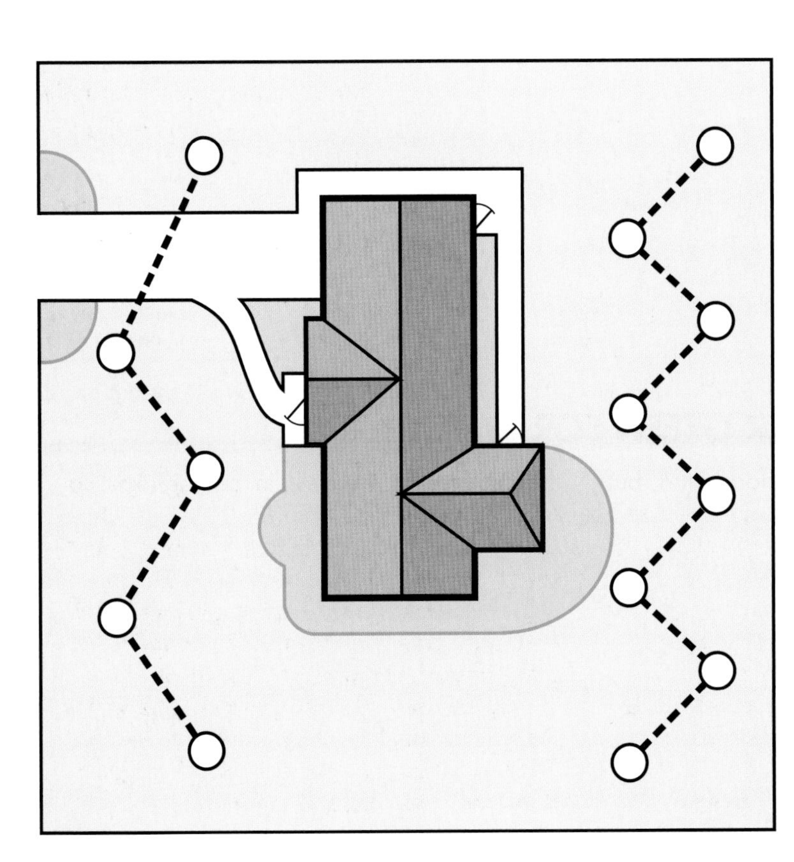

Take soil samples from all parts of your lawn for an accurate test.

CARE

Don't put the mower away. The grass may not be growing except in the warmer areas of the state, but weeds can be growing anywhere. A mowing every few weeks keeps the unwanted greenery under control and the mower in good shape.

WATERING

It's winter, a dry time of year. If the grass is brown or not making much growth, it's using very little water. Turn off the automatic system and check the soil to determine water needs. When the upper inch of soil becomes dry to the touch or the grass blades are beginning to fold and turn gray-green, it's time to water:

- Apply between 1/2 and 3/4 inch of water.
- Water during the early-morning hours.
- Make sure the soil is moist before expected freezes.

Turn off the water during the freeze.

FERTILIZING

January is usually a fertilizer-free month for permanent lawn grasses. Most have been well fed during the fall and early winter months. If the winter is quite mild and the grass begins to grow, some yellowing might be noted. You can apply iron or half the normal rate of a lawn fertilizer just to renew the green.

PROBLEMS

Don't expect a lot of pest problems during winter. Most insects are slowed by the cooler weather. Some, like sod webworms, have been killed back to South Florida by the cold. If the weather is warm, some gardeners might spot the disease brown patch, a disease caused by a fungus living in most soils. The disease prefers warmish weather, moist soil, and spots with poor air movement. It causes large, brown, circular areas to develop. Control with a fungicide available at garden centers.

Weeds grow at all times of the year. The cool-season weeds are quite vigorous and should be controlled to prevent competition with the turf.

- Mow out the weeds as much as possible.
- Dig out persistent weeds.
- Spot-kill with a nonselective herbicide that will permit replanting.

Most selective weed control should be delayed until later in the year when the turf is less likely to be affected.

QUICK GREEN FOR BARE SPOTS

Ryegrass is not a permanent Florida turf, but it can be planted during the cooler seasons to fill in bare spots and regreen brown lawns. It gives a rich green color but requires regular care.

Any **rye** seed can be used. Here are the steps to success:

1. Remove weeds from the areas to be planted. Rake out brown grass blades and clippings near the soil surface.
2. Sow up to ten pounds of **ryegrass** for every 1,000 square feet. Rake the seed into the ground, or water it in among existing grass.
3. Keep the soil moist, and the **rye** should be up within a week.
4. Feed monthly with a lawn fertilizer at half the normal rate. Mow as needed at the height of the permanent grass (or 2 inches).

Ryegrass should grow through the early spring, then decline as hotter weather returns. Other cool-season grasses are **bentgrass**, **bluegrass**, and **fescue.**

FEBRUARY

LAWNS

PLANNING

Prepare to enhance your turf where the family plays games and sits in the yard. Plan for a lawn only where it is really needed: in barren areas that are easy to mow, play areas, on banks as anti-erosion ground cover, and in long or short vistas where you want the feeling of wide-open space. Once you have planned grass areas, determine which grass variety to use. Consider shade, soil type, salt conditions, and other factors that affect turf growth. Sometimes you may have to pick another type of ground cover.

PLANTING

Now is the time for establishing a new lawn. Start with the basics and prepare the site for planting. Here are some sodding tips:

- Order the sod to arrive the day it's needed. Sod left on a pallet more than a day or two starts to decline.
- If you are picking up the sod at a garden center, find out when the fresh sod arrives. Be one of the first to get the fresh sod. It may be kept a day or two in the shade if you are not quite ready.

Allow grass to undergo water stress to develop longer roots.

- Soak the prepared soil prior to sodding. This gives the roots a moist cool soil to grow into.
- Fit the pieces of sod closely together. Use a knife to cut off pieces to fill in small spots and create rounded corners.
- Water the sod as it is laid so it never dries out.
- Start a watering program. Apply a half-inch of water daily the first week, a half-inch every other day the second week, and 1/2 to 3/4 inch water every third day the third week If the lawn should show severe stress at any time, additional watering may be needed.

New lawns in shade may need less frequent watering.

- After the third week the sod should be able to be placed on an "as-needed" watering schedule.

CARE

Mow all lawns as needed. If the lawn needs cutting the day it is installed, you can mow it. Most lawns, however, won't need mowing for a week or two after installation. The general rule is to cut the coarse grasses of **St. Augustine** and **bahia** at the highest mower setting (this is usually in the 3- to 4-inch range). The semidwarf **St. Augustines** can be cut at the 2- to 2 1/2-inch height.

WATERING

Established turf won't need a lot of water at this time of year. This is a good time to train your lawn to produce a deep root system. One way you can help the lawn go a few extra days between waterings is to make sure you are cutting it at the highest recommended height. Research

shows that the higher the leaf blade, the deeper the root system, and a deeper root system can absorb more water. Here are a few more tips to help your lawn go longer between waterings.

- Turn off the automatic sprinkler system and water only when needed.
- Allow the lawn to start developing some dry spots.

A little moisture stress encourages a little root growth.

- Wait to water until the leaf blades in some spots begin to take on a gray-green color and fold inward.
- Give the lawn a good soaking at each watering by applying 1/2 to 3/4 inch water.
- Don't water again until the lawn shows a need.

Most home lawns can last five to seven days or more between waterings at this time of year if they have a deep root system.

FERTILIZING

First-of-the-year feedings start in South Florida and work their way northward this month. When the grass blades are dry, apply a fertilizer with a 16-4-8, 13-3-13, 15-0-15, or similar analysis. Distribute the fertilizer uniformly over the lawn. Use a spreader setting as guide, or apply the recommended amount per 1,000 square feet of lawn. Make sure the spreader swaths overlap just a little to avoid yellow strips in the lawn. Water after the application. A few weed-and-feed fertilizers are made to apply to damp lawns-follow label instructions.

PROBLEMS

It's crabgrass-control time throughout much of the state. The trick to eliminating this weed is to prevent seed germination. Most crabgrass begins growth as the weather warms during late winter. Conditions are normally right for seed germination around February 1 in South Florida, February 15 in Central Florida, and March 1 in North Florida. If the winter is unseasonably warm, you may have to make the treatments earlier.

1. Remove all growing crabgrass and dormant runners.
2. Apply a preemergence herbicide made for use with your lawn type. Most are sold as crabgrass preventers. Others just list crabgrass seed control on the label.
3. Follow all label instructions. Most need to be watered-in lightly to begin preventing seed germination.
4. Note repeat treatments needed as specified on the label. Crabgrass does not just germinate at one time of the year-seeds could sprout between late winter and early fall in most areas of the state.

Watch for brown patch in lawns. Look for circular yellowing areas. Often they keep a green spot of grass in the center.

Look for chinch bugs in yellowing spots in **St. Augustine** lawns.

MARCH

LAWNS

PLANNING

Some areas don't grow turf well. Grass may thicken up at some times, then thin and die out. You need to find out what is wrong before you add more grass. Your local Extension Service will test your soil and provide free publications on Florida turf grasses.

PLANTING

The use of plugs was introduced to homeowners during the 1970s. Plugs make starting a new lawn from a known variety convenient for just about everyone. Some advantages are:

- You can purchase what you can plant in a day or two.
- Plugs can keep in their trays for weeks without declining.
- Trays of plugs are easy to transport.
- Trays of plugs are not heavy and create little mess.

Not all turf grasses grow well as plugs. **Bahia**, in particular, is slow to form from the side shoots, often called runners—it's still best planted as sod or seed. Here are some tips for plugs:

- Have the planting site free of weeds and prepared for planting.

You can plant through old turf and even low-growing weeds that have been killed, but it is better to have a site prepared as for sodding and seeding.

- Give the plugs proper planting. Space **St. Augustinegrass** 6 to 12 inches; **centipede** 6 inches; **zoysia** 6 inches; **Bermuda** 12 inches.
- Dig the hole for the plugs with a trowel or use a plugger.

Some gardeners like to add a plug-starter fertilizer in the hole at this time.

- Insert the plug, and firm the soil around the turf.
- Water areas of plugged turf after installing a tray or two.
- Mow as needed and give the first feeding with a lawn fertilizer in three to four weeks.

CARE

Lawns grow rapidly in all areas of the state this month. Begin mowing all grasses at the preferred height. A close cut is not necessary. To remove brown grass blades, you can give the turf a good handraking or rent a power rake. Avoid using vertical mowers to remove brown blades. These mowers can remove runners and more, making it necessary to reestablish the lawn.

WATERING

Rains have been limited since fall, and now that the weather is hotter, check out the irrigation system to make sure it hits all areas of the lawn.

- Make sure sprinkler heads pop up from below the ground. Some may be covered by runners.
- Look for dry areas. Set out cups to catch water, and measure water amounts after running the system.

If there is not 1/2 inch or more for each cycle, change the time operated or adjust the head.

- Check for sprinklers that are watering the street or sidewalks, and adjust.
- Replace heads that are not rotating properly.

FERTILIZING

Complete all spring feedings at this time of year. This is one of two times all lawn types should get a complete fertilizer. Note that some fertilizers contain only nitrogen, or maybe two of the major nutrients. Make sure you get a fertilizer with all three major nutrients except when the soil has adequate phosphorus, in which case a product with a middle number of zero can be applied. This is a good time to select a fertilizer with the minor nutrients including iron and magnesium. Turf grasses use a lot of these minor nutrients.

If your lawn turns yellow immediately after a spring feeding, it could have an iron deficiency. This is a special problem with **bahia** lawn. A fertilizer for this lawn should have at least 1 percent iron in its formula. Here are a few more tips to prevent or correct iron deficiencies:

• Apply a liquid or granular iron-only fertilizer. A number of brands are available at garden centers. Apply as instructed on the label.

• Check the soil acidity. Most iron deficiencies in **bahia** lawns occur in alkaline or slightly acid soils. If possible, adjust the pH to the 5.5 to 6.0 range.

• Soils that are low in iron or have an acidity problem should always receive a fertilizer that contains iron. You can also use acid-forming fertilizers designed to help correct iron and pH problems.

USE THE PROPER FERTILIZER

If weeds are a problem in your lawn, March is the time to use weed-and-feed fertilizers. Do not apply both a regular fertilizer and a weed-and-feed product-apply one or the other. If you use a fertilizer by itself, then liquid weed-control products are available to use as instructed on the label. Have your weeds identified to make sure the product you choose will be effective.

PROBLEMS

It's an old saying: "If you give a chinch an inch, it will take your yard." Chinch bugs are becoming very active in **St. Augustinegrass** lawns. They overwinter in all areas of Florida and begin mounting large populations during spring.

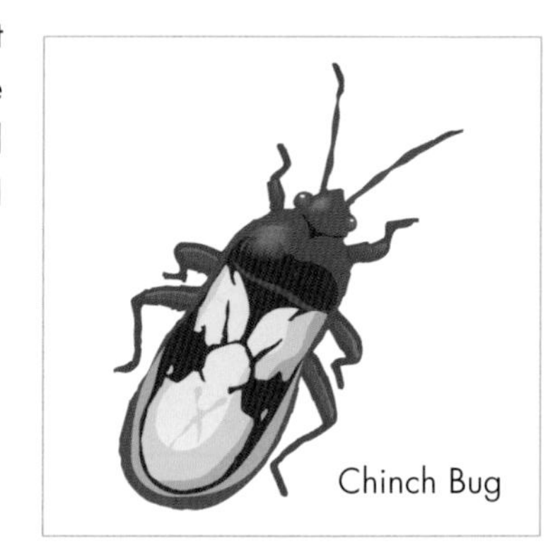

Chinch Bug

April

LAWNS

PLANNING

Part of good lawn planning is deciding what to do about weeds. This is probably the number-one problem about which gardeners complain. Before you even start a lawn, determine which weed problems exist. If they are perennial weeds, pull them out, dig them out, or spot-kill before planting. Other weed problems will pop up throughout the year. Some you can do very little about until spring or fall months when weeds are more susceptible to controls and grass is more resistant to chemicals. If you have a weed problem, have it identified, then design a control program.

PLANTING

Seeding is usually performed during the warmer weather. You will want the seeds to germinate quickly and produce a stand of grass. One problem you may encounter when seeding a lawn is weeds. Plan to create a well-prepared planting site that has been tilled deeply to bury at least some of the seeds. Control all perennial grasses prior to seeding.

- Select a seed with minimal weed content and a good germination percentage of 85 or above. Look for a recent test date on the label.
- Unlike sodding or adding plugs, most seed beds are prepared with a light scatter of fertilizer worked into the soil.
- Seeding rates vary with the grass type. Sow **bahia** seed at the rate of 7 to 10 pounds per 1,000 square feet; **Bermuda** at 2 to 4 pounds; **carpetgrass** at 4 to 5 pounds; **centipede** at .25 pounds.
- Scatter half the seed in one direction and the remaining portion in a perpendicular direction.
- Rake the seed lightly into the soil about 1/4 to 1/2 inch.

Many gardeners like to add a thin layer of weed-free hay or straw to cover 50 to 75 percent of the bare ground.

- Keep the seeded area moist. Light watering may be needed two or three times a day.
- When the seeds begin to germinate, water less frequently but longer to encourage a deep root system.

Give the newly seeded lawn a light feeding three to four weeks after the grass seed begins germinating. Mow when the grass reaches the desired height.

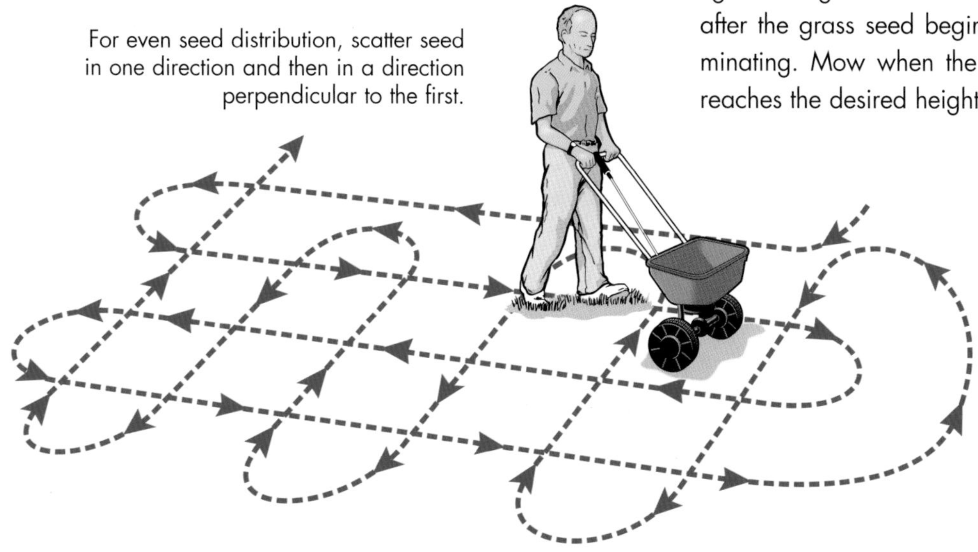

For even seed distribution, scatter seed in one direction and then in a direction perpendicular to the first.

CARE

Some gardeners are concerned about soil aeration, which is sometimes recommended by landscape maintenance companies. It's sort of hard to picture a sandy soil not having enough air, but it may be a problem in clay and very organic soils. Seldom do we aerate sandy soils to let in air, but we may want to let in water. Some home soils consist of various layers of fill soils that aeration can help penetrate and mix together. Use an aerator only if you really have reason.

WATERING

Oh, my—it's the dry time of year. You may wonder why you even have a lawn when the water bills start arriving. Just think-if you didn't water and the lawn declined, it might cost a fortune to replace it.

Lawns are tough, however, and you can put them on a lean diet. Some, like **bahia**, **Bermuda**, and **zoysia**, can survive without water during the dry times—but don't expect a good turf. They will go dormant and then grow back from the rhizomes when it finally rains.

If you do not water **centipedegrass**, **carpetgrass**, and **St. Augustinegrass** lawns, you will lose them during the dry weather. But here is the best way to stretch the time between waterings:

- Wait until spots in the lawn start to turn gray-green and the leaves curl to water the entire lawn.
- Give the lawn a thorough soaking of 1/2 to 3/4 inch water.
- Water during the early-morning hours.
- Stop all feedings during the very dry times.
- Keep your mower at the highest setting for the grass type.
- Do not apply weedkillers to stressed lawns during drought.

FERTILIZING

All spring feedings should be completed early in the month. If the lawn is yellowish, this may be your first hint that you forgot a feeding. There is still time to use a complete fertilizer, but hurry. If the **bahia** turf is showing some yellowing and you applied a spring fertilizer, an iron-only feeding can be applied.

PROBLEMS

This is the last chance to do selective weed control and not affect your turf. Some products specifically say on the label not to apply "when the weather is hot" or "after a certain date." Make sure the lawn is moist and healthy when applying any selective herbicide so there will be no damage to the grass.

Lawn caterpillars may be starting to affect some lawns. The three most common are the sod webworm, armyworm, and grass looper. Army worms and some forms of the sod webworm may be active at this time of year. Others continue through the remaining spring through fall months.

HOW TO MAINTAIN YOUR MOWER

Your lawnmower may be the most important piece of lawncare equipment you own. It takes just a little time to keep this piece of equipment in good shape: Change the oil, lubricate moving parts (not the wheels), clean and oil foam air filters, sharpen the blade monthly, and replace or clean the spark plug once a year. Check safety guards to make sure they are in place.

LAWNS

PLANNING

When you have more than 50 percent weeds, plan for a new lawn. Sometimes you may not have to replace all the grass, only the areas where weeds are out of control. Spot-kill small patches of weeds, and let the good grass fill in. Form squares in problem areas to kill out all growth, or till up and replant. If an area is heavily shaded, consider using another ground cover.

When you have decided where you need grass, choose your variety. Most gardeners are looking for a **bahia** or **St. Augustine** lawn. Don't mix grass types. It's all right to mix varieties of **bahia** or varieties of **St. Augustine**, but not those two grass types. If you cannot water, you most likely need a **bahia**. If an area is shady, choose a shade-tolerant **St. Augustine**.

PLANTING

All grass types can now be added to the landscape. Whether you choose seed, sod or plugs, prepare the soil properly. Shortcuts like laying sod over dead grass or weeds may not work, but good soil preparation always works. Demand good sod or plugs. Don't accept yellow turf for planting.

CARE

Mowing is now one of your major chores. Don't forget to keep the lawnmower blade shape. Why not keep an extra sharp blade handy? This way you always have a ready to use blade as a replacement. When a blade is removed from the mower, take it immediately to be sharpened. Here are a few more mowing tips:

- Scout the lawn to remove bottles, wire, sticks, and similar debris.
- Move children and pets out of the mowing area.
- Wear shoes and clothing that covers the body when operating the mower.
- Mow a dry lawn to prevent slipping and clogging.
- Cut the grass at the same recommended height year-round.
- Mow in a different direction each time to prevent forming ruts in the lawn.
- Leave the clippings on the lawn. Allowing the clippings to fall to the ground returns up to one feeding a year to the turf.

WATERING

The rainy season may return this month, but you can never be sure exactly when it will return. Until the storms start, just water as usual. Now is a good time to recheck the watering system and to look for dry spots. Sometimes watering systems are inadequate during very dry weather. In this case, it's best to do some handwatering or set out some sprinklers at the end of a hose.

FERTILIZING

Some very vigorous and shallow-rooted grasses are ready for

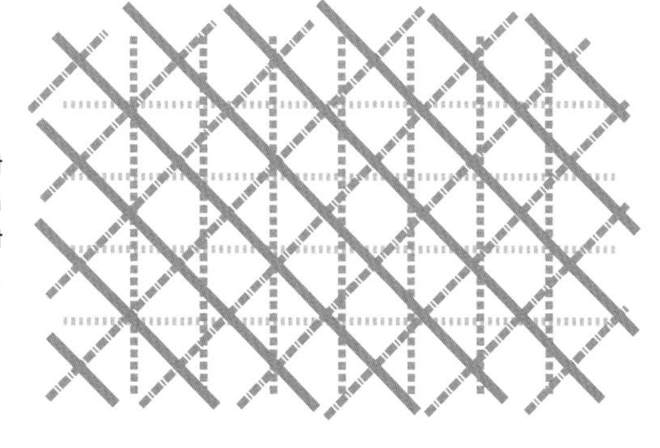

Mow in different directions each time to prevent ruts forming.

another feeding at this time of year. Gardeners keeping to a schedule can give **Bermudagrass** lawns another complete fertilizer application and **zoysia** grass lawns a nitrogen-only feeding.

Many gardeners are not familiar with the nitrogen fertilizers. They are not available at all garden centers, but you should be able to find one or more types. Each is applied to supply 1 pound of nitrogen at each feeding. Some examples: Apply 3 pounds of ammonium nitrate, 5 pounds of ammonium sulfate, or 2 pounds of urea to each 1,000 square feet of turf. These are small quantities of fertilizer and must be applied carefully and watered-in to prevent damage to the lawns. During warmer months, a processed sludge may also be used to supply the needed nitrogen.

THATCH REMOVAL

What is thatch? Most home gardeners have heard about it, but few know what thatch really is in the home lawn. It's not the dry grass blades left over from winter. Dry grass blades can be raked out if needed.

Thatch is the buildup of a peatlike material below the runners of the grass. It is old portions of the grass that have decomposed. Some thatch is normal in all lawns. It's when the thatch becomes too thick that it becomes a problem, limiting water and nutrient movement into the soil. It provides a good spot for insects to hide out of the reach of pesticides.

Grass with thatch layer

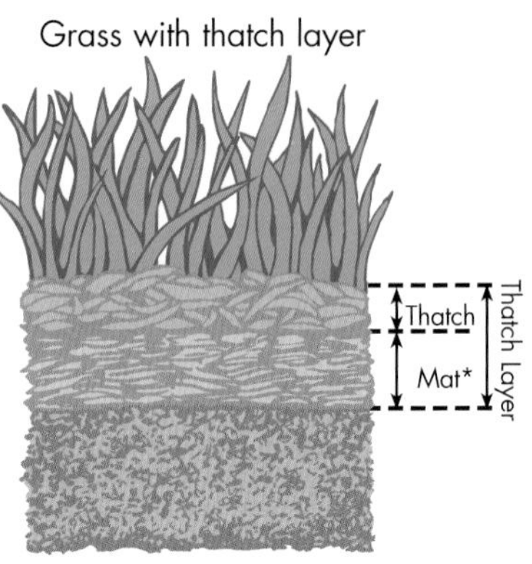

*Old thatch and soil

Most home lawns do not have a thatch problem—the thatch has to be an inch or more in thickness to be considered a real problem. Here are some things you should know about thatch.

- Excessive thatch usually occurs when lawns are overwatered or overfed.
- Keep your lawn on a minimal diet to keep thatch at a safe level.
- Returning grass clippings to the lawn does not promote thatch.
- Thatch removal can be performed using vertical mowers available from rental centers.
- Learn how to properly operate thatch removal equipment or you can permanently damage your lawn.
- If needed, thatch removal is best performed between March and September.

PROBLEMS

It's the beginning of the mole cricket season for **Bermuda**, **bahia**, and **zoysia** lawns. Other lawns can be disturbed by the big brown insects, but damage is usually minimal. The adult mole crickets have been busy laying eggs that can start hatching this month. Other pests may be very active too. Check your lawn for chinch bugs in **St. Augustinegrass** lawns, dollar spot in **Bermuda** turf, lawn caterpillars, mushrooms, and slime mold.

PLANNING

Make note of shady spots where sod won't grow. Your trees may have grown, adding more shade and larger root systems; you might not have the right grass for the shady spots; overwatering can cause root rot problems; and shaded grass wears faster. Sometimes it's a tough decision, but grass may not grow in heavy shade. This means you should consider pavers, mulch, or a shade-tolerant ornamental plant.

PLANTING

During heavy rains, suppliers may not be able to harvest sod, so you may have to wait. Be selective when installing sod during warmer months. Make sure you are buying a high-quality product that is ready to grow. Reject any yellow sod. Don't let it sit more than twenty-four hours on a pallet. Install it over damp, well-prepared soil. Water every day the first week, every other day the second week, and every third day the third week. Then water as needed.

Summer is a great time to fill in a lawn with plugs and seed because Mother Nature often does the watering.

CARE

Keep the mower blade sharp. The blade should be sharpened at least once a month. **Bahia** lawns may be a little tough and can dull a blade in less than a month, and if the mower picks up sand, you may need to check and sharpen the blade more often.

WATERING

Check any brown spots that may indicate inadequate water.

- Don't just reach for a pesticide. Brown areas may not be bugs but just dry soil. Dry spots normally turn uniformly brown with very little yellowing.
- Use a trowel to dig down in the ground. If the soil feels hot and very loose, you have dry soil.
- Run the irrigation system to see how much water is falling on the brown areas. If needed, make sprinkler adjustments or put out a portable sprinkler to water the dry areas.
- If areas get adequate water but are hard to wet, sprinkle a soapy solution over the grass before watering. An aerator may also be used to make holes in the soil that allow water penetration.

FERTILIZING

If you missed feeding this spring, you can catch up with a light application during June. The higher-maintenance grasses may need a feeding if you forgot the May applications.

Some yellowing and lighter-green-colored turf can be expected as the spring fertilizer nutrients are used by the grass. A quick remedy for yellowing can be an iron-only application, or use a product that has iron as one of the major ingredients. Here are a few ways iron can be supplied.

- Liquid iron feedings: Gardeners can apply liquids available from garden centers or make their own. An iron application can be made by mixing 2 ounces of ferrous sulfate in 3 to 5 gallons of water and sprinkling the solution over 1,000 square feet of turf.

PESTICIDE SAFETY

Good lawn care usually means applying pesticides. Only a few natural controls are available to help prevent insects, diseases, and weeds that affect the home lawn. Check at local garden centers for new products that offer natural or low-toxicity solutions to pest problems. Be leery of products that are not university-tested. Often they promise sensational results but there is little proof that they work. Follow extension service recommendations for best results.

When using pesticides, follow all label recommendations. Make sure you are using the proper rates and have the correct application equipment. You cannot be too safe. Here are a few more recommendations when treating pests that affect your lawn:

• Confirm the pest is really the problem in your lawn.

• Consider wildlife and beneficial insects when deciding whether or not to treat.

• Make sure all family members and pets are away from the area to be treated.

• First try the effective pesticide that has the lowest toxicity.

You may have to use a more toxic product if the needed results are not obtained.

• Apply pesticides on a calm day when temperatures are in the proper range for product use.

• Wear pesticide-resistant clothing plus boots, gloves, and a hat.

Some gardeners also like to wear goggles and a respirator for maxi-mum protection.

• Wait until the treatments have dried, and follow label recommendations before returning to a treated area.

Maintain records of your pesticide applications. Mix only the amount of pesticide you need so that all prepared solutions can be used immediately. When the containers are empty, follow label instructions for proper disposal.

• Granular iron formulations: Garden centers offer iron products as granules to apply through a spreader. Follow label instructions to obtain the best results.

PROBLEMS

Mole crickets are becoming more obvious, especially in **bahia** and **Bermuda** lawns. The ground begins to feel soft under the grass, giving the first hint the insects may be present. Check to see if chinch bugs or lawn caterpillars are present in your lawn.

The time for most selective weed control is over. Use of weedkillers during the hot weather may damage the turf. Mow, dig out, or spot-kill weeds with herbicides during the hot time of year.

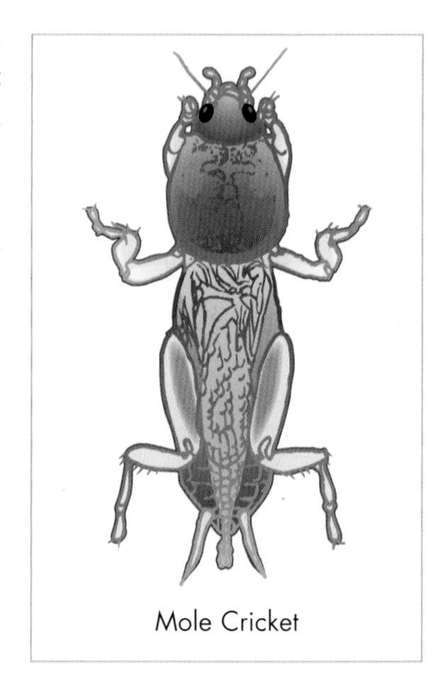

Mole Cricket

LAWNS

PLANNING

To choose the right grass for your lawn, start by determining how much sun the grass will receive. If it's not in the full sun most of the day, choose **St. Augustine**.

Take a look at local lawns to see which varieties do best. Ask the owners what problems have been encountered—their information may help you make a decision.

PLANTING

When adding new turf:

- Give the soil good preparation. Eliminate weeds and till the soil.
- Have the soil acidity tested. Don't start turf off with the wrong pH.

Where needed, adjust the soil acidity with lime or soil sulfur before planting.

- Fertilizer can be added before seeding. It's often delayed until after sodding.
- Keep all new turf and seeded areas moist. Make sure sod in shady locations does not get too much water.
- Check for pests that might be hitchhiking on the new turf.

Caterpillars often arrive with new sod during the summer. Treat as needed.

CARE

Give your mower a midsummer checkup. If it's been a month since the last oil change, renew it. After a month of cutting, your blade should be sharpened. Check the air filter, and oil all cables to keep the mower in good operating condition.

WATERING

Keep track of the rainfall. A rain gauge is a handy item to have in the landscape. Check it after each rain and record the information daily. After a few days without rain, your lawn is probably ready for water. You need to have received 1/4 inch of rainfall to be counted as a significant amount of moisture. If in doubt about water needs, let the grass tell you when it is dry.

- Check the lawn daily
- Water when spots begin to turn gray-green and leaves start to fold.
- Always apply 1/2 to 3/4 inch water.
- Water during the early-morning hours.

FERTILIZING

Has your lawn turned yellow or a lighter shade of green? You might call this a lean lawn, and it's normal this month. Some gardeners don't mind if the turf is a little on the yellow side at this time of year, and it may actually be a more pest-resistant turf.

Most gardeners, however, would like a bright-green to dark-green lawn. One way to change your lawn color is to use an iron-only application. With both **bahiagrass** and **St. Augustinegrass**, a little iron may be helpful during the summer months. Two evenly spaced applications are often recommended for this time of year, using an iron-only that is available at local garden centers, or one with a few additional nutrients. If iron does not renew the green, then a half-strength lawn fertilizer or just a little nitrogen can be added.

Both **zoysia** and **Bermuda** lawns are scheduled for a nitrogen-only feeding at this time of year. They need more nutrients to keep their vigor than do other grasses. Some products that can be applied to supply the needed nitrogen are 3 pounds of ammonium nitrate, 5 pounds of ammonium sulfate, or 2 pounds of urea for each 1,000 square feet of turf. These are small quantities of fertilizer and must be applied carefully and watered-in to prevent damage to the lawns. During warmer months, a processed sludge may also be used to supply needed nitrogen.

CUT YOUR ST. AUGUSTINE SOD BILL IN HALF

If you have money for only half the sod you need, we can help stretch your available **St. Augustinegrass** sod. Prepare the ground as if planting the entire lawn. Then plant rows of sod 12 to 16 inches apart across the lawn. Now all you have to do is wait for the grass to fill in between the rows. You will have to dig shallow trenches to receive the sod so it is even with the ground.

You can also fill in between the pieces with any extra soil. The sod should grow very rapidly during the summer if you follow these instructions:

- Keep the sod and soil moist.
- Feed the new sod three to four weeks after adding the sod. Repeat the feeding during the fall.
- Spot-kill weeds as needed.
- Mow the new lawn as soon as the grass reaches the desired height.
- Control pests, especially lawn caterpillars, as needed.

PROBLEMS

One disease that runs rampant during summer is "Take-All Root Rot." It selects the weaker turf and causes yellowing of the foliage by rotting the root system. Lawns that receive too much water, are competing with other plants, have nematode problems, and have been under general stress are very susceptible.

Many other problems may affect the summer lawn. Check for chinch bugs, lawn caterpillars, and mole crickets during your weekly walks through the landscape.

The time for most selective weed control is over. Use of weedkillers during the hot weather may damage the turf. Mow, dig out, or spot-kill weeds with herbicides during the hot time of year.

AUGUST

LAWNS

PLANNING

Now is a good time to install a **bahia** grass lawn, probably the most carefree of home lawn grasses. Although **bahia** lawns produce tall summer seedheads and may yellow in spring, its low maintenance makes it a good choice for home lawns. Varieties include Argentine, Paraguay, and Pensacola. Argentine produces fewer seedheads and retains a good color, but the seeds are a little more expensive.

Minimal care is just one reason to choose a **bahia** lawn. Here are a few more:

- It's the most pest-free of lawn grasses. Mole crickets are the only major problem, and good controls are available.
- **Bahia** won't mind skipped waterings. It's really the only practical grass for a lawn without irrigation. The turf does turn brown during the drier months when left without water, but it grows back when the rains return.
- A new lawn can be established by seed. Not everyone is good at starting a turf from seed, but if you do, it can be an economical method. Sod is also available.
- It's durable, holding up under neighborhood football games and other family activities.
- Well-grown **bahia** has a good green color and can produce dense growth.

Many gardeners give **bahia** extra consideration during drier months when they are paying big water bills-but bahia has a more open growth habit that gardeners tend to object to in home lawns. When the rain returns, they often stick with the other grasses (usually a **St. Augustinegrass**). If you ever think of establishing a **bahia** lawn, start it during the warmer months.

PLANTING

All lawn grasses can be established during the summer season by seeding, plugging, or sodding. Grasses commonly grown from seed include **Bermuda**, **carpetgrass**, **bahia**, and **centipede**. Give your grass a good start by following these tips:

- Eliminate annual and perennial weeds with a nonselective herbicide that permits planting shortly after the weeds decline.
- Till the soil and rake it free of debris.
- Adjust the soil acidity to the proper level with lime or soil sulfur as needed.
- Apply a light scattering of a 6-6-6 or similar general garden fertilizer and rake it into the ground.
- Divide the seed into two lots and scatter each in different directions across the prepared soil. Use of a spreader is recommended to get the best distribution.
- Rake the seed in lightly. Then add a light scattering of clean hay or straw over the soil.
- Moisten thoroughly. Keep the ground moist during the germination process. Several light waterings may be necessary each day.

CARE

Water newly seeded lawns whenever the surface soil begins to be dry to the touch. Gradually reduce the watering to an as-needed basis after six to eight weeks. Mow the lawn as needed—usually, a vigorous **bahia** lawn requires this three to four weeks after germination. Begin the first feedings at this time as well.

WATERING

The summer rains can be counted on for most of the water. It's not unusual to see rain every day under normal Florida growing conditions. Some days the rain may be just a sprinkle, so check the lawn for dry spots and water if needed.

If you don't have to water, you may forget that the sprinkler system will be needed as we head into fall. It's a good idea to turn it on periodically and make sure it is operating properly. When you do water, remember to apply 1/2 to 3/4 inch and water only during the early-morning hours.

FERTILIZING

Most lawn grasses will not receive a major feeding at this time unless you forgot an earlier fertilizer application. **Carpetgrass** can get a full fertilizer application at this time. If the lawns begin to yellow, you can apply the second iron-only feeding of the summer. This may be all the grass needs to give it a color that is a little brighter green. Use one of the following iron-feeding techniques if needed.

- Liquid iron feedings: Gardeners can apply liquids available from garden centers or make their own. An iron application can be made by mixing 2 ounces of ferrous sulfate in 3 to 5 gallons of water and sprinkling the solution over 1,000 square feet of turf.
- Granular iron formulations: Garden centers offer iron products as granules to apply through a spreader. Follow label instructions to obtain the best results.

Lawns that do not respond to iron treatments as expected can be given a light granular or liquid fertilizer application. If the root system is poor due to disease or other problems, liquid fertilizer application through a sprayer is best.

PROBLEMS

A healthy lawn is more resistant to pest problems, but somehow the sod webworms, root rots, and others still cause some damage. Check the lawn weekly for signs of decline. Look for chinch bugs, lawn caterpillars, mole crickets, and the fungus called "Take-All Root Rot." When early damage is noted take the appropriate control. Delay the use of selective weed-control products another month or two.

CONTROL WEEDS IN HOT WEATHER

Using weedkillers during the hot weather may damage the turf. Mow, dig out, or spot-kill weeds with nonselective herbicides during the hot time of year.

SEPTEMBER

LAWNS

PLANNING

This month brings short days and cooler nights. Complete all lawn seeding so the grass can be well established before cold weather.

Evaluate your lawn. Check for insects, fungal diseases, and weeds. Some areas may now be too shady due to summer tree and shrub growth. Plan to trim plants or change the ground cover. Draw up a timetable for lawn work. By the end of the month, you may be able to start your fall chores.

PLANTING

By the end of October, **bahia** stops producing new shoots, but most lawn grasses grow very well during fall. To fill bare spots, try adding plugs or sections of sod.

- Control all the weeds. Dig them out or spot-kill with a herbicide labeled for lawn renovation.
- Loosen the ground several inches deep. Mix in organic matter if you wish.
- Insert the plugs or lay the sod to cover the soil.
- Water thoroughly as needed to prevent wilting.
- Apply a complete fertilizer in three to four weeks.
- Mow along with the rest of the lawngrasses.

CARE

Don't let up on your mowing. If you go on vacation, have someone do the job. Allowing it to get overgrown and then giving it a severe cutting is a real shock to the grass. When you do mow, leave the clippings on the lawn unless they form piles due to infrequent mowing. If they form piles, the grass should be raked or bagged and added to the compost pile. Returning the grass to the ground adds nutrients that the turf can use for growth—and it won't produce thatch.

WATERING

September is a damp month, at least for the first few weeks. As fall arrives, the drier season starts and you may have to do the watering. All of a sudden you notice dry spots or maybe some declining turf.

- Make sure that when it rains, you are receiving 1/4 inch or more of moisture.
- Look for dry spots that may not be getting adequate water or have limited root systems.
- Water when the grass begins to dry in spots and the grass blades begin to fold together.
- Apply 1/2 to 3/4 inch water each irrigation.
- Water the lawn during the early-morning hours.

St. Augustinegrass

• Check sprinkler heads to make sure they are operating properly.

FERTILIZING

Just about every lawn is now ready for the fall feeding. Many look lean and hungry by this time of year. It is time to apply a complete fertilizer. This is a product with nitrogen, phosphorus, and potassium. In some areas the phosphorus may not be needed, as the soil has a good residual supply. You can obtain a complete soil test through your local extension service office. It will help determine the level of the major nutrients (except for nitrogen, which varies too much anyway and is always added spring and fall). Here are some fertilizing tips:

• Select a product labeled for lawn feeding. A 16-4-8, 13-3-13, 15-0-15, or similar product is quite satisfactory. Get the most from the nutrients by picking a product that has a portion of the nutrients in a slow-release form.

• Apply the fertilizer to a dry lawn.

• Use the proper spreader setting for the product applied, or compute the amount needed.

To figure the fertilizer needed for each 1,000 square feet, divide the first number in the analysis (the nitrogen content) into 100. This is the amount to apply. For example, if the number is 20, you would apply 5 pounds of the fertilizer to each 1,000 square feet of lawn.

• Make sure the fertilizer is evenly distributed across the lawn. Let the sprinklings of fertilizer overlap just a little.

• Water the lawn after feeding.

GET YOUR SOIL ACIDITY TESTED

Soil acidity determines the availability of nutrients in the soil. You can often make nutrients more available to your lawn just by altering the soil pH. The test can be performed at home with kits available from your garden center, or the test can often be made at garden centers for a small fee, or may be made through your local extension service. When you receive the soil test results, you may find there are recommendations for lime or soil sulfur applications. Apply treatments as needed to adjust your lawn to the proper acidity.

PROBLEMS

You can count on summer pests affecting your lawn for at least one more month. Make weekly inspections and look for declining turf. Take the needed steps to control chinch bugs, lawn caterpillars, mole crickets, and "Take-All Root Rot."

Wait until the later part of the month to begin selective weed control. You may want to delay the application of fertilizers with weedkillers until the very end of the month. Until then, pull or spot-treat weeds with a nonselective herbicide.

LAWNS

PLANNING

By this time in most years, the rains become intermittent. **Bahia** grass will gradually slow its growth, but others continue growing. Some pest problems start to decline. While growing conditions are ideal, it's a good time to fill in problem areas with new turf. Here are some spots that may need replacing.

- Areas damaged by pests: Check these carefully to make sure you know what caused the decline. Maybe turf is not the best answer and another ground cover would be a better choice.
- Shady or rooty areas: Select a better turf variety or a different ground cover.
- Dried out lawns: Expand the irrigation system before resodding or plugging.

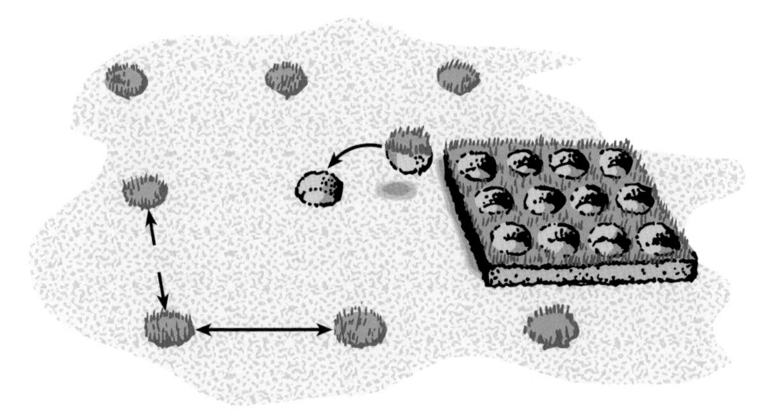

Measure the lawn area that needs to be resodded to determine how much sod or how many plugs you need.

PLANTING

It is already too late to start a new permanent lawn from seed, but you can continue with sodding and plugging. Measure damaged areas to determine how much sod or how many trays of plugs are needed. Sod can be purchased by the piece. A 16-by-24-inch piece makes about $2^1/_2$ feet of usable sod. A pallet holds 400 square feet. A tray of plugs, each plug set 12 inches apart, can reestablish about 18 square feet of turf.

- First make squares or rectangles out of the areas that need replanting.
- Remove all weeds and debris. Weeds can be dug out but are best controlled with a nonselective herbicide that permits replanting.
- Till the planting site or give it a stiff raking.
- Work in organic matter if you wish. It can be done easily with compost. Most gardeners leave larger areas to the on-site soil.
- Adjust the soil acidity if needed.
- Thoroughly moisten the ground.
- Install the new sod or plugs. Some gardeners like to place a light feeding of time-release fertilizer under each plug. Follow label instructions when using products made for this purpose.
- Keep the planted areas moist, and feed in three to four weeks.

CARE

Keep up the mowing. The grass will not stop producing new growth until the weather really gets cool. You can expect to mow most coarse turf types at least once a week and the finer-bladed types twice a week. Now is the time to reexamine the lawnmower blade. It should be sharpened monthly. You may also need to change the oil and air filter on all power equipment used in the yard.

WATERING

It is getting drier, but there will be periods of downpours. Sometimes tropical storms blow by to dump many inches of water on the landscape. But this can all dry up in a matter of days. The short periods of flooding may cause some root damage. If this occurs, be especially attentive to spots that dry out more quickly because of shallow root systems.

- Water whenever spots in the lawn start to dry and fold their leaf blades.

Only light watering may be needed if the rest of the ground is saturated.

- When yellowing occurs due to flooding, try an iron application to renew the green.

Even if the regular rains fail, water as usual. To keep your water bill reasonable, let the lawn tell you when it is dry. If you want a schedule for an automatic system: Most lawns need a good soaking about twice a week. New lawns or renovated areas need more-frequent watering for the first few weeks, and then can be placed on an as-needed schedule.

FERTILIZING

If you forgot the September feeding or have been waiting to apply a weed-and-feed product, now is the time. Most lawns are under less stress and are more resistant to the weedkillers used in turf. If you are applying any of these products to a **bahiagrass** lawn, do it soon, as the grass will soon slow growth.

Bermuda lawns are also ready for a nitrogen-only feeding if you were on schedule with the complete feeding in September. Some products that can be applied to supply the needed nitrogen are 3 pounds of ammonium nitrate, 5 pounds of ammonium sulfate, or 2 pounds of urea for each 1,000 square feet of turf.

- Apply all feedings according to the product label.
- Make sure you cover the lawn uniformly to avoid streaks.
- Most should be applied to a dry lawn.

A few weed-and-feeds recommend applying to a moist lawn.

- Water after feeding.

PROBLEMS

Some pests will be slowing down this time of year. Most leaf spotting of **St. Augustinegrass** lawns is over when the nights become a little cooler and the rainy season ends. "Take-All Root Rot" decreases with the end of the frequent rains. But there are a few pests that linger on for at least a little longer: chinch bugs, lawn caterpillars, and mole crickets.

Mowing, digging out, or spot-killing weeds with nonselective herbicides can continue into the fall months. This is also a time when you can apply some of the selective weed-control products. Follow label instructions carefully to make a safe and effective application. You will be most successful controlling broadleaf weed types.

NOVEMBER

LAWNS

PLANNING

Gardeners often ask if they can install a new lawn during the cooler times of the year. It's not a bad time to do any lawn installation-except for seeding a new permanent turfgrass. One warning: If you normally get winter injury to your lawn, you may be even more likely to receive damage to a new turf. This is because new growth is often encouraged from a recently installed lawn. The risk is small, however, and lawns of all grasses are usually installed year-round. If it's a new neighborhood and a first lawn on the homesite, all you need to do is follow good lawn-installation procedures:

- Start with a soil test you can either make yourself with a kit, receive from a garden center, or receive through your local extension service office. Most lawns like to be in the 6.5 pH range, but **bahia** lawns like the soil just a little more acid (between 5.5 and 6.0).
- Till the soil to remove all weedy growth. Spot-kill the perennial-type weeds.
- Wet the soil and begin laying the sod. Water the turf and ground well as each pallet of sod is installed.
- Keep the new turf moist. Sod installed during the cooler months may not need to be watered as frequently as it would during hotter weather. If the grass begins to wilt, water is definitely needed. To avoid root rot problems, make sure the grass is not overwatered.
- Pests are very few in number at this time of year, but check for caterpillars and mole crickets that might still be active.

PLANTING

Gardeners are often concerned about adding organic matter to the soil when preparing ground for new turf. Much of our soils are sandy and can be improved with compost, peat moss, and similar materials. But this can be costly, and organic-matter additions are only of benefit for short periods of time since they decompose rapidly.

Another way to add water-holding ability to sandy soils is with the addition of colloidal phosphate. This powdery material is mixed with the soil at the rate of 1 to 2 cubic yards for each 1,000 square feet of lawn area to be planted.

Gardeners also like to add fertilizer or work manure into the soil before installing turf. Just make sure any additions are weed-free or you may be adding a problem. If you want to add fertilizer, use a 6-6-6 or similar product at the rate of 10 pounds per 1,000 square feet of prepared soil; it can be tilled in just before seeding, sodding, or plugging.

CARE

One individual suggested that gardeners can take a break from the weekly chore of mowing during November. Well, you might be able to do this in the northern parts of the state, but in the central and southern parts of the state, it's probably mowing as usual. The general rule: When grass grows one third taller, it's time to do the mowing. In most of Florida, we never put the mower to rest.

WATERING

Suddenly it's the dry time of year, with only a few rainy days each month. Luckily, it is a cooler season, and the days are shorter.

- When spots in the lawn begin to dry, water the entire lawn. Look for grass that is a gray-green color with the blades folding together.
- Water until 1/2 to 3/4 inch of moisture has been provided.

Gardeners with automatic systems may need to water only once or twice a week.

FERTILIZING

Zoysia lawns might get an extra nitrogen feeding at this time of year, but the other grasses should be fine unless you have missed a feeding. Many gardeners with **bahia** and **St. Augustine** lawns like to do something to increase winter hardiness. The current recommendation is to apply a potassium-only fertilizer about thirty days before the first frost. (In North Florida, this is around the end of November or early December; in Central Florida, it's around mid-December.) The potassium treatment has to be applied when the weather is cooler so as not to damage the turf. Use 1.6 pounds of muriate of potash or 2 pounds of potassium sulfate for each 1,000 square feet of turf. Water the potassium treatment into the lawn after applying.

PROBLEMS

Have you ever heard of grubs, an immature stage of beetles? They've not been a common Florida pest for years, but recently they have been damaging turf again. Grubs are white with a brown head and have three pairs of legs at the front of the body. They live underground, feeding on roots. Look for chinch bugs in **St. Augustinegrass** lawns. Lawn caterpillars may be chewing leaf blades. Mole crickets are mature and about an inch long at this time.

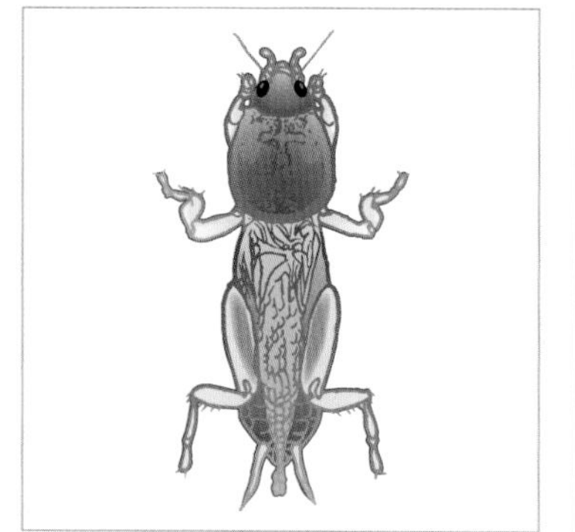

Mole Cricket

Chinch Bug

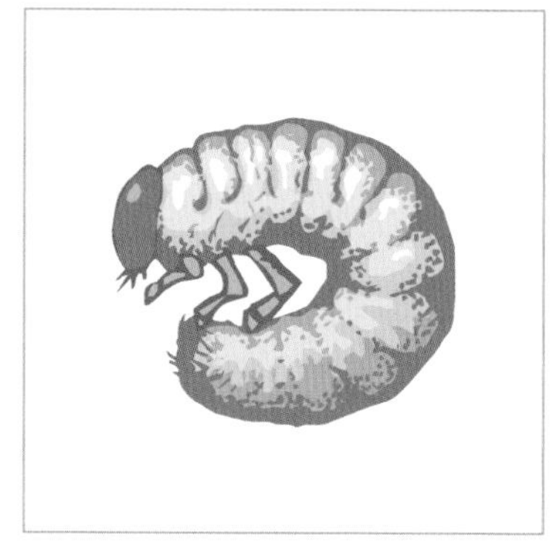

White Grub

DECEMBER

LAWNS

PLANNING

Most gardeners can relax a little during the winter months. Lawn care is really slowing down as the days grow shorter and cooler.

PLANTING

Most temporary winter lawns are planted with **ryegrass**, but **bentgrass**, **bluegrass**, and **fescue** can also be utilized. They are normally not planted until the cool weather is here, and they are mostly planted in the colder sections of Central and North Florida. Here are the steps to success:

1. Remove weeds from the areas to be planted.

Bentgrass

2. Rake out brown grass blades and clippings near the soil surface.

3. Sow up to ten pounds of **ryegrass** for every 1,000 square feet of area to be seeded. Follow label directions for other grasses.

4. Rake the seed into the ground or water it in among existing grass.

5. Keep the soil moist and the **rye** should be up within a week. Others may need two weeks.

6. Feed monthly with a lawn fertilizer at half the normal rate.

7. Mow as needed at the height of the permanent grass, or 2 inches.

CARE

Mowing is continued as needed to maintain the normal height of the lawn. It is also needed to control weeds in many turfgrasses. Do not change the height of the mower blade. Keep it at the same level year-round.

WATERING

It's a dry but cool time of year. Most lawns need only one or two waterings a week. If cold weather is expected, it's best to water the lawn to prevent drying from associated winds. Apply $1/2$ to $3/4$ inch water at each irrigation.

FERTILIZING

Only **Bermuda** lawns normally need a feeding at this time of year. Use a nitrogen-only fertilizer at the label rate to apply 1 pound of actual nitrogen to each 1,000 square feet of turf.

PROBLEMS

Only brown patch is active at this time of year.

Gardeners are more likely to experience frost or freeze damage in cooler areas of the state. This damage occurs after cold nights and appears as a browning of the turf. Here are a few tips to follow when grass is damaged:

- Maintain a moist but not abnormally wet soil.
- Do not apply special feedings to encourage growth.
- Mow the lawn as needed at the normal height.
- Refrain from making pesticide applications.

Fungicides and insecticides do not help cold-damaged lawns.

- Do not panic (most lawns recover with the return of warm weather), but you may have to wait until late winter for good green turf. Some gardeners overseed with **ryegrass** at this time.

CHAPTER SEVEN

PERENNIALS

Just about every landscape should have a flower garden, but you have to decide how much work yours is going to entail. Perennials help make your planning easy by producing new growth and flowers for more than just a few months.

During the 1970s and much of the 1980s, annual flowers ruled, and there was just a sprinkling of perennials at garden centers. Perhaps it was because Florida had so many great annuals, or maybe everyone just forgot about the many flowers that last more than a year—but perennials almost became "extinct." Then all of a sudden, during the early to mid-1990s, perennials were rediscovered. It was almost a plant revolution when gardeners decided they were tired of changing the flower beds every three or four months. They wanted something permanent, and they turned back to perennials.

You are not going to find here many perennial gardens that resemble those of the Northern states, whose gardens are planted along paths or by rocks on the side of a hill with flowers that come into bloom during the early spring months. Florida's perennials are in bloom most of the year and may be intermingled with annuals, trees, and shrubs. (You can add the rocks and a berm or two.)

CHAPTER SEVEN

There is a lot of variety among Florida perennials. Some are quite traditional and grow for years with normal care. Others are treated as long-living annuals, since they may need more cold than Florida can provide. Many are tropical and produce almost continuous bloom for years. Every now and then in North and Central Florida some tropical perennials are severely damaged by cold, but they usually grow back from buds near the ground.

The definition of a perennial is not precise—you probably know it as a plant that lives for more than two years. In this chapter a perennial is broadly defined as a long-living herbaceous plant. We may add a woody plant or two that fits in this category, but we are going to exclude the bulbs, shrubs, roses, and ground covers presented in other chapters.

PLANNING

Just about every landscape should have a flower garden, but you have to decide how much work yours is going to entail. Perennials help make your planning easy by producing new growth and flowers for more than just a few months. This means you can count on an attractive planting for a year or two before major bed renovation is needed.

Decide on where you need color in the landscape and then see where perennials might help. Remember, perennials come in all heights and widths, so they can squeeze into small spaces or be clustered together to fill an entire bed. Here are a few ways to use perennials in the Florida landscape:

- Plant a garden devoted only to perennials.
- Mix perennials and annuals in a garden.
- Add perennials to shrubby borders.
- Edge your walkways with bushy perennials.
- Create small spots of color with just one species along walkways.
- Use the plants to accent water features.
- Fill planters and hanging baskets with perennials, or use them in combination with annuals.
- Add color to shady spots in the landscape.

One thing to keep in mind is that perennials normally give the best displays when clustered together. Try planting groups of three, five, seven, or more of the same type in any one flower bed. Use the taller perennials in the back or center of the bed, and the short or creeping types along the edges.

Here is another thought: Why not use perennials as the base planting for your garden and fill in small areas with annual color throughout the year? This mixes the best of the two plant groups and gives extra seasonal color.

PLANTING

Perhaps you are planting perennials simply because you like the flowers. Many gardeners also add them to the landscape to eliminate having to constantly till and replant flower beds. Whatever your reasons for growing perennials, it makes sense to give the planting site your best care from the beginning.

First check the perennial list on pages 200 to 201. Find a site with the proper light level for the plants you would like to grow. It's important to put the right plant in the right place.

Select a site without a lot of competition: if there are impermeable tree roots in the ground or a runaway hedge nearby, your perennials are probably not going to do well. You need a garden site that can provide years of good growing conditions. Here are the steps to good soil preparation:

1. Control all weeds with a nonselective herbicide that permit replanting. Many weeds can also be dug out, but just a few left-behind sprigs can quickly start a new infestation.

2. Till the soil deeply to disperse weed seeds and pest problems into the ground.

3. Work lots of organic matter into sandy and clay soils. This helps ensure good root growth, some water retention, available nutrients for plant growth, and good drainage to promote attractive perennials. Use peat moss, compost, and similar materials.

4. Many gardeners like to add manure or a light scattering of fertilizer before planting.

Florida perennials can be planted year-round. You can pick them out in bloom at garden centers, use plants shared with neighbors, or grow them from seed. In most cases, it's best to start seeds in containers and move them to the garden when they are an appropriate size.

After planting, most perennials like a mulch to control weeds and maintain a moist soil at a uniform temperature. Keep the mulch back from the base of the plants.

WATERING

Keeping a moist soil is especially important during the establishment period. New garden perennials have a limited root system that needs time to grow out into the surrounding soil. It's best to water daily for the first week or two. After that, the perennial garden can be placed on an as-needed watering schedule.

- Water when the surface soil begins to dry to the touch.
- Use the plants as a guide. If they wilt, a good watering is probably needed.
- Get to know the type of plants you are growing. Some, like blanket flower, butterfly weed, and lantana, are very drought tolerant. Others, including hosta and violets, like a moist soil.
- Maintain a 2- to 3-inch layer of mulch over the soil surface. Some good mulch materials are old hay, pine needles, barks, and coarse compost.
- When water is needed, apply 1/2 to 3/4 inch.
- Use soaker hoses and microsprinklers where possible.

FERTILIZING

Most perennials are not heavy feeders. You can use a general fertilizer, following a schedule, or give the plants a feeding when either growth slows or leaf color begins to fade. Many perennials would rather have frequent feedings at first, then have the diet reduced as they reach maturity. You can also use slow-release fertilizer products to take some of the work out of feeding the plants. Several brands are available at local garden centers.

- When growth is desired, apply a general fertilizer every six to eight weeks, March through November. Use slow-release products according to label directions.
- Place mature plantings on a maintenance schedule of feedings in March, June, and September.
- Scatter the fertilizer over the surface of the soil or mulch, and water-in.

Do not remove the mulch layer to feed the plants.

PEST CONTROL

Perennials are usually very tough and durable. You may experience aphids, leafminers, whiteflies, and/or grasshoppers as noted on other garden plantings. A spray may be needed, or simply tolerance for the few insects. Some plants have scale problems; these are more serious and need immediate control. Get to know your plants, then treat major pest problems as noted.

- Handpick as many pests as possible and destroy them.

You may have to remove some plant portions to control major infestations.

- Control aphids and whiteflies with insecticidal soaps available at garden centers.
- Control scales with oil sprays available at garden centers.
- Control caterpillar infestations with natural *Bacillus thuringiensis* sprays.
- Use synthetic sprays for insects, mites, and diseases only as a last resort and according to label directions.

CHAPTER SEVEN

Perennials

Name	Area of Florida	Common Height (Inches)	Common Width (Inches)	Flower Color/ Season	Light Needed
Angelonia	Throughout	18	12	White, purple/ Year-round	Sun
African Iris	Throughout	24	24	White, blue, yellow/ Year-round	Sun–light shade
Beebalm	NC	36	30	Reddish/April–June	Sun
Bird of Paradise	CS	36	36	Orange, blue/ Year-round	Sun–light shade
Blanket Flower	Throughout	18	18	Yellow, orange, red/ March–Nov.	Sun
Blue Daze	Throughout	12	18	Blue/Year-round	Sun
Blue Ginger	CS	36	24	Blue/May–Oct.	Light shade
Blue Phlox	N	12	12	Blue/Mar.–April	Light shade
Blue Sage	CS	60	30	Blue/Dec.–Mar.	Light shade
Bush Daisy	Throughout	24	24	Yellow/Year-round	Sun–light shade
Butterfly Weed	Throughout	36	36	Yellow, orange/ Year-round	Sun–light shade
Cardinal's Guard	CS	72	48	Scarlet/ May–Oct.	Light shade
Cat's Whiskers	CS	36	30	White, lavender/ Mar.–Nov.	Sun–light shade
Chrysanthemum	NC	18	24	Varied/Sept.–May	Sun–light shade
Coneflower	NC	30	12	White, purple/ April–August	Sun
Coreopsis	Throughout	18	18	Yellow/April–Oct.	Sun
Crossandra	Throughout	12	12	Orange/May–Oct.	Sun– shade
False Dragon Head	Throughout	24	24	White, pink, lavender/Sept.–Oct.	Sun-shade
Firespike	Throughout	72	36	Red/ year-round	Sun–light shade
Four o'clock	Throughout	36	36	White, yellow, red/ April–Oct.	Sun–light shade
Gaura	NC	24	18	White, pink/	Sun year-round
Gerbera Daisy	Throughout	18	18	Varied/Year-round	Sun–light shade
Goldenrod	NC	36	24	Yellow/May–Oct.	Sun
Heliconia	CS	60	24	Yellow, orange, red/ Year-round	Sun–light shade

N = North Florida C = Central Florida S = South Florida

Perennials

Name	Area of Florida	Common Height (Inches)	Common Width (Inches)	Flower Color/ Season	Light Needed
Hosta	NC	18	18	White, lavender/ June–August	Shade
Jacobinia	CS	48	36	White, pink/ Year-round	Shade
Lantana	Throughout	24	24	Cream, yellow, red, lavender/Year-round	Sun
Lion's Ear	Throughout	48	18	Orange/Oct.–April	Sun
Mexican Heather	Throughout	18	18	White, purple/ Year-round	Sun–light shade
Pentas	Throughout	48	36	White, pink, red, lavender/Year-round	Sun–light shade
Philippine Violet	Throughout	48	36	White, lavender/ Sept.–April	Sun–light shade
Poinsettia	CS	72	72	White, pink, red bracts/Dec.–Mar.	Sun–light shade
Rudbeckia	NC	30	18	Yellow/ May–Oct.	Sun
Ruellia	Throughout	36	24	Blue, violet, pink/ April–Nov.	Sun–light shade
Salvia	Throughout	48	48	Blue, red, pink, white, yellow/Year-round	Sun
Shasta Daisy	NC	24	12	White/May–June	Sun
Shrimp Plant	Throughout	60	48	Reddish-brown/ March–Oct.	Sun–light shade
Stokes Aster	Throughout	12	12	White, blue/May–July	Sun–light shade
Veronica	NC	18	18	Blue, white/May–July	sun–light shade
Violet	NC	10	12	White, blue/Mar.–June	Light shade
Yarrow	NC	18	18	Yellow, rose, white/ May–June	Sun
Yellow Alder	CS	24	24	Yellow/Year-round	Sun

N = North Florida C = Central Florida S = South Florida

JANUARY
PERENNIALS

PLANNING

How well the perennial garden is doing this month depends greatly on where you live in Florida. Most of the colder spots have very little color as perennials take a break for the winter. But warmer locations, including most of Central and South Florida, are still enjoying **bush daisy**, **angelonia**, **firespike**, **jacobinia**, and more. One job this month is to make sure cold protection is available for sensitive plants. It takes only a little extra effort to keep a prize **bird of paradise** or cluster of **pentas** from being damaged.

- Bring small plants in containers indoors or to other warm areas.
- Cover plantings with a blanket or similar insulating material to keep out the cold and hold in warmer air. Covers must drape to the ground. Plastic provides very little cold protection.
- Turn a cardboard box or trashcan over plants.
- Line a large flower pot with newspaper and set over smaller plants.
- Use an electric light that is approved for outdoor use under a cover for a little heat.

Make sure the lamp and bulb do not touch the fabric.

Good: Sheets, quilts, or blankets

Better: cloth cover

Make sure you have something on hand to protect cold-sensitive plants.

PLANTING

Winter, with its cool weather, is a good month to prepare beds for planting. This is where having a plan can be helpful. If you know what will be planted in just a month or two, you can do the digging and soil preparation while the climate is comfortable.

In preparing to plant, consider whether or not other plants were previously growing in the ground. If it is untouched land, major tilling and soil enrichment will be needed. Ground that once grew other plants will need all the older stems removed and a check for pests. Here are a few more soil improvement suggestions:

- Control all weeds in the soil to be planted. Some can be pulled out, but most are best controlled with a nonselective herbicide that permits replanting after weeds decline.
- Remove all plant debris.

Take out as much of the root system as possible which could be harboring diseases or nematodes.

- Till the ground deeply to mix soil layers and disperse pests.
- Work liberal quantities of organic matter into the soil.
- Test soil acidity and adjust if needed.

Your soil is now ready to plant. Garden centers are starting to get in a selection of new plants at this time. Select hardy types for your area, or be ready with cold protection.

CARE

Perennials should not be overlooked as a source of bouquet material. Some simply provide greenery at this time of the year, but many have flowers that last as long as or longer than their annual relatives. A little pruning now helps keep the plants in bounds.

WATERING

It's a cool time of year throughout the state, and most plantings need minimal amounts of moisture. Keep track of the rainfall; if a week or so passes without any, most perennials will need water.

- Water when the surface soil feels dry to the touch.
- Give the plantings a good soaking with 1/2 to 3/4 inch of water.
- Make sure the plantings have a 2- to 3-inch mulch layer.
- Water during the early-morning hours.

New plantings need a special watering routine. Keep the soil extra-moist for the first week or two, until roots have time to grow into the surrounding ground. Then gradually reduce the waterings to an as-needed basis.

FERTILIZING

Very little fertilizer is needed this month. Most plants do not produce a lot of growth during cooler weather. Gardeners in the southern parts of the state may notice some yellowing of more-vigorous plants. These can be given a light feeding of a general garden fertilizer as needed. Plants in containers and planters may need an extra feeding or two during the winter months. Use a liquid fertilizer monthly, or apply a slow-release fertilizer, which can feed the plants for months.

PROBLEMS

Sometimes it's difficult to tell a real pest problem from normal plant decline during the winter months. Often gardeners are also dealing with cold damage. Very few pests are active except in the warmer locations. You might find mealybugs, slugs, and snails causing some damage.

Winter damage can be cut from plants to prevent rot problems and improve overall plant appearance.

SAVE A PLANT

Sometimes winters are nasty in Florida, catching gardeners off guard. It may not be possible to save an entire plant, but you may save a portion by first taking cuttings.

- Make your cuttings up to the time the plant freezes.
- Cut stems 4 to 6 inches long from the tip portions and remove flowers.
- Stick the cut ends 1 to 2 inches deep in a pot or tray of vermiculite to root.
- Keep the cuttings and vermiculite moist, and enclose the containers of cuttings in a clear plastic bag.
- Set in bright light but out of direct sun. Most perennial cuttings root in eight to ten weeks.

When the cuttings root, transplant them to small containers.

FEBRUARY

PERENNIALS

PLANNING

February can be quite cold, with frosts and freezes in the central and northern areas. By month's end, however, most areas enjoy consistently warm weather, so plan new plantings.

Stop by your local garden center for new perennials. Try to picture how plants will look in your landscape. Here are some questions to ask:

- How long will the plant bloom? It's nice to have year-round color.
- Is the plant hardy? You may love **pentas**, but it's going to freeze. **African iris** or **rudbeckia** can take more cold.
- What size will it grow? You'll need adequate root space for the plant to grow and flower properly.
- Will the plant need sun or shade? There are perennials for all locations.

PLANTING

Cold-hardy perennials can be planted now. Keep less hardy plants in their containers till after the average last frost date.

First set the plants out over the site to see how they might be arranged. If you are planting more than one type of perennial, draw lines in the soil or use a hose or extension cord to define the boundaries. Then set the plants in place.

- Make sure you have the proper spacing. Look on the label or check with the garden center. A good rule is to space the plants by at least half their expected width.
- Keep tall plants to the back of the bed in one-sided gardens, or in the center of beds that are to be viewed from all directions.
- Plant large clusters of plants-not one of this and one of that.
- Allow creeping or vining plants extra room to grow.
- Leave some extra room between groups of plants to walk between when performing maintenance.
- Allow extra room near walkways or garden accents.

When the plants are in place, you are ready to set them in the ground, using good planting techniques, of course. If containerized, ease them out. When rootballs are heavily entwined, it's good to pull them apart just a little.

1. Open up a large hole and set the rootball in the soil at the same depth it was in the container or original planting site.
2. If the soil is dry, fill the hole with water and allow some to seep into the ground. This is called "mudding in," which makes sure the ground is sufficiently moist.
3. Begin filling in with soil around the root system. Some gardeners like to add more water as the soil is added.
4. Complete the planting with a 2- to 3-inch layer of mulch. Keep the mulch back from the base of the planting to avoid stem and root rot.

Give the planting daily waterings for a week or two, and as needed thereafter to keep the soil moist.

CARE

As winter finishes up, there is bound to be a need for some pruning. Don't be in a big rush to prune out the dead or declining portions, as some cold may linger until the end of the month or even into March. When you sense that winter is over, or if you live in a more southerly section of the state, take out brown plant portions and do any trimming

needed to reshape the plantings. Keep in mind that some, like the **chrysanthemums**, **African iris**, **lantana**, and **jacobinia**, may be getting ready to produce their spring flowers, so trim off only what is needed.

WATERING

As plantings grow, they naturally need more water. It's still a cool time of year, so check about once or twice a week for water needs. When the soil is dry, give the plants a good soaking.

FERTILIZING

Whenever plants are growing is feeding time. It won't hurt to get a little jump on spring anytime during the month. After all, it takes time for nutrients to enter the ground and be utilized by perennials. There are several ways to feed your plants.

PROBLEMS

Bugs and diseases start to become more active this month, mostly in the southerly parts of the state. Look for aphids, mealybugs, slugs, snails, and powdery mildew.

Blanket flower

REDUCE WATER USAGE

Some ways to reduce water usage as we head into the drier months:

1. Install soaker hoses. Wind the hose (which is usually made of recycled rubber) among the plants to allow water to seep into the ground.

2. Set up a microsprinkler system to water individual beds. The sprinklers keep the water close to the ground and take care of only small areas so you won't be wasting water on sidewalks and roads. Ready-to-install systems are available at garden centers.

3. Select drought-tolerant plants, some of which are **blanket flower**, **coreopsis**, **gaura**, **lantana**, and **ruellia**. Keep the drought-tolerant types together and water them less frequently.

4. Maintain a 2- to 3-inch layer of mulch. Some larger-growing perennials can have more mulch added, but no more than a 4-inch layer. Too much mulch may keep water from moving into the root zone during drought.

MARCH

PERENNIALS

PLANNING

Now every Florida gardener can begin perennial plantings. There is some potential for frost until mid-month, but most residents are willing to take a chance. Catalogs and garden centers are full of plants, and many are in bloom. If you grow from seed, plant now as seed can take time to produce a flowering plant. Mail-order may be the only way to get new and unusual varieties. Here are some suggestions when ordering by mail:

- Most plants will be small and need several months of growth to reach flowering size.
- The pictures are pretty, and you might be tempted to buy plants not suited for your climate. Experiment if you like, but choose plants appropriate for your zone.
- When the plants arrive, grow them in pots until they reach garden-center size. Transplant to larger pots for a month or two.
- Keep the plants in filtered sun for a day or two, then give them the normal light level.
- Order the plants for the best planting time for Florida. Make sure the company knows when you want to plant.
- Notify the company about plants that arrive in poor condition and may be yellow, lanky, or broken.

PLANTING

Hurry to complete your spring plantings. Most plants, whether purchased locally or by mail, grow well during the warmish days and cool nights ahead.

When growing plants in the shade, it's not always possible to set them in the ground. Sometimes the soil is too full of roots, and tilling up a major planting site may damage the trees. In any landscape, try to get plants under trees established early, when the trees are young. Here are a few options for shady plantings:

- Plant clusters of perennials by digging a small bed under the tree and removing the roots. Stay as far away from the trunk and larger roots as possible. This should cause minimal damage.
- Add up to 2 inches of soil in the planting site, and choose small plants with shallow root systems.
- Plant in containers and set the plantings on the surface of the soil. You can group several containers together to create a small garden.
- Build a small raised bed under the tree, but don't include the tree trunk. Keep soil away from the trunk to prevent rotting at the base. Fill the bed with potting soil.

Plantings in the shade need extra care. It's so easy to overwater these sites and cause a root problem. Water-in the transplants well, and water every day or two during the first week. Then when the surface feels dry, give the plants a good watering. Maintain a 2- to 3-inch mulch layer.

CARE

Visit your garden several times a week to enjoy the flowers and check for problems. Use this time to direct growth: prune plants that are lopsided to produce a more even shape. If plants look too thin, nip out the tips of developing shoots. Try to avoid trimming shoots that are starting to flower.

WATERING

Try to separate your plantings into heavy-use and low-use areas, and run the irrigation system as needed. Here are some watering tips:

- Check plants for signs of wilting during the day, and water when the leaves begin to go limp.
- Feel the soil and water when the surface becomes dry to the touch. Check container gardens daily and water as needed.
- Drought-tolerant plants can go a day or two more without water when a dry soil is noted.
- Apply 1/2 to 3/4 inch of water. Run soaker hoses until the soil under and around the hose is moist.
- Water during early-morning hours to conserve moisture.

Try to keep the plants on a program of low water usage. It helps them develop a deeper root system, discourages many pests, and saves watering dollars.

FERTILIZING

If you missed the feeding time last month, it is time to give perennial gardens the first feeding of the year. Give new plants extra feedings to encourage growth. Feed the plants monthly with about half the normal rate of a granular fertilizer, or you might use a liquid feeding program as instructed on the label for maximum growth.

- In-ground plantings: Apply a granular general garden fertilizer every 6 to 8 weeks, beginning in February or March and continuing through October or November. You be the judge when the plants stop growing due to cool weather. If plants are active during winter, continue the feedings.
- Container gardens: Feed plants monthly with a liquid fertilizer during periods of active growth, typically March through November.
- Slow-release feedings: Select a fertilizer that slowly releases nutrients to in-ground and container plantings. Follow label instructions. Feedings usually last for 3 or more months. Mark your calendar for the next scheduled feeding.

PROBLEMS

Welcome beneficial insects such as lady beetles, lacewings, and praying mantis, and allow them to feast in your landscape. Try not to spray plants when the "good bugs" are present. But watch for these bad ones: aphids, mealybugs, slugs, and snails.

Mealybug

APRIL

PERENNIALS

PLANNING

Choose most of your perennials this month. Plan your garden so tall plants won't cast shade over smaller selections. Stock up on stakes or similar supports, and plan to stake early so plants will have a natural look as they grow. Here are some planning ideas:

- Plant taller perennials near fences so they can be tied to the wood or wire portions.
- Give each tall growing plant a stake where thinner limbs can be supported as needed.

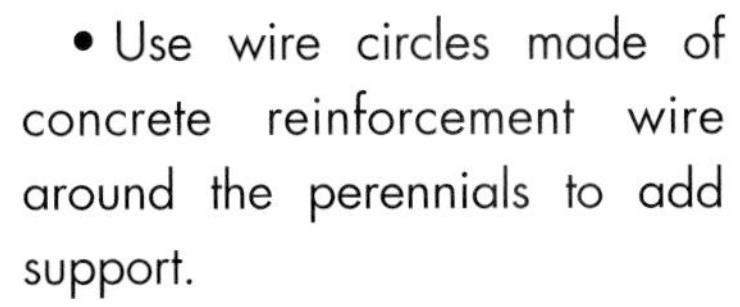

- Use wire circles made of concrete reinforcement wire around the perennials to add support.
- Place a wire tomato cage over each plant to keep the shoots within bounds.
- Form a triangle or square of stakes, and weave a rope mesh enclosure to hold the limbs in place.

PLANTING

Got a large plant that's overgrowing its neighbor? You can either prune or transplant the smaller plant.

- Water the soil the day before the move.
- Dig around the outer edge of the foliage to encircle the plant.
- If the plant is large in diameter and capable of being divided, cut it into two or more sections with a shovel or large knife.
- Lift each section with the rootball intact.
- Give the plant a new garden site with plenty of room to grow.
- Fill in the old hole with compost or good topsoil so the remaining plant can continue growth.

Give the transplanted perennial new-plant care. This includes keeping the soil moist and a first feeding two to three weeks after planting.

CARE

Remove fading flower heads, especially with **bush daisy**, **blanket flower**, **chrysanthemum**, **coreopsis**, **gaura**, **gerbera daisy**, and **jacobinia**. Groom if needed to reshape these plants. Prune lanky limbs.

WATERING

Keeping the soil moist may be one of your main jobs at this time of year. Once perennial gardens establish good root systems, they will draw moisture stored in the ground.

Improve sandy soils to hold extra moisture. Check regularly for water needs.

If a plant is large, it may be divided by cutting with a large knife, shovel, or by separating it using two garden forks.

FERTILIZING

Check your feeding calendar, then look at plant growth. Often if the soil is rich and the plants are not using all the nutrients, a feeding can be skipped. If the foliage is bright green, you can wait a few more weeks; if yellow-green, apply more fertilizer. When growth slows and you need more foliage, try encouraging shoots with another feeding. Young plants producing steady growth need to be kept on a fertilizer program to help them fill the perennial bed. Apply a granular garden fertilizer, liquid fertilizer, or manure.

KEEPING MUMS ANOTHER YEAR

Don't expect the **chrysanthemum**, which gives great displays in Northern gardens, to work as well in Florida landscapes. It can be done, but with considerable effort. Most **mum** plantings produce flushes of growth that are in and out of bloom September through May. Florida **chrysanthemums** are known as **garden mums**. They are planted throughout the year, but mainly when in bloom during late summer through fall. **Mums** in Florida are a bit strange, as our climate, with its warmish winter weather, encourages extra blooms. Here are some **mum** care tips:

- Select the **mums** you like when in bloom and add them to the garden.
- Keep the soil moist and feed lightly every six to eight weeks year-round.
- Prune off faded flower heads as they develop.
- Divide plants in spring to form new beds.
- Plants make good growth during the long days of summer. Give them needed trimmings so they will remain compact. Root the trimmings if needed to start more plants.
- Give the plants a final trimming in mid-August, as they start to form flower buds for fall.

Chrysanthemums often develop leaf diseases during the summer's hot, rainy weather. A fungicide may be needed to prevent major leaf decline.

PROBLEMS

A white form of scale insect is very common on **bird of paradise** and similar plants with thick, persistent foliage. The scale can be rubbed off with your finger or an old toothbrush. You can also use a soap or oil spray to obtain needed control.

An insect that is becoming noticeable on **bush daisy**, **chrysanthemum**, and **lantana** is the garden fleahopper. It's very small and dark colored. The damage looks like yellow pinpricks on the foliage, and the insect is seldom seen, as it hops away very quickly. If present, control with a general synthetic insecticide spray, as natural products are seldom effective.

A few more pests you might find in the April garden are aphids, mealybugs, slugs, snails, and powdery mildew.

MAY

PERENNIALS

PLANNING

Perennials serve as bursts of accent color and provide a backdrop for other garden favorites, such as bulbs. Take a walk through your landscape as some of the spring flowers begin to fade, to see where you might use perennials. Sketch your plans on paper.

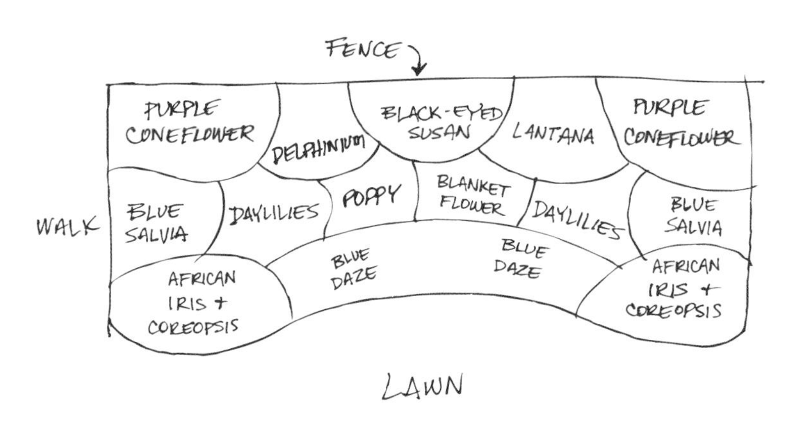

It's helpful to sketch out potential beds before you begin to dig or plant new ones.

• Fill in bare areas with perennials to form a permanent colorful but low-maintenance planting. Consider **African iris**, **heleconia**, **lantana**, and **ruellia**.

• Use perennials as a ground cover for a constant source of color. Good selections are **blue daze**, **coreopsis**, **gaura**, **Mexican heather**, and **salvias**.

• Invite butterflies to visit with **bush daisy**, **butterfly weed**, **firespike**, **lantana**, **pentas**, and **veronica**.

• Add greenery and some color to the shady spots. Try **blue ginger**, **crossandra**, **hosta**, **jacobinia**, **shrimp plants**, and **violets**.

• Fill planters at entrances, along walkways, and near windows with low-growing perennials like **angelonia**, **blanket flower**, **Mexican heather**, **Stokes aster**, **crossandra**, and **yarrow**.

PLANTING

Close to exterior walls, alkaline soil may keep **azaleas** and similar acidity-loving plants from doing well. Overhangs near your house can keep some spots very dry or very wet. If you've had plant failures around your walls, consider new soil preparation before replanting.

• Check for drainage. You may need to install gutters so the water moves away from the bed.

• Consider creating a raised bed next to the home. Check with your termite control company to make sure you are not disturbing their treatments, or you may need another treatment after construction.

• Check the soil acidity. If too alkaline, either use alkaline-loving plants or adjust the pH using soil test recommendations as a guide.

• Improve sandy soils with organic matter.

• Install a microsprinkler irrigation system that keeps the water off the walls of the home and only on the soil under the plants.

• Keep mulch a foot away from the home to prevent termites.

Now pick some of your best perennials for these locations. Most areas need plants that don't grow much over four feet tall. You would probably like plants that are in bloom most of the year. Sounds like a good site for **African iris**, **bush daisy**, **butterfly weed**, **heliconia**, **jacobinia**, **lantana**, **pentas**, **ruellia**, and **yellow alder**.

CARE

Some perennials are not fully awakened from winter dormancy, including **blue ginger**, **crossandra**, **four o'clock**, **heliconia**, **hosta**, **Stokes' aster**, and **yarrow**. These and a few others may die back to a rosette of foliage or buds near the ground and then grow back during the spring season. Make sure each has room to grow or make plans to move them later in the year. This is a good time to give all perennials a label so they won't be forgotten during the dormant seasons.

WATERING

Watering can be a little tricky at this time of the year. You want the plants to have adequate moisture without increasing your water bill. Feeling the soil is still the best way to determine moisture needs.

FERTILIZING

If you did a good job of feeding your plants earlier in the spring, there is no need to apply a fertilizer application yet. But if it's been six to eight weeks since fertilizer was applied or the plants are on the yellow side, give them a feeding. You wouldn't have to feed so frequently if you used a slow-release fertilizer that feeds for three or more months.

PROBLEMS

Leafminers may be found in **chrysanthemum**, **gerbera**, and **rudbeckia** foliage. The insect makes squiggly lines that look bad through the leaves, but cause minimal harm to the plants. Where needed, the leaves may be picked off. If the problem is serious, a synthetic garden spray may be applied. Most gardeners ignore this pest.

One pest will probably be leaving the landscape at this time of the year: powdery mildew. It's not a major pest during hotter weather. Some leaf spots may be taking its place, causing dark spots on plant foliage. Use a copper-containing fungicide, or a synthetic fungicide labeled for flowers, to obtain control as needed.

Aphids, mealybugs, slugs, and snails have not gone away and could be feeding in your gardens.

START NEW PLANTS FROM OLD

From May through early summer is the best time to start new plants to fill in the landscape with favorite perennials. Use tip cuttings taken early in the morning from perennials that have just matured new growth. Some that root very easily are **blue daze**, **bush daisy**, **butterfly weed**, **chrysanthemum**, **firespike**, **jacobinia**, **lantana**, **pentas**, and **yellow alder**.

Make cuttings 4 to 6 inches long and stick them in a pot of damp vermiculite. Place the container with cuttings in a large plastic bag. Use a few dowels to hold the plastic off the foliage and leave the top open just a little. Keep the cuttings moist and in a filtered-sun location. Most root in eight to ten weeks and can be potted and grown to a larger size for use in the garden.

JUNE
PERENNIALS

PLANNING

Some perennials only grow well in certain parts of the state. **Heliconia** are best in Central and South Florida. **Hosta** and **veronica** grow best in the more northerly areas. Temperatures received at these planting sites determine how well and long they grow.

In most instances, plants appropriate for only central and southern portions of the state can still be grown in the north, but in containers that must be protected from cold. Unfortunately, most plants limited to northern and central sections of the state do poorly further south due to the lack of cold during the more dormant winter months.

Experiment a little if you wish, but stick with the basic perennial selection for your area. Maybe you could create just one portion of a garden to try the newer plants along with some that are not zoned for your area.

PLANTING

Perennials are not very fussy and can be dug and divided almost any time of year. This is a very good time to dig and move the **Shasta daisy** to new beds. You might divide **African iris**, **ruellia**, **Stokes' aster**, **violets**, and **yarrow**.

During the hot summer months you have two choices when dividing plants: either move them to a new bed or grow them in containers. In Florida, keeping them in containers for a few months or longer has some advantages. They can be stored in pots until a new bed is prepared. The plants also get off to a vigorous start as you carefully control the growing conditions.

1. Dig the plants and separate them into small clumps.
2. Transplant to a 1-gallon (or larger) container.
3. Use a potting mix in the container and fill to within an inch or two of the top as the perennial is planted.
4. Water until moisture runs out the bottom of the container
5. Feed every other week with a liquid fertilizer solution, or add a slow-release product to the container.

Grow the plants in normal light levels. Keep them in the containers until garden center size and you have a bed ready for planting. Your extra plants also make great gifts for friends.

WATERING

Thank goodness for the start of the rainy season. Stay alert for dry spots, but daily rains should do most of the watering. Keep track of the rainfall. If a day or two passes without $^1/_4$ inch of rain, begin checking the beds.

Shasta daisy

FERTILIZING

Most perennial plantings get a second feeding as the rainy season returns. The extra water encourages new growth, and the plants form more extensive root systems. Even if you have used a time-release fertilizer, check your calendars—it's probably feeding time.

PROBLEMS

Many perennials have toughened up after the spring growth and the bugs don't find them as tasty. Some new pests may include grasshoppers and katydids. Both may be chewing holes in plant leaves. Try to handpick them from the plants, or, if needed, use a synthetic insecticide as instructed on the label for chewing insects.

GROW GERBERA SUCCESSFULLY

It used to be fairly easy to grow **gerbera daisies** in Florida, but the newer fancy varieties just don't seem to have much resistance to root problems. One way to still have attractive plantings is to look for old long-stemmed and single-flowered varieties. You may have to grow them from seed, which is still available. Plan the plantings for either fall or spring. These are the drier times of the year when the **gerbera** can become well established.

- Plant **gerbera** in a well-drained enriched garden soil.
- Set the plants in the ground at the same depth they were growing in their containers, or a little bit higher.
- Add a thin layer of mulch—maybe just an inch or two.
- Keep the soil moist. New plantings may need watering every day for a week or two.
- Feed lightly every four to six weeks for the first few feedings, then follow a regular schedule.
- Control leaf spots and powdery mildew with a synthetic fungicide labeled for flowers.
- Remove old flower heads from the plants.

If you still have trouble with **gerbera**, try growing them in containers. You can have a nice bowl of flowering plants to set along the walkway or patio. The newer varieties seem to grow better when confined to containers.

Aphids are pear-shaped insects that love the summer weather and feed only on new growth. Look for them in buds and new leaves. A soap spray is usually all you need for control. If lady beetles are present, you may not need to spray.

Slugs and snails also love summer weather. They come out on warm days to chew holes in plant leaves. Look for slime trails as the first hint of their presence, then hunt for them at night. Handpick them from plants, or use a snail and slug bait, available at garden centers.

JULY
PERENNIALS

PLANNING

Most gardeners find it very hot and humid outside. It's a time when you hope the winter and spring plantings pay off with good color and little maintenance. Enjoy a walk or two in the landscape to find other areas where you might use perennials.

• Consider problem turf areas as a site for new plantings. Maybe the spot is too shady or the pest problems won't permit good grass growth, but perennials would be ideal.

• Look for hard-to-maintain areas (for example, spots between the road and sidewalk, or little strips of grass in front of shrubs or near an entrance).

• Maybe you are just tired of annuals and want flowers with less work. An old annual bed could be a spot for perennials.

• Areas that are just too dry and look good only during the summer rains are worth considering. Drought-tolerant perennials may be the answer.

You may act now to correct these problem spots, or wait until cooler weather in fall.

PLANTING

Where have all the perennials gone? You might notice the garden centers clearing their shelves of lots of plants as the summer season arrives. Sales are lower as gardening interest declines. This may be a good time to get some good buys.

• Look for sales on unknown perennials that other gardeners may not be using.

• Check for plants that may be a little too large and need a quick home.

• Many garden centers are getting more tropical perennials, often at a good price.

If you make a purchase, you have two choices: the flowers can be added to the garden during the cooler times of the day, or kept in their pots and grown on until fall. Just trim back the overgrown portions and keep the plants well fed until you feel like doing the planting.

CARE

If walkways are overgrown and plant portions are starting to decline, you are going to have to do some pruning. Take a bucket, trash barrel, or wheelbarrow into the garden to begin the trimming.

• Cut off old flower heads to improve the looks of the garden.

• Prune off and discard all dead or pest-infested portions.

• Remove stems overhanging walks.

• Cut back stems interfering with neighboring plants.

• Pinch out the tips of the stems of lanky plants to encourage denser growth.

A good pruning now to spruce up the gardens may save a lot of work later in the year.

Deadheading improves plant growth and the appearance of the garden.

WATERING

Summer rains still provide most water needs. Continue to monitor flower beds and perennial plantings in the landscape. Water as needed if the rains fail to provide adequate water. Check perennials in containers daily. Most may need watering every day as these soils dry very quickly.

FERTILIZING

Summer rains can encourage rapid growth that uses available nutrients. Rains also wash nutrients quickly out of the root zone. Check your calendar—it may be time for another feeding. Monitor plant growth. If the leaves are lighter green and growth a little slower than expected, a feeding may be needed.

Container plants should be receiving regular feedings. If using a liquid fertilizer, apply the solution every other week to encourage growth. When using a slow-release fertilizer, follow label instructions.

PROBLEMS

Some pests are sure to be feeding on perennial plantings. Many can be tolerated if just a few portions of the plants are affected. Some chewing damage can be handpicked as noted, or a cluster of aphids removed and destroyed. If pests are more numerous, you may need an insecticide.

Aphids are pear-shaped insects that feed only on new growth. Look for them in buds and new leaves. They are small and of various colors.

A soap spray is usually all you need for control. If lady beetles are present, you may not need a spray.

Garden fleahoppers are very small, dark insects that hop about the foliage sucking juices from the leaves. They produce pinpoint-sized yellow spots in the leaves.

Control them with a synthetic insecticide labeled for piercing-and-sucking-type insects on flowers.

Grasshoppers are large-legged insects that grow to one inch or longer; when mature, they chew holes in leaves and may be green-brown or multicolored.

Handpick or apply a synthetic insecticide, following label instructions for chewing insects.

Slugs and snails come out on warm days to chew holes in plant leaves. Look for slime trails as the first hint of their presence, then hunt for them at night.

Handpick them, or use a snail and slug bait, available at garden centers.

AUGUST

PERENNIALS

PLANNING

Many perennials may have formed seedheads, and you can save seeds to plant in winter for spring transplants. Plan maintenance this month. Groom to encourage bigger, fuller plants. The following need special care:

Beebalm: Remove the old seedheads. Many need trimming to stay within bounds.

Bird of paradise: Remove old flower heads and declining leaves. Check for scale and control as needed.

Butterfly weed: Trim off lanky stems and encourage new growth. Control aphids feeding in the tips of shoots with a soap spray.

Coreopsis: Trim old flower heads back to near the ground and allow new growth to begin.

Four o'clock: Keep plants inbounds and collect seeds for sowing.

Gerbera daisy: Remove old flower heads and declining leaves. Control fungal leaf spot with a synthetic flower fungicide.

Lantana: Clean out dead portions and trim plants back to renew growth.

Pentas: Prune back overgrown shrubs. Root clippings to start new plants.

Poinsettia: This is the last month to give the plants a needed pruning. Make sure the plants have adequate fertilizer to produce winter blooms.

Shrimp plant

Rudbeckia: Trim off old flower heads and remove declining plant portions.

Shrimp plant: Keep inbounds by pruning back lanky stems or giving entire plants a severe pruning.

Many other perennials may need similar trimming and removal of old flower stems. Some, like the **Philippine violet**, may be just coming into bloom, so delay pruning until winter.

PLANTING

If you started rooting cuttings a month or two ago, they may be ready for a container. Just tug at the plants a little, and if they resist, some roots are forming. Lift a plant out gently, and if the rootball is about the size of a quarter or larger, it's ready for a pot.

1. Give each rooted cutting its own 4-inch (or larger) container.
2. Fill the containers with a good potting soil mix as you transplant each cutting. Allow room at the top of each pot for watering.
3. Moisten the soil until water runs from the bottom of the pot.
4. Set the transplant in a filtered-sun location for a few days to begin growth. Then move it to a normal light level.
5. Feed monthly with a fertilizer solution, or add a slow-release fertilizer to the surface of the soil, following the instructions on the label.

Most transplants should grow rapidly and be ready for the garden in six to eight weeks. This is the last month you can count on the rainy season to help with watering and make establishing new plants a bit easier.

CARE

Have you noticed something besides your favorite perennials growing in the gardens? These too may be perennials, but they are often called weeds. Keeping weeds under control is part of summer chores.

- Hand-pull as many weeds as possible when they are young.
- Spot-kill perennial and annual weeds with a nonselective herbicide that allows use near other plants.
- Maintain a 2- to 3-inch mulch layer over the soil to discourage new weed growth.
- Consider adding a landscape fabric to the landscape at planting time to reduce new weed growth.
- Use a preemergence herbicide in flower beds according to label instructions to reduce seed germination.

Weed control may be a full-time job. Whenever you take a walk in the garden, there may be a weed or two to pull.

SAVING SEEDS FOR SOWING

Many perennials can be started from seeds saved from one season to another, including the **salvias**, **violets**, **ruellia**, **lion's ear**, **gerbera daisy**, **butterfly weed**, and **blanket flower**. Let seeds dry on the plants. When pods begin to open, it's time to harvest. Try gathering the seeds on a dry day.

Bring seeds indoors and let them continue to dry a little longer on a screen or cheesecloth. After a few days, add each type to a plastic bag or a jar and label with the plant name and date. They are then ready for storage.

- Keep the seeds in a vegetable storage section of the refrigerator.
- If you wish, a paper towel containing a handful of dry milk can be added to each bag as a drying agent.
- Use the seeds within a year to get the best germination. Do not store seeds in the freezer.

WATERING

Enjoy the last full month of the rainy season. It's probably been pretty easy having to water only when the rains fail to provide moisture for a few days. Container gardens still need your attention, as do recent transplants.

FERTILIZING

Most gardens are still growing with nutrients applied during previous months. Container gardens need feedings at least monthly with a fertilizer solution, unless fed with a slow-release granular fertilizer. Make sure new transplants in containers get their needed feedings.

PROBLEMS

Check for poor drainage. Fungicides can be used to control root rot, but are relatively expensive when used to treat a few plants, and difficult to obtain. Correcting the conditions that encourage root rot is the best control.

Aphids, garden fleahoppers, grasshoppers, slugs, and snails are active and may need control. Use daily or at least weekly walks to stay ahead of insects and diseases in the gardens.

PERENNIALS

PLANNING

Early September starts off hot, but by the end of the month you should feel like getting outdoors. You will be welcomed by the fall-blooming **goldenrod**, **Philippine violet**, and many other perennials just showing their colors. Decide on what needs to be replaced, pruned, and divided. Take out your original planting diagram and see if there should be some changes made.

- Some perennials may have gotten much taller that you expected. Mark these perennials to be cut back and perhaps moved to the rear of the garden.
- A few plantings may have declined. Maybe it was the wrong location or not a variety suitable for the local climate. These areas have to be tilled and enriched before replanting.
- Often the perennial plants just need some trimming to make them attractive again. **Butterfly weed** is forever lanky and **cat's whiskers** grows out-of-bounds. Often it's best to cut them back to near the ground and let the new growth begin.
- Make note of areas that need a new mulch layer.
- Some of your perennial garden problems may be due to other plants. If trees and shrubs are interfering, schedule them for trimming, too.
- Note areas where you wish you had used perennials. Many new plants will begin appearing soon at the garden centers for fall planting.

With some ideas in mind, you are now ready to take on the fall season, which arrives around mid-month. It's still hot outside, so do most of the work during cooler portions of the day.

PLANTING

It's out with the old and in with the new. A long, hot summer is hard on plants, and many spots are ready for renovation. Some plants have died, and others are just too weak to continue. Yes, even perennials decline in Florida. Sometimes they just wear out. It's a good idea to have some replacement plants ready to be produced either from cuttings, divisions, or seed. When something happens to an older plant, you will be ready with a new start.

1. Dig or pull older declining plants from the beds. Try to get rid of as much of the root system and rotting stems as possible. Spot-kill or dig out weeds that may have invaded the garden.
2. Till the soil deeply to disperse plant pests. Revitalize the soil with liberal additions of organic matter. Compost is especially good, as are peat moss and manure. Work in a light application of a general garden fertilizer.
3. Begin fall plantings.

CARE

Lots of pruning is in order. Take your bucket or barrel to the garden and fill it up with unwanted trimmings. When pruning, make cuts back to a branch angle or bud, or to the ground. If you want a plant to fill in from the base, make the cut about one foot above where you want the new branches to begin. Remove old flower heads and seedpods. Save any seeds you want for later sowing. Cut out dead and declining portions. Remove insect-infested branches. Clippings and trimmings can be added to the compost pile. A good pruning now prepares the plantings for growth during the milder fall climate.

WATERING

Gradually the summer rainy season fades away. The change might catch you off guard, and your plants may suddenly start to wilt. Take more-frequent walks through the garden and inspect the plants and soil for signs of drier growing conditions. New plants will need extra watering, and plants in containers need a good soaking every day until cooler weather.

FERTILIZING

All perennials should be ready for a fall feeding. Try to schedule it just as the rainy season ends, around mid- to late September. This way, the nutrients get down into the soil just about the time the cooler fall weather starts to arrive and plants begin producing sturdy growth.

- Apply a granular fertilizer at the label rate or use a 6-6-6 at one to two pounds for each 100 square feet of garden.
- Check your calendar and reapply slow-release fertilizer products if needed. Most have been depleted by the summer rains and plant growth.
- If using manures, make a sidedressing over the root system of bed plantings. Follow suggested rates on the bags of manure or use a few pounds for each 100 square feet of bed.

Water after all feedings to get nutrients into the soil surrounding the roots. Continue to feed container plantings monthly.

PROBLEMS

The weather is a little cooler in some areas of the state this month, but the pests are not going to take a break. One pest you might notice increasing on some perennials is the mite, which is about the size of a pinpoint. These arachnids like the hot, dry weather and can turn over a new generation in about seven days. They cause small yellow dots to form on leaves due to their piercing-and-sucking activity. Where a control is needed, apply a soap spray following label instructions. Some more pests that have been active during the summer can be expected to continue through fall: aphids, garden fleahoppers, grasshoppers, slugs, and snails.

Cut out the bottom of a gallon container and use the container as a shield when you spot-kill weeds in your perennial beds.

OCTOBER

PERENNIALS

PLANNING

Plan to add fall colors with **chrysanthemums**. Many gardeners use these plants as short-season perennials, fall through early winter. Called **mums** for short, they grow well in full sun or light shade. To keep them for more than one season, improve sandy or clay soils with organic matter.

1. Set the **mums** in the ground within a few inches of each other to create a dense planting. They can be spaced 6 to 8 inches apart if you don't mind the open space and are planning to let the plants continue to grow.

2. Keep them moist, especially during the hot, dry days ahead. Add a 2- to 3-inch mulch layer.

3. Enjoy the flowers, but remove them from the plants when they fade, cutting the stems back near the foliage.

Mums can also be displayed in planters, large pots, or hanging baskets. If given good care, they will produce additional blooms.

Some other plants with fall colors are **butterfly weed**, **coreopsis**, **firespike**, **goldenrod**, **lion's ear**, **pentas**, and **salvias**.

PLANTING

Prepare beds for fall planting. With new plants, be conscious of water needs, because this season is dry.

You might consider using perennials in large pots of varying sizes. They can be brought into a protected area when cold warnings are sounded. Good perennials choices for containers include **angelonia**, **gaura**, **blue daze**, **lantana**, **pentas**, **Mexican heather**, and **salvias**.

- Select a large container. You might use perennials as the focal point and fill in with annuals and herbs.
- Clean old containers with a mild bleach solution before use, and allow the container to air-dry.
- Fill the container about halfway full with a good potting mix.
- Add the perennials, placing taller plants in the center or back of the container. Use smaller-growing types and any addi- tional plants around the outsides and as fillers.
- Keep the plantings moist and feed every other week with a fertilizer solution or add a slow-release granular product to the surface of the soil.

Container gardens can last for months, but gradually the plants run out of room. When this happens, remove the perennials and add them to the landscape.

CARE

Poinsettias form their flower buds this month if they have no nighttime light. Take note of where your plants are growing. If they are located where they might get light during the evening hours, even for just a few minutes, it could be enough to stop or delay flowering.

- Move container plants to an area without nighttime lights.
- Resist turning on outdoor lights near **poinsettias**.
- Cover plants near streetlights or other lights over which you have no control. Covers must be applied before sundown and left on the plants until sunrise.

Keep the **poinsettias** moist and continue scheduled feedings.

WATERING

The dry weather has really just begun. Sure, there will be periods of rainfall, but only a few inches per month. This may be enough for many perennials as

the weather becomes cooler, but until then, check the garden frequently. Many plantings can last up to a week or more without water if they have good mulch.

- Select a mulch that is easy to obtain, nice-looking, and reasonably priced. Some include pine needles, composted leaves, and bark. Weed-free hay or straw also makes a good mulch.
- Create layers of mulch 2 to 3 inches thick. Larger plantings can have a 3- to 4-inch layer.
- Keep the mulch back from the base of the plants to prevent root rot.
- Renew the mulch layers as they decompose. Never remove the mulch unless redoing the beds. Feed the plants by applying fertilizer or manure to the surface of the mulch.

Continue to check container plantings daily for water needs. Some may even need a twice-daily soaking.

CHECK PRUNERS AS A SOURCE OF DISEASE

Pruners are meant for one job only: removing plant portions. They are not meant to spread plant disease. Give your pruning equipment a good cleaning to make sure you are not moving pests between plants.

- Allow the shears to sit in a mild bleach or similar disinfectant solution after use.
- Rub down the pruners with rubbing alcohol between each plants.
- If you know a plant is infected and you are removing diseased wood, disinfect the pruners between cuts. You might take an extra pair into the field to have one soaking while you are using the spare.
- Never put pruning equipment away dirty. Clean it and apply a light coating of oil.

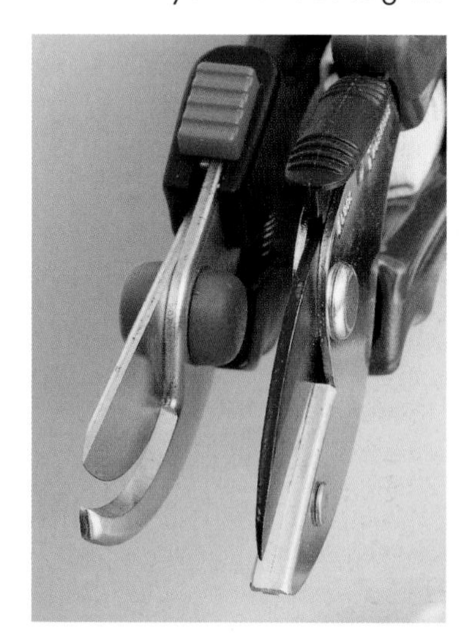

Good pruners are invaluable; keep them clean and disinfect between each use.

FERTILIZING

If you skipped the September feeding, now is the time to complete fertilizer applications for in-ground plantings. Use a granular general fertilizer, slow-release fertilizer, or manure application to provide the needed nutrients. Plants in containers, planters, and hanging baskets receiving liquid applications should be fed every other week.

PROBLEMS

Some pests will be fading from the landscape. You can probably say good-bye to most of the grasshoppers that have been chewing on plant foliage. Root rot problems should decrease as the weather becomes much drier. Stay alert to the presence of aphids, garden fleahoppers, mites, slugs, and snails.

PERENNIALS

PLANNING

Continue perennial plantings into the fall months. This is actually a great time to be adding plants to the landscape. Just make sure you know which are hardy and which you will have to protect if you live in the central and northern areas of Florida. Some perennials know very well that the days have become shorter and start to decline. Look for **blue ginger**, **coneflower**, **crossandra**, **four o'clock**, **hostas**, and similar plants to die back, either to the ground or to a cluster of foliage. You may want to mark these plantings with stakes to know where they are located. Some might need to be divided or relocated during the winter or spring months. Gardeners throughout the state should plan to spend a few hours with their perennial plantings.

- Remove declining plant portions and trim back out-of-bounds shoots.
- Cut off old flower heads and seedpods.
- Renew the mulch in order to maintain a 2- to 3-inch layer.
- Remove declining plants and add new selections to the garden.
- Divide and transplant perennials that have formed clumps larger than their allotted space.
- Design new beds to help reduce landscape maintenance problems.
- Plan cold-protection strategy in the northern parts of the state.

PLANTING

It's really a pleasure to be planting the garden at this time of year. The weather is much milder in all areas of the state and the outdoor chores much easier to perform. Any perennial can be added to the landscape at this time, but you may want to consider keeping new cold-sensitive types in containers in northern areas until the winter is over. Some of these are **angelonia**, **bird of paradise**, **crossandra**, **firespike**, and **pentas**.

- If the plants are outgrowing their containers, move them to a pot one size larger.
- Keep them in normal light levels needed for growth.
- Check the soil daily for water needs, and moisten when the surface soil becomes dry to the touch.
- Feed every other week with a liquid fertilizer solution during periods of active growth. Feedings can often be reduced during winter when growth slows.
- Be ready to move the plants to a warm location if frost and freeze warnings are sounded.

Plants added to the landscape should set in the ground following normal planting procedures. You may not need to water as often during the fall months, but check the soil frequently. When the surface dries, give the plants the normal $1/2$ to $3/4$ inch of water needed to rewet the soil.

- Mulches can be very important during the fall and winter months. Even plants in the warmer locations might be subject to surprise periods of winter cold. Keeping a loose mulch near the plants can provide cold protection that keeps the buds near the stems alive, even when the uppermost stems are killed by frosts and freezes.
- Pine needles and weed-free hay make excellent protective mulches.

You may want to keep a bale or two handy to apply around plants when cold weather is predicted.

CARE

A little edging can make the perennial beds look a lot more attractive and better organized. This is one chore you can perform at any time of the year, but is a lot easier during the cooler months. Good edging defines a bed and helps you keep the plants inbounds. It limits the growth of lawns into the beds and makes maintenance easier.

- Use a hose, rope, or similar material to form the edge of the bed. Then create the edge with a nursery spade or other digging device. Create the edge of the bed by removing soil from along the bed to form a slight depression in the ground.
- Leave the edge open or add bricks, treated wood posts, plastic, or similar materials to obtain a more formal edged look.

Refresh the edge at least once a month using a shovel or power equipment.

WATERING

Not much water is needed during the cooler months. You might be surprised that existing perennials can go a week or more without a sprinkling. Keep track of soil conditions and water only when needed.

FERTILIZING

Feeding time is over in North Florida. If you forgot the fall feeding, you can still apply a general garden fertilizer at half the normal rate. Gardeners in Central Florida should hurry to complete their feedings. Gardeners in South Florida can continue on a regular schedule but stretch the time a little longer between applications as follows.

- Feed in-ground plantings every other month with a general garden fertilizer to maintain growth.
- Stretch the time between container feedings to every three to four weeks, using a liquid fertilizer solution.
- Gardeners using slow-release garden fertilizers can usually allow maximum time between feedings to elapse before making another application.

PROBLEMS

Pests don't go away, but their activity is greatly reduced during the cooler months. Expect most insect feedings in the warmer portions of the state. Check perennial beds weekly for aphids, garden fleahoppers, mites, slugs, and snails.

Edging a bed can be done anytime but during cooler weather is ideal.

DECEMBER

PERENNIALS

PLANNING

Beware of freezing temperatures by month's end. More perennials will sneak into dormancy as the cooler temperatures arrive. These include **goldenrod**, **rudbeckia**, some **salvias**, **Stokes' aster**, **veronica**, **violets**, and **yarrow**. You can expect good color from **poinsettias** as long as the cold allows. Most garden centers will be clearing their shelves, so look for good buys to plant and keep warm until spring weather. Gardeners in South Florida can often ignore this cold talk, but they must stay alert to surprise freezes.

PLANTING

Perennials can be planted at any time. Prepare beds now:

- Remove old plants and weeds. Spot-kill weeds with a nonselective herbicide that permits replanting.
- Till the soil deeply and work in liberal quantities of organic matter.
- Test the soil acidity and adjust to the proper pH if needed.
- Add a mulch to keep weeds down and give an attractive look to the landscape. The mulch can be raked back to allow planting as needed.

CARE

Keep cold protection ready for the sensitive perennials. These are usually the succulent types and those considered tropical. Just a few are the **bird of paradise**, **blue daze**, **firespike**, and **Philippine violet**.

WATERING

It's a dry but cool time of the year, and most plants need minimal watering. Only plants in pots should be of real concern and checked daily. When the surface soil begins to dry, it's time to water. Check plants in the ground every three or four days. Most can last a week or more without a watering if they have a mulch layer over their roots.

Mulch can be just about anything, including rocks as well as plant materials.

FERTILIZING

Feeding time is over, and very few plants in northern and central portions of the state are making growth. Fertilizer applications can continue as normal in the south:

- Feed in-ground plantings every other month.
- Apply a liquid feeding to container plantings monthly.
- Reapply slow-release fertilizers according to label instructions. Check your calendar to determine when the next feeding will be needed.

PROBLEMS

Gardeners often ask if cold can stop insect pests in Florida landscapes. It's probably best to say that cooler weather just slows them down. When plant growth begins, pests always seem to be present. Gardeners in North and Central Florida can probably relax a little and check only the growing plants for pests. Plants in protected locations and in warmer areas of the state may find some aphids, mites, slugs, and snails are still active.

CHAPTER EIGHT

SHRUBS

Often growing between ground covers and trees, shrubs build unity in the landscape design with repeating foliage color and leaf shape. Shrubs may bear attractive flowers, colorful berries, and unique leaf shapes. Some only offer seasonal interest; when the show is over, they fade into the background with other landscape plantings. Others are on display year-round. These are often permanent accents given a prominent spot where they are sure to be noticed by visitors.

There are so many ways to use shrubs:

• Tall shrubs make good view barriers. Select denser-growing varieties if you want complete blockage.

• Use shrubs to exclude sounds. A thick, small-leafed sound barrier can silence busy streets or active neighbors.

• Plant shrubs to form hedges, large or small, natural or formal in growth habit, that direct or limit movement.

• Shrubs can be used to form a backdrop for other garden features. Flower gardens, sundials, birdbaths, and statuary look great displayed against the greenery.

• Use shrubs as foundation plantings. They can hide ugly home features and soften architecture.

• Cluster shrubs together to create seasonal color. Use familiar types to help bring spring,

summer, fall, and winter to the landscape.

• Plant a shrub just because you like it. A "specimen plant" is one you add to the landscape because it has some feature you really appreciate. Try to work it into an accent spot or cluster several together for a color backdrop.

You can probably think of many other reasons to plant shrubs in your landscape.

PLANNING

Shrubs are fairly permanent plantings. They can be dug up and moved, but it's not a fun job and you will lose all the growth that has occurred developing your design. For this reason, you should try to make as many firm decisions about your shrub plantings as possible.

The state of Florida is long and quite varied in the climatic conditions that affect plant growth. It can be divided into three regions, North, Central, and South Florida. In our shrub tables (pages 229 to 231), we have tried to make the selection of shrubs easy by noting the best regions for each. Some areas may be colder than is normal during the winter, others hotter than normal during summer, both of which limit shrub growth. Check with your local garden center, your Extension Service, or even a gardening friend to determine whether or not a shrub is suited to your area.

Think about what types of shrubs you would like in the landscape, and have a purpose in mind for each. Should they be tall or small? Do you want flowers? Here are a few more factors to consider when planning shrub plantings:

• How many shrubs do you need? It is usually best to plant a cluster, using odd numbers to avoid symmetrical designs. Use the eventual width of the plants as a guide when deciding how many to plant in a space (half to three-quarters the width is the best between-plant spacing).

• Arrange plants according to light requirements. Don't allow tall plants to hide smaller shrubs. Make sure that plants preferring lower light levels have a shady spot.

• Place shrubs with year-round interest in key spots. Use them near entrances and patios, and along walkways. Plant larger shrubs at the end point of a view, creating a focal point.

• Check your soil. Some shrubs, like azaleas, need an acid soil, but most like a pH in the 6.5 to 7.0 range, which is slightly acid to neutral.

• Select hardy shrubs most often. If you want a few that are more cold sensitive, realize that they may be frozen back to the ground or completely killed during a severe winter. Just about every gardener wants a hibiscus or tibouchina shrub, but in Central and North Florida they may not be permanent plantings due to sudden winter freezes.

PLANTING

Most shrubs grow well in sandy soil, but you can make care a lot easier by enriching these sites (and clay sites) with organic matter. Till the entire bed and work in the peat moss, compost, and manures. Check the soil pH and adjust before planting if needed.

Make sure the ground has good drainage. If in doubt, mound up the planting site a bit to help extra moisture move away from the root system. In some wet locations, you may consider using more formal raised beds, or developing swales to move moisture to other areas of the landscape. To prevent soil from washing away, avoid planting shrubs near the dripline of a roof. In these spots you may consider guttering.

• Open up a hole that is at least twice as wide as the rootball, but no deeper.

• Ease the new plant from the pot. If the root system is tightly woven together, gently pry some of the roots loose.

• Position the plant in the soil at the same depth it was growing in the container, or just 1 to 2 inches out of the ground.

• Fill in around the new shrub with soil removed from the hole. If possible, add water to the hole as the soil is added. This is especially important with larger shrubs.

• Form a 4- to 6-inch berm of soil around the edge of the rootball to hold water and direct it down through the rootball. Thoroughly moisten the shrub.

• Add a 3- to 4-inch mulch layer over the ground. Keep the mulch back a few inches from the base of the shrub.

CARE

Part of caring for shrubs is taking periodic walks through the landscape to notice how well they are growing. If growth is normal, just pass on by. If you notice wilting foliage, yellow leaves, or pests, however, immediate attention is needed.

Shrubs also need direction, whether a light pruning to keep limbs from reaching out over paths, or a full seasonal pruning to renew vigor. Make sure you prune the plants at the best time so as not to remove flower buds from the more colorful types.

WATERING

Newly planted shrubs need regular attention. How long this period of scrutiny lasts depends on the time it takes the plants to develop roots in the surrounding soil. Some, like azaleas, may not be able to live on their own using normal landscape maintenance techniques for a year or two.

Maintaining a moist soil is critical. Hand watering is best. Fill the berm with water so it thoroughly wets the rootball and moves out into the surrounding soil. Hand-water for at least several weeks until the plants begin to adjust and grow in their new site. Reduce the waterings to an as-needed schedule, then follow these tips:

• Water when the surface soil below the mulch begins to feel dry. For drought-tolerant shrubs, allow several additional days between waterings. Some, once established, may not need special waterings at all.

• Apply 1/2 to 3/4 inch water at each irrigation.

• Water in the early morning.

• Install soaker hoses or microsprinklers, which put the water directly where it is needed.

FERTILIZING

One way to promote growth is by using fertilizer. During good growing weather, shrubs can quickly convert nutrients into new stems and foliage. You may want to feed newer shrub plantings a little more often to help them fill in.

Commercial fertilizers are applied in liquid or granular form. Liquids can be applied through a sprinkling can or hose-end applicator. Granules can be tossed out by hand or applied with a rotary spreader.

Some gardeners like to use natural products. Manures can be applied to the surface of soils or over mulches. They can also be made into teas for drenching the ground. Some natural products are being formulated into granular fertilizers for surface applications.

Here are some options to use when feeding shrub plantings:

New plantings: Feed lightly every six to eight weeks, March through October, with either liquid or granular general garden fertilizers

Established plantings: Feed two to four times a year. Apply a feeding in March and one in September to maintain growth and good plant color. If needed, additional feedings may take place in June and August. Use a general-garden fertilizer or a 16-4-8 product at label rates.

Water to begin moving nutrients into the root zone. There is no need to remove mulch—watering moves the nutrients off the granules and into the ground. You may notice some carrier portions of the fertilizer straying behind.

PEST CONTROL

All shrubs have pests, some more than others. Often you do not know you have a problem until the plant starts to decline. Maybe you'll notice some yellow foliage, then find scale insects on the underside of leaves. With other shrubs, you may only notice a declining limb as the first indication of a fungal infection.

Some insect damage is very noticeable in the early stages. You cannot miss azalea leaf caterpillars or large grasshoppers. Handpick them from the plants. Following are a few pests you might find on shrub plantings:

Aphids: Small pear-shaped insects of varying colors, aphids live in new growths. Their sucking juices from the leaves produces sap and excreta that encourage the growth of black sooty mold. Control as needed with a soap or oil spray following the label instructions.

Caterpillars: The immature stage of moths or butterflies that chew plant foliage, stems or flowers, they are of varying sizes and colors. It is best to handpick them from plants and destroy them, or the plants can be treated with a *Bacillus thuringiensis*-containing natural insecticide.

Leaf spots: Various-shaped yellow to brown spots caused by fungal activity on leaves, many leaf spots are normal and can be ignored since the fungus attacks older plant foliage as it declines and drops. Where new and healthy leaves are infected or the fungus is affecting the quality of the plant, a fungicide should be applied according to label instructions.

Scale insects: Insects covered with a white to dark waxlike coating, they may range from the size of a pinhead to that of a dime. Most can be easily scraped off the leaf or stem with the fingernail to reveal the insect under the covering. Where needed, control with an oil spray, following label instructions.

CHAPTER EIGHT

Shrubs

Name	Average Size Hgt. (ft.)	W. (ft.)	Area of Florida	Flower Color	Season	Light Needs
Abelia	4 – 6	4 – 6	NC	White	Summer	Sun, light shade
Allamanda, Bush	4 – 6	4 – 6	CS	Yellow	Year-round	Sun, light shade
Anise	8 – 10	6 – 8	NCS	*		Sun, shade
Aucuba	5 – 6	2 – 3	N	*		Shade
Azalea, Indian	6 – 8	4 – 6	NC	Varied	Spring	Light shade
Azalea, Kurume	3 – 4	2 – 3	NC	Varied	Spring	Light shade
Azalea, native	5 – 6	4 – 6	N	Varied	Spring	Light shade
Banana Shrub	10 – 12	6 – 8	NC	Yellow	Spring	Sun, light shade
Barberry, Japanese	5 – 6	3 – 4	N	Yellow	Spring	Sun, light shade
Barberry, Wintergreen	5 – 6	3 – 4	N	Yellow	Spring	Sun, light shade
Beautyberry	5 – 6	4 – 5	NC	Lilac	Spring	Sun, light shade
Bottlebrush	8 – 10	8 – 10	NCS	Red	Spring	Sun
Brunfelsia	6 – 8	4 – 6	CS	Purple	Spring	Sun, light shade
Butterfly-bush	4 – 6	4 – 6	NC	Varied	Spring-fall	Sun
Camellia, Japonica	10 – 12	6 – 8	NC	Varied	Winter	Sun, light shade
Camellia, Sasanqua	10 – 12	6 – 8	NC	Varied	Winter	Sun
Cape Jasmine	6 – 8	6 – 8	CS	White	Spring-summer	Sun, light shade
Cassia	6 – 8	6 – 8	CS	Yellow	Fall	Sun
Chaste Tree	10 – 12	10 – 12	NC	Blue	Summer	Sun
Cleyera, Japanese	8 – 10	4 – 6	NCS	Yellow	Spring	Shade
Cocculus	10 – 12	6 – 8	CS	*		Sun, light shade
Cocoplum	10 – 15	10 – 15	S	White	Year-round	Sun, light shade
Coral Ardisia	3 – 4	1 – 2	NC	*		Shade
Crape Myrtle	6 – 15	8 – 10	NC	Varied	Summer	Sun
Crape Myrtle, Dwarf	2 – 4	3 – 4	NC	Varied	Summer	Sun
Croton	6 – 8	4 – 6	CS	*		Sun, light shade
Euonymus, Creeping	1 – 2	3 – 4	N	*		Sun, shade
Euonymus, Japanese	6 – 8	4 – 6	N	*		Sun, light shade
Fatsia	5 – 6	2 – 3	NCS	*		Light shade
Feijoa	8 – 10	6 – 8	NCS	White, red	Spring	Sun, light shade
Firebush	6 – 8	6 – 8	CS	Red	Year-round	Sun, light shade
Firecracker Plant	4 – 5	3 – 4	CS	Red	Year-round	Sun, light shade

CHAPTER EIGHT

Shrubs

Name	Average Size Hgt. (ft.)	W. (ft.)	Area of Florida	Flower Color	Season	Light Needs
Florida Privet	8 – 10	6 – 8	CS	White	Spring	Sun
Florida Yew	8 – 10	8 – 10	NC	*		Light shade
Fortune's Mahonia	3 – 4	2 – 3	N	Yellow	Spring	Light shade
Gardenia	6 – 8	4 – 6	NCS	White	Spring	Sun, light shade
Hibiscus	8 – 10	6 – 8	CS	Varied	Year-round	Sun, light shade
Holly, Chinese	10 – 12	6 – 8	NC	White	Spring	Sun, light shade
Holly, Dwarf Burford	5 – 6	4 – 5	NC	*		Sun, light shade
Holly, Dwarf Yaupon	3 – 4	3 – 4	NCS	*		Sun, shade
Holly, Japanese	2 – 4	2 – 3	N	*		Sun, light shade
Holly Malpighia	1 – 2	1 – 2	CS	Pink	Spring-summer	Shade
Hydrangea, French	5 – 6	4 – 5	NC	Blue-Pink	Spring-summer	Light shade
Hydrangea, Oakleaf	5 – 6	4 – 5	NC	White	Summer	Light shade
Indian Hawthorn	3 – 4	3 – 4	NCS	White, pink	Spring	Sun, light shade
Ixora	4 – 6	3 – 4	CS	Red, yellow	Year-round	Sun, light shade
Jasmine, Arabian	4 – 5	3 – 4	S	White	Summer-fall	Sun, light shade
Jasmine, Downy	5 – 6	4 – 6	CS	White	Spring-fall	Sun, light shade
Jasmine, Primrose	5 – 6	5 – 6	NC	Yellow	Spring-	Sun summer
Jasmine, Shining	4 – 5	4 – 5	CS	White	Spring-	Sun, light shade summer
Juniper, Chinese	4 – 6	4 – 6	NC	*		Sun
Juniper, Shore	1 – 2	4 – 6	NCS	*		Sun
Juniper, Spreading	1	3 – 4	N	*		Sun
Japanese Boxwood	3 – 4	2 – 3	NC	*		Sun, shade
King's Mantle	4 – 6	4 – 6	CS	*	Summer	Sun, light shade
Ligustrum, Japanese	10 – 12	6 – 10	NCS	White	Spring	Sun, light shade
Ligustrum, Sinense	6 – 8	4 – 6	NCS	White	Spring	Sun, light shade
Loropetalum	6 – 8	4 – 6	NC	White,	Spring pink	Sun, light shade
Nandina	3 – 5	2 – 3	NC	White	Spring	Light shade
Natal Plum	6 – 8	4 – 6	CS	White	Spring	Sun, shade
Oleander	10 – 12	6 – 8	NCS	Varied	Year-round	Sun

Shrubs

Name	Average Size Hgt. (ft.)	W. (ft.)	Area of Florida	Flower Color	Season	Light Needs
Orange Jessamine	10 – 12	6 – 8	CS	White	Spring-fall	Sun, light shade
Philodendron, Selloum	6 – 10	8 – 10	CS	*		Sun, shade
Pittosporum	8 – 10	8 – 10	NCS	White	Spring	Sun, light shade
Plumbago	4 – 6	4 – 6	CS	Blue	Year-round	Sun, light shade
Podocarpus, Yew	20 – 25	8 – 10	NCS	*		Sun, light shade
Powder Puff	8 – 10	8 – 10	CS	Red	Winter	Sun, light shade
Pyracantha	8 – 10	6 – 8	NC	White	Spring	Sun
Red-tip Photinia	6 – 8	5 – 6	NC	White	Spring	Sun
Reeves Spirea	5 – 6	4 – 5	NC	White	Spring	Sun
Rose of Sharon	8 – 10	6 – 8	NC	Varied	Summer	Sun, light shade
Sea Grape	12 – 20	10 – 12	CS	*		Sun, light shade
Serissa	1 – 2	1 – 2	NCS	White	Spring- summer	Sun, light shade
Silverthorn	10 – 12	8 – 10	NC	Tan	Winter	Sun
Simpson Stopper	10 – 12	6 – 8	CS	White	Spring	Sun
Snowbush	4 – 6	4 – 5	CS	White	Summer	Sun, light shade
Surinam Cherry	10 – 12	8 – 10	CS	White	Spring	Sun, light shade
Sweet Osmanthus	10 – 12	6 – 8	NC	White	Winter	Light shade
Texas Sage	5 – 6	4 – 5	NCS	Lavender	Spring-fall	Sun, light shade
Thryallis	5 – 6	4 – 6	CS	Yellow	Summer	Sun, light shade
Ti Plant	4 – 6	3 – 4	CS	White, pink	Fall	
Tibouchina	8 – 10	6 – 8	CS	Purple	Summer	Sun
Viburnum, Black Haw	6 – 8	5 – 6	NCS	White	Spring	Sun
Viburnum, Laurestinis	6 – 8	4 – 5	NC	White, pink	Winter	Sun
Viburnum, Sandankwa	5 – 6	4 – 5	NCS	White	Spring	Sun, light shade
Viburnum, Sweet	10 – 12	6 – 8	NCS	White	Spring	Sun
Wax Myrtle	10 – 12	6 – 8	NCS	*		Sun, light shade

* = Inconspicuous Flower Color N = North Florida C = Central Florida S = South Florida

PLANNING

It's good weather for getting out into the garden and deciding where you need shrubs. Make sure you are picking the right shrub for the location.

- Look at the eventual height and width.
- Select lower-growing types for under window areas. What good is a window if you cannot look through it?
- Select shrubs with lots of greenery for backdrops. Florida does have some shrubs that lose their leaves during the winter. These are not good choices if you need green growth year-round.
- Pick one or more shrubs with lots of interest to plant in easily seen spots near patios, along walkways, and at entrances. Pay attention to leaf shape, flower color, and bark types when making the selections.
- Make sure the shrubs are well suited to your climate. You can grow a few of the tropicals in cooler areas of the state, but try to stick to hardy types.

PLANTING

Winter is a great planting time for all shrubs. Garden centers are filling with new plants as they close out the holiday season. Shop early to get a good selection. If the planting site is not quite ready, you can keep plants in containers if you give them plenty of water. This is a good time of year to move plants from one area of the landscape to another. There is a lot less stress on you and the plants. Here are the steps to making transplanting successful:

1. Decide where you want to plant and have the soil ready. If you can't decide, you can put the plant in a container until it can be planted or shared with friends.
2. Thoroughly moisten the soil before digging. If the soil is dry, begin wetting the ground a few days before the planned move.
3. Start digging by making downward cuts with a shovel around the shrub to form a rootball. Get a good-sized rootball that you can still lift.
4. After the rootball is formed, dig under the plant to separate it from the ground.
5. Lift the plant by the rootball or slip a cloth underneath to move it from the hole to the new site or a container.

Watering is the secret to a successful transplant. Keep the ground moist to encourage growth as the weather begins to warm.

Rejuvenate shrubs by proper pruning and thinning.

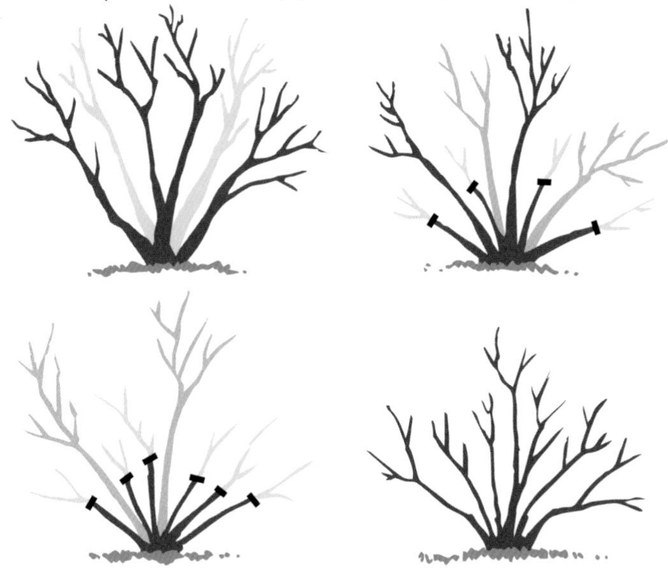

CARE

Plants that bloom during summer are usually ready for a winter pruning. Most form their flower buds on new growth. One exception is the **hydrangea**, which won't flower until summer but already has buds on its stems. A few you can prune now are **crape myrtle**, **tibouchina**, **thryallis**, **butterfly bush**, and **Texas sage**.

1. Remove some of the older wood to the ground to allow new shoots to develop.
2. Trim away all dead or declining plant portions.
3. Remove seedpods. With **crape myrtles**, this may be all the pruning that is needed. Cut back the stems to a point about 1/2 inch in diameter.
4. Reshape the plants, preserving their natural appearance.
5. Thin out shoots that are competing with established main limbs.

SELECTING CRAPE MYRTLES

Some **crape myrtles** are small, others quite tall. It's important to know what you are buying when you make your purchase. If a plant is too tall for your space, you will be doing lots of pruning, which often ruins the plant's shape. Here are some **crape myrtle** buying tips:

- Look for plants that are the size you want: dwarf means less than 4 feet; semi-dwarf means under 12 feet; intermediate means under 20 feet; and trees are greater than 20 feet.
- Check out powdery mildew resistance. Most shrubs that have American Indian tribal names have good resistance to this disease.
- Look for a single-trunk plant if you want a formal **crape myrtle** tree, or one with three to five limbs from the base for a small to large shrub
- Pick a **crape myrtle** with the bark color you like, which can range among tan, light brown, cinnamon, and reddish.
- Pick your plant when it's in bloom to make sure you have the desired flower color.

WATERING

Shrubs are not heavy users of water. Get to know your plantings and try to group shrubs according to their water use. **Azaleas**, **hydrangeas**, and **gardenias** are heavy water users, but **crape myrtles**, **viburnum**, and **ligustrums** need few special waterings. All, however, need water in order to become established and produce growth. Even drought- tolerant plants look their best only when provided with adequate water.

- Check soil periodically for moisture. Note when rains are received and how much rain falls.
- Water when the surface inch of soil begins to dry.
- Water during the early-morning hours and, when possible, use low-volume sprinklers that put the water near the plants.
- Apply 1/2 to 3/4 inch of water each irrigation.
- Maintain a 3- to 4-inch mulch layer.

FERTILIZING

Wait about one more month to feed plants in the ground. Most are producing limited growth due to short days and cool weather.

PROBLEMS

Now is a good time to check shrub plantings for scale insects and the sooty mold that often accompanies them. Two other pests you may find during the warmer days of winter are aphids and mealybugs.

FEBRUARY

SHRUBS

PLANNING

Cold damage may occur this month. Leave damaged plants alone for a few weeks so you can see clearly what is still alive and what is not. Prune tropical leaves that give off a sulfurous smell after a freeze. Give plants the water needed to resume growth, but do not apply fertilizer until growth begins or the normal feeding time rolls around. If plants are frozen to the ground, wait till late spring before making replacements. They might recover.

PLANTING

Garden centers have great selections in easy-to-plant containers so make your choices, and follow good planting methods. Sandy and clay soils can be improved with lots of organic matter. Peat moss, compost, and similar materials supply nutrients and help soil retain moisture. A few areas of Florida have rock as the main planting material. You may want to bring in soil to get the plants off to a good start, creating a raised bed over the rocky ground.

CARE

As plants send out new shoots, you can direct their growth by trimming stems back to a bud pointed in the direction you want new growth to begin. Don't waste a plant's energy by allowing it to produce lots of growth on a stem you plan to take out later-remove it now.

If plants need more dense growth, just pinch out the tip of the shoots with your fingers or with hand-pruners. This technique works well for hedges and backdrops.

WATERING

New growth means the plants are using water. Luckily, it's still cool, and not much moisture will be lost to evaporation. Wait until shrubs tell you they need water. It won't hurt if you allow the foliage to wilt just a little.

New plantings need the most care. Just a day or two without water can cause the rootball to begin drying. More plants are lost during the first few months due to a lack of water than to any other problem. In Florida sands, water is pulled out of the rootball by surrounding soils, leaving the plants dry.

- Make sure the rootball is remoistened at each watering.

One effective measure is to create berms around the rootball to catch and direct water into the soil, thoroughly wetting the root system.

- Don't depend on an irrigation system to water new plants.

A hand-held hose is the best way to soak the soil for at least the first few weeks.

- Check new plantings frequently for water needs. The plants will not be established for at least several months. Some, like **azaleas**, may need two years.
- Use soaker hoses and microsprinklers where possible to put water where it is needed—at the root system.
- Maintain the mulch layer to hold in moisture.

FERTILIZING

Spread your fertilizer uniformly over the surface of the soil under the shrubs. Here are some ways to feed your plants:

New plantings: Feed lightly every six to eight weeks March through October to encourage growth. Apply either liquids or granular general-garden fertilizers.

Established plantings: Feed two to four times a year. Apply two-times-a-year feedings in March and September to maintain growth and good plant color. If needed to encourage, additional feedings could be made in June and August. Use a general-garden fertilizer or a 16-4-8 type product at label rates.

Water after all feedings to move the nutrients into the root zone. There is no need to remove mulches. The watering moves the nutrients off the granules and into the ground. You may notice some carrier portions of the fertilizer remaining behind.

PROBLEMS

Pests may start to show up on new shrub growth. One that loves the tender shoots is the aphid. It appears at the same time leaves start to open. Look for the small pear-shaped bodies found in several different colors. They often produce lots of sap and excreta that attract ants and encourage the growth of sooty mold. Sometimes ladybugs can be seen feeding on the aphids; they may provide adequate control. Where needed, aphid infestations can be controlled with soap sprays. You might also notice mealybugs, leaf spot, and scale insects.

HIBISCUS PRUNING

Is there ever a good time to prune the **hibiscus**? Most plants are in bloom year-round unless affected by cold. When the plants are pruned, it could be six months before flowers reappear. Here are a few tips to help you keep the plants in bloom:

- Wait until late February or early March to do the pruning in cooler locations.
- Cut back or remove tall, lanky shoots to branch angles or trunks within the plants. Some may be cut back to the ground.
- To allow new shoots to develop and renew growth, trim back up to one third of the older stems to the ground or to branches within the plant.
- Remove any dead or declining shrub portions.
- Give the plants a light feeding of low-nitrogen blossom-booster fertilizer.
- Keep soil moist with normal waterings.

Hibiscus

SHRUBS

PLANNING

Plan ahead for color. Determine which shrubs bloom in summer, fall, and winter, and find spots in your landscape where they can be featured.

PLANTING

Good care starts with proper planting. Suppose you just want to plant a shrub or two and you are not preparing a whole bed. How do you get these plants off to a good start?

1. First, remove weeds from the planting site. You may need to use a nonselective herbicide for perennial-type weeds that permits replanting shortly after use. Many can also be hand-pulled or dug out of the ground.
2. Till the soil. Try to work up as much of the ground as possible.
3. Work organic matter into sandy and clay soils.
4. Plant the new shrub as you would any new bare-root or container-grown plant.

The new plant will need special attention. It's very easy to forget one of a few plants among others in the landscape. Be sure to keep up the watering. It will take several months before the plant can grow well with normal maintenance.

CARE

Complete all winter pruning at this time. Get the brown out of the shrubs, cutting declining portions back into the healthy stems. If the plants suffered a lot of winter damage, some reshaping may also be needed.

Winter-flowering shrubs, including **camellias** and **azaleas**, can be given needed trimming as they finish blooming. Try to prune before they jump into new growth, so as not to waste the plant's energy.

WATERING

March welcomes spring, and with it comes warmer weather. Expect plants to use more water as temperatures rise. Keep in mind that most shrubs are fairly drought tolerant. One way to make sure plants have adequate water is to feel the soil. If the upper inch of soil is moist, watering is not needed.

Some gardeners like to put the irrigation system on automatic. If this is the case, a good watering once or twice a week is usually adequate for established plantings. The very best way to conserve water and help the plants develop an extensive root system, however, is to water when needed.

New plants need frequent watering, of course. Check them daily; if the soil is dry, remoisten the ground. Be sure you wet the rootball. This often requires hand-watering.

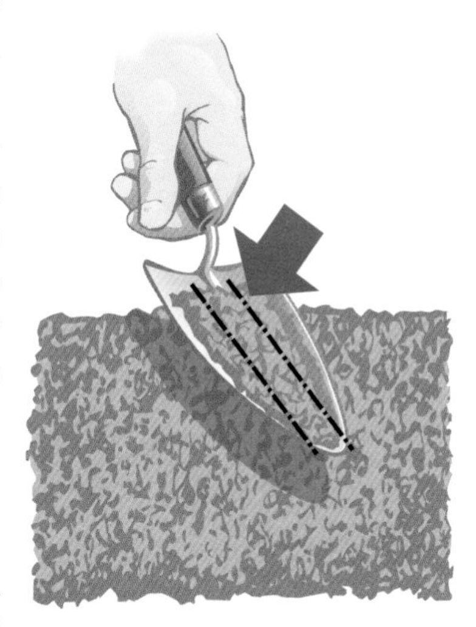

Check soil moisture by digging down with a trowel and feeling the soil. If the upper inch is moist, do not water.

FERTILIZING

If you fell a little behind last month, or you just delayed fertilizing until now, it's time for the spring feeding. You can choose just about any fertilizer. Some gardeners like special products that have an individual plant pictured on the bag. These may have some advantages, as they are made specifically for the individual plant.

- **Azalea** fertilizers help keep the soil acid.
- **Hibiscus** fertilizers contain one or two of the specific minor nutrients this plant needs.
- **Gardenia** fertilizers often contain more magnesium.

You can use one of these products if you wish, but a good general-garden fertilizer usually works fine. Many gardeners are choosing products with a high nitrogen content such as a 16-4-8 or similar. You don't have to carry as much fertilizer home, and it promotes good vigorous growth. You may also want to look for a fertilizer with some of the minor nutrients added. Some such as iron, magnesium, and manganese are important for the health and vigor of many shrubs.

PROBLEMS

Bring on the insects and diseases along with good spring growth. Perhaps you noticed some browning of **azalea** flowers during the damper weather. This is caused by a fungus living on the flowers. Fungicides can be used, but it's quite a chore to spray all the plants, which has to be done frequently during the flowering period. Most gardeners just choose to lose a few blooms to the disease. A few pests you may want to control during spring are aphids, mealybugs, leaf spots, and scale insects.

FALL-BLOOMING AND FRUITING SHRUBS

Select some fall-blooming or fruiting shrubs to add to the landscape next to their spring-blooming cousins. You will be happy you did as the seasons change.

- **Beautyberry** provides light flower interest during the spring but lots of purplish berries in fall.
- **Camellias** offer a selection of species that can be in bloom October through March.
- **Cassia** is good green shrub throughout the year that bursts into yellow blooms in fall.
- **Firecracker plant** is in bloom much of the year and has reddish flowers, especially in summer.
- **Ixora** offers good orange and yellow blooms most of the year, especially during the warm months.
- **Loropetalum** offers good spring color, and many varieties have colorful foliage.
- **Philodendron** has attractive foliage for year-round interest.
- **Pyracantha** flowers during the spring and has attractive berries in fall.
- **Texas sage** offers silvery foliage throughout the year and lavender flowers during the summer.
- **Thryallis** has good yellow summer and fall color.

SHRUBS

PLANNING

Most shrubs are very drought tolerant, and many can go several weeks without special watering. Only some, like **azaleas**, **gardenias**, and **hydrangeas**, need lots of water, and they can be planted in a kind of "oasis." A "transition zone" in your landscape can be filled with plantings that need watering only occasionally, perhaps every week or two. Hedges may fall in this category, along with water-conserving perennials. A "fringe area" can contain your most drought-tolerant shrubs, those that can rely on natural rainfall.

PLANTING

This month, garden centers are full of shrubs. If you buy plants and need to keep them in containers for a while, here's how:

- Keep the soil moist by checking daily. Water until moisture runs from the bottom of the pot. Lift the plants periodically. If water runs down the sides without wetting the rootball, push the soil against the edges of the container with your fingers; then water again.
- Apply a liquid fertilizer every other week, or add a slow-release fertilizer to the soil surface.

Sometimes plants are kept in containers a bit too long at the nursery or at your home when they are waiting for planting. When this happens, they develop a rootbound condition. This means the roots are tightly wrapped, taking the shape of the container. Try to avoid rootbound plants, but sometime you have no choice.

1. Prune off any extra-long roots growing through the pot as you get ready for planting.
2. Ease the plant out of the pot and gently loosen the outer layer of roots. You cannot untangle all the roots, just some that might begin new growth.
3. Add the new plant to the land- scape, following normal transplanting techniques.
4. Keep the plant moist until new roots grow out into the surround soil. This may be an extended period of time for severely rootbound plants.

Unless severely rootbound plants are given this special treatment, they may never grow out into the surrounding soil; they will make limited growth and often decline.

CARE

Spring growth is popping out wherever you look. Some of the growth may be unwanted weeds. A portion can be pulled and others spot-killed with a nonselective herbicide that permits use with growing plants. Here are some other ways to help control weeds.

- Periodically freshen the mulch layers to bury seeds and control growth.
- Apply a preemergence herbicide to stop weed growth, following label instructions for shrubs.
- Install a landscape fabric at planting time to keep weeds from growing up around the shrubs. Add a mulch to improve the appearance.
- Periodically hoe or rake the soil to control new seedling growth.

WATERING

It's the hot and dry time of year, and this means extra waterings. Walks among the plantings are a necessity if you are controlling the watering. Look for drying foliage. It does not hurt the plants to wilt just a little. When noted, it is time to turn on the irrigation.

Here are some tips for conserving water.

• Only water plantings that need to be watered. Plants grouped in the oasis or frequent-watering zone need more attention.

Some plantings may be drought tolerant and need watering only during very dry weather, if at all.

• Water during the early-morning hours.

• Apply 1/2 to 3/4 inch of water.

• Adjust sprinklers so they put the water only where it's needed. Keep water off the streets and walkways.

FERTILIZING

Fertilizer is optional at this time of year. If for some reason you forgot a feeding, now is the time to make a fertilizer application. You may want to encourage extra growth from newly planted shrubs with an extra feeding, or give plants recovering from pruning or winter injury some extra nutrients.

PROBLEMS

Your **gardenias** may be coming into bloom shortly; with the pure-white flowers come some easy-to-see thrips. This is the real spoiler for the flower, causing the petals to turn brown and ruining the display value of the blooms. Good thrip control starts before the buds open with insecticidal sprays. No good natural controls are available at this time but the synthetic insecticide Orthene has been controlling this pest. Apply the insecticide as instructed on the label. Keep a lookout for leaf spots, aphids, caterpillars, mealybugs, and scale insects.

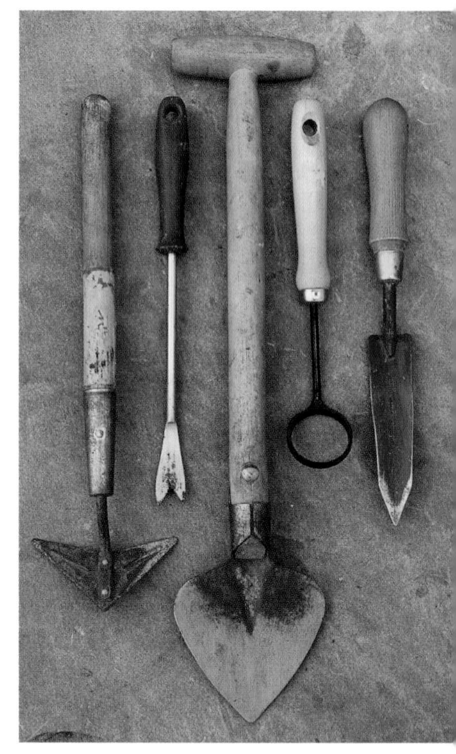

It's helpful to have a variety of weeding tools on hand.

SHAPING A HEDGE

Are formally pruned hedges old-fashioned? They may be, just because it takes a lot of work to keep a nice shapely hedge. Many gardeners are choosing plants that block a view and reduce noise but have limited growth. They also choose plants that are naturally dense and need little trimming. But if you do have a formal hedge and want it to look good:

• Prune when new growth becomes 6 to 8 inches long.

• Trim back growth, leaving an inch or two of new growth.

• Shape the hedge so it's obviously narrow at the top and wide at the bottom. This helps keep the foliage exposed to the sun and growing near the ground.

• Give hedges a little extra watering and fertilizing attention if needed to promote growth.

MAY

SHRUBS

PLANNING

The **azaleas** are gone and the **gardenias** are losing their color too. What is left for summer? Try to find shrubs that keep the landscape full of greenery and pop out some color as well. Nothing beats the **crape myrtles**, often called the **southern lilacs**. And try the standard **hibiscus**, often called **Chinese hibiscus**, or some of the other species such as **fringed hibiscus**, **rose-of-Sharon**, or **sea hibiscus**. They are easy-to-grow plants that can be used as a backdrop for other landscape plantings or featured as accents. Gardeners in colder portions of the state can either treat them as annuals or give them winter protection. Chemically **dwarfed hibiscus** are available at garden centers; they keep their size for about a year before growing to maturity.

PLANTING

Continue planting the shrubs you need to complete your landscape. You may want to add an entire bed of shrubs or just a plant here and there. Good soil preparation is one of the keys to a successful transplant. Work in lots of organic matter with sands and clays.

Some gardeners may want to move plants at this time of year, but it is difficult. Try to put off transplanting until the cooler time of year. If you must move plants, pick the small ones. These are likely to transplant more successfully.

CARE

After spring growth, some shrubs are likely to be overgrowing sidewalks and competing with their neighbors. It won't hurt to do some needed trimming at this time. One plant you should be trying to complete trimming is the **azalea**. You don't have to do a heavy pruning every year, but at least see if some grooming is needed.

- Check for dead or declining wood and remove it from the plants.
- Nip back extra-long or lanky shoots to promote good sturdy growth.
- Periodically remove some of the oldest wood back to the ground so new shoots can sprout from within to form a vigorous shrub.

Up to one-third of the old wood can be removed during any spring pruning.

- Every few years, cut the plants back to a foot or more below the desired height.

WATERING

Hot and dry is the best way to describe the month of May. Some rains may possibly begin by the end of the month—but until then you have to do the watering. Check the plants regularly. Some may not be getting the proper amount of water for many reasons.

- Sprinklers may not be hitting the shrub plantings.
- New growth may be hiding the sprinklers.

Trim the new growth or raise the sprinkler head above the shrubs.

- Plants at the end of a sprinkling system often get some water but not enough.

You may have to move the heads or create a separate zone for these plantings.

- Some soils repel moisture. If you have such a soil, be sure to give it a mulch, which helps keep the soil uniformly moist.

Also try wetting the soil with a weak detergent solution before sprinkling.

Automatic watering systems are probably run once or twice a week for most established shrub plantings. But if you monitor the plantings, you may have to

CHANGING HYDRANGEA COLOR

Do you like the blue or pink **hydrangeas**? The standard florist **hydrangea**, sometimes called the **French hydrangea**, can bloom in either color. The secret is soil acidity. At a low pH, the flowers are blue, and at an alkaline pH, they are pink. In the middle, they may look like dirty dishwater.

Have your soil tested at a local garden center or extension service. Then adjust the soil acidity for the hydrangea color you want.

- Blue **hydrangeas** require a soil pH below 6.5. Add soil sulfur to maintain an acid pH. Aluminum sulfate is available at some garden centers, but use it sparingly to prevent aluminum toxicity in local sands.
- Pink **hydrangeas** require a soil pH above 7.0. Use dolomitic lime as needed, following a soil acidity test, to produce the alkaline growing conditions.

Pink hydrangea

water only once a week or even less.

FERTILIZING

Wait—don't make a feeding application quite yet. The rainy season is just ahead, and the plants will begin making additional growth. If you delay feedings for another month, you will probably get better use of the fertilizer and the natural rainfall will water it in.

If you notice some plants on the yellow side, then a feeding may be needed. Any shrubs in planters or pots waiting for planting may need a fertilizer application at this time. But if the plants are good and green, wait just a little longer.

PROBLEMS

Plant pests love summerlike weather. You may be starting to see more of the grasshopper. Many have hatched out recently and are chewing holes in the plant foliage. Unless you find them constantly attacking one plant, they are very difficult to control. Try catching the critter and removing it from the plants. If needed, a synthetic insecticide for chewing insects can be applied following label instructions. A few more summer shrub pests are aphids, caterpillars, mealybugs, and scale insects.

PLANNING

Most gardeners dream a little during the hot summer season. Use this time of year to develop landscape plans. Decide where you need additional shrub plantings. Or maybe you need to move some shrubs to different locations. Here are some things to consider:

• Find spots where you need additional color. Maybe you have only a season or two of color. Try to fill in with some shrubs that add new interest.

• Some shrubs may be thinning due to shade. You may have to replant with a more-tolerant type.

• Did you pick the wrong shrub for a certain spot? Sometimes they get too tall and either need lots of pruning or replacement.

• In some instances, a variety may not have performed well in your landscape.

Maybe you need to pick another type.

• Do you need privacy? Views change and so do neighbors. A new hedge or view barrier may be in your future.

Finalize new landscape plans at this time and take time during the summer to pick the plants.

PLANTING

In Florida we add landscape plantings year-round, but it's a lot more stressful for you during the summer months. Try doing the work during the early-morning or early-evening hours. Make sure you have the right plant for the proper light level. If not, the summer sun is sure to produce some burns.

• Check plant tables to make sure the light level is adequate for growth.

• Shade-loving plants may be able to withstand some morning sun but need midday and afternoon shade.

• Pick the right shade level.

Light shade means the plant is getting some filtered sun. This may be necessary for good growth and flowering.

• Check for root competition.

Light levels may be just right in the shade but if the plant cannot compete, it's going to decline. You may have to find yet another spot for planting.

Crape myrtle

CARE

Hurry to complete all **azalea**, **camellia**, and **gardenia** pruning at this time. These plants are forming their buds for next year. Trim out the dead and declining portions and then cut back the plant portions that are out of control.

Delay pruning any plants that flower during the summer. Do remove the forming seedheads on **crape myrtles** as they complete flowering. Cut them back to points along the stem about 1/2 inch in diameter. With periodic seedhead removal, **crape myrtles** can be kept in bloom through September.

WATERING

The summer rains may be doing most of your watering. But check often, and when a few days pass without water, it may be your turn to provide the moisture. At least a 1/4 inch of rain should fall to provide significant water for shrub plantings. Keep track of the rainfall with a rain gauge.

FERTILIZING

A second feeding can be provided to encourage additional growth or maintain shrub color. Use a granular fertilizer or a liquid feeding as preferred. Some gardeners also like to use manure and similar natural products.

PROBLEMS

Keep your eye open for summer insects. Here are a few of the hot-weather problems and suggested controls.

Aphids are small pear-shaped insects of varying colors living in new growths. Their sucking of juices from the leaves produces sap and excreta that encourage the growth of the black sooty mold fungus.

Control as needed with a soap or oil spray, following label instructions.

Caterpillars are the immature stage of moths or butterflies, and they chew plant foliage, stems, or flowers. They are of varying sizes and colors.

They are best handpicked from the plants and destroyed, or the plants can be treated with a *Bacillus thuringiensis*-containing natural insecticide.

Grasshoppers are large-legged insects up to 2 inches long and green to brown in color. They chew plant foliage.

Some damage can be ignored; otherwise, pick off and destroy, or control with a synthetic insecticide following label instructions.

Scale insects are usually small and covered with a white to dark waxlike coating. With their coating they may range in size from a pinhead to a dime.

Most can be easily scraped off the leaf or stem with the fingernail to reveal the insect under the covering. Where needed, control with an oil spray, following label instructions.

Leaf spots are various-shaped yellow to brown spots caused by fungal activity on leaves. Many are normal and can be ignored; the fungus attacks older plant foliage as it declines and drops.

Where new and healthy leaves are infected and the fungus is affecting the quality of the plant, a fungicide can be applied, following label instructions.

JULY
SHRUBS

PLANNING

Think tropical during the summer months. It's certainly hot and humid, just as you would expect in a jungle-type climate. The plants are making lots of growth, filling in the voids rather quickly. Shrubs can help create a tropical feeling, and you will find many being offered at garden centers. If you live in South Florida you can add all you want, but Central and North Florida residents should beware of overplanting because of the winter cold.

• Add plants with large flowers to the landscape, such as **hibiscus**, **tibouchina**, **king's mantle**, **allamanda**, and **oleanders**.

This adds a tropical look when staged against a green background.

• Look for shrubs with exotic leaf colors. Some that can help are the **croton** and **ti plants**. They come in various sizes and color patterns.

Plant entire beds or mix them with other greenery.

• Look for exotic leaves. The **philodendrons** are ideal, providing deeply cut leaves to feature as backdrops or accent clusters.

• Use the shrubs in combination with other tropical **palms**, ground covers, and trees to complete the design.

Tropical gardens are best created as part of the patio, along walks, or at rest areas in the landscape.

PLANTING

Nothing is keeping you from planting except the heat. If you are adding some of the tropical plants, they won't mind the heat one bit. Just make sure you are following good planting techniques.

1. Prepare the soil by tilling as deep as possible.
2. Work in lots of organic matter.
3. Set the plants in the ground at the same depth they were growing in the pots.
4. Build a 4- to 6-inch-high berm of soil around the edge of the rootball to fill with water.
5. Add a mulch and keep the soil moist.

CARE

Hydrangeas are in bloom now and will be ready for a trimming in a few weeks or so. Remove the old flower heads as the color begins to fade. Perform any needed trimming to reshape the plants. They will form their flowers for next year later in the fall.

Complete all **azalea** and **gardenia** pruning early this month. It's probably already too late to do additional pruning of **camellias** without affecting some flowering.

Keep up with your weeding. This is the time when they make good growth too. Handpull or spot-kill with a nonselective herbicide that allow use near growing plants. Renew mulch layers to help prevent germinating seeds.

WATERING

You probably won't have to do a lot of watering. Summer rains normally occur at least every few days. If you fail to get a good rain within four or five days, you had better check the higher-water-use plantings. Remember that some like **azaleas** and **hydrangeas** can go only a few days without water in sandy soils during the really hot weather.

FERTILIZING

If you missed the June feeding, there is still time left to apply fertilizer during the summer months. Your plants are making lots of growth, which can take some extra nutrients. Apply a complete granular garden fertilizer or a liquid feeding.

- Scatter the nutrients over the surface of the soil under the plants out past the dripline.
- Water after feeding to move the nutrients into the root zone.
- Plants on a low-maintenance program do not need the summer feeding.

There are many different types of fertilizers, including granular and liquid.

PROBLEMS

The rainy season helps control some pests but encourages others. There are very few mite problems on shrubs at this time of year, but other pests are quite active.

You might see aphids building up high populations on **crape myrtles**.

Often ladybugs will keep them under control and a spray will not be needed.

One new pest you might look for is the lacebug on **azaleas**. These insects suck the juices out of the leaves to turn them a yellowish color. They have lace-like wings and leave dark deposits on the bottom of the leaves.

Control with an oil spray as needed, following the label instructions.

Caterpillars are the immature stage of moths or butterflies, and they chew plant foliage, stems, or flowers. They are of varying sizes and colors.

They are best handpicked from the plants and destroyed, or the plants can be treated with a *Bacillus thuringiensis*-containing natural insecticide.

Grasshoppers are large-legged insects up to 2 inches long and green to brown in color. They chew plant foliage.

Some damage can be ignored; otherwise, pick off and destroy, or control with a synthetic insecticide following label instructions.

Leaf spots are various-shaped yellow to brown spots caused by fungal activity on leaves. Many are normal and can be ignored; the fungus attacks older plant foliage as it declines and drops.

Where new and healthy leaves are infected and the fungus is affecting the quality of the plant, a fungicide can be applied, following the label instructions.

SHRUBS

PLANNING

Try looking ahead to your future landscape needs. Check your landscape plan and note where more of the same shrubs you already have or a neighbor might have are going to be needed. Duplicating shrub types builds unity in the design by repeating like foliage types. If you find some big needs and you don't want to purchase the plants, try your hand at propagating them during summer. You might be surprised how rapidly the **pittosporum**, **viburnums**, **jasmine**, **hibiscus** and others root during the warmer times of the year.

- Take cutting material during the early-morning hours from the tip portions of stems.
- Fill 6-inch or larger pots or trays that have drainage with vermiculite, and moisten.
- Make the cuttings 4 to 6 inches long and remove some of the bottom leaves.
- Dip the cut end in a rooting powder available at local garden centers.
- Stick the end of the cutting about 2 inches deep into the containers of vermiculite with the foliage just touching.
- Place the containers of cuttings in a shady spot and surround with plastic held off the foliage.
- Keep the cuttings moist and most should root in ten to twelve weeks.

When the cuttings form roots 1 to 2 inches long, they can be potted and then raised to a landscape size. Keep them moist, and after a few weeks move them into a normal light level. Feed every other week with a liquid fertilizer or add a slow-release fertilizer to the surface of the containers, following label instructions.

PLANTING

Perhaps the early-morning or early-evening hours are a good time to get beds ready for planting. Maybe you decided to replace some turf with more care-free shrubs or replace some plantings that have failed for some reason.

- Remove all unwanted plants and weeds from the planting site.
- Till the soil deeply and add organic matter to sandy or clay soils.

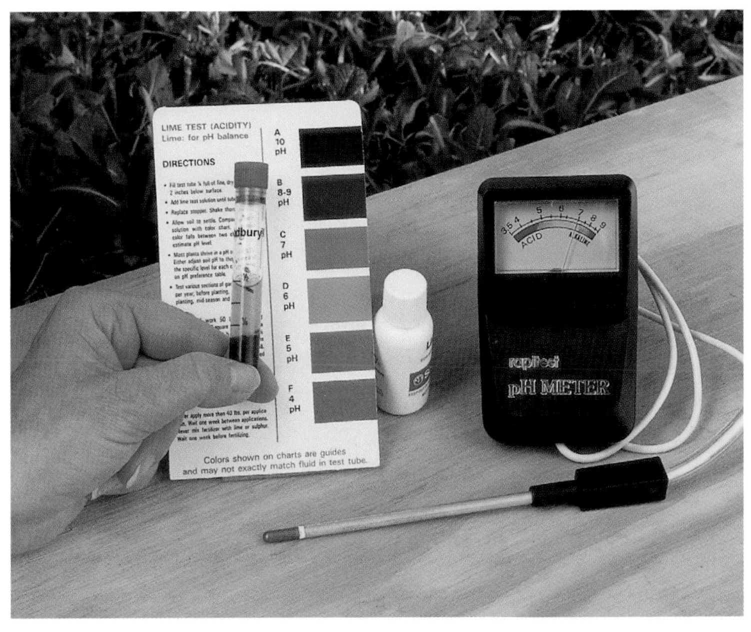

This is a good time to take a soil test to check the pH level.

• Test the soil acidity and adjust to the proper pH with lime or soil sulfur if needed.

• Mix the soil well and let it settle to await planting.

CARE

Continue to do needed hedge pruning during summer. The general rule is to allow the new shoots to grow 6 or more inches long, then do the shearing. Cut them back to within an inch or two of the previous cuts. This allows the hedge to grow a little each time it is trimmed. In a few years a major pruning to reduce the height and width will be needed.

WATERING

It's the last full month of the rainy season. You probably won't have to do a lot of watering at this time. Just monitor the rainfall and if the plants do not receive significant water in 3 to 5 days, irrigation may be needed. Rainfall has to provide at least one-quarter inch of moisture to begin wetting the soil. When you water, apply 1/2 to 3/4 inch.

FERTILIZING

Gardeners trying to get the most growth from their shrubs may want to apply a third feeding of the year now. Also, some plantings are starting to show some nutrient deficiencies by this time if other feedings were skipped. It's not unusual to find some yellowing of older leaves and then leaf drop that can be prevented with a feeding at this time of year. Any one of a number of feeding techniques can be used.

• Apply granular fertilizers under the spread of the plantings.

• Use liquid fertilizers as a spray or drench over the plants. Wash off the foliage if applied during the heat of the day or suggested on the label.

• Apply manures as a topdressing, or make a manure tea to apply to the soil.

PROBLEMS

Don't forget to use pesticides only when destructive insects are out of control. There are many beneficial insects working in the landscape too, including ladybugs, lacewings, and mantids. Leave them to help control pests living on your plantings. Following are some pests that you may have to control this summer.

Caterpillars are the immature stage of moths or butterflies, and they chew plant foliage, stems, or flowers. They are of varying sizes and colors.

They are best handpicked from the plants and destroyed, or the plants can be treated with a *Bacillus thuringiensis*-containing natural insecticide.

Grasshoppers are large-legged insects up to 2 inches long and green to brown in color. They chew plant foliage.

Some damage can be ignored; otherwise, pick off and destroy, or control with a synthetic insecticide following label instructions.

Lacebugs are lacy-winged insects about 1/8 inch long that suck juices from plant leaves. They are most likely to be found on **azalea** and **pyracantha** shrubs. During feeding, they turn leaves yellow and produce a brown excreta on the bottom of the foliage.

Control with an oil spray as needed.

Leaf spots are various-shaped yellow to brown spots caused by fungal activity on leaves. Many are normal and can be ignored; the fungus attacks older plant foliage as it declines and drops.

Apply a fungicide where new and healthy leaves are infected and the fungus is affecting the quality of the plant. Follow label instructions.

SEPTEMBER

SHRUBS

PLANNING

As you recover from the intense summer heat, think about new shrubs for fall color. Many shrubs make great backdrops to hide fences or walls, and in fall, their color bursts out. Plants like **pyracantha**, **beautyberry**, **shrubby hollies**, and **nandina** provide accents for weeks or months.

You can also display standalone shrubs as specimen plants. Two for fall color are the **cassia** shrub and **sasanqua camellia**.

No matter what you decide to grow, it's about time to complete the landscape plans you started in summer.

PLANTING

Adding new shrubs should get easier as the weather becomes cooler. By late September, the moderating temperatures might coax you outdoors to begin planting. If you haven't gotten the soil ready yet, take a weekend or two to do the tilling.

- Remove all weeds and declining plant portions.
- Till the soil as deeply as possible.
- Work liberal quantities of organic matter into sandy and clay soils.
- Test the soil pH and adjust if necessary with lime or soil sulfur.

Don't apply lime without a test, as gardeners may in other areas of the United States. In Florida, we test the soil first.

- Give the soil one more good tilling and you are ready to plant.

Many shrubs are arriving at garden centers and are ready for planting. When the soil is ready, all you have to do is slip the plants out of the pots and add them to the soil. Planting a shrub bed can be a family affair that makes quick work of landscaping.

CARE

It's time to get out into the landscape and do some fall pruning. You would like the plants to produce some extra growth over the next few months, filling voids left by limb and shoot removal. Here are some pruning tips:

- Pruning time for **azaleas**, **camellias**, and **gardenias** is long gone. But if you see a few lanky shoots, they can be removed at this time.
- If you remove seedheads from **crape myrtles** early in the month, you may get one more bloom.
- Make all pruning cuts back to a branch angle, back to buds along the stems, back to the trunk, or back to the ground.
- Give formal hedges a final reshaping of the year. All plantings should be recovered from pruning by winter.
- Do not use pruning paints to cover wounds. They may only impede wound healing.

WATERING

You have to watch the weather this month to know when to pick up on the watering. Most of early September should have adequate water as the rainy season gradually comes to an end. By the end of the month, watering may be your complete responsibility.

• Check the plantings often.

Feel the soil below the mulch, and when the surface starts to dry, it's time to water.

• When water is needed, apply between 1/2 and 3/4 inch.

• Check the irrigation system.

Look for overgrown heads, stuck sprinklers, and major leaks that could affect watering.

FERTILIZING

You could begin feedings during late September, but most gardeners wait just a little longer. If plants are showing sign of deficiencies, a fertilizer application is needed. Use either a granular fertilizer or a liquid feeding to renew the green color and encourage fall growth. Water the fertilizer into the soil after an application.

PROBLEMS

We do have bugs and plenty of them. Most develop large populations during the summer that keep on feeding into the early fall months. Develop a pest control strategy for fall.

EDIBLE LANDSCAPING

Why not produce a little food for the table? Edible landscaping is simple. Instead of ornamental plantings, choose shrubs that produce fruits or other harvests. See if your garden has room for some of these:

• **Blueberry** needs an acid soil and is limited to central and northern areas of the state. Plants form large bushes and open attractive white spring flowers. The fruits mature in late spring. The plants are deciduous and develop good fall color.

• **Feijoa** is also called the **pineapple guava**. This shrub can be used as a hedge and is very drought tolerant. It has attractive spring flowers and in late summer matures green edible fruits. Scoop out the insides and eat them fresh or add to salads.

• **Natal plum** is a nice dark-green small-to-medium-growing hedge plant. It produces red plumlike fruits that can be made into a jelly.

• **Pyracantha** makes a good view barrier and all-purpose shrub. It opens white flowers in spring and produces fruits for fall that can be made into jellies.

• **Surinam cherry** makes a nice hedge for central and southern portions of the state. Plants flower in spring and produce red early-summer fruits.

• Walk the landscape at least once a week looking for plant problems. Turn over some leaves and check for insects living under the foliage and along stems.

• Look for beneficial insects including ladybug, lacewing, mantids, and spiders that may be providing pest control.

• Pick off any beginning infestations of caterpillar, grasshopper, and others.

• Try to use the least-toxic spray first when pests are spotted, and treat the plants promptly.

During your walks you may find aphids, caterpillars, grasshoppers, leaf spots, and mites.

OCTOBER

SHRUBS

PLANNING

In October through May you can count on only a few inches of rain each month, and it often comes as a downpour. This is where a drought-tolerant landscape really pays off.

Shallow-rooted and tropical shrubs suffer most during dry periods. Try to group your plantings into three major areas: the oasis for frequent watering, transition zone, and fringe area. Plants in the transition and fringe areas should be the drought-tolerant. Luckily, most shrubs can go at least a week or two without special waterings.

• Make sure the plantings have a good mulch layer. Three to 4 inches of mulch is adequate—any more and the mulch may keep water from reaching the root system when the rains return.

• Put the water where it is needed, at the base of the plants.

Use soaker hoses and microsprinklers to do the watering for you.

• Avoid frequent waterings that develop shallow root systems. When plants are under a little stress, they tend to grow deeper roots.

• Reduce feedings during periods of drought.

Supplying nutrients encourages water-using growth.

• Wait until the surface inch of soil dries to do the watering.

PLANTING

Fall is a great time to add new plants. The milder weather allows the root system to grow out into the surrounding soil with little stress on the foliage. Follow good planting procedures to be successful. New plantings need moisture daily for the first few weeks. Thereafter, use the soil moisture as a guide. If soil under the mulch starts to feel dry, it's time to water. Don't expect a lot of growth during the fall. Green foliage on a plant usually means the plant is establishing properly.

CARE

Hurry to complete all fall pruning in the central and northern portions of the state. Ideally, you would like the plants to produce growth that matures before the winter weather. Now is also a good time to test the irrigation system.

WATERING

You are on watering duty for the next seven or so months. Make at least weekly walks in the landscape to determine water needs. It's best to let the plants tell you when they need water. If you wish to use an automatic system, watering once or twice a week should be adequate.

• Run the irrigation system during the early-morning hours.

• Apply between 1/2 and 3/4 inch water.

• Operate the manual irrigation system when the surface inch of soil below the mulch layer begins to dry. Drought-tolerant plants may not need water at all.

FERTILIZING

It's feeding time for all shrub plants. If you have waited until October, it's time to give the plantings the last feeding of the year. There are many ways to apply fertilizer. One of the easiest is with a rotary fertilizer spreader. Many can be handheld, and some can be strapped on for when you walk through the plantings. If there is plenty of walking room you might also use a rotary lawn fertilizer spreader

to do the feeding. Most shrub plantings can be fertilized in 15 to 20 minutes with a rotary spreader.

Just as there are many ways to feed your plant, there are numerous fertilizers. All can most likely provide adequate nutrients for plant growth. Select the technique that is best for you.

• Apply a granular general-garden fertilizer at label rates.

• Select a granular slow-release fertilizer to feed the plants for several months.

• Use a liquid fertilizer through a hose-end applicator.

• Side-dress the plantings with manure, or use drenches of manure tea.

• Use fertilizer stakes pushed into the ground near the plants, following label instructions.

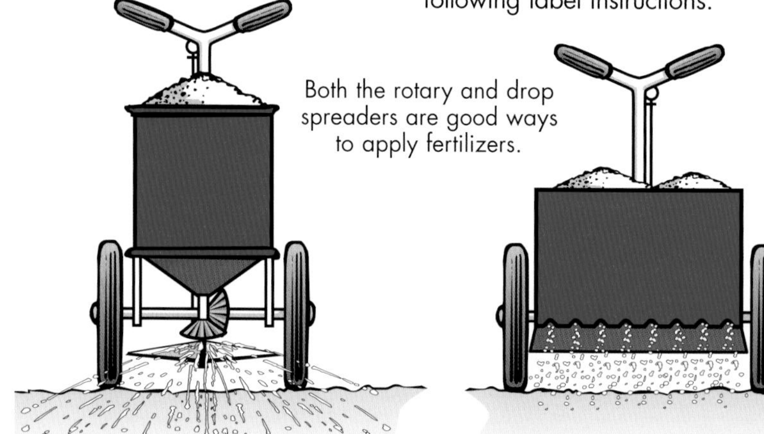

Both the rotary and drop spreaders are good ways to apply fertilizers.

PROBLEMS

Most gardeners will be fighting some pests for a month or two longer before cooler weather slows their growth. One pest that may be increasing is mites. The dry fall weather allows them to remain on the foliage to suck juices from the plants. Mites are small, often the size of a pinpoint. Some are reddish and others are almost colorless. Where needed, control with a soap or oil spray, following label instructions. Check your landscape plantings for caterpillars, grasshoppers, lace bugs, and leaf spots as well.

LARGE OR SMALL: WHAT IS BEST?

Do you buy the big plant or settle for the small one? How much money you have to spend on the landscape may help you decide. But make sure the plant in the big pot is really larger—sometimes a plant has been recently stepped up to a larger container and it is still the same size as the one in the smaller. Here is some more information to help you decide which is the better buy:

• Small plants often establish more rapidly than the larger ones, catching up in size with new growth by the end of the season.

• Plants in small pots may be rootbound, and you will have to break the roots apart, which can lead to slower growth.

• Larger plants may be several times more expensive and greatly increase the cost of the project.

• Larger plants give the instant landscape look, producing a more attractive design sooner.

• Smaller plants usually need less water to become established.

• Larger plants may flower sooner to provide desired color.

NOVEMBER

SHRUBS

PLANNING

Would you like to heat up the landscape during the winter or cool it down during summer? You can by picking shrubs to create a theme garden. Just by selecting flower colors, you can set the mood in any landscape. Whites and pastels are very relaxing, while yellows, oranges, and reds stimulate action.

Now shrubs cannot do it all alone. You might add annuals and perennial flowers plus plant foliage to help set the mood. For example, if you wanted to warm up the landscape during the winter, you might choose red **camellias**, **powderpuff**, **hibiscus**, **ixora**, and **firecracker plant**. Add to this the red **dianthus**, **petunias**, and **pentas**, and you will have a really hot landscape.

If you want to cool down the landscape in late spring, you might look for **gardenia**, **jasmine**, **golden hydrangea**, **oleanders**, and **ligustrum**. Some other plants to include are the white-leaf **caladiums** and **Aztec liriope** as well as the flowering linear-leaf **zinnias**, **pentas**, and **gingers**. Are you cool yet?

There is no reason you cannot create colored gardens of pink, blue, yellow, and orange. How about a garden with a fall theme, with flowers and berries reflecting the leaf drop of Northern landscapes?

PLANTING

Adding plants is enjoyable during the month of November. There is less stress on you and the shrubs. Visit the garden center to find plants with fall and winter seasonal interest. This is the best time to make the selections while you can see how well they are performing.

Keep in mind that there are no shortcuts to good soil preparation. But what do you do if you are only adding one shrub to a site? Maybe it's a replacement for a shrub that declined, or you just need one more plant to complete the collection. Is it a waste of time to add organic matter to the soil for just one plant? Probably not, if it's a shrub.

Oakleaf hydrangea

1. Dig a large hole and save the soil on a tarp. Make the hole wider but no deeper than the rootball.

2. Mix in lots of organic matter with the fill soil. Choose from peat moss, compost, manures, and similar materials.

3. Position the plant in the hole at the same depth it was in the container or slightly higher out of the soil.

4. Fill in around the rootball with the enriched soil, watering while you do so.

5. Create a 4- to 6-inch berm of soil to hold water and direct it down through the rootball at each watering. Then add a mulch.

Improving the soil is not a waste of time for many shrubs that slowly grow out of the rootball. The enriched soil will hold some moisture and provide some nutrients for plant growth until the roots grow out beyond the planting site.

CARE

Pruning time is over for all shrubs in central and northern portions of the state. It's just too risky to do major trimming that will encourage growth that might be damaged by winter cold. You can feel free to remove any dead limbs or shoots that are starting to decline. Shrubs in South Florida landscapes can be trimmed as needed; these are seldom damaged by cold and often continue to grow during the winter months.

WATERING

It is a dry month, but the weather is a bit cooler. Continue to check at least weekly for water needs. If you find some dry spots, that may be due to a faulty watering system. Turn on the system and check it for some possible problems.

- Look for sprinkler heads damaged while performing other landscape maintenance.

Make sure shrubs and other vegetation have not obstructed the water flow.

- Look for heads that are stuck and watering only part of the landscape.

Determine if more heads are needed or if a system should be divided to increase the pressure.

Most shrubs (except those that are heavy water users) can last a week or more between periods of irrigation at this time of year. The very drought-tolerant types obtain most of what they need from seasonal rainfall.

FERTILIZING

Feeding time is about over in northern and central portions of the state. Hurry to complete any last-minute fertilizer applications. Try to allow shrubs adequate time to mature the foliage before winter weather arrives. If you have forgotten a feeding or the plants are not quite as green as desired, a light feeding may be applied.

Gardeners in South Florida can continue to feed plantings as needed. Most will not need an extra feeding to make it through the winter except for very tropical types that are continuing growth.

PROBLEMS

Pest activity starts to slow down this month, but don't give up regular checks on the landscape. Suspect any plant that has yellow leaves, sooty mold, and leaf spots. It may have a pest problem. Some plants will be losing leaves naturally, but only a few, like the **crape myrtles**, **beautyberry** and **spirea**. Others should keep their good green color. Expect the following pests to stay active on warm days: aphids, caterpillars, grasshoppers, leaf spots, and mites.

DECEMBER

SHRUBS

PLANNING

Shrubs such as **anise**, **feijoa**, **ligustrum**, **oleander**, and **viburnum** can serve as substitutes for trees in the landscape. A large shrub can fill the space of a small tree if you provide a little training. Select one or more trunks to form the structure of a tree. Gradually remove the lower limbs as the shrub grows taller. Over a period of several years, form the tree shape you want from the shrub by thinning out the upper limbs to create a canopy. Encourage growth with frequent, light feedings throughout the growing season.

PLANTING

Winter arrives this month, and it's a great time to add shrubs to the landscape. If you have some plants in the wrong places, it's also a good time to relocate them. When moving plants, make sure the soil is moist, and try to get a large intact rootball.

CARE

Be prepared for possible cold warnings. Some protection can be provided for the more sensitive shrubs when freeze warnings are sounded:

Anise

- If the shrub is small, it can be dug and potted to move to a warmer location.
- Blankets can be used as coverings, hanging to the ground to hold in heat and keep out cold.
- Soil can be mounded up around the lower stems to protect buds near the ground.
- Covers can be constructed over prize shrubs and outdoor-approved electric lights added to provide heat. Keep the covers above the foliage and place lights so they won't touch the plant foliage or covers.

WATERING

Take weekly inventory of moisture needs. Most plantings can go a week or more during the cooler months without rainfall or irrigation. When the soil starts to dry under the mulch, it's time to turn on the irrigation system.

FERTILIZING

Feeding time is over for most shrub plantings. Even if you missed a fertilizer application, it is probably best to wait until the late-winter or spring application time. Only shrubs producing growth and exhibiting deficiencies should be fed this month.

PROBLEMS

Only in the warmer locations are pests usually active—but this is a good time to look for scale insects and apply a control if infestations are spotted. Make sure sprays are applied when temperatures are above 40 degrees Fahrenheit and below 85 degrees. Look for leaf spots and scale insects on warm days.

CHAPTER NINE

TREES & PALMS

Perhaps there is nothing more sacred in the landscape than trees. Maybe it's because you can relate to them. They can be hugged and climbed and we often watch them grow one year at a time. Many gardeners planted trees when they were young and still go back to check on their progress.

It takes time to grow a tree, and it should be the first addition to the landscape. But don't plant too many trees—deciding where to plant a tree takes careful consideration. Once the tree is in the ground, it's not easily moved. And don't decide to plant just any old tree—decide carefully on the type you might like. Here are just a few considerations:

1. Should the tree be evergreen or deciduous? Evergreen trees keep their foliage most of the year. Some drop the leaves very quickly and get new growth, and others just drop some leaves throughout the year. But for the most part, the evergreen tree provides constant shade. Deciduous trees lose their leaves for a large part of the win-

ter months. Sun passes through the branches and can have a needed warming effect during the cooler weather.

2. Do you want a flowering tree? All trees flower, but we are referring to eye-catching blooms that make you stop and look. Maybe you want a tree to accent the yard, at least at a certain time of the year.

3. How tall do you want the tree to grow? Be sure you plant a small tree under utility wires. And make sure the tree is not going to produce branches than interfere with other plantings and provide excessive shade.

4. Will fruits be of benefit or a problem? Some fruits are edible, others are nice to look at, and others simply create a mess. If you feel that fruits might stain a walkway or be hard to clean up, select a tree with small or dry pods.

Just about every homeowner wants a shade tree, but make sure it's the right choice. Use our table (pages 260 to 263) to select a favorite or two, then check it out at local garden centers and botanical gardens. Palms are not really trees even though many have thick trunks and grow quite tall. They are more closely related to grasses. We include them in this chapter because they are often tree lookalikes, and are often called "palm trees."

One way palms differ from trees is they cannot heal wounds. If a palm trunk is nicked, the wound is there forever. Many palms have only one bud at the top of the stalk. If it's damaged, the entire palm will die. Some have shoots that grow from the base to produce a multistemmed or -trunked plant, but if the bud in one of these stems declines, the entire stem is usually lost.

PLANNING

Pick the right tree for the right place. Take a look at your yard and decide where you want shade. Should it be light shade or filtered? If it is too dense, you may not be able to grow grass—and most shady areas are a problem when it comes to growing flowers and vegetables. Try to decide what areas of the landscape should have the sun or shade, and you will then know where to plant a tree.

But this is only the beginning. Trees have numerous uses in the landscape. Here are a few more good uses for trees:

- Plant trees to block views. If you don't want to look across the street or at a building down the street, plant a tree. It has to be the right potential size, growing to a height and width to obscure the objectionable feature. It may take some time, but most trees grow faster than you think, so you don't always have to start with large trees.
- Add interest to the landscape with trees. Some trees have attractive flowers and others colorful fruits. A few Florida trees also offer fall color or attractive barks. Even some of the foliage can be unusual enough to attract attention.
- Use trees to frame a home or view. Large trees at least are best kept to the sides of the home and back of the property. You do not want to hide the entrance to the house with trunks or limbs of trees. If there is a view in a distance such as a lake, open field, or a garden, it can be enhanced by framing with trees.
- Keep the wind out of your yard with trees. Yes, Florida landscapes can get some gusty, cold winds during the winter. A barrier of trees on the northwest side of the yard can keep the home and landscape just a bit warmer. Trees around the yard also help to keep down dust and other debris that may blow in from neighboring yards.

Florida gardeners love their palms, which add a tropical look to home landscapes. Check the palm chart (page 262) and you will find there are species to grow in every part of the state. Try to find ways to use palms in your landscape.

- Cluster several tall palms together to provide a lightly shaded area.
- Use groups of palms to frame a home as substitutes for trees.
- Add an interesting palm planting near the patio as an accent feature.
- Plant palms as replacements for street trees.
- Plant small palms in containers to set on patios or near entrances.

PLANTING

Adding a tree to the landscape is not very difficult, but make sure you have the right spot before you do the digging. For one thing, keep large trees 15 to 20 feet from the home. You don't need roots approaching the foundation to cause cracks. By giving the tree some growing room, you won't have to remove as many limbs that might overhang a roof.

In the same manner, you want to keep any tree a good distance from septic systems and drainage pipes. Roots grow best where the soil is moist. Any drain field or leaking pipe provides an ideal water source where roots can grow and affect drainage.

Another concern is overhead wires. Use only small trees under utility lines, or make sure larger trees are some distance to one side of the wires.

As you locate the tree, make sure it is not in the middle of the yard. A tree can block a clear view of the home for police and emergency personnel should they be needed.

Underground utilities should be located. A few calls to the electric, telephone, and cable TV companies are all it takes to have the lines marked so you won't cut the wires to interrupt service.

Unlike shrubs, trees do not require a big, prepared planting site. In most cases, it is only necessary to dig a hole two or more times wider than the rootball and no deeper. Then just following these steps to complete the planting:

1. Position the tree in the hole at the same depth it was in the container or slightly higher out of the ground.
2. Begin filling the hole with water and soil at the same time. We normally do not improve the fill soil unless you just want to.
3. When the hole is filled with soil, create a 4- to 6-inch berm of soil around the outer edge of the rootball to catch and direct water down through the root system.
4. Add a 3- to 4-inch mulch layer over the root system and water.
5. If a tree might be affected by winds, it should be staked at this time.

Palms are planted in a manner very similar to trees, with the exception that the rootballs are often much smaller. And the very best planting time for dug palms is March through August. Palms make the best root and top growth when the weather is warm. If the palm is moved into the landscape in a container, it can be planted at any time. Tall palms will likely need staking. This is performed by strapping short 2-by-4-inch boards to the trunks, cushioned by burlap or a similar material. Support boards are then nailed to the boards strapped to the palm trunk.

Unlike trees, palms dug from the ground and moved should often have about half the older leaves removed at planting time. The leaves left on the palm are usually drawn up above the bud and tied in place to retard water loss from the foliage and bud. The leaves are left tied in place for about sixty days. Cabbage palms often have all the leaves removed during the transplanting process. Palms transplanted from containers do not need special pruning.

CARE

New plantings need different care from the care received by older trees that are well established. You will want new trees to quickly root into the surrounding soil to become well

anchored in the ground. A healthy, vigorous root system can absorb needed moisture and nutrients to keep the tree green and pest resistant. All trees lose lower limbs as they grow older, as these limbs are crowded or shaded out by the growths above. But here are some signs the tree may need other attention:

• Growth slows and leaves are not replaced each year, resulting in thinning of the limbs.

• Leaves lose their good green color during the normal growing season (fall leaf drop and color loss are, of course, normal for deciduous trees).

• Spanish moss or ball moss begins excessive growth on tree limbs. This often indicates the tree is not as vigorous as it should be.

• Large limbs develop dead sections or hollow areas.

• Sap flows from trunks and branch angles.

• Hollow or rotten areas are noted in the trunk of the tree.

If any of these signs and symptoms are noticed, a closer inspection of the tree may be needed to determine problems and decide on corrective action. Certified arborists are available in local communities and inspect trees for a fee.

When palms are planted during the proper time of the year, transplanting is very successful. It usually takes several seasons before the palm establishes roots in the surrounding soil.

WATERING

New trees and palms need plenty of water. You should be filling the berm surrounding the tree daily for the first month or more. Some horticulturists suggest daily waterings for larger trees for more than four months in a well-drained soil. They also recommend keeping palm plantings moist for a similar period of time.

After that, the trees are placed on an every-other-day watering program for several additional months. To a certain extent, you have to be the judge of root growth in the surrounding soil and determine when the tree can grow on its own. Here are a few watering thoughts:

• Some trees are very slow to become established. Dogwoods and magnolias appear to be two of the worst. They develop their root systems slowly and may take two years to become well established. Most trees are established after a year.

• The time needed to become established can depend on tree size. Small trees of 6 to 8 feet anchor in the ground and appear to be on their own much more quickly than taller and older trees. Be ready to give older trees more care during drier weather for well over a year .

• Fill the basin formed from the berm of soil around the rootball full of water. Make sure enough water is being applied to wet the rootball at each irrigation.

• Don't count on the irrigation system to do the watering. Hand watering is best during the establishment period.

• Keep a 3- to 4-inch mulch over the root system to keep the ground moist and conserve water.

Once the trees and palms are established, very few need frequent watering. Only some trees, like the dahoon holly, dogwood, loblolly bay, red maple, and others need a moist soil for good growth as older trees. They should be given special waterings during dry weather in sandy soils.

FERTILIZING

Most gardeners are surprised to learn that shade and flowering trees need fertilizer only during the establishment period. This is the time when they are forming new roots and making rapid stem and leaf growth. Three to five years after planting, most special feedings can be discontinued in home landscapes. It

should be noted that trees grown for their fruit crops are given special feedings every year. Their needs will be covered in separate chapters.

No fertilizer is normally added to the planting hole. Trees often come with an adequate supply of fertilizer for at least a few months of growth, then the intense watering for the first month or two washes the nutrients out of the ground. The first limited feeding is normally applied 4 to 6 weeks after planting. Just a light scattering over the surface of the soil of a general-garden fertilizer is usually all that is needed.

There are many fertilizers available for tree growth. Studies show the those high in nitrogen give the best results for shade and flowering trees. Try a 12-4-8, 16-4-8, or similar product found at a local garden center. The fertilizer is used at the rate to supply 1 pound of nitrogen over each 1000 square feet of soil surface under the limbs and out past the dripline. Here are some feeding suggestions:

1. Feed trees becoming established once in the spring and once in fall. Some gardeners who want to promote extra growth may also add an early-summer feeding.

2. Apply the fertilizer at 1 pound of nitrogen per 1,000 square foot. For a 12-4-8, the amount is 8 pounds; for a 15-5-15, the amount is 6.5 pounds; for a 16-4-8, the amount is 6 pounds. Usually this is the lawn rate shown on the bag.

3. Use a handheld or push spreader to apply the fertilizer under the trees. Just tossing out the fertilizer by hand may not give good distribution. Fertilizer should be applied to the surface of the soil or over a mulch; it is no longer placed in the ground.

4. Water the fertilized area to begin moving the nutrients into the soil.

5. Feedings can be continued on a regular schedule for three to five years. Thereafter, most shade and flowering trees obtain adequate nutrients from nearby lawn and shrub feedings.

If for any reason a tree declines in growth, is affected by construction, or becomes injured, regular feedings can be resumed for short periods of time.

Palms should be fertilized on a regular schedule throughout the life of the plant. Most gardeners forget that palms are not trees, and they skip feedings. Current Extension Service recommendations call for feeding palms three to four times a year with a slow-release palm fertilizer. If a slow-release product is not utilized, a regular palm fertilizer should be applied lightly but monthly during the growing season. A suggested rate is 1 to 2 pounds of a standard palm fertilizer for each 100 square feet of area under the spread of the palm.

PEST CONTROL

Trees and palms do have pests, but most established plantings are resistant and can withstand some holes in the leaves and defoliation. Most of the real concern for pests is associated with the young trees and with new palm plantings that are becoming established. A pesticide may be applied where insects, mites, or diseases appear to be causing major damage. Because of their size, very few large established trees or palms are sprayed.

Check your young trees and palms during walks in the yard for pest problems. If noted, many can be hand-picked from the plants and destroyed. Some of the more common problems found in home plantings are aphids, borers, caterpillars, palmetto weevils, powdery mildew, scale insects, and thrips. See pages 317 to 320 for descriptions and controls. Other insects and diseases may be noted as they occur during the growing year, but they usually affect just a few trees. Also see page 321 for details on cycads.

CHAPTER NINE

Trees

Name	Area of Florida	Ht/Wd (Feet)	Soil Type	Flowers/ Season	Fruits	Best Uses
African Tulip Tree	S	50/50	Average	Orange, yellow/Winter, spring	Not showy	Accent, shade
American Holly	NC	40/20	Average	White/Spring	Red/Fall	Accent, street, shade
Attenuate Holly	NC	30/15	Average	White/Spring	Red/Fall	Street, shade
Bald Cypress	NCS	80/30	Wet or dry	Inconspicuous	Green/ Summer	Street, shade
Black Olive	S	40/40	Average	Inconspicuous	Black/Fall	Shade, street
Bottlebrush	CS	15/15	Average	Red/Spring	Not showy	Accent, street
Camphor	CS	50/60	Average	Yellow/Spring	Black/Fall	Shade
Cattley Guava	S	20/15	Average	White/Spring	Red/ Summer	Accent, shade, street
Cherry Laurel	NC	35/30	Average	White/Spring	Black/Fall	Shade, street
Chickasaw Plum	NC	20/20	Average	White/Spring	Reddish/ Summer	Accent, shade, street
Chinese Elm	NC	35/40	Average	Greenish/Fall	Not showy	Shade, street
Chinese Pistache	NC	25/25	Average	Greenish/ Spring	Orange/Fall	Shade, street
Crape Myrtle	NC	20/20	Average	Various/ Summer	Brown/Fall	Accent, shade, street
Dahoon Holly	NCS	25/10	Moist	White/Spring	Red/Fall	Accent
Dogwood	NC	30/20	Moist	White/Spring	Red/Fall	Accent, shade
Frangipani	S	20/20	Average	White,pink/ Summer	Not showy	Accent, street
Fringe Tree	NC	12/10	Average	White/Spring	Not showy	Accent, under story
Geiger Tree	S	25/25	Average	Orange/Spring	Not showy	Accent, shade, street
Golden Rain Tree	NC	30/30	Average	Yellow/Fall	Pink pod/ Fall	Accent, shade, street
Golden Shower Tree	S	40/40	Average	Yellow/ Summer	Pod/Fall	Accent, shade, street
Italian Cypress	NCS	30/10	Average	Inconspicuous	Not showy	Accent, hedge
Jacaranda	CS	40/50	Average	Purple/Spring	Not showy	Accent, shade
Jerusalem Thorn	NCS	20/20	Average	Yellow/ Summer	Not showy	Accent
Laurel Oak	NCS	60/50	Average	Inconspicuous	Acorn/Fall	Shade, street

CHAPTER NINE

Trees

Name	Area of Florida	Ht/Wd (Feet)	Soil Type	Flowers/ Season	Fruits	Best Uses
Lignumvitae	S	15/10	Average	Blue/ Year-round	Yellow/ Year-round	Accent
Ligustrum	NCS	15/15	Average	White/Spring	Black/Fall	Accent, shade
Live Oak	NCS	60/100	Average	Inconspicuous	Acorn/Fall	Shade, street
Loblolly Bay	NC	40/15	Moist	White/Summer	Not showy	Accent, shade
Loquat	NCS	25/20	Average	White/Fall winter	Orange/Fall,	Shade, fruit
Mahogany	S	50/50	Average	Green/Spring	Brown/Fall	Shade, street
Orchid Tree	CS	25/25	Average	Purple, white/ Year-round	Not showy	Accent, shade, street
Pigeon Plum	S	30/20	Average	White/Spring	Red/Fall	Accent, shade, street
Queen's Crape Myrtle	S	30/30	Average	Purple/ Summer	Not showy	Accent, shade, street
Redbud	NC	25/20	Average	Pink/Spring	Not showy	Accent, shade, street
Red Maple	NCS	40/30	Moist	Red/Winter	Reddish/ Spring	Shade, street
River Birch	NC	40/30	Moist or dry	Inconspicuous	Not showy	Accent, shade, street
Royal Poinciana	S	40/50	Average	Orange, red/ Summer	Not showy	Accent, shade, street
Saucer Magnolia	NC	25/20	Average	Pink/Spring	Not showy	Accent
Sea Grape	CS	20/12	Average	White/Spring	Purple/ Summer	Accent, shade, street
Shumard Oak	NC	60/60	Average	Inconspicuous	Acorn/Fall	Shade, street
Silk Tree	NC	30/30	Average	Pink/Spring	Not showy	Accent, shade
Silver Buttonwood	S	15/15	Average	Inconspicuous	Not showy	Accent, shade, street
Slash Pine	NCS	60/40	Average	Inconspicuous	Cone	Shade
Southern Magnolia	NCS	80/40	Moist or dry	White/Summer	Green pod/ Summer	Accent, shade, street
Southern Juniper	NCS	30/30	Average	Inconspicuous	Blue/Fall	Shade, street, hedge
Sugarberry	NC	50/50	Moist	Inconspicuous	Red/Fall	Shade, street
Sweet Acacia	CS	15/20	Average	Yellow/ Year-round	Brown/ Year-round	Accent, street
Sweetbay Magnolia	NCS	40/20	Moist	White/Spring	Not showy	Shade

CHAPTER NINE

Trees

Name	Area of Florida	Ht/Wd (Feet)	Soil Type	Flowers/ Season	Fruits	Best Uses
Sweet Gum	NC	60/30	Moist or dry	Inconspicuous	Brown/Fall	Shade, street
Sycamore	NC	80/60	Average	Inconpicuous	Brown/Fall	Shade, street
Tabebuia	CS	25/25	Average	Yellow, pink/ Spring	Not showy	Accent, shade
Tulip Tree	NC	80/30	Average	Yellowish/ Spring	Not showy	Shade, street
Water Oak	NCS	50/60	Average	Inconspicuous	Acorn/Fall	Shade, street
Wax Myrtle	NCS	15/20	Moist or dry	Inconspicuous	Blue/Fall	Accent, street
Weeping Fig	S	50/70	Average	Inconspicuous	Not showy	Shade
Winged Elm	NC	30/25	Average	Inconspicuous	Not showy	Shade, street
Yaupon Holly	NC	20/15	Average	White/Spring	Red/Fall	Accent, street
Yellow Poinciana	CS	50/50	Average	Yellow/	Not showy Summer	Accent, shade
Yew Podocarpus	NCS	40/20	Average	Cream/Spring	Purple/ Summer	Accent, hedge

Palms

Name	Area of Florida	Height (Feet)	Light Needs	Growth Habit	Best Uses
Areca	S	10 – 20	Sun, filtered sun	Multistemmed	Accent, patios
Australian Fan	CS	40 – 50	Sun	Single trunk	Clusters
Butia	NCS	10 – 20	Sun	Single trunk	Accent, patios
Cabbage	NCS	30 – 40	Sun	Single trunk	Clusters, streets
California Washington	NCS	50 – 60	Sun	Single trunk	Clusters, streets
Canary Island Date	NCS	30 – 40	Sun	Single trunk	Accent, streets
Chinese Fan	CS	20 – 30	Sun	Single trunk	Clusters, patios
Date	NCS	40 – 50	Sun	Single trunk	Accent, streets
Dwarf Palmetto	NCS	3 – 6	Sun	Single trunk	Accent, natural areas
European Fan	NCS	6 – 8	Sun, filtered sun	Multistemmed	Accent, patios
Florida Silver	S	15 – 20	Sun, filtered sun	Single trunk	Accent, patios

CHAPTER NINE

Palms

Name	Area of Florida	Height (Feet)	Light Needs	Growth Habit	Best Uses
Gru-Gru	S	30 – 40	Sun	Single trunk	Clusters, streets
Jamaica Thatch	S	10 – 20	Sun	Single trunk	Clusters
Lady	CS	8 – 10	Filtered sun	Multistemmed	Foundations, patios
Licuala	S	6 – 8	Filtered sun	Single trunk	Accent, patios
MacArthur	S	20 – 25	Sun, filtered sun	Multistemmed	Accent, patios
Malayan Dwarf Coconut	S	40 – 60	Sun	Single trunk	Clusters, street
Mexican Washington	NCS	80 – 90	Sun	Single trunk	Streets
Needle	NCS	4 – 5	Light shade	Multistemmed	Accent, natural areas
Paurotis	CS	15 – 20	Sun, light shade	Multistemmed	Accent, patios
Puerto Rico Hat	CS	40 – 50	Sun	Single trunk	Clusters
Pygmy Date	S	8 – 10	Sun, filtered sun	Single trunk	Accent, patios
Queen	CS	25 – 30	Sun	Single trunk	Clusters, streets
Royal Palm	S	80 – 90	Sun	Single trunk	Clusters, streets
Saw Palmetto	NCS	4 – 6	Sun, filtered sun	Multistemmed	Accent, natural areas
Senegal Date	S	20 – 25	Sun	Multistemmed	Accent, patios
Solitaire	S	15 – 20	Sun, filtered sun	Single trunk	Accent, patios
Windmill	NC	10 – 15	Sun, filtered sun	Single trunk	Accent, patios

N = North Florida C = Central Florida S = South Florida

JANUARY

TREES & PALMS

PLANNING

January is the start of the tree-planting season. Florida kicks it off with its own Arbor Day celebration on the third Friday of each year. Now is the time to decide where you could use a new tree. Try to find a spot where you need shade first. Remember the hot summer days to come. The weather might feel good now, but as the warmer days return you are going to want some cooling shade.

PLANTING

Trees in all forms can be planted during the cooler times of the year, but **palm** plantings should be delayed until warmer weather. Florida sets aside January especially for bare-root plants. These are often offered as seedlings during Arbor Day festivities. Many gardeners also order trees that arrive bare root, and some are dug from landscapes and shared between friends.

Small dormant trees are the best size to select for bare-root planting. They should be set back in the ground shortly after they are dug or received. It's important the roots stay moist during transporting from one location to another. Once the trees are at the site, planting is simple.

1. Dig a hole that is wider but not deeper than the root system.
2. Construct a small mound of soil in the center of the hole.
3. Spread the roots out over and down the sides of the mound of soil.
4. Add soil from the hole and water to fill in around the roots. It's not necessary to amend the soil unless you would like to.
5. Build a 4- to 6-inch berm of soil around the edge of the planting hole.
6. Add a 3- to 4-inch mulch layer over the root system and planting site.
7. Water one more time.
8. Stake large trees that might be affected by winds.

Your new tree will need frequent waterings to keep the soil moist. It may not be on its own for a year or more, until the roots grow out into the surrounding soil.

CARE

Start the pruning of all shade trees. Don't perform major pruning of flowering trees that produce their blooms during spring. Fruiting trees need special trimming. But just about any tree can have dead limbs removed, suckers trimmed off, old seedpods removed, lanky growths trimmed, and crisscrossing limbs controlled.

When needed, **palms** can be trimmed during winter. Remove old seed stalks and declining leaves from the trunks.

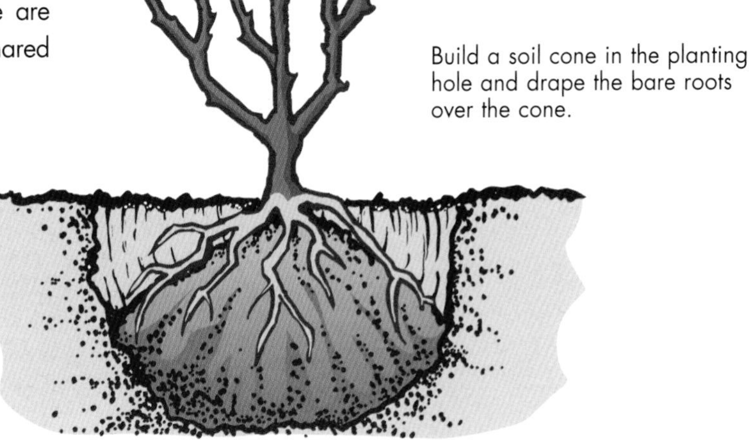

Build a soil cone in the planting hole and drape the bare roots over the cone.

WATERING

Few established trees and **palms** need special waterings, but gardeners do need to be concerned about new plantings. Most should be watered every day for the first few months after planting in a well-drained soil. Generally, the larger the tree, the longer watering is needed before the tree is left on its own. After a period of daily waterings, most trees are irrigated every other day for several additional months.

- Water adequately to thoroughly wet the rootball.
- Trees are best watered by hand during the first few months to make sure the berms are filled each irrigation.
- Maintain a mulch over the root system to keep the soil uniformly moist and control competing weeds.

FERTILIZING

Shade and flowering trees are often fertilized for the first three to five years. Thereafter, the root systems will allow the trees to remove nutrients from the ground in nearby areas that have been fertilized because of lawns and shrub plantings. Nutrients can also be used from decomposing mulches and leaf litter. For new trees, scatter fertilizer over the surface of the soil two or three times a year (try 12-4-8, 15-5-15, or 16-4-8 at the rate of 1 pound nitrogen for each 1,000 square feet of area under the tree). Water after feeding. **Palm** feedings should be delayed until warmer weather.

LIMB REMOVAL MADE EASY

How many times have you removed a limb only to see bark strips down the side of the tree? Now you have a larger wound than you really wanted to deal with. Removing a tree limb is not difficult, but it's a lot easier if you go by the numbers.

1. Make the first cut on the underside of the limb a foot or more from the trunk of the tree. This is just a shallow cut about an inch or so deep through the bark.
2. Cut number two is 4 to 6 inches farther out on the limb, past the first cut but on the upper side of the limb. Cut all the way through the limb to remove it from the tree.
3. Make a third cut to remove the stub of a limb left on the tree. Make this cut just outside the branch collar near the trunk.

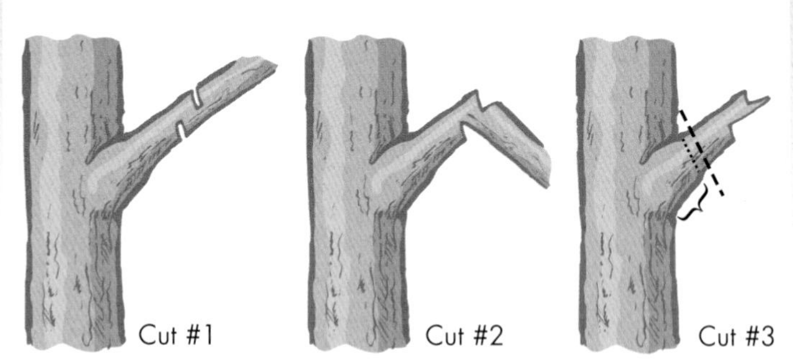

PROBLEMS

Luckily, insects are not very active during the winter months in most areas of the state. But you should still check your trees for possible insect damage. Some, like the scale insects, are often easy to spot on the surface of leaves or attached to the limbs. Other insects that might be active, especially in the warmer areas of the state, are aphids, caterpillars, and thrips.

FEBRUARY

TREES & PALMS

Redbud

PLANNING

If your landscape is full of shade, you may want to add small accent trees to the front yard or near a patio. **Chickasaw plum**, **dogwood**, **orchid tree**, **fringe tree**, **redbud**, and **tabebuia** should be coming into bloom this month. The trees feature flowers, foliage, or fruits, with year-round interest.

Place accent trees where visitors will enjoy them near the driveway, entrance, or path to the back yard. Set accent trees beside the patio to invite visitors to stop and rest. Place them as focal points outside a kitchen or dining-room window or porch.

PLANTING

When visiting your local garden centers, here are some things to look for:

• Select a tree that has a straight trunk. Avoid trees that have twin trunks and branches with sharp "V" angles.

• Look for trees with good branching. Make sure limbs alternate up the trunk and are present on all sides.

• Check for trees that have roots growing out of the pot and into the ground. These have been in the container too long and may take extra time to establish in your soil.

• Make sure most limbs are alive. A few small limbs may be dry and can be removed, but the bigger ones should be ready to grow.

• Look for any signs of disease or insect pests. You don't need to take home a disaster.

• If leaves are present, they should be green or normal for the time of the year. Poor leaf quality may indicate nutritional problems or an old tree.

• Don't always go for the biggest tree. A small compact tree may be faster to take root and may catch up and surpass an older specimen.

Make sure you can conveniently get your new tree home. A tree that has to be strapped to the car may be damaged during transport. Again, a smaller tree may be best-or make arrangements for delivery.

CARE

It's time to renew the mulch layers around the trees and **palms**. Winter rains, winds, and natural decomposition may be causing the ground to become a bit bare. Select a mulch that is best for your landscape. Some choose mulches by color, and others look for types that will last the longest. Actually, just about any mulch is fine. Most gardeners

like the looks of the barks best, but all types can keep the soil moist and help control weeds.

• Maintain a 3- to 4-inch mulch layer over the root systems of the trees and palms.

• Keep the mulch back a few inches to a foot from the trunk.

• Control weeds that may sprout through the mulch by hand-pulling or spot-weed control.

• Apply water and fertilizer to the surface of the mulch.

• Add new mulch over the old as needed.

WATERING

All new trees need water. This is still a cooler time of year, and you can be a little lax on the watering schedule, but it is best if new trees get a daily soaking. Apply the water to fill the berms to make sure the rootballs are thoroughly moistened. Late-winter and spring plantings will need constant attention to keep them moist and growing for four to five months.

Existing well-established trees and **palms** do not normally need special waterings—the nearby irrigation of lawns, shrubs, and flower beds normally supply adequate moisture. Some exceptions may be **dogwood**, **loblolly bays**, and **red maples** in sandy soils.

FERTILIZING

It's feeding time for trees just about everywhere, but delay **palm** feedings for one more month. For trees, you can pick the time to apply the fertilizer: either now or next month. Perhaps the easiest way to feed trees is with a soil-surface application. It's as simple as running the lawn spreader over the ground and applying 1 pound of nitrogen for every 1,000 square feet of ground under the trees. This is normally the lawn rate found on most fertilizer bags. Other feeding alternatives are tree spikes, liquid fertilizers, and manures.

Most shade and flowering trees receive feedings for the first three to five years. Some may also receive a special feeding if they are in poor health or in areas of construction where roots have been damaged. Older trees normally obtain adequate nutrients from nearby feedings of lawns and shrubs.

PROBLEMS

Caterpillars may start appearing in trees as the new leaves start to unfold from the buds. Look for **oaks** and **plums** to have late-winter and spring infestations. Most can be ignored, but if the infestation is heavy, it can be pruned out. A natural control of a spray containing the *Bacillus thuringiensis* organism can be applied. Most trees are too tall to spray, and if it's needed, you can contact a tree-care company. Healthy trees can usually survive a caterpillar attack. Some additional insects to look for this month are aphids, scales, and thrips. Seldom are controls applied except with small trees.

HELPFUL HINT

Nothing kills a tree more quickly than damage during construction. If you are building a home, installing a pool, installing an underground utility cable, or trenching for irrigation, you will destroy roots. Heavy equipment near trees can cause trunk damage and soil compaction. Protect your trees during construction.

MARCH

TREES & PALMS

PLANNING

Trees make good barriers to block the view of a neighbor's shed, parked cars, or a busy street.

- Select trees that grow tall and wide enough to fill the spot.
- For a year-round screen, pick an evergreen.
- To block the view completely and dampen noise, select a tree with dense growth.
- Plant understory shrubs to fill in as trees lose lower limbs.
- For a screen in a hurry, select a fast-growing, good-sized tree.

Plan for new **palms**. They can substitute for trees. Many can be used along streets or as accent plantings. Tall **palms** planted in clusters 10 or more feet apart can provide light shade.

PLANTING

If you buy a tree or **palm** in a container, it should have a good root system. Cut off any roots that may be growing out of the holes to make it easier to remove the tree. If the soil in the container is dry, give the tree a good soaking.

- Dig a hole that is twice as wide and as deep as the rootball.

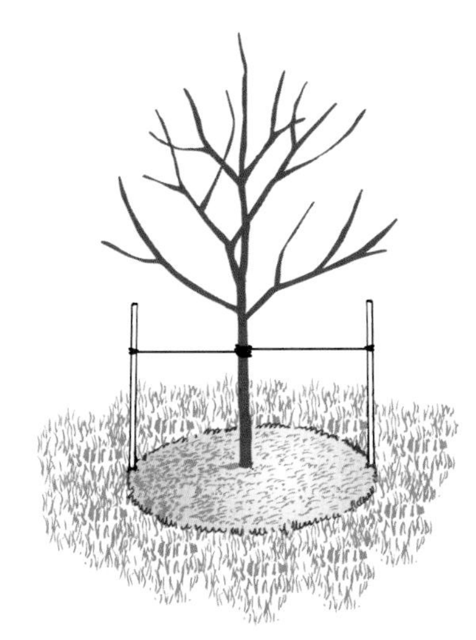

You may stake (or attach guy lines) a newly planted tree if winds are a concern.

- Remove the plant from the container, and position it in the ground at its proper depth. Use a board to make sure the top of the rootball is level with or a few inches above the soil line. In sands, trees and **palms** may sink a few inches into the ground, encouraging root rot problems.
- Mix organic matter with the fill soil if you wish. Begin filling in around the rootball, adding water at the same time.
- Fill the hole and form a 4- to 6-inch berm around outer edge.
- Add a 3- to 4-inch layer of mulch. Water one more time.

If winds are of concern, add some staking to prevent the plant from blowing over.

CARE

Make sure your younger trees maintain a straight trunk as new growth begins. Remove all limbs that may be competing with the central leader. Most shade trees are trained to a single trunk until they grow well above head high. Then some major branches may be allowed to develop a rounded tree, especially when the modified leader system is utilized. In this latter case, there is no central leader as the tree grows older, but side branches grow up to form the limbs that shape the tree.

- Make all pruning cuts back to a bud, branch angle, or the trunk.

HIRING AN ARBORIST

Anytime you have doubts about the condition of a tree, you may want to consider hiring an arborist to obtain another opinion. These are tree specialists skilled in helping to diagnose and correct tree problems. You may obtain the help of an arborist associated with a tree-care company, or one that only does consultation work. Check through the neighborhood to see if anyone has knowledge of an arborist who has worked in the area. (Satisfied customers are the best advertising.)

- Make all trunk cuts just outside the branch collar. This is an area of slightly swollen tissue around the limb, usually within inches of the trunk.
- Do not paint wounds when pruning plants. Studies have shown that coating wounds may impede wound healing.
- Remove at least one portion of any crisscrossing limbs that may produce wounds for pests to enter.

Palms need very little guidance. Keep the buds of plants dug from the nursery covered with leaves for about 60 days. If the ropes holding the leaves together do not break naturally, they can be cut and the foliage released to assume a normal position. Where needed, dead leaves can be removed anytime.

WATERING

Keep up scheduled watering. March is a dry month, and it would take only a few days without water for new trees and **palms** to dry.

FERTILIZING

If you missed the February feeding or planned the first feeding of the year for March, now is the time to do it. It can be as simple as running the fertilizer spreader under the new trees with the amount of fertilizer needed. Use a 12-4-8, 15-5-15, or 16-4-8 at the label rates for lawns, or calculate the amount of fertilizer that will supply 1 pound of nitrogen to 1,000 square feet of area under each tree. (The amount can be obtained by dividing the first number on the fertilizer label into 100.) After feeding, water thoroughly.

Palms should have a "palm special" applied over the root system under the spread of the fronds. Where possible, use a product that has slow-release properties. Unlike trees, **palms** should receive regular feedings every year. If the fertilizer does not have slow-release qualities, make light monthly applications during the warmer months.

PROBLEMS

Trees under any stress may be susceptible to borers. These are immature stages of beetles that attack weak trees. In nature, they are very beneficial, helping to reduce the litter in the woodland areas. In your yard, they may attack some of your prize shade and flowering trees that have come under stress.

Palms may be affected in a similar manner by the palmetto weevil. This insect can cause a quick decline of new **palms** and **palms** under stress. Contact your local Extension Service office for control recommendations.

APRIL

TREES & PALMS

PLANNING

Oaks are always popular, but landscapes need variety to create interest. Visit your garden center and consider many types of trees before making a selection. Consider tall evergreen trees such as **camphor tree**, **cherry laurel**, **mahogany**, **loquat**, **southern magnolia**, and **hollies**.

• You may not want a big tree but would like just a little shade. How about a **black olive**, **tree ligustrum**, **silver buttonwood**, or **yaupon holly?** These, too, are evergreen.

• Maybe you want summer shade but would not mind some warming winter sun coming through. Take a look at the **Chickasaw plum**, **Chinese elm**, **orchid tree**, **redbud**, **river birch**, and **winged elm**.

PLANTING

When you have a tree or **palm** in mind, all you have to do is find the right location and add it to the landscape. The time for planting bare-root plants is over, but you can still add balled-and-burlapped and container-grown plants to the landscape. In fact, this is national Arbor Day month, and during the last Friday of April, many communities will be conducting tree plantings. This occasion is not quite as big in Florida as in other states, since many neighborhoods held a local Arbor Day celebration in January. Still, there is plenty of planting going on.

Most balled-and-burlapped trees and **palms** are planted by nurserymen, not homeowners, these days. Smaller trees and palms for homeowners normally come in containers. If you do obtain a plant with burlap, however, here's how it is installed:

1. Open the hole several times wider but not deeper than the rootball.

2. Position the plant at the same depth it was growing in the field or just a little higher out of the ground.

3. Check the wrapping material around the rootball. Is it natural burlap or a synthetic material? If it burns, it's probably true burlap; if it melts, it's probably a synthetic material that deteriorates very slowly and could affect root growth. Remove synthetic burlap before filling the hole.

4. Begin filling the hole, adding fill soil and water. When you get within a foot of the surface of the ball, pull the natural burlap down a few inches below the top of the ground. The excess can be

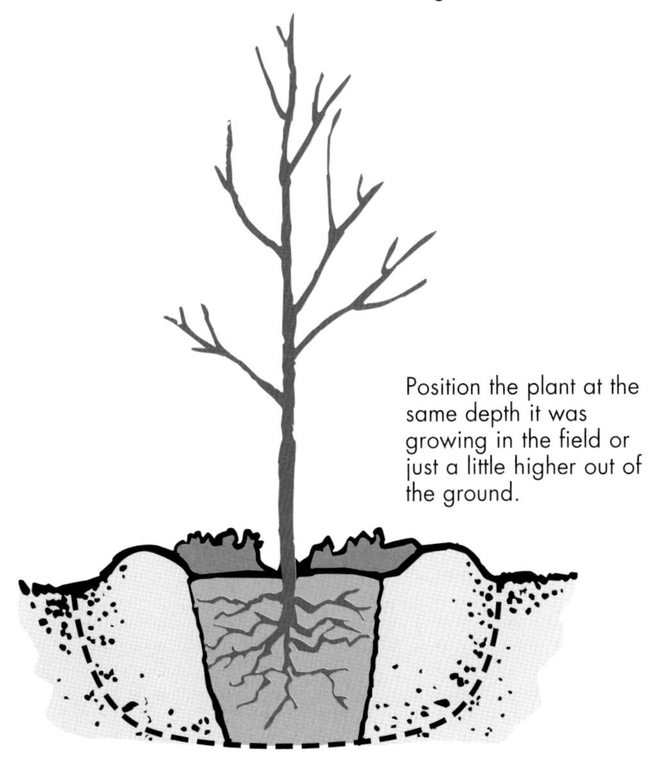

Position the plant at the same depth it was growing in the field or just a little higher out of the ground.

cut off if you wish. Then continue filling the hole.

5. Add soil up to the top of the rootball, then build a 4- to 6-inch berm of soil around the outer edge.

6. Spread a 3- to 4-inch layer of mulch over the surface of the soil and water one more time.

Your tree or **palm** is planted. But if it's tall and could be affected by winds, add stakes to secure the trunk in the ground.

CARE

Check your new trees weekly and older trees at least once a month for possible problems. Limbs can be damaged or may be starting to decay. Sometimes just a little pruning during a walk can prevent severe problems later in the life of a tree. Look for limbs growing out-of-bounds that should be tipped back, and shoots competing with a central leader that should be trimmed.

WATERING

It's a dry time of year—don't forget the regular waterings. If you are thinking of taking a vacation soon, maybe a neighbor or family member could help. A few days to a week can be critical in the care of a new tree or palm. Most older trees and **palms** are fine and can exist with the seasonal rains.

FERTILIZING

Feeding time is over for most shade and flowering trees in the landscape. If you forgot the spring feeding, there is still time. The next scheduled feeding for new trees is in June, an optional feeding time, and then in September or October. Unless under stress, older trees usually do not need special feedings. They can obtain needed nutrients from fertilizers applied to nearby lawns and shrub plantings. Continue feeding **palms** as needed during the spring months.

PROBLEMS

Treehoppers may appear in some trees. Often they are found in **oaks**, but some forms can be found in just about any tree. These insects are sometimes called thorn bugs or sharpshooters. All adult stages have wings held like a roof over their backs. Most are less than 1/2 inch long. They can be quite colorful and are often found clustering on tree limbs when they first hatch. They are piercing, sucking-type insects, but the damage appears to be minimal. When laying eggs in the limbs, they can leave scars that cause the limbs to break. But most damage is minimal, and these insects are usually ignored.

Caterpillar may be extra-heavy this month. They especially like **oak**, **mahogany**, **redbud**, and **sweet gum** trees. Most can be ignored or treated with a natural spray. Look for aphid, borer, and scale infestations. A palm leaf skeletonizer may be found feeding in the **palm** foliage.

Oak trees often develop a puckering of the leaves known as oak leaf blister during the spring months. It's usually not noticed until the leaves are already affected. This is a fungus that makes the leaves look bad but causes minimal damage. It is usually ignored. Control is not possible until the following year if it is needed before infection during late winter or early spring.

TREES & PALMS

PLANNING

Let's take a tour of your landscape to find out where you may need trees. It's becoming quite warm, and a shade tree would be nice. Not only might you like to sit under a tree, but it can be used to shade the side of your house. Most homes have lots of insulation in the ceilings, but older homes may lack good insulation in the walls. A little afternoon shade would not hurt. Just make sure you keep tall-growing trees 15 to 20 feet from the home. This will give plenty of room for shade to be cast on the side of the home without worrying about meandering roots. Here are some other ways to use trees:

- Use trees to create a screen. Block out the unwanted views or noise.
- Cluster several trees in a rest area or private spot in the landscape. You can add a sandbox for the kids or maybe a hammock just for you.
- Add trees for color. It's nice to look at a tree in full bloom. Select a tree for the different seasons. You can also select a tree for its leaf color or fruits.
- Plant a tree just because you like it. We all have our favorite tree. Just make sure you find the best location for it.
- Make sure you keep tall-growing trees out from under overhead wires.

If you need a tree in these locations, select a small-growing species.

PLANTING

There is still plenty of planting time. Most trees planted now come in containers, and there should be lots to choose from at your local garden center. But hurry, as they will be reducing inventory as summer approaches. If you get the tree home and you are not quite ready for planting, give it a little extra care:

- Keep the tree in the normal light level that it will receive in the landscape.
- Check daily for water needs. Most will need daily waterings.
- If plants are stored for a long period, feed with a liquid fertilizer solution every other week, or apply a slow-release fertilizer to the containers, following label instructions.
- To plant, use normal planting procedures.

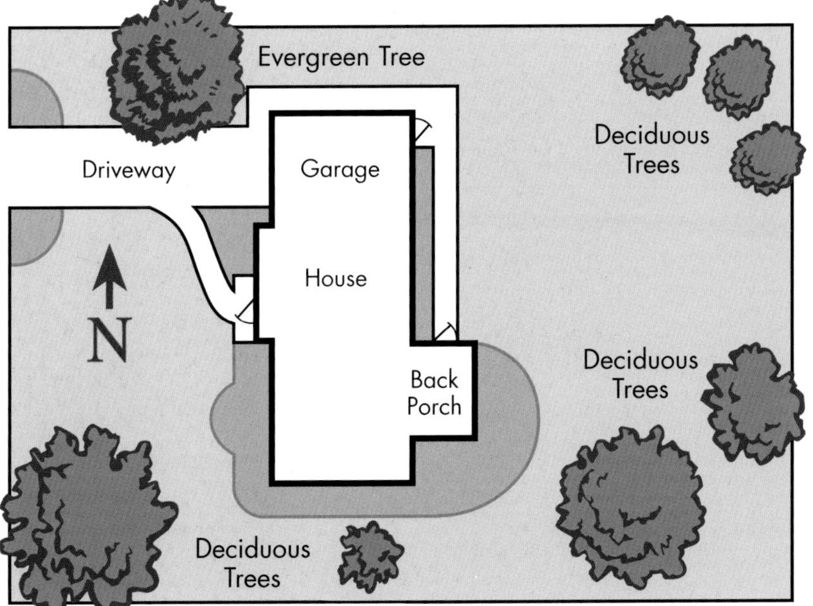

Use trees to create a screen to enhance your view, and to shade your home from the sun.

Now is the ideal time to add **palms** to the landscape. The root systems make lots of growth to become established much quicker at this time of the year. **Palms** can be added balled-and-burlapped or from containers.

CARE

Continue good grooming of all trees and **palms** in the landscape. Remove limbs and fronds that may be interfering with landscape maintenance. These can be taken back to the trunk. If some lower limbs need to be removed on a younger tree, try shortening the limbs instead. The trees use the limbs with foliage to produce food that develops strong trunks.

It's also time to adjust the ties of stakes supporting trees that might be affected by winds. Make sure the ties are not cutting into the trunks. Allow enough movement so the trunks can develop and strengthen to support the trees.

WATERING

Watering is important during this very hot month. Keep watering the new plantings on a regular schedule. Fill the berms formed around the rootballs so the moisture will thoroughly moisten the ground.

- Water new trees daily for the several months following planting.
- After monthly waterings are over, water every other day for three to five months.
- Keep **palms** on a similar schedule, making sure the soil remains moist at all times.

The above schedule applies to plantings in well-drained soil. Soils that remain moist will not need watering as frequently. Instead, water when the surface inch of soil begins to be dry to the touch.

FERTILIZING

There's just one more month to go before the optional feeding for trees. Wait until June if you can to apply the fertilizer application. Too much fertilizer encourages weak lush growth. Only if you are going to be away in June should you proceed with a May feeding. This is an optional feeding and needed only if you want to speed up limb and leaf development.

Palms can be fed now if you are using a slow-release palm fertilizer following the normal rate. If using a product with normal qualities, a light feeding is recommended on a monthly schedule during the warmer months.

PROBLEMS

Powdery mildew loves the mild spring months. The fungus covers leaves on many trees with a white film of mycelium and is especially noticeable on **crape myrtle**, **dogwood**, and **sycamores**. The disease will not cause major decline but will cause leaves to become contorted and much smaller in size. It can prevent flowering in **crape myrtles**. **Dogwoods** can be weakened after repeated attacks and made susceptible to other pests. With a young tree still developing a basic tree structure, control powdery mildew with a natural copper fungicide or one of the synthetic fungicides, following label instructions. Other pests may be active during May. Look for borers, caterpillars, thrips, palm leaf skeletonizers, and scale insects.

Many gardeners notice **magnolia** trees dropping their leaves during spring. This is normal, as they replenish the foliage. Some of these trees lose most of their leaves before putting on new growth.

JUNE

TREES & PALMS

PLANNING

Summer storms pack a powerful punch. Winds can reach hurricane force to toss about trashcans, blow over poolside furniture, and damage your trees. Older trees are the most susceptible because they often have hollow trunks, insect-infested limbs, and poor branching habits. You have only to take a drive through older neighborhoods after a storm to find trees that have lost limbs or blown over, sometimes damaging homes and automobiles. And most of the damage could have been prevented, starting with a simple inspection.

First get to know your trees. Some, including **weeping willows** and **silver maples**, are notorious for their weak wood and may be damaged during even mild storms. All trees reaching the end of their life span are suspect. It's probably a good idea to give trees over fifty years of age a quick check every few months for the common indicators of weakening wood.

- Look for holes in the trunks and larger limbs.
- Examine trees with twin trunks or sharp branch angles that may split apart.
- Check for sap flowing from trunks that could indicate a disease or insect infestation.
- Suspect limbs with wounds or deadwood, even if most of the branches are alive.
- Look for mistletoe growing in older limbs; it can cause wounds and weak wood.
- Make sure trees near roads and walkways are firmly rooted in the ground; sometimes roots are cut during construction.

You can often spot many of these problems from the ground. If any are noticed, contact a consulting arborist or tree company for a more-thorough inspection. With older trees, especially those that could affect buildings or other neighboring property, consider having a professional inspection every five years.

Palms are much more resistant to the winds than are true trees. Fronds can be torn off, but most **palms** are left standing after all but the most severe storms. Remove declining fronds and check for hollow trunks. If

Willow

the trunks are heavily damaged by rot problems, the **palm** is best removed before the stormy season.

PLANTING

In Florida, the planting never stops. Add a container-grown tree or **palm** to the landscape if you wish. When you do, make sure it gets off to a great start. Summer is arriving this month with temperatures consistently in the 90s Fahrenheit. If you cannot give a tree good care, delay the planting until fall. All **palm** plantings are best made at this time.

CARE

Gardeners checking their **oaks** may find some strange-looking growths that are some- times round and greenish, brown and fuzzy, or dark and hard as a rock. They may be attached to the stems or leaves. What are the growths? They are galls made by mites, wasps, or similar insects living with the trees. Many have beneficial stages, and this is where they raise their young. **Oaks** are one of their favorite trees. Since they cause minimal harm, just enjoy and forget about sprays.

WATERING

With a little luck, Mother Nature will help with the watering. The rainy season should begin, providing lots of moisture to help with tree and **palm** growth. Still, the new plantings need daily waterings that wet the soil. If you do not get at least 1/2 inch or more of water from rain, you should fill up the berms around new trees and **palms**. It won't hurt to do it anyway, just as a little insurance.

Trees and **palms** on an every-other-day or longer watering schedule may receive all they need from the rainfalls. But make sure the rain wets the ground. If in doubt, give these plantings a good soaking as well. Established trees and **palms** should love the summer rains, and many will produce another flush of growth.

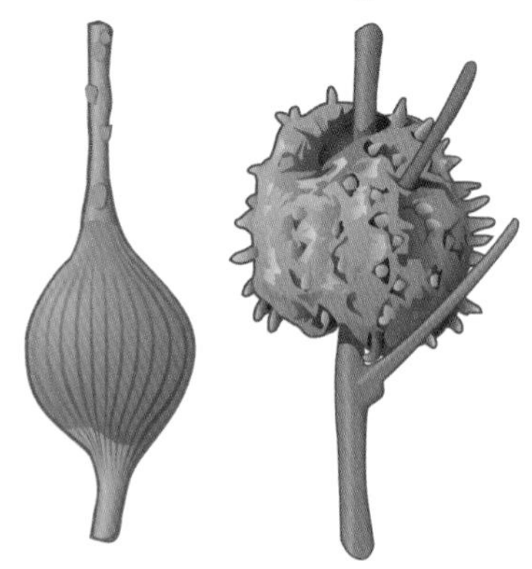

Insects living in oak trees often form galls to raise their young; the galls are harmless or cause minimal damage.

FERTILIZING

New trees, or trees that have been weakened or may not be making the growth you feel they should, can receive a special feeding this month. Use any general-garden fertilizer or lawn fertilizer at the rate of 1 pound nitrogen per 1,000 square feet of area under the branches and out past the dripline. Some products you might use are a 12-4-8, 15-5-15, or 16-4-8. Follow the lawn application rates on the label, and water after spreading the fertilizer.

If you missed the **palm** feeding last month, you can provide a slow-release fertilizer application. If you are on a monthly schedule, now is the time for a light fertilizer application.

PROBLEMS

Pests may be noticed in many trees. If you look hard, you can probably find more than you ever knew lived in trees. But their damage is minimal and seldom are sprays needed. Some to look for are aphids, borers, mites, oak leaf blister, powdery mildew, and scales. In **palms**, check for skeletonizers and leaf spots.

PLANNING

Crape myrtle trees are known as the lilacs of the South. If you don't have a **crape myrtle**, now would be a good time to add one.

If it grows to the 15-foot-plus range, you will have to decide whether to train it to a single or multiple trunks. Most gardeners seem to prefer the **crape myrtles** with three to five trunks.

Crape myrtles are easy to grow. All they need is a sunny site. They can exist with less light, but don't count on good flowering. Make sure they have adequate room to grow. Most get just about as wide as tall. When selecting a **crape myrtle**, look for your favorite features:

- **Crape myrtles** may have white, pink, red, or lavender flowers. Some white-and-red blends are also available.
- Select **crape myrtles** by size as well as color. A plant of a certain color may be small, medium, or tall.
- Consider bark color. Some are whitish, beige, cinnamon, or orange.
- A few **crape myrtles** have unique growth habits. Some are very upright and at least one, 'Acoma', has the **Japanese maple** shape with horizontal branching.
- Make sure your **crape myrtle** has some powdery mildew resistance. Plants with American Indian tribal names usually have good resistance.

If you need a list of **crape myrtles** as a guide, contact your local Cooperative Extension Service office. The Florida researchers maintain plantings of most varieties and have published their evaluations. Unfortu- nately, the common **crape myrtles** grow only in central and northern portions of the state. But South Florida can enjoy the **queen's crape myrtle** that forms a small tree too, with large flower clusters.

If you find the tree or **palm** you want, don't be afraid to add it to the landscape. University of Florida research suggests summer is a good time for tree and **palm** plantings. It appears the root systems make lots of growth during the hot weather. But you do have to provide good care. Make sure you find the right location for planting.

- Keep tall trees and **palms** out from under utility wires.
- Call utility companies before you dig to locate underground wires.
- Make sure the soil has adequate drainage. Some trees and **palms** like moist soils, but most want soils that do not stay overly wet.
- Keep trees and **palms** away from buildings and septic systems. A good rule is to keep the plantings 15 to 20 feet from a building.

CARE

Summer pruning can be made on trees that flower during winter. But don't delay much longer. Most cool-weather and spring-flowering trees form their buds during summer. Pruning is normally limited to limbs that might be in the way of maintenance and branches that are growing out-of-bounds. Don't forget to remove dead or declining limbs.

If you want to keep the **crape myrtles** blooming, remove the seed-heads that form during summer. Cut the limbs with seed clusters back to a point about the size of your finger. New growths start almost immediately and in six to eight weeks will be back in bloom. With good pruning, you can keep **crape myrtles** in bloom through September.

Now is a good time to check out the **palm** fronds. Some of the older leaves can be removed at this time, but don't remove too much of the good green foliage. **Palms** use their leaves to produce food needed for growth. Many gardeners overprune their **palms**. Now is a good time to

remove old flower and seed stalks plus the remains of stems close to the trunks.

WATERING

Hope the summer rainfalls continue during the next few months. If they do, the care of trees and **palms** will be a lot easier. You still have to give the new plants extra care, but you may be able to skip a watering or two if you get a good soaking rain. Otherwise, water new trees and **palms** daily for the first few months and then every other day for several additional months.

FERTILIZING

Forget the tree feedings for another month or two unless you are a little behind. If you missed the optional June feeding for new trees, you still have time to apply the fertilizer. You can make quick work of the chore by applying a lawn fertilizer at the turf rate and watering. Make the application under the spread of the tree and out past the dripline.

If you are on a monthly feeding program for **palms**, remember that a light application is all you need. Scatter 1 to 2 pounds of a standard palm fertilizer under the spread of the trees for each 100 square feet of area.

Cabbage palm

PROBLEMS

Sycamores will look brown in many neighborhoods because of lacebugs. These piercing, sucking insects feed on the underside of foliage and leave dark deposits, but they have cute lace-like wings. Look closely—they may be a little hard to see at first. Few gardeners can spray large trees, so you may have to tolerate lacebugs.

Thrips feed on **sweet gums**. Their rasping mouth parts turn the leaves light brown. Oil sprays can help, but it's difficult to spray large trees. Other insects feeding in summer include the aphids, caterpillars, and scales.

AUGUST

TREES & PALMS

PLANNING

As you sit under your shade trees, you may notice one thing missing: there may not be a lot of understory plantings. Shade trees and some **palms** create a lot of competition for light, water, and nutrients. Fortunately, some plants don't mind the challenge. It is best to try to establish the shade trees, **palms**, and associated plants together if at all possible. Some will need shade, so you have to wait a few years to plant these, but the sooner you plant them, the better. Here are some categories of plants and suggestions to complete the landscape.

Shrubs: Look for those that won't mind the low-light locations. A few are **anise**, **azalea**, **Indian hawthorn**, **ligustrum**, **suspensum viburnum**, and **yaupon holly**. Some, like the **azaleas**, need an acid soil, so have the pH of the site tested.

Ground covers: Fill in bare areas with plants that spread out over the soil or create grasslike effects. Some that creep out over the ground or produce underground rhizomes are the **Algerian ivy**, **Asiatic jasmine**, **bromeliads**, **cast-iron plant**, **English ivy**, **ferns**, and **wandering Jew**. For a grasslike effect, choose **mondo grass**. If you use creeping and climbing types, make sure they don't become attached to the tree trunks.

Flowers: Only a few really like the shade. Choose from **begonias**, **coleus**, **jacobinia**, and **impatiens**. Most have to be replanted throughout the year and may be affected by cold.

Foliage plants: Many plants you grow in the home also like the outdoor life. They usually find the shade of a tree the ideal spot and can be planted in the ground or grown in containers. In the coolor locations, container plantings can be moved indoors for the winter. Some are **dieffenbachia**, **dracaena**, **ficus**, **grape ivy**, **peace lily**, and **spider plant**.

Grass may be an alternative for the shade, but only some of the **St. Augustines** tolerate light shade. Often the sites have a light level that is too low for grass.

Pygmy date palm

PLANTING

Continue to add container-grown trees and **palms** to the landscape. This may be the best time to find out where you really need shade and would like a few **palms**. Remember, the sun

patterns do change throughout the year. About now the sun is directly overhead. During the winter it stays in the southern horizon.

The rains help to make planting easier. The soil is moist and digging is easy. After planting, rainfall can keep the soil moist and increase humidity to reduce evaporation from the foliage. Follow good planting procedures when adding new trees and **palms**.

CARE

Continue to remove the old seedheads from **crape myrtle** trees throughout this month to encourage additional blooms. Look for limbs that may have become extra-long and now interfere with landscape maintenance or walks along pathways.

- Cut unwanted limbs back to a branch angle or to the trunk.
- Remove old fronds and seed stalks from **palms**.
- Remove shoots on new trees that may be competing with the central leader.
- Trim back limbs that are out-of-bounds and ruining the shape of the tree.
- Look for diseased or damaged limbs that should be removed.
- Do not apply paints or wound coverings to pruning wounds. Let them heal naturally.

WATERING

With a little luck, the summer rains will do some of the watering for at least one more month. August can be a very rainy month. When you get 1/2 inch or more of rainfall, you can probably skip that watering for all but the most recently planted, and for these it's still best to fill the berms with water. Remember, when you have new plantings, don't rely on the irrigation system to do the watering. It may never completely wet the rootball, and the plants may start to dry.

FERTILIZING

No feeding of trees is needed for another month or two. It's best to allow the trees to use the nutrients already in the soil. Overfeeding pushes topgrowth that may produce a lanky tree. It could also put stress on the root system, which would have to supply the extra foliage with moisture. It's best to stick with scheduled feedings.

Palms are ready for another feeding of a slow-release fertilizer or a light feeding of a standard **palm** fertilizer. Scatter the fertilizer under the spread of the **palms** and water to begin moving the nutrients into the soil.

PROBLEMS

If you notice some chunks removed from tree leaves, this could be due to grasshoppers, katydids, or beetles. They are all chewing insects that like to feed on tree foliage. Unless the trees are small, the damage is minimal and will not affect the growth of the tree. It's as if it has extra foliage to share. When a young tree is affected, you may want to handpick the pests from the tree or apply a synthetic insecticide for chewing insects available at the local garden center- follow label instructions.

A number of insects will continue throughout the summer and into fall. Look for aphids, caterpillars, lacebugs, thrips, scale, and whitefly insects on local trees. **Palms** may have skeletonizers and leaf spots present.

SEPTEMBER

TREES & PALMS

PLANNING

If you enjoy fall leaf color, plan to add deciduous trees such as **bald cypress**, **Chickasaw plum**, **crape myrtle**, **redbud**, **red maple**, **river birch**, **sugarberry**, **sweet gum**, and **winged elm**.

You might also plant fruiting trees with attractive fruits and pods: **black olive**, **camphor**, **dogwood**, **golden rain tree**, **hollies**, **southern juniper**, and **wax myrtle**. For fall flower color, try **golden rain tree**, **loquat**, **orchid trees**, and **sweet acacia**.

River birch

PLANTING

Tree and **palm** planting can continue during summer and early fall with container-grown material. Just make sure you give the plants good care when they are transported to the home. Leaves blowing about in a car or truck can dry out very quickly. If you cannot move the tree or **palm** properly, ask to have it delivered.

Make sure the planting site has the proper moisture level for your new tree or **palm**. Most like a well-drained site. If the area is moist, either select a different species or add the plant to a raised bed. By planting the tree or **palm** in a mound of soil you will ensure good drainage for the roots, even if the surrounding soil remains moist.

CARE

Eliminate competition from weeds, grass, shrubs, and similar plants around the base of the tree. A covering around the trunk can often encourage foot rot and similar diseases. It also gives insects a good place to hide. Trim back shrubs, vines, and flowers encroaching on the trunk. Handpull weeds and clip grass. Be careful when using mechanical weed-cutting equipment. Some can easily damage the trunk. If needed, non-selective herbicides for use around growing plants can also be used to control weeds.

WATERING

In most years the rainy season ends by mid-month. If you have new trees and **palms**, keep up the daily waterings. More-established plantings need every-other-day waterings for a few more months. Trees and **palms** that have been in the landscape for a year or more can most likely exist with the seasonal rains.

FERTILIZING

Fall feeding time is here for trees, but you don't have to hurry. Most gardeners who feed new trees up to three to five years old make the fertilizer applications this month or the next.

- Apply 1 pound of nitrogen over every 1,000 square feet of ground under the spread of the trees and out past the dripline.
- Use a general-garden fertilizer of a 12-4-8, 15-5-15, or 16-4-8 analysis.

DEALING WITH WOUNDS

Pruning, lightning, animals, and mowing equipment can wound trees. No longer do we rush to make major repairs. Instead, we rely on the healing abilities of the tree:

1. Clean the wound of all loose bark and shattered wood.
2. Trim the wound to a rounded to oblong shape with smooth edges.
3. Leave the wound exposed. Do not apply paints or other coverings.
4. If the tree appears weakened and borers may affect the tree, a borer control spray may be applied.
5. Encourage normal growth with good watering and feeding practices.
6. Add fencing, tree guards, or other barriers to prevent damage to trunks as needed.

Remember, **palms** cannot heal wounds—the cuts and damaged bark will never heal. It is no use trying to help a **palm** cover its wounds.

Use the lawn rate recommendations, or divide the first number into 100 to get the amount needed.

- Use a handheld spreader or lawn spreader to get an even application.
- Wet the soil after feeding to begin moving the nutrients into the root zone.
- Apply the fertilizer over the mulch.

Do not remove the mulch to feed the tree.

Palm feedings of a slow-release fertilizer should be delayed one more month. If you are applying a light monthly feeding of a standard **palm** fertilizer, you can continue the application.

PROBLEMS

Every so often you may notice the ends of your trees have died back—but don't be too alarmed. This may be borer damage, but it causes minimal harm to the trees. In fact, many gardeners just consider it a good pruning. The little dark-colored twig beetles that make their home in the end of stems may be at work. Trees most likely to be affected are **dogwoods**, **maples**, **magnolias**, and **oaks**. The stem ends often snap at the point where the beetle enters to raise the next generation. Since the trees are often tall, the pests are usually ignored. Where possible, prune them from the trees to eradicate the population.

Twig girdlers, large gray beetles with long horns and sharp mandibles, may also be at work in some trees in the landscape. They cut off the ends of branches which then drop to the ground. Pick up the twigs and destroy to control the next generation.

Gardeners with **palms** often notice rows of small holes around the trunks. Some gardeners also notice the damage on tree trunks. Don't worry, these holes are made by a bird—the sapsucker. The minor damage causes no harm to the plantings and can usually be ignored.

Other insects are sure to continue into the fall. Just a few are caterpillars, scales, and whitefly.

TREES & PALMS

PLANNING

Review your landscape plan, and plant trees first. They require many more years than shrubs, vines, or ground covers to reach a mature size.

Gardeners may want instant shade, but big trees are usually more expensive and take more initial care and watering. If they don't become quickly established, smaller trees may outgrow them.

This is not the time to plant **palms**. They make very little root growth at this time of the year and have to live with stored moisture and foods in the leaves and trunks. **Palms** in containers can still be added, but do not expect much growth until spring.

PLANTING

Planting gets easier during the fall because of the cooler weather. It's still recommended that you follow the good steps to planting, but you can do it with less effort:

- Find the ideal site away from buildings, some distance from homes and septic systems, and in a well-drained soil.
- Open a planting hole wider but not deeper than the rootball.
- Position the tree or container-grown palm in the hole so the top of the rootball is even with the surface of the ground or a little higher.
- Fill in around the rootball with soil and water at the same time.
- Build a 4- to 6-inch berm of soil around the outer edge of the rootball.
- Add a mulch layer, and water.

Now that was easy. You may have to add several stakes for support if the tree or **palm** may be affected by winds. Allow the trunk a little freedom to move so it continues to strengthen.

CARE

Tree and **palm** care begins to wind down during fall. Continue to check for storm-damaged limbs and fronds, and declining portions. These can be removed anytime. Try to complete major

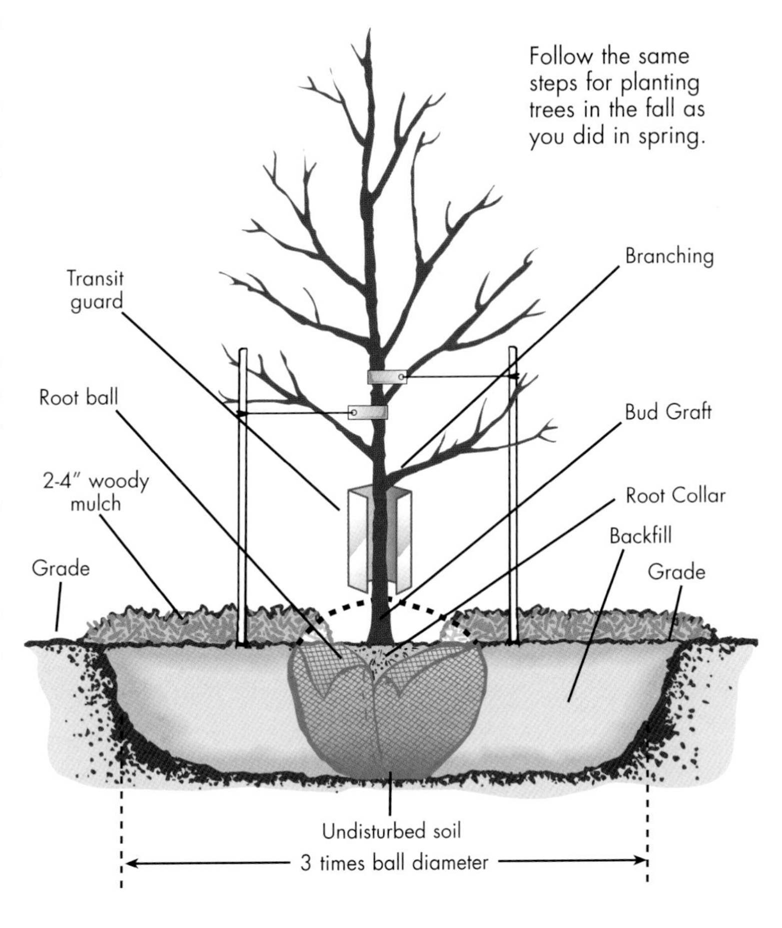

Follow the same steps for planting trees in the fall as you did in spring.

pruning in the colder portions of the state. Where possible, the plantings should be dormant or growth slowed during winter. This appears to help protect trees from winter damage—new shoots growing through frost and freezing weather are more susceptible to damage.

WATERING

You do not have to be quite as conscientious about watering new trees and **palms** this month, but it's best if they remain moist until established. The month does start the drier time of the year. Where possible, continue the daily waterings for trees and **palms** that have been a month or two in the ground. Then begin the every-other-day program for several additional months. If a day or two is skipped it probably won't make a difference, except with the extra-large trees that need the special care.

FERTILIZING

If you missed the September tree feeding, there is still time. Just scatter a lawn fertilizer under the trees' spread. Make sure you are using a fertilizer without a weed-killer. Use the fertilizer at the lawn rate to feed the turf and tree. Only trees up to three to five years of age need the special feedings. Others obtain nutrients from the feeding of landscape plantings.

This is the last feeding of the year for **palms** if you are using either the slow-release or standard fertilizers. The plants won't need additional feedings as growth slows for winter. The fall feeding is important, as it helps to promote winter hardiness.

PROBLEMS

Pests begin to slow their feeding habits as cooler weather arrives. Twig girdlers usually continue to feed on the ends of branches, and lacebugs damage the remaining **sycamore** leaves. You can expect some caterpillars among the foliage of some shade trees. In general, the damage from all these pests is ignored and fallen tree portions are collected and added to the compost pile. Some leaves or fallen limbs with the insects present may also be destroyed.

TEST YOUR TREE I.Q.

• Most trees growing in home landscapes do not have taproots. True or False? The answer is True. When trees are transplanted, the taproots are often lost.

• Tree roots grow mainly under the spread of the branches. True or False? This is False. Over half of a tree's roots may grow past the dripline.

• Most feeding roots are in the upper foot of soil. True or False? The answer is True. Most of the water- and nutrient-absorbing roots are in the upper 6 inches of soil for many trees. This is why we put the fertilizer on the surface of the ground.

• Established trees need a good feeding once a year. True or False? If you have been reading this chapter, you know this is False. Most shade and flowering trees over three to five years of age in your yard can make adequate growth with nutrients supplied by mulches and other nearby landscape plantings.

• Topping creates a hazardous tree. True or False? It's True. Cutting the tops out of trees may result in weak growth and wounds that can lead to rotting limbs that break during storms.

NOVEMBER

TREES & PALMS

PLANNING

Most trees available at garden centers do not like wet feet. If you have an area where water accumulates, be sure you select a tree that won't mind the damp soil.

If you obtained a home during the drier time of the year, the ground may appear dry but is flooded when the summer rainy season returns. If you are not sure about the drainage in the landscape, you can test the soil:

1. Dig a hole in the ground about a foot deep.
2. Check the color and smell of the soil. If it is gray in color and has a bad odor, the ground is probably poorly drained.
3. Fill the hole with water.
4. If the water leaves the hole dry in a hour or two, your soil is likely to be a well-drained site. If the water remains in the hole, it's probably a poorly-drained site.

Soils that hold water need special trees. You can find some of them growing in the wet areas along the road. Some of these are in cultivation and can be purchased at garden centers. Try **bald cypress**, **Dahoon holly**, **loblolly bay**, **palms (cabbage**, **paurotis**, and **royal)**, **red maple**, and **river birch**.

Other trees that grow best in a moist soil include **dogwood**, **southern magnolia**, **sweet gum**, and **wax myrtle**. Many gardeners try to grow the **weeping willow**, which must have a damp site. This tree can be grown in northern and central portions of the state but has numerous diseases and pests that mar the beauty of the tree.

PLANTING

Adding trees to the landscape never stops in Florida, thanks to container production. As the weather turns a bit cooler, it becomes easier to move trees both balled-and-burlapped and bare root. The planting techniques are about the same for all.

1. Make sure the tree is positioned at the original depth or with the rootball level or slightly above the surface of the soil.
2. Check the burlap-wrapped plants to make sure the material is a natural type that will decompose. If it is not, the burlap material should be removed at planting.

Check drainage in a potential planting site before you position your tree or palm.

3. Turn down natural burlap at planting time. If left above the ground, it may act like a wick and remove water from the rootball.
4. All plantings should have a 4- to 6-inch berm created to hold water that directs the moisture down through the root system and then out into the surrounding soil.
5. Add a 3- to 4-inch mulch over the root system to control weeds and conserve moisture.

Late fall and winter are not the best times to add **palms** to the landscape. If necessary, con-

tainer-grown plantings can be added in the warmer areas of the state.

CARE

Some trees are going to need staking after they are planted. These are usually the taller trees and trees with a large canopy that may be affected by winds. Don't stake a tree if it's not needed. The natural movement of the tree trunk helps produce a sturdier tree.

- Trees less than 3 inches in diameter can be secured with wood stakes driven into the ground at the edge of the rootballs. Use two stakes for a tree under 2 inches in diameter and three stakes for the larger trees. Secure the trunk to the stakes with fabric or a hose-covered wire. Leave the tie just a little loose to allow some trunk movement.

- Trees over 3 inches can be supported with additional stakes or guy wires. Use three or more guy wires that extend from one spot on the trunk to the ground and are attached to stakes driven in the ground. Paint the stakes and wires with a bright color or use flags to mark them so as to avoid accidents.

Trees should not need the supports for more than a year. Remove the stakes and wires as soon as the tree appears to be rooted in the surrounding soil.

WATERING

It's a drier but cooler time of year. Watering is not quite as necessary as during the hotter weather. Some trees will be dropping their leaves and will not need as much moisture. Do make sure the soil stays moist with newer trees. If you skip a scheduled watering, it probably won't be missed. But for best tree growth, try to follow a recommended watering program.

Newly planted trees: Water daily for the first month or two.

Establishing trees: Water every other day for three to four months.

Rains may do the watering for you when $1/2$ inch or more rainfall is measured. At this time of year, use your judgment about when to apply water. If the soil is moist, scheduled waterings can be skipped. Give new **palms** a similar watering program. At this time of year, most only need a moist soil.

FERTILIZING

Feeding time is over for the year for all landscape trees and **palms**. The next scheduled feeding is during February or March. If you are keeping trees in containers, a light feeding may be applied if they are making growth at this time.

PROBLEMS

Gardeners notice lots of what appear to be problems on trees, but **Spanish** and **ball moss**, **lichens**, and peeling bark are all normal and seldom need attention.

DECEMBER

TREES & PALMS

PLANNING

Trees and **palms** make nice gifts that last for generations. Just make sure the person receiving the gift really wants a tree or **palm**.

PLANTING

If you need to transplant trees from one area to another, make sure the soil is moist at the time of digging. Dig a large rootball, about a foot in diameter for each inch of trunk diameter measured 6 inches above the ground. Make downward cuts around the tree to form the rootball. When the ball is shaped, dig under the tree to loosen it from the ground. Wrap the ball in burlap, and gently move the tree to the new site. Follow normal planting practices, and keep the soil moist to ensure root growth.

Delay all **palm** plantings till warmer weather, March through midsummer.

CARE

Make sure the area under trees and **palms** remain weed-free. Even though winter arrives this month, Florida has winter weeds. Pull the weeds by hand or spot-kill with a nonselective herbicide that permits use around growing plants. Renew mulches as needed to maintain a moist soil and help control weeds.

WATERING

After a tree is first planted, adhere to the watering schedules for at least a week or two. If the soil is moist, you can probably skip a watering. Otherwise, make sure drying soils receive the needed moisture.

FERTILIZING

Feeding time is over for the rest of the year. Most trees and **palms** are dormant and have received all the nutrients needed for growth. The next feeding time for trees of up to three to five years of age is in February or March. Feeding time for **palms** begins in March. Make sure all leftover fertilizer is stored in a sealed bag to keep it from clumping and becoming difficult to spread.

PROBLEMS

Most pests are not very active at this time of the year.

One tree disease that can cause major loss at any time is mushroom root rot. **Leyland cypress** is especially sensitive to the disease. Others that frequently have problems are **maples**, **crape myrtles**, **yew podocarpus**, and **cherry laurel**—but the fungal organism may affect any tree. When infected, the tree rapidly loses leaves or turns brown and declines. The fungus lives in the soil and waits for trees to come under stress. There is no control except to keep the landscape plantings, including shrubs, in good health.

Palms have a similar disease called butt rot where mushrooms form on the lower portions of the trunk. When affected, the only remedy is to remove the **palm** and not plant in the same location.

CHAPTER TEN

VINES, GROUND COVERS, & ORNAMENTAL GRASSES

An area may be too small for trees or too narrow for shrubs, or you may want some plants to spread out rather than grow upright. You may want something green and durable in an area, but it may be too shady for turfgrass. These are all spots for a vine, ground cover, or ornamental grass.

You are probably familiar with vines and ground covers. Vines grow in trees, and they also cover walls and climb trellises. Ground covers hide bare spots, fill in for turf, and make easy maintenance out of the more-difficult-to-care-for areas of the landscape. Both can be colorful and at times are eye-catching accents.

But what about ornamental grasses? They have been around for a long time, but many gardeners just don't know what to do with them. In fact, you can use them like shrubs or ground covers, they add a natural look to the landscape, and many are quite colorful. Most are also low maintenance, which makes them of real value in modern landscaping.

PLANNING

An area may be too small for trees or too narrow for shrubs, or you may want some plants to spread out rather than grow upright. You may want some-

thing green and durable in an area, but it may be too shady for turfgrass. These are all spots for a vine, ground cover, or ornamental grass.

Vines: Nature gave these plants the ability to reach for the sun. Very few really like the shade, and all love sunny sites. In fact, all vines grow best when given some support, usually a trellis or a wire or wood support. They can be trained to be free-standing or attached to a wall. Vines tend to grow very quickly during the warmer months.

- Put vines to use hiding a wall or fence. Green plants are much easier to look at than wire, wood, or concrete.
- Many vines produce colorful flowers. Some can be in bloom just about year-round, while others are seasonal.
- Use vines trained to a trellis or fence to separate areas of the landscape. Create the rooms of the landscape with vines.
- Plant vines as accent features. Use the flowers and fruits to attract attention. Use them at the end of a view or to create a focal point.
- Vines are ideal where you have limited space but need some height. They can grow in a container and still climb a wall or trellis.
- Use vines to create overhead cover on an arbor or similar structure.

Ground covers: Some grow very upright, and others spread out across the surface of the soil. Ground covers provide extra greenery in the landscape, often becoming transition plantings. They form a bridge between the trees, shrubs, and lawn areas.

- Many grow in the shady spots where grass, shrubs, and flowers can't survive.
- Use them under trees to compete with the roots.
- Fill in the hard-to-mow spots or areas in which it is just difficult to maintain plantings.
- Use ground covers in the dry spots, areas of poor soil, and on banks.
- Some make excellent seaside plantings in areas where salt levels prevent other plant growth.
- Add them to containers for a spot of greenery or in combination with flowers.
- Use ground covers to fill in large open areas where a low-maintenance planting is needed.

Ornamental grasses: You are familiar with the turfgrasses—now meet their relatives. These are grasses with a clumping growth habit that like to grow tall and often have attractive inflorescence. They add a prairie and meadow look to the landscape, and are often used in naturalist settings. Ornamental grasses are usually low maintenance and provide food and a home for wildlife.

- Create a view barrier or hedge from the taller-growing grasses.
- Use the plants as an edging, or plant in a mass as a ground cover.
- Create accent features with the grasses that sport showy inflorescence or colorful foliage.
- Mix together wildflowers and grasses.

PLANTING

Vines, ground covers, and ornamental grasses aren't very particular about planting sites. Most do like a well-drained soil, but it can be sandy, clay, or peaty. Care is made a lot easier if the sand or clay are enriched with organic matter, but in fact you can pop these plants in the ground just about anywhere. When their roots systems become established, most are very drought tolerant. Here are just a few tips to give the soil the best preparation for your new plantings:

- Spot-kill weeds with a non-selective herbicide that permits replanting.
- Till compost, peat moss, and manures into sandy or clay sites.

• Check the soil acidity and adjust to a slightly acid pH.

• Level the planting site . . . and you are ready to plant.

It is important to learn a little about the plant to be added to the landscape. If you are going to use more than one vine, give them adequate room to grow. The same can be said for ground covers and ornamental grasses. Make sure you learn which is going to spread out and will need more room. Most of this information is found on plant labels or can be obtained from garden center employees. Now you can put the plants in the ground:

• Open a hole big enough to hold the root system plus some growing room.

• Position the plant so the rootball is even with the surface of the soil.

• Fill in around the rootball with water and soil.

• Add a 2- to 3-inch layer of mulch to conserve water and prevent weeds.

• Keep the planting site moist with frequent waterings.

CARE

Primary care involves guiding the growth of the new plants and keeping older plants inbounds. Periodically *check* the new growths from beginning vines to make sure they are filling in the trellis. *Direct* the runners of creeping ground covers across the soil. If needed, vines and creeping ground covers can have their ends pinched back to cause branching and new growth.

Ground covers may also need periodic trimming to stay inbounds. Some seem to want to invade other plants, cross walkways, or climb trees. You may need to check these planting monthly for errant growth during warm weather.

Grasses usually get a major trimming during the winter months, after the stems have turned brown and flowering is over. Most can be cut back to near the ground to await spring growth.

WATERING

Vines, ground covers, and ornamental grasses are a hardy bunch. Once established, most can exist with seasonal rains. After planting, however, you should give each enough water to establish a root system and begin growth out into the surrounding soils.

• Handwater individual plants to maintain a moist rootball and surrounding soil. In water-resistant soil, it may be necessary to build small berms around the plants to catch and hold water.

• Apply 1/2 to 3/4 inch water at each irrigation.

• Water daily for the first few weeks. Then reduce the waterings to every other day for a few more weeks.

Gradually reduce the waterings to an as-needed schedule.

• Maintain a 2- to 3-inch mulch layer over the root system.

• Water during the early-morning hours.

When the plants begin growth and roots can be found in the surrounding soil, watering can be reduced to an as-needed schedule. Too much water can cause many vines, ground covers, and grasses to develop root rot problems. Feel the soil, and if it's dry in the upper inch, it may need watering. Reapply the 1/2 to 3/4 inch of water.

FERTILIZING

Feeding is needed only to encourage growth, usually during the establishment period. After the vines fill a trellis, ground covers grow together, and grasses produces spring growth, little fertilizer is needed. All can be fed lightly about three times a year to help the plantings produce new shoots, leaves, and flowers.

• Apply a 6-6-6, 10-10-10, or 16-4-8 fertilizer at the general rate for garden use once in March, July, and September if needed to encourage growth.

• Scatter the fertilizer over the surface of the soil or mulch in the planted area.

Do not place the fertilizer near the stems.

• Water after feeding to move the nutrients into the soil.

Feedings can be continued on a yearly schedule as needed to maintain growth. If the plantings are making adequate growth, feedings can be skipped. Many vine, ground cover, and ornamental grass plantings are never fertilized. They obtain nutrients from decomposing mulches and fertilizer applied to nearby plantings.

PEST CONTROL

Many vines, ground covers, and ornamental grasses grow pest free. Seldom do you have to spray, as they can tolerate the few leaf spots and holes made by pests. Sometimes a few get out of control, and these hot spots can be spotted during walks in the landscape. *Handpick* from the plants or treat with natural sprays.

• Aphids: Small pear-shaped insects of numerous colors usually feeding in new growths and flower buds. They may be associated with ants that feed on their excreta. Small populations can be tolerated and may be controlled by beneficial insects. Where needed control with a soap spray following the label instructions.

• Caterpillars: The immature stage of moths and butterflies, of many different colors and sizes. May be found feeding on foliage and stems. Best handpicked or controlled with a natural Bacillus thuringiensis spray available at garden centers.

• Grasshoppers: Large brown to green insects with big legs that hop or fly between plants. They chew large holes in leaves or entire plant portions. Best controlled by handpicking or use of synthetic insecticides.

• Leaf spots: Yellow to brown spots forming on plant foliage, usually caused by a fungus. Often prevalent on weakened plants and at leaf drop time. Can usually be ignored.If needed control with a natural copper-containing fungicide or a synthetic fungicide following label instructions.

• Mealybugs: White to gray scale-related insects to 1/8 inch long. Often associated with sooty mold. The insects reduce plant vigor and cause decline. Control with a soap or oil spray as needed, following label instructions.

• Mites: Small pinpoint-size arachnids that suck juices from foliage. May be clear or of tan to reddish color. They cause leaves to yellow and drop. Control with a soap or oil spray as needed.

• Powdery mildew: A white fungal growth on the surface of plant foliage. Most prevalent during the spring season. Can cause yellowing and leaf drop. Usually ignored unless excessive and plant damage is noted. If needed control with a natural copper-containing fungicide or a synthetic fungicide, following the label instructions.

• Scale insects: Brown to white specks to bumps the size of a dime on leaf surfaces and stems. Many are associated with the dark sooty mold fungus living on excreta from the insects. If minor they can be removed by hand, but most need an oil or synthetic insecticidal treatment to obtain control.

CHAPTER TEN

Vines

Name	Area of Florida	Climbing Height (ft.)	Foliage Type	Flowers Color/Season	Light Needed
Allamanda, Purple	CS	Variable	Evergreen	Purple/Summer-fall	Sun
Allamanda, Yellow	CS	Variable	Evergreen	Yellow/Year-round	Sun, light shade
Bengal Clock Vine	CS	20 – 30	Evergreen	White, blue/Summer	Sun
Bleeding Heart	CS	12 – 15	Evergreen	White&red/ Spring-fall	Sun,light shade
Bougainvillea	CS	10 – 20	Evergreen	Numerous/ Year-round	Sun
Bower Vine	CS	15 – 20	Evergreen	White&pink/Spring	Sun, light shade
Calico Flower	CS	12 – 15	Evergreen	White&brown/ Summer	Sun, light shade
Cape Honeysuckle	CS	6 – 10	Evergreen	Orange/Summer-fall	Sun
Cat's Claw Vine	NCS	20 – 30	Evergreen	Yellow/Spring	Sun, light shade
Ceriman	CS	15 – 20	Evergreen	Green/Summer	Light shade, shade
Chinese Wisteria	NC	20 – 30	Deciduous	Lavender/Spring	Sun
Confederate Jasmine	NCS	15 – 20	Evergreen	White/Spring	Sun, shade
Coral Vine	CS	30 – 40	Evergreen	Pink/Spring-fall	Sun
Flame Vine	CS	30 – 40	Evergreen	Orange/Winter	Sun
Garlic Vine	CS	20 – 30	Evergreen	Lavender, pink, White/Spring-fall	Sun, light shade
Japanese Clematis	NC	10 – 15	Evergreen	White/Summer	Sun
Mandevilla	CS	15 – 20	Evergreen	Pink/Spring-fall	Sun
Mexican Flame Vine	CS	15 – 20	Evergreen	Orange/Spring-summer	Sun, light shade
Painted Trumpet	NCS	15 – 20	Evergreen	Lavender/Spring	Sun
Passion Flower, Red	CS	15 – 20	Evergreen	Red/Spring-summer	Sun
Pothos	CS	20 – 30	Evergreen	Inconspicuous	Shade
Queen's Wreath	S	20 – 30	Evergreen	Purple/Spring-summer	Sun, light shade
Rangoon Creeper	CS	15 – 25	Evergreen	White, red/Summer	Sun, light shade
Showy Combretum	CS	15 – 20	Evergreen	Red/Fall-spring	Sun
Stephanotis	S	10 – 15	Evergreen	White/Summer	Sun, light shade
Trumpet Creeper	NC	20 – 30	Deciduous	Orange/Summer	Sun
Trumpet Honeysuckle	NC	15 – 25	Evergreen	Orange, yellow/ Spring-summer	Sun
Yellow Jessamine, Carolina	NC	20 – 30	Evergreen	Yellow/Winter	Sun, light shade

N = North Florida C = Central Florida S = South Florida

CHAPTER TEN

Ground Covers

Name	Area of Florida	Height (Inches)	Light Needed	Flowers Color/Season	Best Uses
Asiatic Jasmine	NCS	8 – 12	Sun, shade	Seldom flowers	Under trees, open areas
Asparagus Fern	CS	12 – 18	Sun, light shade	Whitish/ Summer	Banks,open areas
Beach Morning Glory	CS	4 – 60	Sun	Purple/ Summer-fall	Banks, seashores
Beach Sunflower	NCS	12 – 24	Sun	Yellow/ Year-round	Open area, seashores
Bromeliads	CS	6 – 36	Light shade	Variable/ Year-round	Under trees
Bugleweed	NC	6 – 10	Sun, light shade	Purple/Summer	Under trees, edging
Cast-iron Plant	CS	18 – 30	Shade	Purple/Spring	Under trees
Confederate Jasmine	NCS	10 – 18	Sun,shade	White/Spring	Under trees, open areas
Coontie	NCS	12 – 24	Sun, light shade	Inconspicious	Under trees, open areas
Creeping Fig	NCS	8 – 12	Sun, light shade	Inconspicious	Banks, open areas
Daylily	NCS	12 – 24	Sun, light shade	Numerous/ Spring-summer	Open area
Dichondra	NCS	1 – 2	Sun, light shade	Inconspicious	Under trees, open areas
Dwarf Gardenia	CS	6 – 12	Sun, light shade	White/Spring	Under trees, open areas
Holly Fern	CS	12 – 18	Shade	None	Under trees
Ivy, Algerian	NCS	6 – 10	Light shade, shade	Inconspicious	Under trees, banks
Ivy, English	NC	6 – 10	Light shade, shade	Inconspicious	Under trees, banks
Juniper, Chinese	NC	12 – 24	Sun	Inconspicious	Banks, open areas
Juniper, Shore	NCS	12 – 24	Sun	Inconspicious	Banks, open areas
Lantana, Common	CS	36 – 60	Sun	Numerous/ Year-round	Banks, open areas
Lantana, Trailing	CS	18 – 24	Sun	Lavender	Banks, open areas
Leatherleaf Fern	CS	18 – 24	Light shade, shade	None	Under trees
Lily Turf	NCS	12 – 24	Sun, light shade	Purple-white/ Summer	Under trees, edging
Lily Turf, Creeping	NCS	6 – 18	Sun, light shade	Purple-white/ Summer	Under trees,edging
Mexican Heather	CS	12 – 18	Sun, light shade	Purple/ Year-round	Edging, open areas
Mondo Grass	NCS	6 – 12	Light shade, shade	Inconspicious	Under trees, edging
Oyster Plant	CS	18 – 24	Sun, light shade	White/ Year-round	Under trees, banks

Name	Area of Florida	Height (Inches)	Light Needed	Flowers Color/Season	Best Uses
Purple Heart	CS	18 – 24	Sun, light shade	Pink/Year-round	Under trees, open areas
Society Garlic	CS	18 – 24	Sun, light shade	Purple/ Spring-fall	Edging, open areas
Sword Fern	NC	12 – 36	Light shade, shade	None	Under trees, open areas
Wandering Jew	CS	6 – 12	Light shade, shade	Pink/Year-round	Under trees
Wedelia	CS	8 – 12	Sun, light shade	Yellow/ Year-round	Banks, open areas
Winter Creeper	N	18 – 24	Sun, light shade	White/Spring	Banks, open areas

Ornamental Grasses

Name	Growth Habit	Height (Inches)	Inflorescence Color/Months	Best Use
Chalky Bluestem	Upright	12 – 18	White/Sept. – Oct.	Ground cover
Elliott Lovegrass	Mounded	12 – 24	Silver/Aug. – Sept.	Ground cover
Fakahatchee Grass	Arching	24 – 36	Gold/June – Sept.	Ground cover
Florida Gammagrass	Arching	12 – 24	Gold/Sept. – Oct.	Ground cover, accent
Fountain Grass	Arching	36 – 48	Purple/Aug. – Oct.	Ground cover, view barrier
Giant Plumegrass	Upright	24 – 30	Pink, purple/ Sept. – Oct.	Ground cover, accent
Great Dame	Upright/ creeping	6 – 12	Green/Year-round	Ground cover
Lopsided Indiangrass	Upright	12 – 24	Gold/Sept. – Oct.	Ground cover
Muhly Grass	Mounded	24 – 30	Pink/Sept. – Oct.	Ground cover, accent
Pampas Grass	Upright	72 – 96	White, pink/Aug. – Oct.	Accent, view barrier
Pineland Dropseed	Mounded	18 – 24	Maroon/June – July	Ground cover
Purple Lovegrass	Mounded	12 – 24	Pink/Aug. – Sept.	Ground cover, accent
Sand Cordgrass	Upright	48 – 60	Brownish/May – June	Ground cover, view barrier
Short-spike Bluestem	Arching	12 – 24	Golden/Sept. – Oct.	Ground cover
Wiregrass	Upright	12 – 18	Bronze/June – Oct.	Ground cover

N = North Florida C = Central Florida S = South Florida

JANUARY
VINES, GROUND COVERS, & ORNAMENTAL GRASSES

PLANNING

Most gardeners like a lot of greenery between major plantings. Fences and walls may need a covering, too. Walk through the landscape and decide where you can use the vines, ground covers, and ornamental grasses. Draw your landscape plan, and get ready to plant soon.

PLANTING

Most vines grow quite tall and wide. Try to determine the maximum width of the vine and then space the plants so the shoots just grow together at maturity. You can do some pruning on vining plants, but it can limit flowering. It's not really necessary to dig up a large area when just a small spot will do for a vine or two. Choose a site near a wall, next to a fence, or at the base of a trellis. Then you are ready to plant.

- Remove all weeds. If perennial weeds are present, spot-kill them with a nonselective herbicide that allows replanting.
- Loosen the soil in an area several feet wide and long. Work in organic matter if you wish, but it's not necessary for just a plant or two.
- Open a hole a foot or two larger than the diameter of the root system but no deeper.
- Set the plant in the ground so the rootball is level with or slightly above the ground.
- Position the plant so the new shoots can easily reach the trellis or fence.
- Fill in around the rootball with soil and water. Build a 4- to 6-inch berm of soil around the outer edge of the rootball, and add a mulch.
- Tie any shoots in place on the fence or trellis

Keep the soil moist and apply a light feeding in four to six weeks.

CARE

January is the start of pruning time for most landscapes. Like most landscape plantings, vines, ground covers, and ornamental grasses may need some grooming. Gardeners can reduce the height and width of most plants that do not flower until later in the season or if pruning helps promote better spring flowering. Here are a few general pruning tips:

- Remove all dead and declining plant portions.
- Trim off stems affected by insects or disease if controls are not possible.
- Trim the tops of brown grasses to the basal clumps. (This is usually to within 6 to 12 inches of the ground.)
- Remove extra-long shoots that are growing out-of-bounds.
- Edge ground covers beginning to creep out over walkways.

Plants that flower during the late-winter or spring months usually have pruning delayed until after the blossoms fade.

WATERING

It's a cool but dry time of year. New plantings need water daily for the first few weeks, then you can water every other day for several additional weeks. Vines, ground covers, and ornamental grasses usually become established very quickly.

Watering established plantings is usually needed only during periods of drought. If the plants fail to obtain adequate water from rainfalls over several weeks, irrigation may be needed. Follow good watering practices.

FERTILIZING

In South Florida, many plants may begin growth and the spring feedings can begin. Feed plantings only where you want to encourage growth. Use a general garden fertilizer at the

recommended rate. Scatter the product across the surface of the soil, and water to move the nutrients into the root zone. Gardeners in Central and North Florida usually wait until February or March to make the first feeding.

PROBLEMS

Insects do not become active in most plantings until new growth begins. You can, however, spot scale insects at any time of the year. Sometimes they are easier to spot on the older growths as the scales mature. You may also notice sooty mold developing on the foliage where soft scales are present. Winter is a good time to control scales with an oil spray. It coats the insects to cause their decline. Where possible, remove heavily infested plant portions. Apply an oil spray to upper and lower portions of the leaves plus the stems, applying when temperatures are above 40 degrees Fahrenheit. Follow label instructions. Scale insects and sooty mold slowly flake off the plant portions. Do not expect clean foliage for a month or more.

FORCING WISTERIA BLOOMS

Wisterias form large vines but are often reluctant bloomers. It usually takes several years of special care to produce the pendulous purple clusters in spring. Develop a trellising plan. It's better to keep the growth to a central trunk with a few main stems, often called arms, that develop lots of shoots. **Wisterias** grow rapidly and usually fill a trellis in one to two years. When a plant reaches the desired size, eliminate the frequent feedings and waterings. Place the vine on a lean diet to encourage flowering.

- Water only during an extended drought.
- Feed lightly in spring and early summer with a low-nitrogen fertilizer often sold as a blossom booster.
- Prune during summer to keep the plants in-bounds. Complete all summer pruning by the end of August.
- During January or February, cut back all side shoots originating from the main arms, leaving six to eight buds on each shoot. Spring flowers are found within the remaining buds and open when warm weather arrives.

Wisteria

FEBRUARY

VINES, GROUND COVERS, & ORNAMENTAL GRASSES

PLANNING

Ornamental grasses attract attention, require low maintenance, and have many positive features:

- Grass is durable and can withstand hot sun and dry weather.
- The plantings have very few pests and you won't have to do a lot of pest control.
- Grasses have attractive inflorescence, starting in midsummer and lasting through fall when other plants may not be in bloom.
- The leaves and seeds provide food for wildlife plus nesting material.
- Grasses can add fall color to the landscape in a Southern climate where there is little leaf change.

Grasses are great fillers for the large open areas, hillsides, and banks, and look nice along walkways and drive-ways. Grasses can grow tall or stay small. Some create view barriers and become accents.

Now see if you need some vertical interest. Vines can help add the greenery and seasonal color. Many of Florida's residents are enjoying the **yellow jasmine**, **bougainvillea**, and **flame vine** during winter.

Put ground covers to good use. Fill large areas where grass won't grow. Some even produce flowers.

PLANTING

This is the most stress-free planting time of the year. The weather is warming, and garden centers are filling. Most vines, ground covers, and ornamental grasses need very little preplanting site preparation. You could just open up a hole, pop them in the ground and expect good survival—they are usually that tough. But you'll have more certain results if you follow normal preplanting soil preparation:

- Clear the weeds from the planting site.
- Till in organic matter if you have sandy and clay soils.
- Test the soil acidity and adjust to a slightly acid pH.
- Add your new plants by opening up a hole bigger but not deeper than the root system.
- Fill in around the root system with soil and water.
- Add a mulch layer over the surface of the ground.

CARE

Prune ornamental grasses just before their spring growth. You don't have to prune every year, but if there is a lot of brown among the plants, do a major pruning to allow new growth.

- Prepare for pruning by covering your arms and legs.

The grass blades are often sharp and can cut the skin.

- Use hand pruners or loppers to cut the stems to a few inches to a foot above the ground.

The bigger the plant, the higher above the ground the plant can be pruned.

- Remove any dead portions to allow new growth to begin.
- Provide a spring feeding, and renew the mulch layer to encourage growth.
- Water thoroughly.

WATERING

Water new plantings every day for the first week or two. Then for the next few weeks, water every other day or two. Sometimes water does not wet the rootball and the plants begin to dry. Here are a few tips:

- Maintain a 2- to 3-inch mulch layer over the rootballs.
- Build a 4- to 6-inch berm of soil around the edge of the rootballs.
- Handwater the plants to make sure the moisture runs through the root system and out into the surrounding soil.

• Install soaker hoses or microsprinklers to put the water at the base of the plants.

Established plants usually do not need special waterings at this time. If drought conditions are present, water every week or two.

FERTILIZING

Many vines, ground covers, and ornamental grasses get the nutrients they need from decomposing mulches, but they'll benefit from a spring feeding. Use a general granular garden fertilizer at the lower rates, or use some alternative feeding techniques:

1. Manures can be applied to the surface of the soil.
2. Select a slow-release fertilizer that gradually supplies nutrients to the plants.
3. Liquid fertilizers can be drenched around the plants following label instructions.

PROBLEMS

It's not abnormal to find aphids associated with new growth on vines and ground covers. Some can be ignored, but these pests are up to no good. They suck juices from the new stems and can cause contorted growth and stunted plantings. Aphids are small, so you have to look carefully within the tips of the plants. They are often brightly colored and are pear-shaped. When high populations are noted, you may need to apply an insecticidal soap or synthetic insecticide following label instructions. Sometimes beneficial insects are present and providing adequate control, so you can skip the sprays. Other pests to look for this month are mites, mealybugs, scale, and powdery mildew. If pests are found, a heavy treatment may be needed.

KEEP VINES OUT OF TREES

Vines naturally latch on to the limbs and trunks of trees. But you are not going to get full enjoyment of the vine with its flowers and foliage mingled with those of the trees. And they compete with the trees for light, often causing a thinning of the tree branches. Thick vining growths around trunks can also provide a home for insects and disease. Give vines their own spots:

• Create a trellis for vines to climb.
• Train the shoots up stakes onto an overhead arbor
• Send them up and over a wall with some support for foliage.

Vines can quickly cover a tree.

MARCH

VINES, GROUND COVERS, & ORNAMENTAL GRASSES

PLANNING

Take time to draw a landscape plan. A simple drawing will do. Sketch your existing plants, then fill in with plants you want to add. Draw new plants at mature size. A landscape plan is a visualization of what your home site will look like at maturity.

If you have bare spots where turf won't grow, consider adding a ground cover. Most ground covers grow just a foot or two in height. They fill in areas between trees and shrubs and make transitions between turf and flower beds. Here are other possibilities:

- Fill in shady spots where other plants won't grow.
- Use plantings to edge walkways.
- Hang creeping ground covers over walls.
- Grow as a covering over banks and hillsides.
- Fill large open areas where you do not want to use grass or other shrubs.
- Plant as a covering for any bare area where vegetation is needed.

PLANTING

Make sure your plants have the right light level at planting time. Not all need to grow in full sun. That's the good part of growing many of the ground covers that can survive in the shady spots. **Bromeliads**, **Asiatic jasmine**, **lily turf**, **ivy**, and many more produce great greenery in the shady areas.

Very few vines or grasses like the shade. If given a light level that is too low, they rapidly decline or produce just spindly growths. Vines in shady areas also begin seeking out the sun, which means they may not fill the trellis or wall as intended.

Once you have the right spot, planting is easy. If you are only setting one plant in the ground, just open up the hole and loosen the surrounding soil. Then add the plant. When preparing a large planting site, it's best to loosen the soil in the entire area and then add lots of organic matter.

Once the soil is prepared, follow good planting procedures to install the plants. Then start a good watering program to keep the soil moist.

CARE

Vines need some guidance at this time as they begin new growth. Try to direct them onto a trellis so they can form a complete covering for walls or create a solid view barrier. Some as they make new growth may need trimming to keep them inbounds. Pinching back the vines just above the buds will cause branching and produce additional shoots.

Some ground covers need trimming to keep them off walkways and other plants. Trim them back 6 inches to a foot or more to avoid frequent pruning.

WATERING

You are entering the dry time of the year. Keep track of new plantings to make sure they have adequate moisture. The first month or two is usually the critical period when the plants need extra moisture until the roots grow out into the surrounding soil. If there is any doubt about the root growth, dig down in the soil and take a peek.

- Water recent plantings daily for the first week or two, and then every other day for several additional weeks.

HELPFUL HINTS

Here are some sources of organic matter you might find in your area.

- Compost: Can be purchased at local garden centers or obtained free from many municipal landfills. Can also be made at home from yard waste.
- Peat moss: Available at garden centers and some local landscape material suppliers.
- Manures: A source of organic matter and nutrients for plant growth. May be obtained composted at garden centers or fresh from stables with bedding material.
- Organic soils: Vary as to the amount of organic matter. May have weeds and other pest problems.
- Potting soils: Can be used to fill beds or improve planting sites. May be relatively expensive to add to large planting sites.

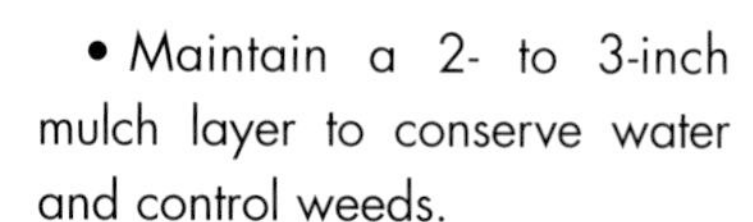

- Maintain a 2- to 3-inch mulch layer to conserve water and control weeds.
- Water during the early-morning hours to conserve moisture.
- Apply 1/2 to 3/4 inch water at each irrigation.

Older established plants will only need water during severe drought or when the plants show signs of wilting.

FERTILIZING

If you missed the spring feeding, it's not too late to make a fertilizer application. Most plantings that need additional growth can be fed with a granular general garden fertilizer. Scatter the fertilizer over the surface of the soil and water. Gardeners can also use slow-release fertilizer, liquid products, and manures to feed their plantings.

PROBLEMS

Mites are often a problem on ornamental plants during the drier times of the year. Check leaves that might be yellowing or developing brown spots for signs of mites. These are arachnids the size of a pinpoint. Some are reddish and others almost clear. You may also find some producing a web. Use a hand lens to spot the mites and the egg stages living on the foliage. If present, they can often be washed off the foliage, or a soap spray can be used to obtain control.

Other pests becoming active in the landscape on vines and ground covers include aphids, caterpillars, powdery mildew, and scales. Properly identify the pests and then apply a treatment if needed.

APRIL

VINES, GROUND COVERS, & ORNAMENTAL GRASSES

PLANNING

Selections of vines and ground covers offer varying flower colors, leaf types, and plant heights. The **trumpet creeper** is usually orange, but the variety 'Flava' has orange-yellow flowers. The **lily turf** includes 'Evergreen Giant', an extra-tall type, 'Variegata', with variegated foliage, and many more. Some other vines and ground covers with interesting varieties are **cape honeysuckle**, **lantana**, **Mexican heather**, **bugleweed**, and **bougainvillea**. Some are more resistant to pests or cultural conditions.

- Dwarf forms may be used in small places where the full-sized plants could not grow.
- Pick a new color that might better fit your outdoor decor.
- Select a variety that stays inbounds a little better.
- Look for new leaf shapes and colors. Some may have yellow or white stripes and others reds and burnt colorings.
- Cluster ground covers that have a unique growth habit along pathways and near statuary to form mini-accents.
- Add a plant with a different feature just because you like it.

Plants of different varieties are not always available at your local garden center. Sometimes you have to shop gardening catalogues or visit company web sites.

PLANTING

Adding vines, ground covers, and ornamental grasses can continue throughout the year, though it's best to buy vines and creeping ground covers early in the season. They can become entangled while waiting at the nursery. If you do obtain a vine later in the season, try to find one on a trellis so the shoots can be easily switched over to your growing area. Where plants have become entangled, you may trim to remove the problem portions. You can also divide ground covers and some vines that produce shoots at the base of the plants:

1. Find a large clump of a plant that produces offshoots like **lily turf**, **day lilies**, **cast-iron plant**, or **leatherleaf fern**.
2. Dig the entire plant or just a portion to divide.
3. Use a knife or shovel to separate the plant into small clumps or individual plants.
4. Trim off any dead or damaged portions.
5. Set the plant portions in the new site or in containers of soil at the same depth they were growing in the garden.

Bougainvillea

6. Water the site or containers to thoroughly wet the soil.

7. Add a 2- to 3-inch mulch layer to in-ground plantings.

Keep the planting moist and begin feedings in two to three weeks.

CARE

Check vines to make sure they are filling the trellis or climbing a wall properly. The ideal planting produces shoots in all directions to establish a solid-green covering as quickly as possible.

- Tie shoots to a trellis with garden tape or pieces of cloth.
- Position shoots so they fill voids on the wall or trellis.
- Pinch the tips of shoots to cause branching where needed.
- Trim back shoots that are too vigorous and growing out of proportion to the plant.

WATERING

Established plantings can often go a week or two without irrigation. But during dry weather, make sure new plantings have adequate moisture. If the rootball of any new plant dries, it may be lost. This can easily happen in a sandy soil when you water the plant, the moisture runs around the outside of the rootball. The plant dries, wilts, and dies.

- Dig down and check wilting plants for dry rootballs.
- Use a handheld hose to wet the rootball and surrounding soil.
- Build a berm of soil around the edge of the rootball to catch and direct the water down through the rootball.
- If you cannot wet the rootball, lift the plant and repot. Keep it potted until it is revived and ready again for the landscape.

FERTILIZING

No fertilizer is really needed by vines, ground covers, and grasses at this time. If you want to push growth a little, however, you could give plants fed over a month or two ago a light application. Most gardeners wait for the summer feeding time to apply more fertilizer.

If you are growing transplants in containers, you should be feeding the plants monthly. Use a general-garden fertilizer at the container rate. Many gardeners like to use liquids that can be applied through a sprinkling can. Others are using the granular slow-release fertilizers that feed the plants for months with one application.

PROBLEMS

Some insects and diseases are becoming active. Check for powdery mildew on the surface of foliage. Look for grasshoppers chewing on the leaves of all plantings. You may also find mites, scales, and mealybugs active at this time.

STRETCH YOUR GROUND COVER DOLLARS

When purchasing ground covers, look for plants that completely fill the pot, with shoots growing in all directions. **Ferns**, **lily turf**, **mondo grass** and others may fill pots with lots of new shoots. These can be divided when you get them home:

- Prepare the planting site and have it ready when the plants arrive.
- Slip the plants from their pots and check the growth.
- Use a knife to make two or more plants from the clump.
- Set the plants in the ground at the same depth they were in the container.
- Water and mulch to begin new growth.

MAY

VINES, GROUND COVERS, & ORNAMENTAL GRASSES

PLANNING

When planting vines, it helps to check out the growth habits. Some climb and grow by themselves. Others need assistance to fill a trellis or mount walls. It's not that they could never do the climbing on their own, but if you want them in a certain spot, it's best to provide assistance.

• **Clinging vines:** Some vines have rootlike structures that grasp on to buildings and walls. The roots appear to have an adhesive ability that grabs hold of surfaces. Some vines in this group include the **English ivy**, **ceriman**, and **creeping fig**. Many gardeners send these up masonry walls to create complete cover. Remember that they can with time loosen concrete and the plants may be hard to remove.

• **Twining vines:** New growths of these vines rotate until they find a surface to climb. It may be a stick, tree limb, or trellis. Many twine in one direction that should be noted when trying to train them onto a structure. Some vines with this habit are the **Bengal clock vine**, **Confederate jasmine**, **mandevilla**, and **trumpet honeysuckle**.

• **Tendril-forming vines:** Tendrils are modified leaves that twist around limbs, wires, and sections of wood. They hold very tight. Gardeners often notice the tendrils on the edible **grape vines**, but they also form on the ornamental **cat's claw vine** and **painted trumpet**. It's best to give these training in the early stages so you won't have to cut loose the firmly affixed tendrils.

Choose a support that the vine can easily adhere to in the landscape. Solid walls are useful only for a few. Most grow best with a wire or wood trellis to provide a grid for climbing.

Confederate jasmine

PLANTING

Continue planting any of the vines, ground covers, and ornamental grasses you might like. Plants in containers make it easy. Just be sure you have a water source available, as this is a dry month. You don't have to give the soil special preparation, but if planting a large bed, the addition of organic matter helps stretch the time between waterings and feedings.

CARE

Not only will your new plants grow well-so will the weeds. You can help reduce weeds before planting by controlling the perennial types with a nonselective herbicide that permits rapid replanting. Once the new plants are in the ground, weed control is up to you.

• Adding a 2- to 3-inch mulch layer helps retard weeds during the establishment period.

• Check out landscape fabrics that can be used with all but ground covers that spread underground.

Cover with a mulch after applying the fabric to the surface of the soil.

• Use a preemergence weed-control product for landscape plantings according to the label instructions to prevent seed germination.

• Spot-kill weeds with a nonselective herbicide that permits use near growing plants.

• Look for over-the-top herbicides that remove certain weeds. Check the label to make sure they can be used with your plants.

• Don't forget that hoeing and pulling are still good ways to control weeds.

WATERING

We have one more month of dry weather. Keep up a regular watering schedule for newly planted vines, ground covers, and ornamental grasses. Once they are established, make periodic checks. If the soil appears dry and the plants show signs of wilting, it's time to turn on the water. (Even though it is dry, you may not have to water well-established plantings.)

English ivy

FERTILIZING

Delay all feedings until summer. There is no use pushing growth during the dry times of the year. The plants don't need the fertilizer, and if they did, the new growth initiated would only require water. Hold off another month or two to give the plantings a feeding if needed for growth.

PROBLEMS

Caterpillars and aphids may be your two worst pests at this time of the year. They both like the new growths. Look for the pear-shaped and small aphids in the very tips of the new shoots. They may be one of many colors. Where needed, use a soap spray.

LOOK FOR CATERPILLARS

Caterpillars are often the same color as the plant foliage. They may not be spotted until portions of leaves have been chewed from the plants. Those like the bougainvillea caterpillar drop off the foliage when gardeners approach the plants. If caterpillars are seen or suspected, try the natural *Bacillus thuringiensis*-extract spray available at garden centers.

JUNE

VINES, GROUND COVERS, & ORNAMENTAL GRASSES

PLANNING

Some areas of Florida have need of vines, ground covers, and ornamental grasses that can grow in the seaside locations.

Pampas grass

These are usually locations with salty water, salty soil, and salty spray from the sea. Some inland neighborhoods also have deposits of salty water below the ground that at times affects irrigation water. Salt-resistant plants may be needed in these landscapes too. Following are just a few plants in each category you might look for at local garden centers and nurseries when planning your seaside landscapes.

- **Vines: Allamanda**, **flame vine**, **bougainvillea**, **Confederate jasmine**.
- **Ground covers: coontie**, **ivy**, **dichondra**, **mondo grass**, **beach morning glory**, **purple heart**, **wedelia**.
- **Ornamental grasses: sand cordgrass**, **muhly**, **pampas grass**. One additional grass often used specifically on the beach is **sea oats**, a native Florida plant.

PLANTING

Continue plantings as needed. If you are replacing dead or declining plants, some special soil preparation may be needed, as these plants have often developed pest problems in the soil.

- Remove the affected plants plus as much of the root system as possible.

If there was a major root rot problem, you may also need to remove some of the soil.

- Improve the planting site with organic matter and till it deeply.
- Set the new plant in the ground at the proper depth, and water as new soil is added.
- Create a 4- to 6-inch berm of soil around the edge of the rootball, and water.
- Complete the planting with a 2- to 3-inch mulch layer.

Pull the mulch back from the base of the plant to expose the stems.

CARE

Check vines and ground covers that may be growing out of control. The start of the rainy season is when you can expect a flush of new shoots. Keep plants off walkways and out of trees. Some ground covers can climb trunks and should be trimmed back from the base a foot or more.

Continue to control weeds that make some of their best growth during the hot humid weather.

WATERING

Most plantings make good growth as the rainy season returns. You may not have to do any watering of even newly established plantings. Check the ground between storms to make sure recently added plants have a moist soil. Older established plantings like the moist growing conditions and should begin additional growth at this time.

FERTILIZING

It's now or next month for feeding. If the plantings appear to be making normal green growth or you want to limit shoot and leaf development, you can skip this feeding. New plantings should probably receive the fertilizer to encourage filling in the bare spots and covering the trellis.

• Apply a 6-6-6, 10-10-10, or 16-4-8 fertilizer at the general rate for gardens. Make sure the foliage is dry at the time of the application.

Apply fertilizer only to plants that have adequate soil moisture.

• Scatter the fertilizer over the surface of the soil or mulch in the planted area.

GROWING IN SALTY PLACES

Just because a plant does not have major tolerance to salt doesn't mean it cannot be used in seaside plantings. But you do have to make sure it does not receive salt spray and will be watered only with low-salt water.

• If well water is salty, mix it with half city water as needed to obtain a suitable and economical water source when irrigating sensitive plants.

• Use salt-sensitive plants in protected areas of the landscape shielded from seaside winds.

• Plant salt-sensitive plants in containers to move as needed to protected spots.

• Feed sensitive plants with fertilizers low in salts, including manure and sludge.

Do not place the fertilizer near the stems.

• Handheld spreads can be used to spread the fertilizer in most beds to ensure uniform application.

• Water after feeding to move the nutrients into the soil.

Make sure granular fertilizers are washed off the surface of large leaves.

PROBLEMS

Summertime means lots of rain, and with it the chance of rot problems. Most vines, ground covers, and ornamental grasses can have problems when the soil is excessively damp. If a plant appears to be wilting and you know it has adequate water, you can suspect a rotting root system. Dig down and take a look for brown mushy roots. Unfortunately, there is probably little you can do for rotting root systems to save the plants. Root rot control fungicides are relatively expensive, and by the time you notice the decline, the plant is usually severely damaged. Do note the wet spots, and provide better drainage and new soil before replanting.

Leaf spots may also be a problem on many plants. They are usually caused by a fungus encouraged by the hot rainy weather. Where needed, a copper-containing fungicide or synthetic product made for leaf spots on your plants can be applied. Quite often, leaf spots are minor and can be ignored. Summer pests often include aphids, caterpillars, grasshoppers, and scales.

JULY

VINES, GROUND COVERS, & ORNAMENTAL GRASSES

PLANNING

Perhaps you don't have a lot of room but you still want to enjoy vines, ground covers, and ornamental grasses. You can use just a small area of tilled soil in the landscape, or you might try growing some of these plants in containers. One nice thing about container plantings is that you are in charge of just about everything. You can give the plant the best soil, watering, and feedings. You can also spot the insects and other pests affecting the plants much more quickly, and many container gardens can be moved from one area of the landscape to another.

• Add container gardens to the patio. You might try using a ground cover alone or combine it with flowering annuals and perennials.

• Set a vine in a container and allow it to climb a wall or add a trellis to create a stand-alone display.

• Grow vines on a balcony in containers, and allow them to climb railings or hang down over the edge.

• Grow ground covers and ornamental grasses in containers to set at entrances or along walkways.

If you wish, a nice container planting can be brought indoors during parties. Let the visitors try to figure out how you grew this plant inside. Tropical plants in containers can be protected from the cold that often affects central and northern portions of the state.

PLANTING

Container plantings are fun to create. Just select your favorite plants at the local garden center, and pick out a pot that can contain the rootball plus some room to grow. You will most likely want a 5-gallon or larger container. If you want to combine several plants, a much larger container should be selected.

• Obtain a good potting soil. Select one that is loose and well drained.

Avoid backyard soils or mixtures that compact easily.

• Remove the plants from their pots.

If potbound, loosen the roots before planting.

• Set in the pot so the top of the rootball is 1 to 2 inches below the surface of the rim.

• Add soil to fill in around the roots.

• Water thoroughly to obtain good soil-to-root contact.

• Add a slow-release fertilizer to take some of the work out of plant care.

Mandevilla in patio containers

Most gardeners feed the plants for several months.

• Find the best location for your container garden. You need to make sure it has the proper exposure to light.

Many will have to provide protection from drying or salty winds.

CARE

Keep up with the growth of your landscape plantings. There is always trimming to do with the vines and ground covers to keep them inbounds. If you feel a lot of trimming is needed for the vines, maybe they do not have adequate room to grow. Consider expanding the trellis or just allowing them to ramble a little more.

Many ornamental grasses begin flowering during the early-summer months. The inflorescence is the attractive portion and should be left on the plants until it turns a brown color that is sometimes objectionable. Many gardeners like to cut and dry the flowering grassy portions to use in dried arrangements.

WATERING

Mother Nature is probably helping with the watering. You do have to check the more recent plantings for water needs or possibly overwatering. Where plants are flooded by the rains, consider gutters, swales, or other means of drainage to move the water away from the plantings. You may also consider building raised beds to keep the root systems dry.

Very few established plantings need special waterings at this time of the year. They are very busy making growth using the seasonal rains.

FERTILIZING

If you delayed or missed a planned feeding for summer, now is the time to apply the fertilizer. Most gardeners apply a general garden fertilizer to plantings where they would like to increase growth. You do have several other options when it comes to feeding the plantings:

1. Apply a light layer of composted manure over the surface of the soil or mulch. Fresh manure with bedding from farms may also be used. This supplies the mulch and nutrients needed for growth.

2. Select a liquid fertilizer product to drench over the soil or mulched beds.

3. Make manure tea to drench over the planted sites.

For container gardens, apply slow-release fertilizer at planting, then note on the calendar when another application will be needed. Feed them monthly with a liquid fertilizer at the container plant rate.

PROBLEMS

Plants making new growth are always susceptible to grasshoppers and caterpillars. It's best to check the plants during walks to look for these pests. If seen, they can be handpicked from the plants and destroyed. Most plantings can tolerate some defoliation from insects before pesticides are needed.

Some scale insects may also be active. The soft scale that hug the underside of leaves and stems are often active during the warmer months, sucking juices from plants. They are often first spotted by black sooty mold forming on the surface of leaves. Take a close look, and you may spot the brown to green insects on the plant portions. Where needed, scales and sooty mold can be controlled with an oil spray following label instructions.

AUGUST

VINES, GROUND COVERS, & ORNAMENTAL GRASSES

PLANNING

Many homeowners have pools, patios, and similar areas where low-growing plants and vertical vines are needed. You can quickly spot some of these areas, like the walls that have only a little space between the building and the sidewalk, or the area between the pool and the grass. What better places to use some of the plants featured in this chapter?

Just pick the lower-growing ground covers to fill in the small spaces where you would still like to look out over the landscape or see the kids at play. You might include **Asiatic jasmine**, **ivies**, **lily turf**, **Mexican heather**, **wandering Jew**, **mondo grass**, and **wedelia**. Some of the ornamental grasses might fill in these areas, too, including **chalky bluestem**, **Elliott lovegrass**, and **great dame**.

Cover the walls in the small spots with plants that climb on their own, or give them something to cling to like a small trellis. Try to pick the smaller vines for a wall of the home, or make sure you have a wall with plenty of width. It's always best when constructing a trellis next to the home to keep it a few inches from the wall. This allows good air circulation, keeping moisture out of the inner rooms. Here are a few more suggestions when selecting the best plants for small areas:

- Pick a plant for the proper light level.
- Decide if you really want a plant with flowers that can attract bees or wasps. Bees and wasps can be a problem, especially near pools.
- Select plants that will stay inbounds and not need a lot of trimming.
- If quick cover is needed, select a plant that has lots of shoots beginning to climb or creep out over the ground.

PLANTING

Don't let the hot summer months keep you from adding plants to the landscape. Just be sure you have a well-prepared planting site. When digging the soil, examine the moisture content. If extra-dry, it may repel moisture and be hard to wet. If so, you need to perform a little more preparation than normal.

Work lots of organic material, especially compost, into the planting sites.

• Lower soil levels may be moist and more receptive to water. Till the soil deeply to mix layers of soil.

• Work lots of organic matter, especially compost, into the ground.

• Wet the area well before planting.

If the soil surface is still resistant to water, add a tablespoon of mild dish detergent to a gallon of water and sprinkle it over every 10 to 15 square feet of soil to be planted. Then water the ground.

• Build a 4- to 6-inch berm of soil around the new plants to catch and direct water into the ground through the rootballs.

• Form a mulch layer 2 to 3 inches thick over the surface of the soil.

• Water these plants individually as needed.

CARE

It's the last-of-the-season pruning time for **bougainvillea**. Give the plantings any trimming needed to keep them inbounds. The **bougainvillea** plants will be forming buds for winter bloom shortly, and all new growths should be near maturity. Other vines and ground covers that bloom during the spring should also get their last trimming of the year at this time.

WATERING

New plants need watering attention. Make sure the soil remains moist. Even though the summer rains produce lots of moisture, they may not occur every day. New plantings need water daily the first few weeks, then every other day for the following few weeks.

• Check to make sure rootballs are being moistened. A shriveling plant may simply be dry.

• When water is needed, apply $1/2$ to $3/4$ inch at each irrigation.

• Water during the early-morning hours.

FERTILIZING

Most plantings have adequate fertilizer to get them through the summer season. The next scheduled feeding for in-ground plantings is in September. If plants begin to yellow, you may have a moisture or pest problem. Where a plant appears to lack adequate fertilizer or you want to push growth, a light feeding or liquid fertilizer may be applied. Continue to feed container plantings at this time with a liquid fertilizer. Where slow-release fertilizers are being used, check the calendar for the next scheduled application.

PROBLEMS

Mealybugs often build up in the tips of growing plants and at the bases of leaves. They are not a major pest, but they may be found in tropical plants. The insects are small and a white to grayish color. They build white-covered egg masses among the foliage. Where present, they can be controlled with oil or synthetic insecticides, following label instructions.

Other pests feeding on the landscape plantings include grasshoppers, caterpillars, and scale insects. You may also notice some leaf spots and root rot problems encouraged by summer rains.

SEPTEMBER

VINES, GROUND COVERS, & ORNAMENTAL GRASSES

Train vines to a support to create a dramatic focal point in your garden.

PLANNING

Mailboxes are always spots in the landscape that could use some attention. What have you done to beautify yours? Maybe you have added a shrub or two. Others just let the grass grow around the area. How about a vine that climbs a trellis or the concrete portion of some boxes?

Select a small vine or creeping ground cover. Some that have been used are the **allamanda**, **mandevilla**, **Confederate jasmine**, and **Asiatic jasmine**. What's important is that the plantings be kept confined to a relatively small area. If you wish, a trellis can be built in back of the mailbox or as a feature to enclose the box for bigger vines.

Vines can also be used on arbors at the entrances to gardens. Just think about walking into your landscape through a vine-covered path. It would certainly have a cooling effect during the summer season. Some gardeners also like to use vines at entrances and over patios.

• Make sure you use only the number of plants needed to fill a trellis or arbor.

A number of vines may look good in the beginning, but they will eventually become quite entangled and compete for growing room.

• Give the vines needed support, and direct the growth to fill the desired area as quickly as possible.

• Avoid vines that produce large fruits or have flowers that might produce stains and debris over patios and other areas where you do not want a cleaning problem.

• Make sure the trellis is strong and of rot-resistant material.

You will not want to be replacing or repairing the structures too often.

PLANTING

The weather is becoming a little cooler, and it's easier to spend some time outdoors performing needed plantings. The garden centers are restocking plants for the fall season. Any of the vines, ground covers, and ornamental grasses can be planted at this time of the year. Just review the best planting techniques:

• Control weeds that have grown during summer by hand-pulling or spraying with a nonselective herbicide that permits replanting shortly after use.

• Loosen soil in the area where one or more plants will be added.

• Work in lots of organic matter if you have sandy or clay soils.

• Set the plant in the ground at the same depth it was in the container, with the top of the rootball even with or slightly above the ground.

• Fill in around the rootball with water and soil at the same time.

• Water well, and apply a mulch over the soil surface.

CARE

Sometimes the vines just get completely out of control. They overgrow a fence or climb a tree, and it's time to do some major pruning. The best time to do rejuvenation pruning is probably after they flower, but you can actually do the trimming just about anytime the plants are making growth.

- Remove all dead and declining vine portions.
- Cut back the vines well beyond the edge of the trellis.
- If all the growth is at the top of the vine, trim it back a foot or more to where you want the new foliage to begin.
- Make needed repairs to the trellis or other support structure.

Such a heavy pruning may delay flowering for a year. Try to perform the trimming so much of the growth will reach maturity before severe winter weather in central and northern portions of the state.

WATERING

The rainy season comes to an abrupt end in September. You may have to take over the watering around mid-month or earlier if the rains fail. The only plants that usually need special waterings are recent transplants and container plants. When watering, make sure the soil is thoroughly moistened.

FERTILIZING

Check your calendar—it's time for the last feeding of the year if it's needed to maintain growth and green leaf color. Many vines, ground covers, and ornamental grasses receive adequate nutrients from decomposing mulches and feedings given nearby plants. If the plantings are growing vigorously, you might think of skipping this feeding. You can use one of several feeding techniques.

- Scatter a granular general garden fertilizer over the surface of the soil or mulch within the planted areas.
- Use a slow-release granular fertilizer among the plantings.
- Apply a layer of manure following rates on the bag, or use fresh manure with bedding to create a mulch layer.
- Apply a liquid fertilizer over the plants and soil as instructed on the label. Gardeners may also use a manure tea in this manner.

After feeding, most products are best watered into the soil to move the nutrients into the root zone.

PROBLEMS

Caterpillars are often heavy during the fall months. Many have been building large populations during the summer. Check for chewed leaves. Some caterpillars can be hard to see, as they may drop from the leaves or hide during the day. Where needed, handpick and destroy, or apply a *Bacillus thuringiensis*-containing insecticide following label instructions. Other pests active in the landscape include grasshoppers, mites, leaf spots, and scales.

OCTOBER

VINES, GROUND COVERS, & ORNAMENTAL GRASSES

PLANNING

Look for areas under trees that might support shade-tolerant ground covers. These plants thrive in the lower-light areas and grow enough roots to absorb needed water and nutrients. Some, like **bromeliads**, have limited roots systems, but they also have special cups of foliage that collect water and nutrients. Others, like the **wandering Jew**, **purple heart**, and **oyster plant**, exist with a root system that is close to the surface.

- Keep new plantings back from the base of the tree. Give them 2 to 4 feet of growing room before they reach the trunk.

Use mulches up close to the tree.

- Space the plants so they have plenty of room to grow.

Many have creeping growth habits, and just a few plants can fill a large space after a season or two of growth. Plants with more upright growth should be planted with the leaves just about touching.

- A 2-inch layer of soil can be added over a protruding root system. This extra soil may give the new plants some competition-free growing room to get started.
- Keep the new plantings moist but not too wet.

In shade, it is easy to overwater and encourage root and stem rot organisms.

- Maintain a 2- to 3-inch layer of mulch to control weeds and keep the soil moist.

Many ground covers can be planted in containers to use in the shade locations. Tropical types can be used in the cooler regions and moved to a protected area when frosts or freezes are expected.

PLANTING

There is no excuse not to get outdoors and enjoy the landscape, and it's an ideal time to make any needed plantings. You may have divided some plants earlier and added them to containers, or you may have made a few purchases and just left them in the pots. Use the cooler stress-free planting time to add them to the landscape. If some of these plants will be replacements, make sure you know why the previous plants were not appropriate, or why the plants declined and died. Was it due to poor drainage or maybe a disease? Did a plant just grow too large and out of control? Make sure you are not just repeating a problem.

Purple heart

- If the site was poorly drained, add new soil to the planting site to create a raised bed. Consider changing the drainage pattern by adding gutters or swales to the area.
- When a plant dies in the area to be replanted, determine the cause. Then consider adding a different type of plant. Diseases often build up in a soil and may reinfect new plantings of the same type.

The best way to prepare a previously planted site is by tilling the soil deeply. If soilborne organisms were at fault, consider removing the soil from the root zone. Work in lots of organic matter to rejuvenate the planting site. Then you are ready to plant, using good transplant procedures.

CARE

Complete all needed trimming this month. Many of the ornamental grasses will be making their fall display. If you wish, cut some of the long inflorescence to dry or use in fall displays. When the flower stalks fade, many turn brown and can be cut from the plants as needed.

WATERING

Check new plantings regularly for needed moisture. When the soil feels dry to the touch, it's time to water. Make sure the water is wetting the rootballs. If a plant dries too quickly, you may need to give it extra attention. One good way of making sure it gets the needed water is with a 4- to 6-inch soil berm built around the edge of the rootball. This catches and directs the water through the rootball and out into the soil.

- Water during the early-morning hours.
- Apply 1/2 to 3/4 inch of water.
- Use soaker hoses or microsprinklers that put the water where it is needed.
- Maintain a mulch over the root system.

FERTILIZING

If you missed the September feeding or just delayed the application, there is still time to supply needed nutrients to the plants. You can make quick work of the feeding by using a handheld spreader. Just walk among the plants to apply the needed amount of a general garden fertilizer. It can be performed so quickly you can make the treatment during a football game's half-time intermission. A number of fertilizers are available. Just follow the rate on the bag for general landscape or lawn use. After feeding, it's a good idea to water the plantings to wash granules off the foliage and begin moving nutrients into the soil.

PROBLEMS

Gardeners may begin noticing a lot of leaf spots on the deciduous vines during the fall. Some, like the **trumpet creeper** and **Chinese wisteria**, are getting ready for winter, and some leaf spotting as the leaves begin to drop is normal. Even some of the evergreen types, including **mandevilla** and **coral vine**, are not as vigorous during fall and may develop brown to yellow portions. This is normal, and no control is needed. Pests you might be more concerned about are the grasshoppers, caterpillars, mites, and scale insects.

NOVEMBER

VINES, GROUND COVERS, & ORNAMENTAL GRASSES

PLANNING

Banks are always problem areas in a landscape, especially in Florida's sandy soils. You cannot plant these areas as you do others, and turf is always a problem to mow. Ground covers are one of the best solutions. Obviously, it's best not to till up a bank and then add the ground cover. The loose soil would wash away with the next rainfall. Planting on banks should occur with the least amount of soil preparation.

Start by picking your most durable ground covers. You want one that is going to grow quickly and form a dense covering. You also want a drought-tolerant plant with an extensive root system. Some to choose from are **Asiatic jasmine**, **beach morning glory**, **beach sunflower**, **Confederate jasmine**, **trailing lantana**, and **wedelia**.

- If the bank or slope has an established covering of grass or similar vegetation, apply a nonselective weed control product that permits replanting shortly after use.
- Mow or cut the declining vegetation to within a few inches of the ground.
- Where banks and slopes consist of bare ground, consider a covering of landscape fabric or a mesh-type product to prevent erosion.
- Determine the best spacing, and plant the new ground covers. Just open the holes, and set the plants in the ground at the proper depth.
- Add a hay or pine straw mulch that resists washing away.
- Until they are established, keep the plants moist with frequent handwatering.

PLANTING

It continues to be a good time for planting. Where possible, till up a planting site to add a number of ground covers or ornamental grasses. Sometimes you are only adding one or two plants to the landscape, and with these plants a lot of soil preparation is really not needed. For a single vine or a grass used as an accent, make planting as simple as possible.

- Dig a hole a little bigger than the rootball.

If the soil is compacted and of poor quality, then a larger hole is needed.

- Remove the plant from the pot, and check for a rootbound condition. If the roots are entangled, loosen some around the outer edge of the ball.
- Set the plant in the ground with the top of the rootball even with the surface of the soil. Fill in with water and soil at the same time.
- Build a 4- to 6-inch-high berm of soil around the edge of the rootball.
- Water and add a 2- to 3-inch layer of mulch.

Now, wasn't that easy?

CARE

Most landscape plant growth is slowing. If it's not the cool weather, it's the shorter days that are reducing the growth. Your job is to remove ground cover growths and vines that may be interfering with landscape movement or affecting other plantings. Very little pruning is needed at this time. Weeds don't stop, however, and gardeners have to get ready for a whole new group of cool-season annuals. You can get the jump on these weeds.

Check soil dryness by feeling it—you be the judge, not the timer.

- Maintain mulch layers at the 2- to 3-inch thickness.
- Handpull or hoe out the weeds before they grow too large.
- Apply a preemergence herbicide before seeds begin to germinate.
- Spot-kill with a nonselective herbicide that permits use near growing plants.

WATERING

Cool weather means less watering will be needed. Do check the new plantings, and make sure the soil remains moist. Waterings can probably be reduced to every few days. You be the judge—when the surface soil begins to dry, turn on the irrigation. Well-established plants seldom need watering, except for container plantings. Check the plants in containers daily, and water when the surface soil begins to be dry to the touch.

FERTILIZING

Feeding time is over for the year except for container plantings. Continue feedings on a monthly schedule using a liquid fertilizer. If slow-release granules were applied during fall, another feeding will not be needed until spring.

PROBLEMS

Mites can remain a pest during the fall months. These arachnids love the dry weather. Luckily, most vines and ground covers are fairly resistant. Unless you have a major infestation, these pests can be ignored. Mealybugs may develop as growth slows for fall. Plantings in the shady spots are more likely to become affected. Soap sprays are often all you need for both mites and mealybugs. Do keep an eye out for caterpillars and a few remaining grasshoppers during fall.

DECEMBER

VINES, GROUND COVERS, & ORNAMENTAL GRASSES

PLANNING

If you need winter color, select vines and ground covers that bloom year-round. Vines like the **yellow allamanda** and **bougainvillea**, plus ground covers **beach sunflower**, **common lantana**, **Mexican heather**, and **wedelia** can bloom in warmish winter weather.

Allamanda

Place these plants in special spots:

- Along walkways where you rest and sit a while
- Near a patio where the plants can be easily seen by visitors
- In view of a window where the bright flowers bring a bit of the outdoors inside
- On a balcony to brighten the winter months

PLANTING

Shop your garden center early because they often reduce general stock in December to display holiday plants. You can keep plants in containers for a while if the time is not right for planting.

CARE

Old flowers provide food for wildlife and nesting materials for birds. Some gardeners like the meadow look of the browning flower stems and leaves as they head into the cooler months, but if you think they're ugly, you can cut them back. Very little pruning is needed except for vines that may blow off a trellis or arbor.

WATERING

When it's a little cooler outside, it's a lot easier to skip the waterings. Check all plantings for adequate water. Days may add up to weeks, and all of a sudden you may see that some of the plants are dry. This is a good time to check the irrigation system.

Water as needed to maintain a moist soil among new plantings. Older plantings can usually go weeks between waterings. Container plantings can usually skip a day or two.

FERTILIZING

Don't feed in-ground plantings. If you have container plantings, you can stretch the time between feedings to four to six weeks. Skip feedings if plants are dormant.

PROBLEMS

Scale insects may be quite evident in winter on older growths. Look for the white to brown flecks or bumps on foliage and stems to signal scale infestations. The cooler months are a good time to control these pests with an oil spray. Just make sure the temperatures are above 40 degrees Fahrenheit at the time of application. Coat all portions of the plant to achieve the best control.

In warmer locations of the state where plants are continuing growth, check for mites, mealybugs, and aphids that may need control.

FLORIDA PEST CONTROL

Aphids are small pear-shaped insects, variously colored, that feed only on new growth. Look for them in buds and new leaves. They often produce lots of sap and excreta that attract ants and encourages growth of the black sooty mold fungus. A soap spray is usually all that is needed for control. If lady beetles are present, a control may not be needed.

Blackspot produces dark spots, often with a yellow halo, on roses; affected leaves drop and plant vigor is affected. You can help keep this disease under control by watering only during the early-morning hours to allow the foliage to dry during the day. Control with fungicides as needed especially during rainy weather.

Borers are insects or insect larvae that feed in the woody parts of plants. Borers may be an indication of more severe problems like diseases that affect roots and trunks to weaken the plants. Check for sap or sawdust around the trunks of trees and dying branches. If only minor, the damage from borers can be ignored—the plant may have the problem under control. When borer activity appears severe, some control can be achieved with sprays obtained at garden centers. Follow label instructions. Look for major causes of plant stress and correct while controlling the borer attacks. If borers persist, have the plants checked by a specialist. Severe damage or infections may make plant removal necessary.

Brown patch is a turf disease caused by a fungus living in most soils. The fungus is active during warmish late-fall and early-spring weather in moist soils and locations with poor air movement. The disease causes large, brown, somewhat circular areas to develop. Control with a fungicide available at local garden centers if severe.

Caterpillars are the immature stages of moths or butterflies. They chew plant foliage, stems, or flowers, and are of varying sizes and colors. They are best handpicked from the plants and destroyed, or the plants can be treated with a *Bacillus thuringiensis*-containing natural insecticide or a synthetic product, following label directions. Some gardeners allow caterpillars to feed on their plants, as many turn into attractive moths or butterflies.

Chinch bugs, common in St. Augustinegrass, are insects that cause yellow spots in the lawn that gradually enlarge. Adults are 1/5 inch long, and black with white crossed wings. Immature stages are red and the size of a pinpoint. Check sunny warm areas for small yellowing patches that start to turn brown and enlarge. Look for the chinch bugs at the edge of a yellow-and-green area. They overwinter in all areas of Florida and begin mounting large populations in spring. When the insects are damaging the turf, treat just the affected areas and a few feet around them with a lawn insecticide labeled for chinch bugs. The damage usually continues for two weeks after the pests are under control due to toxins placed in the runners by the bugs. Replace severely damaged turf.

Cutworms are the larvae of various moths. They feed on and destroy a wide variety of plants, often chewing through stems near the ground as if cutting them off. Check for cutworms when preparing

new beds. If present, handpick from the beds or treat the soil with a general insecticide labeled for preplant application. A paper or cardboard collar placed at the base of the plant around the stem can also help control cutworms.

Dollar spot is a fungal disease that can attack any lawn but is often seen in the Bermuda turf. It's often an indication of a weak turf affected by drought or pest problems. Usually a fertilizer application helps the grass outgrow the fungus.

Garden fleahoppers are 1/16-inch-long black insects that will suck juices from marigold, globe amaranth, verbena, and similar flowers plus some vegetables and herbs. The damage resembles mite injury, so look for the little black bugs. Use a general garden insecticide for piercing-and-sucking-type insects labeled for your plants as needed.

Grasshoppers are large-legged brown-to-bright-green insects up to 2 inches long that chew plant foliage. Some damage can be ignored. Otherwise, handpick them or apply a synthetic insecticide labeled for chewing insects on your plants.

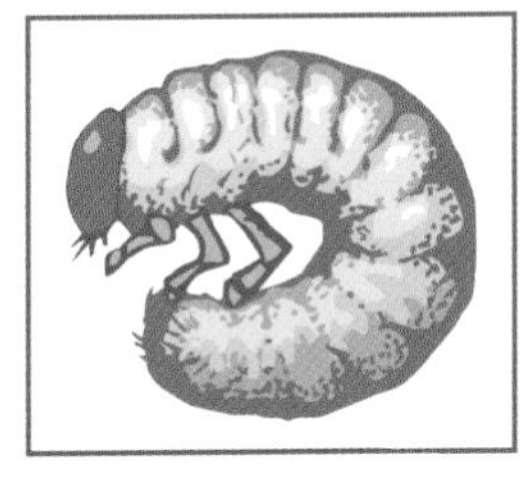

Grubs have not been a common Florida pest for years, but recently this immature beetle stage has been damaging some turf. The grubs are white with a brown head and have three pairs of legs at the front of the body. They live underground feeding on roots. Look for grass that is yellowing in patches. Use a shovel to dig up a layer of sod an inch or two below the surface. Sometimes the sod just rolls back when affected. Look for the white grubs. If two or more are present per square foot of turf, you need a control. Apply a granular or liquid insecticide labeled for grubs that is available at your garden center. Note products generally have to be watered into the soil to be effective . . . but follow the instructions on the label.

Lawn caterpillars chew grass blades, making a lawn appear as if it has been closely mowed. Several types might be active. The three most common are the sod webworm, armyworm, and grass looper. Check the grass blades—if they appear to be chewed, you most likely have a lawn caterpillar. Armyworms and grass loopers feed on the blades during the day and sod webworms at night. During the day, sod webworms hide in the grass near the ground. When caterpillars are at work, try a natural control containing the *Bacillus thuringiensis* organism. Synthetic pesticides for lawn caterpillar control are also available. Treat only the infested area and a few feet around it. Keep damaged areas moist and the grass will usually grow back.

Leaf spots are various-shaped yellow to brown spots caused by fungal activity on leaves. Many are normal and can be ignored, as the fungus may attack older plant foliage as it declines and drops. Where new and healthy leaves are infected and the fungus is affecting the quality of the plant, control with a copper-containing fungicide or synthetic fungicide according to label directions for your plants. Ligustrums and pittosporums are notorious for having cercospora and other fungal problems. Some have to be tolerated, as just about all these plantings seem to have a little of the fungus present.

Leafminers are the immature stages of a moth or fly that tunnel between the leaves of plants. Some damage should be tolerated. Some control can be obtained by hanging sticky boards near plantings in flower, vegetable, or herb gardens. Where needed, apply a properly labeled synthetic insecticide.

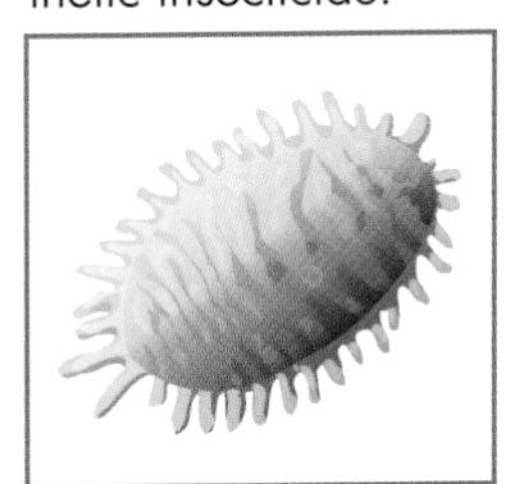

Mealybugs are white insects about 1/8 inch or smaller, often found in the buds and leaf angles of plants. They suck juices from plants and encourage the growth of sooty mold. Look for a general decline in plant vigor. Wash off with a soap solution, daub with rubbing alcohol on a swab, or treat with a natural insecticidal soap product. You may also control with an

oil or synthetic insecticide as needed, following label instructions for your plants.

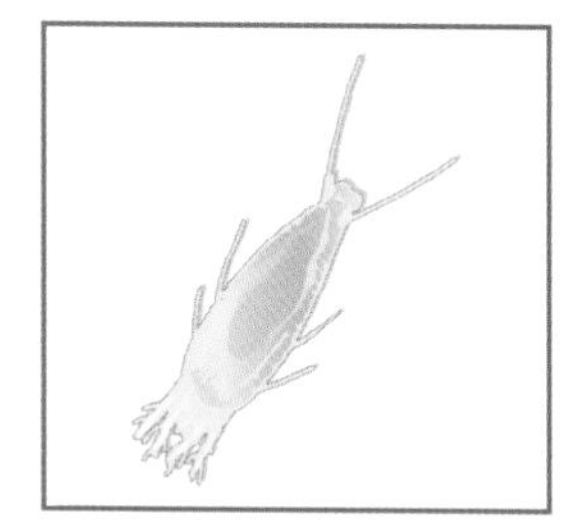

Mites are small pinpoint-sized arachnids that are prevalent during warm, dry weather or on plants kept in the home. They suck juices from plant foliage. Damage is often first noted as a yellowing to browning of the foliage. You need a hand lens to see these pests but can often spot the transparent skins on the leaves with the unaided eye. Check for mites under leaves. They are often found near the veins of the leaves at first and then they spread out. They may be clear or orange in color; some make webs. Control with a strong stream of water, soapy solution, or soap spray. Oil and synthetic sprays may also be used on some plants, following label instructions.

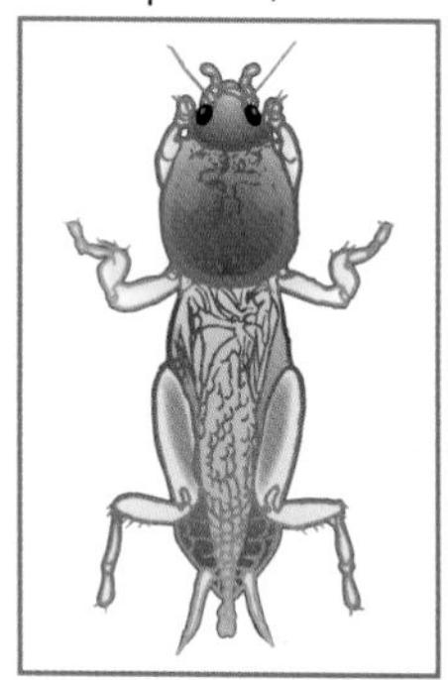

Mole crickets are often found in all lawns but are especially damaging to bahia and Bermuda lawns. The adult mole crickets lay eggs that start hatching in May. When the ground begins to feel soft under the grass, it's the first hint the insects may be present. Monitor the populations in your lawn with a soap flush starting in May. Mix $1^1/2$ tablespoons of a mild dish detergent in 2 gallons of water, and sprinkle over 4 square feet of turf. If the young crickets are present, they will scramble to the soil surface in a matter of minutes. When two or more mole crickets are spotted in a square foot of lawn, it's time to apply a control. Apply a mole cricket bait or liquid control available from garden centers, following label instructions. They should be applied in late afternoon after any rains. The mole crickets come to the surface of the soil at night to feed. Sprays are also available. Follow label instructions for effective control. Note that some sprays should be watered into the soil but others are left on the surface.

Mushrooms and toadstools may produce fruiting bodies on the surface of the soil during damp weather. Don't worry too much when you see them. They cause no harm and can be picked from a lawn and garden or knocked over to shrivel.

Palmetto weevil is a large beetle-like insect that usually attacks transplanted cabbage, Canary Island date, Mexican fan, and a few other palm species, causing death. The pest can also attack any palm under stress due to poor growing conditions or other pests. Contact your local Extension Service office to obtain the latest control recommendations.

Powdery mildew is a common disease of many landscape plants that can be seen as a white covering on the surface of foliage and buds. The disease affects the appearance of the plants, reduces vigor, and can distort growth. Most plants are susceptible to this powdery-looking fungus, but only a few including roses, gerbera and some crape myrtles have a real problem. When it becomes severe, try a copper fungicide or one of the synthetic fungicides available at local garden centers, following label instructions.

Root knot nematodes are microscopic roundworms that feed on plant roots causing swollen portions to form. Nematodes reduce plant vigor and cause the plants to decline. Many vegetables and annual flowers are affected. Try planting nematode-resistant varieties or practicing soil solarization during the summer in gardens. Check with your Extension Service for new products that might be developed for nematode control.

Scales are yellow, green, or dark-colored insects that have a waxy coating and cluster on leaves and stems. They range in size from a pinhead to a dime. Most can be easily scraped off a leaf or stem with a fingernail to reveal the insect under the

covering. They are often hard to see and may be hidden under foliage. Some contribute to a black sooty mold. Wash off or control with a soap, oil, or synthetic insecticide spray. Follow label instructions to determine which plants can be treated with each product. When using oils, make sure you cover all portions of the plant and especially under the leaves. Winter is a good time to use oil sprays for scale insect control. The products are of low toxicity and are very effective at eliminating scale populations. Use oils when temperatures are above 40 degrees Fahrenheit and below 85. Oil sprays also remove the sooty mold that frequently accompanies scale infestations, but do not expect the scale or sooty mold to drop rapidly from the plants. Each is firmly attached and wears away with time.

Slime mold is a fungus present on turf during damp periods, usually in late spring or early summer. It is scary looking, producing a gray covering over the surface of the leaves, but it is harmless. Just use a broom to sweep it off, or wash it away with water.

Slugs and snails are slimy pests that may or may not have a shell. They love leafy crops and come out during warm moist weather to chew holes in plant leaves. Look for slime trails in the morning as the first hint of their presence, then hunt for them at night. Handpick from the plants, lure into shallow containers of beer, or use a synthetic snail and slug bait purchased at a garden center following label instructions.

Sooty mold is a gray to black fungus associated with aphids, mealybugs, scale, and other piercing-sucking insects. Loosen with a soap spray or treat with an oil spray to control the pests associated with the sooty mold following label instructions for your plant type.

Stem cankers appear on the stems of your plants as gray to brown dead areas. Sometimes the bark is loose or cracked in the affected areas. This is where the fungus is living and causing the stem to decline. Prune out all canker portions, cutting back into healthy growth. Sterilize your pruning shears between cuts. Apply a fungicide made for your plant after pruning.

Take-all root rot is a fungus that affects stressed lawns. No fungicides have been found effective, and the disease may run rampant during the summer months. Lawns that receive too much water, are competing with other plants, have nematode problems, and have been under general stress are very susceptible. Here is the best way you can fight this disease: Make sure the lawn is mowed at the proper length. This is normally the highest setting. If take-all root rot is diagnosed, apply light but frequent liquid fertilizer applications. When turf declines due to the disease, remove the old grass, till the soil deeply, and reestablish new sod. Try to eliminate any cultural problems that may weaken the turf.

Thrips are very small insects, about the size of a thread, that attack flowers and some plant foliage. Your first hint of damage may be buds not opening properly and developing brown edges. Thrips are real spoilers of gardenias and roses. Remove a flower and pull it apart to see the very small clear to brownish thrips. Select an insecticide labeled for thrip control to treat the flower buds.

Whiteflies are small fly-like insects, snow-white in color, that live among foliage. They have a yellowish immature stage that forms on the underside of the leaves. Control with a soap or oil spray according to label instructions for your plants. Repeat sprays are usually needed.

CYCADS OF FLORIDA

Gardeners often call cycads "palms." The plants do look like palms, but they are in a group all by themselves. This is an ancient group of plants many of which were present when the dinosaurs roamed the earth.

It may be hard to believe but cycads are more closely related to pines, cypress, junipers, and podocarpus than the palms; at best, palms are very distant relatives. Still, gardeners usually refer to cycads as palms and they are treated like palms.

What really amazes many gardeners is the flowering habits of the cycads, which is most noticeable in the larger-growing species including the dioon and king and queen sagos. All cycad plants are either male or female and produce unique flowers after a maturation period of as many as 8 to 10 years. At this time the male plants produce a cream-to-yellow pinecone-shaped inflorescences, often several feet tall. They last only a few weeks and then shrivel. The female plants produce a rounded-to-oblong brown cone up to a foot

or more in diameter that remains for up to a year until the seeds mature.

Taller growing cycads are best used as accent plants. Give them plenty of room as they usually grow as wide as they are tall. As noted in the table, many also have very sharp leaf portions. So keep them away from walkways plus areas frequented by children and family pets. Lower growing selections are often planted in clusters and used as ground covers or small accent features.

Considering many cycads have grown on Earth for millions of years, they are survivors. Care consists of feedings with a general garden fertilizer or palm fertilizer up to three times a year—usually once in spring, summer, and early fall. Some cycads appear to have a high need for manganese and develop shriveling brown growths and spots on the leaves when deficient. A one-time use of a product containing manganese found at garden centers usually corrects this decline.

Cycad plants are drought tolerant and once established can usually exist with natural rainfall. All make the best growth when watered during the very dry weather. It's also best to keep the soil mulched.

Pests usually consist of mealy bugs and scales. In recent years, cycad scale has attacked the king sagos and caused major decline. Gardeners have been able to gain some control with repeated natural oil sprays. New products are being released for this scale so contact your local Extension Agent to learn more about the available controls

Common Cycads of Florida

Name	Area of Florida	Leaves	Height (Feet)	Light Needs	Growth Habit	Best Uses
Cardboard Plant	CS	Feather-shaped cardboard-like to 3 feet	2–3	Sun, filtered sun	Multiple stems	Ground cover
Dioon	CS	Feather-shaped sharp to 4 feet	6–8	Sun,	Single trunk	Accent
Florida Coontie	NCS	Feather-shaped leathery to 3 feet	2–3	Sun,	Multiple stems	Ground cover
King Sago	NCS	Feather-shaped sharp to 4 feet	10–12	Sun,	Multiple trunks	Accent
Queen Sago	CS	Feather-shaped flexible to 5 feet	10–15	Sun,	Single trunk	Accent

BIBLIOGRAPHY

Black, Robert J. and Edward F. Gilman. *Your Florida Guide to Bedding Plants: Selection, Establishment and Maintenance.* Gainesville, FL: University Press of Florida, 1996.

Black, Robert J. and Kathleen C. Ruppert. *Your Florida Landscape, a Complete Guide to Planting and Maintenance.* Gainesville, FL: Institute of Food and Agricultural Sciences, University of Florida, 1995.

Brandies, Monica Moran. *Herbs and Spices for Florida Gardens.* Wayne, PA: B. B. Mackey Books, 1996.

Broschat, Timothy K. and Alan W. Meerow. *Betrock's Reference Guide to Florida Landscape Plants.* Cooper City, FL: Betrock Information Systems, Inc., 1991.

Chaplin, Lois Trigg and Monica Moran Brandies. *The Florida Gardener's Book of Lists.* Dallas, TX: Taylor Publishing Company, 1998.

Editors of Sunset Books and Sunset Magazine. *Sunset National Garden Book.* Menlo Park, CA: Sunset Books, 1997.

Ferguson, Jim. *Your Florida Dooryard Citrus Guide.* Gainesville, FL: Institute of Food and Agricultural Sciences, University of Florida, 1995.

Gilman, Edward F. and Robert J. Black. *Your Guide to Shrubs: Selection, Establishment and Maintenance.* Gainesville, FL: University Press of Florida, 1999.

Gilman, Edward F. *Betrock's Florida Plant Guide.* Hollywood, FL: Betrock Information Systems, 1996.

Gilman, Edward F. *Trees for Urban and Suburban Landscapes.* Albany, NY: Delmar Publishers, 1997.

Hoyer, Mark V., Daniel E. Canfield, Jr., Christine A. Horsburgh, and Karen Brown. *Florida Freshwater Plants: a Handbook of Common Aquatic Plants in Florida Lakes.* Gainesville, FL: Institute of Food and Agricultural Sciences, University of Florida, 1996.

BIBLIOGRAPHY

Koehler, Philip G., Donald E. Short, and William H. Kern Jr. *Pests in and around the Florida Home.* Gainesville, FL: Institute of Food and Agricultural Sciences, University of Florida, 1998.

MacCubbin, Tom. *Florida Home Grown: Landscaping.* Orlando, FL: Sentinel Communications, 1987.

MacCubbin, Tom. *Florida Home Grown 2: The Edible Landscape.* Orlando, FL: Sentinel Communications, 1989.

MacCubbin, Tom and Georgia B. Tasker. *Florida Gardener's Guide.* Franklin, TN: Cool Springs Press, 1997.

McCarty, L. B., Robert J. Black, and Kathleen C. Ruppert, editors. *Florida Lawn Handbook.* Gainesville, FL: Institute of Food and Agricultural Sciences, University of Florida, 1995.

Meerow, Alan W. *Betrock's Guide to Landscape Palms.* Cooper City, FL: Betrock Information Systems, Inc., 1992.

Ogden, Scott. *Garden Bulbs for the South.* Dallas, TX: Taylor Publishing Company, 1994.

Stephens, James M.. *Vegetable Gardening In Florida.* Gainesville, FL: University Press of Florida, 1999.

Taylor, Walter Kingsley. *The Guide to Florida Wildflowers.* Dallas, TX: Taylor Publishing Company, 1992.

Watkins, John V. and Thomas J. Sheehan. *Florida Landscape Plants, Native and Exotic.* Revised Edition. Gainesville, FL: University Press of Florida, 1975.

PHOTOGRAPHY & ILLUSTRATION CREDITS

ILLUSTRATIONS

Bill Kersey, Kersey Design

PHOTOGRAPHY

Thomas Eltzroth: pages 7 (mandarin, top of page); 24 (viola, top of page, and cosmos, bottom of page); 32; 40; 44; 55 (calla lily, top of page); 63; 74; 78; 81 (lemon, top of page, and citrus planters, bottom of page); 96; 100; 106; 111; 113 (mango, top of page, and apple tree landscape, bottom of page); 126; 131; 138; 141 (tomato, top of page, and harvest bench landscape, bottom of page); 149; 155; 158; 169 (close-up view of zoysia, top of page, and Bermuda lawn landscape, bottom of page); 190; 196; 197 (bird of paradise, top of page); 212; 216; 225 (ixora, top of page, and camellia, bottom of page); 235; 241; 242; 274; 277; 278; 300; 302; 303; 304; 316

Neil Soderstrom: pages 36; 48; 71; 77; 80; 104; 128; 150; 165; 166; 208; 221; 223; 224; 239; 245; 246; 299; 308; 315

Jerry Pavia: pages 53; 68; 197 (tropical garden landscape, bottom of page); 205; 252; 266; 280; 284; 287 (mondo grass, top of page); 310; 312

Liz Ball and Rick Ray: pages 82; 125; 254; 287 (wintercreeper and fern landscape, bottom of page); 297

Andre Viette: pages 295; 306

Lorenzo Gunn: page 255 (southern magnolia, top of page); page 321 (sago palm, bottom of page)

Pam Harper: page 255 (live oak landscape, bottom of page)

Charles Mann: page 55 (crocosmia and dahlia, bottom of page)

Dency Kane: page 7 (orchid, middle of page)

Netherlands Bulb Association: page 60

PLANT INDEX

INDEX

INDEX

INDEX

INDEX

INDEX

INDEX

INDEX

INDEX

MEET TOM MACCUBBIN

Tom MacCubbin

Tom MacCubbin is known to gardeners in Florida through his radio, television, and newspaper contributions. An extension environmental horticulturist with the University of Florida in Orange County, MacCubbin has degrees in Horticulture from the University of Maryland. Readers are familiar with his question-and-answer gardening columns and feature articles for *The Orlando Sentinel,* while others may recognize him as a co-host of *Orange County Gardening* on cable television and weekly horticulture reports on Central Florida News 13. His radio program *Better Lawns & Gardens* is broadcast over twenty-three Florida stations.

The National Association of County Agriculture Agents has recognized his media contributions with numerous awards, including awards for the best state personal column, best news photo story, best news column, and best television program. Most recently, his *Better Lawns & Gardens* radio program was judged best in the nation for 1998; in 1999, he was presented the AT&T Communications Award in the Best Videotape/Television category as a regional winner for his role as co-host of *Orange County Gardening.* He has been honored with the Best Horticulture Writer Award by the Florida Nurseryman and Growers Association, and was granted the Garden Communicators Award by the American Nurseryman's Association.

MacCubbin is the author of two other books, *Florida Home Grown: Landscaping* and *Florida Home Grown 2: The Edible Landscape.* He is co-author of *Florida Gardener's Guide* published by Cool Springs Press.

Active in their community, MacCubbin and his wife Joan live near Apopka.

ENJOY THESE OTHER HELPFUL BOOKS FROM COOL SPRINGS PRESS

Cool Springs Press is devoted to state and regional gardening and offers a selection of books to help you enjoy gardening and bird watching where you live. Choose Cool Springs Press books with confidence.

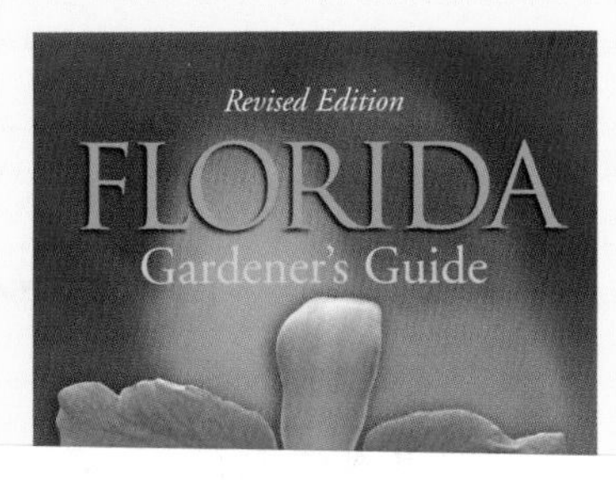

Tough Plants for Florida Gardens

Low Care, No Care, Tried and True Winners

Felder Rushing

Tough Plants for Florida Gardens
ISBN# 1-59186-120-9 • $24.99

Florida Bird Watching

A Year-Round Guide

Bill Thompson, III and the staff of Bird Watcher's Digest

Florida Bird Watching
ISBN# 1-59186-097-0 • $16.99

Cool Springs Press
A Division of Thomas Nelson Publishers
Since 1798
www.coolspringspress.net

See your garden center, bookseller, or home improvement center for these Cool Springs Press titles. Also, be sure to visit www.coolspringspress.net for more great titles from Cool Springs Press.

NATO
The Entangling Alliance

Robert Endicott Osgood

Never before, in times of peace, has a group of nations been so inextricably committed to a common interest as are the members of the North Atlantic Treaty Organization. For the United States, in particular, such deep entanglement with the affairs of other nations marks a revolution of foreign policy. Since its creation in 1949, NATO has been the outstanding political instrument of American security, but the extensive military and political collaboration it demands is a source of trouble as well as of strength.

Robert Osgood, in this book, concerns himself primarily with the military-strategic sources of NATO's troubles. But military strategy has become, he holds, far more than "the science and art of fighting battles." With the present hesitation to resort to open warfare, the political and psychological consequences of the disposition of armed forces may be the primary function of military strategy. Such vexing problems as the stabilization of deter-

Acknowledgments

I want to thank the Librarians and Curators at the following places for their help: Stanford University Library; The Library, Merton College, Oxford; Princeton University Library; Houghton Library, Harvard University; William Andrews Clark Memorial Library; Berg Collection, New York Public Library; University Library, University of California at Los Angeles; Humanities Research Center, University of Texas at Austin; Ashmolean Museum; Tate Gallery; National Portrait Gallery, London; Victoria and Albert Museum. I am grateful to Harvard University and Stanford University for financial assistance in preparing this book, and to the following people for other kinds of aid and advice: Sir John Rothenstein, David Magee, Julius Barclay, J. G. Riewald, Mrs. Nellie Guedalla. I am particularly grateful to Sir Rupert Hart-Davis for generously allowing me to consult his files on Beerbohm's caricatures, and for correcting several points in the manuscript, and to Robert H. Taylor for sharing his fine Beerbohm collection with me. For their comments on part or all of the book, I thank Harry Levin, Jerome Buckley, Peter Stansky, Bliss Carnochan, Claude Simpson, Ian Watt, David Levin, Gordon Ray. I was helped immensely by the attentive, constructive criticisms of Robert Polhemus, Craig Comstock, Wilfred Stone, and Barbara Gelpi, and by Herbert Weinstock's careful editing and shepherding. No kind of thanks can express the value of what my wife, Mary

Lowenthal Felstiner, brought to this book, while also doing her own work; we discussed virtually every paragraph as well as the general ideas, and she often saw when I could not see that the book was worth writing.

Grateful acknowledgment is made to Eva Reichmann for permission to quote from unpublished and previously published material now in the Estate of Sir Max Beerbohm, and to the following for permission to quote from the sources listed below:

Dodd, Mead & Company, Inc., and The Bodley Head, Ltd., London: From *Works* and *More,* by Max Beerbohm. From *Zuleika Dobson* by Max Beerbohm, copyright 1911 by Dodd, Mead & Company. Copyright renewed 1938 by Max Beerbohm.

E. P. Dutton & Co., Inc.: From *And Even Now* by Max Beerbohm. Copyright 1921 by E. P. Dutton & Co., Inc. Renewal 1949 by Max Beerbohm. From *A Christmas Garland* by Max Beerbohm.

Faber and Faber, Ltd., London: "Brennbaum," in *Collected Shorter Poems* by Ezra Pound.

The Stephen Greene Press, Vermont: From *Max in Verse: Rhymes and Parodies,* edited by J. G. Riewald.

William Heinemann, Ltd., London: From *Observations, Rossetti and His Circle, Seven Men,* and *Fifty Caricatures,* all by Max Beerbohm, published by William Heinemann, Ltd. Also for small quotations and captions by Beerbohm from various published sources.

Hutchinson Publishing Group, Ltd., London: From *Herbert Beerbohm Tree* by Max Beerbohm.

Alfred A. Knopf, Inc.: From *Yet Again* by Max Beerbohm, published 1923, 1951 by Alfred A. Knopf, Inc. From

Mainly on the Air by Max Beerbohm, copyright 1946 by Max Beerbohm. From *A Variety of Things* by Max Beerbohm, copyright 1928 and renewed 1956 by Max Beerbohm.

J. B. Lippincott Company, and Rupert Hart-Davis, Ltd., London: From *Max Beerbohm's Letters to Reggie Turner,* edited by Rupert Hart-Davis. Letters copyright © 1964 by Eva Reichmann.

Methuen & Co. Ltd., London: From *A Book of Caricatures* by Max Beerbohm © 1907 by Methuen & Co. Ltd.

New Directions Publishing Corporation: "Brennbaum," in *Personae* by Ezra Pound. Copyright 1926 by Ezra Pound.

R. Lang, Rye, New York: For a verse inscription by Max Beerbohm in a copy of *Caricatures of Twenty-Five Gentlemen* by Max Beerbohm.

Taplinger Publishing Co., Inc., and Rupert Hart-Davis, Ltd., London: From *Around Theatres,* copyright © 1969 by Eva Reichmann; from *Last Theatres,* copyright © 1970 by Eva Reichmann; from *More Theatres,* copyright © 1969 by Eva Reichmann. All by Max Beerbohm.

Acknowledgment is also made to the following for permission to use material from libraries and private collections:

Henry W. and Albert A. Berg Collection, The New York Public Library (Astor, Lenox, and Tilden Foundations); Harvard College Library; Princeton University Library, Rare Books and Special Collections; Charlotte Ashley Felton Memorial Library, Stanford Libraries, Stanford University; Robert H. Taylor Collection; University Library, University of California; William Andrews Clark Memorial Library, University of California, Los Angeles.

Contents

Illustrations

Asterisks appear in the text to indicate that a given illustration under discussion can be found in one of the plates listed below.

Plates *following page 170*

The following illustrations appear in the body of the text:

Grateful acknowledgment is made to Eva Reichmann and the Estate of Sir Max Beerbohm for their generous cooperation and for giving general permission to use the illustrations in this book, as well as particular permission for the following:

drawing (top), p. 30; p. 47 (orig. pub. in *Adam* Magazine); p. 99; Plate II, top (*Caricatures of Twenty-Five Gentlemen*); Plate II, bottom (Alfred Douglas: *Oscar Wilde and Myself*); Plate X, top and bottom (*Caricatures of Twenty-Five Gentlemen*); Plate XI, top and bottom (ibid.); Plate XIII, bottom right (*Yellow Book*); Plate XIV, top (*The Poets' Corner*); Plate XIV, bottom (*Caricatures of Twenty-Five Gentlemen*); Plate XVI, top and bottom (ibid.); Plate XVIII, bottom (*Cartoons: The*

Second Childhood of John Bull); Plate XIX, bottom (*The Poets' Corner*).

Special acknowledgment is also made to the following for the illustrations indicated:

Sir Cecil Beaton: Photograph of Max Beerbohm (Frontispiece)
Saul Steinberg: Drawing Hands © 1954 by Saul Steinberg, from *The Passport;* reprinted by permission of The Julian Bach Literary Agency, Inc.
Ashmolean Museum, Oxford: drawing, p. 211; Plates I, XVII, XXI (bottom), XXII
Berg Collection, New York Public Library: p. 145
Houghton Library, Harvard University: Plate XXI (top left)
The Humanities Research Center, The University of Texas at Austin: p. 193; Plate XXIV (top and bottom)
Merton College, Oxford University: p. 99; Plate XXI (top right)
Methuen & Co. Ltd., London: p. 108; Plates III (bottom) and XX (both from *A Book of Caricatures*)
National Gallery, London: Plates IV–V (top)
National Portrait Gallery, London: Plates IX, XV
Robert H. Taylor Collection: pp. 30 (bottom), 31, 35, 109, 119, 172, 173, 178, 215; Plates VII, X, XI, XVI
Robert Montgomery Collection: Plate XII
Stanford University Library: Plate XXIII
Tate Gallery, London: Plate VI
Victoria and Albert Museum, London: Plate IV (bottom)
William Andrews Clark Memorial Library, University of California at Los Angeles: p. 117
William Heinemann, Ltd., London: Plate VI (*Rossetti and His Circle*); Plates VIII (top and bottom), XV, XVIII (top) (all from *Fifty Caricatures*); Plate XIX (top) (*Observations*)

The two vignettes of Max Beerbohm by Aubrey Beardsley (pp. 39 and 41) are taken from *Bon-Mots* by Walter Jerrold (London: J. M. Dent; 1893–4). The portrait of Henry James by John Singer Sargent (Plate XIII, top right) originally appeared in *Academy* Magazine, London (1886).

The image of the finished dandy, the perfect stylist, the elfin wit, the incomparable Max, suggests that extended study can only overinterpret him. I want to put forward a different (though not entirely exclusive) image of Beerbohm's writings and drawings.

It was part of his creative economy to set up mirrors that have somewhat stymied criticism. He tells us that his "gifts are small," totally self-controlled, and do not bear much looking into; that his unphilosophic nature and limited experience inhibit any fundamental teaching about life; that he is an "ex-Arcadian," a focus for our own nostalgia; and that in watching himself write, he is his own best critic. We might feel these things even without his advertising them, but they are not necessarily the whole approach to Beerbohm. I have looked instead for the inner frame of his art.

In the way that assumptions and answers can become questions again, I found that organizing my views led me farther into understanding Beerbohm, and I have tried to make the structure demonstrate the argument of this book. While I take up his work more or less chronologically, I am convinced that the whole of it reveals a progression, an order that is peculiar not only to him but to much of comic literature. The three parts or stages of the book correspond to the way Beerbohm evolved, as well as to kinds of comic writing. First, pure invention or creation, in the form of prophecy, hyperbole, hoax, lying. Then criticism, analysis—that is, exposing the means of illusion, sorting out the artist from his work. And growing out of both stages, the parody of literature: of particular authors, and of everything from letter-writing manuals to modern slang, from the artist's illusions to the audience's.

These modes of writing—creation, criticism, parody—form a comic scheme. A trivial but exact illustration of it occurs in Beerbohm's 1893 letter to Reggie Turner, trying to persuade him to come to Oxford and stay in some modern rooms rather than some "lonely, loathsome, over-old rooms":

> I know a man called Fergusson who lived for two years in the latter. . . . He told me that people living there spend their time in prolonged gloom and discomfort and despair: that they can think of nothing but food decently cooked and decently served, and have a perpetual craving for hot water laid on, which never leaves them even in after-life. I know no such person as a matter of fact, but I am sure that all I have written has a large measure of truth.

Beerbohm was given to exuberant invention all his life, but schematically, the steps from "a man called Fergusson" to "no such person" to "a large measure of truth" can stand for a dialectic order in his writing between 1893 and 1918, an order which I trace in the three parts of the book.

A parody contains the whole comic scheme within itself, generating criticism within a creative, exaggerative act. And Beerbohm stands out by virtue of his parodies: those of James, Shaw, and others, as well as the protean voices he assumes for any purpose, everywhere in his writing, and the generic parody of fiction in his later work. Parody's range and force go beyond the usual function of criticizing a specific style: they epitomize literature as a whole. Like parody, any work of fiction begins by inventing a Fergusson and, with a more or less apparent technique, moves toward a measure of truth. Writers and what they wrote were Beerbohm's dominant theme. This preoccupation, this literary angle of vision, coinciding with his parodic talent, makes him a unique kind of feedback within literature. I do not think it misuses Beerbohm to see him this way, though it may mean neglecting some of his most appealing essays, such as "Hosts and Guests" or "Going Out for a Walk." His view of these subjects seems to me less characteristic than his view of his own vocation.

Alongside the discussion of his formal literary production and his preoccupation with art and artifice, which occurs mostly in chapters 1, 3, and 5, I deal with Beerbohm's other center of attention: namely, himself, and the idea of selfhood. Chapters 2, 4, and 6 trace his early self-advertising, his role as portrait caricaturist, and the writer/actor colluding in his own fictions.

Commentary on Beerbohm has divided the mask and the man. What we really have to consider is one person. An ironist, certainly: his caricatures and his dandyism put aesthetic in place of moral criteria, and as a writer he practiced giving away his own technique. But from all the published, private, and uncollected writing and drawing, which I run together in this study, one comic imagination emerges. The things I emphasize in Beerbohm's work may look unfamiliar. For instance, the review of *When We Dead Awaken* discussed in chapter 3 is only one of his many reviews of Ibsen, among nearly five hundred theater reviews that are less well known than his other writing. But Beerbohm's imagination entered into any occasion, however small or trivial: perhaps his enigmatic personality, which has puzzled biographers and critics, is to be found in the whole set of these verbal and visual occasions.

Various things have kept Beerbohm from being fully recognized: the brevity and the light, casual aspect of his writings, the divided sense one gets of him as writer and caricaturist, the lack in English of a critical approach to caricature, the topicality of caricature and of specific parody, and our own history since the end of the First World War, when he stopped writing. He was stuck by reputation in the fin-de-siècle and Edwardian eras, so our sense of him depends partly on how we regard those years—end, beginning, transition, interlude. The cultural history of the nineties especially needs more study, and I have not provided as much background as I would have liked. But I think Beerbohm himself helps organize our view of the time between Wilde's paradoxical *Intentions* in 1891 and the writing of *Ulysses*—that is, our view of what can be called both late-Romantic and modernist consciousness. Beerbohm enlivens things that were and still are problematic: the agency of the artist, the integrity of his work, its relation to a possible subject, and the active audience. It is no surprise to say that his graphic art takes the form of caricature. I mean to be almost as categorical in showing that his literary art, including novels, stories, essays, hoaxes, and casual pieces, takes the comprehensive and illuminating form of parody.

PART ONE

1

Masks

"A Defence of Cosmetics"

> Nay, but it is useless to protest. Artifice must queen it once more in the town . . . For behold! The Victorian era comes to its end and the day of sancta simplicitas is quite ended. The old signs are here and the portents to warn the seer of life that we are ripe for a new epoch of artifice.

The rhetoric is that of apocalypse, of the trembling of the veil, and it sweeps protest away with the cadences of prophecy. Max Beerbohm published "A Defence of Cosmetics" in the first number of the *Yellow Book,* April 1894, making an extravagant claim for the transfiguring power of artifice:

> For the era of rouge is upon us, and as only in an elaborate era can man, by the tangled accrescency of his own pleasures and emotions reach that refinement which is his highest excellence, and by making himself, so to say, independent of Nature, come nearest to God, so only in an elaborate era is woman perfect. Artifice is the strength of the world, and in that same mask of paint and powder, shadowed with vermeil tinct and most trimly pencilled, is woman's strength.

Beerbohm borrows the language of religious and political enthusiasm, elaborating a "renascence of cosmetics," a "revival," a "resurgence," a "rising tide." To carry his point he adds example upon example, dealing with gambling, the

Roman Empire, the court of Louis XVI, Victorian womanhood, physiognomy, stained glass. Masks will mean perfect individual realization, and Englishwomen beautifully made up will transform the world's taste and behavior, though old England may "lose her martial and commercial supremacy." Cosmetics, under Beerbohm's impetus, are made to seem the unacknowledged hope of civilization. He originally meant to call his first major publication "The Philosophy of Rouge." Changing to "A Defence of Cosmetics" got the polemic tone he wanted. The title enlists Sidney's and Shelley's defenses of poetry to imply that cosmetics manifest the creative imagination, and that those who use them are inspired "makers" of truth.

Beerbohm speaks of a "day," an "era," an "epoch," as if the eighteen-nineties were a distinct period with its own fate in its hands. With a kind of radical exclusiveness, he assumes that a late-Victorian spirit, an exhausted earnestness, can be identified simply and thus changed by a single force. The news in Beerbohm's essay comes in the language of revolution: artifice returns from exile to the kingdom, driving out the monarch herself. Like many twentieth-century cultural manifestoes, "A Defence of Cosmetics" gains its modernity by putting away the dull past.

Throughout his harangues, proofs, and digressions, Beerbohm holds to a principle of the mask, the face made by art. For Yeats, who developed the principle more fully and whose life was shaped by it, masks could serve to hide the inner self of the artist from a vulgar age, or to carry him beyond himself. They could also aestheticize experience, and crystallize man's personality. "Make yourself a work of art" was what Pater and Wilde were saying. Beerbohm follows them in describing the "combinations of line and colour" by which women will realize their moods. He stresses the formal power of cosmetics, a word that derives from *cosmos* and its root meaning of order and harmony.

The leading idea of masks has a corollary. With the

advent of cosmetics, "surface will finally be severed from soul." We will not degrade the face aesthetically by staring into it as if it were a barometer of emotion or character. Beerhohm says, in effect, that the surface is not superficial, and artifice is not artificial, if "superficial" and "artificial" are meant to imply the existence of some deeper, truer element in persons or in works of art. His notion is partly a defense, partly an affirmation. It avoids the demand for moral sincerity and high seriousness, and also argues the autonomy of man's creations, their freedom to stand only for themselves.

Cosmetics were a perfect choice to join the teachings of the moment, aestheticism and decadence. Midway in "A Defence of Cosmetics" occurs what I take to be both its principle and a good example of its method: "So fascinating an art too! So various in its materials from stimmis, psimythium and fuligo to bismuth and arsenic, so simple in that its ground and its subject-matter are one." To identify the ground with the subject—the form of a face with the content of cosmetic art—points conspicuously to the idea of art for art's sake. In 1894, sacred evidence for the identity of form with content lay in Théophile Gautier's sculptural images, and in Walter Pater's use of music as the type to which all art aspires. Beerbohm links the idea instead to a list of exotic ingredients for rouge. Max Nordau had just cited exotic detail as a symptom of diseased, decadent literature, in his fanatic and extremely popular diagnosis, *Degeneration.* And the process of making up was regarded as effete, nasty, something for actresses, harlots, and transvestites. So Beerbohm's argument comes in lurid, indefensible terms.

The essential gesture of the essay is hyperbole, a fantastically affected idea of aesthetic form. For Beerbohm, twenty-one years old and an undergraduate at Oxford, the gesture itself counted as much as the idea. It is impossible to separate the two in his presentation. At the time, the

Yellow Book represented a considerable venture, with a long opening story by Henry James and art work by Sir Frederick Leighton, President of the Royal Academy, as well as by Aubrey Beardsley. Against the assurances of the editor and publisher, in their prospectus, that the magazine would "preserve a delicate, decorous, and reticent mien," Beerbohm's essay stands out gaudily. It does have inherent faults; the layers of examples, the mannered prose, begin to pall after twenty pages, even if you read it as a spoof. Still, the gesture in "A Defence of Cosmetics"—that is, the attitude toward an idea—set Beerbohm in motion.

To regard his essay only as a jeu d'esprit or a spoof misses the point: it was a joke in which an idea resided. Beerbohm was impressionable, and attracted to aestheticism. At the same time, he was too independent to fall in wholeheartedly with the pretensions of Wilde's followers or to take an ethical position against them. It hardly matters that his mother and sisters would never have tolerated makeup, and that he had just fallen out of love with a young comedienne because she took to wearing rouge and powder. In the "Defence of Cosmetics" he found a mask to project the roles of aesthete and counter-aesthete at once. The ways in which art changes nature and the technique of parody both went on to supply Beerbohm's imagination in writing and caricature.

The Background

Before publishing in the *Yellow Book,* Beerbohm had written a short, anonymous appreciation of Oscar Wilde as well as an essay inspired by him. He had known Wilde since 1893, and Wilde's sayings had been current for years:

> In all unimportant matters, style, not sincerity, is the essential. In all important matters, style, not sincerity, is the essential.

> It is only the superficial qualities that last. Man's deeper nature is soon found out.
>
> The first duty in life is to be as artificial as possible. What the second duty is no one has as yet discovered.
>
> Only the shallow know themselves.

An impulse for the "Defence of Cosmetics" starts in these paradoxes. And the essays from Wilde's *Intentions* (1891), one of the few books Beerbohm admitted to reading at Oxford, all turn on kindred themes: "The Truth of Masks," on the illusionary and expressive power of stage costume; "The Decay of Lying," on the notion of exaggeration and the primacy of art over experience; "Pen, Pencil and Poison," on beauty as the criterion of ethics; "The Critic as Artist," on the importance of being and saying something interesting rather than doing it.

In his first piece on Wilde, Beerbohm managed as few people did to identify the nature of Wilde's wit, to comprehend "his sayings as ideas." The "Defence of Cosmetics" then made a program out of those ideas. Both men, writing about the place of art in the rest of human experience, stand at the end of a long swing from Blake on, a swing away from the accepted authority of the artist within society. Wilde's paradoxes and Beerbohm's exclusiveness about cosmetics compensate for this alienation. But by emphasizing the primary expressive power of art, they also represent the narrow channel of the Romantic imagination into the twentieth century. What separates Beerbohm from Wilde, who died in 1900, is the difference between paradox and parody. Wilde's reversal of norms and his personal embodiment of a mask tied him to the system he opposed, whereas in the wild exaggeration of "A Defence of Cosmetics" Beerbohm was riding out an idea.

With Aubrey Beardsley, he also shared a fin-de-siècle timeliness. Although nothing came of a book of "Masques" they planned to do together, Beerbohm was closely aware of Beardsley's work. Beardsley's 1894 drawings for Wilde's *Salome* took off from their model in the same way that Beerbohm's *Yellow Book* essay did. The first drawing for "The Toilette of Salome" was a delicate scene, irrelevant to the play, of beautiful slave boys, a masked Pierrot-coiffeur, rouge-pots, puffs, and on a bookshelf, Zola and *Les Fleurs du mal.* Beardsley had two figures in masks on the cover of the *Yellow Book*'s first number, and Volume III showed a courtesan making herself up. He did toilet scenes for *The Rape of the Lock, Lysistrata,* and his own *Venus and Tannhäuser.* A slightly insulting, languid poise marks these drawings, with their carved bottles, excessive robes, servile attendants, all surrounding the act of *maquillage.*

There is a kind of tableau vivant in the "Defence of Cosmetics," in which Beerbohm pictures a Roman lady at her toilet. The passage is tantamount to a verbal enactment of Beardsley's *Salome* designs, which had just been published:

> The slave-girls have long been chafing their white feet upon the marble floor. . . . Scaphion steps forth from among them, and, dipping a tiny sponge in a bowl of hot milk, passes it lightly, ever so lightly, over her mistress' face. . . . Now Calamis dips her quill in a certain powder that floats, liquid and sable, in the hollow of her palm. Standing upon tip-toe and with lips parted, she traces the arch of the eyebrows. . . . But why does Psecas abase herself? She is craving leave to powder Sabina's hair with a fine new powder. It is made of the grated rind of the cedar-tree, and a Gallic perfumer, whose stall is near the Circus, gave it to her for a kiss.

To want to trace out a picture in words, handle what had been imaginary, animate and sample each detail in turn, seems prurient in itself. The language here sounds like that of erotic daydreams materializing Beardsley's intricate shapes and rhythms. In 1894 Beardsley himself was beginning a similar piece of writing, *Venus and Tannhäuser*. His slightly sickening description of a toilet-scene, with its "tiny silver tongs, warm from the caresses of the flame," comes close to Beerbohm's style. Finally, Beardsley as a graphic artist looks less free than Beerbohm in dealing with cosmetics, perhaps because his technical intensity drove him farther into the world on the paper. His vision stayed with him, he could only keep or reject it.

Cosmetics inevitably call to mind a demimonde of courtesans and perverse sensuality shared in by Beardsley's drawings and the minor English verse of the period. Beerbohm on the theme is subtle and lively, in contrast with Arthur Symons mustering up weary urban passions: "Divinely rosy rouged, your face/Smiles, with its painted mouth,/Half tearfully, a quaint grimace." Symons wrote another, slightly less insipid poem called "Maquillage." When a reviewer objected that his poetry had an unwholesome smell of perfume, he replied (Beerbohm's defense had appeared by this time) with "A Word on Behalf of Patchouli" and the licitness of rouge as a literary subject. Years later Beerbohm parodied erotic, hothouse verse in his fictional character Enoch Soames, who writes to a young woman:

> Pale tunes irresolute
> And traceries of old sounds
> Blown from a rotted flute
> Mingle with noise of cymbals rouged with rust . . .

Behind the feverish attempt to reverse nature and spiritualize the tactile world, behind Symons, Soames, and "A Defence of Cosmetics," is the presence of Baudelaire. Though Beerbohm seldom mentioned him, it is striking how close Baudelaire's claims and his style come to Beerbohm's in this and other passages from "Éloge du Maquillage" ("Praise of Makeup," 1863):

> Who cannot see that the use of rice powder, so foolishly anathematized by naïve philosophers, has the aim and

> effect of removing from the complexion every spot that nature outrageously sowed there, and of creating an abstract unity in the grain and color of the skin—a unity which . . . makes the human figure like a statue, that is to say, a divine, superior being?

"A Defence of Cosmetics" has it that man can, "by making himself, so to say, independent of Nature, come nearest to God." Beerbohm's "Nature," capitalized, refers to something inactive, taken for granted, and "so to say" adds to one's sense that a concept is being entertained, not insisted upon. Baudelaire's praise of makeup, like his dandy's stoicism, consciously rejects the ugly impulses of nature.

In an aesthetic context, the two writers agree that artifice perfects man, and their tone is equally ironic. The difference between them is that Baudelaire really depends on his metaphysics. He begins with a conviction of original sin, and thus spiritualizes the art that overcomes sin. The "Éloge du Maquillage" asserts that "crime, whose taste the human animal gets in his mother's belly, is by origin natural. Virtue, on the contrary, is *artificial,* supernatural." In "A Defence of Cosmetics," however, soul is an antonym of artifice. Predictably, the cosmetics in Beerbohm's essay make an enamel mask, "beautiful and without meaning," while Baudelaire imagines a black mascara circle "making the eye seem more like a window open to infinity."

Though women will be the ones to wear cosmetics, they are a troubling idol for both writers. With perfume and metal adornments (the two repeatedly artificial elements in *Les Fleurs du mal*), women are beautiful for Baudelaire; otherwise they are abominable. In Beerbohm's hands the condition of women is a matter for oblique satire. To keep their rouge from cracking, they have got to stay in place and refrain from hard thinking, tennis, bicycles, politics, and novel-writing. (Virginia Woolf extends this picture in her diary comment on a meeting with Beerbohm: "In spite of

October 1899

Dear Mr. Denselow
I have much pleasure
in sending you my
autograph; also a
faithful portrait of
myself, as a warning to
you not to become a
caricaturist when you grow
up.
Yours very truly
Max Beerbohm

I

OVERLEAF:
Self-caricature, 1899

Aubrey Beardsley, 1896

Oscar Wilde
and Alfred Douglas

"Rudyard Kipling's Soul"

John Davidson, 1907

"Ho-Tei," by Hokusai

"Death of St. Peter Martyr," by Giovanni Bellini

"The Small Hours in the 'Sixties at 16, Cheyne Walk.
—Algernon reading 'Anactoria' to Gabriel and William," 1916

"Genus Beerbohmiense:
Species Herbertica Arborealis, Species Maximiliana," 1909

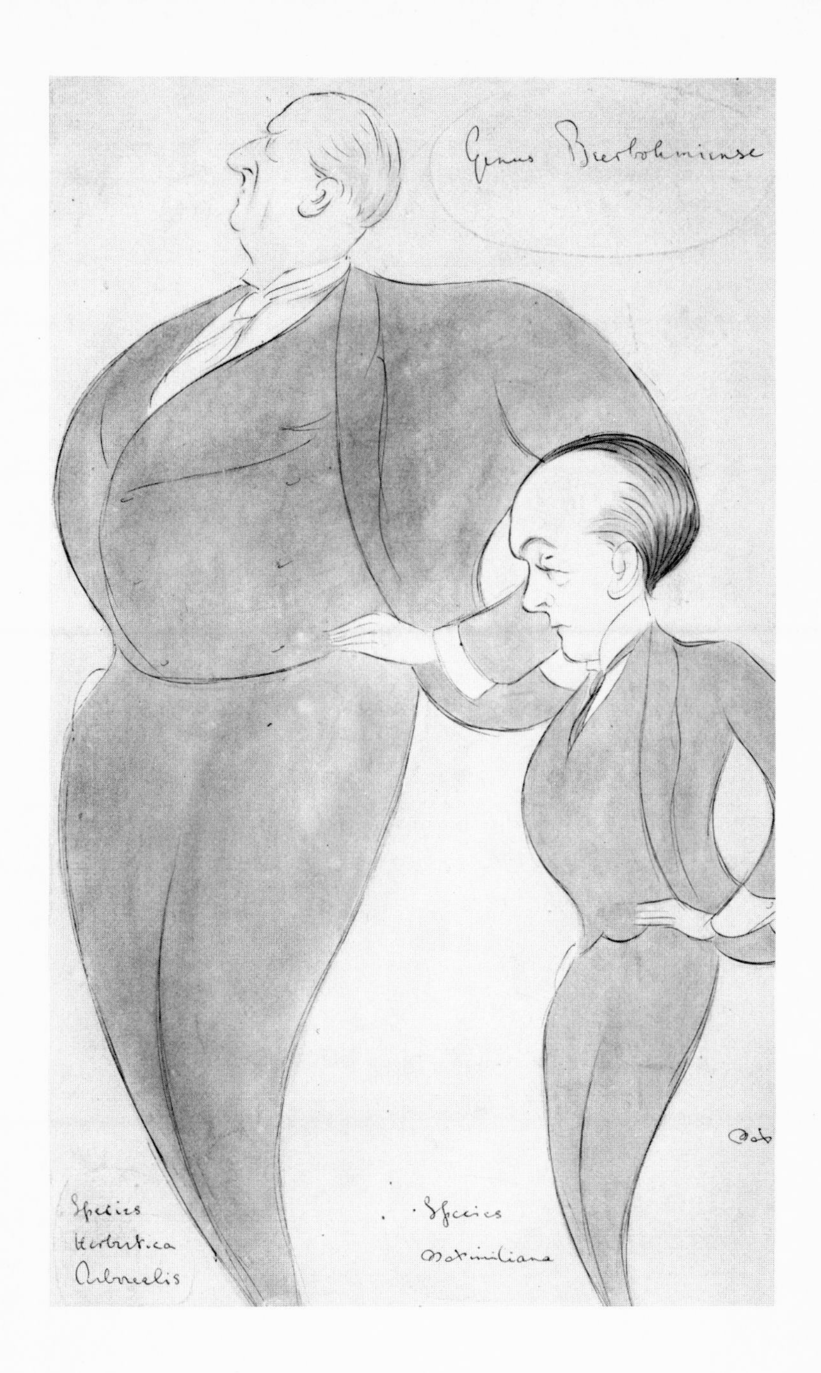
Genus Beerbohmiense
Species Herbertica Arborealis
Species Maximiliana

George Bernard Shaw and Max Beerbohm, 1913

"Mild surprise of one who, revisiting England after long absence, finds that the dear fellow has not moved"

"Cecils in Conclave," 1913 —Robert, Edward, Hugh

Max's brilliance, and idiosyncrasy, which he completely realises, and does not overstep, this was a surface evening; as I proved, because I found I could not smoke the cigar which I had brought. That was on the deeper level.") In place of the womanly woman and the Dickensian "dear little creature," Beerbohm's "Defence of Cosmetics" advocates a decorative woman, and camouflages under the praise of rouge his genuine distaste for feminism.

Satirists traditionally have abused women for using cosmetics. In Juvenal, Ben Jonson, and Congreve, powder and paint are ridiculed for what they conceal, not praised for what they express, and Swift's poem "The Lady's Dressing Room" moves from disgust at natural foulness to bare toleration of cosmetic illusion as an "order from confusion sprung." *The Rape of the Lock* approaches Beerbohm's tone and perspective more nearly. In Belinda's toilet scene, "cosmetic powers" awaken graces and call forth a purer blush, keener lightnings in her eyes. Pope is ridiculing affectation, but not the order and brilliance of Belinda's world.

The structure of mock-encomium in "A Defence of Cosmetics" puts it also in the tradition of Swift's *Modest Proposal* and *The Praise of Folly*. In Erasmus's title, Folly does the praising and is also the subject of praise. You have to credit her authority to praise herself, but you discredit anything said by Folly. Beerbohm's artificial defense of artifice also goes this way. The tone of the essay conveys that aesthetes and decadents sound ridiculous, but there is a residual irony: today, Beerbohm implies, only foolish instances are available to assert what is true—namely, that English culture suffers from an incapacity to make new forms, new fictions, out of the substance of modern life.

We still want to know whether or not he cares about cosmetics, but the point is that he countenances both attitudes. The essay is circular, its style justified from the outset by a theory it goes on to develop. The perfect emblem for this collusiveness is M. C. Escher's picture and a similar one by Saul Steinberg of a hand with a pen, drawing and being drawn by another pen and hand. One hand, either of them, is the artist's; the other is what he has drawn. As neither is definitely responsible for the other, anything goes, and it is precisely this freedom from being arraigned that "A Defence of Cosmetics" aims for. Finally the joke in Steinberg's drawing is that both the "real" hand and the "image" are on paper; in wondering which is which we have already accepted the artist's convention of representing reality. Every subject and style in literature is an invention, Beerbohm demonstrates. His essay is a pun on "making up."

"Nobody has any idea where these decadents will stop"

Reviewers, and readers who found the magazine on a newsstand, were expecting other kinds of interest in the *Yellow Book*. The opening of "A Defence of Cosmetics"—"Nay, but it is useless to protest"—acknowledges a decent British audience and half encourages their protest. Beerbohm takes for granted a natural distrust of cosmetics, a distrust which in 1894 would pertain to such things as hedonism, French cleverness, and softening of the national character. It was not that the article actively violated canons of taste in sex, religion, or politics. It merely threatened the public weal in a vague way, by its frivolity almost more than by its doctrine. And in a year of growing imperialist sentiment, Beerbohm was subversive in turning to the "waning time" of the Roman Empire when "unguentaria reached its zenith."

Some of the *Yellow Book*'s first volume was easily acceptable, such as Henry James's story and an article on reticence in literature, which the press applauded for satirizing the vices of modernity that the rest of the magazine exemplified. Though James noted the "horrid aspect and company" of Volume I, he published in later volumes. In fact, the magazine mainly dealt in the vein of naturalism

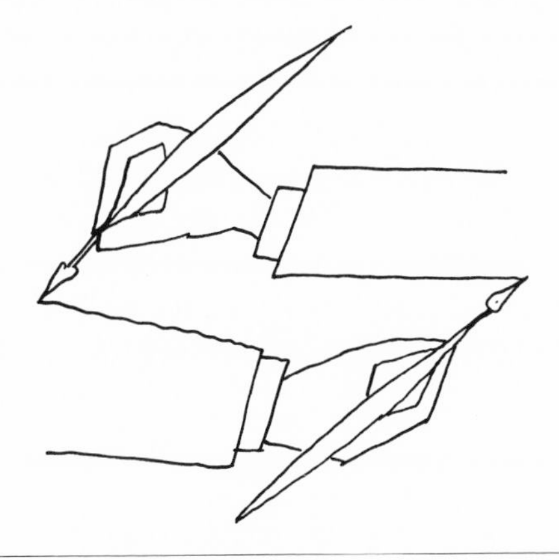

Drawing Hands,
by Saul Steinberg

and realism, but Beerbohm's essay became and has remained the epitome of the *Yellow Book*. Most reviewers in London and New York genuinely disliked it, some thought it pure nonsense. "A Defence of Cosmetics" seemed to them typical because the magazine had announced, along with its "ret-icent mien," its mission of providing only art for art's sake.

Underneath the insistent phrasing of Beerbohm's defense, I feel him slightly jaded with the topic. Blake and Keats could assert the overwhelming truth of art more freshly: to see how far the issue had shifted by 1890, we can try to think of "imagination" in place of "artifice" in Beerbohm's essay. Through lectures by Ruskin, Arnold, and Morris, art had become topical and problematic. Whistler's libel trial in 1878 won him a farthing's damages for defending the autonomy of painting, and Wilde spent the year 1882 in America propagandizing for aesthetics. Coming when he did, Beerbohm found already prepared the role of the artist in challenging society. It was more and more a symbiotic relation.

The *Yellow Book*'s reception was played out first within a contentious journalistic establishment. Aline Harland, the wife of the editor, wrote to an American critic that the first number went into four editions within a month, and added:

"It is impossible to tell you the bitterness, hatred and malice rife in the London art world—how each big fish lives by devouring the little fishes." *Punch* had long since set itself against novelty; it "grins and squeaks and bludgeons only in the cause of law and order," Beerbohm wrote in 1897. Following the *Yellow Book*'s appearance, *Punch* printed a poem on him, "Ars Cosmetica":

> How deftly he dabs on his grease,
> How neatly spreads his wax;
> And finds in dirty aids like these
> The charm that Nature lacks.

The *Spectator,* typically a voice of militant gentility, described most of the volume in familiar terms: "not merely indecent and indecorous, it is also inartistic and untrue to Nature, and offends the moral sense." American periodicals showed more specific indignation, calling Beerbohm's essay intemperate, impertinent, vulgar, revolting, intolerable, and mentioning its excessive style only as further incrimination. This conditioned reflex, that immoral literature must be inartistic as well, runs through British and American criticism of the "Defence of Cosmetics." Beerbohm offended "not only . . . by declaring that all women should paint their faces, but . . . by the tortured use of words." Whether phrased in terms of pleasure and profit, or literary merit and redeeming social content, it is a perennial issue, which Wilde greatly popularized and Beerbohm's essay exacerbated.

The first reviews of "A Defence of Cosmetics" were righteous and humorless, like the Dutchman who wrote to Erasmus after reading *The Praise of Folly,* saying that now he must write a praise of wisdom. Erasmus answered that it was Folly who had spoken, not he, and in a sense Beerbohm did the same to his critics. He felt that the public's negative reaction had to be corrected, and published a letter in the second volume of the *Yellow Book,* the gist of which was that his critics had mistaken him:

> Indeed, it seems incredible to me that any one on the face of the earth could fail to see that my essay, so grotesque in subject, in opinion so flippant, in style so wildly affected, was meant for a burlesque upon the "precious" school of writers. If I had only signed myself D. Cadent or Parrar Docks, or appended a note to say that the MS. had been picked up not a hundred miles from Tite Street, all the pressmen would have said that I had given them a very delicate bit of satire. But I did not.

The fact is, he did not; and referring familiarly to Tite Street in Chelsea, where Oscar Wilde lived, probably implicated him a little more.

Confronted with Beerbohm's explanation in the second issue, most journals merely agreed that the "Defence of Cosmetics" should not have been taken seriously, and let it go at that. *Punch* eventually produced a hodgepodge of ineffective pastiche, but the *National Observer* drew more of a lesson: "That his 'Defence of Cosmetics' was taken as an expression of sincere decadence only shows that nobody has any idea where these decadents will stop." This leaves in doubt whether he is or is not one of "these decadents," and thus identifies Beerbohm accurately, if inadvertently. His letter supposedly disavowing cosmetics had only intensified the doubt. At one point in it he had asked, "May I . . . assure the affrighted mob that it is the victim of a hoax? May I also assure it that I had no notion that it would be taken in?" Beerbohm keeps juggling the issue. What is a hoax if it doesn't take people in? That he meant the original essay to have two degrees of freedom is confirmed by the drift of his letter, which moves through some general scathing of the critics into a peroration that picks up the extravagant rhetoric of the original work. Before republishing the essay in 1896, he revised it to make a more nearly perfect argument for cosmetics. A new title, "The Pervasion of Rouge," dropped the defensive posture and pointed to an accomplished fact in society. After several rhetorical questions Beerbohm now put an exclamation point instead of the original question mark. And he cut out a paragraph that associated cosmetics with hermaphrodites, dandies, and homosexuals.

The essay, the following letter, and the revisions amount to a tightrope walk in which Beerbohm plays form against content in art, and passionateness against skepticism in his view of art. What he really wanted was his own vantage point in the crisis of art and its audience. By 1890, according to the *Encyclopedia of the Social Sciences,* the term "degenerate" was extended beyond criminals and the feeble-minded to include "egotists, clever liars, eccentrics and men of genius." Beerbohm's letter, in describing the critical reception he got, creates a radical, avant-garde image that serves him better as a point of personal identity than as a proof of how the critics erred:

> The mob lost its head, and, so far as any one in literature can be lynched, I was. In speaking of me, one paper dropped the usual prefix of "Mr." as though I were a well-known criminal, and referred to me shortly as "Beerbohm." . . . [My essay] was a bomb thrown by a cowardly decadent, another outrage by one of that desperate and dangerous band of madmen.

Edward Lear's limericks present a similar image of what society's "they" does to the foolish man; and a contemporary limerick is remarkably apt:

> A young expert in matters cosmetic,
> Wrote some words that were rash and heretic;
> They read what he said,
> Then they cut off the head
> Of that expert in matters cosmetic.

Beerbohm's letter clearly exceeds the occasion in trying out the uses of antagonism between writers and society, the way in which artistic and philistine attitudes help create each other.

Dandyism

The conspicuous performance of Beerbohm's early work derives from his idea of cosmetics and dandyism, arts that identify form with subject in the individual person. Sometimes his writing is explicitly dandified, so that words like "spiflicate," "obtund," "accrescency," "secern," and "cinct" echo what he occasionally wore: primrose gloves, a claret-colored dress shirt, or a green baize waistcoat. There is no doubt about his exquisite dress, as often sober as gaudy. The only thing he knew more intimately than men's costume was the English language.

Though Beerbohm was not at all rich, as were Brummell and Baudelaire when they became dandies, his poise gave him a dandy's prerogatives. He seemed to have mastered life by an exclusive concentration of effect among people and as an artist, scarcely ever writing, drawing, saying, or wearing anything that did not represent him perfectly. Clearly dandyism offered the great opportunity for significant personal advertisement, whereas cosmetics limited Beerbohm to a theoretical defense. The dandy, he wrote, "presents himself to the nation whenever he sallies from his front door."

In the nineties an inherent part of his dandyism was to play with the role. He caricatured himself constantly in a top hat longer than his torso, exceedingly high collar, and narrow trousers that tapered away invisibly, as if free of gravity.* Beerbohm's papers include a set of typed notes, jokingly arranged as if for ten articles on himself in some American paper. The notes come from his three-month trip in 1895 to several U.S. cities with the theater company of his brother Herbert Beerbohm Tree, and they express a fantasy he had of himself there. Some excerpts:

*Asterisk, here and throughout, denotes picture included in book.

FIRST ARTICLE—The best dressed man in London, Mr. Max Beerbohm.

SECOND ARTICLE—The surprising new creation of Mr. Beerbohm . . . A single-breasted frock coat . . . Will the Prince of Wales adopt it? . . . A remarkable garment which is a complete revelation to the swells of the West End . . . Important information for New York Dudes.

THIRD ARTICLE—Will he revolutionise prevailing fashions?

FOURTH ARTICLE—Mr. Beerbohm's valet interviewed . . . How the great man performs his toilet . . . He has sixty-eight pairs of trousers, seventy boots . . . and four hundred and sixty-nine different cravats.

. . .

SIXTH ARTICLE—The modern Beau Brummell interviewed.

SEVENTH ARTICLE—How he discovered a man of exquisite taste in Hoboken.

. . .

TENTH ARTICLE—His bitter criticism of the silk hat . . . A plea for art in dress.

In essence the notes announce a creation, a revelation, and a revolution. They caricature the dandy as a type of superman or cultural prophet discovering and embodying a great new mode of life. Four essays that Beerbohm published between 1893 and 1896 in Oxford, London, Chicago, and New York, and gathered in the *Works* as "Dandies and Dandies," argue that the art of costume is not merely a phase of the dandy's temperament, but "the very core of his existence." It is an odd figure for outer dress, "the very core," and signifies that dandyism was a whole way of life. It subsumed qualities Beerbohm liked: precision, economy, distinctiveness, surprise.

"Dandies and Dandies" in its style is not so recherché as the "Defence of Cosmetics," because dandyism engaged

Beerbohm much more thoroughly than rouge did. The unexpected thing about the essay is its repeated and sober characterization of ideal dress, particularly Beau Brummell's, as quiet, reasonable, plastic, economical, scrupulous. This insistence on utter simplicity (and stoicism, in Baudelaire's dandy) characterizes dandyism as much as the occasional showy dress or language that Beerbohm used. He writes of the symmetry, austerity, subtlety, and somber restraint of the ideal dandy, chastened of all flamboyance, free from folly or affectation. Beau Brummell was the "Father of Modern Costume" because he expelled a "Byzantine spirit of exuberance" from the Regency. The dandy that Beerbohm imagines (and *was*, to judge from photographs and paintings) is a disciplined individual, someone whose "tightly buttoned coat" exalts style over life.

That kind of dandyism, with its congruities of black and white and gray, shocks us by upsetting our placement of values, by conforming aesthetically to an ethical bias. A figure of the counterculture, the dandy dresses instead of living in earnest and rejects useful behavior. In 1892 a friend applied Baudelaire's aphorism on "Le Dandy" to Beerbohm: "'Max' doit aspirer à être sublime sans interruption. Il doit vivre et dormir devant un miroir." With Arnold and Pater as well as Baudelaire and Wilde behind him, Beerbohm fell easily into what might be called an aesthetic heresy of individualism: that being, not doing, is the aim of life; that one should look and also live like a work of art.

He asserts the timeliness of dandyism by refuting two earlier writers on the subject, Carlyle and Barbey d'Aurevilly, even though one hated and the other praised dandyism. Beerbohm treats Carlyle's *Sartor Resartus* not as transcendental philosophy but as a clumsy attempt by a bad dresser to write something important about men's clothes. He quotes Carlyle's sardonic definition of the dandy as one "heroically consecrated" to wearing clothes, calling it "the only true words in *Sartor Resartus*." And where Carlyle coined the word "dandiacal" to have an ugly, maniac sound, Beerbohm uses it genially. He takes issue in a different way with Barbey d'Aurevilly, a brilliant, vehement dandy and writer. Barbey's *Du Dandysme et de G. Brummell* (1845) is a finely written analysis of "a consummate Dandy . . . a man who bears in himself something superior to the visible world." Barbey treats Brummell as a cool, indifferent dandy of the spirit, whose wit consisted in perfect self-possession. Dress and material visibility were only aspects of the dandy's intelligence. Just this depreciation of appearance led Beerbohm to refute Barbey by making costume the "very core" of Brummell's existence. Years later on the BBC he made the same point, reminiscing that the man about town was "not necessarily interesting in himself; but fraught with external character and point: very satisfactory to those for whom the visible world exists."

Dandyism involves the whole person in public. Because it "has its own aims and laws, and knows none other," as Beerbohm says, the dandy himself is a work of art, and a kind of poster displaying a new image of society. Once again, Baudelaire sees him almost obsessively, as providing an epiphany, a resistance to the fallen, material world. In "Dandies and Dandies," simply by stressing the pure art of costume, Beerbohm can insist on the critical, oblique relation of the dandy to society and on the dandyism of the artist. "Like the single-minded artist that he was, he turned full and square towards his art and looked life straight in the face out of the corners of his eyes." This is Beerbohm on Beau Brummell, and on himself. Ellen Moers, in *The Dandy: Brummell to Beerbohm,* writes of Wilde and Beerbohm as the decadence and epilogue of dandyism in England. She describes the phenomenon as it lapsed into flamboyant social impudence, but does not fully account for Beerbohm. In reasserting Brummell's fundamental principles, he rescues dandyism from the stigma of *Dorian Gray* and Wilde's homosexuality. "Dandies and Dandies" also deflects Fabian arguments against the self-indulgent individualism of free enterprise.

In keeping with his harlequin posture, Beerbohm published in the *Yellow Book* and then the *Works* "A Note on George the Fourth," which argues for the gaudy hedonism of the dandy. The essay overrichly reinstates George after the "brilliant denunciation" by Thackeray, one of Beerbohm's favorite authors. George's life, Beerbohm writes, was "a poem in the praise of Pleasure," "beautifully ordered" among the pleasures of food, gambling, women, and the "little pomps and foibles of . . . the finest collection of clothes that has been seen in modern times." Except for an unseemly involvement in politics, he was a dandy of the fullest mold. This image of deliberate dissoluteness also happened to fit Albert Edward, then Prince of Wales, and a figure who fascinated and repelled Beerbohm; and the caricature of George IV that Beerbohm originally published with his essay can be recognized as an even more corpulent Oscar Wilde. As in the "Defence of Cosmetics," he ties his essay to images of dubious morality. The details of George's profligate life are much the same as those Thackeray cited righteously in *The Four Georges,* but Beerbohm turns them all into a picture of uninhibited individualism. Where Thackeray attacked George's failure to serve in the Army, Beerbohm claims that serving would have made his kingship less "ornamental" than it was. Thackeray ridiculed the auction of George's wardrobe after his death; Beerbohm praises the King for never forgetting a suit of clothes. Beerbohm creates an image of gusto, a complement to Brummell's austere manner, and carries the example of aesthetic individualism to ridiculous lengths without destroying it. Looking back on the age of George IV, forty years after writing about him, Beerbohm found the dandy "a now extinct species, a lost relic of the eighteenth century and of the days before the great Reform Bill of 1832." As Beerbohm's nineties receded, his sense of the possibilities for cultivated illusion gave way with them. But he had conveyed the idea that shaping one's own person and actions aesthetically is the key to shaping human consciousness at large.

"Not until nudity be popular," he wrote in the essay on dandies, "will the art of costume be really acknowledged." Beerbohm's mannered language need not obscure a point of view that Huizinga and Lévi-Strauss, among others, have also brought to the study of human culture. As in the "universal instinct" for face-painting, "the first kind of painting man can have known," Beerbohm saw, in man's desire to add on to nature by dressing up, a "free will" at work—"the liberty of all expression."

2

The Beerbohm Period

"Max"

In Beerbohm's early essays and caricatures, his reviews and occasional controversy, we see an act of self-presumption. His presumption has drawn attention away from Beerbohm's ideas, but these two elements are part of each other. The mask and the dandy he wrote about come together as an accurate image of the process of making a personality and displaying it in public. In a sense, *Homo faber* was the theme of Beerbohm's early writing, *Homo ludens* the person who emerged in it.

As a young, free-lance artist Beerbohm was also responding to the logic of literary journalism. New magazines proliferated, London's papers took day-by-day notice of cultural phenomena, and the artist was more visible than before. In this atmosphere, it was important to make oneself recognizable. Beerbohm's success at this can be measured by comparing the *National Observer*'s first review of the "Defence of Cosmetics," lumping him with "these decadents," to the paper's review of his *Works* two years later: "Mr. Beerbohm writes with such nicely affected conviction of the claims of dandyism and cosmetics that for the critic to call him *poseur* or coxcomb would be but to hiss the Adelphi villain, a recognized form of the highest compliment." To say that Beerbohm's early essays were a convincing act comes very close to the mark. He was able to imagine himself and perform in the role of writer and caricaturist without implying another, opposed self behind the role. The mask or anti-self of Yeats differs significantly, in its qualities of intensity and overcoming. Beerbohm's mask was antic self-advertisement. In 1894 he began signing his caricatures "Max," in the tradition of "Oscar" and "G.B.S." Like the stage villain, he took on the cachet of a unique popular institution.

He had the run of the press. His caricatures of London club types appeared in 1892 in the newly founded *Strand,* an illustrated monthly with immense circulation, aimed at middle-class households. Soon after, Beerbohm wrote for Lord Alfred Douglas's *Spirit Lamp* a dandified essay on "The Incomparable Beauty of Modern Dress," at a time when he was also drawing gross, unforgiving caricatures of Oscar Wilde. He moved in 1896 from publishing in the *Yellow Book* and the only true avant-garde journal of the time, the *Savoy,* to the new halfpenny *Daily Mail* for busy men. His essays there commented disenchantedly on the social conventions that readers of the paper were still disposed to accept. Somehow Beerbohm's ironic poise began to carry with it an immunity from serious reprisal (by the same token, his caricatures were not always taken at full strength) and a freedom from being identified with any of the different journals and papers he published in.

Raymond Williams notes that in the mid-nineties, after a major economic depression, advertising took on a new importance in industry. Alfred Harmsworth's *Daily Mail* was the first to capitalize on this development. By 1900, partly because of its vigorous support of the Boer War, the paper had run its sales up to one million. Late in 1901, Beerbohm gave Harmsworth six drawings to publish from a group entitled *The Second Childhood of John Bull.* The image of a ridiculously swollen and stupid John Bull was not what Harmsworth's public was used to. Some reader must have asked what the artist looked like, for three weeks later a self-caricature appeared in the paper, showing him in casually elegant morning dress with a cane and a tiny Elizabethan beard beneath his lower lip. It was hardly the man behind those rude, sarcastic drawings. The caption—"Regretting that I live in this self-advertising age, I respond to the invitation to portray myself"—keeps Beerbohm's irony intact. If it was an age of self-advertising, in art as well as in business, he had certainly helped make it so.

Beerbohm had a superabundant literary milieu in which to realize himself as caricaturist, personal essayist, and critic. To have a point of view in the nineties was to think of bringing out a magazine. His father founded two commercial papers, and at Oxford for a while Beerbohm put out a weekly, *The Clown*. His first books were published by the Bodley Head, the chief outlet for decadent writers, and Leonard Smithers—"known," Beerbohm later wrote, "to have been engaged in the sale of disreputable books"—brought out *Caricatures of Twenty-Five Gentlemen* in 1896. *Punch* had signed its second parody "Max Mereboom," but the implication of flash talent was not borne out. His notoriety allowed him to develop freely in various kinds of writing and to keep in touch with people not always in touch with each other, like Wilde, Yeats, Shaw, Beardsley. By 1900 his work had been published in more than forty journals and newspapers. His caricatures in the *Daily Mail* reached the largest audience for anything he ever did, excepting some World War II BBC broadcasts. He was drama critic for the *Saturday Review*, and kept the job for twelve years while writing dozens of humorous, semi-topical essays, articles, book reviews, parodies, parts of two novels, and giving four exhibitions of caricature.

"The *World* is rude about me this morning. . . . But so long as I attract notice I am happy." This is only a private flippancy about the "Defence of Cosmetics," but it points up Beerbohm's easy attitude toward a growing component of the writer's profession, public visibility. He had done two personal interviews for London journals by the time the

Yellow Book started coming out—one of a music-hall comedienne, the other a superb interview of a famous Oxford cricketer. Then he was himself interviewed twice, by women. Though we take it for granted now, the practice of interviewing artists marks the reduced condition of late-Romantic literature: it is hard to imagine William Blake interviewed. After Wordsworth's *Prelude,* Arnold's criticism, Pater's *Marius the Epicurean,* and Wilde's dialogues, personal interviews seem a last resort for securing general confidence in the artist's perspective. Beerbohm used them ironically, to baffle that kind of confidence. Being interviewed on his George IV article: "I meant all I said about George, but I did not choose to express myself quite seriously."

In interviews and in personal essays, he had a habit of making up things about himself that reveal more than the truth would. He said, for example, that he had read only three books at Oxford: Thackeray's *Four Georges,* Wilde's *Intentions,* and Edward Lear's *Book of Nonsense.* Besides suggesting a matrix for some of Beerbohm's leading impulses—satire, paradox, and fantasy—his statement creates a guise of frivolity and idleness. The personal myths he establishes are always in some sense designed to lessen himself. "Diminuendo," a short essay he put at the end of the *Works,* concerns his choice at the age of eighteen to withdraw into contemplation. Beerbohm treats Walter Pater's doctrine of experience as if it were purely literal advice, as Symons and others did, walking the crowded streets in London. He says it may be well enough for the Prince of Wales to hunt and sail and dance and drink, to be (in Pater's words) "present always at the focus where the greatest number of forces unite in their purest energy." But Beerbohm cannot abandon himself to life, and decides instead for monotonous simplicity, a little villa in the suburbs where "no vital forces unite." Behind the pretense is a truth that became more apparent as he retired in 1910 to the villa in Rapallo, Italy, where he lived until his death in 1956. He was never the "seer of life," as "A Defence of Cosmetics" put it, but the spectator. Beerbohm's essay ends, "I shall write no more. Already I feel myself to be a trifle outmoded. I belong to the Beardsley period. Younger men, with months of activity before them," and so on. "Diminuendo" has a kind of pop-art contemporaneity: nothing is more definitively modern than superseding oneself.

In announcing his retirement at the end of "Diminuendo," Beerbohm wrote that despite his precocious success, "the stress of creation soon overwhelmed me." His only specific self-parody, "A Vain Child" (1896), appeared a few months after the *Works,* just as he began writing for the *Saturday Review.* It deprecates and promotes him at the same time:

> I write for a weekly paper, and call myself "We." But the stress of anonymity overwhelms me. I belong to the Beerbohm period. I have tumbled into the dark waters of current journalism, and am glad to sign my name.

The title and substance of the piece are based on Heinrich Hoffmann's *Struwwelpeter*—in particular, on Johnny Head-in-Air, who walks along watching birds in the sky and falls headlong into a river, losing his writing-book. "A Vain Child" borrows from the *Works* for an effect of superfluous literary flavor: Greek, Latin, and French tags, curious phrases ("it has indeed the sentiment of style") and diction ("furial," "fugient"), and precious intrusions ("for lo!"). Stylistically the parody is disappointing, an inferior version of the original, like *Punch*'s skits on Beerbohm. His early essays call more than enough attention to their own ingenuity, and "A Vain Child" reads like something he felt he ought to do.

The irony of *The Works of Max Beerbohm* grew with his successive books of essays, which he called *More, Yet Again, And Even Now,* as if to say, "Don't worry, it's only Max." He stayed within a circle of literary discretion and control. One critic of the *Works* found "neither amusement in their folly nor in their precocity the symptoms of salubrious growth"—phrases that sound very much like Samuel Johnson. In fact, Beerbohm wrote them himself. Any occasion would do to make up an ironic image of himself. Zuleika Dobson, the heroine of his novel, explains why her way of speech has a literary flavor: "Ah, that is an unfortunate trick which I caught from a writer, a Mr. Beerbohm, who once sat next to me at dinner somewhere." In his essays and dramatic reviews, he also had the habit of breaking in with apologies for ignorance and mannerism. The opening, for instance, of "Laughter": "M. Bergson, in his well-known essay on this theme, says . . . well, he says many things; but none of these, though I have just read them, do I clearly remember." Confessions like this became part of Beerbohm's mask. They include their own reinstating power, for our response is to say, Maybe you're foolish or overliterary or unphilosophical, but we trust you more for telling us.

The kind of reflexive writing Beerbohm practiced was a source of poise, even of strength. Anthony Eden once asked him to address the Oxford Uffizi Society, but he wrote back declining to address them on any topic. "I am quite easy to dispense with. . . . I don't know of any subject on which I am *not* ignorant. My ignorance extends even so far as that!" When, in 1921, Bohun Lynch began a study of him and asked for help, Beerbohm replied:

> My gifts are small. I've used them very well and discreetly, never straining them; and the result is that I've made a charming little reputation. . . . Avoid such phrases as "It was at or about this time that the young Beerbohm" etc. My life (though to me it has been, and is, extremely interesting) is without a single point of general interest. . . . Note that I am *not* incomparable. Compare me. . . . Point out how much less human I am than Lamb, how much less intellectual than Hazlitt. . . . Tend rather to *under*rate me.

Possibly Beerbohm's self-reductive impulse stemmed from anxiety about not amounting to much, but the manner of writing throughout this letter (which as preface to Lynch's book became the most interesting part of it) is resilient, at times almost elated.

Beerbohm found his readiest mask in self-caricature. None of the people he drew almost by second nature—Wilde, James, Shaw, and others—appears half so much as he himself does. The catalogue Sir Rupert Hart-Davis is preparing of Beerbohm's caricatures records more than seventy self-caricatures so far. This includes only things more or less deliberately planned, not the countless sketches he did of himself in letters, manuscripts, books, and elsewhere. He drew himself most often as a lithe dandy, then later as many other things: cricketer, clubman, fat veteran, Bismarck, Apollo, Praxiteles' Hermes, an indolent fireside chap, a professor of caricature, or a scourge being implored to stop by the men he caricatured. Because Beerbohm never physically distorts himself as he does other men, these drawings make fun without being hostile. What matters is the number of times he set his hand to the job, not to study his face but to trace his own survival.

The self-caricatures on the covers of Beerbohm's first two books of caricature express his relation to late-Victorian culture. For *Caricatures of Twenty-Five Gentlemen,* he makes himself a heavy-lidded, somewhat portly clown in a top hat, holding a quill pen as a staff. The quill itself has a wry face and a battered top hat at the pen's point, but the clown stands intact. His expression is ambiguous: mild and self-deprecating, yet totally assured, acquainted with human illusions. It is as if the art, not the man, carried the burden of satire. For *The Poets' Corner* in 1904, Beerbohm is a small citizen with a pocket torch, shining it upward to admire the bust of a great writer. The angle of vision he has toward literary success catches it least flatteringly, lighting up a chin and nose from underneath, while a bland

The Poets' Corner, *cover, 1904*

Self-caricature ca. 1890

Caricatures of Twenty-Five Gentlemen, *drawing for cover, 1896 (opposite)*

stream of light comes down onto the poet's brow from a stained-glass window. And Beerbohm's countenance is perfectly modest, implying that his own deficiencies are what keep him from recognizing greatness.

Conceiving himself was an ongoing job. It meant steady immunization against other people's intolerance and his own doubts, by doses of self-criticism. He had actual limitations; he could not, for example, comprehend Goethe or Whitman, who are trivially caricatured in *The Poets' Corner*. But self-irony gave him leverage. He says at the end of an impressionistic essay on the eighteen-eighties, in the *Works*: "To give an accurate and exhaustive account of that period would need a far less brilliant pen than mine." This mock of humility points ahead to the strong voice in his later stories and essays. As a gesture in the nineties, the pretense of insignificance mainly freed Beerbohm from being accurate and exhaustive—freed him, in effect, from responsibility, from unimaginativeness.

Controversies

Among some notes for an essay on "Preciosity" occurs the phrase, "Myself when young—foolscap—words, words." Collecting his writings in 1922 for what was called the Harlequin edition, Beerbohm did little substantive revising, leaving intact "the young coxcomb in the distance." These images—foolscap, harlequin, coxcomb—were not inventions of Beerbohm's maturity. He acted them out in the mid-nineties, and his standpoint of self-awareness seemed proof against any need for correction. He had grown up in a benevolent, somewhat quirky upper-middle-class family, with no oppressive atmosphere of religious duty. Julius Beerbohm, sixty-two at the birth of Max, his last child, was a liberal man who was "very well content," Beerbohm remembered later, "that his sons should do as they willed." It is partly this absence of a strong father, and partly his own precocious success, that account for Beerbohm's air of cockiness in the mid-nineties.

"When I started writing," he said in 1920, "I delighted in being rude to eminent elder men. And oh, my delight when (as frequently happened) I 'drew' them!" In 1896 and 1897, his presumptuousness consisted of the dandy's discipline: not to be caught out, or off guard; not to be moved, but to astonish others without losing one's own poise. Wilde's remark about Max's "gift of perpetual old age" was a commonplace at the time. Several of Beerbohm's targets tried to point out the childishness underneath his self-assurance. Robert Buchanan, who years before had attacked Rossetti and the "Fleshly School of Poetry," talked about Beerbohm's capers and "cheeky comments on the men and manners of the day." Whistler called him a curly-headed boy. There was some truth and some defensiveness in these attitudes. Reviewing the most successful authors controversially was in fact an inverted *rite de passage* for Beerbohm, the novice attacking his elders, even the dead ones such as Carlyle and Thackeray, to reach a new stage in life.

The popular novelists Arthur Conan Doyle and Hall Caine were his easiest game. Doyle had turned to the Sherlock Holmes stories from an unsuccessful medical practice, so Beerbohm addressed him as Doctor, calling his attempt to write romance a pitiable mistake—"I never regard him as anything but a medical man." Doyle responded solemnly in two letters to the *Saturday Review,* and soon after, Beerbohm wrote about Doyle's next novel that it was "told with force and sentiment, and with a literary style which no imitator of Stevenson need blush to acknowledge as his own." Hall Caine's moralistic novels were a phenomenal success. When *The Christian* came out in 1897, Beerbohm saw it as "a false, garish farrago . . . chaotic, journalistic, pseudo-propagandistic diatribe." Two years later Caine turned *The Christian* into a play, which Beerbohm thought might be better as ballet: its "dialogue would lose nothing by being conducted as dumbshow." He also published a caricature of Hall Caine, "with frenzied eyes and hair," as Beerbohm later described it, "bearing a sandwich-board on which his name was inscribed in lavish capitals." Apparently it gave the novelist trouble. He told Beerbohm that during an American lecture tour, the caricature had followed him from city to city, appearing in the local papers.

No one was "drawn" by Beerbohm more than Clement Scott, a sentimental poet and essayist, enemy of Wilde, apoplectic opponent of Ibsen, and drama critic of the *Daily Telegraph*. He was disgusted with Scott at their first meeting: "Possibly I may have seen commoner and stupider men but I can't at this moment recall any such. His fat fingers were loaded with huge glassy-looking jewels and he wore two bracelets." In September 1896 Beerbohm published anonymously a critique of Scott's *Lays and Lyrics*, quoting admiringly (and occasionally misquoting) Scott's jingling verse. "There is no living man, save Scott, who could have written such poetry as this." He analyzed a love poem called "Violet" as if it were addressed pseudonymously to some coastal resort, and he kindly advised Scott to retire from drama criticism and give up London for the seashore, where he might be happier. Scott answered with a furious, confused challenge to the anonymous criticism, "Come out of your hole, Rat!" to which Beerbohm replied calmly. A year later Scott published some essays, *Sisters by the Sea*. Beerbohm duly wrote an "appreciation" that is heady with irony, quoting from the "careless rapture" of Scott's book so as to make him look like a writer of advertising copy for the Brighton Chamber of Commerce. Oscar Wilde thought the review was "very dainty and witty," and Scott kept quiet. As if acting under the primitive power of satire, he had recently spoken up against the evil profession of acting. He was soon forced to resign his job as drama critic, whence he retired to the Continent.

Beerbohm was fascinated by Whistler, whose signature

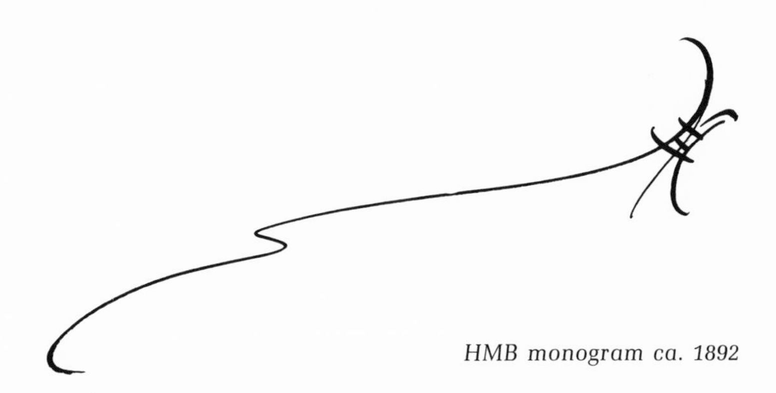

HMB monogram ca. 1892

was a butterfly in the air, trailing a long, gracefully drawn tail with a barb at the end. For his own monogram before 1894, Beerbohm took the initials of his name—Henry Maximilian Beerbohm, HMB—and superimposed them, lengthening the central spike of the M so as to form a butterfly with a long tail. Whistler set a model for controversy. He and Wilde used to send sparring telegrams and letters through the daily press, and eventually Whistler published them in *The Gentle Art of Making Enemies* (1890). In one article, Beerbohm took on the "gay, but terrible, antagonist," and when Whistler replied from Paris to the "simple youth," he returned with a note about the artist's antiquated impertinence.

Beerbohm seized the occasion when William Heinemann announced a new edition of *The Gentle Art of Making Enemies* in 1897. His review begins by quoting Heinemann: "The continued demand for this unique work has enabled the publisher to induce Mr. Whistler to consent to the issue of another edition," and then converts this truckling sentence into a verbal caricature of Whistler, "lordly recumbent on a sofa," and Heinemann, "pale with diffident resolve. . . . He is about to take a chair near the door, but another glance from Mr. Whistler causes him to start violently and change his mind." He continues jesting at Whistler's success, asking why the painter has always been contentious rather than "indifferent, aloof, unruffled" by popular opinion, and why recently he seems to demand popular recognition. Beerbohm's unconscious strategy calls for joking at Whistler for behavior that he himself has invested in. In one passage, Beerbohm's prose seems more weighted than usual, almost as if Whistler were a text for brooding on himself; the level tone has an uncanny echo, every word returning back on Beerbohm:

> Mr. Whistler has never tried conclusions with life. . . . His nocturnes are beautiful as fantasies, beautiful as decorations. . . . When, nowadays, art critics prate of his "marvelous knowledge of the limitations of his medium," they mean really that marvelous knowledge of his own limitations, that divine caution, which has ever withheld him from (perhaps) higher tasks and has left him content with absolute monarchy in his own sphere. . . . I doubt whether Mr. Whistler has ever suffered greatly in the pursuit of his art.

By the time Whistler died in 1903, Max was established and could write a serious, enthusiastic essay on the art of Whistler's writing, the "Autolycine style" in the letters particularly: "The voice drawls slowly, quickening to a kind of snap at the end of every sentence, and sometimes rising to a sudden screech of laughter. . . . the very lack of coherence in the style, as of a man gasping and choking with laughter, drives the insults home with a horrible precision." Beerbohm sees him as a more terrible antagonist than he really was. But the point of the essay, that Whistler was a great amateur writer as well as an artist, also projects Beerbohm's expectations of himself.

His controversial prose, however self-serving, reflects some of the forces operating in the eighteen-nineties, and representative personalities can be seen through Beerbohm's writing and caricature. What he sees is of course highly selective; it leaves out the movements of philosophy, religion, and science, as well as what was in newspaper headlines. But then, any analysis of culture is selective. Throughout almost all the literature on the eighteen-nineties, the decade has been what he called it in 1895, the Beardsley period. There were many affinities between Beerbohm and Beardsley, and where they separate, we can see a split in consciousness that is typical of the period and tells a great deal about Beerbohm.

The two artists were satirized together in *Punch,* and the *World* linked them as leaders of decadent nonsense:

> 'Twas rollog, and the minim potes
>   Did mime and mimble in the cafe;
> All footly were the Philerotes,
>   And Daycadongs outstrafe.
>
> Beware the Yallerbock, my son!
>   The aims that rile, the art that racks,
> Beware the Aub-Aub bird, and shun
>   The stumious Beerbohmax.

One of the first things Beardsley wrote was "The Art of the Hoarding," a short piece on London's need for posters: "May not our hoardings claim kinship with the galleries? . . . London will soon be resplendent with advertisements, and against a leaden sky skysigns will trace their formal arabesque. Beauty has laid siege to the city." This appeared three months after "A Defence of Cosmetics," in close imitation of Beerbohm's style. Both artists also caricatured Wilde, though Beardsley was the one drawn into range of Wilde's scandal when it broke, and dismissed as art editor of the *Yellow Book.*

They were born within the same week, became friends in 1893, and had early success at the same time. Both were influenced by Kate Greenaway's illustrations for children's books, but their use of her clear outlines and even coloring diverges sharply. In Beerbohm's caricature, lines and shapes and contrasts are meant to exaggerate what is latent in the subject; in Beardsley it is the medium itself that is distorted—black becoming blacker, one small design breeding many. The difference is that between simplifying and involving, between exaggerating and metamorphosing appearances. In any case, Beardsley right away liked Beerbohm's work as a caricaturist, and Beerbohm at Oxford attempted imitations of Beardsley's black-and-white style. In an 1897 article, he praised Beardsley's exuberance and was disgusted that "criticasters" found the "black blots and cobweb lines" ugly. "They will never realise that, in art, subject is the least important of all things. . . . The important thing in these drawings is their decorative value." I doubt that this expresses Beerbohm's whole feeling in the matter, but at the time it probably seemed most important simply to defend Beardsley's art.

A humorous exchange between them in caricature made sharper criticism than either of them ventured in other ways. In 1893, Beardsley drew more than a hundred vignettes—grotesque figures and designs to illustrate a series of anthologies. Most are abstract or purely imaginary, but one of them depicts a tiny figure in stylish evening dress and high collar, with sunken eyes and mouth and the bulbous, bumpy profile of a foetal head that also resembles an old man's head. It is almost surely Max Beerbohm. About Beardsley's obsession with foetuses, Brian Reade thinks that he had "witnessed a miscarriage of his sister's and one for which he himself had been responsible." In any event, Beardsley was dying of consumption and had good cause to see life as aborted, age jammed into youth. Whether his obsession was indiscriminate or Beerbohm's head really reminded him of a foetus, the vignette makes a powerful image of what troubled people about the dandy playing aged skepticism against childish ingenuousness.

Vignette of Max Beerbohm, by Aubrey Beardsley, 1893

Another of the vignettes is unquestionably Beerbohm, and though not a foetus, it is in profile again, with a bald swelling head and comically small top hat. The figure is a girlish child seen naked from behind, wearing wings and leading by a string a delicate miniature dog in a jacket. Beerbohm reacted with a caricature which is almost a recipe for hyperaestheticism, showing Beardsley's flat, pale features, arms and legs crossed, in a curtained chair. Another drawing, for *Caricatures of Twenty-Five Gentlemen,* got the same wispy, bloodless quality in Beardsley's figure. The hands hang down like limp worms, and the iconography of the caricature indicates a complex of ruling motives: Beardsley is in the act of languidly curbing a toy dog on wheels, a female French poodle.* This not only answers the vignette, but depicts Beardsley's inspiration as a childish and falsely Gallic dirtiness. Thanking Beerbohm for a copy of the book, Beardsley wrote "Of course I like my own portrait best," and wrote again soon afterwards that he was proud of the "brilliant" 1897 review Beerbohm had done of his work.

It is not easy to see into Beardsley. Much about him is indeed like Beerbohm: the impertinence, the primary care for baroque elegance. Yet Beardsley's style has the nervous energy and precision of someone desperate not to let anything go by him. His self-portrait as a dying Pierrot, or tied to a phallus, incorporates a fatal sense of himself that Beerbohm never experienced. The generous obituary that Beerbohm wrote in 1898 recalls an afternoon spent with Beardsley:

> He was in great form, and showed even more than his usual wit and animation, as he paced up and down the room, talking, with all his odd, abrupt gestures, about one thing and another, about everything under the sun. I am a very good listener, and I enjoyed myself very much. Next day I heard that his mother and his sister and a doctor had been sitting up with him till daybreak. He had been seized, soon after I had left, with a terribly violent attack of haemorrhage, and it had been thought, more than once, that he could not live through the night.

Whether Beerbohm felt it or not, a sense of parasitism comes into this account.

In the same essay he plays down Beardsley's grotesque vision, emphasizing that, contrary to the public's notion of a monster, he was a "devoted son and brother." Not surprisingly, Beerbohm leaves out any mention of *Venus and Tannhäuser* in the essay, or of the *Lysistrata* drawings. They would weaken his insistence that Beardsley "became gradu-

Vignette of Max Beerbohm, by Aubrey Beardsley, 1893

ally more 'human,' less curious of horrible things." And though the *Salome* and *Yellow Book* drawings had some influence on him, he always cited Beardsley's more predictable *Rape of the Lock* illustrations as his favorites. He explains in the essay that Beardsley's drawing was morbid because he was just out of a schoolboy stage of brooding, a normal phase that found "abnormal outlet through premature skill in art. I think, too, that he had a boyish delight in shocking people, and that it was often in mere mischief that he chose, as in many of his grotesques for the *Bon-Mots* series, to present such horribly ugly notions." The boyish delight and premature skill are true, but hardly locate Beardsley's impact. They could as well refer to Beerbohm.

Unlike Yeats, he had trouble attuning himself to Beardsley's vision, to the transformation on paper of morbid, unconscious perception.

In Beerbohm's critique of some kinds of artists, a certain identification with them shows up, a form of projected questioning of what is lost and gained between an artist and his work. He says in 1898 that despite Beardsley's high spirits he was "detached from ordinary conditions, a kind of independent spectator. He enjoyed life, but he was never wholly of it." He ends the obituary by identifying what isolated Beardsley: "No man ever *saw* more than Beardsley. . . . All the greatest fantastic art postulates the power to see things, unerringly, as they are." It is a brilliant notion, but undercut by the previous dismissal of Beardsley's morbidness and horror as a product of mere boyishness. Beerbohm lived out of touch with what Beardsley's fantasy saw in things as they are.

The overtones of his critique of artists, the passages of feeling he was not perfectly conscious of, come out most in relation to Beardsley, Whistler, Wilde, and Henry James—those who put the greatest faith in art. As in the parodic "Defence of Cosmetics," his sympathy splits. With Beardsley, he understands the talent and precocious success, even the remoteness from actuality, as parallel to his own, but not the vision of evil. Along with his irony and self-caricature, this kind of projection makes up Beerbohm's surmise about himself.

Oscar Wilde

Beerbohm had very little antagonism toward Beardsley, partly because his friend did not loom over him as an example. Oscar Wilde did, however, and a revealing mixture of skepticism and allegiance, direct and reflexive feelings, develops in Beerbohm's many writings about him:

1891—"Ballade de la Vie Joyeuse," a poem on *Dorian Gray*

1893—"Oscar Wilde," Beerbohm's first article, published anonymously

—"The Incomparable Beauty of Modern Dress," an essay in imitation of Wilde

1894—"A Peep into the Past," a hoax on Wilde

—"A Defence of Cosmetics"

1896—*The Happy Hypocrite,* a takeoff on *Dorian Gray*

1900—obituary article

1902 to 1909—reviews of *The Importance of Being Earnest* (two), *Lady Windermere's Fan, Salome, A Florentine Tragedy*

1905—review of *De Profundis*

In addition, there are two early fairy tales somewhat in the manner of Wilde, notes for a later essay, annotations and drawings in copies of Wilde's books, a number of published and unpublished caricatures, and a short talk on Wilde's superb conversation for the 1954 centennial ceremony.

Making fun of Wilde became a British institution while Beerbohm was growing up. One of his early memories was of being taken in 1882 to the offices of *Punch* by his brother Herbert. Wilde had just arrived in the United States, and Tree turned in a lush, overwritten parody of his being interviewed in New York, where he had come to "reap the scorching harvest of self-love." In *Punch,* Beerbohm also followed George du Maurier's caricatures of aesthetes, which were based on Wilde's appearance. At Oxford in 1891 he got into the habit of drawing satirically in his own copies of books and those he gave to friends. *Intentions* is the most elaborately decorated, with sixteen different designs. The drift of these illustrations, most of which are childishly drawn in comparison with Beerbohm's later work, is to make Wilde a ridiculous figure; yet they do represent a commitment to him. Some of them are undergraduate clichés, like the one of Wilde holding a model of the Parthenon and flying through the air above a gross John Bull, who has just shot a feeble, twisted arrow. But several of Beerbohm's drawings make considerably more interesting comment on Wilde than *Punch* and the daily press were offering. On the title page to "The Decay of Lying" Beerbohm drew a chimera, as if agreeing that the truth is fabulous. And on the flyleaf of *Intentions* there is a scene of Wilde looking over a hedge down a beautiful garden path with a closed gate in it.

At first, Wilde might as well have been acting in a comedy for Beerbohm, who reacted to him exuberantly and sympathetically but not seriously. When *Salome* was banned in 1892, he wrote to Reggie Turner:

> I have designed a great picture in which King Bull makes a great feast and when they have feasted the daughter of Mrs. Grundy dances before them and pleases the King—insomuch that he promises her whatsoever she shall desire. After consultation with her mother she demands that "they bring unto her by and by the head of Oscar the Poëtast on a charger."

The same kind of amused recognition of Wilde's prophetic role in British culture appears in Beerbohm's first article, in which he regrets "that people have not flocked into the desert to hear him." He tries not to be completely charmed by "the Master (as his disciples call him)." While recounting epigrams and sketching him as "a perfect type and a personality without flaw," he also gives a vivid picture of Wilde's corpulence, a dubious quality in Beerbohm's scheme. He comments, "Mr. Wilde is indolent and so his writings are few. . . . He is so versatile that he has hardly ever attempted two things of a like kind," and adds that Wilde ought not to write plays because he is "far too charming for self-effacement." The irony here is sometimes out of focus because Beerbohm means what he says but also feels sardonic towards Wilde, and does not want to praise him straightforwardly.

His early article, defining Wilde's ideas and personality, was after all a bid for recognition and a veiled challenge that Wilde clearly felt. He congratulated Beerbohm on having a style "like a silver dagger." Soon afterwards Beerbohm wrote "The Incomparable Beauty of Modern Dress." Eventually part of "Dandies and Dandies," it came out first in the *Spirit Lamp,* in the same issue as a prose poem by Wilde about the mutual narcissism between disciple and master. Beerbohm's essay put various conceits about costume together with some direct echoes of Wilde's epigrams on the amorality of art. He had moved from exposition and defense to pastiche of Wilde's ideas. Later, in "A Defence of Cosmetics" and other pieces, he had a much better sense of how to take off from those ideas and form an integral work of his own. When he rewrote the essay on modern dress in 1896, he omitted all allusions to Wilde.

Beerbohm made his discipleship a process of individuation. But then so did Wilde, in stories he told about himself and Pater. Some notes of Beerbohm's contain these phrases about Wilde: "Day of announcement of Pater's death—Laughed—cut off in flower of middle age." He deflected Wilde's influence on him through caricature and parody, as in an early drawing of Richard Le Gallienne, small and vapid, imitating Wilde in dress, pose, hair, and cane. The best drawing of this sort concerns Wilde and Douglas, one talking and the other listening. They are seated opposite each other at a café table, Wilde hunching forward with the ring and cigarette Beerbohm always gave him, and his hand gesturing. Douglas is small, slouched against his chair, also holding a cigarette. His face is the key to the insight in Beerbohm's drawing: stretched up toward Wilde and concentrating, frowning a little, rapt but almost belligerent.* Douglas himself published the caricature in one of his self-vindicating books, and also mentioned a dinner at the Café

Royal with "Mr. Max Beerbohm, who giggled prettily at everything either Wilde or I said." Sometime before 1895 Beerbohm did another sketch, including Wilde, himself, Douglas, and Reggie Turner. Four profiles are arranged in that order from left to right as a collage, with each head smaller than the last, so that Wilde's contains the other three and seems to control their angle of vision—a beautiful emblem of involvement with the Master.

When Beerbohm met Wilde in early 1893, he began to see him with the caricaturist's eye, possessively:

> I am sorry to say that Oscar drinks far more than he ought: indeed the first time I saw him, after all that long period of distant adoration and reverence, he was in a hopeless state of intoxication. He has deteriorated very much in appearance: his cheeks being quite a dark purple and fat to a fault.

In fact, Beerbohm's drawings of Wilde were invariably cruel—a bloated torso, fat white hands and fingers "not soigné," and "Oscar's coy, carnal smile." The artist in Beerbohm, as distinct from the writer, saw Wilde plainly, undisguised by the verbal gift. Beerbohm's hardness appears in his joking reaction to hearing that Wilde had complained about some caricatures: "He is simply an unpaid model of mine and as such he should behave." On the other hand, Beerbohm in his letters through 1895 continued happily imitating Wilde's wit, even when his intentions toward Wilde were satirical. From an August 1893 letter:

> Apropos of my former self, Oscar was at the last night of the Haymarket: with him Bosie and Robbie [Alfred Douglas and Robert Ross] and Aubrey Beardsley. The last of these had forgotten to put vine-leaves in his hair, but the other three wore rich clusters—especially poor Robbie. Nor have I ever seen Oscar so fatuous: he called Mrs. Beere "Juno-like" and Kemble "Olympian quite" and

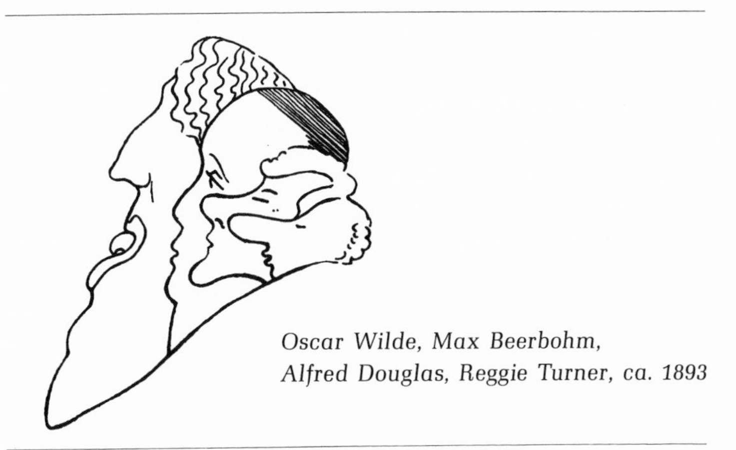

Oscar Wilde, Max Beerbohm,
Alfred Douglas, Reggie Turner, ca. 1893

> waved his cigarette round and round his head. Of course I would rather see Oscar free than sober, but still . . . I have just been reading *Salome* again: terribly corrupt but there is much that is beautiful in it, much lovely writing: I almost wonder Oscar doesn't dramatise it.

The full outline of a caricature comes out, an image of Wilde waving his cigarette and somehow victimized by his own genius. The two paradoxes about *Salome*, modeled on Wilde's paradoxes, are a kind of implicit homage. And the phrase, "I would rather see Oscar free than sober," a parody on "Ireland sober is Ireland free," still says something penetrating, even compassionate, about Wilde.

After the mixed adulation of his first article and the pastiche on modern dress, Beerbohm's next writing had a new distance and certainty—in a letter he tells an anecdote that is certainly the germ of "A Peep into the Past":

> Bobbie has offended Oscar most *fearfully* by telling him that whatever his shortcomings may be—and they are many—no one can deny that he is a gentleman of the old school. Isn't it exquisitely funny? There *is* something rather Georgian in Oscar's deportment.

Out of this notion came a short, perfectly composed hoax about Wilde, then at the top of his success in the theater and the beau monde, as "the survivor of a bygone day . . . always interested to hear oral news of the present." A hoax is the logical extreme of fiction: once you take the original lie for granted, you have, as Beerbohm said, "a large measure of truth." In "A Peep into the Past," written in the voice of an interviewing journalist, Beerbohm reverently visits the "old gentleman" in quiet retirement on Tite Street to verify some facts about the early Victorian era. His tone is unbeatably modest, and respectful of Wilde solely on account of his old age—"many of us are fated to outlive our reputations." He pictures Wilde rising at 4:30 A.M. and "bending over the little spirit-kettle, at which he boils himself his cup of hot cocoa," or pacing his bedroom at night still working out a joke he had sketched to his wife that evening.

By Dickensian reiteration of "the old gentleman" and "the old journalist," Beerbohm releases Wilde into the past. If the Master is outmoded, the disciple must have come into his own. Moreover, Beerbohm erases his own literary dependence by describing Wilde's writings as "a book of parodies upon Rossetti, a few fairy-tales in the manner of Hans Andersen, an experimental novel in the style of Poe, a volume of essays, which Mr. Pater is often obliged blushingly to repudiate." Wilde himself once remarked about his relation to Flaubert, "Remember—Dans la littérature il faut toujours tuer son père," and in a sense this advice sanctioned "A Peep into the Past."

The hoax gave Beerbohm full freedom of invention, and this is certainly one of his surest and funniest pieces of writing. His note at the top of the manuscript says it was intended for the first number of the *Yellow Book,* but "A Peep into the Past" was published only in an unauthorized American edition of 1923. Probably he withheld the hoax in 1894 and substituted "A Defence of Cosmetics" because Wilde's reputation was becoming too lurid. Near the beginning of the visit, he notes a certain quality in his host: "He is something of a martinet about punctuality in his household and perhaps this accounts for the constant succession of page-boys, which so startles the neighbourhood." The last phrase and the word "perhaps," later emendations by Beerbohm, carry a sexual innuendo and yet keep him innocent of it, as another passage also does:

> As I was ushered into the little study, I fancied that I heard the quietly receding *frou-frou* of tweed trousers, but my host I found reclining, hale and hearty, though a little dishevelled upon the sofa. With one hand, re-adjusting the nut-brown Georgian wig that he is accustomed to wear, he motioned me with a courteous gesture of the other to an armchair.

Beerbohm was skilled enough in joking about pederasty. Within the small London circle of homosexuals, made up of Wilde, Alfred Douglas, Robert Ross, Reggie Turner, and others, he seems to have moved easily. He could write to Turner, "Please give [Ross] some mulierastic equivalent for my love"—"mulierast" being Ross's term for heterosexual; or could invent a scene in another letter a few months before Wilde's scandal: "Oscar has at length been arrested for certain kinds of crime. He was taken in the Café Royal (lower room). Bosie escaped, being an excellent runner, but Oscar was less nimble." This might be the tone Beerbohm would use if he were sexually involved with these men. But despite some aspects of taste and demeanor, he seems to have had no homosexual experience and not much heterosexual drive either.

By 1895 Wilde was a criminal, arrested while Beerbohm was in New York. Wilde's trial and imprisonment troubled but did not threaten Beerbohm; there was no complicity. During the trial he spent an evening at the home of the Leversons, Wilde's good friends. He described the scene in a letter as "quite absurd": Mr. Leverson explaining it was not "anything unnatural" he liked in Oscar, but the plays and personality; Alfred Douglas "ashen-pale"; and finally "I myself exquisitely dressed and sympathising with no one." Behind the phrase "sympathising with no one," you see the involuntary cruelty of the clown on the cover of *Caricatures of Twenty-Five Gentlemen.*

When Wilde was about to be released from prison in 1897, he named some friends, Max among them, who might send books to be waiting for him. Beerbohm sent his *Works* and *The Happy Hypocrite. The Happy Hypocrite,* published while Wilde was in prison, takes off Wilde's fairy tales, such as "The Happy Prince." It is about Lord George Hell, an ugly, dissolute Regency nobleman whose cheeks, like Wilde's, are a deep purple. George buys a special mask of saintly beauty to win the hand of Jenny Mere, a pure-hearted young actress. She accepts him as Lord George Heaven, and they leave the city to live on seedcakes and dewberry wine, playing the flute and stringing daisy chains. *The Happy Hypocrite* draws a proper nineties moral: "As days went by, he grew reconciled to his mask. No longer did he feel it jarring on his face. It seemed to become an integral part of him." One day George's jealous former mistress finds them and rips the mask off, "but lo! his face was even as his mask had been."

A close model for this tale existed in Wilde's parable (circulated but not published) about a wicked, ugly girl who buys a mask for a dance, charms a young man, takes off the mask and is beautiful. *The Happy Hypocrite* goes farther only in elaborating improbable detail about George and Jenny. Beerbohm's title also hits sarcastically at Wilde's hedonistic creed, and George Hell's mask reverses the morality of *The Picture of Dorian Gray,* in which human character alters a work of art. Wilde read the story immediately and wrote to Beerbohm, admiring it except for the "philistine" satire of himself in the title. He chides Beerbohm for "picking up a brickbat and wearing it as a buttonhole," but adds: "The implied and accepted recognition of *Dorian Gray* in the story cheers me. . . . How useless it is for gaolers to deprive an artist of pen and ink. One's work goes on just the same, with entrancing variations." To Reggie Turner he wrote that he had read *The Happy Hypocrite* "beginning at the end, as one should always do"—a ploy that would nullify the satire and make Wilde into the tragic figure he styled himself.

He always treated Beerbohm gingerly, because of the "silver dagger" of ironic prose, the power of caricature, and because he recognized an elusive personality like his own. "When you are alone with him," Wilde asked a woman friend, "does he take off his face and reveal his mask?" Among all the reactions to "A Defence of Cosmetics" in 1894, Wilde's was the best: "Max on Cosmetics in the *Yellow Book* is wonderful: enough style for a large school, and all very precious and thought-out: quite delightfully wrong and fascinating." This catches everything. Beerbohm in turn was Wilde's only truly intelligent disciple. "Many a young man," Wilde had said in the "Decay of Lying," "starts in life with a natural gift for exaggeration which . . . by the imitation of the best models, might grow into something really great and wonderful." The outcome of this conceit had to be Beerbohm's hoaxes and burlesques, his form of boutonnière, and Wilde stayed out of the way to enjoy the flattery without controversy. His only published token of association with Beerbohm is found at the climax to *The Importance of Being Earnest,* where the hero is leafing wildly through Army lists to find the full name of his father: "Generals . . . Mallam, Maxbohm, Magley, what ghastly names they have."

In the fall of 1900, as Oscar Wilde was dying in Paris, Beerbohm dramatized *The Happy Hypocrite.* There is a final irony in his writing to commiserate with Reggie Turner, who was tending Wilde, while also reporting jubilantly the success of his play. The death of Wilde brought a turn in Beerbohm's attitude, marked by his sober obituary tribute in the *Saturday Review.* An instance of this new seriousness is the caricature he did in 1911 to illustrate a book on Wilde.

He asked the author not to publish a "cruel" 1894 drawing, and sent one instead that had none of the early traits—ring, cigarette, overblown conceit. But the 1911 caricature is lifeless and ineffectual, and the cruel view has been regularly reproduced.

After 1900 Beerbohm's interest in Wilde turned almost exclusively to the plays, and the kind of comedy Wilde would have developed. When *The Importance of Being Earnest* was revived for the first time in 1902, Beerbohm reviewed it, stressing the blend of poetic dignity and absurdity in what Wilde's characters have to say: "They speak a kind of beautiful nonsense—the language of high comedy, twisted into fantasy. Throughout the dialogue is the horse-play of a distinguished intellect and a distinguished imagination—a horse-play among words and ideas." In this review and in later ones, Beerbohm takes nonsense to be Wilde's essential quality. What he understood by it can be inferred from his criticism of an actress in the play for acting her part in the direction of burlesque: "By displaying a sense of humour she betrayed its limitations." He also criticizes an actor for trying to make his part serious, "instead of taking the part seriously for what it is." The point is that Wilde sees life as neither foolishness nor importance, but as the inevitable coincidence of the two, which nonsense expresses. Beerbohm comments on his favorite scene:

> I noted several faults of textual omission. When Lady Bracknell is told by Mr. Worthing that he was originally found in a handbag in the cloak-room of Victoria Station, she echoes "The Cloak-room at Victoria Station?" "Yes," he replies; "the Brighton Line." "The line is immaterial," she rejoins. . . . Now, in the present revival "the line is immaterial" is omitted. Perhaps Mr. Alexander regarded it as an immaterial line.

Nonsense can be thought of as a parody of the world's sense. By emphasizing fantasy and nonsense instead of the social masquerade in Wilde's plays, Beerbohm brings out qualities he thinks will last, and ones that will inform his own writing. He also means to separate the gift for nonsense from the solemn, tragic image created by Wilde's *De Profundis* and *Ballad of Reading Gaol.*

In 1905, reviewing *De Profundis,* he set himself against the notion that this letter from prison was a tragic document, the naked heart-cry of a transformed person:

> Nothing seemed more likely than that Oscar Wilde, smitten down from his rosy-clouded pinnacle, and dragged through the mire, and cast among the flints, would be *diablement changé en route.* Yet lo! he was unchanged. He was still precisely himself. He was still playing with ideas, playing with emotions.

In a sense Beerbohm was right: Wilde still had an artist's freedom. *De Profundis* manifests that prison, a place in which nothing happens but emotions, literalized the imaginative writer's world. "What I suffered then, and still suffer, is not for pen to write or paper to record." Beerbohm quotes this in his review, and continues, "Yet pen wrote it, and paper recorded it, even so." He sees Wilde as a man for whom everything occurs in the words and the self-consciousness of the artist. In *De Profundis,* Wilde decides he was too much society's victim, not enough the agent of his own fall. Remembering the prosecution's "appalling denunciation . . . and being sickened with horror at what I heard," Wilde says: "Suddenly it occurred to me, '*How splendid it would be, if I was saying all this about myself!*' "

Beerbohm's awareness of this gambit rises directly from his own self-immunizing. The difference of scale and intensity in Wilde's case did not trouble him. His easy habit of reflexive writing led him to give too much credit to wordplay and joy in *De Profundis* and not enough to the artist's vulnerability. It is revealing to compare Beerbohm's review with one Gide wrote, which, though it puts quotation marks around Wilde's "humility," ends by accepting the fatality of his encounter with experience. Beerbohm keeps insisting that Wilde was "still himself—still with the same artistry in words, still with the same detachment from life." Something both tough and delicate in Beerbohm kept him uncommitted yet reluctant to see Wilde's sensibility deepened by circumstance. To admit radical change in the man might entail damage to Beerbohm's own literary genesis, which was bound up in him.

In the lucid, unforgiving views of caricature, Beerbohm's physical aversion to Wilde did the work of moral judgment, and also yielded truer images of Wilde than George du Maurier's or Thomas Nast's. An honest estimate of Wilde occurs in some random notes—both a caricaturist's and an essayist's notes—made by Beerbohm around 1910, when both his debt and his aversion were thoroughly assimilated. The mind's eye shows him Wilde's weakness, and then goes deeper into intuitive, for once totally unironical, notations of a great personality: "hair curled—Assyrian—vast malmaison—enormous dowager or schoolboy—way of laughing with hand over mouth—stroking chin, looking up sideways—But real vitality—Effeminate, but vitality of twenty men—magnetism—authority—Deeper than repute or wit."

In the eighteen-nineties Beerbohm took the instigation of Wilde's aesthetic ideas, exaggerating and deflecting them. His first sense of himself as "Max" entailed getting free of Wilde, whose presence evoked the whole progression of Beerbohm's comic responses, from adulation and pastiche to hoax and parody. Most of what makes his later writing distinctive stems from his passage with Wilde—the mock of impressionism, the criterion of dramatic illusion, the play of fiction and history, and of art and actuality—but all these go far beyond what Wilde could do as a writer.

PART TWO

3

Mirrors

The Exposure of Illusion

The critical impulse, the impulse to question artistic means and ends, runs all through Beerbohm's writing between 1897 and 1910, when he stopped reviewing theater, married, and left England. Earlier, in the *Works,* the strategy had been pretense, pure surmise—"Artifice is the strength of the world." His doctrine on cosmetics and his pieces on Whistler, Conan Doyle, and others created a flagrant posture for him. Life had to imitate art: at first, Beerbohm's skepticism about this claim was hard to recognize, a matter of taking his exaggerated arguments as parody. Even after he shifted the point of balance of "A Defence of Cosmetics" by writing a letter to the *Yellow Book,* few people took the essay that way. Through 1896, his irony was weighted on the aesthete's side of the issue of art for art's sake.

Toward the turn of the century, he dropped the harlequinism of the *Yellow Book* period. Enoch Soames, the fin-de-siècle poet in a story from *Seven Men,* disappears from sight in 1897: he is presented as Max Beerbohm's alter ego, and that date can mark the end of Beerbohm's attentiveness to English decadent aesthetics. The job as a critic, and more simply, the fact that he was not so young a man, gradually altered his disposition. More of his subjects came from common experience, his style ran more evenly. He was no longer trying to juggle words and opinions faster than the eye could follow. Wilde had talked about the "shackles of verisimilitude": Beerbohm began examining them, looking directly at the play between art and actuality.

Criticism, understood as the vision of that play, took various forms. The essays in *More* (1899) and *Yet Again* (1909) expose deceptions, some deliberate and some in the nature of things, scattered throughout an urban existence. A series called *Words for Pictures* (1898–1901) relates literature and art, a painting and the characters within it, the characters and us, or explores patterns imposed by the artist on life and by the critic on a work of art. As a drama critic, Beerbohm looks for an illusion of reality, not for reality itself, and objects to Shaw's inartistically opinionated characters. In 1913, in *The Mirror of the Past,* he sets Pater's gospel of the "hard, gemlike flame" against his timid existence, and the caricatures in *Rossetti and His Circle* show a romantic artist at odds with circumstance. From this circle of instances, no one decision about adjusting art to life will emerge. Like a number of writers who follow him, Beerbohm in his criticism takes the flux between illusion and reality, or between literary means and ends, as a theme in itself rather than a problem to be solved.

The writing collected for *More,* his second book, almost always has to do with artifice or illusion. At times he wants to keep them in force, and will consider the "unintelligent realism" of photography. At other times he focuses on the false conventions of *Punch*'s cartoonists or asks for the fatuous old tunes of the music hall to come back in place of today's aesthetically demanding performances. The other subjects in *More* are such things as Madame Tussaud's, actors, and "Pretending," while an essay on royalty suggests that wax robots would do much better. Most of the pieces in the book are slight compared to "Dandies and Dandies" and the "Defence of Cosmetics," but they consistently expose what was hidden in the *Works*—namely, the traps of aestheticism. The rhetoric has changed from defending to explaining, from "Gracious goodness! why do not we have masks upon the stage?" to an 1897 formula: "The Actor's medium is himself." One piece in *More* resembles Wilde's argument for poisoning ugly people, but Beerbohm breaks down the aesthetic posture. He urges that fires are beautiful to behold, then says that he is organizing an Artists' Corps to go about slitting firemen's hoses and carrying its own filled with oil. Throughout *More* he alternately undercuts and asserts the influence of art in life, in order to rescue a comic question from what Pater treated solemnly and Wilde flamboyantly.

The essays in *Yet Again*, published mostly between 1900 and 1906, concern things likely to be met with by the average Londoner. On the subject of some waxen effigies shown to visitors in Westminster Abbey, Beerbohm argues carefully that lifelike art depends upon an illusion not a replica of life. He also urges the Dean to replace the Abbey's monotonous guides by parrots chained to each tomb and bust. Another essay describes a dejected nag he saw, and then reveals it to be a discarded rocking-horse. Or in civil courts he finds more of the excitement of the theater than in the theater itself. The key essay in *Yet Again*, "Seeing People Off," also derives from Beerbohm's drama criticism. In Euston Station one day, after the emotionally awkward and unsuccessful business of seeing someone off, Beerbohm spots a man, an ex-actor whom he had known, in the midst of fervent goodbyes with a woman. Both are in tears but it seems a rich experience. After she has left, Beerbohm learns that his friend is now working for a bureau that hires out people to see Americans off. The twist (recalling Hamlet's question about the tragedian: "What's Hecuba to him, or he to Hecuba,/that he should weep for her?") is doubly funny and characteristic because it implicates Beerbohm: his friend offers to give him lessons, and though the fee is steep, he decides to accept.

While each of these essays has a point to make, their fundamental design is not to foster a choice between authentic and inauthentic events, any more than the parables of Jorge Luis Borges mean to say: this view of things is true, that untrue. Beerbohm's questions about the structure of consciousness turn into answers. In finding civil courts better than theater, he neither downgrades theater nor takes human trouble lightly, but discovers play at the heart of human behavior and belief.

"Madame Tussaud's," written in 1897, epitomizes all the essays of this period. It speculates on the waxworks as stiff, morbid, barren puppets, obscene images with tallowy faces, glass eyes, "smooth, nailless, little hands." The statues "were not life-like. They gave me no illusion. . . . Though these wax-works are made in so close an imitation of life, they have, indeed, less verisimilitude than the outcome of any fine art." Coleridge had illustrated his central principle by calling waxwork figures mere likenesses: genuine art, for him, displayed both likeness and unlikeness to nature. This distinction served Beerbohm as a critic, and it defines as well the exaggerating and thus life-giving technique of caricature.

In Madame Tussaud's he roams on through the halls, feeling an increasingly oppressive lassitude, and ends on a pitch of Gothic horror:

> . . . why should Garibaldi and those others all stare at me so gravely? Had they some devil's power of their own, some mesmerism? It flashed upon me that, as I watched them, they were stealing my life from me, making me one of their own kind. My brain seemed to be shrinking, all the blood ceasing in my body. I would not watch them. I drooped my eyelids. My hands looked smooth, waxen, without nerves. I knew now that I should never speak nor hear again, never move. I took a dull pride, even, in the thought that this was the very frock-coat in which I had been assassinated. . . . With an effort, I pulled myself together. Looking neither to the right nor to the left, I

> passed, through that morgue of upstanding corpses, to the entrance, down the marble staircase, out into the street. . . . Ah! it was good to be in the street!

He comes to the Wax Museum anticipating a show, but the curve of anticipation turns to disillusion. After making himself vulnerable to the stopping power that any kind of art has, waxwork or Grecian urn, he finally breaks out. This essay belongs to the central current of imagination in Beerbohm: his movement from aesthetic idealism through the testing of illusion to a new opening on life. The episode is a dream of escape from the trap of art.

"Words for Pictures"

The issue in which *Punch* printed "Ars Cosmetica" against Beerbohm also reviewed a New English Art Club Exhibition, noting the "surprising wickedness" of Aubrey Beardsley's faces, "a charming little chip of wood by Mr. R. E. Fry," and the absence of "home-truths" in the painting of Wilson Steer, one of the impressionists Beerbohm knew and admired. A British intolerance of unfamiliar technique in art, of unlikeness as a criterion, survived the nineties. What the Attorney General had asked Whistler years before about his nocturne "Battersea Bridge," still applied to any decent artist: how were those vague figures up on the bridge going to get down? The passage between actuality and art was not something to be confused or played with.

This is precisely what Beerbohm does in a totally neglected group of writings: fascinating, unexpected pieces called *Words for Pictures*. Between 1898 and 1901 he published these fifteen short prose sketches based in various ways on paintings he had seen, by Uccello, Giovanni Bellini, Velázquez, Rubens, Corot, and Gainsborough among others. The "words for pictures" are nothing like Rossetti's poems for paintings or Ruskin's word-pictures. They are critical conceits, reveries about what is going on in a painting and why. Beerbohm will take off from an equestrian portrait by Velázquez or Rubens's "Garden of Love" into a supposition about them that hovers between plausibility and fantastic inappropriateness.

His thinking starts from the difference between words and pictures. He says that Corot's painting of Macbeth approaching the witches succeeds only because it is remote from Shakespeare and does not try to copy the action of *Macbeth.* Then Beerbohm's essay winds so far into the painting that he can consider interfering personally before Macbeth hears the fatal prophecy. Time is stopped in Corot, but words move through time. The idea of joining prose to painting may have begun as a parody of Pater's impressionism in *The Renaissance,* and of the synthesis of the arts that appealed so strongly in the nineties. But in setting one art off against another and against the life they are supposed to portray, *Words for Pictures* carries deeper than Pater and with a gaiety Pater never attempted. Beerbohm's is an offhand version of the classical *ecphrasis,* "speaking out": the description of visual or plastic art in words, as in Homer's shield of Achilles and Keats's Grecian urn. *Words for Pictures* brings mute, motionless works of art to life again in language, changing space into time—how are those figures to get down?

The best of the sketches is "Peter the Dominican" (1898), based on Bellini's *Death of St. Peter Martyr* in London's National Gallery.* Bellini's painting shows the Inquisitor Peter of Verona just attacked by a rival, Cavina. According to a Dominican record Beerbohm has read, Peter as he died began writing *Credo in Dominum* in the dust:

> Here, before this picture by Bellini, one looks instinctively for the three words in the dust. They are not yet written there; for scarcely, indeed, has the dagger been

> planted in the Saint's breast. But here, to the right, on this little scroll of parchment that hangs from a fence of osiers, there are some words written, and one stoops to decipher them . . . JOANNES BELLINUS FECIT.

The anachronistic scroll is the juncture of a martyrdom with an artist's consciousness, so that the event, the painting, and the writing about them all connect—act and image and idea at once. Beerbohm goes on:

> Now, had the Saint and his brother Dominican not been waylaid on their journey, they would have passed by this very fence, and would have stooped, as we do, to decipher the scroll, and would have very much wondered who was Bellinus, and what it was that he had done. The woodmen and the shepherd in the olive-grove by the roadside, the cowherds by the well, yonder—*they* have seen the scroll, I dare say, but they are not scholars enough to have read its letters.

Once the anachronism is set up in Beerbohm's prose, we see "the Saint and his brother Dominican" like an optical illusion, in history and in art at once. Their actions, stooping and deciphering, depend on not being waylaid, but also on being painted by Bellini.

The painting is both pattern and action. Through literature's power to release the physical and emotional movement caught in visual art, Beerbohm turns from the scroll to the whole phenomenon of the martyrdom:

> Cavina stands now over the fallen Saint, planting the short dagger in his heart. The other Dominican is being chased by Cavina's comrade, his face wreathed in a bland smile, his hands stretched childishly before him. Evidently he is quite unconscious how grave his situation is. He seems to think that this pursuit is merely a game, and that if he touch the wood of the olive-trees first, he will have won, and that then it will be his turn to run

> after this man in the helmet. Or does he know perhaps that this is but a painting, and that his pursuer will never be able to strike him, though the chase be kept up for many centuries?

The scene has that slowness, as in Faulkner, of history compressed into a moment. Ruskin used this painting as an example of "serenity in state or action," one of the four essentials of the greatest art. What Beerbohm does with the gentleness of the scene is to make a dreamlike game of tag, with the subjunctive "if he touch" and the innocence of "this man in the helmet." The event becomes a ritual played out for the sake of Bellini, and the Dominican's innocence is the comic-strip kind all fictional creatures enjoy.

"Does he know perhaps that this is but a painting?" By an arrest of motion, the pursuer forever pursuing, Beerbohm catches the Dominican in an element somewhere between the event, the painting, and the writing—an element of questions about the forces shaping experience. Then he moves to a final paradox, the one that was implied all along:

> Even we, posterity, think far less of St. Peter than of Bellini when we see this picture; St. Peter is no more to us than the blue harmony of those little hills beyond . . . The little screed on the fence is no mere vain anachronism. It is a sly, rather malicious symbol. PERIIT PETRUS: BELLINUS FECIT, as who should say.

The difference between "Peter the Dominican" and Wilde's conversational technique—a sunset "a very second-rate Turner"—shows how far Beerbohm had come in a few years. His particular talent here is to imagine the things a critic would deal with ordinarily—act, image, and artist—in extraordinarily lively relation to each other. We go to the heart of criticism's perennial subject, the interpenetration of art and experience, in trying to conceive the dimension in which Bellini kills Peter.

In 1939 Beerbohm wrote (but did not publish) a six-paragraph story called "Ten Years Ago," occasioned by a painting hanging in the Surrey cottage he lived in during the war. This painting, showing an oddly constructed house and five graceless people, made him want to explain this modern scene. He did it in the form of "words for pictures," describing how the five people—two unemployed and malformed clerks, a Borstal boy, a discharged cook, and a woman with a tin apron—came to this house on the edge of the world but could not go in because it was too small. They are still there, unhappy and dull. Now and then a Mr. Oepts comes and says to them brightly that they make a nice pattern. When I first saw this manuscript essay without any identification, it seemed an unexpected parable or fairy tale of ugly, vacant life—something attributable to "school of Kafka" and not at all what Beerbohm would sit down to write. It made sense then to find that a painting had acted as catalyst for Beerbohm's spiritual critique of the modern spirit. The strongest effects in "Ten Years Ago" are visual. Everything is badly formed, as if to stress the null or negative effect the artist has in these empty, isolated lives. In fact, Beerbohm was writing out his impression of modern poetry, represented particularly by T. S. Eliot. A month before, he had received a copy of Eliot's poems and had written to a friend about how little pleasure they gave him. As parts of *Four Quartets* came out between 1939 and 1942, he commented several times by quoting a favorite nineties' music-hall lyric,

> Wot's the good o' trying to earn a living nowadays? . . .
> Wot's the good of *ennyfink?* Why, *nuffink!*,

that seemed to him to summarize Eliot's poetry. "Oepts" must be an anagram for "poets," and "Ten Years Ago" forms an inspired gloss on the link in *Four Quartets* between the poetic and the human "pattern."

Critics as Artists

In Walter Pater and his disciples, Beerbohm found the fullest example of personal impressions and works of art flowing in and out of each other. Pater's book *The Renaissance* (1872) had several strong tendencies. Saying that each art could "pass into the condition of some other art," it obscured the border between painting and prose, a border that *Words for Pictures* keeps clear by calling attention to it. And where Beerbohm plays with his critical response to paintings, Pater's impressions actually displace the work of art and turn into a romantic absolute—in Wilde's words, "more creative than creation . . . the highest criticism is that which reveals in the work of Art what the artist had not put there." Wilde's essays are the ones "Mr. Pater is often obliged blushingly to repudiate," in Beerbohm's 1894 hoax, and one of the last sketches in *Words for Pictures,* "Ho-Tei," involves not only Pater's work as a critic but also the influence of Pater on Wilde and George Moore.

In 1901 Beerbohm produced this piece of ecphrastic writing that embraces much of late nineteenth-century art criticism. "'Ho-Tei': A Coloured Drawing by Hokusai" begins, "What monster have we here . . . swathed in his abominable surplusage of bulk," and imitates that surplusage by parodying what critics might say about Hokusai's drawing.* Beerbohm did not have to invent an interest in the prolific Japanese painter and caricaturist, whose work reached France and England soon after his death in 1849 and was still popular among the artists Beerbohm knew. Hokusai's exuberance in treating all kinds of life and his bold economy meant, for Beardsley and others, a newfound freedom of representation. Whistler refers to him at the climax of his "Ten O'Clock" lecture in 1885, and George Moore's *Confessions of a Young Man* (1888) declares his "readiness to decapitate all the Japanese in Japan and elsewhere, to save from destruction one drawing by Hokusai." Wilde's "Decay of Lying" claims that real Japanese do not exist at all except in the pictures of Hokusai, and for Beerbohm, a troupe of Kabuki players he reviewed in 1901 seemed to come "incarnate from the conventions of Utamaro and Hokusai."

The first description of Ho-Tei follows closely the way Hokusai drew the Japanese god of increase and good fortune:

> Wide his nose, narrowly-slit his eyes, and with little teeth he smiles at us through a beard of bright russet—a beard soft as the russet coat of a squirrel, and sprouting in several tiers according to the several chins that ascend behind it from his chest. . . . He seems to be very happy, sprawling here in the twilight. The wine oozes from the wine-skin; but he, replete, takes no heed of it. On the ground before him are a few almond-blossoms, blown there by the wind. He is snuffing their fragrance, I think.

The gratuitous sentence at the end calls to mind George Moore's whimsical, self-conscious style in art criticism, and Moore had several fleshy word-portraits of Ingres's figures resembling this description of Ho-Tei. In a biographical sketch of Moore, Beerbohm wrote that "no one but Ruskin has written more vividly than he, more lovingly and seeingly, about the art of painting." But the drawing by Hokusai was already a caricature, and "Ho-Tei" is overcharged with words. There is a point at which fastidious attention to the features of experience no longer vivifies them, as Pater thought, but embalms them.

Ho-Tei's complacence satirizes the egotistic impressionism of Pater and Moore:

> He is far too fat to care for humanity, too gross to be divine. I suspect he is but some self-centred sage, whom Hokusai beheld with his own eyes in a devious corner of Yedo. . . . we revel as whole-heartedly as he in his monstrous contours. "I *am* very beautiful," he seems to

> murmur. And we endorse the boast. At the same time, we transfer to Hokusai the credit which this glutton takes all to himself. It is Hokusai who made him, delineating his paunch in that one soft summary curve, and echoing it in the curve of the wine-skin that swells around him. Himself, as a living man, were too loathsome for words; but here, thanks to Hokusai, he is not less admirable than Pheidias' Hermes, or the Discobolus himself.

"Ho-Tei," like "Peter the Dominican," constructs a criticism out of four elements: the artist, the actual subject, the technique, and the viewer: "Hokusai beheld," "I *am* very beautiful," "that one soft summary curve," "We endorse the boast." But there is no movement here, no questioning, only passive appropriation of the drawing. And it is Praxiteles' Hermes, not Pheidias': Beerbohm has in mind Wilde's knowing allusion to Pheidias in "The Decay of Lying," and also Moore's casual grasp of facts. For the image of complacent aesthetic appreciation, he could have gone to a review by Moore of Charles Keene's drawings. Moore describes Keene's "fat farmer . . . the great stomach, how well it is drawn," and the drawing of a big artist "who thinks of nothing but his art, who lives in it, who would not be thin because fat enables him to sit longer out of doors . . . to me that man never really existed until I looked upon this drawing." A 1903 review by Beerbohm makes it clear that Ho-Tei, the "self-centred sage," stands for Moore's and Pater's kind of critic. He talks in the review about Pater, Anatole France, and the school of "temperamental" criticism: "As with the masters, so with the disciples. They seem quietly greedy . . . self-centred." The word "temperament" had occurred twice in "Ho-Tei," and was revised to "fatness."

Beerbohm really liked elaborate prose, but what struck him in Pater was the spiderlike preservation of every perceived shape and motion, and the resulting enervation. The sentence in Pater's "Mona Lisa" passage which begins, "She is older than the rocks among which she sits," accumulates nine successive "and"-clauses: "like the vampire she has been dead many times, and learned the secrets of the grave; and has been a diver in deep seas, and keeps their fallen day about her; and trafficked for strange webs and . . ." This passage hung in the air during the nineties. Beerbohm adapted it farcically in describing Queen Victoria, the Prince of Wales, and Robert Ross, as if agreeing with Pater that Mona Lisa contained all modes of experience. He quotes Pater's passage, with one extra word stuffed in, to reflect on the beauty of Ho-Tei:

> "It is a beauty," like that of Mona Lisa, "wrought out from within upon the flesh, the" adipose "deposit, little cell by cell, of strange thoughts and fantastic reveries and exquisite passions." It is the beauty of real fatness—that fatness which . . . makes a man selfish, because there is so much of him, and venerable because he seems to be a knoll of the very globe we live on, and lazy inasmuch as the form of government under which he lives is an absolute gastrocracy—the belly tyrannising over the members whom it used to serve, and wielding its power as unscrupulously as none but a promoted slave could.

He had reviewed *Coriolanus* the month before publishing "Ho-Tei," and picked up the play's metaphor for the body politic. It serves here as expansive material, grotesquely unwinding a more and more imperceptive sentence. And the word "adipose," pasted into Pater's prose like the Dadaist moustache put on "Mona Lisa" by Marcel Duchamp, is meant to carry the last deposit of fat after four centuries of admiration.

It obsessed Beerbohm to portray one writer's reliance on another. Moore's umbilical attachment to Pater explains the insinuations of *The Renaissance* in "Ho-Tei," and appears again in one of the funniest *Christmas Garland* parodies, "Dickens." The parody arises from Moore's own essays on

Balzac and French Impressionism. It wanders through his habitual critical landscape of harmless gaffes, digressions, vagueness, trivia, misplaced eroticism, and unconscious plagiarism. In the parody he calls Tintoretto Flemish, Renoir's palette somber, wonders what narrow-flanked girl inspired Palestrina, suggests Franz Hals's skill at deciduous and wistful aspens and Manet's delight in red cheeks. Finally he praises "the disengaging of the erotic motive" in *Pickwick Papers'* Nathaniel Winkle and Arabella Allen (though in fact Moore was not fond of Dickens) and lapses into musing on Arabella's timelessness:

> Strange thoughts of her surge up vaguely in me as I watch her—thoughts that I cannot express in English . . . Elle est plus vieille que les roches entre lesquelles elle s'est assise; comme le vampire elle a été fréquemment morte, et a appris les secrets du tombeau; et s'est plongée dans des mers profondes, et conserve autour d'elle leur jour ruiné; et . . .

We get Moore's pride in a fin-de-siècle Parisian idiom, and the joke that he cannot express in English thoughts that are originally in English. Pater's images of "Mona Lisa" surge up to be pre-empted by Moore as his own. It is parody of the finest complexity.

Moore himself claimed to have seen an irony in the "Mona Lisa" passage. Behind the mask Pater could not lift, he wrote, "was a shy, sentimental man, all powerful in written word, impotent in life." Beerbohm went a step farther. Pater, he felt, wrote like a widower hanging over the sepulchre. The gospel of impassioned experience which Pater drew from art fascinated Beerbohm only in contradiction with Pater's tepid, withdrawn existence. In private, Beerbohm called him an "old woman," a "humpback *manqué.*" As a kind of warrant, he put a presentation note into his copy of Pater's *Miscellaneous Studies*—"For Max Beerbohm ingenioso et audaci"—and also some "opinions of the Press":

> Preaches the doctrine of work with less perhaps than Carlyle's persuasiveness but with possibly more than Carlyle's rude vigour. . . . —*Daily Telegraph*

> Something of raucousness but much of virility . . . Mr. Pater does not mince his words. —*Spectator*

Another paper cites his "robust faith in the industrial system." These "opinions" reflect Pater's fastidious, retiring character; yet Beerbohm himself disliked Carlyle, work, raucousness, overvirility, the industrial system. He cultivated their opposites, and stayed at one with himself by taking Pater's contradictions as comic material.

Beerbohm's sharpest critique comes via the narrator of a projected novel, *The Mirror of the Past.* Sylvester Hethway reports that Pater

> earnestly counselled the young to be—what was the famous phrase?—to "be present always at the focus where the greatest number of vital forces unite in their purest energy." And he himself could not stand Kensington High Street. He very solemnly warned the young that "to form habits is failure in life." I suggested to him one day that in the next edition of his book he ought to add a foot-note: "In life, however, there are worse things than failure: for example, not having one's cup of tea, with a slice of thin bread and butter, at five o'clock *punctually.*" He laughed gently and said, "That is a shrewd jest at *me,* Hethway; but not at the sincerity of my doctrine."

Beerbohm gets evident joy in conceiving this scene. Having parodied Pater and his school in "Ho-Tei," he now separates the man from his own ideas. The last incarnation of the critic as artist is the comic writer like Beerbohm who rebuilds a whole structure connecting actuality, art, and criticism.

Rossetti and The Mirror of the Past

"The past is a work of art," Beerbohm wrote at the age of seventy. It was therefore doubly desirable to him: open to the critical imagination as well as to nostalgia. Two of his major works during the First World War, *The Mirror of the Past* and *Rossetti and His Circle,* move back to the eighteen-sixties and seventies, to the nature and condition of the artist then. They move back, they do not look back: at its best, Beerbohm's criticism, like his parody, re-creates what it has to consider. In a 1955 BBC broadcast, he introduces some excerpts from *The Mirror of the Past* as "Hethway Speaking," an older man's reminiscences. By deliberately removing the point of view on Pater, Rossetti, Meredith, Morris, Carlyle, and Whistler to the past, he objectifies his sense of these artists. Hethway's reports as an eyewitness are authentic. Not until the end of the broadcast does Beerbohm reveal that Sylvester Hethway existed "only in my imagination. . . . I thought that he as a real person would be likelier than I as a fabricator to impress and please you."

The Mirror of the Past, begun in 1913 and never completed, was to have been a fantasy arising from the powers of a circular, convex Regency mirror hanging in Sylvester Hethway's drawing room—a mirror that ceased reflecting the present and began to reflect things long past, people Hethway had known. It had, Beerbohm said, "a *temps perdu* of its own." He actually had a Regency mirror from his nursery and kept it with him throughout his life. Its properties fascinated him, not as a funhouse piece so much as a clue to aesthetics: "There is no poetry in a straight mirror—just a reproduction of life. But what one sees in a convex mirror is a complete picture, a composition, an *intérieur.* By miniaturizing, it concentrates and essentializes."

The hundred pages of drafts, diagrams, and illustrations for Beerbohm's projected novel provide a sense of his complex visual and literary imagination. He planned to write the book in his own person, as a friend of Hethway and inheritor of the mirror. The notes detail Hethway's discovery that "reflections in a mirror are not mere illusions nor mere momentary films: they are films that stack themselves, one above the other, behind the surface of the glass," at a rate of one thousand per second. These are held by the pressure of new films, but in 1889 Hethway's experiments release them. Everything in the convex mirror is reversed in space as well as time, so that Hethway lights candles "by merely puffing his cheeks at them," and Whistler, Pater, and others walk backwards into the drawing room. To confirm his fantasy for this book, Beerbohm made diagrams showing the lapse of time in both directions, and long notes on the nature of reflection, the constant succession of multitudinous, disintegrating images somehow preserved in the quicksilver of the mirror. These ruminations, untypical of Beerbohm, might be the rationale for perceptual experiments that Virginia Woolf and James Joyce were to make.

For *The Mirror of the Past* he meant to use his speculations, and what the notes call a "dreadful little talent for parody," to develop apocryphal memoirs or vignettes. There are sketches for several episodes, including a jaunty letter from Whistler to Hethway, and exact biographical data on the Pre-Raphaelites. The outcome of it all, however, was a book of caricature. Interrupting *The Mirror of the Past* (it became "too complicated," Beerbohm said later, "I couldn't understand it myself"), he began drawing *Rossetti and His Circle*. These two works clearly belong together: the draft for the novel has drawings of Rossetti, Swinburne, Ford Madox Brown, Elizabeth Siddal, Ruskin, and others who appear in Beerbohm's set of caricatures; and one incident that he invented, between Rossetti and George Meredith, occurs in both works. The preface to *Rossetti and His Circle* suggests the most important link. Beerbohm says that in preparing this book he has used, besides old drawings and paintings, early photographs, and eyewitness accounts, "another and surer aid, of the most curious kind imaginable. And some day I will tell you all about it, if you would care to hear." This is not exactly whimsy. There is even a convex Regency mirror on the wall in the last Rossetti caricature. Certainly Beerbohm was talking about this particular form of his imagination, and about the novel that would embody it.

A niece of Rossetti's said that no one within their circle had given so good a picture of the Pre-Raphaelites, physically and spiritually, as Beerbohm. The convex mirror represents a capacity to reflect details and still create a single, essential vision. Each caricature was prepared with enough pictorial and historical accuracy to support its hypothetical situation. He did trial drawings of the various artists at different stages of their lives and put plausible replicas of Rossetti's and John Millais's paintings into the background of the caricatures. One scene shows Rossetti, at work on his Arthurian fresco at the Oxford Union, approached by the academician Benjamin Jowett: "And what were they going to do with the Grail when they found it, Mr. Rossetti?" In the background of this Victorian confrontation, Rossetti's fresco is exactly reproduced, down to pencil sketching for parts of the design he had not painted yet. Beerbohm follows Rossetti's whole career, beginning with his "queer indifference to politics" as a young boy sprawled under a table, drawing, among his father's Italian patriot friends, and ending with Wilde's annunciation of Rossetti in America in 1882, the year the painter died.

The humor in *Rossetti and His Circle* comes from a historical divination that collapses the generalities, the illusion of logical process, with which we keep the past in order. Beerbohm reanimates specific situations to feel their contradictions. One set of drawings concerns the ménage of Rossetti, Swinburne, and Meredith that Rossetti set up after his wife's death in 1862. William Rossetti's 1895 memoir describes the depressed condition of his brother then, and his

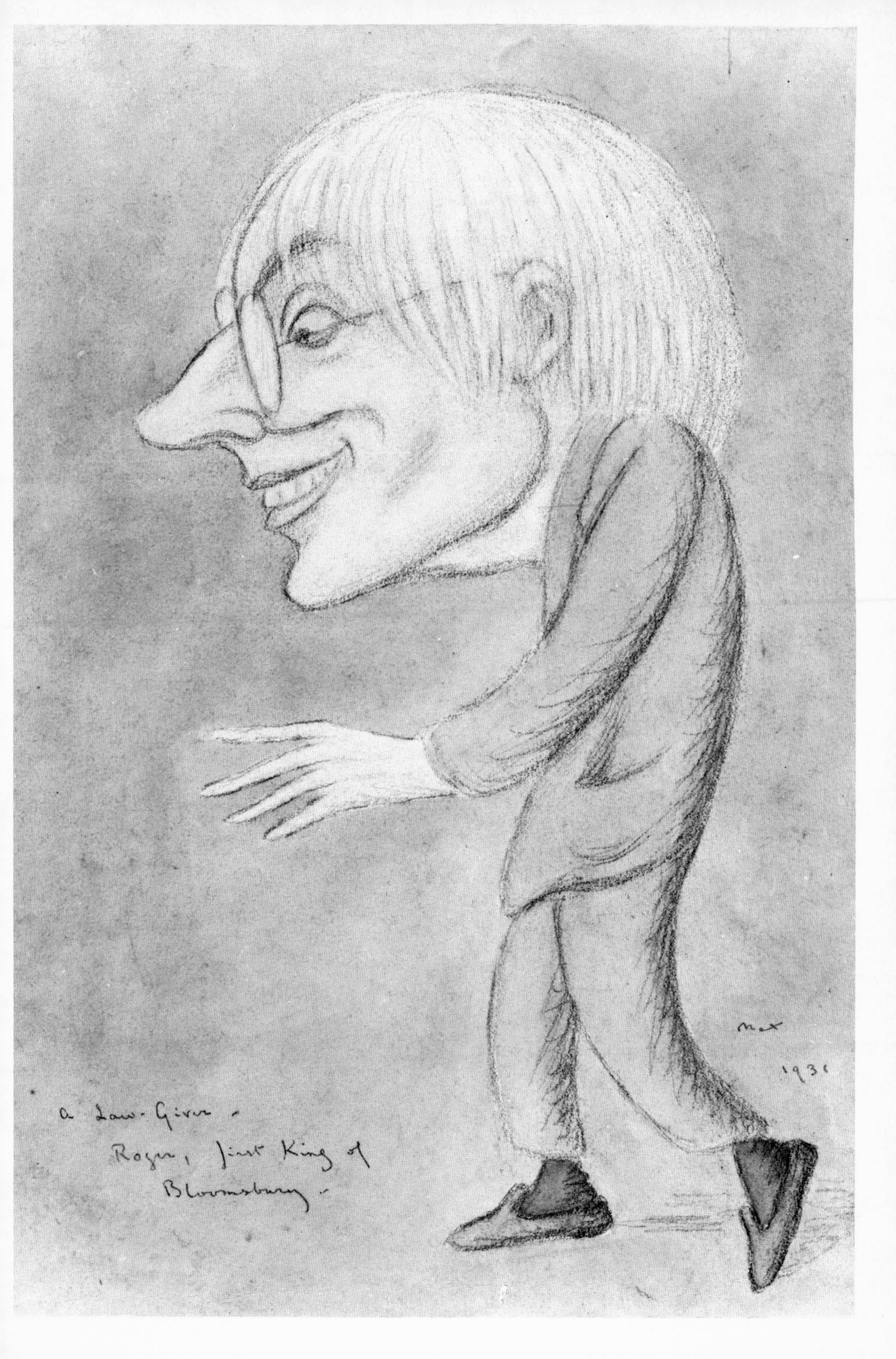
Max
1931
a Law-Giver –
Roger, first King of
Bloomsbury –

IX

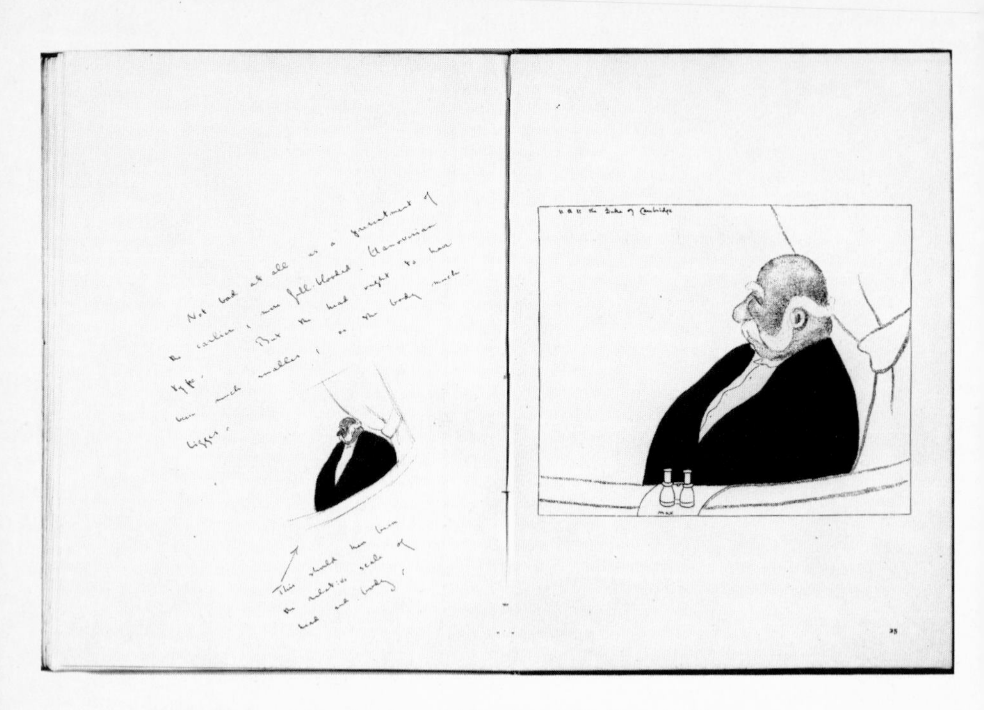

The Duke of Cambridge and Rudyard Kipling, 1896,
from CARICATURES OF TWENTY-FIVE GENTLEMEN, *emended 1920*

OVERLEAF: *Roger Fry, 1931*
"A Law-Giver—Roger, first King of Bloomsbury"

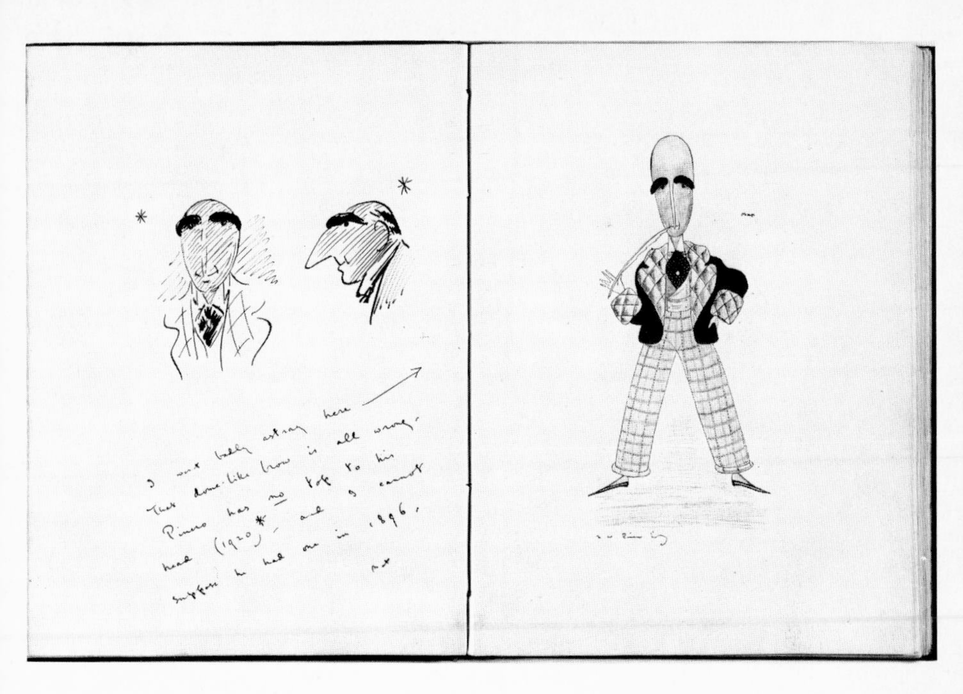

Arthur Wing Pinero and Lord Rosebery, 1896,
from CARICATURES OF TWENTY-FIVE GENTLEMEN, *emended 1920*

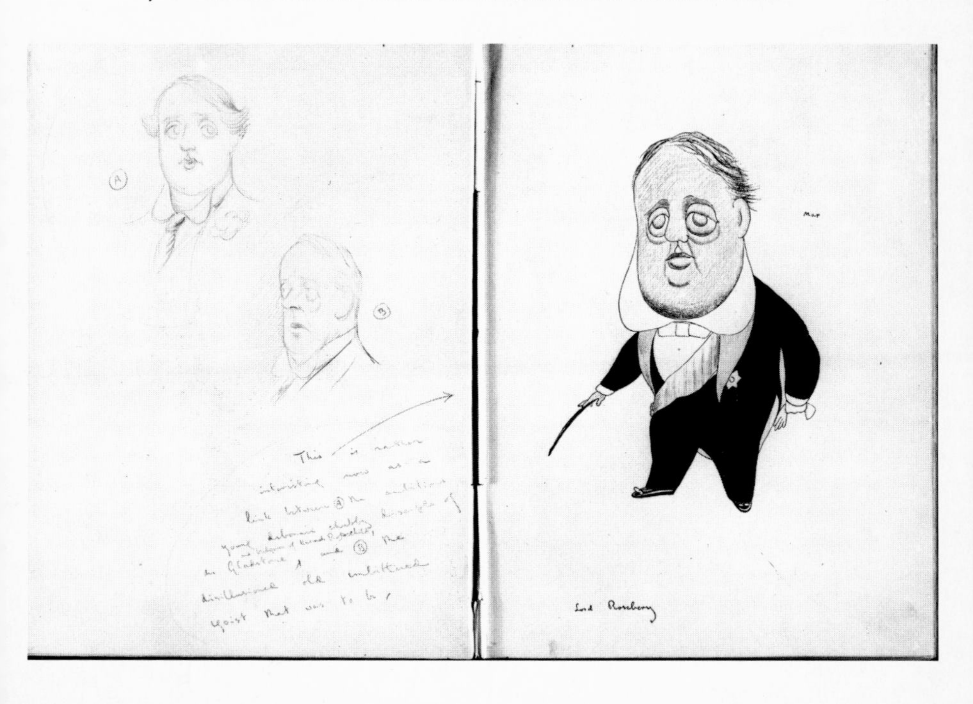

"One fine morning, or, How they might undo me," 1911

LEFT TO RIGHT:

L. V. Harcourt, G. K. Chesterton, Lord Kitchener, W. J. Locke, W. L. Courtney, Arthur Balfour, Lord Curzon, Israel Zangwill, Wilson Steer, Henry Tonks, F. E. Smith, Lord Ribbesdale, Andrew Lang, J. S. Sargent, A. B. Walkley, Lord Burnham, Lord Spencer, A. W. Pinero, Alfred Sutro, George Moore, Arnold Bennett, Rudyard Kipling, William Rothenstein, Hall Caine, Lord Haldane, G. B. Shaw, R. J. Campbell, Lord Rosebery, Marquess de Soveral, Herbert Asquith

Henry James,
by John Singer Sargent, 1886

Henry James, 1898

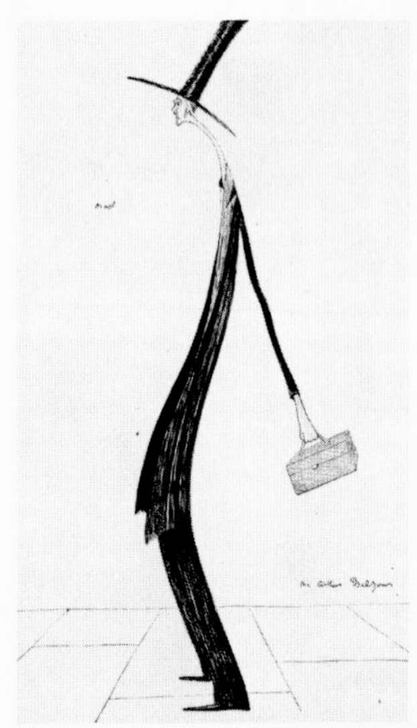

"Mr W. B. Yeats,
presenting Mr George Moore
to the Queen of the Fairies," 1904

Arthur Balfour, 1896

Sir Edward Carson, 1912

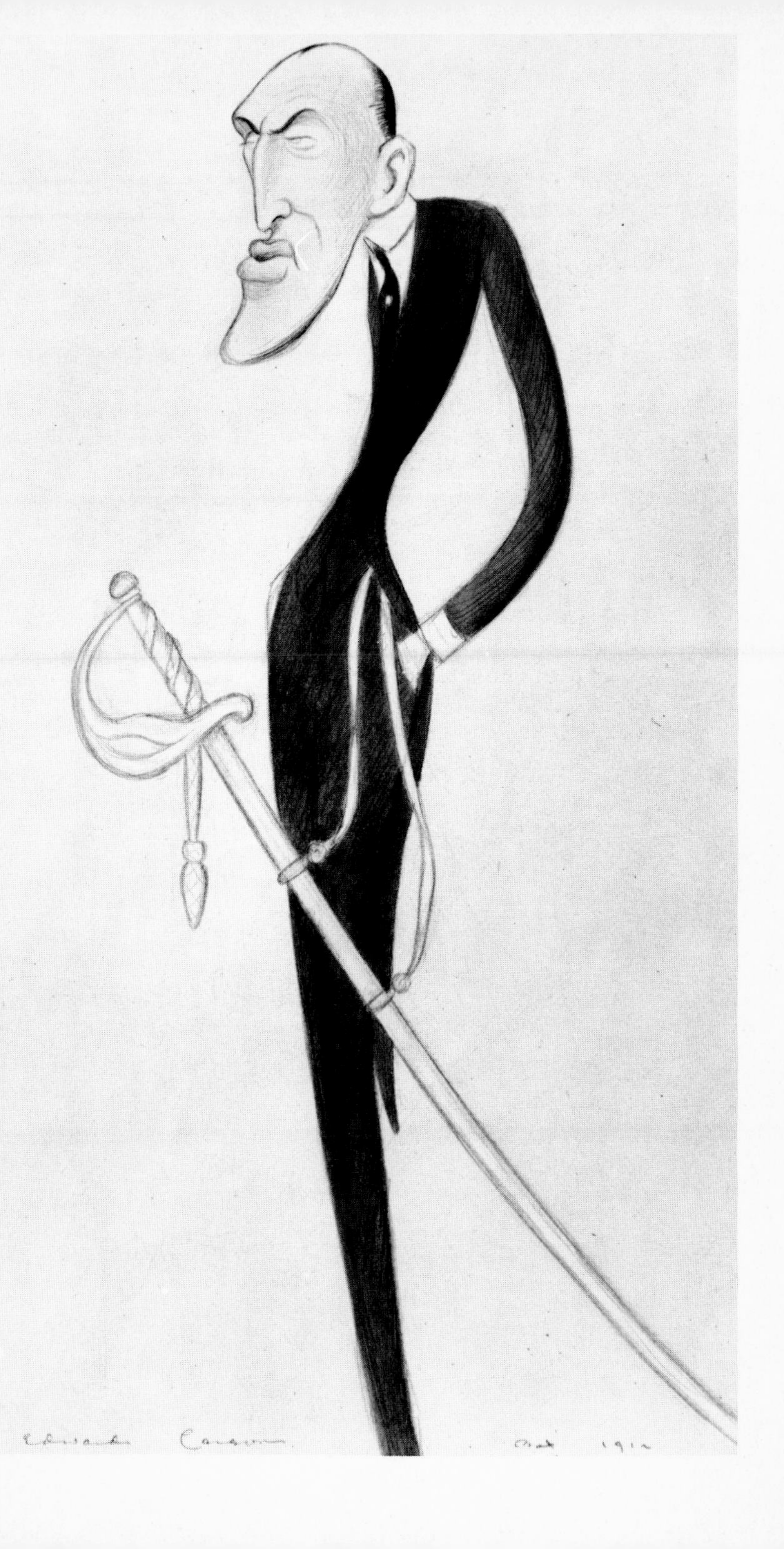

XV

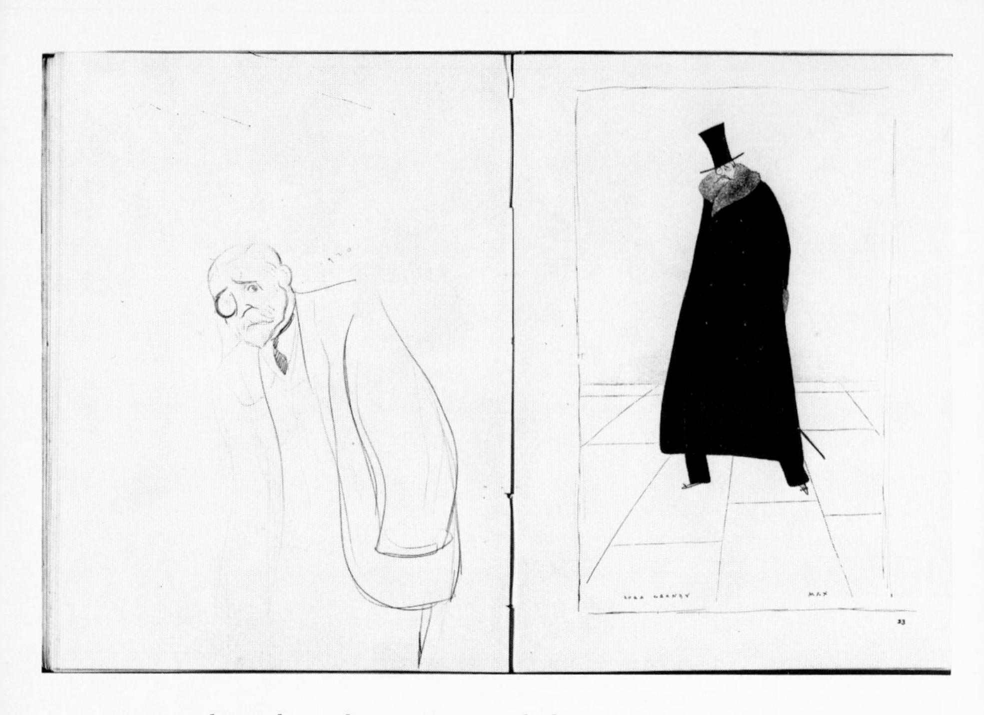

Lord Granby and George Bernard Shaw, 1896,
from CARICATURES OF TWENTY-FIVE GENTLEMEN, *emended 1920*

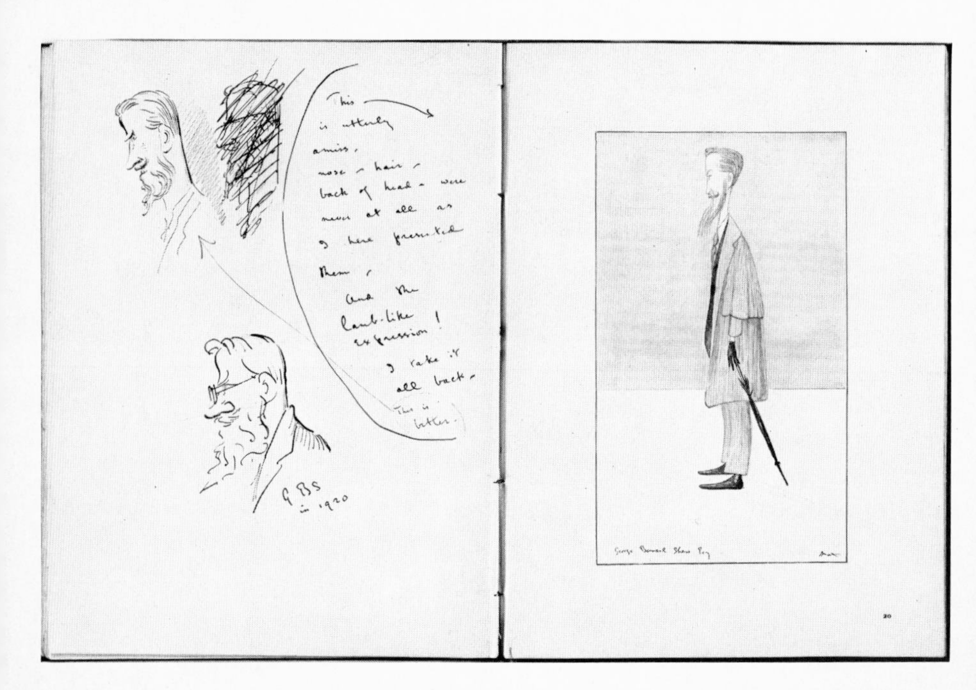

need for distraction. Beerbohm, who read the memoir, dates at "Autumn 1862" a caricature in which Meredith exhorts Rossetti to come on a brisk long walk to Hendon and beyond, but he shows Rossetti sullenly trying to ignore Meredith and go on painting. The similar scene from "Hethway Speaking" has Rossetti say to Meredith, "if you brought Hendon to me in your hand, I wouldn't look at it." William Rossetti also mentions that his brother particularly wanted Swinburne with him, because "he needed some inspiriting association." Beerbohm transforms this into Swinburne, under a head of wild red hair, reading to the two brothers from "Anactoria," a sapphic poem he wrote in 1862 with lines such as "Ah, ah, thy beauty like a beast it bites!" William is sitting dead somber; the widower Gabriel slumps on a chaise longue, scowling painfully.*

These caricatures resolutely locate the artist at odds with his personal circumstances. In what Beerbohm calls "Rossetti's Courtship," a long, disorderly period of cohabitation, Miss Siddal looks severe, delicate; Rossetti is sloppy and bored; a portfolio of sketches is strewn over the floor. Later in the book he is shown introducing a new friend to a new model, John Ruskin to Fanny Cornforth. That she was an uneducated, voluptuous girl and that Ruskin, who encouraged the Pre-Raphaelites, had recently had his marriage annulled on the grounds of impotence, accounts for the dubiousness in Rossetti's face. Other drawings in the book point to Rossetti's distance from social issues. The most surprising scene has John Morley bringing a pale, intellectual John Stuart Mill to Rossetti in 1869, for their common "interest" in women. Morley, plucking at Rossetti's coat, wants him to do a series of paintings illustrating Mill's *Subjection of Women,* while Rossetti, with a dreamy, sensuous female on the wall behind him, looks dark and suspicious.

Rossetti's career may have meant for Beerbohm the last time an artist could be "complex and elusive," as the preface puts it, and not deal himself out to society like Whistler,

Wilde, Shaw, and Beerbohm himself. To be interesting, a man should be "born outside his proper time and place"; Rossetti shone with an ambiguous light "in London, in the great days of a deep, smug, thick, rich, drab, industrial complacency." In the midst of wartime, Beerbohm partly settles his own emotions on Rossetti, and ignores the shrewd, bouncy, comical side of the artist. Rossetti's troubled posture in the drawings and his gloomy, careless dress are a figure for estrangement. Yet the Pre-Raphaelite faces, in contrast to Beerbohm's usual caricatures, are barely distorted, and the complete watercoloring he did for the book romanticizes Rossetti's milieu. Two colors, gold and blue, suffuse these drawings with life. They were important in Pre-Raphaelite painting, and predominate throughout *Rossetti and His Circle* almost as motifs for Arcadian vividness and innocence.

Rossetti had an artist's conviction that drew Beerbohm to him. In a *Yellow Book* essay, Beerbohm had described the Pre-Raphaelites as a "band of shy artificers." Later, with a firmer sense of what he valued in art, he began to see the period as a lost time back before beauty had to be advertised. The convex mirror of imagination in *Rossetti and His Circle* secured and composed that time.

Illusion in Plays

In the only job he ever had, writing on theater, Beerbohm produced nearly five hundred articles between 1898 and 1910. Eric Bentley calls his reviews the best weekly dramatic criticism in English next to Shaw's, and Edmund Wilson describes them as courageous and free from prejudice. Unlike the earlier essays, they are firm in tone. If a concerted body of opinion emerges from what Beerbohm wrote, it is around the question of aesthetic illusion, for the action, characters, and conversation in drama make it potentially the most lifelike form of art.

"I don't care a damn about the theatre," he said in a letter to Shaw when Shaw asked him to take over on the *Saturday Review*. His casual attitude stemmed from childhood; through his brother, Beerbohm had easy, constant access to the theater and as early as 1895 he published a multiple parody of London's five major theater critics. He brought a jaded faith to the *Saturday Review* job. Four times in one paragraph of his first official article, "Why I ought not to have become a dramatic critic," Beerbohm asserts a lack of love for the theater. This is partly self-protection; he was not likely to commit himself fully in a realm his older brother already dominated. But the job's prestige and regular pay were welcome, and in any event Beerbohm's interest was such that he never stopped doing caricatures of stage people. As a critic he remained flexible enough to cope with everything that came along—Aristophanes, Gorki, stage censorship, Ibsen in Italian. Sometimes the play under review comes in on a tangent and disappears a few sentences later while Beerbohm continues on his own theme. In any case there is plenty of humor and intelligence, if no deep faith in the use of criticism and no zeal like that of his friend Gordon Craig for the central, saving experience of theater.

What Beerbohm wrote for the Thursday deadlines, shutting himself in his room while his mother kept the house quiet, does not have the resonance of writing like *Words for Pictures,* which finds a comic subject in the difference between art and actuality. As a drama critic, he ordinarily could only analyze that difference. He felt that a critic "has to regard the story as a work of art, all the time, and is thus precluded from the rapture of illusion." When the play at hand was not good enough to be enjoyed, though, he often went to parody as a way of resolving the analyst's task. In one case he entirely re-conceived a miserable play in the idiom of a Sherlock Holmes tale. Or to help explain *The Devil's Disciple* he invented a suitable passage from Shaw's forthcoming preface.

A review of Arthur Wing Pinero begins with some clogged and stilted writing, in Pinero's style, to make a point about the theater. Modern drama has become realistic, Beerbohm says, and its characters must not sound like books, or conversely, like verbatim reports of ragged, irrelevant human speech. What is needed is unobtrusive "selections, compressions, sharpenings," somewhat the work of the convex mirror. This is the substance of Beerbohm's demand, in review after review, for realism, not reality. He makes the demand in a sober language of "must," "ought," and "should" that occurs nowhere else in his writing.

A series of opinions from various reviews will show how his mind ran: a child should not play the part of a child; cardboard horses would have been more convincing in *Cyrano de Bergerac* than real horses, whose "hoofs fall with a series of dull thuds"; public and historical figures well known to us seem strangely unreal as characters on the stage, or else they show up the rest of the play; Salome should have stayed in the shadows with the cardboard head of John the Baptist—instead she "brought the head briskly down to the footlights, and in that glare delivered to it all her words and kisses." Reviewing a performance of *Samson Agonistes* in 1908, Beerbohm complained about a Chorus entering down through the audience:

> After Samson's first speech our attention was attracted by a weird twittering noise at one of the entrances. The twitter developed into a murmur of feminine voices. Are the militant Suffragists upon us? we wondered, gazing up towards the door. A score of vaguely Phrygian figures came in view, and began to pick their way (very slowly, for fear of tripping up) down the steep gangway, ululating all the while, in our midst.

About the performer of tragedy: "If a mime lose not himself or herself in his or her part, he or she leaves us unilluded." Despite their awkwardness Beerbohm regularly used these two words—"mime" in place of "actor" or "actress," and "illude" for what drama should do. They both carry the sense not so much of reproducing as of playing on life.

Beerbohm's argument for an illusion of reality was steady though not exclusive. Although the kind of drama he had in mind was far from being in force, he was consistently fair to other kinds. A review of Maxim Gorki's *Lower Depths* shows about where Beerbohm's sympathies end. He tries to make his chief complaint against formlessness, not against theme. The play is not even a slice of life, "it is chunks, hunks, shreds and gobbets, clawed off anyhow, chucked at us anyhow." But his inevitable distaste for the life Gorki wrote about appears a year later when he reviews Tolstoy's play of peasant life, *The Power of Darkness,* and contrasts it favorably with Gorki. He finds in Tolstoy a pattern with a moral idea, and thus "we are compensated for the hideousness of [the] material." Gorki, says Beerbohm, is not an artist and merely "snap-shots his wastrels." "I dare say the characters in *The Lower Depths* are closely observed from life. But so are the figures in the lower depths of Madame Tussaud's quaint establishment [where the famous murderers are]. I defy you to leave the Chamber of Horrors . . . conscious of an aesthetic impression." Gorki's play was not performed again in England for fifty years.

Beerbohm's aesthetic rules and personal taste cut him off from much of early-twentieth-century literature, including Joyce and Eliot. About an author like Galsworthy, who was more congenial, he could write with interest. Shortly before retiring in 1910, he reviewed Galsworthy's *Justice,* still focusing on the problems of verisimilitude as he had been twelve years earlier in recommending cardboard horses:

> If the cinematograph were chromatic and stereoscopic, and free from vibration, and gramophonic into the bargain, Mr. Galsworthy might—no, even then, as I shall presently show, he would not have a dangerous rival. . . .

> The curtain rises on the second act; and presently we have forgotten the foot-lights, and are *in* a court of law. At a crucial moment in the cross-examination of a witness, somebody at the reporters' table drops a heavy book on the floor. An angry murmur of "sh!" runs round the court, and we ourselves have joined in it. . . . In the third act, we arrive at a prison. Gloomily producing a special pass signed "John Galsworthy," we are shown over the interior. We interview the governor, the chaplain, the doctor.

The cinema had not advanced far beyond mechanical realism in 1910; Beerbohm had probably seen films of such things as a prizefight or a group of employees leaving for lunch, and dramatic illusion could do better than that. *Justice* troubled him. This sense of being *in* a courtroom and *in* a prison abused "the game of producing an absolute illusion of reality."

Galsworthy had done a great deal of prison research for *Justice,* and Beatrice Webb praised the play's relevance to her "Minority Report of the Poor Law Commission." Soon after seeing *Justice,* the Home Secretary, Winston Churchill, announced a program of prison reform. Beerbohm's first-night review had predicted some such effect, but without much interest in the social consequences of Galsworthy's art. He appreciated the drama of capital against labor in *Strife,* but felt that the playwright belonged on the side of privilege, and had "sold his birthright for a pot of message." The pull of Galsworthy's birthright against his social conscience forms the subject of "Endeavour," Beerbohm's *Christmas Garland* parody about the anguish of a well-bred couple. If they dole out crumbs to a starving robin, will they be degrading it, or interfering with the collective action of the State? The robin dies, testifying to Galsworthy's misconceived responsibilities and to the futility of tendentious art.

Several times in 1907 and afterwards, Beerbohm made a point of studying dramatizations of the life of women and the middle class—social elements that he had trouble portraying in caricature. He asked why modern drama neglected the drab, perforce uncultivated middle class, and concluded, only halfheartedly, that really they were richly interesting characters. Another review contemplated the cold, lightless, lower-middle-class Ballard family: "Do such people as the Ballards really exist? I would fain hope not." A 1907 caricature of St. John Hankin, whose themes came from middle-class life, had him dressed in a loose, nondescript business suit and leaning unevenly against a straight, simple chair. In sum, Beerbohm's criteria were aesthetic, not sociological. The importance of getting this class into drama did not concern him, but rather the usual questions of illusion and meaningful action. In Elizabeth Robins's play *Votes for Women,* he ironically praised a Trafalgar Square rally whose "reality is overwhelming enough to be almost inartistic." One of his ruling social beliefs was that the element of play pervades life: after attending the 1908 trial of the suffragettes Christabel and Emmeline Pankhurst, he wrote a genuinely reasoned article on their movement as comic theater, with society playing the buffoon.

Instead of propaganda or raw slices, Beerbohm called for intellectual realism, like Ibsen's *Hedda Gabler* and *Rosmersholm.* But realizing that they were out of reach for British theater, he looked for the realistic comedy of ideas—a play that had something of Wilde and Shaw but was like life. Even this kind of drama was in short supply. A 1901 cartoon from *The Second Childhood of John Bull,* titled "De Arte Theatrali," shows the prospect he felt Edwardian drama really had: John Bull is waving aside Melpomene, muse of tragedy, and allowing Thalia, the muse of comedy, to remain as long as she does not try to "get Ideas" into her head. Beerbohm had enough John Bull in him to agree at least with the choice of muse. He himself wrote a one-act comedy of manners, *A Social Success* (1913), about a man who cheats at cards in a vain attempt to get free of upper-class smugness. As a critic, he rated the treatment of social mores by Henry Arthur Jones higher than that of any other British playwright. After Wilde's brilliant moment, Jones in 1898 was "the only dramatist of any intellectual force." That this estimate partly reflected the poor state of drama Beerbohm admitted tacitly when, in 1924, he included only one of his fourteen reviews of Jones in a large selection, *Around Theatres*. Beerbohm's criticism gave a great deal of attention but little encouragement to Pinero, the "tailor" to the West End who "keeps abreast of all the latest improvements in ideas" and is very good at stagecraft. From 1898 on, noting Pinero's attempts at intellectual drama, Beerbohm urged him to leave off pastiches of Ibsen and return to ingenious farces and the comedy of manners; for which Pinero called him "a scorpion in the guise of a scholar."

Beerbohm's criterion for drama, the illusion of reality, aligns his criticism with his other writing of the period. Often the reviews will fool with that criterion, as when he begins by reporting an absurd series of events that turns out to be nothing but the summary of a play's absurd plot. At bottom—and this is the key to his drama criticism—he enjoyed the workings of illusion more than the image of reality. The prose he wrote promoting Granville Barker, St. John Hankin, and other realists sounds constrained. An article at the end of his reviewing career, called "Confessional," admits that despite the years of urging ideas and contact with actual life, what he longs for is fantasy, joy, theatricality.

He got that pleasure from a range of things: *Charley's Aunt, The Importance of Being Earnest,* the "uproarious fun" of James Barrie's "modern fantasy" *The Admirable Crichton,* as well as the unimproved vulgarity of the music halls. The addiction to music halls in the nineties had the force, for Beerbohm, of a vital aesthetic convention. He wrote an early essay, various reviews, and a 1942 reminiscence about the Pavilion, the Tivoli, names like Albert Chevalier, Gus Elen, Dan Leno, Marie Lloyd, George Robey, and he had by heart whole stanzas of songs. What he liked about music halls was the fatuous, bawling humor, the talentless rendition of song after song "instilling a sense of deep beatitude—a strange sweet foretaste of Nirvana." The music hall may have been a kind of brothel for the man who did not want exactly that, and a place to catch life's sordidness in humorous, unpretentious form. Beerbohm also liked the grotesquerie of Punch and Judy, and a Barrie pantomime about harlequins—"the longer and the better they mimic, the more deeply do they absorb into their private souls their public semblance." He reviewed three different productions of *A Midsummer Night's Dream,* "the most impressive of all the plays." And from the beginning he responded to the dreamlike element in Maeterlinck, the dim emotional poignancy and remoteness. He thought Gordon Craig's towering, limitless sets perfect for fantasy, and another kind of strangeness that appealed to him was the Celtic drama of Yeats and Synge. Reading through Beerbohm's years of drama criticism, we come to see that his rational, persuadable, professional self carried on its job above another self that could be thrilled, terrified, bored, overjoyed, convulsed with laughter, transported.

George Bernard Shaw

"When Mr. Shaw is not morally purposeful, he is fantastic and frivolous, and it is then that his plays are good." In a May 1898 *Saturday Review* with Shaw's valedictory, which introduced "the incomparable Max" stepping sprightly in, Beerbohm wrote about *Mrs. Warren's Profession* as an implausible tragedy that should have been a farce. He instructed Shaw simply to be Paddy the stage Irishman. "If he will do that," the review ends, "he has a great future in

English drama." It was part of Shaw's personal economy to make his cocky critic his successor, and to announce him with the fatal line from Ibsen, "The younger generation is knocking at the door." Beerbohm's blessings were all thinly disguised curses, Shaw said, and he told a biographer: "Max only enjoyed my tricks. When I turned an intellectual somersault he rolled in his seat and when I did a bit of cerebral conjuring he had convulsions. He would have liked me best as a music-hall turn, dancing a mental tight-rope or producing endless japes by sleight-of-brain." There is more to it, however. Beerbohm's mixed attitudes in opening-night reviews and caricatures exemplify the response Shaw has evoked ever since.

Shaw loomed over the British theater from the mid-nineties on, and Beerbohm at the beginning had to have him his own way, someone he could cope with. In his copy of *Plays, Pleasant and Unpleasant,* he retouched a frontispiece photo by putting in the crinkly eyes, the canted, Mephistophelian brows and perky mouth that mark all his early caricatures of Shaw. Privately Shaw was not so amused by Beerbohm's sprightliness as the *Saturday Review* introduction suggests. His carefully preserved home has no Beerbohm caricature on the walls, and at an exhibition Shaw's wife bought a drawing in which Shaw looked slightly tipsy, only to tear it up in Beerbohm's face. Beerbohm's preference for frivolity, for the mental tricks, was shadowed by another feeling. Until 1905 he tended to consider Shaw's mind an "exquisite machine" and to talk about "the loud, rhythmic machinery of this brain at work." The characters in *Mrs. Warren's Profession* were "disputative machines." Even describing the brilliant dialogue of *Man and Superman,* in which "every phrase rings and flashes," Beerbohm made it sound mechanical. In all respects his image of Shaw puts Beerbohm's own qualities into relief.

At bottom he felt that Shaw was not an artist: Shaw failed to put the play itself ahead of everything else, and broke the integrity of his work by thrusting Shavian talk and opinion into it. *Man and Superman,* Beerbohm said in 1903, was "infinitely better . . . than any play." Since he had as little taste for Shaw's religious, political, and economic philosophy as for his play-writing, there was no way to approach him, as is evident in Beerbohm's caricature of himself tentatively coming upon "the dear fellow" standing on his head.*

"For art's sake alone, I would not face the toil of writing a single sentence." Beerbohm picked this from the preface to *Man and Superman* as an axiom; it explains why he had trouble dealing with Shaw, and not with Wilde and James. Shaw would use any form he could lay his hands on to make people listen, Beerbohm said, including melodrama and farce. Beerbohm faulted him for this, but in fact Shaw used the hackneyed Victorian forms as a decoy for radical moral questioning. Although Shaw fascinated him as a phenomenon, Beerbohm's twenty or so criticisms make very little case for the man in his vocation. He admits only a few convincing characters and brilliant debates, a great second act in *Major Barbara,* and occasional fun. The caricatures always display Shaw in sloppy dress, which for Beerbohm meant that he was inartistic. Another sign was Shaw's lack of empathy with the writers and artists in his plays. Comparing him with Henry James, Beerbohm criticized Shaw's use of real paintings to show the work of Louis Dubedat in *The Doctor's Dilemma:* they only reveal an inability to imagine the artist's genius for us. Generally Beerbohm attributed Shaw's failure in creating living characters to a lack of sympathy with human nature which he also found in other socialists, Sidney Webb and H. G. Wells. This charge appears in some manuscript notes on Shaw ("uncomfortable—never playing with dog or child . . . no joy") and throughout the reviews. Shaw's characters were inhuman because overly self-conscious and full of talk, Beerbohm said. As sometimes happened, the fault he found pointed indirectly to a strength in Shaw's art. You could not have Aesop's fables unless the animals talked, as Shaw once put it; in order to express forces we are not normally aware of, his characters have powers they would not possess in real life.

Still, in a 1905 review of *Major Barbara,* Beerbohm states an important principle: "to deny that he is a dramatist merely because he chooses, for the most part, to get drama out of contrasted types of character and thought, without action, and without appeal to the emotions, seems to me both unjust and absurd." Better than any criticism at the time, this answers the objection to Shaw's inhuman characters and identifies Shaw's dramatic form. But we have to allow, as Beerbohm did not, that thinking was a mode of action and emotion for Shaw. The 1907 performance of *Don Juan in Hell* he found superb but only as philosophic dialogue, as wit and logic, not as human drama. *Getting Married* (1908) was arid and *Misalliance* (1910) gave Beerbohm the sensation of walking up Praed Street (a street of squalid shops) on an empty Sunday morning against a wind that "drove into my eyes and mouth and ears dry particles of refuse. Bits of trampled paper careered wildly past me along the gutters. Orange peel and wisps of straw . . . There was a faint odour of staleness everywhere."

A random note that he made to himself traces pretty well the course of his criticism of Shaw: "My own first hostility—came round full circle. . . . He was best of his time—I fell under influence. My waning pleasure in his work—out of love with it." It took some nerve to say in 1898 that Henry Arthur Jones was the only dramatist of any intellectual force. For Beerbohm, the dramatist in Shaw was lacking, not the intellectual force. He kept to this position except for the years 1904–1907 and the Court Theatre's fine productions of *John Bull's Other Island* and *Major Barbara.* In the Irish play, he finds humor and serious interest blended, real characterization, and a relaxation of Shaw's dogmatism into "something almost like dubiety." He identifies Shaw with the disillusioned Larry Doyle, in contrast with "an unfrocked priest, a mystic, who touches a note of visionary wisdom that makes every other character seem cheap and absurd." But this is all Beerbohm says about Keegan, the mad alienated priest; for some reason he does not name him, or perceive that Keegan is a true figure of Shaw as much as Doyle is. Similarly, in reviewing *Major Barbara,* over which he recants his earlier dissatisfaction with Shaw, Beerbohm sees Barbara's spiritual beauty, her religious fanaticism, and her agony as a serious subject. But he mentions "her father" only in passing, without indicating that the figure of Undershaft, a man of the world, also embodies Shaw's passion. At various times he recognized either the idealist or the tough-minded streak in Shaw, but he found it difficult to grasp Shaw's strategies for reconciling them.

If the playwright never finally took hold on Beerbohm, the personality did. There are more caricatures of Shaw than of anyone except Beerbohm himself and King Edward. They cover a range of Shaws and pseudo-Shaws and Shaws-despite-himself: fop, capitalist, vegetarian, "sleek and portly" newlywed, self-advertiser, iconoclast, peddler of second-hand Schopenhauer and Ibsen and Nietzsche. Some of the drawings get their laugh too easily or merely incarnate a cliché. For the impulse behind Beerbohm's critique of Shaw, you need to look at his grotesque "improvements" on photographs. He kept at Archibald Henderson's 1911 biography of Shaw for more than a year, doctoring every photo and adding burlesque notes in Henderson's style. Many of the changes make Shaw a cunning clown or an idiot. Others have less animus in them. A photograph of Shaw's home at Ayot St. Lawrence had the usual note in small type at the bottom, "Facing p. 418." Beerbohm wrote in a caption saying that Shaw was "imprévoyable . . . the ordinary successful man chooses a country house facing South. Shaw chose one Facing p. 418." And for Rodin's bust of Shaw, this editorial note:

> The bust, as first conceived by Rodin, was to be a great noble mass of rough bronze, with just the tip of one eyebrow protruding somewhere near the summit, amidst several impressions of Rodin's own thumbs. "C'est comme ça," he said, "que je vois cet illustre poète et dramaturge."

The whole production is extremely funny, yet it exposes a helpless obsession with Shaw. The wit and intelligence that Beerbohm brought to Shaw very early as a critic displaced a deeper attitude, a need to neutralize Shaw's tremendous rhetoric and impressive, though vulnerable, personality.

Beerbohm's disgust with the exposures of sex and marriage in *Getting Married* and *Misalliance* can be seen partly in the light of his own sex life. He had had two engagements broken: a long one with a minor Irish actress in his brother's company, the second with a full-throated leading lady who allegedly felt that life with him would be carpet slippers. Then for six years he carried on a quiet friendship with a rather nervous American actress, Florence Kahn, before marrying at the age of thirty-seven and moving to the Italian Riviera. Nothing could have been farther from the mood of Shaw's bizarre relationships with the actresses Ellen Terry and Mrs. Patrick Campbell. Beerbohm produced some elaborate satiric drawings about the latter affair when the letters between Stella and Joey, as they called themselves, were published in 1922. He made them a childish music-hall duo, deceiving each other and themselves.

He was also sensitive to the egoism in Shaw which took the form of bluff gibing at others and at himself. When G. K. Chesterton's study of Shaw came out in 1909, Beerbohm caricatured its concluding sentence, about the man "whose spear was never broken" defending life itself against "the Spirit who Denies." The fun of the drawing is that both figures in it—a stage clown jousting with a cushioned wand against a stage devil—look like Shaw, as if to say that his idealism is really vanity. Beerbohm is reported to have taken Landor's famous quatrain and devised an epitaph for Shaw:

I strove with all, for all were worth my strife.
Nature I loathed, and, next to Nature, Art.
I chilled both feet on the thin ice of Life.
It broke, and I emit one final fart.

This is not vintage Max, but it brings out what separated him from Shaw. Shaw's reformism and his rough honesty with himself were paralleled in Beerbohm by a clear conscience, an acceptance of the shape of things. Once, however, by means of a parody, he caught Shaw's contradicted optimism profoundly, and from within the man.

In 1906, at the height of Shaw's first major accomplishment, Beerbohm wrote "A Straight Talk" as preface to an imaginary Shavian play called *Snt George*. He thought that Shaw was difficult to parody because there was no beauty in his style, yet the preface to *Snt George* is an uncanny document. "Flatly, I stole this play" from the Christmas mummers, it begins—as Shaw in one of his own prefaces announces his plagiarism of William Blake. The author admits that trapping his customers in barbed-wire dialectic and then "training my moral machine guns" on them used to be his method. Now he is not sure what it takes to reform humanity, perhaps dynamite (a presage of the desperate remedy in *Heartbreak House*). "I believe in the future; but this only makes the present—which I foresee as going strong for a couple of million years or so—all the more excruciating by contrast." In the parody, Shaw's optimism and self-reference have an increasing undertone of desperation as he describes the action of the play around England's patron saint. A Saracen knight, the body politic, rules in England with three attendant monsters, Good, Beauty, and Truth—that is, the current forms of Religion, Art, Science. Snt George slays them, but they are revived at the end by a Physician, who stands for

> that irresistible force of human stupidity by which the rottenest and basest institutions are enabled to thrive in the teeth of the logic that has demolished them. Thus, for the author, the close of the play is essentially tragic. But what is death to him is fun to you, and my buffooneries wont offend any of you. Bah!

Beerbohm in his reviews was used to making fun of Shaw for basing his plays on the fallacy of "life as logic." "A Straight Talk" gives that crucial judgment to Shaw to make, as he always does, in his own voice. So the parody creates an act of self-recognition without losing objective force against the man: it is "essentially tragic." The turn at the end—"what is death to him is fun to you"—places Shaw's idealism almost compassionately, as parody can, in the whole drama he set himself.

Henrik Ibsen

If Shaw had created Hedda Gabler, she would have been utterly different, Beerbohm guessed. Instead of the slow, subtle revelation of a psychology, as natural as if we had known her for years, she would talk too much about herself, understand her place in the universal scheme, and be turned inside out neatly by another character. Ibsen, however, was profoundly and meticulously an artist, and on the surface "no more explanatory or moralistic than Nature herself." This would have been a brave point on which to center his whole response to Ibsen. But the playwright's satiric inspiration skewed Beerbohm's judgment. Having decided that frivolity was Shaw's dramatic gift, he saw a specter in Ibsen, an example of pessimism and misanthropy. "Death and disease, disaster / And downfall were our joy, / . . . While Ibsen was our Master," runs a song he wrote about the nineties. Did Ibsen hate corrupt social conditions and also his own ignoble characters? Against his image of Ibsen an image of Beerbohm emerges: the skeptical innocent, aware of the world but not disposed to fight it.

The faith of Shaw and other disciples in Ibsen's redemptive philosophy put Beerbohm off, and his copy of *When We Dead Awaken* has a warm presentation note from Ibsen, written by Beerbohm in crude, heavy pen strokes. Two caricatures show Ibsen being worshipped by William Archer, his earliest advocate and translator in England: Ibsen is on a pedestal in one drawing; the other, from *The Poets' Corner,* has him scowling while Archer kisses his feet in a room papered with replicas of Ibsen's whiskery face. He also appears as an unlovable master in the *Christmas Garland* parody of Edmund Gosse, who excitedly brings Ibsen to Robert Browning, translating "God's in His heaven, all's right with the world" into Norwegian as they go. When Browning and Ibsen meet, Gosse has to intercede with mistranslations of the conversation in order to conceal Ibsen's insensitivity. The whole parody is overspread with a slight fear of what Gosse calls his "strange, crustacean genius."

Herbert Tree had produced Ibsen in the nineties (in matinees at first, to be safe), and at that time it was important to support Ibsen because Clement Scott and others were shocked by his indecency. By the time Beerbohm began reviewing, controversy over Ibsen in England had subsided. Certainly James Joyce's grandiloquent essay in 1900 on *When We Dead Awaken* is anticlimactic, historically if not for Joyce: "The shadow of a great change is stalking close in the morning silence. . . . Henrik Ibsen is one of the world's great men before whom criticism can make but feeble show." Beerbohm's early reviews take it for granted that Ibsen is the best dramatist of the century; the question is whether he will have false imitators like Pinero or "exceedingly good pastiches" by Shaw.

Florence Kahn had made a slight reputation playing Ibsen in New York before she married Beerbohm. This connection complicated Beerbohm's judgment a little, not only because he distrusted the Ibsenite New Woman but because Florence was definitely not one, and acted Ibsen peculiarly. After he had known Florence for four years, he applauded a London performance of *Rosmersholm* in which she played Rebecca: the characters "have been meticulously thought out by their creator, and are all full and vital"; while social conflicts are sharply presented, at heart the play unfolds mysteriously. Beerbohm devoted much of the review to carefully analyzing Miss Kahn's moving portrayal of secret emotion and her power "in the rare moments when Rebecca breaks through her reserve." But another reviewer who also liked the play thought Florence Kahn was inadequate: "a quiet, subdued voice and a self-repressed manner are all she gives us, except a few ebullitions of emotion." Reports about Florence's acting are generally mixed, and Beerbohm had to hedge when he praised her or her roles in plays he found extremely problematic.

The strangest of these plays was *When We Dead Awaken,* to which Florence as Irene, a New York reviewer said, brought only her "delightful elocution." It is Ibsen's last work, a slow-moving, symbolic, autobiographical epilogue about an old sculptor, Rubek, trying to regain the vital joy he has forfeited to art. ("When is a man not a man?" Shem asks in *Finnegans Wake*—to which one of the answers is, "when wee deader walkner.") At the end of the play Rubek and Irene, a former model whom he had spurned, climb upwards on a mountain at dawn and disappear suddenly in an avalanche of snow as a nun cries "Pax vobiscum!" Both Gosse and William Archer considered Ibsen's play a senile self-caricature, and *Punch* parodied it immediately. It is an awkward work in comparison with Ibsen's best plays. The feeling that Beerbohm developed for *When We Dead Awaken* tells us a great deal about himself.

When Florence Kahn did the play in New York, he wrote to her that Irene was a beautiful part, that Ibsen's meaning was beautiful too, and "as plain as a pikestaff." But his review in 1903, when the play was first performed, flatly says that it is feebly executed, and that the critics have been belaboring themselves seeking the meaning of *When We Dead Awaken*—there is nothing mysterious in it. Ibsen's moral is simply that a "great artist is always inhuman" and misses the greater joy of life. Beerbohm is unimpressed by the sublime ending in the mountains, which are, "obviously, symbols for freedom and reality of life." In "this business of the avalanche" and the death of the couple, he finds no awakening—only a tired old man's admission, "as clear as it can be," that now it is too late to change. The review ends: "Ibsen speaks to us, I doubt not, of himself."

Beerbohm introduces this critique in a cool way that reveals more about himself than about Ibsen. He sets up a pair of approaches to Ibsen's epilogue, saying in the opening paragraph that there are two kinds of critic. The first labors under a burden of profound insight, pretending that some quite obvious work is "fraught with all manner of brain-wracking and heart-breaking obscurities." The other critic, faced with a truly complex work of art, is "terribly at ease in Zion," disguising his bewilderment with "the pretence that all is as clear as noontide." The second kind is the "more plausible rogue," Beerbohm says, and he goes ahead with his criticism on that basis. His response to *When We Dead Awaken* is an impersonation, trying for a sensible as against a prophetic view of the cost of great art, choosing to be "at ease in Zion," aware, yet free of Ibsen's trouble.

The phrase he chooses to mark himself was originally an angry warning from the prophet Amos against profane, self-indulgent living in a time of trouble—"Woe to them that are at ease in Zion!" Carlyle used the phrase in the same vein, but Matthew Arnold reinterpreted it in *Culture and Anarchy*—Socrates is "terribly at ease in Zion"—to mean the critical spirit, the Hellenic clarity and flexibility of mind that perceive the right shape of life without being thwarted by a dark Hebraic sense of sin. In "The Critic as Artist," Wilde turns the phrase again to describe "ordinary people" who propose to walk comfortably among great poets without a sense of mystery and sanctity. Out of three nineteenth-century prophets Beerbohm derives his mask.

Several years later, Chesterton in his study of Shaw advised him to "be at ease in Zion"—that is, to relax his zeal and let a frivolous second self come out, "more real than the real person." Beerbohm had been saying the same thing to Shaw, and to himself in the 1903 Ibsen review. He meant to finesse or to mimic the steepest question: whether self-exposure finally defeats or transforms an artist. There were comic means to imagine an answer for Oscar and G.B.S. But Ibsen's severity really was troubling. When he died in 1906, Beerbohm's obituary came back powerfully to the question: "Throughout his life an artist essentially, he wrote in *When We Dead Awaken* a savage attack on the artistic nature which he exemplified. . . . he reserved his most vicious kick for himself." If Ibsen had been a clown like Shaw, or an inadequate artist like Gorki and Madame Tussaud, a conventional one like Bellini, an odd spectacle like Moore and Pater, an alien like Rossetti—that is to say, if Beerbohm had found room between the writer and his work, then he would not have been horrified by Ibsen. But what comic criticism cannot deal with, if it thrives on the play between art and actuality, is the artist's negation of his own creative will.

4

Caricature

The Impulse to Caricature

To render other men in caricature is an exposed, inherently controversial act of skill and criticism for the visual artist. Living in a city charged with images from politics and entertainment, the caricaturist comes forward as someone with a special grasp of personality, a shaping power over it. Beerbohm's drawings, from the first ones published at school in 1888 through his last exhibition in 1952, present a fascinating anatomy of selfhood in British cultural and political elites: what it is to be and to observe certain people. If he had not been a brilliant writer, the wit and original graphic qualities of his caricature alone would have distinguished him.

In understanding Beerbohm as an artist, we have to allow full play to the fact that he got from drawing an immediate joy that he did not get from writing. Vyvyan Holland, Wilde's son, remembered going to Beerbohm's home in London and watching him draw caricatures: "He would chuckle to himself all the time he was doing them." From the beginning, caricature was a habit and a pleasure for him. He started drawing and painting at the age of six, sometimes with his older brother Herbert—"What he excelled me in was Mr. Gladstone and Lord Beaconsfield." Beerbohm used to color in *Punch*'s cartoons every week, and Herbert would draw people he had recently met: "'This is Whistler, the painter,' he would say . . . or 'Here's Oscar Wilde, the poet.'" When he was a child, Beerbohm owned the early books illustrated by Randolph Caldecott and Kate Greenaway. He knew page for page the English version of Heinrich Hoffmann's *Struwwelpeter, or Pretty Stories and Funny Pictures for Children,* with its illustrations by the author stressing his characters' evil traits—Peter's hair hanging to his feet, his disgusting long nails. Beerbohm also had a book by Lewis Carroll with Henry Holiday's grotesque drawings for *The Hunting of the Snark.* Like Thackeray, he was known as a good caricaturist at Charterhouse; he drew his teachers, and read in Thackeray's *Paris Sketch Book* a chatty essay that suggested the centrality of caricature in Parisian culture. At Oxford, Beerbohm hung his room with prints by the caricaturist Carlo Pellegrini, *Vanity Fair*'s "Ape." Though he liked the Warden of Merton College, he drew him ruthlessly, in the likeness of a mad baboon, and once gave his tutor an essay with caricatures of the tutor on it.

Caricature is "a recreation to me," Beerbohm said in a 1903 interview. "To sit down to write is a business requiring thought and conscience. Caricaturing, on the other hand, is pure, natural instinct without any trouble at all." For twelve years he did drama reviews on Thursdays, putting them off until the last moment, laboring painfully over them, feeling perfect release when they were done. Caricatures, however, he often drew after coming home from parties, sketching face after face of the people he had met there. This distinction between the two arts associates one of them (at least in Beerbohm's mind) with the world of work and responsibility, the other with a world of play.

Beerbohm often drew while he wrote, as a way of self-inspiration. He almost never illustrated his published prose, but a great number of his manuscripts have impromptu illustrations in them, caricatures rapidly drawn in the margins and on the backs of sheets—"to refresh the fatigued scribe," he once said, thinking of the margins of medieval manuscripts. The fair copy of "A Peep into the Past" is decorated with caricatures of Wilde, taking him from infancy through old age to prove that his span of years is completed. While writing essays on Andrew Lang and George Moore, Beerbohm sketched their faces several times, as if that released his understanding of them. Some of his points in prose actually translate elements from his caricatures of Moore. He opens the essay talking about "that quality of luminous vagueness which Moore's presence always had," and describes his manner in conversation: "Limply there hung over his brow a copious wisp of blond hair, which wavered as he turned the long white oval of his face from one speaker to another." Then when Moore talked, "a sort of ripple passed up over the modelling of the flaccid cheeks; the chin suddenly receded a little further. . . ." The visual is not Beerbohm's only kind of perception in this essay, but it does seem to animate his interest in Moore. The same holds for his written notes on Clement Scott's bracelets and fat fingers, and on Wilde as a heavy dowager or a lush waving his cigarette round and round. Even in his reading, mostly memoirs, letters, and biography, Beerbohm would notice foibles, predicaments, incongruous meetings, and self-contradictions as situations for caricature. He wrote to Edmund Gosse about John Morley's *Recollections* as if the book were a source for captions: "I liked the comedy of the scene between Carlyle and Chamberlain. Morley's frantic dash down to Brighton, when Herbert Spencer made some sign of wavering in strict agnosticism, pleased me much."

He relied on the truth of his visual imagination. Among the many books he improved by interpolating caricatures was Herbert Read's *English Prose Style*. On the half-title page of his copy, Beerbohm drew a gaunt, beaked old man frowning through tight spectacles. Next to this he wrote that he had always been repelled by Read's political and aesthetic views, and thought him a dry, disgruntled man. He could not believe the photograph he once saw of him young and beautiful: "The camera can lie. My pencil can't. Having read parts of this book I am more than ever sure that Herbert Read is as he here appears"—that is, in the caricature.

Beerbohm had an equally strong imagination in writing and drawing, words and lines. His 1903 essay on Whistler argues that no one has taken the painter's prose seriously enough. "When a man can express himself through two media, people tend to take him lightly in his use of the medium to which he devotes the lesser time and energy." He says this has also delayed appreciation of Disraeli's novels and Rossetti's painting. Beerbohm himself is a rare case of equivalence between one talent and the other. Thackeray, Lewis Carroll, Mark Twain, G. K. Chesterton, D. H. Lawrence never carried their talent as artists very far; Whistler and Beardsley were sporadic writers, and not so accomplished as Beerbohm liked to think. In varying ways, Blake, Rossetti, Edward Lear, and James Thurber managed an equal realization in verbal and visual form. Beerbohm belongs in this list, and though he insisted that his gifts were small, they made him absolutely distinctive in the arts of figure caricature and parodic writing.

Caricature gave him a grasp of life from his own perspective. The earliest self-caricature he did is actually a set of caricatures: the perplexed schoolboy in the center, surrounded by images of what he might become—lawyer, scholar, theatergoer, artist. Vis-à-vis the world around him, particularly the literary world, Beerbohm sometimes proved himself by altering portraits and title pages from his library. In one book he sketched side whiskers over a photograph of Yeats to make him look genteel and early Victorian. The frontispiece portraits in collections of Lord Tennyson's and Sir William Watson's poetry are ingeniously altered. In another book, Beerbohm's bête noire, Kipling, has a cleft chin, idiot sneer, and eyes jerking sideways as if in panic. Above the altered portrait Beerbohm wrote in—after the name Rudyard Kipling—"'s Soul."* We begin to recognize the true aim of caricature.

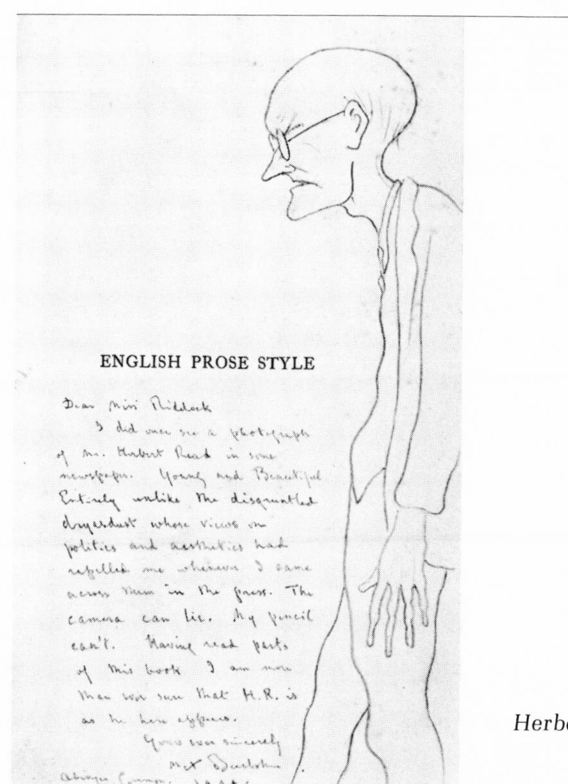

Herbert Read, 1944

Beerbohm's alterations and improvements were more private than public, however. He worked assiduously with an erasing knife, ink, and watercolor on the nineteen photographs in Henderson's biography of Shaw. The result is wildly funny in places. Plates are altered to narrow Shaw's head, make his eyes squint, put on kid gloves and clown's nose, turn his family into cockeyed idiots, him into a coarse nouveau riche, a fop, or a pig. Besides this primitive whimsy of Beerbohm's, the time and painstaking care spent on a private joke betray an obsession as well as a playing within aesthetic convention.

None of the alterations in Beerbohm's library is odder or more gratuitous than his job on a book about his half-brother, Beerbohm Tree. Photographs showing Tree in his dramatic roles have various silly things done to them, but one theme runs all through—Beerbohm changing his brother's appearance to that of a woman. In one view of Tree as Nero, the robe becomes a dress, streamers are drawn on a hat. In other photographs, Tree gets long hair, and his waist is cut in by shading to give him a full bodice. I do not know whether Beerbohm showed this kind of play to other people; it would seem less bizarre if he had. Why was he impelled to feminize Tree? It may have been a way of nullifying the man's potency and success. Beerbohm's feeling for his brother, twenty years his senior, was hero-worship at first. Tree had introduced him to London and taken him to America. But someone once described their relationship as one of "armed neutrality."

Sometimes an emotion twists the artist's pen without his fully knowing why. Beerbohm in 1920 made a point of recanting the sourness expressed in an early caricature of Tree: "My brother looked abstracted, but not disagreeable or aggressive. This drawing is one of my failures." Tree had died recently, and Beerbohm had put a lot of work into editing a memorial volume: he regretted the effect he had gotten in 1896. If Tree came out disagreeable and aggressive, it was probably because his less heroic brother instinctively felt that way about him. Another caricature, done when Tree was knighted in 1909, is drawn skillfully enough and still shows the same expression as in 1896. It depicts the brothers together, Herbert looming very large and puffing his chest grandly, Max much smaller and puffing in imitation.* "I do believe," Beerbohm once wrote, "he took as much pride in my little career as I took in his big one." One of his memories of Tree bears out the suggestion that Beerbohm felt himself overshadowed, even outmanned, by his brother's heroic posture. He remembers as a schoolboy being presented by Tree to a famous actress in her dressing room; she lay on a sofa eating hothouse grapes, and one immense, important-looking man in the room laughed at the smallness of "Beerbohm Tree's brother." The idea of size was always fundamental to Beerbohm's art and thinking. Anything large-scale—corpulence, egotism, universal ideas—repelled him. He was unusually small when young, and later, though of normal height, continued to create an impression of himself as small. To say of Tree, as he did, "Things on a small scale, however exquisite, did not satisfy him," points to the trouble. Degrading his brother (as Beerbohm would have regarded it) to a woman was a way of getting on even terms and distinguishing his own figure in the world.

Beerbohm theorized in 1901, as Freud did later, that caricature lets us expend our contempt and hostility. This formula would apply to artist and viewer alike, and it partly explains Beerbohm's treatment of his brother. The action of altering portraits, which is both playful and aggressive, occurs at a deeper level than Beerbohm's other kinds of drawing. These private alterations stand for the impulse beneath the art of caricature.

Artist and Subject

When you look at a sketch or even a photograph of yourself, you may instinctively feel at odds, trifled with, misrepresented. That feeling must be far stronger with a caricature unless you are perfectly free of vanity and self-consciousness. Most of the men Beerbohm drew were not. There is no record of anyone's having said he positively liked seeing his features and expression distorted in a Beerbohm drawing. More likely his subjects swallowed their uneasiness for the esteem that came with it. Better to be caricatured by Beerbohm than not to be.

A number of them felt drawn in effigy by Beerbohm's caricature as if the artist had some primitive power in which the image *is* the face. Even unexercised, that power resided in him, so that Wilfred Owen, meeting Beerbohm at a reception, wrote that "when he looked at me, I felt my nose tip-tilting in an alarming manner; my legs warped; my chin became a mere pimple on my neck." At one point Beerbohm even took up sculpture for a while, using Plasticine to mold the people he was used to caricaturing. The brooding, Nietzschean poet John Davidson reacted to a 1907 caricature as if Beerbohm's thumbs were actually working at him. Beerbohm had drawn him harmlessly enough as a somewhat shabby, smug gentleman.* If one did not know Davidson, the figure might seem that of a semi-prosperous provincial banker. Yet when the *Morning Chronicle* published the caricature, Davidson, already suffering from mania about his desperate mission in the world, wrote to a friend:

> Curious that it should have selected my caricature for reproduction. It is, doubtless, one of the cleverest—a presentation of the terrible intellectual disease, swelled head. The face and skull are entirely disfigured by the turgidity of the brain, of the thyroid gland, and of the pharyngeal organs; the eye crushed out of position; the nose is extended and spread like an inverted snout; the hat has to be carried in the hand as it is much too small for the head; the body becomes stunted; the other extremities small in sympathy with the cranium, and a constant vertigo requires the assistance of a staff to maintain an erect posture.

Davidson's sickness affords a classic image of the plastic force of caricature. The verbs he uses—swelled, disfigured, extended, crushed, stunted—all assume a man who actually perpetrated that violence. But somehow Davidson decided that only the caricature implied a deep insult, not the artist. Soon afterwards, he said that Beerbohm was "the only writing person in London out of all the crowd whom I seem to care for at all."

A torsion similar to what Davidson felt occurs in the

artist too, though not so intimately or immediately. Beerbohm liked to sign single-figure caricatures in a way that suggested his efficacy in them. Instead of displacing his signature to the bottom right or left corner, he would sometimes put it into the space of the drawing itself, between the subject's legs or beside his face. During the nineties, he was disingenuous about the effect of his drawings, and whether people were hurt by them: "I never pretend that my caricatures are meant for portraits. And I do not think that the men themselves whom I have drawn have ever been offended." This was unlikely in 1895, and became more so as time went on. Wilde and Hall Caine were offended; James, according to Lady Ottoline Morrell, feared "that terrible power of caricature" in Beerbohm. H. G. Wells on one occasion responded publicly, unlike the others. In answer to Beerbohm's 1903 caricature of him as president of a "patent mechanical New Republic," Wells sent to the *Sketch* a picture called "Body and Soul," an awkwardly drawn child with a round head, leading a tiny black monkey on a string.

George Moore's troubled private reactions expose caricature as more than merely an aesthetic convention whose subject becomes "the joy of his creator," as Beerbohm liked to claim. For Moore or any model, attached to himself, the leaps from reality to image and from likeness to unlikeness could be painful. Supposedly the two men were friends: all Beerbohm's published comments on Moore are benevolent, and show that he enjoyed him personally. He drew Moore constantly, from *Caricatures of Twenty-Five Gentlemen* until his very last caricature, done in 1955: always the same shapeless creature, with a wispy moustache, bemused expression, and one limp hand gesturing. As Moore aged, he even grew to resemble the person Beerbohm had been drawing. Successive photographs show the chin receding, the look getting blanker. In his letters, Moore said that Beerbohm's technique robbed him of his humanity. "Max Beerbohm has caricatured everybody ferociously; his representation of me hardly resembles a human being; I have never complained." Evidently his not complaining cost Moore something. Another time he said that caricature should not aim to make one "physically repulsive": "Max and others have caricatured me out of all human resemblance but I never objected." It begins to look as though caricature can have the effect a camera sometimes has on the superstitious. It distorts a man's individuality, it threatens to divide him from himself.

For a third person, on the other hand, someone neither artist nor subject, the response to a caricature will be different. In the nineties there was speculation that we tend to perceive visual art physiologically, by moving with and imitating the shapes and rhythms of a painting. Applied to caricature, this would suggest that the spectator slouches or puffs up as he follows such a figure. In any event, the interested witness will get a moral impression from the physical terms of caricature. Thus a recent book on the social functions of art can say that Beerbohm's caricatures of aristocrats reveal them as "decadent freaks," though the case is quite different. A casual comment Oscar Wilde made on one of Beerbohm's drawings of Moore has in its words the whole kinetic structure of caricature. He called it "a most brilliant and bitter rendering of that vague formless obscene face." "Brilliant" describes Beerbohm's skill, but "bitter" carries Wilde's response to Moore. Again, it was Beerbohm who rendered the face vague and formless, and Wilde who saw it as obscene.

Beerbohm's pre-emptive innocence and the aesthetic doctrine he adopted in his early career led him to disavow anything moralistic in caricature. "The caricaturist merely passes his subject through a certain grotesque convention," he said in 1895. Or, to a man who asked him how he managed to make his people look so absurd and yet so like: "I see them as caricatures." And Beardsley said the same sort of thing about his monstrous figures, putting technique in place of emotion. Beerbohm understood that caricature, as the word implies, carries a charge of some kind. What can be said at this point is that his drawing of men does tend to bear out whatever imperfect drift their faces have, yet so as to celebrate their distinctiveness rather than condemn their vices: Wilde at his worst in Beerbohm's caricatures is Wilde at his most fascinating.

Distortion

Caricature transforms, as parody does; it creates a specific difference. Beerbohm was aware of caricature's active relation to normal portraiture. He did one drawing in which Shaw shows him a favorable oil portrait of himself and asks, "Why can't you do me like that?" "Most men are not at all like themselves," Beerbohm wrote, introducing a book of portrait drawings. "The test of fine portraiture is in its power to reconcile the appearance with the reality—to show through the sitter's surface what he or she indeed is." In the second number of the *Yellow Book,* John Singer Sargent's pencil drawing of Henry James appeared, a mild, slightly idealized profile with a strong brow and serious eyes.* Three years later Beerbohm did a caricature of James, also in profile.* *Academy* magazine published the two drawings on facing pages, making it obvious that Beerbohm's, with its bunched brow and glaring eyes, was based on Sargent's. The effect of that confrontation, surprisingly enough, is not to depreciate Beerbohm's caricature, but to suggest that Sargent's finesse, like a waxwork replica, loses the particular vitality James had.

The *Academy* gave a full page to Sargent's drawing of James and less than a quarter page to Beerbohm's, thereby measuring not only the artists' relative stature, but also a supposed distinction between serious or fine art and caricature. That distinction, which the work of Hokusai and Daumier should have disproved, reflects the state of British caricature when Beerbohm began drawing. To see his achievement accurately, then, calls for some acquaintance with the tradition he knew.

"A profoundly humiliating period," Philip Guedalla called British caricature's high-Victorian phase, compared with Hogarth and Gillray, and with the French political and social satirists who learned from them. Manners, sports, domestic comedy were the topics of Victorian caricature, as seen from *Punch*'s middle-class standpoint. "Certainly the pages of *Punch* do not reek with pessimism," Henry James said in an essay on Daumier. The work of George du Maurier, John Leech, Charles Keene is infused with a sense of hearty confidence that England's all right. What dissatisfied Beerbohm in nineteenth-century British caricature was its lack of true critical energy, which meant a lack of style. His predecessors and most of his contemporaries were not caricaturists at all, but cartoonists dealing in false conventions. Keene's popular drawings of life's contretemps Beerbohm considered merely illustrated jokes. The same held for du Maurier's indoor scenes. As to John Tenniel and Carruthers Gould, Beerbohm found their political allegories worthless cartoon-mongering. About *Punch*'s Linley Sambourne, he said, with a kind of contempt for his own silliness as a child, that he used to wait eagerly each week to see whether Sambourne had "made Gladstone into a shark or a canary or a buffalo or what?"

In 1901 Beerbohm wrote that England had no pure caricature at all. The critical energy he looked for belonged to portrait caricature, the significant distortion of features and gestures. Only Carlo Pellegrini satisfied this criterion, and Beerbohm wrote that even his work succumbed to the English atmosphere after a while, becoming "mild and gentlemanly" like that of his successor, Leslie Ward ("Spy"). From Pellegrini, to whom he dedicated his first book of caricature, Beerbohm had taken chiefly the emphasis on a single figure rather than a scene. Distending or eliminating features to reveal personality was his own addition. His caricatural technique is apparent by contrast with an imitation he did of Pellegrini's style. In 1896 he drew George Meredith with just the design, coloring, and slight charge that Spy and Pellegrini would have used. The picture is benign, nothing like the rest of Beerbohm's work. By making his basic technique the distortion of salient features in a single figure without a background, he distinguished himself from nearly all previous caricature in England. He wanted a purity and beauty of line not found in English journalistic caricature, and his instinct as well as his artistic talent was for satirizing individual character.

He drew from memory, as Baudelaire says Guys and Daumier did—from the distortion in the mind's eye, not from life. This technique gives his best caricatures their free expressiveness. When Beerbohm had trouble caricaturing Walter Pater, Will Rothenstein offered to show him his own faithful lithograph of the man. "No thanks," Beerbohm said, "I never work from photographs." Occasionally he did use photographs, to do people he had never seen or those no longer alive, such as the Pre-Raphaelites for *Rossetti and His Circle*. Usually he preferred to observe a man in Parliament or in society and to draw him later. His 1901 essay argues that there must be time for imagination, for the "unconscious process of exaggeration to work."

It is above all his extravagant line that distinguishes Beerbohm from nineteenth-century caricature. In one of his best collections, the 1907 *Book of Caricatures*, we see an immense slope for Count Benckendorff's nose, Ray Lenkester's floating jowls, Lord Ribbesdale's reedy legs. He will trace a single line around the entire contour of a head from crown to collar, and another from collar to feet, or let the curve of G. K. Chesterton's belly go on endlessly, in the manner of Beardsley and Hokusai.

Beerbohm liked his simplest, quickest caricatures. The

Lord Tweedmouth, 1907

"best drawing in [the] book," he said about Lord Tweedmouth in *A Book of Caricatures.* He did not say why, but as one of several in that volume done with a quill pen, it seems perfectly unstudied, a moment's inspiration. Tweedmouth's face is a few brief marks, his hair a few more. Any one line alone would be random and insignificant: the single vague curve for the brow and eyes, the semicircle for the nose, the twist for spectacles, two scratches for the mouth. There is no more abbreviated face in all of Beerbohm's published work, but its character is complete. One effect of this rough sketch is to present the old man unaware, in a moment of inwardness, not posing as Beerbohm's subjects often are. It happens that at the time Beerbohm drew him,

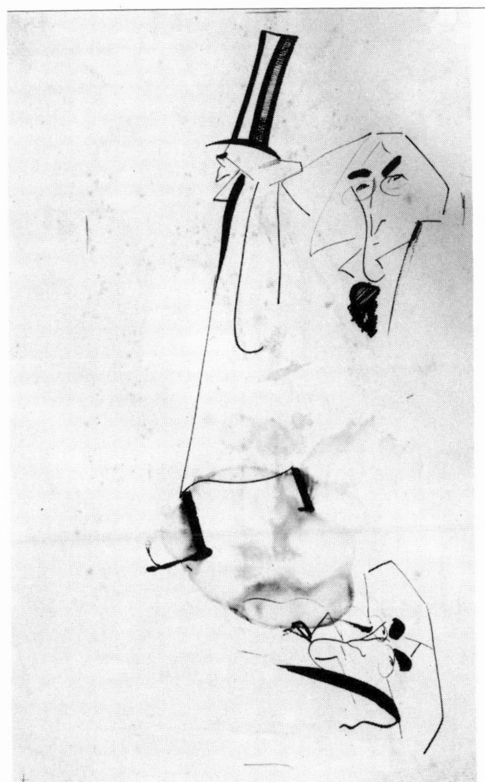

Henry Irving, ca. 1893

Tweedmouth was going out of his mind. The frizzled hair, rumpled clothes, forehead, and mouth suggest some pain that Beerbohm caught, though he liked the caricature because no convention had intervened. It was genuine.

Unlike pencil drawing, using a quill pen commits you to the original impulse of a line, without check or correction. In a pen-and-ink drawing Beerbohm did of Swinburne in June 1899, just after lunching with the poet, there are only a couple of dozen strokes for the entire figure. The springy movement from domed head to wispy beard, fluttering hands, slight potbelly, and slippers contains far more life than Pellegrini's finished caricature of Swinburne in *Vanity Fair*. Swinburne reportedly looked weak but vivid, birdlike, an astonishment to the eye: the 1899 caricature gets precisely those traits.

That Beerbohm trusted ease and rapidity in drawing is clear from his liking for Sem, the French artist who he said could do "instantaneous caricatures of living, moving people." And in "A.B." (1897), the only essay he published on a caricaturist, Beerbohm praised Alfred Bryan, of whose "simple, swift, and slap-dash" work he estimated he saw about eleven hundred new examples a year. Though Sem and A. B. sketched single figures, they did not try for Beerbohm's minimal economy.

During his 1913 exhibition, he remarked on his favorite drawings: "These are caricature in its finest purity—caricature brought to a pitch of such simplicity and of beauty as you won't find except in very good Japanese prints." In Japanese painting and drawing, the fewest strokes are enough if an idea is present. Translated into caricature, this implies a saving—That's all there is to him, it takes only a few lines!—even when Beerbohm loved the man; witness Reggie Turner's nose, in another 1907 quill drawing. Minimal lines do not inhibit the distortion of a figure: they make it possible, for simplifying to the essentials inevitably discriminates some features above others. For the tenth Earl of Chesterfield, Beerbohm said he first drew a cravat and buttonhole, "and the rest was exhaled corollarily from them." The exuberance and economy of his technique conduced as easily to stylization as to distortion. He singled out Sir George Lewis, the fashionable solicitor, as the best thing in the 1896 book, "a really good synthesis and simplification." It is the most stylized drawing in the book: three loops for the head, collar, and coat.

Beerbohm never had any lessons in art beyond the age of about twelve, and people who liked his caricatures always added that of course he was not a draftsman. "It was obvious that in the accepted sense Max could not draw at all. His technique was naïve and childish," David Low wrote. It is true he hardly tried articulating the joints of a body or modeling hands and feet, yet Beerbohm could do everything with the mobile human face and with total bodily gesture. Unlike Thurber, whose humor stemmed directly from technical awkwardness, he had perfect flexibility with a pen or pencil.

Unfortunately he was not well served by available methods of reproduction. Lithography was not very popular in England or suitable for Beerbohm. When he began publishing caricatures, the woodcuts used by *Punch* and the photomechanical process of reproduction were good mainly for the solid masses and sharp lines of artists like Phil May and Aubrey Beardsley, but not for shadows or subtle tones. The caricatures in Beerbohm's first volume were done to be easily reproduced by wood engravings with halftone tint applied, and are slightly unpleasant to look at on account of their hard, mechanical texture. He went on more and more to use pen and pencil with washes of pale color. *The Poets' Corner* and *Rossetti and His Circle* depend entirely on watercolor technique. So his caricature was seen at its best only in gallery exhibitions and private homes, by the people likely to be in such places, whereas Beardsley's style in drawings, posters, and book illustration suffered very little from mass reproduction. Beerbohm used a special ribbed paper and made his drawings fairly large. Thus the small, fuzzy, gray- or sepia-tinted cheap paper plates in his books scarcely indicate what he drew. They have no liveliness or subtlety, and his finely written captions become microscopic, altering the drawings' true proportions. *A Survey* (1921) is especially bad, with its brownish tinted drawings mounted on yellowish-brown pages. In *Rossetti and His Circle,* the blues, reds, and golds are dead compared with their originals in the Tate Gallery. Luckily the plates in *The Poets' Corner* are lithographed actual size, and their color is fairly authentic. They, along with the few quill drawings in *A Book Of Caricatures,* give the best sense of Beerbohm's style.

It is typical of Beerbohm that his own technique of significant distortion in caricature, embodying a central principle of early-twentieth-century art, did not open him up toward that art. He ridiculed Sargent's superficiality, but also the breakup of ideal form in modern art. In the background of a 1913 caricature about Roger Fry's enthusiasm for primitive art, he drew burlesques of a cubist and a postimpressionist painting. Three times during the Bloomsbury period he caricatured Fry with a manic light in his eyes,* and he told Virginia Woolf he had once heard Fry lecture on aesthetics and been disappointed: "He kept on turning the page—turning the page." When someone suggested that Graham Sutherland paint his portrait, Beerbohm refused to sit. He said he himself had once been "a ruthless monstrifier of men," but he distrusted Sutherland's impressionistic portrait of Somerset Maugham: "Maugham looks in it as if he had died of torture." These are the attitudes of a man whose particular skill crystallized early, but in fact he was a daring artist within the scope of caricature.

Beerbohm had London exhibitions in 1901, 1904, 1907, 1908, 1911, 1913, and his caricatures belong in part to the movement of modern art at the time. For Kenneth Clark they were "the first nonrealistic works of art I ever enjoyed," and Roger Fry found them "perfectly amazing." Fry was looking to modern art to "dispense once for all with the idea of likeness to Nature . . . and consider only whether the emotional elements inherent in natural form are adequately discovered." This can speak for Beerbohm, who in returning to his 1896 version of Moore found it "untrue" physically and yet "really *very* like" the man's temperament. After looking at the Swinburne long enough, we incorporate its distortion into our sense of the man, so that in photographs Swinburne then looks less like himself. The caricature of Tweedmouth totally reconstitutes our vision, much as Braque and Picasso do, by abstracting the model's inherent form. "Being so drastic in its methods," Beerbohm said, caricature "demands in its beholders a keen faculty of imagination." As with the cubists, the implicit subject of his art was that very transit, or metaphor, between the original and the figure drawn. "I see them as caricatures": Beerbohm is part of the revolution in visual art of his time.

Visual Metaphor

In its transformations, caricature often works by creating a visual metaphor—Gladstone a shark, Chesterton a stomach—and it entails unlikeness as well as likeness, as a metaphor does. The classic example is Charles Philipon's gross, pear-shaped face of Louis Philippe (*poire* is slang for "fathead"). Philipon was accused of treason for it, but defended himself by showing how he had arrived at a pear. He drew four versions of the King, starting with a likeness and reducing him step by step to a bulging pear. Each transformation being plausible, Philipon was acquitted. This story, which appears in, among other places, Thackeray's *Paris Sketch Book,* interested Beerbohm enough to form the basis for two caricatures. One refers directly to the French incident. The other is a drawing in four stages, turning Whistler into a snuffed-out bedtime candle. Like Philipon's *poire,* it is a visual pun or metaphor.

The *poire* and the candle are explicit, schematic examples. Typically, Beerbohm's caricature transforms from within. Exaggerate what is salient: this formula enabled him to show men both to their own satisfaction and to our detached view, whence the mixture of reverence and ridicule in his caricatures. "H.R.H. The Duke of Cambridge," from *Caricatures of Twenty-Five Gentlemen,* is a good example.* The man was a cousin of the Queen's, and commander in chief of the Army until forced to resign in 1895 because he was an obstacle to reform. Beerbohm drew him as a heavy oval form settled in a theater box, with closed eyes and jowls sunk in his collar. The honorific title and public setting create the outside point of view the world has. At the same time, the Duke's complacence expresses his own view of himself. Depending on how we feel, we can see him as uselessly pompous or as august, and his own outlook can be either bloated or full of dignity. Years later, Beerbohm drew the figure over again to make its torso even heavier and more immovable, thus removing the ambivalence—he can only seem pompous—and proving the power of caricature to release a moral through a visual perception.

"The whole man must be melted down, as in a crucible," Beerbohm's 1901 recipe has it, "and then, as from the solution, be fashioned anew. He must emerge with not one particle of himself lost, yet with not a particle of himself as it was before. . . . And he will stand there wholly transformed." The violent, reductive image of melting a man down counters a popular notion, which Beerbohm occasionally followed, that caricature merely pulls one feature out of shape. The key phrase in his recipe is "wholly transformed," for caricature can be a radical and integrating process. In his finest portraits, Beerbohm manages to shape an entire person—his appearance and role in the world—as a metaphor for his essential nature. By being unjournalistic, he gets a longer span into his critique of men, a truer drift and a figure that will hold. The first drawing he did of Arthur Balfour, in 1894, is a single long curve connecting hat and shins, and he held to that afterwards, emphasizing stooped shoulders and adding a drooping moustache and sad eyes.* Balfour's sloping body is a visual figure for patrician uncertainty, and combines with his height (twice too tall for the proportions, in a 1907 drawing) to exaggerate the man's uneasy Olympian attitudes. Beerbohm also drew Edward Carson, the Irish statesman and lawyer who prosecuted Wilde, in a long curve,* but Carson's has the tenseness of a whip, Balfour's the looseness of a question mark.

Some of the other truly caricatural figures that come to

mind are Frank Harris preened and inflated like a fighting cock, as if to signify his sexual activity and self-confidence, and the bluntness of Balfour's rival, Bonar Law. Nothing demonstrates the metaphoric vision more clearly than the brief emendations and notes Beerbohm made in 1920 on his 1896 drawings of Rudyard Kipling and Pinero.* He took care to correct the back of Kipling's neck and make it "more brutal," because that detail bore out his opinion of the man. It was equivalent to the overmuscular language and the actual brutality in Beerbohm's *Christmas Garland* parody of Kipling. Of course Kipling's jaw bore the brunt of distortion in all the caricatures Beerbohm drew of him, and if we look at the jaw and the neck in paintings or photographs of Kipling, we can see that Beerbohm's judgment of the man determined his technique before the technique conveyed a judgment. For changing the 1896 Pinero, Beerbohm had similar cause. As a critic he had persistently exposed the playwright's intellectual weaknesses, so the "dome-like brow" seemed "all wrong" and he redrew Pinero leaving "*no* top to his head." This technique is far subtler than the common journalistic habit of drawing verbal clichés—something Beerbohm did once, for example, by putting William Archer's head in clouds because he hoped for a national theater. The drawings of Balfour and Harris undergo the same transition from physical to moral terms as words like "devious," "upright," "overblown," "eccentric," or "supercilious." This identity between the process in words and the process in pictures lies at the heart of the language of caricature.

Sometimes in relying on a salient feature to express the whole man, Beerbohm developed signs for the people he drew: Pinero's eyebrows, "like skins of some small mammal," Beerbohm said, "just not large enough to be used as mats." Making preliminary sketches, he could draw a face three or four times and keep to an identical configuration. Also, after many years of not having done a man, particularly one toward whom his attitude had not changed, he would produce precisely the kind of distortion he had originally made. He kept the sign in his mind's eye, partly as a matter of technique and partly because his own example led him to expect that men essentially settle in themselves. If they do not, if men can change from mean to generous, arrogant to humble, sloppy to scrupulous, then the art of caricature may lose its attaching power. Beerbohm did an elaborate drawing illustrating this possibility, "One fine morning, or How they might undo me."* In it he stands at the side, recoiling from a file of thirty men winding past him. Each of them has altered in some point from the way Beerbohm habitually drew him: Balfour has a goatee, Pinero's eyebrows are shaved off, Moore's upper lip is clean, Rothenstein smiles instead of scowling, Kipling's jaw does not jut out, Shaw sports a high collar, buttonhole, tiepin, cufflinks, and spats, Rosebery wears a walrus moustache, and Hall Caine without his moustache is passing closest to Beerbohm and glaring in panicky anger. They all look wrong, distressed, and seem to want to revert to the way Beerbohm drew them. Besides pointing out the economy he relied on in grasping men by their salient features, "How they might undo me" contains a reverse wisdom—namely, that these eminent men themselves rely on outer props and costume to realize a personality.

Beerbohm was "undone" by recognizing something new in William Butler Yeats, a man whose temper changed dramatically, and scarcely went on drawing him at all. He met Yeats in 1896, forming an impression of something intense and mysterious in his verse and physical appearance, "some sort of mood enclosed in a vacuum far away." Several times between 1899 and 1904 he caricatured the poet, lanky and wavering, with thin hands and a shock of dark hair,* and after that did him only in groups, making him a fatter version of the early mystic. Beerbohm ended an essay on Yeats with this explanation of the problem:

Pencil sketches

> As years went by, the visual aspect of Yeats changed a little. His face grew gradually fuller in outline, and the sharp angles of his figure were smoothed away . . . those very long, fine hands did seem to have lost something of their insubstantiality. . . . I found it less easy to draw caricatures of him. He seemed to have become subtly less like himself.

"Less like himself": an intuition of Yeats's mask. The truth is that he had become more like himself. Beerbohm continued to think him "sombrous and psychic," but Yeats had by an evolving discipline made his themes and his style more tough-minded, idiomatic, accountable—a process that was bound to disable Beerbohm's caricature.

"Do you notice that schoolmasters never change?" he remarked during an interview about his caricature. It is likely that he kept a childish attitude toward men he had no sympathy for, and that they remained fixed in his art because he could not tolerate or encompass them otherwise. He did draw, however, an ironic series for his last collection in 1925, called "The Old and the Young Self." The caricatures are double presentations playing on various kinds of earnestness and disillusion. The Shaw has an excellent caption: Old to Young Self, "Strange! You strike me as frivolous, irreligious, and pert; full of a ludicrous faith in mankind and in the efficacy of political propaganda . . . And I used to think you quite perfect!" The Young Self of H. G. Wells appears as an ambitious biologist, the complacent Old Self as a monger of the future. Arnold Bennett's Old Self is huge and swaggering: "All gone according to plan, you see"—the Young Self answering, "*My* plan, you know." Caricature could evidently compass the varieties of delusive change, if not Yeats's real self-transformation.

Two questions come to mind, then, in thinking about caricature. First, what is the interplay between vision and judgment, between aesthetic and moral perception? Second, does the art depend on arresting, or mean to arrest, the development of the person it depicts? Both these questions and a good deal else are illuminated by a copy of *Caricatures of Twenty-Five Gentlemen* in which more than half the portraits were redrawn on facing pages and annotated by Beerbohm years after publication. This particular book thus spans his career, and couples the verbal and visual strains of his imagination. What happened was that Mr. Mark Hyam lent his copy to Beerbohm, who inadvertently kept it a very long time, periodically adding self-caricatures, notes of apology, and in 1920, new portraits. The self-caricatures seem to enjoy rather than excuse Beerbohm's delays. The

Self-caricature, 1903

first, done in 1903 in the midst of his active London theater- and party-going, shows a dandy nonchalantly turning his back. The brim of his top hat has an impossible snap to it, his legs taper to virtually no feet. Beerbohm did the sketch rapidly, with a thick quill pen, and wrote the inscription rapidly too. He may well have been slightly drunk at the time, connecting his words with a deep scoop, pressing hard enough to separate the tip, and going on even after the point was empty of ink. By 1909, tired of the London theater and engaged for the third time, he drew himself turned half towards us, in Edwardian dress and no longer a dandy, while his script was small and precise. Finally in 1920, having married and settled in Italy, returned for the war, and then left England again, he faces us with gray hair and a plain collar, serenely balanced on a hill in full sunlight over the blue Adriatic. During 1920 Beerbohm felt his impulse to draw giving out; by picking up the 1896 book to regenerate his first subjects, he was fulfilling his commitment to the caricaturist's vision of people.

The title, *Caricatures of Twenty-Five Gentlemen,* stresses style and subject equally, and that pet issue of the nineties arises crucially when it comes to caricature: Is it the artistic convention or the innate deformity of human nature that we are made aware of? In Hyam's book, Beerbohm calls Sir William Harcourt "a good pattern," but the run of his notes and changes makes it clear that visual and moral observation coincide in caricature. All the later views mentioned in this chapter—Cambridge's torso, Kipling's neck, Pinero's head—as well as the comments on Lewis and on Tree's disagreeableness, derive from this copy. The concerted revisions of Bernard Shaw show Beerbohm indirectly defining himself by establishing another man in his imagination. To judge from contemporary photographs, the original was not really so "utterly amiss" as Beerbohm says, but he felt he had to rework its "lamb-like expression" into the bristling and vital G.B.S. he always drew. That the nose and beard in 1920 only reiterate the eager iconoclasm of 1896* marks a defeated idealism in Shaw that Beerbohm did not have to suffer.

Several kinds of change are exposed in this quarter-century delay. The pages of self-caricature trace Beerbohm from an exuberant, conspicuous, urbane Londoner to a late-middle-aged, postwar, quietly retired artist. And his pen, brush, and pencil additions point up the rapid, subtle hand he developed. One quite remarkable thing about the book is the phenomenon of self-criticism it presents, admitting that the finished dandy of the nineties made mistakes and had far to go. "I went badly astray here," he says, or "This is utterly amiss. . . . I take it all back." This is not the straw man

Beerbohm often makes himself in writing and caricature. The return upon himself entails a rare access of strength, a capacity for real self-correction without loss of integrity.

Beerbohm was equipped to follow change in some of the antique Victorian statesmen who survived with him into the lamentable twentieth century. Henry John Brinsley Manners (1852–1925), eighth Duke of Rutland and Marquis of Granby, perhaps had little but his class to rely on. In Beerbohm's caricatures he comes out poignantly. The 1896 figure looks debonair and self-composed to an extreme degree, with a hint in his expression that nothing in the world comes quite up to scratch.* The second time Beerbohm merely set down an image with no comments—the only case in which he did that. Granby's body is disappearing. His monocle is still in place, the set of the shoulders and even the expression are the same as before, but in 1920 they now seem to convey profound sadness, even fear.

Behind the exhibitions and books of caricature lies this manifold activity of annotating, decorating, correcting, sometimes subverting books. Beerbohm kept another copy of the *Caricatures of Twenty-Five Gentlemen* at Rapallo all his life, adding comments, coloring, a few new versions, and an epitaph—"Some dead, some living unremember'd—all/ Ruthlessly changed by busybody Time!" This cannot be classified as merely anecdotal material. Above all, the act of adding and changing kept him in living relation to the published matter we normally take for granted. The Mark Hyam book manages what works of art seldom do: that is, to come alive off the page, to enter the pull of time. The caricaturist locates himself in the scheme of aging and failing. Granby, Shaw face themselves across the center of the book. And Beerbohm brings art and morality into focus together, finding judgments simply by checking himself as an artist. Redeeming the blankness of the facing page, these activities of the comic imagination are the richest traces of Beerbohm's confidence in caricature.

Society

During his seventy years as an artist, Beerbohm drew two thousand formal caricatures and probably as many informal ones. A computer analysis of them might reveal things otherwise hidden: that ninety-five percent of his scenes, say, take place indoors, or that all of the women are expressionless. Short of using a computer, a simple conspectus of Beerbohm's caricature—the milieu, nature, and activity of the people he drew—is the way to arrive at his direct opinions.

When he first began to draw, he was fascinated by the great Liberal and Conservative statesmen of the eighties: Gladstone, Sir William Harcourt, Lord Randolph Churchill, Balfour, Lord Rosebery, and Joseph Chamberlain, who "always stepped out of F.C.G. or Tenniel." It is hard to tell which depended on the other, his love for statesmen or his love for caricature. Being a strong Tory on the example of his father, Beerbohm thought Gladstone's Cabinet "wicked—but great." Early in 1885 someone took him to hear Gladstone speak in the House, and for the next several years, during school vacations, he frequented Downing Street to watch the titans come and go. They were a race apart, remote in great town and country houses, mysterious, rich, powerful. He did a series of caricatures later on called "Men Who Matter." The quality he liked in these statesmen and aristocrats was the one that made it interesting to caricature them: their individuality. You could see them because they walked slowly and wore their hair, whiskers, moustaches, beards, and clothes distinctively. "Each one of them was a law unto himself," Beerbohm reminisced. After the turn of the century, he began to be invited to fashionable homes. He talked casually about this world and his "mere disinterested flunkeyism" in it, but it gave him a chance to meet and draw the men in it.

Coming from an eccentric, well-off, but hardly wealthy family, he caricatured these men on half-satiric, half-snobbish impulses: he would not have minded being in their shoes. The caricatures display them at once as spectacles and as self-contained individuals. Possibly this self-containment explains a peculiar and consistent feature in the portraits of men of class position or vested power. Almost without exception they have their eyes shut: Sir Edward Carson, the Duke of Cambridge at theater, or the globular face of Viscount Haldane, which seems to be meditating on its extra flesh. Queen Victoria's puffy eyes are closed disgustedly against the scandalous Prince of Wales in Beerbohm's famous picture. In a late series called "Studies in the Eighteen-Seventies," he drew a judge, a lord, a general, a foreign count, and others with their eyes shut or obscured behind monocles and top hats. All three Cecil brothers standing "in conclave," where we would expect them at least to be looking at each other, show the same motif of disdain for us and for a world becoming less considerable than it was.* In *Caricatures of Twenty-Five Gentlemen*, Henry Chaplin's eyes are closed, above a self-satisfied smile. He was a man who considered politics important but secondary to horses, who at Oxford hunted six days a week, and whom the Queen telegraphed for advice when her ponies had pinkeye. "Ultimus Victorianiorum," Beerbohm called him when he returned to the book in 1920. Chaplin was eighty then; his eyes were still shut and he had remained the sporting man by dyeing his hair a deep golden brown against time.

Balfour and Rosebery had a greater valence for Beerbohm and turn up repeatedly, though not with the closed eyes he gave to men he looked at with awe. Born before 1850 and living to over eighty, they were both scions of the landed oligarchy, brilliant statesmen in their ways yet susceptible to doubts about their vocation. In Balfour, Beerbohm sensed more real strength: "unlike Rosebery, he *poses* as a dilettante." This made it easier to joke at his devotion to philosophy or tennis. And Balfour lasted marvelously in politics:

he was all right, and not someone in whom any difficult emotion need be vested. Rosebery conceivably embodied something more mysterious, the ultimate failure of a brilliant but not wholly committed man. Beerbohm was stirred by failure and obliquely identified with it, either in real persons or imaginary ones like Enoch Soames, which accounts for the ingenious double page devised for Rosebery in the emended *Caricatures of Twenty-Five Gentlemen*. There is nothing else quite like it in Beerbohm's work, though he did once exhibit three caricatures of Rosebery together, showing him in 1885, 1897, and 1912. The set in Mark Hyam's book covers a longer span, and it links the insouciant bridegroom of 1878, the recently defeated Prime Minister of 1896, and the long-since-bypassed old man of 1920 in a paradigm of time and chance.* The three views, seen next to photographs or Millais's idealized portrait, bear out gradually a disposition to fleshiness, a downward setting of cheeks, mouth, and lidded eyes—what Rosebery's biographer calls his self-enfolding, self-pitying tendency. Beerbohm's comment on the "embittered egoist" of 1920 is somewhat harsh, in light of the fact that Rosebery had recently lost his younger son in the war and suffered a paralytic stroke. But the pencil drawing of the face is superb, particularly the averted cast of the eyes. And it is not really harsh. If we follow from first to last the look in Rosebery's eyes, including the distress in "How they might undo me" (1911), it reveals a tragic drift that is too strong to quarrel with.

When Beerbohm found things in a face that interested him, he went on drawing it, with or without changes. For his bedroom at Rapallo he painted a mural on dry plaster of "faces that have always come easiest to me—lines of least resistance for the budding frescoist": Rosebery, James, Chamberlain, Moore, Kipling, and others in a sort of parade, led by Edward VII. No one else but Shaw has quite the status of Edward VII in Beerbohm's caricature. There are sixty-two caricatures of him, and what is remarkable is not merely the number but the variety of situations (two of the caricatures are sets of eight or nine scenes). From 1896 to 1953 Beerbohm went on imagining Edward's adolescence, trouble with his mother, gout, drinking, marriage, ties with Jews, and so forth. A body as wide as it is tall, a ravaged face, a sidelong leer, and a cigar come back again and again. This was the first British monarch to be accessible to the public. Beerbohm, having watched him expand socially, was fascinated by Edward as he had been by George IV—by his gusto, materialism, fear of boredom, quick temper.

Just after Edward's accession, pictures of a new coin with his idealized profile and bare bust were circulated. True to the caricatural instinct, Beerbohm mounted two of these images together, leaving one clear and reworking the other into the "real" Edward VII, bald with a beak nose and fat creases in his neck. The next year the King paid a round of ceremonial visits in Europe—"The Edwardyssey," as it turned out in a series of burlesques that were not exhibited until 1945. "The Edwardyssey" is elaborate and brutally irreverent.

On May 6, 1910, the King died, just after Beerbohm had left for his honeymoon and Italy. He still drew the man. A 1921 caricature, "The rare, the rather awful visits of Albert Edward, Prince of Wales, to Windsor Castle" has the grim tone of the second half of Victoria's reign. Beerbohm's Queen is an epitome of herself, not amused, the woman who blamed her son for the Prince Consort's death. Another drawing, "Edward VII of Blessed Memory," retains the usual face with milder lines and no satiric bite. And a third is as exuberant as "The Edwardyssey." It follows through the seven decades in which Edward lived and his first in heaven, from the pudgy boy flanked by tall black guardians, to the dandy, the dissolute playboy among aging society ladies, and finally the fat, haloed angel. When these were exhibited in 1923 (to a gathering including the Duchess of Westminster, Oswald Mosley, Sinclair Lewis, and Aldous Huxley), the

London press exploded—"scarifying . . . Teutonically brutal . . . dastardly attack . . . infamous bad taste"—and New York magazines dramatized the controversy. It was a more delicate predicament than being attacked for ridiculing Labour, as Beerbohm had been two years before. While probably enjoying the controversy, he had the offensive caricatures of Edward withdrawn (they are now in the Royal Collection at Windsor) so as not to be misunderstood by the public. The truth is, the public had understood perfectly well his contempt for royal figures as such. What it could not appreciate was that Edward VII was in a sense a hero of Beerbohm's art, beyond judgment or respect. In 1953 Beerbohm was still setting down, with a tiredly written caption and shaky, spidery outlines, "The Old Familiar Figure." Caricaturing him had passed from fascination and critique into ritual.

In drawings of notables, dandies, and other fashionable men, and in most of Beerbohm's self-caricatures, there is a motif even more common than closed eyes. Instead of ending in feet placed on the ground, the legs of these types, looking like delicately shaped awls, taper away finely to a pinpoint without any interruption by an ankle or a heel. It is not enough to say he was unable to draw feet, in the sense that Thurber had trouble drawing cows' and horses' hooves and stood his animals in grass whenever possible. These tapering legs signify the dandy's poise on his own point of balance, free of gravity and sexual commonness. The 1913 caricature of Beerbohm contemplating Shaw works partly by a contrast between Beerbohm's pointed legs and Shaw's obviously large and practical shoes* (Shaw happens to be standing on his head and his trouser legs have slipped down). There is a similar drawing of that year, "Lord Alexander Thynne enchanting the Labour Party." * Thynne's feet are impossibly constricted and fastidious, like ballet slippers, while the Labourites have on clumsy, anomalous boots: a basic distinction in scores of Beerbohm caricatures.

The Labour members gathered around Lord Alexander

Thynne are rough, ignorant creatures, but in 1913 are still looking ineffectual. Then just after the war Beerbohm wrote an essay on "Servants"; its tone is whimsical, but full of doubt about "the Spirit of the Age"—he has seen a butler pouring out wine in a hostile manner and actually humming to himself. The image of a working class that appears in Beerbohm's caricatures around 1919–1920 differs very little from Matthew Arnold's image a half-century earlier, in *Culture and Anarchy*. Arnold had spoken of the Populace as a playful giant, a large, coarse, threatening fellow, and this describes precisely the stock figure that began to impinge on Beerbohm's mind. In 1919 he wrote "Something Defeasible," a humorous parable on the erosion of England's comfortable polity: "We are at the mercy of Labour, certainly; and Labour does not love us." A later caricature answers this fear, with an enormous proletarian holding two tiny society ladies in his palm: "and if I destroyed *them* I should destroy myself *with* 'em."

A Survey (1921) includes a large portion of topical political cartoons, some of which drew criticism from London's press. The *Daily Herald* objected to the vulgar inference of "The Patron," which anticipated (Labour did not come in until 1924) a porcine Minister of Education bellowing at a wispy poet who had imagined that under Labour the arts might be encouraged: "Wot! You'll dedicate your mon-you-mental translation of Pett Rark's sonnits to me . . . You're a worker? . . . OUT!" In fact, the first Labour Minister of Education was C. P. Trevelyan, Harrow and Trinity College, Cambridge, grandnephew of Lord Macaulay. The *Manchester Guardian* asked whether Beerbohm was losing touch with English affairs, if he could draw the cartoon "When Labour Rules," which shows another oaf—this time a new Secretary for Foreign Affairs—greeting the prim French Ambassador, "Glad to see you Moossoo . . ."

Except for a flatly cynical cartoon on "Communist Sunday School," "Pupils learning that they must not shrink from shedding blood in order to achieve starvation," Beerbohm left revolution alone in his next-to-last volume, *Things New and Old* (1923). When Labour finally did take power in 1924 and lost it the same year, he did a cartoon entertaining the notion that British good sense had pulled the country through again, though Communism and Anarchism were still dangers. *Observations* (1925) contains a good deal of topical commentary in which Beerbohm's earlier complaints are settling into irony. "Civilisation and the Industrial System": the lumpy, beastlike jailer with a diamond in his navel, to the pure damsel, "You took me for better or wuss in younger and 'appier days, and there'll be no getting away . . ."* The threatening force is more absurdly exaggerated than ever, and what there is to counter that force looks false. In a cartoon of the Governing Classes and Communism, Beerbohm's ironic detachment from the struggle seems greater than it actually was: another beast, with pointed ears, assaults a disdainful, desiccated figure made up unbelievably of every Establishment emblem—epaulettes, riding boots, a cross, chancellor's wig, silk hat, and umbrella. The caption asks, "Too proud to fight . . . or too short-sighted?—or too liberal-minded? or what?" This kind of satire recalls the mode of James Gillray but is not so penetrating.

Beerbohm had little sense of who the members of the working class were, except to suppose realistically (as he does in a 1925 drawing) that the class-consciousness they would "like ter have" was that of the nobility. Some of his sharpest criticism in caricature went against other groups as well: fashionable modern women, captains of industry, militarists, advertising magnates. Essentially, what bothered him was the emergence of modern social groups and classes. Well before becoming preoccupied with Labour, he found in middle-class Englishmen the stigma of urban existence: the "uniform dreariness," "shuffling gait," and "petty tasks" of women out shopping and men who come home on the Tube at night. He found no technique in caricature for expressing bourgeois nature, as Daumier did. His average man is banal to look at, never triumphantly mediocre. In the mid-thirties, when in England giving nostalgic BBC talks, he did caricatures contrasting Victorian and modern personality. One of them, "If they were flourishing in this our day," puts a group of well-known Victorians into efficient suits and haircuts. Rossetti and Disraeli look like tired shopkeepers. Beerbohm means to say that costume still makes a difference, and that colorful, distinctive personality is not to be expected in 1936. But the caricature also suggests that without the visual signs he was accustomed to, he would hardly recognize the value of a man. As the century wore on, he linked his own distinctiveness more and more to the past, drawing a double self-caricature in 1938 with the elaborate costume and coiffure of a nineteenth-century artist on one side and a standardized business suit and short haircut on the other. The elements of twentieth century life that displeased him, industrialization and collectivization, also threatened his caricature. He tried to draw the twentieth-century man in the street, with a baggy trench coat and scruffy shoes, rushing along smoking a cigarette. The trouble is, his drawing of "the Demon of Uniformity in his drastic democratic stride" is itself aesthetically nondescript. The task of doing a both typical and modern man defeated him.

Women, Jews, and Americans are represented scantily or by unfair stereotypes. There are little more than a dozen drawings in which women are prominent, for not many figured in the public life of either politics or culture. Actresses attracted Beerbohm and occasionally he caricatured them; apart from that, he grew up accepting the Victorian notion of reticent, home-encircled womanhood. At home, school, college, or the Café Royal, he had little chance to see women as equal agents, and they did not stir him to draw. "They are uncaricaturable," he said, "they are too elusive, and they have no features—and if they have, they are hideous"—a statement that recalls the plea in "A Defence of Cosmetics" for women to keep their masks beautiful and expressionless. He felt perhaps that the softer features and lack of distinguishing facial hair would leave less to caricature. But Beerbohm was not pleading delicacy in being unable to draw women. Instinctually he could feel threatened by them. He had a habit of redoing fashion advertisements in the newspaper. Women's shoes became clodhoppers, dresses and hats were altered and women generally made fun of—in some places Beerbohm uglified them or drew them over as dwarfs.

When he caricatured Jews, he unfailingly stressed a large, distasteful nose: in his friend Reggie Turner, who was half-Jewish; in the Rothschilds, and other Jewish financiers tiptoeing into Buckingham Palace; even slightly in Disraeli, and in London's orthodox Jewry being painted by William Rothenstein. Two other, unpublished caricatures have real animus in them. One, entitled "Jermyn Street," depicts a slobbish store owner, obviously rich and beckoning with fat, oily hands. The other is a grotesque, four-nosed monster in kiss-curls, called "Messrs Carfax," sitting on a bag of "Percentages" (stereotyped humor again: Beerbohm gave his first exhibitions at the Carfax Gallery, which was run by friends of his). Malcolm Muggeridge, looking for some stripe across Beerbohm's life, said that he was in panic flight from his Jewishness, and Ezra Pound suggested the same. In fact, there is no evidence of Jewish background in Beerbohm's family, and one sister took orders in an Anglican priory. But Beerbohm married an American Jew and when she died, a German-Jewish woman came to live with him during the last years, marrying him on his deathbed. In London he had mixed easily with what he called its "cosmopolosemitics," but when asked if he was a Jew, he always denied it politely. I doubt he was particularly defensive. The distaste that comes out in caricatures is a matter of temperament, like Beerbohm's other opinions.

With the exception of Teddy Roosevelt ("The Prince of

Bores") and Woodrow Wilson, the Americans whom Beerbohm drew regularly were expatriates in England, or in Rapallo, where he knew Ezra Pound. Pound in a 1934 caricature has wild arms blowing in the wind and a deep, open collar. "Crazy," Beerbohm later called him. He did revealing caricatures of the Americans who succeeded in a cultural milieu familiar to him: Whistler, Sargent, James, Henry Harland, editor of the *Yellow Book,* Frank Harris, and the art critic Joseph Pennell. In addition, there is a drawing of Whitman and two good ones of Mark Twain. It is when Beerbohm has to draw typical Americans that an easy colonialist bias emerges. They are usually rough frontiersmen or vulgar nouveaux riches. Oscar Wilde announces the name of Rossetti to an American audience made up of mutations on Abraham Lincoln. In a drawing of Woodrow Wilson addressing Congress, the President is austere and academic, while all eleven Congressmen in the picture are coarse plutocrats staring bestially at him.

Beerbohm did not mind selling his work to Americans, but his curiosity extended no farther than the burlesque—the cigar-chewing capitalist, the pioneer. Soon after the Rhodes Scholarship bequest was announced, he did a caricature combining one blind spot in his imagination with another. He drew Charles Boyd, administrator of the Rhodes Trust, receiving a bug-eyed, thick-lipped American Negro with gaudy clothes under cap and gown, looking expectant but mindless. In *Zuleika Dobson,* the Rhodes Scholar Abimelech V. Oover is just as fantastic, though with good cause in that context. Beerbohm never traveled to America when his wife did, and to an American impresario offering him $12,000 for a short speaking tour of the United States, he replied that the conditions were not right:

> If you will guarantee an absolutely smooth Atlantic (forfeit of $500 to be paid by you for the least ripple observed by me) and will build an exquisite little marble hall on

> Ellis Island, a hall warranted to hold not more than twenty-five persons, to whom, on one night only and for not more than twenty minutes, and for a fee of twenty-five million dollars, I shall utter very quietly whatever nonsense may come into my head, do let me hear from you again.

Beerbohm caricatured Americans, the working class, and the bourgeoisie automatically as part of the impending degradation of civilization and the arts. This preoccupation stems from the Boer War cartoons of 1901, in which vulgar, decrepit John Bull asks painters for a good lesson, poets for a wholesome "toon." Beerbohm did the fifteen drawings in *The Second Childhood of John Bull* (his only collection labeled "cartoons") out of frustration at national degeneracy. The first cartoon is an "ideal" John Bull—"I'm going to see this thing through"—and the others bitterly undermine that smugness. Although not strikingly beautiful to the eye, they have a loose energy Beerbohm sometimes found outside his own native dimension. John Bull is the crucial figure throughout, shaming himself in Europe, vilely drunk or helpless in the face of heavy British losses, and deeply Philistine.* On the evidence of these cartoons, Shaw called Beerbohm "the most savage Radical caricaturist since Gillray." This judgment (made in 1917) partly reflects Shaw's own exasperation with England, and his personal sensitiveness to Beerbohm's caricature. Yet *The Second Childhood of John Bull* does have some of the angry invention of Gillray. In the later part of 1901, when the cartoons were drawn, nearly everyone was sick of a prolonged, humiliating, costly war. What angered Beerbohm during the Boer War was not Britain's damaged empire—he was indifferent to that: "the only feeling that our Colonies inspire in me is a determination not to visit them." It was the self-delusions and debasement of conduct at home, the slavish reliance on grandiose national myths.

The Boer War cartoons give a disproportionate sense of how Beerbohm conceived his role as a caricaturist in England. During the First World War, his letters reverted to sentimental patriotisms about dear old England. He decided not to allow any exhibition of his caricatures because their tone was inappropriate and inevitably they belittled the ruling class. He did no war cartoons, though Charles Masterman of the Propaganda Office and others asked him to, and Arnold Bennett insisted that "the absence of war-cartoons by you is generally *felt.*" Beerbohm sensed that his work had nothing to do with crisis and disaster. Caricature was ultimately part of his own aesthetic and psychological economy, not the nation's.

Britain's leaders are not charged with national decay in the caricatures of Max Beerbohm. He never imagined any radical reform of government. Along with John Bull he caricatured the conservative 1901 Cabinet and leaders of the Opposition under a title, "Pillars of Our State and Stewards of Our Greatness," that mocks them without questioning their legitimacy. This point above all separates Beerbohm from Gillray, or from George Grosz's scathing caricatures of militarism and capitalism in the nineteen-twenties. Beerbohm's Chamberlain in 1901, jigging wildly with a Union Jack and a bottle of vitriol, and Rosebery, out of office at the time, are seen and enjoyed with an eye for what men are individually—for their conceits, contradictions, deadlocks, excesses. Beerbohm drew more for fun than in the hope of changing attitudes or behavior. In fact, he depended as man and artist on the survival of the context he satirized.

The principle that history is the biography of great men satisfied him. He copied out long excerpts from books of biography and autobiography, and his kind of caricature was designed to signalize individuals rather than the historical pressures on them. Beerbohm deplored the gradual decay of the individualist idea since his youth. It frightened him that life was being destroyed for the Tory Anarchist, as he called himself, who would "like every one to go about doing just as he pleased—short of altering any of the things to which I have grown accustomed." Society after the war was being arranged by Ramsay MacDonald and his "wild men" for the "rabble of dreadful creatures" on the streets of London. There was no place for the intentional play with culture that began in Beerbohm's writing of the nineties, no place any more for the tempo and substance of his work.

In 1928 he traveled from Rapallo to London to arrange an exhibition called "Ghosts." It was a retrospective show of 109 drawings dating from 1896 on. "I have abandoned all hope of being 'topical,'" he wrote in the catalogue, and exhibited all his old reliable subjects—Wilde, Beardsley, Chamberlain, James, Shaw, Rosebery, Kipling—kept as they were in caricature. The tone of the show was nostalgic, as his letters of that period were becoming. Although he felt untopical, Beerbohm was a striking financial success. In 1901 his drawings had sold for four or five pounds apiece, and now they sold for forty or fifty pounds, and one for seventy-three: the entire show grossed over £2,000. Beerbohm brought back the past, and people liked that. By 1928 at least half a dozen books on the fin de siècle had appeared, stressing his affinity with the period, and he himself did nothing to alter that impression. Through *Rossetti and His Circle* and "Studies in the Eighteen-Seventies," he had fostered the anachronism by linking himself imaginatively with a lost age.

A remarkable shift occurred toward the end of Beerbohm's career as an active caricaturist. His drawings were no longer satirical exaggerations but mild likenesses, benevolently disposed toward their subjects. He could write to a friend in 1924, "If you don't approve of the presentment of yourself in the Theatre Exhibition drawing, you must tell me—and I'll do another and a better when I see you again." Among drawings from 1926 there are two sorts. The "Memory of Henry Irving" keeps a satiric sharpness of outline in the face, making Irving look sly and sinister.* But a drawing of Meredith is gentle,* and one of Whistler has little boldness or satire in it, as if Beerbohm were reconciled to this old antagonist. In 1928, he drew two self-caricatures unlike his previous ones. Although he never had distorted himself painfully in self-caricature, these were just pictures of himself. He had lost his primary impulse for the métier of caricature. Having been away from England since 1910, Beerbohm no longer responded to current figures; many he had drawn earlier were now dead or inactive, and he rendered new subjects, such as Stanley Baldwin, more or less faithfully. Mildness of treatment is the first impression you get from *Heroes and Heroines of Bitter Sweet* (1931), and in very late caricatures of Edward VII and Moore, the original signs recur in a softened form. Reconcilement had taken away Beerbohm's means for caricature, an art that flourishes between tolerance and ridicule of the way things are.

Caricature and Parody

If caricature is to mean anything, you must "really see," Beerbohm said. Its visual nature above all distinguishes caricature from parody, the other art Beerbohm's genius led him into. Chesterton's girth and Moore's vague gestures give a strong impression of who they are—*present* them—whereas the parodies Beerbohm did of these men only *represent* them through language. Thus another difference: parody attaches to a man's style, caricature to the man himself. Possibly Beerbohm always called caricaturing an easy, natural habit so the men he drew would not feel themselves under serious attack. His drawings could have a damaging and a rudely direct effect. They constituted a form of unprotected opinion, in contrast to the baffles of irony in "A Defence of Cosmetics" or "A Peep into the Past."

Essentially, however, the two arts have in common that

they work from within their subject. By empathy Beerbohm gets in to what it feels like to be Rudyard Kipling (at least that is his presumption) and draws or verbalizes aggressiveness. Caricature and parody try to discover a man in the line of his strength, to take his standpoint, and then to produce a laugh. They make a strong bond out of hostile and creative impulses. As distinct from satire, which is analytic and breaks up things from outside, they are literally *expressive*. And because all art entails some exaggeration of neutral fact, caricature and parody exemplify the larger genres they fall within. Daumier, it can be said, was a prerequisite for Edvard Munch. Beerbohm's parodies of James are, in a way, paradigms of James's theoretical prefaces.

The parodies direct our attention to style and to literature itself. With a few exceptions, the generic dimension is a different sort in Beerbohm's caricatures, which deal with persons rather than with aesthetics or the creative process. He tended to depict the public hazards of talent—Sargent besieged by foreign lady sitters, Shaw with his eulogists or critics, Whistler in dispute over the fee for a portrait. Or in *The Poets' Corner*: "Mr. Tennyson reading *In Memoriam* to his sovereign" with his long legs splayed on an elegant carpet that extends between him and the remote Queen; and "Mr. Robert Browning taking tea with the Browning Society," in which the poet stands out ruddily from a circle of pale, obsequious faces. Indeed it is hard to imagine how caricature could present inward, solitary work. Beerbohm did try at times to get at the screened-off inspirations of art. These drawings are funny, but seldom particularly revealing. He drew Wordsworth "at cross-purposes in the Lake District," in the rain looking at an unexpressive country girl; Lytton Strachey staring at a bust of Queen Victoria; Kipling posturing as an Elizabethan poet while composing a ballad to raise money for soldiers' wives; Conrad on a desolate beach looking promisingly at a human skull; "Mr. W. B. Yeats, presenting Mr. George Moore to the Queen of the

Fairies."* The background of "Mr. Thomas Hardy composing a Lyric," a blasted hill under lowering skies, only visualizes a critical commonplace about Hardy. But Beerbohm gives the poet a beautifully musing expression, which is probably what Mrs. Hardy had in mind when she wrote later that Beerbohm's caricatures of her husband "show greater insight than any other portraits."

The innovation that only Beerbohm was capable of making and sustaining was to bring the dynamics and sometimes the language of parody into caricature. He drew Beardsley in the style of Beardsley, Phil May in Phil May's style, and himself once, exactly as he appears in a portrait by William Rothenstein. In the caricature from *Rossetti and His Circle* of Whistler showing blue china to Thomas Carlyle, Carlyle's mournful profile, meant to express distaste, is the same as in Whistler's portrait of him. At about the turn of the century, Beerbohm began to conceive situations as well as single figures, and to add captions. We see these drawings and their words bifocally, in a way that resolves academic doubts (raised over Blake and Rossetti) that the two media can be joined. As a natural parodist, Beerbohm located the subjects of these caricatures in plausible circumstances (Henry James in a "to him so very congenial" blind London fog) and then let them react with characteristic excess (James's sudden dismay that he *can,* "with an almost awful clarity," see his hand in front of his eyes).* Another drawing has James kneeling tensely outside a hotel bedroom with his ear, not his eye, pressed to the keyhole.* Caricatures like these create for their subject a quintessential situation that just might occur, say, in a dream or a failure of discretion. Compared with Tenniel's allegory, du Maurier's social vignettes, the bestiary figures of F. Carruthers Gould, and the endless borrowing from *Alice in Wonderland,* Beerbohm's infusion of parody marks a profound change in the mimetic grasp of English caricature.

What he did for British art and society was to witness

critically part of the cultural life from Rossetti on, through images of painters, novelists, poets, playwrights, actors, managers, journalists, critics, dons, entrepreneurs, and consumers of art. All these make up an anatomy of British culture which has shaped our sense of the period. It is only after looking through the entire range of his caricatures on every subject that we can see what an achievement they represent. Judging from their continued use in reviews, biographies, autobiographies, and histories, and their display in homes and museums all over England and the United States, his drawings amount to more than a quarter century's comic documentary. Caricature is usually considered an ephemeral art, limited to its topical relevance. Sometimes this holds for Beerbohm. But most often his caricatures and his parodies brim with an expressive energy that lasts.

PART THREE

5

Parody

Henry James

Beerbohm began by defending, in the person of his own style, the exclusive creative agency of art. In drama criticism and other writing around the turn of the century, such as *Words for Pictures*, his angle of vision shifted to what would directly expose the working of artistic illusion. Then a new form of expression, fusing those two impulses, emerged in *A Christmas Garland*, *Zuleika Dobson*, and *Seven Men*. Parody, the quintessence of that new form, is at once a creative and a critical act. It resolves, without quite deciding, the problem raised by Ibsen—whether art is worth it.

At the head of *A Christmas Garland*, Beerbohm placed his parody of Henry James. James's work stood for the whole of fiction, and Beerbohm imagined James rather than Wilde or Shaw as an example of the accomplished artist. His attention to James lasted throughout sixty years, in parodies, essays, reviews, letters, poems, caricatures, alterations, and a last reminiscence written in 1954. All together they present Beerbohm's fullest image of a writer, and a reflection of himself.

When, in 1896, he had the idea of parodying various writers (including himself) on the subject of Christmas, he thought of doing "Henry James never mentioning Xmas by name." But he did not write a parody of James then, and he preserved only one of that first group, with considerable revision, for publication in book form. It was not until ten years later that he had the literary experience and stylistic capacity for successful parody. And James's later, fuller manner made him more worth parodying. In December 1906 Beerbohm published "The Mote in the Middle Distance," a fetish for anyone who either loves or disparages James.

The finely involved, central intelligence of the parody is Keith Tantalus, wondering with his sister Eva what the Christmas stockings at the foot of their beds contain, and whether to investigate them. What Beerbohm re-creates is the way every utterance, every human option in James is swaddled in layers of awareness. Keith at one point has reached out as if to touch his stocking:

> The gaze she fixed on her extravagant kinsman was of a kind to make him wonder how he contrived to remain, as he beautifully did, rigid. His prop was possibly the reflection that flashed on him that, if *she* abounded in attenuations, well, hang it all, so did *he*! It was simply a difference of plane. Readjust the "values," as painters say, and there you were! He was to feel that he was only too crudely "there" when, leaning further forward, he laid a chubby forefinger on the stocking, causing that receptacle to rock ponderously to and fro. This effect was more expected than the tears which started to Eva's eyes, and the intensity with which "Don't you," she exclaimed, "see?"

Keith and Eva do see the obsessive mote in the middle distance, the thing that complicates our moral perspective. Beerbohm's title and the rest of his parody develop the way of registering perceptions which James developed in his later novels. All the turns of style Beerbohm invents for Keith and Eva can be found in *The Wings of the Dove* and *The Golden Bowl*. They sometimes seem to be done better by Beerbohm, sometimes less well done: the broken sentences, roundabout simplicities, syntactical quibbles, colloquialisms made genteel by inverted commas, italics for delicate intonation, stunning double negatives, accumulated homely adjectives, abruptly placed, vague adverbs, banal metaphors worried and reworried, the narrator's unsettling glances into the future and his intimacy with "our friend" Keith, the exasperating, magnified scruples, and, at last, the vibrant moral renunciation by Keith and Eva—"One doesn't violate the shrine—pick the pearl from the shell!"

"The Mote in the Middle Distance," with its discriminations and qualifications, displays a perverse subtlety. One can compare Keith and Eva to the brother and sister in *The Turn of the Screw*, but really Beerbohm's children are a burlesque reduction of Merton Densher and Kate Croy in the final scene of *The Wings of the Dove*. Densher decides it would be better to return unopened an envelope containing his inheritance: Keith says finally, "One doesn't even peer" into the Christmas stockings. An undertone of frustration runs through the generally benign stylistic parody of James. For one thing, Beerbohm makes the children brother and sister, yet Keith thinks about Eva as nervously as one of James's lovers would: "his fear of what she was going to say was as nothing to his fear of what she might be going to leave unsaid." And the name Eva Tantalus clearly implies that some kind of sexual frustration lies behind James's imagining of his characters and their experiences.

Beerbohm was involved enough in that imagining to come back to his parody in 1922 and write a new passage for it, which he meant to come closer to "the great dark glow of the later manner." Keith and Eva are talking about the unknown contents of the stockings:

> "In respect, you mean, of what's in either of *them*?"
> "In respect," she rose at it, "of what's in *both* of them."
> Well, he had got, *tout bonnement*, the measure of it now. But he had not yet covered, as was to appear, the span of his insistence. "You know, then, by blest induction, what there *is* in them?"

> "I know," she had a high gesture for it, "*only* that."
> He hardly hesitated. "*What*'s in them?"
> "Everything," she gave back to him. She had closed her eyes. "More than everything," she passionately, she all but inaudibly now breathed.

And she resists Keith's vision that they might look into their stockings:

> "Ah, the vision!" It was as though, with a courage that matched his, she could hang and brood over that too. But she presently turned from it. "What we have to hold on to—but with a tenacity!—is not so much what you perhaps saw as what you have all along, *caro,* foreseen—the impossibility, simply, of our *not* being able not to. *That's* all that counts. It's the lamp in our darkness and the seal of our good faith. It's the end of the journey and the garland at the feast."

It is hard to imagine anything closer to the toils and renunciations of James's moral consciousness. You have in Beerbohm's parody the sense of being present at the first few cell divisions of *The Wings of the Dove.*

Beerbohm never used this passage in later editions of *A Christmas Garland.* By the time he had an opportunity to do so, "The Mote in the Middle Distance" was a recognized work of art. Revising it would have called into question the integrity of the parody. Although his parodies are indeed criticism, he did not think of them as tools that might be improved. "The Mote in the Middle Distance" is a form of discourse in itself with Henry James for a theme, along with the theme of knowledge and renunciation. In fact, Beerbohm's addition has totally assimilated James. The finest parody may only erase its original, like dubbing over an entire tape.

James recognized this kind of danger, and it could be disastrous to let him know that he had been parodied.

Henry James and Max Beerbohm, ca. 1911

Apparently he felt inhibited from writing just after reading "The Mote in the Middle Distance." He said jokingly that Beerbohm's book of parodies had destroyed the trade of literature because "no one, now, can write without incurring the reproach of somewhat ineffectively imitating—you!" No response could have been more flattering, short of James's eventually believing the parody to be his own work.

Beerbohm's ability to conceive "The Mote in the Middle Distance," and his love for James, whom he came to know personally in the nineties, do not seem to have been affected by the clear contrasts between them: by James's passionate absorption in the art of fiction, and the great formal culmination, as against Beerbohm's versatility dwindling to a piece every few years; James's dense emotion and Beerbohm's lightness; James's massive aesthetic impersonality and Beerbohm's self-insinuations. Remaining aware of these disparities may even have been Beerbohm's way of accommodating himself as an artist. An informal caricature by him contains one view of the personal relation. The novelist is in profile, glaring at Beerbohm; his mouth is moving and his hand gesturing remonstratively. Opposite, the slighter figure of Beerbohm—hands half-raised, eyes bland and attentive, tie-pin in place. Besides confronting parodist with victim, this drawing suggests the lower pitch at which Beerbohm existed, in contrast with James.

He never seemed deeply troubled in his private or professional existence, yet his critique of James touches on topics that pertain also to himself. James's celibacy is one of these. Just as Wilde's sexual affinities gave "A Peep into the Past" its oblique satiric force, Beerbohm wrote in 1909 another hoax involving the personal circumstances of James's seclusion in the town of Rye. The hoax itself consists of an imaginary book, *Half Hours with the Dialects of England*, from which Beerbohm produces a title page and a specimen chapter on Rye. His example of Rye dialect is a sonnet by Miss Alice Peploe, who, Beerbohm's introductory notes explain, is a dressmaker smitten by love for the novelist. The sonnet, number 153 of JAEMES: A ZONNET-ZEQUENCE, begins "Jaëmes! Thou dost be för bein' egregious / To never discommode the heart o' me." Miss Peploe chides him "för bein' damsel-coy," and ends:

> . . . as Thou dost be för bein ztrong,
> Do be för bein' merciful. Ahoy!
> Wings o' the Dove! No dove do be för bein'
> Möre dove than me when I do thee be zeein'.

The editor supports this sonnet with footnotes on the peculiar, roundabout speech of Rye people, and on Shakespearean influences in the couplet, remarking only briefly that he hopes the sonnet "may chance to meet the eye of Mr. James, and so, perhaps, pave the way to Miss Peploe's future happiness."

Beerbohm could not have laughed at James's privation, or invented the copious editorial paraphernalia, if he had not otherwise found James's art complete and convincing. Much earlier, before the three last novels, he had not been entirely sympathetic to James's "fastidious coyness" as a writer, his "fear of penetrating into the passions" of his highly civilized world. But when *The Golden Bowl* appeared in 1905, Beerbohm copied into his notebook some passages that stirred him; for instance, one between Charlotte and the Prince: "Their lips sought their lips, their pressure their response and their response their pressure; with a violence that had sighed itself the next moment to the longest and deepest of stillnesses they passionately sealed their pledge."

The caricatures on James's sexual condition are more probing than the writing. In one drawing, exhibited but not collected in book form, James brings the Man in the Iron Mask and the Mona Lisa together for an ideal marriage, and glares at Mona Lisa as if sensual beauty was the hardest thing to coerce into his discipline. There are other caricatures implying, as Eva Tantalus and Miss Peploe do, that James's whole style is founded on some obscure sexual need. On the title page to Beerbohm's copy of *The Aspern Papers*, he drew the author doubled up in pain, with the caption, "Mr. Henry James in the act of parturiating a sentence." The caricature of James kneeling next to the men's and ladies' boots outside a bedroom door* satirizes *The Sacred Fount*, whose narrator, curious about the flow of vitality between man and woman, says that while psychological diagnosis is acceptable, "what's ignoble is the detective and the keyhole." In making a caricature of voyeurism, Beerbohm was also using against James an essay on D'Annunzio in which James says that a novelist can tell us nothing distinctive about human passions by merely conducting us vulgarly among "the boots and shoes that we see, in the corridors of promiscuous hotels, standing, often in double pairs, at the doors of rooms." The angle on James depended partly on what audience Beerbohm had in mind. He withheld this caricature, drawn just after his own marriage, until long after James's death. And while devising Miss Peploe's sonnet, also unpublished, he could praise James in his weekly theater column, stressing the superb moral conscience of the novels rather than their avoidance of primitive emotion.

About America Beerbohm was skeptical in any case, so

James's return there in 1904 after twenty years away evoked an elaborate caricature. "Mr. Henry James revisiting America" predicts the thickly qualified attitudes that were to emerge in James's book *The American Scene*. Beerbohm draws him confronting a group of stereotyped Americans welcoming the novelist in their peculiar idioms. Among them, an Indian with his eyes shut—"Hail, great white novelist! Tuniyaba—the spinner of fine cobwebs!", and an Aunt Jemima with open arms—"Why, it's Masser Henry! Come to your old nurse's arms, honey!" The other figures, a banker, a frontier scout, a Harvard snob, a cakewalking nigger, seem to be burlesque abstractions from Oscar Wilde's tour of the United States and Beerbohm's short, sheltered visit in 1895. They crudely embody James's dismay at American vulgarity and vernacular style. If the drawing is not as inquiring as *The American Scene*, a parody within the drawing points to the crucial uncertainty behind James's book—that is, whether he can really understand who and what these people are. James is holding back from the improbable scene in Beerbohm's caricature, musing:

> So that, in fine, let, without further beating about the bush, me make to myself amazed acknowledgement that, but for the certificate of birth which I have, so very indubitably, *on* me, I might, in regarding, and, as it somewhat were, overseeing, *à l'oeil de voyageur*, these dear good people, find hard to swallow, or even to take by subconscious injection, the great idea that I am—oh, ever so indigenously!—one of them.

A year later Beerbohm was moved again, by James's story "The Jolly Corner," to stress the expatriate's predicament and the artist's dissociation from America. He wrote to James praising "The Jolly Corner," and did a fine drawing visualizing the idea that if James had stayed in New York he would have become an overdressed, red-faced plutocrat.

In the "Jolly Corner" caricature and in all the others,

James's eyes are his one brilliant trait. Beerbohm habitually drew statesmen and actors with their eyes closed, but James's are always bulging with perception, with what Beerbohm called his "awful vision" of life. "Your fine eyes, blurred like arc-lamps in a mist," Beerbohm wrote in a sonnet to James. There is an extremely funny drawing of James at the moment of getting the notion for *The Turn of the Screw*, as he says he did, from the Archbishop of Canterbury, E. W. Benson. Where Benson appears perfectly serene, James is starting violently, gripping the arms of the chair. His eyes are glaring with astonishment and insatiable curiosity. They are like that outside the hotel bedroom,* and in the London fog*—a beautiful study of shades of gray in which only James's eyeball and Beerbohm's signature are clearly visible. The novelist is "overseeing, *à l'oeil de voyageur*," Beerbohm's American scene, and also the middle distance of Keith and Eva Tantalus. James himself called the writer "a figure with a pair of eyes" at one window in the house of fiction. The eyes as Beerbohm drew them are in every sense filled with apprehension.

Next to *The Wings of the Dove*, he was most attracted to James's fiction about the condition of the writer, and wrote in 1954 a reminiscence of that kind, about choosing to read a new story by James rather than spend an afternoon with him. Nearly all James's stories about novelists were written during the eighteen-nineties. Two of them appeared with Beerbohm's work in the early volumes of the *Yellow Book*. Later he praised James's way of imagining paintings or sculpture and his loving, cunning analysis of the artist's condition. In a 1914 essay, "Books Within Books," he carefully discusses the nonexistent canon of James's imaginary novelists: Ray Limbert's *The Hidden Heart*, for instance, "'the shortest of his novels, but perhaps the loveliest,' as Mr. James and I have always thought."

One claim Beerbohm cannot make, however, is that James re-creates the writing of his authors. We take Vereker's "finest fullest intention" in "The Figure in the Carpet" and Dencombe's "fine talent" in "The Middle Years" to be very much like James's, but the value of their art must be felt through someone else—the public or an admiring narrator. In contrast, Beerbohm in the stories from *Seven Men* takes every chance for parody. We get a lively sense of Enoch Soames's writing, and not of Dencombe's, because Beerbohm was not tied exclusively to his own sacred Muse. What is more, in James's style the sentences build literally by exaggeration: if he were imitating rather than merely describing a talent comparable to his own, he would have trouble knowing where to begin. The rare moments when James can be said to parody himself occur when he is immensely moved or gratified, often about some small matter. Beerbohm's letter to him about "The Jolly Corner" evoked a letter of thanks that blooms with incipient self-parody: "I can only gather myself in and up," wrote James, "arching and presenting my not inconsiderable back—a back, as who should say, offered for any further stray scratching and patting of that delightful kind. . . . it charms me to think—or rather so authentically to know, that my (I confess) ambitious Muse does work upon you; it really helps me to believe in her the more myself."

Several stories from *Seven Men* have their inspiration in James, with the difference that Beerbohm's writers are talentless. James's are as good as they try to be; it is the world's taste that is at fault. "Poor Dencombe," as "The Middle Years" calls him, faints when caught revising his own newly published book (*The Middle Years*), and dies on the brink of a splendid "last manner." The evocation of his death by James is a triumph, in Beerbohm's view: "It rises and glows and gladdens," he wrote in "Books Within Books." "It is more exquisite than anything in *The Middle Years*." This easy illusion of familiarity with Dencombe's imaginary book marks a quality that let Beerbohm mix freely among Soames and the others in *Seven Men*, as both author and character. James scrupulously kept himself out of his stories, as his notebook entries during the nineties show. He took more precautions settling the point of view in his stories of novelists than in any others.

There is not much explicit recognition by Beerbohm of the long crisis—two novels failing and then his plays—behind James's tales of artists' isolation and ghostly disaster in the eighteen-nineties. But he followed and welcomed James's later development of a complex and demanding technique. Early in 1902 he had called James "that perfect master of a small method." Then after *The Wings of the Dove* and *The Golden Bowl*, he wrote that reading James was like climbing slowly up a mountain with gradually expanding views until at last one saw the "large and luminous whole"—a hint, also, of the element of duration in a novel, which parody can hardly reproduce. Beerbohm liked the rich difficulties of James's vision. He caricatured him in 1908, subpoenaed as psychological expert in a cause célèbre, listening gravely in the witness box to a gross, impatient cross-examiner: "Come, Sir, I ask you a plain question, and I expect a plain answer!"

The change in James is marked clearly in Beerbohm's drawings before and after the turn of the century. At first James is bearded and strongly contained: in 1895, Beerbohm said, he "had looked rather like a Russian Grand Duke." After the nineties, and without a beard, he looked more like "a lay Cardinal." Beerbohm drew him heavier set, though according to Edith Wharton the novelist resented "any suggestion that his silhouette had lost firmness and acquired volume." He was drawing James's body as a figure for James's aesthetics. Where Shaw looks springy and graceless and Wilde overblown, James is never corpulent: his expansiveness fits him.

The double selves of James, younger and older, appear twice in Beerbohm's caricature. One set, in his copy of James's *Notebooks*, is now published in the paperback edition of that book. The other, possibly the most ingenious fusion of parody and caricature Beerbohm ever managed, was done to improve a book by Constant Coquelin, *Art and the Actor* (1915). Because the book's introduction, by James, was based on a much earlier essay, the publishers added a note on the first page: "The substance of this paper appeared in the Century Magazine for January, 1887." Beerbohm, seeing more in it than that, added another note in pencil: "and was very obviously—or rather, deviously and circuitously—revised in the great dark rich fullness of time, for republication in 1915." Leading away from this brief parody, he drew an arrow pointing to a caricature on the facing page. There, in pale blue wash and dark ink, two portraits face each other: on the right, a thickset, bearded, early James; on the left, a heavy-chinned, balding, clean-shaven later James with hair trailing back over his collar. The older man is making a gesture of reproof, the younger one is stubborn. Their words to each other share one balloon containing the phrase, "How badly you . . ."—completed by later James with "wrote!" and by early James with "write!"*

Self-transformation could be a disquieting thing for Beerbohm to watch. He ignored it in Yeats, denied it in Wilde, urged it innocently in Whistler. For himself it was never an option: he deepened and extended his original concerns, clarified his style, and let his notoriety in the nineties give way to modest popularity in the twentieth century. Through parody, caricature, and the private game of hoaxes, annotations, altered portraits, he fixed himself in relation to more salient forces in the culture around him. He was unwilling to see those forces modified, so his openness to James is impressive.

What Beerbohm did object to (as the Coquelin book demonstrates) was James's revising earlier work in the later style. "How badly you wrote!" looks a little trivial beside James's grandiose apology for revision—"the act of seeing it again"—in the preface to *The Golden Bowl*. But Beerbohm's point is well taken. He compared the revising to "patching pale grey silk with snippets of very dark thick brown velvet" and called it "a wanton offense against the laws of art." Evidently the idea of making one's lifework cohere in a new perspective was no excuse. He himself revised his earlier writing only once, for "The Mote in the Middle Distance," and then apologized: "I hold, with you," he wrote to Edmund Gosse, "stern views on the folly of re-writing anything that one wrote in the past. But since H.J. himself so unaccountably indulged in the folly, surely the humble and loving parodist of him might follow in his misdirected footsteps." Beerbohm also disliked James's prefaces for the collected New York Edition because of the objective, analytic consciousness they applied, calling them "a solecism—a sin against the art of fiction and against illusion, against the illudibility of the reader." He might have been expected to respond enthusiastically to this unique unfolding of literary process. But in one sense Beerbohm's parodies come closer to the experience of fiction as we have it now. No matter how discreetly James keeps his preface from impinging on the novel to come, we still feel his anxiety about adjusting means to ends. On the other hand, "The Mote in the Middle Distance" preserves the reader's illusion, and absorbs that pressure of means against ends into its own mimetic vision.

Of course the substance of the parody still owes itself to James, as Beerbohm's second full parody emphatically proves. He wrote "The Guerdon" in 1916, when James on his deathbed became a British citizen and received the Order of Merit. Although "The Mote in the Middle Distance" has been reprinted more than any other parody of Beerbohm's, "The Guerdon" is finer, almost too fine, its movements of thought articulated enough, its phrasing precise enough, to be sheer communion with James, never broadening into farce as other skits and parodies on James always do. "The Guerdon" is an ecstasy of tact, doubt, and release from doubt, all in the fine conscience of "poor decent Stamfordham," the King's Private Secretary on his way to the palace with a prospective Honors list containing one name that he has omitted to identify.

> This omission so loomed for him that he was to be conscious, as he came to the end of the great moist avenue, of a felt doubt as to whether he could, in his bemusement, now "place" anybody at all; to which condition of his may have been due the impulse that, at the reached gates of the palace, caused him to pause and all vaguely, all peeringly inquire of one of the sentries: "To whom do you beautifully belong?"

In 1909 Beerbohm had reviewed a play by James, and though he thought the drama was no vehicle for James's genius, he was gratified by Forbes-Robertson's speaking of one line from the play: "I mean, to whom do you beautifully belong?" He described the actor's intense rendition as "irony kneeling in awe" of James, and the same holds for "The Guerdon." Stamfordham's words belong to James, and under that auspice they purify the substance of the parody.

The subject of "The Guerdon," a novelist's precarious fame, saves it from turning into flattery. Stamfordham's delicacy keeps him from giving away to the King "his whole dim bland ignorance of the matter in hand," and he fears but will not expose the King's dimness. What is dim, throughout "The Guerdon," is precisely the identity and accomplishment of "Henry James." As the Honors list comes down to this name, Stamfordham wonders if the King, living also "on the great grey beach of the hesitational and renunciational," will be afraid to look in *Who's Who*:

> Our friend held, as for an eternity, his breath. He was to form, in later years, a theory that the name really *had* stood in peril of deletion, and that what saved it was that the good little man, as doing, under the glare shed

> by his predecessors, the great dynastic "job" in a land that had been under two Jameses and no less than eight Henrys, had all humbly and meltingly resolved to "let it go at that."

The joy of this climax is that it rises on the novelist's perfected idiom while bringing out the fantastic possibility that James got the Order of Merit solely because he was a British citizen, and that he may never get real recognition as a writer.

Beerbohm was among the first to speak intelligently and seriously about James, and he kept on returning to his copies of "The Death of the Lion" and "The Middle Years" all his life. "The Guerdon," coming as it does in the war, represents in a way his gratitude for the great Jamesian effort at holding Western civilization together by the grip of conscious art. And in 1937, when that effort had failed, Beerbohm read *Daisy Miller* and had "pangs of longing for the dear delicate un-panic-stricken world of sixty years ago."

He wrote once that James's amazing method would perish because no one else could handle it. The prediction is ironical, as parody would help that process along. But Beerbohm was irrevocably engaged with James. He brought himself into a continuum in which their disparities of background, temperament, demeanor, and vocation could be justified in comic forms. In Beerbohm, parody acted as a safe-conduct for exposing himself to the artist's passionate task, in the person of James, without losing himself to it. Keith and Eva also brought him closer to expressing moral passion than anything he wrote in his own voice.

Partly through parody, and less obviously in casual forms, Beerbohm meditated on James. The famous oil portrait that Sargent did in 1913 was "a dead failure," he thought, "a good presentment of a butler on holiday; but no more"—in contrast with the intense imaginative power that one finds expressed in Beerbohm's caricatures and parodies of James. It would, inevitably, be a caricature that caught the tragic cast of James's imagination. Done as a memory in 1920, it may refer to James's late story about the disaster of a solitary, empty life, "The Beast in the Jungle." In this sketch of a few lines, James is old, hunched forward with his hands in front of his face as if to ward off something, and staring in blank, pure dread.*

A Christmas Garland

When Beerbohm first thought of the Christmas parodies, in 1896, he imagined a title, "'Seasonable Tributes' Levied by Max Beerbohm." The pun on "tribute" comes from a root ambiguity: that the act of parody both celebrates and undermines literary invention. It works by empathy with an author's way of conceiving things, and yet by distortion creates a distance, a freedom from his vices. Beerbohm's note to *A Christmas Garland* says he used contemporary writers as models and also, "it must be admitted, in the hope of learning rather what to avoid." Most of the writers were both warnings and models, so the empathic distortion of parody had the effect of stretching the salient parts of a style to show where it went wrong, and what might have been possible in its own terms. The purely patricidal impulse of parody was spent for Beerbohm when Wilde died.

Modern parody has not been well understood in theory. Usually it is defined as burlesque, the ridiculing of a style by means of an incongruous substance, and considered merely the tool of the larger genre, satire. In Beerbohm, parody becomes its own genre. His schooling with Wilde to regard surface and manner as ends in themselves lies behind this genre, as does his instinct for trying out any sort of verbal expression, even one he disliked. A parody of his may well have satiric effect, but we do not sense the butt of satire as much as we do, say, in Swift's *Modest Proposal.*

Parody imagines a subject rather than an object. The parodies in *A Christmas Garland*, composed in 1906 and 1912 as if for a Victorian family Christmas album, confirm this proposition with James, Shaw, Conrad, Bennett, Galsworthy, Kipling, Chesterton—seventeen authors in all.

On the basis of *Anna of the Five Towns* (1904) and *The Old Wives' Tale* (1909), Beerbohm wrote a parody of Arnold Bennett, "Scruts." Like "A Straight Talk," the Shaw parody, "Scruts" has an entirely probable subject. It passes in and out from the insistent provincial environment of the Five Towns to the narrow psychological compass of Emily Wrackgarth:

> She would not try to explain, to reconcile. She abandoned herself to the exquisite mysteries of existence. And yet in her abandonment she kept a sharp look-out on herself, trying fiercely to make head or tail of her nature. She thought herself a fool. But the fact that she thought so was for her a proof of adult sapience. Odd! She gave herself up. And yet it was just by giving herself up that she seemed to glimpse sometimes her own inwardness. And these bleak revelations saddened her. But she savoured her sadness. It was the wine of life to her. And for her sadness she scorned herself, and in her conscious scorn she recovered her self-respect.

Parody cannot cope with the slow evolution of character through experience, which Beerbohm came to appreciate in *The Old Wives' Tale*. "Scruts" exposes instead a cross-section, the immediate limits of a technique.

With G. K. Chesterton, he set his parody in an argumentative posture. By coincidence the parody, "Some Damnable Errors About Christmas," appeared in the *Saturday Review* on the day when an essay on Christmas by Chesterton himself appeared in the *Illustrated London News*. The two have the same air of paradox and ready generalization, ridding men of their illusions: "Christmas is essentially a *dies irae*," the parody says. While Chesterton in his article argues down Shaw's vegetarian pity for the Christmas turkey, Beerbohm ends his parody with the startling paradox that spiritually, Christmas occurs seven times a week, so "roast turkey and plum-pudding shall be the staple of our daily dinner." Not only that, Shrove Tuesday occurs every day, and "every day pancakes shall be eaten, either before or after the plum-pudding." In Beerbohm's caricatures, Chesterton's huge stomach stands partly for this love of food, partly for another quality that the parody brings out—his faith in his own girth as the measure of things.* The verbal exuberance in "Some Damnable Errors About Christmas" belongs to the over-blown confidence: parody can get both the virtue and the defect of a man's style in one writing.

Beerbohm had nothing good to say for H. G. Wells. His 1896 parody is cheerful, but "Perkins and Mankind" (1912) develops a callous humanitarianism and a mind which, in its distaste for the present, becomes ambitiously utopian instead of nostalgic as Beerbohm's mind would. Perkins, an angry commoner at a country house party, wonders whether the "huge nasty mess" of the human race will be reformed by his plan for a Provisional Government of England by the Female Foundlings, and he tells himself, "This regeneration of mankind business may still be set going—and by *you*." Here, as in caricatures of Wells, Beerbohm hits off a crass, ego-centered social engineering. In a parody within the parody, Perkins pulls himself together by reading H. G. Wells on General Cessation Day, an annual holiday when everyone who has ceased to be of use to the state will proceed to the Municipal Lethal Chamber to "make way" for the rising generation. By this point, "Perkins and Mankind" has broken down into burlesque.

Being out of sympathy does not always prevent Beerbohm from using a writer's momentum, as a kind of judo, for significant and consistent parody. Rudyard Kipling stood nearly opposite James in Beerbohm's imagination, but the

Kipling parody in *A Christmas Garland*, "P.C., X, 36," is a brilliant one. In order to find Kipling out, Beerbohm chooses his situation pointedly: an encounter between the most obsequious of narrators and Judlip, a brutal policeman looking for business on Christmas Eve. Judlip's language gives the piece its tone, along with an improvised police station ditty at the head of the parody: "Wot, 'e *would*, would 'e? Well, / Then yer've got ter give 'im 'Ell, / An' it's trunch, trunch, truncheon does the trick!" That Kipling brought the Cockney voice into literature is an achievement easily forgotten in the bullying air of "P.C., X, 36." The parody's real insight into Kipling comes not through Judlip but through its narrator, the admiring civilian who fills notebooks with Judlip's authoritarian remarks and his jingoist pride in the Force ("which same is the jool Britannia wears on 'er bosom as a charm against hanarchy"). The narrator's worship of Judlip manifests an essentially submissive personality that Beerbohm saw in Kipling, a virility that works by proxy. After Judlip gets Santa Claus down from a rooftop, knuckles his spine, and drags him off, the parody closes. "Hold him. He's a German," shouts the narrator, and dances after them shrieking "Frog's-march him! For the love of heaven, frog's-march him!" This is the cruelest sentence Beerbohm ever wrote.

The same insight explains both Beerbohm's suggestion elsewhere that "Rudyard Kipling" may be a woman's pseudonym and the inevitable aspect of Kipling in Beerbohm's caricatures—a belligerent jaw thrust out above a jerky, inadequate body. Yet it takes the *Christmas Garland* parody to show how Kipling's authoritarian sympathies came out in fiction. Beerbohm regularly hounded "the schoolboy, the bounder, and the brute," and felt that Kipling prostituted his moral intelligence and his talent. This is the sense of a caricature in *The Poets' Corner*, a cocksure midget with a war helmet on, prancing along "for a day on th' blasted 'eath" next to a tall, dignified figure of Britannia.* Another drawing (in *The Second Childhood of John Bull*) has Kipling dressed as a schoolboy, listening to John Bull, who dilates on the lack of wholesome poets in England and congratulates him on his talent for providing the kind of information Alf Harmsworth does in the imperialist *Daily Mail*. Kipling's militarist inspiration also prompted a verse parody by Beerbohm in 1918, "The Old Volunteer"—"I can hear the bugle calling/ and it don't want me." Kipling's stoic rhythms come round to a final quatrain:

> But there'll be a better judgment for
> The Last Relay:
> I shall hear the bugle calling,
> And I'll march *that* day.

In manuscript Beerbohm set the poem under his drawing of *The Times*'s masthead for May 27, 1918, and added a note from the next day's paper to the effect that Rudyard Kipling had written in disowning the verses: "We apologise to Mr. Kipling and to our readers, and we are investigating the forgery." What is remarkable here and in "P. C., X, 36" is how closely Beerbohm managed to forge Kipling's manner, considering their total separation as writers.

A writer Beerbohm was prepared to resist even more than Kipling was Dostoevsky (he shares this opinion with James and Vladimir Nabokov). The British cult for Dostoevsky that began with the translation of *The Brothers Karamazov* struck him as contemptible, so in "Kolniyatsch" (1913), he adopts the voice of a toadying journalist. "Kolniyatsch" (the name of Beerbohm's Russian author derives from Colney Hatch, a mental asylum outside London) is a truckling appreciation of anguished souls from the Continent "plucking out their vitals for exportation," and of the Russian author whose style "compasses a broken rhythm that is as the very rhythm of life itself, and a cadence that catches you by the throat." This journalist also admires the writer's message, "too elemental, too near to the very heart of naked Nature, for exact definition." Beerbohm's dislike of Dostoevsky could be described as provincial and fastidious, but his journalist and a critic whom the journalist quotes are inane:

> As one of the critics avers, "It is hardly too much to say that a time may be not far distant, and may indeed be nearer than many of us suppose, when Luntic Kolniyatsch will, rightly or wrongly, be reckoned by some of us as not the least of those writers who are especially symptomatic of the early twentieth century and are possibly 'for all time' or for a more or less certainly not inconsiderable period of time." That is finely said. But I myself go somewhat further. I say . . .

and it goes on. Beerbohm could estimate the passion and the cost of literature in James, but he saw Kolniyatsch, the critics, and the journalists engaged only in a senseless fraud.

Traditionally the drift of parody has been in two directions: working against outworn modes or, as in "Kolniyatsch," against new vagaries of culture. Beerbohm was independent of these roles; he did not parody James or Meredith as obsolete, nor was he, like *Punch*, a watchdog of national interests. In 1928, H. M. Paull's remarkable book called *Literary Ethics* discussed parody as part of "the growth of the literary conscience," placing it somewhere between the "crimes" of forgery and plagiarism on the one hand, and on the other, hoaxes, pseudonyms, and the use of actual persons in fiction, classed as "misdemeanors." The book sees parody as unoriginal, degrading, parasitic. One way or another, Beerbohm is guilty of all the literary misdemeanors and some of the crimes. In aping contemporary authors, he can spoil the innocence with which we pick them up and read them. But he had little motive to degrade these authors. Essentially his parody was mimetic, not satiric, with the motive that literary representation itself has—to try out a form of expression. Moore and Bennett, like James, said they felt disturbed on sitting down to write after reading Beerbohm's parodies of them. And a parody he did of Maurice Baring moved Baring to say, "Its only fault is that it is so much better than anything I could have done myself, and reveals a higher intelligence and a better craftsman." This follows from Beerbohm's having taken an inferior model. More important, it illustrates the tendency of his parody to originate the very process of literary invention.

The Parodic Voice

On the basis of *A Christmas Garland*, Beerbohm became recognized as the finest parodist of his time in English. This has tended to draw attention away from the whole range of parody in his work. The parodies of contemporary writers are only one expression of a general, or generic, talent. Beerbohm liked to say that parody was "for the most part, a specialty of youth," to be grown out of. "Occasionally, however," he wrote in 1904, "a man retains the knack even in his prime, and even though he has a distinct individuality. In him, and in him only, we behold the complete mimic."

The voices scattered throughout Beerbohm's writing constitute a complete mimicry, a pantomime, imitation of all things. Whatever the occasion, for publication or not, he is ready to parody anything: *Who's Who*, Regency memoirs, Victorian diaries, Christmas keepsake volumes for family reading, parliamentary reports, American or English journalese, Midwestern or London slang, Samuel Johnson's talk and his prose, Whistler's letters, Walter Pater, the verger of Westminster Abbey, the poetry of Wordsworth, Byron, Tennyson, Landor, Yeats, Hardy, Housman, dialect verse, Surrey proverbs, phonetic spelling, obituaries, crossword puzzles, Slavophiles, Baconians, letter-writing manuals, authorial inscriptions, press cuttings, popular romance, Shakespeare and neo-Shakespearean blank verse, Queen Victoria's handwriting, and (once, with less than usual success) himself.

Parody was second nature for Beerbohm, not merely the exercise of one more literary talent alongside his essays, stories, novels, fairy tales, criticism, biography, and light verse. The element of parody pervades all these and his caricature as well; it is too habitual for only the "cleansing, exorcising," style-making function that Proust speaks of in *Pastiches et Mélanges*. In his first year at Charterhouse, Beerbohm wrote to the school paper complaining about its dullness and illustrating his point with brief parodies. His first formal publication there was a mock-heroic poem in Latin elegiacs, accompanied by textual notes in the full vein of classical scholarship. The "Peep into the Past" of 1894 adopts journalistic jargon, as does the mock of London's theater critics in 1895. Whatever idea he had, it was likely to translate into parody. Beerbohm's occasional parodies often came from an impulse to enact some common mode of language, like the obituary clichés on "Euphemia Lady Warburton" or the "Surrey Saws and Sayings" he wrote while waiting out the Second World War ("It's poor grass that cannot be cropped under a waning moon," "He that hath no teeth hath no toothache"). As a form of marginalia, he sometimes interpolated ridiculous notions into a book he was reading, extending the syntax and style of the original. His incidental parodies, such as the verse of Enoch Soames, form the liveliest part of Beerbohm's characterizations. Or they function as argument in reviews of Pinero, W. S. Gilbert, Shaw, and William Archer, and he seems more at home in the functional parody than in the rest of the review.

Although Beerbohm and many of his admirers held that reverence was the basis of parody—"on se moque de ce qu'on aime"—he saw through what he hated as well as what he loved, Kipling's vulgarity as well as James's scrupulousness. This is also true of the informal parodies, which proceed beyond personal and aesthetic preferences. He intensely disliked professional literary women, parodying two of them in 1896 and responding to John Oliver Hobbes (Pearl Mary

Teresa Craigie) with a heavily sarcastic parody. It may have been out of impotence to do anything else about her, but in any case the verbal empathy was there. Beerbohm had a copy of *The Artist's Life* by Mrs. Craigie, an American who published in the *Yellow Book* and issued a successful novel a year during the nineties. On the flyleaves of the book he wrote down a mock-lecture on the model of her essay "Balzac, Turner and Brahms." Beerbohm's parody, "Isaiah, Watteau, and Strauss," begins by having her explain that she has grouped these three together because she has nothing new to say about any one of them. She remarks parenthetically, "My hat, at which so many of you are looking, cost 17 guineas," and comes to her subject:

> There have been very few feminine prophets. . . . But Isaiah was not a woman. Isaiah was a man. About his parentage and his early education little is known. It is likely enough that, in his boyhood, people did not foresee his future eminence. There were people who did not foresee mine. And yet here I am. Watteau, when he grew up, was essentially a *Court* painter. He delighted in all that is graceful and gay and distinguished in the outer aspects of life. In this he was very different from Rembrandt, who probed deep into character. That is what *I* do, but then I don't only do that, you bet your bottom dollar: I've got culture but I'm a right smart Amurrican gurl.

Beerbohm hates the phenomenon of John Oliver Hobbes and enjoys writing it out, but the combination of a woman writer and an American finally breaks down the integrity of his parody.

A stronger passage of energy from personal distaste into the gladness of parody occurs in a paragraph of slang Beerbohm wrote in the nineteen-forties or -fifties, to judge by the shaky handwriting. It is a detail not only of locutions but also of elements in modern consciousness that disgusted him:

> Ladies and Gentlemen, It is up to us Britishers to get together and get busy and get a move on and face up to what we are up against. That is what we are out for. That is our job. Let us go *to* it, each one of us doing his bit to better the lot of the underdog, instead of staying put with cold feet and exchanging wisecracks with highbrow escapists and leftist glamour girls who have inferiority complexes in their unconscious and are not motivated by an urge to make good. It is not enough to be gadget-minded these days. In order to do our stuff, and put it across, and have it okayed, we have got to be streamline-conscious. Otherwise we shall have something more than a spot of bother and a big headache. We shall be told off, dressed down, beaten up—and perhaps even shot up, done in, and checked up on. And even if we *are* able to make a get-away, I have a hunch that we shall not be able to stage a come-back.

Worse than being shot up or done in, it seems, is to be checked up on. The parody's crazy logic shows how tenuously Beerbohm felt the good sense of civilization holding together, and it recalls the last, degenerate stages of James Joyce's "Oxen of the Sun" episode in *Ulysses*. Beerbohm is a "bawd of parodies" like Joyce's Shem the Penman, with the difference that Joyce truly was a willing vessel for all styles, whereas Beerbohm knew perfectly well that he approved of some and not of others.

An impossible crossword puzzle, published in the *Times* in 1940, is Beerbohm's purest concatenation of words. For some reason—his age, or the war—he added a letter explaining that its clues, with the exception of six very simple ones, signified nothing whatsoever. In the letter he also imagined a nightmare scene in a club before lunchtime, as if the puzzle had appeared without explanation: "In the armchairs men with blank, set, fixed, pale, just-not-despairing faces . . . one of them perhaps rising unsteadily and lumbering out to the library and asking the librarian 'Have we a Wordsworth concordance?'" The clues themselves are uncanny: "1 Across, A Victorian statesman lurking in a side lair," "24 Across, Acknowledgement of debt in a vessel," "6 Down, Wordsworth's fan mail?," "7 Down, And yet sugar *can* be refined."

Given the kind of subjects Beerbohm chooses for his essays, parody often seems inevitable. Writing about his visits to the House of Commons, he naturally illustrates its oratory:

> "It seems to me that the Right—the honourable member for—er—er (*the speaker dives to be prompted*)—yes, of course—South Clapham—er (*temporising*) the Southern division of Clapham—(*long pause; his lips form the words 'Where was I?'*)—oh yes, the honourable gentleman the member for South Clapham seems to me to me—to *be*—in the position of one who, whilst the facts on which his propo—*supposition* are based—er—may or may not be in themselves acc—correct (*gasps*)—yet inasmuch—because—nevertheless . . . I should say rather—er . . ."

and so forth. It is clear that Robert Benchley's "Treasurer's Report" and much else that he wrote descend from Beerbohm.

He devised one essay in *And Even Now* (1920), his last major collection, solely as a vehicle for parody. "'How Shall I Word It?'" was based on an actual letter-writing manual of that name. It begins by describing the discreet and easy style in the letters "reproaching Fiancée for being a Flirt" or "replying to Undesirable Invitation for her Child." Responding to a broken engagement, one model letter-writer says, "it was honest and brave of you to write to me so straightforwardly . . . I give you back your freedom only at your desire. God bless you, dear." Beerbohm is annoyed that the author of the manual (and presumably his public) should retain this unfazeable sweetness in face of intolerable injury.

So the essay continues with his own models of letters for angry, unrighteous people. There is a carefully phrased blackmail note in which James Gridge says he has found an adulterous love letter and wishes to return it: "I would prefer to hand the document to you personally. I will not ask you to come to my attic, where I could not offer you such hospitality as is due to a man of your wealth and position," etc. There are letters for refusing to pay a tailor bill, and for acknowledging a "small, cheap, hideous" wedding present. The most strongly felt model letter is for someone who wants to write "to member of Parliament unseated at General Election":

> Dear Mr. Pobsby-Burford,
>
> Though I am myself an ardent Tory, I cannot but rejoice in the crushing defeat you have just suffered in West Odgetown. There are moments when political conviction is overborne by personal sentiment; and this is one of them.

It ends on a note of sympathy for the defeated politician's wife, "a woman whose spirit was well-nigh broken by her conjunction with you," because now she will have more of his time:

> Only, remember this: chattel of yours though she is, and timid and humble, she despises you in her heart.
>
> I am, dear Mr. Pobsby-Burford,
> Yours very truly,
> HAROLD THISTLAKE

James Gridge and Harold Thistlake are as authentic as Shaw and James, and at the same time they are comic characters, a release for Beerbohm, like putting on a carnival mask. Encountering them and all his other dramatis personae, one gradually comes to forget what Beerbohm's own raison d'être was. This may be what Chesterton meant by

"Max's queer crystalline sense" and by saying, "he does not indulge in the base idolatry of believing in himself." Although Beerbohm does stand for certain qualities—beauty and economy in art, personal honor, modesty, grace—these seem to vanish behind the bitterness of Thistlake or the incoherence of the Member of Parliament. Despite the "Max" of the personal essays, "Going Out for a Walk," "Hosts and Guests," etc., it is hard to assign a "distinct individuality" to Beerbohm in his character as a writer. His parodies form a freehand circle of voices, drawn without reference to a fixed center.

Beerbohm could not have been a man of absolute and organized opinion and still have disposed himself so surely among various kinds of discourse. Take a caricature he did of Boswell and Johnson in 1915, when Johnson's house was presented to the nation. Boswell asks him if he isn't pleased, and won't the house tend to promote happiness and virtue. "JOHNSON: Nay, Sir, let us have no more of this foppishness. The house is naught. Let us not *sublimify* lath and plaster." And then Beerbohm adds another parodic exchange between them, on the opposite hypothesis that Johnson would have been pleased.

The casual and momentary parodies, along with the specific ones on Shaw, James, and the others, define a literary motive that is tantamount to philosophical principle. Keats described the character of the "camelion Poet" in a way that also suggests the nature of parody: "It is not itself—it has no self—it is everything and nothing . . . continually in for—and filling some other body." The more absorbed he is in his skill the sooner the habitual parodist may turn into a writer without ideas, like Beerbohm and Nabokov. Keats also felt an anxiety in this condition. "It is a wretched thing to confess," he wrote in an often-omitted section of the camelion Poet letter, "but is a very fact that not one word I ever utter can be taken for granted as an opinion growing out of my identical nature."

Certainly Beerbohm held his own opinions on private and public events, good and bad art. But he never made single-minded doctrine, and this has created the false impression of his writing as witty dilettantism. In fact, he meant any voice he could take. The catalogue of his parodies demonstrates a potentially unlimited imagination, primed by his ear for prose tempo and idiom. While such a flexible style implies an absence of motive, a loss of self, it also locates the parodist in the center of available forms of expression. It is as if Beerbohm gradually encountered the world as a play made up of various kinds of speech and writing, and took the role of dramatist.

Zuleika Dobson

What may have been Oxford mythology or superstitious humor—that a really seductive girl would drive its undergraduates mad—blows up to fantastic tragedy in *Zuleika Dobson* (1911). Beerbohm's novel brings forward an irresistibly pretty orphan and ex-governess who has parlayed her cheap conjuring tricks and secondhand patter into a world reputation, "the toast of two hemispheres." Soon after Zuleika's arrival in Oxford, the entire university is madly in love, but she has never been able to love a man who prostrated himself. In Judas College, the Duke of Dorset spurns her at first, then deeply disappoints her by falling in love. When she will not accept him, he imagines he must take his own life, and announces this at a dinner of the Junta, a club so exclusive that at one time he was its president and sole member. A telegram from his family estate, reporting the traditional omen of a reigning duke's death, confirms his decision. After the next day's boat races he leaps into the Thames, and because Dorset is Oxford's paragon, all the undergraduates follow him in a mass suicide. Zuleika orders a special train for Cambridge.

Zuleika Dobson is written as if on a dare: Watch this! The principle of the book is stylization, in small ways and over all. On the eve of the Duke's death, he and a Scotsman confront each other over who will escort Zuleika home. They seem about to fight, and it occurs to her—"a vague memory of some play or picture—that she ought to be holding aloft a candelabrum of lit tapers." The entire story is played out under the various lights of classical tragedy, romantic love, and the ceremonial ethos of Oxford itself. Everything is stylized: prose, structure, characters, incidents, milieu.

Zuleika Dobson's opening pages advertise that in one way or another the entire novel has quotation marks around it. Undergraduates are waiting at the railway station, which, in the vein of Matthew Arnold's rhapsody on Oxford's towers, "does yet whisper to the tourist the last enchantments of the Middle Age." Zuleika steps out of the train—"A hundred eyes were fixed on her, and half as many hearts lost to her"—and looks for her grandfather, the Warden of Judas College: "Him espying, the nymph darted in his direction." Beerbohm's prose watches itself in a mirror: each sentence of the narrative is substance and manner at the same time. This conscious heightening can be appropriate when the Duke of Dorset puts on his robes of the Garter, or gratuitous when Zuleika empties a waterjug on his head: "Full on the face crashed the cascade of moonlit water, shooting out on all sides like the petals of some great silver anemone." *Zuleika Dobson* moves on a cushion of prose. Describing the heroine's peculiar kind of passion: "But would she ever meet whom, looking up to him, she could love—she, the omnisubjugant?" This construction parodies no particular narrative style but is an act of style itself, like a tightrope walk.

At times the novel sounds more like Joyce's *Ulysses* than Beerbohm's *Yellow Book* writing or *The Rape of the Lock*. Zuleika Dobson's name divides her into heroic and mundane proportions, like Odysseus-Bloom, and Beerbohm introduces

"Lord Alexander Thynne enchanting the Labour Party," 1913

"Lest we forget ourselves," 1901

"Kimberley—Ladysmith—Mafeking.
J.B. 'What I shay ish thish:
A man'sh ash young
ash 'e feelsh, an' ash dignified.'

'We are often taunted with being a phlegmatic & unemotional race; but the nature and extent of the recent rejoicings will convince even our neighbours' etc, etc. (See Contemporary Historians, passim.)"

OVERLEAF:
G. K. Chesterton, 1912

"Civilisation and the Industrial System," 1924

"HE: 'No, my dear, you may've ceased to love me, but you took me for better or wuss in younger and 'appier days, and there'll be no getting away for you from me, ever.' "

"Mr Rudyard Kipling takes a bloomin' day aht, on the blasted 'eath, along with Britannia, 'is gurl," 1904

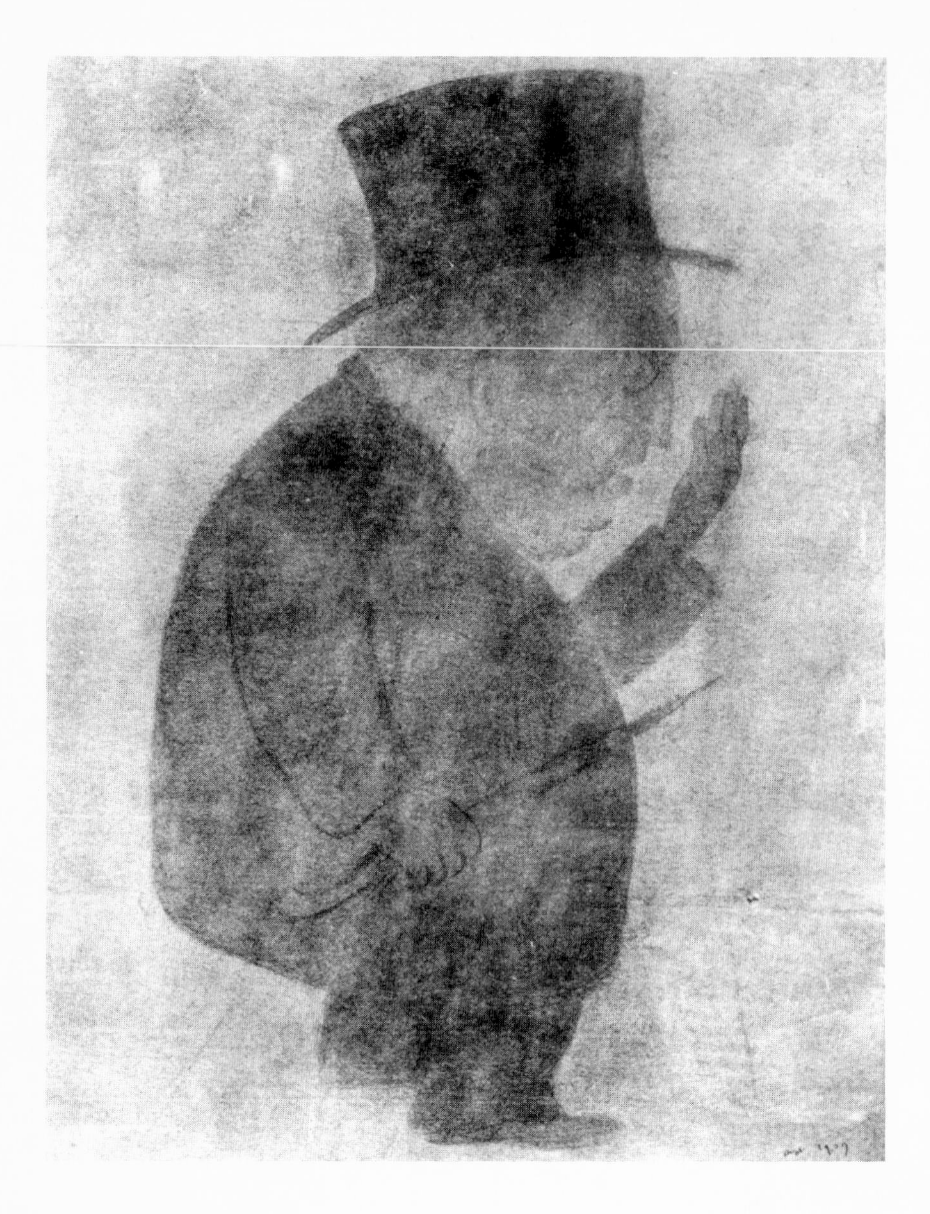

"London in November, and Mr Henry James in London," 1907

"... It was, therefore, not without something of a shock, that he, in this to him so very congenial atmosphere, now perceived that a vision of the hand which he had, at a venture, held up within a inch or so of his eyes was, with an almost awful clarity, being adumbrated ..."

Henry James, 1936
Old Self and Young Self

Henry James, 1920
"A Memory"

Henry James, ca. 1910

"A Memory of Henry Irving," 1926

George Meredith, 1926

"Box Hill—a memory"

Max Beerbohm
and Enoch Soames, 1919

Enoch Soames
and William Rothenstein, 1919

"Seen at the Café Royal"

her and Dorset in the heroic prose and catalogue form that Joyce was to use in his Cyclops and Nighttown episodes. On Zuleika's career:

> from the Vatican, the Pope launched against her a Bull which fell utterly flat. In Petersburg, the Grand Duke Salamander Salamandrovitch fell enamoured of her. Of every article in the apparatus of her conjuring-tricks he caused a replica to be made in finest gold. . . . Zuleika was conducted across the frontier, by an escort of love-sick Cossacks. On the Sunday before she left Madrid, a great bull-fight was held in her honour. Fifteen bulls received the *coup de grâce*, and Alvarez, the matador of matadors, died in the arena with her name on his lips. He had tried to kill the last bull without taking his eyes off *la divina señorita*. A prettier compliment had never been paid her, and she was immensely pleased with it.

She takes on the universality of the *femme fatale*, the Mona Lisa who for Pater expressed "what in the ways of a thousand years men had come to desire."

Dorset too is described as a legendary phenomenon, the last heir of privilege, composite of all admirable qualities. At Oxford "the Duke had already taken (besides a particularly brilliant First in Mods) the Stanhope, the Newdigate, the Lothian, and the Gaisford Prize for Greek Verse. . . . He was adroit in the killing of all birds and fishes, stags and foxes. He played polo, cricket, racquets, chess, and billiards as well as such things can be played." When Zuleika turns down his proposal of marriage, the Duke argues from nobility:

> I, John, Albert, Edward, Claude, Orde, Angus, Tankerton,* Tanville-Tankerton,† fourteenth Duke of Dorset, Marquis of Dorset, Earl of Grove, Earl of Chastermaine, Viscount Brewsby, Baron Grove, Baron Petstrap, and

*Pronounced as Tacton. †Pronounced as Tavvle-Tacton.

Zuleika Dobson and the Duke of Dorset, from manuscript of novel, ca. 1908

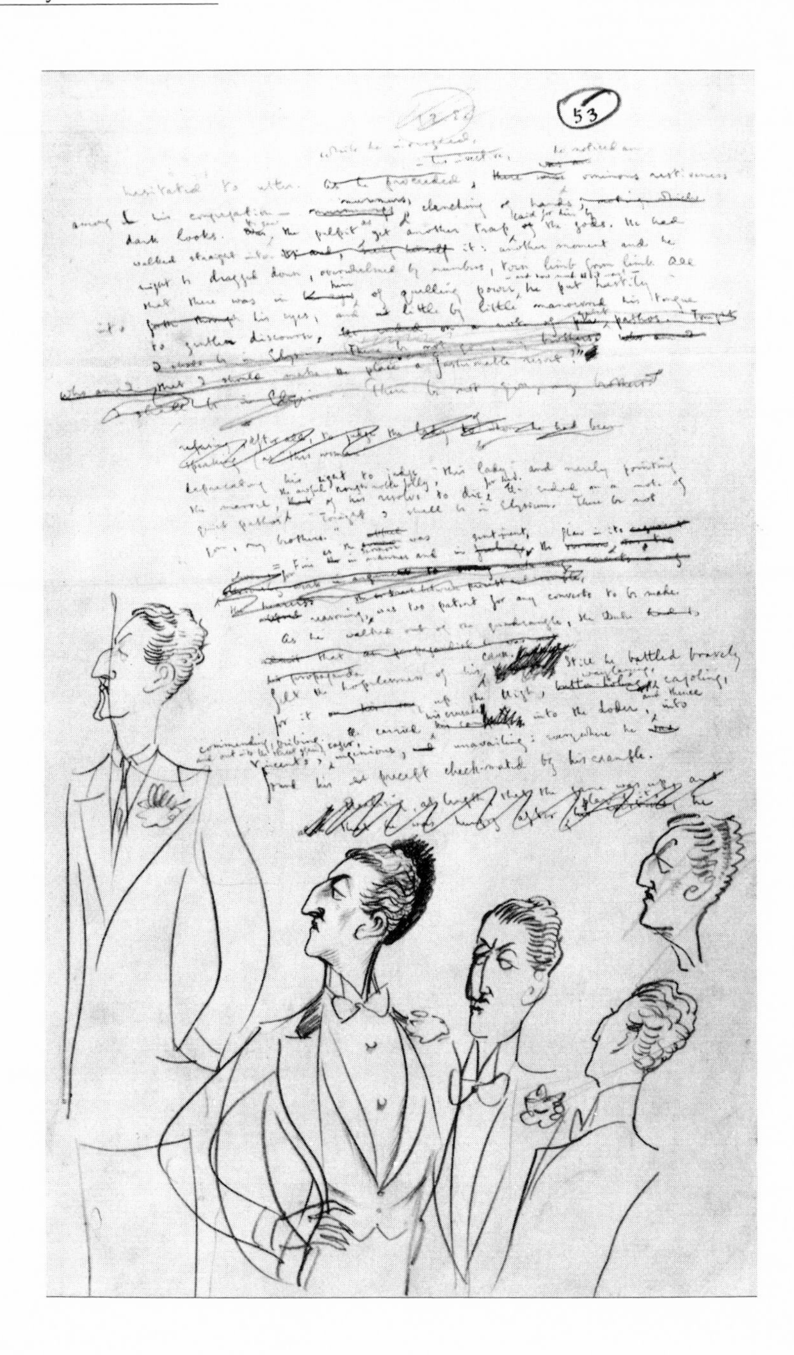

> Baron Wolock, in the Peerage of England, offer you my hand. Do not interrupt me. . . . Tankerton, of which you may have seen photographs, is the chief of my country seats. . . . Round the house runs a wide paven terrace. There are always two or three peacocks trailing their sheathed feathers along the balustrade, and stepping how stiffly! as though they had just been unharnessed from Juno's chariot. . . . There are many twisting paths, and sudden aspects, and devious, fantastic arbours. Are you fond of horses? In my stables of pinewood and plated-silver seventy are installed. . . . On the eve of the death of a Duke of Dorset two black owls come and perch on the battlements. They remain there through the night, hooting. At dawn they fly away, none knows whither.

He has titles in the peerages of Scotland, Ireland, Wales, and France—"Louis Napoleon gave the title to my father for not cutting him in the Bois. I have a house in the Champs Élysées. There is a Swiss in its courtyard. He stands six-foot-seven in his stockings." Wherever the Duke of Dorset goes, he has two chefs who fight each other with rapiers when one of them is complimented; also "a third chef, who makes only soufflés, and an Italian pastry-cook; to say nothing of a Spaniard for salads, an Englishwoman for roasts, and an Abyssinian for coffee."

Although *Zuleika Dobson* is not pitched continually at hyperbole, any more than *Ulysses* is, this piling of words and images does mark the exuberant parodic forces in Beerbohm's novel. Like Joyce, he passes naturally in and out of various styles. The first description of Zuleika follows slavishly a quasi-classical technique of double negatives and ironic understatement: "No apple-tree, no wall of peaches, had not been robbed, nor any Tyrian rose-garden, for the glory of Miss Dobson's cheeks. . . . She had no waist to speak of"—a passage analyzed by William Empson as an advanced type of ambiguity, expressing the opposite of what it says.

Early in the novel Beerbohm inserts a description of Oxford's bells, beginning: "Some clock clove with silver the stillness of the morning. . . . The air was confused with the sweet babel of its many spires." Always quoted as an example of Beerbohm's love for Oxford, it is above all a deliberate purple passage, a tour de force.

In *Zuleika Dobson*, parody also takes the form of dramatic characterization; for example, we see the ridiculous American Rhodes Scholar Abimelech V. Oover wholly through his own talk. He is the first to speak after Dorset tells his friends they need not follow his example in dying for Zuleika: "Duke, I guess I am voicing these gentlemen when I say that your words show up your good heart, all the time. Your mentality, too, is bully, as we all predicate." Oover says they won't be budged from Miss Z. Dobson's feet, "not for bob-nuts." Beerbohm also has occasion to reproduce the writings of the Duke of Dorset, whose dandyism includes an over-impressive literary capacity. Dorset writes in French when living on the Champs Élysées, Sanskrit in flights of contemplation, Greek in hours of mere joy. Recovering from Zuleika's jug of water, he takes his anger out in Juvenalian hexameters, an epistle to his heir presumptive:

> Vae tibi, vae misero, nisi circumspexeris artes
> Femineas . . .

The afternoon of his death, he gives a testimonial to his landlady, a sonnet courteously written in Oxfordshire dialect:

> Zeek w'ere thee will in t'Univürsity,
> Lad, thee'll not vind nôr bread nôr bed that matches
> Them as thee'll vind, roight züre, at Mrs. Batch's.

Beerbohm quotes nothing more, he says, because the low style is uncongenial to Dorset, and the command of dialect "seems to me based less on study than on conjecture."

Beerbohm ought to know. His privileged criticism of Dorset's sonnet betrays the relation he has to events in *Zuleika Dobson*—a relation on which very much depends. At the book's exact midpoint, Beerbohm announces that he is primarily a historian. He interrupts Zuleika's impromptu magic show, wondering if he can "fob off on his readers just one bright fable" to the effect that Zuleika suddenly became inspired, "cast a seed on the ground, and that therefrom presently arose a tamarind-tree which blossomed and bore fruit and, withering, vanished." As Clio's servant he must be factual, and admits that the climax of Zuleika's entertainment was only the Magic Canister that spirits away an audience's rings and cufflinks. Then, in the classic interlude tradition, Beerbohm's next chapter suspends the action to relate that the book is being written by a historian who also has the novelist's invisible presence at human events and emotions. Clio had been jealous of Melpomene for a long time because tragedy was more philosophic and spiritual than history, but all she could do was refrain from reading the works she inspired and secretly read poetry or, after a while, novels. One day Zeus fell in love with her, and "flashed down in the semblance of Kinglake's *Invasion of the Crimea* (four vols., large 8vo, half-calf)." She saw through him, but he learned of her addiction to novels and began wooing her as the year's latest fiction. Finally she consented on condition that he just once grant the novelist's privileges to a writer of history. Clio then saw Zuleika "stepping from the Paddington platform into the Oxford train. A few moments later I found myself suddenly on Parnassus," Beerbohm writes. "In hurried words Clio told me how I came there, and what I had to do. . . . And then, lo! I was on the platform of Oxford station."

Zuleika Dobson stands between Beerbohm's *Yellow Book* period, with its quasi-historical essays "George IV" and "1880," and his mature work, *The Mirror of the Past* and *Seven Men*, in which he mediates as a character between the given and the improbable. In his novel he claims to fall for the elaborate pageant of Dorset and Zuleika. He calls attention to the reality of his story ("They are still vivid to us, those headlines") instead of tacitly taking it for granted as normal fiction does. An artifice like this tends to prejudice the credibility of the story, and at the same time to rediscover the assumptions behind any technique in literature. Clio with Melpomene's powers is always the novelist's muse. The difference between reporting events and writing fiction ("what had been" and "what might be," as Beerbohm puts it in the interlude) is only one between systems of myth-making. Bringing these systems together in himself, he creates a point of view that gets beyond the alternatives of fact and fantasy.

The novel was begun in 1898, then put off, and completed between 1908 and 1911—a delay that conditioned the book and Beerbohm's tactic of introducing himself as historian-novelist. He left off after writing the first third of the book (as the handwriting and certain changes and additions indicate), and only the later part, which he called "stronger and suppler," advertises Clio's special dispensation. The interlude particularly shows up in manuscript as a separate composition, probably done in 1910. Several things can account for the way Beerbohm shaped his book: the years of drama criticism, with his ridicule of stock romantic melodrama and his underlying impatience with realism; the essays on illusion and actuality around the turn of the century; James's great achievement in the novel and the 1906 *Christmas Garland* parodies; the remoteness of Victorian Oxford; and Beerbohm's three engagements to actresses. At the very least, this intervening experience made a straight novel impossible for him.

The epistemology of *Zuleika Dobson* permits a complex attitude toward Oxford itself. In the ordinary run of the narrative, Oxford's sanctified customs, places, and personalities are satirized. But just after the interlude, Beerbohm

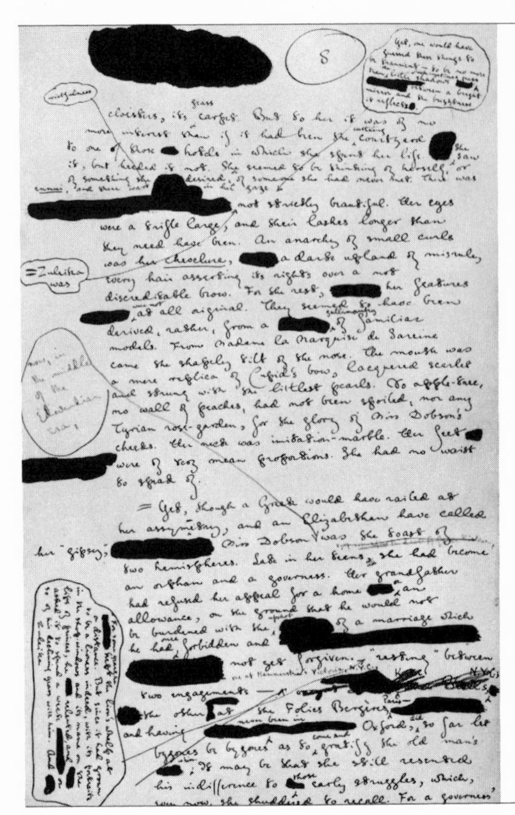

Manuscript of Zuleika Dobson, *1898–1908*

floats into Merton, his old college, and then out into the mist over the meadows between Merton and the river Isis, as the Thames at Oxford is called. A long paragraph resembling Matthew Arnold's tribute to Oxford the adorable dreamer, home of lost causes, exposes Beerbohm's and indeed Oxford's divided allegiance to what is and what might be, in human affairs. The Colleges are permeated by a "mild, miasmal air" that obscures their sense of reality in a way that Beerbohm can neither accept nor reject. Oxford fosters "her peculiar race of artist-scholars, scholar-artists." She is aware of the "exigent realities of the outer world" but not touched by them.

Beerbohm's particular experience there—coming of age

quickly as a man and an artist, and not bothering to finish a degree—disposed him to write neither eulogy nor criticism of the place. He loved Oxford, but the kind of wit the university fostered in him discouraged loving anything very seriously. In *The Works* he had said that the city struck him as "a bit of Manchester through which Apollo had once passed." But as twentieth-century civilization invaded it, particularly in the form of the Morris automobile works, Beerbohm's irony dissolved. He clung to the lush, playful, and ritualistic Oxford of his own experience, and *Zuleika Dobson*, which describes that Oxford, began to look more like an attempt to preserve the nineties' milieu and spirit than to satirize them. In a 1947 edition, Beerbohm notes that all fantasy should have a solid basis in reality. Although mid-twentieth-century readers of his book may think its image of Oxford life "a wild infraction of that law," he assures them that "the old Oxford" was far closer to his fantastic image than to the present motorized place.

The same note claims that *Zuleika Dobson* is not what people had thought it at first, a satire on the herd instinct, feminine coquetry, snobbishness, and legerdemain. "I myself had supposed it was just a fantasy," Beerbohm says. The book is satiric nevertheless. Beerbohm means to release it from that functional role and bring out instead the domain he created. The busts of the Roman Emperors in Broad Street sweat, frown, and relax, according to what they see happening, and pearls and studs, given the expressive power of costume, change color symptomatically with their owners' emotions. The book's essential fantasy consists in the way history and fiction mix. What happens in Beerbohm's world derives from the ruling image of Clio reading novels. In the first few chapters we get Latimer, Ridley, Mommsen, Aristotle, Watteau, Holbein, Beerbohm: we also get Mrs. Suetonius X. Meistersinger in New York, and Meg Speedwell, the dairy-maid who married Dorset's great-great-grandfather. We get Merton and Balliol, and also Judas College. Beerbohm urges us to forget Mr. Sargent's portrait of the Duke in trying to imagine him (it has nothing but "the astounding slickness of Mr. Sargent's technique"). Another mixture, practically unnoticeable, comes about when Zeus woos Clio in the guise of Kinglake's *Crimea*, a book that it turns out was written in the house Beerbohm's family came to occupy while he was at Oxford. The jostling in *Zuleika Dobson* between fact and fantasy makes us think we can unite them as easily as Dorset walks from Balliol to Judas.

Fantasy inevitably offers itself as an alternative to realism. *Zuleika Dobson*'s realistic milieu is Mrs. Batch's lodgings, where the Duke lives with his plebeian friend Noaks and is served with unrequited love by Katie, the landlady's daughter. Reggie Turner wrote to Beerbohm that Katie Batch's suffering stood out too poignantly from the book's fantasy, and Beerbohm replied that he had wanted his characters "to *behave like* real people, within the limits of the absurdity conditioned. . . . But it never occurred to me that while I was trying to do this I was giving to the characters anything in the nature of a *real*, as opposed to a fantastical-humorous reality." His remark implies that he saw everything in the book as protected within the element of fantasy. The Junta dinner at which Dorset announces his decision ends with cartoon-strip violence—Dorset leaping out a window, followed by Oover, splintering a window-box, and Mr. Trent-Garby, "who, catching his foot in the ruined flower-box, fell headlong, and was, I regret to say, killed." Beerbohm advised the producers of a musical *Zuleika Dobson* in 1954 to keep all the action unreal, especially the mass suicide. In comic fantasy, the suffering and violence and death are meant to slide by innocently, though they may have stemmed from things that Beerbohm obscurely desired to happen to Oxford.

The fantasy reaches its center of gravity when the Duke receives news of the traditional omen in his family. He has been on the point of defying Zuleika and choosing life, when a prepaid telegram arrives from his steward at Tankerton:

> Deeply regret inform your grace last night two black owls came and perched on battlements remained there through night hooting at dawn flew away none knows whither awaiting instructions.
>
> Jellings

> Jellings Tankerton Hall
> Prepare vault for funeral Monday
>
> Dorset

This ends a chapter. In the beginning of the next, the author intervenes for a few paragraphs and deflects the fatalism of the two telegrams. He has the reader question him about the Duke's reaction, and replies, "Please don't interrupt me again. Am *I* writing this history, or are you?" Beerbohm knew that the action in stage fantasy should be believed to get the fun out of it. Here he deliberately disregards that advice by trifling with the already mock-heroic exchange of telegrams. In the 1947 edition he cut out "Am *I* writing this history, or are you?," so as not to push the reader too far away and skew the lines between fiction and history.

We have no real point of balance in this book between the style-ridden parody of romantic love stories and the self-parody Beerbohm fosters by insisting on the authenticity of his characters and action. He always inclined to romantic irony, the arbitrary destruction of literary illusion. And here, like Cervantes who in the second part of *Don Quixote* refutes a false sequel to the first, he sets one parody against another, a mock teller against a mock tale. *Zuleika Dobson* remains fascinating to read, but unsettling too, unless we look on through the incompatible structure and style.

Beerbohm chose the great theme of the Western world, tragic love. In 1902, when the book was in abeyance, he mentioned in a weekly article that Oxford had never been made the background for a serious novel because of the novelist's fear of eliminating sex. *Zuleika Dobson* was no solution but the gross caricature of a solution, the fantasy of what happens when Young Oxford, which Beerbohm calls "one great passive monster," meets the Duke's "hyena woman." Yet in comparison with previous jocular or sentimental treatments, he could claim to have given "a truer picture of undergraduate life." His book points to real elements of conformity and sexual repression. The contagion of madness is developed beautifully: when Zuleika shows herself outdoors, it is to a "mob of hoarse infatuate youths," or to "boyish faces, all fused and obliterated," or to the "dense mass of the disorganised procession" on her last march to the river. By chance the river itself has the name of Isis, Egypt's greatest goddess, all things to all men. So what emerges is an allegory of Youth forsaking Alma Mater, the Benign Mother, for the consummating love of Woman. At this level the book re-enacts a romantic theme, but not without local detail undercutting the allegory. When Dorset finally plunges into the river and others follow: "'Brave fellows!' shouted the elder men, supposing rescue-work. . . . Shouts and screams now from the infected barges on either side. A score of fresh plunges. 'Splendid fellows!'"

Zuleika's justification as the goddess of a cult, alluring to all men, lies not in her but in what is said and believed about her, mainly by Beerbohm. On various occasions she is described or alluded to as a nymph, a madonna, a nun, a gypsy, a shepherdess, a prima donna, and a basilisk, the fabulous serpent whose look and breath are fatal. Noaks is infatuated, and says she "looks like a foreigner." The Duke considers introducing her conjuring act as that of a "she-wizard," and actually does introduce her as the master of "an art which, more potently perhaps than any other, touched in mankind the sense of mystery and stirred the faculty of wonder; the most truly romantic of all the arts." This is the prose to support a Gothic romance. And Beerbohm, in his first appearance as Clio's servant, wants the "spirit of the higher thaumaturgy" to descend on Zuleika like a flame.

In basic outline she is like the *anima*, man's psychic image of the woman he desires or fears: dangerous, irresistible, associated with the waters of the unconscious, and omnivorous in her decision to go on to Cambridge at the end. She may have been modeled in part on Adah Menken, the fabulously popular bareback rider whom Swinburne knew and who wrote free verse lamenting her failure to find the perfect lover. But unlike Dorset, whose dandyism over-exemplified a romantic tradition, Zuleika falls short in many ways, and embodies the *femme fatale* chiefly in the number of men accounted for. Physically unlike Salomé, Lamia, or the demimondaine of eighteen-nineties minor verse, she is not sinister or even sexy. Her hair is dark, but curly; she has violet eyes, but they are bright rather than mysterious. She moves lightly and attracts men as an extremely accomplished *vedette*, not as some languorous creature from the dark side of the moon. Marginal, but not strange, she is the offspring of a curate and a circus-rider, and her access to the supernatural consists in doing tricks. The Mona Lisa was laden with experience, but Zuleika's glittering past makes her like a child always looking forward to each "new toy."

In a sense the portrait of Zuleika gets away from Beerbohm. Her main traits push courtly love to obsession. As a governess she loses job after job by flirting with the grown-up son and then refusing his offer of marriage. After stealing the Magic Canister and other amateur trappings from one of these sons, she becomes increasingly popular and flattered. "As the homage of men became for her, more and more, a matter of course, the more subtly necessary was it to her happiness. The more she won of it, the more she treasured it." Zuleika's profession is only a means. She is a Volpone of self-conceit: her mirror is her world. This megalomania produces a paradoxical bitterness and loneliness: all the world's youth is prostrate with love, but she can only love a man who will spurn her. The image she has, and the language she consistently uses, are those of a slave seeking a master. Her helpless rapture when the Duke first brusquely ignores her—"I had longed for it, but I had never guessed how wonderfully wonderful it was. It came to me. I shuddered and wavered like a fountain in the wind"—sounds like the joys of flagellation. The Duke even finds himself wanting to "flay" her with Juvenalian verses. "He would make Woman (as he called Zuleika) writhe." At the end she worships Noaks: "I bow to your will, master. Chasten me with your tongue." Zuleika is a virgin whose relation to men is at bottom sado-masochistic, and the parodic nature of the book does not alter Beerbohm's queer idea of what a woman wants.

His account of her ("She had no waist to speak of") can be heard to undercut femininity. And this novel, like the "Defence of Cosmetics," incidentally satirizes the New Woman. It is possible to see Zuleika as the outcome of two emotions working in Beerbohm: his tacit preference for the submissive, motherly Victorian woman as servant in the home, and his anxiety about independent, dominating, professional women. Zuleika's presence in Oxford gives him the occasion to say that there are now two colleges ("virgincules") for women, "but beauty and the lust for learning have yet to be allied." The extreme unlikeliness of Zuleika makes sport of feminist images of woman, but that is not finally the scale on which Beerbohm's irony works.

On his own terms he wrote, in *Zuleika Dobson*, a history of romantic love. Dorset's view of love and death as the dandy's sacraments, and Zuleika's obsessiveness, evolve under an aura of dozens of scattered allusions to mythology, religion, literature, music, history—to what Western culture has experienced or imagined as exemplary, mostly tragic sexual love. These allusions, coming as if from the collective unconscious, pervade the narrative in the form of similes.

No single one stands out, but in sum they put an immense frame around the story. Above all there is Zeus' passion for Clio. Then in one way or another Isis and Osiris appear (a don bores Zuleika by telling her about the Temple of Osiris), Achilles and Briseis, Cervantes's shepherdess Marcella and Chrysostom, who died for love of her, the Song of Songs, Juvenal, the Greek pastoral poets, the Elizabethan sonneteers, and perhaps a totally bizarre Christian heresy, in that Judas bumps Magdalen on the last day of the boat races—or does this allude to a different Oxford affair, Judas having been Walter Pater's nickname at Oxford, and Magdalen Wilde's college? At one point Beerbohm compares Zuleika to the wife of Giacopone di Todi, a man who took holy orders when he found at his wife's death that she had been wearing a hairshirt under her fine clothes. Alcestis, Helen of Troy, Lot's wife, Faust's Gretchen, Ophelia, and Clarissa Harlowe all enter the narrative at different times, and Chopin with George Sand. Zuleika's French maid Mélisande is engaged to a café waiter named Pelléas (Beerbohm reviewed Maeterlinck's *Pelléas et Mélisande* in 1898 and 1900). There is a poignant romance between a gentleman and a country girl in the history of the Junta, and another in the Duke's family. Beerbohm alludes once to the *Liebestod* music for Wagner's heroines, and to Strauss (whose *Salome* was first performed in 1905); Dorset resists the "despicable maundering" of the German Romantics Novalis and Friedrich Schlegel. In Beerbohm's grand farewell to dandyism, Dorset, whose name Mélisande mispronounces as "D'Orsay," is related to the French dandy of many accomplishments and a tragic marriage, Alfred D'Orsay. And through it all there is the image of Dorset's counterpart, Byron, who was at Cambridge, not Oxford, was promiscuous in love and politics where Dorset was chaste, and was a swimmer of the Hellespont, which Dorset swam twice. Two of the romantic allusions remain tacit. The pious heroine who dies of a broken heart in Byron's *Bride of Abydos,* and also

Potiphar's wife, who failed to seduce Joseph in Egypt, are named Zuleika.

There are no allusions to nineteenth-century novels, as if Zuleika Dobson already summed up their eponymous heroines—Emma, Jane Eyre, Tess. The classics that Beerbohm does allude to frame an otherwise unclassical story whose climax fails to go according to form: it rains before the Duke jumps, and Noaks hides in his room during the drowning. Dorset and Zuleika, the capstone of romantic love, carry the stock of allusions completely away with them. Yet the parody in *Zuleika Dobson*—the aura of allusions, the narrator's double muse, his hyperbole and euphuism—leaves the art of fiction finally intact, if less firmly settled in its aims and techniques. Zuleika's Magic Canister remains as an image of Beerbohm's own conjuring with all our love stories. Her act always climaxes with the Magic Canister: "Well, this is rather queer!" she says after the audience's rings and cufflinks disappear. But you know you will get them back.

6

The Seventh Man

"Where the yellow spot is I'm pointing to, that's where it hurts"

This note appears on a drawing by Albrecht Dürer, a self-portrait evidently for consultation by an out-of-town physician. Dürer drew himself naked, with one hand pointing to a mark on the left side of his abdomen. The spot is the spleen, seat of melancholy. He identifies his ruling humor, and bases on his art a cure for what hurts him.

During Beerbohm's active literary career—1893 to 1918—two phenomena became more and more significantly intermixed: the presentment of himself, and the displaying of aesthetic technique. By analogy with Dürer, we have the image of a writer confessing inherent inadequacy by means of an adequate act of writing. Beerbohm could comprehend the language of *De Profundis*, if not the apocalyptic symbolism of *When We Dead Awaken*. In his own early prose, the rudimentary form of reflexive irony occurs when he excuses mannerisms by advertising them. He went on to change this coyness into a technique, a condition that alters the ends of literature by building in and questioning the means, including the writer himself.

"A Relic," written in 1918, illustrates this technique. Beerbohm deliberately placed the essay at the beginning of *And Even Now*, a collection otherwise arranged chronologically, 1910 to 1920. The "relic" is a broken-off butt from a cheap fan, dropped near him in a café at Dieppe in 1891 and left behind by a bitterly quarreling French couple, whose psychological drama led Beerbohm to begin his writing career with a *conte* modeled after Guy de Maupassant. He would be an "impersonal *je*" sitting at a table; "four or five short sentences would give the whole scene. One of these I had quite definitely composed. . . . 'Down below, the sea rustled to and fro over the shingle.'" But all he had was that one sentence, which was to recur quietly amidst emotional stress. He could get nowhere in trying to re-create their whole story. Perhaps the man kept a once-prosperous fan shop, now destitute because this woman always smashed his presents: "'Ah, monsieur . . . the fan she broke tonight was the last—the last, monsieur—of my stock.' Down below . . ." The story failed to be written, yet "A Relic" paradoxically reaches what Maupassant was after. Between author and inadequate refrain, we glimpse an act of life that will not be made into something else.

With "A Relic" in mind, we can speak interchangeably, as Roland Barthes does, of the analysis and the creation of literature. Indeed, in more than half the essays of *And Even Now*, it is artists and works of art—of literature, above all—that activate Beerbohm's imagination: model letters, books within books, Swinburne, Slavic writers, a woman novelist's novel about a woman novelist, an unfinished painting, a veiled statue. The essay on laughter makes its points by means of Bergson, *Henry IV,* Tom Moore's life of Byron, and Boswell's *Johnson.* Limiting and secondhand as it seems, this recourse to literature, to Kolniyatsch's "broken rhythm," for instance, filters a richer consciousness of reality than some impartial viewpoint would. Parody is also an obvious filter, and the coincidence between Beerbohm's specific talent for parody and his habitual literary themes marks the true center of his inspiration.

A meditation on Boswell's biography of Johnson (the best book in the English language, Beerbohm thought), and a parody of Johnson's style, coexist in "'A Clergyman'" (1918). "A Clergyman" is merely Boswell's heading for the only remark made on April 7, 1778, at Thrale Hall by a man whose name he cannot remember. Beerbohm quotes the close of an exchange on the English preachers:

> BOSWELL: What I want to know is, what sermons afford the best specimen of English pulpit eloquence.
> JOHNSON: We have no sermons addressed to the passions, that are good for anything; if you mean that kind of eloquence.
> A CLERGYMAN: Were not Dodd's sermons addressed to the passions?
> JOHNSON: They were nothing, Sir, be they addressed to what they may.

This germinates into a beautiful surmise, a fiction, on the man who "solicits my weak imagination," as Beerbohm says. The conditional tense pervades this essay, along with constructions that emphasize how difficult it is to find the human truth behind the fact of events: "I suppose," "We may assume," "I think we can guess," "It is probable," "On no other hypothesis can we account," and so forth. Towards the end, Beerbohm shifts to constructions such as "I see him" and "I'm sure of it."

The dim, forgettable clergyman (pale face, receding chin, mouse-colored hair) must have come from the local church, felt himself a small actor among the great divines, and sat nervously waiting to make an impression on Doctor Johnson. Judging then from the cadence of his question, Beerbohm imagines that it was delivered in an irritatingly shrill voice, and that Johnson roared back deeply. "Boswell does not record that there was any further conversation. . . . Perhaps the whole company had been temporarily deafened." Toward the end of the essay, one sentence occurs as if by an act of primitive possession—"Every man illustrious in his day, however much he may be gratified by his fame, looks with an eager eye to posterity"—and goes on reproducing

Johnson's diction and balance perfectly. Then Beerbohm finishes speculating on the fate of the clergyman:

> A robust man might have rallied under the blow. Not so our friend. Those who knew him in infancy had not expected that he would be reared. Better for him had they been right. . . . 'A Clergyman' never held up his head or smiled again after the brief encounter recorded for us by Boswell. He sank into a rapid decline. Before the next blossoming of Thrale Hall's almond trees he was no more. I like to think that he died forgiving Dr. Johnson.

The clergyman has, in effect, been killed, taken out of the minimal circumstances of Boswell's report and released into the freedom of an invented life so completely that he can die. It is the radical act of fictional creation and yet nothing but surmise.

Seven Men

The book that realizes the potential of "A Relic" and "'A Clergyman,'" indeed the potential of all Beerbohm's previous writing, is *Seven Men*. It was written during the First World War, when Ezra Pound was writing his own engaged critique of aestheticism, *Hugh Selwyn Mauberley*. *Seven Men* is a book of narratives about imaginary late-Victorian and Edwardian characters: a poet, a playwright, two novelists, a gambler, and a compulsive liar—six men in all. Beerbohm is the seventh, narrating the stories and participating as a ludicrously naïve version of himself.

He asked his publishers to give *Seven Men* (and *Zuleika Dobson* as well) an essaylike format. The reader should feel he has a book of actual memoirs in his hand, and these narratives do take that form. Their circumstances are autobiographical and depict Beerbohm's own sphere before his marriage: the Café Royal, a restaurant in Soho, the British Museum, a country estate, a seashore hotel, a casino in Dieppe. With narratives verging on the supernatural, he takes care to make the texture realistic. Arthur Balfour mingles with the guests in one story, and Beerbohm's early journalistic career forms part of another. To illustrate "A. V. Laider" for the American edition, he had special notepaper printed with the name of the hotel he and his character stayed at, and on it he made a rough sketch of Laider, done as if at the time of the story. Beerbohm had remarked hopefully to Reggie Turner that the realistic elements of *Zuleika Dobson* would make it "something to be worried about, something rather baffling." What marks *Seven Men* is again this desire to keep the reader's mind moving, reverberating, checking among alternatives.

"A. V. Laider" concerns Beerbohm's encounter, while recuperating from influenza at a sleepy hotel by the sea, with another man who suffers from influenza. Being English, they remain aloof from each other, but on the last evening of Beerbohm's stay they happen to talk. The subject is reason, faith, free will, and, in particular, palmistry. Laider with some pain says that he will never look at a hand again, for fear of the "awful things" he might see there, and he tells Beerbohm why. Palmistry used to be a passionate hobby with him, though he had seen in his own hand that at about age twenty-six he would have a narrow escape from violent death. Just after turning twenty-seven, he happened to travel in a railway carriage with five acquaintances. As a favor to them, he read their hands, and discovered that all of them showed signs of a violent death at about their present ages. Laider began to understand the fatal coincidence, but could not find the nerve to stop the train and tell the guard there was going to be a collision. There *was* a collision, Laider says, and the others died. He escaped alive with a severe concussion.

After leaving the hotel, Beerbohm decides that Laider's

brain, recovering from concussion, may actually have invented the whole occurrence, and he writes him back a letter suggesting as much. A year later by chance they both return to the same hotel, again after influenza, and then Laider has to apologize nervously: he has never believed in palmistry, and no collision ever occurred. Whenever he is sick, he says, his "imagination stampedes." Beerbohm wonders if his friend may really have been telling the simple truth a year before, about the collision, and now is telling an ingenious lie. On the last evening of this second stay, he happens to mention seeing a great number of sea gulls that afternoon flying close to shore, and the story closes:

> "Sea-gulls?" said Laider, turning in his chair.
>
> "Yes. And I don't think I had ever realised how extraordinarily beautiful they are when their wings catch the light."
>
> "Beautiful?" Laider threw a quick glance at me and away from me. "You think them beautiful?"
>
> "Surely."
>
> "Well, perhaps they are, yes; I suppose they are. But—I don't like seeing them. They always remind me of something—rather an awful thing—that once happened to me." . . . .
>
> It was a very awful thing indeed.

The flip of the wheel in Beerbohm's last sentence invites a nightmarish return into unreality, something like Zuleika's special train to Cambridge at the end of the novel. Beerbohm was disturbed that the printer of *Seven Men* left out the full seven dots before "It was a very awful thing indeed"—a crucial matter of timing the narrator's and our reaction. Remembering that Laider is again recovering from influenza, we—unlike Laider's friend Beerbohm—break out of the delusion. Laider turns out after all to be one of the creative artists in *Seven Men*. His tale of the train-wreck is referred

A. V. Laider

to as "invention," "preposterous fable," "sheer improvisation." It is the raw action of imagination, and with Laider's subsequent exposure of the tale, followed by the sea gulls, we have a full comic gesture: illusion, the breaking of illusion, and a new venture.

The most extraordinary inventions in *Seven Men*, "'Savonarola' Brown" and "Enoch Soames," concern a playwright and a poet. As in "A. V. Laider," Beerbohm makes himself vulnerable to their delusions—in this case, delusions about the value of their writing. Everything about literature comes into play in these two stories: creative process, friendship between writers, a text itself, publishers, literary criticism, the reader's share, posterity. And Beerbohm as a character changes the nature of the fiction. He said in 1900 that an essayist should obtrude his personality, but that in a story, the author effaces himself to preserve an illusion of life. *Seven Men* complicates that simple distinction. The seventh man and the author behind him make it clear that believing in literature is an endlessly self-correcting process. The stories are fictions exploring fiction, generic parodies.

"Savonarola" Brown is a meager type whose "extraordinarily unimaginative" parents named him Ladbroke because they happened to live in Ladbroke Crescent in London. He and Beerbohm met at Charterhouse, where the boys persecuted him—Trafalgar Brown, Tottenham Court Brown, Bond Brown—and thus pushed him in the direction of literature. He has no interest in religion or human character, only in words, books, and plays, so Beerbohm is surprised when Brown tells him he means to write a play about Savonarola:

> He made me understand, however, that it was rather the name than the man that had first attracted him. He said that the name was in itself a great incentive to blank-verse. He uttered it to me slowly, in a voice so much deeper than his usual voice, that I nearly laughed.

In keeping with this purely verbal inspiration, Brown avoids historical fact for his tragedy. And he decides not to invent a plot in advance: "I don't want puppets on wires. . . . What I've got to do is to make Savonarola *live*." From time to time Brown reports to Beerbohm on his progress. Savonarola has come on alive, and other characters insist on appearing. After nine years, Brown announces one evening, walking back from the theater, that the Fourth Act is finished. But he has no notion how Savonarola is to die. Beerbohm urges him that in tragedy, the catastrophe must have been led up to logically.

> "I don't see that," he said, as we crossed Piccadilly Circus. "In actual life it isn't so. What is there to prevent

> a motor-omnibus from knocking me over and killing me at this moment?"
>
> At that moment, by what has always seemed to me the strangest of coincidences, and just the sort of thing that playwrights ought to avoid, a motor-omnibus knocked Brown over and killed him.

Brown has made his friend the literary executor, as Hethway passed on the convex mirror, so Beerbohm has an unfinished play on his hands. After so many years of heroic devotion from its author, he still finds it somewhat disappointing. Brown, with all his displeasure in the work of living playwrights and the efforts of the Elizabethans, should have been "more immune from influences" than he was. And leaving his characters unfettered he has made Savonarola sound merely improvised. The hero seems utterly inconsistent, though he may be "just complex, like Hamlet." Nevertheless Beerbohm is not blind to the play's "great merits. . . . Here is a play that abounds in striking situations, and I have searched it vainly for one line that does not scan." Then he prints the four acts of *Savonarola*.

In composing "'Savonarola' Brown," Beerbohm began by inventing the parodic text of a blank-verse tragedy, *Savonarola*, just as Nabokov wrote the poem "Pale Fire" before the book. Then around the play he built a frame story, for which there are marginal notes in the drafts of *Savonarola*. Parody is usually a secondary art; here it generated an original fiction around itself. The play's metrical inertia ("Savonarola looks more grim today / Than ever," it begins) carries it along in a mediocre, sometimes brilliantly mediocre vein. It is a distillation of Shakespeare and of the pseudo-Elizabethan blank verse dramas by Tennyson, Browning, Wilde, Stephen Phillips, Arthur Symons, Swinburne, and others. In Swinburne's *Duke of Gandia* (1908), Lucrezia and Cesare Borgia and the Pope appear, as they do in *Savonarola*, and in fact lines from Swinburne could easily go into Beerbohm's parody. The consistency with which Ladbroke Brown falls into iambic pentameter results sometimes in small but memorable absurdities. Thus St. Francis to Dante (they somehow have insinuated themselves into Act One) upon learning that Beatrice is dead:

> If the condolences of men avail
> Thee aught, take mine.

Just as often, the virtue of having no line that does not scan gives the play a demented, clocklike energy. Savonarola is spurned by Lucrezia Borgia:

> SAV. And this is all thou hast to say to me?
> LUC. It is.
> SAV. I am dismiss'd?
> LUC. Thou art.
> SAV. 'Tis well.

Beerbohm said this was one of the few works he wrote with joy. His own comic force carries to its extreme in Act Three, when "the foul and greasy plebs" of Florence surge around the major characters, to be swayed one way and then the other by their rhetoric. No doubt Beerbohm's feelings about "the sovereign people," as he called them elsewhere, are at work in the stage directions for this mob. But so is the language of a manic release from probability, akin to Joyce's Nighttown fantasy in *Ulysses*. The piazza is filled with a rude crowd in which "cobblers predominate," as Beerbohm notes. Lorenzo de Medici captures the crowd first:

> Citizens!
> [*Prolonged yells and groans from the crowd.*]
> Yes, I am he, I am that same Lorenzo
> Whom you have nicknamed the Magnificent.
> [*Further terrific yells, shakings of fists, brandishings of bill-hooks, insistent cries of "Death to Lorenzo!" "Down with the Magnificent!" Cobblers on fringe of*

crowd, down C., exhibit especially all the symptoms of epilepsy, whooping-cough, and other ailments.]
You love not me.
[The crowd makes an ugly rush. LOR. *appears likely to be dragged down and torn limb from limb, but raises one hand in the nick of time, and continues:]*
Yet I deserve your love.
[The yells are now variegated with dubious murmurs. A cobbler down C. thrusts his face feverishly in the face of another and repeats, in a hoarse interrogative whisper, "Deserves our love?"]

With the mob on his side, Lorenzo lets them know that their true enemy is Savonarola:

His twin bug-bears are
Yourselves and that New Learning which I hold
Less dear than only you.
[Profound sensation. Everybody whispers "Than only you" to everybody else. A woman near steps of Loggia attempts to kiss hem of LOR.*'s garment.]* . . .
Take the Dialogues
Of Plato, for example. You will find
A spirit far more truly Christian
In them than in the ravings of the sour-soul'd
Savonarola.
[Prolonged cries of "Death to the Sour-Souled Savonarola!" Several cobblers detach themselves from the crowd and rush away to read the Platonic Dialogues. Enter SAVONAROLA. *The crowd, as he makes his way through it, gives up all further control of its feelings.]*

As Ladbroke Brown had said to Beerbohm, drama shows us "what men *would* do, not just what they *did*."

Act Four opens on Savonarola in prison and a long soliloquy ending with his anxiety about life after prison:

Why, the very Novices
And callow Postulants will draw aside
As I pass by, and say, "That man hath done
Time!" And yet shall I wince? The worst of Time
Is not in having done it, but in doing it.

Besides the meter and the slang, which are Ladbroke Brown's, the quibble on time is the kind of thing Beerbohm felt came much too easily to Shakespeare. The fragments of Shakespeare embedded in this parody express Brown's lack of imagination and Beerbohm's boredom. He thought there was hack-work in the comedies and histories, and, swayed perhaps by his brother's many grand productions, he asked for a thirty-year moratorium on *Macbeth*, *Hamlet*, *Romeo and Juliet*. The first utterance of Pope Julius as he stands over the dead body of the Gaoler, thinking it is Savonarola, comes from the end of *King Lear*, and he then slips into the closing lines from *Coriolanus* and *Julius Caesar*. The Fool too is a compound of Feste and Touchstone, though his senseless songs and business fit the already manic world of *Savonarola*. *Hamlet* finally provides the wildest touches, as Cesare Borgia discovers that the dead body is not the Gaoler, but the Fool he had had to dismiss from his household:

I deem'd him no good riddance, for he had
The knack of setting tables on a roar.
What shadows we pursue! Good night, sweet Fool,
And flights of angels sing thee to thy rest!

The playwright has reached his highest moment, and it does not matter that "What shadows we pursue" comes from an election speech by Edmund Burke.

Beerbohm then explains that he did his best to get this play produced, but while theater managers were all "very kind," they could not take a play without an ending. So as literary executor he provides a scenario for Act Five. At dawn, Savonarola and Lucrezia have fled from the Pope up Mount Fiesole:

> SAV. *has a speech to the rising sun*—Th' effulgent hope that westers from the east / Daily. *Says that* his *hope, on the contrary, lies in escape* To that which easters not from out the west, / That fix'd abode of freedom which men call / America!

Machiavelli, who has slept the night on Mount Fiesole, betrays them and as the Pope approaches, Savonarola and Lucrezia take deadly nightshade. With this, Beerbohm's memoir is virtually complete, except for a final word by him which slightly but radically alters the whole story. In attempting to incarnate Act Five from his skeleton scenario he "failed wretchedly," he admits. "I saw that Brown was, in comparison with me, a master." The confession gives back Ladbroke Brown his dignity: his bizarre talent looks authentic, almost fulfilled. He and his play already amounted to a striking conception: now they seem even more authentic in proving too much for Max Beerbohm. There is immense gain in this story over a purely analytic criticism of neo-Shakespearean drama. We move back and forth between Brown and Shakespeare, the narrator and Brown, the play and the scenario, Beerbohm and himself, until everything about drama looks completely different. As Beerbohm put it in describing caricature, not one particle of the man lost, yet not a particle as it was before. The distortions and improprieties in "'Savonarola' Brown" end up by giving us an active sense, even as drastic a sense, of the domain of drama as Lewis Carroll gives us of childhood.

"Enoch Soames," written in 1915, portrays a man with even less genius than Ladbroke Brown, and Beerbohm's insinuations go far deeper than friendly collaborating. This memoir of London in the mid-nineties develops the relationship between Soames, a nonvirulent follower of the English imitators of Verlaine and Baudelaire, and the young narrator, Beerbohm. Soames sips absinthe in the right cafés and says that Milton converted him to Catholic Diabolism. But he seems weak-minded. Talking with Rothenstein and Beerbohm in the Café Royal,* he asserts:

> "Of course in Art there is the good and the evil. But in Life—no. . . . In Life there are illusions of good and evil, but"—his voice trailed away to a murmur in which the words "vieux jeu" and "rococo" were faintly audible. . . . Anyway, he cleared his throat and said *"Parlons d'autre chose."*

He leaves, and Beerbohm, a novice writer, tries to find the *mot juste* for him. He settles on "dim," but Rothenstein calls Soames utterly nonexistent. Soames's first book, *Negations*, has a preface that begins, "Lean near to life. Lean very near—nearer. Life is web, and therein nor warp nor woof is, but web only." He writes a *conte* about the murder of a mannequin, which seems to Beerbohm like a story by the ultradecadent Catulle Mendès in which the translator has cut out every other sentence. As Soames's bit in the pseudo-pagan Catholicism of the nineties, there is a dialogue between Pan and St. Ursula, lacking, Beerbohm feels, in "snap." All the literary forms in *Negations*

> had evidently been wrought with much care. It was rather the substance that eluded me. Was there, I wondered, any substance at all? It did now occur to me: suppose Enoch Soames was a fool! Up cropped a rival hypothesis: suppose *I* was. I inclined to give Soames the benefit of the doubt. I had read "L'Après-midi d'un Faune" without extracting a glimmer of meaning.

Soames tells Beerbohm that the poems in his next book, *Fungoids*, will be like that—strange growths, wild, exquisite, full of poisons—though apparently the poet has a low opinion of Baudelaire, "a *bourgeois malgré lui*." Beerbohm, pleased to be able to buy the book of a friend, buys *Fungoids* immediately and finds things that seem very good:

TO A YOUNG WOMAN

Thou art, who hast not been!
Pale tunes irresolute
And traceries of old sounds
Blown from a rotted flute
Mingle with noise of cymbals rouged with rust,
Nor not strange forms and epicene
Lie bleeding in the dust,
Being wounded with wounds.

For this it is
That in thy counterpart
Of age-long mockeries
Thou hast not been nor art!

A certain inconsistency between the first and last lines may only indicate his failure, Beerbohm says, to see the depth of Soames's meaning. And "as for the craftsmanship, 'rouged with rust' seemed to me a fine stroke, and 'nor not' instead of 'and' had a curious felicity." Every irony that Beerbohm practices against himself rebounds onto Soames. Within the contorted, unmoving, semi-erotic, and falsely sinister verse, there is a parody of what Symons and others also imported from French Symbolism: a hermetic circularity and, in the pale tunes, traceries of sounds, and rouged cymbals, an infusion of literature with visual and musical experience.

Beerbohm had spoken in the *Works* about "lurid verses written by young men who, in real life, know no haunt more lurid than a literary public-house," and as early as 1892 he caricatured the Rhymers' Club poets for their decadent affectation. Several of them can be suggested as models for Soames. The closest is Theodore Wratislaw, whom Beerbohm knew. Besides a feeble book on Swinburne, Wratislaw published *Orchids*, with lines such as "Odour of women faintly wrought" and "Nor musk nor heliotrope it is." Symons, Victor Plarr, and John Gray form part of the composite. Beerbohm prints another poem from *Fungoids* in which the petty Satanism of the period falls under a title that ought to suggest a pensive, impressionist scene:

NOCTURNE

Round and round the shutter'd Square
I stroll'd with the Devil's arm in mine.
No sound but the scrape of his hoofs was there
And the ring of his laughter and mine.
We had drunk black wine.

I scream'd, "I will race you, Master!"
"What matter," he shriek'd, "to-night
Which of us runs the faster?
There is nothing to fear to-night
In the foul moon's light!"

Then I look'd him in the eyes,
And I laughed full shrill at the lie he told
And the gnawing fear he would fain disguise.
It was true, what I'd time and again been told:
He was old—old.

Beerbohm admires the swing of the first stanza, and while stanza two may be "slightly hysterical," the third is quite heartening and shows the Diabolistic side of Soames to be his best.

A doubleness in the story begins to come out as, between 1894 and 1896, Soames falls into deeper neglect and Max Beerbohm rises (vulgarly, he feels, compared with Soames) from *Yellow Book* notoriety to the *Saturday Review* and the *Daily Mail. Fungoids* gets only one review (from Soames's home town) and sells three copies; his third book goes unreviewed and Beerbohm cannot remember the name of it. One afternoon in June 1897, the two men lunch together.

Soames anguishes over missing worldly recognition: if he could only be projected into the British Museum reading-room a hundred years hence—

> "just for this one afternoon! I'd sell myself body and soul to the devil, for that! Think of the pages and pages in the catalogue: 'SOAMES, ENOCH' endlessly—endless editions, commentaries, prolegomena, biographies."

At that moment a stranger who has been sitting nearby during lunch, "a tall, flashy, rather Mephistophelian man," joins them. Against Beerbohm's desperate pleading, Soames makes his bargain.

The trip into the future, reversing a scheme Beerbohm was then working on for *The Mirror of the Past,* allows some anti-utopian satire. On returning from 1997, Soames reports that he made quite a stir in the reading-room. Everyone else was dressed in a Shavian wool uniform and wore a numbered metal disc on the left sleeve. Unfortunately the SN-SOF volume of the catalogue had only the three little slips he already knew. Soames could find nothing except one trivial mention of himself, in a late-twentieth-century literary history, which he copied out for Beerbohm. It is from T. K. Nupton's *Inglish Littracher 1892–1900,* "published bi th Stait" in 1992:

> Fr egzarmpl, a riter ov th time, namd Max Beerbohm, hoo woz stil alive in th twentieth senchri, rote a stauri in wich e pautraid an immajnari karrakter kauld 'Enoch Soames'—a thurd-rait poit hoo beleevz imself a grate jeneus an maix a bargin with th Devvl in auder ter no wot posterriti thinx ov im! It iz a sumwot labud sattire but not without vallu as showing hou seriusli the yung men ov the aiteen-ninetiz took themselvz.

Soames is outraged, and Beerbohm insists desperately that it must be some idiotic mistake or coincidence.

> Again I examined the screed. "Immajnari"—but here Soames was, no more imaginary, alas! than I. And "labud"—what on earth was that? (To this day I have never made out that word.) "It's all very—baffling," I at length stammered.
>
> Soames said nothing, but cruelly did not cease to look at me.

Here, with Soames threatened as Beerbohm was in Madame Tussaud's, the narrative begins to oscillate. Soames accuses Beerbohm of not being a good enough artist: "so far from being able to imagine a thing and make it seem true, you're going to make even a true thing seem as if you'd made it up. You're a miserable bungler." Beerbohm protests that T. K. Nupton is the bungler, and besides, "I'm an essayist, an observer, a recorder." Finally Soames, with more dignity than Beerbohm had ever seen in him, says, "I see the whole thing. *Parlons d'autre chose.*" Beerbohm frantically suggests an escape to Calais, but the poet is soon called for and gone. "In the blinding glare of the near Jubilee" of Queen Victoria, no one notices his disappearance. Later, on a street one day in Paris, Beerbohm runs into the Devil and despite his anger cannot help nodding and smiling politely. The Devil stares haughtily without acknowledging him and Beerbohm is furious.

The possible sources for "Enoch Soames" do not help much in defining its form: *Faust* and Wells's *Time Machine* are mentioned in the narrative; Pater's *Imaginary Portraits* and James's stories of frustrated writers both lack Beerbohm's easy obtrusiveness. The closest analogues are those that come after "Enoch Soames," in the involutions of Nabokov and Jorge Luis Borges. As in Borges, the delusion of linear time runs through Beerbohm's story. At the beginning he mentions that he has no option, he must write this memoir about Soames. Later we learn why. After Soames vanishes, Beerbohm decides that the extract from Nupton's repulsive book proves only that Nupton, a sloppy scholar, will not read far enough into the memoir to see his mistake. (What awaits T. K. Nupton, of course, is the kind of nullity which Soames had to confront.) And Beerbohm realizes that Soames made a stir in the reading-room because the people there, on the afternoon of June 3, 1997, must have been prepared by this memoir for a ghostly visitation: "In his first visit, Soames was a creature of flesh and blood . . . in a building that was itself an illusion. Next time, that building and those creatures will be real." Unavoidably we want to know in what dimension of time the first and second visits can be distinct and yet the same.

Beerbohm's presence, like his signature in a caricature, qualifies the whole story. A collusion between author and participant makes it hard to say which of them lives within the aura of failure around Soames. Liking "rouged with rust" is harmless enough, but the very structure of the narrative implies that Beerbohm, near the height of his success when he wrote *Seven Men*, may be imagining his own limits in Soames's. Unlike Soames and the "tragic generation" that Yeats saw die or commit suicide or go mad, he "woz stil alive in th twentieth senchri." But he never felt at home in it. He used to say that Soames was lucky in his period if in nothing else.

The two characters cannot both exist at once, so reading the story is like turning a Möbius strip, and the ambiguity involves some risk. Taking Soames seriously entails a possibility that he may be the other side of Beerbohm, a secret sharer. Among the extra illustrations Beerbohm did for this story is one that shows Soames very tired and empty-eyed, opposite Beerbohm sitting straight-backed in an immaculate top hat, innocent but unreal.* Soames is a literary nonentity, the part of himself which Beerbohm fears. But if Soames does exist, as they both claim, and the Devil exists also, cutting Beerbohm as if he did not see him, then by the terms of the action Beerbohm is indeed a nonentity. Within the action there is no fixed point, like Laider's influenza or the street outside Madame Tussaud's, to relieve the ambiguity. We have to tolerate and understand both readings simultaneously, so that Beerbohm is both a success and a failure—fiction does and does not tell the truth.

The trouble with this kind of writing can be that, like an optical illusion, it delights you until it does not. What remains then is the efficacy of parody—we have exact, vivid evidence that Soames is third-rate—and the double agency of self-parody, Beerbohm's equivalent to the apotheosis of Rubek in *When We Dead Awaken*. He believes in Soames to the extent of admitting that he could never make out one word, "labud," in the excerpt from T. K. Nupton. Tell him what it means, and it's as if a sculpture reached out to jostle you, or the actor in a play laughed at you. Beerbohm's helplessness reverts to power: he wrote the satire, which is anything but "labud." You are left with a Cheshire Cat disappearing behind the smile, and with Soames's last words to Beerbohm as the Devil takes him roughly away: "*try* to make them know that I did exist!"

We are used to thinking about how the artist shapes his subject. "Enoch Soames" makes the most drastic case for that. Periit Soames: Beerbohm fecit. The irony is that the poet, like the clergyman, perishes when he attains most life, in the heroic, existential "I see the whole thing." Usually, in our imagination, fictional characters reach for more of the life that literature can give them. Here Soames is claiming actual life. He is a fiction struggling against fiction, and against the bungler, the man who stopped living for a while to write about him. We begin to feel a tension on the puppet strings and control being reversed. The story moves back to its own point of origin and on past.

Beerbohm urges that literature is no more and no less stylized than life. His writing institutes a primary world, something even he as character can appear in. If art survives in this century by the game of questioning itself, an essential part of this game finds its shape in Beerbohm's parody of literature.

At Ease in Zion

With "Enoch Soames" Beerbohm had come a long way from the "Defence of Cosmetics," which he said perhaps should have been signed D. Cadent or Parrar Docks. In both works, he plays off against the reader's bafflement his own relation to decadent aesthetics. The change is from having to publish a corrective letter in the *Yellow Book* to inventing a "labud" story and the "curious felicity" of Soames's verse. He had come by way of Shaw, Ibsen, James, *Zuleika Dobson*, and *The Mirror of the Past*, enacting the contradictions he had to live with.

The comic artist, as described by Baudelaire in his essay on laughter, is consciously himself and another at the same time, while his characters are unaware of their nature. In Beerbohm's case, the artist often doubles as his own character. There was a nineteenth-century anecdote of the Harlequin actor who went, out of costume, to a doctor, complaining of deep melancholy. For a cure he was advised, Visit the theater and watch Harlequin perform. Beerbohm gained from that predicament. Part of his equipment was an instinct for splitting himself imaginatively. In a number of drawings he appears as caricaturist, and at a loss—the "veteran exile," for example, "doddering on" at the drawing table in Rapallo. And he wrote reflexively. At times this resulted in static mannerisms or attitudes, as with the coxcomb-criminal of the "Defence of Cosmetics." But in his later, familiar essays, Beerbohm gets sharp perceptions out of appearing vulnerable. In the comedy of *Seven Men* he is outside and inside his role at the same time, in contrast with writers like James and even Wilde, who seem more bound to themselves. The best gloss on Max Beerbohm lies in a key remark about acting. He said that the tragic actor must lose himself in his role, but that the actor in a comic part "may, and should, exercise a critical as well as a creative faculty."

There is a shield of Perseus in his art. Self-doubt reflects in the critique of other artists or changes to capability in works like "A Relic" and "'Savonarola' Brown." Usually Beerbohm settled his sense of himself by changing the matter of anxiety into comic invention. Shortly before the battle of Jutland in the First World War, when Alexander Woollcott urged him to give a public recital of poetry, he declined, suggesting how unfit he was: "Yesterday I received a charming letter from Sir John Jellicoe [Commander of the Fleet]. He said there was going to be a great action in the North Sea next month, and he particularly wanted me to be in command of one of the battleships." During the war Beerbohm flourished as an artist. *Seven Men* and *Rossetti and His Circle* released the energy of nostalgia and took him away from the catastrophe. More than that, Rossetti's romantic alienation and the failed writers in *Seven Men* stabilized his own identity.

A social revolutionary in one of Edmund Wilson's novels is said to "shudder at the sight of a handful of volumes of Max Beerbohm." Although in some sense he converted his limitations to virtues, Beerbohm was still disregarding the pain and dirt at the bottom of his society. Alongside Shaw and Wilde, whose disgust with poverty stemmed from a humane anger, he seems defensive if not beside the point in looking only at the artistic aspect of social realism. I do not mean that he was insensitive to the condition of the mass of men: in fact, he used unworldliness, doubleness, and anachronism to insulate himself.

In contrast with Dostoevsky, Nietzsche, Freud, Strindberg, Proust, the troubled Hebraic spirits whom he began to hear about after the nineties, Beerbohm was "at ease in Zion." He could explain why his friend the writer John Davidson had committed suicide: "Davidson was very poor, and was weighted with heavy responsibilities. Also, he was a man of intense emotional temper, with as much capacity for despair as for joy. Also, he was a man of genius; and he believed—rightly or wrongly, but in every fibre of his being—that he had an indispensable message for mankind." Free of all these burdens and acutely aware of them, Beerbohm lived in an eddy of sympathetic imagination. What makes his relation to Davidson even more ironic is that in 1906 he had parodied his friend as a philosopher-clown stabbing himself. After the suicide in 1909, he left the parody out of *A Christmas Garland*. Like his caricature of Davidson, the parody had disastrous knowledge that Beerbohm himself did not have.

His innocence can be measured against a law of nature he expressed in the essay on Swinburne. Talking of the poet's lifelong palsy, the fluttering hands visible in Beerbohm's caricature, he says: "I have known no man of genius who had not to pay, in some affliction or defect either physical or spiritual, for what the gods had given him." Beerbohm's own affliction, that he was not a man of genius, helped him in writing *And Even Now* and *Seven Men*, and in getting perspective on some of the major artists of his time. "No. 2. The Pines" (1914), a lively, gentle memory of meetings with Swinburne in 1899, leans, as Beerbohm always did, toward the time just before his own. The essay is beautifully constructed to show Beerbohm perceptive but slightly callow, and Swinburne buoyant but pathetic. It ends by imagining Swinburne not with the sparse, straggling gray hair he had when Beerbohm met him, but plunging into the Elysian waters "quite, quite young, with a full mane of flaming auburn locks, and no clothes to hinder him." When, in 1918, Edmund Gosse circulated a confidential paper on Swinburne's drunkenness and sado-masochism, Beerbohm protested: "how definitely dreary and ghastly and disgusting the whole thing becomes. . . . Why not let the lovers of his poetry hereafter be immune from *definite* knowledge?" I sense that he wanted to relieve Swinburne as well as himself of that knowledge, just as he later protested Frank Harris's "raking-up of the old Sodomitic cesspool" around Wilde.

Personal circumstances rarely disabled Beerbohm. The strongest blow came in 1904, when Constance Collier broke their engagement to be married. He wrote to Reggie Turner:

> It *is* a pity I was not born either rich or the sort of solid man who could be trusted and who could trust himself to make his way solidly in the world. Of course I am a success in a way . . . but that is in virtue of certain qualities in my defects: it is in virtue of a sort of nimble fantastic irresponsibility; for solid worldly success this is no good at all. And I now, for the first time clearly, see myself as on the whole a failure.

In his caricature of her, Constance Collier's strong chin, thick neck, and formidable bosom suggest a way in which Beerbohm felt unequal, but it hardly worked on him as an affliction.

The letter implies that he was born with his nimble fantastic irresponsibility. The closer the focus on him, however, the more it appears his easiness was not wholly a natural gift. You see this clearly in his working manuscripts, in which corrections are made by crossing out and then thoroughly inking over, as if to remove any sign of imperfectness, any chance of being second-guessed. He was also obsessively careful in getting printers to follow his directions about type, margins, title-page, binding, cover, etc., and in getting proofreaders to respect the purity of his punctuation—"My choice of stops is as important to me . . . as my choice of words." His work was not capacious enough to tolerate misprints, Beerbohm said. Fantasy especially required accuracy in small things, and he wrote exuberantly to the publishers of *Zuleika Dobson* about some typographical problems:

Constance Collier

I am quite ready and glad to believe that all those swaying lines, those letters bobbing up, those letters slipping down . . . were due merely to "a slight inequality in the alignment of this particular fount." In all friendliness, then, I implore Messrs Ballantyne to seal up this particular fount (which is evidently our old friend the *fons et origo malorum*) for ever and ever, or to set it playing only on very special occasions—as when they are called on to print *The Confessions of a Dancing Dervish*, for example, or *The Random Memories of a Palsied Hottentot*.

Constance Collier's description of Beerbohm tallies with his fastidiousness in literary matters: "so neat and debonair, his collar very high, and abnormally tight cuffs." His liking for small, clear, contained things rather than things large and loose formed part of a creed evidently achieved at some cost in personal ease. The sexual aspect of this creed comes out in the Duke of Dorset's celibate dandyism and in the threat that professional women writers posed to Beerbohm. Rebecca West once described him at a party of literary women: a white Chinese porcelain dragon with a rounded forehead, small hands and feet, blue eyes, skin clear as a child's, and looking more "perilously fragile" as more ladies arrived. The same kind of delicacy affects what Beerbohm felt about Lytton Strachey, the only writer to emerge after the First World War whom he really liked: "There's the wittiest mind of the age, and the virtue of it guarded even more strictly and puritanically than I have guarded the virtue of mine."

The continence of Beerbohm, which is not what we always get in his writing, stems in part from native physical and temperamental qualities. In his childhood, his sister was far more adventurous, "something even of a tomboy," he said. "I was fairly fond of swinging rather slowly on a trapeze in the nursery." It is tempting to look for a childlike nature in many elements of his life and work: in the poking at established figures, the criterion of make-believe in theater criticism, the role-playing in parody; in his self-sufficiency and private game of "improving" books, his readiness, in caricature and elsewhere, to alter the given fact, his avoidance of abstractions; in his insulation from the world, his two care-taking wives, and the recurrent descriptions of his baby face and eyes. Like Beerbohm's general easiness, these qualities took shape consciously. He elaborated his childlikeness within a frame of complex skills. To be accurate about the personality he worked with as an artist, we can point to the difference between Beerbohm's caricatures and a child's naturally distorted drawings. And in his writing, a circle of parodic voices developed in place of a creed.

About children specifically he wrote almost no fiction,

and the two sentimental fairy tales of 1897 derive from Wilde. He had no particular love for children, but a kind of respect for their imperfectness which made him reject the late-Victorian cult of the romantic child, the dear simple little thing. In 1896 he parodied himself as "A Vain Child," and in another piece wrote sarcastically, "The public . . . knows me to be a child author, and likes to picture me at my desk, dressed in black velveteen, with legs dangling towards the floor." Publishing "Diminuendo" and his complete works at the age of twenty-three, and linking himself with the Regency and Pre-Raphaelitism, Beerbohm carried out a wish to be dated, to be not young, which outlasts his early cheekiness. His nostalgia has more to do with this wish than with any desire to recover home and childhood, like that of James Barrie and Lewis Carroll. He reviewed the first *Peter Pan* with barely veiled sarcasm at Barrie's childishness, and several years later wrote about it again with even greater sarcasm. Towards C. L. Dodgson he was sympathetic, emphasizing the difference between Dodgson's personal child-worship and the imagination of *Alice in Wonderland* and *Through the Looking Glass*—books that were filled with queer, grotesque dream creatures far more convincing to children than Barrie's sentimentality. Beerbohm's delight in the Punch and Judy show conformed to his idea that violence and amorality were good to see when presented on the plane of comic art. During the First World War he saw a performance on a London street corner: if Punch still survived "in our changed city and in our tragic world," maybe England could. Children understood Punch, but as the audience seemed to be made up of Boy Scouts, Beerbohm remembers, this humpbacked "wife-beater, with his homicidal and infanticidal ways, rather shocked them."

He always had in mind the fantasies of "wrong's horrible results" in *Struwwelpeter*. "Elements of terror were lurking everywhere" in the book, he said. When some playwrights adapted it, leaving out the various punishments for sin, he objected: it was a mistake "that Harriet should not really be burnt, that Augustus should retain his former bulk, that the sucked thumb should not really be cut off." What persuaded him was the logic of fantasy rather than morality. He liked early-nineteenth-century cautionary verse, and believed that children were fascinated by the confrontation with guilt. Beerbohm's maturity is childlike in that he imagines the dark things the way a child does. Guilt, sin, punishment, amorality, the grotesque, violence, death—his own writing explores them under the comic supervision of parody, fantasy, and nonsense.

Aware of what he called "the Mosaic conscience"—bent on self-conquest and doing right, and thwarted by imperfection—Beerbohm substituted dandyism and self-irony for it. In "Brennbaum," a lyric of *Hugh Selwyn Mauberley*, Pound got the dandy's discipline but none of his play:

The sky-like limpid eyes,
The circular infant's face,
The stiffness from spats to collar
Never relaxing into grace;

The heavy memories of Horeb, Sinai and the forty years,
Showed only when the daylight fell
Level across the face
Of Brennbaum 'The Impeccable'.

Innocence and anxiety, at odds in this view, come together in the self that Beerbohm's writing fosters. His comic work transforms potential sources of anxiety—sexual anomaly in Wilde, James, and Swinburne, failure in Soames and Brown—and the stiffness does relax into grace.

"Stil alive in th twentieth senchri"

Beerbohm once told Oscar Wilde's son Vyvyan that he had been born "with a small head and large hands and feet but,

Self-caricature ca. 1907

by dint of making countless drawings of himself and by continual concentration, he had achieved his ambition, which was to have a large head and very small hands and feet." It was, he said, "the world's example of the triumph of mind over matter." If Beardsley's big embryo heads hint at the unviability of a precocious spirit, this image suggests that man invents himself, and indeed Beerbohm made his art and personality equally vital conditions of each other. He arrived at a disabused form of romantic individualism, caricaturing himself more than any other subject and entering ironically into his essays and stories. Virginia Woolf called him "the triumph of style," saying that we cannot tell the essayist from the man. His work in general joins two sources of interest, Max Beerbohm and the art in question. We see the caricaturist being shown Shaw's true portrait, the seventh man reading poems from *Fungoids*.

The imagination experiments between actual experience and illusionary or artistic experience. It is a movement from the purely inventive to the critical and the parodic action of the imagination, throughout Beerbohm's writing and conjoined in single works, that makes him worth reading. He started outright by defending the aesthetic image, in cosmetics and costume, and by embodying it in various personal fabrications. Then, as a victim in Madame Tussaud's and a witness of Bellini's painting or London's theater, he set himself to expose the workings of mimetic art, particularly the disparity between image and fact which caricature also builds upon. It was a turn, in large measure, from assuming that words are in true ways bound up with things, to testing how language represents the world.

Beerbohm reached the limit of his vision in coupling these two activities. Parody sustains them both, taking the form of synthesis rather than analysis. *Zuleika Dobson* fuses history with fiction, and the structure of the later stories assimilates what is inadequate or laughable about literature. It is not surprising that Beerbohm loved the puppet scene from *Don Quixote*, in which Quixote attacks a show of pasteboard Moors. An analogy from it occurs in the "Defence of Cosmetics," and on his deathbed he read the scene aloud. In *Seven Men*, he maintains his heroes' (and his own) illusions against the disenchantment he also sponsors.

He is a pivotal figure historically. The major essays, criticism, parodies, and stories, *The Poets' Corner* and *Rossetti and His Circle*, taken together with private and uncollected sketches, notes, jokes—they all present images of art and the artist and, like a convex mirror, reflect modern literature from within. In questioning the value of the imagination and its constructions, Beerbohm belongs to the Romantic movement of thought. Whether deliberately or whimsically does not matter so much: he joined Arnold's and Pater's aesthetic idealism to the self-consciousness of James and Wilde in a generic parody of literature. As parody by its nature thoroughly pervades whatever form it takes, Beerbohm's writing is like an intake of breath or a shudder. It has all the signs of a literature breaking up and perhaps reconditioning itself. The writer abnegates himself, the process of composing essays and stories becomes a spectacle, and many of them express the precarious relation of form to content. Where ordinarily we neglect or take for granted the connections between an artist, a work of art, and ourselves, Beerbohm literalizes, energizes those connections—pretentiously, with "A Defence of Cosmetics," and in crucial ways later on. Paintings or characters come alive out of their frames; imitation and illusion take over as subjects, instead of remaining the means for conveying a subject. The author turns up in his own work, sometimes even a victim of it. Bits of actual life contend with invented things in narrative, and the reader is drawn in off balance. The mirror of art now generates light and images, and as in Lewis Carroll's books, language gets back something of its primordial life.

I do not mean that Beerbohm's writing is experimental in the sense that *Ulysses* forms a series of experiments. His comic vision works within structures of traditional symmetry and recurrence, and the skepticism in "Enoch Soames" or *A Christmas Garland* is of a different order from the gratuitous, subversive nonsense in Dada or the crumbling style of Samuel Beckett. Just as Beerbohm's taste for modern art stopped at the first stage of harmonious impressionism, he kept his preference for form and beauty in prose. He parodied facile realism and the Edwardian novel years before Joyce or Virginia Woolf began to break up conventional forms of narrative, yet his parody treats the methods of Bennett and Galsworthy as still negotiable. Virginia Woolf called for throwing them away entirely. In "Mr. Bennett and

Mrs. Brown" (1924), thinking of the impact of England's first postimpressionist show, she said that human character had changed in 1910: a narrative that respected the surface of events could no longer comprehend the multifold perceptions we have of a Mrs. Brown, or the disorder of feelings she has. Beerbohm denied this view, while conceding to Virginia Woolf that her own novels left him feeling beaten, "with an acute sense of disgrace . . . half-dead . . . bemused and miserable."

He was uncompelled to follow the winding path of modern consciousness, even though his writing under its own terms locates the otherness of events and people, the emptiness of culture and the self. A final, paralyzing awareness of these things did not seem to him the province or purpose of literature. As an instinctual parodist, Beerbohm says what Beckett's exhausted speaker says, "I can't go on, I'll go on," but with exuberance and a decided love for the order of language. He is still alive in the twentieth century because he wrote himself into a parody of literature that invents and conserves radical criticisms of itself, asking us not to stop the lies of art but to see through them and with them.

Notes

The notes are without exception merely citations for facts, references, and quotations. They are keyed by page numbers from this book and by a pertinent phrase from the item being annotated. For short essays, reviews, and parodies, only the first reference has been noted. The place of publication of books and articles is assumed to be London unless specified otherwise. The following locations of Beerbohm materials are abbreviated in the notes:

Ashmolean	Print Room, Department of Western Art The Ashmolean Museum, Oxford
Berg	Berg Collection, New York Public Library
Clark	William Andrews Clark Memorial Library University of California, Los Angeles
Hart-Davis	Private collection of typescripts, manuscripts, and photographic copies of caricatures Sir Rupert Hart-Davis, Richmond, Yorkshire
Houghton	The Houghton Library, Harvard University
Merton	Beerbohm Collection The Library, Merton College, Oxford
Taylor	Robert H. Taylor Collection, deposited in Department of Rare Books and Special Collections Princeton University Library, Princeton, New Jersey
UCLA	Department of Special Collections The University Library University of California, Los Angeles

Preface

Page ix

"gifts are small": Bohun Lynch, *Max Beerbohm in Perspective* (1921), p. viii.

"ex-Arcadian": Beerbohm, letter to William Rothenstein, 21 May 1942, in Houghton.

Page x

"I know a man called Fergusson": Beerbohm, *Letters to Reggie Turner,* ed. Rupert Hart-Davis (1964), 15 May 1893, p. 41.

Page xi

"Hosts and Guests," "Going Out for a Walk": Beerbohm, *And Even Now* (1920).

review of *When We Dead Awaken:* Beerbohm, *More Theatres, 1898–1903,* ed. Rupert Hart-Davis (1969), 7 Feb. 1903, pp. 532–5.

Chapter 1

Page 3

"Nay, but": Beerbohm, "A Defence of Cosmetics," *Yellow Book,* I (April 1894), 65–83.

Page 4

"The Philosophy of Rouge": Beerbohm, *Letters,* p. 87.

Page 5

Degeneration: first English edition, 1895; rpt. New York, 1902, p. 305.

Page 6

"preserve a delicate": Katherine Lyon Mix, *A Study in Yellow: The Yellow Book and Its Contributors* (Lawrence, Kansas, 1960), p. 78.

a young comedienne: Beerbohm, *Letters,* p. 72.

appreciation of Oscar Wilde: "Oscar Wilde," *Anglo-American Times,* 25 Mar. 1893; repub. in Beerbohm, *Letters,* pp. 285–92.

essay inspired by him: "The Incomparable Beauty of Modern Dress," *Spirit Lamp,* June 1893, 90–8.

Wilde's sayings: from Wilde, "Phrases and Philosophies for the Use of the Young," *Chameleon,* December 1894; repub. in Wilde, *Miscellanies* (New York, 1909), pp. 176–8.

Page 7

comprehend "his sayings as ideas": Beerbohm, "Oscar Wilde," in *Letters,* p. 291.

book of "Masques": *The Letters of Aubrey Beardsley,* ed. Henry Mass, J. J. Duncan, W. G. Good (Fairleigh Dickinson Univ. Press, New Jersey, 1970), p. 52.

Page 8

The slave girls: *Yellow Book,* I, 74.

Page 9

Venus and Tannhäuser: (New York, 1927), first published as "Under the Hill," *Savoy,* January 1896, 160.

"Divinely rosy rouged": quoted in Holbrook Jackson, *The Eighteen Nineties* (1913; rpt. 1931), p. 162.

"A Word on Behalf of Patchouli": Arthur Symons, *Studies in Prose and Verse* (1904), p. 281.

"Pale tunes irresolute": Beerbohm, "Enoch Soames," in *Seven Men* (1919), p. 16.

"Who cannot see": in Charles Baudelaire, *The Painter of Modern Life and Other Essays,* trans. and ed. Jonathan Mayne (New York, 1964), p. 33. I have altered the translations from Baudelaire, using the *Oeuvres Complètes* (Paris, 1961).

Pages 10–11

"In spite of Max's brilliance": Virginia Woolf, *A Writer's Diary* (New York, 1954), p. 295 (1 Nov. 1938).

Pages 11–12

Escher: "Drawing Hands," in *The Graphic Work of M. C. Escher* (New York, 1961; 2nd ed. 1967), pl. 69. Steinberg: in Steinberg, *The Passport* (New York, 1954); repub. in E. H. Gombrich, *Art and Illusion* (1960), p. 200.

Page 12

the press applauded: cf. *The Nation,* 24 May 1894, 390.

"horrid aspect": Henry James, *The Letters of Henry James,* ed. Percy Lubbock (New York, 1920), I, 222.

Page 14

"It is impossible": Aline Harland, letter to E. C. Stedman, 21 May 1894, in Stanford University Library, Department of Special Collections.

"grins and squeaks": Beerbohm, "Punch," in *More* (1899), p. 25.

"How deftly": *Punch,* 5 May 1895, 210.

"not merely indecent": *Spectator,* 19 May 1894, 695.

"not only . . . by declaring": *Critic* (New York), 26 May 1894, 360.

Dutchman who wrote to Erasmus: Walter Kaiser, *Praisers of Folly* (Cambridge, Mass., 1963), p. 23.

Page 15

"Indeed, it seems incredible": "A Letter to the Editor," *Yellow Book,* II (July 1894), 282.

Punch eventually produced: "A Phalse Note on George the Fourth," 27 Oct. 1894, 204.

"That his 'Defence' ": *National Observer,* 18 Aug. 1894, 359.

"The Pervasion of Rouge": Beerbohm, *The Works of Max Beerbohm* (1896), pp. 99–124.

Page 16

"degenerate": Frank H. Hankins, "Degeneration," in *Encyclopedia of the Social Sciences,* ed. Edwin Seligman (New York, 1935), V, 55.

Page 17

"presents himself to the nation": Beerbohm, "Dandies and Dandies," in *Works,* p. 17.

typed notes: UCLA, Box 959, #33.

Page 18

Four essays: "Dandies and Dandies," in Beerbohm, *Works,* pp. 3–29; reworked from "The Incomparable Beauty of Modern Dress," *Spirit Lamp,* June 1893; "Dandies and Dandies," *Vanity,* Feb. 1895; "Notes in Foppery," *Unicorn,* Sept. 1895; "De Natura Barbatulorum," *Chap-Book,* Feb. 1896. For more detailed reference, see J. G. Riewald, *Sir Max Beerbohm: Man and Writer* (The Hague, Netherlands, 1953), p. 215.

Page 19

" 'Max' doit aspirer": on flyleaf of Beerbohm's copy of James

McNeill Whistler, *The Gentle Art of Making Enemies* (1890), in Clark.

Page 20

Barbey's *Du Dandysme:* (Caen, France, 1845), p. 116.

"not necessarily interesting": Beerbohm, "London Revisited" (broadcast 29 Dec. 1935), in Beerbohm, *Mainly on the Air,* enl. ed. (1957), p. 6.

Baudelaire sees him: "The Dandy," in *The Painter,* pp. 26–9.

Ellen Moers: pub. New York, 1960.

Page 21

"A Note on George the Fourth": *Yellow Book,* III (April 1894), 247–69; repub. as "King George the Fourth," in *Works,* pp. 59–96.

Thackeray: William Makepeace Thackeray, "George the Fourth," in *The English Humorists* and *The Four Georges* (New York, 1867), pp. 410–49.

"a now extinct species": Beerbohm, "London Revisited," p. 11.

Page 22

Huizinga and Lévi-Strauss: cf. Johan Huizinga, *Homo Ludens: A Study of the Play-Element in Culture,* trans. R. F. C. Hull (1949); Claude Lévi-Strauss, "A Native Society and Its Style," in *Tristes Tropiques,* trans. John Russell (1961), Ch. 17.

Chapter 2

Page 23

"Mr. Beerbohm writes": *National Observer,* XVI, No. 402, 337.

Page 24

London club types: *Strand,* Sept., Nov., Dec., 1892.

Savoy: Beerbohm, "A Good Prince," *Savoy,* Jan. 1896, 45–7; repub. in *Works,* pp. 33–7.

Daily Mail: Between 5 Dec. 1896 and 17 April 1897 Beerbohm published a weekly essay in the *Daily Mail.* See Riewald, *Sir Max Beerbohm,* p. 272.

Raymond Williams notes: *The Long Revolution* (rev. ed., 1961; rpt. New York, 1966), pp. 199–207.

six drawings: Beerbohm, *Letters,* 4 Dec. 1901, p. 148. The entire group was on exhibition at the Carfax Gallery, Nov.–Dec. 1901.
self-caricature: *Daily Mail,* 27 Dec. 1901; repub. in J. A. Hammerton, *Humorists of the Pencil* (1905), p. 68.

Page 25
His father founded: Riewald, p. 1.
The Clown: Beerbohm, letter to an Oxford journal, Jan. 1954, in Merton.
"known to have been engaged": Beerbohm, *Mainly on the Air,* p. 98.
"Max Mereboom": "1894," *Punch,* 2 Feb. 1895, 58.
World War II BBC broadcasts: pub. in *Mainly on the Air.*
"The *World*": Beerbohm, *Letters,* 24 April 1894, p. 94.

Page 26
music hall comedienne: Cissey Loftus; Beerbohm, *Letters,* 9 Aug. 1893, p. 42.
Oxford cricketer: C. B. Fry; "Fry of Wadham," *English Illustrated Magazine,* Aug. 1894, 1057–62.
interviewed twice: Ada Leverson, "A Few Words with Mr. Max Beerbohm," *Sketch,* 2 Jan. 1895, 439; Isabel Brooke Alder, "Max Beerbohm," *Woman,* 29 April 1896, 8–9.
"I meant all I said": Leverson interview.
three books at Oxford: William Rothenstein, *Men and Memories: Recollections of William Rothenstein, 1872–1900* (1931), p. 146.
"Diminuendo": pp. 149–160. First pub. as "Be It Cosiness," *The Pageant* (1895), pp. 230–5.

Page 27
"A Vain Child": *Saturday Review,* Christmas, 1896, 11; repub. in *Parodies: An Anthology from Chaucer to Beerbohm—and After,* ed. Dwight MacDonald (1960), pp. 460–2.
Struwwelpeter: pub. in Germany, 1845, trans. 1848; 12th English edition, 1863. Mark Twain's 1891 translation was published in the United States in 1935: Justin Kaplan, *Mr. Clemens and Mark Twain* (New York, 1966), p. 315.
"neither amusement in their folly": MS note in Merton.

Page 28
"Ah, that is an unfortunate trick": Beerbohm, *Zuleika Dobson: or An Oxford Love Story* (1911), p. 100.

"M. Bergson": Beerbohm, *And Even Now,* p. 303.

"I am quite easy": Beerbohm, letter to Anthony Eden, 25 Mar. 1922, in Taylor.

"My gifts are small": Lynch, *Max Beerbohm in Perspective,* p. viii.

Page 32

"To give an accurate": Beerbohm, "1880," in *Works,* p. 55.

"Myself when young—foolscap": in UCLA, Box 959, #34.

Harlequin edition: A. E. Gallatin and L. M. Oliver, *A Bibliography of the Works of Max Beerbohm* (1952), p. ix; Desmond MacCarthy, *Memories* (1953), pp. 192–8.

"the young coxcomb": Beerbohm, *Works,* Vol. I of the *Collected Edition* (1922), xiv.

"very well content that his sons": *Herbert Beerbohm Tree: Some Memories of Him and of His Art,* ed. Max Beerbohm (New York, 1920), p. 188.

Page 33

"When I started writing": Beerbohm, letter to Gordon Craig, 2 Oct. 1920 (probable date), in Bibliothèque Nationale, Paris (courtesy of Mme. Marie-Claire Hamard).

"gift of perpetual old age": Vincent O'Sullivan, *Aspects of Wilde* (1936), p. 68. See also Rothenstein, *Men and Memories* (1931), p. 144.

"cheeky comments": "Max Nobiscum!," *Saturday Review,* 19 June 1897, 690.

Whistler called him: "An Acknowledgement," *Saturday Review,* 27 Nov. 1897, 592.

"I never regard him": "Doctor Conan Doyle's Latest Case," *Saturday Review,* 26 Dec. 1896, 665.

Doyle responded: *Saturday Review,* 2 Jan. 1897, 15–16, and 9 Jan. 1897, 40–1.

"told with force": "Chromoconanography," *Saturday Review,* 10 July 1897, 31.

"a false, garish farrago": *More Theatres,* 21 Oct. 1899, p. 200.

Page 34

"dialogue would lose nothing": *More Theatres,* 21 Oct. 1899, p. 201.

"with frenzied eyes": caricature pub. in *Sketch,* 28 Sept. 1898, copy, Hart-Davis; described by Beerbohm in *Mainly on the Air,* p. 67.

"Possibly I may have seen": Beerbohm, *Letters,* 3 Dec. 1893, p. 83.

"There is no living man": "An Unhappy Poet," *Saturday Review,* 12 Sept. 1896, 282.

"Come out of your hole": *Era,* 3 Oct. 1896; cf. Beerbohm, *Letters,* p. 112.

Beerbohm replied: "Hold, Furious Scot!," *Saturday Review,* 10 Oct. 1896, 395–6.

"careless rapture": "An Appreciation," *Saturday Review,* 4 Sept. 1897, 254.

"very dainty and witty": Oscar Wilde, *The Letters of Oscar Wilde,* ed. Rupert Hart-Davis (New York, 1962), 15 Oct. 1897, p. 659.

he had recently spoken up: cf. Laurence Irving, *Henry Irving: The Actor and His World* (1951), pp. 614–16.

Page 35

"gay, but terrible, antagonist": "Papillon Rangé," *Saturday Review,* 20 Nov. 1897, 546.

"simple youth": *Saturday Review,* 27 Nov. 1897, 592.

antiquated impertinence: Unsigned note, *Saturday Review,* 4 Dec. 1897, 609.

"The continued demand": "Papillon Rangé," *Saturday Review,* 20 Nov. 1897, 546.

Page 36

"Autolycine style," "The voice drawls": Beerbohm, "Whistler's Writing," in *Yet Again* (1909), pp. 115–17.

Page 37

The two artists were satirized: *Punch,* 21 April 1894 through 21 Dec. 1895.

"'Twas rollog": Lynch, *Max Beerbohm,* p. 22.

"The Art of the Hoarding": *New Review,* July 1894; repub. in Albert Gallatin, *Aubrey Beardsley* (New York, 1945), pp. 110–11.

Kate Greenaway's illustrations: Brian Reade, *Aubrey Beardsley, 1872–1898* (1967), p. 14.

Page 38

Beardsley right away liked: Rothenstein, *Men and Memories* (1931), p. 182.

an 1897 article: Beerbohm, "Mr. Beardsley's Fifty Drawings," *To-morrow,* Jan. 1897, 28–35.

Beardsley . . . vignettes: pub. in three books of *Bon-Mots,* ed. Walter Jerrold (J. M. Dent, 1893 and 1894).
tiny figure: Reade, pl. 211.
"witnessed a miscarriage": Reade, p. 22.

Page 39
Another of the vignettes: Reade, pl. 232.
Beerbohm reacted: *Pall Mall Budget,* 7 Jan. 1894; copy, Hart-Davis.
Another drawing: pl. 12.

Page 40
"Of course I like": Beardsley, *Letters,* p. 227.
"brilliant" 1897 review: Beardsley, *Letters,* p. 241.
"He was in great form": Beerbohm, "Aubrey Beardsley," in *A Variety of Things* (1928), p. 225.

Page 41
Rape: cf. Beerbohm, letter to Holbrook Jackson, 30 Oct. 1913, in Taylor.

Page 42
Unlike Yeats: cf. *The Autobiography of William Butler Yeats* (New York, 1953), p. 199.

Page 43
"Ballade de la Vie Joyeuse": written in copy of Oscar Wilde, *The Picture of Dorian Gray* (1891), now in Houghton; pub. in *Max in Verse: Rhymes and Parodies,* ed. J. G. Riewald (Brattleboro, Vt., 1963), p. 7.
"Oscar Wilde": [Max Beerbohm,] "Oscar Wilde," by An American, *Anglo-American Times,* 25 March 1893; repub. in Beerbohm, *Letters,* pp. 285–92.
"A Peep into the Past": Privately printed (New York, 1923), with facsimile of MS.
The Happy Hypocrite: Yellow Book, XI (Oct. 1896), 11–44; repub. as *The Happy Hypocrite: A Fairy Tale for Tired Men* (1897; rpt. 1936); Beerbohm, *A Variety of Things,* pp. 309–53.
obituary article: as part of "A Satire on Romantic Drama," *Saturday Review,* 8 Dec. 1900, 719; repub. in Beerbohm, *Letters,* p. 136.
reviews [in *Saturday Review*]: *The Importance of Being Earnest:* 18 Jan. 1902, repub. in Beerbohm, *Around Theatres* (1953), pp. 188–91; 11 Dec. 1909, repub. in Beerbohm, *Last Theatres,* pp. 508–11; *Lady Windermere's Fan:* 26 Nov. 1904, repub. in *Last Theatres,* pp. 101–5; *Salome:* 13 May 1905, repub. in *Around*

Theatres, pp. 377–80; *A Florentine Tragedy:* 16 June 1906, repub. in *Last Theatres*, pp. 249–252.

De Profundis: "A Lord of Language," *Vanity Fair*, 2 March 1905, 309; repub. in *Oscar Wilde: The Critical Heritage*, ed. Karl Beckson (New York, 1970), pp. 248–51.

fairy tales: "The Story of the Small Boy and the Barley Sugar," "Yai and the Moon," pub. in 1897, repub. in *A Variety of Things*, pp. 277–88, 291–305.

notes: two pages of Holograph Notebook, in Berg.

annotations and drawings: particularly in Houghton and Clark.

short talk: Clark.

One of his early memories: *Herbert Beerbohm Tree*, ed. Max Beerbohm, p. 190.

"reap the scorching harvest": *Punch*, 14 Jan. 1882, 14.

George du Maurier: Beerbohm, "Punch," in *More*, p. 17.

Intentions: (1891) Beerbohm's copy in Clark.

Page 44

"I have designed": Beerbohm, *Letters*, June 1892, p. 22.

"that people": "Oscar Wilde."

Page 45

"like a silver dagger": Beerbohm, *Letters*, 21 April 1893, p. 37.

"Day of announcement": Holograph notes in Berg.

drawing of Richard Le Gallienne: pub. in Rothenstein, *Men and Memories, 1872–1900*, p. 238.

drawing of . . . Wilde and Douglas: pub. in Lord Alfred Douglas, *Oscar Wilde and Myself* (New York, 1914).

Page 46

"Mr. Max Beerbohm, who giggled": Douglas, *Oscar Wilde*, p. 57.

1895 . . . sketch: pub. in *Adam*, Nos. 241–3 (1954), viii.

"I am sorry to say": Beerbohm, *Letters*, 12 April 1893, p. 35.

"not soigné": Holograph notes in Berg.

"Oscar's coy, carnal smile": Beerbohm, letter to William Rothenstein, 1896, in Houghton.

"He is simply": Beerbohm, *Letters*, 2 Oct. 1893, p. 73.

"Apropos of my former self": Beerbohm, *Letters*, 19 Aug. 1893, pp. 52–3.

Page 47

"Bobbie has offended Oscar": Beerbohm, *Letters,* 29 Sept. 1893, p. 72.

Page 48

"the survivor": Beerbohm, "A Peep into the Past."

"a large measure": Beerbohm, *Letters,* 15 May 1893, p. 41. Cf. Preface, above.

"Remember": Rothenstein, *Men and Memories, 1872–1900,* p. 184.

Page 49

"Please give [Ross]": Beerbohm, *Letters,* 23 Aug. 1898, p. 131.

"Oscar has at length": Beerbohm, *Letters,* 12 Aug. 1894, p. 97.

"quite absurd": Beerbohm, *Letters,* 3 May 1895, p. 104.

Page 50

Wilde . . . named some friends: Wilde, *Letters,* 6 April 1897, p. 521.

"As days went by": Beerbohm, *The Happy Hypocrite* (1897; rpt. 1936), p. 56.

Wilde's parable: *Adam,* Nos. 241–3 (1954), 5.

"picking up a brickbat": Wilde, *Letters,* 28 May 1897, p. 576.

Page 51

"beginning at the end": Wilde, *Letters,* 27 May 1897, p. 575.

"When you are alone with him": Oscar Wilde, *Letters to the Sphinx from Oscar Wilde: with Reminiscences of the Author by Ada Leverson* (1930), p. 42.

"Max on Cosmetics": Wilde, *Letters,* ?20 April 1894, p. 355.

"Many a young man": *Intentions* (New York, 1909), p. 9.

writing to commiserate: Beerbohm, *Letters,* 11 Dec. 1900, p. 138.

Page 52

He asked the author: Stuart Mason, *Bibliography of Oscar Wilde* (1914), p. 214.

"They speak": *Around Theatres,* 18 Jan. 1902, p. 190.

Page 53

"Nothing seemed more likely": Beerbohm, "A Lord of Language," p. 309.

"appalling denunciation": Wilde, *Letters,* "De Profundis" letter to Alfred Douglas, Jan.–March 1897, p. 502.

Gide wrote: *Ermitage,* 15 April 1905; repub. in André Gide, *Oscar Wilde* (1951).

Page 54
random notes: Holograph Notebook, in Berg.

Chapter 3

Page 57
"shackles of verisimilitude": "The Critic as Artist," in *Intentions,* p. 143.

Page 58
Words for Pictures: partially collected for publication in *Yet Again.*
The Mirror of the Past: about 100 pages of notes, drafts, diagrams, and a twelve-page synopsis made between 1913 and 1916, in Taylor.
Rossetti and His Circle: drawn 1916–17, published 1922.
"unintelligent realism": *More,* p. 48.
Punch's cartoonists: "Punch," in *More,* pp. 15–26.
music hall: "The Blight on Music Halls," in *More,* pp. 117–26.
Madame Tussaud's: "Madame Tussaud's," in *More,* pp. 37–44.
actors: "Actors," in *More,* pp. 27–36.
"Pretending": in *More,* pp. 55–62.
essay on royalty: "Some Words on Royalty," in *More,* pp. 1–14.
"Gracious goodness!": "The Pervasion of Rouge," in *Works,* p. 109.

Page 59
"The Actor's medium": *More,* p. 30.
One piece in *More:* "An Infamous Brigade," pp. 63–72.
waxen effigies: "A Ragged Regiment," in *Yet Again,* pp. 235–44.
Another essay: "A Study in Dejection," in *Yet Again,* pp. 75–80.
civil courts: "Dulcedo Judiciorum," in *Yet Again,* pp. 265–80.
"Seeing People Off": in *Yet Again,* pp. 19–26.
"What's Hecuba": *Hamlet,* II, ii, 585–6.

Page 60
Coleridge: "On Poesy or Art" (1818), in *Criticism: The Major Texts,* ed. Walter Jackson Bate (New York, 1952), p. 395.

Page 61
New English Art Club: *Punch,* 5 May 1894, 208.

Attorney General: during the 1878 libel trial against John Ruskin. William Gaunt, *The Aesthetic Adventure* (New York, 1945), p. 109.

Page 62

portrait by Velázquez: "Don Baltasar Carlos in the Riding School," *New Liberal Review,* July 1901, 762–4.

Rubens's "Garden": in *Yet Again,* pp. 285–9.

Corot's painting: "Macbeth and the Witches," in *Yet Again,* pp. 301–6.

The Renaissance: The Renaissance: Studies in Art and Poetry (1872).

"Peter the Dominican": in *Yet Again,* pp. 295–8.

Page 64

"serenity in state": John Ruskin, *The Lamp of Beauty,* ed. Joan Evans (1959), p. 117.

"very second-rate Turner": Wilde, *Intentions,* p. 43.

Page 65

"Ten Years Ago": Manuscript in Merton. Cf. Edward Beddington-Behrens, *Look Back Look Forward* (1963), p. 125. Copy of painting, Hart-Davis.

Eliot's poems: Letter to Sydney Schiff, 15 Feb. 1939, in Merton.

"Wot's the good": "Music Halls of My Youth," in *Mainly on the Air,* p. 38; Beddington-Behrens, *Look Back,* p. 126.

Page 66

"pass into the condition": in "The School of Giorgione."

"more creative": Oscar Wilde, "The Critic as Artist," Part II, in *Intentions,* p. 223.

"'Ho-Tei'": originally pub. in Mrs. Aria, *The May Book* (1901); repub. in *Yet Again,* pp. 310–14.

"Ten O'Clock": Whistler, *The Gentle Art,* p. 159.

"readiness to decapitate": *Confessions of a Young Man* (1888; rpt. 1928), p. 119.

"Decay of Lying": Wilde, *Intentions,* p. 47.

Page 67

"incarnate": *Around Theatres,* 22 June 1901, p. 156.

fleshy word portraits: George Moore, *Modern Painting* (1893), p. 74.

"no one but Ruskin": "George Moore," in *Mainly on the Air,* p. 78.

Page 68

Wilde's knowing allusion: in *Intentions,* p. 34.

"fat farmer," "who thinks of nothing": Moore, *Modern Painting,* p. 217.

A 1903 review: *Around Theatres,* 31 Oct. 1903, pp. 290–3.

"She is older": Walter Pater, "Leonardo da Vinci," in *The Renaissance.*

Page 69

Queen Victoria: *Around Theatres,* 9 July 1904, p. 332.

Prince of Wales: "Diminuendo," in *Works,* p. 154.

Robert Ross: *Robert Ross, Friend of Friends,* ed. Margery Ross (1952), p. 58.

Coriolanus: More Theatres, 27 April 1901, pp. 366–7.

"Dickens": originally pub. in *Saturday Review,* 15 Dec. 1906, 737–8; repub. in Beerbohm, *A Christmas Garland* (1912), pp. 179–85.

Page 70

Balzac and French Impressionism: "Balzac," in Moore, *Impressions and Opinions* (1891); Moore, *Reminiscences of the Impressionist Painters* (Dublin, 1906). Moore sent Beerbohm a copy of *Reminiscences* in 1906: Sotheby and Co., *The Library and Literary Manuscripts of the Late Sir Max Beerbohm* (1960), Lot 157.

"was a shy": George Moore, *Avowals* (New York, 1919), p. 215.

widower: "Diminuendo," in *Works,* p. 150.

an "old woman": Beerbohm, *Letters,* 20 Oct. 1898, p. 133.

"humpback *manqué*": Beerbohm, *Letters,* 8 March 1894, p. 90.

Miscellaneous Studies: (1895); Beerbohm's copy in Clark.

Page 71

"earnestly counselled": "Hethway Speaking" (an episode from *The Mirror of the Past,* given as a 1955 BBC broadcast), in *Mainly on the Air,* p. 117.

Page 72

"The past": Beerbohm, "Lytton Strachey," The Rede Lecture (Cambridge, Eng., 1943), p. 12; repub. in *Mainly on the Air,* pp. 173–92.

"Hethway Speaking": *Mainly on the Air,* pp. 109–18.

"a *temps perdu*": S. N. Behrman, *Portrait of Max* (New York, 1960), p. 41.

"There is no poetry": Behrman, p. 41.

The hundred pages: in Taylor.

Page 73

"too complicated": Behrman, p. 41.

began drawing Rossetti: the original drawings are in The Tate Gallery.

"another and surer aid": *Rossetti and His Circle*, p. vii. Further references will give plate number only.

Page 74

niece of Rossetti's: William Rothenstein, *Men and Memories, 1900–1922* (1932), p. 314.

trial drawings: in Merton.

"And what were they": pl. 4.

"queer indifference": frontispiece.

Wilde's annunciation: pl. 22.

One set: pls. 11, 13.

William Rossetti's 1895 memoir: *Dante Gabriel Rossetti: His Family-Letters, With a Memoir*, ed. William Michael Rossetti, 2 vols. (1895), p. 227.

Page 75

"Autumn 1862": pl. 13.

"if you brought Hendon": "Hethway Speaking," p. 111.

"he needed": *Dante Gabriel Rossetti*, p. 234.

"Anactoria": pl. 11.

"Rossetti's Courtship": pl. 2.

John Ruskin to Fanny Cornforth: pl. 7.

John Morley: pl. 18.

"complex and elusive": *Rossetti and His Circle*, p. vi.

Page 76

"band of shy artificers": "1880," in *Works*, p. 46.

Eric Bentley: *The Playwright as Thinker: A Study of Drama in Modern Times* (New York, 1946; rpt., 1955), p. 288.

Edmund Wilson: *Classics and Commercials: A Literary Chronicle of the Forties* (New York, 1950), p. 440.

Page 77

"I don't care a damn": *More Theatres,* p. 12.

multiple parody: "Press Notices on 'Punch and Judy,'" *Sketch,* 16 Oct. 1895, 644.

"Why I ought not": *Around Theatres,* 28 May 1898, p. 1.

"has to regard": *Around Theatres,* 17 Aug. 1907, p. 471.

Sherlock Holmes: *Around Theatres,* 6 May 1905, p. 373.

The Devil's Disciple: Around Theatres, 7 Oct. 1899, p. 40.

Page 78

Pinero: *Around Theatres,* 24 Oct. 1903, p. 286.

a child: *More Theatres,* 25 June 1898, p. 41.

cardboard horses: *Around Theatres,* 9 July 1898, p. 7.

historical figures: *Around Theatres,* 27 Jan. 1900, p. 55.

"brought the head": *Around Theatres,* 13 May 1905, p. 378.

"After Samson's": *Around Theatres,* 19 Dec. 1908, p. 530.

"If a mime": *Around Theatres,* 24 May 1902, p. 206.

Page 79

Gorki's *Lower Depths: Around Theatres,* 5 Dec. 1903, pp. 302–5.

Tolstoy's play: *Last Theatres,* 31 Dec. 1904, pp. 113–16.

"I dare say": *Around Theatres,* pp. 304–5.

Galsworthy's *Justice: Around Theatres,* 5 Mar. 1910, pp. 565–8.

Page 80

Webb . . . Churchill: Samuel Hynes, *The Edwardian Turn of Mind* (Princeton, New Jersey, 1968), p. 130.

Strife: Last Theatres, 20 Mar. 1909, pp. 440–3.

"sold his birthright": William Rothenstein, *Since Fifty: Men and Memories, 1922–1938* (1939), p. 129.

"Endeavour": *A Christmas Garland,* pp. 103–14.

Page 81

He asked why: *Around Theatres,* 23 Feb. 1907, p. 452.

Another review: *Last Theatres,* 15 June 1907, p. 300.

St. John Hankin: Beerbohm, *A Book of Caricatures* (1907), pl. 19.

"reality is overwhelming": *Around Theatres,* 13 April 1907, p. 461.

Pankhurst: *Last Theatres,* 24 Oct. 1908, pp. 392–6.

Hedda Gabler: Last Theatres, 9 Mar. 1907, pp. 279–82.

Rosmersholm: Around Theatres, 15 Feb. 1908, pp. 497–501.

"De Arte Theatrali": Exhibited 1901, pub. in *Cartoons: The Second Childhood of John Bull* (1911).

Page 82

A Social Success: pub. in *A Variety of Things,* pp. 234–73, and in *The Modern Theatre,* ed. Eric Bentley (New York, 1960), VI, 235–54.

Jones . . . "the only dramatist": *More Theatres,* 5 Nov. 1898, p. 76.

Pinero . . . "keeps abreast": *More Theatres,* 9 April 1898, p. 20.

leave off pastiches: *Around Theatres,* 7 July 1900, p. 96.

"a scorpion": note in UCLA.

begins by reporting: *Last Theatres,* 8 Feb. 1908, p. 341.

"Confessional": *Last Theatres,* 19 Feb. 1910, pp. 530–3.

Charley's Aunt: More Theatres, 29 July 1899, p. 178.

The Importance of Being Earnest: Around Theatres, 18 Jan. 1902, pp. 188–91.

Admirable Crichton: Around Theatres, 15 Nov. 1902, p. 232.

early essay: "The Blight on the Music Halls," in *More,* pp. 117–26.

various reviews: e.g., *Around Theatres,* 3 Dec. 1898, p. 11.

1942 reminiscence: "Music Halls of My Youth," in *Mainly on the Air,* pp. 33–42.

Page 83

"instilling a sense": *Mainly on the Air,* p. 41.

Punch and Judy: Beerbohm, Introductory essay to Russell Thorndike and Reginald Arkell, *The Tragedy of Mr. Punch* (1923), pp. 5–10.

Barrie pantomime: *Last Theatres,* 15 Apr. 1905, p. 152.

A Midsummer: More Theatres, 18 Feb. 1899, pp. 113–16; 20 Jan. 1900, pp. 230–3; *Last Theatres,* 29 Feb. 1908, pp. 346–7.

"the most impressive": *More Theatres,* p. 230.

Maeterlinck: *More Theatres,* 25 June 1898, pp. 38–42.

Gordon Craig: *More Theatres,* 25 April 1903, p. 563.

Celtic drama: *More Theatres,* 13 May 1899, pp. 140–4.

"When Mr. Shaw": *More Theatres,* 21 May 1898, p. 25.

Shaw's valedictory: *Saturday Review,* 21 May 1898, pp. 682–3.

Page 84

"The younger generation": Henrik Ibsen, *The Master Builder,* in *Eleven Plays* (New York, n.d.), Act One, p. 310.

Beerbohm's blessings: Stephen Winsten, *Jesting Apostle* (1956), p. 129.

"Max only enjoyed my tricks": Hesketh Pearson, "Max Beerbohm and the Stage," typescript in UCLA, Box 959, #38.
Plays, Pleasant and Unpleasant: (1898), in Merton.
Shaw's wife: Katherine Lyon Mix, "Max on Shaw," *Shaw Review,* VI, No. 3 (Sept. 1963), 100.
"exquisite machine": *Last Theatres,* 1 July 1905, p. 167.
"the loud": *Around Theatres,* 2 Nov. 1901, p. 172.
"disputative machines": *More Theatres,* 21 May 1898, p. 25.
"every phrase": *Around Theatres,* 12 Sept. 1903, p. 270.

Page 85
"infinitely better": *Around Theatres,* 12 Sept. 1903, p. 268.
Beerbohm's caricature: *Fifty Caricatures,* pl. 8.
"For art's sake": *Around Theatres,* 12 Sept. 1903, p. 269.
Shaw would use any form: *More Theatres,* 8 June 1901, p. 385; *Around Theatres,* 12 Sept. 1903, p. 270.
Major Barbara: Around Theatres, 9 Dec. 1905, p. 412.
The Doctor's Dilemma: Around Theatres, 24 Nov. 1906, p. 445.
"uncomfortable": Holograph notebook, in Berg.
Shaw's characters: *More Theatres,* 21 May 1898, p. 25; *Last Theatres,* 9 Mar. 1907, p. 280.
Aesop's fables: Bernard Shaw, *Sixteen Self Sketches* (New York, 1949), p. 156.

Page 86
"to deny": *Around Theatres,* 9 Dec. 1905, p. 412.
Don Juan in Hell: Last Theatres, 8 June 1907, p. 296
Getting Married: Around Theatres, 23 May 1908, pp. 508–12.
Misalliance: Around Theatres, 26 Feb. 1910, p. 561.
"My own first hostility": Holograph notebook, in Berg.
"something almost like dubiety": *Around Theatres,* 12 Nov. 1904, p. 356.

Page 87
fop: "One fine morning," *Colophon,* Part 10 (1932).
capitalist: copy, Hart-Davis.
vegetarian: copy, Hart-Davis.
"sleek and portly": cf. Beerbohm, *Letters,* p. 297.
self-advertiser: *Vanity Fair,* 28 Dec. 1905.
iconoclast: "The Iconoclast's one friend": copy, Hart-Davis.
peddler: *A Survey,* pl. 44.

Archibald Henderson: *George Bernard Shaw: His Life and Works* (1911); Beerbohm's copy in Berg.

Page 88

Irish actress: Grace Conover.

leading lady: Constance Collier; see her autobiography, *Harlequinade: The Story of My Life* (1929).

carpet slippers: Mix, *A Study in Yellow*, p. 249.

satiric drawings: exhibited at the Victoria and Albert Museum, Feb. 1968.

Chesterton's study: *George Bernard Shaw* (1909; rpt. New York, 1956), p. 190. Caricature pub. in *Daily Mail*, 20 Nov. 1909.

Page 89

"I strove with all": reported by Ezra Pound; pub. in *Max in Verse*, p. 124.

"A Straight Talk": *Saturday Review*, 22 Dec. 1906, 769; repub. in *A Christmas Garland*, pp. 155–63.

difficult to parody: Holograph notebook, in Berg.

plagiarism of William Blake: Preface to *Three Plays for Puritans*, in Bernard Shaw, *Complete Plays with Prefaces* (New York, 1963), III, 1.

Page 90

"life as logic": *More Theatres*, 29 Dec. 1900, p. 336.

Shaw . . . Hedda Gabler: *Last Theatres*, 9 Mar. 1907, p. 280.

"Death and disease": "Playgoing," in *Mainly on the Air*, p. 58.

Page 91

Ibsen's redemptive philosophy: *More Theatres*, 22 July 1899, p. 173.

When We Dead Awaken: trans. William Archer (1900), first English edition; in Merton.

on a pedestal: *Chap-book* (Chicago), 1 Oct. 1896.

The Poets' Corner: [pl. 5].

Christmas Garland parody: "A Recollection," in *A Christmas Garland*, pp. 133–43.

Tree . . . produced Ibsen: Miriam A. Franc, *Ibsen in England* (Boston, Mass., 1919), p. 168.

"The shadow": James Joyce, "Ibsen's New Drama," *Fortnightly Review*, 1 April 1900, 585.

imitators like Pinero: *More Theatres*, 9 April 1898, p. 20.

"pastiches" by Shaw: *Around Theatres,* 26 Jan. 1901, p. 120.

Page 92

Rosmersholm: Around Theatres, 15 Feb. 1908, pp. 497–501.

"quiet, subdued": *The Athenaeum,* 15 Feb. 1908, pp. 203–4.

"delightful elocution": *Theatre,* V, No. 50 (April 1905), 82.

"When is a man": James Joyce, *Finnegans Wake* (New York, 1939), p. 170.

Gosse and . . . Archer: Edmund Gosse, *Henrik Ibsen* (1907), p. 208; Charles Archer, *William Archer: Life, Work and Friendships* (1931), p. 261.

Punch: F. Anstey, "When We 'Figures of Speech' Philander," *Punch,* 18 April 1900, 285–8.

Page 93

"as plain as a pikestaff": Beerbohm, two letters to Florence Kahn, April 1905; copies, Hart-Davis.

review in 1903: *More Theatres,* 7 Feb. 1903, pp. 532–5.

"Woe to them": Amos 6:1.

Carlyle . . . Arnold: Matthew Arnold, "Hebraism and Hellenism," in *Culture and Anarchy [1869] with Friendship's Garland and Some Literary Essays,* ed. R. H. Super, *The Complete Prose Works of Matthew Arnold,* V (Ann Arbor, Mich., 1965), p. 168. Arnold attributes the entire phrase to Carlyle, who in fact said Plato, not Socrates. Beerbohm used the phrase again: *Last Theatres,* 16 Feb. 1907, p. 278.

Page 94

"ordinary people": Oscar Wilde, *Intentions,* p. 160.

Chesterton: *George Bernard Shaw,* pp. 32–4.

"Throughout his life": "Ibsen," in *Around Theatres,* 26 May 1906, p. 436.

Chapter 4

Page 95

"He would chuckle": Vyvyan Holland, letter to Elisabeth Beerbohm, 22 May 1956, in Merton.

"What he excelled me in": Max Beerbohm, "From a Brother's

Standpoint," in *Herbert Beerbohm Tree,* ed. Max Beerbohm, p. 189.

Page 96

Caldecott . . . Greenaway . . . Lewis Carroll . . . Thackeray: copies in Merton.

Hoffmann's *Struwwelpeter:* twelfth English edition, 1863.

a chatty essay: "Caricature and Lithography in Paris" (1886).

Warden of Merton: *Caricatures of Twenty-Five Gentlemen,* pl. 18.

Caricature is "a recreation": "The Art of Caricature: A Talk with Mr. Max Beerbohm," by Raymond Blathwayt, *Cassell's Magazine,* Feb. 1903, 279.

almost never illustrated: with the exception of *Seven Men,* American edition (1920), and a set of drawings for *Zuleika Dobson,* published after Beerbohm's death.

"to refresh": Beerbohm, pencil draft of letter to Mr. Samuel, Jan. 1935, in Taylor.

"A Peep": in Berg.

Page 97

Lang . . . Moore: "Andrew Lang," draft in Merton. George Moore: Sotheby and Co., Lot 330.

"that quality": "George Moore," in *Mainly on the Air,* pp. 74–89.

"I liked the comedy": Beerbohm, letter to Edmund Gosse, 26 Jan. 1917, in Ashley Library, British Museum.

Read's *English Prose Style:* (1931), in Merton.

Page 98

"When a man": "Whistler's Writing," in *Yet Again,* p. 109.

earliest self-caricature: pub. in Bohun Lynch, *Max Beerbohm,* p. 106.

photograph of Yeats: H. S. Krans, *William Butler Yeats* (New York, 1904), in Merton.

Tennyson, Watson, Kipling: Sotheby and Co., Lots 224, 237, 139.

Page 99

Henderson: *George Bernard Shaw* (1911), in Berg.

Page 100

Photographs showing Tree: Mrs. George Cran, *Herbert Beerbohm Tree* (1907), in Merton.

"armed neutrality": *Herbert Beerbohm Tree,* ed. Max Beerbohm, p. 200.

"My brother": 1920 note in copy of *Caricatures of Twenty-Five Gentlemen* (1896), in Taylor.

memorial volume: *Herbert Beerbohm Tree.*

Another caricature: "Genus Beerbohmiense," in Taylor.

"I do believe": *Herbert Beerbohm Tree,* p. 200.

memories of Tree: *Herbert Beerbohm Tree,* p. 191.

Page 101

theorized in 1901: "The Spirit of Caricature," in *A Variety of Things,* pp. 205–17.

as Freud did: Sigmund Freud, *Jokes and Their Relation to the Unconscious* [1905], trans. James Strachey (1960), pp. 194–209.

Page 102

"when he looked at me": Wilfred Owen, *Collected Letters,* ed. Harold Owen and John Bell (1967), p. 529.

Plasticine: *Robert Ross,* ed. Margery Ross, p. 71.

John Davidson: Beerbohm, *A Book of Caricatures,* pl. 26.

"Curious that it": Benjamin J. Townsend, *John Davidson: Poet of Armageddon* (New Haven, Conn., 1961), p. 384.

"the only writing person": Townsend, p. 395.

Page 103

"I never pretend": Leverson, "A Few Words," p. 439.

"that terrible power": Lady Ottoline Morrell, *Ottoline: The Early Memoirs of Lady Ottoline Morrell,* ed. Robert Gathorne-Hardy (New York, 1964), p. 118.

"patent mechanical": pub. in *Bookman,* Aug. 1911.

"Body and Soul": pub. in *The Sketch,* Christmas 1958, pp. 26–7.

"the joy of his creator": "The Spirit of Caricature" (1901), p. 214.

last caricature: owned by Mrs. Eva Reichmann, London.

"Beerbohm has caricatured": Joseph Hone, *The Life of George Moore* (1936), p. 287.

Page 104

"Max and others": Hone, p. 307.

perceive visual art: Vernon Lee, "Art and Life, III," *Contemporary Review,* LXX (July 1896), 64; and "Beauty and Ugliness, I,"

LXXII (Oct. 1897), 544. See also E. H. Gombrich, "The Mask and the Face: The Perception of Physiognomic Likeness in Life and Art," unpub. lecture, 1968.

"decadent freaks": Alan Gowans, *The Unchanging Arts: New Forms for the Traditional Functions of Art in Society* (Philadelphia, Pa., 1971), p. 373.

"a most brilliant": Oscar Wilde, *Letters,* p. 778.

"The caricaturist merely passes": Leverson, p. 439.

"I see them": Robert Hichens, *Yesterday* (1947), p. 86.

Page 105

Shaw shows him: "A Counsel of Perfection" (1907); copy, Hart-Davis.

"Most men": "Prefatory Note" by Beerbohm in William Rothenstein, *Six Portraits of Rabindranath Tagore* (1915), pp. ix–x.

caricature of James: *The Academy,* LV (26 Nov. 1898), 339; repub. in Beerbohm, *Max's Nineties,* ed. Rupert Hart-Davis and Allan Wade, intro. Osbert Lancaster (1958), pl. 26.

Page 106

"A profoundly humiliating": Philip Guedalla, *Masters and Men* (1923), p. 101.

"Certainly the pages of *Punch*": Henry James, *Daumier: Caricaturist* (1954), p. 4.

Keene . . . du Maurier . . . Sambourne: Beerbohm, "Punch," in *More,* pp. 15–23.

no pure caricature: "The Spirit of Caricature," p. 205.

Page 107

George Meredith: *Vanity Fair,* 24 Sept. 1896; repub. *Vanity Fair* Supplement, 24 Feb. 1909.

Baudelaire: Baudelaire, *The Painter,* p. 16 (Guys), p. 179 (Daumier).

"No thanks": Rothenstein, *Men and Memories, 1872–1900,* p. 146.

Page 108

"best drawing": pl. 10; written in Beerbohm's copy, in Merton.

Page 109

Swinburne: owned by Mrs. Philip Guedalla; pub. in Bohun Lynch, *A History of Caricature* (1926), pl. XIV.

Pellegrini: *Vanity Fair,* 21 Nov. 1874, p. 284.

Swinburne reportedly looked: T. Earle Welby, *A Study of Swinburne* (New York, 1926), p. 74.

Page 110

"instantaneous caricatures": Behrman, p. 239.

"A.B.": in *More*, pp. 143–9.

"These are caricature": Beerbohm, *Letters*, 22 April 1913, p. 225.

"and the rest": A. E. Gallatin, *Whistler's Pastels and Other Modern Profiles* (1913), p. 47.

"a really good synthesis": note in copy of *Caricatures of Twenty-Five Gentlemen*, in Taylor.

"It was obvious": David Low, *British Cartoonists, Caricaturists and Comic Artists* (1942), p. 35.

Page 112

Sargent's superficiality: *Zuleika Dobson* (1911), Ch. XVIII, p. 273.

1913 caricature: "We needs must love the highest when we see it," in Beerbohm, *Fifty Caricatures* (1913), pl. 43.

he caricatured Fry: "Significant Form" (1920–1), pub. in Clive Bell, *Old Friends* (1956); "A Law-Giver" (1931), in National Portrait Gallery, London.

"He kept on turning": Virginia Woolf, *A Writer's Diary*, p. 294.

"ruthless monstrifier": Behrman, p. 148.

"the first non-realistic works": in Beerbohm's 1952 Birthday Book, Merton.

"perfectly amazing": Virginia Woolf, *Roger Fry* (New York, 1940), p. 118.

"dispense once for all": Roger Fry, "Essay in Aesthetics," in *Vision and Design* (New York, 1947), p. 25. See also Arthur Koestler, "Caricature and Satire," in *The Act of Creation* (New York, 1964; rpt. 1967), p. 71.

"untrue" physically: 1920 note in copy of *Caricatures of Twenty-Five Gentlemen*, in Taylor.

"Being so drastic": "The Spirit of Caricature," p. 214.

Page 113

Philipon's . . . Louis Philippe: E. H. Gombrich, *Art and Illusion*, p. 291.

two caricatures: "La poire reversée" [sic] (1912), owned by Philip Hofer; Whistler: copy, Hart-Davis.

Page 114

Years later: 1920, in copy of *Caricatures of Twenty-Five Gentlemen,* in Taylor.

"The whole man must be melted down": "The Spirit of Caricature," p. 214.

Balfour: "Two Eminent Statesmen," *Pall Mall Budget,* 5 July 1894; copy, Hart-Davis.

a 1907 drawing: *A Book of Caricatures,* pl. 43.

Edward Carson: Fifty Caricatures, pl. 10; Beerbohm, *A Survey* (1921), pl. 12.

Page 115

Frank Harris: *Caricatures of Twenty-Five Gentlemen,* pl. 8.

Bonar Law: *Fifty Caricatures,* pl. 1.

Kipling and Pinero: in copy of *Caricatures of Twenty-Five Gentlemen,* in Taylor.

William Archer: in Ashmolean.

Pinero's eyebrows, "like skins": Edward Marsh, *A Number of People* (1939), p. 103.

Page 116

"One fine morning": (1911), pub. in *Colophon,* Part 10 (1932).

"some sort of mood": Beerbohm, "First Meetings with W. B. Yeats," in *Mainly on the Air,* p. 96.

he caricatured the poet: *Max's Nineties; The World,* Christmas 1900; *The Poets' Corner.*

Page 117

"As years went by": "First Meetings with W. B. Yeats," p. 101.

"sombrous and psychic": Beerbohm, letter to Mabel Beardsley, 2 Feb. 1914, in the J. Harlin O'Connell Collection of the Eighteen Nineties, Department of Rare Books and Special Collections, Princeton University Library.

Page 118

"Do you notice": "The Art of Caricature," p. 277.

"The Old and the Young Self": Beerbohm, *Observations* (1925), pls. 34–51.

copy of *Caricatures of Twenty-Five Gentlemen:* in Taylor.

Page 121

another copy: Sotheby and Co., Lot 5.

Page 122

"always stepped out of F.C.G.": Holograph notes (28 folio pages), in Berg.

"wicked—but great": Holograph notes, in Berg.

to hear Gladstone: Beerbohm, "A Small Boy Seeing Giants," in *Mainly on the Air,* p. 30.

"Men Who Matter": in *The Bystander,* XXIV and XXXV (1 May–14 Aug. 1912).

"Each one of them": Beerbohm, "A Small Boy Seeing Giants," p. 26.

"mere disinterested flunkeyism": Beerbohm, *Letters,* 4 Dec. 1901, p. 149.

Page 123

Haldane: *A Book of Caricatures,* pl. 46.

Queen Victoria's puffy eyes: Beerbohm, *Things New and Old* (1923), pl. 10.

"Studies in the Eighteen-Seventies": Beerbohm, *Things New and Old,* pls. 34–49.

three Cecil brothers: *Fifty Caricatures,* pl. 24.

Henry Chaplin . . . "Ultimus Victorianiorum": pl. 14; copy in Taylor.

"unlike Rosebery": Holograph notebook, in Berg.

Page 124

1885, 1897, and 1912: *Catalogue of an Exhibition Entitled "Ghosts" by Max Beerbohm* (Leicester Galleries, 1928), Nos. 96–8.

Millais's: copy, Scottish National Portrait Gallery, Edinburgh.

Rosebery's biographer: Robert Rhodes James, *Rosebery* (New York, 1964), p. 489.

"faces that have always": note on sketch for mural; copy, Hart-Davis.

Page 125

Beerbohm went on imagining Edward: copies, Hart-Davis. Very few of these have been published; see *Fifty Caricatures,* pl. 47.

a new coin: pub. in *Bandwagon,* June, 1902; owned by Mrs. Philip Guedalla.

"The Edwardyssey": copy, Hart-Davis.

"The rare, the rather awful": *Things New and Old,* pl. 10.

"Edward VII of Blessed Memory": copy, Hart-Davis.

seven decades: "Proposed Illustrations for Sir Sidney Lee's forthcoming biography" (1921); copy, Hart-Davis.

Duchess of Westminster . . . "scarifying": Riewald, *Sir Max Beerbohm,* p. 26.

Page 126

ridiculing Labour: Cecil, *Max,* p. 387.

"The Old Familiar Figure": copy, Hart-Davis.

The 1913 caricature: "Mr. Bernard Shaw," in *Fifty Caricatures,* pl. 8.

Thynne: *Fifty Caricatures,* pl. 29.

Page 127

"Servants": (1918), in *And Even Now,* pp. 161–82.

"Something Defeasible": Beerbohm, *And Even Now,* pp. 215–23.

enormous proletarian: "Our Complex World." Exhibited at Leicester Galleries, May 1921.

The *Daily Herald* objected: Cecil, *Max,* p. 387. "The Patron": pl. 30.

The *Manchester Guardian:* 21 January 1922. "When Labour Rules": pl. 16.

"Communist Sunday School": pl. 25.

Page 128

British good sense: "Recurrent Alarms," in *Observations,* pl. 24.

"Civilisation and the Industrial System": pl. 6. Governing Classes and Communism: pl. 16.

class consciousness: *Observations,* pl. 32.

"uniform dreariness": Beerbohm, "Unattractive, Undramatised," in *Around Theatres,* 23 Feb. 1907, p. 452.

Page 129

"If they were flourishing": (1936), pub. in *Manchester Guardian,* 13 May 1936, p. 7. See also "Eminent personage," Holograph notebook, in Berg.

double self-caricature: copy, Hart-Davis.

"the Demon of Uniformity": *Strand,* Oct. 1946, pp. 51–5.

"They are uncaricaturable": "The Art of Caricature" (Feb. 1903), p. 277.

Page 130

redoing fashion advertisements: Items in Merton.

he caricatured Jews: Turner—in *A Book of Caricatures,* pl. 18, and in Beerbohm, *Letters,* p. 176; Jewish financiers—"Are we as welcome as ever?" in *Fifty Caricatures,* pl. 47; London's orthodox Jewry—Robert Speaight, *William Rothenstein* (1962), p. 165; cf. also Beerbohm's caricature, "A Quiet Morning in the Tate Gallery," with replica of Rothenstein's "Jews Mourning in a Synagogue," in Tate Gallery.

"Jermyn Street": copy, Hart-Davis.

"Messrs Carfax": (1901), copy, Hart-Davis.

Malcolm Muggeridge: "A Survivor," *New York Review,* V, No. 8 (25 Nov. 1965), 31.

Ezra Pound suggested: in "Brennbaum," *Hugh Selwyn Mauberley* (1920).

German-Jewish woman: Elisabeth Jungmann, former secretary of Gerhart Hauptmann.

"cosmopolosemitics": *Around Theatres,* 15 Nov. 1902, p. 232.

always denied it: Beerbohm, letter of 12 Mar. 1954; copy, Hart-Davis.

Teddy Roosevelt: in "Men Who Matter," *Bystander,* XXXV, 325. Woodrow Wilson: *A Survey,* pl. 50.

Page 131

Pound: "Mr. Ezra Pound"; copy, Hart-Davis.

"Crazy": Behrman, p. 280.

Americans: Whistler—in *Max's Nineties, Rossetti and His Circle;* Sargent—in *Observations;* James—see Ch. V, below; Harland, Harris—in *Caricatures of Twenty-Five Gentlemen;* Pennell—in *Fifty Caricatures;* Whitman—in *The Poets' Corner;* Mark Twain—copies, Hart-Davis.

Oscar Wilde announces . . . Rossetti: *Rossetti and His Circle,* pl. 22.

Woodrow Wilson: "President Wilson addressing Congress" (1913), *A Survey,* pl. 50.

Rhodes Scholarship: *A Book of Caricatures,* pl. 45.

"If you will guarantee": Beerbohm, letter to Mr. Reid, 18 Jan. 1926, in Merton; quoted in Cecil, *Max,* p. 414.

Page 132

The Second Childhood of John Bull: Exhibited in 1901 at the Carfax Gallery, published in 1911.

"the most savage Radical": George Bernard Shaw, *Pen Portraits and Reviews* (1932), p. 235.

"the only feeling that our Colonies": Beerbohm, "General Elections," in *Yet Again,* p. 145.

Page 133

dear old England: Beerbohm, *Letters,* 6 Sept. 1914, pp. 234 ff.

not to allow any exhibition: Oliver Brown, *Exhibition* (1968), p. 189.

Charles Masterman: Rothenstein, *Men and Memories, 1900–1922,* p. 312.

Arnold Bennett insisted: Bennett, letter to Beerbohm, ca. 1918, in Merton.

Beerbohm sensed: Beerbohm, letter to Arnold Bennett, 1 Dec. 1915, in Berg.

"Pillars of Our State": Catalogue, *One Hundred Caricatures by Max Beerbohm* (Carfax & Co., Ltd., Nov. 1901).

Chamberlain: on exhibit, the Beerbohm Room, Merton College.

Tory Anarchist: "Servants," in *And Even Now,* p. 185.

Page 134

"wild men": Beerbohm, letter to William Rothenstein, Oct. 1929, in Houghton.

"rabble": Cecil, *Max,* p. 388.

"I have abandoned": *Catalogue of an Exhibition entitled "Ghosts" by Max Beerbohm* (Leicester Galleries, Nov.–Dec. 1928), p. 7.

sold for four or five pounds: as per notations in 1901 Catalogue, in Merton; sold for forty or fifty: notes on sales in UCLA, Box 959, #6.

"If you don't approve": Beerbohm, letter to Martin Hardie, 8 Sept. 1924, in UCLA, Box 940.

"Memory of Henry Irving": in Ashmolean.

Page 135

drawing of Meredith: in Department of Special Collections, Stanford University Library.

one of Whistler: pub. in Hesketh Pearson, *The Man Whistler* (1952).

two self-caricatures: in his copy of Lady Margaret Sackville, *Hundred Little Poems* (1928), in Merton.

Stanley Baldwin: *Observations*, pl. 17.

Edward VII and Moore: owned by Eva Reichmann, London.

"really see": "The Art of Caricature," p. 277.

Page 136

Sargent: *Fifty Caricatures*, pl. 41. Shaw: *passim*. Whistler: with Sir William Eden, pub. in Pearson, *The Man Whistler*.

"Mr. Tennyson," "Mr. Robert Browning": *The Poets' Corner*, [pls. 10 and 2].

Wordsworth: *The Poets' Corner*, [pl. 9].

Lytton Strachey: *A Survey*, pl. 6.

Kipling: (1903), *Things New and Old*, pl. 19.

Conrad: *A Survey*, frontispiece.

"Mr. W. B. Yeats . . . Mr. George Moore": *The Poets' Corner*, [pl. 14].

Page 137

"Mr. Thomas Hardy": *Fifty Caricatures*, pl. 25.

"show greater insight": Beerbohm, letter to Edmund Gosse, 19 Sept. 1919, in Berg.

He drew Beardsley: *Caricatures of Twenty-Five Gentlemen*, pl. 12.

Phil May: (1894); *Max's Nineties*, pl. 3.

himself, once: "Sir Max" (1939), in Clark; Rothenstein: in William Rothenstein, *Twenty-Four Portraits* (1920), [pl. 2].

to conceive situations: cf. the series "Mr. Gladstone goes to Heaven" (1899), in *Max's Nineties*, pls. 35–45.

Henry James in . . . fog: *A Book of Caricatures*, pl. 11.

James . . . kneeling tensely: (probably 1910–11), in Ashmolean.

Chapter 5

Page 141

parody of Henry James: "The Mote in the Middle Distance," *Saturday Review*, 8 Dec. 1906, 702–3; repub. in Beerbohm, *A Christmas Garland* (1912).

"Henry James never mentioning": Rothenstein, *Men and Memories* (1931), p. 290.

Page 142
The Wings of the Dove: (New York, 1902).
The Golden Bowl: (New York, 1904).

Page 143
a new passage: a single page, rough draft, in Clark; four pages sent with Beerbohm's letter to Edmund Gosse, 30 July 1925, in O'Connell Collection, Princeton University Library.

Page 144
could be disastrous: Edith Wharton, *A Backward Glance* (New York, 1964), p. 189.

Page 145
he felt inhibited: Desmond MacCarthy, *Memories,* p. 195.
"no one, now, can write": indirect quotation, letter of Edmund Gosse to Beerbohm, Christmas Eve 1912, in Evan Charteris, *The Life and Letters of Sir Edmund Gosse* (1931), p. 350.
informal caricature: in Beerbohm's Diary, Berg Collection; Sotheby and Co., title page.
Half Hours with the Dialects of England: in *Max in Verse,* pp. 20–5.

Page 146
"fastidious coyness": *More Theatres,* 10 May 1902, p. 462.
"Their lips": Holograph notes, in Berg; from Henry James, *The Golden Bowl* (1905), p. 220.
Man in the Iron Mask: "Ideal," pub. in *The Bookman,* Aug. 1911, 208.

Page 147
"Mr. Henry James in the act": Behrman, p. 306.
James kneeling: (probably 1910–11), in Ashmolean; exhibited in 1928.
"what's ignoble": Maxwell Geismar, *Henry James and the Jacobites* (Boston, Mass., 1963), p. 209.
essay on D'Annunzio: Henry James, "Gabriele D'Annunzio," *Quarterly Review,* CXCIX (April 1904), 383–419; repub. in James, *Notes on Novelists* (1914) and James, *Selected Literary Criticism,* ed. Morris Shapira (New York, 1964), pp. 265–96.
praise James: *Around Theatres,* 27 Feb. 1909, p. 542.

Page 148

"Mr. Henry James revisiting": (1905), in *A Book of Caricatures,* pl. 48.

The American Scene: (New York, 1907).

He wrote to James: Beerbohm, *Letters,* 22 Dec. 1908, p. 178.

a fine drawing: copy, Hart-Davis.

Page 149

"awful vision": Holograph notes, in Berg.

"Your fine eyes": from a sonnet in which Beerbohm and Edmund Gosse wrote alternate lines; *Max in Verse,* p. 19.

notion for *The Turn of the Screw:* copy, Hart-Davis.

London fog: *A Book of Caricatures,* pl. 11.

"a figure with a pair of eyes": Henry James, Preface to *The Portrait of a Lady,* in *The Art of the Novel,* ed. Richard P. Blackmur (New York, 1934), p. 46.

a reminiscence: "An Incident," in *Mainly on the Air,* pp. 119–20.

Yellow Book: Henry James, "The Death of the Lion," I; "The Coxon Fund," II.

imagining paintings: *Around Theatres,* 24 Nov. 1906, p. 444.

"Books Within Books": in *And Even Now,* pp. 101–13.

Page 150

"The Figure in the Carpet": in *Embarrassments* (1896); "The Middle Years," in *Terminations* (1895).

"I can only gather": Beerbohm, *Letters,* 19 Dec. 1908, p. 178.

Page 151

notebook entries: Henry James, *The Notebooks of Henry James,* eds. F. O. Matthiessen and K. B. Murdock (New York, 1947).

"that perfect master": *More Theatres,* 10 May 1902, p. 462.

"large and luminous whole": *Around Theatres,* 27 Feb. 1909, p. 542.

psychological expert: sketch for this caricature in Humanities Research Center, University of Texas at Austin.

"Grand Duke . . . Cardinal": written in Beerbohm's copy of James's *Notebooks,* in Houghton.

"any suggestion": Wharton, *A Backward Glance,* p. 175.

his copy of James's *Notebooks:* in Houghton.

Page 152
Art and the Actor: (New York); Beerbohm's copy in Houghton.

Page 153
"patching pale grey silk": Beerbohm, "From of Yore," *Observer,* 13 Nov. 1949, 7.
"I hold, with you": 30 July 1925, in O'Connell Collection, Princeton University.
"a solecism": Beerbohm, letter to Theodora Bosanquet, 8 Nov. 1946, in Houghton.
"The Guerdon": Autograph manuscript in Houghton; first separate, unauthorized edition, 1925; repub. in *A Variety of Things,* pp. 133–8.

Page 154
reviewed a play by James: "The High Bid"; *Around Theatres,* 27 Feb. 1909, p. 540.

Page 155
kept on returning: see notes in Beerbohm's copy of James, *Terminations,* in Merton.
"pangs of longing": Beerbohm, *Letters,* 18 Nov. 1937, p. 280.
James's amazing method: *Around Theatres,* 27 Feb. 1909, p. 542.
"a dead failure": Beerbohm, letter to Simon Nowell-Smith, 24 Sept. 1946, in Taylor.

Page 156
a memory in 1920: in Beerbohm's copy of James, *The Finer Grain* (1910), in Merton.
"'Seasonable Tributes'": Rothenstein, *Men and Memories* (1931), p. 289.
defined as burlesque: cf. Gilbert Highet, *The Anatomy of Satire* (Princeton, N.J., 1962), pp. 13, 67; also Koestler, "The Trivial and the Exalted," in *The Act of Creation* (New York, 1964), p. 69, and W. H. Auden, *The Dyer's Hand* (New York, 1962), p. 382.

Page 157
"Scruts": *A Christmas Garland,* pp. 85–99.
"Some Damnable Errors About Christmas": *A Christmas Garland,* pp. 51–7; first pub. as "Christmas Day," *Saturday Review,* 29 Dec. 1906, 798–9.

Page 158

1896 parody: "The Defossilized Plum-Pudding," *Saturday Review,* Christmas 1896, p. 9; repub. in *Parodies,* ed. MacDonald, pp. 207–9.

"Perkins and Mankind": *A Christmas Garland,* pp. 33–47; first pub. as "General Cessation Day (Chapter V. of 'Sitting Up For the Dawn')," in *Saturday Review,* 29 Dec. 1906, 797–8.

judo: cf. *Parodies,* ed. MacDonald, p. xiii.

Page 159

"P.C., X, 36": *Christmas Garland,* pp. 13–20; first pub. in *Saturday Review,* 15 Dec. 1906, 736–7.

"Rudyard Kipling": *Around Theatres,* 14 Feb. 1903, p. 245.

"the schoolboy": Beerbohm, letter to Holbrook Jackson, 30 Oct. 1913, in Taylor.

cocksure midget: [pl. 20].

Another drawing: "De Arte Poetica," [pl. 13].

Page 160

"The Old Volunteer": in UCLA, Box 959, #5.

translation of *The Brothers Karamazov:* by Constance Garnett, 1912.

"Kolniyatsch": in *And Even Now,* pp. 47–54.

Page 161

"the growth of the literary conscience": p. 136.

Moore: see Beerbohm's presentation inscription to Moore in *A Christmas Garland;* copy owned by Joseph Bransten, San Francisco.

Bennett: Highet, *Anatomy,* p. 146. This may not be true.

Page 162

Maurice Baring: "All Roads—," first pub. in *John o' London's Weekly,* Christmas, 1939; repub. in *A Christmas Garland,* enl. ed. (1950).

"Its only fault": Baring, letter to Beerbohm, 14 Dec. 1939, in UCLA, Box 959, #21.

"a specialty of youth": *Last Theatres,* 11 June 1904, p. 67.

Page 163

"cleansing, exorcising": *Parodies,* ed. MacDonald, p. 501.

the school paper: Beerbohm, letter to the *Carthusian* (Oxford), Dec.

1886; repub. in Charles Evans, "A Note on 'Carmen Becceriense,'" *Book Collector,* Winter 1952, pp. 215–16.
first formal publication: "Carmen Becceriense" (1890); repub. in *Max in Verse,* pp. 1–3.
"Euphemia Lady Warburton": in UCLA, Box 959, #5.
"Surrey Saws and Sayings": *Abinger Chronicle* (Dorking, Surrey), April 1940, pp. 42–3.
literary women: Marie Corelli and Alice Meynell, in *Saturday Review,* Christmas 1896, pp. 8–11; and in *Parodies,* ed. MacDonald, pp. 201–4.

Page 164
The Artist's Life: (1904); Beerbohm's copy in Berg; repub. in Vineta Colby, *The Singular Anomaly: Women Novelists of the Nineteenth Century* (New York, 1970), pp. 227–8.
paragraph of slang: in UCLA, Box 959, #33.

Page 165
"bawd of parodies": Joyce, *Finnegans Wake,* p. 296.
crossword puzzle: 9 Mar. 1940, repub. 23 Aug. 1952.

Page 166
"It seems to me": "The House of Commons Manner," in *Yet Again,* p. 189.
"'How Shall I Word It?'": in *And Even Now,* pp. 13–26.

Page 168
"Max's queer crystalline sense": Maisie Ward, *G. K. Chesterton* (1944), p. 135.
"he does not indulge": G. K. Chesterton, *Autobiography* (1936), p. 98.
"Going Out for a Walk," "Hosts and Guests": in *And Even Now,* pp. 187–93, 125–46.
Boswell and Johnson: *Things New and Old,* pl. 33.
"camelion Poet": Keats, letter to Richard Woodhouse, 27 Oct. 1818, in *The Complete Poetical Works and Letters of John Keats* (Boston, 1899), pp. 336–7.

Page 169
"the toast of two hemispheres": *Zuleika Dobson,* Ch. II, p. 10. All further citations will be by chapter and page number in the first edition.

Page 170
"a vague memory": X, 172.
Arnold's rhapsody: Preface to *Essays in Criticism: First Series* (1865).
"does yet whisper": I, 1.
puts on his robes: XVIII, 271.
"Full on the face": X, 176.
"But would she ever": II, 23.

Page 171
"from the Vatican": II, 17.
"the Duke had already taken": III, 29.
"I, John, Albert": V, 57.

Page 174
"Louis Napoleon": V, 62.
"a third chef": V, 62.
"No apple-tree": II, 10.
William Empson: *Seven Types of Ambiguity,* 3rd ed. (1930; rpt. New Directions, n.d.), pp. 176–7.

Page 175
"Some clock clove": IV, 39.
"Duke, I guess": VIII, 132.
"Vae tibi": XIII, 201.
"Zeek w'ere": XVIII, 264.

Page 176
"fob off on his readers": X, 165.
"flashed down": XI, 181.

Page 177
"They are still vivid": XI, 178.
"what had been": XI, 180.
begun in 1898: Beerbohm, *Letters,* 27 June 1898, p. 130.
put off, and completed: Cecil, *Max,* p. 295; MS. of entire novel (written out between 1898 and 1911) and pencil draft of Chs. IX–XXIV (written in Italy, 1910–11), in Taylor.
"stronger and suppler": Beerbohm, *Letters,* 15 Feb. 1911, p. 194.

Page 178
"mild, miasmal air": XII, 189.

Page 179
"a bit of Manchester": "Diminuendo," p. 152.
"a wild infraction": in "Note" to 1947 edition, signed "M.B. 1946."

Page 180
"the astounding slickness": XVIII, 273.
written in the house: Leverson, "A Few Words."
Reggie Turner wrote: Beerbohm, *Letters,* 29 Oct. 1911, p. 208.
"to *behave like* real people": Beerbohm, *Letters,* 3 Nov. 1911, p. 209.
"who, catching his foot": VIII, 139.
Beerbohm advised the producers: letter, Hart-Davis.

Page 181
"Deeply regret": XIV, 217.
"Please don't interrupt": XV, 219.
action in stage fantasy: *Around Theatres,* 18 Jan. 1902, p. 190.
Don Quixote: Part Two, Ch. LIX.
a weekly article: *Around Theatres,* 4 Oct. 1922, pp. 224–5.

Page 182
"one great passive monster": X, 162.
"hyena woman": XIII, 204.
"a truer picture": Beerbohm, letter to Edmund Gosse, 15 Oct. 1911, in Taylor.
"mob of hoarse"; "boyish faces"; "dense mass": VII, 113; X, 162, XIX, 282.
"'Brave fellows!'": XIX, 288.
"looks like a foreigner": IV, 42.
"she-wizard": X, 160.

Page 183
"spirit of the higher thaumaturgy": X, 165.
Adah Menken: Jean Overton Fuller, *Swinburne: A Critical Biography* (1968), pp. 163–6.
"new toy": II, 20.
"As the homage": II, 15.

Page 184
"I had longed for it": IV, 52.
"flay" her: XIII, 201.

"I bow to your will": XXII, 325.
"virgincules": VII, 94.

Page 185
Walter Pater's nickname: Thomas Wright, *The Life of Walter Pater* (1907; rpt. New York, 1969), II, 119.
Pelléas et Mélisande: More Theatres, 25 June 1898, p. 38; *Around Theatres,* 30 June 1900, p. 91.

Page 186
Potiphar's wife: Genesis 39.
"Well, this is rather queer!": X, 167.

Chapter 6

Page 187
"Where the yellow spot is": Erwin Panofsky, *The Life and Art of Albrecht Dürer* (Princeton, New Jersey, 1955), p. 171.
"A Relic": in *And Even Now,* pp. 3–12.

Page 188
Roland Barthes: "The Structuralist Activity," *Partisan Review,* XXXIV, No. 1 (Winter, 1967), 83.
"'A Clergyman'": in *And Even Now,* pp. 233–41.

Page 190
essaylike format: *Seven Men*—Beerbohm, letter to The Century Company, 1919, in Houghton; *Zuleika Dobson*—Beerbohm, *Letters,* 10 July 1911, p. 204.

Page 191
Arthur Balfour: "Hilary Maltby and Stephen Braxton," p. 92.
journalistic career: "Enoch Soames."
illustrate "A. V. Laider": Beerbohm, letter to The Century Company.
"something to be worried about": Beerbohm, *Letters,* 3 Nov. 1911, p. 209.
"A. V. Laider": in *Seven Men,* pp. 139–71. Further references to this story by page number.
"awful things": p. 151.

Page 192
"imagination stampedes": p. 167.
"Sea-gulls?": p. 170.
seven dots: see manuscript of "A. V. Laider" in Houghton.

Page 193
"invention," "fable," "improvisation": pp. 164, 167, 168.

Page 194
He said in 1900: *More Theatres*, 10 Feb. 1900, p. 235.
"Savonarola" Brown: "'Savonarola' Brown," in *Seven Men*, pp. 175–219. Further references to this story by page number.
"extraordinarily unimaginative": p. 175.
"He made me understand": p. 178.
"I don't want puppets": p. 180.
"I don't see that": p. 182.

Page 195
"more immune": p. 184.
In composing: see two drafts of "'Savonarola' Brown," in Berg.
"Savonarola looks more grim": p. 185.
Wilde: cf. *A Florentine Tragedy* (1908); reviewed in *Last Theatres*, 16 June 1906, pp. 249–52.
Phillips: cf. *Paolo and Francesca* (1902); reviewed in *More Theatres*, 15 Mar. 1902, pp. 444–8.
Symons: cf. *Cesare Borgia* (1912), *Tristan and Iseult* (1917).

Page 196
"If the condolences": p. 189.
"SAV. And this is all": p. 197
Beerbohm said: Behrman, p. 140.
"the foul and greasy plebs": p. 198.
"the sovereign people": "Stage Crowds," in *Last Theatres*, 23 Oct. 1909, pp. 496–9.
"Citizens!": p. 200.

Page 197
"what men *would* do": p. 179.

Page 198
"Why, the very Novices": p. 209.
thirty-year moratorium: *Around Theatres*, 1 Oct. 1898, p. 8.

"I deem'd him": p. 215.
Burke: Speech at Bristol on Declining the Poll, 1780.
"very kind": p. 216.

Page 199
SAV. *has a speech:* p. 217.
"failed wretchedly": p. 219.
describing caricature: "The Spirit of Caricature," p. 215.
"Enoch Soames": in *Seven Men*, pp. 3–48. Further references to this story by page number.

Page 200
"Of course in Art": p. 8.
"Lean near": p. 11.
"a *bourgeois*": p. 15.

Page 201
"To A Young Woman": p. 16.
"lurid verses": "Diminuendo," p. 157.
Rhymers' Club: Beerbohm's satiric illustrations in *Book of the Rhymers' Club* (1892), Reginald Turner's copy; in Houghton.
Orchids: (1896).

Page 202
"Nocturne": p. 17.

Page 203
"just for this one afternoon!": p. 27.
"Fr egzarmpl": p. 39.

Page 205
"In his first visit": p. 46.
Soames was lucky: Beerbohm's note written in copy of *Cornhill Magazine*, June 1916, 55, in Clark. "Enoch Soames" first appeared in England in this issue.
extra illustrations: in Humanities Research Center, University of Texas at Austin.

Page 206
"try to make them know": p. 43.

Page 207
Baudelaire . . . on laughter: "The Essence of Laughter," in *The Painter*, pp. 164–5.

Harlequin actor: this anecdote, usually told about the clown Joseph Grimaldi, also appears in Thackeray, *The English Humorists,* p. 5.

"veteran exile": *Things New and Old,* pl. 21.

remark about acting: *Around Theatres,* 24 May 1902, pp. 206–7.

Page 208

"Yesterday I received": Beerbohm, letter to Woollcott, 10 March 1916, typescript in Houghton.

"shudder at the sight": *I Thought of Daisy* (New York, 1967), p. 99.

"Davidson was very poor": *Last Theatres,* 26 June 1909, p. 473.

Page 209

parodied his friend: *Saturday Review,* 8 Dec. 1906, pp. 203–4.

"I have known no man": "No. 2, The Pines" (1914), in *And Even Now,* p. 66.

"how definitely dreary": Fuller, *Swinburne,* p. 444.

Page 210

"raking-up": Beerbohm, letter to John Middleton Murry, 7 Aug. 1920, in Taylor.

"It *is* a pity": Beerbohm, *Letters,* 12 April 1904, p. 159.

Constance Collier's strong chin: in Ashmolean.

"My choice of stops": Beerbohm, letter to editor of *The Century Magazine* (New York), 6 March 1916, in Taylor.

Page 211

"I am quite ready": letter to Sidney Pawling, 16 Nov. 1911, in Beerbohm, *Letters,* p. 213.

"so neat and debonair": Constance Collier, *Harlequinade,* p. 152.

Page 212

Rebecca West: "Notes on the Effect of Women Writers on Mr. Max Beerbohm," in *Ending in Earnest* (New York, 1931), pp. 66–74.

"There's the wittiest mind": Cecil, *Max,* p. 370.

"something even of a tomboy": from Beerbohm's account of his sister Dora, written at her death in 1940; in Beerbohm, *Letters,* p. 293.

Page 213

fairy tales: "The Story of the Small Boy and the Barley Sugar," "Yai and the Moon"—see Ch. II, 3 above.

"The public . . . knows me": "A Cloud of Pinafores," in *More,* p. 175.

Peter Pan: Around Theatres, 7 Jan. 1905, pp. 357–61; *Last Theatres,* 28 Dec. 1907, pp. 334–7.

difference between Dodgson's: "Pantomime for Children," in *Last Theatres,* 14 Jan. 1905, pp. 116–20.

"in our changed city": Introduction to Thorndike, *The Tragedy of Mr. Punch,* p. 6.

"wrong's horrible results": *Last Theatres,* 14 Jan. 1905, p. 120.

"Elements of terror": *More,* p. 178.

playwrights adapted: *More Theatres,* 29 Dec. 1900, p. 338.

Page 214

cautionary verse: especially, that of Ann and Jane Taylor, which Kate Greenaway illustrated in 1883—*More,* p. 177; *Last Theatres,* 14 Jan. 1905, p. 120; *Yet Again,* p. 321.

"the Mosaic conscience": Speaight, *William Rothenstein,* p. 165.

"The sky-like limpid eyes": "Brennbaum" (1920), in *Personae: Collected Shorter Poems* (1952), p. 203.

"with a small head": Vyvyan Holland, *Son of Oscar Wilde* (1954), p. 191.

Page 215

"the triumph of style": Virginia Woolf, "The Modern Essay," in *The Common Reader* (1925; rpt. 1962), p. 275.

Page 216

Don Quixote: puppet scene—Part Two, Ch. XXVI; analogy—*Works,* p. 110.

on his deathbed: Behrman, p. 303.

Page 217

"Mr. Bennett and Mrs. Brown": in *The Captain's Death Bed* (1950), pp. 90–111.

Page 218

"with an acute sense": Beerbohm, letter to Virginia Woolf, 30 Dec. 1927, in Taylor.

"I can't go on, I'll go on": Samuel Beckett, *The Unnamable* (New York, 1958), p. 179.

Bibliographical Note

When Lord David Cecil's *Max* came out in 1964, it was reviewed by W. H. Auden, S. N. Behrman, Ian Fletcher, Stanley Kauffmann, Frank Kermode, Malcolm Muggeridge, V. S. Pritchett, George Steiner, Philip Toynbee, Evelyn Waugh, Stanley Weintraub, and others. The impression from reading them was that Beerbohm commanded a definite and enthusiastic, though not an organized, public, one not used to hearing itself heard. There is only a very small body of criticism on his work. The best-known books are biographies: *Max* and S. N. Behrman's *Portrait of Max* (1960). Cecil's is an official biography with a great deal of pertinent information, an acute, sympathetic view of Beerbohm, with little interpretation of the writings and caricatures. Behrman's sketches, first published serially in *The New Yorker,* are suggestive and charming. The reports of Beerbohm's attitudes and conversations are valuable to have, though a wry, gentle image of Max in his eighties does not represent his stature as an artist.

There are three books of criticism. Bohun Lynch, himself a caricaturist, had little to say about Beerbohm's writing in *Max Beerbohm in Perspective* (1922). His book makes perceptive remarks about caricature in general and about technical aspects of Beerbohm's drawings, but does not relate the two areas or discuss the psychology of caricature; he makes no attempt to bring any data from the life or writings to bear on the caricature, or to discuss the coexistence in Beerbohm of the kindred forms, caricature and parody. J. G. Riewald's *Sir Max Beerbohm: Man and Writer* (1953) includes a brief, informative life and character and a definitive bibliography; the book is invaluable for any student of Beerbohm.

It surveys his writings, emphasizing in particular his ancestry as an essayist and the stylistic parallels between him and Wilde. Riewald does not discuss caricature, and Beerbohm's unpublished writings were unavailable in 1953. Bruce J. McElderry's *Max Beerbohm* (1971) is a well-presented introductory survey.

Critical writing on Beerbohm in the twenties, thirties, and forties contains isolated perceptions, but always in passing, never developed. The tone is mostly discreet, well-turned, and careful not to bore the reader. This is especially true in reminiscential surveys of the eighteen-nineties. The chapters on Beerbohm in general surveys of British caricature are less adequate than Lynch. On the writing, Virginia Woolf has the most authoritative remarks, three pages on Beerbohm's essayistic personality and style, in *The Common Reader* (1925). Louis Kronenberger wrote a good essay in 1947, "The Perfect Trifler," but was caught, as most critics were, between asserting Beerbohm's artistic perfection and eschewing a claim of greatness. Edmund Wilson in a 1948 article (and another in 1963) avoids that catch by simply taking Beerbohm seriously, like any artist. Both articles are filled with aperçus, and an evident faith in Beerbohm's freshness. F. W. Dupee's essay-introduction to *Zuleika Dobson* is excellent, though he does not mention the structure of history and fiction that I find central to the novel. And W. H. Auden's review of *Max* is very much worth looking up.

Among still unpublished work and work in progress: a volume of uncollected essays, edited by Sir Rupert Hart-Davis; a collection of Beerbohm's letters to William Rothenstein, edited by Mary Lago; a catalogue of Beerbohm's caricatures, being compiled by Sir Rupert Hart-Davis; a volume of collected criticism on Beerbohm, edited by J. G. Riewald, to be published for the Beerbohm centennial in 1972; a manuscript on Beerbohm's dramatic criticism by Roy Huss.

The present bibliography is a personal one, including books and articles that were useful to me. Some peripheral items cited once in the Notes are not included. The major locations of unpublished Beerbohm materials are indicated at the beginning of the Notes.

Bibliography

Note: A Collected Edition of Max Beerbohm's writings was published by William Heinemann, London, 1922. It includes: I. *The Works;* II. *More;* III. *Yet Again;* IV. *And Even Now;* V. *A Christmas Garland;* VI. *Zuleika Dobson;* VII. *Seven Men;* in addition, in 1924, VIII. *Around Theatres,* Vol. I; IX. *Around Theatres,* Vol. II; and in 1928, X. *A Variety of Things.*

I. Bibliography on Max Beerbohm

Gallatin, A. E. *Sir Max Beerbohm: Bibliographical Notes.* Cambridge, Mass.: Harvard University Press, 1944.

——— and L. M. Oliver. *A Bibliography of the Works of Max Beerbohm.* London: Rupert Hart-Davis, 1952.

Riewald, J. G. *Sir Max Beerbohm, Man and Writer: A Critical Analysis With a Brief Life and Bibliography.* The Hague, 1953, pp. 213–333.

Sotheby and Co. *The Library and Literary Manuscripts of the Late Sir Max Beerbohm.* London, 1960.

II. Writings of Max Beerbohm

1. First Editions of Books:

And Even Now. London: William Heinemann, 1920.

Around Theatres. 2 vols. London, 1924; later ed., London: Rupert Hart-Davis, 1953.

A Christmas Garland. London: William Heinemann, 1912.

The Happy Hypocrite: A Fairy Tale for Tired Men. Orig. pub. in *Yellow Book*, Oct. 1896, pp. 11–44. Repub. in Beerbohm, *A Variety of Things*.

Herbert Beerbohm Tree: Some Memories of Him and of His Art, Editor. London: Hutchinson & Co., 1920.

Last Theatres. Ed. Rupert Hart-Davis. London: Rupert Hart-Davis, 1970.

Letters to Reggie Turner. Ed. Rupert Hart-Davis. London: Rupert Hart-Davis, 1964.

Mainly on the Air. London: William Heinemann, 1946; enl. ed. 1957.

Max in Verse: Rhymes and Parodies. Ed. J. G. Riewald. Brattleboro, Vt.: The Stephen Greene Press, 1963.

More. London: John Lane, The Bodley Head, 1899.

More Theatres, 1898–1903. Ed. Rupert Hart-Davis. London: Rupert Hart-Davis, 1969.

A Peep into the Past. New York: Privately Printed, 1923.

Seven Men. London: William Heinemann, 1919.

A Variety of Things. London: William Heinemann, 1928.

The Works of Max Beerbohm, with a Bibliography by John Lane. London: John Lane, The Bodley Head, 1896.

Yet Again. London: Chapman and Hall, 1909.

Zuleika Dobson: or An Oxford Love Story. London: William Heinemann, 1911; later ed. 1947.

2. Uncollected Articles, Reviews, Prefaces to books by other authors, etc.:

"A.B.W. 'Pastiche and Prejudice.'" *Times* (London), 15 Sept. 1921, p. 6a.

"Another 'Real Conversation.'" *Saturday Review*, 13 Feb. 1904, pp. 200–1.

"An Appreciation." *Saturday Review*, 4 Sept. 1897, p. 254.

"The Art of Caricature: A Talk with Mr. Max Beerbohm." by Raymond Blathwayt. *Cassell's Magazine*, Feb. 1903, pp. 277–9.

"Chromoconanography." *Saturday Review*, 10 July 1897, p. 31.

"Contempt for Ideas." *Saturday Review*, 28 Nov. 1903, pp. 668–9.

"Ex Cathedra V—Mr. Beardsley's Fifty Drawings." *To-Morrow*, Jan.-June 1897, pp. 28–35.

"From of Yore." *Observer*, 13 Nov. 1949, p. 7 [review of Henry James, *A Little Tour in France*].

"'Fry of Wadham.'" *English Illustrated Magazine,* Aug. 1894, pp. 1057–62 [interview].
"A Gallery of Significant Pictures." *Saturday Review,* 18 April 1903, pp. 483–5.
"Hold, Furious Scot!" *Saturday Review,* 10 Oct. 1896, pp. 395–6.
"The Incomparable Beauty of Modern Dress." *Spirit Lamp,* June 1893, pp. 90–8.
"Introduction." Dixon Scott. *Men of Letters.* London, 1916.
"A Letter to the Editor." *Yellow Book,* July, 1894, pp. 281–4.
"A Lord of Language," *Vanity Fair,* 2 March 1905, p. 309. [review of Oscar Wilde, *De Profundis*]. Repub. in Karl Beckson, ed. *Oscar Wilde: The Critical Heritage.* New York, 1970.
"Max Beerbohm in Italy." *Daily Mail,* Nov. 8, 9, 14, 15, 21, 27, 1906; Dec. 3, 11, 17, 27, 1906.
"Meditations of a Refugee." *The Book of the Queen's Dolls' House Library.* Ed. E. V. Lucas. London, 1924.
"Mr. Punch." Introduction to Thorndike, Russell and Reginald Arkell. *The Tragedy of Mr. Punch: A Fantastic Play in Prologue and One Act.* London, 1923.
"A Needed Noun." *Academy,* 8 Feb. 1902, pp. 149–50.
"A Note on 'Patience.'" London, [1918?].
"Old Surrey Saws and Sayings. Collected and communicated by Sir Max Beerbohm, P.R.A. (Professor of Rural Archaeology)." *Abinger Chronicle* (Dorking, Surrey), April 1940, pp. 42–3.
"Oscar Wilde, by An American." *Anglo-American Times,* 25 March 1893; repub. in Beerbohm, *Letters,* pp. 285–92.
"Papillon Rangé." *Saturday Review,* 20 Nov. 1897, p. 546.
"The Power of Inexpert Criticism." *Saturday Review,* 14 Dec. 1901, pp. 739–40.
Preface. John Rothenstein. *The Portrait Drawings of William Rothenstein, 1889–1925: An Iconography.* London, 1926.
Prefatory Letter. Ronald Searle. *The Female Approach, with Masculine Sidelights.* London, 1950.
Prefatory Note. William Rothenstein. *Six Portraits of Rabindranath Tagore.* London, 1915.
"An Unhappy Poet." *Saturday Review,* 12 Sept. 1896, p. 282.
"Vague Hints from the Author to the Company." George Arliss. *Up the Years from Bloomsbury.* Boston, 1927.
"A Vain Child." *Saturday Review,* Christmas, 1896, p. 11; repub. in *Parodies.* Ed. Dwight MacDonald. London, 1960.

III. Caricature by Max Beerbohm

1. Collections:

A Book of Caricatures. London: Methuen & Co., 1907.
Caricatures of Twenty-Five Gentlemen. London: Leonard Smithers, 1896.
Cartoons: The Second Childhood of John Bull. London: Stephen Swift & Co., 1911.
Fifty Caricatures. London: William Heinemann, 1913.
Heroes and Heroines of Bitter Sweet. London: [Leadly], 1931.
Max's Nineties: Drawings 1892–1899. Ed. Rupert Hart-Davis and Allan Wade. Intro. Osbert Lancaster. London: Rupert Hart-Davis, 1958.
Observations. London: William Heinemann, 1925.
The Poets' Corner. London: William Heinemann, 1904; later ed. King Penguin, 1943.
Rossetti and His Circle. London: William Heinemann, 1922.
A Survey. London: William Heinemann, 1921.
Things New and Old. London: William Heinemann, 1923.

2. Catalogues:

One Hundred Caricatures by Max Beerbohm. London: Carfax & Co., Ltd., Nov. 1901.
Caricatures by Max Beerbohm. London: Carfax & Co., [1904]; no copy available.
Catalogue of Caricatures by Max Beerbohm. London: Carfax & Co., April 1907.
Catalogue of Caricatures by Max Beerbohm. London: Carfax & Co., April–May 1908.
Catalogue of an Exhibition of One Hundred Caricatures by Max Beerbohm. London: The Leicester Galleries, April–May 1911.
Catalogue of an Exhibition of Cartoons by Max Beerbohm. London: The Leicester Galleries, April–May 1913.
Catalogue of Another Exhibition of Caricatures by Max Beerbohm. London: The Leicester Galleries, May–June 1921.
Catalogue of an Exhibition of a Series of Drawings, "Rossetti and His Friends," by Max Beerbohm. London: The Leicester Galleries, Sept. 1921.

Catalogue of Another Exhibition of Caricatures by Max Beerbohm. London: The Leicester Galleries, June 1923.

Catalogue of Another Exhibition of Caricatures by Max Beerbohm. London: The Leicester Galleries, April–May 1925.

Catalogue of an Exhibition entitled "Ghosts" by Max Beerbohm. London: The Leicester Galleries, Nov.–Dec. 1928.

Catalogue of the Philip Guedalla Collection of Caricatures by Sir Max Beerbohm. London: The Leicester Galleries, Sept.–Oct. 1945.

Catalogue of an Exhibition of Drawings by Sir Max Beerbohm entitled 'Max' in Retrospect. London: The Leicester Galleries, May 1952.

Catalogue of a Memorial Exhibition of Drawings by Sir Max Beerbohm (1872–1956). London: The Leicester Galleries, June 1957.

Catalogue of the Caricatures of Max Beerbohm by Rupert Hart-Davis. London: Macmillan Ltd., 1972.

IV. Books and Articles by Other Authors

* = specifically about Beerbohm

Archer, Charles. *William Archer: Life, Work and Friendships.* London, 1931.

Archer, William. *Masks or Faces?* London, 1888; rpt. New York, 1957.

Arnold, Matthew. *Culture and Anarchy* (1869), with *Friendship's Garland and Some Literary Essays.* Ed. R. H. Super. Vol. V of *The Complete Prose Works of Matthew Arnold.* Ann Arbor, 1965.

Ashbee, C. R. *Caricature.* London, 1928.

Auden, W. H. *The Dyer's Hand.* New York, 1962.

*———. "One of the Family." *The New Yorker,* 23 Oct. 1965, pp. 227–44.

Barbey d'Aurevilly, Jules. *Du Dandysme et de G. Brummell.* Caen, France, 1845.

Barthes, Roland. *Essais Critiques.* Paris, 1964.

———. "The Structuralist Activity." *Partisan Review,* XXXIV, No. 1 (Winter 1967), 82–8.

Baudelaire, Charles. *Oeuvres Complètes.* Paris, 1961.

———. *The Painter of Modern Life and Other Essays*. Trans. and ed. Jonathan Mayne. New York, 1964.

Beardsley, Aubrey. *The Letters of Aubrey Beardsley*. Eds. Henry Maas, J. J. Duncan, W. G. Good. Rutherford, N.J., 1970.

———. *Venus and Tannhäuser*. New York, 1927.

Beckson, Karl, ed. *Aesthetes and Decadents of the 1890's: An Anthology of British Poetry and Prose*. New York, 1966.

Beddington-Behrens, Edward. *Look Back Look Forward*. London, 1963.

*Behrman, S. N. *Portrait of Max: An Intimate Memoir of Sir Max Beerbohm*. New York, 1960.

Bendz, Ernst. *The Influence of Pater and Matthew Arnold in the Prose-Writings of Oscar Wilde*. Gothenburg, Sweden, 1914.

Bentley, Eric. *The Playwright as Thinker: A Study of Drama in Modern Times*. New York, 1946; rpt. 1955.

*Bergonzi, Bernard. "Books." *Commonweal*, 25 June 1965, pp. 452–3.

Boas, George. "The Mona Lisa in the History of Taste." *Wingless Pegasus: A Handbook for Critics*. Baltimore, Maryland, 1950.

*Bottome, Phyllis. "Max Beerbohm." *From the Life*. London, 1944, pp. 32–46.

Brown, Oliver. *Exhibition: The Memoirs of Oliver Brown*. London, 1968.

Burdett, Osbert. *The Beardsley Period: An Essay in Perspective*. London, 1925.

Butor, Michel. *Les mots dans la peinture*. Geneva, Switz., 1969.

Cazamian, Madeleine L. *L'Anti-intellectualisme et l'Esthétisme (1880–1900)*. Vol. II of *Le Roman et les Idées en Angleterre*. Paris, 1935.

*Cecil, David. *Max*. London, 1964.

Cecil, Robert. *Life in Edwardian England*. London, 1969.

Charlesworth, Barbara. *Dark Passages: The Decadent Consciousness in Victorian Literature*. Madison, Wis., 1965.

Charteris, Evan. *The Life and Letters of Sir Edmund Gosse*. London, 1931.

Chesterton, Gilbert Keith. *Autobiography*. London, 1936.

———. *George Bernard Shaw*. London, 1909; rpt. New York, 1956.

The Child's Part. Ed. Peter Brooks. *Yale French Studies*, 43 (1969).

Coleridge, Samuel Taylor. "On Poesy or Art." *Criticism: The Major Texts*. Ed. Walter Jackson Bate. New York, 1952, pp. 395–6.

Collier, Constance. *Harlequinade: The Story of My Life*. London, 1929.

Coquelin, Constant. *Art and the Actor*. New York, 1915.

Coveney, Peter. *The Image of Childhood, The Individual and Society: A Study of the Theme in English Literature*. 1957; rev. ed. Baltimore, Md., 1967.

Craig, Gordon. *The Mask*. Florence, Italy, March 1908.

Douglas, Lord Alfred. *Oscar Wilde and Myself*. London, 1914.

Du Maurier, George. *Social and Pictorial Satire: Reminiscences and Appreciations of English Illustrators of the Past Generation*. London, 1898.

*Dupee, F. W. "Beerbohm: The Rigors of Fantasy." *New York Review of Books*, VI, No. 10 (9 June 1966), 12–17.

Edel, Leon. *Henry James: The Treacherous Years: 1895–1901*. Philadelphia, Pa., 1969.

Elliott, Robert C. *The Power of Satire: Magic, Ritual, Art*. Princeton, N.J., 1960.

Ellmann, Richard. "Romantic Pantomime in Oscar Wilde." *Partisan Review*, Fall 1963, 342.

Empson, William. *Seven Types of Ambiguity*. 3rd ed., London, 1930; rpt. New York, n.d.

Ensor, R. C. K. *England 1870–1914*. Vol. XIV of *The Oxford History of England*. London, 1936.

*Epstein, Joseph. "The Beerbohm Revival." *New Republic*, 27 June 1964, pp. 32–3.

Escher, M. C. *The Graphic Work of M. C. Escher*. 2nd ed., New York, 1967.

*Evans, Charles. "A Note on 'Carmen Becceriense.'" *Book Collector*, Winter 1952, 215–16.

Farmer, A. J. *Le Mouvement esthétique et 'décadent' en Angleterre (1873–1900)*. Paris, 1931.

*Felstiner, John. "Changing Faces in Max Beerbohm's Caricature: An Account of Beerbohm's Notes and New Versions Twenty-Four Years After in Mark Hyam's Copy of *Caricatures of Twenty-Five Gentlemen*." Princeton University Library Chronicle, Feb. 1972.

*———. "Max Beerbohm and the Wings of Henry James." *Kenyon Review*, Sept. 1967.

Fletcher, Ian. "The 1890's: A Lost Decade." *Victorian Studies*, IV, No. 4 (June 1961), 345–54.

*———. Review of Cecil, *Max. Victorian Studies*, IX, 277.
Forster, E. M. *Aspects of the Novel*. London, 1927.
Foucault, Michel. *The Order of Things: An Archaeology of the Human Sciences*. New York, 1970.
Franc, Miriam A. *Ibsen in England*. Boston, Mass., 1919.
Freud, Sigmund. *Jokes and Their Relation to the Unconscious*. Tr. and ed. James Strachey. New York, 1963.
Fry, Roger. *Vision and Design*. London, 1920; rpt. New York, 1947.
Fuller, Jean Overton. *Swinburne: A Critical Biography*. London, 1968.
Gallatin, Albert. *Aubrey Beardsley*. New York, 1945.
*———. "'Max': Caricaturist." *Whistler's Pastels and Other Modern Profiles*. New ed. London, 1913.
Gaunt, William. *The Aesthetic Adventure*. London, 1945.
Geismar, Maxwell. *Henry James and the Jacobites*. Boston, Mass., 1963.
George, M. Dorothy. *English Political Caricature*. 2 vols. Oxford, 1959.
Gide, André. *Oscar Wilde*. London, 1951.
Gombrich, E. H. *Art and Illusion: A Study in the Psychology of Pictorial Representation*. London, 1960.
——— and Ernst Kris. *Caricature*. Harmondsworth, Engl., 1940.
———. "The Mask and the Face: The Perception of Physiognomic Likeness in Life and in Art." Unpub. lecture, 1968.
———. *Meditations on a Hobby-Horse*. London, 1963.
———. "Moment and Movement in Art." *Journal of the Warburg and Courtauld Institutes*, XXVII, 293–306.
Gordon, D. J. "Aubrey Beardsley at the V. & A." *Encounter*, Oct. 1966, pp. 3–16.
Gosse, Edmund. *Henrik Ibsen*. London, 1907.
Gowans, Alan. *The Unchanging Arts: New Forms for the Traditional Functions of Art in Society*. Philadelphia, Pa., 1971.
Gross, John. *The Rise and Fall of the Man of Letters: A Study of the Idiosyncratic and the Humane in Modern Literature*. New York, 1969.
Guedalla, Philip. *Masters and Men*. London, 1923.
*———. "Sophia Swinburne: From Max Beerbohm, 'No. 2 (bis) The Pines'" [a parody of Beerbohm]. *Bonnet and Shawl: An Album*. London, n.d., pp. 195–7.

Halévy, Elie. *A History of the English People in the Nineteenth Century.* Trans. E. I. Watkin. Vol. IV: *Victorian Years 1841–1895.* London, 1951. Vol. V: *Imperialism and the Rise of Labour.* 2nd ed. London, 1951.

Hamerton, Philip Gilbert. "The Yellow Book. A Criticism of Volume I." *Yellow Book,* II (July 1894), 179–90.

* Hammerton, J. A. "Max Beerbohm." *Humorists of the Pencil.* London, 1905, pp. 68–73.

Harris, Frank. *Contemporary Portraits.* London, 1924.

Henderson, Archibald. *George Bernard Shaw, His Life and Works: A Critical Biography.* London, 1911.

Hichens, Robert. *The Green Carnation.* London, 1894.

———. *Yesterday: The Autobiography of Robert Hichens.* London, 1947.

Hicks, Granville. *Figures of Transition.* New York, 1939.

Highet, Gilbert. *The Anatomy of Satire.* Princeton, N.J., 1962.

* Hillebrand, Harold Newcomb. "Max Beerbohm." *Journal of English and Germanic Philology,* April 1920, pp. 254–69.

Hillier, Bevis. *Cartoons and Caricatures.* London, 1970.

Hoffmann, Heinrich. *The English Struwwelpeter, or Pretty Stories and Funny Pictures for Little Children.* 1845; 12th English ed., London, 1863.

Hofmann, Werner. *Caricature from Leonardo to Picasso.* London, 1957.

Holland, Vyvyan. *Son of Oscar Wilde.* London, 1954.

Hone, Joseph. *The Life of George Moore.* London, 1936.

Huizinga, Johan. *Homo Ludens: A Study of the Play-element in Culture.* Trans. R. F. C. Hull. London, 1949.

* Huss, Roy. "Max Beerbohm's Drawings of Theatrical Figures." *Theatre Notebook,* XXI, 2, pp. 75–86; XXI, 3, pp. 102–19; XXI, 4, pp. 169–180.

Hynes, Samuel. *The Edwardian Turn of Mind.* Princeton, N.J., 1968.

Ibsen, Henrik. *Eleven Plays of Henrik Ibsen.* Intro. H. L. Mencken. New York, n.d.

———. *When We Dead Awaken: A Dramatic Epilogue in Three Acts.* Trans. William Archer. London, 1900.

Irving, Laurence. *Henry Irving: The Actor and His World.* London, 1951.

Jackson, Holbrook. *The Eighteen Nineties: A Review of Art and*

Ideas at the Close of the Nineteenth Century. London, 1913; rpt. 1931.

James, Henry. *The Art of the Novel: Critical Prefaces*. Ed. Richard P. Blackmur. New York, 1934.

———. *Daumier: Caricaturist*. London, 1954.

———. *The Letters of Henry James*. Ed. Percy Lubbock. New York, 1920.

———. *The Notebooks of Henry James*. Ed. F. O. Matthiessen and Kenneth B. Murdock. New York, 1947.

———. *Selected Literary Criticism*. Ed. Morris Shapira. New York, 1964.

———. *Stories of Writers and Artists*. Ed. F. O. Matthiessen. New York, 1954.

James, Robert Rhodes. *Rosebery: A Biography of Archibald Philip, Fifth Earl of Rosebery*. New York, 1964.

Joyce, James. *Finnegans Wake*. New York, 1939.

Kaiser, Walter. *Praisers of Folly*. Cambridge, Mass., 1963.

Kampf, Louis. *On Modernism: The Prospects for Literature and Freedom*. Cambridge, Mass., 1967.

*Kauffmann, Stanley. "Maximum Max." *New Republic*, 10 April 1965, pp. 19–22.

Kermode, Frank. *Romantic Image*. London, 1957.

*———. "Whom the Gods Loathe." *Encounter*, March 1965, p. 74.

Kiremidjian, G. D. "The Aesthetics of Parody." *Journal of Aesthetics and Art Criticism*, XXVIII, No. 2 (Winter 1969), 231–42.

Kitchin, George. *A Survey of Burlesque and Parody in English*. Edinburgh, 1931.

Klingender, F. D., ed. *Hogarth and English Caricature*. London, 1944.

Koestler, Arthur. *The Act of Creation*. New York, 1964; rpt. 1967.

Kris, Ernst. "The Psychology of Caricature" and "The Principles of Caricature" (with Ernst Gombrich). *Psychoanalytic Explorations in Art*. London, 1953, pp. 173–203.

*Kronenberger, Louis. "The Perfect Trifler." *Saturday Review of Literature*, 21 June 1947, pp. 9–10.

*Layard, George Somes. "Max Beerbohm; or, Art and Semolina." *Bookman*, Aug. 1911, pp. 201–8.

Le Gallienne, Richard. *The Romantic '90s*. London, 1926.

Lester, John A., Jr. *Journey Through Despair: 1880–1914. Transformations in British Literary Culture.* Princeton, N.J., 1968.

* Leverson, Ada. "A Few Words with Mr. Max Beerbohm." *Sketch,* 2 Jan. 1895, p. 439. Repub. in Violet Wyndham. *The Sphinx and Her Circle.* London, 1963, p. 45.

Levin, Harry. *Contexts of Criticism.* Cambridge, Mass., 1957.

Lévi-Strauss, Claude. *Tristes Tropiques.* Trans. John Russell. London, 1961.

* Lewis, Naomi. "Tale of Max." *New Statesman,* 68 (20 Nov. 1964), 789.

Low, David. *British Cartoonists, Caricaturists and Comic Artists.* London, 1942.

Lynch, Bohun. *A History of Caricature.* London, 1926.

* ———. *Max Beerbohm in Perspective.* London, 1921.

MacCarthy, Desmond. *Memories.* London, 1953.

Marsh, Edward. *A Number of People.* London, 1939.

Mason, Stuart. *Bibliography of Oscar Wilde.* London, 1914.

———. *Oscar Wilde: Art and Morality.* London, 1912.

* McElderry, Bruce J. *Max Beerbohm.* New York, 1971.

Minney, R. J. *The Edwardian Age.* London, 1964.

* Mix, Katherine Lyon. "Max on Shaw." *Shaw Review,* VI, No. 3 (Sept. 1963), 100–4.

———. *A Study in Yellow: The Yellow Book and Its Contributors.* Lawrence, Kansas, 1960.

Moers, Ellen. *The Dandy: Brummell to Beerbohm.* New York, 1960.

Moore, George. *Avowals.* New York, 1919.

———. *Confessions of a Young Man.* London, 1888; repub. 1928.

———. *Impressions and Opinions.* London, 1891.

———. *Modern Painting.* London, 1893.

———. *Reminiscences of the Impressionist Painters.* Dublin, 1906.

Morrell, Lady Ottoline. *Ottoline: The Early Memoirs of Lady Ottoline Morrell.* Ed. Robert Gathorne-Hardy. New York, 1964.

* Muggeridge, Malcolm. "A Survivor." *New York Review of Books,* 25 Nov. 1965, pp. 31–3.

Nordau, Max. *Degeneration.* London, 1895.

Nowell-Smith, Simon, ed. *Edwardian England, 1901–1914.* London, 1964.

Oreglia, Giacomo. *The Commedia dell'Arte.* New York, 1968.

O'Sullivan, Vincent. *Aspects of Wilde.* New York, 1936.

Owen, Wilfred. *Collected Letters*. Eds. Harold Owen and John Bell. London, 1967.

Panofsky, Erwin. *The Life and Art of Albrecht Dürer*. Princeton, N.J., 1955.

Parodies: An Anthology from Chaucer to Beerbohm—and After. Ed. Dwight MacDonald. London, 1960.

Pater, Walter. *Imaginary Portraits*. London, 1887; a new collection, ed. Eugene J. Brzenk. New York, 1964.

———. *The Renaissance: Studies in Art and Poetry*. London, 1872. 4th ed., 1890.

Paull, H. M. *Literary Ethics*. London, 1928.

Pearson, Hesketh. *The Man Whistler*. London, 1952.

Poggioli, Renato. *The Theory of the Avant-garde*. Trans. Gerald Fitzgerald. Cambridge, Mass., 1968.

Pound, Ezra. *Personae: Collected Shorter Poems*. London, 1952.

Praz, Mario. *The Romantic Agony*. 2nd ed., Oxford, 1951.

———. *Mnemosyne: The Parallel Between Literature and the Visual Arts*. Princeton, N.J., 1970.

*Pritchett, V. S. Review of Cecil, *Max*. *New York Times Book Review*, 11 April 1965, p. 1.

Reade, Brian. *Aubrey Beardsley, 1872–1898*. London, 1967.

*Riewald, J. G. *Sir Max Beerbohm, Man and Writer: A Critical Analysis with a Brief Life and Bibliography*. The Hague, 1953.

*Roberts, S. G. *Zuleika in Cambridge*. Cambridge, England, 1941.

Romanticism and Consciousness: Essays in Criticism. Ed. Harold Bloom. New York, 1970.

Romantic Mythologies. Ed. Ian Fletcher. London, 1967.

Roosbroeck, G. L. von. *The Legend of the Decadents*. New York, 1927.

Rosenberg, Harold. *The Anxious Object: Art Today and Its Audience*. New York, 1964.

Ross, Margery, ed. *Robert Ross, Friend of Friends: Letters to Robert Ross, Art Critic and Writer*. London, 1952.

Rossetti, William Michael, ed. *Dante Gabriel Rossetti: His Family-Letters, With a Memoir*. 2 vols. London, 1895.

Rothenstein, John. *A Pot of Paint: The Artists of the 1890's*. New York, 1929.

———, ed. *Sixteen Letters from Oscar Wilde*. London, 1930.

———. *Summer's Lease. Autobiography 1901–1938*. London, 1965.

Rothenstein, William. *Men and Memories: Recollections of William Rothenstein, 1872–1900.* London, 1931.

———. *Men and Memories: Recollections of William Rothenstein, 1900–1922.* London, 1932.

———. *Since Fifty: Men and Memories, 1922–1938.* London, 1939.

———. *Twenty-Four Portraits, With Critical Appreciations by Various Hands.* London, 1920.

Ruskin, John. *The Lamp of Beauty.* Ed. Joan Evans. London, 1959.

* Russell, Bertrand. "'The Faultless Max' at 80." *New York Times Magazine,* 24 Aug. 1952, pp. 18–19.

Scott, Dixon. *Men of Letters.* Introduction by Max Beerbohm. London, 1916.

Seaman, Owen. *Borrowed Plumes.* London, 1902.

Shaw, George Bernard, ed. *Fabian Essays in Socialism.* London, 1920.

———. *Pen Portraits and Reviews.* London, 1932.

———. *Sixteen Self Sketches.* New York, 1949.

Sizeranne, Robert de La. "Le Rôle de la Caricature." *Le Miroir de la Vie.* Paris, 1912, pp. 75–146.

Speaight, Robert. *William Rothenstein.* London, 1962.

Spitzer, Leo. "Linguistic Perspectivism in the *Don Quixote.*" *Linguistics and Literary History: Essays in Stylistics.* Princeton, N.J., 1948.

Squire, J. C. *Collected Parodies.* New York, 1925.

* Steiner, George. "Mask Behind the Face." *Times Literary Supplement,* 26 Nov. 1964, p. 1056.

* Stevenson, David H. "The Critical Principles and Devices of Max Beerbohm." Diss. University of Michigan, 1954.

Symons, Arthur. *Aubrey Beardsley.* London, 1898.

———. *Studies in Prose and Verse.* London, 1904.

———. *The Symbolist Movement in Literature.* London, 1899.

Thackeray, William Makepeace. *The English Humorists* and *The Four Georges.* New York, 1867.

[———]. *The Paris Sketch Book,* by Mr. Titmarsh. London, 1886.

Townsend, J. Benjamin. *John Davidson: Poet of Armageddon.* New Haven, Conn., 1961.

* Toynbee, Philip. "The Inscrutable Max." *The Observer Weekend Review,* 8 Nov. 1964.

Trilling, Lionel. "Kipling." *The Liberal Imagination*. London, 1951, pp. 118–28.

Tuchman, Barbara. *The Proud Tower: A Portrait of the World Before the War 1890–1914*. New York, 1966.

* Updike, John. "Rhyming Max." *The New Yorker*, 7 March 1964, pp. 176–81.

Veth, Cornelius. *Comic Art in England*. London, 1930.

* Waugh, Evelyn. "The Max Behind the Mask." *The Sunday Times*, 8 Nov. 1964.

Webb, Sidney. *The Difficulties of Individualism*. Fabian Tract No. 69. London, June 1896.

* Weintraub, Stanley. "Alone with His Wit." *Saturday Review*, 17 April 1965, pp. 46–7.

Welby, T. Earle. *A Study of Swinburne*. New York, 1926.

Welsford, Enid. *The Fool: His Social and Literary History*. London, 1935.

West, Rebecca. *Ending in Earnest. A Literary Log*. New York, 1931.

Wharton, Edith. *A Backward Glance*. New York, 1964.

Whistler, James McNeill. *The Gentle Art of Making Enemies*. New York, 1890.

Wilde, Oscar. *Intentions*. London, 1891. Repub. as Vol. VII, *Complete Writings of Oscar Wilde*. New York, 1909.

———. *The Letters of Oscar Wilde*. Ed. Rupert Hart-Davis. New York, 1962.

———. *Letters to the Sphinx from Oscar Wilde: with Reminiscences of the Author by Ada Leverson*. London, 1930.

———. *The Picture of Dorian Gray*. London, 1891.

Williams, Raymond. *Culture and Society 1780–1950*. London, 1958; rpt. 1966.

———. *The Long Revolution*. Rev. ed. New York, 1961; rpt. 1966.

* Wilson, Edmund. "An Analysis of Max Beerbohm." *Classics and Commercials: A Literary Chronicle of the Forties*. New York, 1950, pp. 431–41.

———. *I Thought of Daisy*. New York, 1929.

———. "The Kipling That Nobody Read." *The Wound and the Bow*. London, n.d., pp. 105–81.

*———. "A Miscellany of Max Beerbohm." *The Bit Between My Teeth: A Literary Chronicle of 1950–1965*. New York, 1965, pp. 41–62.

Woolf, Virginia. *The Captain's Death Bed*. London, 1950.
———. *The Common Reader*. London, 1925; rpt. 1962.
———. *Roger Fry: A Biography*. New York, 1940.
———. *A Writer's Diary: Being Extracts from the Diary of Virginia Woolf*. Ed. Leonard Woolf. New York, 1953.
Worcester, David. *The Art of Satire*. New York, 1940; rpt. 1960.
Wright, Thomas. *The Life of Walter Pater*. 2 Vols. London, 1907; rpt. New York, 1969.
Yeats, William Butler. *The Autobiography of William Butler Yeats*. New York, 1953.
Yellow Book, I–IV (April 1894–Jan. 1895).

Index

Note: Underlined numbers indicate illustrations.

A Note About the Author

John Felstiner received his Ph.D. from Harvard University in 1965. The winner of the Kenyon Review Award for Criticism, he is presently Assistant Professor of English at Stanford University, and is now at work on a comparative study of Pablo Neruda and T. S. Eliot.

A Note on the Type

The text of this book was set in Medallion, the film version of Melior, a typeface designed by Hermann Zapf and issued in 1952. Born in Nürnberg, Germany, in 1918, Zapf has been a strong influence in printing since 1939. Melior, like Times Roman, another popular twentieth-century typeface, was created specifically for use in a newspaper. With this functional end in mind, Zapf nonetheless chose to base the proportions of its letterforms on those of the Golden Section. The result is a typeface of unusual strength and surpassing subtlety.

Composed by York Graphic Services, York, Pa. Printed by Halliday Lithograph Corporation, West Hanover, Mass. and bound by H. Wolff Book Manufacturing Co., New York, N.Y. Typography and binding design by Betty Anderson.